THE YEAR'S WORK
IN ENGLISH STUDIES 1986

The Year's Work
in English Studies

Volume 67 · 1986

Edited by
LAUREL BRAKE

and
SUSAN BROCK
DAVID BURNLEY
MAUREEN MORAN
JOHN THIEME
(associate editors)

JACQUELINE HOOI
(editorial assistant)

Published for
THE ENGLISH ASSOCIATION

by
JOHN MURRAY, LONDON
HUMANITIES PRESS, ATLANTIC HIGHLANDS, N.J.

© The English Association 1989

First published 1989
by John Murray (Publishers) Ltd
50 Albemarle Street
London W1X 4BD

Typeset by Colset Private Ltd
Printed and bound in Great Britain by
Biddles Ltd, Guildford and King's Lynn

British Library Cataloguing in Publication Data

The Year's work in English studies.
  Vol. 67 (1989)
  1. English literature—Critical studies—Serials
  I. Brake, Laurel
  820.9

ISBN 0-7195-4567-6

The Library of Congress has cataloged this
serial title as follows:

The Year's work in English studies. v.[1]- 1919/20-
  London. Published for the English Association
  by John Murray [etc.]

  v. 23 cm.

  Annual.
  ISSN 0084-4144 = Year's work in English studies.
  ISBN 0-391-03645-9

  1. English philology—History.   2. English philology—
Bibliography.   3. English literature—History and criticism.
4. English literature—Periodicals.
I. English Association.
PE58.E6   22-10024
                                                 MARC-S

Library of Congress   [8503r80]rev4

Preface

YWES is a selective, comprehensive, and evaluative narrative bibliography of scholarly writing in the fields of English language and literature in English in Britain, America, Africa, Australia, Canada, the Caribbean, and India.

It may help the user of this work to remember that books are sometimes published a year later in the U.S.A. than they are in the U.K. and vice versa, that the year of publication is not always that which appears on the title-page of the book, and that the inevitable inadvertent omissions of one year are made good in the next; thus, the search for a notice of a book or article may have to extend to the volume after the expected one and sometimes to that which precedes it. Reports of important omissions are welcomed.

Offprints of articles are always useful, and editors of journals that are not easily available in the U.K. are urged to join the many who already send us complete sets. These should be addressed to The Editor, *YWES*, The English Association, The Vicarage, Priory Gardens, London W4 1TT. We are grateful to the authors and publishers who have made our task easier by supplying books and articles for Volume 67, and to the editors of *ASE* and *MLA International Bibliography* for proofs of their annual bibliographies. In drawing the reader's attention at the beginning of chapters to the main bibliographical aids, we presuppose in each case a reference to the *MLA International Bibliography* and the *Annual Bibliography of English Language and Literature* published by the MHRA.

The editors and the English Association announce the winner of the first annual Beatrice White prize for the outstanding scholarly article in the field of English Literature before 1590 to be noticed in this volume as Rosalind Field for her essay 'The Heavenly Jerusalem in *Pearl*' (*MLR*). The prize commemorates a distinguished past editor of *YWES* whose encouragement of younger colleagues informed the subject of the prize as outstanding articles by, whenever possible, younger scholars.

Change continues to characterize the volume. You will find this year, in the preliminary list of journal abbreviations and in a pilot Chaucer chapter, the kind of additional bibliographical information which will appear in full next year – the volume or issue numbers of the journals covered and the pagination of journal articles. Perhaps as momentous for *YWES* is a change of publisher: with this volume we end a long and happy publishing connection with John Murray, our publisher for twenty-five years, and begin with the next volume to publish with Basil Blackwell. The many improvements and innovations discernible in the Murray years attest to an impressive degree of co-operation and joint endeavour between publisher, editors, and the English Association.

Laurel Brake
University College of Wales
Aberystwyth

for the Editorial Board

Susan Brock (The Shakespeare Institute)
David Burnley (University of Sheffield)
Maureen Moran (West London Institute of HE)
John Thieme (Polytechnic of North London)

The English Association

This bibliography is an English Association publication. It is available through membership of the Association; non-members can purchase it through any good bookshop.

The object of the English Association is to promote the knowledge and appreciation of English language and literature.

The Association pursues these aims by creating opportunities of co-operation among all those interested in English; by furthering the recognition of English as essential in education; by discussing methods of English teaching; by holding lectures, conferences, and other meetings; by publishing a journal, books, and leaflets; and by forming local branches overseas and at home.

Publications

The Year's Work in English Studies. An annual bibliography. Published by John Murray (U.S.A.: Humanities Press).

Essays and Studies. An annual volume of essays by various scholars assembled by the collector covering usually a wide range of subjects and authors from the medieval to the modern. Published by John Murray (U.S.A.: Humanities Press).

English. The journal of the Association, *English* is published three times a year by the Oxford University Press.

News-Letter. A *News-Letter* is published three times a year giving information about forthcoming publications, conferences, and other matters of interest.

Benefits of Membership

Institutional Membership

Full members receive copies of *The Year's Work in English Studies, Essays and Studies, English* (3 issues) and three *News-Letters.*

Ordinary Membership covers *English* (3 issues) and three *News-Letters.*

Schools Membership covers two copies of each issue of *English*, one copy of *Essays and Studies* (optional), three *News-Letters* and preferential booking for Sixth Form Conference places.

Individual Membership

Individuals take out basic membership, which entitles them to buy all regular publications of the English Association at a discounted price.

For further details write to The Secretary, The English Association, The Vicarage, Priory Gardens, London W4 1TT.

Contents

College, University of London; Trevor R. Griffiths, B.A.,
M.A., Ph.D., Principal Lecturer in the School of Literary
and Media Studies, Polytechnic of North London; Audrey
E. McMullan, M.A., Samuel Beckett Research Fellow,
University of Reading

Material in German: E. Anthony McCobb, B.A., Ph.D., Lecturer in   .
German, University of Hull. Reviews are marked E.A.M.

Abbreviations

1. Journals, Series, and Reference Works

A&E	*Anglistik und Englischunterricht*
ABäG 24–5	*Amsterdamer Beiträge zur älteren Germanistik*
ABC 7	*American Book Collector*
ABELL 58	*Annual Bibliography of English Language and Literature*
ABMR 13	*Antiquarian Book Monthly Review*
ABR 37	*American Benedictine Review*
AC	*Archeologia Classica*
ACLALSB 7	ACLALS Bulletin
Acta	Acta (Binghamton, N.Y.)
ADS	*Australasian Drama Studies*
AEB 10	*Analytical and Enumerative Bibliography*
AF	Anglistische Forschungen
AfrSR 29	*The African Studies Review*
Agenda 24	*Agenda*
AH 9	*Art History*
AHR 91	*The American Historical Review*
AI 43	*American Imago*
AJES 11	*Aligarh Journal of English Studies*
AJS	*American Journal of Semiotics*
AKML	*Abhandlungen zur Kunst-, Musik- und Literaturwissenschaft*
AL 58	*American Literature*
ALA	African Literature Association Annuals
ALASH 36	*Acta Linguistica Academiae Scientiarum Hungaricae*
AlexS	Alexander Shakespeare
ALH	*Acta Linguistica Hafniensia: International Journal of Linguistics*
ALLCB 14	*Association for Literary and Linguistic Computing Bulletin*
ALR 19	*American Literary Realism, 1870–1910*
ALS 12	*Australian Literary Studies*
ALT 14	*African Literature Today*
AmerP 33/4	*American Poetry*
AmerS 27	*American Studies*
AmLS	*American Literary Scholarship: An Annual*
AMon 257–8	*The Atlantic Monthly*
AmRev	*The Americas Review: A Review of Hispanic Literature and Art of the USA*
Amst 31	*Amerikastudien/American Studies*
AN 19	*Acta Neophilologica*
AN&Q 24/5	*American Notes and Queries*

AnBol 104	*Analecta Bollandiana*
ANF 101	*Arkiv för Nordisk Filologi*
Anglia 104	*Anglia: Zeitschrift für Englische Philologie*
Anglistica	Anglistica
AnH	Analecta Husserliana
AnL 28	*Anthropological Linguistics*
AnM 26	*Annuale Mediaevale*
AntColl 57	*The Antique Collector*
AntigR	*Antigonish Review*
APR 15	*The American Poetry Review*
AQ 38	*American Quarterly*
AR 44	*The Antioch Review*
ArAA 11	*Arbeiten aus Anglistik und Amerikanistik*
Archiv 138	*Archiv für das Studium der neueren Sprachen und Literaturen*
ARCS 16	*The American Review of Canadian Studies*
ArdenS	Arden Shakespeare
ArielE 17	*Ariel: A Review of International English Literature*
Arnoldian 13	*The Arnoldian: A Review of Mid-Victorian Culture*
ArQ 42	*Arizona Quarterly*
ARS	Augustan Reprint Society
ArtB 68	*Art Bulletin*
ArthL 6	*Arthurian Literature*
AS 61	*American Speech*
ASch 55	*The American Scholar*
ASE 15	*Anglo-Saxon England*
ASInt 24	*American Studies International*
ASoc	*Arts in Society*
ASPR	*Anglo-Saxon Poetic Records*
Assaph 3	Assaph: Studies in the Arts *(Theatre Studies)*
ATQ 59–62	*American Transcendental Quarterly: A Journal of New England Writers*
AuBR	*Australian Book Review*
AuJL 6	*Australian Journal of Linguistics*
AUMLA 65–6	*Journal of the Australasian Universities Language and Literature Assoc.*
AWR 82–4	*The Anglo-Welsh Review*
BakhtinN	*Bakhtin Newsletter*
BALF 20	*Black American Literature Forum*
BASAM 3	*BASA Magazine*
BB 43	*Bulletin of Bibliography*
BBCS 33	*The Bulletin of the Board of Celtic Studies*
BBCSh	BBC Shakespeare
BBN	*British Book News*
BBSIA 38	*Bulletin Bibliographique de la Société Internationale Arthurienne*
BC 35	*The Book Collector*
BCS	*B. C. Studies*
BDEC	*Bulletin of the Department of English* (Calcutta)
BDP	Beiträge zur Deutschen Philologie

BFLS	*Bulletin de la Faculté des Lettres de Strasbourg*
BGDSL 108	*Beiträge zur Geschichte der Deutschen Sprache und Literatur*
BHI	*British Humanities Index*
BHL	*Bibliotheca hagiographica latina antiquae et mediae aetatis*
BHR 48	*Bibliothèque d'Humanisme et Renaissance*
BI 44–5	*Books at Iowa*
Biography 9	*Biography: An Interdisciplinary Quarterly*
BIS 14	*Browning Institute Studies: An Annual of Victorian Literary and Cultural History*
BJA 26	*British Journal of Aesthetics*
BJCS 1	*British Journal of Canadian Studies*
BJDC 21	*The British Journal of Disorders of Communication*
BJECS 9	*British Journal for Eighteenth-Century Studies*
BJHS 19	*The British Journal for the History of Science*
BJPS 37	*The British Journal for the Philosophy of Science*
BJRL 68/9	*Bulletin of the John Rylands University Library of Manchester*
Blake 19/20	*Blake: An Illustrated Quarterly*
BLE 87	*Bulletin de Littérature Ecclésiastique*
BLJ 12	*The British Library Journal*
BLR 12	*The Bodleian Library Record*
BN 21	*Beiträge zur Namenforschung*
BNB	*British National Bibliography*
Boundary 14/15	*Boundary 2: A Journal of Postmodern Literature and Culture*
BP	*Banasthali Patrika*
BPMA 349–53	*Bulletin* (Philadelphia Museum of Art)
BPN	*The Barbara Pym Newsletter*
BRH 87	*Bulletin of Research in the Humanities*
BRMMLA	*Bulletin of the Rocky Mountain Modern Language Association*
BSANZB 10	*The Bibliographical Society of Australia and New Zealand Bulletin*
BSE	*Brno Studies in English*
BSEAA	*Bulletin de la Société d'Etudes Anglo-Américaines des xviie et xviiie siècles*
BSJ 36	*The Baker Street Journal: An Irregular Quarterly of Sherlockiana*
BSLP 81	*Bulletin de la Société de Linguistique de Paris*
BSNotes 15/16	*Browning Society Notes*
BSRS 4	*Bulletin of the Society for Renaissance Studies*
BST 19	*Brontë Society Transactions*
BSUF 27	*Ball State University Forum*
BuR 30	*Bucknell Review*
BurlM 128	*The Burlington Magazine*
BurnsC 11	*Burns Chronicle*
BWVACET	*The Bulletin of the W. Virginia Assoc. of College English Teachers*

ByronJ 14	The Byron Journal
CABS	Contemporary Authors Bibliographical Series
CahiersE 29–30	Cahiers Élisabéthains
CAIEF 38	Cahiers de l'Association Internationale des Études Françaises
Caliban 23	Caliban [Toulouse, France]
Camobs	Camera obscura
CamR 107	The Cambridge Review
CanD 12	Canadian Drama
C&L 35/6	Christianity and Literature
C&M 37	Classica et Medievalia
CanL 108–11	Canadian Literature
CanPo 18–19	Canadian Poetry
CapR	Capilano Review
CARA	Centre Aixois de Recherches Anglaises
CarR 15	Caribbean Review
Carrell	The Carrell: Journal of the Friends of the University of Miami Library
CBEL	Cambridge Bibliography of English Literature
CCRev	Comparative Civilizations Review
CCrit 8	Comparative Criticism: An Annual Journal
CDCP	Comparative Drama Conference Papers
CdL	Cahiers de Lexicologie
CE 48	College English
CEA	CEA Critic
CEAfr 26	Cahiers d'études Africaines
CE&S 8/9	Commonwealth Essays & Studies
CentR 30	The Centennial Review
CFM	Canadian Fiction Magazine
ChauR 20/1	The Chaucer Review
ChildL 14	Children's Literature
ChiR 35/6	Chicago Review
ChLB 53–6	Charles Lamb Bulletin
CHLSSF 79–80	Commentationes Humanarum Litterarum Societatis Scientiarum Fennicae
CHum 20	Computers and the Humanities
CI	Critical Idiom
CILT	Amsterdam Studies in the Theory and History of the Language Sciences IV: Current Issues in Linguistic Theory
Cithara	Cithara: Essays in the Judaeo-Christian Tradition
CJ 81/2	Classical Journal
CJE 16	Cambridge Journal of Education
CJIS 12	Canadian Journal of Irish Studies
CJL 31	The Canadian Journal of Linguistics
CL 38	Comparative Literature (Eugene, Oregon)
CLAJ 29/30	CLA Journal
ClarkN 10–11	The Clark Newsletter: Bulletin of the UCLA Center for 17th- and 18th-Century Studies
CLC 35/6	Columbia Library Columns

ClioI 15/16	*Clio: A Journal of Literature, History, and the Philosophy of History*
CLQ 22	*Colby Library Quarterly*
CLS 23	*Comparative Literature Studies*
Clues	*Clues: A Journal of Detection*
CMCS 11–12	*Cambridge Medieval Celtic Studies*
CML 6/7	*Classical and Modern Literature*
CN 8	*Chaucer Newsletter*
CNew 7	*The Carlyle Newsletter*
CNIE	*Commonwealth Novel in English*
ColF	*Columbia Forum*
CollG 19	*Colloquia Germanica*
CollL 13	*College Literature*
CompD 20	*Comparative Drama*
ConL 27	*Contemporary Literature*
ConnR	*Connecticut Review*
Conradian 11	*The Conradian*
Conradiana 18	*Conradiana: A Journal of Joseph Conrad Studies*
ContempR 248–9	*Contemporary Review*
CP 19	*Concerning Poetry*
CQ 15	*The Cambridge Quarterly*
CR 28	*The Critical Review*
CRCL 13	*Canadian Review of Comparative Literature*
CRev 12	*The Chesterton Review*
Crit 28/9	*Critique: Studies in Modern Fiction*
CritI 12/13	*Critical Inquiry*
Criticism 28	*Criticism: A Quarterly for Literature and the Arts*
Critique 42	*Critique* (Paris)
CritQ 28	*Critical Quarterly*
CRNLE	*The CRNLE Reviews Journal*
CRUX 20	*CRUX: A Journal on the Teaching of English*
CSLBull 17/18	*Bulletin of the New York C. S. Lewis Society*
CSR 15/16	*Christian Scholar's Review*
CTR 46–9	*Canadian Theatre Review*
CulC 2–5	*Cultural Critique*
CUNY	*CUNY English Forum*
CV2	*Contemporary Verse 2*
CVE 23–4	*Cahiers Victoriens et Edouardiens*
CWAAS	*Transactions of the Cumberland and Westmorland Antiquarian and Archaeological Society*
DA	*Dictionary of Americanisms*
DAE	*Dictionary of American English*
DAEM 42	*Deutsches Archiv für Eforschung des Mittelalters*
DAI 46/7	*Dissertation Abstracts International*
Daphnis 15	*Daphnis: Zeitschrift für Mittlere Deutsche Literatur*
DC	*The Dickens Companions*
DerbyM 11	*Derbyshire Miscellany*
DHLR 18	*The D. H. Lawrence Review*
Diac 16	*Diacritics*
Dialogue 25	*Dialogue: Canadian Philosophical Review*

Dickensian 82	*The Dickensian*
DicS 59–60	*Dickinson Studies*
DLB	Dictionary of Literary Biography
DLN 10	*Doris Lessing Newsletter*
DM	*The Dublin Magazine*
DN 17	*The Dreiser Newsletter*
DNB	*Dictionary of National Biography*
DOE	*Dictionary of Old English*
DownR 104	*The Downside Review*
DQ 20/1	*Denver Quarterly*
DQR 16	*Dutch Quarterly Review of Anglo-American Letters*
DQu 3	*Dickens Quarterly*
DR 66	*Dalhousie Review*
DSA 15	*Dickens Studies Annual*
DU 38	*Der Deutschunterricht: Beiträge zu seiner Praxis und wissenschaftlichen Grundlegung*
DUJ 47/8	*Durham University Journal*
DVLG 60	*Deutsche Vierteljahrsschrift für Literaturwissenschaft und Geistesgeschichte*
EA 39	*Études Anglaises*
EAL 21	*Early American Literature*
E&S 39	*Essays & Studies*
E&Soc 15	*Economy and Society*
EAS	*Essays in Arts and Sciences*
EB	*Euralex Bulletin*
EC 23	*Études Celtiques*
ECCB 8	*Eighteenth Century: A Current Bibliography*
ECent 27	*The Eighteenth Century: Theory and Interpretation*
ECLife 10	*Eighteenth Century Life*
ECr 26	*L'Esprit Créateur*
ECS 19/20	*Eighteenth-Century Studies*
ECW	*Essays on Canadian Writing*
EDAM	*Early Drama, Art, and Music Newsletter*
EDH 44	*Essays by Divers Hands*
EdL	*Études de Lettres*
EdN	*Editors' Notes: Bulletin of the Conference of Editors of Learned Journals*
EDSL	*Encyclopedic Dictionary of the Sciences of Language*
EHR 101	*The English Historical Review*
EI 11	*Études Irlandaises* (Lille)
EIC 36	*Essays in Criticism*
EinA 13	*English in Africa*
EiP 11	*Essays in Poetics*
EIRC 12	*Explorations in Renaissance Culture*
Eire 21	*Éire-Ireland*
EiT 4/5	*Essays in Theatre*
EJ	*English Journal*
ELangT 40	*ELT Journal: An International Journal for Teachers of English to Speakers of Other Languages*
ELH 53	[*Journal of English Literary History*]

ELN 23/4	*English Language Notes*
ELR 16	*English Literary Renaissance*
ELS	*English Literary Studies*
ELT 29	*English Literature in Transition*
ELWIU 13	*Essays in Literature* (Western Illinois University)
EM	*English Miscellany*
Emblematica 1	*Emblematica: An Interdisciplinary Journal of English Studies*
English 35	*English: The Journal of the English Association*
ES 67	*English Studies*
ESA 29	*English Studies in Africa*
ESC 12	*English Studies in Canada*
ESP	The English Satirical Print 1600–1832
ESQ 32	*ESQ: A Journal of the American Renaissance*
ESRS	*Emporia State Research Studies*
ESTC	*Eighteenth Century Short Title Catalogue*
EWIP	*Edinburgh University, Department of Linguistics, Work in Progress*
EWN 20	*Evelyn Waugh Newsletter*
EWW 7	[*English World-Wide*]
Expl 44/5	*The Explicator*
FCEMN	*Mystics Quarterly* (formerly *Fourteenth-Century English Mystics Newsletter*)
FDT	Fountainwell Drama Texts
FH	*Die Neue Gesellschaft/Frankfurter Hefte*
FJS 19	*Fu Jen Studies: Literature and Linguistics* (Taipei)
FLH 7	*Folia Linguistica Historica*
Florilegium	*Florilegium: Carleton Univ. Annual Papers on Classical Antiquity and the Middle Ages*
FMLS 22	*Forum for Modern Language Studies*
FoLi 20	*Folia Linguistica*
FR 22–4	*Feminist Review*
FreeA 4–7	*Free Associations*
FS 40	*French Studies*
FSt 12	*Feminist Studies*
GaR 40	*Georgia Review*
GEFR 17	*George Eliot Fellowship Review*
GeM 22	*Genealogists' Magazine*
Genre 19	*Genre*
Gestus	*Gestus: A Quarterly Journal of Brechtian Studies*
GHJ 9/10	*George Herbert Journal*
GissingN 22	*The Gissing Newsletter*
GJ 61	*Gutenberg-Jahrbuch*
GL 26	*General Linguistics*
GL&L 39/40	*German Life and Letters*
Glossa	*Glossa: An International Journal of Linguistics*
GLS	*Grazer Linguistische Studien*
GR 61	*The Germanic Review*
GrandS 5–6	*Grand Street*
Greyfriar 27	*Greyfriar: Siena Studies in Literature*

GRM 36	*Germanisch-Romanische Monatsschrift*
GSE	Gothenberg Studies in English
GURT	*Georgetown University Round Table on Language and Linguistics*
HC 23	*The Hollins Critic*
HEdQ 26/7	*History of Education Quarterly*
HEI 7	*History of European Ideas*
HeineJ 25	*Heine Jahrbuch*
HEL	*Histoire Épistémologie Langage*
Hermathena 140–1	*Hermathena: A Trinity College Dublin Review*
HeyJ 27	*The Heythrop Journal*
HistJ 29	*The Historical Journal*
History 71	*History: The Journal of the Historical Association*
HJR 7/8	*The Henry James Review* (Baton Rouge, La.)
HL 13	*Historiographia Linguistica*
HLB 34	*Harvard Library Bulletin*
HLQ 43	*The Huntington Library Quarterly*
HNR	Harvester New Readings
HOPE 18	*History of Political Economy*
HPT 7	*History of Political Thought*
HQ 13	*The Hopkins Quarterly*
HRB	*Hopkins Research Bulletin*
HSci 24	*History of Science*
HSE 19	*Hungarian Studies in English*
HSELL 31	*Hiroshima Studies in English Language and Literature*
HSJ 12	*Housman Society Journal*
HSL 18	*University of Hartford Studies in Literature*
HSN	*Hawthorne Society Newsletter*
HSSN 4–7	*The Henry Sweet Society Newsletter*
HSt 8	*Hamlet Studies*
HT 36	*History Today*
HTR 79	*Harvard Theological Review*
HudR 38/9	*Hudson Review*
HumeS 12	*Hume Studies*
HumLov 35	*Humanistica Lovaniensia: Journal of Neo-Latin Studies*
HUSL 14	*Hebrew University Studies in Literature and the Arts*
HWJ 21–2	*History Workshop*
HWS	History Workshop Series
IAN 45	*Izvestiia Akademii Nauk S.S.S.R.* (Moscow)
I&C	*Ideology & Consciousness*
ICS 11	*Illinois Classical Studies*
IF 91	*Indogermanische Forschungen*
IFR 13	*The International Fiction Review*
IJES	*Indian Journal of English Studies*
IJPR	*International Journal for the Philosophy of Religion*
IJSL	*International Journal of the Sociology of Language*
IJWS	*International Journal of Women's Studies*
ILS	*Irish Literary Supplement*
IMB	*International Medieval Bibliography*
IndL 111–16	*Indian Literature*

Inklings 4	*Inklings: Jahrbuch für Literatur und Asthetik*
IowaR 16	*The Iowa Review*
IRAL 24	*IRAL: International Review of Applied Linguistics in Language Teaching*
IS 41	*Italian Studies*
ISh 24	*The Independent Shavian*
ISJR 60/1	*Iowa State Journal of Research*
IUR 16	*Irish University Review: A Journal of Irish Studies*
JAAC 44/5	*Journal of Aesthetics and Art Criticism*
JAAR	*Journal of the American Academy of Religion*
JAF 99	*The Journal of American Folklore*
JAfM	*Journal of African Marxists*
JAMS 39	*Journal of the American Musicological Society*
JAmS 20	*Journal of American Studies*
JArabL 17	*Journal of Arabic Literature*
JBeckS	*Journal of Beckett Studies*
JBS 25	*Journal of British Studies*
JCA	*Journal of the College of Arts* (King Saud University)
JCanL	*Journal of Canadian Literature*
JCC	*Journal of Canadian Culture*
JCF 35/6	*Journal of Canadian Fiction*
JChL 13	*Journal of Child Language*
JCL 21	*The Journal of Commonwealth Literature*
JCSR	*Journal of Canadian Studies/Revue d'Etudes Canadienne*
JCSt 5	*Journal of Caribbean Studies*
JDHLS	*Journal of the D. H. Lawrence Society*
JDJ 5	*John Donne Journal*
JEDRBU	*Journal of the English Dept, Rabindra Bharati Univ.*
JEGP 85	*Journal of English and Germanic Philology*
JEH 37	*The Journal of Ecclesiastical History*
JEn	*Journal of English* (Sana'a University)
JEngL 19	*Journal of English Linguistics*
JENS	*Journal of the Eighteen Nineties Society*
JEP	*Journal of Evolutionary Psychology*
JEPNS 18/19	*Journal of the English Place-Name Society*
JES 16	*Journal of European Studies*
JETS	*Journal of the Evangelical Theological Society*
JFR 23	*Journal of Folklore Research*
JGE 37/8	*JGE: The Journal of General Education*
JGH 6	*Journal of Garden History*
JHI 47	*Journal of the History of Ideas*
JHLP	*Journal of Historical Linguistics and Philology*
JIES 14	*The Journal of Indo-European Studies*
JIL 15	*Journal of Irish Literature*
JIPA 16	*Journal of the International Phonetic Association*
JIWE 14	*Journal of Indian Writing in English*
JJB 19–21	*James Joyce Broadsheet*
JJQ 23/4	*James Joyce Quarterly*
JL 22	*Journal of Linguistics*

JLP	*Journal of Linguistics and Politics*
JLS 15	*Journal of Literary Semantics*
JLVSG	*Journal of the Loughborough Victorian Studies Group*
JMemL 25	*Journal of Memory and Language*
JMH 12	*Journal of Medieval History*
JML 13	*Journal of Modern Literature*
JMMLA	*Journal of the Midwest Modern Language Assoc.*
JMRS 16	*Journal of Medieval and Renaissance Studies*
JNPH 2/3	*Journal of Newspaper and Periodical History*
JNT 16	*Journal of Narrative Technique*
JP 83	*The Journal of Philosophy*
JPC 19/20	*Journal of Popular Culture*
JPCL 1	*Journal of Pidgin and Creole Languages*
JPhon 14	*Journal of Phonetics*
JPJ 10	*Journal of Psychology and Judaism*
JPrag 10	*Journal of Pragmatics*
JPRS 6/7	*Journal of Pre-Raphaelite Studies*
JQ 63	*Journalism Quarterly*
JR 66	*Journal of Religion*
JRH 14	*The Journal of Religious History*
JRMMRA 7	*Journal of the Rocky Mountain Medieval and Renaissance Assoc.*
JRSA 134/5	*Journal of the Royal Society of Arts*
JRUL	*Journal of the Rutgers University Libraries*
JSA 8	*Journal of the Society of Archivists*
JSaga 18	*Journal of the Faculty of Liberal Arts and Science, Saga Univ.*
JSAS 12/13	*Journal of Southern African Studies*
JSSE 6-7	*Journal of the Short Story in English*
JTheoS 37	*The Journal of Theological Studies*
JWCI 49	*Journal of the Warburg and Courtauld Institutes*
JWIL 1	*Journal of West Indian Literature*
JWMS 6/7	*The Journal of the William Morris Society*
JWSL	*Journal of Women's Studies in Literature*
KanQ 18	*Kansas Quarterly*
KJ 60	*The Kipling Journal*
KN 33	*Kwartalnik Neofilologiczny* (Warsaw)
KompH 13-14	*Komparatistische Hefte*
KPAB	*Kentucky Philological Association Bulletin*
KR 8	*Kenyon Review*
KSJ 35	*Keats-Shelley Journal*
KSMB	*Keats-Shelley Memorial Bulletin*
Kuka	*Kuka: Journal of Creative and Critical Writing* (Zaria, Nigeria)
Kunapipi 7/8	*Kunapipi*
KWS	*Key-Word Studies in Chaucer*
L&C 6	*Language and Communication*
Landfall 40	*Landfall: A New Zealand Quarterly*
L&H 12	*Literature and History*
L&P 32	*Literature and Psychology*

L&S 29	*Language and Speech*
Lang 62	*Language: Journal of the Linguistic Society of America*
Lang&S 19	*Language and Style*
LangQ 24/5	*USF Language Quarterly*
LangR	*Language Research*
LangS 8	*Language Sciences*
LanM 80	*Les Langues Modernes*
LB 75	*Leuvense Bijdragen*
LCrit 21	*The Literary Criterion* (Mysore, India)
LCUT 34–7	*The Library Chronicle of the University of Texas at Austin*
LeedsSE 17	*Leeds Studies in English*
Legacy 3	*Legacy: A Journal of Nineteenth-Century American Women Writers*
LeS 21	*Lingua e Stile*
Lexicographica 2	*Lexicographica: International Annual for Lexicography*
LFQ 14	*Literature/Film Quarterly*
LH 7	*Library History*
LHY 27	*The Literary Half-Yearly*
Lib 8	*The Library*
LibrQ 56	*The Library Quarterly*
LingA 16	*Linguistic Analysis*
Ling&P 9	*Linguistics and Philosophy*
LingB 101–6	*Linguistische Berichte*
LingI 17	*Linguistic Inquiry*
LingInv 10	*Lingvisticæ Investigationes*
Lings 24	*Linguistics*
Lingua 68–70	*Lingua: International Review of General Linguistics*
Linguistique 22	*La Linguistique*
LitH	*Literary Horizons*
LitR 29/30	*The Literary Review: An International Journal of Contemporary Writing*
LJGG 27	*Literaturwissenschaftliches Jahrbuch im Auftrage der Görres-Gesellschaft*
LMag 25/6	*London Magazine*
LockeN 17	*The Locke Newsletter*
LongR 31	*Long Room: Bulletin of the Friends of the Library, Trinity College, Dublin*
Lore&L 4	*Lore & Language*
LR 40	*Les Lettres Romanes*
LRB 8	*London Review of Books*
LSE	Lund Studies in English
LSoc 15	*Language in Society*
LST	Longman Study Texts
LTP 5	*LTP: Journal of Literature Teaching Politics*
LTR 6	*London Theatre Record*
LWU 19	*Literatur in Wissenschaft und Unterricht*
MÆ 55	*Medium Ævum*
M&H 14	*Medievalia et Humanistica*
M&L 67	*Music and Letters*

Manuscripta 30	*Manuscripta*
MaRDiE 3	*Medieval and Renaissance Drama in England*
MarkhamR	*Markham Review*
MBL	*Modern British Literature*
MC&S 8	*Media, Culture and Society*
MCJNews	*Milton Centre of Japan News*
McNR 31	*McNeese Review*
MCRel 4	*Mythes, Croyances et Religions dans le Monde Anglo-Saxon*
MCV	Modern Critical Views
MD 29	*Modern Drama*
Meanjin 45	*Meanjin*
MED	*Middle English Dictionary*
MESN 14–15	*Mediaeval English Studies Newsletter*
METh 8	*Medieval English Theatre*
MFS 32	*Modern Fiction Studies*
MHRev 73–4	*The Malahat Review*
MichA 18	*Michigan Academician*
MiltonQ 20	*Milton Quarterly*
MiltonS 22	*Milton Studies*
MinnR 26–7	*Minnesota Review*
MissQ 39	*Mississippi Quarterly*
MJLF 12	*Midwestern Journal of Language and Folklore*
MLAIB	*Modern Language Assoc. International Bibliography*
MLJ 70	*The Modern Language Journal*
MLN 101	[*Modern Language Notes*]
MLNew 17–18	*Malcolm Lowry Review*
MLQ 47	*Modern Language Quarterly*
MLR 81	*The Modern Language Review*
MLS 16	*Modern Language Studies* (a publication of the Northeast Modern Language Association)
MMG	Macmillan Master Guides
ModA 30	*Modern Age: A Quarterly Review*
ModSp 30	*Moderne Sprachen*
Month 21	*The Month: A Review of Christian Thought and World Affairs*
Moreana 89–92	*Moreana: Bulletin Thomas More* (Angers, France)
Mosaic 19	*Mosaic: A Journal for the Interdisciplinary Study of Literature*
MP 83/4	*Modern Philology*
MPHJ	*Middlesex Polytechnic History Journal*
MPR 20	*The Mervyn Peake Review*
MQ 27/8	*Midwest Quarterly*
MQR 25	*Michigan Quarterly Review*
MR 27	*Massachusetts Review*
MRTS	Medieval and Renaissance Texts and Studies
MS 48	*Mediaeval Studies*
MSE 10	*Massachusetts Studies in English*
MSh	Macmillan Shakespeare
MSpr 80	*Moderna Språk*

MSR	Malone Society Reprints
MSSN 17–18	*Medieval Sermon Studies Newsletter*
MT 127	*The Musical Times*
MTJ 24	*Mark Twain Journal*
MW 76	*The Muslim World* (Hartford. Conn.)
NA 2157–60	*Nuova Antologia*
Names 34	*Names: Journal of the American Name Society*
N&Q 33	*Notes and Queries*
NB 74	*Namn och Bygd*
NCaS	New Cambridge Shakespeare
NCBEL	*New Cambridge Bibliography of English Literature*
NCF 40	*Nineteenth-Century Fiction* (now *Nineteenth-Century Literature*)
NCL 41	*Nineteenth-Century Literature*
NConL 16	*Notes on Contemporary Literature*
NCS	New Clarendon Shakespeare
NCTR 14	*Nineteenth Century Theatre Research*
NDQ 54	*North Dakota Quarterly*
NegroD	*Negro Digest*
Neoh 13	*Neohelicon*
Neophil 70	*Neophilologus*
NEQ 59	*The New England Quarterly*
NewA 220–31	*New African*
NewBR 2/3	*New Beacon Review*
NewR	*New Republic*
NewSt	*Newfoundland Studies*
NfN 1–2	*News from Nowhere*
NGC 37–9	*New German Critique*
NGS 14	*New German Studies*
NH 22	*Northern History*
NJL 9	*Nordic Journal of Linguistics*
NL	*Nouvelles Littéraires*
NLH 17/18	*New Literary History: A Journal of Theory and Interpretation*
NLR 155–60	*New Left Review*
NLRev	*New Literature Review*
NLWJ 24	*The National Library of Wales Journal*
NM 87	*Neuphilologische Mitteilungen*
NMAL	*NMAL: Notes on Modern American Literature*
NMer	New Mermaids
NMS 30	*Nottingham Medieval Studies*
NN	*Nordiska Namenstudier*
NNER	*Northern New England Review*
Nomina 10	*Nomina: A Journal of Name Studies Relating to Great Britain and Ireland*
NoP 9	*Northern Perspective*
NOR 13	*New Orleans Review*
Novel 19/20	*Novel: A Forum on Fiction*
NOWELE 7–8	*NOWELE (North-Western European Language Evolution)*

NPS	New Penguin Shakespeare
NRF 388–91	La Nouvelle Revue Française
NS 85	Die Neueren Sprachen
NSS	New Swan Shakespeare
NTQ 2	New Theatre Quarterly
NVSAWC 12	Newsletter of the Victorian Studies Assoc. of Western Canada
NwJ	Northward Journal
NWR 24	Northwest Review
NYH 67	New York History
NYLF	New York Literary Forum
NYRB 32/3	The New York Review of Books
NYT	New York Times
NYTBR 91	The New York Times Book Review
OA	Oxford Authors
OB	Ord och Bild
OBSP	Oxford Bibliographical Society Publications
OED	Oxford English Dictionary
OENews 19/20	Old English Newsletter
OET	Oxford English Texts
OH 6	Over Here: An American Studies Journal
OHEL	Oxford History of English Literature
OhR 36–7	The Ohio Review
OL 41	Orbis Litterarum
OLR 8	Oxford Literary Review
OPBS	Occasional Papers of the Bibliographical Society
OpL	Open Letter
OPLiLL	Occasional Papers in Linguistics and Language Learning
OS	Oxford Shakespeare
OSS	Oxford Shakespeare Studies
Outrider 18	The Outrider: A Publication of the Wyoming State Library
Overland 102–5	Overland
PA	Présence Africaine
PAAS 96	Proceedings of the American Antiquarian Society
Paideuma 15	Paideuma: A Journal Devoted to Ezra Pound Scholarship
P&L 10	Philosophy and Literature
P&P 110–13	Past and Present
P&R 19	Philosophy and Rhetoric
PAPA 12	Publications of the Arkansas Philological Association
PAPS 130	Proceedings of the American Philosophical Society
Parabola 12	Parabola: The Magazine of Myth and Tradition
Paragraph 7–8	Paragraph: The Journal of the Modern Critical Theory Group
ParisR 99–101	The Paris Review
Parnassus 13/14	Parnassus: Poetry in Review
PastM	Past Masters
PaterN 17–18	Pater Newsletter
PAus	Poetry Australia

PBA 71	*Proceedings of the British Academy*
PBerLS 11	*Proceedings of the Berkeley Linguistics Society*
PBSA 80	*Papers of the Bibliographical Society of America*
PCL 12	*Perspectives on Contemporary Literature*
PCLAC	*Proceedings of the California Linguistics Association Conference*
PCLS	Proceedings of the Comparative Literature Symposium (Texas)
PCP 21	*Pacific Coast Philology*
PEAN 2	*Proceedings of the English Association North*
PELL	*Papers on English Language and Literature* (Japan)
Peritia 5	*Peritia: Journal of the Medieval Academy of Ireland*
Persuasions 8	*Persuasions: Journal of the Jane Austen Society of North America*
PHOS	Publishing History Occasional Series
PhT 30	*Philosophy Today*
PIL 19	*Papers in Linguistics*
PJCL 6–7	*The Prairie Journal of Canadian Literature*
PLL 22	*Papers on Language and Literature*
PLPLS 20	*Proceedings of the Leeds Philosophical and Literary Society, Literary and Historical Section*
PM	Penguin Masterstudies
PMLA 101	*Publications of the Modern Language Association of America*
PNotes 17	*Pynchon Notes*
PNR 12/13	*PN Review*
PoeS 19	*Poe Studies*
Poetica 23	*Poetica: Zeitschrift für Sprach-und Literaturwissenschaft* (Amsterdam)
PoeticaJ 24	*Poetica: An International Journal of Linguistic-Literary Studies* (Tokyo)
Poetics 15	*Poetics: International Review for the Theory of Literature*
PoetryR 75/6	*Poetry Review*
PoetryW 21/2	*Poetry Wales*
PostS 5/6	*Post Script: Essays in Film and the Humanities*
PoT 7	*Poetics Today*
PowysR 18–19	*The Powys Review*
PP	Penguin Passnotes
PP 68	*Philologica Pragensia*
PPMRC	*Proceedings of the International Patristic, Mediaeval and Renaissance Conference*
PPR 46/7	*Philosophy and Phenomenological Research*
PQ 65	*Philological Quarterly*
PQM	*Pacific Quarterly* (Moana)
PR 53	*Partisan Review*
PrairieF 7	*Prairie Fire*
Praxis	*Praxis: A Journal of Cultural Criticism*
Prépub 98–104	*(Pré)publications*
PRIA 86	*Proceedings of the Royal Irish Academy*

PRIAA	Publications of the Research Institute of the Åbo Akademi Foundation
PRMCLS	*Papers from the Regional Meetings of the Chicago Linguistics Society*
Prospects 9	*Prospects: An Annual Journal of American Cultural Studies*
Proteus 3	*Proteus: A Journal of Ideas*
Proverbium 3	*Proverbium*
PrS 60	*The Prairie Schooner*
PSt 9	*Prose Studies*
PTBI	Publications of the Sir Thomas Browne Institute
PubH 19-20	*Publishing History*
PULC 46/7	*Princeton University Library Chronicle*
PURBA 17	*Panjab Univ. Research Bulletin (Arts)*
PVR 14	*Platte Valley Review*
PY 3	*Phonology Yearbook*
QI 7	*Quaderni d'Italianistica*
QJS 72	*Quarterly Journal of Speech*
QLing	*Quantitative Linguistics*
QQ 93	*Queen's Quarterly*
Quadrant 30	*Quadrant* (Sydney)
Quarendo 16	*Quarendo*
RAL 17	*Research in African Literatures*
RALS 16	*Resources for American Literary Study*
Ramus 15	*Ramus: Critical Studies in Greek and Roman Literature*
R&L 18	*Religion and Literature*
Raritan 5/6	*Raritan: A Quarterly Review*
RBPH 64	*Revue Belge de Philologie et d'Histoire*
RCEI	*Revista Canaria de Estudios Ingleses*
RCF 6	*Review of Contemporary Fiction*
RDN 6/7	*Renaissance Drama Newsletter*
RE 13-15	*Revue d'Esthétique*
ReAL 12/13	*Re: Artes Liberales*
REALB 4	*REAL: The Yearbook of Research in English and American Literature* (Berlin)
RECTR 1	*Restoration and Eighteenth-Century Theatre Research*
RedL 18-20	*Red Letters: A Journal of Cultural Politics*
REED	Records of Early English Drama
REEDN 10	*Records of Early English Drama Newsletter*
Ren&R 10	Renaissance and Reformation
Renascence 38/9	*Renascence: Essays on Value in Literature*
RenD 17	*Renaissance Drama*
RenP	*Renaissance Papers*
RenQ 39	*Renaissance Quarterly*
Rep 13-16	*Representations*
RES 37	*The Review of English Studies*
Restoration 10	*Restoration: Studies in English Literary Culture, 1660-1700*
Rev 8	*Review* (Blacksburg, Va.)
Revels	Revels Plays

RevelsCL	Revels Plays Companion Library
RFEA 11	*Revue Française d'Etudes Américaines*
RH 18	*Recusant History*
Rhetorica 4	*Rhetorica: A Journal of the History of Rhetoric*
Rhetorik 5	*Rhetorik: ein internationales Jahrbuch*
RHL 86	*Revue d'Histoire Littéraire de la France*
RHT	*Revue d'Histoire du Théâtre*
Ricardian 7	*The Ricardian: Journal of the Richard III Society*
RL	Rereading Literature
RLC 60	*Revue de Littérature Comparée*
RLMC 39	*Rivista di Letterature Moderne e Comparate*
RMR 40	*Rocky Mountain Review of Language and Literature*
RMS 30	*Renaissance and Modern Studies*
RMSt 12	*Reading Medieval Studies*
RomN 26/7	*Romance Notes*
ROO	*Room of One's Own: A Feminist Journal of Literature and Criticism*
RORD 29	*Research Opportunities in Renaissance Drama*
RPT	Russian Poetics in Translation
RQ	*Riverside Quarterly*
RRDS	Regents Renaissance Drama Series
RRestDS	Regents Restoration Drama Series
RSQ 16	*Rhetoric Society Quarterly*
RUO 56	*Revue de l'Université d'Ottawa*
RuskN 30/1	*Ruskin Newsletter*
SAC 8	*Studies in the Age of Chaucer*
SAF 14	*Studies in American Fiction*
SagaB 22	*Saga-Book (Viking Society for Northern Research)*
Sagetrieb 5	*Sagetrieb: A Journal Devoted to Poets in the Pound-H.D.-Williams Tradition*
Sal 69–72	*Salmagundi: A Quarterly of the Humanities and Social Sciences*
SAntS 4	*Studia Anthroponymica Scandinavica*
SAP 19	*Studia Anglica Posnaniensia*
SAQ 85	*South Atlantic Quarterly*
SAR	*Studies in the American Renaissance*
SatR	*Saturday Review*
SB 39	*Studies in Bibliography*
SBHC 14	*Studies in Browning and His Circle*
Scan 25	*Scandinavica: An International Journal of Scandinavian Studies*
ScanS 58	*Scandinavian Studies*
SCent 1	*The Seventeenth Century*
SCER	*Society for Critical Exchange Report*
SCJ 17	*The Sixteenth Century Journal*
SCL	*Studies in Canadian Literature*
ScLJ 13	*Scottish Literary Journal: A Review of Studies in Scottish Language and Literature*
ScLJ(S) 24–5	*Scottish Literary Journal Supplement*
SCN 44	*Seventeenth-Century News*

SCR 18/19	*The South Carolina Review*
SCRev	*South Central Review*
Scriblerian 18/19	*The Scriblerian and the Kit Cats: A Newsjournal Devoted to Pope, Swift, and their Circle*
Scriptorium 40	*Scriptorium: International Review of Manuscript Studies*
SDR 24	*South Dakota Review*
SECC 15	*Studies in Eighteenth-Century Culture*
SED	*Survey of English Dialects*
SEL	Studies in English Literature
SEL 26	*Studies in English Literature 1500–1900* (Rice University)
SELing	*Studies in English Linguistics* (Tokyo)
SELit 61	*Studies in English Literature* (Japan)
Semiosis 41–4	*Semiosis: Internationale Zeitschrift für Semiotik und Ästhetik*
Semiotica 58–62	*Semiotica: Journal of the International Assoc. for Semiotic Studies*
SER	*Studien zur Englischen Romantik*
SF&R	*Scholars' Facsimiles and Reprints*
SFic	*Science Fiction: A Review of Speculative Literature*
SFNL 10/11	*Shakespeare on Film Newsletter*
SFQ	*Southern Folklore Quarterly*
SFR 10	*Stanford French Review*
SFS 13	*Science-Fiction Studies*
SH	*Studia Hibernica* (Dublin)
ShakB	*Shakespeare Bulletin*
ShakS 18	*Shakespeare Studies* (Tennessee)
ShawR 6	*Shaw: The Annual of Bernard Shaw Studies*
ShJE 122	*Shakespeare Jahrbuch* [East Germany] (Weimar)
ShJW	*Deutsche Shakespeare-Gesellschaft West Jahrbuch* (Bochum)
ShN 36	*The Shakespeare Newsletter*
SHR 20	*Southern Humanities Review*
ShS 39	*Shakespeare Survey*
ShStud 23	*Shakespeare Studies* (Tokyo)
SIcon	*Studies in Iconography*
Signs 11/12	*Signs: Journal of Women in Culture and Society*
SiHoLS	Studies in the History of the Language Sciences
SIM 20	*Studies in Music*
SIR 25	*Studies in Romanticism*
SJS 12	*San José Studies*
SL 40	*Studia Linguistica*
SLang 10	*Studies in Language*
SLitI 19	*Studies in the Literary Imagination*
SLJ 18/19	*Southern Literary Journal*
SLRev 3	*Stanford Literature Review*
SLSc 16	*Studies in the Linguistic Sciences*
SMC	Studies in Medieval Culture
SMed 27	*Studi Medievali*

SMLit	*Studies in Mystical Literature* (Taiwan)
SMRH 8	*Studies in Medieval and Renaissance History*
SMy	*Studia Mystica*
SN 58	*Studia Neophilologica*
SNew	*Sidney Newsletter*
SNNTS 18	*Studies in the Novel* (North Texas State University)
SOÅ	*Sydsvenska Ortnamnssällskapets Årsskrift*
SoAR 51	*South Atlantic Review*
SocN 16	*Sociolinguistics*
SocT 7	*Social Text*
SohoB	Soho Bibliographies
SoQ 24/5	*The Southern Quarterly*
SoR 22	*The Southern Review* (Louisiana)
SoRA 19	*Southern Review* (Adelaide) .
Soundings	*Soundings: An Interdisciplinary Journal*
Southerly 46	*Southerly: A Review of Australian Literature*
SovL 454–65	*Soviet Literature*
SP 83	*Studies in Philology*
Spectrum	*Spectrum*
Speculum 61	*Speculum: A Journal of Medieval Studies*
SPELL	Swiss Papers in English Language and Literature
Sphinx	*The Sphinx: A Magazine of Literature and Society*
SpM	*Spicilegio Moderno*
SpNL 17	*Spenser Newsletter*
Sprachwiss 11	*Sprachwissenschaft*
SPWVSRA 11	*Selected Papers from the W. Virginia Shakespeare and Renaissance Assoc.*
SQ 37	*Shakespeare Quarterly*
SR 94	*The Sewanee Review*
SRen	*Studies in the Renaissance*
SRSR 85–8	*Status Report on Speech Research* (Haskins Laboratories)
SSEL	Stockholm Studies in English
SSELER	Salzburg Studies in English Literature: Elizabethan and Renaissance
SSELJDS	Salzburg Studies in English Literature: Jacobean Drama Series
SSELPDPT	Salzburg Studies in English Literature: Poetic Drama and Poetic Theory
SSELRR	Salzburg Studies in English Literature: Romantic Reassessment
SSEng 11/12	*Sydney Studies in English*
SSF 23	*Studies in Short Fiction*
SSL 21	*Studies in Scottish Literature*
SSMP	Stockholm Studies in Modern Philology
SSt 6	*Spenser Studies*
SStud 1	*Swift Studies: The Annual of the Ehrenpreis Center*
STC	*Short-Title Catalogue*
StHum 13	*Studies in the Humanities*

StIn	*Studi Inglesi*
StLF 12	*Studi di Letteratura Francese*
StQ 19	*Steinbeck Quarterly*
StR	*Structuralist Review*
StTCL 10/11	*Studies in Twentieth Century Literature*
Style 20	*Style* (De Kalb, Ill.)
SUAS	Stratford-upon-Avon Studies
SubStance 49–51	*SubStance: A Review of Theory and Literary Criticism*
SUS	*Susquehanna University Studies*
SVEC 242	*Studies on Voltaire and the Eighteenth Century*
SWPLL	*Sheffield Working Papers in Language and Linguistics*
SWR 71	*Southwest Review*
TA	*Theatre Annual*
T&P	Text and Performance
TCBS 9	*Transactions of the Cambridge Bibliographical Society*
TCE 18/19	*Texas College English*
TCL 32	*Twentieth Century Literature*
TCS 3	*Theory, Culture & Society: Explorations in Critical Social Science*
TD 8	*Themes in Drama*
TDR 30	*The Drama Review*
TEAS	Twayne's English Authors Series
TEBS	*Edinburgh Bibliographical Society Transactions*
Telos	*Telos: A Quarterly Journal of Post-Critical Thought*
Text	*Text: Transactions of the Society for Textual Scholarship*
TH	*Texas Humanist*
THA 4	*Thomas Hardy Annual*
ThC	*Theatre Crafts*
Theoria 67–8	*Theoria: A Journal of Studies in the Arts, Humanities and Social Sciences* (Natal, S. Africa)
THES	*Times Higher Education Supplement*
THIC	*Theatre History in Canada*
THJ 2	*The Thomas Hardy Journal*
ThoreauQ 18	*The Thoreau Quarterly: A Journal of Literary and Philosophical Studies*
Thought 61	*Thought: A Review of Culture and Ideas*
Thph	*Theatrephile*
ThR 11	*Theatre Research International*
ThreR 7	*The Threepenny Review*
ThS 27	*Theatre Survey: The American Journal of Theatre History*
THStud 6	*Theatre History Studies*
THY	*The Thomas Hardy Yearbook*
TiLSM	Trends in Linguistics Studies and Monographs
TJ 38	*Theatre Journal*
TJS	*Transactions* (The Johnson Society)
TkR	*Tamkang Review*
TLS	*The Times Literary Supplement*

TN 40	*Theatre Notebook*
TP	*Terzo Programma*
TPLL	*Tilbury Papers in Language and Literature*
TPS	*Transactions of the Philological Society*
Traditio 42	*Traditio: Studies in Ancient and Medieval History, Thought, and Religion*
TRB 4	*The Tennyson Research Bulletin*
TRHS 36	*Transactions of the Royal Historical Society*
TriQ 65-7	*TriQuarterly*
Trivium 21	*Trivium*
TSAR 4/5	*The Toronto South Asian Review*
TSB 174-7	*Thoreau Society Bulletin*
TSL 30	*Tennessee Studies in Literature*
TSLang	Typological Studies in Language
TSLL 28	*Texas Studies in Literature and Language*
TSWL 5	*Tulsa Studies in Women's Literature*
TTR	*Trinidad and Tobago Review*
TUSAS	Twayne's United States Authors Series
TWAS	Twayne's World Authors Series
TWN 10	*The Thomas Wolfe Review*
TYDS	*Transactions of the Yorkshire Dialect Society*
UCrow 6	*The Upstart Crow*
UCTSE	*University of Cape Town Studies in English*
UDR	*University of Dayton Review*
UE 37/8	*The Use of English*
UEAPL	*UEA Papers in Linguistics*
UES	*Unisa English Studies*
ULR 28-9	*University of Leeds Review*
UMSE 7	*University of Mississippi Studies in English*
UOQ 56	*University of Ottawa Quarterly*
USSE	*University of Saga Studies in English*
UTQ 55/6	*University of Toronto Quarterly*
UWR 19	*The University of Windsor Review*
VCT	Les Voies de la Création Théâtrale
VEAW	Varieties of English Around the World
Verbatim 12/13	*Verbatim: The Language Quarterly*
VIA 8	*VIA: The Journal of the Graduate School of Fine Arts, Univ. of Pennsylvania*
Viator 17	*Viator: Medieval and Renaissance Studies*
VIJ 14	*Victorians Institute Journal*
VN 73-4	*Victorian Newsletter*
VP 24	*Victorian Poetry*
VPR 19	*Victorian Periodicals Review*
VQR 62	*The Virginia Quarterly Review*
VS 29/30	*Victorian Studies*
VSB 10	*Victorian Studies Bulletin*
WAL 20/1	*Western American Literature*
W&I 2	*Word & Image*
W&L	*Women and Literature*

WascanaR	*Wascana Review*
WBEP	Wiener Beiträge zur Englischen Philologie
WC 17	*The Wordsworth Circle*
WC	World's Classics
WCR 20/1	*West Coast Review*
WCSJ	*Wilkie Collins Society Journal*
WCWR 12	*William Carlos Williams Review*
Westerly 31	*Westerly: A Quarterly Review*
WF 45	*Western Folklore*
WHR 40	*Western Humanities Review*
WLT 60	*World Literature Today* (formerly *Books Abroad*)
WLWE 26	*World Literature Written in English*
WolfenbüttelerB	*Wolfenbütteler Beiträge: Aus den Schätzen der Herzog August Bibliothek*
Word 37	*WORD: Journal of the International Linguistic Assoc.*
WQ 10	*The Wilson Quarterly*
WS 12/13	*Women's Studies: An Interdisciplinary Journal*
WSIF 9	*Women's Studies International Forum*
WSJour 10	*The Wallace Stevens Journal*
WTJ 48	*The Westminster Theological Journal*
WTW	Writers and their Work
WVUPP 31	*West Virginia University Philological Papers*
WWR 3/4	*Walt Whitman Quarterly Review*
XUS	*Xavier Review*
YCC	*Yearbook of Comparative Criticism*
YeA 4	*Yeats Annual*
YER 8	*Yeats Eliot Review*
YES 16	*The Yearbook of English Studies*
YFS 70-1	*Yale French Studies*
YNS	York Notes Series
YPL 12	*York Papers in Linguistics*
YR 75/6	*The Yale Review*
YULG 60/1	*Yale University Library Gazette*
YWES 64	*The Year's Work in English Studies*
ZAA 34	*Zeitschrift für Anglistik und Amerikanistik*
ZCP 41	*Zeitschrift für Celtische Philologie*
ZDA 115	*Zeitschrift für Deutsches Altertum und Deutsche Literatur*
ZDL	*Zeitschrift für Dialektologie und Linguistik*
ZGKS 10-11	*Zeitschrift der Gesellschaft für Kanada-Studien*
ZGL 14	*Zeitschrift für Germanistische Linguistik*
ZPSK 39	*Zeitschrift für Phonetik, Sprachwissenschaft und Kommunikationsforschung*
ZSpr 5	*Zeitschrift für Sprachwissenschaft*
ZVS 99	*Zeitschrift für Vergleichende Sprachforschung*

Volume numbers of journals for 1986 have been supplied where they exist and where they have been ascertainable. A dash between the figures represents more than one consecutive volume for the year, an oblique volumes which straddle the turn of the year.

2. Publishers

AAAH	Acta Academiae Åboensis Humaniora, Åbo, Finland
A&B	Allison & Busby, London
A&R	Angus & Robertson, North Ryde, N.S.W.
A&U	Allen & Unwin, now Unwin Hyman
A&UA	Allen & Unwin, North Sydney N.S.W.
A&W	Almqvist & Wiksell International, Stockholm
AarhusU	Aarhus UP, Aarhus, Denmark
AberdeenU	Aberdeen UP, Aberdeen
Abhinav	Abhinav Pubns, New Delhi
Abingdon	Abingdon Press, Nashville, Tenn.
ABL	Armstrong Browning Library, Waco, Texas
Ablex	Ablex Pub., Norwood, N.J.
Åbo	Åbo Akademi, Åbo, Finland
Abrams	Harry N. Abrams Inc., New York
Academic	Academic Press, London and Orlando, Fla.
Academy	The Academy Press, Dublin
AcademyC	Academy Chicago Publishers, Chicago
AcademyE	Academy Editions, London
ACarS	Association for Caribbean Studies, Coral Gables, Fla.
ACCO	ACCO, Leuven, Belgium
ACS	Assoc. for Canadian Studies, Ottawa
Addison-Wesley	Addison-Wesley, Reading, Mass.
Adosa	Adosa, Clermont-Ferrand, France
AF	Akademisk Forlag, Copenhagen
AFP	Associated Faculty Press, New York
Africana	Africana Pub. Co., New York
AIAS	Australian Institute of Aboriginal Studies, Canberra
Ajanta	Ajanta Pubns, Delhi
AK	Akadémiai Kiadó, Budapest
Al&Ba	Allyn & Bacon, Boston, Mass.
Albion	Albion, Appalachian State Univ., Boone, N.C.
Alderman	Alderman Press, London
Allen	W. H. Allen, London
AM	Aubier Montaigne, Paris
AMAES	Association des Médiévistes Angliciste de l'Enseigne-ment Supérieur, Paris
AmberL	Amber Lane, Oxford
AMS	AMS Press Inc., New York
AMU	Adam Mickiewicz Univ., Posnan
Anansi	Anansi Press, Toronto
Anvil	Anvil Press Poetry, London
APA	APA, Maarssen, Netherlands
APL	American Poetry and Literature Press, Philadelphia
Appletree	Appletree Press, Belfast
APS	American Philosophical Society, Philadelphia
Aquarian	The Aquarian Press, Wellingborough, Northants.
ArborH	Arbor House Pub., New York
Archon	Archon Books, Hamden, Conn.

ArchP	Architectural Press Books, Guildford, Surrey
Ardis	Ardis Pubs., Ann Arbor, Mich.
Ariel	Ariel Press, London
Ark	Ark Paperbacks, London
Arkona	Arkona Forlaget, Aarhus, Denmark
Arnold	Edward Arnold, London
Arrow	Arrow Books, London
ASECS	American Society for Eighteenth-Century Studies, c/o Ohio State Univ., Columbus
Aslib	Aslib, London
ASLS	Assoc. for Scottish Literary Studies, Aberdeen
ASP	Applied Science Pubs. Ltd, London
ASU	Arizona State Univ., Tempe
ATCAL	Association for the Teaching of Caribbean and African Literature
Atheneum	Atheneum Pub., New York
Athlone	Athlone Press, London
AucklandU	Auckland UP, Auckland
AUG	Acta Universitatis Gothoburgensis, Sweden
AUP	Associated University Presses, London and Toronto
AUPG	Academic & University Pubs. Group Ltd, London
AUU	Acta Universitatis Umensis, Umeå, Sweden
AUUp	Acta Universitatis Upsaliensis, Uppsala
Avebury	Avebury Pub., Amersham, Bucks.
Avero	Avero Pubns, Newcastle upon Tyne
A-W	Arnold-Wheaton, Leeds
AWP	Africa World Press, Trenton, N.J.
BA	British Academy, London
Bagel	August Bagel Verlag, Düsseldorf
Bamberger	Bamberger Books, Flint, Mich.
B&B	Boydell & Brewer, Woodbridge, Suffolk
B&E	Buchan & Enright, London
B&H	Bell & Hyman, London
B&J	Barrie & Jenkins, London
B&N	Barnes & Noble, Totowa, N.J.
B&O	Burns & Oates, Tunbridge Wells, Kent
B&S	Benskin and Samuels, Univ. of Edinburgh
BAR	British Archaeological Reports, Oxford
Barnes	A. S. Barnes, San Diego, Calif.
Batsford	B. T. Batsford, London
BBC	British Broadcasting Corporation, London
BClark	Bruccoli Clark Pub., Columbia, S.C.
BCP	Bristol Classical Press, Bristol
Beacon	Beacon Press, Boston, Mass.
Beck	C. H. Beck'sche Verlagsbuchhandlung, Munich
Becket	Becket Pubns, Oxford
Belknap	Belknap Press, Cambridge, Mass.
Belles Lettres	Société d'Edition les Belles Lettres, Paris
Bellflower	Bellflower Press, Case Univ., Cleveland, Ohio

Benjamins	John Benjamins, Amsterdam
BenjaminsNA	John Benjamins North America, Philadelphia
Benn	Ernest Benn, London
BennC	Bennington College, Bennington, Vt.
Berg	Berg Pub., Leamington Spa
BFI	British Film Institute, London
BGUP	Bowling Green Univ. Popular Press, Bowling Green, Ohio
BibS	Bibliographical Society, London
Bilingual	Bilingual Press, Arizona State Univ., Tempe
Bingley	Clive Bingley, London
Binnacle	Binnacle Press, London
Biografia	Biografia Pub., London
BL	British Library, London
Black	Adam & Charles Black, London
Black Cat	Black Cat Press, Blackrock, Eire
Blackie	Blackie & Son, Glasgow
Black Moss	Black Moss, Windsor, Ont.
Blackstaff	Blackstaff Press, Belfast
Blackwell	Basil Blackwell, Oxford
BlackwellR	Blackwell Reference, Oxford
Blackwood	Blackwood, Pillans & Wilson, Edinburgh
Bl&Br	Blond & Briggs, London
Blandford	Blandford Press, Dorset
Bloodaxe	Bloodaxe Books, Newcastle upon Tyne
Bloomsbury	Bloomsbury Pub., London
BM	Bobbs-Merrill, New York
BMP	British Museum Pubns, London
Bodleian	The Bodleian Library, Oxford
Bodley	The Bodley Head, London
Bogle	Bogle L'Ouverture, London
BoiseU	Boise State UP, Boise, Idaho
Borealis	Borealis Press, Ottawa
Borgo	Borgo Press, San Bernardino, Calif.
BostonAL	Boston Athenaeum Library, Boston, Mass.
Bouma	Bouma's Boekhuis, Gröningen, Netherlands
Bowker	R. R. Bowker Co., New York
Boyars	Marion Boyars, London and Boston, Mass.
Boydell	The Boydell Press, Woodbridge, Suffolk
Boyes	Megan Boyes, Allestree, Derby.
Bran's Head	Bran's Head Books, Frome, Somerset
Breakwater	Breakwater Books, St John's, Newfoundland
Brentham	Brentham Press, London
Brewer	D. S. Brewer, Woodbridge, Suffolk
Bridge	Bridge Pub., S. Plainfield, N.J.
Brill	E. J. Brill, Leiden
Brilliance	Brilliance Books, London
Browne	Sinclair Browne, London
Brownstone	Brownstone Books, Madison, Ind.
BrownU	Brown UP, Providence, R.I.

BSB	Black Swan Books, Redding Ridge, Conn.
BSP	Black Sparrow Press, Santa Barbara, Calif.
BSU	Ball State Univ., Muncie, Ind.
BuckU	Bucknell UP, Lewisburg, Pa.
Bulzoni	Bulzoni Editore, Rome
Burnett	Burnett Books, London
Buske	Helmut Buske, Hamburg
CA	Creative Arts Book Co., Berkeley, Calif.
CAAS	Connecticut Academy of Arts and Sciences, New Haven, Conn.
Cadmus	Cadmus Editions, Tiburon, Calif.
Cairns	Francis Cairns, Univ. of Liverpool
Calaloux	Calaloux Pubns, Ithaca, N.Y.
Calder	John Calder, London
Camden	Camden Press, London
C&G	Carroll & Graf, New York
C&W	Chatto & Windus, London
Canongate	Canongate Pub., Edinburgh
Cape	Jonathan Cape, London
Capra	Capra Press, Santa Barbara, Calif.
Carcanet	The Carcanet New Press, Manchester, Lancs.
CaribB	Caribbean Books, Parkersburg, Iowa
Carleton	Carleton UP, Ottawa
Cass	Frank Cass, London
Cassell	Cassell & Co., London
Cave	Godfrey Cave Associates, London
CBA	Council for British Archaeology, London
CCP	Canadian Children's Press, Guelph, Ont.
CCS	Centre for Canadian Studies, Mt Allison Univ., N.B.
CDSH	Centre de Documentation Sciences Humaines, Paris
Century	Century Pub., London
Ceolfrith	Ceolfrith Press, Sunderland, Tyne and Wear
CESR	Société des Amis du Centre d'Etudes Superieures de la Renaissance, Tours
CFA	Canadian Federation for the Humanities, Ottawa
C-H	Chadwyck-Healey, Cambridge
CH	Croom Helm, London
Champaign	Champaign Public Library and Information Center, Champaign, Ill.
Champion	Librairie Honoré Champion, Paris
Chand	S. Chand, Madras
ChelseaH	Chelsea House Pub., New York
Christendom	Christendom Pubns, Front Royal, Va.
Chronicle	Chronicle Books, San Francisco
ChuoUL	Chuo University Library, Tokyo
Churchman	Churchman Pub., Worthing, W. Sussex
Cisalpino–Goliardica	Cisalpino–La Goliardica, Milan
Cistercian	Cistercian Pub., Kalamazoo, Mich.
CL	City Lights Books, San Francisco
CLA	Canadian Library Association, Ottawa

Clarendon	The Clarendon Press, Oxford
Clarion	Clarion State College, Clarion, Pa.
Clark	T. & T. Clark, Edinburgh
Clarke	James Clarke, Cambridge
Clunie	Clunie Press, Strathtay, Perthshire
CMERS	Center for Medieval and Early Renaissance Studies, Binghamton, N.Y.
CML	William Andrews Clark Memorial Library, Los Angeles
CMST	Centre for Medieval Studies, Univ. of Toronto
Colleagues	Colleagues Press, East Lansing, Mich.
College-Hill	College-Hill Press, San Diego, Calif.
Collins	William Collins Sons & Co., London
ColU	Columbia UP, New York
Comedia	Comedia Publishing Group, London
Comet	Comet Books, London
Compton	The Compton Press, Tisbury, Wilts.
Constable	Constable & Co. Ltd, London
Contemporary	Contemporary Books, Chicago
Continuum	Continuum Pub., New York
Corgi	Corgi Books, London
CorkU	Cork UP, Cork, Eire
Cormorant	Cormorant Press, Victoria, B.C.
CornU	Cornell UP, Ithaca, N.Y.
Coronado	Coronado Press, Lawrence, Kansas
Cosmo	Cosmo Pubns, New Delhi
Cowley	Cowley Pubns, Cambridge, Mass.
Cowper	Cowper House, Pacific Grove, Calif.
Crossroad	Crossroad Pub., New York
Crown	Crown Pub., New York
Crowood	The Crowood Press, Marlborough, Wilts.
CSU	Cleveland State University, Cleveland, Ohio
CUAP	Catholic Univ. of America Press, Washington, D.C.
Cuff	Harry Cuff Publications, St John's, Newfoundland
CUP	Cambridge University Press, Cambridge
Currey	James Currey, London
CV	Cherry Valley Editions, Rochester, N.Y.
CVK	Cornelson-Velhagen & Klasing, Berlin
CWU	Carl Winter Universitätsverlag, Heidelberg
Da Capo	Da Capo Press, New York
Dacorum	Dacorum College, Hemel Hempstead, Herts.
Dalkey	Dalkey Archive Press, Elmwood Park, Ill.
D&C	David & Charles, Newton Abbot, Devon
D&M	Douglas & McIntyre, Vancouver, B.C.
Dangaroo	Dangaroo Press, Mundelstrup, Denmark
Dawson	Dawson & Sons, Folkestone, Kent
DBP	Drama Book Pub., New York
De Graaf	De Graaf, Nieuwkoop, Netherlands
Denoël	Denoël S.A.R.L., Paris
Dent	J. M. Dent, London
DentA	Dent Australia, Vic.

Deutsch	André Deutsch, London
Didier	Didier Erudition, Paris
Doaba	Doaba House, Delhi
Dobson	Dobson Books, Durham
Dolmen	Dolmen Press, Portlaoise, Eire
Donald	John Donald, Edinburgh
Donker	Adriaan Donker, Johannesburg
Doubleday	Doubleday, New York
Dove	Dove, Sydney
Dover	Dover Pubns, New York
Drew	Richard Drew, Glasgow
Droz	Librairie Droz S.A., Geneva
DublinU	Dublin UP, Dublin
Duckworth	Gerald Duckworth, London
DukeU	Duke UP, Durham, N.C.
Dundurn	Dundurn Press, Toronto and London, Ont.
Duquesne	Duquesne UP, Pittsburgh
Dutton	E. P. Dutton, New York
DWT	Dr Williams's Trust, London
EA	English Association, London
Eason	Eason & Son, Dublin
Ebony	Ebony Books, Melbourne
Ecco	Ecco Press, New York
ECNRS	Editions du Centre National de la Recherche Scientifique, Paris
ECW	ECW Press, Downsview, Ont.
Eden	Eden Press, Montreal and St Albans, Vt.
EdinU	Edinburgh UP, Edinburgh
Eerdmans	William Eerdmans, Grand Rapids, Mich.
EETS	Early English Text Society, Oxford
Ember	Ember Press, Brixham, South Devon
EMSH	Editions de la Maison des Sciences de l'Homme, Paris
Enitharmon	Enitharmon Press, London
Enzyklopädie	Enzyklopädie, Leipzig
EPNS	English Place-Name Society, Notts.
Eriksson	Paul Eriksson, Middlebury, Vt.
Erskine	Erskine Press, Harleston, Norfolk
ESI	Edizioni Scientifiche Italiane, Naples
ESL	Edizioni di Storia e Letteratura, Rome
EUL	Edinburgh University Library, Edinburgh
Europa	Europa Pubns, London
Exile	Exile Editions, Toronto, Ont.
Eyre	Eyre Methuen, London
FAB	Free Association Books, London
Faber	Faber & Faber, London
FAC	Fédération d'activités culturelles, Paris
FACP	Fremantle Arts Centre Press, Fremantle, W.A.
FALS	Foundation for Australian Literary Studies, James Cook Univ. of N. Queensland
F&F	Fels & Firn Press, San Anselmo, Calif.

F&S	Feffer & Simons, Amsterdam
F-B	Ford-Brown, Houston, Texas
FDU	Fairleigh Dickinson UP, Madison, N.J.
FE	Fourth Estate, London
Feminist	Feminist Press, New York
FictionColl	Fiction Collective, Brooklyn College, Brooklyn, N.Y.
Fine	Donald Fine, New York
Fink	Fink Verlag, Munich
Flammarion	Flammarion, Paris
FlindersU	Flinders Univ. of South Australia
FlorSU	Florida State Univ., Tallahassee, Fla.
FOF	Facts on File, Oxford
Folger	The Folger Shakespeare Library, Washington, D.C.
Fontana	Fontana Press, London
FordU	Fordham UP, New York
Foris	Foris Pubns, Dordrecht
Forsten	Egbert Forsten Pub., Groningen, Netherlands
Fortress	Fortress Press, Philadelphia
Francke	Francke Verlag, Berne
Franklin	Burt Franklin, New York
FreeP	Free Press, New York
FreeU	Free UP, Amsterdam
Freundlich	Freundlich Books, New York
Frommann- Holzboog	Frommann-Holzboog, Stuttgart
FSP	Five Seasons Press, Madley, Hereford
FW	Fragments West/Valentine Press, Long Beach, Calif.
FWP	Falling Wall Press, Bristol
Gale	Gale Research Co., Detroit, Mich.
Galilée	Galilée, Paris
Gallimard	Gallimard, Paris
G&M	Gill & Macmillan, Dublin
Garland	Garland Publishing Co., New York
Gasson	Roy Gasson Associates, Wimborne, Dorset
Girasole	Edizioni del Girasole, Ravenna
GL	Goose Lane Editions, Fredericton, N.B.
GlasgowDL	Glasgow District Libraries, Glasgow
Gleerup	Gleerupska, Lund
Gliddon	Gliddon Books Pubs., Norwich
GMP	GMP Pub., London
GMSmith	Gibbs M. Smith, Layton, Utah
Golden Dog	The Golden Dog, Ottawa
Gollancz	Victor Gollancz, London
Gomer	Gomer Press, Llandysul, Dyfed
GothU	Gothenburg Univ., Gothenburg
Gower	Gower Pub., Aldershot, Hants.
Grafton	Grafton Books, London
Granada	Granada Pub., London
Granville	Granville Pub. Co., London
Grasset	Grasset & Fasquelle, Paris

Grassroots	Grassroots, London
Graywolf	Graywolf Press, St Paul, Minn.
Greenhalgh	M. J. Greenhalgh, Eastcote, Middlesex
Greenwood	Greenwood Press, Westport, Conn.
Groos	Julius Groos Verlag, Heidelberg
Grove	Grove Press, New York
Grüner	B. R. Grüner, Amsterdam
Gruyter	Walter de Gruyter, Berlin
Hale	Robert Hale, London
Hall	G. K. Hall, Boston, Mass.
Hambledon	Hambledon Press, London
H&I	Hale & Iremonger, Sydney
H&M	Holmes & Meier, London and New York
H&S	Hodder & Stoughton, London
H&W	Hill & Wang, New York
Hansib	Hansib Pub., London
Harbour	Harbour Pub., Madeira Park, B.C.
Harper	Harper & Row, New York
Harrap	Harrap Ltd, London
Harvard	Harvard UP, Cambridge, Mass.
Harvester	Harvester Press, Brighton, Sussex
HarvesterM	Harvester Press Microform Pubns, Brighton, Sussex
HBJ	Harcourt Brace Jovanovich, New York and London
Heath	D. C. Heath & Co., Lexington, Mass.
Heinemann	William Heinemann, London
HeinemannA	William Heinemann, St Kilda, Vic.
Herbert	Herbert Press, London
HH	Hamish Hamilton, London
Hilger	Adam Hilger, Bristol
HM	Harvey Miller, London
HMSO	HMSO, London
Hogarth	Hogarth Press, London
HoughtonM	Houghton Mifflin, Boston, Mass.
Howard	Howard UP, Washington, D.C.
HRW	Holt, Rinehart & Winston, New York
Hueber	Max Hueber, Ismaning, W. Germany
HUL	Hutchinson University Library, London
HullU	Hull UP, Univ. of Hull
Humanities	Humanities Press, Atlantic Highlands, N.J.
Huntington	Huntington Library, San Marino, Calif.
Hutchinson	Hutchinson Books, London
IAAUS	Institut für Anglistik und Amerikanistik, Univ. of Salzburg
Ian Henry	Ian Henry Pub., Hornchurch, Essex
IAP	Irish Academic Press, Dublin
ICA	Institute of Contemporary Arts, London
IHA	International Hopkins Assoc., Waterloo, Ont.
Imago	Imago Imprint Inc., New York
IndU	Indiana UP, Bloomington, Ind.
Inkblot	Inkblot Pub., Berkeley, Calif.

IntUP	International Universities Press, New York
Inventions	Inventions Press, London
IOWP	Isle of Wight County Press, Newport, Isle of Wight
IP	In Parenthesis, London
Ipswich	Ipswich Press, Ipswich, Mass.
ISU	Iowa State UP, Ames, Iowa
IULC	Indiana Univ. Linguistics Club, Bloomington, Ind.
IUP	Indiana Univ. of Pennyslvania Press, Indiana, Pa.
Ivon	Ivon Publishing House, Bombay
Jacaranda	Jacaranda Wiley, Milton, Queensland
JadavpurU	Jadavpur Univ., Calcutta
James CookU	James Cook Univ. of North Queensland
Jarrow	Parish of Jarrow, Tyne and Wear
Jesperson	Jesperson Press, St John's, Newfoundland
JHall	James Hall, Leamington Spa, Warks.
JHU	Johns Hopkins UP, Baltimore, Md.
JLRC	Jack London Research Centre, Glen Ellen, Calif.
Joseph	Michael Joseph, London
Journeyman	The Journeyman Press, London
JT	James Thin, Edinburgh
Junction	Junction Books, London
Junius–Vaughan	The Junius–Vaughan Press, Fairview, N.J.
Jupiter	Jupiter Press, Lake Bluff, Ill.
JyväskyläU	Jyväskylä Univ., Jyväskylä, Finland
Kaibunsha	Kaibunsha, Tokyo
K&N	Königshausen and Neumann, Würzburg, W. Germany
K&W	Kaye & Ward, London
Kardo	Kardo, Coatbridge, Scotland
Karia	Karia Press, London
Karnak	Karnak House, London
Karoma	Karoma Pub., Ann Arbor, Mich.
Kenkyu	Kenkyu-Sha, Tokyo
Kennikat	Kennikat Press, Port Washington, N.Y.
Kensal	Kensal Press, Bourne End, Bucks.
KenyaLB	Kenya Literature Bureau, Nairobi
Kerr	Charles H. Kerr, Chicago
Kestrel	Viking Kestrel, London
K/H	Kendal/Hunt Pub., Dubuque, Iowa
Kinseido	Kinseido, Tokyo
Klostermann	Vittorio Klostermann, Frankfurt-on-Main
Knopf	Alfred A. Knopf, New York
Knowledge	Knowledge Industry Pubns, White Plains, N.Y.
Kraus	Kraus International Pubns, White Plains, N.Y.
KSUP	Kent State UP, Kent, Ohio
LA	Library Assoc., London
Lake View	Lake View Press, Chicago
LAm	Library of America, New York
Lamboll	Lamboll House
Lancelot	Lancelot Press, Hantsport, N.S.
Landesman	Jay Landesman, London

L&W	Lawrence and Wishart, London
Lane	Allen Lane, London
LaneA	Allen Lane, Ringwood, Vic.
Lang	Peter D. Lang, Frankfurt-on-Main and Berne
LC	Library of Congress, Washington, D.C.
LCP	Loras College Press, Dubuque, Iowa
LeedsU	Leeds UP, Leeds
LeicsCC	Leicestershire County Council, Libraries and Information Service, Leicester
LeicU	Leicester UP, Leicester
LeidenU	Leiden UP, The Hague
LeuvenU	Leuven UP, Leuven, Belgium
Lexik	Lexik House, Cold Spring, N.Y.
LF	LiberFörlag, Stockholm
LH	Lund Humphries Pub. Ltd, London
Liberty	Liberty Classics, Indianapolis, Ind.
Liguori	Liguori, Naples
LittleH	Little Hills Press, N.S.W.
Liveright	Liveright Pub., New York
LiverU	Liverpool UP, Liverpool
Loewenthal	Loewenthal Press, New York
Longman	Longman Group Ltd, London
LongmanP	Paul Longman, Auckland
Longspoon	Longspoon Press, Univ. of Alberta, Edmonton
Lowell	Lowell Press, Kansas City, Mo.
LSU	Louisiana State UP, Baton Rouge, La.
LundU	Lund Univ., Lund, Sweden
LUP	Loyola UP, Chicago
Lymes	Lymes Press, Newcastle, Staffs.
MAA	Medieval Academy of America, Cambridge, Mass.
Macdonald	Macdonald Pub., Edinburgh
MacdonaldCo	Macdonald & Co., London
Macmillan	Macmillan, London
MacNutt	R. MacNutt Ltd, Hartfield, Sussex
Mainstream	Mainstream Pub., Edinburgh
M&E	Macdonald & Evans, Estover, Plymouth, Devon
M&S	McClelland & Stewart, Toronto
Maney	W. S. Maney & Sons, Leeds
Mansell	Mansell Pub. Ltd, London
ManU	Manchester UP, Manchester
Mayflower	Mayflower Books, London
MB	Mitchell Beazley Ltd, London
McG-Q	McGill-Queen's UP, Montreal
McGraw-Hill	McGraw-Hill, New York
McPheeG	McPhee Gribble Pubs., Fitzroy, Vic.
McPherson	McPherson & Co., Kingston, N.Y.
ME	M. Evans, New York
Meany	P. D. Meany Pub., Port Credit, Ont.
Meckler	Meckler Pub., Westport, Conn.
Mellen	Edwin Mellen Press, Lewiston, N.Y.

Mercer	Mercer UP, Macon, Ga.
Methuen	Methuen, London
MethuenA	Methuen Australia, North Ryde, N.S.W.
MethuenC	Methuen, Toronto
MGruyter	Mouton de Gruyter, Berlin
MH	Michael Haag, London
MHRA	Modern Humanities Research Association, London
MI	Microforms International, Pergamon Press, Oxford
Micah	Micah Pubns, Marblehead, Mass.
MichSU	Michigan State UP, East Lansing, Mich.
MidNAG	Mid Northumberland Arts Group, Ashington, Northumb.
Milner	Milner, London
Minuit	Editions de Minuit, Paris
MIP	Medieval Inst. Pubns, WMU, Kalamazoo, Mich.
MITP	Massachusetts Inst. of Technology, Cambridge, Mass.
MLA	Modern Language Association of America, New York
MlM	Multilingual Matters, Clevedon, Avon
MLP	Manchester Literary and Philosophical Society
Moonraker	Moonraker Press, Bradford-on-Avon, Wilts.
Moorland	Moorland Pub., Ashbourne, Derby.
Moreana	Moreana, Angers, France
MorganS	Morgan State Univ., Baltimore, Md.
Morrow	William Morrow & Co., New York
Mosaic	Mosaic Press, Oakville, Ont.
Mouton	Mouton Pub., New York, The Hague, and Paris
Mowbray	A. R. Mowbray, Oxford
MR	Martin Robertson, Oxford
MRS	Medieval and Renaissance Society, North Texas State Univ., Denton
MRTS	MRTS, Binghamton, N.Y.
MS	Malone Society, c/o King's College, London
MSU	Memphis State UP, Memphis. Tenn.
MtAllisonU	Mount Allison Univ., Sackville, N.B.
Muller	Frederick Muller, London
Murray	John Murray, London
NAL	New American Library, New York
Narr	Gunter Narr Verlag, Tübingen
Nathan	Fernand Nathan, Paris
NBB	New Beacon Books, London
NCP	New Century Press, Durham
ND	New Directions, New York
NDT	Nottingham Drama Texts, c/o Univ. of Nottingham
NEL	New English Library, London
NeWest	NeWest Press, Edmonton, Alberta
N-H	Nelson-Hall, Chicago
NH	New Horizon Press, Far Hills, N.J.
NHPC	North-Holland Publishing Co., Amsterdam and New York
Niemeyer	Max Niemeyer, Tübingen

Nightwood	Nightwood Editions, Toronto
Nijhoff	Martinus Nijhoff, Dordrecht
NIU	Northern Illinois UP, De Kalb, Ill.
NLB	New Left Books, London
NLC	National Library of Canada, Ottawa
NLP	New London Press, Dallas, Texas
NLS	National Library of Scotland, Edinburgh
NLW	National Library of Wales, Aberystwyth, Dyfed
Northcote	Northcote House Pubs. Plymouth
NorthU	Northeastern University, Boston, Mass.
Northwestern	Northwestern UP, Evanston, Ill.
Norton	W. W. Norton & Co. Inc., New York and London
NPF	National Poetry Foundation, Orono, Maine
NPG	National Portrait Gallery, London
NPP	North Point Press, Berkeley, Calif.
NSP	New Statesman Pub. Co., New Delhi
NSWUP	New South Wales UP, Kensington, N.S.W.
NUC	Nipissing Univ. College, North Bay, Ont.
NUP	National Univ. Pub., Millwood, N.Y.
NUU	New Univ. of Ulster, Coleraine
NWAP	North Waterloo Academic Press, Waterloo, Ont.
NWP	New World Perspectives, Montreal
NYPL	New York Public Library, New York
NYU	New York UP, New York
O&B	Oliver & Boyd, Edinburgh
Oasis	Oasis Books, London
O'Brien	The O'Brien Press, Dublin
OBS	Oxford Bibliographical Society, Bodleian Library, Oxford
Octopus	Octopus Books, London
OdenseU	Odense UP, Odense
OE	Officina Edizioni, Rome
OEColl	Old English Colloquium, Berkeley, Calif.
Offord	John Offord Pubns, Eastbourne, Sussex
OhioU	Ohio UP, Athens, Ohio
Oldcastle	Oldcastle Books, Harpenden, Herts.
Olschki	Leo S. Olschki, Florence
Open Books	Open Books Pub. Ltd, Shepton Mallet, Somerset
OpenU	Open University Press, Milton Keynes and Philadelphia
OPP	Oxford Polytechnic Press, Oxford
Orbis	Orbis Books, London
Oriel	Oriel Press, Stocksfield, Northumberland
Oryx	Oryx Press, Phoenix, Ariz.
OSU	Ohio State UP, Columbus, Ohio
OTP	Oak Tree Press, London
OUP	Oxford University Press, Oxford
OUPAm	Oxford University Press, New York
OUPAus	Oxford University Press, Melbourne
OUPC	Oxford University Press, Toronto
OUPI	Oxford University Press, New Delhi

OUPNZ	Oxford University Press, Auckland
Outlet	Outlet Book Co., New York
Owen	Peter Owen, London
Pacifica	Press Pacifica, Kailua, Hawaii
Paget	Paget Press, Santa Barbara, Calif.
PAJ	PAJ Pubns, New York
Paladin	Paladin Books, London
Pan	Pan Books Ltd, London
Pandora	Pandora Press, London
Pantheon	Pantheon Books, New York
Parousia	Parousia Pubns, London
Paternoster	Paternoster Press, Exeter
Paulist	Paulist Press, Ramsey, N.J.
Pavilion	Pavilion Books, London
Peachtree	Peachtree Pub., Atlanta, Ga.
Peepal Tree	Peepal Tree Press, Leeds
Pembridge	Pembridge Press, London
Penguin	Penguin Books, Harmondsworth, Middx.
PenguinA	Penguin, Ringwood, Vic.
Penkevill	The Penkevill Pub. Co., Greenwood, Fla.
Penumbra	Penumbra Press, Moonbeam, Ont.
Pergamon	Pergamon Press, Oxford
Permanent	Permanent Press, Sag Harbor, N.Y.
Perpetua	Perpetua Press, Oxford
Pevensey	Pevensey Press, Cambridge
PH	Prentice-Hall Inc., Englewood Cliffs, N.J.
Phaidon	Phaidon Press, Oxford
PHI	Prentice-Hall International, Hemel Hempstead, Herts.
PhilL	Philosophical Library, New York
Pickwick	Pickwick Pubns, Allison Park, Pa.
Pilgrim	Pilgrim Books, Norman, Okla.
PIMS	Pontifical Institute of Mediaeval Studies, Toronto
Pinter	Frances Pinter Pub., London
Plenum	Plenum Pub., London and New York
Ploughshares	Ploughshares Books, Watertown, Mass.
Pluto	Pluto Press, London
Polity	Polity Press, Oxford
Polygon	Polygon, Edinburgh
Poolbeg	Poolbeg Press, Swords, Co. Dublin
Porcepic	Press Porcepic, Victoria, B.C.
Potter	Clarkson N. Potter, New York
Princeton	Princeton UP, Princeton, N.J.
PrincetonUL	Princeton University Library, Princeton, N.J.
PRO	Public Record Office, London
Profile	Profile Books, Ascot, Berks.
ProgP	Progressive Pubns, Calcutta
PSU	Pennsylvania State UP, University Park, Pa.
Pucker	Puckerbrush Press, Orono, Maine
PUF	Presses Universitaire de France, Paris
PurdueU	Purdue UP, Lafayette, Ind.

Pushcart	Pushcart Press, Wainscott, N.Y.
Pustet	Friedrich Pustet, Regensburg
Putnam	Putnam Pub. Group, New York
PWP	Poetry Wales Press, Ogmore by Sea, Mid Glam.
QED	Q.E.D. Press of Ann Arbor, Mich.
Quartet	Quartet Books, London
RA	Royal Academy of Arts, London
R&B	Rosenkilde & Bagger, Copenhagen
R&L	Rowman & Littlefield, Totowa, N.J.
RandomH	Random House, New York
Ravan	Ravan Press, Johannesburg
Ravette	Ravette, Horsham, W. Sussex
Rebel	The Rebel Press, Bideford, Devon
Reference	Reference Press, Toronto
Regents	Regents Press of Kansas, Lawrence, Kansas
Reichenberger	Roswitha Reichenberger, Kessel, W. Germany
Reidel	Reidel Pub. Co., Dordrecht, Boston, and London
Reinhardt	Reinhardt, London
Remak	Remak, Alblasserdam, Netherlands
RenI	Renaissance Institute, Sophia Univ., Tokyo
RETS	Renaissance English Text Society, Chicago
RH	Ramsay Head Press, Edinburgh
RIA	Royal Irish Academy, Dublin
RiceU	Rice UP, Houston, Texas
Richarz	Hans Richarz, St Augustin
RKP	Routledge & Kegan Paul, London
Robinson	Robinson Pub., London
Robson	Robson Books, London
Rodopi	Rodopi, Amsterdam
RoehamptonI	Roehampton Institute of Higher Education, London
Royce	Robert Royce, London
RS	The Royal Society, London
RSC	Royal Shakespeare Co., London
RSL	Royal Society of Literature, London
RSVP	Research Society for Victorian Periodicals, Univ. of Leicester
Running	Running Press, Philadelphia
Russell	Michael Russell, Salisbury
Rutgers	Rutgers UP, New Brunswick, N.J.
SA	Sahitya Akademi, New Delhi
SAI	Sociological Abstracts Inc., San Diego, Calif.
Salamander	Salamander Books, London
S&D	Stein & Day, Briarcliff Manor, N.Y.
S&J	Sidgwick & Jackson, London
S&M	Sun and Moon Press, Los Angeles
S&P	Simon & Pierre, Toronto
S&S	Simon & Schuster, New York
S&W	Secker & Warburg, London
Sangam	Sangam Books, London

Sangsters	Sangsters Book Stores, Kingston, Jamaica
SAP	Scottish Academic Press, Edinburgh
S-B	Schwann-Bagel, Düsseldorf
Scarecrow	Scarecrow Press, Metuchen, N.J.
Schäuble	Schäuble Verlag, Rheinfelden, W. Germany
Schocken	Schocken Books, New York
Scholarly	Scholarly Press, St Clair Shores, Mich.
Schwinn	Michael Schwinn, Neustadt, W. Germany
Scolar	Scolar Press, London
SCP	Second Chance Press, Sag Harbor, N.Y.
Scribner	Charles Scribner's Sons, New York
Seafarer	Seafarer Books, London
Seaver	Seaver Books, New York
Segue	Segue, New York
Semiotext(e)	Semiotext(e), Columbia Univ., New York
Serpent's Tail	Serpent's Tail Pub., London
Seuil	Editions du Seuil, Paris
7:84 Pubns	7:84 Pubns, Edinburgh
Severn	Severn House, London
SF&R	Scholars' Facsimiles and Reprints, Delmar, N.Y.
SH	Somerset House, Teaneck, N.J.
Shearwater	Shearwater Press, Lenah Valley, Tasmania
Sheba	Sheba Feminist Pubs., London
Sheed&Ward	Sheed & Ward, London
Sheldon	Sheldon Press, London
SHESL	Société d'Histoire et d'Épistemologie des Sciences du Langage, Paris
Shinozaki	Shinozaki Shorin, Tokyo
Shire	Shire Pubns, Princes Risborough, Bucks.
Shoe String	Shoe String Press, Hamden, Conn.
SIL	Summer Inst. of Linguistics, Academic Pubns, Dallas, Texas
SingaporeU	Singapore UP, Singapore
SIU	Southern Illinois UP, Carbondale, Ill.
SJSU	San Jose State Univ., San Jose, Calif.
Skilton	Charles Skilton Ltd, Edinburgh
Sleepy Hollow	Sleepy Hollow Press, Tarrytown, N.Y.
SLG	SLG Press, Oxford
Smythe	Colin Smythe, Gerrards Cross, Bucks.
SNLS	Society for New Language Study, Denver, Colo.
SOA	Society of Authors, London
Soho	Soho Book Co., London
Solaris	Solaris Press, Rochester, Mich.
SonoNis	Sono Nis Press, Victoria, B.C.
Sorbonne	Pubns de la Sorbonne, Paris
Souvenir	Souvenir Press, London
SPCK	SPCK, London
Sphere	Sphere Books, London
Spokesman	Spokesman Books, Nottingham

SRC	Steinbeck Research Center, San Jose State Univ., Calif.
SRI	Steinbeck Research Institute, Ball State Univ., Muncie, Ind.
SriA	Sri Aurobindo, Pondicherry, India
SSA	John Steinbeck Society of America, Muncie, Ind.
SSAB	Sprakförlaget Skriptor AB, Stockholm
Stanford	Stanford UP, Stanford, Calif.
Staple	Staple, Matlock, Derby.
Star	Star Books, London
Starmont	Starmont House, Mercer Island, Wash.
Station Hill	Station Hill, Barrytown, N.Y.
StDL	St Deiniol's Library, Hawarden, Clwyd
Steiner	Franz Steiner, Wiesbaden
Sterling	Sterling Pub., New York
SterlingND	Sterling Pub., New Delhi
St James	St James Press, London
St Martin's	St Martin's Press, New York
Stockwell	Arthur H. Stockwell Ltd, Ilfracombe, Devon
Stoddart	Stoddart Pub., Don Mills, Ont.
StPB	St Paul's Bibliographies, Winchester, Hants.
STR	Society for Theatre Research, London
Strauch	R.O.U. Strauch, Ludwigsburg
Studio	Studio Editions, London
Sud	Sud, Marseilles
Suhrkamp	Suhrkamp Verlag, Frankfurt-on-Main
Summa	Summa Pubns, Birmingham, Ala.
SUNY	State University of New York Press, Albany, N.Y.
SusquehannaU	Susquehanna UP, Selinsgrove, Pa.
SussexU	Sussex UP, Univ. of Sussex, Brighton
Sutton	Alan Sutton, Gloucester
S-W	Shepheard-Walwyn Pub., London
Swallow	Swallow Press, Athens, Ohio
SWG	Saskatchewan Writers Guild, Regina
SydneyU	Sydney UP, Sydney
Syracuse	Syracuse UP, Syracuse, N.Y.
Tabb	Tabb House, Padstow, Cornwall
TamilU	Tamil Univ., Thanjavur, India
T&H	Thames & Hudson, London
Tantivy	Tantivy Press, London
Tarcher	Jeremy P. Tarcher, Los Angeles
Tate	Tate Gallery Pubns, London
Tavistock	Tavistock Pubns, London
Taylor	Taylor Pub., Bellingham, Wash.
TaylorCo	Taylor Pub. Co., Dallas, Texas
TCG	Theatre Communications Group, New York
TCP	Three Continents Press, Washington, D.C.
TCUP	Texas Christian UP, Fort Worth, Texas
TEC	Third Eye Centre, Glasgow
Tecumseh	Tecumseh Press, Ottawa
Telos	Telos Press Ltd, St Louis, Mo.

Temple	Temple UP, Philadelphia
TennS	Tennyson Soc., Lincoln
TexA&M	Texas A & M UP, College Station, Texas
TextileB	Textile Bridge Press, Clarence Center, N.Y.
The Smith	The Smith, New York
Thimble	Thimble Press, Stroud, Glos.
Thornes	Stanley Thornes, Cheltenham
Times	Times of Gloucester Press, Gloucester, Ont.
TMP	Thunder's Mouth Press, New York
Tombouctou	Tombouctou Books, Bolinas, Calif.
Toucan	Toucan Press, St Peter Port, Guernsey
Touzot	Jean Touzot, Paris
TPF	Trianon Press Facsimiles, London
Tragara	Tragara Press, Edinburgh
Transaction	Transaction Pub., New Brunswick, N.J.
Transcendental	Transcendental Books, Hartford, Conn.
TrinityU	Trinity UP, San Antonio, Texas
TTP	Texas Technical Press, Lubbock, Texas
Tuduv	Tuduv, Munich
TulaneU	Tulane UP, New Orleans, La.
TurkuU	Turku Univ., Turku, Finland
Turtle Island	Turtle Island Foundation, Berkeley, Calif.
Twayne	Twayne Publishers, Boston, Mass.
UAB	Univ. of Aston, Birmingham
UAdelaide	Univ. of Adelaide
UAla	Univ. of Alabama Press, University
UAlberta	Univ. of Alberta Press, Edmonton
UAntwerp	Univ. of Antwerp
UAriz	Univ. of Arizona Press, Tucson
UArk	Univ. of Arkansas Press, Fayetteville
UBarcelona	Univ. of Barcelona
UBC	Univ. of British Columbia, Vancouver
UBergen	Univ. of Bergen
UBrno	J. E. Purkyne Univ. of Brno, Brno, Czechoslovakia
UBrussels	Univ. of Brussels, Brussels
UCA	Univ. of Central Arkansas Press, Conway
UCal	Univ. of California Press, Berkeley
UCalgary	Univ. of Calgary Press, Calgary, Alberta
UChic	Univ. of Chicago Press, Chicago
UCopen	Univ. of Copenhagen Press, Copenhagen
UDel	Univ. of Delaware Press, Newark
UDur	Univ. of Durham, Durham
UEssex	Univ. of Essex, Colchester
UExe	Univ. of Exeter, Exeter, Devon
UFlor	Univ. Presses of Florida, Gainesville
UGal	Univ. College, Galway
UGeo	Univ. of Georgia Press, Athens
UGhent	Rijksuniversiteit, Ghent
UGlas	Univ. of Glasgow Press, Glasgow
UHawaii	Univ. of Hawaii Press, Honolulu

UIll	Univ. of Illinois Press, Champaign
UInnsbruck	Univ. of Innsbruck
UIowa	Univ. of Iowa Press, Iowa City
UKan	Univ. of Kansas Press, Lawrence
UKen	Univ. Press of Kentucky, Lexington
UKL	Univ. of Kentucky Libraries, Lexington
ULaval	Les Presses de l'Université Laval, Quebec
ULille	Presses Universitaires de Lille, Lille
Ulster	Univ. of Ulster, Coleraine
U–M	Underwood/Miller, Los Angeles
UMalta	Univ. of Malta, Msida
UMass	Univ. of Massachusetts Press, Amherst
Umeå	Umeå Universitetsbibliotek
UMI	Univ. Microfilms International, Ann Arbor, Mich.
UMich	Univ. of Michigan Press, Ann Arbor
UMinn	Univ. of Minnesota Press, Minneapolis
UMIRes	UMI Research Press, Ann Arbor, Mich.
UMiss	Univ. of Missouri Press, Columbia
UMissip	UP of Mississippi, Jackson
UMysore	Univ. of Mysore, Mysore, India
UNancy	Presses Universitaires de Nancy, France
UNC	Univ. of North Carolina Press, Chapel Hill
UND	Univ. of Notre Dame Press, Notre Dame, Ind.
Undena	Undena Pubns, Malibu, Calif.
UNeb	Univ. of Nebraska Press, Lincoln
Ungar	Frederick Ungar, New York
UNICOPLI	Edizioni UNICOPLI, Milan
Universa	Uitgeverij Universa, Wetteren, Belgium
UNM	Univ. of New Mexico Press, Albuquerque
UNott	Univ. of Nottingham, Nottingham
Unwin	Unwin Paperbacks, London
Unwin Hyman	Unwin Hyman, London
UOkla	Univ. of Oklahoma Press, Norman
UOslo	Univ. of Oslo, Oslo
UOtago	Univ. of Otago Press, Dunedin, N.Z.
UOttawa	Univ. of Ottawa Press, Ottawa
UPA	UP of America, Lanham, Md.
UParis	Univ. of Paris, Paris
UPenn	Univ. of Pennsylvania Press, Philadelphia.
UPitt	Univ. of Pittsburgh Press, Pittsburgh, Pa.
UPNE	UP of New England, Hanover, N.H.
Uppsala	Uppsala Univ., Uppsala
UProvence	Univ. de Provence, Aix-en-Provence
UPValery	Univ. Paul Valery, Montpellier
UQP	Univ. of Queensland Press, St Lucia
URouen	Univ. de Rouen, Mont St Aignan
USalz	Univ. of Salzburg, Salzburg
USC	Univ. of South Carolina Press, Columbia
USheff	Univ. of Sheffield, Sheffield
Usher	La Casa Usher, Florence

USzeged	Univ. of Szeged, Hungary
UTas	Univ. of Tasmania, Hobart
UTenn	Univ. of Tennessee Press, Knoxville
UTex	Univ. of Texas Press, Austin
UTor	Univ. of Toronto Press, Toronto
UVerm	Univ. of Vermont, Burlington
UVict	Univ. of Victoria, Victoria, B.C.
UVirginia	Univ. of Virginia, Charlottesville
UWales	Univ. of Wales Press, Cardiff
UWAP	Univ. of Western Australia Press, Nedlands
UWash	Univ. of Washington Press, Seattle
UWaterloo	Univ. of Waterloo Press, Waterloo, Ont.
UWI	Univ. of the West Indies, St Augustine, Trinidad
UWisc	Univ. of Wisconsin Press, Madison
UWiscM	Univ. of Wisconsin, Milwaukee
UYork	Univ. of York, York
Valentine	Valentine Publishing & Drama Co., Rhinebeck, N.Y.
V&A	Victoria and Albert Museum, London
V&R	Vandenhoeck & Ruprecht, Göttingen
Vantage	Vantage Press, New York
Vehicle	Vehicle Press, Montreal
Verso	Verso Editions, London
Viking	Viking Press, New York
Virago	Virago Press, London
Vision	Vision Press, London
VLB	VLB Editeur, Montreal
VR	Variorum Reprints, London
Vrin	J. Vrin, Paris
W&N	Weidenfeld & Nicolson, London
Water Row	Water Row Press, Sudbury, Mass.
WB	Wissenschaftliche Buchgesellschaft, Darmstadt
W/B	Woolmer/Brotherson Ltd, Revere, Pa.
Webb&Bower	Webb & Bower, Exeter, Devon
Wedgestone	Wedgestone Press, Winfield, Kansas
Wesleyan	Wesleyan UP, Middletown, Conn.
West	West Pub., St Paul, Minn.
Whiteknights	Whiteknights Press, Univ. of Reading, Berks.
Whitston	Whitston Pub. Co., Troy, N.Y.
Whittington	Whittington Press, Andoversford, Glos.
WHP	Warren House Press, North Walsham, Norfolk
Wiener	Wiener Pub., New York
Wildwood	Wildwood House, London
Wiley	John Wiley & Sons, Chichester, New York, and Brisbane
Wilson	Philip Wilson, London
Winthrop	Winthrop Publishers Inc., Cambridge, Mass.
WIU	Western Illinois Univ., Macomb, Ill.
WL	Ward Lock, London
WLU	Wilfrid Laurier UP, Waterloo, Ont.
WMP	World Microfilms Publications, London
WMU	Western Michigan Univ., Kalamazoo, Mich.

Wo-No	Wolters-Noordhoff, Gröningen, Netherlands
Wolfhound	Wolfhound Press, Dublin
Wombat	The Wombat Press, Wolfville, N.S.
Women's	The Women's Press, Toronto
Woolf	Cecil Woolf, London
Words	Words, Framfield, E. Sussex
WP	Women's Press, London
WSU	Wayne State UP, Detroit, Mich.
WVU	West Virginia UP, Morgantown
W-W	Williams-Wallace, Toronto
WWU	Western Washington University, Bellingham
Xanadu	Xanadu Pubns, London
Yale	Yale UP, New Haven, Conn., and London
Yamaguchi	Yamaguchi Shoten, Kyoto
YorkP	York Press, Fredericton, N.B.
Zed	Zed Books, London
Zephyr	Zephyr Press, Somerville, Mass.
Zomba	Zomba Books, London
Zwemmer	A. Zwemmer, London

Reference, Literary History, and Bibliography

H. R. WOUDHUYSEN

This chapter has three sections: 1. Reference Works; 2. Literary Histories: (a) General Works, (b) Anthologies; 3. Bibliography: (a) Theory, (b) Reference Works, (c) Printing and Publishing History, (d) Institutional and Private Library History, (e) Attribution Studies. Exhibition catalogues and studies in medieval manuscripts have not been included.

1. Reference Works

Weighty tomes continue to pour out of the Book Tower in Detroit which houses the Gale Research Company. This year's offerings include two volumes of *Literature Criticism from 1400 to 1800*[1]; each entry consists of a general biographical and critical introduction, followed by a list of principal works, then excerpts of criticism from the writer's own time up to the present, and finally an annotated list for further reading. The twelve authors featured in the first of these volumes are with two exceptions English and belong mainly to the eighteenth century. They include Dryden and Pope: criticism of Pope begins with Wycherley and ends in 1985 with Laura Brown. The second volume has eleven authors mainly from a slightly earlier period; nine of them wrote in English – George Buchanan was an interesting writer to include and the entry for him is quite well done. It is still hard to know for whom these reference works are compiled and what, if any, use is ever made of them: on the whole, while the choice of critics on writers is good many of the extracts themselves are too short to be very stimulating. Similar and further reservations apply to the two volumes of *Nineteenth-Century Literature Criticism*[2] which appeared in 1986. It is undoubtedly useful to have forty or so pages of criticism from over thirty different sources on John Forster (from Landor to John J. Fenstermaker), but none is long enough to give the reader real food for thought. Furthermore, serious literary scholars will want to do their own reading and research, rather than have it predigested for them. All the same, these nineteenth-century volumes are more coherent in their scope than the wider series (where P'u Sung-ling comes between Pope and Smart) and include Russian, German, and American as well as English authors.

1. *Literature Criticism from 1400 to 1800*, ed. by James E. Person. Gale. Vol. III. pp. 584; Vol. IV. pp. 567. $85 each.

2. *Nineteenth-Century Literature Criticism*, ed. by Laurie Lanzen Harris and Cherie D. Abbey. Gale. Vol. XI. pp. 557; Vol. XII. pp. 576. $88 each.

Other volumes from Gale presumably continue to meet some sort of need: the 117th volume of *Contemporary Authors*[3] means that it has now covered some eighty-five thousand 'prominent individuals in media, the lively arts, and related fields'. Not many of the authors covered are exactly familiar names; to take one example at random, Anne Hampson, who was specially interviewed by telephone at her home on the Isle of Man, has produced about a hundred romances for Mills & Boon and gets nearly seven columns of attention: most entries barely stretch to half a column. Gale is heavily committed to supplying information about children's literature. *American Writers for Children Since 1960: Fiction*[4] is made up of more substantial material with well-illustrated accounts of among others Russell Hoban, Randall Jarrell, Ursula Le Guin, and Isaac Bashevis Singer: this seems a much better thought-out work with some useful original material in it. Less detailed biographical information can be found in the latest two volumes of *Children's Literature Review*[5], which is mainly concerned with the reprinting of reviews and critical accounts of the work of a small number of writers: Raymond Briggs and R. L. Stevenson (twice) are among the better-known authors who feature in these two works.

Gale's newest series *Something About the Author: Autobiography Series*[6] provides autobiographical essays by authors and illustrators of books for children and young adults; two volumes have appeared covering about forty subjects, none of whom could be said to be in the first rank of literary fame. Their essays are generally accompanied by innocently revealing photographs from their family albums. The main *Something About the Author*[7] series supplies 'facts and pictures about authors and illustrators of books for young people'; four volumes have appeared this year, so that the series covers well over six thousand men and women, including in the latest offerings Karen Blixen, Dick Bruna, Robert Graves, and Mordecai Richler; the books are well illustrated and make sporadically rather charming reading.

The 1985 *Dictionary of Literary Biography*[8], which Gale produced, contains the usual mixture of biographies, obituaries, and more general articles on the literary events of the year in question; the John Carter Brown library is the literary archive described this year. While the volume in question contains interesting and useful material for browsing in, it is hard to imagine turning to it as a first resource for information. Gale are also responsible for publishing the second edition of *Allusions*[9]; a work which attempts to explain concisely nearly nine thousand 'cultural, literary, biblical, and historical' allusions classified under about seven hundred headings: under 'eroticism' we are told, among

3. *Contemporary Authors*, ed. by Hal May. Vol. CXVII. Gale. pp. 511. $88.

4. *American Writers for Children Since 1960: Fiction*, ed. by Glenn E. Estes. Vol. LII. Gale. pp. xiv + 488. $88.

5. *Children's Literature Review*, ed. by Gerard J. Senick. Gale. Vol. X. pp. 276; Vol. XI. pp. 293. $78 each.

6. *Something About the Author: Autobiography Series*, ed. by Adele Sarkissian. Gale. Vol. I. pp. 368; Vol. II. pp. 381. $50 each.

7. *Something About the Author*, ed. by Anne Commire. Gale. Vol. XLII. pp. 291; Vol. XLIII. pp. 302; Vol. XLIV. pp. 295; Vol. XLV. pp. 304. $64 each.

8. *Dictionary of Literary Biography Yearbook: 1985*, ed. by Jean W. Ross. Gale. pp. xiv + 486. $92.

9. *Allusions – Cultural, Literary, Biblical, and Historical: A Thematic Dictionary*, ed. by Laurence Urdang and Frederick G. Ruffner. Second edn. Gale. pp. 634. $68.

other things, that the *Ars Amatoria* is 'Ovid's treatise on lovemaking' and that *Playboy* is a 'monthly magazine renowned for nude photographs'; an index makes the work a little more serviceable and may help readers to solve odd puzzles from time to time. Apart from Gale's many and substantial offerings, this has not been a very remarkable year for reference works. It is therefore worth drawing attention to an unusual compilation based on material held in the National Art Library at the Victoria and Albert Museum: in *The Country House Described*[10] Michael Holmes provides a short guide to what has been written by architectural historians and antiquaries about more than four thousand country houses in the British Isles – details of auction sales are also included. Given the amount of interest critics and historians have in literary topography and geography this volume should provide them with a very useful starting-off point for their researches.

2. Literary Histories

(a) General Works

Last year's Everyman history of English literature by Peter Conrad set a standard which it would be hard to match. In *A Prologue to English Literature*[11] Wallace Robson has written a far shorter book, of a more conventional kind, divided into chapters covering familiar periods, with plenty of dates, and banal, as well as boldly striking, opinions. This is where it is at its best and most stimulating, for Robson is not afraid to tell the reader the obvious, or what he thinks: 'Chaucer was an excellent narrative poet' but also 'he is fundamentally unromantic', he writes at the beginning of the volume, and ends it by challenging the literary critic and historian to know what to make of Churchill's prose. There are signs of the strain of compression in some of what Robson writes, but he gives a challenging outline, in a pleasingly old-fashioned Oxford way, of what is immediately worth reading and what can be safely left for the future.

Some of the same concerns animate a new collection of Leavis's essays[12], which spans the whole period of his life from a 1929 piece on T. S. Eliot to undated and previously unpublished pieces again on Eliot (with no explanation of their origins or provenance), 'Standards of Criticism', 'The Problem of Value Judgment', and 'Notes on Wordsworth'. The selection gives a fair impression of Leavis's range of concerns and power as a writer; his admirers will be glad to have the new pieces, which contain some interesting personal remarks. Practical criticism is the main object of attention in John Garrett's *British Poetry Since the Sixteenth Century*[13], which after some bland general

10. *The Country House Described: An Index to the Country Houses of Great Britain and Ireland*, by Michael Holmes. StPB. pp. viii + 328. £30.

11. *A Prologue to English Literature*, by W. W. Robson. Batsford. pp. 254. hb £12.95, pb £4.95.

12. *'Valuation in Criticism' and Other Essays*, by F. R. Leavis, ed. by G. Singh. CUP. pp. viii + 309. hb £27.50, pb £9.95.

13. *British Poetry Since the Sixteenth Century: A Student's Guide*, by John Garrett. Macmillan. pp. vii + 248. hb £18, pb £5.95.

remarks on how to read poetry, confines itself to what amount to 'worked examples' of commentary and analysis of twenty-three poems (or extracts) from the works of writers from Sidney to Ted Hughes; it is quite well done, but it is alarming to think that students might have to rely on this book to teach them how to read and write about English poetry.

Three brief general critical books and two collections of essays deserve to be mentioned. In *British Poets and Secret Societies*[14] Marie Roberts considers the attraction which Freemasonry, the Rosicrucians, the Golden Dawn, and other such societies had for Smart, Burns, Shelley, Kipling, and Yeats: it is hard to share Roberts's enthusiasm for the subject, which is not very coherently explained (why poets and not novelists or playwrights?), or to feel that she makes as much of her claim to investigate secrecy in the works of these poets as she might have. Rana Kabbani's argument in *Europe's Myths of Orient*[15] that Westerners (among others Richard Burton, E. W. Lane, C. M. Doughty, Elias Canetti, and V. Ŝ. Naipaul), have consistently misrepresented the Near East in terms of its eroticism and exoticism for imperialist purposes is more polemical: this is an interesting subject, but her book is too short for such a vast and complicated subject, and marred by errors ('Charles Algernon Swinburne' appears in the text and index), to give more than a brief and not entirely convincing taste of her argument. Finally, Stoddard Martin's *Art, Messianism and Crime*[16] looks at some of the odder 'messianic' characters from European history of the last two hundred years, ranging from de Sade to Hitler to Jim Morrison and Charles Manson. It is a bold venture, which produces some striking ideas and connections, but it is sometimes beyond even Martin's powers to make sense of these distinguished but highly unpleasant people.

The Wolfson College Lectures for 1985 were on the subject of literacy[17]: among the distinguished contributions, Walter J. Ong considered the effect that writing has on the expression of thought, and Adam Hodgkin looked at the way that new technologies have changed how authors write and books are published. Keith Thomas's piece on 'The Meaning of Literacy in Early Modern England', in which he examines the problems and significance of the undoubted spread of literacy between 1500 and 1750, is probably of most interest to readers of *YWES*. The essays on the subject of realism in European literature collected in honour of J. P. Stern[18] form, as these collections go, a remarkably coherent group, ranging from the abstractly theoretical considerations of the topic by Erich Heller, Stephen Heath, and Richard Brinkmann to more concrete accounts of realism in Shakespeare's last plays by Anne Barton and Graham Hough on 'Language and Reality in *Bleak House*'. Especially in the context of the volume as a whole these two essays repay particular attention.

For its 1986 'Literary Periodicals Special Number' *YES* has replaced its

14. *British Poets and Secret Societies*, by Marie Roberts. CH. pp. 181. £17.95.

15. *Europe's Myths of Orient: Devise and Rule*, by Rana Kabbani. Macmillan. pp. ix + 166. £25.

16. *Art, Messianism and Crime: A Study of Antinomianism in Modern Literature and Lives*, by Stoddard Martin. Macmillan. pp. vi + 218. £25.

17. *The Written Word: Literacy in Transition: Wolfson College Lectures 1985*, ed. by Gerd Baumann. Clarendon. pp. x + 197. £20.

18. *Realism in European Literature: Essays in Honour of J. P. Stern*, ed. by Nicholas Boyle and Martin Swales. CUP. pp. ix + 206. £25.

familiar orangey-brown cover with one of positively funereal blackness. The tone of some of the articles within, especially Karl Miller's radiantly gloomy piece on *LRB*, matches the cover. The project as a whole is a fascinating one, covering the whole range of literary journalism from David Bromwich on the *Edinburgh Review*'s treatment of the Romantic poets, to Stephen Fender on the origins, practices, and New York politics of *NYRB*. Jeremy Treglown contributes a particularly stimulating essay on the discrepancy between the accepted view of Pound's treatment at the hands of the English literary establishment and what the reviews of his work in the *TLS* actually said; he calls at the end of his account for a revised literary history of the century which would draw on the archives of the most widely influential of all reviewing journals. The *TLS*'s past practice of printing unsigned reviews was inherited from the apparently rigid conventions of the Victorian press; Robert H. Tener briefly examines just how uniform was the code of anonymity in Victorian journalism and considers some cases in which the *Spectator* broke its habitual rule of unsigned pieces in the second half of the nineteenth century.

Among the other more general essays, Laurel Brake contributes a thoughtful piece using much heterogeneous material on 'Literary Criticism and the Victorian Periodicals' in which she shows that a body of largely neglected criticism (much of it anonymous) awaits detailed investigation, and that the type of criticism authors produced was often effectively determined by the characteristics and the editors of the journals for which they wrote. The changing face of Victorian publishing is discussed by Linda Dowling in a rather relaxed piece 'Letterpress and Pictures in the Literary Periodicals of the 1890s', which is mainly concerned with *The Yellow Book* but which also uses *The Century Guild Hobby Horse* as a means of comparison. Bernard Bergonzi peers about in *The Calendar of Modern Letters*, successfully finding several items of interest in the short-lived journal, which anticipated some of Leavis's critical ideas and standards. Donald Davie reflects on the not very happy fortunes of *PNR* in a contribution which edges towards the higher gossip, while Ralph Cohen provides an imn odest advertisement for his journal *NLH*.

A survey of historical drama from Shakespeare to Brecht is, under the best of circumstances, an ambitious undertaking: Matthew H. Wikander[19] bravely attempts it, but his book is undeniably broken-backed with a first part devoted to Shakespeare and later English dramatists up to the Restoration, who are handled briefly and sensibly, and a second part which concentrates on Schiller, Strindberg, Musset, Büchner, and of course Brecht. *Textual Analysis*[20] published by the MLA contains two dozen essays on literature and is perhaps best sampled from the first sentence of its preface: 'Of the difficult and controversial craft called, at various times, close reading, explication de texte, or textual commentary . . .'; the collection of essays shows how 'textual analysis' can work on texts as diverse as Manuel Puig's *Kiss of the Spider Woman* and Elizabeth Barrett Browning's poems: one of the essays has a glossary of terms used and there is an index of them to the whole volume. It would be hard to

19. *The Play of Truth and State: Historical Drama from Shakespeare to Brecht*, by Matthew H. Wikander. JHU. pp. 287. £19.65.
20. *Textual Analysis: Some Readers Reading*, ed. by Mary Ann Caws. MLA. pp. viii + 327. hb $29.50, pb $15.

overestimate the pretentiousness of this enterprise. Two collections of David Lodge's essays and reviews *Working With Structuralism*[21] and *The Novelist at the Crossroads*[22] have come out in paperback.

Finally, a new history of Irish literature has appeared by Seamus Deane[23]. There are problems with the whole enterprise, of which Deane is well aware – he chooses to omit Swift's poetry, Congreve and Sterne altogether, and much of Shaw – yet he writes easily, without sentimentalizing his subject, although he is evidently most at home in the literature of this century. His passages on Yeats and Joyce are unpretentious and Patrick Kavanagh is, for Deane, the leader of postwar Irish poetry. Deane's is a good and quite readable introduction to a subject about which students of literature are bound to hear more in the future.

(b) Anthologies

Two major anthologies have appeared this year, each aimed at a quite different kind of audience. John Wain's three volumes of *The Oxford Library of English Poetry*[24] is pleasantly produced (apart from its lurid covers): it is intended for the general reader who reads poetry for pure pleasure, and is meant to replace the familiar five-volume anthology compiled for the old WC series by W. Peacock. Wain's choice of poems, from Spenser to Heaney, with large extracts from Shakespeare's plays, about sixty pages from *Paradise Lost* and the whole of *The Waste Land* (but not Eliot's Notes), is conventional and eminently sensible; there are few surprises here (and no indication from where Wain has taken his generally modernized texts), but the balance between contemporary and older poetry is well maintained.

The Norton anthologies[25] are, of course, aimed at the American undergraduate market, which needs 'course' books. These new editions include some new selections, particularly relating to women, and within their five thousand pages contain a wealth of material, which has been well chosen, sensibly edited, and clearly presented for readers to whom England and Englishness are now perhaps rather foreign. The question to ask is, if you read through these two volumes would you be well read in English literature? The answer must clearly be in the negative since they cannot deal with the problem of fiction: Dickens is represented by a short passage from *Hard Times*, and then Conrad by *Heart of Darkness* which presumably gets in, as does Joyce's 'The Dead' accompanied by fifty pages from *Ulysses*, because these are 'modernist' texts; there is no more fiction except for short stories by women – Katherine Mansfield, Doris Lessing, Edna O'Brien, and Susan Hill. It is hard to make useful extracts from novels, but an anthology with no prose by Defoe, Richardson, Fielding, Sterne,

21. *Working With Structuralism: Essays and Reviews on Nineteenth- and Twentieth-Century Literature*, by David Lodge. Ark. pp. xii + 207. pb £3.95.

22. *'The Novelist at the Crossroads' and Other Essays on Fiction and Criticism*, by David Lodge. Ark. pp. xi + 297. pb £3.95.

23. *A Short History of Irish Literature*, by Seamus Deane. Hutchinson. pp. 282. pb £6.95.

24. *The Oxford Library of English Poetry*, ed. by John Wain. OUP. Vol. I. pp. xx + 443; Vol. II. pp. xiii + 511; Vol. III. pp. xvi + 476. £27.50.

25. *The Norton Anthology of English Literature*, ed. by M. H. Abrams. Fifth edn. Norton. Vol. I. pp. xxxvii + 2616; Vol. II. pp. xlvi + 2578. pb £12.95 each.

Jane Austen, Thackeray, George Eliot, Trollope (the Brontës are represented by six of Emily's poems), D. H. Lawrence, and so on can hardly be called an anthology of English literature. The Norton 'digest' volume[26] is perhaps a little more excusable in what it omits (though it is sad to find Sidney excluded), but is still bound to give a highly misleading impression of what English literature consists of to many thousands of American (and no doubt other) undergraduates throughout the world; the fault lies as much with the practice of making these kinds of anthologies as with the editors themselves.

At the less academic end of the market OUP continues to lead the field in the wholesale production of literary anthologies. There is no doubt that they make attractive presents, but some of them have an air of desperation on the part of the publisher to get books out, no matter on what subject. *The Oxford Book of English Ghost Stories*[27] is an interesting collection, with some really unpleasant tales and a brief but serviceable bibliography. According to this selection the ghost story begins with Scott's *The Tapestried Chamber* of 1829, but only really gets going with Amelia B. Edwards's *The Phantom Coach* of 1864. The anthology is oddly arranged by date of first publication, so that the last story in the book is T. H. White's *Soft Voices at Passenham*, written in the 1930s but first published in 1981; the editors do not give any indication of whether the stories were ever revised or rewritten by their authors.

In its way *The Oxford Book of Sea Songs*[28] is a much more successful volume. Its editor, Roy Palmer, is an experienced anthologist, and he has produced a collection of 159 songs and shanties which is refreshingly original. The texts are all modernized and glossed, many being printed with music: each one has a paragraph after it putting the poem in some sort of context and there are notes on sources ('The Loss of *The Evelyn Marie*' in 1975 was sung 'by an unnamed Irish woman on a tape' communicated from Ballydavid, Co. Kerry). The last of the current batch of Oxford books is *The Oxford Book of Travel Verse*[29], which might really have been called *The Oxford Book of English Poems About How Ghastly Abroad Is*. Most of the poems describe how horrid the rest of Europe seems (there are eleven on Switzerland), but there are gestures of one kind or another made towards Africa, America, Asia, and Australia. A good many of the poems and extracts are familiar, but there are some unusual eighteenth-century pieces; it is a harmless and sporadically entertaining anthology.

The same cannot be, and has not been, said of Tom Paulin's *The Faber Book of Political Verse*[30], which attracted both hostile and committedly admiring reviews, largely on account of its polemical introduction. The poems Paulin chooses are mainly British with a fair bias towards the Irish and the Scottish; there are a few Americans and some Eastern Europeans later on, but France,

26. *The Norton Anthology of English Literature: The Major Authors*, ed. by M. H. Abrams. Fifth edn. Norton. pp. xxx + 2656. hb £18.95, pb £14.50.

27. *The Oxford Book of English Ghost Stories*, ed. by Michael Cox and R. A. Gilbert. OUP. pp. xvii + 504. £12.95.

28. *The Oxford Book of Sea Songs*, ed. by Roy Palmer. OUP. pp. xxx + 343. £9.95.

29. *The Oxford Book of Travel Verse*, ed. by Kevin Crossley-Holland. OUP. pp. xxxiv + 423. £12.50.

30. *The Faber Book of Political Verse*, ed. by Tom Paulin. Faber. pp. 482. hb £17.50, pb £8.95.

Germany, and Italy before 1900 are represented by about a hundred lines of Dante, and odd poems by André Chenier, Goethe, Heine, and Rimbaud. The notes to the volume are contemptibly thin and lazy; there is no indication from where texts have been taken. It is unclear what Paulin understands either by a 'political' or a 'non-political' poem. Another anthology which has attracted a certain amount of attention because of its unusual subject matter and method of compilation is *A Lycanthropy Reader: Werewolves in Western Culture*[31]. This has a wide range of texts in English from the Renaissance to modern times viewing the subject, which is never really properly defined, from a variety of perspectives including the medical and anthropological. The anthology is certainly morbidly interesting (there are some quite revolting photographs in it), but while it raises interesting topics it supplies few answers to them; it needed a much firmer editorial hand to make it a better piece of work.

Without much of an introduction or explanation, Esther Menascé[32] rather puzzlingly collects four plays on the theme of Don Juan in English literature: Shadwell's *The Libertine*, Shaw's *Don Giovanni Explains*, Flecker's *Don Juan*, and Arnold Bennett's *Don Juan de Marana* (these last two appear never to have been reprinted until this edition).

3. Bibliography

(a) Theory

In many ways 1986 was, with a few major exceptions, a thin year for bibliographical studies. This may prove to be an anomaly, or it may mark the beginning of a change in the structure of the subject: bibliography as it has been taught in universities is moving away from departments of literature into librarianship, where theoretical and historical bibliography provide few opportunities for employment or commercial reward. Specific bibliographical and textual points in specific authors continue to attract the attention of literary scholars, but their investigations rarely range beyond these limits. Book-trade history, which is of interest to members of other disciplines such as historians and economists, may provide a lifeline to the subject, but while it develops (often rather sprawlingly) in that direction bibliography still leaves too many fundamental questions and areas of interest unexplored.

Don McKenzie's inaugural set of three Panizzi lectures at the British Library[33] could be taken as a fair example of what is happening to bibliography. McKenzie's argument is that bibliography needs to be considered as 'the study of the sociology of texts' if it is to hold on to its intellectual status and usefulness. Above all it must focus on the history of the book, to move the bibliographer's task from the consideration of the mechanics of book production to an understanding of authorial production and consumption, not just of manuscript and print, but of all systems of signs, from maps to photographs to

31. *A Lycanthropy Reader: Werewolves in Western Culture*, ed. by Charlotte F. Otten. Syracuse. pp. xvi + 337. hb $32.50, pb $14.95.

32. *Minor Don Juans in British Literature*, ed. and intro. by Esther Menascé. Cisalpino–Goliardica. pp. 286. pb L 20,000.

33. *Bibliography and the Sociology of Texts*, by D. F. McKenzie. BL. pp. x + 70. pb £10.

comic strips, to, inevitably, films. The indeterminacy of texts, their incompleteness before consumption, means, according to McKenzie, that they constantly have to be re-edited, redefined, and reconstructed: it is bibliography alone, not history, nor criticism, nor sociology, which can present the 'reader' with the materials with which to do this. McKenzie's is a powerful voice in bibliographical studies; we shall undoubtedly hear a great deal more from other writers about 'the sociology of texts': it will be surprising if their contributions are as lively and energetic as these lectures.

Two further contributions to this subject appeared in *LH* with John Feather's 'The Book in History and the History of the Book' calling for a full technical and cultural history of the book which would pay special attention to the history of the role of libraries. In the same journal in 'The History of the Book: New Questions? New Answers?' David D. Hall argues for the importance of the study of the history of reading in its relations with popular culture and for the close relationship between social history and the history of the book; both of these articles put their cases sensibly and clearly, but once again one may well feel that the idea of the history of the book is more appealing than the vast amount of new research work that needs to go into its writing.

The only major theoretical offering from the school of Bowers this year was G. Thomas Tanselle's long review essay in *SB* on 'Historicism and Critical Editing'. Tanselle considers how bibliographers and editors have responded to modern ideas about the nature of literary production; the recent writings of among others D. F. McKenzie, Jerome J. McGann, Hershel Parker, and Hans Walter Gabler are found wanting by Tanselle, who concludes rather blandly that 'Recent writings on editorial theory . . . provide the basis both for exasperation and for hope'.

In a pleasantly informal piece, 'A Portrait of the Author as a Bibliography' (*BC*), Dan H. Laurence, the bibliographer of George Bernard Shaw, meditates on the relationship between author-bibliography and biography and pays due attention to the success of the Soho Bibliographies.

A helpful account of the theory of fingerprinting books, which among other uses allows reprints to be distinguished from their originals, is given by P. C. A. Vriesema in 'The STCN Fingerprint' (*SB*), in relation to work on *The Short-Title Catalogue, Netherlands*.

AEB did not appear in 1985 or 1986.

(b) Reference Works

It has taken ten years for the first volume of the revised edition of the *Short-Title Catalogue*[34] covering A to H to appear, since the second volume was issued in 1976; it has been worth waiting for. The new *STC* is such an improvement on the old one, contains so much new information and material, is so much better organized and arranged, that it must be counted as one of the greatest scholarly achievements of the century. It is hard to speak too highly of it. Literary students and bibliographers now have, uniquely for a country of this size and productivity, a complete and accurate list of books, pamphlets,

34. *A Short-Title Catalogue of Books Printed in England, Scotland, & Ireland and of English Books Printed Abroad 1475–1640*, first comp. by A. W. Pollard and G. R. Redgrave. Second edn begun by W. A. Jackson and F. S. Ferguson, completed by Katharine F. Pantzer. Vol. I: *A–H*. BibS. pp. liii + 620. £125.

broadsheets, even bookplates printed in the British Isles or abroad in English before 1641. Additions and corrections will inevitably need to be made to the new *STC* but its basic form and plan are so sound that a complete revision need never again be undertaken; when a third volume of indexes and appendixes is issued, the scope for research into printing, publishing, and literary production between 1475 and 1640 will be further expanded.

The advances bibliography has made in the field of the cataloguing and study of printed books have for long left our knowledge of literary manuscripts far behind. There are signs that this is now changing and a very welcome witness to this development is the publication of another volume of the *Index of English Literary Manuscripts*[35]. The latest part covers the period 1700 to 1800 and lists the manuscripts of authors from Addison to Fielding (for good reasons Blake is dealt with only cursorily). The entries range from the one John Dennis item to four connected with Fielding to the ten associated with Mark Akenside, right up to 1,297 Burns manuscripts, each of which is meticulously described, after concise but extremely useful general introductory remarks on each of the twenty-one authors included in this marvellous volume.

John Feather's *Dictionary of Book History*[36] is a more curious compilation; in plain and sometimes humorous terms it tells the reader, in a more or less alphabetical sequence (from 'Abbey, John Roland' to 'Yellowbacks') about the mechanics of book production, something of the history of printing, publishing, the book trade, collecting, and modern bibliography; but that something is not always sufficient and it is a pity that Feather's work is not both longer and fuller – a second edition, much enlarged, with some badly needed corrections, would make this a more useful and reliable reference book.

Two bibliographies have been re-issued by StPB in corrected and new editions. As one would expect of Philip Gaskell his revision of the bibliography of the Foulis Press[37], which he first issued in 1964, is thorough and painstaking; in a new section of the book he lists 221 additions and amendments to the original work, including over fifty entirely new entries, and the index has been revised to include all of these. J. Howard Woolmer has extended his coverage of the productions of the Hogarth Press[38] from 1938 to 1946 bringing the total number of titles issued by the Press from its inception in 1917 to 525. This is confessedly a plain checklist, not a bibliography, but it includes some production and sales details, although it says very little about reprints of books other than Virginia Woolf's own. Woolmer's book seems aimed more at collectors than literary historians of the productions of one of the most popular and influential publishers of the first half of this century; there is certainly plenty of room for further investigation of the Hogarth Press. Woolmer has also published a brief bibliography (which is again scarcely more than a checklist), of the Samurai Press[39], founded at Ranworth Hall, near Norwich in

35. *Index of English Literary Manuscripts.* Vol. III: *1700–1800.* Part 1: *Addison–Fielding.* Mansell. pp. xx + 357. £120.

36. *A Dictionary of Book History*, by John Feather. CH. pp. 278. £25.

37. *A Bibliography of the Foulis Press*, by Philip Gaskell. Second edn. StPB. pp. 484. £35.

38. *A Checklist of the Hogarth Press 1917–1946*, by J. Howard Woolmer. StPB. pp. xxxiv + 250. £30.

39. *The Samurai Press 1906–1909: A Bibliography*, by J. Howard Woolmer. W/B. pp. xix + 70. $25.

1906 by Maurice Browne in association with, among others, Harold Monro; in its short life it mainly issued austerely designed volumes of poetry, including three books by W. W. Gibson and one by John Drinkwater.

Archer Taylor's *Book Catalogues: Their Varieties and Uses*[40] is a well-known work, first issued in 1957, to be consulted rather than read through; full of useful and obscure information not easily available elsewhere, it is a historical survey of book catalogues, which has now been re-issued in a reprint with appended new material: the largest number of corrections and additions are supplied for the highly valuable list of 'Catalogues of Private Libraries Recommended by Bibliographers'.

Having completed the publication of the index cards to the manuscripts in the British Library, Chadwyck–Healey have turned their attention abroad and quickly and apparently effortlessly delivered eight substantial volumes containing the card catalogues of most of the manuscripts of the libraries at Harvard[41]. As with the BL volumes a certain amount of editing seems to have gone on, but of course for historical reasons the standard of the cataloguing on the Harvard cards is far higher overall than for the London ones. The advantages of having these card catalogues of great British and American collections made widely available do not need to be explained.

LongR has published an index to its first thirty numbers from 1970 until 1985.

(c) Printing and Publishing History
Detailed scholarly work of a high standard continues to be done on the history and methods of English book production and publishing from the early sixteenth century to more recent times. In *Quaerendo*'s 'Jan van Doesborch (?–1536), Printer of English Texts' P. J. A. Franssen usefully attends to the Anglo-Dutch business career of van Doesborch, who between 1505 and 1530 printed at Antwerp some twenty-two English texts including *Frederyke of Jennen* and *Tyll Howlegles*.

For all the theorizing that bibliography attracts, looking at marks on a page still lies at the heart of the matter. Eric Rasmussen's short article in *SB* on 'The Relevance of Cast-Off Copy in Determining the Nature of Omissions: Q2 *Hamlet*' offers some juicy food for thought by suggesting that where a text has been cast-off and set by formes 'The presence or absence of page-filling expedients at the end of a compositor's stint may be of use in distinguishing accidental omissions from intended ones': certainly his example from *Hamlet* where Q2 and F can be compared is convincing. Rasmussen's piece is followed in *SB* by Antony Hammond's long account of '*The White Devil* in Nicholas Okes's Shop', which should be of great interest not just to Webster scholars. Hammond is mainly concerned with compositor-analysis and his conclusions are provocative: that an examination of the width of the type-line in the quarto, shows that since much verse was set as if already justified in the compositor's stick, verse cannot always, as has often been thought, be taken as a reliable witness for discriminating spelling patterns; that analysis by spacing after a mark of punctuation (*pace* Don McKenzie) is a good discriminator, as are

40. *Book Catalogues: Their Varieties and Uses*, by Archer Taylor, rev. by Wm. P. Barlow Jr. Second edn. StPB. pp. xxxvii + 284. £28.
41. *Catalogue of the Manuscripts in the Houghton Library, Harvard.* C-H. Vols. I–VII. pp. 464; Vol. VIII. pp. 454. £995.

spelling tests, but that analysis of this kind is dangerous since in the case of Webster's play different compositors sometimes worked on the same page; and finally that the analysis of damaged type (*pace* Peter Blayney) needs to be undertaken with extreme rigour and that while it is 'a bibliographical tool of value, it will not in itself suffice to determine the compositors, or without some ambiguity, the precise order of setting' of the formes. Hammond's article is long, but clearly and lightly written: textual scholars will need to pay attention to its methods as well as its conclusions. Paul Mulholland in *Lib* further investigates Nicholas Okes's shop in his account of the rare practice of the use of multiple running titles in rotation as one of the several puzzling features connected with the printing of 'Thomas Middleton's *The Two Gates of Salvation* (1609)'.

Valuable work on the history of the book trade before the Civil War continues: Gerald D. Johnson in 'John Trundle and the Book-Trade 1603–1626' (*SB*) writes on the career of Trundle, who among some rather undistinguished titles issued Q1 of *Hamlet*, Middleton and Rowley's *A Fair Quarrel*, and some works by Dekker and John Taylor.

Without attempting headline-analysis or compositor identification Kim Walker in *LongR* simply examines the 'Press Variants and Proof Correction in [James] Shirley's *The Dukes Mistris* (1638)', his last play for the Phoenix theatre: a collation of twenty copies revealed no evidence of authorial proof reading or revision and showed that printing house correction was mainly concerned with the play's punctuation. *Periodical Publications 1641–1700*[42] is a useful survey which pays welcome attention to the technical problems of their production and acts as a foretaste of the authors' *A Short-Title Catalogue of British Serials, 1641–1700*, expected to appear shortly. In a rather diffuse article in *PubH*, 'Print-World Ideology and the Double Natured Stage. Towards an Alliance 1660–1700', Julie Stone Peters looks at the relationship between the theatre and publishers after the Restoration, paying particular attention to Congreve and Jacob Tonson, but has little new to report.

Using *Eighteenth-century British Books* John Feather presents a 'preliminary subject analysis' of books and pamphlets in 'British Publishing in the Eighteenth Century' (*Lib*). Feather analyses the results of his researches in several different and useful ways, but realizes that they provide only a partial and incomplete picture of publishing activity. One expanding area of publishing during this period was that intended to supply the financial markets with commercial information: this new development is briefly surveyed for the first time by John J. McKusker in *Lib* in 'The Business Press in England before 1775'.

The format and nature of the early periodicals, in particular *The Spectator*, are rather too generally considered by Charles A. Knight in 'Bibliography and the Shape of the Literary Periodical in the Early Eighteenth Century' (*Lib*): he too has little new to report. On the other hand, E. W. Pitcher continues to investigate minutely the world of eighteenth-century journalism with two brief notes in *PBSA* firstly on 'Further Remarks on Arbitrary Signatures in Smollett's *British Magazine* (1760–67)', showing the magazine's use of false names and initials to disguise the unoriginal nature of articles, and secondly on

42. *Periodical Publications 1641–1700: A Survey with Illustrations*, by C. Nelson and M. Seccombe. OPBS. BibS. pp. 109. pb £10.

the deceptive publishing history of the short-lived mid-1770s journal *The Monthly Magazine* in 'Problems with Eighteenth-Century Miscellaneous Publications'; and two more such notes in *Lib* on 'Reprintings of Literary Prose in the Final Years of the *Town and Country Magazine*', which freely helped itself to material from earlier journals, and on *The London Magazine*'s borrowings of essay serials from the *British Magazine*.

This has not been such a rich year for studies in Victorian publishing. Using the vast Chiswick Press archive in the British Library, Janet Ing in *PBSA* looks in some detail at the workings and productions of Charles Whittingham's influential publishing house between 1852, when it moved from Chiswick to central London, and 1859, when Whittingham went into partnership with his manager and retired from the business. The career of 'Henry Colburn, Publisher', one of the first users of 'hype', and one of the most disliked of Victorian bookmen, is re-assessed with characteristic energy and insight by John Sutherland in *PubH*. Sutherland also contributes to this year's *VPR* with an article on the '*Cornhill*'s Sales and Payments: The First Decade', based on a notebook in NLS. Periodical history continues to attract other original and useful contributions to research: the same volume of *VPR* contains Monica Fryckstedt's account of 'Douglas Jerrold's *Shilling Magazine*', 'a short-lived, but interesting radical monthly, sponsored by *Punch*' to which she adds an analysis of the contents of its seven volumes which appeared between 1845 and 1848; a piece by Ann Parry, 'The Grove Years 1868–1883: A "new look" for *Macmillan's Magazine*', on the changes that George Grove brought as editor to *Macmillan's* after the resignation of David Masson; and a rather thinner piece by Bruce A. White on 'Elbert Hubbard and *The Philistine: A Periodical of Protest* (1895–1915)' to which Stephen Crane contributed.

The question of which books really were in demand continues to fascinate. In *SB* Richard D. Altick provides 'Nineteenth-Century Best Sellers: A Third List', based on contemporary and later references. Simon Eliot in *Lib* goes to published public library catalogues to survey 'Public Libraries and Popular Authors, 1883–1912': as Eliot realizes there are problems with the methods he has adopted, and the samples he has chosen are too much subject to different sorts of variation, but his inquiry opens up a new field for research, which may possibly one day yield some answers to a topic which clearly worries literary historians.

Just when you thought you had sorted out American issues of British books, Bruce Whiteman comes along in *PBSA* to alert bibliographers to 'Canadian Issues of Anglo-American Fiction': authorized editions of novels by Kipling, Forster, Huxley, and Wells (whose particular case Whiteman briefly investigates) began to appear after the Chase Act of 1891, and if they are not of textual significance they are, as Whiteman correctly argues, a significant part of an author's publishing history.

(d) Institutional and Private Library History
The publication of a facsimile of the 1605 printed catalogue of the Bodleian Library in Oxford[43] compiled by Thomas James marks an important milestone

43. *The First Printed Catalogue of the Bodleian Library 1605: A Facsimile.* Clarendon. pp. xvi + 651. £40.

in the reconstruction of the Bodleian's history, but it also gives a wonderful insight into the resources available to an inquisitive mind at a key point in English and European intellectual history. The Bodleian was in the words of the anonymous author of the Introduction to this facsimile 'the first institutional library to produce a substantial and widely distributed record of a collection which had, from its foundation, world-wide fame'.

Cambridge has not been idle in recording the history of its own magnificent collections. Two large and beautifully produced volumes cover the history of the University Library. The first of these by J. C. T. Oates[44] takes the story from the Library's beginnings in about 1350, through its most important and acquisitive times in the late sixteenth century and the mid seventeenth century, down to the Copyright Act of 1710. As one would expect, the story is expertly told with a good balance between the history of the gradual growth and development of the Library as a whole, the record of individual bequests, and the immediate problems faced by the different University Librarians. This is quite simply a volume which no historian of English literature can afford to ignore. Further work on Cambridge libraries and individual collectors in the town have appeared during the year, but have not been available for review. In *TCBS* David Pearson helpfully supplements with a full catalogue Philip Gaskell's account of 'The Books of Peter Shaw in Trinity College, Cambridge', donated at the beginning of James I's reign; on the whole Shaw's books reflect the usual interests of a Cambridge don at this period, most of them being theological with a bias towards Calvinists and Swiss reformers, with only one work in English (by a recusant), but including a Hebrew Old Testament.

Less familiar collections have also received some welcome attention. The importance of J. M. Blatchly's 'Ipswich Town Library: Unfamiliar Libraries XXVI' in *BC* lies partly in its description of an interesting collection made between 1599 and 1773 and partly in its cracking of the code widely used by early seventeenth-century booksellers to price their books: it is a simple letter for number code written in ink on the title-page of the book. This modest article contains material which will be of great value to those working on English books, their collectors, and prices in the first part of the seventeenth century. For Durham, David Pearson[45] has produced a pioneering study, based on the Cathedral Library and neighbouring archives, of local bookbinders and booksellers from 1660 to 1760: his work has much to say about the provincial trade at this time and about the sort of everyday bindings which have not yet received the attention they deserve.

The papers in *Bibliophily*[46] range from Mirjam Foot's survey of 'Bookbinding Patronage in England', which is perhaps a little too general to be of much new interest, to Katherine Swift's important piece on the 'Bibliotheca Sunderlandia: The Making of an Eighteenth-Century Library', which contains much original research, as does Anthony Lister's account of the difficult relationship between the second Earl Spencer and his unofficial 'librarian'

44. *Cambridge University Library: A History: From the Beginnings to the Copyright Act of Queen Anne*, by J. C. T. Oates. CUP. pp. xviii + 510. £50.

45. *Durham Bookbinders and Booksellers 1660–1760*, by David Pearson. OBS. pp. xi + 61. pb £7.50.

46. *Bibliophily*, ed. by Robin Myers and Michael Harris. PHOS. C–H. pp. x + 172 with three microfiche. pb £25.

Thomas Frognall Dibdin. Other articles in this rather uneven volume include Michael Harris on the British Museum's problems in collecting newspapers in the nineteenth century, Brian North Lee on the uses to which bibliographers can put the study of bookplates, Robin Myers on the characteristically expansive Caxton celebrations of 1877, and Murray McLaggan on the vast private library collected at Merthyr Mawr by the Nicholl family in the last century.

In 'John Twyne of Canterbury (d. 1581)' (*Lib*) Andrew G. Watson presents more of the results of his investigations into early English collectors of medieval manuscripts with an account of the books owned by Twyne: Watson is able to associate him with some fifty manuscripts and to indicate his interest in Anglo-Saxon studies.

The libraries of English men of letters are always fascinating even when only slight evidence of their contents survives. For Sir Thomas Browne we are exceptionally lucky that the 1710 auction catalogue of his and his son's library was printed and has now been reproduced in facsimile by Jeremiah S. Finch[47] with an introduction, notes, and an invaluable index to the identifiable titles, which number just under two and a half thousand. Since only one extant book can be shown to have been in Browne's library, this auction catalogue is the prime source for our knowledge of what books he owned – Finch's notes are mainly concerned with the use to which Browne put the works listed in the catalogue in his writings. Pope's library has had to be reconstructed piecemeal mainly by Maynard Mack: in 'Pope's Books: A Postscript to Mack' (*N&Q*) Graham Cartwright returns to the subject and reports in detail on the Hurd Library at Hartlebury, where he finds that one of Pope's books has been lost since Mack was there and that four books ascribed to Pope's ownership by Mack are not in fact his, but he is able to ascribe a copy of Denham's *Poems* 1703 certainly and a copy of Etherege's *Works* 1704 possibly to Pope's collection.

From a later and more heroic period of book collecting Robert Curzon's adventures in search of manuscripts in the Near East in the 1830s and in trying to keep his estate at Parham together for nearly forty years are chronicled, largely through his amusing letters to his friend Walter Sneyd, in Ian H. C. Fraser's original study based on much unpublished material in *The Heir of Parham*[48].

The considerable riches of the Dunston collection and the background to its formation in Wiltshire are well described in two sympathetic and evocative articles in *BLR*, 'The Dunston Collection' and 'Background to a Collection: The Dunston Family', by Clive and Veronica Hurst: it was begun by F. W. Dunston (1850–1915), included many editions of Browning, Samuel Butler, Byron, Pope, Scott, Stevenson, and Tennyson, and is now in the Bodleian Library, Oxford.

(e) Attribution Studies

The ghost of John Payne Collier may be heard gently laughing at the end of Joel H. Kaplan's investigation ('Thomas Middleton's Epitaph on the Death of

47. *A Catalogue of the Libraries of Sir Thomas Browne and Dr. Edward Browne, his Son: A Facsimile Reproduction with an Introduction, Notes, and Index*, by Jeremiah S. Finch. PTBI N.S. 7. Brill. pp. xiv + 177. Fl 52.

48. *The Heir of Parham: Robert Curzon Fourteenth Baron Zouche*, by Ian H. C. Fraser. Paradigm (now Erskine). pp. xviii + 230. £19.50.

Richard Burbage, and John Payne Collier' in *PBSA*) into whether Middleton's epitaph, first printed by Collier, is genuine or not: Kaplan cannot prove it was forged, but by looking at Collier's use of it in his various publications strongly suggests that it is not authentic. The same journal has two further intriguing contributions to attribution studies: 'What if Defoe Did Not Write the *History of the Wars of Charles XII*?' by P. N. Furbank and W. R. Owens argues forcibly on stylistic and political grounds against Defoe's authorship of the *History of the Wars of Charles XII* (1715); and 'Who Wrote Bertrand Russell's *Wisdom of the West*?' by Carl Spadoni on how modern publishing techniques played down that Paul Foulkes 'ghostwrote' the whole of Bertrand Russell's popular *Wisdom of the West* of 1959.

Almost the whole of one issue of *RES* was given over to a three-cornered debate as to who wrote the poem 'The Barberry-Tree' until now known only from a manuscript copy at Christ Church, Oxford, in a private letter written by Charles Abraham Elton. John Beer challenged its usual ascription to Wordsworth, putting the case, based on verbal echoes, that it could be by Coleridge; J. C. C. Mays announced the discovery of a new text of the poem in *Felix Farley's Bristol Journal* for 1807, investigated the poem's Bristol associations and suggested that it might be either by Elton himself or by Thomas Beddoes; Jonathan Wordsworth replied in defence of his attribution and continued to argue that the poem was by Wordsworth. From the point of view of attribution studies Mays's article was the most interesting, because of his investigation of the textual background and origins of the poem. A debate over attribution which rises no higher than arguing about verbal echoes and their relation to borrowings and parody is not a very useful one.

Literary Theory

TONY PINKNEY, NICK ROYLE,
MAKIKO MINOW, and RACHEL BOWLBY

This chapter has the following sections: 1. General; 2. Poetics and Narratology; 3. Semiotics; 4. Rhetoric and Deconstruction; 5. Hermeneutics; 6. Psychoanalysis; 7. Feminism; 8. Historical and Materialist Criticism. Tony Pinkney has contributed sections 1, 2, 3, 5, and 8, Nick Royle section 4, Makiko Minow section 6, and Rachel Bowlby section 7.

1. General

'We're now in one of those moments', Francis Mulhern remarked at the 1986 Oxford English Limited conference on 'The State of Criticism', 'when the Humanities is forced to discover the difference between itself and actual, empirical, heterogeneous humanity.' It's therefore not surprising that the vexed question of humanism should have come to the fore in this year's general discussions of the state of literary criticism and theory. In *The Humanistic Heritage*[1] Daniel R. Schwarz seeks to spell out the theoretical assumptions of an Anglo-American 'humanistic formalist' novel criticism, from James to Hillis Miller, that has usually been too immersed in close textual analysis to do the job itself, and which has thus ceded unnecessary ground to such theoretically articulate challengers as Marxism and deconstruction. However, one ends this book wondering why a summary of this tradition, however judicious and lucid, should be supposed to constitute a *defence* of it; an altogether tougher brand of argumentation, surely, would be in order here. Moreover, Schwarz's claims for continuity between his humanistic formalism and Marxism and deconstruction are made suspect by his plumping for 'soft' options (Raymond Williams, J. Hillis Miller) rather than the hard cases (Macherey, Eagleton, de Man) which would really test out the contention. Lionel Trilling, surprisingly, doesn't get a chapter to himself in Schwarz's study, but is well served by Mark Krupnik's *Lionel Trilling and the Fate of Cultural Criticism*[2]. The major American disciple of Matthew Arnold, Trilling remains of interest to us today because at various periods his work tries to take on board cultural forces incompatible with Arnoldianism. Krupnik's key theme is the 'two Trillings': urbane man of the Attic centre but also advocate of

1. *The Humanistic Heritage: Critical Theories of the English Novel from James to Hillis Miller*, by Daniel R. Schwarz. Macmillan. pp. viii + 282. £27.50.
2. *Lionel Trilling and the Fate of Cultural Criticism*, by Mark Krupnik. Northwestern. pp. x + 207. $21.95.

'positive Jewishness', of the ethnic margins; humane liberal but also enthusiast
for a modernism that was mostly reactionary and sometimes Fascist. Unlike
Schwarz's, this book is an object lesson in how to make relevant a figure that
contemporary theory might be inclined to dismiss too easily. A similar 'return'
to a powerful American precursor is evinced in the recent revival of interest in
the work of Kenneth Burke; its latest manifestation is Timothy W. Crusius's 'A
Case for Kenneth Burke's Dialectic and Rhetoric' in *P&R*. Edward Said makes
a similar move in his 'The Horizon of R. P. Blackmur' in *Raritan*.

Two impressively sophisticated defences of some key humanist notions are
Reconstructing Individualism[3] and Stanley Corngold's *The Fate of the Self*[4],
both of which acknowledge the force of the theoretical challenge to the notion
of the subject in our century, yet seek to salvage something from the rubble.
Reconstructing Individualism is a massive interdisciplinary collection. Of most
interest to the literary theorist will perhaps be Stephen Greenblatt's 'Fiction and
Friction' which reflects on the relation between cultural discourses on sexuality
and notions of individual identity, Christine Brooke-Rose's somewhat
pedestrian 'The Dissolution of Character in the Novel', and Nancy
Chodorow's 'The Mediation of the Self through Psychoanalysis'. Werner
Hamacher's subtle analysis of 'Nietzsche on the Individual and Individuality'
anticipates Stanley Corngold's project of finding a defence of the self in those
very writers commonly assumed to have dismantled it – Nietzsche, Kafka,
Freud, and Heidegger among others. He shows how our view of the 'poetic self'
must be subtilized, being now reconstructed from elusive effects of meaning
and style rather than assumed *a priori*; in this way, he cannily takes on many of
the interpretative insights of contemporary French theory, but then turns them
against it. His effective readings of key modernist writers serve to demonstrate,
as Marxist theorists have also tended to argue, that poststructuralism wilfully
fetishizes the moments of negativity, rift, and rupture (which had, in their turn,
been wilfully overlooked by classical humanism).

In his *Intellectuals in Power*[5] Paul A. Bové sketches 'A Genealogy of Critical
Humanism'. The book offers finely diagnostic accounts of I. A. Richards and
Erich Auerbach, but seems curiously divided in its loyalties as it approaches the
present. Bové's admiration for Edward Said, who is seen to extract the
maximum politically oppositional mileage out of the old 'critical humanist'
paradigm, is evident throughout – at times movingly and even embarrassingly
so. Yet he also has strong Foucauldian antihumanist allegiances, and reverts
over and over to the claim that the 'leading intellectual' necessarily posited by
humanist discourse, even in its most politicized forms, is an inherently anti-
democratic figure; Foucault's 'specific' rather than humanism's 'universal'
intellectual then seems the only palatable alternative. Such ambivalences are, of
course, hardly unique to Bové. The attempt to problematize unduly transcendentalist or totalizing versions of Theory without endorsing a politically

3. *Reconstructing Individualism: Autonomy, Individuality, and the Self in Western
Thought*, ed. by Thomas C. Heller, Morton Sosna, and David E. Wellbery. Stanford.
pp. xiv + 365. hb $39.50, pb $11.95.

4. *The Fate of the Self: German Writers and French Theory*, by Stanley Corngold.
ColU. pp. xv + 279. $28.50.

5. *Intellectuals in Power: A Genealogy of Critical Humanism*, by Paul A. Bové.
ColU. pp. xx + 340. $27.50.

debilitating relativism or 'localism' is the dilemma of all of us; and Bové's sustained exploration of it makes this a powerfully representative work. Since Bové has long been associated with the journal *Boundary*, we might here mention, belatedly, that it has a 1985 special issue on 'The Institutions of Humanism'. The intellectuals who 'man' (*sic*) such institutions are the subject not only of Paul Bové's book but also of a special issue of *Sal*, with contributions by (among many others) Said, George Steiner, Christopher Lasch, and Conor Cruise O'Brien.

Humanists are – or at least *see* themselves as being – pluralists, but 'pluralism' points also towards those more radical forms of poststructuralist heterogeneity which are usually taken to be antihumanist. This tension enlivens the issue of *CritI* on 'Pluralism and its Discontents', where some of the contributors (Wayne Booth, W. J. T. Mitchell) seek to rescue the notion for traditional liberalism, while others (Ihab Hassan, Hayden White) are more inclined to push it to and beyond its academic limits; Hassan's aim is to 'limn a region of postmodern "indetermanences" (indeterminacy lodged in immanence) in which critical pluralism takes place'. But the shrewdest contributions are those which take the tension itself as the object of analysis, as with Bruce Erlich's 'Amphibolies: On the Critical Self-Contradictions of "Pluralism"'. Another central humanist concept, the 'canon', is canvassed in a special issue of *Sal*. In 'Aiming a Canon at the Curriculum', Robert Scholes attempts to fight off current moves (by E. D. Hirsch among others, in his view) to establish a 'core curriculum' for the humanities in America. Hirsch thereafter complains of being misrepresented, and perhaps – technically speaking – he is; but clearly the conservative notion of an ahistorical cultural 'core' is built into his famous meaning/significance dualism. In 'An Intellectual Impasse' Marjorie Perloff interestingly finds Scholes's liberal generosity just as worrying as the conservative canon itself, and in a passionately argued rejoinder Elizabeth Fox-Genovese speaks on behalf of those marginalized sexual, social, and racial forces that the traditional canon has either excluded (Hirsch) or admitted only as it were negatively and agnostically (Scholes). Any canon of course presupposes criteria of *value*, and W. J. T. Mitchell takes up this aspect of the debate in his 'Three Theories of Value' in *Raritan*; Harold Osborne deals with the question in more philosophical vein in 'Aesthetic Experience and Cultural Value' in *JAAC*.

The assailants, as well as defenders and ambivalent genealogists, of humanism are well represented this year. Nietzsche's *Human, All Too Human*[6] is now available in CUP's excellent Texts in German Philosophy series; the two volumes are here printed as one, and at a pleasantly modest price. *The Nouveau Roman Reader*[7] reminds us of the vigour and variety of this militantly anti-humanist 'school' of novelists, and the editors contribute a helpful introductory overview. Kate Soper's *Humanism and Anti-Humanism*[8] extends the debate into philosophical terrain, dealing with the challenge posed to humanist categories by contemporary French theory. This is an excellent, accessible

6. *Human, All Too Human: A Book for Free Spirits*, by Friedrich Nietzsche, trans. by R. J. Hollingdale. CUP. pp. xix + 395. pb £7.95.

7. *The Nouveau Roman Reader*, ed. by John Fletcher and John Calder. Calder. pp. 255. pb £6.95.

8. *Humanism and Anti-Humanism*, by Kate Soper. Hutchinson. pp. 159. pb £5.95.

survey of arguments around humanism from German Idealism on, often achieving minor miracles of condensation in its accounts of difficult thinkers (Hegel, early Marx, Foucault, Lacan). Soper's own preference is for a socialist or existentialist humanism which rejects any transcendental human 'essence' in arguing for the historical situatedness of human beings, and yet wants to retain a sense of history as irreducibly the product of human acts, meanings, projects – and not as a ballet of dehumanized structures. She claims and persuasively demonstrates that the 'theoretical anti-humanisms' of recent years have flattened out the subtleties of such a stance in the violence of their polemics. My own 'Nineteenth-Century Studies: As They Are and As They Might Be' in the Oxford English Limited journal, *NfN*, offers a historical genealogy of the Arnoldian classicist humanism that was (and is) Oxford's distinctive contribution to English studies and which has been constantly neglected in favour of Cambridge and *Scrutiny*; I also sketch a countertradition centred upon Clough, Ruskin, Lewis Carroll, and William Morris. In a complementary article on 'Dancing in the Dark: The Practice of Theory at Oxford', Ken Hirschkop examines the impact (and impasses) of modern theory among the Arnoldian dreaming spires. Vexed and vast as the question of humanism is, we can at least say that the time has come to venture beyond the sterile antinomies of a simple 'for' or 'against' – even if, as Paul Bové's book testifies, the nature of that 'beyond' is far from clear.

The theme of postmodernism, around which this section was organized last year, remains important. Andreas Huyssen's *After the Great Divide*[9] is a powerful contribution to this debate. Inspired by Peter Bürger's *Theory of the Avant-Garde*, Huyssen argues that we must firmly distinguish between 'modernism' and the 'avant-garde' – the former sealing itself hermetically against the contaminations of mass-culture, the latter breaking open the closed sphere of the 'aesthetic' in order to return it to everyday social praxis. Only with this distinction in place, he contends, can we properly situate *post*modernism. Huyssen's polarity enables him to avoid a more familiar polarization of recent theoretical debate. If much French theory celebrates the postmodern as a radical break with the modernist heritage and much Habermas-inspired German theory laments it as an assault on the rationalistic 'project of modernity', Huyssen proposes a third possibility – that postmodernism continues the project, not of modernism, but of the historical avant-garde (and this in a less negative sense than Bürger's own work suggests). He demonstrates this thesis with a series of compelling readings of such cultural phenomena as Hollywood, Wagner, pop art, the TV series 'Holocaust', which together comprise a rich, multifaceted study. In *NGC* David Roberts joins the critical debate around Bürger's work with a study of '*Marat/Sade*, or the Birth of Postmodernism from the Spirit of the Avantgarde', and in *PLL* Peter G. Christensen extends the argument to other theorists of the avant-garde in his 'The Relationship of Decadence to the Avant-Garde as Seen by Poggioli, Bürger, and Calinescu'.

Related issues are less successfully canvassed in *Postmodernism and Politics*[10], a collection of essays more heterogeneous than its title suggests.

---

9. *After the Great Divide: Modernism, Mass Culture, Postmodernism*, by Andreas Huyssen. IndU. pp. xii + 244. hb $29.95, pb $9.95.

10. *Postmodernism and Politics*, ed. by Jonathan Arac. ManU. pp. xliii + 171. pb £8.95.

Interesting pieces on Raymond Williams, John Berger, Ezra Pound, and reader-response criticism have little to do with the general theme (or at best engage only the '. . . Politics' half of it). Rainer Nägele moves closer in the course of a subtle analysis of 'Theodor W. Adorno's Negative Dialectic in the Context of Poststructuralism', but only Paul Bové and the editor, Jonathan Arac, confront it head on. Bové examines the work of Stanley Aronowitz as one possible model for a postmodernist, 'counterhegemonic' critic, while Arac trenchantly situates the journal *Boundary* (of which this book was initially a double issue) in relation to the broader context of postmodernist polemics and, heroically but not quite convincingly, seeks to forge a unity from his contributors' efforts.

In *The End of Art Theory: Criticism and Postmodernity*[11] Victor Burgin takes up one of the options that Andreas Huyssen had sought to rule out of bounds. 'Art theory' for him denotes those intertwined practices of criticism, art history, and aesthetics which are born in the Enlightenment and come to maturity in 'high modernism'; postmodernity then breaks radically with all this, initiating a general theory of representations rather than an aesthetics. Burgin develops this theme in a series of lively essays, including two fine studies of Roland Barthes: 'Re-reading *Camera Lucida*' and 'Diderot, Barthes, *Vertigo*'. But while it may still be important to bait and refute the traditionalists, there's a sense of untimeliness about this project at a moment when so many strands of radical theory are moving tentatively away from a general semiotics and *towards* a renewed concern with aesthetic questions. *After Truth: A Post-Modern Manifesto*[12] is more a symptom of the postmodern than an analysis of it. This document of the 'new pluralism' cavalierly sacrifices truth on its first page, yet remains fixated on the relativism that is presumed to afflict us when epistemological guarantees are kicked away. 'We can tell whatever political stories we wish', its authors inform us; and so they can, but who will be there to listen? Jeffrey Herf's *Reactionary Modernism* (1984)[13], now in paperback, is a timely reminder where all such blithe dismissals of Enlightenment rationality risk ending up. To reject the Enlightenment and yet enthuse over modern(ist) technology: this Lyotardian vision ends in a fateful *rapprochement* with Nazism, which itself paradoxically combines robust modernism with the cultural nostalgia of *Blut und Boden*. The figures Herf examines include both intellectuals like Oswald Spengler and Ernst Jünger but also, illuminatingly, German engineers of the period. This impressive study reminds us of just how much, in the lonely hour of the last instance, depends on our current debates over modernism and its successors. *Telos* this year provides much relevant material. In 'The Crisis of Post-Modernity in France' Claude Karnoouh tries to shift the term 'postmodernism' from critical to cultural theory, looking at the shifts in recent French social experience by which it was once funded but on which it now founders. In 'Marxism and the Post-Modern Condition' Gérard Raulet evokes Marxism's ambivalent response to modernity to suggest that it may in some ways anticipate the postmodernist critique of the

---

11. *The End of Art Theory: Criticism and Postmodernity*, by Victor Burgin. Macmillan. pp. x + 221. hb £20, pb £6.95.
12. *After Truth: A Post-Modern Manifesto*, by The Second of January Group. Inventions. pp. 31. pb £1.50.
13. *Reactionary Modernism: Technology, Culture, and Politics in Weimar and the Third Reich*, by Jeffrey Herf. CUP. pp. xii + 251. pb £8.95.

latter; in a brief, sharp rejoinder Jean-François Lyotard objects to Raulet's reading of his relation to the Kantian sublime. Christa Bürger takes the debate across the Atlantic, suggesting that in the light of recent political and economic developments the postmodernist celebration of the demise of 'high' or 'auratic' art may be culpably premature.

Two books which should also be noticed in the postmodernist pigeonhole are Jonathan Goldberg's *Voice Terminal Echo*[14] and Arthur C. Danto's *The Philosophical Disenfranchisement of Art*[15]. Goldberg attempts the interesting experiment of reading English Renaissance texts through the grid of post-modernist theoretical concerns. The result is a set of dense, challengingly revisionist accounts of Marvell, Spenser, Herbert, Milton, and Shakespeare, and a vertiginous sense – as with Barthes's modernist reading of Balzac in *S/Z* – that if this can be done, the very literary periodization that allowed post-modernism to become visible as a concept in the first place is breaking down. When, we now feel inclined to ask, were we *not* postmodern? Yet another 'always-already' seems to have set in. Danto's book is concerned with that shifting, vexed border between art and philosophy which postmodernism and poststructuralism have both sought to break down. Danto concedes much of the case in favour of the irreducibly figural dimension of philosophical texts, and does so with a clarity and precision we should expect from the analytical philosopher he is, but which is rare in this particular theoretical domain, where a murky apocalypticism tends to be the order of the day.

Theory and pedagogy remains a pressing concern, at two levels. In terms of commercial publishing, the rush is now on to produce the ultimate anthology of literary theory and the ultimate student's guide to the entire field. Robert Con Davis's *Contemporary Literary Criticism*[16] makes an impressive stab at being the former. One can always haggle over particular choices, but in this case two more substantial objections can be brought. A section on 'The Historical Dialectic' which includes Jameson, Eagleton, Williams, Hayden White (!) but *not* Lukács, Benjamin, or Adorno is grossly overloaded in favour of the present. The 'Depth Psychology and the Scene of Writing' bracket, which includes Jerry Aline Flieger, Isaiah Smithson, and Con Davis himself but *not*, say, Freud, Lacan, Leo Bersani, or Shoshana Felman, is simply inadequate. Still, this is a handy collection to be getting on with, and one looks forward to its publication in paperback. The second edition of Ann Jefferson and David Robey's *Modern Literary Theory* (1982)[17] probably now *is* the ideal student's guide. This new edition supplements what was already an excellent book with accounts of 'reading and interpretation' by Ian Maclean and feminist literary criticism by Toril Moi – both essays achieving the high standards of compression and clarity set by their predecessors.

But 'theory and pedagogy' can also be conceived as a theoretical, rather than

14. *Voice Terminal Echo: Postmodernism and English Renaissance Texts*, by Jonathan Goldberg. Methuen. pp. x + 194. pb £7.95.

15. *The Philosophical Disenfranchisement of Art*, by Arthur C. Danto. ColU. pp. xvi + 216. $25.

16. *Contemporary Literary Criticism: Modernism through Poststructuralism*, ed. by Robert Con Davis. Longman. pp. xiii + 511. £19.95.

17. *Modern Literary Theory: A Comparative Introduction*, ed. by Ann Jefferson and David Robey. Second edn. Batsford. pp. 240. pb £6.95.

pedagogico-commercial, issue, as in Cary Nelson's *Theory in the Classroom*[18]. Most of the writers here are concerned about the consequences of interpretative plurality for teaching – whether it is seen as good in itself, merely the starting point of an interventionist politics of reading, or as something to be overcome in a patient striving towards consensus. Vincent Leitch's 'Deconstruction and Pedagogy' and Paula Treichler's 'Teaching Feminist Theory' are the key contributions here. However, this debate tends to leave the 'canon' firmly in place and to be confined to different ways of treating it – an assumption that is welcomely contested in Lawrence Grossberg's 'Teaching the Popular'. In an interestingly different approach, Susan Wells examines the relevance of central Habermasian concepts – 'communicative competence', 'intersubjective discourse' – to the teaching of 'technical discourse'.

Rex Gibson's *Critical Theory and Education*[19] is a narrower book than the Nelson collection in that 'critical theory' here denotes mainly the Frankfurt School. Gibson effectively uses the Frankfurt critique of 'instrumental reason' to expose the increasing vocationalism of recent education policy and, by marrying Frankfurt and Foucault, stresses that questions of sexuality, the body, and desire must be built centrally into any adequate theory of education. *The Creating Word*[20] is the proceedings of a conference devoted to 'the learning and teaching of English in the 1980s', and might well have been inserted above under the rubric 'humanism'. For it attempts to re-affirm humanist traditions (and pretty unreconstructed ones at that) in the light of the challenges posed by computer technology, language arts methodology, and of course literary theory. The key essays addressing this latter concern are M. H. Abrams's 'Construing and Deconstructing', which compares Derrida to Hume and yet again resumes the old polemic with Hillis Miller, and Louise M. Rosenblatt's 'The Literary Transaction', which offers a lucid survey of her 'transactional theory' of literature. The final book to be considered here is Victor J. Lee's *English Literature in Schools*[21]. This ranges, at its upper academic reaches, from straight literary theory (with, say, Rex Gibson on 'Structuralism and Literature' or Rosenblatt on 'Efferent and Aesthetic Transactions'), to a more direct concern with the cultural politics of reading. An excessively eclectic anthology, it none the less circles round an increasingly pressing practical problem: how, as it percolates down from the universities, is literary theory to be taught at A-level or earlier? I once heard Jacques Derrida remark that teaching deconstruction to twelve-year-olds was much easier than getting it across to eighteen-year-olds who were by then already overburdened with 'metaphysical' prejudices. What are the rest of us doing wrong . . .?

As always, a handful of texts come in which prove difficult to classify. These include *American Formalism and the Problem of Interpretation*[22], in which

18. *Theory in the Classroom*, ed. by Cary Nelson. UIll. pp. xvi + 272. £17.95.

19. *Critical Theory and Education*, by Rex Gibson. H&S. pp. x + 192. pb £6.95.

20. *The Creating Word: Papers from an International Conference on the Learning and Teaching of English in the 1980s,* ed. by Patricia Demers. Macmillan. pp. viii + 215. £25.

21. *English Literature in Schools*, ed. by Victor J. Lee. OpenU. pp. xv + 437. hb £22.50, pb £8.95.

22. *American Formalism and the Problem of Interpretation*, by J. Timothy Bagwell. RiceU. pp. xiv + 130. pb $14.95.

J. Timothy Bagwell offers a defence of aspects of New Critical literary theory, seeking to reformulate 'intention' in terms of literary meaning and taking issue with current theories which blur the boundaries between literary and 'ordinary' discourse. *Murray Krieger and Contemporary Critical Theory*[23] celebrates a theorist who has never made much impact on this side of the Atlantic. Vincent Leitch, in 'Saving Poetry', shrewdly diagnoses Krieger's formalism as an attempt to shore up a precarious Arnoldian-humanist legacy, while Sandor Goodheart, in an essay that could have been titled 'Saving Krieger' rather than 'After *The Tragic Vision*', valiantly tries to rescue his mentor from Frank Lentricchia's assault in *After the New Criticism*. Other contributions examine more specialist aspects of Krieger's work; Richard Berg interviews him, and Wolfgang Iser chairs a colloquy on his work in the University at Konstanz. Two exercises in traditionalist literary-theoretical concerns are Richard Keller Simon's *The Labyrinth of the Comic*[24], which surveys a range of comic theory and practice, particularly Freud's book on jokes, and Mary Mothersill's *Beauty Restored* (1984)[25], which now appears in paperback; in it she meticulously pursues the key themes of aesthetics – the relation of beauty to the sublime, the question of the objectivity or relativism of aesthetic value, the relation between aesthetic and ethical discourse. These are all issues at the very centre of theoretical debate, but are set out here in strangely abstract guise, with a poise and elegance that is the attractive 'other side' of the book's complete ahistoricity. Clive Bloom's *The 'Occult' Experience and the New Criticism*[26] raises expectations which it then sorely disappoints. According to the blurb, Bloom 'examines the work of many key twentieth-century theorists – including Freud, Lacan, Foucault, Derrida and Barthes'. In fact, Barthes, Foucault, and Lacan are all cited only once in the index, and on the indicated pages get only the most fleeting of mentions; Derrida fares rather better, with four pages, but this is mostly summary of his account of Freud's Mystic Writing Pad. There is no doubt an intriguing book to be written on occultist, mystic, Gnostic, and Kabbalistic themes in contemporary theory, but this is certainly not it.

A few writers ambitiously attempt a total survey of contemporary theoretical trends. Julian Patrick, in a very substantial review-article in *UTQ*, reflects ruefully on the need for 'continuing mastery of a bewilderingly varied set of interpretative discourses', and concludes that 'the result is somewhat poor in hard knowledge'. Colin Falck, in *EIC*, has a much simpler answer, counselling a brisk move 'Beyond Theory'.

2. Poetics and Narratology

A. E. Dyson's *Poetry Criticism and Practice*[27] claims to anthologize 'Developments Since the Symbolists', but fails lamentably to do so. Though the

23. *Murray Krieger and Contemporary Critical Theory*, ed. by Bruce Henrickson. ColU. pp. xvi + 307. $32.50.

24. *The Labyrinth of the Comic: Theory and Practice from Fielding to Freud*, by Richard Keller Simon. FlorSU. pp. xii + 260. $27.95.

25. *Beauty Restored*, by Mary Mothersill. Clarendon. pp. vii + 438. pb £12.50.

26. *The 'Occult' Experience and the New Criticism: Daemonism, Sexuality and the Hidden in Literature*, by Clive Bloom. Harvester. pp. x + 133. £27.50.

27. *Poetry Criticism and Practice: Developments Since the Symbolists*, ed. by A. E. Dyson. Macmillan. pp. 217. hb £20, pb £6.95.

subtitle evokes Russian Formalism's brusque dismissal of symbolist mystical waffle in favour of a precise, would-be scientific analysis of poetic devices, Formalist criticism is not represented in this book; nor are its latter-day inheritors such as Michael Riffaterre. Of Harold Bloom's copious and crucial writings on the poetic 'anxiety of influence', we are treated to a single page. And the choice of extracts from poets of the nineteenth and twentieth centuries firmly implies that not a single woman has written or pronounced upon poetry for the last 150 years. This is, in short, a peculiarly superannuated book. R. A. York's *The Poem as Utterance*[28] is a much more worthy affair. Invoking the theory of pragmatics, York seeks to take the study of poetic language out of the windless closure in which stylistics had locked it and into its extralinguistic context of facts and values – from which it draws and into which it intervenes. York gives a very lucid exposition of pragmatic theories of language, deftly weaving his way through such key concepts as presupposition, speech act, *deixis*, register, sentence function, and then applying the theory illuminatingly in a set of discussions of modern poets from Baudelaire on; in this neat dovetailing of poetics and literary history, an intense concern for the pragmatic dimensions of poetry comes to seem characteristic of cultural modernity itself. We should probably also mention here Roger Fowler's *Linguistic Criticism*[29], which continues to be marked by Fowler's own past as a stylistician and therefore does not quite break into the general semiotic theory that it seems constantly on the verge of. If the older stylistics successfully identified objective linguistic structures in the texts it examined but was then unable to give interpretations of their significance that were other than subjectivist, intuitive, or even circular, Fowler's concern here to push stylistics towards pragmatics takes him at least some way out of this impasse. The book has all the virtues that we have come to associate with his writing, and will serve as an excellent student textbook on the uses of linguistic methodology in criticism.

Both York and Fowler see pragmatics as having swallowed up the smaller project of stylistics, as constituting a kind of general theory of relativity to its Newtonianism, and this case is reinforced by the *Bibliography of Stylistics*[30], which has a distinctly retrospective – not to say funereal – feel about it. This is an impressively full annotated bibliography, to which ease of access is ensured by its four indexes (Terms, Authors and Works Studied, Critics Discussed, Contributors). But given that literary discourse no longer can be studied in the abstract, reified way dear to stylistics, it is also something of a dinosaur. *Poetry and Epistemology*[31], a collection of papers from an International Poetry Symposium at Eichstätt in 1983, is inevitably a mixed bag. The essays have little coherence, despite the announced theme (though the occasional brave soul sticks doggedly to it, as with George S. Lensing on 'Wallace Stevens's Epistemology of Form'). The best single essay is probably J. Hillis Miller on 'The Rhetoric of Ruskin', which argues in classically deconstructive fashion that 'a more or less explicit theory of figurative language emerges not only as

28. *The Poem as Utterance*, by R. A. York. Methuen. pp. 214. pb £5.95.

29. *Linguistic Criticism*, by Roger Fowler. OUP. pp. 190. pb £4.95.

30. *Bibliography of Stylistics and Related Criticism, 1967–83*, by James R. Bennett. MLA. pp. 405. hb $35, pb $17.

31. *Poetry and Epistemology: Turning Points in the History of Poetic Knowledge*, ed. by Ronald Hagenbüchle and Laura Skandera. Pustet. pp. 439. pb $17.

crucial to what Ruskin is trying to propose about art, but also as the place where Ruskin's lack of grounds for that proposing, its incoherence and baselessness, most comes into the open'.

Also in retrospective vein, Stephen Rudy has compiled *Roman Jakobson: A Complete Bibliography* (Mouton); unfortunately it has not been possible to see a copy.

If poetics has had rather a lean year, narratology at least has fared better. Claude Lévi-Strauss's *The Raw and the Cooked* (1970)[32] now appears in paperback, as does Gérard Genette's *Narrative Discourse* (1980)[33]. Lévi-Strauss's book is a stunningly encyclopaedic demonstration of his methods of narrative structural analysis, X-raying some 250 South American myths and constantly drawing illuminating comparisons with European customs and traditions. Genette's book established itself on publication as an instant classic; all the general works on narratology noted in this section over the last few years have taken it as a foundation to be built on. Yet the book effects an intriguing marriage of hermeneutic *and* narratology, proposing both a scientific grid of narrative concepts (achrony, anisochrony, and so forth) *and* a reading of Proust's *Recherche*; and this latter dimension of the work has perhaps not yet been sufficiently attended to. Genette's concept of 'rhetoric' is discussed in relation to Paul de Man's by Christopher Harlos in *P&R*.

Also in paperback is David Lodge's *Working with Structuralism* (1981)[34], in which an eminent English 'practical critic' negotiates his way lucidly but a little timorously around these unnerving European theories (see *YW* 62.42). Wallace Martin's *Recent Theories of Narrative*[35] has no such reservations and constitutes a splendid survey of the field. Remarkably evenhanded in its expositions of competing theories, it none the less has a modest axe of its own to grind, being interested above all in the move beyond a 'narrow' structuralist narratology to more encompassing accounts of narrative discourse, reader response, and problems of interpretation. Its pedagogical value is enhanced by its consistent application of the range of theories discussed to four accessible fictions (including *Huckleberry Finn*) and by its extensive annotated bibliographies. A more modest survey is Thomas M. Kavanagh's 'Uneasy Theories: The Ethics of Narration in Contemporary French Criticism' in *Criticism*, which summarizes recent work by Jean-Paul Aron, Luc Ferry and Alain Renault, and Michel Serres, calling 'for a new understanding of narrative as the privileged vehicle for a recentering of the concerns of literary criticism and philosophy on the question of value'. Another overview is offered in *Semiotica* by Michel Grimaud in a so-called 'candid conversation' with Wendy Wellesley on 'French Poetics'. 'Candid'? Are there State secrets in this field?

Nathaniel Wing's *The Limits of Narrative*[36] resourcefully combines

32. *The Raw and the Cooked*, by Claude Lévi-Strauss, trans. by John and Doreen Weightman. Introduction to a Science of Mythology 1. Penguin. pp. ix + 369. pb £5.95.

33. *Narrative Discourse*, by Gérard Genette, trans. by Jane E. Lewin. Blackwell. pp. 285. pb £8.95.

34. *Working with Structuralism: Essays and Reviews on Nineteenth- and Twentieth-Century Literature*, by David Lodge. Ark. pp. xii + 207. pb £3.95.

35. *Recent Theories of Narrative*, by Wallace Martin. CornU. pp. 242. pb $8.95.

36. *The Limits of Narrative: Essays on Baudelaire, Flaubert, Rimbaud and Mallarmé*, by Nathaniel Wing. Cambridge Studies in French. CUP. pp. x + 155. £22.50.

narrative theory and cultural history. Examining the ambivalences of the notion of narrative coherence, which is both a 'utopian' literary goal and a repressive check on the more anarchically utopian energies of fantasy, in works by Baudelaire, Flaubert, Rimbaud, and Mallarmé, Wing offers us little less than a new theory of cultural modernity, stressing the survivals and traces of more archaic modes of writing in what we've taken to be the very canon of French literary modernity. This is a slim book, but suggestive out of all proportion to its size.

Much relevant material is available in 'special issues' of journals, and it's a matter of much regret that these on the whole tend *not* to become available later in book form. *PoT* devotes an issue to the 'Theory of Character', that terrain so fiercely contested between humanistic brands of criticism and their semiotic or narratological challengers. In his 'Characters and Narrators: Filter, Center, Slant, and Interest-Focus', Seymour Chatman helpfully addresses some of the thorny terminological issues that arise here; in 'The Doer and the Deed' Uri Margolin seeks to dissolve character into its 'actantial' basis, into a Narrative Agent which is then further reduced to the grisly acronym N.A.; John Frow in 'Spectacle Binding' resourcefully draws upon aspects of film theory (*suture*, the gendered nature of the gaze) to probe the mysteries of literary character; and Christopher Gill ranges even further afield, examining ancient classical thought on character for its possible relevance to today's debates. The *PoT* issue on 'Poetics of Fiction' works narratological issues through in terms of particular literary texts. K. R. Ireland examines the grammar of narrative sequence in relation to John Fowles's *The French Lieutenant's Woman*, Carl Malmgren authorial narration as exemplified in *The Mill on the Floss*, Leona Toker 'Self-Conscious Paralepsis' in texts by Nabokov, and Koenraad Kuiper and Vernon Small 'Constraints on Fictions' in relation to M. K. Joseph's *A Soldier's Tale*. In more abstract vein, Ruth Ronen sets out a theoretical grid for thinking about 'Space in Fiction'. Related contributions also appear in *Raritan*, where Millicent Bell takes up Frank Kermode's recent demonstrations of the hiatuses in texts in her 'Narrative Gaps/Narrative Meaning', and in *Semiotica*, where Gerald Prince offers a trenchant account of Greimassian narratology.

JLS seems to remain little known, though it contains much interesting theoretical work. B. P. R. Hazenwindt writes on 'The Concept of "Narrative Mass" and the Construction of Narrative Texts', Christopher Norris is at once stringent and appreciative on Greimas's 'structural semantics', Timothy R. Austin ponders poetic ambiguity, unravelling serious discrepancies between critical and linguistic understandings of the phenomenon (this is probably the place to mention Timothy Bahti's excellent 'Ambiguity and Indeterminacy: The Juncture' in *CL*), while Roger Hawkins strives to relate 'Human Linguistic Processing Possibilities and Two Kinds of Experimental Writing'. With a little more polemical energy (which would involve collecting some of their seminal essays into a book), the proponents of 'literary semantics' could doubtless stake out a respectable position for themselves in the current theoretical battlefield. Another journal which occasionally takes up similar concerns is *Word*, which this year has a special issue on 'The Text as a Convergence of Concerns'.

3. Semiotics

On the evidence of this year's publications, semiotics seems to be treading water rather than advancing boldly forwards. David Sless is *In Search of Semiotics*[37], aiming 'from the start to build as simple a way of talking about semiotics as I could' and producing a lively and irreverent guide to the field. Whether his 'new student of semiotic' is going to fork out for a hardback introduction may, however, be doubted. All the more so since that new student can now lay hands on Robert E. Innes' *Semiotics: An Introductory Reader*[38], which brings together fifteen major statements on the subject, each prefaced by a helpful introduction by the editor. Respectable choices from C. S. Peirce, Saussure, Lévi-Strauss, Jakobson, Barthes, and Eco alternate with less familiar pieces by Karl Bühler (an excellent account of 'The Key Principle: The Sign-Character of Language'), Suzanne Langer, Gregory Bateson, and René Thom. While some of these papers are less 'introductory' than the book's subtitle promises, this will none the less surely, with a little tutelary guidance, prove a highly useful teaching text.

A further sign of treading water is the gradual translation and consolidation of Roland Barthes's later writings. *The Rustle of Language*[39] reprints many old favourites – despite the blurb's extraordinary claim that 'all but two [of the essays] appear for the first time in English'. If the attention to the 'rustling' rather than functioning of language bespeaks Barthes's devotion to those 'pleasures of the text' which exceed all articulated meaning-systems, so too does the very form of his book, for many of its contents can hardly any longer be called 'essays'. While 'The Death of the Author' and 'From Work to Text' are extraordinarily compact summaries of the theory of textuality, the pieces here on 'Bloy', 'What Becomes of the Signifier', or even 'Kristeva's *Semeiotike*' are glancing, ephemeral enactments of it, hardly more than a few pages in length. This is less true of *The Responsibility of Forms*[40], where Barthes's attention shifts from the order of the sign to the domains of the visible and the audible. Five essays from the earlier collection *Image–Music–Text* are here reprinted (including 'The Photographic Message', 'The Third Meaning', 'Rhetoric of the Image'), but their new (or is it their old, their original?) context reveals them in a new light – as a trenchant methodological ground-clearing for the more specific studies which here follow. Simultaneously developing and transcending semiology, Barthes ranges across works by Cy Twombly, Schumann, Erté, Requichot, and others in search of that 'third meaning' that escapes all codes and is source of the text's value and eroticism. Neither of these collections offers us much that is new, but they do stress once more the extraordinary fertility and resource of this most necessary – and paradoxical – of semioticians. Barthes's work is the subject of several pieces in *Semiotica*, where Irene A. Webley in 'Professional Wrestling: The World of Roland Barthes Revisited' takes issue with perhaps the most famous of his mass-cultural

37. *In Search of Semiotics*, by David Sless. CH. pp. 170. £19.95.

38. *Semiotics: An Introductory Reader*, ed. by Robert E. Innes. Hutchinson. pp. xvi + 331. pb £9.95.

39. *The Rustle of Language*, by Roland Barthes, trans. by Richard Howard. Blackwell. pp. ix + 373. hb £27.50, pb £8.95.

40. *The Responsibility of Forms: Critical Essays on Music, Art, and Representation*, by Roland Barthes, trans. by Richard Howard. Blackwell. pp. viii + 312. £19.50.

analyses, Joseph Adamson offers a critical account of Stephen Ungar's *Roland Barthes: The Professor of Desire* (1983), and George H. Bauer surveys recent Barthes studies in a lively, substantial review-article.

In the Problemata Semiotica series, Karl Josef Höltgen investigates *Aspects of the Emblem* [41]. If the title evokes Benjaminian expectations, it must be confessed that this arcane little study doesn't live up to them. As if to emphasize the current 'stocktaking' mood of the discipline, we now have the *Bibliography of Semiotics, 1975-1985* [42], which is an impressively thorough compilation with a truly global perspective. But what it desperately needs is a line or two of summary beneath the alphabetical computer print-out entries: just how much does a title like 'La Ville et ses Cartes' really tell one? No doubt bibliographical convenience and publishing economics have fought a pitched battle here; but surely a compromise was possible with a phrase or two under all titles that are not self-explanatory?

The once imperialistic ambitions of semiotics have in recent years suffered severe setbacks, and the discipline now approaches its own frontiers in more chastened mood, being more prepared for comradely exchanges than instant colonization. *Semiotica* is much preoccupied with the relation between semiotics and its 'others'. It offers special issues on 'Semiotics and History', whose highpoint is Alexandros-Ph. Lagopoulos's 'Semiotics and History: A Marxist Approach' (Armando Plebe also works this vein in his 'Entwurf eines semiotischen Materialismus' in *Semiosis*), and on 'Semiotics and Sociology', which is less rewarding; Marc E. Blanchard's useful critique of Hans Robert Jauss in 'Reception Theory and the Semiotics of Literary History' is, however, worth turning up. Another instance of such tentative interchanges is Linda Hutcheon's resourceful deployment, in *Diac*, of the theory and practice of metafiction to 'review' important books on semiotic theory by Teresa de Lauretis and Kaja Silverman.

It is, of course, deconstruction that has brought about this relative loss of nerve on the part of the semiotic enterprise, and semioticians are accordingly scuttling back to their founding father to think through once again the full complexity of the relation of his work to its Derridean critique. Robert Hodge and Gunther Kress ponder 'Rereading as Exorcism: Semiotics and the Ghost of Saussure' in *SoRA*, while James I. Porter's 'Saussure and Derrida on the Figure of the Voice' in *MLN* leads us conveniently into our next section.

4. Rhetoric and Deconstruction

Derrida's *Memoires: For Paul de Man* [43] is a very strange text, comprising three lectures ('Mnemosyne', 'The Art of *Memoires*', and 'Acts: The Meaning of a Given Word') written a few weeks after the death of de Man, in January and February 1984. Structurally and stylistically singular among Derrida's writings, and bearing a relation at once oblique and deeply grafted to the

41. *Aspects of the Emblem*, by Karl Josef Höltgen. Problemata Semiotica. Reichenberger. pp. 205.

42. *Bibliography of Semiotics, 1975-1985*, ed. by Achin Eschbach and Viktória Eschbach-Szabó. Benjamins. 2 vols. pp. 948. $140.

43. *Memoires: For Paul de Man*, by Jacques Derrida, trans. by Cecile Lindsay, Jonathan Culler, and Eduardo Cadava. ColU. pp. xv + 153. £13.40.

structure and style of de Man's texts, these lectures offer the fullest, most vigilant and sympathetic account to date of de Man's work. This account, however, is explicitly opposed to the thought of any totalization; it is rather a series of meditations on 'an oeuvre that has so often uncovered, analyzed, denounced, and avoided it'. Seeing de Man as the 'great thinker and theorist of memory' for whom 'there is only memory but, strictly speaking, the past does not exist', *Memoires* explores some of the ways in which deconstruction is related to notions of memory, death and mourning, promises and affirmation, 'the coming of the future', the proper name and signature, prosopopeia, and autobiography. That de Man and Derrida's work, together or independently, represents a powerful reformulation of 'autobiography' in terms of death is illuminated by Gregory S. Jay's 'Freud: The Death *of* Autobiography' (in *Genre*) and Jane Marie Todd's 'Autobiography and the Case of Signature: Reading Derrida's *Glas*' (in *CL*). As Derrida observes in *Memoires*: '*already* you are *in memory of* your own death; and your friends as well, and all the others, both of your own death and already of their own through yours'. The memorization or memorialization works most profoundly by way of the name since 'In calling or naming someone while he is alive, we know that his name can survive him and *already survives him*', and since, according to Derrida, 'We cannot separate the name of "memory" and "memory" of the name'. What emerges from this is, on the one hand, a fascinating elaboration of the relation of deconstruction to the proper name and signature and, on the other, a critique and displacement of notions of 'memory' wherein it becomes possible to formulate 'deconstruction' as a kind of 'memory-work'.

'Deconstruction' is in fact formulated in a number of (provokingly incommensurable) ways in *Memoires*. 'To risk a single definition', Derrida at one point proposes: '*plus d'une langue* – both more than a language and no more of *a* language.' It is a question of translation and of 'transference'. '"Deconstruction in America"', Derrida notes, 'would not be what it is without Paul de Man.' This year sees the publication of a second posthumous collection of de Man essays [44], which contains 'The Resistance to Theory' (*YW* 63.492–3), 'The Return to Philology', 'Hypogram and Inscription', 'Reading and History', '"Conclusions": Walter Benjamin's "The Task of the Translator"' (*YW* 66.40), 'Dialogue and Dialogism', and (for the first time in English) 'An Interview with Paul de Man' conducted by Stefano Rosso in 1983. There is also a slightly revised version of Tom Keenan's 'Bibliography of Texts by Paul de Man' (*YW* 66.40). 'The Return to Philology' advocates 'a change by which literature . . . should be taught as a rhetoric and a poetics prior to being taught as a hermeneutics and a history'. 'Hypogram and Inscription' assesses the work of Michael Riffaterre, identifying its 'blind spot' as the 'refusal to acknowledge the textual inscription of semantic determinants within a non-determinable system of figuration'. This essay also contains, among other things, the extraordinary proposal that 'in linguistic terms . . . it is impossible to say whether prosopopeia is plausible because of the empirical existence of dreams and hallucinations or whether one believes that such a thing as dreams and hallucinations exists because language permits the figure of prosopopeia'. 'Reading and History' is an examination, focused on the work of Hans Robert

---

44. *The Resistance to Theory*, by Paul de Man. UMinn. pp. xviii + 138. hb $25, pb $10.95.

Jauss, of the ways in which hermeneutics and poetics 'have a way of becoming entangled': 'One can look upon the history of literary theory as the continued attempt to disentangle this knot and to record the reasons for failing to do so'. '"Conclusions"', as published in *YFS* (1985), is here supplemented with a transcript of the discussion following its original delivery as a lecture. 'Dialogue and Dialogism' is a short but challenging account of the work of Bakhtin. Rosso's interview with de Man offers some coverage of the question of the relations between his own and Derrida's work; de Man suggests, for example, that they share a recognition that 'only what is, in a sense, classically didactic, can be really and effectively subversive'. All of the pieces in *The Resistance to Theory* have, in one form or another, appeared previously elsewhere and some are already justly celebrated; but it is extremely useful to have them all together here, especially with Wlad Godzich's foreword, 'The Tiger on the Paper Mat', stressing as it does the context and development of de Man's late writings. *The Resistance to Theory* is a valuable but slim volume, necessarily shadowed by the thought of the essays on Burke, Kierkegaard, and Marx which de Man never lived to write.

CL has a special issue 'dedicated to the memory of Paul de Man', containing Jane Marie Todd's 'Framing the *Second Discourse*', which concentrates on his reading of Rousseau and argues that he neglects 'both the frame of the *Second Discourse* and the problem of sexual difference in Rousseau'; Jean-Pierre Mileur's 'Allegory and Irony: "The Rhetoric of Temporality" Re-examined', which pursues the recognition that 'For de Man, how to understand Romanticism is not just *the* historical question, it is *the* theoretical question as well'; and, as the most stimulating and clarifying of the contributions, Peggy Kamuf's 'Monumental De-Facement: On Paul de Man's *The Rhetoric of Romanticism*', which shows how this de Man text 'proceeds as a deconstruction of the concept of romanticism'. This year has seen the publication of other essays on de Man, including Tilottama Rajan's 'The Supplement of Reading' (in *NLH*) and Juliet Flower MacCannell's 'Portrait' (see below), but the best is undoubtedly Cynthia Chase's 'Giving a Face to a Name: De Man's Figures', which occupies central place in her *Decomposing Figures*[45], a collection of otherwise previously published pieces on Wordsworth, Keats, Hegel and Baudelaire, Kleist, George Eliot, Freud, and Baudelaire and Rousseau. The prevailing conceptual motif of this collection is 'decomposition' or '*disfiguration*', which, in naming both a rhetorical and physical process or effect and leaving uncertain the relationship between them, exemplifies the interpretive predicament it would describe'. In the acknowledgments, Chase notes that her 'debt to de Man for the thinking he made possible much exceeds what this book could acknowledge'; her readings of Romantic texts in this volume are a good example of the kind of rigorous and imaginative work which de Man's texts seem so capable of generating. 'Giving a Face to a Name' is itself a deeply absorbing delineation of his work, providing very helpful coverage of, among other things, prosopopeia, apostrophe, and anthropomorphism, the notion of positing, hypograms and inscription, and the phenomenality and materiality of the sign.

45. *Decomposing Figures: Rhetorical Readings in the Romantic Tradition*, by Cynthia Chase. JHU. pp. 234. £20.35.

Deconstruction is *plus d'une langue* ('Paul de Man'?) – it is a kind of memory-work, it is rhetorical figural analysis and decomposition, it is transference and translation. . . . But 'deconstruction' is not a proper name; in an important way, it *is not anything*. This is partly why, at one point in *Memoires*, Derrida has to retract a remark: he has been considering the question of 'deconstruction in America' and is led to hypothesize that, simply, 'America *is* deconstruction'. How might such a hypothesis be risked transatlantically? Britain *is* deconstruction. While a piece such as Christopher Norris's 'Home Thoughts from Abroad: Derrida, Austin, and the Oxford Connection' (in *P&L*) is concerned to emphasize the importance of Derrida's 'constant dialogue' with British philosophy (and with the 'English' language), it is not the same. As Derrida observes, following a remark made by Umberto Eco, 'deconstruction in Europe is a sort of hybrid growth and is generally perceived as an American label for certain theorems, a discourse, or a school'. Deconstruction in Britain, with *and* without a Marxist orientation, would have to be conceived differently – otherwise.

Meanwhile, the 'program' of deconstruction in the United States – most tendentiously, perhaps, as an updated, 'user-friendly' version of New Criticism – continues. *Rhetoric and Form: Deconstruction at Yale*[46] is a collection of rather disappointing essays bearing witness to, and in part attempting to interrogate, this fact. One of the problems here, as with *The Yale Critics* (*YW* 64.609), is the tendency to identify the work of de Man, Hartman, and Hillis Miller collectively under the rubric of 'deconstruction', another is the evident failure to conceive the 'political' dimensions of deconstruction in sufficiently rigorous terms: most generally, it is the problem of a paradoxical lack of the 'close reading' conventionally (if somewhat erroneously) identified with New Criticism. The book is divided into three parts: 'Part One: The Yale Critics' comprises Hillis Miller's 'The Search for Grounds in Literary Study', which makes nice points about the 'nihilism' of such critics as Eugene Goodheart, Walter Jackson Bate, and René Wellek; Hartman's '"Timely Utterance" Once More', which offers 'a mildly deconstructive reading' of Wordsworth's 'Intimations' Ode; Juliet Flower MacCannell's 'Portrait: De Man', which contains a very useful critique of Suzanne Gearhart's work on de Man (in *Diac*, 1983) and is especially evocative on the notion of 'neutral intonation' in de Man's texts; and a symposium on 'Marxism and Deconstruction' with Barbara Johnson, Louis Mackey, and Hillis Miller, which takes off, in part, from Barbara Johnson's highly dubious formulation of the question, 'Why not actually translate what deconstruction has done on texts into the realm of historical and political action?' Johnson is perhaps more interesting when, as in her piece on 'Apostrophe, Animation, and Abortion' in this year's *Diac*, she is considering the proposal that 'the undecidable *is* the political. There is politics precisely because there is undecidability.' 'Part Two: Controversies' comprises Johnson's 'Gender Theory and the Yale School', which highlights some of the male-oriented aspects of that 'School'; Barbara Foley's 'The Politics of Deconstruction', which is a Marxist–Leninist attack not only on Derrida and the other Yale critics but also on what she sees as the 'kind of leftist

46. *Rhetoric and Form: Deconstruction at Yale*, ed. and intro. by Robert Con Davis and Ronald Schleifer. UOkla (1985). pp. xii + 251. $16.95.

pluralism' of Gayatri Spivak and Michael Ryan; and Robert Con Davis's 'Error at Yale: Geoffrey Hartman, Psychoanalysis, and Deconstruction', which explores sympathetically the ways in which Hartman's work can be seen as 'testing and then retreating from the dangers of deconstruction'. 'Part Three: Theory and Practice' comprises Herman Rapaport's 'Geoffrey Hartman and the Spell of Sounds', which has some engaging things to say about Hartman and notions of voice; Robert Markley's *'Tristram Shandy* and "Narrative Middles"': Hillis Miller and the Style of Deconstructive Criticism', which focuses on the question of style, on how deconstruction 'must manifest itself as a convincing rhetoric, a seductive style, and not simply as a political program'; Christopher Norris's 'Some Versions of Rhetoric: Empson and de Man' (see *YW* 66.38); and Ronald Schleifer's 'The Anxiety of Allegory: De Man, Greimas, and the Problem of Referentiality', which argues that 'de Man's distinction between the possibility and certainty of reference seems somewhat naïve'.

The pedagogical dimensions of 'deconstruction in America' remain crucial. This is in part reflected in an article such as Phillip K. Arrington's 'Tropes of the Composing Process', in *CE*, which argues for the importance of making 'rhetoric, its study and practice, central to education once more'. It is shown more clearly and more extensively in two books which arrived too late for consideration last year, *Writing and Reading Differently*[47] and *Applied Grammatology: Post(e)-Pedagogy from Jacques Derrida to Joseph Beuys*[48]. *Writing and Reading Differently* is concerned, as its subtitle suggests, with 'Deconstruction and the Teaching of Composition and Literature', and includes essays, all of which have appeared elsewhere, by Vincent B. Leitch, Gayatri Spivak, and Geoffrey Hartman. The editors observe candidly that 'the assumption of the essays collected here is that the strategic principles of deconstruction are accessible, that one need not be grounded in Continental philosophy in order to comprehend them'. Indeed they wish to 'question the assumption that an univocal and "proper" deconstruction exists'. This is all well and good, and has been said before. 'Univocal and "proper"' or not, however, there is a difference between, on the one hand, the notion of deconstruction implied by Barbara Johnson in her contribution, 'Teaching Deconstructively', in which she asserts that 'Because deconstruction is first and foremost a way of paying attention to what a text is doing – *how* it means not just *what* it means – it can lend itself very easily to an open-discussion format in a literature seminar', and, on the other, the notion of 'deconstructive' teaching one might be encouraged to conceive on the basis of Leitch's 'Deconstruction and Pedagogy', which provides a brief but very useful sketch of ways in which Barthes and Derrida have variously considered questions of pedagogy and institutions. The most innovatory essay in *Writing and Reading Differently* is Gregory Ulmer's 'Textshop and Post(e)pedagogy'; and this leads us to consider his work in its more extended form, in *Applied Grammatology*.

Applied Grammatology should constitute a significant intervention in any debate about deconstruction and pedagogy. It proceeds by strategically

47. *Writing and Reading Differently: Deconstruction and the Teaching of Composition and Literature*, ed. and intro. by G. Douglas Atkins and Michael L. Johnson. UKan (1985). pp. x + 216. hb $25, pb $12.95.

48. *Applied Grammatology: Post(e)-Pedagogy from Jacques Derrida to Joseph Beuys*, by Gregory L. Ulmer. JHU (1985). pp. xiv + 337. hb £23.55, pb £8.60.

bracketing off the term 'deconstruction'. Ulmer writes: 'Grammatology (I have no illusions about the status of this term, either) is a more inclusive notion, embracing both deconstruction and "writing" (understood not only in the special sense of textualist *écriture*, but also in the sense of a compositional practice).' There are undeniably problems with Ulmer's general approach, for example in the very way that he develops this notion of 'writing', whereby it rapidly ceases to bear any relation to 'writing' as 'arche-writing' in Derrida's use of that term (see below). But these are easily outweighed by the many extremely stimulating and highly original aspects of what Ulmer is doing. Ulmer concentrates on Derrida's 'experimental texts' and on his 'readings of art texts', exploring their potential for rethinking pedagogy in general. His argument is partly derived from an earlier essay, 'Op Writing: Derrida's Solicitation of Theoria' (*YW* 64.610). It is especially exciting in its elaborations of the question of the signature and of the place of the chemical senses in Derrida's work. Part 2 of the book is an attempt 'to clarify the pedagogical principles associated with applied grammatology'. He explains that the 'post(e)-pedagogy' in the title is intended to indicate 'both a move beyond conventional pedagogy and a pedagogy for an era of electronic media (with *poste* meaning in this context television station or set)'. In his final chapter, he considers the films and theories of Sergei Eisenstein, arguing that 'Derrida and Eisenstein together offer a way to achieve filmic writing'. The importance of Ulmer's book for all aspects of 'deconstruction' and pedagogy must remain, for the moment, very pleasurably incalculable. It may be suggested, in passing, that it is disappointing that Ulmer's sense of 'taking chances' (see *YW* 65.782-3) is not comparably manifested in a book which appears this year and is specifically concerned with chance, namely William Beatty Warner's *Chance and the Text of Experience: Freud, Nietzsche, and Shakespeare's 'Hamlet'* [49].

It is some way, also, from the dizzy (and dizzying) levels of Ulmer's explorations to the oddly laboured *Philosophy Beside Itself: On Deconstruction and Modernism* [50], by Stephen W. Melville. Stylistically marred by the recurrent use of such formulations as 'what I want to say', 'what we want to say', and so on, Melville's book nevertheless contains useful things. In particular, there is a chapter entitled 'A Context for Derrida', which presents this context as that of Hegel's *Phenomenology of Spirit*, and goes on to provide related accounts of Heidegger, Lacan, and Georges Bataille. There is also a first chapter on modernism and painting, a chapter on psychoanalysis (including Abraham and Torok) and deconstruction, and a chapter on Paul de Man. The precise nature of Melville's engagement with the work of Derrida and de Man remains unclear. It seems he wishes to isolate a discourse called 'criticism' – a discourse which, he asserts, 'owns itself anasemically', and which is 'an activity intimately bound to the ways in which we do and do not belong in time and in community'. One wonders what such a criticism would look like. The closing paragraphs inform us that it would refuse 'the temptation to speak a truth of literature or of philosophy or of literary criticism' and that it would be 'finally justificatory only of its own writing'. If *Philosophy Beside Itself* is an example

49. *Chance and the Text of Experience: Freud, Nietzsche, and Shakespeare's 'Hamlet'*, by William Beatty Warner. CornU. pp. 308. $32.95.

50. *Philosophy Beside Itself: On Deconstruction and Modernism*, by Stephen W. Melville. ManU. pp. xxix + 188. pb £8.95.

of the kind of criticism it advocates, it is not difficult to feel a preference for the sort of 'performance criticism' of Gregory Ulmer.

There are several extremely good books this year which clarify deconstruction (or Derrida's work in general) in its more specifically 'philosophical' context. Rodolphe Gasché's long-awaited *The Tain of the Mirror*[51], quite simply the finest, most lucid and precise account of Derrida's work yet published, opens by declaring its corrective aims with regard to American literary criticism's 'appropriation of a philosophically purged notion of deconstruction' and with regard to the 'many philosophers' misreadings of Derrida as literary humbug'. The book is divided into three parts. Part 1, 'Towards the Limits of Reflection', explains the importance of the concept of 'reflection' in Western philosophy up to and including Hegel's 'speculative overhauling of the metaphysics of reflection'; it examines the work of Dilthey and Nietzsche, most pointedly in terms of their thinking of 'a *constitutive heterogeneity* of self-reflection and self-consciousness', before moving on to Werner Flach's notion of 'pure heterology' and, finally, to Derrida's philosophy. Part 2, 'On Deconstruction', begins by showing how deconstruction 'can and must be retraced' to the concepts of *'Abbau* (dismantling) in the later work of Husserl and *Destruktion* (destruction) in the early philosophy of Heidegger'; it then proceeds, extremely carefully, to the notion of 'deconstructive methodology' ('deconstruction is also the deconstruction of the concept of method (both scientific and philosophical) and has to be determined accordingly'), focusing on such terms as 'ground', 'origin', 'centre', and 'inscription', and elaborating the notion of 'infrastructure' (which is, like 'deconstruction', 'irremediably plural'). Part 2 concludes with a long chapter entitled 'A System beyond Being', providing excellent expositions of what he calls 'the infrastructural chain' – the arche-trace, différance, supplementarity, iterability, and the re-mark as infrastructures – and of 'the general system'. Part 3, 'Literature or Philosophy?', consists of two chapters: the first, 'Literature in Parentheses', argues that 'the genuine impact that Derrida's philosophy could have on literary criticism has not been, or at best has hardly been, noticed'; it also argues that 'the very future of the institution of literary criticism hinges on its deconstruction'. The final chapter, 'The Inscription of Universality', outlines Derrida's formulations of 'writing' (which is clearly to be distinguished from such formulations as Ulmer's), 'text', and 'metaphor'; it concludes with a consideration of the difficult question of the status of 'infrastructures' as 'quasi-transcendentals'. For the study of both philosophy and literature, *The Tain of the Mirror* is a brilliant and indispensable book.

Irene E. Harvey's *Derrida and the Economy of Différance*[52] is largely confined to treatment of Derrida's earlier texts, in particular *Of Grammatology* and *Speech and Phenomena*. It is not a beautifully written book, but it is undeniably one of the best expository works on Derrida yet to have appeared. It contains an introductory chapter on 'Derrida's Kantian Affiliation or Prolegomena to the Deconstruction of Metaphysics and the Recognition of *Différance*' and is then divided into three sections: 'The

51. *The Tain of the Mirror: Derrida and the Philosophy of Reflection*, by Rodolphe Gasché. Harvard. pp. viii + 348. £19.95.
52. *Derrida and the Economy of Différance*, by Irene E. Harvey. IndU. pp. xv + 285. £24.95.

Principles and the Practice of Deconstruction', 'Derrida and the Concept of Metaphysics', and 'Re-Cognizing *Différance* as the Apocalyptic Play of the World'. These include very good accounts of what deconstruction *is not*. One of the most tantalizing moments in Harvey's text is where she suggests a link between what Derrida calls the 'point of non-replacement' or 'point of orientation' and what she describes as 'the idiom, the subject, the writer, the non-authorized authority, the illegitimate father, who in fact has never left his text': here, in particular, the lack of any sustained confrontation with Derrida's later work on the signature (in *Glas* and *Signsponge* for instance) is disappointing. Finally, *Derrida and the Economy of Différance* contains a reasonably well updated version of the Derrida bibliography to be found in the English translation of the *Origin of Geometry* (1978).

Gasché's and Harvey's are quite fat books; John Llewelyn's *Derrida on the Threshold of Sense*[53] is comparatively thin (130-odd pages), but is also well worth obtaining. At the end of Chapter 5, Llewelyn draws attention to 'the desire to "place" [Derrida] and his writings in the context of the History of Western Thought, a desire that has been indulged so far in the chapters of this book, will motivate the chapter to come, and will doubtless survive its recapitulation'. There are chapters, accordingly, on Hegel ('Dialectical Semiology'), Husserl ('Transcendental Phenomenological Semiology'), Heidegger ('Fundamental Ontological Semiology'), on Lévi-Strauss and Saussure ('Structuralist Semiology'), Austin and Searle ('Rhetorological Semiology'), Nietzsche, Mallarmé, and Freud's 'The Uncanny' ('Anasemiology'), on Wittgenstein, Frege, and Quine ('The Divided Line'), and finally a postscript entitled 'Glassification', and a short bibliography. The most curious and least graceful aspect of the book is perhaps the recurrence of the term 'semiology' in the chapter titles; but, for the most part, it is an extremely enjoyable study, with clear, strong exposition, as well as an ironizing playfulness.

Derrida on the Threshold of Sense also provides some useful observations about the relations between analytical and continental philosophy. Indeed, however brief, it is in some respects clearer and more penetrating than Vincent Descombes's *Objects of All Sorts: A Philosophical Grammar*[54], a book which appears to promise to concern itself with this subject but which in fact tends to lack 'the merit of deigning to provide an example' (to cite Descombes's own rather sarcastic praise of Ducrot and Todorov's *Encyclopedic Dictionary of the Sciences of Language* (1981)). There is a general, quite lengthy attack on 'semiology', and a specific one launched against Lacan, which concludes that 'The doctrine of the signifier suffers from a confusion that appears irremediable'; but there is very little indeed directly focusing on the work of Derrida or Foucault or Blanchot, for example, and nothing whatsoever on such contemporary thinkers as Habermas, Jean-François Lyotard, Philippe Lacoue-Labarthe, Jean-Luc Nancy, or Michel Serres.

The influence of the work of Derrida, Lacoue-Labarthe, and Nancy is to be

53. *Derrida on the Threshold of Sense*, by John Llewelyn. Macmillan. pp. xiii + 137. hb £25, pb £8.95.

54. *Objects of All Sorts: A Philosophical Grammar*, by Vincent Descombes, trans. by Lorna Scott-Fox and Jeremy Harding. Blackwell. pp. 231. £25.

felt throughout Christopher Fynsk's *Heidegger: Thought and Historicity*[55], an excellent expository study of Heidegger, especially in its account of 'The Origin of the Work of Art' and, more generally, of Heidegger's relation to Nietzsche. (This year witnesses the publication in English of Volume II (*The Eternal Recurrence of the Same*) of Heidegger's *Nietzsche*[56].) Fynsk's book also forms a useful complement to Gasché's on the notion of finitude: Fynsk notes that 'The notion of finitude I attempt to elaborate in this book points to the necessary "tracing" or "inscription" of thought. . . . The movement to which I am referring is perhaps properly named deconstruction, in the sense of this term developed by Jacques Derrida.' Reference may here be made to other work this year on Heidegger or on Heidegger and Derrida. Firstly, in *P&L*, there is a piece by Derrida himself, entitled 'Interpreting Signatures (Nietzsche/Heidegger): Two Questions' and concerned with 'the *name* Nietzsche' and 'the concept of totality'. Secondly, *MLN* publishes a very fine article by Timothy Clark, entitled 'Being in Mime: Heidegger and Derrida on the Ontology of Literary Language'. *PPR* contains an essay by Patrick Bigelow on 'The Indeterminability of Time in "Sein und Zeit"', and *JP* a symposium on 'Hermeneutics and Deconstruction', with pieces by John D. Caputo ('Telling Left from Right: Hermeneutics, Deconstruction, and the Work of Art'), Alexander Nehamas ('What an Author Is') and Hugh J. Silverman ('Authors of Works/Readings of Texts'). The work of Richard Rorty comes under Gasché's hammer in a single sentence in *The Tain of the Mirror*: 'Taking "writing" in Derrida to mean the scriptive and wordly practice of writing, a practice that would differ from its usual philosophical interpretation to the extent that the object it is about is no longer the world but texts, Rorty, for instance, in "Philosophy as a Kind of Writing", is bound to misunderstand it as literary writing.' This critique can be set alongside Charles B. Guignou's 'On Saving Heidegger from Rorty' in *PPR* and, more specifically, Charles Eric Reeves's 'Deconstruction, Language, Motive: Rortian Pragmatism and the Uses of "Literature"', in *JAAC*, which argues that Rorty's 'game' requires 'a particular sort of opposition, viz., that between philosophical "closure" and literary "openness"', and which concludes: 'Steering his own artful and intelligent way between the various disturbing dilemmas he sees confronting Derrideans, Rorty has yet to make his seem a road worth taking.'

Derrida's relation to other individual philosophers or thinkers is the subject of two or three further journal articles this year: *PhT* contains a piece by Timothy J. Stapleton, entitled 'Philosophy and Finitude: Husserl, Derrida and the End of Philosophy', which questions whether Derrida has 'really passed *through*, or only *around*, the transcendental reduction'; James I. Porter's 'Saussure and Derrida on the Figure of the Voice' in *MLN* asserts, *pace* Derrida, that 'Despite its apparent formalism Saussure's system could be shown to open up new theoretical possibilities regarding the material dimensions of language'; and Jeffrey Barnouw's 'Peirce and Derrida: "Natural Signs" Empiricism Versus "Originary Trace" Deconstruction', in

PoT, argues that 'what is of value in the deconstructive critique of metaphysics and in corresponding criticism of texts can be carried through more consistently [*sic*] by an empiricism which is grounded in the Peirceian conception of natural signs as the basic terms of perception and thought'.

What would be the implications for the institution and structure of *YWES* of Derrida's *Schibboleth*? This text is published in French[57] this year, and is now for the first time also widely available in English, in a collection of essays entitled *Midrash and Literature*[58]. Dated 14 October 1984, and originally given as a lecture, in French, at a conference at the University of Washington, Seattle, on the work of Paul Celan, 'Schibboleth' is an astonishing meditation on dates, on anniversaries, on the structure of singularity and repeatability which constitutes them. While also focusing on the notions of schibboleth and circumcision, Derrida's text is of most obvious and exceptional interest for an understanding of the notion of signature and the idiom and for any theory of poetry. Through a provoking reading of 'dates' in Celan's poetry, Derrida proposes that 'What dating comes to is signing': 'In its essence, a signature is always dated and only has value on this account. It dates and is a date.' He goes on to describe how 'The initiative is with the date and the poet is constituted by it. It is thence that he appears to himself.' That 'A date marks itself and becomes readable only in freeing itself from the singularity which it nonetheless recalls' links it, like the name itself, to what Derrida calls a 'destiny of ash': 'It may always become no one's and nothing's date, the essence without essence of ash in which one no longer even knows what one day, one time, under some proper name, was consumed.' (Here, among other places, the force of *Memoires* returns.) Such 'ash' can be praised; indeed, Derrida suggests that this is where 'religion begins, in the blessing of dates, of names and of ashes'.

Finally, nuclear criticism. In an issue of *SoRA* which also contains 'Jacques Derrida on the University: An Interview', Christopher Norris's 'On Derrida's "Apocalyptic Tone": Textual Politics and the Principle of Reason' proposes that it is in the 'present situation of a radical instability affecting all the discourses of knowledge and power that deconstruction finds itself tactically aligned with the purposes of "nuclear criticism"'. Norris's is a helpful account of recent Derrida texts such as 'The Principle of Reason' (*YW* 64.587-8), 'Of an Apocalyptic Tone Recently Adopted in Philosophy', and 'No Apocalypse' in relation to this new field of 'nuclear criticism' (see *YW* 65.783). Other contributions in this field have appeared this year: there is, for example (though technically a 'review article'), Richard Klein and William B. Warner's piece on KAL 007 in *Diac*; Peter Schwenger's 'Writing the Unthinkable' in *CritI*; George Kateb's 'Thinking about Human Extinction: (1) Nietzsche and Heidegger', in *Raritan*; and, in *JP*, a symposium entitled 'Nuclear War'. But there is a sense that nuclear criticism is still very much in its formative stages, and that it is a field susceptible to more radical and imaginative representations and transformations. One could wonder, for instance, how the notion of 'la cendre' in Derrida's recent work might be articulated onto its concerns; or how this field is affected by a recent and characteristically difficult but uncanny

57. *Schibboleth: pour Paul Celan*, by Jacques Derrida. Galilée. pp. 126. Ffr 62.

58. *Midrash and Literature*, ed. by Geoffrey H. Hartman and Sanford Budick. Yale. pp. xvii + 412. £27.50.

text by Maurice Blanchot, now available in English, *The Writing of the Disaster*[59].

5. Hermeneutics

This year sees the publication of a mammoth anthology edited by Kurt Mueller-Vollmer, *The Hermeneutics Reader*[60]. This judicious selection contains both well-known figures such as Schleiermacher, Dilthey, Heidegger, Gadamer, and the lesser-known scholars who constitute the developing context from which such seminal contributions emerge: Johann Martin Chladenius, Johann Gustav Droysen, Philip August Boeckh, among others. What is especially welcome is the generosity of the individual selections, which allows considerable elaboration of each thinker's position. All of these are in turn subjected to a great *Aufhebung* in the editor's magisterial account of the development of German hermeneutics 'from the Enlightenment to the Present' with its Gadamer–Habermas dispute. More modestly, Susan J. Hekman's *Hermeneutics and the Sociology of Knowledge*[61] seeks to bring Gadamerian hermeneutics into relation with Karl Mannheim's sociology of consciousness. Both writers, she argues, insist on the historically situated and relative nature of all human meanings; there are no Archimedean standpoints. If Mannheim traces the relationship between world views and particular social groups, Gadamer demonstrates, at a more fundamental level, the linguistically mediated nature of all human standpoints, including that of the sociological investigator him- or herself. But while Hekman excellently maps the convergence of hermeneutics and sociology in that interdisciplinary space which is virtually constitutive of 'critical theory' itself, she perhaps too readily assumes that 'objectivity' and 'objectivism' are the same. When the 'relativity' of truth turns into relativism *tout court*, one has not so much escaped foundationalism as become its mirror-image, fixated on precisely that which one had claimed to be rejecting.

In *JAAC* John M. Connolly offers to restate the Gadamerian account of the hermeneutic circle in Wittgensteinian terms, turning it into 'a Language-Game Approach', while Ian MacKenzie has an intriguing article on 'Gadamer's Hermeneutics and the Uses of Forgery'. We could, he claims, 'use forgeries or possible forgeries as an extremely useful tool towards Gadamer's project of understanding the present through the past, and *vice versa*'. *JBSP* devotes an issue to 'Bachelard, Gadamer and Heidegger'. Francis J. Ambrosio's 'Gadamer and the Ontology of Language' offers a well-nigh Machereyan 'immanent' critique of 'What Remains Unsaid' in *Truth and Method*, but perhaps the most challenging contribution is Gregory Schufreider's 'Heidegger's Contribution to a Phenomenonology of Culture', which broaches 'the entire issue of the nature of culture as the site of historical unconcealment'.

---

59. *The Writing of the Disaster*, by Maurice Blanchot, trans. by Ann Smock. UNeb. pp. xiii + 150. hb £16.95, pb £6.75.

60. *The Hermeneutics Reader: Texts of the German Tradition from the Enlightenment to the Present*, ed. by Kurt Mueller-Vollmer. Blackwell. pp. xi + 380. hb £29.50, pb £12.50.

61. *Hermeneutics and the Sociology of Knowledge*, by Susan J. Hekman. Polity. pp. vi + 224. £22.50.

John D. Caputo follows this up in a later issue on 'The Philosophy of Jacques Derrida' with 'Heidegger and Derrida: Cold Hermeneutics', which intelligently analyses the consequences of the Derridean critique of 'postal eschatology' for hermeneutic practice. The relation between deconstructionist emphases on 'rhetoric' and the hermeneutic tradition is also the subject of Massimo Marassi's 'The Hermeneutics of Rhetoric in Heidegger' in *P&R*.

One writer not represented in Mueller-Vollmer's collection but who (more in the spirit of Hekman's book) gives a substantially sociological twist to hermeneutic questioning is Peter Szondi, many of whose major essays are now posthumously translated in *On Textual Understanding and Other Essays*[62]. The relevance of Szondi's work for us is its attempt to mediate between German and French, hermeneutic and poststructuralist critical traditions. This effort is most apparent in the last of the essays collected here, 'The Poetry of Constancy', in which Szondi links his own and Walter Benjamin's theories of language to those of Foucault and Derrida, and, through a meditation on Celan's translation of Shakespeare's Sonnet 105, proposes virtually a whole theory of postmodern poetry based on 'a determinate negation of discursiveness'. A set of searching essays on German Romanticism and on aspects of Benjamin's work is also included, in all of which the hermeneutic method is turned against the tradition itself to the point where the text becomes a potent source of questions about the intersection of language, the literary, and history. Given that this work is intended to serve as a belated introduction to the scope of Szondi's thought, we can only lament the fact that it does not include a bibliography of his writings, which would have greatly enhanced its usefulness.

Unlike most other branches of literary theory, hermeneutics has never been successfully naturalized in Britain, with the result that homegrown contributions to this field tend to be erratic, even inconsequential – 'provincial' in the old Arnoldian sense. Stephen Prickett's *Words and 'The Word'*[63] investigates the intersection of 'language, poetics and biblical interpretation'. He focuses upon a kind of dissociation of sensibility in our interpretative modernity whereby, from the late eighteenth century on, hermeneutics and literary criticism set out on increasingly separate paths – the former subsequently becoming afflicted by grave problems of method, the latter by irremediable anxieties about meaning. This genealogy of the split is followed by the suggestion that the reunion of these long lost partners may be a way out of the impasses of critical theory today. Well yes, one agrees, but *how*? K. M. Newton, in his *In Defence of Literary Interpretation*[64], similarly feels that a criticism which has renounced hermeneutic preoccupations has lost its way in the sands. But he is also hostile to an E. D. Hirsch-style objectivist hermeneutics that seeks the single 'true' meaning of the text. He accordingly seeks to demonstrate, through both theoretical argument and analysis of a set of texts including *Anna Karenina*, *Great Expectations*, and *Daniel Deronda*,

62. *On Textual Understanding and Other Essays*, by Peter Szondi, trans. by Harvey Mendelsohn. ManU. pp. xxi + 224. pb £8.95.

63. *Words and 'The Word': Language, Poetics and Biblical Interpretation*, by Stephen Prickett. CUP. pp. xii + 305. £27.50.

64. *In Defence of Literary Interpretation: Theory and Practice*, by K. M. Newton. Macmillan. pp. vi + 246. £27.50.

that interpreters are engaged in a struggle for power, in eristics rather than logic. These are both lively and useful books, to be sure, but we still await a British contribution that would have steeped itself fully in – and by doing so rise to the full challenge and stature of – that Continental hermeneutic tradition that Mueller-Vollmer's anthology celebrates.

The United States came closer to producing a native hermeneutics in the work of E. D. Hirsch. In *CritI* his most recent attempt to reformulate his central but vulnerable distinction of 'meaning' and 'significance' is critically examined by James L. Battersby and James Phelan, and Michael Leddy; Hirsch then responds to their objections.

6. Psychoanalysis

If in semiology (and perhaps in Marxism) the return to the texts of the Founder denotes a loss of confidence, a temporizing or 'treading water', in psychoanalysis it more often seems to entail a bold desire to move theoretically forward. Leo Bersani's *The Freudian Body*[65] and Sarah Kofman's *The Enigma of Woman*[66] are cases in point. Bersani's book is a study of the 'speculative turbulence' of Freud's texts – both internally, in the struggle for dominance of competing logics in them, and externally, when brought into relation with works by Beckett, Mallarmé, Henry James, and the Assyrian palace reliefs which preoccupied Bersani in *The Forms of Violence* (see *YW* 66.44–5). Subtle readings of *Civilization and its Discontents*, *Three Essays on Sexuality*, *Beyond the Pleasure Principle*, and *The Ego and the Id* demonstrate, in a by now familiar argument, that Freud's writings anxiously seek to repress their own most unsettling insights. Bersani then attempts to reconstruct, beyond its domestication by teleological narratives, that threatening 'sub-text'. For him, it lies in Freud's suggestion that sexuality is originally constituted as precisely that which defeats coherent psychic structure, i.e. as masochistic impulse. This thought is then put illuminatingly to work in his literary-critical engagements with modernist texts. Brief but pregnant, this book throws out many lines of speculation for further research. So too does Sarah Kofman, though the delay in translating her work (published in French in 1980) means that many such paths have already been trodden by subsequent feminist critics. She admirably charts Freud's complexly ambivalent relations to women in his earlier years, noting his often liberal attitude to some independent women acquaintances, his tentative openness to the mythic power of the Mother, and to the so-called 'feminine' side of his own nature. Through meticulous analyses of such essays as 'On Narcissism' and 'Femininity', she shows this receptive stance as shot through by impulses of fear and panic – which then become increasingly dominant in later life. Studiously refusing a stark binary choice over psychoanalysis (for or against feminism), Kofman's book insists on the need for a more differentiated analysis of this issue. At lower levels of theoretical intensity, the rereading of Freud is continued by Stephen Marcus on 'The Psychoanalytic Self' in *SoR*, Gregory S. Jay on 'Freud: The Death *of*

65. *The Freudian Body: Psychoanalysis and Art*, by Leo Bersani. ColU. pp. 126. $17.50.

66. *The Enigma of Woman: Woman in Freud's Writings*, by Sarah Kofman, trans. by Catherine Porter. CornU (1985). pp. 225. pb $12.95.

Autobiography' in *Genre*, and by an excellent reading of 'The Veiled Woman in Freud's "Das Unheimliche"' by Jane Marie Todd in *Signs*.

Pragmatism's Freud[67] announces a similar blend of old and new, commentary and innovation, but doesn't really achieve it. The key essay here is Richard Rorty's 'Freud and Moral Reflection', which focuses on Freud's decentring slogan: 'the ego is not even master in its own house'. In Rorty's view, the Freudian account of human beings as 'centreless assemblages of idiosyncratic needs' allows us to shift from transcendentalist notions of human 'essence' to a more 'aesthetic' relation to ourselves and our own possibilities. In the other seven pieces in the book a number of Rorty fans expand upon this position or reflect more generally upon his antifoundationalism. Bersani's and Kofman's Freud provokes one into a new look at the classic texts, but Rorty's Freud is just an occasion for him to make his familiar pragmatist points in a new register. One's response to the book will depend on one's view of the new pragmatism (see *YW* 66.25-6), which has always had much less kudos in Britain than it does in the U.S.A.

Two neglected post-Freudian writers are beginning to come back into critical focus. In *Formalism and the Freudian Aesthetic*[68], Linda Hutcheon gives an admirable account of Charles Mauron's *psychocritique*; she is particularly good on its relation to cognate developments among the Bloomsbury group. But a more important 'revival', much more embedded in the native culture, concerns a major analyst who worked in England from 1926 to her death in 1960. Phyllis Grosskurth's *Melanie Klein*[69] is perhaps short on theoretical acumen, but affords an extremely informative overview of Klein's life and work – including her bold, pioneering developments in child analysis and the 'play technique'. In the *Sal* issue on 'Intellectuals', Grosskurth discusses Klein as a 'Creative Intellectual of Psychoanalysis' and briefly debates her work with Christopher Lasch in 'Psychoanalysis and Politics'. In Juliet Mitchell's *The Selected Melanie Klein*[70] we have exactly what is needed to supplement the big Grosskurth book – a handy, cheap anthology of almost all Klein's crucial theoretical essays, including 'Infantile Anxiety Situations Reflected in a Work of Art and in the Creative Impulse' and 'The Importance of Symbol Formation in the Development of the Ego', in which she most directly confronts aesthetic concerns. The journals too seem to show that Melanie Klein's moment has come. In *FreeA* Barnett J. Sokol writes on '*Lolita* and Kleinian Psychoanalysis'; in *MLN* Angela Moorjani discusses 'Käthe Kollwitz on Sacrifice, Mourning and Reparation: An Essay in Psychoaesthetics'; even Leo Bersani is tempted into this field in *CritI* with his 'Marcel Proust and Melanie Klein', which neatly brings together modernist redemptive aesthetics and the Kleinian account of art as reparation. For too long the ghost of Melanie Klein has been hovering on the margins of a Lacan-dominated theoretical debate. Now, however, we can guess that the Imaginary and the Symbolic will soon be facing

67. *Pragmatism's Freud: The Moral Disposition of Psychoanalysis*, ed. by Joseph H. Smith and William Kerrigan. JHU. pp. xxi + 184. $19.25.

68. *Formalism and the Freudian Aesthetic: The Example of Charles Mauron*, by Linda Hutcheon. CUP (1984). pp. xv + 249. £22.50.

69. *Melanie Klein: Her World and her Work*, by Phyllis Grosskurth. H&S. pp. x + 515. £19.95.

70. *The Selected Melanie Klein*, ed. by Juliet Mitchell. Penguin. pp. 256. pb £4.95.

tough competition from Klein's 'paranoid-schizoid' and 'depressive' positions.

But for the moment Lacan still rules, and his dominance may for a while even be reinforced by the appearance of two excellent introductory guides to his work. In *The Works of Jacques Lacan*[71] Bice Benvenuto and Roger Kennedy take the reader step by step through most of Lacan's crucial essays. Despite the authors' rueful remark that 'expression of his ideas without his style is like spaghetti without its sauce', they remain accessible but never condescending, lucid but not excessively reductive. They seem, in fact, to have discovered exactly the kind of 'Student's Guide' format that contemporary theoreticians would most benefit from; a volume like this on Derrida would be very welcome. Commentary on individual essays keeps the 'tutor-text' firmly in view, while the chronological structure means that the developing twists and turns of a difficult thought are not packaged into a misleading homogeneity. Juliet Flower MacCannell's *Figuring Lacan*[72], though still an introduction of sorts, is a more ambitious study, since 'I have tried not so much to follow Lacan's path as to come before and after him'. The book focuses on Lacan's relevance to literary studies, and the 'cultural unconscious' of the subtitle, with its Jamesonian echoes, implies its polemical stance. MacCannell sees Lacan as *historicizing* concepts and themes which in Freud himself are mythic, universalist. While this is certainly a workable appropriation of Lacan's thought, it underplays those conservative dimensions of it – installing the Phallus as master signifier – which feminist critics above all have emphasized. Colin MacCabe's *The Talking Cure*[73], an excellent collection of essays working broadly within the ambit of Lacanianism, is now available in paperback. In *Rep* John Rajchman rewardingly ponders Lacan's claim that 'the status of the unconscious is ethical' ('Lacan and the Ethics of Modernity'), while Carolyn Dean elucidates the function of 'images of decapitation, corporal dismemberment and mutilation' in recent theory in her 'Law and Sacrifice: Bataille, Lacan and the Critique of the Subject'.

Three studies meditate on the vexed relations between psychoanalysis and philosophy. Or rather, the first of them, Ellie Ragland-Sullivan's *Jacques Lacan and the Philosophy of Psychoanalysis*[74], does not see the relation between the two fields as one of 'vexation' at all. Drawing heavily on Lacan's Seminars but also enterprisingly offering much *empirical* material to back up his theoretical positions, Ragland-Sullivan extrapolates from his work a new epistemology and metaphysics, and draws out some of its implications for such areas as developmental psychology and theory of mind. This is an impressively, even monumentally, self-confident edifice, and yet one is reminded uneasily of Bersani's contention that psychoanalysis always seeks to flatten out all that is most uncanny about its own discoveries. Jacques Derrida once denied that deconstruction was a 'psychoanalysis of philosophy'; but at least that phrase

71. *The Works of Jacques Lacan: An Introduction*, by Bice Benvenuto and Roger Kennedy. FAB. pp. 237. hb £20, pb £8.50.

72. *Figuring Lacan: Criticism and the Cultural Unconscious*, by Juliet Flower MacCannell. CH. pp. xxi + 182. hb £18.95, pb £7.95.

73. *The Talking Cure: Essays in Psychoanalysis and Language*, ed. by Colin MacCabe. Macmillan. pp. xiii + 230. pb £8.95.

74. *Jacques Lacan and the Philosophy of Psychoanalysis*, by Ellie Ragland-Sullivan. CH. pp. xxii + 358. £25.

conveys a much better sense of the subversive (and sometimes just plain baffling) dimensions of Lacanianism than Ragland-Sullivan's bland 'philosophy of psychoanalysis'. Our two next authors accept and even thrive on this 'vexation'.

Shoshana Felman's *Writing and Madness*[75] at last appears in English, though some of its contents – especially the enormous essay on *The Turn of the Screw* – have been familiar and influential for several years. For Felman, literature is closely allied to a 'madness' that dominant discourses seek to repress. But this position, which so far sounds aligned with the incipient primitivism of Foucault's *Madness and Civilization*, is given an original twist by Felman's focus on the *rhetorical* dimensions of madness in the text: madness is here not the pathos of a thematic content, but rather a literary speech act or power of performance in its own right. It is as if, in this book, the Dionysiac enthusiasms of Foucault are crossbred with the cool, canny gaze of a Paul de Man – a conjunction of strengths which is put to fine use in the powerful readings of Nerval, Flaubert, Balzac, and James.

Ned Lukacher's *Primal Scenes*[76] has the same subtitle as Felman's book – 'Literature, Philosophy, Psychoanalysis' – but its heroes are rather different: Freud and Heidegger rather than Lacan and Derrida. Our current over-investment in the latter pair has led, in Lukacher's view, to a grave neglect of the radicalism of their great precursors. He shrewdly maps onto each other Freud's notion of the primal scene and Heidegger's account of the history of Being – two powerful theoretical schemas which centre on concepts of memory and forgetting. Memory thus becomes textual rather than transcendental, and Lukacher has forged an interpretative weapon which enables him to negotiate the tensions between an occasionally formalist deconstructionism and the occasionally reductionist 'new historicism' that seeks to move beyond it. He flings down a gauntlet to Felman *en passant*, hinging the first part of his book on a reading of *The Turn of the Screw*, and in the second part analyses a set of intertextual primal scenes: Heidegger and Derrida, Hegel and Shakespeare, Marx and Balzac, Freud and Dickens. Theoretical subtlety and literary erudition combine here to produce a deeply exciting critical study. Another contribution to the debate on psychoanalysis and philosophy is Stephen Melville's 'Sexuality and Convention: On the Situation of Psychoanalysis' in *SubStance*. Examining Derrida's critique of Lacan, he works towards conclusions 'similar to those drawn by Barbara Johnson in her reading of the debate, but mine will bear on ontological rather than epistemological matters, eventuating in an acknowledgement of finitude rather than an espousal of skepticism'. The topic also comes up in Edith Kurzweil's 'Interview with Julia Kristeva' in *PR*.

Formations of Fantasy[77] reprints two crucial essays on its announced theme: Laplanche and Pontalis's 'Fantasy and the Origins of Sexuality' and Joan Rivière's 'Womanliness as a Masquerade' – the latter with a helpful introduction by Stephen Heath. The contributors argue for the constitutive, rather

75. *Writing and Madness (Literature/Philosophy/Psychoanalysis)*, by Shoshana Felman. CornU. pp. 255. $24.95.

76. *Primal Scenes: Literature, Philosophy, Psychoanalysis*, by Ned Lukacher. CornU. pp. 342. $24.95.

77. *Formations of Fantasy*, ed. by Victor Burgin, James Donald, and Cora Kaplan. Methuen. pp. ix + 221. pb £8.95.

than derivative or supplementary, role of fantasy in the construction of both sexual and political identities: John Fletcher explores the ambivalent functions of fantasy in lyric poetry, Cora Kaplan uses Colleen McCullough's *The Thorn Birds* to raise questions about fantasy and romance in the construction of femininity, Francette Pacteau offers an intriguing analysis of androgyny as both utopia *and* regression, Chris Turner and Erica Carter review Klaus Thewelweit's *Male Fantasies* in some depth. Janet Sayers's *Sexual Contradictions*[78] reviews the whole range of psychoanalytic theories that have a bearing on the construction of femininity; it will provide an admirable overview for the inexperienced reader.

With *Memory and Desire*[79], we move from social *con*struction to the natural *de*struction of identity in the processes of ageing and death. This is a sensitive, stimulating collection, bringing a variety of psychoanalytic perspectives to bear on a wide range of texts. Norman Holland considers 'Not So Little Hans', examining both Freud's case study and a memoir written by Hans some sixty-four years later after a career as stage director at the Metropolitan Opera House; to those of us who know only the boy of Freud's text, this essay makes fascinating, uncanny reading. Ellie Ragland-Sullivan offers a Lacanian view of Wilde's *Picture of Dorian Gray*, Carolyn Asp writes on 'Freud, Aging, and *King Lear*', Gabriele Schwab probes 'The Intermediate Area between Life and Death' in Beckett's *The Unnameable*, and there is much besides. The special issue of *L&P* on 'Feminism and Psychoanalysis' offers a similar mix of Freudian rereadings and literary extensions. Sara Van den Berg picks over the 'Dora' case history yet again, Martine Aniel re-examines the theory of penis-envy, while, on the literary side of the fence, Elizabeth A. Hirsh and Joan Lidoff write perceptively about '"New Eyes": H.D., Modernism, and the Psychoanalysis of Seeing' and 'Virginia Woolf's Feminine Sentence: The Mother–Daughter World of *To the Lighthouse*' respectively.

Some useful attempts are made to bring psychoanalysis into productive relationships with other literary-theoretical emphases in *Semiotica*, where Neal H. Bruss offers a survey of 'Hybrids of Psychoanalytic Structuralism and Literary Criticism', Eugene Bauer writes on 'Freud: A Man of Letters' and Juliet Flower MacCannell has a particularly useful study of 'Kristeva's Horror'; and in *CritI* where Norman Holland stitches it together with reader-response theory in his 'I-ing Film', which considers audience response to the film of *The Story of O*. Holland and David Bleich expand upon the principles of 'intersubjective' or 'transactive' reading in *NLH*, and in *The Art of Listening*[80] Norbert H. Platz offers a 'Critical Survey of Recent Psychoanalytical Theories of Reading'.

Diac has played an important role in winning a hearing for the work of Nicolas Abraham. This year it reprints a lecture in which he reflects on 'Psycho-analytic Esthetics: Time, Rhythm, and the Unconscious' or 'the genesis of time in the psychoanalytic sense', and a translation of the postscript to his book

---

78. *Sexual Contradictions: Psychology, Psychoanalysis and Feminism*, by Janet Sayers. Tavistock. pp. x + 214. hb £15, pb £6.95.

79. *Memory and Desire: Aging–Literature–Psychoanalysis*, ed. by Kathleen Woodward and Murray M. Schwartz. IndU. pp. 219. $24.95.

80. *The Art of Listening*, ed. by Graham McGregor and R. S. White. CH. pp. 220. £19.95.

Rythmes by Nicholas Rand and Maria Torok. Some of Torok's own work is represented in *CritI*, in Rand's translation. 'Unpublished by Freud to Fliess' speculates on absences in the published texts of Freud's letters to query whether his renunciation of the seduction theory was as wholehearted as later followers have suggested.

Finally, there seems every year to be at least one iconoclastic exercise which seeks to blow away the very possibility of psychoanalysis and/or psycho-analytic criticism. This year's instance is Frederick Crews's *Skeptical Engagements*[81]. Once a noted Freudian critic, Crews now turns his consid-erable sarcastic powers against the psycholiterary enterprise; it represents, he claims, a 'fear of facing the world, including its works of literature, without an intellectual narcotic at hand'. Starting out with a positivist definition of science, Crews happily proves that psychoanalysis is, in these terms, not 'scientific'. Yes indeed, one murmurs, but so what?

7. Feminism

If 1985 was the year for anthologies of feminist criticism, 1986 saw the publi-cation of three collections of essays written by leading feminist critics over the past ten years or so, most of them already published. Mary Jacobus's *Reading Woman*[82], Cora Kaplan's *Sea Changes: Culture and Feminism*[83], and Jacqueline Rose's *Sexuality in the Field of Vision*[84] all argue for the importance of theory, and specifically of psychoanalytic theory, to feminism; in different ways they all want to emphasize the complications and difficulties in ready appeals to either a given nature of sexual difference, or a feminism based only on the fact of women's evident social subordination. Through psychoanalytic concepts, they seek to go beyond the redundancy of the 'biology versus culture' debate, while still hanging on to the political force and urgency of feminist demands.

In an American context, Mary Jacobus stresses the value of theoretically informed feminist readings against 'the finally untheorized, experiential, and literary-herstorical tendency of much feminist criticism in the United States'. In Britain, Jacqueline Rose insists on the uses of psychoanalysis for feminism (and vice versa), as indispensable to a more complex understanding of what are nonetheless 'our fully political selves'. And in a related move, Cora Kaplan argues that social and psychic modes of analysis must be taken together. A traditional language of social subordination is inadequate for an analysis of women's oppression, but nor can the psychic construction of femininity be divided from its specific social inflections, from differences between women of different social groups, or from the oppressions that operate in terms of race and class rather than of sex.

Despite their general titles, each book consists in the main of detailed and

81. *Skeptical Engagements*, by Frederick Crews. OUPAm. pp. xx + 244. £17.50.
82. *Reading Woman: Essays in Feminist Criticism*, by Mary Jacobus. Methuen. pp. xvi + 316. £25.
83. *Sea Changes: Culture and Feminism*, by Cora Kaplan. Verso. pp. 232. hb £19.95, pb £6.95.
84. *Sexuality in the Field of Vision*, by Jacqueline Rose. Verso. pp. 256. hb £24.95, pb £7.95.

disparate studies of particular texts or issues. Kaplan – by design – is the least academic and the liveliest writer. *Sea Changes* includes studies of particular women writers and feminist critics (Wollstonecraft, Dickinson, Charlotte Brontë, Rossetti, Colleen McCullough, Alice Walker, Kate Millett, and others), with some more theoretical and autobiographical pieces. In her blending of genres and disciplines, Kaplan matches a looser style to her running argument in terms of 'the contradictory elements that make female subjectivity such a vertiginous social and psychic experience', and to her claim that a politics of subjectivity must take into account issues of pleasure and fantasy. (Interestingly, the only chapter where Kaplan renounces her distinctive personal style for straight exposition is the one on the interest of Lacan's account of subjectivity for feminist readings of poetry.)

In highlighting literature and psychoanalytic theory as places where sexual difference is to the fore, while at the same time emphasizing that this cannot be considered apart from issues of race and class, Kaplan raises the question of the priority, structurally and politically, of sexual over other forms of social and psychic differentiation. In general she follows the contention built into psycho-analytic theory that sexual difference comes first, but she also has a habit of putting 'race, class and gender' together in the more neutral, sociological style of the 'triple oppression' of separate but equally significant categories. Jacqueline Rose's book addresses this problem of the conceptualization of sexual difference from within a history of debates between psychoanalysis and feminism. She relates them to parallel debates about the source and specificity of social as well as sexual forms. In addition to psychoanalytic writings (Freud's 'Dora' case, the work of Julia Kristeva, Lacanian theory and its implications for feminism), Rose also looks at literature (readings of *Hamlet*, George Eliot), and at the application of psychoanalytic theory to readings of film and art.

Rose is concerned to hold on to the political force of feminism, but also to the disruptive concept of the unconscious, which renders problematic any simple appeal to a unified political subject, whether masculine or feminine. This leads her to stress, as does Kaplan, the difficulties of feminine subjectivity, and the fact that femininity is never fully attained, while also arguing against those who (in Rose's opinion) would dissolve the concept of the subject altogether as just a textual illusion. Rose walks similar tightropes in relation to other issues. She is anxious to avoid the reductiveness of a purely psychic account of women's distresses (which makes the social irrelevant), but also to avoid an account only in terms of social determination (which ignores the significance of fantasy in structuring perceptions of social reality). She does not want to see femininity as a suppressed 'good nature', but also criticizes the reverse side of this view, that femininity (or sexual difference) can be considered as nothing more than a form of false consciousness. Rose's is a book of questions rather than definitive answers, and all the stronger for that.

Mary Jacobus is also an indefatigable questioner, pursuing her explorations of an elusive femininity through the texts of psychoanalysis (especially Freud and Breuer on hysteria) and literature (especially Mary Wollstonecraft). Jacobus approaches femininity and psychoanalysis from a more overtly literary ('reading') angle than either Kaplan (who concentrates more on politics and history) or Rose (who concentrates more on psychoanalysis as an institution and a therapeutic practice, and resists what she regards as its too easy translation into 'a reading and writing effect'). 'Reading Woman' invokes several layers of connotation: the woman reading; the question of the separate identity of 'women' (apart from a masculinist structure of meaning); the problem of reading itself, and its necessarily unending nature, once the indeterminacy of the text, and notably of the 'woman' it both focuses and obscures, is acknowledged. Rather than argue against more conventionally political feminist criticism, Jacobus defends her own 'textual' exploration of the question of femininity as equally and differently useful. But at the same time, she does demonstrate the weak points in other approaches: the book includes incisive readings between the lines that show up the implicit assumptions, and often the unacknowledged naturalizations of sexual identities of various shapes, in the writings she discusses, including those of fellow feminist critics. Jacobus's deconstructions – her distinctive deployment and interrogation of the texts of psychoanalytic theory – are invaluable exercises in the feminist criticism she rereads or redesignates as 'reading woman'.

Many of these debates about the relation of feminism, or feminist theory, to psychoanalysis, politics, and literature are further played out in journal and conference collections. *m/f*'s self-proclaimed 'Last Issue' begins with an interview in which its editors, Parveen Adams and Elizabeth Cowie, discuss the journal's aims and interests over the eight years of its existence, including whether or not a psychoanalytic frame of reference is generalizable to all feminist issues; and including, once again, the difficulty of holding together both psychic and cultural forms of analysis while also questioning the form of the opposition on which the distinction is based. The final *m/f* also contains an important piece by Maud Ellmann, using Yeats's 'Leda and the Swan' to look at 'the violence of non-coincidence' implied in what psychoanalytic theory describes as drives to knowledge and mastery, and as the forcible imposition of an asymmetrical differentiation of the sexes.

OLR is devoted to the proceedings of its 1985 conference, held in conjunction with Southampton University, on 'Sexual Difference'. The heterogeneity of topics and the multiplicity of approaches gathered under this ambiguous umbrella provides food for frustration as well as curiosity; at the very least, diversity renders hopeless any attempt to synthesize or summarize the many brief contributions as manifestations of some single or general tendency. For the purposes of this review, concerned with the relations between psychoanalysis, sexual identity, and forms of writing, the section on hysteria (with articles by Jacqueline Rose and Parveen Adams) is especially worthy of note. Rose's piece takes the diary of Alice James as an exemplary case for the study of the connections between hysteria, writing, and femininity; Adams, in a companion piece to her contribution to *m/f* on the category of the body in psychoanalysis, draws out the implications for theories of identification and sexual difference of what she demonstrates to be Freud's two models of symptom-formation in hysteria. On feminist criticism, Lisa Jardine looks at the sexist history of literary studies in Britain and Elaine Showalter presents a witty overview of various forms of resistance to feminist studies. Gayatri Spivak examines the complicity of feminist criticism with imperialist exclusions: 'much so-called cross-cultural disciplinary practice, even when "feminist", reproduces and forecloses colonialist structures'.

The Poetics of Gender, edited by Nancy K. Miller[85], is the record of a

85. *The Poetics of Gender*, ed. by Nancy K. Miller. ColU. pp. xv + 303. $27.50.

conference that took place at Columbia. The introductions and concluding remarks celebrate a spirit of conviviality and co-operation at this event, and provide a marked contrast to the hints of acrimony in the 'Sexual Difference' volume. This raises the question of whether consensus should be considered preferable to dispute in matters of gender, and this is not only because the ladies' protestations of harmony sound at times suspiciously excessive. Agreement might mean the end of productive argument; while utterly different approaches may present the appearance of a Babel without any common language in which to have a real dispute.

But in any case, *The Poetics of Gender* itself contains a wide variety of approaches; their unity, by comparison with the *OLR* volume, is rather in terms of a shared focus on literature (except for Nancy J. Vickers's piece on a feminist story buried in the sculptures of Fontainebleau). Several pieces combine textual readings with explorations of psychoanalytic theories of sexual difference, especially in light of the American importing of French feminist theory, and reflect upon changes in the assumptions and aims of feminist critics interested in these issues. Thus in 'Reading Double' Naomi Schor, after showing how George Sand's *La Petite Fadette* anticipates psychoanalytic theory, ends with a call for historical specificity in considering accounts of femininity, including psychoanalytic ones. And in 'Difference on Trial' Domna C. Stanton, having criticized (in somewhat old-fashioned terms) 'the maternal metaphor' in French feminist theory, concludes with an innovative proposal as to the necessary deferral of final feminist solutions aiming to explain femininity or liberate women once and for all. Other essays (such as Catharine R. Stimpson on 'Gertrude Stein and the Transposition of Gender' and Ann Rosalind Jones in 'Surprising Fame' on French Renaissance lyric poetry) start from avowedly historical premises and concerns, and then use sophisticated techniques of reading to analyse strategies of women's writing which are at once political and rhetorical. In a related vein, Sandra M. Gilbert and Susan Gubar in 'Tradition and the Female Talent' look at turn-of-the-century writing by men as a response to what they perceived as the threat posed by 'scribbling women', leading towards what should now be seen as 'the sexual crisis that underlies modernism'. Taken together, the essays in this volume interrogate the relations between historical, formalist, and psychoanalytic ways of feminist reading. The shared questions (there is no one answer) make this a stimulating collection.

Paragraph – like *OLR*, not a journal whose reputation in based on its feminist interests – gives a whole issue to 'Feminism'. (The relation of 'feminism' and 'sexual difference' is an open question, and the definition of the first is another problem, noticeably unilluminated by a book tantalizingly entitled *What Is Feminism?*[86].) In accordance with what Diana Knight's introduction calls the 'tactic' of 'separatism' in this issue entirely written by women, some of the articles address a problem of masculine appropriations of feminism or feminist theory, and other threats to a cohesiveness or coherence conceived as desirable for feminism. Nancy K. Miller, in 'Parables and Politics: Feminist Criticism in 1986', discusses the difficulties and problematic implications of getting women writers onto an American 'Great Books' syllabus, and suggests

---

86. *What Is Feminism?*, ed. by Juliet Mitchell and Ann Oakley. Blackwell. pp. ix + 252. hb £25, pb £6.95.

that 'it may well be that it is precisely the "diversity that characterises feminist criticism" that undermines its effects outside its own sphere of influence'; while Margaret Atack, writing in 'The Other: Feminist' on Kristeva, objects to her subject's objections to feminism, and asks 'what of Kristeva's philosophy can be appropriated for the (very diverse) feminist theorizations of the social construction of gender and identity positions, when its boundaries are policed by the division between woman and feminist?' From different angles, both statements imply that feminist diversity may go too far. Their institutional and social references point up the problem addressed in Jacqueline Rose's book of how to maintain the political import of feminism at the same time as engaging in a thoroughgoing and inevitably divisive theoretical analysis of psychic and social forms.

Kristeva's work has become a focus for this debate, and the publication of *The Kristeva Reader*, edited by Toril Moi[87], is thus to be welcomed in making accessible a good selection of her work in a single volume. This year also at last sees the translation of *The Newly Born Woman*, by Hélène Cixous and Catherine Clément[88], previously available only in frequently quoted extracts of Cixous's contribution. Sandra M. Gilbert's elegant introduction presenting the text to American readers is also a tacit supplement, adding the figure of the woman writer (exemplified by Emily Dickinson) to Clément and Cixous's gallery of female witches and hysterics and 'feminine' male writers. Gilbert's reading makes the case for *écriture féminine* by tying it to actual women and by stressing the shared resistance of all women to patriarchal culture (this is what Dickinson, the WASP poet of Amherst, has in common with Cixous, the French Algerian Jew). But this defence has the effect of shifting the emphasis of Cixous's concept of feminine writing (defined by its subversion of patriarchal codes rather than by the sex of its author), as if there were risks in undoing what should be seen as a natural tie between femininity, feminist protest, and women.

Maggie Humm's *Feminist Criticism: Women as Contemporary Critics*[89] is divided into one section which analyses different contemporary approaches to feminist theory, and another which looks at the criticism of Virginia Woolf, Rebecca West, and Adrienne Rich. The first part crams in too much all at once, tending to criticize the approach under discussion by appealing to arguments which will only be explained later on, or to utilize terms from several theoretical languages at the same time. The second part suffers from similar confusions at times, but contains some interesting points.

Another book which in a different way falls victim to its attempt to cover the field is Mary Eagleton's reader in *Feminist Literary Theory*[90]. The book is divided into five topics or questions, each with a helpful introduction. But the selections themselves are so truncated (no doubt in part because of copyright

87. *The Kristeva Reader*, by Julia Kristeva, ed. by Toril Moi. Blackwell. pp. viii + 327. hb £25, pb £7.95.
88. *The Newly Born Woman*, by Hélène Cixous and Catherine Clément, trans. by Betsy Wing. ManU. pp. xviii + 169. hb £26.50, pb £6.95.
89. *Feminist Criticism: Women as Contemporary Critics*, by Maggie Humm. Harvester. pp. xii + 218. hb £20, pb £7.95.
90. *Feminist Literary Theory: A Reader*, ed. by Mary Eagleton. Blackwell. pp. xiv + 237. hb £22.50, pb £7.95.

difficulties) that it is hard to see how they can provide the basis for informed discussion which the editor intends.

Gender and Reading, a collection of essays edited by Elizabeth A. Flynn and Patrocinio P. Schweickart, is another relatively disappointing book[91]. The concept of reading here is a long way from Mary Jacobus's: most of the contributors are involved in the task of eradicating what they identify as the gender-neutral but actually masculine assumptions of reader-response criticism, while not questioning that frame of analysis (a subject/object or reader/text distinction, with varying versions of 'context' added in). The chapters which deal with empirical studies of gender differences in reading tend to be circular in their arguments: insisting on the social (not natural) construction of gender characteristics, predictably finding these norms confirmed in patterns of response to texts, but treating as given the equally normative categories of analysis ('critical detachment' or 'empathy'; 'dominance' of or 'submission' to the text) according to which these distinctions are perceived. The essays by Schweickart ('Reading Ourselves') and Jean E. Kennard ('Ourself behind Ourself') are both interesting attempts to account or allow for women's identification with male characters in the first case, and lesbian readers' pleasure in heterosexist texts or heterosexual characters in Kennard's case. But Schweickart ends up by reinstating a natural difference of the sexes, based on women's allegedly more relational disposition, and by calling for the application of different feminist reading strategies to texts by men and women (which again takes for granted the difference which was initially problematized). The volume also includes readings of texts about reading (Judith Fetterley), studies of popular reading in relation to gender (Kathryn Shevelow's 'Fathers and Daughters', Madonne M. Miner's 'Guaranteed to Please'), and a piece by Susan Robin Suleiman ('Malraux's Women') on the results of rereading Malraux with an eye to the lack of women in his texts.

8. Historical and Materialist Criticism

David McLellan's *Ideology*[92] and Robert Bocock's *Hegemony*[93] offer brief, lucid guides to two of the key, and much contested, concepts of a Marxist literary or cultural theory; both will afford an excellent entry to these issues for students. Thomas Sowell's *Marxism: Philosophy and Economics*[94] is a trenchant survey of major areas of doctrine: peculiarly schizophrenic, the book combines sober exposition with occasional venomous spasms of anti-Marxist rhetoric. Jon Elster's *Making Sense of Marx*[95] has already been recognized as a major classic of Marx interpretation and has inaugurated the new theoretical paradigm of 'analytical Marxism'. Since modern Marxist criticism has always developed in the wake of the burgeoning of what Martin Jay once called our

91. *Gender and Reading: Essays on Readers, Texts, and Contexts*, ed. by Elizabeth A. Flynn and Patrocinio P. Schweickart. JHU. hb £21.60, pb £8.60.

92. *Ideology*, by David McLellan. OpenU. pp. 99. hb £16, pb £4.95.

93. *Hegemony*, by Robert Bocock. Tavistock. pp. 136. hb £8.50, pb £4.25.

94. *Marxism: Philosophy and Economics*, by Thomas Sowell. Unwin. pp. x + 226. pb £3.95.

95. *Making Sense of Marx*, by Jon Elster. CUP (1985). pp. xv + 556. hb £32.50, pb £10.95.

century's 'series of adjectival Marxisms', it remains to be seen what the literary consequences of the new epithet 'analytical' will be. Another work of great interpretative power is Paul Ricoeur's *Lectures on Ideology and Utopia*[96], which for the first time extends his concerns to social and political issues. Ranging widely over Marx, Althusser, Weber, Habermas, and Mannheim, Ricoeur's focus on the couplet ideology/utopia articulates a concern close to the heart of contemporary Marxist criticism: how to move beyond demystification, from ideology *to* utopia, from a purist sociology of art to something like a materialist aesthetics. Carefully teasing out the tangled significations of both these key terms, seeking a utopian moment within the concept of ideology itself, Ricoeur's book will certainly clarify the theoretical – though not the political – issues involved.

In his *Western Marxism*[97] J. G. Merquior offers a caustic analysis of the whole field of what he deridingly abbreviates as 'WM'. His fertilely polemical pen generates many pungent phrases and many shrewd theoretical insights, but constantly runs the danger of overkill. His final denunciation – 'all in all, the age of WM (1920–1970) was just an episode in the long history of an old pathology of western thought: irrationalism' – is surely overstated; and not least because 'WM' itself powerfully demonstrated that the notion of 'rationality' that underpins such judgements has its own pathological dimensions. The founder of 'WM', Georg Lukács, makes a curious appearance this year as personal correspondent rather than political militant and theorist. His *Selected Correspondence: 1902–1920*[98], which includes letters to and from such figures as Max Weber, Georg Simmel, and Ernst Bloch, gives a fascinating glimpse of the turn-of-the-century 'crisis' in bourgeois culture and of the long painful path (in Michael Löwy's phrase) 'from romanticism to Bolshevism'. Lukács's *History and Class Consciousness* receives sophisticated analysis in Andrew Feenberg's *Lukács, Marx and the Sources of Critical Theory*[99], which works through a sustained comparison of the Lukács text and Marx's *Paris Manuscripts*; the book aims in particular to rebuff the accusation (repeated by Merquior) that the theory of reification is irrationalist. In a series on 'Leading Thinkers' in *Praxis*, Mihailo Marković gives a trenchant synopsis of 'The Critical Thought of György Lukács', while a subsequent article under the same rubric is devoted to 'The Concept of Community in the Thought of Lucien Goldmann'. This is a brave attempt to redeem Lukács's Rumanian disciple, whose theory of 'genetic structuralism' has put him almost beyond the pale of contemporary (including Marxist) theory; there is much more in his work, Morton Kaye suggests, than just that. In an account of 'Forms of Longing' in Lukács's work in *Criticism*, Debra A. Castillo throws out the tantalizing suggestion that Marxism for Lukács represents 'if the word is used guardedly, an erotics'.

Lukács's Frankfurt successors are well served by paperback reprints:

96. *Lectures on Ideology and Utopia*, by Paul Ricoeur. ColU. pp. xxxvi + 353. $35.
97. *Western Marxism*, by J. G. Merquior. Paladin. pp. viii + 247. pb £3.95.
98. *Georg Lukács: Selected Correspondence 1902–1920*, ed. by Judith Marcus and Zoltan Tar. ColU. pp. 318. $25.
99. *Lukács, Marx and the Sources of Critical Theory*, by Andrew Feenberg. OUP. pp. xii + 286. pb £8.95.

Marcuse's *One-Dimensional Man*[100] is again available, as – for the first time – is Adorno's *Aesthetic Theory*[101], a work that is already having a major impact on the current revival of interest in aesthetics among radical critics. In a subtly argued essay on 'Adorno, Post-structuralism and the Critique of Identity' in *NLR*, Peter Dews contends that Adorno's critique of 'identity thinking' escapes the abstract opposition of bare immediacy and conceptual determination that funds much of the Nietzschean and poststructuralist critique of the modern subject. The Lukácsian and Frankfurt heritages inform the collection *Reconstructing Aesthetics* (Blackwell), edited by Lukács's former pupils, Agnes Heller and Ferenc Feher; however, it has not been available for review. The major event within Western Marxist studies this year, at least in terms of sheer bulk, is the translation into English of the three volumes of Ernst Bloch's *The Principle of Hope* (Blackwell). Conceived on a truly monstrous scale, the book will only properly be assimilated across the years to come. But we can predict even now that it will strongly reinforce the trend within Marxist cultural studies – already noted in relation to Paul Ricoeur's book – away from the critique of ideology towards a deciphering of the utopian potential, however distorted, of literary and other texts.

Walter Benjamin continues to fascinate. His *Moscow Diary* (Harvard) is now in English, and will provide further grist to the commentators' mill. Not that the mill is idle, however, for *NGC* has its 'Second Special Issue on Walter Benjamin', a rich haul indeed. Based on a conference on 'Walter Benjamin et Paris' in 1983, the contributions here not surprisingly focus on Benjamin's 'Arcades project'. Irving Wohlfarth, the editor, offers 'Re-Fusing Theology. Some First Responses', and essays by Burkhardt Lindner ('The *Passagen-Werk*, the *Berliner Kindheit*, and the Archaeology of the "Recent Past"') and Bernd Witte ('Paris–Berlin–Paris') set Benjamin's fascination with Paris in the context of his general interest in the great European capitals. Phillipe Ivornel, in 'Paris, Capital of the Popular Front or the Posthumous Life of the Nineteenth Century', analyses the political context in which Benjamin wrote as a determinant of his Parisian investigations, and Chryssoula Kambas expands the Popular-Frontist theme into a general meditation on 'Walter Benjamin's Concept of History'; Wolfgang Fietkau then moves back some twenty years to consider the problematic of the 'Lost Revolution' in Benjamin's work. In characteristically subtle and profound essays, Susan Buck-Morss inserts the figure of the 'sandwichman' into the Benjaminian urban equation of *flâneur* and whore, while Irving Wohlfarth examines 'The Historian as Chiffonier'. Rounding off the collection is H. D. Kittsteiner's meticulously argued study of 'Walter Benjamin's Historicism', which proposes that we consider Benjamin – 'not to his disadvantage' – as a materialist historicist rather than a historical materialist. In *PR* Edouard Roditi gives a brief account of his 'Meetings with Walter Benjamin' in Berlin in 1930–31. One of the intermediate links turns out to be Jean Ross, real-life model for Christopher Isherwood's Sally Bowles; might we see Benjamin get a bit part in a post-Minnelli version of *Cabaret*?

100. *One-Dimensional Man: Studies in the Ideology of Advanced Industrial Society*, by Herbert Marcuse. Ark. pp. xvii + 260. pb £3.95.

101. *Aesthetic Theory*, by T. W. Adorno, trans. by C. Lenhardt, ed. by Gretel Adorno and Rolf Tiedemann. RKP. pp. x + 526. pb £7.95.

The death of Jean-Paul Sartre in 1980 has led to a revival of interest in his status within Western Marxism, as evidenced by an issue of *YFS*, 'Sartre after Sartre' (1985). Philip Wood, in 'Sartre, Anglo-American Marxism and the Place of the Subject in History', asserts the continuing relevance of Sartre's work in our own poststructuralist climate; Ronald Aronson has a valuable account of the second, as yet unpublished, volume of Sartre's *Critique*, 'Sartre and the Dialectic', while Juliette Simont, in '*The Critique of Dialectical Reason*' defends the function of the concept of 'need' in the first volume against Aronson's criticisms of it in his book on Sartre; essays by David Gross on 'Sartre's (Mis)Reading of Flaubert's Politics', and Pierre Verstraeten on 'The Negative Theology of Sartre's *Flaubert*', on *The Family Idiot*, are accompanied, most welcomely, by Sartre's own notes towards its fourth volume; Alexandre Leupin ('A New Sartre') reviews Denis Hollier's study of Sartre, *Politique de la Prose*, whose translation is forthcoming. A tribute of another kind is Simone de Beauvoir's *Adieux: A Farewell to Sartre*[102]. The first part of the book is a bleak biographical account of Sartre's failing physical powers in the last ten years of his life; it is followed by a set of wide-ranging, sometimes incisive, sometimes meandering but always interesting set of 'interviews' with Sartre by de Beauvoir herself. Ronald Hayman's *Writing Against*[103] is the first full-scale intellectual biography of Sartre in English. Well paced and highly readable, it gives an effective sense of the great range of Sartre's achievement, of the fertile integration of his life and thought. In briefer compass in *PR*, Hayman gives a conspectus of Sartre's career which applies Sartrean biographical methods to their own inventor. *SocT* also offers preliminary accounts of the mass of manuscript Sartre left behind him – accounts which tend to stress the *ethical* dimension of his work. All in all, this body of work points to a significant revival of Sartre's fortunes in the world of critical theory.

One other body of Western Marxist work that has been increasingly invoked in the attempt to move beyond certain impasses in poststructuralism is that of Jürgen Habermas. Rick Roderick's *Habermas and the Foundations of Critical Theory*[104] is now probably the best short guide to the *œuvre*. It centres on two crucial questions in Habermas: the problems of justifying the normative dimensions of critical social theory, and of connecting theory with political practice – both of which involve what Roderick terms the 'problematic of rationality'. Having finished Roderick's book, which finally takes Habermas to task for having too readily abandoned Marx's 'productive paradigm' in favour of a 'communication paradigm', the reader might then move on to the collection of interviews with Habermas edited by Peter Dews[105], which has a splendid introduction in which Dews mobilizes Habermas's defence of the project of the Enlightenment against poststructuralism in general and Lyotard in particular. The interviews range illuminatingly across the whole range of the

102. *Adieux: A Farewell to Sartre*, by Simone de Beauvoir, trans. by Patrick O'Brian. Penguin (1985). pp. 453. pb £4.95.

103. *Writing Against: A Biography of Sartre*, by Ronald Hayman. W&N. pp. xxxix + 487. £14.95.

104. *Habermas and the Foundations of Critical Theory*, by Rick Roderick. Macmillan. pp. xi + 194. hb £20, pb £6.95.

105. *Habermas: Autonomy and Solidarity*, ed. by Peter Dews. Verso. pp. viii + 219. hb £18.95, pb £6.95.

oeuvre, as well as Habermas's own personal and political formation in postwar Germany, and present in attractively informal manner a thinker whose writings can be unwieldy (macrostructurally) and stodgy (microstructurally). Another valuable collection is *Habermas and Modernity*[106], in which the most relevant essays for the literary theorist will be Richard Rorty's 'Habermas and Lyotard on Post-modernity' and Martin Jay's excellent 'Habermas and Modernism'. Jay notes Habermas's implicit dependence on Walter Benjamin's 'mimetic' theory of language to found a Schillerian 'redemptive' aesthetic which in many ways runs counter to his general stress on reason, evolution in history, and the non-identity of subject and object. Habermas himself contributes an account of the 'affirmative feature of Herbert Marcuse's negative thinking' and, in a concluding overview, responds to Jay's challenge to define what he means by 'aesthetic rationality'. Habermas's concern to provide a normative foundation for critical social theory is set in a broader Frankfurt context in John Torpey's 'Ethics and Critical Theory: From Horkheimer to Habermas' in *Telos*, while in the same journal Peter U. Hohendahl ponders 'Habermas's Philosophical Discourse of Modernity', whetting one's appetite for the forthcoming translation of Habermas's *magnum opus* on this topic.

Studies of Mikhail Bakhtin and his 'school' proceed apace; for he has come to figure centrally in the Marxist engagement with poststructuralism. The 1983 issue of *CritI* devoted to Bakhtin is now re-issued, together with later contributions to the debate, as *Bakhtin: Essays and Dialogues on his Work* (Chicago), edited by Gary Saul Morson, but it has not been available for review. In it, Morson replies to Ken Hirschkop's reply to the original forum (see *YW* 66.53), and this polemic rumbles on with Hirschkop's 'Bakhtin and Liberalism' in the *BakhtinN*, in which he re-iterates his claim that Morson's attempt to use Bakhtin to move beyond the sterile antinomy of social and individual fails lamentably; Morson is no doubt by now sadly lamenting the day that he provoked the ire of as indefatigable and hard-hitting a polemicist as this. Hirschkop expounds his own *positive* conception of Bakhtin's relevance in his 'Bakhtin, Discourse and Democracy' in *NLR*. This powerfully synoptic piece celebrates Bakhtin as combining – unusually within twentieth-century Marxism – a commitment to both modernism and populism, and Hirschkop aims in particular to spell out the institutional preconditions of a 'dialogic', democratic culture – a dimension underdeveloped in Bakhtin's own work. In *The Politics and Poetics of Transgression*[107] Peter Stallybrass and Allon White sketch an account, inspired by Bakhtin and Kristeva, of the 'cultural imaginary' of the European bourgeoisie from the seventeenth century on. Subtly analysing a series of key cultural motifs – the fair, the pig, the city, servants – they demonstrate that as the bourgeois élites withdrew from popular culture, the 'carnivalesque' forces they renounced later re-emerged as objects of both disgust and desire in the fields of literature and psychoanalysis. There's a faint whiff of the old 'dissociation of sensibility' about this thesis, which certainly lacks a Habermasian sense of the *necessity* of the differentiation of the spheres in cultural modernity. Yet, despite this, the book remains exemplary in

106. *Habermas and Modernity*, ed. by Richard J. Bernstein. Polity (1985). pp. x + 243. pb £6.95.

107. *The Politics and Poetics of Transgression*, by Peter Stallybrass and Allon White. Methuen. pp. xxii + 228. hb £13.95, pb £7.50.

its attempt to weld together theoretical meditation, historical analysis, and recommendations for contemporary cultural politics – spheres of work which are themselves all too often 'dissociated' in today's debates. Raymond Williams, in his 'The Uses of Cultural Theory' in *NLR*, also draws contemporary cultural-political lessons from Bakhtin; he uses the Bakhtin school's critique of Russian Futurism and Formalism to mount an impassioned assault on the nihilistic tendencies within our own avant-garde movements. Jay Caplan's *Framed Narratives*[108] has a more limited aim, applying Bakhtinian concepts to the interpretation of Diderot (though by implication the analysis bears upon early bourgeois literature in general). For Caplan, the narrative device of 'tableau' sets up a dialogical relationship between reader, author, and characters; this linkage of theoretical concept and narrative motif then leads to a set of subtle interpretations across the whole range of Diderot's multigeneric *œuvre*. In *UTQ* Charles Lock similarly puts Bakhtinian concepts to literary-critical work in a piece on 'Polyphonic Powys', while in *Genre* Craig Howes explores 'Rhetorics of Attack: Bakhtin and the Aesthetics of Satire'. In a substantial review-article in *E&Soc* Keith Tribe assails the limitations of the Clark and Holquist Bakhtin biography (*YW* 66.53); 'Bakhtin's life', he argues (rather like Hayman on Sartre), 'would have to be written as a dialogic text.' On a more iconoclastic note, Richard M. Berrong's *Rabelais and Bakhtin*[109] tries to upset the Bakhtinian boat by demonstrating both the historical and textual weaknesses of *Rabelais and his World*; he argues in particular that Rabelais's attitude to popular culture is notably more ambivalent, even on occasion negative, than Bakhtin suggests. While such claims need not affect the general theoretical suggestiveness of Bakhtin's arguments, it will be interesting to see how the Bakhtinians – and above all the doughty Hirschkop – rise to this challenge.

Contemporary Marxist work on the whole remains preoccupied with the question of poststructuralism. Terry Eagleton's *Against the Grain*[110] reprints many of the essays noted individually in *YWES* over recent years. Ranging widely over such figures as Macherey, Derrida, Bakhtin, Wittgenstein, Perry Anderson, and Brecht, Eagleton's collection is preoccupied with the attempt to invent a 'modernist Marxism' which would take on board central insights from deconstruction, feminism, postmodernism, while not renouncing the classical canons of class struggle. Perhaps the exemplary essay in this respect is 'Wittgenstein's Friends', which sees Bakhtin's work as mediating between the abstract extremes of a Derridean stress on the 'materiality' of the signifier divorced from the material conditions in which it moves and a Wittgensteinian emphasis on precisely those conditions but with little sense of semiotic potential in his 'studied linguistic "ordinariness"'. 'The Critic as Clown' is a lesser but engaging piece, shifting away from Eagleton's long combat with *Scrutiny* to discover and celebrate a certain radical populist iconoclasm in the writings of William Empson (Colin MacCabe, we might note here, covers some of the same

108. *Framed Narratives: Diderot's Genealogy of the Beholder*, by Jay Caplan. ManU. pp. 134. pb £7.95.

109. *Rabelais and Bakhtin: Popular Culture in 'Gargantua and Pantagruel'*, by Richard M. Berrong. UNeb. pp. xiii + 156. $21.50.

110. *Against the Grain: Essays 1975–1985*, by Terry Eagleton. Verso. pp. 199. hb £18.95, pb £5.95.

ground in his 'The Cambridge Heritage: Richards, Empson and Leavis' in *SoRA*). Eagleton gives a substantial interview on his work in *Thesis Eleven: A Socialist Journal* (1985), which also includes Tony Bennett on 'A Political Critique of Aesthetics' and Richard Wolin on 'Communism and the Avant-Garde'; but, alas, this fine journal is extremely difficult to find in Britain and the 1986 issues have not come to hand. In another interview in *SocT*, conducted by Andrew Martin and Patrice Petro, Eagleton again surveys many aspects of his recent thought.

John Frow's important *Marxism and Literary History* [111] is a less combative, more systematic book than Eagleton's, but belongs to the same overall project, being 'part of a semiotically orientated intervention in cultural politics'. A critique of Lukács, Macherey, Eagleton, and Jameson is organized around Frow's dissatisfaction with the categories of representation and ideology, i.e. the epistemological categories, in which the operations of literary discourse have often been thought within Marxist theory. This is by now a familiar argument, often leading to attempts to develop a materialist aesthetics based on concepts of pleasure and value, but this is not the path Frow follows. He reformulates the notions of both ideology and discourse: the former is conceived non-representationally as a *state* of discourse, while the latter is seen as the structured regulation of practices, in the spirit of Bakhtin, Halliday, and Foucault. This general reformulation of 'discourse' is then the basis for reworking the concepts of 'literary system' (drawing effectively upon Russian Formalism), 'intertextuality', 'text', and 'reading'. This is a meticulously argued work, perhaps becoming a little too agnostic about the 'real' in its insistence on a necessary semiotic mediation, and will surely have a major impact upon Marxist cultural argument.

Diane Macdonell's expository *Theories of Discourse* [112] deals with that bastard child of poststructuralism and Marxism, 'post-Marxism'. Unpretentiously and with great clarity, she expounds the work of Althusser, Michel Pêcheux, Barry Hindess and Paul Hirst, and Foucault, arguing for the ideological relativity of meaning, its enmeshment in power-relations and institutional contexts. The book will be a boon to students, and while a full-scale polemical engagement with its theorists would obviously be out of place in a work of this kind, it does none the less offer pointers towards a critique of their occasional lapses into pragmatism. Also in expository vein, Mary Louise Pratt's 'Ideology and Speech Act Theory' in *PoT* helpfully supplements the Macdonell book. For the full-blooded polemic, we can turn to *From Prague to Paris* [113], in which J. G. Merquior, fresh from his demolition of Western Marxism, turns his attention to its (in his view) equally irrationalist successors. Merquior concentrates on Lévi-Strauss, Barthes, and Derrida, seeing the latter as representing 'the final consequence of the surrender of philosophy to the literary ideology forged by High Modernism'; but perhaps his most interesting suggestion is that structuralism need not, in fact, have undergone its Parisian degeneration. For in the work of the Prague School of the 1930s, Merquior sees

111. *Marxism and Literary History*, by John Frow. Blackwell. pp. ix + 275. £19.50.
112. *Theories of Discourse: An Introduction*, by Diane Macdonell. Blackwell. pp. viii + 146. hb £22.50, pb £6.95.
113. *From Prague to Paris: A Critique of Structuralist and Post-structuralist Thought*, by J. G. Merquior. Verso. pp. xi + 286. hb £18.95, pb £6.95.

the development of a structuralism *not* afflicted by *rive gauche* formalism; Mukařovský, rather than Jakobson and his Parisian progeny, is the hero of this account. Merquior's critique of structuralism *et al.* is often compelling, its swingeingly sarcastic tone eventually becomes tiresome. It's high time, one feels, that he devoted as much energy to a *positive* intellectual project as he does to his screeds and comminations. In a shrewd essay on 'Marxism and Post-Marxism' in *SocT*, Richard D. Wolff and Stephen Cullenberg argue that much of the poststructuralist critique of Marxism is misjudged or, rather, that it applies to the Marxist tradition rather than to Marx himself – that tradition having simplified the originality and power of its founder's thought.

As might be expected from a critic who has made the concept of genre so central to his work, Fredric Jameson continues to produce outstanding essays mediating between high theory and critical practice. In a discussion of 'On Magic Realism in Film' in *CritI*, he expands on the themes of his chapter on romance in *The Political Unconscious*, while his 'Third-World Literature in the Era of Multinational Capitalism' in *SocT* sketches a 'theory of the cognitive aesthetics' of Third-World literature, in an essay that clearly forms a pendant to his celebrated account of postmodernism (see *YW* 66.19). There is now so much seminal but scattered work by Jameson in the journals that we very urgently need his – just as much Terry Eagleton's – *Selected Essays*.

Michel Foucault, object of Merquior's blistering polemical attention last year (*YW* 66.50), receives more measured, though never reverent, treatment in *Foucault: A Critical Reader*[114]. Martin Jay's 'In the Empire of the Gaze' situates Foucault's 'Denigration of Vision' in the history of twentieth-century French attempts to deprivilege vision as an epistemological metaphor. Jürgen Habermas trenchantly argues in 'Taking Aim at the Heart of the Present' that Foucault cannot justify the normative standards presupposed in any critique of the present. Richard Rorty sees *The Archaeology of Knowledge* as the odd man out in Foucault's *œuvre*, mistakenly attempting to make 'archaeology' the successor subject to epistemology. In Rorty's view, Foucault cannot escape the charge of epistemological relativism, but Charles Taylor, in his 'Foucault on Freedom and Truth' disagrees, arguing that Foucault gets lost in his own paradoxical stance towards truth. Truth and reason are also central to the article 'What Is Maturity?' by Hubert Dreyfus and Paul Rabinow, which helpfully contrasts Habermas and Foucault on the Enlightenment 'project', and to Barry Smart's 'The Politics of Truth and the Problem of Hegemony'. In a more political vein, David Couzens Hoy and Edward Said debate Foucault's account of power. This rich collection also contains interesting essays by Ian Hacking, Michael Walzer, Mark Poster, and Arnold Davidson. Mike Gane's *Towards A Critique of Foucault*[115] collects essays which had previously appeared in *E&Soc*. Once again, the *Archaeology* is seen as the weak link in the theoretical chain by Beverley Brown and Mark Cousins in 'The Linguistic Fault', while questions of politics are here much to the fore: Jeff Minson ('Strategies for Socialists') and Gary Wickham ('Power and Power Analysis') discuss the ways in which Foucault's work can enrich – but also on occasion

---

114. *Foucault: A Critical Reader*, ed. by David Couzens Hoy. Blackwell. pp. 246. hb £27.50, pb £8.50.

115. *Towards a Critique of Foucault*, ed. by Mike Gane. RKP. pp. vii + 179. pb £6.95.

undermine – socialist conceptions of 'strategy' and power. But the highlight of the anthology is Peter Dews's 'The *Nouvelle Philosophie* and Foucault', which charts the dilution and ideological appropriation of Foucauldian themes at the hands of André Glucksmann, Bernard-Henri Lévy, and others.

Numerous articles on Foucault have appeared. John Bowen reflects on his definitions of the 'intellectual' in *LTP*, while the *Telos* issue on 'French Politics and Culture' contains Richard Wolin on 'Foucault's Aesthetic Decisionism'. Wolin argues that Foucault's 'ubiquitization' of Enlightenment panopticism ultimately compels a Nietzschean 'leap' to 'extricate himself from the theoretical *cul de sac* in which he finds his position immobilized. This is the leap of aesthetic decisionism'. In the same issue Maria Daraki's 'Foucault's Journey to Greece' reflects intriguingly on the general cultural functions of the 'discourse on Greece' in contemporary France ('The Greek experience has for several years challenged the structuralist determinism which prevailed in France') and on Foucault's self-insertion into it in his last writings. Rebecca Conway aims at 'Excavating the Repressive Hypothesis' from its burial in *The History of Sexuality*, and Keith Gandal once again considers the problem posed for 'Foucault's Politics' by its apparent lack of normative foundations. John Rajchman also addresses this problem in his 'Ethics After Foucault' in *SocT*. *E&Soc* translates Foucault's 'Kant on Enlightenment and Revolution', with a weighty introduction by Colin Gordon; this issue also includes 'Michel Foucault (1926–84): The Will to Knowledge' by Pasquale Pasquino, in which a co-worker considers research projects which will now not be concluded. In *TCS* Alex Callinicos reflects briefly on the second and third volumes of *The History of Sexuality*. Finally, a new anthology of the master's own writings has appeared, *The Foucault Reader*[116]. While much of this is familiar territory (with the 'archaeological' period strangely excluded), we can be grateful for the translation of one crucial essay, 'What Is Enlightenment?', and several illuminating interviews.

At the grey, confused borderline between literary theory and cultural studies, we get a fruitful symbiosis of what Colin MacCabe terms *High Theory/Low Culture*[117]. MacCabe makes a preliminary attempt at 'Defining Popular Culture', Laura Kipnis's lively '"Refunctioning" Reconsidered' re-assesses the Brechtian concept, Andrew Tolson discusses cultural studies itself in 'Popular Culture: Practice and Institution'; other essays offer analyses of speci fic forms from film music to video games and need not be noticed here. A similar blend of theory and practice is on offer in *Popular Culture and Social Relations*[118], but is here organized under the motif of a 'turn to Gramsci'. In 'The Politics of the "Popular"' Tony Bennett examines the function of the notion of 'the people' in the Marxist tradition of cultural theory, seeing it as all too often flawed by an essentialism which obscures the need for precise conjunctural analyses of the field of 'the popular'; Stuart Hall then offers a model instance of such work, charting shifting relations in 'Popular Culture and the State' in three areas: law, the nineteenth-century press, and the BBC. In a

116. *The Foucault Reader*, ed. by Paul Rabinow. Penguin. pp. viii + 390. pb £5.95.

117. *High Theory/Low Culture: Analysing Popular Television and Film*, ed. by Colin MacCabe. ManU. pp. x + 171. hb £23.50, pb £6.50.

118. *Popular Culture and Social Relations*, ed. by Tony Bennett, Colin Mercer, and Janet Woollacott. OpenU. pp. xix + 243. pb £7.95.

suggestive essay, 'Complicit Pleasures', Colin Mercer explores the inter-relations between recent theories of the mechanisms of cultural pleasure and the Gramscian concept of 'consent'. The other essays in the book are more applied, local analyses; but even so their stress on a Gramscian problematic rescues them from the vague eclecticism which occasionally afflicts the MacCabe collection. Brian Dutton's *The Media*[119] is a useful brief introductory text, featuring worked practical exercises as well as theoretical exposition, while Iain Chambers in *Popular Culture*[120] gives a very lively account of urban popular culture since the 1880s; long on historical detail, it might perhaps have done more towards theorizing the richly diverse phenomena it surveys. *Popular Fictions*[121] collects essays which have appeared in *L&H* and which have all the virtues customarily associated with that journal: lucidity, historical precision, scholarly tenacity. The obverse of all this, however, is a certain lack of theoretical adventurousness. The only sustained theoretical meditation here is Tony Bennett's 'Marxism and Popular Fiction', which sees Marxism's neglect of such artefacts not just as a contingent defect or oversight, but as 'symptomatic of a faulty conception of the Marxist critical project, which has proved debilitating even for [its] study of canonized texts'. One brand of cultural theory somewhat neglected in all these publications is the work of Pierre Bourdieu: its impact on British cultural theorists will now surely be accelerated by the publication in *TCS* of Axel Honneth's 'Reflections on Pierre Bourdieu's Sociology of Culture' and a long interview with Bourdieu himself.

Much fine theoretical work with an orientation towards history is also being done outside the Marxist tradition. In 'Disfiguring History' in *Diac*, Peter De Bolla gives a thoughtful critique of the work of Hayden White and Dominick LaCapra in his effort to answer (or, more modestly, properly pose) the question: 'can there be a post-structuralist history?' The *NLH* issue on 'Studies in Historical Change' shares similar concerns. In 'The Revenge of Literature: A History of History' Linda Orr shows that historiography is always caught up in the 'literariness' it would fain deny. Shuli Barzilai and Morton W. Bloomfield tease out the implications of the concept of 'novelty' in 'New Criticism or Deconstructive Criticism, or What's New?', Berel Lang in 'Postmodernism in Philosophy' ponders postmodernism's own historiographic practices in such powerful recent rewritings of the history of philosophy as those of Heidegger, Derrida, and Richard Rorty, and Murray Krieger operates at a 'meta-theoretical' level in exploring 'Literary Invention and the Impulse to Theoretical Change'. *PoT* has an issue on 'Literature in Society', whose key texts for our purpose are perhaps Nuritz Gertz's 'Social Myths in Literary and Political Texts' and Mary F. Robertson's fine 'Deconstructive "Contortion" and Women's Historical Practice'. Stanley Fish's notion of 'interpretative communities' is another non-Marxist opening of theory to history, and in 'Accounting for the Changing Certainties of Interpretative Communities' in *MLN* Reed Way Dasenbrock seeks to fine-tune the concept by bringing it into relation with Wittgenstein's philosophy.

119. *The Media*, by Brian Dutton. Longman. pp. 106. pb £3.25.

120. *Popular Culture: The Metropolitan Experience*, by Iain Chambers. Methuen. pp. xii + 244. hb £13.95, pb £5.95.

121. *Popular Fictions: Essays in Literature and History*, ed. by Peter Humm, Paul Stigant, and Peter Widdowson. Methuen. pp. xiv + 265. hb £15, pb £6.95.

Finally, a set of diverse texts which certainly belong in this section, but which prove uncommonly difficult to classify within it. Terence Hawkes criticizes our culture's 'processing' of its national Bard in *That Shakespeherian Rag*[122]. Materialist in intent, the book effectively deconstructs any notion of an 'essential' Shakespeare into the historically varied constructions of the meaning of his work; and yet its stance and tone – lively, sportive, nimble, and restless – though affording a welcome break from academic solemnity, mean that in the end it is not materialist enough. Suggestive rather than exhaustive, the book is too brief to unpack 'Shakespeare' into the full complexity of his (over)determinations; the chapters on Bradley and Raleigh, for instance, say far too little about the institutional context, the fledgeling Oxford English Faculty, in which their Shakespearean interpretations were elaborated (Hawkes would do well to turn up the accounts of these matters in *NfN*). José Maravall's *Culture of the Baroque*[123] operates in the tradition of Lucien Goldmann, writing the 'history of mentalities' and seeing literature in relation to Goldmann's 'collective mind'. In a massive analysis of the beginnings of mass-culture in seventeenth-century Spain, Maravall argues for the centrality of culture in the formation of the 'modern' State. Olivia Smith's excellent study, *The Politics of Language, 1791-1819*[124], demonstrates the imbrication of linguistic theory in wider social processes – thus in a sense constituting an applied study in that 'discourse theory' that Diane Macdonell surveyed. Smith demonstrates both the theoretical mechanisms whereby 'vulgar' English was marginalized by the 'polite' culture, and the subsequent radical politico-linguistic challenges to such mechanisms of exclusion. Sander L. Gilman's *Difference and Pathology*[125] is a study in similar vein, an 'investigation into the history of perceiving difference'. He exposes the cultural strategies of exile and projection whereby such powerful stereotypes as sexuality, race, and madness are associated with 'marginal' groups such as Jews, blacks, women, and the lower classes. Gilman does not mention Bakhtin, and yet his demystification of the 'cultural imaginary' covers much of the same ground as the Peter Stallybrass and Allon White study noted above. Another book which belongs in this context is René Girard's *The Scapegoat*[126], which investigates, from a largely anthropological perspective, one of the central themes of modern theory: the projection of one's own violence onto its very victims, who thereafter become feared precisely in proportion to their marginality and impotence. This is a powerful study of what Girard terms the 'stereotypes of persecution', and suggests that Girardian anthropology may be as relevant to literary theory today as the Lévi-Straussian version of it was thirty years ago; and the book makes a very welcome addition to an increasingly impressive Athlone critical theory list.

122. *That Shakespeherian Rag: Essays on a Critical Process*, by Terence Hawkes. Methuen. pp. x + 131. hb £10.95, pb £4.95.

123. *Culture of the Baroque: Analysis of a Historical Structure*, by José Maravall, trans. by Terry Cochran. ManU. pp. xxxvii + 330. hb £29.50, pb £14.50.

124. *The Politics of Language, 1791-1819*, by Olivia Smith. Clarendon. pp. xvi + 269. pb £9.95.

125. *Difference and Pathology: Stereotypes of Sexuality, Race, and Madness*, by Sander L. Gilman. CornU. pp. 292. hb $34.95, pb $12.95.

126. *The Scapegoat*, by René Girard, trans. by Yvonne Freccero. Athlone. pp. 216. £29.95.

Scenes and Actions [127] is a selection from Christopher Caudwell's unpublished manuscripts: novels, short stories, letters, and some theoretical writing on fantasy and 'Heredity and Development'. The book perhaps presages a modest revival in its author's fortunes as a precursor of contemporary British Marxist criticism. An excellent, off-beat venture is Norman Geras's *Literature of Revolution* [128]. Well known as a superbly intelligent political theorist, Geras here reprints some of his already famous exercises in Marxist interpretation, above all his 'Aspects of Fetishism in Marx's *Capital*' and 'Althusser's Marxism'. But the volume also represents a lively departure in his work: here he puts on his literary-critical hat and offers a spirited defence of Trotsky's *œuvre* as an indispensable *literary* resource for the Marxist tradition. At a time when so many literary theorists are trespassing into the domains of political theory and sociology, it's good to see that the traffic is also running the other way.

127. *Scenes and Actions: Unpublished Manuscripts*, by Christopher Caudwell, ed. by Jean Duparc and David Margolies. RKP. pp. viii + 241. pb £9.95.
128. *Literature of Revolution: Essays on Marxism*, by Norman Geras. Verso. pp. xix + 271. hb £18.95, pb £6.95.

English Language

RICHARD COATES, MICHAEL K. C. MacMAHON, KENNETH
TURNER, FRAN COLMAN, DAVID DENISON, and
PAUL SIMPSON

1. Introduction

The chapter has ten sections: 1. Introduction; 2. General; 3. History of English Linguistics; 4. Dialectology and Sociolinguistics (Including Creolistics); 5. Phonetics, Phonology, and Orthography; 6. Morphology; 7. Syntax; 8. Vocabulary and Semantics; 9. Onomastics; 10. Stylistics. The work of our new team is apportioned as follows: sections 2, 5 and 9 are by Coates, section 3 by MacMahon, section 4 by Turner, sections 6 and 7 by Colman, section 8 by Denison with some brief material on Present-Day English by Coates, and section 10 by Simpson. We have occasional forays outside our own patches.

2. General

This was the year in which the English language hit the television screen in a big way. There was a thirteen-part tour of the anglophone world, profusely illustrated, of course, and the book of the series emerged at the same time as the earlier transmissions[1]. There was considerable fascination in hearing, for the first time, such dialects as that of Tangier Island (Virginia) actually being spoken, after long being driven towards incredulity by the phonetic transcriptions on offer. We may, in the long run, find this chapter reviewing computer programs, videotapes, and microfiche more than books, but for the time being we are content to note other books-of-the-TV/radio-programme. A Scottish multi-media series on *The Mither Tongue*[2] appears in book form, dealing largely with the external history of Scots. Although done in a popular fashion, it is informed and up to date, and well worth reading as a preliminary to the more formidably academic *Focus on: Scotland* volume reviewed last year (*YW* 66.70) and the Murison Festschrift of 1983 (*YW* 64.32). Decidedly less serious is the compilation by Jeffrey Miller and Graham Nown entitled *Street Talk*[3]; the purpose of this is to steer the more parochial among us through a bout of culture-shock should we happen to turn on 'Coronation Street'.

1. *The Story of English*, by R. McCrum, W. Cran, and R. MacNeil. Faber/BBC. pp. 384. £14.95.

2. *Scots: The Mither Tongue*, by Billy Kay. Mainstream. pp. 191. £9.95.

3. *Street Talk: The Language of Coronation Street*, comp. by Jeffrey Miller and Graham Nown. WL. pp. 96. pb £3.95.

Glaswegian was the topic of Michael Munro's *The Patter*[4], a book of not dissimilar intent to the one just mentioned. Among popular books on English, Randolph Quirk's *Words at Work*[5], a series of entertaining lectures, delivered in Singapore, should be noted. Which should remind us of the recent prominence of works on English as spoken far from its western European cradle; this literature is extended by Braj B. Kachru's *The Alchemy of English: The Spread, Functions and Models of Non-Native Englishes*[6]. For him the term *alchemy* is an allusion to the changes in power-relations benefiting those who master the art. Kachru sees the learning and institutionalization of English abroad as a powerful political tool, and this book complements his already well-known work in this area. Loreto Todd and Ian F. Hancock's encyclopaedia of *International English Usage*[7] is in some ways a strange compilation, its entries including descriptions of the phonological peculiarities of extra-territorial dialects, definitions of technical terms, accounts of differing social mores in different regions, lists of confusable words, and disquisitions on the syntactic and semantic properties of individual words. It is not always clear to me how one would decide what to look up in pursuit of some particular piece of information (except trivially, by scouring the index!), because it is not easy to see what the criteria for inclusion are; why, for instance, is *apposition* there when it is merely a technical term of general linguistics and when it shows no variable realization in all the Englishes of the world? The diversity of modern English (or *Englishes*, to use the now widely accepted plural form) is a topic more amply documented in section 4 below. It accounts for the increasing bulk of this chapter more than any other single topic since the rise of generative linguistics using English as its major language of exemplification. A sidelight on the multiplicity of Englishes is provided by Jean D'Souza, who wonders 'Codification of Non-Native English: Is It Necessary/Possible?' (*SLSc*) and concludes in some doubt about the enterprise.

The 'theme of the year' appears to be the need to understand the diversity of English in the world in relation to a more differentiated ancestor language; or, as John Harris (see section 4) puts it succinctly, we should 'expand the superstrate'. Related to this concern is the idea that distinctive local, especially extraterritorial, dialect developments may take their impetus from variability in the language spoken in its original homeland, rather than from substrate influences in the new homeland, however obvious these may seem. Examples are given from South Africa and Ireland in section 5. Nonetheless there is still a vigorous New World research tradition which seeks to link North American dialect peculiarities with particular areas in the Old Country. This has all the marks of an important debate in the making.

Dictionaries are well to the fore this year, and significant milestones in the lexicography of the medieval and the modern language are reported in sections 5 and 8. As David Denison notes in the latter section, the imminent availability of large-scale easily accessed lexical databases is one of the most exciting

4. *The Patter*, by Michael Munro. GlasgowDL (1985). pp. 84. pb £3.50.

5. *Words at Work*, by Randolph Quirk. SingaporeU/Longman. pp. 137. pb £5.75.

6. *The Alchemy of English: The Spread, Functions and Models of Non-Native Englishes*, by Braj B. Kachru. Pergamon. pp. xi + 200. pb £11.50.

7. *International English Usage*, by Loreto Todd and Ian F. Hancock. CH. pp. viii + 520. £16.95.

prospects for the study of English for some time. Harmless drudges can now shed the quill-and-filing-card image for ever. Our 'best buys' for 1986 would include some of these major dictionaries, if we personally could ever afford to buy them. Another very useful source of information is *Irregularities in Modern English*[8], which has been circulating in Danish for some years now. It covers irregularities at all levels: phonological, orthographic, morphological, etc., and attempts to provide historical explanations for their existence without fighting shy of saying that some development is inexplicable. This is a book marked by an impressive degree of care and clarity of presentation; a useful handbook for the scholar in a hurry looking for an example of some exotic or exceptional process. An old friend running to its fourth edition is Bruce Mitchell and Fred C. Robinson's *A Guide to Old English*[9]; it differs from previous editions in including verse texts. It remains, of course, the leading introduction to the topic, and will doubtless run to several further editions. Well recommended also are John Harris's book reviewed in section 5, and Seán Ó Mathúna's in section 3.

There are no major Anglistic conference proceedings this year, but this deficiency is amply made up for by the Festschrift for the fiftieth birthday of the Polish Anglicist Jacek Fisiak[10]. It can surely be no exaggeration to suggest that this is one of the most handsome offerings ever presented to anyone in the academic life – two massive volumes on both general and Anglistic themes, stuffed with goodies by a whole battery of prominent scholars. Numerous papers from it are reviewed in the pages that follow. It is a fitting tribute to a man of great ability across a whole range of theoretical and practical sub-disciplines and a tireless organizer/editor of conferences and proceedings. A further magnificent collection is that assembled for the sixty-fifth birthday of Charles Ferguson, who has made a memorable contribution to general socio-linguistics; this is reviewed in section 4. The general linguist R. H. Robins also receives a volume, from which the papers of relevance to English linguistics are reviewed in section 3. Less happily, it is the death of the eminent dialectologist Raven I. McDavid Jr in 1984 that occasions a special issue of *JEngL* devoted to his memory; and we also have to report the premature death in late 1985 of Alan J. Bliss, who made a major contribution to the study of the English language in Ireland as well as to OE metrics.

In general linguistics, we note helpful new textbooks from CUP on *Lexical Semantics*[11], *Statistics in Language Studies*[12], and *Intonation*[13]. D. A. Cruse's

8. *Irregularities in Modern English*, by Erik Hansen and Hans Frede Nielsen. *NOWELE* Supplement 2. OdenseU. pp. ix + 359. pb Dkr 220.

9. *A Guide to Old English*, by Bruce Mitchell and Fred C. Robinson. Fourth edn. Blackwell. pp. 368. hb £24.50, pb £8.50.

10. *Linguistics across Historical and Geographical Boundaries: In Honour of Jacek Fisiak on the Occasion of his Fiftieth Birthday*, ed. by Dieter Kastovsky and Aleksander Szwedek, assisted by Barbara Płocińska. Vol. I: *Linguistic Theory and Historical Linguistics*. Vol. II: *Descriptive, Contrastive and Applied Linguistics*. Mouton de Gruyter. pp. xxiv + xiv + 1543 (continuous pagination). DM 535/$240. (Hereafter *Fisiak*.)

11. *Lexical Semantics*, by D. A. Cruse. CUP. pp. xiv + 310. pb £8.95.

12. *Statistics in Language Studies*, by Anthony Woods, Paul Fletcher, and Arthur Hughes. CUP. pp. xii + 322. hb £27.50, pb £9.95.

13. *Intonation*, by Alan Cruttenden. CUP. pp. xiv + 214. pb £7.95.

work on lexical semantics is based solidly on traditional scholarship, and he avoids both the formalisms of modern semantics and the rigour of the definitions derivable from them in his largely taxonomic exposition of relations among vocabulary items. His style, and his assumptions about what a student audience will have taken on board, are somewhat ambitious; I suspect that those who can feel their way through the issues hinted at in the early pages will have no real need for the more elementary aspects of the subject-matter presented in the same pages. Nonetheless this is a useful reference work which is full of examples and whose analytical battery is more fine-grained than that offered in John Lyons's classic *Semantics* (*YW* 58.31), though it does not have the philosophical sophistication of the latter. I missed having a proper account of relations other than sense-relations, e.g. attitudinal/stylistic relations, holding between lexical items. Alan Cruttenden's book on intonation gives a clear introduction to prosody in general and devotes three fairly large chapters to intonation in particular. Of most interest to readers of *YWES* may well be the sections on the abstract meanings of nuclear tones, and patterns more generally, a highly topical and controversial area; and the smaller sections which point to intonational variability within English. The book breaks new ground in several ways, not least by attempting to provide a basis for the discussion of intonation cross-linguistically; as Cruttenden says, this is certainly the first textbook ever to do this, even if earlier collections of essays have pointed in this direction. Whilst on the subject of intonation, we need to notice the collection *Intonation in Discourse*, edited by Catherine Johns-Lewis[14]. The papers in this most interesting and very technical collection are primarily intended as contributions to the theoretical understanding of the workings of intonation, but several advertise themselves as being specifically about the prosody of English, and these are noticed in section 5 below. Even those without a notice may be read with interest by English language specialists, however, with the possible exception of the chapter on Welsh.

1986 saw the publication of 'the new Chomsky', which is noted in section 7. Those interested in the state of the art of GB will also be pleased to inform their students about a major new textbook by the leading proponents of neo-Chomskian syntax, Henk van Riemsdijk and Edwin Williams[15]. A major theoretical work which has already excited a considerable amount of interest and spawned numerous articles and conference papers is Dan Sperber and Deirdre Wilson's *Relevance*[16], which has as its goal the uniting and re-interpretation of H. P. Grice's disparate conversational maxims under a single over-riding principle (called *relevance*, in a technical, but not counterintuitive, sense) and of offering a theory of cognition with a linguistic basis. And finally we note the massive new introduction to historical linguistics by Hans Henrich Hock[17], which gives more space than is customary to the role of the social in linguistic

14. *Intonation in Discourse*, ed. by Catherine Johns-Lewis. CH/College-Hill (1985). pp. xxxvi + 302. £21.

15. *Introduction to the Theory of Grammar*, by Henk van Riemsdijk and Edwin Williams. MITP. pp. xvi + 366. hb $35, pb $17.50.

16. *Relevance*, by Dan Sperber and Deirdre Wilson. Blackwell. pp. 229. hb £27.50, pb £8.50.

17. *Principles of Historical Linguistics*, by Hans Henrich Hock. Mouton de Gruyter. pp. xiii + 722. hb $127/DM 266, pb $27.75/DM 58.

change (especially Chapters 14–16, 20), and draws its illustrative material from a wide range of languages. There is a more balanced account than we have come to expect either from its proponents or its opponents of the contribution of generative phonology to the study of phonological change. A must for the serious bookshelf. Peter Trudgill's new book is also of prime importance to theorists of the social transmission of change, having at its core the notion of *accommodation*; as is Peter Mühlhäusler's on creolistics (both reviewed in section 4).

3. History of English Linguistics

1986 has seen the publication, apart from a number of journal articles, of three books dealing with linguistic historiography relevant to English. Firstly, there is the Festschrift for R. H. Robins [18], which contains a wealth of material, much of it to do with English linguistic thought. (The other items deal mainly with Greek, Latin, Renaissance, nineteenth century, and European topics.) Secondly, there is the monograph by Seán Ó Mathúna on William Bathe [19], the sixteenth/seventeenth-century Jesuit priest and linguist, which is a translation of the Irish-language version published in 1981. And thirdly, we have the set of papers on lexicography [20], edited by Reinhard Hartmann, which stem from Exeter's Dictionary Research Centre seminar in 1986; twenty-three of the twenty-five papers that were presented are published here. Many have to do with English lexicography; the others deal with a dozen or more other languages, sometimes in conjunction with English. All three books are important contributions to the literature, and deserve the attention of the student of historiography. Their contents, as well as those of the journal articles, will be dealt with below.

There is little to report on 'large' theoretical issues. Herbert Brekle (*Robins* [18]) gives us a brief excursus on an old theme in his 'What Is the History of Linguistics and to What End Is It Studied? A Didactic Approach'. He ranges over a number of possible answers, especially Nietzsche's by-now famous distinction between 'monumental', 'antiquarian', and 'critical' studies of the past.

In view of the contents of the Hartmann volume, lexical matters will be treated together in this review. Frederic Dolezal ('How Abstract Is the English Dictionary?') considers the question of how some lexicographers have selected and defined their vocabulary, and Tom McArthur ('Thematic Lexicography') argues in favour of greater attention being paid in future to thematic rather than alphabetic ordering of lexical entries. The paper by Werner Hüllen ('The Paradigm of John Wilkins' Thesaurus') discusses such a tradition of thematic ordering in Wilkins, Roget, and Johann August Eberhard in Germany. An area for further research, according to Robert Ilson ('Lexicographic Archaeology:

18. *Studies in the History of Western Linguistics in Honour of R. H. Robins*, ed. by Theodora Bynon and F. R. Palmer. CUP. pp. x + 285. £27.50. (Hereafter *Robins*.)

19. *William Bathe, S.J., 1564–1614: A Pioneer in Linguistics*, by Seán Ó Mathúna. SiHoLS. Benjamins. pp. xiii + 218 + 2 endplates. Fl 85/$34.

20. *The History of Lexicography: Papers from the Dictionary Research Centre Seminar at Exeter, March 1986*, ed. by R. R. K. Hartmann. SiHoLS. Benjamins. pp. viii + 265. Fl 110/$44.

Comparing Dictionaries of the Same Family'), is the changing style of different editions of the same dictionary and of different dictionaries from the same publishing house. The background to the various editions of the *COD* is described by Robert Allen ('A Concise History of the *COD*'). Allen Read's 'Competing Lexical Traditions in America' focuses on the differences between the Webster and Joseph Worcester approaches to dictionary-writing. An important paper is that by Noel Osselton ('The First English Dictionary? A Sixteenth-Century Compiler at Work'). One of the Rawlinson manuscripts in the Bodleian contains three pages of material for a monolingual dictionary of English. Its author is unknown, but if the work had been completed, it would undoubtedly have predated Cawdrey (1604). Osselton suggests an approximate date for it in the last quarter of the sixteenth century, and argues in favour of a Latin–English dictionary as the source of the work. Douglas Kibbee looks at the methodologies of John Palsgrave in England and Robert Estienne in France in their respective works ('The Humanist Period in Renaissance Bilingual Lexicography'). Palsgrave figures also in Gabriele Stein's paper 'Sixteenth-Century English-Vernacular Dictionaries', where the focus is on a comparison of five such dictionaries on the basis of features like the handling of non-standard language and literary references. The subject of pronouncing-dictionaries from Nathan Bailey (1727) to the present is reviewed by Arthur Bronstein, although he places greater emphasis on twentieth-century dictionaries than on the earlier ones. Bilingual lexicography is considered in two papers: Roger Steiner's 'The Three-Century Recension in Spanish and English Lexicography', which surveys the field from 1591 to 1900, and Nawal El-Badry's 'The Development of the Bilingual English–Arabic Dictionary from the Mid Nineteenth-Century to the Present'. Finally, one can note the useful, albeit brief, survey by Reuven Merkin ('Four Remarks on the Prehistory of Historical Lexicography') of the predecessors to the three great historical dictionaries of the nineteenth century, James Murray, Emile Littré, and Jacob Grimm. The works of Samuel Johnson, John Jamieson, Charles Richardson, and George Wheelwright are touched on.

It is unusual to find scholars who will reveal in detail their publication plans: better to surprise the world than give the competition a head start. But the paper by David Jost and Stephen Lappert, 'A Proposal for a Textbook about the History and Methodology of British and American Lexicography' (*PIL*), makes a healthy change from some of the cloak-and-dagger business that can surround proposals for books. They announce, in quite some detail, their ideas for a work – which they have still to write – on the history and methodology of British and American lexicography. Their qualifications for such a large-scale undertaking include associate editorships with the *Middle English Dictionary* and teaching of university courses on lexicography. One wishes them well in their work, and, from the résumé that they have presented, one can look forward to reading in due course an important contribution to both linguistic historiography and the methodology of lexicography.

We turn now to grammar and the Middle Ages. Michael Covington, in his 'Grammatical Theory in the Middle Ages' (*Robins*[18]), provides an elegantly written account of the work of the medieval grammarians, including such English ones as William of Ockham and William of Sherwood. No attempt is made to introduce new material or a new point of view: the virtue of the article lies in its lucid structure – it is, in short, a valuable summary of what we currently understand by medieval grammatical theories. Roger Bacon's inter-pretation of how pragmatics, syntax, and semantics interact is discussed by Irène Rosier and Alain de Libéra in 'Intention de Signifier et Engendrement du Discours chez Roger Bacon' (*HEL*), one of a number of papers given at the 1985 Paris colloquium on enunciation. Vivien Law's article 'Late Latin Grammars in the Early Middle Ages: A Typological History' (*HL*) touches on the work of various linguists, including, for English purposes, Aldhelm, Boniface, and Alcuin. Rather more is said about Boniface, especially about the preface to his grammar, in her 'Originality in the Medieval Normative Tradition' (*Robins*[18]). The work of Bede is discussed by Martin Irvine in his 'Bede the Grammarian and the Scope of Grammatical Studies in Eighth-Century Northumbria' (*ASE*), in which he argues the case for widening the intellectual context in which we view Bede and his three grammatical treatises. Irvine emphasizes the importance of an early eighth-century Northumbrian commentary on Donatus' *Ars minor* for a better appreciation of the climate in which Bede was working. This is a long and scholarly contribution, and the references to forthcoming publications by himself and other scholars presage further interesting studies in the area of medieval linguistic historiography.

For students of seventeenth-century studies, the appearance of an English translation by Seán Ó Mathúna of his 1981 study[19] (in Irish, but under the English alias of Seán O'Mahony) of the life and work of the applied linguist William Bathe is most welcome. Bathe, the author of *Ianua Linguarum* (1611), is still little known outside the specialist area of historical education studies, and Ó Mathúna's study, including as it does a detailed account of the man's family background, his life as a Jesuit priest and teacher, as diplomat and linguist will re-establish Bathe's reputation in linguistic studies, for long overshadowed by the work of his younger contemporary Jan Comenius. Among much else, there is a valuable chapter on the historical and educational background to Bathe's work. Also included is an English translation of the preface to the *Ianua Linguarum*.

Vivian Salmon reveals her considerable knowledge and expertise in seventeenth-century linguistic studies with a useful bird's-eye view of the state of linguistic studies in seventeenth-century England, 'Effort and Achievement in Seventeenth-Century British Linguistics' (*Robins*[18]). The major names, however, such as Wallis and Wilkins, are deliberately omitted: instead, she gives us brief summaries of the work done by other linguists on, for example, the Germanic languages, non-Indo-European languages, applied linguistics, and 'sociolinguistics'. For those who require an authoritative summary of the stages that were reached in seventeenth-century linguistic studies, this paper is a must. Another article by Mrs Salmon, 'Missionary Linguistics in Seventeenth Century Ireland and a North American Analogy' (*HL*, 1985), escaped mention last year. In it, she draws parallels between the activities of various Christian missionaries in Virginia, having to confront the problems of describing and learning indigenous Amerindian languages (and dialects of the same language), with a comparable situation in Ireland. The work of William Bedell, an English Protestant clergyman who had the foresight and common sense to learn Irish before attempting any proselytizing work, is singled out for attention.

The article by Robert Markley, 'Robert Boyle on Language: *Some Considerations Touching the Style of the Holy Scriptures*' (*SECC*, 1985) considers, mainly from a philosophical rather than a linguistic point of view, this relatively little-known work (1661) by an F.R.S. For Boyle, scriptural language should be taken as the yardstick with which to measure human utterances. He emphasizes thereby the contrast between the perfection of a divine creation and the imperfections and irregularities of a language that is employed to describe this creation. The place of The Royal Society and linguistic work surfaces again, this time in a paper by Brian Vickers, unnoted in 1985, 'The Royal Society and English Prose Style'[21]. Vickers calls into question the views of Richard Foster Jones, expressed during the course of more than forty years of scholarship between 1919 and 1963, about the attitudes of and reactions to the Society's famous committee for 'improving the English tongue'.

A further contribution by Frederic Dolezal, touching on the theme of his paper in the Hartmann volume, is his 'John Wilkins' and William Lloyd's *Alphabetical Dictionary* (1668): Towards a Comprehensive, and Systematically Defined, Lexicon' (*PIL*). The *Alphabetical Dictionary* by Wilkins and Lloyd was appended to Wilkins's *Essay* of 1668. Dolezal discusses the attention that both scholars paid to defining the 'definitional terms' in their Dictionary – a technique which remained uncopied in lexicography until the twentieth century.

Erik Hansen, in his 'John Locke and the Semantic Tradition' (*ES*) provides an extended review of Hans Aarsleff's *From Locke to Saussure* (1982), describing it at one point as 'clearly one of the major works in intellectual history since 1945'. He emphasizes the importance of certain figures in the post-Lockean tradition (e.g. Taine and Michel Bréal) for an understanding of the sources of some of Saussure's ideas, and draws our attention to the significance of Condillac's work in particular for a proper understanding of aspects of English Romantic literature. Norman Blake's lengthy article 'Jonathan Swift and the English Language' (*EAS*) reconsiders the traditional view of Swift's ideas about language in terms of the famous *Proposal* of 1712, and argues in favour of a less specialized approach: three other works need to be taken into account, he says, as well as the social, political, and religious circumstances of Swift's day.

The only item to do with late eighteenth-century work is James Mulvihill's 'A Tookean Presence in Peacock's *Melincourt*' (*ES*), which sets out the evidence for John Horne Tooke being the model for Mr Simon Sarcastic.

As ever, work on various aspects of nineteenth-century linguistics has continued apace. Winfred Lehmann offers an interesting short article, 'Fick and Kleuker on Jones – Riga 1795' (*HL*) on the part played by Georg Fick and Johann Kleuker (but notably the latter) in introducing some of Sir William Jones's views on Asia and the East to the attention of a German audience, thus preparing part of the ground for an understanding of comparative philology. Back to England, and an excellent background study on Cobbett is that by Flor Aarts, 'William Cobbett: Radical Reactionary and Poor Man's Grammarian' (*Neophil*). He notes not only the importance of the *Grammar* (1818) in

---

21. In *Rhetoric and the Pursuit of Truth: Language Change in the Seventeenth and Eighteenth Centuries: Papers Read at a Clark Memorial Library Seminar, 8 March 1980*, by Brian Vickers and Nancy S. Struever, ed. by Thomas F. Wright. CML (1985). pp. v + 121.

establishing a different approach to grammatical description from that of Lowth and Murray, but also that of other works on grammar and language teaching which have tended to be overlooked by most readers of Cobbett. The views on language of Joseph de Maistre, as set out in his *Soirées de Saint-Pétersbourg* (1821), are discussed by Hans Aarsleff in 'Joseph de Maistre and Victorian Thought on the Origin of Language and Civilisation' (*Robins*[18]). He compares them with somewhat similar views held by the cleric-linguists Richard Chenevix Trench and Richard Whately.

Moving beyond mid-century, it is worth mentioning *en passant* Anny Sadrin's article 'Langage des Origines, Origines du Langage dans *The Origin of Species*' (*CVE*), which focuses on the lack of precision – and resulting misunderstandings – with which Darwin defined his metalanguage in *The Origin of Species*. Bizarrely, critical terms such as *species*, *varieties*, and *genera* lacked any conscious, careful definition.

Maria Bologna's paper 'Whitney in Italia' (*HL*) is concerned with influences: that of Whitney on the Italian linguist Francesco D'Ovidio, who translated *The Life and Growth of Language* into Italian and published several papers strongly imbued with Whitney's outlook on language and language analysis. The article by Patrizia Pierini, 'Language and Grammar in the Work of Henry Sweet' (*LeS*), emphasizes the modernity of Sweet's views on such subjects as diachrony and synchrony and the importance of speech in linguistic study. It also provides us with one of the first lengthy discussions to date of Sweet's views on grammar – in the sense of both morphology/syntax and the total description of the language. John Ferguson's 'Of Spooner, Spoonerisms and Other Matters' (*Verbatim*, 1985) is a light but amusing piece of work on the man and his behaviour.

There are a number of items dealing specifically with American linguistics. The paper by William Woods, 'The Cultural Tradition of Nineteenth-Century "Traditional" Grammar Teaching' (*RSQ*, 1985), gives a useful historical summary of attitudes towards grammar and the place of grammar in the educational curriculum. What role should traditional grammar teaching now play in American secondary education? he asks. The note by Stephen Murray and Wayne Dynes 'Edward Sapir's Coursework in Linguistics and Anthropology' lists the courses that Sapir took *en route* to his M.A. thesis in 1905. The article by Myron Tuman, 'From Astor Place to Kenyon Road: The NCTE and the Origins of English Studies' (*CE*) discusses the background to the early years of the National Council of Teachers of English and its role in encouraging the teaching of composition as a school and university-level subject. On a similar topic, Donald Stewart's 'NCTE's First President and the Movement for Language Reform' (*CE*) looks at the personality and healthily liberal attitudes to language of the first president, Fred Newton Scott. And finally, bringing us completely up to date is the second edition of Frederick J. Newmeyer's study of linguistics in the United States[22], which discusses the generative linguistics period from the 1950s right up to 1986. For those who require a well-written, level-headed account of the ups and downs in generative work, this book has much to recommend it. The style of presentation, furthermore, is very much historical – seeing the broader issues, as well as the specific detail, and putting them into a proper intellectual perspective.

4. Dialectology and Sociolinguistics (Including Creolistics)

This year I confine my attention to the modern and present-day English language; the monumental *Linguistic Atlas of Late Medieval English* is reviewed in section 5.

My predecessor observed last year that 1986 promised to be a good year for pidgin and creole studies. The observation was accurate, but, as the year progressed, it became increasingly understated. The year will in retrospect probably be seen as the beginning of a new *belle époque*, for both descriptive achievements and theoretical ambitions. Scholarly production is already very high – motivated no doubt by the implications of Derek Bickerton's Language Bioprogram Hypothesis – and there are signs that it has yet to reach its peak. There is, first, from the Benjamins stable, a new journal, the *Journal of Pidgin and Creole Languages* (*JPCL*). In the first volume Salikoko S. Mufwene examines 'Restrictive Relativization in Gullah'. He isolates three relative clause strategies and presents persuasive and amply documented evidence to suggest that English superstrate influence has played the most significant role in the selection of these strategies. In a slightly different vein Priya Hosali and Jean Aitchison discuss classificatory criteria in 'Butler English: A Minimal Pidgin?' Their data is the speech of seven speakers which reveals, under analysis, 'that attempts to "pidgin-hole" pidgin-like linguistic systems are doomed to failure'. Mark Sebba, in 'Adjectives and Copulas in Sranan Tongo', attempts to make a case for treating Sranan predicate adjectives as a type of stative verb. Pieter A. M. Seuren, in 'Adjectives as Adjectives in Sranan: A Reply to Sebba', gives his reasons why the attempt, as presented, fails. In addition to these articles the journal also contains a section called 'Creole Classics' in which important historical works are serialized. The first offering is Part One of William Greenfield's 1830 'A Defence of the Surinam Negro-English Version of the New Testament' and further instalments are impatiently awaited; there is a mysterious but irresistible attraction in *lectio interrupta*.

Accompanying and complementing the journal is a new series of books, again from the Benjamins stable, appearing under the rubric of Creole Language Library. The first volume, edited by Pieter Muysken and Norval Smith, bears the title *Substrata versus Universals in Creole Genesis*[23], and consists of papers from the 1985 Amsterdam Creole Workshop, which, my creolist colleagues tell me, has been the most significant recent event in their calendar. Ian Hancock's 'The Domestic Hypothesis, Diffusion and Componentiality: An Account of Atlantic Anglophone Creole Origins' presents evidence and argues for the refutation of two theses which enjoy a wide subscription, that anglophone Atlantic creole originated in the western hemisphere and not in Africa, and that it was only introduced into that continent with the Jamaican Maroons who went to Freetown in 1800. He documents a suggestion that a range of creolized varieties of English became

---

23. *Substrata versus Universals in Creole Genesis: Papers from the Amsterdam Creole Workshop, April 1985*, ed. by Pieter Muysken and Norval Smith. Benjamins. pp. vii + 311. $60.

established in settlements along the Upper Guinea coast at the beginning of the seventeenth century in the family situations resulting from the contacts between English speakers and Africans and that African slaves awaiting shipment to the western hemisphere had ample time to acquire some knowledge of creole from the grumettoes who tended them.

The theoretical issue is further addressed by John R. Rickford in 'Social Contact and Linguistic Diffusion: Hiberno-English and New World Black English (*Lg*) and by John Harris in 'Expanding the Superstrate: Habitual Aspect Markers in Atlantic Englishes' (*EWW*). Rickford argues, uncontroversially to some minds, for the diffusion of (*does*) *be*, as a marker of habitual or iterative aspect, from Hiberno- or Irish-English to New World Black English (including the West Atlantic English-based creoles and American Vernacular Black English). This is not the first time that this suggestion has been raised but what distinguishes Rickford's case is his detailed excavation of the socio-historical context: would that other diffusionist arguments were similarly documented. Harris adds a twist to the course of the debate by remarking that accounts of creole origins have frequently neglected to take into consideration the sociolinguistic diversity that characterizes a superstrate language in colonial conditions – a remark which is underscored by Rickford in a 'Short Note' in *JPCL* – and suggests that the role of substrate languages may be preservative or selective of sociolinguistic options that fall beyond the perimeter of evidence which is almost entirely restricted to the ancestor varieties of present-day Standard English. Kean Gibson in 'The Ordering of Auxiliary Notions in Guyanese Creole' (*Lang*) disputes Bickerton's claim that a Tense–Modal–Aspect ordering is obligatory in creole language and presents a re-analysis which indicates that a Modal–Tense–Aspect ordering is more correct. In 'Tense/Aspect Variation in American Indian English' (*NJL*) H. G. Bartelt presents some morphological characteristics regarding tense and aspect found in Apachean English interlanguage and suggests, since they cannot be traced to either the English superstrate or the Western Apache substrate, that they be regarded as evidence for the bioprogram. There is every reason to believe that this debate will continue to find a forum in the future.

The local situation is more than adequately represented in *The Language of the Black Experience: Cultural Expression through Word and Sound in the Caribbean and Black Britain*[24], in which Pastor L. A. Jackson added to my collection of prepatterned speech with his 'Proverbs of Jamaica'. The representation is continued by Mark Sebba and Shirley Tate in 'You Know What I Mean?: Agreement Marking in British Black English' (*JPrag*), by Viv Edwards in *Language in a Black Community* (MlM), which, by a stroke of poor luck, I have been unable to see, and particularly by Roger Hewitt's *White Talk Black Talk: Interracial Friendship and Communication amongst Adolescents*[25]. This book is based on intensive and long-term participant observation in two South London communities, and with extensive verbatim transcriptions of the interviews that he conducted, Hewitt is able to detect and document the linguistic

24. *The Language of the Black Experience: Cultural Expression through Word and Sound in the Caribbean and Black Britain*, ed. by David Sutcliffe and Ansel Wong. Blackwell. pp. x + 214. hb £19.50, pb £5.95.

25. *White Talk Black Talk: Inter-racial Friendship and Communication amongst Adolescents*, by Roger Hewitt. CUP. pp. x + 253. hb £25, pb £8.95.

and discursive parameters of the negotiation and management of racial identity and racism. The ethnography and accompanying analyses – among the most sensitive and probing that I have encountered, and a model to those preferring qualitative to quantitative strategies – finds inspiration both in the American school of ethnography and, to return to the creole situation for a moment, in Robert Le Page and Andrée Tabouret-Keller's *Acts of Identity: Creole-Based Approaches to Language and Ethnicity*[26]. This latter, inadvertently missed last year, conveniently summarizes and refers to much of the authors' previous empirical work in the Caribbean and their theory of language which interprets a speaker's positioning within 'linguistic space' as constituted by numerous linguistically expressed 'acts of identity'. This perspective prefers a phenomenological approach to the strict definitions of purely linguistic boundaries and is gaining enthusiasts like Hewitt who recognize that it provides greater accuracy and flexibility in dealing with very fluid linguistic situations such as those which obtain amongst some black adolescents. In addition, the second chapter of the book, 'Some Pidgin- and Creole-speaking Communities and their Histories', provides demographic background to the settlement history of the Caribbean and is required in order to throw light upon disputed aspects of what has gone into the making of regional culture. The trend is one in which pidgin and creole studies has become increasingly colonial towards its disciplinary neighbours, in particular demography, and seeks solutions to well-defined linguistic problems in the broader sweeps of social history. In this connection I cannot fail to recommend Sidney W. Mintz's *Sweetness and Power: The Place of Sugar in Modern History*[27] which ought to be on every (substratist?) creolist's bookshelf.

Le Page and Tabouret-Keller's work on the Caribbean might profitably be compared with that from a more orthodox perspective in an edited collection by Manfred Görlach and John A. Holm called *Focus on: The Caribbean*[28]. In an ambitious but tantalizingly brief history lesson Holm documents 'The Spread of English in the Caribbean Area'; Dennis R. Craig, in 'Social Class and the Use of Language: A Case Study of Jamaican Children', examines, with daunting statistical evidence, how socialization shapes educational achievement; and John Roy in 'The Structure of Tense and Aspect in Barbadian English Creole' disputes the widely held view that Bajan is not a creole but rather a regional non-standard variety of English by demonstrating that the verb system used in certain areas of rural Barbados remains basically creole in structure. Salikoko S. Mufwene's 'Notes on Durative Constructions in Jamaica and Guyanese Creoles' is an invitation to reconsider certain recent proposals about the origins of *de*, *da*, and *a*. The paper is less concerned with making a positive empirical contribution than with reminding the reader of the many parameters that require analytical consideration before conclusions can be confidently asserted. Frederic G. Cassidy's 'Etymology in Caribbean Creoles' makes the very same point although, unlike Mufwene, he fails to include mention of sociolinguistic

26. *Acts of Identity: Creole-Based Approaches to Language and Ethnicity*, by Robert Le Page and Andrée Tabouret-Keller. CUP (1985). pp. x + 275. pb £9.95.

27. *Sweetness and Power: The Place of Sugar in Modern History*, by Sidney W. Mintz. Penguin. pp. xxx + 274. pb £3.95.

28. *Focus on: The Caribbean*, ed. by Manfred Görlach and John A. Holm. VEAW. Benjamins. pp. ix + 209. pb Fl 75/$30.

diversity as a source of etymological light. The editors modestly regard this collection as an interim report: it does, however, accurately reflect the current state of play. One notes, before leaving the Caribbean, Mufwene's 'Number Delimitation in Gullah' (*AS*), which is a searching analysis of about fifteen hours of conversations on a variety of topics with about twenty speakers, and which suggests that Gullah shares more of its number delimitational system with Jamaican creole than with its English acrolect. Such detailed work, quite typical of this author, is particularly welcome at a time when Gullah appears to be under extreme sociolinguistic pressures and is feared to be disappearing; see Patricia Jones-Jackson's 'Gullah Since Turner 1949' in the biannual *JHLP* (1985).

A single-authored and less diffuse reflection on the field in general can be found in Peter Mühlhäusler's *Pidgin and Creole Linguistics*[29]. In addition to the basic ingredients essential in a book designed for students, the author also argues that the study of pidgins and creoles requires us to question many of our culture-specific views on the nature of human language and verbal communication and forces us to rethink many aspects of the discipline. Perhaps Mühlhäusler has here provided an explanation for the recent explosive popularity of this kind of inquiry; a scholarly community dissatisfied with its conceptual currency turns to pidgin and creole situations for inspiration about replacements. Whatever the diagnosis, it is safe to conclude that creole studies have entered into the mainstream of linguistics and English language studies and that they perhaps justify the removal of the parenthesis in the title of this section.

As far as dialectology is concerned, student, and more seasoned, readers are excellently served by Volume X in Blackwell's Language in Society series, which is *Dialects in Contact*[30] by Peter Trudgill. The author is recognized as one of the most articulate in the field and in chapters on the topics of accommodation between dialects, dialect contact, dialect mixture, and the growth of new dialects and koineization in colonial English he displays his skills. Those readers who prefer a theoretical orientation to a purely descriptive one may experience a mild irritation with Trudgill's self-confessedly 'very ad hoc' attempts at providing explanations for the phenomena he examines. On the other hand, those whose tastes draw them to chapters that are packed with data and examples will be amply satisfied with *Varieties of English: An Introduction to the Study of Language*[31]. I am not normally one with such tastes but I found much in this book to keep my attention. The collection *Problems of Standardization and Linguistic Variation in Present-Day English*[32] edited by Gerhard Nickel and James C. Stalker did not fare so well, although it will find an interested audience in the language teaching community.

29. *Pidgin and Creole Linguistics*, by Peter Mühlhäusler. Blackwell. pp. xii + 320. hb £29.50, pb £8.95.

30. *Dialects in Contact*, by Peter Trudgill. Blackwell. pp. vii + 174. hb £22.50, pb £7.95.

31. *Varieties of English: An Introduction to the Study of Language*, by Dennis Freeborn, with David Langford and Peter French. Macmillan. pp. xiii + 222. hb £18, pb £5.95.

32. *Problems of Standardization and Linguistic Variation in Present-Day English*, ed. by Gerhard Nickel and James C. Stalker. Groos. pp. vi + 95. pb DM 48.

Two papers in *AS* are of general interest beyond their subject, English dialects in the U.S.A. Timothy C. Frazer enters a methodological protest about the size of the communities chosen for analysis in the *Linguistic Atlas of the North Central States*, and shows a good deal of micro-level variation, a diagnostic test for this being the incidence of essentially northern place-name types as islands in dialectally midland areas ('Microdialectology: Internal Variation in a LANCS Community'). Craig Carver, in 'The Influence of the Mississippi River on Northern Dialect Boundaries', uses lexical evidence to support his contention that dialect is shaped by settlement, i.e. the standard Kurathian view of things; other writers this year are leaning towards the alternative view that the origin of dialectalisms can be sought in specific extra-territorial locations (see above and section 5 in particular).

It is much to be regretted that Wolfgang Viereck's collection of essays *Focus on: England and Wales*[33] was not reviewed in 1985, but at least we can mention its companion in the now well-established VEAW series: Martyn F. Wakelin's survey volume *The Southwest of England*[34]. It is unusual in that series in being primarily a commentary on a large number of individual texts (some given on an accompanying cassette) representing places scattered throughout the West Country, containing a vast amount of valuable linguistic detail. Wolfgang Viereck re-examines 'Dialectal Speech Areas in England: Orton's Lexical Evidence' (*Fisiak*[10]). He is concerned to make generalizations where his predecessors only collected and collated forms, and hence to establish broad dialect areas (taking a gentle swipe at Wakelin as he goes). Lexical evidence allows him to establish marked heteroglosses from the Ribble to the Humber, across Cumberland, around Lincolnshire, on the eastern border of Devon and that of Hampshire, and around Cambridgeshire, to mention just the most striking ones. He identifies some of the enclosed areas as 'relict areas'.

Several papers in David Sankoff's collection *Diversity and Diachrony*[35] are about variation in English dialects, mainly in North America. In 'More Evidence for Major Vowel Change in the South' Crawford Feagin adds to the evidence for a rapidly spreading Southern U.S. vowel chain-shift with his investigations in rural Alabama. William Labov and Wendell A. Harris observe 'De Facto Segregation of Black and White Vernaculars' in Philadelphia and chart those characteristics of the local black English vernacular which are pulling it away from the norms of local white speech. The features themselves are by now pretty familiar. The same authors, this time with David Graff, investigate a vocalic chain-shift in the white vernacular of Philadelphia and show how it is used as a marker of ethnic identity in 'Testing Listeners' Reactions to Phonological and Ethnic Identity: A New Method for Sociolinguistic Research'. They are able to test their views of its social significance by collecting informants' responses to appropriately synthesized stimuli. The complex patterns of elision and reduction of *of*, especially in BEV, are investigated by

33. *Focus on: England and Wales*, ed. by Wolfgang Viereck. VEAW. Benjamins (1985). pb $40.
34. *The Southwest of England*, by Martyn F. Wakelin. VEAW. Benjamins. pp. xiv + 231. pb Fl 90/$36.
35. *Diversity and Diachrony*, ed. by David Sankoff. CILT. Benjamins. pp. xi + 430. Fl 130/$52.

Francisca Sánchez in '*Of*-Reduction in Black English: A Quantitative Study'. There are two papers on the variability of the third person singular present tense marker in verbs; John Myhill and Wendell A. Harris emphasize and refine the now well-known view that the use of *-s* forms typifies narrative contexts in 'The Use of the Verbal *-s* Inflection in BEV', while in 'Contrastive Use of Verbal *-z* in Slave Narratives' Walter Pitts examines the numerous theories of its nature that have been proposed, and analyses its occurrences in narrations of ex-slaves. There are other papers in this volume on questions of syntactic variation. Curiously, the papers on English lexicology/syntax (see section 8) are all by Scandinavians and those on phonology/morphology by Americans.

In *JEngL*, the McDavid memorial volume, Lawrence M. Davis discusses and is not complimentary about 'Sampling and Statistical Inference in Dialectology', whilst H. B. Allen concludes, with Part 2 on pronunciation and Part 3 on grammar, his trilogy on 'Sex-Linked Variation in the Responses of Dialect Informants'. The findings of his inquiry into the influence of an informant's sex upon the response to a field-worker are the expected ones but they are offered with full and detailed statistical support. Bent Preisler's *Linguistic Sex Roles in Conversation: Social Variation in the Expression of Tentativeness in English*[36] continues the exploration of sex-linked variation with a statistical sanction. Jennifer Coates's *Women, Men and Language: A Sociolinguistic Account of Sex Differences in Language*[37] is the first volume of a new series from Longman entitled Studies in Language and Linguistics and will be appreciated by those who prefer their accounts of sex differences with more transparent quantification. In an interesting paper Janet Holmes explores the 'Functions of *you know* in Women's and Men's Speech' (*LSoc*) and from a corpus of spontaneous speech found that although there was no difference in the total number of occurrences of *you know* produced by men and women there appeared contrasts in the most frequent functions expressed. She also discusses the ever present danger that negative stereotypes may distort perceptions of women's usage. An inadequately researched area is sensitively discussed, with data from America and Austria, by Ruth Wodak and Muriel Schulz in *The Language of Love and Guilt: Mother–Daughter Relationships from a Cross-Cultural Perspective*[38]. And one notes with gratitude the edited collection by Harold B. Allen and Michael D. Linn, *Dialect and Language Variation*[39], which conveniently assembles, with pedagogical intent, thirty-nine previously published central texts on regional and social linguistic difference.

Charles A. Ferguson's sixty-fifth birthday is marked with the appearance

36. *Linguistic Sex Roles in Conversation: Social Variation in the Expression of Tentativeness in English*, by Bent Preisler. Mouton de Gruyter. pp. xviii + 347. DM 128.

37. *Women, Men and Language: A Sociolinguistic Account of Sex Differences in Language*, by Jennifer Coates. Longman. pp. vii + 178. pb £5.95.

38. *The Language of Love and Guilt: Mother–Daughter Relationships from a Cross-Cultural Perspective*, by Ruth Wodak and Muriel Schulz. Benjamins. pp. xiv + 253. hb £50/$35, pb £14.95/$15.

39. *Dialect and Language Variation*, ed. by Harold B. Allen and Michael D. Linn. Academic. pp. x + 616. pb £18.50.

of two massive volumes[40] edited by J. A. Fishman, A. Tabouret-Keller, M. Clyne, Bh. Krishnamurti, and M. Abdulaziz and bearing a meteoritically suggestive title. Volume I is entitled *From Phonology to Society* and Volume II, *Sociolinguistics and the Sociology of Language*. Of note is 'Riddling and Lying: Participation and Performance' by the ubiquitous John Rickford who makes a further contribution, with data drawn from a Sea Island community off the coast of South Carolina, to my now healthy collection of conversational routines, and especially the paper by John Sandefur and John Harris who, in what they overmodestly describe as 'a very tentative outline', discuss 'Variation in Australian Kriol'. The seventy-eight papers contained in the two volumes will provoke a severe headache if attempted in one sitting but they and the 'Charles Ferguson Bibliography 1945–1985' at the end of Volume II leave the reader in no doubt as to the extent of that impact. A seminal sociolinguistic career is drawing to a close.

A notoriously difficult, and consequently rarely addressed, problem is courageously approached by Gregory Guy, Barbara Horvath, Julia Vonwiller, Elaine Daisley, and Inge Rogers (safety in numbers?) in 'An Intonation Change in Progress in Australian English' (*LSoc*). They detect what has been called Australian Questioning Intonation – phonetically, a high rising terminal contour – which occurs in declarative clauses but does not convert the declaration into a polar interrogative. Its significance is interactional, rather than propositional, and is understood as requesting verification of the listener's comprehension. The authors show that AQI has the patterns of social distribution that are frequently associated with a change in progress, with higher rates of usage among working-class speakers, teenagers, and women. Your humble bibliographer was fascinated by this paper and looks forward to more of the same. Another difficult topic is treated, this time single-handedly, by Anna Wierzbicka in 'Does Language Reflect Culture? Evidence from Australian English' (*LSoc*). The answer is of course in the affirmative, but the problems encountered in *proving* it to be so against the disbeliever have brought the debate into a severe state of disrepute. Wierzbicka does not escape some of these even though she does succeed in painting a persuasive picture of Australian linguistic culture. The more respectable matter of morphophonemic variation is discussed by Michael R. Huspek in 'Linguistic Variation, Context, and Meaning: A Case of ing/in' Variation in North American Workers' Speech' (*LSoc*). His voice is one which prefers ethnographic observation and interpretive sensitivity to conjectures on the significance of statistical correlations between linguistic variant and social or stylistic variables. In the same ethnographic spirit we note Volume 10[41] in the excellent Cambridge Studies in Oral and Literate Culture, by Richard Bauman, which is based on a corpus of Texan oral narratives that the author has collected over the past fifteen years. And a little further south Margarita Hidalgo provides a window, albeit a small one, on the question of 'Language Contact, Language Loyalty and Language

40. *The Fergusonian Impact: In Honor of Charles A. Ferguson on the Occasion of his Sixty-Fifth Birthday*, ed. by J. A. Fishman, A. Tabouret-Keller, M. Clyne, Bh. Krishnamurti, and M. Abdulaziz. 2 vols. Mouton de Gruyter. pp. xv + 545 and pp. xv + 598. DM 435.

41. *Story, Performance, and Event: Contextual Studies of Oral Narrative*, by Richard Bauman. CUP. pp. x + 130. hb £20, pb £7.50.

Prejudice on the Mexican Border' (*LSoc*). It is to be hoped that we can expect more studies from situations where the First World touches the Third.

Finally, the vexed question of method. The year's fruits are not going to extinguish any of the previous controversies and may well excite a few new ones. John Rickford gives an excellent reflection on the methodology of sociolinguistics in 'The Need for New Approaches to Social Class Analysis in Sociolinguistics' (*L&C*). He observes that the predominance of functional models of society can be explained by their compatibility with structural techniques in linguistics but that conflict models of society may provide insights that would otherwise be left obscured. He illustrates this suggestion with an example of his own field-work. Additional reflections on methodology are provided by Dennis R. Preston in 'Fifty Some-Odd Categories of Language Variation' and Dell H. Hymes in 'Discourse: Scope without Depth' (both *IJSL*). And finally in this section Charles L. Briggs broaches a methodological matter in *Learning How to Ask: A Sociolinguistic Appraisal of the Role of the Interview in Social Science Research*[42] which is the first volume in a series from Cambridge called Studies in the Social and Cultural Foundations of Language. There has been much dissatisfaction with the interview format almost since it became a methodological instrument and Labovian strategies for easing this are by now familiar. Briggs is honest about his own initial inadequacies in the field and his book is distinguished from many others, as its title announces, in its inclusion of sociolinguistic concerns. It will be most informative to those who have yet to embark on empirical research.

5. Phonetics, Phonology, and Orthography

Old English phonology this year looms as large as ever. It usually looms large because some of the leading – and productive – experts in theoretical phonology have a background in Anglistik, e.g. Morris Halle, Roger Lass, Paul Kiparsky, Samuel J. Keyser, Jerzy Rubach, and John M. Anderson. Only two of these have written on OE this year, however: Anderson investigates 'The Status of Voiced Fricatives in Old English' (*FLH*), and comes up with a highly interesting reductionistic argument about the archiphonemic relations among these notoriously problematic sounds, within the framework of dependency phonology. Consonants are also attacked by Rubach in *Fisiak*[10]; the connection between 'Degemination in Old English and the Formal Apparatus of Generative Phonology' is that only given formalisms such as the rule-collapsing conventions of GP is it possible to determine which of the pair of geminate consonants is deleted. I am not sure whether to be impressed or amused. Jerzy Wełna does battle with 'The Old English Digraph ⟨cg⟩ Again' in the same volume, worrying about the detail of the changes in pronunciation which it masks, especially in degemination contexts. Fran Colman has 'A

cǣġ to Old English Syllable Structure' (same volume); she starts from the well-known paradox of the ordering of palatalization and *i*- umlaut in OE (neither order accounts for the facts, supposedly), and salvages a solution (proposed and rejected) by Richard Hogg by suggesting that the recalcitrant words in fact fall into two groups differing in syllable structure. Palatalization before

42. *Learning How to Ask: A Sociolinguistic Appraisal of the Role of the Interview in Social Science Research*, by Charles L. Briggs. CUP. pp. xv + 155. hb £20, pb £7.95.

umlaut, the old orthodoxy, is rescued. Raymond Hickey argues in 'On Syncope in Old English' (also in *Fisiak* [10]) that the process is restricted not just by phonological conditions, but also by the grammatical class and morphological structure of the words affected – i.e. that syncope is not a classic 'neogrammarian' sound-change. Ana Pinto proposes, uncertainly to judge by the question mark, 'A New Origin for the English /ʃ/ Phoneme?' (*Word*). One would not deduce from the title that the article is really about the vexed origin of the present pronunciation of the word *she*; the author rejects the view that /ʃiː/ arose in certain subject-inverted constructions in early medieval Northumbrian, suggesting instead (following an ancient view of Henry Sweet's) that it is a direct reflex of the OE feminine demonstrative pronoun *seo*, and that some phonological and lexical features of medieval Danish acted as a catalyst for this and other changes. Joseph P. Crowley reviews the evidence available for 'The Study of English Dialects' (*ES*). It is a chastening document in that it undermines some traditional certainties, but it disappointingly makes use of precious little scholarship since 1980; the work of Gillis Kristensson is barely mentioned and that of Thomas S. Toon not at all, though their attacks on the notion of 'dialectal consistency' are directly germane to Crowley's theme, centring as it does on the history of research into isoglosses. It remains a modestly useful 'how-much-do-we-know?' survey. Hans Frede Nielsen offers a very stimulating insight of principle 'On the Origin of Emigrant Languages with Special Reference to the Dialectal Position of Old English within Germanic' (*JEngL*), based on the research which went into his book *Old English and the Continental Germanic Languages* (UInnsbruck), of which both the first (1981) and the second (1985) editions were regrettably missed by *YWES*. Nielsen gives special prominence to what he sees as compromise forms; i.e. he is interested in the mismatch between dialectal patterning and settlement history. He affirms persuasively that it is undesirable to argue from unknown sociolinguistic conditions to explanations of similarities (shared innovations or common inheritances?) and differences within and among the Germanic languages. His conclusion, leading away from the notion that innovations can be geographically localized, is especially interesting in view of the small rash of papers making specific claims based on this notion, dealt with below. Frederik Kortlandt also writes on 'The Origin of the Old English Dialects' (*Fisiak* [10]), but his view is that the differences stem from differences in departure time from north Germany rather than from difference in geographical area. He notes certain archaisms in West-Saxon and Kentish in contrast with innovations which Anglian shares with continental dialects. Elsewhere (*ES*), Angelika Lutz explores 'The Syllabic Basis of Word Division in Old English Manuscripts', arguing, on a statistical basis and controversially, that scribal habits divided polysyllabic words in line with universal syllable structure preferences.

We find three papers of interest on OE metrics this year. In *NM* O. D. Macrae-Gibson's 'The Metrical Entities of Old English' is a thorough critique of the late A. J. Bliss's system propounded in his standard work *The Metre of Beowulf*. 'Syllable Theory and Old English Verse . . .' come together in '. . . A Preliminary Observation' by Seiichi Suzuki (*Fisiak* [10]); in the terms of current Metrical Phonology, alliteration is importantly linked to a syllable-initial *w*-branch. Suzuki feels able to explain the alliterative behaviour of *s* + consonant clusters by juggling *s*'s and *w*'s under the *w* characterizing syllable-initial position. See Chapter 4, p. 124 for Edwin Duncan's scepticism (also in *NM*) that the age of an OE text can be deduced from a syllable-count of the word *frea*: syllabicity is in fact determined by the morphosyntactic environment in which the word occurs. Old English poetry is also the subject of Alfred Bammesberger's student-oriented *Linguistic Notes on Old English Poetic Texts*[43].

Manfred Görlach returns to the old chestnut 'Middle English — a Creole?' (*Fisiak*[10]), and, after careful discussion, concludes that ME cannot be so called without bleaching the term *creole* of all usefulness. But Andrei Danchev, in the same collection, argues that the drastic reduction of the OE vowel inventory which characterizes ME can be traced to the convergence of ME, French, and Anglo-Danish ('Interlanguage Simplification in Middle English Vowel Phonology?'). This is a further contribution in the current drive to blame the Danes for ME (*YW* 66.75). Now we find out why Roger Lass has not written on OE this year: he has been thinking about ME instead, and indeed also PrE, as we shall see below. In 'Minkova *noch einmal*: MEOSL and the Resolved Foot' (*FLH*), he amplifies the argument of Donka Minkova's revolutionary text on M(iddle) E(nglish) O(pen) S(yllable) L(engthening) (*YW* 63.32). She relates the change in question to an overriding principle of foot-weight preservation; he rejects the view of lengthening as a compensatory change in favour of one dependent on the notion of an alternative foot type, arguing in support of a consistent Germanic change-direction along a hierarchy of foot-type preferences. James Noble, in *NM*, argues that 'The 4-Stress Hemistich in Laȝamon's *Brut*' is not, after all, the norm for this text; rather, it supports particular types of narrative detail and mood. Still on the *Brut*, Haruo Iwasaki argues that the case of certain line-end nouns is determined by considerations of rhyme ('Case and Rhyme in Laȝamon's *Brut*' (*Fisiak*[10])).

The greatest publishing event for many years in Middle English studies — to be equalled in importance only when *MED* is finally completed — is the appearance of *A Linguistic Atlas of Late Mediaeval English*[44], edited by Angus McIntosh, M. L. Samuels, Michael Benskin, and their collaborators. Thirty years in the making, these splendidly produced volumes defy one to use the reviewers' clichés about any other books. It is a feeble understatement to say that any future study of English during the years 1350–1450 will start from the database provided by the *Atlas*. Volume I contains the general introduction to the work, an index of sources (two hundred pages of them!), and a battery of dot-maps on which classes of variants are conflated to bring out certain general patterns; the uncollapsed data is presented in Volume II on the item maps, where the geographical origins of all the attested scribal variants of sixty chosen words are displayed. Volume III presents scribal profiles for each of the chosen texts, displaying graphic idiosyncrasies within the standardized battery of keywords, while Volume IV is organized by the keywords themselves; the distribution of their attested forms is analysed county by county. For some areas, e.g. Sussex, the *Atlas* incidentally provides the first reliable characterization of the dialect during the later ME period that there has ever been. Further review is premature; its value will be tested as it is used over a period of years. There are

43. *Linguistic Notes on Old English Poetic Texts*, by Alfred Bammesberger. CWU. pp. 124. DM 30.

44. *A Linguistic Atlas of Late Mediaeval English*, by Angus McIntosh, M. L. Samuels, and Michael Benskin, assisted by Margaret Laing and Keith Williamson. 4 vols. AberdeenU. pp. ix + 569; xxiii + 388; xxiv + 700; xxii + 345. £225.

only occasional production lapses; e.g., where the dots representing linguistic forms do not coincide with the dots marking places, the reader has the sense of being subjected to Rorschach tests (Vol. I, p. 317, map 52, for instance). But this is of little account; I already wish I had had this tool for years, and I now know what I have been missing. It would be a shame to allow Gillis Kristensson's paper on 'A Middle English Dialect Boundary' to disappear in the shadow of such a mighty work, so it is treated in section 9.

Martyn F. Wakelin is especially worried about the general lack of interest in the dialectology of early Modern English. Fittingly, his contribution to *Fisiak*[10], 'The "Exmoor Courtship" and "Exmoor Scolding"': An Evaluation of Two Eighteenth-Century Dialect Texts', is the only paper in 1986 in this area. It is essentially a piece describing the phonology of these texts.

The entire phonological history of English is the subject matter of Karl Hubmayer's Salzburg *Habilitationsschrift* entitled '*Natürliche Diachronie*': *Untersuchungen zur phonetischen Motivation historischer phonologischer Prozesse im Englischen*[45], whose title is surely self-explanatory. The early part makes rather heavy weather of discussing some commonplace background notions, but the real meat of the book is a survey of the findings of recent work in phonology and (especially) phonetics, giving some substance, in a critical way, to the notion of 'naturalness'. A wide range of familiar historical changes is put under the spectrograph. Hubmayer pleads in the end for a serious reconsideration of the view that changes have their impetus in variation in the chain of speech and in the interplay between the activities of speaking and hearing.

The phonetics of the present-day language is the concern of Leigh Lisker in his paper '"Voicing" in English: A Catalog of Acoustic Features Signaling /b/ versus /p/ in Trochees' (*SRSR*; also in *L&S*). He and his collaborators have isolated no less than sixteen different acoustic features which may cue the ostensibly unitary distinction mentioned in his title. He stresses the need for these to be understood in terms of the fine detail of articulatory movements. A further detailed phonetic report is Daniel Hirst's 'Phonological and Acoustic Parameters of English Intonation', in *Intonation in Discourse*[14]. I have unfortunately not seen Charles-James N. Bailey's *English Phonetic Transcription* (SIL/UTex, 1985). The flyer suggests that it deals with the problems of transcribing narrowly a fairly large number of English accents worldwide. Equally, I have not seen Jonathan Dalby's IULC monograph on the *Phonetic Structure of Fast Speech in American English*. Wiktor Jassem has conducted a computer-aided analysis of 'Vocalic Oppositions in Monosyllabic English Words'[46], showing the unexpected conclusion that as many as 40% of such words enter into no minimal pairs in respect of their vowels. It also appears that the most heavily loaded oppositions concern pairs of long or pairs of short vowels; why on earth has Jassem made nothing of this theoretically potentially very interesting finding? Bernhard Diensberg turns his attention from medieval borrowings (*YW* 66.76) to 'The Phonology of Modern French Loanwords in Present-Day English' (*Fisiak*[10]), taking into account especially what integrative

---

45. '*Natürliche Diachronie*': *Untersuchungen zur phonetischen Motivation historischer phonologischer Prozesse im Englischen*, by Karl Hubmayer. USalz. pp. 337. pb.

46. In *In Honor of Ilse Lehiste/Ilse Lehiste Pühandusteos*, ed. by Robert Channon and Linda Shockey. Foris. pp. xxii + 542. £55.

changes might be predicted from considering the differences between the phonological systems of the languages in question.

Suzanne Romaine studies 'The Effects of Language Standardization on Deletion Rules: Some Comparative Germanic Evidence from *t/d*- Deletion' (*Fisiak*[10]); given the norms of the writing-based culture of western Europe, her conclusion that standardization in general inhibits consonant deletion processes is not terribly surprising.

Dialect phonology is much in evidence in 1986. The third volume of the Scots section of *The Linguistic Atlas of Scotland*[47] is published. The editors insist that its primary purpose is comparative, and they therefore introduce the pragmatically defined structural notion of a *polyphoneme*, a unit broadly comparable with the *diaphoneme* of some recent works on English dialects (criticized in *YW* 65.38–9). The first part consists of very extensive data-tables for each of the localities outwith the Highland Line and in the east of Northern Ireland, giving a clear idea of the lexical distribution of particular phones in each place. There follow systemic maps, showing, for each locality, how many phonemes there are in the local phonological system and also how many phonemes represent each polyphoneme in a particular phonetic environment. The subsequent word maps give a conventional representation of how given words are pronounced in each locality. The maps are of excellent quality. The survey reveals itself to have been a traditional older-rural-male based type of investigation, restricted in principle to one informant per locality; the methodology has been extensively criticized over recent years and that criticism will not be rehearsed here. Since the survey was set in motion many decades ago, and set up in a way which did not allow online modification, it is more charitable to accept the findings for what they are worth, which is a good deal; we learn a lot about a type of broad Scots which may well no longer exist, or whose days are numbered, from this handsome *Atlas*.

A couple of papers seek to show that details of pronunciation in one dialect can be traced to some other, extraterritorial one (compare and contrast the notes on Nielsen's paper, above). Rudolf C. Troike claims to be able to trace 'McDavid's Law' (*JEngL*), i.e. /z/ → /d/ in certain environments, to Cornwall. Likemindedly, William Kirwin and Robert Hollett link 'The West Country and Newfoundland . . .' on the basis of '. . . some *SED* evidence' (*JEngL*), though they allow for the possibility of independent development in some cases. Roger Lass and Susan Wright come to compatible conclusions for a modern set of dialects in 'Endogeny vs. Contact: "Afrikaans Influence" on South African English'; they affirm that contact is likely to have had only a facilitating role in establishing the distinguishing traits of SAE, which were at least embryonically present in the dialects of south-east England in the nineteenth century (*EWW*). (Lass by himself presents a similar argument against recently proposed Irish influence on the syntax of Hiberno-English ('"Irish Influence": Reflections on "Standard" English and its Opposites, and the Identification of Calques' (*SAP*)).

There is a fair amount, as we have been seeing, on recent variation and change in the English language; and what there is is good. Top of the list is John Harris's excellent book *Phonological Variation and Change: Studies in*

47. *The Linguistic Atlas of Scotland: Scots Section*. Vol. III: *Phonology*, ed. by J. Y. Mather and H. H. Speitel with cartography by G. W. Leslie. CH. pp. xviii + 398. £175.

Hiberno-English[48], which places the findings of the linguistic survey of Belfast at the disposal of general historical linguistics. Harris focuses on the competing variants (essentially Scots and essentially English) of certain front vowels, and establishes that their distribution is governed by sociolinguistic trends, though phonological environment plays a catalysing role. The most interesting part of a most interesting work deals with the notion of phonological merger: whether its effects can be undone, how it is implemented, and how it may be avoided. For a key change in Belfast English, Harris argues that it is being effected by gradual lexical class-transfer and not classical neogrammarian sound-change. And mergers may be avoided by adjustment, either qualitative or quantitative, of morae peripheral to the vocalic nucleus. The book is backed by a fine grammatical article in *EWW*, 'Expanding the Superstrate', discussed in section 4. Still *within* English, Raymond Hickey is at pains to make a good case for the view that the 'Possible Phonological Parallels between Irish and Irish English' (*EWW*) are not to be ascribed to Irish influence without a searching critical examination of other dialects of English and of natural phonetic tendencies. More on sociophonological matters is provided by Harold B. Allen in *JEngL*, who investigates 'Sex-linked Variation in the Responses of Dialect Informants. Part 2: Pronunciation'. He finds limited evidence for a 'female phonology', involving, almost inevitably, some conservatism and some spelling-influence – not necessarily the same thing, of course. His findings are backed with adequate statistical evidence.

Apart from the intonation paper mentioned in section 4 above, the Australian scene, strongly featured last year, is represented by just one paper missed during the glut; Barry J. Blake analyses 'The Status of "Short *a*" in Melbourne English' (*JIPA*, 1985), concluding that the contrast /æ/ ~ /æ:/ has marginal phonemic status in the relevant dialect. Laurie Bauer provides the first reasonably thorough 'Notes on New Zealand English Phonetics and Phonology' that I have seen (*EWW*). U.S. English pronunciation features in an article in *AS* by Ann Pitts, who establishes the existence of 'Flip-flop Prestige in American *tune, duke, news*'. The relevant feature is the prevocalic glide, being re-introduced into Northern dialects as spoken by people in the media, among others, as a result of elocution, she claims, and being deleted from the speech of those Southerners who conservatively possessed it on the basis of (now clearly obsolescent) Northern models. A most interesting paper by J. K. Chambers and Margaret F. Hardwick analyses the 'Comparative Sociolinguistics of a Sound Change in Canadian English' (*EWW*). They catalogue the incipient break-up of the unitary dialectal feature commonly referred to as 'Canadian raising'; younger people in two urban centres are heard to be phonologically Americanizing their speech, while in Vancouver an alternative realization of the /au/ diphthong is spreading, apparently of indigenous origin. Nigeria's linguistic heterogeneity contributes to the continuing use of English, whose sociolinguistic relations with local languages are explored in two papers. V. O. Awonusi examines 'Regional Accents and Internal Variability in Nigerian English' (*ES*), concluding that not all the observed variety is caused by substrate interference; different missionary traditions of teaching English have also had a hand in the matter. Munzali Jibril also writes on 'Sociolinguistic Variation in

48. *Phonological Variation and Change: Studies in Hiberno-English*, by John Harris. CUP (1985). pp. xiii + 379. £25.

Nigerian English' (*EWW*), emphasizing the inadequacy of models developed for the description of urban dialects in the industrialized world in dealing with Third-World sociolinguistics. Ethnicity, rather than social class, correlates strongly with phonological variables in Nigerian English, according to his statistical study. Although this point of view is worthy of further pursuit, some readers may wish to see this part of the argument elaborated before giving it credence.

The collection of theoretical papers *Dependency and Non-Linear Phonology*[49], edited by Jacques Durand, is a welcome addition to the bookshelf because it is the first easily accessible and wide-ranging book exploring dependency phonology and its relation to other models (especially in the introductory essay by John M. Anderson and the editor). It includes some papers specifically devoted to English. Charles Jones is able to demonstrate, using 'A Dependency Approach to Some Well-Known Features of Historical English Phonology', that certain changes have more in common than might at first be thought; specifically breakings and smoothings in OE and ME before a variety of consonants. His conclusions resemble somewhat the theorizing about 'conspiracies', i.e. goal-directed clusters of changes, which was current in the early 1970s; one group of changes promoted overall 'palatality', another overall 'velarity', while both groups may be characterized as having augmented duration of vocal-cord vibration. Ken Lodge argues, in 'The English Velar Fricative, Dialect Variation and Dependency Phonology', that the said phone has different histories in different dialects, and that, while its underlying presence should not be postulated in the Southern and U.S. dialects described in *The Sound Pattern of English* (*YW* 50.52), there is a stronger argument for its retention in the lexicon of certain Northern dialects (cf. also *YW* 65.38-9). Charles T. Scott's paper in *SAP*, 'English Front Round Vowels: A Synchronic and Diachronic Interpretation', is an intriguing attempt within a GP framework to argue for the persistence, in the underlying forms of the modern language, of rounded front vowel segments such as /y(:)/, and shows how the *SPE* glide-insertion rule can be simplified and generalized under his assumptions. John M. Anderson questions the usual assumptions about what he takes to be 'The English Prosody /h/' (*Fisiak*[10]), treating it as a syllable prosody rather than as a phoneme. He gives an account of a number of words that appear exceptional to his formulation, using principles that are already fairly well discussed.

Theoretical questions within a generative framework are also well to the fore. Jeri J. Jaeger writes in *PY* 'On the Acquisition of Abstract Representations for English Vowels'. She argues that she can find no psychological basis for the idea that the 'rules' of the Great Vowel Shift in the synchronic phonology of PrE are subparts of a single rule, nor for the idea that they are all of equal validity. She finds – surely surprising no one by now, but she sets it all out well – that those vowel-shift rules which have some psychological validity are mediated by spelling, i.e. they are not purely phonological constructs in the minds of real speakers at all. Essentially similar in direction is the paper by H. Samuel Wang and Bruce L. Derwing in the same periodical entitled 'More on English Vowel Shift: The Back Vowel Question'; they conclude that all

49. *Dependency and Non-Linear Phonology*, ed. by Jacques Durand. CH. pp. [xvii] + 333 £29.95.

hypotheses about vowel-relatedness enshrined in the idea of a synchronic vowel-shift rule fail to gain empirical confirmation on at least one count. The empirical bases of phonological theory are also explored in Arnold M. and Elizabeth D. Zwicky's 'Imperfect Puns as a Source of Evidence about Phonological Similarity' (*FoLi*).

On a specific issue in current Lexical Phonology, K. P. Mohanan argues, on the basis of a familiar range of English data, that the notion of the cyclicity of lexical strata is not to be regarded as a theoretical postulate, but as a parameter, and that English is not marked by strict cyclicity. Not all nonfinal strata are cyclic, he argues in this revisionist account. This paper, 'Syllable Structure and Lexical Strata in English', is in *PY*, and other papers in this journal touch on similar issues.

Anne Cutler continues her work on the structure of the phonological aspect of the mental lexicon with a typically provocatively titled piece: '*Forbear* Is a Homophone: Lexical Prosody Does Not Constrain Lexical Access' (*L&S*). She argues that supposedly phonemic stress differences are irrelevant in the accessing of lexical material during speech recognition; a disturbing conclusion for structural linguists of any persuasion, but a well-motivated one on the evidence she presents.

1986 is a good year for non-verbal aspects of English. In addition to the general works on intonation mentioned in section 2 above, there is an impressive crop of material specifically on English. First in line is a significant new textbook: Elizabeth Couper-Kuhlen's *An Introduction to English Prosody*[50]. It presents an attempt at a unified descriptive system, giving due weight to competing viewpoints, on the basis of a highly impressive battery of sources. Very much to be welcomed is the chapter-by-chapter presentation of the issues involved in the relation of intonation to other aspects of the linguistic system, which are notoriously confounded by other commentators: information structure, discourse structure, grammar and illocutionary force, and speaker's attitude. Couper-Kuhlen is especially at pains to tease apart from each other the grammatical and pragmatic senses of terms like *question*, the confusion of which must be ended before a proper approach to prosody can begin. An impressive book, which gives more than it promises: there is material on other languages, and comparative and typological questions are raised. Still on prosody, Merle A. Horne's paper in *SL*, 'Focal Prominence and the "Phonological Phrase" within Some Recent Theories', argues that we can dispense with the notion of a phonological phrase, espoused by some, if phonology is allowed direct access to semantico-pragmatic notions such as *focus*. Elisabeth O. Selkirk also argued in her recent book (*YW* 65.41–2) that we could do without it. Focus is also the subject of William H. G. Wells's rather sophisticated contribution to *Intonation in Discourse*[14] entitled 'An Experimental Approach to the Interpretation of Focus in Spoken English'. His experiment leads him to believe that focus and contrast are phenomena realized purely phonologically in English. In the same collection, Carlos Gussenhoven describes 'The Intonation of "George and Mildred": Post-Nuclear Generalisations', and is able to validate an important generalization about sentence accent placement: that it falls on an argument in a focus domain. It

50. *An Introduction to English Prosody*, by Elizabeth Couper-Kuhlen. Niemeyer/Arnold. pp. viii + 239. hb £25, pb DM 36/£9.95.

may be that this is the groundwork of an answer to the puzzle presented by some perennially troublesome cases first isolated by Dwight Bolinger and Susan Schmerling. His wide-ranging paper also covers the analysis of focus in relation to comic effects. I have regrettably not seen Kathleen Bardovi-Harlig's *Pragmatic Determinants of English Sentence Stress* (IULC). The said Bolinger contributes a paper to a recent volume in the Studies in Descriptive Linguistics series [32] (the supplement series of *IRAL*) entitled 'The English Beat: Some Notes on Rhythm', where he underlines the importance of recognizing the rhythmical consequences of the existence of an unstressed vowel system in English, i.e. one where the vowels in question are not derived from underlying full vowels.

An Antwerp research report published in 1986 is Ronald Geluykens's *Questioning Intonation* [51]. He sets out in this corpus-based analysis to test the common-currency idea that there is a significant relation between rising nuclei and the pragmatic category of *questions*. Surprisingly, and impressively, he shows the common belief to be untrue. Rather than nucleus-type, he argues, it is the pragmatics of situation which is likely to determine whether hearers judge a given utterance to be a question, in defiance of the intonational structure where this leads in the opposite direction. J. K. Local, J. Kelly, and W. H. G. Wells have a paper striving 'Towards a Phonology of Conversation: Turn-Taking in Tyneside English' (*JL*). It is good to see a paper whose ultimate intentions are theoretical using data from a non-standard dialect, and also good to have the pragmatic functions of prosodic features explored in detail. They conclude that, at least as far as marking of the ends of conversational turns is concerned, the categories linguists are wont to set up for the description of intonation are at variance with those which may be inferred from the observed behaviour of native users. The authors also believe that standard accounts of these phenomena are based on observationally inadequate premises, a point returned to by Wells and Local in separate papers in *Intonation in Discourse* [14].

Orthographic papers this year include 'Medieval English Scribal Practice: Some Questions and Assumptions' (*Fisiak* [10]), by Gero Bauer, who makes a renewed appeal for writing systems to be considered as something more than a mere representation of phonological systems, from which they may depart for reasons rather more interesting than failure to adhere to the phonemic principle. Bauer sees the state of affairs epitomized in the new *Atlas* [44] as representing a writing system of emergent autonomy; but he reaffirms (not surprisingly) that writing is the sole source of information for the historical phonologist at most periods. Vivian Salmon contributes a piece on 'The Spelling and Punctuation of Shakespeare's Time' to the original-spelling edition of *The Oxford Shakespeare* [52]. This is a concise, comprehensive, thoroughly exemplified, and mildly sceptical overview of the current state of knowledge about the topic. Sidney Greenbaum reviews the surprising number of 'Spelling Variants in British English' (*JEngL*), especially in learned vocabulary, and attributes some of them to American sources. (John Algeo revisits H. L. Mencken's prediction about the ultimate Americanization of British English in a rather light-hearted paper in the same journal; he finds the prediction borne out up to a point.)

51. *Questioning Intonation*, by Ronald Geluykens. UAntwerp. pp. 92. pb.

52. *The Oxford Shakespeare*, ed. by Stanley Wells and Gary Taylor. Original spelling edn. Clarendon. pp. lxiii + 1456. £75.

6. Morphology

Papers on morphology offer something on both inflectional and derivational problems, from a range of historical periods: I'll start from the 'beginning'. I would not find myself compelled by a revival of claims simplistically blaming the Danes for the loss of inflections in English; but Dieter Stein, in 'Old English Northumbrian Verb Inflection Revisited' (*Fisiak* [10]), while suggesting an 'ensemble of factors' to account for the third person singular -*s*, winningly returns us to the influence of Scandinavian inflections – at least to reinforce already independently existing drifts. Based on a not-unreasonable re-adjustment of data previously assembled by Rolf Berndt on second person plurals with -*s*, Stein makes good sense of the earlier hypothesis by Erik Holmquist, of an extension of -*s* from second singular to second plural (and then to other persons), invoking well-attested evidence for the special status of the third person singular to account for the retention of -ð where it is so. Here we are shown 'how theory changes data and leads to the refinement of old and the formulation of new hypotheses'. In 'On Some Morphological Formatives in Old English' (*FLH*, 1985), Fran Colman questions Bauer's classification of certain phonological sequences (see *YW* 64.49) as ones which must be included in the morphological analysis, while not necessarily representing a morph (called 'empty formatives' by Colman). From an analysis of selected OE declensional and conjugational paradigms, based on an extended word and paradigm model (the presentation of which, in all its braces, represents something of a triumph for the printers), she concludes that, at least for the data treated here, every phonological sequence represented in the orthography may be accounted for as 1. part of the lexical part of the word, 2. a phonologically predictable phonological sequence (allomorphy), or 3. a correlate with the expression of some morphological property; no evidence here forces acceptance of the concept 'empty formative'. Though Raymond Hickey's title 'On Syncope in Old English' (*Fisiak* [10]) suggests its focus on phonology, its burden is not unrelated to the question of morphological formatives, claiming morphological conditioning for certain instances of syncope, and, crucially, a morphological basis for distinguishing epenthesis from lack of syncope: vowel insertion characterizes compounds, while vowel deletion occurs in morphologically complex forms.

On inflectional inconsistencies in ME, Hanna Mausch's 'A Note on Late Middle English Gender' (*SAP*) offers an elegantly subtle interpretation of detailed data: i.e., forms of bird names from the *c.* 1493 print of the allegorical 'Branches of the Appletree'. Mausch convinces that the inconsistency of gender reflected by pronominalizations is not explicable by invoking influence of natural gender, or by tracing the original (French) of which her text is a translation. Instead, she suggests *enallage*: 'a distortion of formal grammatical relationships in a text by the employment of a different grammatical form than would normally be expected': here the influence of the gender of the nearest subject is a possible cause of *enallage*, and of 'unaccountable' shifts in gender. Haruo Iwasaki, in 'Case and Rhyme in Laʒamon's *Brut*' (*Fisiak* [10]) explores instances of case inflections, such as 'unnecessary' final -*n*, strong nouns declined as weak, mutated dative plural forms, arguing for the possible influence of the rhyme patterns on choice of morphological form: though it is not clear whether this can be extended beyond the *Brut* as part of a theory about syncretism in diachronic inflectional morphology.

'The analysis of words is a subject which is momentarily out of fashion': with
this quotation from Peter Matthews (*YW* 55.71) Georges Bourcier opens his
'Remarques sur les dérivés chez Richard Rolle: Où en est la morphologie?'
(*Fisiak* [10]), which explores Rolle's use of various derivational morphemes, and
their collocations with particular inflectional suffixes, and with roots of particular word-classes. It seems that the 'moment' is past, since we have enough on
morphology for a section in *YWES*, which will now turn to more recent
English, via Knud Sørensen's 'Phrasal Verb into Noun' (*NM*), where a detailed
survey of stylistic usage and semantic fields of an inventory of deverbal nouns
consisting of verb stem plus particle denoting movement (based on statistics
assembled by Lindelöf in 1938) suggests various putative causes of the increased
occurrence of nominalizations of phrasal verbs during the eighteenth and
nineteenth centuries. Invoked here are the disuse by ME of the OE prefix plus
verb type of 'compound verb', the rise of conversion, seen as a concomitant of
inflection loss, and the tendency of phrasal verbs to develop many sense-
differentiations, several of which become nominalized.

Frans Plank, in 'How disgrace-ful' (*ALH*), explores the adjacency constraint
on conditioning of allomorphy, viz., 'morphemes must be adjacent (and
perhaps within the same word) to be able to influence the selection of
allomorphs'. The testing of such a constraint by analysis of *dis–ful* adjectives in
English, specifically *disgraceful*, invokes analysis of *able* as two suffixes: weak-
boundary + *able* and strong-boundary #*able*. Negation of *able* adjectives by *in*
and *un* fits the requirement of the adjacency constraint, which requires prefix
allomorphy to mirror the + *able*/#*able* distinction. There is, however, no
formal evidence for splitting *ful* into two suffixes, weak- and strong-boundary,
and the well-argued conclusion (implied by the title of the paper) favours a
structure in which the suffix *ful* is attached to the prefixed stem *disgrace*. A very
readable paper which illuminates the immediate constituent structure of a range
of derivational morphological constructions in English. (The same author
engages attention again in 'Paradigm Size, Morphological Typology, and
Universal Economy' in *FoLi*, this time on inflectional morphology.)

Another highly readable paper on derivational morphology is Dieter
Kastovsky's 'The Problem of Productivity in Word Formation' (*Lings*),
gratifyingly concerned with formalization of generalizations, and here in
particular with distinctions between derivational morphological and syntactic
processes, and between aspects of word-formation itself. A major aspect of the
problem of productivity concerns the consequences for acceptability of new
formations; i.e. that the outputs of word-formation processes, viz., lexical
items, tend to be incorporated in the lexicon (unlike the output of syntactic
rules): a neologism, even if coined on the basis of a regular productive pattern,
may be rejected, if it is not part of the mental lexicon of the hearer. Inversely,
neologisms may not be produced if an equivalent lexical item is in existence, and
an interplay of competence and performance results. After a brief historical
note on the role of productivity in earlier word-formation studies, Kastovsky
advocates a functional point of view for keeping apart competence and
performance in word-formation. Functions of word-formation patterns are
characterized as 1. labelling (operating under pragmatic restrictions) and
2. syntactic recategorization (under genuinely linguistic restrictions); and these
two types are to be regarded as basically different phenomena, especially if
approached from a semantic, and not purely morphological, angle. This paper
appeals, however, for recognition of the 'interdependence of function, scope of

a rule and productivity in the sense of actual application', with respect to the labelling and recategorization functions, whose co-operation is illuminatingly illustrated in the same author's analysis, in 'Diachronic Word-Formation in a Functional Perspective' (*Fisiak*[10]), of instances of changes in English derivational morphology. *Sit in* type words evidence the pattern of change from labelling to syntactic recategorization; the reverse is seen in what has happened to the *–ee* suffix; and the discussion closes with the observation of shift towards recategorization, going on under our very eyes, which may end up providing English with a new word-formation category: compound verbs.

Perhaps an apt title is 'Legible but not Readable: On the Semantics of English Adjectives in *ble*' (*SN*), in which Göran Kjellmer correlates frequency of occurrence of the relevant adjectives, with their semantic classifications, based on 'various desk dictionaries', as A: 'those which present in a neutral way the potentiality for the concept contained in the stem' (e.g. *legible*) or B: 'those which go beyond that and suggest an attitude to this potentiality' (e.g. *readable*), and concludes that 'frequency as such seemed to be the best key to semantic variation in the A:B dimension'. Kjellmer's addition to the not very remarkable generalization that frequency of occurrence is likely to be associated with non-compositionality is that the denotations of the B types involve subjective evaluation. Some quite subtle argumentation, based on a search of two one-million word corpora of modern English, compared with a Shakespearean corpus, leads the same author to predict the loss of determinative *its*, in 'On "Pattern Neatening" in the English Pronominal System' (*SL*): such loss would remove the irregularity in a system in which independent possessives tend to have human reference, and which lacks independent *its*. If only languages behaved themselves. On the other hand, Kjellmer regards prediction of loss of nominative forms of pronouns as rash, in '"Us Anglos are a Cut above the Field": On Objective Pronouns in Nominative Contexts' (*ES*): a paper which relates the invasion of Standard English by such objective pronoun + noun phrase constructions as exemplified in the title to loss of subject/object marking on nouns, and to the colloquial drift of personal pronouns towards objective forms in nominative contexts.

The not surprising conclusion in Janet H. Randall's *Morphological Structure and Language Acquisition*[53], is that the greater the distance between the base- and derived form, the fewer subcategorizations will be inherited. Its interest lies in the way it is reached: it treats certain derivational regularities as part of a description of 1. the nature of the adult system being acquired, 2. the pre-adult grammar of the language learner, and 3. a model of learnability which provides a mapping between them. The generalization of the Case Complement Restriction formulated by G. Carlson and T. Roeper, that a complex verb can have at most a direct object as its complement in its subcategorization, is explained in terms of an Inheritance Principle, whose formulation (regrettably with a misprinted 'unchanged' in Fig. 6, p. 63; but printed correctly in Fig. 4, p. 200) rests on a distinction between levels of operation of various rules which map subcategorization structures onto either identical or different subcategorization structures. A level two rule changes both meaning and category, and the derived form can inherit only unmarked subcategorizations (i.e. only a

---

53. *Morphological Structure and Language Acquisition*, by Janet H. Randall. Garland. pp. 250. $26.

direct object NP); a level one rule changes either meaning or category or neither, and allows inheritance of other subcategorizations of the base verb. Lexical-semantic and pragmatic factors are, unsurprisingly, invoked to account for apparent exceptions to the Inheritance Principle: the failure, for instance, of some verbs (e.g. *think, smoke*) to take *re-*, a level one rule. I have not seen Robert Beard, *On the Separation of Derivation from Morphology: Toward a Lexeme/Morpheme Based Morphology* (IULC), or W. N. Francis, 'Proximity Concord in English' (*JEngL*). M. Sebba argues in 'The *-ex* ending in Proper Names' (*AS*) that the function of this quasi-element is precisely that of a marker of proper names.

Kazuo Kato proffers evidence in 'Gradable Gradability' (*ES*) for gradability of allegedly non-gradable adjectives, such as *dead, married* (though this gradability is also gradable); metaphorical uses of *pregnant* (*pregnant pause*) are supposedly excluded, but the literal interpretation of *very pregnant, too pregnant* as grades of pregnantness rather than metaphors conveying impressions of weight or size suggests a breakdown of a binary opposition with which many are perhaps more at ease. But as Bernard Comrie concludes, with more on tense (see *YW* 66.82–3) in 'Tense in Indirect Speech' (*FoLi*), aiming to show clearcut arguments that *was* is used in 'Arthur said that he was sick' because it follows a main clause verb in the past tense (and not that it has past time reference): 'the choice of one analysis rather than another is not, or at least not always, a question of esthetics or personal preference'.

7. Syntax

(a) Old English and Middle English

1986 has been an 'impersonal' year, *noch einmal*. Although individual verbs have been described as 'impersonal', and show morphological peculiarities (see especially Anderson, below), the 'impersonal construction' seen as a syntactic unit pushes a treatment of this area into the present section.

As the bulkiest work on impersonals, Michiko Ogura's book, *Old English 'Impersonal' Verbs and Expressions*[54] gets first mention. The relevant verbs (whose occurrences are meticulously noted) are subcategorized according to largely superficial syntactic behaviour, viz. occurrence with or without 'formal *(h)it*' as subject, with or without other arguments marked for dative or accusative, and possibility of collocating, in participial or inflected infinitive form, with *beon, wesan, (ge)weorðan*. Each subcategory is accorded a chapter of exemplification and discussion of the individual verbs and their lexical semantics, the latter seen to be relevant to the primary concern of the book: putative causes for the demise of 'OE "impersonal" verbs and expressions'. These may be summarized thus: 1. co-occurrence of 'rival expressions' ousted certain lexical items; and with the development of *sculan* and *motan* as auxiliaries, those 'impersonal' verbs which had similar meaning and function died out; 2. occasional 'personal' use of the 'impersonal' verbs, as well as parallel uses of personal and 'impersonal' verbs establish a pattern favouring personal constructions; 3. syntactic environments which make dative and

54. *Old English 'Impersonal' Verbs and Expressions*, by Michiko Ogura. Anglistica 24. R&B. pp. 310.

accusative ambiguous destroy one of the syntactic criteria for identifying impersonal verbs and constructions. I pre-empted what must be the obvious question of how to identify 'impersonal', largely because I have to admit defeat by the initial definition 'tentatively' offered (p. 16), which involves distinctions between uses of both 'impersonal' and 'personal' with and without inverted commas, as well as the terms 'expressions with formal *(h)it*', and 'nominative-less expressions'. I leave the reader to seek out the book, whose detailed presentation of data makes it a valuable successor to W. Elmer and W. Van der Gaaf, but whose claims are the more difficult to grasp in the absence of an overt theoretical model. The same quotation delineating 'impersonal' etc., appears in section 4 of Ogura's 'Old English "Impersonal Periphrasis", or the Construction "Copula + Past Participle" of "Impersonal" Verbs' (*PoeticaJ*), containing much material also in her book, but focusing on verbs of its Group C(2), with semantically and syntactically based subdivisions (inclusion of *beon/wesan* in sections 2 and 6 as verbs with past participle forms seems strange). Again, the range of data, from glosses, homilies, translations and verse, is impressive, and the interesting results of comparisons with Latin constructions suggest that while, for instance, the occurrence of *he is/wæs gepuht*, may be influenced by Latin, among other factors, other structures, such as *is/wæs gelumpen*, occurring outwith glosses, represent native OE stylistic variants of the simple form (see more on languages in contact in Nagucka and Lass, below). Ogura's 'Old English "Impersonal" Verbs Denoting "to happen", "to befit" or "to belong to"' (*Senshu Jimbun Ronshu*, 1985) is a reworking of another section of her book.

Yet another paper by the same author, 'Old English Verbs of Thinking' (*NM*), on specific lexical items, may be included here, since one of them at least, ðyncan, is an impersonal verb; and again the concern is with the loss of items. The conclusion that OE verbs of thinking seem to be distinguishable from each other by their syntactic features allows the deduction of a general principle: the greater the restriction of a verb to a single syntactic feature, the more likely its falling into disuse. The relevance of other factors, such as loans, phonological, and semantic changes is of course acknowledged.

'Reconsidering the History of *like*' (*JL*) by Cynthia Allen, in a LFG framework, introduces a verb at least marginally a candidate for 'impersonality', by virtue of having a dative-marked experiencer and accusative experiencee as well as a nominative, which provides twelfth-century counter-evidence to David Lightfoot's claims for syntactic re-analysis in the history of English. The difference between Modern English *like*, which 'subcategorizes for a cause, which takes the grammatical role of object, and an experiencer, which plays the role of subject' and OE *lician*, for which 'the semantic roles were assigned to the opposite grammatical roles', is attributed to the introduction of a new subcategorization frame which ousted the old one. This wide-ranging discussion pays detailed attention to existing accounts, notably by Jespersen in relation to *lician*, and Fischer and van der Leek (*YW* 64.54) on the history of verbs with dative experiencers in OE, and argues, on the basis of the behaviour of subjects with respect to concord-control and the co-ordinate subject deletion constraint, for the possibility of dative subjects in OE. (I am not sure how convinced to be by the association of 'the more careful proof-reading of modern printing houses' with continued exceptions to the deletion constraint in the Early Modern English period.) 'Dummy Subjects and the

Verb-Second "Target" in Old English' (*ES*), by the same author, is a very neat piece, happily complementing the treatment of dative experiencers in the longer paper. Addressing the question of a possible conditioning factor for presence or absence of subject *hit* in OE, dealing compactly with John Haiman's invocation of the verb-second requirement, and agreeing with data presented by Nils Wahlén in 1925 as support for strong preference for *hit*, Allen remarks on the infrequency of the dummy subject in the presence of an experiencer. For the experiencer to be assigned the role of subject would explain both the very high frequency of its preverbal position, as well as the lack of dummy *hit*. A connection between case marking and semantic roles, rather than merely grammatical relations, finds yet more support.

A paper to be noted here is Rolf H. Bremmer Jr's 'The So-Called "Impersonal Verb"'-construction in Old Frisian' (*NOWELE*), as an expansion on the non-English early Germanic 'impersonal' data given in Ogura (see above), for the nice array of Old Frisian, and for its definition of 'impersonal verb' constructions as 'subjectless verb' ones, in which the predicate usually occurs in the third person singular. Here *it*, 'though formally the subject, really is empty because it has no referent'; but dative 'pseudo-subjects' are accorded a place. Verbs available for 'impersonal' constructions are said to be determined not lexically, but semantically.

John M. Anderson's 'A Note on Old English Impersonals' (*JL*) gives the strongest definition of a true impersonal verb, as one which appears in finite predications, but shows no variation in person/number, always inflected for third person singular. Such verbs can show none, one, or two (non-nominative) arguments; 'quasi-impersonal' constructions combine such a verb with the semantically empty (nominative) *hit*. The argument against an analysis assuming idiosyncratic properties of individual subcategorization-frame entries for such verbs as *of-hreowan* (Elmer's RUE class), pursued overtly in terms of the GB framework adopted by Fischer and van der Leek (*YW* 64.54), leads the reader, almost unawares, to the classic Case Grammar conclusion that the grammatical category of subject is non-contrastive, thereby providing a more generalized, strong claim, uniting groups of verbs otherwise apparently idiosyncratic.

The rocky ground of Lightfoot's syntactic re-analysis arguments is a fertile source of contention (see Allen above), harvested again by Linda Thornburg in two papers in *PBerLS*. 'The History of the Prepositional Passive in English' (1985), which may be set alongside David Denison's treatment of the topic (*YW* 66.86), addresses the problem of the existence in OE of sentences that appear to satisfy the SD of the transformational passive, but yet unaccompanied by any instances of prepositional passives. Focusing on relative clauses, Thornburg argues for a chronological progression from structures with preverbal prepositions in OE, to late OE/early ME preposition stranding, to subsequent postverbal position available for all prepositions, with the prepositional passive emerging by 1300 (cf. Lightfoot's fifteenth century). One or two generalizations here are questionable: that in OE 'when the pronoun is clearly dative, the adposition is in post-verbal position' would be tenable the other way round; and that 'dative pronouns always index animate NPs', if true, may simply reflect concerns of the narratives which survive. 'The Development of the Indirect Passive in English' is claimed (in preference to Lightfoot's theories) to have been motivated by the universal tendency for clauses to adhere to the pragmatic prototype of information flow: so, OE and ME regular passives with fronted indirect objects and postverbal subjects topicalize the highly animate and definite indirect object NP. Against well-known claims that the indirect passive arose as the result of syncretism in expression of case in NPs, and re-analysis of the original (fronted) indirect object as subject, Thornburg cites ME data which she assumes, unconvincingly to my mind, to illustrate means of disambiguating subjects: e.g. in *The Duke Mylon was geven hys lyff. And fleygh out of the land with hys wyff* (*c*. 1300) the absence of a surface subject in the co-ordinate clause is taken as evidence that *Duke Mylon* must be the subject of the former. Thornburg argues for independent re-analysis of fronted pronouns as early as OE, in passive constructions with *that*- clauses or infinitives functioning as direct objects, such as *he ne wæs forlæten þeodum godcunde lære to bodienne* (perhaps begging the question as to the analysis of OE constructions with *beon/wesan* plus participle/adjective as passives), to conclude that there is little evidence for the ordering of acquisition of syntactic properties earlier than that of coding properties: rather, they may occur simultaneously, given that, according to Thornburg, clause-initial pronouns possess the pragmatic properties of subject.

Two papers deal with OE word order, one each on prose and verse. David Denison's 'On Word Order in Old English' (*DQR*), about the importance of synchronic analysis as a preliminary to understanding change, presents a meticulous and appropriate 're-working' of some of the *Chronicle* data presented by Bean (*YW* 64.52), questions the ability of 'monolithic' approaches to word-order change to handle the variety of patterns in OE, and explores weight ordering, aptly linked with 'rhematicity', as one of a range of possible interacting factors in word-order selection, and change. The weighty and detailed analysis in Daniel Donoghue's 'Word-order and Poetic Style: Auxiliary and Verbal in the Metres of Boethius' (*ASE*) takes us through the metrical 'laws' of Kuhn and Sievers, and discovers that, in the work under discussion, principal clauses are distinguished by the preverbal position of the auxiliary, while dependent clauses must have a stressed auxiliary, and that the order (1) stressed auxiliary − (2) verbal is therefore common to both types. Comparison of the prose and verse versions supports the suggestion that exigencies of metre can here override normal syntactic patterns; and the difference between the *Metres* and *Beowulf*, where the auxiliary position is determined by introductory particles rather than the grammatical function of the clause, suggests that the former may represent a continuation of the tradi-tion of lays, distinct from the epic. Another significance of Donoghue's work is its delicate but firm querying of the use of very early poetic texts as evidence for basic Germanic word order.

Other papers (all in *Fisiak*[10]) relating directly to OE fall less clearly under themes and theories in this section, but a couple relate to concerns of papers reviewed in subsequent ones. Ruta Nagucka's 'Complementation in *Ælfric's Colloquy*' (relevant to her treatment of putative Latin influence on accusative and infinitive constructions: see *YW* 66.84) is sympathetic to theories of languages in contact, but claims that parallel or identical patterns in two languages need not result from influence of one on the other, even where contact is known to have occurred (cf. sections 4 and 5 above). Similarities between OE and Latin in the chosen text may be attributable to, for instance, lexical-semantic ones; instances of supposedly Latin-influenced constructions (e.g. accusative-infinitive) are found in OE texts without Latin models (notably verse); and the various types of complementation in the *Colloquy* can be understood in terms more general than language-specific. The well-argued claims here are nicely complemented by those in Lass (see below). From data from four manuscripts of the *OE Chronicle*, Veronica Kniezsa's sophisticated 'Temporal Relationships from OE to Early ME' argues that the increase in prepositional phrases was not an 'automatical' outcome of inflectional syncretism; it is associated, rather, with the function of the phrases (in complementary distribution with simple case) to express more detailed and subtle time relations. I am not clear what conclusions are reached in Hiroshi Fujiwara's rather disappointing paper from the same Festschrift, 'The Relative Clauses in *Beowulf*', which asks whether these clauses can contain any 'apokoinu' constructions. I have problems, too, with another paper in this volume, but more because of my remaining unconvinced about the application of the particular 'theory' to OE texts: so perhaps this is not fair. In 'More about the Textual Function of the Old English adverbial *pa*', Nils Erik Enkvist rehearses the claim that since *þa* is used with clauses describing actions it collocates with action, rather than stative, verbs; since actions tend to be fore-grounded, *pa* is used as a foregrounding device; therefore the use of *þa* with non-action verbs is, among other functions, as a foregrounding marker. Leaving aside the observation that any adverb of time is more likely to collocate with action verbs, not stative ones, the perverse reader could see the relegation to background of, for instance, the Beormas and Terfinnas in the *Ohthere* passage cited, as out of accord with the length of description accorded these peoples, their languages, their walruses, and so on, in the continuation of the text in both manuscripts containing the story, which, incidentally, with OVS order in *Fela spella him sædon þa Beormas*, could be interpreted as focusing on the stories of the Beormas.

Analyses of selected ME data involving *see* – NP – S in Roman Kopytko's 'Perception Verb Complements and Diachronic Syntax' (*SAP*) lead us to treatments within, and some criticisms of, theories of autonomous syntax. Kopytko concludes that the constituent structure approach (with its dependence on intuitions, accessibility of linguistic data, and constituent structure tests) seems insignificant for diachronic analyses, and favours a synchronic theory with general linguistic principles, rules, linguistic universals, and so on, equipped with the 'diachronic projection principle' questioned in *YW* 66.86.

(b) Modern English

Since much this year is informed, not unusually, by the influence of Chomskian autonomous syntax, we may note first the appearance of *Barriers* [55] by the linguist himself: a monograph that leads the reader on a tour of explora-tion of issues related to Universal Grammar, particularly the theories of government and bounding, in attempts to determine what might constitute barriers to various types of movement. And speaking of islands . . .

At last *Constraints on Variables in Syntax* in hard covers, with its working title changed to that of the published version, John Robert Ross's *Infinite*

55. *Barriers*, by Noam Chomsky. MITP. pp. 92. hb $17.50, pb $7.95.

Syntax![56]. The present title is elucidated in the 'after words' which some may find to their taste. But I need scarcely comment on the contents of the book, familiar for twenty years to students of Chomskian syntax, and neatly reviewed in the foreword by Paul M. Postal, concluding: 'while few works in the transformational tradition would merit consideration a dozen years after their writing, *CVS* is unquestionably among them'. Disappointingly, I have not seen Postal's own *Studies of Passive Clauses* (SUNY).

Jane B. Grimshaw's *English 'Wh'-Constructions and the Theory of Grammar*[57] proposes a semantic theory of complement selection for the two types of *wh*-constructions (those with phrasal structure with *wh*-phrases as heads, e.g. free relatives, and those with sentential structure, e.g. questions), in a model positing distinct syntactic selection frames and semantic frames, as evidence for strong autonomy of syntax. Adherents to the theory will be interested.

Noël Burton-Roberts's *Analysing Sentences: An Introduction to English Syntax*[58] provides clear and workable definitions of the terms syntax, semantics, morphology, and phonology, pointing also in the introduction to the relationship between the first two components, pursued throughout the book. Here the novice is led happily through a perspicuously connected sequence from the notion of constituents, and their functions, to Subject and Predicate and the kinds of phrases (crucially NP and VP) functioning as such, to modifier-head relationships within constituents, to combinations of phrases in complex sentences. Major word classes are appropriately identified with respect to their members' participation in particular constructions, as well as to morphological criteria. For members of both NP and VP we find definitions and discussions of labels (gratifyingly notionally based). Exercises throughout are comprehensive (and comprehensible), accompanied by answers and discussion, and works for further reading are detailed. This book knows its audience, and addresses it: though I ought to remark that some of my first year students have found the progressions in presentation of arguments and concepts in the opening chapters perhaps too 'obvious'. This, however, worries me less than some of the complexities, such as the feature 'ditransitive', imposed by the (essentially EST) framework upon the treatment of verbs with two NP arguments. Nevertheless, I would continue to recommend, and use, Burton-Roberts for introductory courses, and for reference, on English syntax. The *Introduction to the Theory of Grammar* by Henk van Riemsdijk and Edwin Williams[15] is not confined to English data, but, pursuing in more detail concepts and issues treated in Burton-Roberts, is to be strongly recommended as the most comprehensive introduction to yesterday's state of the art in GB.

Christopher Lyons builds on his claim in 'A Possessive Parameter' (*SWPLL*) that by virtue of filling the Determiner position, preposed genitives allow the NP to be understood as definite, arguing in 'The Syntax of English Genitive Constructions' (*JL*) that postposed genitives occur freely in indefinite

---

56. *Infinite Syntax!*, by John Robert Ross. Ablex. pp. xxi + 312. $45.

57. *English 'Wh'-Constructions and the Theory of Grammar*, by Jane B. Grimshaw. Garland. pp. 239. $32.

58. *Analysing Sentences: An Introduction to English Syntax*, by Noël Burton-Roberts. Longman. pp. 265. pb £6.95.

containing NPs, and, following a little history of Chomsky's treatments since 1981 of *the destruction of the city* (more on this in *Barriers*[55]), that *of* in such constructions may correspond to any of a variety of θ-roles, functioning not as a marker of case-assignment, but as nothing but a preposition. The notion of definiteness is further revised by Aimo Seppänen and Ruth Seppänen in 'Notes on Quantifiers and Definiteness in English' (*SN*), prompted by detailed exemplification from English, supported by comparisons with Swedish, as evidence that a surface analysis with phrase structure rules handles anomalies such as those presented by numerals + NP and presence or absence of *of* + definite article better than earlier deep structure analyses such as that by Ray S. Jackendoff. Crucially, it allows a treatment of the definite/indefinite interpretation as a semantic problem, instead of a syntactic phenomenon. A treatment of *want* and *like* in terms of syntactic configuration and associated θ-roles, forms the basis for Richard J. Watts's defence of Chomsky (perhaps contra Chomsky?) against 'asemantic' charges in 'Complementation and Meaning' (*SAP*), claiming that the GB framework offers an opportunity to integrate semantico-syntactic properties with 'what appear to be purely syntactic principles'. Interestingly, once again the unwary reader is led to a Case Grammar conclusion (see Anderson, above), but here this is presented as one of several 'developments' of the GB model, based on suggestions taken from 'case grammar (in all its ramifications)': 'Theta roles, such as Agent, Place, Theme etc., are projected onto the complement of the verb at the level of D-structure'. However, since Watts cites no other CG work than Charles F. Fillmore's classic *The Case for Case*, and since he leaves open the question as to primitive and universal status of semantic roles, it might appear that not all the 'ramifications' of CG have been considered. James P. Thorne's 'Because' (*Fisiak*[10]), so concise as to be barely reduced by summary, provides evidence that *because*-clauses which are S-daughters involve two propositions, those which are VP-daughters only one, and dissects the striking nature of the ambiguity of *because*-clauses falling within the scope of a negative in the main clause.

John A. Hawkins, in *A Comparative Typology of English and German: Unifying the Contrasts*[59], cites Chomsky *et al.* as pursuing the search for universals through the study of one language in depth, and compares their approach with subsequent comparative-universal approaches. Hawkins continues the search by way of a large number of variant linguistic properties in a small number of languages, in the descriptive generalization uniting contrasting rules in English and German. This fascinating work attaches importance to semantic aspects of morphological and syntactic variation: note, for instance, the account, acknowledging unpublished work by Frans Plank, of the tighter selectional restrictions imposed by German predicates, as compared with the collapse in English of semantic distinctions within a given lexical field (Chapter 2 section 5). Resuscitation of the Sapirian view of case syncretism as an explanation for the fixing of word order in English is convincingly balanced by the author's insistence that syncretism played a sufficient (if not necessary) role in English, and on the possibility of other causes also. A subtle and tightly argued account of the relevant literature on word-order change in Chapter 3 section 3 entices the reader to the view that the phonological changes in English

---

59. *A Comparative Typology of English and German: Unifying the Contrasts*, by John A. Hawkins. CH. pp. xiv + 244. £17.95.

which destroyed the case system acted as a trigger for the syntactic changes leading to contrasts between English and German.

Now I turn to Functional Grammar, and to Michael Hannay's view that an existential construction represents a specific discourse device in *English Existentials in Functional Grammar* [60], a book which is, as it claims, both a study of English existentials and an exercise in FG. Based on a restrictive definition of an existential as a *there + be* construction, a subset of presentative constructions, it firmly distinguishes this *there* from the demonstrative adverb, and elaborates on accounts of the source of the former. A detailed and elegant appraisal of previous literature addresses problems of the syntactic properties of presentative *there*. Hannay separates E-existentials (in which what is asserted to exist is a first-order entity) from state-of-affairs existentials (with copula + participle, analysed as embedded predications, not 'small clauses'), and does away with both the Definite restriction and the Predicate one, proposing a re-analysis in terms of a pragmatic ('focality') condition on the appropriateness of the postcopula term ('definite terms may occur naturally in existentials if their referents are salient in the given communicative setting'). This is a well-ordered, clearly argued presentation of a particular theoretical framework, and its handling of a phenomenon of present-day English is of interest also to historical linguists. Another Foris book, Martin Everaert's *The Syntax of Reflexivisation*, is out of print: I hope to review it for *YW* 68.

Functional conclusions are reached also by Elizabeth Wieser, in 'On the Splitting of the *of*-genitive' (*ES*), to account for the construction-type: head noun + parenthetic material + *of*-postmodifier (e.g. *The dubbing into English of Fellini's 'La Dolce Vita'*). A consideration of such factors as semantic subclasses of nouns available for the construction, constituent status of nominals and parenthetic material, complexities such as subordination and co-ordination concomitant with the construction, sees this construction-type in the light of structural complexity and the constraints that go with it. The split *of*-genitive saves structurally weak, but interesting, material from deletion; it thus reduces functionally undesirable (though structurally possible) complexity in English syntax.

Functional-semantic changes in the development of OE '*hæbban* Object past participle' to Modern English '*have* past participle Object' and '*have* Object past participle' are accounted for by an appeal to a drift in English towards agentivity (exemplified by, for instance, the shift from impersonal to personal constructions), and dynamicization of the verb, in Yoshihiko Ikegami's 'The Drift toward Agentivity and the Development of the Perfective Use of *have* + pp. in English' (*Fisiak* [10]), pursuing his concern with ergativity; and Sölve Ohlander, giving yet more on *wh-* clauses (see *YW* 66.88), argues that differences in grammatical behaviour between two types of dependent interrogative clauses may be captured by a characterization of their semantic distinctions, in 'Question-Orientation versus Answer-Orientation in English Interrogative Clauses' (*Fisiak* [10]). The plea for contextual interpretation for denominal adjectives in Michał Post's 'On the Semantic Indeterminacy of Denominal Adjectives' (*SAP*) is pursued, perhaps more coherently, in the same

60. *English Existentials in Functional Grammar*, by Michael Hannay. Foris. pp. xiv + 226. Fl 42/$21.90.

author's 'A Prototype Approach to Denominal Adjectives' (*Fisiak*[10]), in favour
of an infinite-number-of-relationships view, rather than a meaning-based
theory. Here non-derived nouns and denominal adjectives are assigned core, or
prototype, meanings to which extensions are possible in a 'dynamic and flexible
classificatory matrix', and cognitive bases are invoked for the interpretation of
denominal adjectives.

Function appears, along with much data-counting, in various guises in *SL*.
Aimo Seppänen's 'The Syntax of *seem* and *appear* Revisited' continues, as the
title implies, the debate with a reworking and restating of earlier claims,
including a critique of earlier works by Rudanko and Olsen. The behaviour of
that-clauses after these verbs with respect to processes of passivization, *what*-
questioning, and pseudo-clefting, depends, it is argued, on sentence functional
factors, rather than categorial ones (the three processes apply to objects, but
not to predicate complements). That such clauses fail to undergo topicalized
fronting is explained by their non-factivity. While structurally, the *that*-clauses
are within VP (rather than analysed as S-daughters), it seems that their
functional equivalence with NPs (*It seems (appears) that he is a serious student*
and *He seems (appears) a serious student*) is taken as evidence of their categorial
status as NPs. *Seem* and *appear* feature also, along with the use of progressive
forms and *as*, in U. Bäcklund's 'Toward "Perfective" Co-Time' (*CdL*).
Bäcklund argues that language-study is 'trapped' in mechanistic linguistics and
must be freed by holistic linguistics, which recognizes the study of language as a
humanistic science. Pertti Hietaranta's consideration of a generous selection of
sentences in 'A Functional Constraint on Topicalization' accepts the view that
topicalized NPs must be either definite or generic, and seeks to account for this
in terms of the Gricean requirement that the referent of the topic be identifiable, associated with the function of the topic to enable the speaker to
preserve the old–new information flow. In 'Another Look at Negatively
Conditioned Subject–Operator Inversion in English', Bengt Jacobsson details
previous works and their proposals, notes the inadequacy of analyses based on
a one-to-one correspondence between inversion and sentence negation, and
non-inversion and constituent negation. He concludes that regularization of
negatively conditioned inversion has been happening for some centuries, and
that it involves both the semantic effect of making the clause non-affirmative
(thus avoiding the undesirable sequence of negative opener plus affirmative
S + V) and the syntactic effect of a closer connection between negative and
verb ('negative attraction' revised, as 'connectedness'). J. W. Ney's (*GL* 1983)
interpretations, and omissions, of earlier works on possible semantic bases for
sequences of prenominal adjectives, as well as his data-analyses, are unpicked
by Lorenz Sichelschmidt's careful piece 'Optionality and Choice in the Analysis
of Adjective Order: Comments on Ney'.

More function, in discourse perspective, in two papers in *SLang*. Taking into
account the relevance of a diachronic view of semantic change, Elizabeth Closs
Traugott's paper 'On the Origins of "and" and "but" Connectives in English'
details an instance of Kronasser's Law (relating to the development of 'logical
connective' meanings from spatial and temporal ones), with respect to listing
connectives (the 'and' type) and contrastive ones (the 'but' type), and posits a
meaning of asymmetry (and temporal sequence) as a fundamental condition for
the development of both types of connectives. These have arisen in English
from spatials, temporals, numerals, and quantifiers: only those terms that

express a proximal–distal or a linear configuration are eligible for selection. Given 'rules' about particle movement to the right of the direct object of a phrasal verb, in accordance with whether the object-type is 'heavy' or not, Ping Chen hypothesizes in 'Discourse and Particle Movement in English', that such movement is more likely in proportion to the 'participant continuity' (i.e. predictability) of the direct object. The analysis of data from two twentieth-century literary sources confirms Paul Hopper's earlier claim that of all object participants (including the particle), the one with the high topicality takes the grammaticalized direct object slot. (I take it that the abrupt end to the final page (93) preceding the bibliography: 'order out of chaos and' is not the intended conclusion?)

Peter Erdmann, 'A Note on Reverse *wh*-Clefts in English' (*Fisiak*[10]), correlates differences between the behaviour of reverse clefts (which may take a variety of *wh*-forms) and that of *wh*-clefts (restricted to *what* and *where*) with function in discourse: reverse clefts focus on something in the immediate context to be treated as topic in the further discourse; the latter focus on something yet to appear, not yet specified. Charles F. Meyer adopts the notion of empathy as relating to the speaker's identification, with varying degrees, with the participant in the event described by the speaker, and investigates three empathy constraints in 'Grammatical and Pragmatic Effects on Empathy Constraints' (*SL*): the ban on conflicting empathy foci, the surface structure empathy hierarchy, and the speech-act participant empathy hierarchy. He formulates a hierarchy of relative strengths of various pragmatic principles: 1. no empathy constraints override obligatory rules of the grammar; 2. all empathy constraints override optional rules of the grammar; 3. empathy constraints apply inconsistently when reacting to other pragmatic principles (here exemplified by principles of end-weight and end-focus), thereby accounting for apparent exceptions to earlier formulations, and providing further welcome systematization in the treatment of empathy as a pragmatic factor. I have not seen Marit R. Westergaard's *Definite NP Anaphora: A Pragmatic Approach* (CUP).

The basis for Richard G. Warner's examination of connectives such as *otherwise*, *but*, *like*, *so*, etc., in *Discourse Connectives in English*[61], is the claim that levels of structure above the sentence are of grammatical interest, and that it is appropriate to adapt the tools of generative semantics at the sentence level. Following a survey of discourse studies to date, structural descriptions of various discourse fragments (here defined as two sentences plus a discourse connective), and derivations for the surface structures, are used to support an analysis of the connectives as realizations of syntactic relations between sentences. Some of the same lexical items are the focus of Herbert Pilch, in 'The Tag Syntagm of Spoken English' (*Fisiak*[10]), where the question 'what is their syntax', as tags, is addressed in terms of dependency relations between tags and nucleus constituents, and of commutation classes and restrictions on compatibility of members of the different classes, with a plea for the inclusion of intonation in a description of the syntax of spoken language. Without turning (as recommended here) to Pilch's earlier work, however, the reader who doesn't 'remember having heard' the intonation types exemplified here

61. *Discourse Connectives in English*, by Richard G. Warner. Garland. pp. 193. $26.

might regret the deliberate lack of explicit formalism in their presentation. GPSG is the model again for Ron Verheijen (see *YW* 66.87), this time for 'A Phrase-Structure Syntax for English *self*-Forms' (*Lings*), in which he distinguishes three types of *self*-forms used non-reflexively (here labelled 'intensifiers' rather than 'emphatics'), as head-bound intensifiers (those inside the NP that also contains their head), as after-Aux intensifiers, and as end (of sentence) intensifiers, and argues for an explicit syntax for English intensifiers.

Eirlys Davies's argument in *The English Imperative*[62] for a class of imperatives as a syntactic class (rather than a verbal category associated with 'mood', or a description of meaning), identifies the imperative's propositional type as presentative (as distinct from declarative and interrogative types) and appropriately stresses the role of pragmatic rather than syntactic explanations for supposed anomalies in the behaviour of imperatives: with respect to e.g. use of the perfect, passive imperatives, distribution of *please* and vocative *someone*, and co-ordinate constructions (see also the final chapter on the *Let* construction). This syntactic class of imperatives is homogeneous, with no motivated subclasses, and may be identified by syntactic properties characterizing imperative constructions: crucially, optionality of subject (and restriction of what subject is possible), their behaviour with respect to whether they need *do* for negation and emphasis (even with *be* or auxiliary *have*). Though affecting to eschew any particular framework, Davies's book consistently eschews the *ad hoc* (and previous treatments of imperatives are both soundly covered and soundly chided for descriptions left unspecified and not general enough), and satisfyingly invokes consistently the notion of contrast (and of the significance of contextual factors), and aims for both the specific and general strong claim.

Rosemarie Gläser enters 'A Plea for Phraseo-Stylistics' (*Fisiak*[10]), meaning that greater emphasis should be placed on the study of lexical units larger than the word. To this end she has produced a textbook on English, *Phraseologie der englischen Sprache*[63], covering idiomatic and non-idiomatic expressions, a syntactic taxonomy of idiom-types, allusions, and conversational routines.

David Banks's 'Getting by with *get*' (*Linguistique*) offers observations on the *get* passive, which ought to have got along with *YW* 66.88. *Ought* in the past has appeared under Vocabulary and Semantics (*YW* 65.58), where works on this verb are seen to be very much alive – and kicking. For the verb itself, however, Martin Harris accepts a more dire, if well-documented, prognosis in a carefully argued and readable attempt to explain its supposed demise in terms of its failure to be fully assimilated to the morphosyntactic class 'auxiliary verb' (note its retention of the *to*-construction), and problems with interrogative and negative structures (hence my inclusion of 'English *ought (to)*' (*Fisiak*[10]) in this section). My only difficulty here, is that my intuitions, and those of others I know, do not see *ought* as 'on its last legs' . . . though perhaps they *should*. Intuitions which do accord with mine (for what those of an albeit partially educated Wagga Wagga lass ought to be worth) support Roger Lass's typically delightful dissection of Raymond Hickey's claims (*SAP*, 1983) for Irish influence as a source for certain Hiberno-English syntactic constructions:

62. *The English Imperative*, by Eirlys Davies. CH. pp. 275. £25.
63. *Phraseologie der englischen Sprache*, by Rosemarie Gläser. Niemeyer. pp. 201. pb DM 24.

constructions used quite happily in varieties of English outwith HE. Lass's claim in '"Irish Influence": Reflections on "Standard" English and its Opposites, and the Identification of Calques' (*SAP*), that contiguity of languages is not necessarily evidence that influence of one of them on the other is responsible for identity of common feature(s), complements that of Nagucka (above), but in this instance, evidence is drawn from Afrikaans structures which, for all they look like possible results of English influence, are attested elsewhere in Germanic languages. American influence is one of the reasons adduced by Åge Lind, in 'The Variant Forms *aim to do/aim at doing*' (*ES*), for the replacement in British English of the latter by the former construction. Other reasons include analogy with verbs used synonymously with *aim*, and the tendency for the more 'purposive' *aim* to take *to*, whereas a more tentative attitude is expressed by *at* + *ing*.

This is a review of works on English syntax, and, as such, focuses primarily on those which aim at elucidating aspects of structure evidenced in present-day and earlier English (while acknowledging that some works escape, including, as well as some already cited, F. R. Palmer's *Mood and Modality* (CUP)). But nothing much can be said about the structure of English (or any language) outwith an explicitly formulated theoretical model. So while the piece I conclude with may be regarded as an exercise in theory, if that is ever considered a drawback for the present audience (cf. the remarks of Stein, above, on theoretical interpretations of linguistic data), the theory it advances has repercussions for many of the recurrent issues in English Language studies. The Structural Analogy Assumption formulated by John M. Anderson in 'Structural Analogy and Case Grammar' (*Lingua*), viz. that 'structural differences between the levels and planes . . . of linguistic representation are severely constrained: . . . we expect the same properties to recur on different levels and planes', hitherto invoked with reference to dependency phonology in *ALH* (1985), supports the strong Case Grammar claims that semantic case relations are syntactically primitive and, as relations, are uniquely basic to the syntax; that basic elements are contrastive; and that only four contrastive case relations need be invoked (the last representing the specifically localist viewpoint). Analogies drawn between the planes of syntax and phonology include: analysis of circumstantial arguments of verbs as stray arguments, so extra-clausal arguments may violate the one-instance-per-clause constraint on CRs, compared with the stray segment convention whereby extra-metrical segments may violate the sonority hierarchy; the possibility of establishing a set of semantic elements appropriate to the description of language, compared with the universal phonetic alphabet; raising as a cyclic structure-changing rule (some delicate un-limbing of the unaccusative hypothesis here) plus the possibility of the same rules applying cyclically and postcyclically, compared with the strict cycle condition in phonology (as formulated by Kiparsky, and here exemplified by trisyllabic shortening). From this exploration of the notion of contrast, a lot is seen (once again, in some instances, for the CG devotee) to be redundant, non-contrastive: notably, assignment of grammatical relations and of phrasal configurations (such as VP), and linearity, are all derivative. Constraints are therefore imposed on individual lexical entries, and on the character of lexical as well as syntactic rules. A theory in which CRs are basic, making available to the syntax semantically characterizable elements, is more tightly constrained than, and so preferable to, any which denies syntax access to concisely delineated, contrastive, semantic relations.

8. Vocabulary and Semantics

Two historical dictionaries passed important milestones in 1986, and there was a flurry of publication, particularly from Germany, on etymology and historical semantics.

(a) Old English

The first fascicle of the *Dictionary of Old English*, covering the letter *D*[64], has now been published in microfiche, keeping the cost reasonable and allowing for running revision of earlier fascicles as later ones come out. Three fiche contain 951 pages of dictionary, while a fourth contains a preface, also provided as a booklet, and the *List of Texts and Index of Editions* previously issued in book form with the two microfiche concordances (*YW* 61.35–6, 65.54). Generous spacing and varied typefaces make the dictionary easier to read than the concordances, and there have been a few improvements of detail over the printed samples already published (*YW* 66.93). Citations, usually untranslated, are plentiful without being overwhelming, and proliferation of subsenses is avoided. Some knowledge of OE is useful, for example to see that *don (to/togædere)* 'to add' in the *don* entry conflates two syntactically different constructions. Readers hardened to existing OE dictionaries will value the consistent policy of registering Latin equivalents in the manuscript, the full indexing of OE material in all major historical, dialect, and place-name dictionaries, and other helpful features of what seems to be a well-planned and well-executed project. Another promising project is discussed in a short contribution by Jane Roberts and Christian Kay, called 'An Old English Thesaurus: A Progress Report' (*MESN*). Words from the field of weaving are used to exemplify connections and continuities not visible in *OED*. The project is both an offshoot of, and a pilot study for, the main *Historical Thesaurus of English* under way at Glasgow.

A number of pieces touch on the Indo-European and Germanic background to English. Patrick Stiles concludes a series of papers with Parts 2 and 3 of 'The Fate of the Numeral "4" in Germanic' (*NOWELE*). There is a shorter piece of numeric philology, 'On the Germanic Decads from "20" to "60" '[65], in which Alfred Bammesberger tries to bring in both ordinals and cardinals, though the latter prove more troublesome. His proposed etymology is Gmc **tegunp-* < pre-Gmc **dekm̥t-*. The same author gives a succinct account of 'The Adjectival Stem **kwikwa-* in Germanic' (*GL*), suggesting that this etymon of OE *cwic* 'alive' was derived by back-formation from the reduplicated ancestor of the verb *cwician*, to replace a regular form without *-k-* (**kwiwa-* < IE **g*^{w}*i(ǝ)-wó-*) which might have fallen in with (for instance) OE *cū* 'cow'. Although Bammesberger and others have taken the glossary word 'Ae. lǣ

64. *Dictionary of Old English*. Fascicle *D*, by Angus Cameron, Ashley Crandell Amos, Antonette diPaolo Healey, Sharon Butler, Joan Holland, David McDougall, and Ian McDougall. PIMS for the Dictionary of Old English project, CMST. 4 fiche. $5.95.

65. In *Germanic Dialects: Linguistic and Philological Investigations*, ed. by Bela Brogyanyi and Thomas Krömmelbein. Benjamins. pp. ix + 693. Fl 215/$86.

"Haupthaar"' to be a ghost word, Karl Toth (*Anglia*) does some lengthy ghost-busting and pronounces it *echt*. In *Sprachwiss* (1985) Lucio Melazzo examines 'Ae. scirde "auctionabatur" ', an entry in the *Corpus Glossary*. After accusing previous scholars of various errors he concludes that the entry in Bosworth-Toller under *sciran* III 'to bring a charge' should be altered to '*löschen*' (whose English equivalent is perhaps 'discharge'). Alan Crozier looks at 'Old West Norse *íþrótt* and Old English *indryhtu*' (*SN*) and denies any connection between them. He would account for the OE noun **indryhtu* and adjective *indryhten* on the basis of an unattested noun **indryht* 'household troop, king's comitatus'. Sherman M. Kuhn makes a magisterial contribution to *JEngL*, 'Old English *macian*, its Origin and Dissemination'. Following up an earlier piece of his which I have been unable to trace (the reference given is spurious), he now uses the *Microfiche Concordance* for late OE and also samples other Germanic languages. He suggests that *macian* 'make' was borrowed into Alfredian OE from Old Saxon, in turn from Old High German. Ever the lexicographer, Kuhn gives citations for many (sub)senses of *macian* and records its distribution by manuscript.

Now for three offerings made to Jacek Fisiak in a Festschrift[10]. Raimo Anttila offers 'An Etymology for the Aquatic "*Acker/Aiker*" in English, and Other Grains of Truth?' What I think Anttila is postulating is two IE roots which have merged and then separated again into, *inter alia*, the *acre* of standard English with its land-based meaning and the dialect word of the title, meaning 'ripple, eddy, etc.' Both are claimed to have a common antecedent with the meaning 'driving' (whether cattle or water). Anttila gallops past *acorn*, *massacre*, and much else in his reference-free discussion. Eric P. Hamp has a note on 'German *Baum*, English *Beam*', which he traces to Gmc **bargmaz* '(high) growth' < IE **bhorǵh-mó-s*. Roger Lass writes incisively on 'Words without Etyma: Germanic "tooth" '. He finds that the consonantal segments can be reconstructed conventionally as IE **dVnt-*, but that vocalism and declension class of Gothic and other Germanic forms cannot imply common descent from a single etymon (in the sense of string of segments).

Michiko Ogura considers 'OE Verbs of Thinking' (*NM*) in a piece very similar in style and layout to her dissertation on impersonals (see section 7 above). Her classification is based on meaning and on the forms of complementation allowed. Ogura suggests that *wenan* was lost because it was used only in one context (with a *þæt*-clause), whereas *þencan* survived because it was the least specific in meaning and in syntactic subcategorization; compare Louis Goossens (*YW* 66.94) on lack of specificity in OE words for speaking. Curiously Ogura does not mention Higuchi's interesting work on the semantics of *wenan* (*YW* 64.64). R. D. Eaton lets us into his confidence on 'Anglo-Saxon Secrets: Rūn and the Runes of the Lindisfarne Gospels' (*ABäG*). He argues that OE *run* does not mean 'secret' and that runes are not in themselves carriers of secrets: both are more to do with literacy and bookishness. Eaton's point is real and his argument nice, and he guesses that it will hold not just for the *Lindisfarne Gospels* but more widely in OE as well. In 'The Old English Alcoholic Vocabulary – A Re-examination' (*DUJ*) Bill Griffiths gives a learned but inconclusive survey, spending most of his time on *beor* and *ealu*. Jürgen Strauss's discussion of 'Concepts, Fields, and "Non-Basic" Lexical Items' (*Fisiak*[10]) concerns the relationship between lexical fields and conceptual fields. Brief consideration of some OE and ME fields is used to argue against componential analysis of their non-basic members. In the same volume Torben Thrane does careful, detailed work 'On Delimiting the Senses of Near-Synonyms in Historical Semantics: A Case-Study of Adjectives of "Moral Sufficiency" in the Old English *Andreas'*. Thrane homes in on adjectives whose meaning depends explicitly or otherwise on the þegn:þeoden relation. Altogether an interesting exercise.

(b) Middle English

The *Middle English Dictionary*[66] issued three 128-page parts in 1986 compared to four in 1985, ending up at *sē* 'sea'. Can the project be completed this decade? Progress remains slow but steady.

Lister M. Matheson points out that '*Licere*: A Ghost Word in the *Middle English Dictionary*' (*N&Q*) arose from a typo in a text edition whereby ð dropped out of *swiðlicere*. Hans Peters supplements *MED*'s citations for 'Middle English *fals*' (*Archiv*), in order to show that most extensions of meaning from its purely legal use in OE had already taken place in early ME, probably as a result of both Anglo-Latin influence and indigenous development. In the same journal Stephen Morrison looks at 'Early Middle English *oferrswifenn*' − a spelling which makes obvious which text it occurs in. Morrison identifies Orm's source for the passage concerned and infers that Orm wanted an equivalent for Latin *vincere*. His word is based on the common OE *oferswiðan*, Morrison decides, but modified because of homonymic clash with a Norse borrowing, ME *(for)swipen* 'burn'. John A. Rea has a note on 'Foxfire' in *ELN*, arguing unconvincingly that it is based on an Old French spelling *fox* for ModF *fou* 'fool, foolish'. Michael Murphy adds 'More on *quaint* and *quondam* Words' (*AS*) to the speculations of Zacharias P. Thundy on 'The Etymology of *condom*' (*AS*, 1985). (The latter went unnoticed last year in the welter of publicity about AIDS.) W. F. Bolton finds some 'Middle English in the Law Reports and Records of 11−13 Richard II' (*ELN*), using occasional English words within French and Latin texts to antedate *OED* and even *MED* (e.g. *doublet* 'counterfeit jewel').

Michael Peverett argues that ' "Quod" and "seide" in *Piers Plowman*' (*NM*) are not synonymous. *Quod*, he claims, is equivalent to *seide panne* in that it emphasizes the act of speaking, whereas *seide* draws attention to what is said.

Only three pieces rise above this mass of fine detail, and two are largely descriptive. Xavier Dekeyser's 'Romance Loans in Middle English: A Reassessment' (*Fisiak*[10]) (of counts done by Jespersen and Baugh) is a statistical exercise based on 2,250 items in *MED*, contrasting native words with words derived from French, Latin, or both. Dekeyser offers generally greater precision, for instance dating the beginning of a decline in French borrowing to the last quarter of the fourteenth century. K. E. M. George presents 'Forenames as Common Nouns in English and French' (*SN*) in the form of a long list split into conceptual categories like fool, rogue, profession, parts of the body. There are some remarks on tendencies shown by the data, especially parallels between English and French. More fundamental questions are addressed by Elizabeth Closs Traugott, who offers interesting speculations 'On

---

66. *Middle English Dictionary*. Parts *R.6* and *S.1-2*. Editor-in-chief Robert E. Lewis, review editor John Reidy. UMich.

the Origins of "and" and "but" Connectives in English' (*SLang*) in iconic terms. A closed-field relation involves face to face interaction, whereas an open-field type involves objects facing the same way and with no final barrier: one or other of these configurations must be present in the meaning of a term for it to be able to become a contrastive (e.g. *but*, *yet*, *while*) or listing (e.g. *and*, *then*, *again*) connective.

(c) Modern and Present-Day English

The major contribution to the study of English vocabulary is the fourth and final volume of the new *Supplement* to *OED*[67] (earlier volumes reviewed in *YW* 53.38, 57.16, 63.38), edited by R. W. Burchfield. Since further praise is superfluous, some minor deficiencies can be illustrated from two examples. The *theta-* or *θ-role* of Chomskian linguistics is ignored (though a meaning for *theta* within Scientology is generously exemplified), conceivably reflecting a contempt for contemporary linguistics aired in Dr Burchfield's recent book (*YW* 66.59) and again at irrelevant length in the *Supplement* preface. Although *up* 'in working condition' (of a computer) is recorded, the obvious cross-reference to (*gone*) *down* 'not working' is absent, presumably because that sense of *down* did not get into Volume I. The unhelpful distinction of two separate adverbs *up* is inherited from the parent work, together with the idiosyncratic pronunciation key, and of course much that is excellent. When *Supplement* and *OED* have been merged into one electronic database (see *YW* 66.99–100) with cross-references complete, the possibility of sorting other than just alphabetically, and continual updating – *what* a research tool we will have then. But in the meantime, carping aside, the *Supplement* in its beautiful printed form is a magnificent piece of work.

Two other Oxford dictionaries have undergone Alice-like transformations of size. *The Concise Oxford Dictionary of English Etymology*[68], edited by T. F. Hoad, is both shorter than and an improvement in detail upon its parent work (*YW* 47.46) edited by C. T. Onions. Onions also first produced *A Shakespeare Glossary* as long ago as 1911, and an enlarged edition is now offered by Robert D. Eagleson[69], tapping modern scholarship and modern technical aids to ensure greater precision and comprehensiveness. This helpful work now gives at least one quotation for every entry and offers fuller cross-referencing.

The minutiae of lexicography this year include the usual lists in *N&Q*: P. J. Gabriner's splendidly ambiguous 'Antedatings, Postdatings, and Additions from Pope's Translation of the *Iliad* for *OED*'; R. R. Dunn's 'Additions to *OED* from William Camden's *Remains* 1605, 1614, 1623'; R. W. McConchie's (mere six) 'Further Additions to *OED* from John Cotta's *Ignorant Practisers of Physicke* (1612)'; and the appropriately named E. W. Pitcher on '*Moonshine* "illicit spirit" in *OED*'.

Klaus Dietz makes a detailed study of 'Modern English *cruive* "wicker salmon-trap" ' (*Fisiak*[10]) a dialect word found in Scotland and elsewhere. His

67. *A Supplement to the Oxford English Dictionary*. Vol. IV: *Se–Z*, ed. by R. W. Burchfield. Clarendon. pp. xxiii + 1409 + 45. £90.

68. *The Concise Oxford Dictionary of English Etymology*, ed. by T. F. Hoad. Clarendon. pp. xvi + 552. £13.95.

69. *A Shakespeare Glossary*, by C. T. Onions. Third edn enlarged and rev. by Robert D. Eagleson. Clarendon. pp. xvii + 326. hb £17.50, pb £5.95.

(admittedly incomplete) etymology brings in Old Irish *cró* and Old Norse *kró*. David L. Gold writes 'Still More on the Origin of New York City English *Sliding Pond*' (*LB*), a term for a children's slide which is likely to be a partial calque of Dutch *glijbaan*. Much of the piece is a complaint about unfair treatment by Marge E. Landsberg of his previous contributions, bringing to light a squabble hitherto neglected by *YWES* (see *AS*, 1981; *LB*, 1984, 1985).

Knud Sørensen considers the change 'Phrasal Verb into Noun' (*NM*) which produces words like *comedown, lockout*. As his title implies, verbal combinations usually precede nominal ones, though in some cases it is apparently the noun which comes first. The discussion moves fluently from one topic to another and offers much interesting information, though not a systematic treatment. Garland Cannon has a methodical piece on 'Blends in English Word Formation' (*Lings*), mainly a survey of scholarly literature and an analysis of 132 (written English) blends like *chunnel, stagflation* culled from recent dictionaries (actually most of them are American). Cannon concludes a long contribution with the announcement that blending, however frequent a source of short-lived neologisms, is a very unimportant element in word formation. I have not seen the same author's monograph on *Historical Change and English Vocabulary* (Lang).

Pejorative semantic change is the subject of Grzegorz Kleparski's monograph[70]. A brief survey of work on semantic change (Traugott's recent research is missing) is followed by a rather plodding analysis of such words as *harlot, knave, knight*. Meanings abstracted from dictionary citations (and beware, 'M.E.' here means 'Modern English') are translated into componential analyses, and developments from one set of features to another are then described in the terms of Rolf Berndt's *History of the English Language*[71] (a book which seems to have escaped *YWES*'s net). A process which can lead to pejoration is euphemism, the subject of an interesting compilation by D. J. Enright, *Fair of Speech*[72]. Among the (mostly serious) contributions, the most academic in approach is Robert Burchfield's 'An Outline History of Euphemisms in English'. Burchfield apologizes that a definitive treatment is impossible because of the alphabetic organization of dictionaries, though he covers a surprising amount of ground and gives copious illustrations. Perhaps he will revise his already worthwhile paper when the tools become available.

Your reviewer for the rest of this section (Coates) is not a specialist in semantics or lexicology. What follows is a stopgap report on some writings published in 1986 on (mainly) present-day English vocabulary, semantics, and discourse/text phenomena. Where the intentions of a book or article appear to me to be entirely theoretical, even if based entirely on English-language data, I have usually disqualified it from mention. No works having a principally comparative intention are covered. Items that actually appear here are eye-catchers, and mention of them in these pages in itself implies no value-judgement.

70. *Semantic Change and Componential Analysis: An Inquiry into Pejorative Developments in English*, by Grzegorz Kleparski. Pustet. pp. 112. pb DM 32.

71. *A History of the English Language*, by Rolf Berndt. Enzyklopädie (1982). pp. 240. M 25.

72. *Fair of Speech: The Uses of Euphemism*, ed. by D. J. Enright. OUP (1985). pp. vi + 222. hb £9.95, pb (1986) £4.95.

Facets, Phases and Foci[73] is an investigation whose point turns on the relations of hyponymy holding between lexical items and their morphological derivatives, and in passing useful attempts are made to bring order into the chaos of such problems as how to decide whether a particular lexical relation is one of polysemy or homonymy. The book is yet another example of the painstaking attention to lexical detail that is the hallmark of Scandinavian English studies. Lexical relations are the implicit subject matter of Leonhard Lipka's 'Semantic Features and Prototype Theory in English Lexicology' (*Fisiak* [10]).

Jaap Hoepelman's *Action, Comparison and Change*[74] presents a formal-semantic account of verbs and adjectives which he claims allows him to achieve a clear characterization of the notion of comparison. Adjectives also feature as the topic of Boris Hlebec's 'Sources of Shared Polysemy in English Spatial Adjectives' (*SAP*), in which parallel development in antonyms each of which is polysemous is charted. In the same journal, Michał Post argues ('On the Semantic Indeterminacy of Denominal Adjectives') that denominal derivation is accompanied by only a crude semantic specification, and that identifiable pragmatic principles contribute the detail of the meaning of the derivative. He has a piece on a related topic in *Fisiak* [10]. Adjectives are also the topic of Edna Andrews's 'A Synchronic Semantic Analysis of *de-* and *un-* in American English' (*AS*).

The collection edited by Gunnel Tottie and Ingegerd Bäcklund, entitled *English in Speech and Writing*[75], includes four papers contrasting written and spoken realizations of a variety of categories (conjunctions, verbless clauses introduced by a conjunction, modals, and focusing adverbials), and four essentially on the spoken usage of four individual (or small groups of) lexical items (*actually*, you know). A final paper deals with improvements in the quality and utility of elicited speech. The immediate ancestor of PrEONLY features also in Terttu Nevalainen's 'The Development of Preverbal *Only* in Early Modern English' (*Diversity and Diachrony*[35]).

Major works on individual lexical items include an entire monograph on the semantics of TURN by Marijke van Remortël (*Literalness and Metaphorization: The Case of 'Turn'*[76]). Metaphor is also the topic of Dumitru Chitoran's contribution to *Fisiak* [10] entitled 'Metaphor in the English Lexicon: The Verb'. Smaller pieces include the identification of OE *'Undergytan* as a "Winchester" Word' by Shigeru Ono (*Fisiak* [10]), while in the same work, Alfred Bammesberger reflects 'On Old English *gefrægnod* in Beowulf 1333a', arguing that the archetype cannot have had this particular form.

The semantics of items of the present-day language are discussed in *Fisiak* [10] by James P. Thorne ('Because') and Johan van der Auwera ('The Possibilities of *May* and *Can*'). The same pair of lexical items are also discussed by Merja

73. *Facets, Phases and Foci: Studies in Lexical Relations in English*, by Ulf Magnusson and Gunnar Persson. AUU (distr. A&W). pp. v + 308. pb Skr 127/£13.

74. *Action, Comparison and Change: A Study in the Semantics of Verbs and Adjectives*, by Jaap Hoepelman. Niemeyer. pp. vi + 194. pb DM 64.

75. *English in Speech and Writing: A Symposium*, ed. by Gunnel Tottie and Ingegerd Bäcklund. AUUp (distr. A*W). pp. 204. pb £11.

76. *Literalness and Metaphorization: The Case of 'Turn'*, by Marijke van Remortël. UAntwerp. pp. 130. pb Bfr 150.

Kytö in 'On the Use of the Modal Auxiliaries *Can* and *May* in Early American English', who shows increasing encroachment of *can* on the contexts formerly occupied by *may*, which she claims to have been the unmarked member of the pair in earlier times (*Diversity and Diachrony*[35]). The quasi-auxiliary 'English *ought* (*to*)' is the subject of Martin Harris's contribution to *Fisiak*[10]. In *LingI* Jaakko Hintikka explores 'The Semantics of *A Certain*', concluding that the popular view that it must have wider scope than other quantifiers in the same clause is unfounded. Fred Shapiro extols the usefulness of online databases in attempts to trace the first uses and etymological origins of recent lexical innovations ('Yuppies, Yumpies, Yaps and Computer-Assisted Lexicology' (*AS*)).

The relation between the English lexicon and that of other languages is explored most prominently in Yoshio Terasawa's 'Hebrew Loan-Words in English' (*Fisiak*[10]).

A new major dictionary also bills itself as unique in several ways. Collins's *COBUILD English Language Dictionary*[77], based on the B(irmingham) U(niversity) I(nternational) L(anguage) D(atabase), flaunts its reliance on 'real' English, i.e. English from sources written (to a historical linguist's eye) within the last twenty-four hours (David Lodge [the Brum connection?], Tom Sharpe, Robert M. Pirsig . . .). It also innovates by expressing its definitions in sentences containing the word to be defined and at least one main verb, which is presumably to endear it to foreigners (especially) and others perplexed by the average dictionary's battery of technical and other abbreviations in the text of the entries and its unrelenting nominal style. Another unique dictionary is *The BBI Combinatory Dictionary of English*, pedestrianly subtitled *A Guide to Word Combinations*[78]. An uncharitable reviewer could describe it as a list of clichés or fixed expressions; a more discerning one will note that it is an invaluable tool for foreign learners for whom the search for idiomaticity in fluent speech is (along with native-like intonation) the last hurdle to jump in second language learning. Here is a sizeable cohort of all the collocations they could ever have wished to know; and it is also a useful database for those theoreticians interested – as I am – in the gradient between expression-coining and the fixity of idiom and the implications of this gradient for the nature of the mental lexicon; a surprising winner.

Other dictionaries not mentioned in the historical section above include Máiri Robinson's *The Concise Scots Dictionary*[79] and Adrian Room's brantubs for the general reader, *Dictionary of True Etymologies*[80] and *Dictionary of Changes in Meaning*[81]. Preparatory studies for dictionaries include Thomas L. Clark's 'Cheating Terms in Cards and Dice' and Thomas E. Murray's 'The Language of Naval Fighter Pilots' (both in *AS*).

77. *Collins COBUILD English Language Dictionary*, ed. by J. Sinclair. Collins. pp. 1728. pb £12.95.

78. *The BBI Combinatory Dictionary of English: A Guide to Word Combinations*, by Morton Benson, Evelyn Benson, and Robert Ilson. Benjamins. pp. xxxvi + 286. pb $20.

79. *The Concise Scots Dictionary*, ed. by Máiri Robinson. AberdeenU (1985). pp. xli + 320. £17.50.

80. *Dictionary of True Etymologies*, ed. by Adrian Room. RKP. pp. 193. £11.95.

81. *Dictionary of Changes in Meaning*, ed. by Adrian Room. RKP. pp. 292. £16.45.

The second volume of *Lexicographica* has as its thematic section twelve papers on a variety of issues concerning bilingual dictionaries. The non-thematic part is entirely concerned with German lexicography except Robert Ilson's paper on 'General English Dictionaries for Foreign Learners'. The same author reports on the Fulbright colloquium on lexicography held at Bedford College, London in 1984.

On the text front: Gerhard Leitner explores 'Reporting the "Events of the Day": Uses and Functions of Reported Speech' (*SAP*). Volume IX, number 1 of *Ling&P* is devoted to various theoretical approaches to the description of 'Tense and Aspect in Discourse'. Douglas Biber compares 'Spoken and Written Textual Dimensions in English: Resolving the Contradictory Findings' (*Lang*). His multidimensional analysis provides a far more sensitive matrix (of forty-one features) than has been achieved before within which to assess the relation between the two media. He criticizes earlier work for jumping to conclusions on the basis of grossly insufficient evidence, but takes pains to render their findings compatible with his own. Sung-Yun Bak argues, in assessing 'The Syntax and Semantics of the *There* Construction in English' (*LangR*), that the grammaticality or otherwise of the construction is pragmatically determined, but I do not find his argument easy to evaluate as the paper is in Korean. I conclude this brief survey by making an exception to my 'no comparative papers' rule by drawing attention to Senko K. Maynard's 'On Back-Channel Behavior in Japanese and English Casual Conversation' (*Lings*), where the author isolates grammatical completion as the single most important context in English eliciting back-channel activity; Japanese auditors, on the other hand, are sensitive to a much wider range of cues.

Finally, there is an interesting little paper on lexical matters in *Fisiak*[10] which is hard to find paragraph-mates for. Matti Rissanen scrutinizes 'Middle English Translations of Old English Charters in the *Liber Monasterii de Hyda*: A Case of Historical Error Analysis'; and shows just how wide was the cultural and linguistic gulf between the compiler of the *Liber de Hyda* and his ME translator.

9. Onomastics

There are no new major academic books on English place-names in 1986, but two familiar texts go to revised editions: *The Names of Towns and Cities in Britain*[82] and *Compliment and Commemoration in English Field-Names*[83]. A. D. Mills has brought out a popular book based on the research for his not yet complete EPNS survey of Dorset[84]. Name-change was the topic of the 1986 Bamberg symposium (*BN*), to which John Insley contributed a paper representing the English language, 'Ortsnamen und Besitzwechsel im Altenglischen und Mittelenglischen'.

Place-name pieces in *Nomina* this year include Denise Kenyon's study on

82. *The Names of Towns and Cities in Britain*, rev. edn by Margaret Gelling, W. F. H. Nicolaisen, and Melville Richards. Batsford. pp. 216. pb £7.95.

83. *Compliment and Commemoration in English Field-Names*, rev. second edn by John Field. Dacorum. pb.

84. *Dorset Place-Names: Their Origins and Meanings*, by A. D. Mills. Gasson. pp. 192. pb £3.95.

'The Antiquity of *hām* Place-Names in Lancashire and Cheshire'. She argues, in line with current thinking on names elsewhere in England, that *ham* does indeed represent a very early usage, but considers that it could have been in use as late as the eighth century in remoter parts of the northern kingdoms. The same writer's 'Notes on Lancashire Place-Names 1: The Early Names' (*JEPNS*) is a wider discussion of early naming patterns in the light of modern theorizing. Another survey of element distributions is Jennifer Scherr's 'Names of Springs and Wells in Somerset' (*Nomina*).

There are two discussions of name-elements. F. M. Griffith suggests, in *Nomina*, that archaeological evidence may represent the only hope of telling apart *'Burh* and *Beorg* in Devon' or elsewhere, and Richard Coates argues in *JEPNS* 'Towards an Explanation of the Kentish – *mondens*', suggesting that an OE **munddenn* 'protected swinepasture' is involved in such names as *Spelmonden*. Etymological pieces on individual names include Richard Coates's '*Mendip*' (*Nomina*), where the second element is taken to be OE *yppe*; Gillis Kristensson's 'The Place-Name *Scugger Ho* (Cumberland)' (*N&Q*), interpreted as 'goblin-marsh houses'; and Paul Coones's 'Euroclydon: A Biblical Place-Name' (*JEPNS*). There is a nice little piece by David L. Shores in *AS* entitled '*Porchmouth* for *Portsmouth*' (the one in Virginia); the non-standard pronunciation has a wider social distribution than its users would care to admit. A real place-name provides an analogical source for a literary one, according to a somewhat laboured argument by Peter J. Lucas. 'Hautdesert in Sir Gawain and the Green Knight' (*Neophil*) is based on *Beaudesert*, the Bishop of Lichfield's palace in Staffordshire. Bang up to date is Karen Koegler's analysis of possible names for one's des. res., 'A Farewell to Arms: The "Greening" of American Apartment Names' (*Names*).

Well to the fore this year is the question of the critical evaluation of sources of ideas about place-names. In *Nomina* John Freeman has a very cautionary piece, 'Some Place-Names of Archenfield and the Golden Valley Recorded in the Balliol Herefordshire Domesday', showing the existence of a period of unstable naming in the eleventh century; while Frank Thorn's 'The Identification of Domesday Places in the South-Western Counties of England' is an eloquent plea for a more critical approach to the problem of identification. The same topic is the subject matter of P. S. Keate's 'Comments on the Location of Some of the Forms in *PN Worcs* pp. 293–303 (Halesowen and its Townships)' (*JEPNS*), where numerous identification errors in the Place-Name Society's volume for that county are exposed. A piece where the intellectual current is in the opposite direction is Joseph P. Crowley's 'The Study of Old English Dialects' (*ES*); Crowley discusses the use of place-names as evidence in dialectology (see Section 5). In this vein, Gillis Kristensson identifies 'A Middle English Dialect Boundary' in the West Midlands, that of the eastern extent of ⟨a⟩ for the *i*-umlaut of **a* before *l* + a consonant, on the basis of onomastic evidence (*Fisiak* [10]), a familiar theme of the author's.

There is a good deal of anthroponymic material for the year in question. I shall omit detailed discussion of the majority, for it is not about names as linguistic objects, but about their social distribution and interpretation. Several articles in *Names, Human Biology, Annals of Human Biology*, and *Sex Roles* cover such topics, and mentions of them can be recovered by interested readers from the Bibliography in *Nomina*. The use of 'Forenames as Common Nouns in English and French' is the subject of a paper by K. E. M. George in *SN*. But the only piece of the year on the etymology of a specifically English personal name is Judith Weise's 'The Meaning of the Name *Hygd*: Onomastic Contrast in *Beowulf*' (*Names*). She argues in this essentially literary piece that this name alone among the one-element names in *Beowulf* is a creation of the poet. (Norbert Wagner discusses 'Das Erstglied von *Ludwig*' in *BN*, which will be of interest to consumers of the previous item.) Of considerable onomastic interest also is David Dumville's study of 'The West Saxon Genealogical Regnal List: Manuscripts and Texts' (*Anglia*); this is the first critical edition of this very important text. It is a companion piece to the same author's 'The West Saxon Genealogical Regnal List and the Chronology of Early Wessex' (*Peritia* (1985, but only just published)). Veronica Smart publishes a survey of 'Scandinavians, Celts and Germans in Anglo-Saxon England: The Evidence of Moneyers' Names'[85], pointing out the perils attending conclusions based on the sometimes highly equivocal inscriptions on coins. Using the evidence of 'Devon Locative Surnames in the Fourteenth Century' (*Nomina*), Margaret Camsell demonstrates that by the time of the Subsidies there had been no substantial movement of people to places far away from their place of origin, at least in rural districts.

As for names in the modern contemporary language, Arthur Scherr has studied 'Change-of-Name Petitions of the New York Courts: An Untapped Source in Historical Onomastics' (*Names*). His chief interest is in the motivations for the adoption of new given names and surnames, which include would-be English ethnicity, and family and pecuniary advantage (or in short, status). Returning to a theme which he pursued several years ago in relation to the male sex, Edwin D. Lawson teams up with Lynn M. Roeder to investigate 'Women's Full First Names, Short Names, and Affectionate Names: A Semantic Differential Analysis' (also in *Names*). They find that female names are in general evaluated further from supposedly 'positive' values of certain personality attributes than those of males; and that men and women appear to suffer from different stereotypical perceptions of names (e.g. affectionate names go down less well, in relation to personality traits, among women than among men). Some fairly predictable psychological speculation ensues. Finally, Philip M. Shaw has a piece in *AS* entitled 'Factors Affecting the Formation of Citizen-Names in the United States': there are some sensible observations on the complicated machinery involved in the creation and selection processes.

10. Stylistics

Roger Fowler's *Linguistic Criticism*[86] provides a useful starting point for a survey of 1986 publications in stylistics. As the title of the book suggests, the ideas, arguments, and techniques developed are rooted firmly in the 'critical linguistics' tradition. In keeping with his own earlier work, Fowler uses linguistic techniques in an interpretative way, as a means of uncovering the value-systems and sets of beliefs that underlie texts. Although the emphasis in the book is on works commonly designated 'literary', the author argues that the

---

85. In *Anglo-Saxon Monetary History: Essays in Memory of Michael Dolley*, ed. by M. A. S. Blackburn. LeicU. pp. 384. £35.

86. *Linguistic Criticism*, by Roger Fowler. OUP. pp. 190. hb £12.50, pb £4.95.

methods employed may be applied more generally. Literature, from this perspective, is viewed as just one kind of creative use of language, and linguistic criticism 'may be practised on any use of language'. Much of the theoretical direction in *Linguistic Criticism* is provided by developments in Prague School structuralism and Russian formalist criticism (notably Victor Shklovsky's notions of *habitualization* and *defamiliarization*), whilst the analytic tool-kit is derived mainly from systemic-functional linguistics. This is much in evidence in Fowler's analyses of cohesion, transitivity, and lexicalization in a variety of texts ranging from the poetry of Keats to Dashiel Hammett's *The Maltese Falcon*. If there is a criticism to be made of the book, it is one that has been voiced elsewhere in relation to the theoretical stance adopted by critical linguists: namely, that their deterministic view of language is not easily reconciled with their functional explanation of linguistic structure. This last point aside, *Linguistic Criticism* is vigorously argued and presents an excellent demonstration of the critical-linguistic technique.

Some of the topics covered in *Linguistic Criticism* have also been the subject of a number of publications in journals this year. In the course of his book, Roger Fowler provides a lucid (and much needed) critique of Jakobson's famous definition of the 'poetic function' in language. The notion of the poetic function also forms the basis of Ruth Ronen's 'Poetical Coherence in Literary Prose' (*Style*). Ronen reformulates and extends Jakobson's definition in order to account for the literary quality of narrative prose. Supporting her argument with examples from Flaubert and Austen, she contends that, in the specific case of literary prose, the poetic function interacts with the referential function in the organization of language. Another ramification of *Linguistic Criticism* concerns the critical-linguistic analysis of non-literary texts. Early in the book, Fowler illustrates how ideological slanting is created in three newspaper reports and media language is also the subject of scrutiny in an article by Gunther Kress, another leading exponent of the critical linguistics approach. In 'Language in the Media: The Construction of the Domains of Public and Private' (*MC&S*), Kress attempts to document the ideological and political forces which are articulated in media texts. Adopting what is almost standard methodology, he analyses two Australian news reports which describe the same event and argues that in one report the event is constructed in terms of a 'private' domain, while in the other, it is constructed in terms of a 'public' domain. Kress then extends the analysis to other genres, such as radio phone-ins, letters to problem pages, and advertisements. The last of these forms the basis of another stylistic analysis of non-literary texts. Donald D. Hook, in 'Spitzer and Key Revisited: The Artfulness of Advertising' (*Lang&S*), provides a rather impressionistic commentary on an advertisement for cognac. ('What is advertising language like? Is it unique? No, in fact it is rather old-fashioned and commonplace.') Although some reference is made to 'the grammar of the text', neither the ideological structure nor the interactive aspects of advertising are touched upon.

In a somewhat different vein, although crucially linked to more general questions of style, is Walter Nash's *English Usage*[87]. In a handbook that deals

87. *English Usage: A Guide to First Principles*, by Walter Nash. RKP. pp. xiii + 167. hb £24.95, pb £4.95.

primarily with written usage, Nash offers a clear – and thoroughly entertaining – guide to some of the stylistic choices that are available to users of English. The orientation is towards communicative, rather than social, acceptability in language and, as such, Nash considers his own stance to be neither descriptive nor prescriptive but 'constructive'. The first and last chapters of the book deal with questions of usage in the general context of language and society, and provide some incisive criticisms of venerated 'authorities' on language. The second chapter explores some of the principal resources of English grammar in relation to questions of style, while Chapter Three contains some 'prescriptions' (in actuality, a set of recommendations) on stylistic practice. The fourth and fifth chapters deal with 'options' and 'punctuations' respectively. Nash supports his argument with examples from a variety of contexts, ranging from the vivid lexical innovations of the author's mother to some of the more opaque passages from 'quality' newspapers. The question of English usage is also taken up in H. Michael Buck's 'Final Free Modifiers: Characteristic of Preferred Style?' (*Lang&S*). In an informant-based analysis, Buck examines the subjective responses of readers to sentence-final non-restrictive structures such as participle and appositive groups and clauses. He concludes that a majority of educated readers are more favourably predisposed towards this type of free-modifier construction than to more 'traditional' simple, compound, and complex sentence structures.

A number of publications in journals this year were concerned with grammatically based stylistic analysis. Of these, two were addressed specifically to tense and aspect in fiction. Bernard Comrie, in 'Tense and Time Reference: From Meaning to Interpretation in the Chronological Structure of a Text' (*JLS*), argues that the chronological interpretation of verb forms in a text is much richer than the context-independent meaning of the verb forms themselves. Working from a short piece of constructed fiction exhibiting a variety of tenses, he demonstrates how different tense forms assume different discourse functions depending, in part, on features of the context, and, in part, on features of the verb. Comrie's argument, although based on the analysis of introspective data, has important implications for the analysis of tense in a variety of text types. An article which presents views not incompatible with those of Comrie – and which draws on some of Comrie's definitions – is Carl Bache's 'Tense and Aspect in Fiction' (*JLS*). Bache proposes a distinction between 'the normal referring mode of communication' and 'the fictional mode of communication' and contends that the grammatical categories of tense and aspect are suspended in the fictional mode. He suggests that this 'category suspension' is evidence of the way in which a stylistic analysis can uncover textual functions which necessitate the modification of grammatical rules. The mediative role of stylistics is also at the forefront of Timothy R. Austin's '(In)Transitives: Some Thoughts on Ambiguity in Poetic Texts' (*JLS*). Austin stresses the importance of the study of ambiguity to both linguists and literary critics and proposes that stylistics should provide a useful interpretative bridge between the two fields. Having provided a detailed transformational-generative analysis of three lines from Shelley's *The Revolt of Islam*, Austin goes on to consider how the results of his analysis would be evaluated from the perspectives of both Empson-influenced literary criticism and orthodox Chomskian linguistics. Poetic texts are also the focus of Colleen Donnelly's 'The Syntactic Counterplot of the Devils' Debates and God's Council'

(*Lang&S*). Acknowledging that, in Miltonic poetry, the speeches of the devils are often more entertaining and compelling than the speeches of the council of heaven, Donnelly seeks to demonstrate that a 'syntactic counterplot' is established in the language of the devils wherein 'the syntactic structure of the sentences . . . work[s] to counter the enticements offered on the semantic level'. The evidence offered in support of this claim is comprehensive, although the general argument is not assisted by numerous comments which conflate linguistic description with more aesthetically motivated responses ('God's language is forthright, truthful, and perlocutionary'). Paul M. Hedeen, in 'Moving in the Picture: The Landscape Stylistics of *In Our Time*' (*Lang&S*), puts forward a highly imaginative, if somewhat tenuous, thesis on the influence of Cézanne on Hemingway's prose style. In an argument that presupposes an exact correspondence between verbal and visual art, Hedeen attempts to demonstrate how the positioning of syntactic elements in certain passages from *In Our Time* generates 'verbal landscapes', landscapes which exhibit the same kind of depth, distance, and space as the paintings of Paul Cézanne. Sentence construction is also of primary concern in P. N. Furbank and W. R. Owens's 'Defoe and the "Improvisatory" Sentence' (*ES*), although this article tends to promise more than it delivers. Despite references to Defoe's 'remarkable syntactic resourcefulness' and 'most beautifully organized and articulated' sentences, all that we are told by way of definition is that 'the effort of the improvisatory sentence is devoted to postponing the end – and what is more, postponing the decision as to how it shall end'.

Turning now to prosodic analyses of poetic texts, two articles merit some comment. Richard D. Cureton, in 'Traditional Scansion: Myths and Muddles' (*JLS*), is highly critical of what he terms traditional methods of foot-substitution scansion. Having isolated seven major failings of the traditional approach, he goes on to propose 'hierarchical phrasal scansion' as an alternative model that can unify the description of rhythmic structuring across literary genres. In 'Punctuation, Contrastive Emphasis, and New Information in the Prosody of Jonson's Poetry' (*Lang&S*), Michael McCanles draws on work on the relation between intonation and meaning in order to demonstrate how Jonson's unusual punctuation articulates significant contrastive emphases in his poetry.

Metaphor and simile are the subject of three articles in *JLS* this year. In 'Some Semantic Features of Cause and Effect Metaphors', Don Jobe claims that standard definitions of 'synecdoche' and 'metonymy' are inadequate as they oversimplify complex symbolization processes, and he outlines a 'general symbolization rule' as a criterion for defining all types of metaphor. Alan Bailin, in 'Metaphorical Extension', examines the effect of a metaphorical interpretation on the extension of words and phrases, supporting his argument with examples of both 'everyday' utterances and utterances from literary texts. Neal R. Norrick's 'Stock Similes' provides an illuminating account of the types of simile that recur regularly in the texts of a linguistic community. Isolating the structural properties of 'object', 'tertium', and 'vehicle', Norrick explores the various textual functions of stock similes and notes how humour can be created through a manipulation of these structures.

In the area of narrative analysis, Russell A. Hunt and Douglas Vipond provide an account of 'Evaluations in Literary Reading' (*Text*). Drawing in part on Labov's work on natural narrative, they identify three types of evaluation in literary narrative: 'discourse evaluations', 'story evaluations', and 'telling evaluations' (although the boundaries between these categories do not appear to be all that discrete). Narrative is also the focus of attention in a special issue of *Poetics*, of which two articles are of particular relevance to stylistics. P. Bange's 'Towards a Pragmatic Analysis of Narratives in Literature' and Wolf-Dieter Stempel's 'Everyday Narrative as a Prototype' both display an interest in the relationship between 'everyday' communication and 'literary' communication. Bange focuses on semiotic and pragmatic aspects of narrative and attempts to solve some of the specific problems associated with literary narratives (genre, fictionality, the role of the narrator), whilst Stempel assesses the differences between oral and literary narratives and suggests how a categorical boundary between the two may be drawn.

Turning now to the representation of speech and thought in texts, Monika Fludernik, in 'The Dialogic Imagination of Joyce: Form and Function of Dialogue in *Ulysses*' (*Style*), undertakes a statistical analysis of the techniques Joyce uses to record characters' utterances. Not intending the term 'dialogic' in the Bakhtinian sense, Fludernik concentrates solely on how the various modes of speech presentation are deployed in the novel. Although the formidable corpus of data restricts her to only a general survey of tendencies, a number of useful observations are made. (Did you know that dialogue makes up 26.8% of the text of *Ulysses*?) Rainer Warning's 'Reading Irony in Flaubert' (*Style*) also deals with modes of speech presentation, focusing on Flaubert's use of free indirect speech as a means of creating irony. In an argument which echoes that presented by Roy Pascal in *The Dual Voice* (1977), Warning contends that FIS creates a discourse in which both character and narrator have a role, thereby opening up 'a wide range of ironic enunciation masquerading as authorial narrative'.

In the general area of discourse stylistics, a number of articles emerge which draw on pragmatic models of analysis. Kripa K. Gautam and Manjula Sharma, in 'Dialogue in *Waiting for Godot* and Grice's Concept of Implicature' (*MD*), seek to demonstrate how the verbal exchanges between Beckett's characters help to create a 'situation of existential despair'. Although they highlight some interesting examples of how characters violate and flout maxims and how breaches in the Co-operative Principle are achieved in the play, the analysis of drama texts within a framework of Gricean implicature is a well-tilled field in discourse stylistics. Speech-act theory is also at the centre of Joseph A. Porter's 'Pragmatics for Criticism' (*Poetics*). Porter reviews the work of the 'first generation' speech-act theorists (Austin, Searle, and Grice), concentrating particularly on the constative–performative distinction and its consequent rejection in favour of a theory of illocutionary acts. He complains that 'second generation' speech-act theorists and literary critics working with pragmatic models have not been aware of important developments in each others' areas and proposes that a fuller integration of the two fields would help develop a 'pragmatic criticism'. Porter makes a special case for the inclusion of speech act theory in current Shakespearean criticism. Beverly Olson Flanigan, in 'Donne's "Holy Sonnet VII" as Speech Act' (*Lang&S*), reviews literary-stylistic applications of speech-act theory before carrying out an analysis of the illocutionary acts that are represented in Donne's poem. She takes as a point of departure I. A. Richards's report of his students' generally negative reactions to this poem and argues that a contextually based speech-act analysis provides a formal procedure for explaining these reactions. In an original adaptation of some of Dan Sperber and Deirdre Wilson's work on pragmatics, Jean Jacques Weber examines 'Inferential and Evocational Processing in Literary Texts' (*GLS*). Basing his analysis on John Fowles's *The French Lieutenant's Woman*, Weber shows how the author is able to manipulate the reading process by creating an illusion of 'evocational' processing. This evocational processing is broken down in the third ending to the novel and the reader is forced to 'retreat from evocational processing back into inferential processing'. Winifred Crombie, in 'Two Faces of Seneca: Metaphysical and Baroque Prose Styles in the Seventeenth Century' (*Lang&S*), sets out a comprehensive semantic-relational framework for the analysis of written discourse. She identifies three major types of discourse relation: 'associative relations' (involving comparison or contrast), 'logicodeductive relations' (involving causality), and 'contiguity relations' (involving contiguity in time and space). Crombie uses her model to define seventeenth century metaphysical and baroque prose styles, but proposes that it should receive wider application within discourse stylistics.

In a special issue of *Text* devoted to text linguistics and written composition, two articles are particularly relevant to stylistics. Nils Erik Enkvist, in his introduction to the volume ('Introduction: Stylistics, Text Linguistics and Composition'), provides an overview of the theoretical problems associated with definitions of style. He argues that style can be defined and explicated using a number of basic concepts and outlines four different types of 'text model' that can be used for this purpose. A comparable multilayered approach to style is in evidence in A. M. Bülow Møller's 'Composition as Utterance'. Møller analyses a short sequence of dialogue from a number of different perspectives, using models developed by, *inter alia*, Halliday, Labov, and Goffman.

And finally, no year's work in stylistics would be complete without at least one analysis of Hemingway's short story 'Cat in the Rain'. This year's contribution is supplied by Oddvar Holmesland in 'Structuralism and Interpretation: Ernest Hemingway's "Cat in the Rain"' (*ES*). Drawing on both Prague School and Saussurean structuralist theory, Holmesland explores familiar themes such as the enigma of the cat's identity and the indeterminacy of the story's ending.

Old English Literature

JOYCE HILL

This chapter has the following sections: 1. Bibliography; 2. Social, Cultural, and Intellectual Background; 3. Literature: General; 4. Beowulf; 5. The Junius Manuscript; 6. The Poems of the Vercelli Book; 7. The Exeter Book; 8. Other Poems; 9. Prose.

1. Bibliography

As ever, students of literature are well served by the classified bibliographies in *ASE*, *OENews*, and the *IMB*. *OENews*, of course, does more than list publications: an appendix of abstracts of conference papers is included in the spring issue, the fall issue reviews work published in 1985, and in both there are reports on conference activity and on research projects worldwide. Each also carries a short article, one by Thomas H. Ohlgren on f. 12 of the Harley Psalter (spring), and one by Paul E. Szarmach on f. 62v of Alcuin's *Liber de Virtutibus et Vitiis* from Cotton Vitellius D iv (fall). Carl T. Berkhout's record of 'Old English Research in Progress 1985–1986' (*NM*) lists what is yet to come. This year one hundred items are noted. The other annual bibliographical resource is the *MSSN*, which continues to cater for a specialized but active field of research.

2. Social, Cultural, and Intellectual Background

For the first time in 1983 the International Congress on Medieval Studies at Western Michigan University included a symposium, ranging over Anglo-Saxon literature, history, art, and archaeology. The papers appear in a volume named, like the symposium, *Sources of Anglo-Saxon Culture*[1]. Those on specific literary works will be reported at the appropriate point in this chapter, but there are many which are relevant in a more indirect way, notably 'The Preservation and Transmission of Greek in Early England' by Mary Catherine Bodden, 'Towards the Identification of Old English Literary Ideas – Old Workings and New Seams' by J. E. Cross, 'Continental Sources of Anglo-Saxon Devotional Writing' by Thomas H. Bestul, 'The Imagery of the Living Ecclesia and the English Monastic Reform' by Robert Deshman, 'The Marvels-of-the-East Tradition in Anglo-Saxon Art' by John Block Friedman, 'The Dictionary of Old English' by Ashley Crandell Amos, and 'A Handlist of Anglo-Saxon Manuscripts' by Helmut Gneuss.

1. *Sources of Anglo-Saxon Culture*, ed. by Paul E. Szarmach with Virginia Darrow Oggins. WMU. pp. xii + 457. hb $38.95, pb $18.95.

Martin Irvine's article 'Bede the Grammarian and the Scope of Grammatical Studies in Eighth-century Northumbria' (*ASE*) is likewise of general interest to students of the vernacular literary tradition in showing how, at an early date, grammar achieved high status as an all-embracing discipline among the *artes*. Also included in *ASE* is Michael Lapidge's 'The School of Theodore and Hadrian', which can be commended as a model of how to write productively and wisely on the basis of scanty evidence. Lapidge's analysis of what we know about the activity of these two scholars in England is supported by his sensitive investigation of the vestiges of their teaching preserved in the Leiden Glossary, whose related texts are listed, with annotation and bibliography, in a detailed appendix.

A much broader view of Anglo-Saxon intellectual history is taken by Helmut Gneuss who, in 'Anglo-Saxon Libraries from the Conversion to the Benedictine Reform' in this year's *Settimane* volume from Spoleto, attempts the ambitious task of surveying the history of Anglo-Saxon libraries up to the first half of the tenth century. Readers who are interested in this topic are directed also to articles by Gneuss and Morrish which are reviewed on pp. 132–3 below. James P. Carley's focus, by contrast, is on the monastic library of Glastonbury, which was fortunately visited by Leland before the Dissolution. In 'John Leland and the Contents of English Pre-Dissolution Libraries: Glastonbury Abbey' (*Scriptorium*) Carley edits for the first time the Glastonbury material from Leland's autograph notebook and annotates each item in great detail. Much of what Leland lists is not, of course, from the pre-Conquest period, but there is no doubt that Anglo-Saxonists will be interested in this investigation of the pre-Dissolution holdings of what had been a major Anglo-Saxon monastery.

Thomas H. Ohlgren's *Insular and Anglo-Saxon Illuminated Manuscripts: An Iconographic Catalogue c. A.D. 625 to 1100*[2] examines the Christian traditions of Anglo-Saxon England from a different viewpoint. With the help of some twelve other scholars he has compiled and edited an iconographic catalogue of 299 insular and illuminated manuscripts from the Anglo-Saxon period which will benefit scholars in a range of disciplines. The detailed indexes enable one to search by manuscript shelf-mark, authors and titles, places of origin and provenance, dates, and iconographic contents.

Art of a different kind is dealt with in *The Sutton Hoo Ship Burial*[3], by Angela Care Evans. Anyone who has been teaching *Beowulf* for a good many years will already have a collection of these British Museum handbooks, which cumulatively record the archaeologists' developing understanding of the site and its artefacts, but the one published this year surpasses them all and can be warmly recommended. The text is more detailed than in any of the previous editions and there are many more illustrations. It has, of course, been written in the light of the work done for the definitive publication of Sutton Hoo and it is enlivened by up-to-date news of modern excavations, in which the author has been personally involved. Further details of recent fieldwork on the site are provided in *ASE* by M. O. H. Carver, who explains, in 'Anglo-Saxon Objectives at Sutton Hoo, 1985', that there is another large ship burial under

2. *Insular and Anglo-Saxon Illuminated Manuscripts: An Iconographic Catalogue c. A.D. 625 to 1100*, comp. and ed. by Thomas H. Ohlgren. Garland. pp. xxvii + 400 + 50 illus. $75.

3. *The Sutton Hoo Ship Burial*, by Angela Care Evans. BMP. pp. 127. pb £5.50.

mound two and that the site as a whole has evidence of a wider range of burial customs than had previously been supposed. *ASE* also contains an article by Carola Hicks on 'The Birds on the Sutton Hoo Purse'.

Turning to extant texts, it is a pleasure to note that this year sees the first publication of a variorum edition of the West Saxon regnal list, for which David N. Dumville draws upon manuscript versions that have effectively remained unknown or unused by scholars. The edition, published in *Anglia* as 'The West Saxon Genealogical Regnal List: Manuscripts and Texts', is accompanied by a description of the manuscripts and an attempt to reconstruct text-history. In the final section of the paper Dumville presents continuations of the list, the tabular extract in BL MS Cotton Tiberius B v, Vol. I, f. 22r, and the East Saxon Royal Genealogies from BL MS Add. 23211, f. 1v. LD. W. Rollason, in 'Goscelin of Canterbury's Account of The Translation and Miracles of St. Mildrith (*BHL* 5961/4): An Edition with Notes' (*MS*), offers another significant first publication. The account is important not only because of the contribution it makes to our knowledge of this Flemish hagiographer who was so prolific a writer of English saints' lives, but also because of the information it contains about the important early Kentish abbey of Minster-in-Thanet and about Canterbury and the abbey of St Augustine. For anyone interested in the end of the Anglo-Saxon period it has, of course, the added dimension of showing the state of the cult of an eighth-century English saint at a time when the English church and English saints' cults were being affected by the influx of ecclesiastics trained in Normandy and elsewhere on the Continent.

For early monastic life in the north of England we have the first-hand testimony of Bede, who lived according to Benedict Biscop's eclectic Rule. It has often been assumed, however, that the Rule of St Benedict was a dominant influence on life at Monkwearmouth and Jarrow, and this seems to be borne out by A. G. P. van der Walt's study of 'Reflections of the Benedictine Rule in Bede's Homiliary' (*JEH*). Bede is also the subject of some of the items in James Campbell's *Essays in Anglo-Saxon History*[4], which collects together the papers published by Campbell in various places between 1966 and 1984. One can usually also look to the annual Jarrow lecture for comment on some aspect of the world of Bede, but this year A. J. Piper's *The Durham Monks at Jarrow*[5] investigated the post-Conquest monastic life at the site. Nevertheless, the persistence of the Benedictines of Durham in maintaining Jarrow as a dependent cell for more than three hundred years may be seen as an impressive practical testimony to the reputation of the original foundation and of its saintly scholar.

Andreas Fischer's *Engagement, Wedding and Marriage in Old English*[6] takes us into another world altogether. It is not, as one might suppose, primarily a sociological study, but a philological investigation of the words and phrases used in OE for engagement, wedding, and marriage, and it is for its definitions of meaning and usage that it is valuable for the reader of OE

    4. *Essays in Anglo-Saxon History*, by James Campbell. Hambledon. pp. xi + 240. £22.

    5. *The Durham Monks at Jarrow*, by A. J. Piper. Jarrow Lecture. Jarrow. pp. 40. pamphlet £1.80.

    6. *Engagement, Wedding and Marriage in Old English*, by Andreas Fischer. AF 176. CWU. pp. 196. hb DM 112, pb DM 84.

literature. There are, nevertheless, sociological implications in what Fischer has to say, and the study of the words is prefaced by a useful survey of Anglo-Saxon marriage law and marriage customs.

The final item in this section is David Fairer's 'Anglo-Saxon Studies'[7], which traces the development of Anglo-Saxon scholarship at Oxford University from 1688 to the end of the eighteenth century. It is in large part an account of the struggles and achievements of such great pioneering scholars as William and Elizabeth Elstob, George Hickes, Humfrey Wanley, and Edward Thwaites, to name but a few. Their work is familiar to all Anglo-Saxonists, but it is not common for their relative places in the development of Anglo-Saxon studies to be defined in relation to the university with which they were associated. It is this perspective which gives Fairer's survey its particular interest.

3. Literature: General

The book which must be mentioned first this year is *A New Critical History of Old English Literature*[8] which, as its title suggests, is designed to replace Stanley B. Greenfield's *A Critical History of Old English Literature*, published twenty-one years ago (*YW* 46.61). Greenfield makes a major contribution to the new book, but he is joined by Daniel G. Calder, who has been responsible for a complete rewriting of the sections on OE prose, and by Michael Lapidge, who has written an excellent survey of the Anglo-Latin background. The addition of a good Anglo-Latin chapter and the need to provide a new approach to OE prose are not so much indications of weaknesses in Greenfield's original *History* as positive responses to exciting new developments in Anglo-Saxon literary scholarship. The chapters on OE poetry, written by Greenfield himself, are more obviously adapted from his original publication, not least because the chapter headings remain the same, pointing to a similar division of subject matter. Even here, however, the changes are marked, as may be seen from the treatment of *Andreas*: twenty-one years ago most of the comment on this poem dealt with the supposed relationship to *Beowulf*; in the *New Critical History* it has more space and much attention is given to expounding its figural and thematic interpretation. The same shifts of emphasis are apparent throughout, and indeed the new book is a good guide to two decades of OE literary criticism. Yet it has to be said that it is often no more than that. While it has its value as an intelligent survey and bibliographical record, the *New Critical History* frequently reads more as a diligent and considered report on the scholarship than as a stimulating response to the literature itself. A notable exception, however, is Michael Lapidge's first-hand account of the Anglo-Latin tradition.

Greenfield's undoubted contribution to OE literary scholarship was publicly recognized this year by a Festschrift[9] containing sixteen essays, most of which,

---

7 In *The History of the University of Oxford*. Vol. V: *The Eighteenth Century*, ed. by L. S. Sutherland and L. G. Mitchell. Clarendon. pp. xix + 949. £75.

8. *A New Critical History of Old English Literature*, by Stanley B. Greenfield and Daniel G. Calder, with a survey of the Anglo-Latin background by Michael Lapidge. NYU. pp. xi + 372 + maps. $30.

9. *Modes of Interpretation in Old English Literature: Essays in Honour of Stanley B. Greenfield*, ed. by Phyllis Rugg Brown, Georgia Ronan Crampton, and Fred C. Robinson. UTor. pp. xxi + 298. £24.50/$40 (in Europe). (Hereafter *Greenfield*.)

in accord with Greenfield's own interests, are concerned with poetry. Those commenting in detail on a particular poem will be discussed at the appropriate point later in this chapter, but there are four which have a general significance. Peter Clemoes, in ' "Symbolic Language" in Old English Poetry', attempts in a short space the large and difficult task of defining the impact that Christianity had on the thought-processes of vernacular writers by showing how, in the pre-Christian tradition, symbol and narrative, name and action coalesce, and how subsequently, under the influence of Latin rhetorical training, traditional socio-cultural expressions became less organic, leading to a natural shift from poetry to rhetorically structured prose. The next article, 'Old English Verse as a Medium for Christian Theology', by George Hardin Brown, examines the Advent lyrics in *Christ I*, focusing on the first two in an attempt to demonstrate the general point that OE verse is a suitable medium for expressing some of the most difficult and paradoxical religious tenets. Alain Renoir, in 'Old English Formulas and Themes as Tools for Contextual Interpretation', confronts the perennial problem of the contextual vacuum of most OE poems and tries to show how patterns of expectation triggered by formulae and themes can act as partial substitutes for the extra-textual contexts that are no longer available to us. Matti Rissanen's ' "Sum" in Old English Poetry' analyses the functions and meanings of the pronoun 'sum' in poetic contexts and offers thereby many worthwhile observations on how a wide range of poetic passages should be read.

Interesting though these and many other contributions are, they stand firmly within a well-established tradition of OE literary criticism, thus representing an approach which has been vigorously, if perhaps a little unfairly, challenged by Allen J. Frantzen and Charles L. Venegoni. In 'An Archaeology of Anglo-Saxon Studies' (*Style*) they note, reasonably enough, that the criticism of OE literature appears remarkably resistant to the influence of contemporary literary theory, even though, as they claim, it has much to learn from postmodern critical methods, particularly from reception criticism. Where they are unfair, I think, is in their characterization of current scholarly work. The approaches that they describe and object to – the attempt to recover 'pure origins', the search for an Ur-text, for first uses of words, and so on – are only part of what modern scholars do, and not always the main part; there are many who are at least as interested in the subsequent transmission of material and its reception by later adapters and audiences. In the same volume of *Style* similar points are made, though less belligerently, by Martin Irvine who questions, in 'Anglo-Saxon Literary Theory Exemplified in Old English Poems: Interpreting the Cross in *The Dream of the Rood* and *Elene*', the apparent self-sufficiency of the source-study methodology. Nevertheless, Irvine's own position is avowedly historical in that he is interested in coming to terms with texts by using a definition of the principles of interpretation and the nature of textuality from within the cultural discourses known to and practised by Anglo-Saxon writers themselves.

With Alfred Bammesberger's *Linguistic Notes on Old English Poetic Texts*[10] we return to traditional methodologies, for it was in working on a new etymological dictionary of OE that Bammesberger found himself disagreeing with

10. *Linguistic Notes on Old English Poetic Texts*, by Alfred Bammesberger. AF 189. CWU. pp. 124. pb DM 30.

particular readings and linguistic interpretations embedded in standard editions and widely accepted by literary critics. The essays offered by Bammesberger in this useful volume comment on particular words and lines in fifteen poems. There is also discussion of the runic inscription on the front of the Franks Casket. Bammesberger makes the firm point that he is concentrating on linguistic issues, in contrast with the focus of much OE poetic scholarship in recent times, which has taken a determinedly literary-critical approach. But of course the two are not separable. Literary critics need an established text or they will be led astray by commenting on what they misunderstand or on what is simply an error of transmission. Bammesberger's *Linguistic Notes* should therefore be frequently consulted.

Another work in the traditional mould but much better than what the tradition has previously supplied is the revised edition of *A Guide to Old English* [11] by Bruce Mitchell and Fred C. Robinson, which now includes not only the original nine prose texts but also five of the most popular OE poems, fifteen riddles, and four extracts from *Beowulf*. The notes and glossary match the grammar in their helpfulness and clarity; here at last is a comprehensive grammar and reader that we can confidently adopt as the standard one-volume introduction to OE language and literature.

The final book in this section is Jane Chance's *Woman as Hero in Old English Literature* [12]. This ranges widely over OE poetry and pays some attention to OE prose and to the Anglo-Latin tradition in exploring the dominant role models governing the literary presentation of Anglo-Saxon women. Not surprisingly, she finds that Mary is a major biblical model, with Eve as the antithesis, but Chance believes that OE writers were also drawn to a third figure within the Christian tradition: the more militant heroic widow Judith, who sums up qualities also found in many of the women saints most popular in Anglo-Saxon England. The model for the secular ideal, as exemplified in Wealhpeow and Hygd, is taken to be the portrayal of women in *Maxims I* and *II*. The survey is a useful one and the detailed bibliography can be recommended, but in her eagerness to categorize and polarize, Chance often simplifies and overstates. It is not true, for example, that peace-weaving women are necessarily peaceful and passive, and it is a convenient rhetorical device rather than an insight into any true relationship to say that the Anglo-Saxon woman's ideal role as peace-weaver or peace-pledge was analogous to the Virgin's role as intermediary between man and God. It is just as difficult to accept the opposite case: that Eve, the antitype, is used for comparison with other 'failed women' both in the elegies and in *Beowulf*. Before one can even begin to entertain that possibility, one needs first to establish whether or not they are presented to us as 'failed women', which many would doubt: if they expose a failure, it surely resides in heroic society, not in them.

There are few articles of general significance, but Hugh Magennis offers one. '*Monig oft gesæt*: Some Images of Sitting in Old English Poetry' (*Neophil*) is an interesting discussion of how and why the action (or rather inaction) of sitting in OE poetry is frequently associated with elegiac or contemplative situations.

11. *A Guide to Old English: Fourth Edition Revised with Prose and Verse Texts and Glossary*, by Bruce Mitchell and Fred C. Robinson. Blackwell. pp. xvi + 354. hb £24.50, pb £8.50.
12. *Woman as Hero in Old English Literature*, by Jane Chance. Syracuse. pp. xvii + 156. hb $25, pb $12.50.

There will be few readers of OE poetry who have not responded to the association unconsciously, but there is much to be said for having the examples drawn together and for having one's perception thereby sharpened. Pauline A. Thompson's 'Æpplede Gold: An Investigation of its Semantic Field' (*MS*) has a much narrower focus, but I mention it here since it deals with three poems, *Elene*, *Phoenix*, and *Juliana*, and cites *in extenso* 'gold' and 'apple' words from the whole of the OE corpus, both singly and in compounds. Her conclusion is that 'æpplede' in the three poems indicates the colour or texture of the gold and that it stands as a metaphorical equivalent of 'read gold', reinforcing the poems' exotic tenor.

There are also few metrical studies this year. In a long and complex article on 'The Metrical Entities of Old English' (*NM*) O. D. Macrae-Gibson subjects the system of metrical analysis set out by A. J. Bliss in *The Metre of Beowulf* (*YW* 39.70–1) to detailed critical examination. He focuses in particular on the proportion of the occurrences of any metrical type which appear in the a-verse and on the proportion of these having double alliteration and argues that it is necessary to consider what syntactic structures create the types, rather than simply considering the types themselves. When the syntactical aspect is taken into account, it is evident that some of Bliss's analysis needs extensive methodological correction before its conclusions can be accepted. More is promised for future articles. Dennis Cronan, in 'Alliterative Rank in Old English Poetry' (*SN*), demonstrates that a high alliteration rate is a reflection of a stylistic quality inherent in certain words, and that the markers of stylistic quality (apart from the high rate of alliteration) are characteristics such as the word's restriction to poetry, its possible descent from a common Germanic poetic tradition, or its use in a figurative or extended meaning. 'Chronological Testing and the Scansion of *Frea* in Old English Poetry' (*NM*) by Edwin Duncan shows that 'frea' was disyllabic when it was the second element of a compound, or when it was preceded by a possessive pronoun, but that it was monosyllabic elsewhere. The implications of this metrical evidence are that, since the syllabic form of 'frea' was determined by its immediate syntactic environment throughout the OE period, we can no longer accept the traditional view that its occurrence in disyllabic form is indicative of an early date for the text in which it occurs. For another technical article, of interest to textual editors, Angelika Lutz's investigation of 'The Syllabic Basis of Word Division in Old English Manuscripts' (*ES*), see Chapter 3, p. 80.

4. Beowulf

Kevin S. Kiernan, author of the controversial *'Beowulf' and the 'Beowulf' Manuscript* (*YW* 64.96–7), has now undertaken an exhaustive study of the transcripts of the manuscripts made by Thorkelin and his scribe, documents which have more than antiquarian interest since they are central to our understanding of the transmission and foundation of the text of *Beowulf* in modern times. The first part of *The Thorkelin Transcripts of 'Beowulf'* [13] describes the circumstances under which Thorkelin discovered the OE poem, which is an interesting story in itself; more gripping still is Kiernan's attempt to identify

---

13. *The Thorkelin Transcripts of 'Beowulf'*, by Kevin S. Kiernan. Anglistica 25. R&B. pp. xiii + 155. pb Dkr 315.

Thorkelin's scribe. The analysis of each transcription is necessarily less of a good read, but here too one's attention is caught by the argument that Thorkelin made his own transcription not, as he claims, in 1787, when his scribe was also at work, but some years later, after consulting the scribe's transcription. As with his book on the *Beowulf* manuscript itself, Kiernan challenges common assumptions. It remains to be seen whether, on this occasion also, he himself will be challenged.

Apart from Kiernan's monograph, all other publications that I have seen on *Beowulf* this year have been in the form of articles. The most rash is that by Zacharias P. Thundy who, in '*Beowulf*: Date and Authorship' (*NM*), claims on the basis of his interpretation of internal evidence that the poem was composed between 927 and 931 by a certain Wulfgar who was a retainer of King Athelstan.

By contrast with Thundy's determined pursuit of a precise location in time, Strother B. Purdy sets out to confront the question of how we can best see the poem for ourselves in the twentieth century. In 'Beowulf and Hrothgar's Dream' (*ChauR*) he argues that the poem's fragmentary, disorganized, and self-contradictory nature is explicable as the survival of mythic dreams, either in the mind of one man or in the collective consciousness of the *Volk*. His preliminary characterization of the poem begs a large question: *is* it fragmentary, disorganized, and self-contradictory? And is it sufficient to proceed, as Purdy does, by summary and assertive comment?

Paul Beekman Taylor's study of 'The Traditional Language of Treasure in *Beowulf*' (*JEGP*) sets off on an apparently more traditional tack, although in the end his approach also draws too heavily on twentieth-century terms of reference, which may well not have been shared by contemporary Anglo-Saxons.

Much livelier is '"Mere" and "Sund": Two Sea-Changes in *Beowulf*', Roberta Frank's contribution to *Greenfield* [9]. Through an investigation of the meanings of 'mere' and 'sund' she attempts to clear up two areas of confusion in our reading of *Beowulf*: what the poet envisaged when he called Grendel's home a 'mere', and whether the contest between Beowulf and Breca involved swimming or rowing. In both cases there are possible differences between the poetic and prosaic uses of the word and Frank shows that in both cases – although in different ways – the poet exploits the inherent ambiguity. For those interested in the role of Unferð, the discussion of 'sund' offers some stimulating insights. Another approach to the Unferð episode, also in this volume, is John C. Pope's '*Beowulf* 505, "gehedde", and the Pretensions of Unferth', which examines the possibility of retaining the manuscript's 'gehedde' at l. 505. His conclusion is that 'gehedde' is acceptable as a derivation of *gehēdan*, 'care for, be concerned about', and that its use here accounts for the genitive plural 'mærða', since *hēdan* (and presumably *gehēdan*) normally takes a genitive object. In the light of this reading Pope sees Unferð as a warrior of some standing who nevertheless falls short of Beowulf, and who has performed at least one morally reprehensible deed, to which Beowulf refers. Pope does not attempt the impossible task of making him into a lovable character, but he certainly argues for his rehabilitation as a respected fighter and privileged spokesman.

Working our way through the poem, the next line to be commented upon is 770a. Carl T. Berkhout and Renëe Medine in '*Beowulf* 770a: *reþe renweardas*' (*N&Q*) argue that the problematic 'renweardas' means specifically 'watchdogs', rather than the more general 'guardian(s) of the house' favoured by editors of *Beowulf*, and that the wrestling match between Beowulf and Grendel is thus presented figuratively as a vicious dogfight. The authors go on to make a case for the authenticity of *renhund*, 'house-dog', as an OE word, although it is not attested before *c*.1220.

The notable crux of 'Earme on eaxle (*Beowulf* 1117a)' is commented upon by G. A. Lester in *SN*. Previous attempts at solving it are summarized and reviewed, but Lester's own solution takes us far from these since he regards the phrase, unemended, as being a reference to Hildeburh's posture as she mourns: 'wretchedly the woman lamented upon her shoulder'. The objection that such a reading produces an extraordinary physical contortion is met by Lester, who cites the posture of grief given to the Virgin Mary in a number of Anglo-Saxon illuminated manuscripts.

Mary Kay Temple, in '*Beowulf* 1258–1266: Grendel's Lady-Mother' (*ELN*), scrutinizes the poet's use of 'ides' to describe Grendel's mother and shows that in this ironic exploitation 'ides' reminds us that the monsters and their realm form an anti-society.

Raymond P. Tripp Jr's '*Beowulf* 1314a: The Hero as *Alfwalda*, "Ruler of Elves" ' (*Neophil*) also examines a particular usage, arguing for the adoption of the manuscript reading 'alfwalda' as a designation of Beowulf in l. 1314a, rather than the common editorial emendation to 'alwalda' as a name for God. The allusion, according to Tripp, is to Beowulf's success in controlling monsters who are among the eotens, elves, orcs, and other such giants who have long warred against God.

The subject of Sarah Lynn Higley's ' "Aldor on Ofre", or the Reluctant Hart: A Study of Liminality in *Beowulf*' (*NM*) is ll. 1368–72, in which Hroðgar describes how the stag refuses to jump into Grendel's mere. Higley argues that the passage should be read as an ironic reversal of the familiar oral-formulaic theme of the Hero on the Beach and that the *Beowulf* poet's exploitation of this theme, negatively here and positively elsewhere, is indicative of the poem's concern with the liminal, that is to say, with the ability or inability to cross thresholds.

The final article on specific lines is 'The Lost Letters of Beowulf 2253a' (*Neophil*) by Kevin Kiernan, who challenges the common editorial 'feormie'. On the basis of a detailed examination of the *Beowulf* manuscript under high intensity light, he claims to have detected enough letter fragments to indicate that 'fægnige' is a better restoration. Further comments on individual lines are to be found in Bammesberger's *Linguistic Notes on Old English Poetic Texts* [10], for which see pp. 122–3 above.

Norma Kroll, in a more general essay entitled '*Beowulf*: The Hero as Keeper of Human Polity' (*MP*), explores the essential similarities between the hero and the monsters, showing that they are, in a sense, identical and opposite enough to be doubles. She argues that the doubles relationship is a key to the poem's moral dilemmas and ambiguities, which allow only for a limited victory.

The last item in this section, 'Rudolf von Raumer: Long Sentences in *Beowulf* and the Influence of Christianity on Germanic Style' (*N&Q*), is by E. G. Stanley, who takes us back, as he has done before, to nineteenth-century German scholarship and shows that there were some critics, such as von Raumer, who had a subtle appreciation of OE literature and whose views, though now largely forgotten, would be readily accepted by modern scholars.

5. The Junius Manuscript

As is often the case, there is little to report here. E. G. Stanley's 'Notes on the Text of the Old English *Genesis*' (*Greenfield*[9]) offers thirty observations on the poem and in most cases translations for the pieces of emended text. Paul Cavill, in 'Notes on Maxims in Old English Narrative' (*N&Q*), examines two maxims embedded in the text of *Genesis B* (ll. 623–5 and 634b in the composite *Genesis* text printed in *ASPR*) and demonstrates that both show clear signs of an Old Saxon origin. He observes, in conclusion, that this exceptional instance of the transference of maxims from one Germanic culture to another indicates the validity of the wisdom tradition in both. Another study of the same poem is Karen Cherewatuk's 'Standing, Turning, Twisting, Falling: Posture and Moral Stance in *Genesis B*' (*NM*), where it is argued that the poet literalizes the idea that to sin is to turn away from God by describing the prelapsarian Adam and Eve as standing upright, and the fallen angels and fallen man as turning, twisting, and falling. It is a neatly presented case, but I suspect that few will be convinced by it unless it could first be demonstrated that the poet's choice of words was entirely free. What Cherewatuk ignores completely is the pressure of a given narrative and the need to express it in language which must draw upon a range of synonyms and near-synonyms to meet the stylistic and metrical demands of OE verse.

I know of no separate studies of the other poems in the manuscript, although of course they are commented upon in the *New Critical History*[8] and there are notes on all four in Bammesberger's *Linguistic Notes on Old English Poetic Texts*[10] (see above pp. 122–3).

With regard to the manuscript itself, J. R. Hall, in 'On the Bibliographical Unity of Bodleian MS Junius 11' (*AN&Q*), writes in support of Barbara Raw's conclusion (*YW* 65.91) that *Christ and Satan* did not constitute part of an independent booklet, as Peter Lucas had earlier claimed (*YW* 60.68), and that the poem can therefore be accepted as having been part of the editor's original programme for the manuscript.

6. The Poems of the Vercelli Book

Readers are again directed to the *New Critical History*[8] and to Bammesberger's *Linguistic Notes on Old English Poetic Texts*[10], which includes comment on several lines in *Andreas* and *Elene*. There are few items otherwise.

In 'Figurative Language and its Contexts in *Andreas*: A Study in Medieval Expressionism' (*Greenfield*[9]) Daniel G. Calder puts forward the novel if perhaps anachronistic view that the incongruities between style and subject matter in *Andreas*, which critics have frequently commented upon unfavourably, were deliberately engineered by the poet in order to draw attention to the poem's metaphorical import, which overrides the limits of time, space, and circumstantial probability.

Edward B. Irving Jr's contribution to the same volume, 'Crucifixion Witnessed, or Dramatic Interaction in *The Dream of the Rood*', adds to the voluminous literature generated by *The Dream of the Rood* a perceptive and sensitive study of the dramatization and psychology of the two main characters, Dreamer and Rood, showing how they interact with each other and, ultimately, with the crucifixion, to produce a poem of unparalleled spiritual and psychological richness. Inevitably, Irving has most to say about the first half of the poem, but the last half, which has often been ignored, is shown to be essential to the poem's dramatic as well as didactic purpose. What we are offered in Part III of *Sources of Anglo-Saxon Culture*[1] is an interdisciplinary approach to the poem developed by a group of three articles. Sandra McEntire, in 'The Devotional Context of the Cross Before A.D. 1000', attempts to reach an understanding of the milieu out of which arose the poem and crosses such as those at Bewcastle and Ruthwell by investigating the personal devotion of the Sign of the Cross, the motif of the Cross as a cosmological symbol, and the theological and devotional meaning of pilgrimage as it relates to the Cross. McEntire's paper is interdisciplinary in itself, since evidence is drawn from a wide variety of historical and cultural sources. Robert T. Farrell, in the following article, 'Reflections on the Iconography of the Ruthwell and Bewcastle Crosses', illuminates the context of the poem-fragments carved on the Ruthwell Cross but does not himself discuss *The Dream of the Rood* directly. Éamonn Ó Carragáin's approach to the poem is similarly oblique, since his examination of 'Christ over the Beasts and the Agnus Dei: Two Multivalent Panels on the Ruthwell and Bewcastle Crosses' is concerned with identifying the spiritual uses to which the crosses may have been put. Since, however, the Ruthwell Cross and *The Dream of the Rood* have a peculiarly intimate, if imperfectly understood, relationship, the editors of the volume were justified in regarding all three papers as contributions to our understanding of the poem.

7. The Exeter Book

As with the other poetic codices, readers are directed to the *New Critical History*[8] and to Bammesberger's *Linguistic Notes on Old English Poetic Texts*[10]. For *Juliana* they should also note Marie Nelson's '*The Battle of Maldon* and *Juliana*: The Language of Confrontation', summarized on p. 131 below. The survey of publications given below follows the order of the items in the manuscript, but is preceded by notice of three articles which take a broader view of the codex.

In his introduction to the facsimile of the Exeter Book (*YW* 14.73–5), Robin Flower had suggested that the colophon of Lambeth Palace Library MS 149 might provide a clue to the provenance of the Exeter Book, which is in the same hand as the Lambeth manuscript. Joyce Hill, in 'The Exeter Book and Lambeth Palace Library MS 149: A Reconsideration' (*AN&Q*), re-examines the colophon and questions Flower's implication that the place of origin was Crediton, an attribution which, given the lack of evidence about the Exeter Book, has been gratefully accepted by editors as a probability. Further consideration of the problem is promised in the light of the colophon's reference to a *monasterium* dedicated to St Mary. 'The Structure of the Exeter Book Codex (Exeter, Cathedral Library, MS 3501)' by Patrick W. Conner (*Scriptorium*) reports the results of a detailed codicological and palaeographical examination of the manuscript, which has revealed that the Exeter Book, like the other three major poetic codices of OE poetry, is a composite. The three booklets that Conner identifies are ff. 8r–52v, 53r–97v, and 98r–130v. As he notes in conclusion, the advantage of recognizing this structure is that it allows students of OE poetry to examine and exploit the juxtaposition of poems within each booklet without having to account for the relationship of apparently disparate texts throughout the codex as a whole. It is the literary grouping which is investigated by Karma Lochrie in *'Wyrd* and the Limits of Human Understanding: A Thematic Sequence in the *Exeter Book' (JEGP)*. Lochrie believes that, in addition to the groupings of poems according to genre and related *topoi*, there are less obvious sequences of poems which present variations on some particular theme or a series of instructions for devotional exercises. The example she discusses is *Judgment Day I*, *Resignation A* and *B*, which she considers form a penitential group. They present three different approaches – a homiletic poem, a prayer, and an elegy – to the common concern with *wyrd* and its effect on mankind, and she believes that they were either written as a group or, more likely, were written down independently of each other and that it was the Exeter Book compiler who arranged them into the thematic sequence that we find in the codex now.

Turning to the individual poems, we note firstly Thomas D. Hill's article in the *Sources of Anglo-Saxon Culture*[1], 'Literary History and Old English Poetry: The Case of *Christ I, II, III* '. The paper divides into two parts, the first being a discussion of the general value of source-study in the study of OE literature, and the second being a demonstration, by a few particular examples, of how comparison between a vernacular text and its source can confirm its uniqueness and the essential difference between its thought-world and the thought-world of other poems with which, for various reasons, it might be closely associated and even physically grouped. It is on the third of these *Christ* poems that Frederick M. Biggs focuses his attention in *The Sources of 'Christ III': A Revision of Cook's Notes*[14]. The poem has not been edited since Albert S. Cook's monumental edition of 1900 and Biggs performs an invaluable service in this revision, incorporating a large body of twentieth-century published scholarship and the results of his own research, which together lead him to discount Cook's claim, often repeated, that an anonymous Latin hymn cited by Bede is the OE poem's principal source.

Karen Swenson, in *'Wapentake*: A Realistic Detail in Cynewulf's *Juliana'* (*N&Q*), provides a literal, historical context for the apparently odd statement that when Africanus and Eleusius meet to discuss Juliana's unwillingness to marry, they do so after leaning their spears together. The detail, which is not in the source, has been interpreted as symbolic of worldly wealth, heathen values, or even as metaphorical counterparts of the spears that have been used to kill the elect. Swenson, however, cites references in Tacitus and in law-codes from Norway and England in support of her argument that the detail was included by Cynewulf to define the men's position in Germanic terms: they are 'voting citizens', who lean their spears together to indicate their essential concord.

In a note on 'Growth and Decay in *The Riming Poem*, Lines 51–54' (*ELN*) Anne L. Klinck argues that 'tinneð' (54b), sometimes translated as 'extends', refers to the process of animal growth and that the poet, in using a normally transitive verb as an intransitive, presents man's decline of glory and increase of sorrow in terms of the processes of nature. Her examination of this passage in *The Riming Poem* involves a discussion also of *The Fortunes of Men* ll. 1–4a.

---

14. *The Sources of 'Christ III': A Revision of Cook's Notes*, by Frederick M. Biggs. OENews Subsidia. CMERS. pp. 48. pb $3.

Morton W. Bloomfield, in *Greenfield*[9], reviews some of the approaches to *Deor* that have been published since 1964 when Bloomfield argued (*YW* 45.60) that the poem had been influenced by the form and content of the charm. In '*Deor* Revisited' Bloomfield takes issue with Murray Markland's 'Boethius, Alfred, and Deor' (*YW* 49.67). Less space is given to Bloomfield's current view of the poem, but it seems to differ little from that of 1964.

Stanley B. Greenfield, in '*Wulf and Eadwacer*: All Passion Pent' (*ASE*), tackles the persistent problem of how to interpret the most enigmatic of OE poems and puts forward a reading (with translation) which re-asserts its status as a poignant poem of love-longing, the first of its kind in the secular literatures of Western Europe.

An edition of the riddles, *Die altenglischen Rätsel des Exeterbuchs: Text mit deutscher Übersetzung und Kommentar*[15] by Hans Pinsker and Waltraud Ziegler, which I was unable to report on last year, has full scholarly apparatus, a useful commentary, and an extensive bibliography. This year comment on the riddles comes from Matti Rissanen. In his study of '*Nathwæt* in the *Exeter Book Riddles*' (*AN&Q*) he examines the semantic and syntactic properties of the *nat + hw-* pronouns and their distribution in the OE riddles, where five of the six occurrences of *nathwæt* and *nathwær* are in the riddles referring to the sexual organ or its location. This observation leads to an examination of the tone of some of these riddles and to the possible connection between this use and Riddle 93, the one occasion when *nathwæt* occurs in a context usually regarded as serious and not at all obscene.

Karma Lochrie's 'The Structure and Wisdom of *Judgment Day I*' (*NM*) vindicates the inclusion of this poem in T. A. Shippey's edition of *Poems of Wisdom and Learning in Old English* (*YW* 57.48) by showing that, while it seems incoherent and lacking in subtlety or purpose if read in the light of its editorial title, it can be seen to have a complex purpose and a unified structure if approached as a wisdom poem. The poet's treatment of the limits of human understanding and knowledge in the face of *wyrd* and Doomsday is what gives the text its cohesion and purpose, according to Lochrie, and the poet's aim was to stimulate the audience's recognition and solemn fear.

Lochrie also writes on *Resignation*. In 'Anglo-Saxon Morning Sickness' (*Neophil*) she examines the common association between morning and misery in OE poetry and argues that the poet of *Resignation* exploits the association by a play on words through which he makes morning-sickness into a metaphor for misery itself.

James E. Anderson, in 'Dual Voices and the Identity of Speakers in the Exeter Book *Descent into Hell*' (*Neophil*), notes that *The Descent into Hell* is one of a group of poems clustered in the Exeter Book which have plural speakers or apparent disunity of thought, and he questions whether this duality, repeated in so many poems so close together in the manuscript, does not have a suspicious air of common and deliberate purpose contributing to a single grand riddling scheme. For *The Descent into Hell* in particular, Anderson detects, through the 'riddling logic' of the poem's last twenty lines, the voice of the liturgical celebrant of solemn Holy Saturday baptism, a reading

15. *Die altenglischen Rätsel des Exeterbuchs: Text mit deutscher Übersetzung und Kommentar*, by Hans Pinsker and Waltraud Ziegler. AF 183. CWU. pp. 422. hb DM 112, pb DM 85.

which supports his startling claim that the six hundred-odd lines of verse from *The Wife's Lament* through to *The Ruin* stand as a *compilatio* which riddles on the liturgical rites and theological meaning of the Easter *triduum*.

A more conservative approach to *The Ruin* is taken by Anne L. Klinck in 'A Damaged Passage in the Old English *Ruin*' (*SN*). The passage in question is ll. 12–20. Careful scrutiny of what can be deduced from the manuscript allows her to add a few words and letters to the damaged text as printed in Roy Leslie's edition and, with more textual material to consider, Klinck suggests that the damaged passage emphasizes not the wreckage of the buildings, as has been assumed, but their remaining impressiveness, which would fit with the poem's alternating pattern of contrast between past glory and present decay.

8. Other Poems

Last year I reported the momentous discovery by H. L. Rogers that the copyist of *The Battle of Maldon* was David Casley and not John Elphinstone (*YW* 66.128), a finding which, as Rogers showed, called into question some of the readings in D. G. Scragg's edition. Another challenge to Scragg is now offered by Fred C. Robinson who, in 'Literary Dialect in *Maldon* and the Casley Transcript' (*AN&Q*), uses Rogers' identification of the copyist to support the copy-manuscript reading of 'ḏon' in l. 33 against Scragg's emendation to 'þonne'. What is particularly satisfying to Robinson is that the identification of the transcriber provides objective evidence to support a reading which he had earlier put forward on literary grounds. Earl R. Anderson's '*The Battle of Maldon*: A Reappraisal of Possible Sources, Date, and Theme' (*Greenfield*[9]), reviews recent scholarship on the poem and opens up the possibility that it may be late enough to have been influenced by the *Encomium Emmae Reginae*, written during the reign of Hardacnut (1040–42), in particular by its description of the Battle of Ashingdon, fought in 1016. This is, as Anderson admits, only one possibility among several, but whether it is accepted or not, the examination of the poem includes a number of interesting observations, notably on the poet's sensitivity to dialect differences and on the problems of ll. 89–90. Virginia Valentine, in a short note on the opening of the poem, 'Offa's *The Battle of Maldon*' (*Expl*), argues that the vignette of Offa's kinsman, who sends his hawk into the wood before preparing to fight, stands as the poem's first example of proper conduct in the face of a challenge and serves to advance the revelation of Byrhtnoð as a leader of heroic stature.

Maldon has also been the subject of comparative studies this year, as in Dolores Warwick Frese's 'Poetic Prowess in *Brunanburh* and *Maldon*: Winning, Losing, and Literary Outcome' (*Greenfield*[9]). The comparison of the two battle poems is carried out in an attempt to define and understand the reasons for their different qualities. Frese argues that these have to do with the *Brunanburh*-poet's responsibilities as a chronicler, and with the differing psychological and sociological networks generated by winning (as in *Brunanburh*) and by losing (as in *Maldon*). The other comparative analysis in *Greenfield*[9] is Marie Nelson's '*The Battle of Maldon* and *Juliana*: The Language of Confrontation'. Here speech-act theory is employed to define the dynamics of the verbal confrontations between Byrhtnoð and the Vikings, and between Juliana and her heathen and diabolic opponents.

Although readers of OE quickly learn to recognize which lexical items are poetic, it is far harder to identify and define poetic syntax. An opportunity to do so, however, is provided by the OE *Metres of Boethius*, which were composed not from the Latin original, but from an OE prose translation. In 'Word Order and Poetic Style: Auxiliary and Verbal in *The Metres of Boethius*' (*ASE*), Daniel Donoghue takes advantage of this in order to define what features in the verse text's ordering of auxiliaries and verbals can be regarded as specifically poetic. He points in conclusion to the contribution that this analysis can make to our understanding of poetic style more generally.

Chadwick B. Hilton, in 'The Old English *Seasons for Fasting*: Its Place in the Vernacular Complaint Tradition' (*Neophil*), argues that the OE poem is a transitional work, perhaps of the early eleventh century, and that, in its complaint against a corrupt priesthood, it marks a shift from doctrinaire support of the church to the distrust and cynicism that we find brilliantly expressed in Langland and Chaucer. The conclusion is much too simplistic: on the one hand the Anglo-Saxon attitude to the clergy was much more likely to be critical than Hilton implies, and on the other the so-called 'shift' towards a Langlandian or Chaucerian 'brilliance' is so slight in *Seasons for Fasting* as to be all but imperceptible. Moreover, the footnotes are astonishingly inaccurate.

My last item in this section relates to the *Rune Poem*, although only indirectly. Stephen E. Flowers's monograph *Runes and Magic: Magical Formulaic Elements in the Older Runic Tradition*[16] explores at great length the whole question of the connection between the elder runic tradition and the practice of magic by the Germanic peoples during the first millenium. The OE poem is not discussed, but Flowers's book provides much useful background material.

9. Prose

Although this section is usually dominated by reports of work on the homiletic prose of the tenth and eleventh centuries, the balance is redressed this year by the publication of a collection of sixteen essays edited by Paul E. Szarmach, which focuses attention on OE prose before the Benedictine Reform[17]. The editor's introductory essay highlights the contributors' principal arguments and an appendix by Carl T. Berkhout lists 'Research on Early Old English Literary Prose, 1973–82', thus continuing from where the Greenfield and Robinson *Bibliography of Publications on Old English Literature* (*YW* 61.61) left off. The volume as a whole is intended to supplement the eleven essays in *The Old English Homily and its Backgrounds* edited by Szarmach and Huppé (*YW* 59.59). The contributions will be discussed at their appropriate place in this section.

Alfred's Preface to the OE *Pastoral Care* regularly attracts scholarly attention, frequently in the form of a discussion about its reliability as an account of the state of learning. This year has seen two such discussions, both of a high standard and both leading outward beyond the Preface itself to a consideration of the manuscript evidence that may or may not support Alfred's

---

16. *Runes and Magic: Magical Formulaic Elements in the Older Runic Tradition*, by Stephen E. Flowers. Lang. pp. xv + 457. Sfr 91.30.

17. *Studies in Earlier Old English Prose: Sixteen Original Contributions*, ed. by Paul E. Szarmach. SUNY. pp. vi + 420. hb $39.50, pb $19.50. (Hereafter Szarmach.)

claims. Helmut Gneuss, in 'King Alfred and the History of Anglo-Saxon Libraries', one of the few contributions to *Greenfield*[9] not to discuss Old English poetry, begins by pointing out that King Alfred does not say that learning in England declined as a result of Viking attacks, as many critics claim, but that learning was in decline before the attacks began in earnest. The accuracy of what Alfred says is tested by Gneuss against what is known of the state of the English church in the eighth and ninth centuries and the survival of manuscripts from this period, with the result that the king is vindicated, even when due allowance is made for the influence of literary *topoi* in the Preface and the accidental loss of manuscripts. The other article, by Jennifer Morrish, takes an altogether more optimistic view than Gneuss of what constitutes a ninth-century manuscript. In 'King Alfred's Letter as a Source on Learning in England in the Ninth Century' (Szarmach[17]), she describes seventeen manuscripts which she considers were copied in England during the ninth century and argues that what we can prove or surmise about the number of codices available undermines Alfred's generalization that all the books were burned by the Vikings. Furthermore, the copying was being done in all parts of England, and the manuscripts being produced were personal books and books containing specialist texts, which suggests that libraries were already stocked with basic materials.

It is the body of the text rather than its preface which is the subject of Dorothy M. Horgan's 'The Old English *Pastoral Care*: The Scribal Contribution' (Szarmach[17]). By examining the manuscripts in chronological order she attempts to assess the contributions of individual scribes whose hands can be detected, and to answer a tantalizing question: was the scribal office that of scholarly amanuensis, careful secretary, sub-editor, or editor-in-chief? What we come to recognize is an interesting variability of practice, which brings us close to 'the hand that pushed the pen'. Richard W. Clement's essay in the same volume attempts to take us back even further, to the collaborative relationship between Alfred and his helpers. By comparing the OE translation and its Latin source he is able to identify the method of translation and to demonstrate that the joint exercise was controlled by a set of what we today would call editorial principles, which Clement attributes to Alfred himself.

Milton McC. Gatch's contribution to Szarmach[17], 'King Alfred's Version of Augustine's *Soliloquia*: Some Suggestions on its Rationale and Unity', deals with another Alfredian text, examining the fundamental problem of the relationship between the OE text and its main source, Augustine's *Soliloquia*, which is freely paraphrased by Alfred in Book I, more distantly used for Book II, and departed from altogether for Book III. Gatch argues that what Alfred does is explicable in terms of the educational and intellectual history of his time and that even when he seems to depart from his major source, he is in fact 'reading' it in the light of his own learning and experience. In other words, the OE text in its entirety expresses the kind of understanding of the *Soliloquia* that would be expected in the ninth century. Also on the same text and in the same volume is Ruth Waterhouse's study of 'Tone in Alfred's Version of Augustine's *Soliloquies*'. What is investigated here is the implicit relationship between writer and audience in the OE version and the way in which this differs from the writer/audience relationship in the Latin original. Since, of course, it is impossible to scrutinize all aspects of the text, Waterhouse selects for particular examination the use made of the dialogue format as compared with the Latin, and the construction of metaphor/analogy complexes expanded from or added to the source. The changes mean that the tone of the OE version is more relaxed and intimate than the original.

The other translation certainly by Alfred is the *Old English Boethius* and this is the subject of W. F. Bolton's 'How Boethian is Alfred's *Boethius*?' (Szarmach [17]). Departures from the Latin original are noted, but Bolton reminds us finally that Alfred's text is not an individual reaction to a pure, original *Consolatio* since, for all practical purposes, no such original was available to him. Direct comparison is therefore misleading. What Alfred rendered into OE was the *Consolatio* as it had come down to the ninth century, and his individual contributions were in the tradition of these by then conventional features.

David Yerkes, likewise writing in Szarmach [17], continues his work on the OE *Dialogues* with an investigation of 'The Translation of Gregory's *Dialogues* and its Revision: Textual History, Provenance, Authorship'. His comparison of three 'unrevised manuscripts' with the Latin text leads to the conclusion that they descended independently from a common exemplar or archetype which was perhaps that circulated by Alfred. A similar close examination of the work of the Revising Scribe of Corpus Christi College Cambridge MS 32 and the Reviser of Oxford, Bodleian Library MS Hatton 116 leads him to propose that the reviser was Aldulf or Ealdwulf, one of the most esteemed followers of Æþelwold, who succeeded Oswald at Worcester. But we know that there was at least one other OE translation of the *Dialogues* in existence. Brigitte Langefeld, in 'A Third Old English Translation of Part of Gregory's *Dialogues*, This Time Embedded in the Rule of Chrodegang' (*ASE*), identifies Gregory's *Dialogues* as a source of the final chapter of the enlarged version of the Rule of Chrodegang of Metz and shows that the OE translation of it, which is found along with the Latin in Corpus Christi College Cambridge MS 191, was made independently of the versions by Werferth and his later reviser. The translation in question is given in full in the course of Langefeld's article.

The OE translation of Bede's *Ecclesiastical History* is the subject of Donald K. Fry's 'Bede Fortunate in his Translator: The Barking Nuns' in Szarmach [17]. Fry focuses on the translation of the miracles at the double monastery at Barking (IV.7–11) and shows that the translator responded sensitively to Bede's account, capturing and even heightening the features of imagery and diction by which Bede unified the series of miracles which are, in essence, somewhat diffuse and unspectacular.

Elizabeth M. Liggins, in 'Syntax and Style in the Old English *Orosius*' (Szarmach [17]), undertakes a stylistic analysis of the OE text, focusing on a number of syntactic elements in order to test the validity of the impression that the style of Book I is simple and somewhat tentative, that of Books II, III, IV, and V more assured, and that of Book VI comparatively monotonous. The results of this investigation lead Liggins to propose that there is nothing inherently unlikely in the view that more than one author shared in the translation of the historical books of Orosius.

Although the last four items noted refer to works not by Alfred, they have long been associated with his educational campaign and contribute indirectly, as his own translations do directly, to our sense of his achievement. Broader but revealing perspectives on Alfred's attitudes and status are given in two historical essays by Janet L. Nelson, which deserve mention here: 'Wealth and

Wisdom: The Politics of Alfred the Great' in the proceedings of the 1984 ACTA conference, edited this year by Joel T. Rosenthal under the general title of *Kings and Kingship* [18], and ' "A King across the Sea": Alfred in a Continental Perspective' (*TRHS*). More obviously literary in its implications is Simon Keynes's study of 'A Tale of Two Kings: Alfred the Great and Æthelræd the Unready' (*TRHS*), where we see how the sense of contrast between the successful Alfred and the unsuccessful Ethelred stems to a large extent from the tenor of the accounts of their reigns in the Anglo-Saxon Chronicle. Style is all.

Before moving on to consider the other publications on the Chronicle, however, I conclude the survey of work on Alfredian translation by referring to Allen J. Frantzen's *King Alfred* [19]. This book, as all others in the series, is aimed at the student, but Frantzen is to be congratulated on making the most of his subject within the obvious constraints. Rather than simply explaining what each OE work is about, he engages with the more complex and interesting issues of manuscript tradition, editorial history, critical approaches, and the forward movement of Alfredian scholarship. The whole is supported by frequent detailed notes and by a useful bibliography.

Turning now to the Anglo-Saxon Chronicle, I am happy to report another excellent contribution to the ambitious collaborative edition. Janet M. Bately's volume *The Anglo-Saxon Chronicle, MS A* [20], which is Volume III in the series although not the third to be published, provides us with a semi-diplomatic edition of Corpus Christi College Cambridge MS 173 (the Parker manuscript), which is the oldest of the surviving copies of the Chronicle but not the source of MSS B, C, D, or E. In fact the manuscript tradition to which A relates is now attested to solely by Latin materials. Bately's detailed and scholarly introduction explores these relationships at length. She also does much to elucidate the manuscript's textual history, not at all a straightforward matter since this is not simply the oldest manuscript, but also physically the most complex. As the general editors rightly note, much of what she says on these and other matters has implications which extend to other branches of Anglo-Saxon studies. Another contribution to the elucidation of the Chronicle's textual relationships is made by Audrey L. Meaney in 'St. Neots, Æthelweard and the Compilation of the *Anglo-Saxon Chronicle*: A Survey' (Szarmach [17]). In a long and detailed argument she examines the origin and development of the earlier versions of the Anglo-Saxon Chronicle and the relationship of Plummer's 'æ' (the 'common original' up to 892) to the annals of St Neots and Æþelweard's *Chronicon*. The evidence of the manuscripts is closely scrutinized, but so also are the theories of previous scholars. Meaney finally offers her own assessment of the compilation history, but also satisfies scholars with a less technical interest by making some observations on the Chronicle's stylistic qualities. Her chief concern, however, is what can be learnt about the preoccupations of the various chroniclers from their use of the materials available to them. By contrast, Karen Ferro's study of the Cynewulf and Cyneheard story, 'The King in the Doorway: The Anglo-Saxon Chronicle, A.D. 755', in Rosenthal [18], is concerned solely with literary criticism in the form of a detailed *explication de texte*, through which she

18. *Kings and Kingship*, ed. by Joel T. Rosenthal. Acta 11. CMERS. pp. 151. pb $15.

19. *King Alfred*, by Allen J. Frantzen. TEAS. Hall. pp. 148. $18.95.

20. *The Anglo-Saxon Chronicle: A Collaborative Edition*. Vol. III: *MS A*, ed. by Janet M. Bately. Brewer. pp. clxxvii + 124. £29.50.

identifies how the chronicler polarizes the protagonists, so emphasizing the clash between Cynewulf's forthright boldness and Cyneheard's more manipulative power.

The final article to be mentioned before surveying the large body of work on homiletic materials is Janet M. Bately's 'Evidence for Knowledge of Latin Literature in Old English'[1], which poses some searching questions about the accessibility of Latin literature to Anglo-Saxon writers: How did the material reach them? In what form? How much did they understand? Her discussion is wide-ranging and points to possible areas for future research, but in the main her attention centres on the evidence provided by four prose texts: the *Old English Orosius*, Alfred's *Boethius*, Alfred's *Soliloquies*, and the Anglo-Saxon Chronicle.

A ninth-century text which stands outside the Alfredian tradition is the *Old English Martyrology*. As in past years, our understanding of it continues to be advanced by the source studies of James E. Cross which, as always, demonstrate the need to go beyond the published Latin hagiographical material and to take into account early unpublished recensions. This year, in his 'Identification: Towards Criticism' (*Greenfield*[9]), he has turned his attention to St Pancras, Saints Julian and Basilissa, the Forty Soldiers of Sebastea, St Sosius, St Lucy of Rome, and St Mammas. In all cases the details in the OE text which appear odd when compared with printed Latin recensions are entirely comprehensible when unpublished manuscripts are consulted. There is therefore impressive cumulative evidence that the OE martyrologist was an altogether more learned man than George Herzfeld had surmised. In another article in Szarmach[17], 'The Latinity of the Ninth-Century Old English Martyrologist', Cross draws upon his extensive knowledge of the *Martyrology*'s sources to show that the author was a competent Latinist. Again this conflicts with the views of George Herzfeld, who commented in the introduction to his edition that the text contained some curious mistakes. Cross, however, accounts successfully for most of the 'mistakes' identified by Herzfeld, showing that some are attributable to Herzfeld's own misunderstanding, others to mistakes by the copyist, and yet others to the fact that Herzfeld was comparing the OE with a version or recension of the saint's life which was too far removed from the one that the Anglo-Saxon writer must have used. The third essay on this text is by Günter Kotzor. In 'The Latin Tradition of Martyrologies and the *Old English Martyrology*' (Szarmach[17]), he maps out, in a detailed and most informative way, the Latin tradition of prose martyrologies before the ninth century and shows that there is no striking relationship between the Latin and OE texts. Such a negative conclusion could well be thought to lead nowhere, but in fact, as Kotzor argues, it helps to define the degree of independence and originality in the vernacular martyrology. It is highly individual in its arrangement, with a tendency towards including narrative entries on 'rare' saints of mainly local interest, and it displays learning as well as independence and originality in selecting details from a large variety of sources. Clearly then, the *Old English Martyrology* deserves the increased attention that it has received in recent years and deserves attention in the years to come from scholars of various disciplines.

A small amount of attention has been paid to the Blickling Homilies this year. Paul Acker, in 'The Going-Out of the Soul in Blickling Homily IV' (*ELN*), suggests that a short eschatological passage on p. 195 of Morris's edition (ll. 6–17), for which a source had not previously been identified, derives ultimately from the *Visio Pauli*, the text long recognized as the source for the exemplum in Blickling IV, to which the material printed on p. 195 as item XVI in Morris's edition properly belongs. Acker also notes other similar examples of the influence of the *Visio Pauli* on the anonymous homilies and thus provides further evidence of the cohesiveness of eschatological *topoi* in this tradition. In 'Blickling Homily XIII Reconsidered' (*LeedsSE*), Mary Clayton elucidates, with admirable clarity, a confused and confusing apocryphal account of the assumption of the Virgin Mary. She identifies for the first time the source for the second section of the homily and discusses how and why the homilist combined this source with the apocryphal sources already known.

More popular this year is the Vercelli collection, for which there is comment on homilies I, IX, XIV, XV, and XXI. When Ælfric declined to produce homilies for the last three days of Holy Week, subsequent users of his collection filled the gaps, in the case of Good Friday by adopting a homily first recorded in the Vercelli MS (homily I). Paul E. Szarmach, in 'The Earlier Homily: *De Parasceve*'[17], examines the nature of this homily, the possible circumstances that influenced its form and content, and its suitability for filling the gap left by Ælfric. There are in fact four other recensions of it, which Szarmach considers briefly, but although the five witnesses exhibit various important differences, Szarmach uses the Vercelli version as the most accessible and the best known. D. G. Scragg, in ' "The Devil's Account of the Next World" Revisited' (*AN&Q*), shows how the imaginative portrayal of the common homiletic contrast between the pains of hell and the sensuous attractions of heaven in item 18 of BL MS Cotton Tiberius A iii is not an original composition, but a skilful compilation, which draws upon Vercelli homily IX. Scragg's investigation shows further that all the surviving OE examples are interrelated. It is also suggested, more tentatively, that there may be an Irish connection. Mary Clayton, in writing on 'Delivering the Damned: A Motif in OE Homiletic Prose' (*MÆ*), begins by noting that Ælfric, in his homily *In Natale Sanctarum Virginum*, rejected as heretical the belief that, at the Last Judgement, Mary and certain other saints would rescue a portion of those condemned by Christ to hell. Two anonymous homilies express this belief, however: Vercelli XV and an Easter homily in Corpus Christi College Cambridge MSS 41 and 304. Clayton discusses their treatment of this motif, the difficult question of the relationship between the two texts, and the possible genesis of the intercession motif, for which no source has yet been found. Finally, in 'Two Notes on the Vercelli Homilies' (*ELN*), Paul E. Szarmach contributes to the identification of sources for homilies XIV and XXI.

For those interested in the Catholic Homilies there is the exciting news that fifty-six manuscript fragments have been discovered and are now published, under the editorship of Else Fausbøll[21]. She describes how they were found in 1980 in the Rigsarkivet in Copenhagen in the bindings of thirteen of the seventeen volumes containing the papers of Peder Charisius, the Danish Resident at The Hague 1651–9. On the evidence of marginal additions it seems that they were read probably as late as the fifteenth or sixteenth centuries. Fausbøll gives a facsimile of each, with facing transcription. She also notes

21. *Fifty-six Ælfric Fragments: The Newly-Found Copenhagen Fragments of Ælfric's 'Catholic Homilies'. With Facsimiles*, ed. by Else Fausbøll. Dept of English, UCopenhagen. pp. 125. pb Dkr 133.

variations from Thorpe's text and provides a descriptive introduction, but she has not attempted to establish the place of the fragments in the tradition of Ælfric manuscripts. Ælfrician scholars will look forward eagerly to the results of such investigation.

Theodore H. Leinbaugh, in 'A Damaged Passage in Ælfric's *De Creatore et Creatura*: Methods of Recovery' (*Anglia*), performs a useful service in restoring nearly all of the damaged text of a hitherto unpublished sermon by Ælfric. The only manuscript witness to the sermon is BL MS Cotton Otho C.i, vol. 2, which was severely burnt in the Cotton fire, but the text in question is related to Ælfrician passages elsewhere, which Leinbaugh draws upon in his restoration. His article is useful also in commenting in detail upon the state of the manuscript and on aspects of its possible history before the fire.

Joseph B. Traherne Jr's brief note 'Ælfric: More Sources for Two Homilies' (*AN&Q*) identifies a text by Cæsarius of Arles as the source for ll. 1–6 of Ælfric's homily on Ascension Eve (Pope XXV), and one by Augustine for part of his homily on the Nativity (Pope I). There is further source-identification, this time for Ælfric's *Sermo de Sacrificio in Die Pascae*, in Theodore Leinbaugh's 'The Sources for Ælfric's Easter Sermon: The History of the Controversy and a New Source' (*N&Q*), but here the author's chief aim is to examine in detail the contribution that Ælfric's sermon made to the debate on transubstantiation once it was published in 1566 or 1567. The article concludes with a valuable bibliographical appendix of authors from the sixteenth century to the present day who have cited Ælfric's stand against transubstantiation. In fact, as Leinbaugh makes clear, the influential text published in the sixteenth century had been moulded by tendentious editing which destroyed Ælfric's fragile synthesis of symbolist and carnal interpretations. The subject of 'The Exegesis of Inebriation: Treading Carefully in Old English' (*ELN*) by Hugh Magennis is homily IV from the Second Series of Catholic Homilies (the Marriage Feast at Cana). Here too Ælfric's source is significant, but in a negative way, in that Ælfric can be seen to omit Bede's imagery of spiritual inebriation. Even though it was used often enough in the Christian Latin tradition, Magennis shows that Ælfric was not alone among vernacular writers in avoiding it. In an immediately following note, 'Water – Wine Miracles in Anglo-Saxon Saints' Lives' (*ELN*), Magennis speculates that this reticence was probably due to the worries of Old English writers about the dangers of literal intoxication. By contrast however, as Magennis shows, Anglo-Saxon hagiographical narratives, both Latin and Old English, frequently refer to miracles of increase of wine and of water being turned into wine, a type of miracle which is given respectability by its powerful association with Christ's miracle at Cana.

Ælfric was always reticent about apocryphal material also, and when he first prepared his collection of Catholic Homilies he did not include an item for the feast of the Nativity of the Blessed Virgin. He wrote a homily later, however, which he intended to form part of his revised edition of the First Series. In an interesting and informative article on 'Ælfric and the Nativity of the Blessed Virgin Mary' (*Anglia*), Mary Clayton examines the possible reasons for the original omission and shows how Ælfric subsequently came to terms with the need to provide a homily for the feastday (8 September). The study as a whole makes a valuable contribution to our understanding of Ælfric's attitude towards apocryphal material and the extent to which he set himself standards which were perhaps more exacting even than those of Winchester, where he had been trained. It is worth noting at this point that in 'Assumptio Mariae: An Eleventh-Century Anglo-Latin Poem from Abingdon' (*AnBol*) Mary Clayton has described and edited a poem on the Assumption from a monastery which had been subjected to the rigorous reforms of Æþelwold. We also owe to Clayton the identification of two further instances of Ælfric's habit of using reminiscences of other texts even when he is using a main source fairly closely. The instances that she cites in '*Ælfric and Cogitis Me*' (*N&Q*) are in the homilies for the Feast of the Purification and of All Saints in the First Series of Catholic Homilies, both of which contain reminiscences of the Pseudo-Jerome text *Cogitis Me*. *Cogitis Me* was used as the principal source for the First Series homily on the Assumption of the Virgin and Ælfric evidently recalled it when writing the other two homilies because they also deal with the Virgin.

In a full and detailed study of 'Contrasting Features in the Non-Ælfrician Lives in the Old English *Lives of Saints*' (*Anglia*) Hugh Magennis demonstrates that vocabulary choices and characteristics of style show clearly that the lives of St Mary of Egypt, St Eustace, St Euphrosyna, and the Seven Sleepers could not have been by Ælfric and that, moreover, each is the work of a different writer. Each of the lives is discussed in turn, but the article is useful also for Magennis's analysis of some of Ælfric's saints' lives, which are referred to for comparative purposes. It is evident, however, that the non-Ælfrician saints' lives are important in themselves, and Colin Chase, in 'Source Study as a Trick with Mirrors: Annihilation of Meaning in the Old English "Mary of Egypt"'[1], uses one of them to illustrate that the culture within which even traditional texts are repeated becomes implicit in their meaning. He invites us to consider the implications that this has for source study: we must not, in dealing with text or source, abstract it from its physical and cultural *Sitz im Leben*.

In 'St George Before the Conquest' (*Report of the Society of the Friends of St George's and the Descendants of the Knights of the Garter*) Joyce Hill assembles the evidence for Anglo-Saxon interest in the cult of St George, noting in particular the form of his legend in circulation, the attitude towards it of Anglo-Latin and vernacular authors, and the apparent rise in the status of the saint towards the end of the period.

J. E. Cross's edition and study of 'An Unpublished Story of Michael the Archangel and its Connections' from Pembroke College Cambridge MS 25 in a Festschrift for Robert Earl Kaske[22] is of a Latin homily, but it is referred to here because of its tangential relevance to the vernacular accounts of St Michael and because, in his opening remarks, Cross draws attention to the connection between this Latin homiliary and a number of Old English homilies, including some from the Vercelli manuscript.

Another saint commented upon this year is Thomas. According to Richard James's seventeenth-century table of contents, BL MS Cotton Vitellius A xv contained as its third item part of the OE legend of St Thomas, which was unaccountably lost by 1705. Although doubts have been expressed, the information is repeated in N. R. Ker's *Catalogue of Manuscripts Containing Anglo-Saxon* (1957) and by Kevin Kiernan in *'Beowulf' and the 'Beowulf'*

---

22. *Magister Regis: Studies in Honor of Robert Earl Kaske*, ed. by Arthur Groos, with Emerson Brown Jr, Thomas D. Hill, Giuseppe Mazzotta, and Joseph S. Wittig. FordU. pp. viii + 292. $50.

Manuscript (*YW* 64.96–7). Roland Torkar, in 'Cotton Vitellius A xv (pt. I) and the *Legend of St Thomas*' (*ES*), examines Part I of this manuscript with great care and shows that no textual losses have been sustained since it came into Cotton's possession, and that what James identified as part of the St Thomas legend was in fact the colophon to King Alfred's *Soliloquies*. The correction of a long-standing misapprehension is valuable in itself, but the investigation also identifies errors in Kiernan's study of the manuscript in connection with his attempts to redate *Beowulf*.

Guthlac and Machutus are more localized saints than George, Michael, and Thomas. Jane Roberts begins her study of 'The Old English Prose Translation of Felix's *Vita Sancti Guthlaci*'[17] by observing that the OE translation is not well known among readers of OE and that, perhaps as a result of the inaccessibility of Paul Gonser's 1909 edition, curiously inaccurate statements are made about this work. Roberts's survey of the surviving texts, the *Life* in BL MS Cotton Vespasian D xxi and the *Homily* which is the final item in the Vercelli manuscript, clarifies the situation admirably. There is, of course, an obvious relevance to the OE *Guthlac* poems, as Roberts repeatedly signals. David Yerkes, in a note on 'The Provenance of the Unique Copy of the Old English Translation of Bili, *Vita Sancti Machuti*' (*Manuscripta*) supplements information contained in his edition of *The Old English Life of Machutus* (*YW* 65.100–1) and strengthens the possibility that the group of texts (Group D) of which the *vita* is one, was copied at Worcester, as were Groups C and E.

The survey of work on saints' lives concludes with articles by Michelle P. Brown and D. W. Rollason. Brown, in 'Paris, Bibliothèque Nationale, lat. 10861 and the Scriptorium of Christ Church Canterbury' (*ASE*), demonstrates that this Anglo-Saxon manuscript containing saints' lives was probably written at Christ Church Canterbury, or at a related southern house, during the first quarter of the ninth century. There are implications here both for the study of Anglo-Latin and OE saints' lives as well as for the study of ninth-century southern English script. Brown expresses the hope, in conclusion, that the dating of this manuscript will have helped in the establishment of a chronology of the important 'Canterbury' or 'Tiberius' group of manuscripts and its associates. Rollason's 'Relic-cults as an Instrument of Royal Policy *c.* 900– *c.* 1050' (*ASE*) is more historical, but his comments on the general issue of the cult of saints in the later part of the Anglo-Saxon period are of interest to anyone working on vernacular hagiographic narratives.

The last three items of all fall into none of the major prose categories. Patrizia Lendinara's study of 'The Third Book of *The Bella Parisiacae Urbis* by Abbo of Saint-Germain-des-Prés and its Old English Gloss' (*ASE*) discusses the vernacular gloss but is in fact principally a study of the poem itself and its fortunes in England, where the verses were rearranged and where we find evidence of a prose version. A manuscript of the poem was among the books given by Æþelwold to the monastery of Peterborough and this fact, as well as the OE gloss from the first part of the eleventh century, is of interest to anyone working on the period of the Benedictine Reform. Lendinara concludes by wondering whether the glossator's choice of words was dictated by poor training or by educational practice, by good sense or by disapproval – akin to Ælfric's – of the hermeneutic style of Abbo's work.

The Regius Psalter, written *c.* 950, possibly but by no means certainly at Winchester, appears to have reached Christ Church Canterbury by the eleventh century. Patrick P. O'Neill's examination of 'A Lost Old-English Charter Rubric: The Evidence from the Regius Psalter' (*N&Q*) strengthens this established Canterbury connection and allows him to suggest that the scribe of the notes on the end flyleaf (f. 198v) had access to the monastery's collection of original charters, now extant only in the form of a thirteenth-century Latin cartulary.

Mary P. Richards, in 'The Manuscript Contexts of the Old English Laws: Tradition and Innovation'[17], attempts to show that collections of laws had various functions which become apparent when one considers them in their manuscript contexts, and that they were not copied and recopied simply as historical records. Their transmission takes us into the twelfth century and thus into the period covered by the following chapter.

Middle English: Excluding Chaucer

T. P. DOLAN, A. J. FLETCHER, and S. POWELL

The chapter has eleven sections: 1. General and Miscellaneous Items; 2. Alliterative Poetry; 3. The Gawain-Poet; 4. Piers Plowman; 5. Romances; 6. Gower, Lydgate, and Hoccleve; 7. Middle Scots Poetry; 8. Lyrics and Miscellaneous Verse; 9. Malory and Caxton; 10. Other Prose; 11. Drama. Sections 1, 4, and 10 are by T. P. Dolan; 3, 8, and 11 by A. J. Fletcher; and 2, 5, 6, 7, and 9 by S. Powell.

1. General and Miscellaneous Items

This year there have been some remarkable contributions which break entirely new ground and indicate the vitality of Middle English studies.

It would be difficult to overpraise Penn R. Szittya's book on *The Antifraternal Tradition in Medieval Literature*[1] or indeed to overestimate its importance in scholarship concerned with Middle English literature. An earlier article in *Speculum* (*YW* 58.75) explained the growth of the perception of the mendicants as forerunners of Antichrist. His present account is an eminently readable study, self-contained and generously supported from every conceivable authority (the footnotes alone comprise a uniquely valuable source-study of the antimendicant problem). In the introduction he unravels what he calls 'The Puzzle of Sire *Penetrans Domos*' and the ensuing seven chapters take us through the early history of the controversy, featuring the contributions of William of St Amour and his *De Periculis Novissimorum Temporum*, the mercurial Richard FitzRalph, John Wyclif and his followers, and the English poetic tradition, culminating with 'The False Apostle' in Chaucer's The Summoner's Tale and *Piers Plowman*. Szittya's command of such disparate material (historical, biblical, polemical, literary) is an awesome achievement. Time and again his phrasing tempers the seriousness of his material – for instance, his felicitous description of Elde in *Piers Plowman* rounding on Will the dreamer, 'running smack over his head like a runaway lawnmower'. There are two appendixes, one setting out the sources of the *Omne Bonum* Article on 'Fratres', and the other collating this Article with the sources of MS Bodley 784, Part 3. The book concludes with two indexes, one general and the other listing the biblical references. The absence of a formal bibliography leaves us with something at which to cavil, but the footnotes healthily defuse that problem. Perhaps one should quibble about the term 'antifraternal' itself, which may appear awkward to purists, or that the different orders of friars, which tend to

1. *The Antifraternal Tradition in Medieval Literature*, by Penn R. Szittya. Princeton. pp. xvi + 316. £26.70.

be treated as a homogeneous unit in the book, should perhaps have been more clearly differentiated according to their diverging Rules. But these are hardly blemishes in such a sumptuous treasure of original scholarship.

'What sort of literature is popular and for what reasons?' is one of the many basic questions asked and answered in an important, original book, entitled *The Popular Literature of Medieval England*[2]. Thirteen major scholars have contributed essays on: the various audiences and occasions for which medieval popular literature was written (by D. W. Robertson Jr), manuals of popular theology (by Leonard E. Boyle), the influence of canonical and episcopal reform on popular books of instruction such as *The Lay Folks' Catechism* (by Judith Shaw), the folkloric sources of medieval popular literature (by Bruce A. Rosenberg), secular life and popular piety in medieval English drama (by Stanley J. Kahrl), the medieval romances (by Edmund Reiss), attitudes to pilgrimage represented by Chaucer and Erasmus (by John V. Fleming), the Middle English *Planctus Mariae* devotional literature and its concern with eliciting compassion (by George R. Keiser), learned and popular eschatology in *Piers Plowman* (by Robert Adams), the influence of Chancery documents on the text of Chaucerian manuscripts (by John H. Fisher), Richard Rolle's debt to Bonaventuran mysticism in the *Melos Amoris* (by William F. Pollard), and the similarity of Margery Kempe's assimilation of the mystical qualities of the Virgin Mary as compared with the practices of the Beguines of Belgium and the Dominican nuns of Germany (by Ute Stargardt). The book is a feast of brilliant insights and represents a watershed in the history of the popular literature of the medieval period since it redefines, with notable success, most of the so-called truisms and received opinions which have been regurgitated so often in the classroom.

Graciela S. Daichman's *Wayward Nuns in Medieval Literature*[3] is not as exciting as its title suggests. It is a chatty, almost gossipy account of a very limited range of nuns – to be precise, the Doña Garoza in the *Libro de Buen Amor* and Chaucer's Madame Eglentyne. These two egregious ladies take the stage in Chapter 4, after three introductory chapters which chase up references to deviances in nunneries all over the place. This book is a delightful read but lacks scholarly rigour: 'What a wonderful touch of fine Chaucerian irony to have Madame Eglentyne wear a wimple as a nun naturally would. . . .' Infelicities creep into the text, such as a blatantly incorrect translation of an extract from the Hiberno-English 'Satire on the People of Kildare' (p. 51). The author has done a lot of worthy research but the result in several respects does not equal the effort.

In his introduction to an anthology of essays on Middle English literature[4] David Aers includes a review of the book by an anonymous reader, with whom he takes issue. It makes for fascinating reading. Following this lively start, nine articles by different scholars sustain the individuality of the introduction. Aers himself contributes a penetrating analysis of the implications of Chaucer's

2. *The Popular Literature of Medieval England*, ed. by Thomas J. Heffernan. UTenn. pp. xii + 330. $28.50.

3. *Wayward Nuns in Medieval Literature*, by Graciela S. Daichman. Syracuse. pp. xvi + 223; 13 illus. $35.

4. *Medieval Literature: Criticism, Ideology and History*, ed. by David Aers. Harvester. pp. vii + 228. £28.50.

Friar's opinion that 'Glosynge is a glorious thyng'. Toril Moi looks at the code of courtly love in a useful essay on Andreas's *De amore*. Margery Kempe's mysticism is sympathetically reviewed in the light of modern feminist studies by Sarah Beckwith. Anthony Gash attempts, with some success, to redefine the 'evaluated effect' of some medieval drama against the background of 'recent historical research into medieval popular culture and belief', which includes Mikhail Bakhtin's *Rabelais and his World*. For Stephen Knight, 'the romances are the ugly ducklings of medieval English studies', but his essay discloses their importance as a 'testimony to the hopes and fears of the medieval English ruling class'. Derek Pearsall's magnificent commendation of the English tradition of literary criticism (with specific reference to Chaucer), as opposed to the anachronistic and dangerously simplistic attitudes fostered by New Criticism, stands out from all the other essays in this volume since it monitors many of the tenets they cite. Mikhail Bakhtin's work on Carnival is used again, with great success, in a wide-ranging essay on the function of laughter in *The Canterbury Tales* by Jon Cook. The final essay in this arresting book is contributed by Bernard Sharratt, who again uses Bakhtin's work (this time his notion of the dialogic 'novel') as a basis for his provocative discussion of Skelton's multilingualism. Any medieval student who is interested in current literary theory will be enriched and sometimes infuriated by this book.

Acta was devoted to the important theme of 'Text and Image' and includes eight papers by a distinguished group of scholars, led by John V. Fleming, who deal in various ways with the relationship between written texts and their illustrations or between 'images in the visual arts and their literary, biblical, patristic, or other sources'.

G. H. V. Bunt provides a great deal of useful information in his paper on 'The Story of Alexander the Great in the Middle English Translations of Higden's *Polychronicon*'[5]. Two translations survive, one by John Trevisa, and the other by an anonymous scholar (extant only in British Library MS Harley 2261). Significant comparisons show the superiority of Trevisa's version.

Stephan Kohl thoughtfully provides a summary in English of his *Das englische Spätmittelalter, Kulturelle Normen, Lebenspraxis, Texte*[6]. He was motivated by the desire to identify the originality of fifteenth-century English literary works, especially those which have been perceived until now as imperfect copies of earlier writings. Certainly such works venerate the past, but they exhibit concerns relevant to their time (e.g. *The Troy Book* as compared with *Troilus and Criseyde*). As well as this type of writing, the author notes works which 'follow new, more pragmatic, more realistic ideas' (e.g. the Prologue to *The Tale of Beryn* as compared with the General Prologue). It is an interesting thesis which helps to clarify specific qualities of fifteenth-century literature.

Mary Dove has written a remarkably original monograph entitled *The Perfect Age of Man's Life*[7], comprising three major sections: 'The Middle Age of Man's Life'; 'The Perfect Age of Man's Life'; and 'The Perfect Age in Ricardian Poetry'. This last section deals in fascinating detail with 'Myddel

5. In *Vincent of Beauvais and Alexander the Great: Studies on the 'Speculum Maius' and its Translations into Medieval Vernaculars*, ed. by W. J. Aerts, E. R. Smits, and J. B. Voorbij. pp. viii + 187. Forsten.

6. *Das englische Spätmittelalter Kulturelle Normen, Lebenspraxis, Texte*, by Stephan Kohl. Niemeyer. pp. viii + 270. DM 78.

7. *The Perfect Age of Man's Life*, by Mary Dove. CUP. pp. xiii + 175. £25.

Age' and 'Hy tyme' in *Piers Plowman*; 'Myghty youthe' in *Confessio Amantis*; 'Hyghe eldee' in *Sir Gawain*; and the 'ryght yong' man and Lady Perfect Age in *The Book of the Duchess*. The author skilfully demonstrates that middle age in the Middle Ages was typically perceived as a 'perfect age'. This perception confronts the *memento mori* conviction of so many other artefacts in medieval art and literature (cf. Philippa Tristram's excellent study on this theme, *YW* 57.60–1).

Following Augustine, Richard Lock asks 'Quid est tempus?' in his interesting study of *Aspects of Time in Medieval Literature*[8], with specific reference to narrative. Concepts of time are closely related to literacy and non-literacy: the former utilizes linear time, and the latter cyclic time. Thus, the action of *The Song of Roland*, for instance, displays a cyclic structure, whereas the style and narrative of *Sir Gawain and the Green Knight* are linear in concept. The analysis considers *Atlamál*, *Atlakviða*, *Beowulf*, *Sir Gawain and the Green Knight*, *Gunnlaugs Saga*, The Shipman's Tale, and *Yvain* in the light of this basic thesis: that 'the invention of the mechanical striking clock and of the fixed hour of sixty minutes' had a profound effect on the way authors organized their narrative sequences.

J. D. Burnley breaks new ground in his searching analysis of the term 'style clergial' in his authoritative article on 'Christine de Pisan and the so-called *style clergial*' (*MLR*). The term has been commonly misapplied.

In an interesting paper Sharon Farmer makes good use of Thomas de Chobham's *Summa Confessorum* (*c*. 1215) to clarify the perception which medieval clerical writers had of the role of women, in particular their function as monitors of the moral and economic behaviour of their husbands (*Speculum*). One among many useful points is an explanation of the value which Thomas placed on women's powers of speech as contrasted with the universal endorsement of monastic silence.

In an important article Debora K. Shuger challenges currently held assumptions about 'The Grand Style and the *genera dicendi* in Ancient Rhetoric' (*Traditio*, 1984), and convincingly identifies differences between the Greek and Roman understanding and realization of the *genus grande*.

Finally, we acknowledge a momentous and long-awaited event in medieval studies. Douglas Gray has accomplished a singularly difficult task in bringing the late J. A. W. Bennett's volume of The Oxford History of English Literature[9] to press. There are ten chapters. The first, on Pastoral and Comedy, deals with a selection of texts exhibiting these two effects, including *The Owl and the Nightingale* and *Dame Sirith*. In the second chapter there is a comprehensive critical survey of didactic and homiletic verse. Chapter 3 is given over entirely to Laȝamon in a persuasive attempt to raise his status and to justify F. Madden's description of the *Brut* as 'semi-Saxon'. Chapters 4 and 5 deal respectively with History in Verse (e.g. Barbour's *Bruce*) and Romances. The poems of the Gawain manuscript are examined in Chapter 6. Then, a happy decision results in about a hundred pages being devoted to a sympathetic appraisal and analysis of medieval prose. The three final chapters deal respectively with Lyrics,

---

8. *Aspects of Time in Medieval Literature*, by Richard Lock. Garland (1985). pp. iii + 270. $35.

9. *Middle English Literature*, by J. A. W. Bennett, ed. and completed by Douglas Gray. Clarendon. pp. xi + 496. £25.

Gower, and Langland. The main study is followed by a useful chronological table and a select bibliography. The volume is a monument of humane criticism and will occupy a prominent place in the distinguished Oxford History. It represents the distillation of a lifetime's study of medieval English literature and may be confidently recommended to all students for its sensitivity, originality and, above all, its incomparable learning.

2. Alliterative Poetry

Recent surveys of the literary development of Arthur will be treated here, although they are, of course, also relevant to sections 5 and 9.

Peter Korrel's chronological survey of Arthur, Guinevere, and Modred [10] is a conscientious and useful summary, unfortunately not sufficiently transmogrified from the Ph.D. thesis it once was. Korrel too has preferred the old to the recent edition and is not as aware of current criticism as he should be (his comments on Malory need revision, certainly). However, he provides us with chapters on the historical records (Gildas, Bede, etc.) and early Welsh poetry; Geoffrey, Wace, and Laȝamon; the alliterative *Morte Arthure*, stanzaic *Morte Arthur*, and *Morte Darthur*; and a somewhat perfunctory epilogue. The chapters provide more than a mere chronicle – Korrel gives his own opinions and comes to his own conclusions: interestingly, for example, that Gildas's Ambrosius Aurelianus may be Arthur himself. Korrel's initial justification for covering somewhat the same ground as Karl Heinz Göller's *König Arthur* (1963) is his additional treatment of Guinevere and Modred and his inclusion of the Welsh material ignored then (but since rectified) by Göller. However, the treatment of the former is less careful than that of Arthur himself, and Korrel's conclusion on the Welsh poetry is expressed in regret that, despite its richness, it had almost no influence on medieval Arthurian literature.

In 1984 James J. Wilhelm and Laila Zamuelis Gross made a valiant attempt 'to bring under one cover some of the richly diverse materials related to the romantic lore of King Arthur' [11] with material on the Latin chronicles, the early Welsh poetry and *Culhwch and Olwen*, Geoffrey, Chrétien's *Lancelot*, *Gawain*, the alliterative *Morte Arthure*, and Caxton's *Morte Darthur*. New translations were commissioned from the contributors, Chrétien and *Gawain* were printed whole with introductory essays, and the other selections were woven into discussions of the subjects treated. The audience throughout would seem to have been educated layman rather than academic. Wilhelm and Gross gushed at the time that 'it was difficult to omit many of the beautiful Arthurian works that one would have liked to have here' and in 1986, after Gross's death, an unexpected Part 2 has appeared [12]. This is altogether better, with many more complete texts provided, and the two volumes together are creditable and useful to layman and academic alike. Part 2 has selections from Wace, Laȝamon, Thomas, the *Prose Merlin* and the *Suite du Merlin*, and complete translations of

10. *An Arthurian Triangle: A Study of the Origin, Development and Characterization of Arthur, Guinevere and Modred*, by Peter Korrel. Brill (1984). pp. viii + 301. Fl 110.

11. *The Romance of Arthur*, ed. by James J. Wilhelm and Laila Zamuelis Gross. Garland (1984). pp. vii + 314. hb $47, pb $15.

12. *The Romance of Arthur*, Part 2, ed. by James J. Wilhelm. Garland. pp. x + 271. hb $45, pb $15.

Peredur, Graelent, Chrétien's *Yvain*, Béroul's *Tristan*, Marie de France's *Chievrefueil*. As in the 1984 volume, there is a short booklist at the end of each section, but the 1984 general booklist has been extended to cover the best-known foreign, as well as English, works.

Also in 1984, Karl Heinz Göller was writing on 'The Figure of King Arthur as a Mirror of Political and Religious Views'[13]. Resoundingly dogmatic, Göller takes us chronologically through the attempts of Church and State to anglicize, vulgarize, and Christianize Arthur, while arguing that 'even today, King Arthur retains both his religious and his political significance, even if the authorities of Church and State object'. There is plenty both to stimulate and irritate in this provocative piece.

In the field of alliterative poetry proper, the alliterative *Morte Arthure* has received most attention this year. Mary Hamel's dissertation on the editorial problems and principles of the poem has resulted in an excellent critical edition[14]. Her justification for a successor to Valerie Krishna's 1978 edition is her use of the Winchester manuscript which she discusses in the introduction and places at the foot of her edited text, but she admits that, while it has provided useful information, her treatment of it has been 'conservative, if not actively suspicious'. The introduction is thorough, sensible, and a pleasure to read. She argues against conjectural emendation based on stylistic assumptions to do with verbal repetition, alliterative irregularities, paratactic and elliptical syntax, formulaic technique, and unusual French lexis – 'scribal blunders there certainly are in this text but there are probably fewer than has often been assumed'. In dating she opts for 1398–1402. While accepting an essentially provincial audience for alliterative verse, she presents a poet 'attached in some capacity to the household of one of the great nobles'. The notes, select bibliography, and glossary are excellent, and there is an appendix on 'Scribal Self-Corrections in the Thornton *Morte Arthure*' (*YW* 64.124). A further appendix is provided by W. G. Cooke's suggestions for interesting and generally plausible readings to replace those of both Krishna and Hamel in 'Notes on the Alliterative *Morte Arthure*' (*ES*).

In 'Sir Gawain in the Alliterative *Morte Arthure*' (*PLL*), Christopher Dean argues that Gawain's significance lies in his relation to Arthur – 'Gawain's role is to complement that of Arthur by displaying those qualities which are praiseworthy in a knight but which would perhaps be unsuitable in a monarch'. Gawain's reputation undergoes whitewashing in order to support Dean's theory of comparisons and contrasts.

David V. Harrington's reaction to the problems posed by two of the best-known alliterative poems is to argue that they are deliberate problems. In 'Indeterminacy in *Winner and Waster* and *The Parliament of the Three Ages*' (*ChauR*), he points out that 'nearly every generic feature in these poems – the irresponsible narrator, the dream vision, the debate, personification allegory – encourages uncertainty rather than assurance', and he contends, not unconvincingly, that through these features the poets aim at 'a more dynamic,

---

13. In *Functions of Literature: Essays Presented to Erwin Wolff on his Sixtieth Birthday*, ed. by Ulrich Broich, Theo Stemmler, and Gerd Stratmann. Niemeyer (1984). pp. vi + 328. DM 192.

14. *Morte Arthure: A Critical Edition*, ed. by Mary Hamel. Garland (1984). pp. xi + 546. $65.

intellectual reception by the intended audience', who are encouraged to seek conclusions for themselves.

In the year prior to his edition of *William of Palerne* (*YW* 66.139), G. H. V. Bunt wrote on the poem in 'Patron, Author and Audience in a Fourteenth-Century Alliterative Poem'[15]. Bunt argues that Humphrey de Bohun was an intended reader of the poem he commissioned (Turville-Petre and others accept that the readership was only his non-French-speaking retainers) and that he might well want an English translation since French would have been 'an acquired language, in which he was less fluent than in his native English'. The Gloucestershire connections of the poem are suspect, Bunt contends, and based on a mistranslation of l. 166. The article is worth reading and the apology for 'very unexciting, if not indeed trivial' conclusions may be read as a modesty topos. In '*William of Palerne* and *Alafekks saga*' (*Florilegium*, 1984), Hubert E. Morgan not unexpectedly finds the saga less sophisticated a work than the romance. His conclusion is that 'even though the works seem structurally homologous the meanings of the transformation allomotifs in them are quite distinct'.

In 'Laȝamon's Welsh Sources' (*ES*), Françoise Le Saux dismisses Herbert Pilch's resurrection of Madden's belief in Welsh sources for the *Brut*, though she thinks it possible that he used one of the Welsh prophetic poems for his account of the discussions at the battle of Lincoln. If so, she prefers to think that the poet was introduced to the Welsh poem by an informant who chose it as least abusive of the English. It is less likely that Laȝamon knew Welsh, though he knew and respected Welsh tradition.

In the more mechanistic fields of Laȝamon study, James Noble writes in 'The Four-Stress Hemistich in Laȝamon's *Brut*' (*NM*) that, notwithstanding the practice of his contemporaries and the assertions of metrists, the poet uses that particular metre only rarely and not exclusively in non-alliterating lines. Where he does employ it, it is for emphasis or to make a dramatic point. From Hans Sauer's 'Laȝamon's Compound Nouns and their Morphology'[16] we learn that the poet is 'fairly conservative in his use of compounding types as far as nouns are concerned: he hardly uses types that are new in Middle English; he also hardly uses those synthetic and verbal-nexus types that go back to Old English and have become very productive in Modern English'.

Two interesting notes end this section. In '"Queme Questis" in *Saint Erkenwald*' (*ELN*, 1985), Thomas A. Ryan suggests that the obscure phrase in l. 133 of the poem is a corruption of the Easter introit, 'Quem quaeritis'. He admits that there is no evidence for the detachment of this particular trope from the Easter liturgy but suggests that the angel's rebuke to the Maries at the tomb resembles Bishop Erkenwald's rebuke to the people of London over the miraculously preserved corpse at St Paul's. William G. Cooke writes on 'The Tournament of Tottenham: An Alliterative Poem and an Exeter Performance' (*REEDN*). Until now the poem has been neglected and there has been no evidence for English mock tournaments of the type it describes. John Wasson's researches for REED in Devon have uncovered a reference to a Tottenham

---

15. In *Mélanges de Civilisation Mediévale Dédiés à Willem Noomen*, ed. by Martin Gosman and Jaap van Os. Bouma (1984). pp. x + 298. $50.

16. In *Historical Semantics: Historical Word-Formation*, ed. by Jacek Fisiak. TiLSM. Mouton (1985). pp. xiii + 607. $121.

tournament at Rougemont Castle in 1432-3 and Cooke speculates interestingly and sensibly on the possible significance of the reference in the Exeter Receiver's Account Rolls.

Also relevant to this section is Jean E. Jost's *Ten Middle English Arthurian Romances: A Reference Guide*, which is reviewed in section 5.

3. The Gawain-Poet

Only one book was published on *Sir Gawain and the Green Knight* this year, and its novelty makes it more conspicuous still. *Approaches to Teaching 'Sir Gawain and the Green Knight'*[17] is the result of an enquiry conducted by the Modern Language Association of America into how *Gawain* is taught in, for the most part, American colleges. Its first section, 'Materials', looks at what editions of the poem are recommended and compares their relative merits, and also at what have proved the most useful items to include in bibliographies. The second section, 'Approaches', comprises short accounts by various scholars on particular angles that can be taken on the poem (for example, '*Sir Gawain and the Green Knight* and a Course in Literary Criticism', 'The Celtic Heritage of *Sir Gawain and the Green Knight*'), and on how scholars go about teaching them. This book is a notable satisfier of curiosity, and its interest on this side of the Atlantic will mainly consist in the picture it draws of how American colleagues face the pedagogical problems raised by this poem. It may also suggest some fresh approaches.

In 'To "Ouertake Your Wylle": Volition and Obligation in *Sir Gawain and the Green Knight*' (*Neophil*), Robert J. Blanch and Julian N. Wasserman investigate the legal role of 'wylle' in medieval contractual tradition and read *Sir Gawain and the Green Knight* in the light of their findings. Their reading, while sometimes informative, tends towards reductive overemphasis, and is not uncontentious in its unguarded acceptance of the 'flawed confession' theory. Peter J. Lucas writes a note on 'Hautdesert in *Sir Gawain and the Green Knight*' (*Neophil*), suggesting that for some members of the poet's audience, Hautdesert may have been reminiscent of either the Beaudesert near Henley-in-Arden or, perhaps even more so, of that near Longdon, the site of an episcopal palace of the Bishops of Lichfield.

In 'The Two Courts: Two Modes of Existence in "Sir Gawain and the Green Knight"' (*ES*), Heinz Bergner suggests an eminently sensible approach to the similarities and differences that mark the courts of Arthur and Bertilak, and discusses their possible consequences for an understanding of the poem. He also offers an intriguing speculation that the counterpointing of the two courts may in its way be a poetic reflex of the perception that an actual provincial court had of itself in relation to court society in the capital. Doreen M. E. Gillam makes a credible case to suggest why in '*Sir Gawain and the Green Knight*, Lines 1020-1066' (*Expl*), the *Gawain*-poet seems to ignore Holy Innocents' day (28 December) in his chronology of the days following Christmas. She believes, however, that the poet has taken over the associations of ill-omen that the day traditionally held, and has drawn on the courtly game of capture in the

17. *Approaches to Teaching 'Sir Gawain and the Green Knight'*, ed. by Miriam Youngerman Miller and Jane Chance. MLA. pp. xii + 256. hb $27.50, pb $14.50.

bedroom by women (the game of *prisio*), the sort of game likely during this season, even on the ominous Childermas.

J. Eadie claims to have found 'A New Source for the Green Knight' (*NM*) in certain details of the descriptions of the characters Eur and Meseur, particularly the latter, who feature in the *Livre de la Mutacion de Fortune*, a work completed by Christine de Pisan in 1403. If Eadie's source be accepted, it has obvious implications for dating *Sir Gawain and the Green Knight*. Moreover, he proposes the years 1414 and 1415 as providing the only dates when the poet, whom he considers to have been a clerk in the *familia* of Thomas Langley, Bishop of Durham, could have had access to the *Livre* (Langley was in Paris on embassies in both these years). These large claims deserve careful consideration. However, I think far too many objections to this thesis have been silently passed over.

'The Idea of the Green Knight' (*ELH*), by Lawrence Besserman, is a fluent but rather periphrastic discussion of the function of the Green Knight in the poem. He considers that the doctrine of the hypostatic union, the idea of Christ as both human and divine, provides a medieval conceptual analogue to the paradoxical Green Knight. He makes the interesting point that not only the Green Knight but Gawain too might be regarded as a double image, as 'the pentangle/girdle knight, the nephew of Arthur/the nephew of Morgan le Fay'. Sidney Wade presents 'An Analysis of the Similes and their Function in the Characterization of the Green Knight' (*NM*) in which he illustrates a neat proportional balance between similes from the world of nature and those from the world of the court in the description of the Green Knight. This balance illustrates in microcosm one of the larger themes of the poem, paradox. The 'Notes on British Library, MS Cotton Nero A.x' (*Manuscripta*) by Sarah M. Horrall add further evidence in support of Ian Doyle's argument that the Cotton Nero A.x manuscript was copied in two stages: first the text itself, dated by Doyle sometime in the last quarter of the fourteenth century, and second the pictures, added even as late as the early years of the fifteenth century. Her evidence rests mainly upon dating the fashions worn in the manuscript illustrations. The pictures, she argues, could not have been copied before 1400, and she shows how they do better justice to the text of the poem than they are usually given credit for.

In '*Patience* and the Ideal of Mixed Life' (*TSLL*), John M. Bowers makes the case that *Patience* is concerned with the mystical apprehension of God's will that leads a man to turn towards some worldly endeavour to share that apprehension; ideally the voluntary act of preaching is the means whereby the mystical apprehension is shared. He considers that *Patience* should be viewed not merely as a parable on the healthy discipline of the mystic, nor as a parable on the proper conduct of the preacher, but also as an illustration of the complementary balance of these two modes of life. '*Patience* – Beyond Apocalypse' (*MP*), by Sandra P. Prior, argues that criticism has neglected the use in *Patience* of apocalyptic traditions which assist in the presentation of a central thematic paradox of active patience. She describes what she sees as constituting the apocalyptic dimension in the poem, and suggests that as the poet reminds his audience of their eschatological hope, he also urges them not merely to look towards a distant future *eschaton* but to bring the Kingdom into their hearts now.

Two articles on *Pearl* conclude this year's *Gawain*-poet section. Rosalind

Field persuasively suggests that the vision of 'The Heavenly Jerusalem in *Pearl*' (*MLR*), though underestimated by critics, provides a fitting climax to the poem. She considers the poem's final scenes in the context of their standard medieval literary and artistic depiction, and finds them to be carefully nuanced and, by the standards of the time, unusual. They are contrived to provoke an exploration of religious mystery through visual and verbal paradoxes. 'A Plum for the *Pearl*-Poet' (*ELN*) by Christoph Manes argues plausibly that the often emended word *blose* in l. 911 of *Pearl* could be interpreted as a syncopated by-form of ME *bolas* derived independently from OF *beloce*, meaning a wild plum tree. This meaning could be easily justified in its context.

4. Piers Plowman

Lavinia Griffiths' monograph on *Personification in 'Piers Plowman'* [18] will prove to be an excellent guide for students and teachers alike, since it contains a lucid reading of the peculiar quality of the poet's use of allegory. The trope is much more than an incidental rhetorical ornament: Langland uses allegory as an agent to stamp homogeneity on the diverse themes and conceits of his poem. Griffiths concentrates on the allegorical function of Holy Church and the Tower of Truth, Meed, the Deadly Sins, the Castle of Love and the Tree of Charity, and Faith, Hope, and Charity. Her analysis shows how the poet uses the trope to keep his audience's mind fixed on the irresolvable aspect of his message: there is no complete answer, only a set of questions.

In an exhilarating and perceptive paper on Passus V of the B Text Nick Gray argues that Clement the Cobbler is to be seen as a figurative mock-confessor to Glutton, whose vomiting may recall Proverbs 18.11 (*LeedsSE*). In 'Langland's Ymaginatif, Kynde and the *Benjamin Major*' (*MÆ*) Hugh White looks at the passage in B XII 14–20 in which Langland ascribes to Ymaginatif the inter-pretation of the vision from Myddelerthe offered Will by Kynde. A passage from Richard of St Victor's *Benjamin Major* which associates the imagination with God's creativity helps to explain the importance of Ymaginatif's role at this point.

Samuel A. Overstreet returns to the question of *mede* and *mercede* in C III in a useful paper entitled '"Grammaticus Ludens": Theological Aspects of Langland's Allegory' (*Traditio*), with due reference to an earlier paper by John Alford (*YW* 63.76–7). In a concise but highly significant note on 'Langland and the Priest's Title' (*N&Q*) R. N. Swanson demonstrates that Langland's knowledge of what made a priest eligible for ordination (in particular, financial security) was very precise in his passage on that topic in C XIII 100–113. In an interesting paper Helen Barr considers 'The Use of Latin Quotations in *Piers Plowman* with Special Reference to Passus XVIII of the "B" Text' (*N&Q*). In that Passus Langland pointedly assimilates the quotations into the line, whereas elsewhere they have been left to stand outside.

J. P. Thorne and Marie-Claire Uhart reconsider the implications of J. N. King's paper on the same topic (*YW* 57.67) in their article on 'Robert Crowley's *Piers Plowman*' (*MÆ*). They stress the conservatism of Crowley's version. Michael Peverett has written a significant note on ' "Quod" and "Seide" in

18. *Personification in 'Piers Plowman'*, by Lavinia Griffiths. Brewer (1985). pp. ix + 125. £17.50.

Piers Plowman' (*NM*). Langland uses these words very carefully, 'quod' much more frequently than 'seide'. A. V. C. Schmidt considers the meaning and purpose of 'The Inner Dreams in *Piers Plowman'* (*MÆ*) which occur in visions three and five respectively.

James Simpson supplies a complicated analysis of the way Langland uses the terms of earthly life to condemn that life in an elaborate paper entitled 'The Transformation of Meaning: A Figure of Thought in *Piers Plowman'* (*RES*). In 'From Reason to Affective Knowledge: Modes of Thought and Poetic Form in *Piers Plowman'* (*MÆ*), which concentrates on Passus II to IV of the B Text, Simpson studies the correlation between cognitive and rhetorical categories as a means to understanding 'the formal, poetic changes in *Piers Plowman'*. In a third article he compares *Piers Plowman* B XV 149–212 with Augustine's *De Trinitate* XV 8–10 and offers reasonably convincing evidence for Langland's acquaintance with the latter (*N&Q*).

5. Romances

Jean E. Jost has produced a bibliography of *Ten Middle English Arthurian Romances* [19], consisting of entries from *c.* 1800 to 1980, arranged chronologically and furnished with comprehensive abstracts. There are three chapters, the first on general works, the second on earlier romances (*Of Arthour and of Merlin, Sir Tristrem, Sir Percyvelle of Galles, Ywain and Gawain*), and the last on late romances (*Morte Arthure, Awntyrs off Arthure, Le Morte Arthur, The Avowynge of King Arthur, The Turke and Gowin, Golagros and Gawain*). The introduction surveys the history of scholarship for each of the ten poems and suggests desiderata for the future. There is a full index.

Derek Pearsall's 'Middle English Romance and its Audiences' [20] will serve as a companion piece to his paper on 'The Alliterative Revival: Origins and Social Backgrounds' (*YW* 63.78). Once again he argues for the importance of qualification and reappraisal – 'premature or oversimplified decisions concerning the audience of a genre such as romance are worse than no decisions at all'. One such decision is that on the minstrel, which Pearsall probes gently but firmly. Minstrels, or *disours*, did exist, formulae suggest improvisation, and textual variation within single romances suggests oral transmission ('there is no ideal text, from which succeeding copies degenerate by a process of scribal corruption and decomposition: rather the text exists in an open and fluid state, the successive acts of writing down being no more than arbitrary stages in the continuously evolving life of the poem'). But most extant manuscripts are for the reading public and by the time of Malory and Caxton the verse romance has shifted to prose, which caters more specifically for the reader, not the listener.

Stephen Knight's essay on 'The Social Function of the Middle English Romances' is coded correctly for David Aers's collection of papers on *Medieval Literature* [4]. Were it not, it would not, of course, have been included in this volume, for Aers is every bit as prejudiced as the third reader of his collection

19. *Ten Middle English Arthurian Romances: A Reference Guide*, by Jean E. Jost. Hall. pp. xxx + 162. $50.

20. In *Historical and Editorial Studies in Medieval and Early Modern English for Johan Gerritsen*, ed. by Mary-Jo Arn, Hanneke Wirtjes, and Hans Jansen. Wo–No (1985). pp. 229. Fl 62.25.

whom he castigates so lengthily and angrily in his introduction. Knight, as usual, prefers to tend to the sparkling and incisive rather than, necessarily, the accurate comment. He gives us 'a brief general account of the inherent and centrally ideological structure of the romances' in which threats and values present 'a self-concept for the powerful and an acceptable image of power to those without it'. This leads on to a more detailed account of three major romance types, the third of which contains the ' "quality" romances' such as *Gawain* and *Morte Darthur* which Knight praises for their 'socially critical role'. Knight writes very ably in a certain way and the essay should be read (so should the introduction).

There are two articles on the Middle English *Prose Merlin* in a tribute to Cedric B. Pickford[21], which reflects his many interests in the development of Arthurian romance. Carol M. Meale writes on 'The Manuscripts and Early Audience of the Middle English *Prose Merlin*' because she feels the need for more research on the production of medieval prose works. She provides the first good description of the two manuscripts and looks to them for evidence of readership. The single leaf of the one manuscript does not provide much (though Meale gamely points out that other works by the same hand had middle-class owners), but she derives much fascinating and useful information from the annotations of her second manuscript. Karen Stern tells us in 'The Middle English *Prose Merlin*' that her work is complementary to Meale's in that both are concerned with the *Merlin*'s oblivion. However, Meale gets to grips with righting that wrong, while Stern merely criticizes the inadequacies of the text's only edition and draws on Meale to inform us that the female annotations of the manuscript reveal an interest in the love relations of women in the *Merlin*.

Roger Dahood's *The Avowing of King Arthur*[22] has grown out of, or perhaps shrunk from, his original Ph.D. dissertation. The introduction consists of conventional chapters on language, manuscript, dialect, date, textual corruption, analogues, metre, and style, some of which would be better not existing in the presumably truncated form in which they exist here ('style' is particularly weak). A select bibliography precedes the text, and there are adequate notes, an appendix listing words with horizontal strokes through looped ascenders(!), a good glossary with line references and etymologies, and an index of names.

Betty Hill, in 'Sir Orfeo 241–56, 102–12' (*N&Q*) compares the four successive quatrains which contrast past happiness and present misery in ll. 241–56 with the same device in ll. 1757–86 of the *Meditations on the Life and Passion of Christ*, and she suggests that Heurodis' description at ll. 102–12 parallels that of the crucified Christ in a thirteenth-century French lyric. In other words, the rhetorical devices of the Passion lyrics are used for both Orfeo's active and Heurodis' passive sufferings. Sandy Feinstein's interest in *Orfeo* (as well as *Havelok* and *King Horn*) is different again. 'Whatever Happened to the Women in Folktale?' (*WSIF*) is sandwiched between 'Women as Keepers and

21. *The Changing Face of Arthurian Romance: Essays on Arthurian Prose Romances in Memory of Cedric B. Pickford*, ed. by Alison Adams, Armel H. Diverres, Karen Stern, and Kenneth Varty. Boydell. pp. xxiv + 168. £25.

22. *The Avowing of King Arthur*, ed. by Roger Dahood. Garland (1984). pp. 157. $26.

Carriers of Knowledge' and 'Behavior of Women Automobile Drivers', but Feinstein's article is surprisingly free of jargon in her comparison of two folk-tales and a ballad with the three romances. Not unexpectedly, she discovers that women's roles are conventional in folktale, while in romance 'women are the movers and shakers, not the passive receptacles of male worship'.

In 'The Celtic Connections of the Tristan Story (Part 1)' (*RMS-t*), W. Ann Trindade reviews critical opinion on the pro- and anti-Celtic sources debate and looks at the extant Welsh material (Part 2 will appear next year). G. D. Burger uses 'Another English *Godefroy of Buillon*?' (*AN&Q*, 1985) to suggest that the only English translation other than Caxton's is not a redaction of Caxton but a condensation from a similar French exemplar which aims 'to focus on the part played by Godfrey of Bouillon and on the usefulness of his history as a guide in conducting an actual crusade'. In 'The Watermarks of Four Late Medieval Manuscripts containing *The Erle of Tolous*' (*N&Q*, 1985), Friedrich Hülsmann takes issue with some previous descriptions of the watermarks. Anne F. Sutton and Livia Visser-Fuchs continue their comments for the Journal of the Richard III Society with 'Richard III's Books: II. A Collection of Romances and Old Testament Stories: 1. *Ipomedon*' (*Ricardian*). They deal with the evolution of *Ipomedon*, its popularity, and the significance of Richard's signature and motto on f. 98v of his book.

Also of interest to readers of this section are the works of Korrel, Wilhelm and Gross, and Göller reviewed in section 2.

6. Gower, Lydgate, and Hoccleve

Last year *Fifteenth-Century Studies* provided a review of recent Gower criticism (*YW* 66.145); this year a full bibliography appears in the revised *Manual of the Writings in Middle English*[23]. The compilers, John H. Fisher, R. Wayne Hamm, Peter G. Beidler, and Robert F. Yeager, express their gratitude to the editors of the forthcoming *Descriptive Catalogue of Manuscripts of the Works of John Gower*, with whose help they have produced manuscript lists of the French, Latin, and English writings. The chronological bibliography covers General Treatments; Place in Social and Intellectual History; Bibliographies; Life; Family and Tomb; Associations with Chaucer and the Court; French Works, Latin works, and English works, with booklists for the individual works up to 1984.

Initial irritation may be felt at Hans-Jürgen Diller's proposition in '"For Engelondes sake": Richard II and Henry of Lancaster as Intended Readers of Gower's *Confessio Amantis*'[13] that literature functions at two levels: Level 1 (author-oriented and reader-oriented) and Level 2 (the socio-cultural system). Certainly, AOF and ROF are off-putting, like most unfamiliar acronyms. But the model Diller proposes is followed coherently and convincingly as he investigates the revisions in the Preface and later part of Book 8, noting a significant change from AOF to ROF (so that the Preface's 'bok for king Richardes sake' has really become the revised 'bok for Engelondes sake') and suggesting reasons for the removal of praise of earthly love and the reference to Chaucer in

23. *A Manual of the Writings in Middle English, 1050–1500*. Vol. VII, ed. by Albert E. Hartung. Archon for CAAS. pp. vii + 2195–2595. $32.50.

the Epilogue. So much for Level 1; at Level 2 Diller finds the function constant since Gower's shift from Richard to Henry does not alter his original aim – to seek acceptance of his social and political ideals, which include the limitation of the King's power.

On *Confessio Amantis*, Katherine S. Gittes writes about 'Ulysses in Gower's *Confessio Amantis*: The Christian Soul as Silent Rhetorician' (*ELN*). She asks why Ulysses, with his reputation as a rhetorician should remain silent for all but one of the five episodes in which he appears. Since this episode is the last, in which he is dying, Gittes suggests that his story represents a pilgrimage of the Christian soul, parallel to that of Amans, and that, like Nebuchadnezzar, Ulysses is dumb through sin until his soul is transformed by his final forgiveness of his son. In 'Gower's Geta and the Sin of Supplantation' (*NM*), Stephen K. Wright plausibly suggests a source in the *Geta* of Vitalis of Blois, and, less plausibly, explains discrepancies in the names of seducer and husband as 'a moment of self-referential comedy' – the story's theme is supplantation, the main characters illustrate supplantation, and even Genius supplants his *auctor*. Judith Davis Shaw provides 'An Etymology of the Middle English *coise*' (*ELN*, 1985), the term applied to the hag in the 'Tale of Florent'. One tends to prefer her derivation from OF *coi*, *what*, i.e., *thing*, to that from OF *cuisse*, *thigh*, i.e. '*butt*, *asshole*'.

Malcolm Richardson is very hard on Hoccleve. His study of 'Hoccleve in his Social Context' (*ChauR*) has shown him that 'as a professional bureaucrat, Hoccleve was exactly what he tells us he was, a bungler, misfit, and perpetual also-ran'. There were certainly disadvantages to the office of Privy Seal clerk, but Hoccleve's contemporaries managed to do well. Moreover, Hoccleve ignored five lucrative options open to him and even worsened his situation by marrying. Richardson has no sympathy for him – 'his laments resemble those of modern students who complain bitterly that they cannot have at the same time a university education, two children, and a new automobile'.

In a densely written and sometimes rather baffling exposition of 'John Lydgate's *Temple of Glas*: "atwixen two so hang I in balaunce"'[24], Anna Torti sees the poem's title as emblematic of the oppositions inherent in the poem (light, dark; continuity, transience; solidity, disintegration). If solidity is represented by the temple, the glass (and, therefore, the mirror – an essential point the reader is expected to accept) is characterized by disintegration and luminosity. Torti investigates the 'obsessive repetition of the mirror metaphor' with this essential dichotomy in as various referents as the temple, Venus, the lady, even the poem itself (not only 'the mirror of a past tradition', but 'a mirror of personal tensions' which make a work imitative of Chaucer essentially unchaucerian).

A. S. G. Edwards provides 'Additions and Corrections to the Bibliography of John Lydgate' (*N&Q*, 1985). The note criticizes the facts that the canon was not re-appraised nor the *Index of Middle English Verse* and its *Supplement* checked in Volume VI of the *Manual of the Writings in Middle English* (1980). He notes foliation errors and provides a list of addenda and emendata.

24. In *Intellectuals and Writers in Fourteenth Century Europe: The J. A. W. Bennett Memorial Lectures, Perugia, 1984*, ed. by Piero Boitani and Anna Torti. Narr/Brewer. pp. 276. $37.

7. Middle Scots Poetry

A new *Reference Guide*[25] covers the same four Middle Scots poets as Vol. IV of *A Manual of the Writings in Middle English* (1976) and for only another seven years (1971–8, despite the more recent date of publication). Moreover, in 1985 *Fifteenth-Century Studies* reviewed the current state of scholarship for three of these poets (*YW* 66.147). Nevertheless, there is use in this book. After an introduction which briefly summarizes the development of critical opinion on each man, five sections, each with its own index, deal with general works and then each of the four poets. Entries (which include dissertations) are arranged chronologically from 1521 to 1978 and are furnished with brief and useful abstracts. James I is limited to *The Kingis Quair*, but Douglas is allowed *King Hart*.

Dieter Mehl's 'Robert Henryson's Moral Fables as Experiments in Didactic Narrative'[13], which I have just seen, would seem to be the same article published elsewhere in 1985 (*YW* 65.106–7, 120).

The playful element is as important as the punitive in 'Mobbing Scenes in Middle Scots Verse: Holland, Douglas, Dunbar' (*JEGP*). David Parkinson summarizes, analyses, and interestingly compares mock punishment scenes in *The Buke of the Howlat*, Douglas's *Palice of Honour*, and Dunbar's 'Ballat of the Fenȝeit Freir of Tungland'. Parkinson's date for the *Buke* is *c*. 1450; in 'Dating *The Buke of the Howlat*' (*RES*), Felicity J. Riddy studies the evidence of the shields on the woodpecker pursuivant's tabard and suggests the summer of 1448.

Alasdair MacDonald writes on 'The Middle Scots Expansion of *Iesu, nostra redemptio*, and a Ghost in the Bannatyne Manuscript' (*Neophil*). The 'ghost' is item D17 in the facsimile volume of the Bannatyne manuscript, which is not a separate item but part of item D14, a poem based on the Latin hymn of MacDonald's title.

8. Lyrics and Miscellaneous Verse

Two latecomers from the Middle English Texts series have arrived for review this year. Rodney Mearns has edited *The Vision of Tundale*[26] from its five extant manuscripts, using the version in BL MS Cotton Caligula A.II for his base text, and adding a full critical apparatus. A transcription of the Latin *Visio Tundali* from MS Bodley 636 (*not* MS Bodley 536 as stated on p. 79) is added at the foot of each page for comparison with the ME version (Bodley 636 is selected as an appropriate witness to the kind of textual tradition of the *Visio* from which it is argued that the ME translator worked). A useful introduction describes the genesis and transmission of the original text: it was composed by an Irishman named Marcus at Regensburg in 1149, and shortened by the chronicler of the Cistercian order, Helinand of Froidmont, for use in his *Chronicon*. This work was in turn drawn on by Vincent of Beauvais in his *Speculum Historiale* (not *Speculum Historialis*, as stated on p. 9), and via Vincent's work the *Tundale* story was widely available to the later Middle Ages,

25. *Middle Scots Poets: A Reference Guide to James I of Scotland, Robert Henryson, William Dunbar, and Gavin Douglas*, by Walter Scheps and J. Anna Looney. Hall. pp. xvi + 292. $60.

26. *The Vision of Tundale*, ed. by Rodney Mearns. CWU (1985). pp. 180. DM 85.

including, indeed, the translator of the ME poem. Mearns questions a recent theory that *The Vision of Tundale* is translated not from a Latin but from an Anglo-Norman version by pointing to the theory's attendant difficulties. The five ME manuscripts are described and a *stemma codicum* justified. It is pleasing to see the competent philological discussion that follows. This edition is a sound one; it is a pity, however, that no glossary was provided for it.

Oliver S. Pickering has put much skill and effort into his work on the *South English Legendary*, and this edition of its *Ministry and Passion*[27] section, edited from St John's College, Cambridge, MS B. 6, runs true to past form. Pickering describes the three manuscripts in which the poem, in whole or in part, is contained, and proceeds to discuss its content and narrative structure. He suggests that since the *Ministry and Passion* is likely to have had no literary model, its author was probably obliged to forge its structure quite unaided, a task to which he was not quite equal. The result is 'unsophisticated . . . a collection of isolated episodes loosely strung together'. The poem has the character of a first draft that subsequent revisers were to refine. Though the content of the poem is largely biblical, there is a significant use of non-biblical sources that Pickering classifies into four kinds: material used to expand the basic narrative; interpretation of or comment on Gospel passages; references to contemporary medieval life and customs; and apostrophes, particularly to Christ. No one source can be identified for these, and although the *Historia Scholastica* of Petrus Comestor comes nearest to claiming such a distinction, the content of the non-biblical material comprises for the most part widely found commonplaces. After a discussion of the poem's relationship with other parts of the *South English Legendary*, the questions of date, area of composition, authorship, and audience are addressed, and the choice of base text justified. Next there follows another, much fuller, description of the base text manuscript (which has the effect of making its earlier description appear somewhat otiose), and its language. Its scribe was evidently trained in a south-east or south-central Norfolk area (to say that this is where the manuscript was 'probably written', p. 69, sounds a little incautious). The rest of Pickering's apparatus is standard, and includes a statement of editorial method, a set of notes on the text, a glossary, and a bibliography. His edition is a distinct contribution to the study of the poem, and is admirably full and lucid.

The decision to include John Stevens's *Words and Music in the Middle Ages*[28] in this section on lyric poetry is made somewhat arbitrary by the fecundity of his book. It ranges from various forms of medieval song in Latin and the vernacular to the liturgical drama with a consecutiveness and cohesion that daunts neat classification. It is organized in three sections. The first, on number in music and verse, considers among other things the *conductus*, the *planctus*, and the *lai*. The second, which examines the relations of speech, action, emotion, and meaning in song, covers a wealth of genres (for example, *carole*, *chanson de geste*, liturgical drama), and the third, on melody, rhythm, and metre, looks at the writings of musical theorists on these topics, as well as at manuscript notation and layout. One of the main concerns of the book is to

27. *The South English Ministry and Passion*, ed. by Oliver S. Pickering. CWU (1984). pp. 256. DM 118.

28. *Words and Music in the Middle Ages: Song, Narrative, Dance and Drama, 1050–1350*, by John Stevens. CUP. pp. xviii + 554. hb £40, pb £15.

suggest the nature of the medieval awareness and appreciation of music, and the technical, musicological aspects of the discussion are clearly presented and explained so as not to alienate readers from other disciplines. The inter-disciplinary approach that Stevens has spent many years acquiring has served us splendidly in this book.

The fourth volume of the collaborative edition of the southern version of the *Cursor Mundi*[29] has come out this year, and continues the promise seen in the previous volumes (see *YW* 59.94 and 66.149). Peter H. J. Mous has edited ll. 17289–21346, which deal with events from the Resurrection onwards and include the fates of the Apostles. A brief introduction describes the sources used in this section, and the text is followed by notes and bibliography.

A survey of 'Lapidary Formulas as Topics of Invention – From Thomas of Hales to Henryson' (*RES*) by Ian Bishop describes the use of formulas akin to those found in medieval verse lapidaries in *Pearl*, Thomas of Hales's *Luve Ron*, the Harley lyrics, and finally in Henryson's fable of the Cok and the Jasp. Bishop discusses persuasively how the formulas are manipulated for poetic effect. In 'The Authorship of *The Owl and the Nightingale*: A Reappraisal' (*ES*) J. Eadie questions and rejects the hypothesis of Nicholas of Guildford as author of the poem. However, perhaps more problems are raised than solved, for the arguments for the counter-hypothesis, that the author may have been Nicholas of Guildford's absent mistress, separated from him for some reason, do not instil much conviction. Thomas D. Hill, in '"Mary, the Rose-Bush" and the Leaps of Christ' (*ES*), argues that the various events mentioned in the 'Mary, the Rose Bush' carol have more in common with the tradition which conceives of Christ as taking a particular series of leaps in redeeming mankind than with the tradition of the Five Joys of Mary. He suggests that the carol is contrived to display Mary's organic connection with the redemptive work of her Son. Valerie Edden has produced a useful study of 'Richard Maidstone's *Penitential Psalms*' (*LeedsSE*), in which she deduces that Maidstone, Carmelite and anti-Lollard propagandist, composed his *Penitential Psalms* to meet a late fourteenth-century need among literate layfolk for devotional, and safely orthodox, material in the vernacular. She also considers the literary form of the *Psalms*, and argues their use as a means of private preparation for the sacrament of penance.

Three articles on the Harley lyrics conclude the section for this year. Michael J. Franklin, in '"Fyngres heo hap feir to folde": Trothplight in Some of the Love Lyrics of MS Harley 2253' (*MÆ*), argues strongly that the expression 'fyngres feyre forte folde', commonplace in several lyrics, connotes a ceremony of 'trothplight', also known as 'handfasting', and that not only does it suggest a sensual anticipation of clasping the mistress's hand, but also a desire for marriage. The article is illustrated from a pleasing variety of medieval literary sources. 'The Fair Maid of Ribblesdale: Content and Context' (*NM*), by Marion Glasscoe, argues that a context of Cistercian asceticism surrounded this Harley lyric, whose tonal extremes are thereby explained. After all, Ribblesdale was rich in Cistercian settlements, and one might appropriately imagine its author to have been a Cistercian monk. A view on the Ribblesdale lyric with somewhat different implications is presented by F. Jones in 'A Note on *Harley*

29. *The Southern Version of 'Cursor Mundi'*, Volume IV, ed. by Peter H. J. Mous. UOttawa. pp. xxii + 170. C.$25.

Lyrics 7' (*NM*). He points out that there are *two* speakers in the poem, only one of whom has seen the fair maid. From this the poem is said to derive its comic strength, and to become the funnier the further away from Ribblesdale the provenance of the young man in its narrative is imagined.

9. Malory and Caxton

The starting point for Terence McCarthy's 'Private Worlds in *Le Morte D'Arthur*' (*EA*) would seem to have been a phrase of Derek Brewer's, 'private virtues and necessities'. For McCarthy, these 'must, in Malory's world, be controlled; the tragedy of that world is that, in the end, they are not'. He writes incisively of an Arthurian public world and its virtues (fellowship, publicity, honour) and argues that 'what goes on in private . . . is not Malory's concern and as historian – as opposed to omniscient narrator – is something to which he has limited access'. In succumbing to private emotions, Arthur brings about his own downfall; Lancelot and Guinevere sin in allowing themselves to be the vehicles for private matters to intrude into public life. But Lancelot is not culpable in his three rescues of the Queen (which McCarthy scrutinizes carefully), because in the end his private cause has become a public one, 'the survival of the Arthurian world itself'.

In an interesting, sometimes tendentious, explication of 'Vestiges of Paradise: The Tree of Life in *Cursor Mundi* and Malory's *Morte Darthur*' (*M&H*, 1985), James Dean alerts the reader to the medieval *curiositas* in the relics of the earthly paradise. Both the withered imprints on Eden's grass in the *Cursor Mundi* and the three spindles on the ship of Faith's bedcanopy in the *Morte Darthur* relate intricately to the tree of knowledge in the Garden of Eden, and hence evoke the loss of paradise and the subsequent degeneration of the world.

It is worth reading Earl R. Anderson's 'Malory's "Fair Maid of Ascolat"' (*NM*), even though some of it is less convincing than other parts. The suggestion that the 'month of May' passage should be the epilogue to the Elaine story is competently handled, and its source in Lydgate's *Pageant of Knowledge* is convincingly illustrated by verbal parallel. The attempt to link the Elaine story and the tournament by, firstly, the figures of 'Charon' and 'Diana', and, secondly, by 'warrior medicine' and 'syncretic medicine' deserves less credence.

The Changing Face of Arthurian Romance[21] contains two essays on Malory. In 'Malory's "Proving" of Sir Lancelot', Derek Brewer criticizes the anachronistic criticism of the *Morte* as a classical modern novel and urges an 'archaic' or 'naïve' reading. Basing his comments on the Tale of Lancelot, he demonstrates the limited importance of character and action, the use of reiteration, the lack of causality, and the inconsistency of the tale. Like McCarthy, he argues succinctly that Malory's interest is in the hero in relation to honour, not love, and he alerts us to 'the indissoluble unity between personal, social, and moral obligation characteristic of Malory's unifying mentality'. Faith Lyons's detailed comparison of 'Malory's *Tale of Sir Gareth* and French Arthurian Tradition' reveals similar elements in both 'dominant and broadly based themes' (e.g. conduct in chivalric combat and anonymity) and 'adventure pure and simple' ('details, brief sketches, and most important, longer sequences'). Her rather pedestrian account reinforces Eugene Vinaver's opinion of *Gareth*, that it draws on common French literary tradition and depends on a French source.

On Caxton, I have only found Richard Hamer's note on Caxton's translation of *The Golden Legend* in 'Jean Golein's *Festes Nouvelles*: A Caxton Source' (*MÆ*). A few items of Arthurian interest may be mentioned here. Richard Barber provides an 'Update. The Manuscripts of the *Vera Historia de Morte Arthuri*' (*ArthL*). Mildred Leake Day has edited and translated the *De ortu Waluuanii nepotis Arturi* [30], although there would seem to be little evidence for her statement that 'at least one copy of the story circulated in England, apparently influencing *Sir Gawain and the Green Knight* and *The Faerie Queene*, Book 1'. Margaret Wright has published a description of the 1985 John Rylands Library exhibition, 'The Arthurian Legend' (*BJRL*, 1985). For those who were unfortunate enough to miss it, the catalogue is still available from the Library.

Also of interest to readers of this section are the works of Korrel, Wilhelm and Gross, and Göller reviewed in section 2.

10. Other Prose

Prose continues to attract a great deal of lively attention but, as usual, the main interest is in the later period. To celebrate the six-hundredth anniversary of John Wyclif's death a series of lectures was given in his old college, Balliol, in 1984. Now edited by Anthony Kenny [31], they illustrate the full range of Wyclif's achievements as one of the foremost thinkers of medieval England. Each of his spheres of influence (history, philosophy, theology, and English language and literature) is covered by a specialist in that particular area. Maurice Keen writes on Wyclif's development into a heresiarch, with a definitive account of the famous attack on transubstantiation. He also contributes an important paper on the impact of Wyclif's ideas over the centuries. Kenny takes the measure of Wyclif's theory of Realism as represented in *De Universalibus*. Norman Kretzman tackles the fundamental issue of Wyclif's attitude towards continuism and indivisibilism. The doctrinal relationship between Wyclif and Hus is carefully analysed by Gordon Leff. For students of literature, Anne Hudson contributes two authoritative articles – one on 'Wycliffism in Oxford 1381–1411', in which she rightly re-opens the question of whether or not Lollardy was a spent force in Oxford at the time of Wyclif's death; the other, on 'Wyclif and the English Language', in which she considers the impetus which Wyclif gave towards the use of the vernacular. This nobly concise volume, which is to be highly recommended as a companion for all studies of Wyclif, concludes with another outstanding paper by Master Kenny on Wyclif's counter-Reformation reputation.

Paul Vincent Spade and Gordon Anthony Wilson have produced a fine critical edition of Wyclif's *Summa insolubilium* [32], which was probably written between 1361 and 1363. The editors describe an *insolubile* as 'a semantic

---

30. *The Rise of Gawain: Nephew of Arthur (De ortu Waluuanii nepotis Arturi)*, ed. and trans. by Mildred Leake Day. Garland (1984). pp. xliii + 131. $30.

31. *Wyclif in his Times*, ed. by Anthony Kenny. Clarendon. pp. iii + 174. £19.50.

32. *Johannis Wyclif 'Summa insolubilium'*, ed. by Paul Vincent Spade and Gordon Anthony Wilson. MRTS 41. CMERS. pp. 1 + 122. $18.

paradox or antinomy like the famous Liar-Paradox', and note that Wyclif put forward an identical theory as part of his discussion of conditional sentences in his *Logicae continuatio*. From the six surviving manuscripts they have selected MS Prague, Státní Knihovna ČSR, 1536 as the base for their edition. Their editorial principles seem unexceptionable except, perhaps, for their decision to normalize the orthography in accordance with Lewis and Short's *Latin Dictionary*. The text is followed by two appendixes, one tabulating parallel passages between the *Summa insolubilium* and the *Logicae continuatio*, and the other containing explanatory comments on textual or doctrinal difficulties in particular passages of the work. The edition concludes with the apparatus, a bibliography, and indexes of manuscripts, persons, and topics. Wyclif's theory, which seems to have been original, had some influence in the late fourteenth and fifteenth centuries. This edition is a useful contribution to the growing interest in the Wyclif canon.

S. J. Ogilvie-Thomson has satisfied a vital need in his excellent edition of Walter Hilton's *Mixed Life*[33], based on Lambeth Palace MS 472. As the title of the work implies, the book discusses the mixed life of action and contemplation. The supporting notes are all exclusively concerned with the relationships between the various surviving manuscripts: there are two separate textual traditions. Otherwise, there are no explanatory notes and the edition, which is not furnished with a glossary, will be mainly of use to textual critics.

Three books published as part of the Middle English Texts series at Heidelberg have arrived for review. Venetia Nelson has edited the prose version of the *Speculum Vitae*, known as *A Myrour to Lewde Men and Wymmen*[34], from British Library MS Harley 45, one of the four extant manuscripts. The text is accompanied by a comprehensive introduction, notes, glossary, and a bibliography. The basic material for both the *Speculum Vitae* and *A Myrour* is mainly derived from the *Somme le Roi*, and this edition provides a useful set of comparisons which demonstrate the main differences in arrangement between the English and French texts. Of particular value is the stylistic comparison which the editor makes between the *Speculum* and the *Myrour* (the former is paratactic, in contrast with the hypotaxis of the latter). There is also a searching analysis of the relationship between *A Myrour* and *Jacob's Well* (cf. Carruthers, below), and a short note on the place of *A Myrour* in the history of late Middle English prose – it is a particularly interesting text because not many examples of unrhymed verse texts have survived in England from the late Middle Ages.

The Book of Tribulation[35] is a previously unpublished fifteenth-century Middle English translation of an Old French prose treatise, the *Livre de tribulacion*. The translation survives in three manuscripts – MSS Bodley 423, British Library Harley 1197, and British Library Arundel 286, none of which contains a complete version. The *Livre de tribulacion* (which is itself a translation from a Latin original) survives in twenty-three manuscripts, and Barratt prints the relevant sections at the foot of each page so as to facilitate

33. *Walter Hilton's 'Mixed Life'*, ed. from Lambeth Palace MS 472 by S. J. Ogilvie-Thomson. SSELER. USalz. pp. xlii + 69. DM 40.

34. *A Myrour to Lewde Men and Wymmen*, ed. by Venetia Nelson. CWU (1981). pp. 306. DM 98.

35. *The Book of Tribulation*, ed. by Alexandra Barratt. CWU (1983). pp. 174. DM 98.

comparisons between the two versions. The volume concludes with a lucid set of notes, a glossary, and a short bibliography. The text itself is remarkably tedious, but it is a pleasure to experience Barratt's flawless editorial procedure, which leads her to choose the Bodley manuscript as the base for her edition.

Sarah M. Horrall has edited, for the first time, the Middle English prose *Lyf of Oure Lady*[36] and its Latin source, the *Vita Sancte Marie* of the English Franciscan, Thomas of Hales. The concise but comprehensive introduction includes a number of important new points about the work and its author, notably that Thomas of Hales was not a famous theologian and debater at Oxford and Paris – he was, above all, a popularizer, with his reputation based firmly in England, not on the Continent. Two fifteenth-century manuscripts of the Middle English version survive: MS St George's Chapel, Windsor Castle, E.I.I. (on which this edition is based), and MS Bodley Laud Misc. 174. The volume concludes with an excellent set of explanatory notes, a selective glossary, and a bibliography.

La Somme le Roi et Ses Traductions Anglaises: Etude Comparée[37], by Leo M. Carruthers, makes a distinguished contribution to the growing number of studies dealing with the wide-ranging influence of *La Somme le Roi*. There are eleven whole or part translations of *La Somme* into English, and also five remodelled versions, including the *Speculum Vitae*, *A Myrour to Lewde Men and Wymmen*, *Jacob's Well*, and Chaucer's Parson's Tale. Much of this book is given over to a detailed analysis of the relationship between *La Somme* and *The Book of Vices and Virtues*, a point which is taken up again in an appendix listing the French words in the latter. A second appendix lists English common nouns (abstract and concrete) which indicate the English author's independence of *La Somme*.

On an allied theme J. D. Burnley has written an important paper on 'Curial Prose in England' (*Speculum*) in which he investigates to what extent English authors had to look to foreign models in order to create their own prose style: by the late fourteenth century there was already an English tradition of curial prose which had no need by that time to assimilate French syntactical patterns. The main change occurred in the adoption of French vocabulary in exchange for English.

Alan J. Fletcher provides an absorbing description of 'The Sermon Booklets of Friar Nicholas Philip' (*MÆ*), an English Franciscan (fl. early fifteenth century), which are contained in MS Bodley Lat. th.d.l. Like Richard FitzRalph's famous sermon-diary, these booklets tell us a great deal about the preacher's interests and travels and help to shed new light on the influence of Franciscan preaching.

Mystical writers continue to attract attention. J. P. H. Clark writes on 'Richard Rolle as Biblical Commentator' (*DownR*) in a substantial and convincing paper in which he sets out principles for dating Rolle's commentaries on biblical matters in relation to some of his other works, taking 1330 as the provisional *terminus post quem*. He provides an acceptable order of

---

36. *The Lyf of Oure Lady: The ME Translation of Thomas of Hales's 'Vita Sancte Marie'*, ed. by Sarah M. Horrall. CWU (1985). pp. 136. DM 68.

37. *La Somme le Roi et Ses Traductions Anglaises*, by Leo M. Carruthers. AMAES. pp. iii + 180. Ffr 100.

composition for that section of Rolle's writings which began with *Super Threnos* and concluded with *The Form of Living* (1348-9).

In a refreshingly clear-sighted paper Dorothea Siegmund-Schultze draws our attention back to essential cultural points in her study of 'Some Aspects of Julian of Norwich's *Revelations of Divine Love*' (*ZAA*). Ritamary Bradley, in 'Perception of Self in Julian of Norwich's *Showings*' (*DownR*), disputes 'the patriarchal view of the self', with reason assigned to the male part of the soul and passion to the female part. For Julian, 'Christ, who is Mother Wisdom, is the perfect exemplar of the unity between these parts'.

In 'From God as Mother to Priest as Mother: Julian of Norwich and the Movement for the Ordination of Women' (*DownR*) David A. Foss strikes a cautionary note against the use of Julian's exploration of the motherhood of God as a justification for ordaining women. His careful analysis, which includes a useful, concise account of the theme of the motherhood of God in the spiritual writings of the High Middle Ages, indicates the orthodoxy of Julian's views about male priests.

In 'Walter Hilton in Defense of the Religious Life and the Veneration of Images' (*DownR*, 1985) J. P. H. Clark analyses Hilton's letter *De Utilitate et Prerogativis Religionis*, which was addressed to Adam Horsley, and argues that Hilton may have been motivated by opposition to Lollard sentiments about image-veneration. Lollard views also feature in an inspiring paper by Christina von Nolcken on 'An Unremarked Group of Wycliffite Sermons in Latin' (*MP*), dating from the fifteenth century.

11. Drama

This section is divided into the following subsections: (a) Editions and General Studies; (b) Chester; (c) Wakefield; (d) Moralities and Non-Cycle Plays; (e) Interludes.

(a) Editions and General Studies

This year has been a good one for the REED series. Two more volumes have appeared, both showing the same careful presentation and attention to detail for which this series has distinguished itself (see *YW* 60.99-100 and *YW* 66.156). In editing the Devon records[38], John M. Wasson has added substantially to our understanding of dramatic and ceremonial activity in this county, yet at the same time he is not deceived about how partial the general picture that results may be; missing documents make generalizing dangerous. Exeter diocese produces the earliest reference in the mid twelfth-century *Penitential of Bartholomew of Exeter*. Later, references are thickest on the ground in borough and parish documents (with only a single item of expenditure appearing in monastic accounts, and that is for a boy bishop in 1475 at Cowick Priory). The second REED volume[39] is the first in the series to treat two different regions between the same covers. Audrey Douglas has researched the records of Cumberland and Westmorland, and Peter Greenfield those of

38. *Devon*, ed. by John M. Wasson. REED. UTor. pp. lxxiv + 623. C$108.
39. *Cumberland, Westmorland, Gloucestershire*, ed. by Audrey Douglas and Peter Greenfield. REED. UTor. pp. ix + 547. C$93.50.

Gloucestershire. Cumberland and Westmorland (modern Cumbria) have some interesting points of comparison, but mainly the two regions contrast in the nature of their dramatic and ceremonial activity. Waits and drummers form the only grounds for direct comparison between them. Otherwise the boroughs of Carlisle (Cumberland) and Kendal (Westmorland) display distinct characteristics: Carlisle, for long in its history a troubled border town, nevertheless marked its calendar, particularly in the seventeenth century, with celebrations from a much older folk tradition; Kendal, a small market town, maintained a ceremonial and dramatic tradition which was linked largely to municipal events. Peter Greenfield's work on Gloucestershire has produced a rather shorter corpus of references, but of these some are of especial interest. For example, Edward I's reward to Gloucester clerks in 1283 for performing the miracles of St Nicholas is a useful addition to the scanty evidence for the existence of a St Nicholas play tradition in England, and Greenfield prints in an appendix R. Willis's justly famous description of the morality play called *The Cradle of Security* which he saw as a youth in Gloucester. Both these REED volumes constitute an indispensable addition to our understanding of British theatrical history and must, like their predecessors, be applauded.

William Tydeman's *English Medieval Theatre, 1400–1500*[40] is a three-part survey of fifteenth-century English staging techniques. Part 1 describes the surviving repertoire of medieval drama, and early on reassures readers less familiar with the medieval dramatic corpus that what survives is 'usually of excellent quality'. Only a few pages later, however, it is unenthusiastic about the surviving English saints' plays, and none of these is discussed in Part 2, the book's core. The first of its five chapters argues that *Mankind* was staged in an inn-yard, in which was erected a simple booth-stage, and follows the narrative of the play, imagining its action in these staging circumstances; the second conjectures a performance of *The Play of the Sacrament* set against the backdrop of All Saints' Church, Croxton, and using three scaffold stages; the third returns to the vexed issues surrounding a production of *The Castle of Perseverance*; the fourth imagines the consequences of performing the Passion sequence of the York cycle after the mode of presentation suggested by Stanley Kahrl in 1974 (see *YW* 55.142) with a few modifications. Tydeman paints a lively picture of people scurrying back and forth to catch the plays they are specially interested in. The fifth chapter reconstructs a possible performance of *Fulgens and Lucres* in the setting of a medieval Great Hall. Part 3 of the book is a broad survey of different kinds of venue available for medieval dramatic productions, different acting styles that different venues would have called for, and medieval *mise-en-scène* and production organization. In all, this book is welcome for its convincing evocation of the sheer variety of medieval performances. It is not uncontentious: a suggested emendation for part of the wording of *The Castle of Perseverance* staging diagram, for example, seems decidedly overbold. Also his account of staging in York leaves a lingering aftertaste of uncertainty about how the cycle there was managed. Nevertheless, it is lucid, well researched, and thoroughly informed by a practical grasp of theatre.

The first of this year's latecomers for review in this section is the excellent

40. *English Medieval Theatre, 1400–1500*, by William Tydeman. RKP. pp. xiv + 221. £25.

short study of *The Early Plays of Robin Hood*[41] by David Wiles. His book traces the way in which the Robin Hood myth changed its meaning at the end of the medieval period and acquired its modern shape and connotations. In this change, drama played an important role. After an introduction, Chapters 2 and 3 describe the interconnections between Robin Hood and the Lord of the May tradition, showing how the Robin Hood game is a variant of the king game. Chapter 4 investigates the combat component of the Robin Hood game, and attempts a convincing reconstruction of the action lying behind the dramatic fragment of Robin Hood from *c.* 1475. Chapter 5 makes a good case for believing that the game could as easily have influenced the Robin Hood ballad tradition as vice versa, and that 'the memory or the reality of combat plays nourished the imagination of minstrel and listener'. The final chapter addresses the question of whether the Robin Hood game in England allowed a formal, if limited, expression to repressed political sentiments, and argues that while the medieval game was an institutionalized expression of egalitarian sentiment, the Elizabethan gentry, intolerant of such sentiment, fashioned Robin Hood in a new image and turned the former plebeian Lord of Misrule into a nobleman and patriot. Five appendixes conclude the book.

The Saint Play in Medieval Europe[42] contains an article, the longest in the collection, by the volume's editor, Clifford Davidson, which will be of interest to students of medieval English drama. 'The Middle English Saint Play and its Iconography' is a wide-ranging account of the evidence for saint plays in the British Isles, and is impressively in touch with what scattered references survive to plays now lost. He also considers in some detail the Digby *Mary Magdalene* play. Davidson also contributes an article on 'The Lost Coventry Drapers' Play of Doomsday and its Iconographic Context' (*LeedsSE*), in which he ingeniously reconstructs the likely dimensions of spectacle present in a now-lost play by recourse to a number of sources, most notably iconographic ones.

William R. Streitberger describes the connection between 'William Cornish and the Players of the Chapel' (*METh*) in a carefully researched article that traces the career of Cornish and his involvement in dramatics. Cornish was probably responsible for establishing the Players of the Chapel, and from at least 1493, he was involved with the Gentlemen of the Chapel in mounting performances. Cornish collaborated with this company throughout the latter part of Henry VII's reign and into the early years of the reign of Henry VIII.

Robert Adams dips into medieval *distinctio* collections in search of clues to help explain 'The Egregious Feasts of the Chester and Towneley Shepherds' (*ChauR*). He suggests that the gluttonous feast in both plays serves to characterize the corrupt spiritual leadership which was a mark of the Old Law, and to present the shepherds, before the Nativity, as the corrupt guardians of the chosen flock. Nevertheless he does not lose sight, gratifyingly, of the way the feasts are in a more literal and anachronistic sense appropriate to medieval shepherds honouring Christ's birth.

41. *The Early Plays of Robin Hood*, by David Wiles. Brewer (1981). pp. 97. £17.25.

42. *The Saint Play in Medieval Europe*, ed. by Clifford Davidson. MIP. pp. x + 269. $15.95.

(b) Chester

Volume II of the Lumiansky and Mills edition of *The Chester Mystery Cycle*[43] has appeared, though due to rising costs of publishing it is much reduced from the scope promised in Volume I. Fortunately, a good deal of the omitted material found publication at another press in 1983 (see *YW* 64.140). In this volume, the commentary on each play is prefaced with a list of its *dramatis personae*, of the stage locations named in it (for example, '*in desertum*', or '*super pinnaculum templi*' of Play XII), and of its costumes and properties. After this material related to production, there follow sections on sources and, wherever necessary, on the wording of play-headings. The remaining commentary aims primarily to aid a reader's understanding of the cycle text and to clarify any difficulties it may pose. This volume is an indispensable accompaniment to the first one.

Chester has also attracted one article missed last year. 'Tudd, Tibbys Sonne, and Trowle the Trewe: Dramatic Complexities in the Chester Shepherds' Pageant' (*SN*, 1985) by Joseph E. Grennen is a curate's egg of an article, excellent in parts, but teasing credulity in others. He aims to salvage the Chester Shepherds' play from critical indifference, and on the whole the attempt works. But to believe, for example, that when the Second Shepherd says 'Therefore will I wayte on this would/upon the wedder, for I am werye', the word 'wedder' may in fact be implying 'wether' (that is, 'Lamb of God') as much as 'weather', an act of faith is required that we will be prepared to make, I think, depending upon how serious-minded about the play we are.

(c) Wakefield

All three articles on Wakefield this year have appeared in the same place, *LeedsSE*, and all show the quality to be expected from this periodical. In hope of stimulating further interest in the pageant, Arthur C. Cawley and Martin Stevens have printed 'The Towneley *Processus Talentorum*: Text and Commentary'. This is the only pageant in any of the cycles entirely concerned with the gambling of the soldiers for Christ's seamless coat, and it appears to be a later addition to Towneley, since the preceding Towneley Crucifixion pageant also contains a briefer treatment of the same theme. The Talents play is given with apparatus and commentary. Further on the same theme, Arthur C. Cawley writes on 'The Towneley *Processus Talentorum*: A Survey and Interpretation', in which he describes the course of secondary literature on the play from its earliest appearance in 1831 until the present day. He then examines, with a delightful lightness of touch, various aspects of the meaning and staging of the Talents, including the presentation of Pilate, the influence of Psalm 21 in the play, the possibilities for number symbolism in the dicing episode, and staging. In '"The Towneley Plays" or "The Towneley Cycle"', David Mills asks the question how meaningful is the concept of the 'cycle' as a generic definition, and focuses his discussion on the Towneley play collection. He believes that Towneley sometimes eludes the Augustinian notion of time (in which memory and expectation are regarded as active in time present), especially in its depiction of 'morally unaligned' actions that trap the characters who deal in them in 'the prison of the present'. Heroes of the plays, conversely,

---

43. *The Chester Mystery Cycle*, ed. by R. M. Lumiansky and David Mills. Vol. II: *Commentary and Glossary*. EETS. pp. xx + 465. £15.

make frequent appeals to the memory of the audience (and hence prompt their expectation too). In this respect Towneley is quite unlike Chester, for example, in placing such an onus on the audience to create meaning.

(d) Moralities and Non-Cycle Plays

This year the play *Wisdom* has attracted the unusual distinction of a volume of essays devoted to it[44]. Three of the volume's five papers have appeared in print before, one of which eluded a *YWES* review (that by Milla Cozart Riggio; for the other two, see *YW* 66.159–60). Riggio's article on 'The Staging of *Wisdom*' is a description of the respective merits of two productions of *Wisdom* staged in Trinity College, Hartford, Connecticut, in 1984. The indoor production, deemed to have been better suited to the play's requirements than the outdoor one, was presented as if to an aristocratic audience which included some clerics, and in the context of a banquet. Riggio's commentary on the elaborate costuming directions in *Wisdom* is particularly interesting. It seems that when Donald Baker asks the question, 'Is *Wisdom* a "Professional" Play?', he loses sight of it in the consideration of similarities and dissimilarities between *Wisdom* and other moralities with which his essay is largely concerned. However, he salvages it near the end by arguing that our reasons for believing a play a 'professional' or 'popular' one are far from clear, and that if plays like *The Castle of Perseverance* and *Mankind* are reckoned to be 'professional', the play *Wisdom*, in being more like them than is generally recognized, should be too. Lastly, in '*Wisdom* and the Records: Is There a Moral?' Alexandra F. Johnston asks whether the choice of setting and occasion for the Trinity College *Wisdom* performance (notionally at the abbey of Bury St Edmunds on the occasion of a visit there of Edward IV) was the right one. Her answer in short is that the rightness of the choice is unprovable either way, for in her view (and it is impressively supported) *Wisdom* could as conceivably have been commissioned by a secular magnate and played in his house to a predominantly courtly audience with some clerics in attendance.

In explaining some of the 'Devotional Themes in the Violence and Humor of the *Play of the Sacrament*' (*CompD*), Richard L. Homan sensitively justifies the play against the criticism that its intentional comedy is irrelevant, while its scenes of violence are unintentionally comic. He argues that the scenes of violence would have been taken seriously by a medieval audience because they incorporate motifs which touch fifteenth-century devotional sensibility closely, and that the comic episode of the Doctor and his boy is thematically integrated with the main plot.

(e) Interludes

The last of this year's latecomers, but a welcome one for all that, is Alan H. Nelson's edition of *The Plays of Henry Medwall*[45]. The introduction comments briefly on the form of Medwall's two plays, and continues with an outline of Medwall's biography. This outline is supported by an appendix that lists all known sources for Medwall's life records. Nelson goes on to consider

---

44. *The 'Wisdom' Symposium: Papers from the Trinity College Medieval Festival*, ed. by Milla Cozart Riggio. AMS. pp. xiii + 110. $27.50.

45. *The Plays of Henry Medwall*, ed. by Alan H. Nelson. Brewer (1980). pp. viii + 237. £22.95.

aspects of the plays which may reflect Medwall's training and personal circumstances, and the possible link between him and Sir Thomas More; the year 1491 is advanced as being as likely a date for the composition of *Fulgens and Lucres* as the more generally held 1497. Prosody and language are discussed, though rather sparsely, and the printing history of Medwall's plays described. The edited play texts themselves are provided with a traditional apparatus, notes, and glossary. For the first time both of Medwall's extant plays are now available together in one reliable edition.

Finally, and still on the topic of Medwall, Alan J. Fletcher has noticed in a description of a Christmas gambol of 1603 a close parallel to the mock joust in *Fulgens and Lucres*. In '"Farte Prycke in Cule": A Late-Elizabethan Analogue from Ireland' (*METh*), Fletcher discusses the parallel which helps confirm a reconstruction of the mock joust mooted by Peter Meredith (see *YW* 65.135), and suggests that Medwall drafted for use in his play what was originally a seasonal game.

Middle English: Chaucer

JOHN J. McGAVIN and DAVID MILLS

This chapter is divided into four sections: 1. General; 2. Canterbury Tales; 3. Troilus and Criseyde; 4. Other Works.

1. General

Bege K. Bowers has compiled 'Chaucer Research, 1985: Report No. 46' (*ChauR* 21.67–83) and 'Chaucer Research in Progress: 1985–1986' (*NM* 87.437–55). Lorrayne Y. Baird-Lange and Bege Bowers with Hildegard Schnuttgen have compiled 'An Annotated Chaucer Bibliography, 1984' (*SAC* 8.279–341). The latest in the useful series of selective interdisciplinary bibliographies from Toronto is *Chaucer: A Bibliographical Introduction*[1]. Offering a considerable range of material, from Alchemy to Nigellus Wireker and from Annual Bibliographies to Philip Ziegler, it is divided into three sections – 'Materials for the Study of Chaucer's Works', 'Chaucer's Works', and 'Backgrounds'; the last begs some critical questions but it has an obvious organizational advantage and accurately reflects the way subjects such as the Peasants' Revolt have been traditionally related to Chaucer's writing. The *terminus ad quem* for selection is 1979, but room is found for some important items from the early 1980s.

The Cambridge Chaucer Companion[2] is 'intended for students approaching Chaucer for the first time' but its essays, by eminent scholars, are original studies, not critical résumés. Paul Strohm examines 'The Social and Literary Scene in England', stressing that Chaucer was a social poet whose juxtaposition of personal and literary styles provides an analogue to contemporary social heterogeneity. David Wallace examines 'Chaucer's Continental Inheritance: The Early Poems and *Troilus and Criseyde*'. The French dream-format is Chaucer's early means of measuring the capabilities of English against Dante's Italian, culminating in the *Parliament of Fowls* where 'a Dantean standard of artful naturalness in vernacular diction' is achieved; in *Troilus* Chaucer turns to Boccaccio, with whose work he had natural affinities, and locates his own poem confidently within the European literary tradition while signalling his continuing heritage as an English romancer. Piero Boitani writes of 'Old Books

1. *Chaucer: A Bibliographical Introduction*, by John Leyerle and Anne Quick. UTor. pp. xx + 321. hb £24.50, pb £12.
2. *The Cambridge Chaucer Companion*, ed. by Piero Boitani and Jill Mann. CUP. pp. x + 262. hb £27.50, pb £8.95.

Brought to Life in Dreams: The *Book of the Duchess*, the *House of Fame*, the *Parliament of Fowls*', offering readings of the three poems as explorations of the processes whereby books generate books; Chaucer's audience is, throughout his works, involved in a game of intertextuality to find the sources. Mark Lambert's account of 'Telling the Story in *Troilus and Criseyde*' emphasizes the poem's 'structure of bilateral symmetry' in which the poetry of grace, moral health, and delight of the first part leads the reader to pleasurable self-discovery and certainty, which then dissolve in the second part into less pleasant discoveries and into uncertainty about the art itself.

Jill Mann offers a revealing new angle on an old topic in 'Chance and Destiny in *Troilus and Criseyde* and the *Knight's Tale*', emphasizing the subjective aspect of the perception of Destiny. Although the ongoing action of *Troilus* is open to chance, it seems inevitable only retrospectively – witness the way the lovers construe the events and shape their attitudes accordingly in Book III; Chaucer has supplemented Boethius's concern with external mutation by including the internal mutations on which those external variables work. In the Knight's Tale events are shown to be directed not by chance but by higher powers, but though we see the hidden causes operating on Destiny, we do so incompletely. This thought-provoking essay concludes by stressing that 'the question of whether the world is governed by "fortunous hap" or by a benign ordering power' is central to all Chaucer's serious poetry.

For C. David Benson in '*The Canterbury Tales*: Personal Drama or Experiments in Poetic Variety?' the answer lies clearly in the poetic individuality of the tales, not the tellers. Four further essays isolate modes in the tales. J. A. Burrow's 'The *Canterbury Tales* I: Romance' finds evidence in some tales of romance potential to suggest that Chaucer was perhaps not easy within that genre. Derek Pearsall's 'The *Canterbury Tales* II: Comedy' offers ground rules for the genre and reasons for excluding the tales of the Friar and Summoner from it. Robert Worth Frank Jr's 'The *Canterbury Tales* III: Pathos' emphasizes the features which led to the popularity of this type of narrative in the later Middle Ages but make it unfashionable today. And A. C. Spearing's 'The *Canterbury Tales* IV: Exemplum and Fable' draws attention to the increasing tension between story and doctrinal truth in the tales of the Friar, Pardoner, Nun's Priest, and Manciple, perhaps illustrative of a growing scepticism of any linking of the two. Morton W. Bloomfield continues his useful discussion of 'Chaucerian Realism' begun in 1964 (*YW* 45.84) by demonstrating Chaucer's use in the *Tales* of an authenticating level to validate or reinforce a story, however unreal, and to encourage the suspension of disbelief. Barry Windeatt suggests that 'Literary Structures in Chaucer' are contextualizing devices which enable different materials to interact; proposing a scale of 'open' to 'close' structures, he argues that Chaucer seeks an open structure for the *Tales* but ends absolutely, in a resolution of faith. Dieter Mehl presents 'Chaucer's Narrator: *Troilus and Criseyde* and the *Canterbury Tales*' as a device to heighten our critical awareness of the processes of composition and transmission, and Derek Brewer, in 'Chaucer's Poetic Style', discusses Chaucer as a literate poet who affects the oral style. An excellent bibliography of 'Further Reading: A Guide to Chaucer Studies' by Joerg O. Fichte concludes this useful and at times stimulating collection of essays.

Two of the 1984 J. A. W. Bennett Memorial Lectures have Chaucerian subjects and, as the title of the lecture anthology – *Intellectuals and Writers in Fourteenth-Century Europe*[3] – might lead one to expect, both provide contemporary intellectual contexts for their evaluations. For Willi Erzgräber in '"Auctorite" and "Experience" in Chaucer', the first-person narrator is a means of realizing the challenge to theological truth offered by Ockhamite concern with cognition through human reason and experience. His series of individual analyses of Chaucer's poems – including from the *Tales* the Wife of Bath's Prologue, the Parson's Tale, and the Retractions – include predictable but intelligent assessments of the validity of the narrator's moral–theological conclusions to *Troilus* and the *Tales*. But the essay's most perceptive insights concern the way the *Book of the Duchess* prioritizes classical virtue and consolatory memory over traditional spiritual consolation, and the cynicism engendered in the *House of Fame* from the opposition of the moral–theological and the 'philosophical–anthropocentric' approaches. Alistair Minnis's essay, 'Chaucer's Pardoner and the "Office of Preacher"', offers abundant evidence of the type of the morally bad preacher with which Chaucer would be familiar and which recognizably underlies the Pardoner. Chaucer is uncompromising in denying his highly intelligent Pardoner the possible excuse that his address effects moral reform because his vice is secret; the reader is left to ponder the power of his superb narrative.

With the North American market in mind, Robert O. Payne provides a replacement for the earlier study by E. J. Howard (*YW* 45.80–1), hence his rather disconcerting and misleading title page, *Geoffrey Chaucer*: Second edition[4]. A personal introduction for beginners, it tends to eschew critical problems and to recognize rather than explore Chaucer's complexity. The book encourages the modern response rather than supposedly medieval ones, a fact evident in its highly selective bibliography. With its nineteen items written before 1960, however, it offers a remarkable contrast to David Aers's *Chaucer*[5]. This short and inexpensive critical investigation will offer undergraduate readers a challenging – though by constraints of space a critically unrepresentative – introduction to Chaucer. The book is refreshing in its preference for reflexive ethical discourse in the historical context over current metapoetical interpretations. In the world Chaucer presents 'al is for to selle', and he accordingly grounds, physicalizes, and literalizes any language or ideology for which transcendental status might be claimed. Aers's readings are often illuminating and even when, as in the area of Chaucer's anti-clericalism, they are not essentially new, they are freshly and valuably stated. The argument is presented with careful qualification and clear demonstration throughout but is inevitably damaged at times by the selectivity built into its critical theory and imposed by the book's format. Aers's own sizable contribution to work in Chaucer has made his sniping at a 'medieval critical establishment' seem dated.

Equally, the critical insecurity manifest in Stephen Knight's *Geoffrey*

---

3. *Intellectuals and Writers in Fourteenth-Century Europe: The J. A. W. Bennett Memorial Lectures, Perugia, 1984*, ed. by Piero Boitani and Anna Torti. Narr/Brewer. pp. 276. £27.95.

4. *Geoffrey Chaucer*, by Robert O. Payne. Second edition. TEAS. Twayne. pp. xiv + 153. £13.95.

5. *Chaucer*, by David Aers. Harvester. pp. xi + 121. pb £4.95.

Chaucer[6] is unnecessary. At a time when Chaucer criticism can benefit from historicist approaches and many students have the theoretical knowledge to deal with them, what is needed is less carping self-justification and more weighty historicism, such as will, for example, give terms like 'feudal' and 'Gothic' a greater dialectical sophistication than they possess in Knight's book. In pressing for a radical re-adjustment of critical responses, he sometimes loses his balance: poems receive too much or too little space for their importance to the argument; the religious dimension – and especially the 'new forces within Christianity' which Knight recognizes – is underexamined, and the conservative implications of comedy demand fuller consideration. In consequence, the Chaucer of the Nun's Priest's Tale becomes a mere 'chucker-out'. But, despite these criticisms, this is an exciting book, with much to value and to argue about. Particularly good is its close analysis of public and private values in *Troilus*, but readers will also find interesting its re-assessment of the Physician's and Manciple's tales and of Melibee, and its claims for the *Book of the Duchess* and the *House of Fame* as analyses of aristocratic failings. Knight's book should succeed in its avowed aim of encouraging us to read Chaucer's work 'in terms of its relation to the dynamic historical forces of its own period'. A general review of critics who have or have not read in this way is provided by Derek Pearsall's essay, 'Chaucer's Poetry and its Modern Commentators: The Necessity of History'[7]. Topics discussed include the unacceptability of seeing literature as 'reflecting' history ('embedding' is Pearsall's final image); the importance of genre in a historical study; the ahistorical approach; and various Marxist approaches. Pearsall's own, historically determined, preference is for the English tradition of language study since textual relations with history seem best discovered in the close analysis of meaning and connotation.

Despite their very different subjects, David Burnley's 'Courtly Speech in Chaucer' (*PoeticaJ.* 24.16–38) and Phillipa Hardman's 'Chaucer's Muses and his "Art Poetical"' (*RES* 37.478–94) perform a similar service by looking at two modern critical preoccupations, respectively language and metapoetics. A complex of courtly markers establishes speech as courtly for Burnley. He locates its characteristics in Chaucer in a combination of the socio-moral (friendliness and approachability) and the aesthetic (elaborated eloquence gently delivered), and illustrates these features from specific examples analysed as 'address', 'message', and 'attitude'. Ciceronian theories of *mutua benevolentia* prove helpful to explain our sense of an underlying stable concept of courtliness. The article concludes with a discussion of courtly euphemism. In her valuable study, Phillipa Hardman reveals the importance of the etymologies of mythographers, especially Fulgentius, for understanding the characterizations of the Muses in *Anelida and Arcite* and *Troilus*, and of Fulgentius's explanation of them as nine stages of literary activity for the *House of Fame*. Departures from this tradition include the affirmative search in Book III of the *House of Fame*, and the Boethian attitude to the Muses in *Troilus* which serves as an index of the narrator's changing attitude to the story. From a rhetorical rather than a mythographical point of view, Marjorie Curry Woods offers a

6. *Geoffrey Chaucer*, by Stephen Knight. RL. Blackwell. pp. xi + 173. hb £15, pb £4.50.

7. In *Medieval Literature: Criticism, Ideology and History*, ed. by David Aers. Harvester. pp. vii + 228. £28.50.

quite different account of the ending of *Troilus* from that which Hardman's researches would support. In her 'Poetic Digression and the Interpretation of Medieval Literary Texts'[8] she argues that the narrator's final judgement in *Troilus* and also Chaucer's Retractions should be seen as examples of rhetorical digression which explores areas related to but distinct from the original subject.

Henrik Specht's discussion of '"Ethopoeia" or Impersonation: A Neglected Species of Medieval Characterization' (*ChauR* 21.1–15) makes brief reference to the *Legend of Good Women* and offers a closer analysis of Criseyde's soliloquy (*Troilus* V.1054–85) to exemplify Chaucer's use of interior monologue for characterization and stylistic heightening. Renate Haas illustrates the variety and artistry of 'Chaucer's Use of the Lament for the Dead'[9], distinguishing the ambiguous tension of lover's and mourner's laments in the courtly poems from the traditional lament-patterns of his religious and didactic works (which, however, also employ ostensibly antithetical structures). This interest in laments for the dead was congruent with Chaucer's experiments in tragedy, a concern activated by the rediscovery of Seneca.

The foundation of Henry Ansgar Kelly's scholarly monograph, *Chaucer and the Cult of Saint Valentine*[10], is that Chaucer would be too much of a realist to permit the inconsistency by which a February 14 date for St Valentine's Day is accompanied by 'full-fledged spring landscape and activity' in poems such as the *Parliament of Fowls*. In addition, the cult of St Valentine, as patron of love-matches, cannot be proved to antedate Chaucer. Prompted either by knowledge gained in Italy or by the betrothal of Richard II to Anne on 3 May 1381, Chaucer developed a cult of St Valentine on the basis of St Valentine of Genoa (festal day 3 May) and offered the royal couple annual Valentine's Day poems, details from which were soon culturally adopted and subsequently transferred to the more widely known saint, despite the climatic inconsistencies which resulted. Although Kelly's book proceeds from a questionable premise to only a possible conclusion, it is succinctly instructive throughout, considering as part of its argument such topics as the terminology of the seasons, the creation of saints' cults, and the relative unpopularity of Valentine as a child's name in England. As critical tradition almost demands, his scholarship begins to get out of hand when he discusses the date 3 May in Chaucer's works, but overall it is well deployed and his argument clearly summed up.

Two important articles which touch upon Chaucer within much wider terms of reference are J. D. Burnley's fine piece on 'Curial Prose in England' (*Speculum* 61.593–614) and John N. King's substantial study of 'Spenser's *Shepheardes Calender* and Protestant Pastoral Satire'[11]. Burnley considers it unnecessary to look beyond native sources for Chaucer's use of curial style in Melibee but analysis of the tale also suggests that Chaucer considered fully curial prose to be less 'a literary stylistic ideal' than an appropriate style for

8. In *Acta Conventus Neo-Latini Sanctandreani: Proceedings of the Fifth International Congress of Neo-Latin Studies, 1982*, ed. by I. D. McFarlane. CMERS. pp. 656. $50.

9. In *Chaucer in the Eighties*, ed. by Julian N. Wasserman and Robert J. Blanch. Syracuse. pp. xxi + 258. hb $37.50, pb $17.50.

10. *Chaucer and the Cult of Saint Valentine*, by Henry Ansgar Kelly. Brill. pp. xii + 185. pb £18.90.

11. In *Renaissance Genres: Essays on Theory, History, and Interpretation*, ed. by Barbara Kiefer Lewalski. Harvard. pp. 512. hb $25, pb $8.95.

discourse where clarity was vital, as in the astronomical works. John N. King finds that the Chaucer of anticlerical satire (who was also the supposed author of the *Plowman's Tale*) 'furnishes Spenser's model for the structures and conventions of the satirical eclogues, as well as the role of the new English poet'. In combination with Virgil, he is praised under the name *Tityrus*, for his radical proto-Protestant morality as much as for his art. In 'Chaucer, Deschamps, and *Le Roman de Brut*' (*Arts* 12 (1984).35–59), Roy J. Pearcy claims Wace's Pandras as the reference of 'la langue pandras' in Deschamps's *ballade* and that it refers to the Trojan founder of Britain, in contradistinction to the reputedly dishonest and shifty Saxons; Deschamps was appropriating Chaucer for the non-Saxon section of English society, building on the idea of Richard II as Trojanly pro-French and Henry of Lancaster as Saxonly anti-French. He deduces from *To His Purse* that Chaucer, though unexceptionable in his comments on the new régime, would not have welcomed a regressive insularity. Ruth M. Ames, in 'Corn and Shrimps: Chaucer's Mockery of Religious Controversy' (*Acta* 8 (1984).71–89) notes the toleration of religious diversity in Richard II's court and points to the allusive treatment of contemporary controversial issues in Troilus's despairing view of freewill and the Host's attitudes to certain clerics; Chaucer's audience would appreciate this oblique humour, she assures us.

Jeanne E. Krochalis supplies poetic and artistic contexts for the innovatory desire for a realistic author-portrait expressed by 'Hoccleve's Chaucer Portrait' (*ChauR* 21.234–45). Memorial realism in royal tomb-effigies is offered as a starting point, though Hoccleve may have had the *ABC* in mind in setting his portrait among the Virgin and saints. Though Hoccleve extends to the literary figure an honorific gesture hitherto reserved for the holy, powerful, or wealthy, Chaucer himself sought no memorial outside his poetry.

Shinsuke Ando traces 'The English Tradition in Chaucer's Diction'[9], drawing upon native romance elements and techniques in translating foreign works. Haruo Iwasaki provides 'Some Notes on the *gan*-Periphrasis' (*KWS* 1 (1984).15–32), listing the frequency of the construction, the verbs involved, frequent patterns, and the problem of '*gan* versus *bigan*'. The same author also enumerates and discusses '"Not worth a straw" and Similar Idioms' (*KWS* 1 (1984).33–49).

Dieter Mehl's *Geoffrey Chaucer*[12] is a revised and expanded translation of his German book of 1973 (*YW* 54.109–10). The major new addition is 'The Storyteller and his Audience: *The Legend of Good Women*' in which the poem is seen to display Chaucer's fascination with Ovid's narrative skill and material; though the challenge was beyond Chaucer's skill, it led to the development of a new form and a characteristic treatment which directed the reader to the problems of literary composition. G. K. Chesterton's 1932 essay, 'The Greatness of Chaucer', is the first of nine essays reprinted by Harold Bloom in the Modern Critical Views volume *Geoffrey Chaucer*[13]. The others are claimed to be in E. Talbot Donaldson's tradition of literary humanism and include two essays by him.

12. *Geoffrey Chaucer: An Introduction to his Narrative Poetry*, by Dieter Mehl. CUP. pp. viii + 243. hb £25, pb £8.95.
13. *Geoffrey Chaucer*, ed. by Harold Bloom. ChelseaH (1985). pp. ii + 149. $19.95.

2. Canterbury Tales

C. David Benson explores *Chaucer's Drama of Style: Poetic Variety and Contrast in the 'Canterbury Tales'* [14]. He prefers this form of drama to the traditional view of the tales as dramatically reflective of their tellers, which he comprehensively undermines. Perhaps because stylistic variety in Chaucer is neither hard to accept nor novel, his readings do not always challenge, but they are always valuable and the book as a whole is full of good sense and clear writing. Benson draws stylistic distinctions between tales and their prologue links; among tales in the same genre; between the Chaucer of the General Prologue and that of Sir Thopas and Melibee; and among different forms of discourse from the same speaker. He finds the Merchant's Tale particularly representative of a variety which Chaucer employed to explore genres and develop themes dialectically as well as for sheer pleasure. His concern to point up contrasts between tales can lead Benson to overestimate uniformity within individual poems and his word-counts can seem mechanical (though they serve rather than lead his argument), but this is certainly the best study of Chaucer this year. In contrast, Roger Ellis's *Patterns of Religious Narrative in the Canterbury Tales* [15] is too long and methodologically introspective for a book which seeks to read with simplicity. Though earnestly written, it is bedevilled by questions of form and content, a lack of critical direction, and an intermittent assumption of realism on Chaucer's part as an aid to critical argument.

William E. Rogers's book, *Upon the Ways: The Structure of The Canterbury Tales* [16], offers a serial reading of the Ellesmere sequence as a 'collection of world views' whose form is determined by dissatisfaction, so that no view is adequate though one responds to another. Honest about its aims and wholly justified in finding support for its personal stance from the circularity underlying all critical interpretation, this book is nevertheless limited by its reductive generality. 'What we learn from the work is to be dissatisfied with this life, and what we learn from that dissatisfaction is to turn to God.' Discussions of individual Fragments – tendentiously or provocatively terse – are subordinated to this thesis and appear under headings such as 'Social Order and Individual Freedom' (Fragment I), 'The Value of Earthly Experience' (Fragments III-V), or 'The Problem of Language' (Fragments VII-X). Although the subtlety of Stephen Knight's reading in 'Chaucer's Religious Canterbury Tales' [17] is considerably greater, Knight shares with Rogers a tendency to structure the *Tales* in a fixed sequence around an implicit psychological drama within its author. While Rogers can point only to a series of dissatisfactions, Knight locates four definite sections. Chaucer first establishes social structures and the historical forces with which they are in tension. He then grounds this dialectic in individual pilgrims (the section between the Wife and the Pardoner inclusive). Next, in gradual retreat from the achievement of

14. *Chaucer's Drama of Style: Poetic Variety and Contrast in the 'Canterbury Tales'*, by C. David Benson. UNC. pp. viii + 183. £17.
15. *Patterns of Religious Narrative in the Canterbury Tales*, by Roger Ellis. CH. pp. 316. £30.
16. *Upon the Ways: The Structure of The Canterbury Tales*, by William E. Rogers. UVict. pp. 144. pb C$6.50.
17. In *Medieval English Religious and Ethical Literature: Essays in Honour of G. H. Russell*, ed. by Gregory Kratzmann and James Simpson. Brewer. pp. vi + 250. £27.50.

the latter section, he reveals a 'steady closing down of the historical imagination' until, finally, a position of orthodoxy is reached in the last four tales. The
article is about more than what the ordinary reader would consider Chaucer's
religious tales but the title is deliberately ambiguous because Knight wishes to
claim, on the basis of other works with which the collection was often bound,
that 'the *Tales* as a whole was seen as having a distinct religious impact'.

In his important discussion of 'The Genre of Chaucer's Fabliau-Tales' [18] Roy
J. Pearcy argues that 'Chaucer's fabliau-tales differ from the traditional
fabliaux according to the degree in which they realize the comedic potential in
the conventional fabliau plots which they appropriate'. He sustains a
meaningful comparison of the Miller's Tale with the *Geta* of Vitalis de Blois
and suggests Chaucer may have known texts of the twelfth-century Latin
comedies; in the tale, the clerical view of love characteristic of fabliau is dismissed and Christian myth substitutes for classical as a means of proposing
comedic values. Those values are sacrificed by the Reeve as he moves the text
away from its French analogue to privilege his own spiteful satiric mode. The
two tales reflect their narrators' personalities and, with the unfinished Cook's
Tale, mark a development through Fragment A. Further comparisons with
French analogues reveal Chaucer's distinctive modifications in other tales; the
Merchant gives mythic significance to marital strife while the Shipman assigns
atypical functions to his characters.

In an interesting, if densely written, account of 'Some Discarnational
Impulses in the *Canterbury Tales*' [17] Penelope Curtis regards the tales of the
Man of Law, the Second Nun, the Clerk, and the Prioress as sharing 'a
purifying, abstracting and disheriting impulse (which in extreme form tends
towards Manicheism)'. They blend legend and literature, corporate transmission and individual creation, and in a variety of ways – not least their
expression of the 'feminine' principle – they appear through Curtis's reading
as very like Shakespeare's last plays (to which she several times refers). A
working definition of 'incarnational' would have helped this unusual and
suggestive article.

Charles A. Owen Jr's wilfully paradoxical title, 'The Tales of Canterbury:
Fictions within a Fiction that Purports not to be a Fiction' [18] indicates his
concern with the *Tales* as fictive autobiography in which the narrator aligns
himself with his pilgrim-creations and cedes control to them, imagining (say) a
Miller listening to a Knight and then insisting on telling his own story. Chaucer
also imagines the experience of the readers as listeners and cedes choice to them
as they stand outside the game, enjoying Chaucer's creativity. The Host,
though judge, is also a comic touchstone of hearing and mishearing who cannot
impose his authority upon the game. Nothing is predictable or fore-
known – 'telling, projection, sharing of experience, however imperfect,
become part of the fiction on every level'.

The title of J. D. Burnley's important and perceptive article, 'Chaucer's
Host and Harry Bailly' [18], sums up the critical positions he explores – the
historical Harry Bailly representing the presuppositions of a familiar reality
that generates psychological consistency, and the Host, the awareness of
literary alterity that emphasizes the devices and ends of moral didacticism.

18. In *Chaucer and the Craft of Fiction*, ed. by Leigh A. Arrathoon. Solaris.
pp. xxv + 430. pb $20.

Burnley demonstrates that, even where there is an overwhelming sense of reality in the *Tales*, the 'integrity of fictive personality' may not be paramount. He traces the means by which Bailly is individualized in Fragment A and, from Fragments A and H – his two dealings with the Cook – illustrates his individuated linguistic usages. But the Host's learned and allusive sententiousness aligns him, not with the Southwark innkeeper, but with the poetic sensibility of Chaucer himself. The medieval aesthetic and the circumstances of literary creation admitted such eclecticism and allowed the writer to transcend the limits of realism.

Musing on 'Chaucer and the Art of Hagiography'[9], Laurel Braswell finds the hagiographical genre, artistically shaped by literary concern, in the Second Nun's Tale – where it is extended by liturgical reference – and the Prioress's Tale – expressing without irony a characteristically Franciscan sentimentality. But the tales of the Man of Law and the Clerk become pseudo-hagiographical and generically ambiguous through their selective evocation of theological detail. William Kamowski discusses 'Varieties of Response to *Melibee* and the *Clerk's Tale*'[9]. The former continues the wide concern in the *Tales* with interpretation and misinterpretation by inviting consideration of Melibee's own interpretative errors, ironically paralleled in the Host's very personal response to the tale. The Clerk's exegetical interpretation of his tale invites resistance and directs attention to the latent ironies within it, inviting the audience to respond more fully to the complexities it raises.

Behind Deschamps's description of Chaucer as *grant translateur* lies the primary sense of *translatio* as the transformation of form and substance, and with it the process of creating and altering meaning. So argues Edmund Reiss in 'Chaucer's Fiction and Linguistic Self-Consciousness in the Late Middle Ages'[18], finding in Chaucer the late-medieval fascination with language and an awareness of its limitations. In the *Tales* Chaucer seeks to challenge the reader's critical self-awareness by revealing, through the complex and paradoxical nature of his transformations of the traditional, the limitations of literary creation. The wide-ranging issues raised by the Nun's Priest's Tale reflect the contemporary intellectual turmoil resulting from a confusion of traditional disciplines and a sense of intellectual bankruptcy. Those issues point to the simple trust in divine will with which the *Tales* end – an ending that is also revealed as an awareness of limitation and a process of transformation.

The manuscript controversy surrounding the *Canterbury Tales* provides the starting point for Derek Pearsall's more widely ranging essay on 'Editing Medieval Texts: Some Developments and Some Problems'[19]. The process by which the editorialized Ellesmere manuscript became the base of the modern standard edition in preference to the intrinsically superior Hengwrt manuscript, 'an early and uneditorialized manuscript', illustrates problems inherent in the quest for a final 'author's text' – so obvious in an unfinished work – and the tyranny of the modern definitive edition.

Two studies of scribal practice have direct bearing on Chaucer this year. R. Vance Ramsey responds to M. L. Samuels (*YW* 64.151) in 'Paleography and Scribes of Shared Training' (*SAC* 8.107–44), one of the more important items in this year's work. A persuasive account of the workings of a scribal shop,

19. In *Textual Criticism and Literary Interpretation*, ed. by Jerome J. McGann. UChic. pp. xi + 239. hb $22, pb $10.95.

based on the attested case of a father and son writing a single manuscript of the *Tales*, is only part of his argument that scribal schooling could produce virtually indistinguishable hands and, consequently, that handwriting alone is inadequate evidence for a claim that two manuscripts were written by the same scribe rather than by two who shared dialect and training. More specifically, Ramsey argues that Hengwrt and Ellesmere were copied by two scribes, not one; that Trinity College, Cambridge, MS R.3.2 was not by the supposed scribe of Hg and El; and that a single scribe was not responsible for both Harley 7334 and Corpus Christi 198. Although Daniel W. Mosser's work on the Cardigan manuscript of the *Tales* reveals a different form of production from that discussed by Ramsey, he also seeks to adduce evidence other than handwriting (viz. pronoun forms) to support his account of scribal practice. In 'The Two Scribes of the Cardigan Manuscript and the "Evidence" of Scribal Supervision and Shop Production' (*SB* 39.112–25) Mosser argues that two rather than three independent craftsmen, unsupervised and self-correcting, wrote the manuscript, one taking over when the other was for some reason unable to continue.

Ralph W. V. Elliott divides the tales of 'Chaucer's Clerical Voices'[17] into two groups on the basis of their time of composition, homogeneity, irony, and other criteria. He regards the chronologically earlier group (Clerk, Monk, Second Nun, and Prioress) as forming almost 'a distinct narrative genre'. Focusing his discussion on the Wife of Bath, Griselda, and Emily – but, sadly, not Criseyde – Brian S. Lee notes a Chaucerian recognition of female individuality in contrast with the traditional theological hierarchy of marriage, continence, and virginity. The word 'feminist' in the title of his article, 'Chaucer's Handling of a Medieval Feminist Hierarchy' (*UES* 1–6), is misleading.

The biblical allusiveness of the Merchant's reference to Esther and the covert allusiveness of the Prologue reference to a mouse in a trap serve Emerson Brown Jr in 'Of Mice and Women: Thoughts on Chaucerian Allusion'[18] as examples of the learning and creative playfulness required to read allusions. Jon Cook applies a wide range of Bakhtin's ideas to the *Tales* in 'Carnival and *The Canterbury Tales*: "Only equals may laugh"'[7]. Among the enemies of carnival are the Pardoner and the Clerk, though, with an inclusiveness typical of the mode, the latter is reclaimed by his remarks to the Wife and by his final song. But Chaucer's Retractions, far from concluding the *Tales*, actually repress its prevailing carnival spirit of anti-authoritarianism. Samuel Schuman takes a common syntactical construction – 'the use of a single statement both as the consequence of a preceding idea and the introduction to a following one' – and sees it as a wider structural principle, 'The Link Mechanism in the *Canterbury Tales*' (*ChauR* 20.200–6). Helen Cooper recognizes similarities between 'Chaucer and Joyce' (*ChauR* 21.142–54) in the naturalism, inclusiveness, and allusiveness of the *Tales* and *Ulysses*.

In '"A Poet Ther Was": Chaucer's Voices in the General Prologue to *The Canterbury Tales*' (*PMLA* 101.154–69) Barbara Nolan argues that none of the three voices identifiable is to be recognized as closest to the poet if we wish properly to appreciate the notion of fictionality. Instead, each offers an image of poetry from 'poetry as philosophy' through the partial and dialogically creative language of 'common humanity' to the Host's conception of poetry as 'distracting merriment'. Michael E. Moriarty responds (*PMLA* 101.859–60), suggesting a Derridean deletion of the term 'voice' and proposing a quasi-syllogistic pattern in the opening forty-two lines of the General Prologue; Nolan replies in turn (*PMLA*: 101.860–1). Lawrence Besserman unravels 'Girdles, Belts and Cords: A Leitmotif in Chaucer's *General Prologue*' (*PLL* 22.322–5) and finds that Chaucer has ironically omitted them from his portraits of ecclesiastics, where they would be of most significance. The Franklin's dagger and pouch are a fashionable affectation from ladies' dress. Yvette Salviati surveys the various interpretations placed upon details of the Prioress's portrait by critics in her commentary on it; setting out from Robertson's Augustinian approach, as might be expected from her title 'Geoffrey Chaucer: *Les Contes de Cantorbéry*: "Charitas" ou "Cupiditas"? Madame Eglantyne Devant la Critique' (*MCRel* 2 (1984).9–29), she concludes in sympathy with the conclusions of Muriel Bowden, which she feels characterize Chaucer's general approach in the *Tales*. In '"This Worthy Lymytour Was Cleped Huberd": A Note on the Friar's Name' (*ChauR* 21.53–7) Warren Ginsberg accepts that his proposal to see the name as an allusion to the patron saint of hunting rests on uncertain ground but makes it nevertheless, because of the imagery of hunting in the Friar's Tale, Chaucer's knowledge of unusual saints, and its contribution to the pattern of equivocation which Ginsberg finds elsewhere. Laurel Braswell studies the importance of the moon in astrological medicine, reminding us in 'The Moon and Medicine in Chaucer's Time' (*SAC* 8.145–56) that Chaucer's Physician is 'grounded in astronomye'.

In 'White and Red in the *Knight's Tale*: Chaucer's Manipulation of a Convention'[9] Robert J. Blanch and Julian N. Wasserman use Chaucerian examples to suggest that the conjunction of the two colours signifies totality, completion, and perfection. In the Knight's Tale this ontological unity is asserted only to be subsequently violated by the 'red versus white' allegiances of the contending lovers, and the motif thus becomes a means of further reinforcing the tale's Boethian vision of unity. Emerson Brown Jr focuses on a particular editorial problem in 'The *Knight's Tale*, 2632: Guilt by Punctuation' (*ChauR* 21.133–41) but raises more general issues about the effects of anachronistic punctuation systems on an unpunctuated Chaucer text. He argues cogently that a text without punctuation should be standard for advanced readers of Chaucer. T. McAlindon examines 'Cosmology, Contrariety and the Knight's Tale' (*MÆ* 55.41–57), finding that 'concept, emotion, character and situation are all subject to a process of contrarious juxtaposition and exchange'. The poem's mingling of optimism and pessimism, and the conflicting forces of order and disorder evident throughout, have their macrocosmic analogue in the *concordia discors* at the heart of various medieval cosmologies. Lorraine Kochanske Stock's article on 'The Two Mayings in Chaucer's *Knight's Tale*: Convention and Invention' (*JEGP* 85.206–21) shows why within the poem's Boethian framework Arcite could not get the girl: he wants Emily less for amatory than for vengeful ends. Chaucer changes the *Teseida* to create connections between Emily's and Arcite's May observances, but while Emily is presented as having mythical affinity with both Flora and Diana, Arcite is discovered by Stock – after some nifty work with the *MED* – to be singing 'an almost obscene request to deflower the flower-like Emelye'.

In 'The Misdirected Kiss and the Lover's Malady in Chaucer's *Miller's Tale*'[9] Edward C. Schweitzer claims that both Arcite and Absolon suffer the physical malady of *amor hereos*; but while Arcite dies, Absolon is cured by the misdirected kiss that dispels the idealized illusion of his disordered imagination. Sandra Pierson Prior discovers Chaucer 'Parodying Typology and the Mystery Plays in the Miller's Tale' (*JMRS* 16.57–73) by showing the inadequacies, confusions, and, ultimately, the punishment of Nicholas, a clerk-cum-drama-producer who 'becomes the focal point, and often the source, of the theological hodgepodge created'. The significant link of the Miller with Pilate adds further irony since he, like the Chaucer-narrator, seeks to wash his hands of responsibility. The article valuably collects the many comic biblical allusions in the tale and shows how they are confusingly overlapped, but it starts from the questionable assumption that typology is a major feature of cycle-plays. Macklin Smith reads '"Or I Wol Caste a Ston"' (*SAC* 8.3–30) of the Miller's Tale (Fragment A, 3712) 'in relation to scriptural stone-casting, the Parson's references to scriptural stone-casting, the rich ambiguity inherent in stone-casting itself, and the actualities of love and sex inside and outside John's window', including the singing of Lauds. 'The Darker Side to Absolon's Dawn Visit' (*ChauR* 20.207–12) is 'the savage survival of the self' according to Raymond P. Tripp Jr, who regards the tale as 'darker rather than unBoethian'. More substantially, Katharina Wilson draws parallels of 'giving' and 'revenge' between the tale and legends of St Nicholas and the Absalom story of 2 Samuel 13. In 'Hagiographical (Dis)play: Chaucer's *The Miller's Tale*' [20] she views them as part of late-medieval secular playing with hagiographical material, an activity possibly furthered by the vernacular drama.

In 'Line 30 of the Man of Law's Tale and the Medieval Malkyn' (*ELN* 24:2.15–20) Alan J. Fletcher stoutly defends the honour of all Malkyns, finding in them an unsophisticated rusticity characteristic of their low social station upon which authors of more learning and higher status might project such vices as they felt congenial. Elizabeth Archibald engages in a motif-analysis which seeks to relate the *Clementine Recognitions* and *Apollonius of Tyre* to the Man of Law's Tale. Marked differences emerge, however, and her article, 'The Flight from Incest: Two Late Classical Precursors of the Constance Theme' (*ChauR* 20.259–72), looks like the first half of an interesting study which would explore more thoroughly why Chaucer alluded to the Apollonius story and another tale of incest but then did not tell a similar one.

The Wife of Bath continues to exert her terrifying power over modern Chaucerians. For John A. Alford, she and the Clerk, as representatives of rhetoric and philosophy (logic), 'define the boundaries of Chaucer's fictional world' and their contrary demands can perhaps be reconciled only in art. His substantial article, 'The Wife of Bath versus the Clerk of Oxford: What Their Rivalry Means' (*ChauR* 21.108–32) outlines the troubled relationship of Rhetoric and Philosophy and the iconography associated with these figures, concluding that Chaucer's characters are not 'composites from a variety of sources' but 'extremely coherent distillations of a single tradition'. The Clerk and the Wife are also linked in Donald C. Green's analysis of 'The Semantics of Power: *Maistrie* and *Soveraynetee* in *The Canterbury Tales*' (*MP* 84.18–23). Chaucer distinguishes between groups of words which relate to individual or role-defined relationships. *Maistrie* and *servyse* express the former,

20. In *Auctor Ludens: Essays on Play in Literature*, ed. by Gerald Guinness and Andrew Hurley. BenjaminsNA. pp. ix + 204. hb $32, pb $19.95.

soveraynetee and *servage* the latter. Thus *maistrie* is not relevant to the role-defined relationship developed in the Clerk's Tale and does not occur in the tale proper; but the Wife confounds *soverayntee* with *maistrie* by seeing one as achievable by means of the other. This also contravenes the natural order of things, in which *soverayntee* derives from one's role in the divine hierarchy. In 'Repetition and Design in the *Wife of Bath's Tale*'[9] Martha Fleming proposes the restoration of order in the Knight's world and the definition of his role within it as the tale's main concern, leaving *mastery* and *sovereignty* open to misinterpretation. Devices of repetition support this reading, as does an examination of the Knight's Tale. Joseph E. Grennen associates 'The Wife of Bath and the Scholastic Concept of *Operatio*' (*JRMMRA* 7.41-8), finding connections between the loathly lady's remarks on *gentilesse* in practice and the Wife's own practicality.

J. K. Bollard studies 'Sovereignty and the Loathly Lady in English, Welsh and Irish' (*LeedsSE* 17.41-59), concluding, first, that the transmission of the 'loathly lady' motif is hard to establish since English versions are quite distinct in meaning from the Irish ones and the case for Welsh and French intervening versions is not strong; and, second, that the considerable differences among the English versions reveal Chaucer's use of the motif as particularly creative. The Wife of Bath's claims that stories by women would be misandric and that the one-sided ideal of female excellence is upheld solely by men are tested in Katharina M. Wilson's '*Figmenta vs. Veritas*: Dame Alice and the Medieval Literary Depiction of Women by Women' (*TSWL* (1985).17-32) against the works of Hrotsvit of Gandersheim and Christine de Pisan which are at the centre of the essay's concern.

Added impetus has been given to scholarship on the Wife and her Tale by modern feminism. In 'Alisoun Weaves a Text' (*PQ* 65.387-401) Peggy A. Knapp studies ll. 248-378 of the Wife's Prologue to show how they can produce different accounts of the Wife as entrepreneur, feminist (of sorts), sinful woman, and social subversive. The tightly woven text is representative of Chaucer's art. In her consideration of 'Chaucer's Working Wyf: The Unraveling of a Yarn-Spinner'[9] Beryl Rowland reads the Wife of Bath's cloth-making activity as a sign, not of her managerial role in the wool-trade, but of her insatiable concupiscence; the reference to *bacon* (418) indicates her joyless promiscuity, a common condition of nymphomania, that explains her desire to subjugate men. 'The Wife as Moral Revolutionary' (*ChauR* 20.273-84) by Walter C. Long is one of a growing number of studies that associate late medieval literature with Ockhamism. Long believes that the Wife radically challenges notions of degree from an Ockhamist position where will to change has been freed from a fixed order of nature. Where she seems to invoke or encourage traditional male views of women, she is being defensively ironic in order to avoid rejection as unvirtuous. Such an approach unwittingly reveals the difficulties of associating the different discourses of literature and philosophical theology and the dangers of oversimplifying the latter.

Martin Puhvel's description of his approach in 'The Wife of Bath's "Remedies of Love"' (*ChauR* 20.307-12) as musings that 'amount in essence to little more than flights of fantasy' which nevertheless might have formed part of Chaucer's intention will have an ominous ring to the true scholar. He is referring to the possibility that Alison used erotic magic on her fourth husband and, failing that, did knowingly administer a noxious substance to his mortal injury or the permanent impairment of his health. Chaucer's vagueness on the matter is presented as dramatic or psychological acuity since the Wife would hardly tell all in public. In contrast, Louise O. Fradenburg generates, in 'The Wife of Bath's Passing Fancy' (*SAC* 8.31–58) a powerful examination of the work's 'experimentation with romance poetics'. Prologue and tale offer 'a strong historical reading of the romance genre: an interpretation of the nature of desire in the age that witnessed the slow death of feudalism'. Drawing on a range of modern theoretical positions, she discusses the cultural ambivalence of romance – its nostalgia, institutional conservatism, and patronizing association with women; but also, its potentially revolutionary character, expressive of fantasy and the creative imagination. This ideologically focused essay is densely written, overfond of phrasal inversions, but repays close reading and contributes significantly to both Chaucer studies and feminist historical criticism. Unlike Fradenburg, Sara Disbrow considers the Wife of Bath's Tale to be more folkloric than romantic. She argues that 'The Wife of Bath's Old Wives' Tale' (*SAC* 8.59–71) is an old-fashioned and inadequate comment on life and is analogous to the Jewish oral tales of superstition, the *aniles fabulas*, rejected by Augustine, referred to in 1 Timothy 4.7, which the Parson alludes to when he refuses to tell such stories. The Wife herself is the foolish woman of Proverbs 9.13 and is constantly trying to disguise her ignorance. Fradenburg's and Disbrow's articles, challengingly juxtaposed in *SAC*, thus have a very different sense of the way the tale relates to late fourteenth-century modernity and to the woman uttering it. Finally, in 'Taking the Gold Out of Egypt: The Art of Reading as a Woman'[21] Susan Schibanoff contrasts the Wife of Bath and Christine de Pisan's literary representative, 'Christine', as paradigms of female reading; the former natural, in a sense illiterate, and unconscious of the idea of a 'fixed' text; the latter reaching female authoritativeness through learning, and discovering as she does so that textual meaning is in part created by readers. Schibanoff, unlike Delany (below), does not consider possible implications of the fact that the authors are of different sex.

Patrick Gallacher's study of 'The *Summoner's Tale* and Medieval Attitudes Towards Sickness' (*ChauR* 21.200–12) seeks to combine medical, theological, and literary issues within a dialectic of the self and the other. The Friar consistently ignores or hypocritically adopts the treatment advised for sick people, and his relationship with Thomas 'strikingly alludes . . . to the six non-naturals of Greek medicine'. Holly Wallace Boucher wisely chooses the Summoner's Tale in her discussion of Chaucer's concept of language. Less wisely, she omits the views on language implied in the Summoner's portrait in the General Prologue. The main contention of 'Nominalism: The Difference for Chaucer and Boccaccio' (*ChauR* 20.213–20) is that later writers such as Chaucer and Boccaccio viewed language as more self-referential and riskier (because cut off from an authorizing truth or reality) than did Dante or the author of *La Queste del Sainte Graal*. This brief, lightly referenced, and generally unpersuasive essay predicates a more substantial investigation of an important, interdisciplinary area. In '"Glosynge is a Glorious Thing, Certeyn": A Re-consideration of *The Summoner's Tale*' (*Acta* 8.89–101

---

21. In *Gender and Reading: Essays on Readers, Texts and Contexts*, ed. by Elizabeth A. Flynn and Patrocinio P. Schweickart. JHU. pp. 368. hb $27.50, pb $10.95.

(1984)), Martha H. Fleming emphasizes the theme of anger in the tale, both as a unifying element and also as a revelation of the Summoner's own irous nature; he is an exemplum of the deadly sin of ire, to be shunned by all his fellows except the Pardoner. Antifraternal satire in the Tale takes conventional forms, but wrath was not a conventional element of complaint.

Bernard S. Levy finds multiplicity in 'The Meanings of *The Clerk's Tale*'[18]. The literal reading of wifely love and obedience is directed to the literally minded Wife of Bath, though a more sophisticated literalism would emphasize Griselda's role as exemplary servant. But simultaneously the tale signals the symbolic purpose of a parallel of husband and wife with Christ and the Church.

The two-part structure of the tale is central to Karl P. Wentersdorf's discussion of 'Imagery, Structure, and Theme in Chaucer's *Merchant's Tale*'[18]. Literary allusions and paired images – some traditionally symbolizing lust and love (notably, the pear-tree) – point the contrast between the favourable surface and the underlying unpleasant reality and indicate the shared responsibility of January and May for the situation. In '"For craft is al, whoso that do it kan": The Genre of *The Merchant's Tale*'[18], Leigh A. Arrathoon characterizes the tale as an apologue, pointing out that Chaucer's allusive devices in it warn about the use and misuse of text. The Merchant's reference to St Thomas of India (Fragment E, 1223) launches a characterization of him as Gnostic, with specific Manichean teachings on sexuality and food that account for his distaste for and fascination with Epicurean January and suggest reference to contemporary Lollard attitudes. The inversion of the teachings of Jerome and Augustine – copiously interpolated – suggests a critique of the unreliable narrator and his creations. The disputational structure becomes a debate between the carnal and patristic views of marriage; the resulting levels of meaning – theological, moral, and mystical – provide a corrective to the theoretical debate and exemplary fabliau of the narrative and to the attitudes of its heretical narrator. Kenneth Bleeth finds analogies and contrasts between the motif of 'Joseph's Doubting of Mary and the Conclusion of the *Merchant's Tale*' (*ChauR* 21.58–66). While his essay extends our sense of the biblical parody in the tale, it suffers from the usual problem in paralleling motifs: the more widespread the motif, the less pointed the comparison. An 'inconsequential amble' is how George Schlesinger unpromisingly describes his article, 'A Tale of Two Cuckolds' (*DUJ* 48.51–8) in which he compares and contrasts love, experience, and marriage in the Merchant's Tale and *Middlemarch*. He reminds us that George Eliot knew her *Tales* and 'could scarcely avoid superimposing the two old men [Casaubon and January] in their gardens'. Robert P. Miller's article, 'Chaucer's Rhetorical Rendition of Mind: *The Squire's Tale*'[18], perceptively reveals Chaucer seeking 'to define the perspective of youth absorbed in the world of appearances'. The Squire exhibits and is engrossed by Art and flaws the whole by local structural and stylistic deviations, trivializing his father's thought and distorting Boethian teaching in the manner of the youthful romantic portrayed in the Prologue. From Donald C. Baker's study of 'William Thynne's Printing of the *Squire's Tale*: Manuscript and Printer's Copy' (*SB* 39.125–32) Thynne emerges as a genuine editor rather than a mere printer of what he found. For his Squire's Tale Thynne used substantially two manuscripts, both now lost, and although his employment of other printed texts is less clear, he probably also used the second Pynson edition and consulted Wynkyn de Worde's, and Caxton's second edition. In '"The Wordes of the Frankeleyn to the Squier"': An Interruption?' (*ELN* 24:1.12–18) David M. Seaman considers the link-passage to be an end-comment since it lacks the distinctive features of other 'interruption-links'; hence it was written either in anticipation of the tale's completion – not achieved in its present form – or to follow an interruption by someone else.

Nowhere is the heterogeneity of Chaucer criticism this year more evident than in writing on the Franklin's Tale. Here, R. A. Shoaf's 'The *Franklin's Tale*: Chaucer and Medusa' (*ChauR* 21.274–90) and an article by Gerald Morgan, 'Boccaccio's *Filocolo* and the Moral Argument of the *Franklin's Tale*' (*ChauR* 20.285–306), could hardly be more different, though both are admirable. The tale is easier to recognize in Morgan's reading, where emphasis in laid on the elucidation of a moral virtue through action rather than through character-psychology. Morgan rejects as unmedieval the notion that the tale is explicable in the light of our opinion of its narrator. Instead, he stresses the careful establishment of a moral context in the story and the rhetorical complaints. Dorigen is trapped into certain moral error through offering Aurelius a tactful escape from his ill-judged request, but she refuses willingly to undertake infidelity or suicide; Arveragus accepts the obligation of her vow, manifesting high generosity in setting honour above shame. Aurelius is the one who deserves our censure. Morgan's critical stance privileges medieval over modern habits of mind; he also conveys an imaginative sympathy with another human mind and time. On the other hand, he could show greater recognition of the gaps and tensions which arise in any reading. R. A. Shoaf's style will not commend him to everyone – in particular, his irritating puns which are less necessary to his genuinely clever argument than might first appear. Substantially, the article offers two broadly familiar lines – the untrustworthiness of the Franklin as narrator, and the tale's capacity to carry metapoetic readings. On the former topic, the Franklin's Tale and narratorial method are intended to distract from his own insecurities and to prevent us moving beyond the meanings he overtly provides. On the latter topic, the tale 'is to be read as an instance of how writers and readers should *not* read and write. It is a figure of the abuses of figuration.' Shoaf also seeks to ground both readings in an inter-textual relationship with Dante's *Inferno* 9 and 10, of which the tale is a partial palimpsest. Chaucer does not suffer from anxiety at this influence but responds buoyantly to the challenge of earlier writing. Judith Ferster's 'Interpretation and Imitation in Chaucer's Franklin's Tale'[7] also makes a worthwhile contribution to the use of theoretical systems in reading a text, not least because she is self-conscious and explicit about the methodology she employs. She recognizes the similarities (and differences) between her application of phenomenological hermeneutics to the tale and the exegetical principles which Augustine followed in taking the meaning he thought right from Scripture. It is thus much easier to entertain Ferster's account of the tale as a demonstration of hermeneutic principles than it is to accept Harwood's comparable view of the Nun's Priest's Tale (below). 'The *Franklin's Tale* is an examination of the interpretation of stories and the imitation that stories often inspire', Ferster writes, and finds more specifically that it shows the contextual prejudgements we make, and our selective acceptance of influences within the interpretative sphere. It also suggests that the hermeneutic circle may not be a vicious one. Source-study and comparison are represented by Douglas A. Burger's article, 'The *Cosa Impossibile* of *Il Filocolo* and the *Impossible* of *The Franklin's*

Tale[18], which shows how Chaucer's changes to Boccaccio's story lead the reader to explore *fin amore* through the strongly emphasized conjugal love of Arveragus and Dorigen, the theological issues raised by the black rocks, and the intrusive Franklin-narrator himself.

William Kupersmith suggests links between 'Chaucer's *Physician's Tale* and the Tenth Satire of Juvenal' (*ELN* 24:2.20–3).

In 'Intention and the Pardoner'[18] Janette Richardson argues that the Pardoner skilfully employs rhetoric for an unsophisticated audience for his sinful personal ends, but the pilgrims are a different audience. Seeking solidarity with them in his Prologue, he miscalculates in offering stylistic skill rather than exemplary morality. He is the living verification of his own theme, and his weak delivery and misapplied incentives to penitence undercut his claims to effect reform in his usual audiences. Frances Bixler finds such 'Links between Chaucer's "Pardoner's Tale" and "Second Nun's Tale"' (*PAPA* 12.1–12) as would suggest that Fragment VI should be placed immediately before Fragment VIII.

Discussing 'Money, Sexuality, Wordplay, and Context in the *Shipman's Tale*'[9], Thomas Hahn establishes the Merchant of the Tale as a financial entrepreneur and locates his activities among contemporary attitudes towards financial transactions designed to avoid the technical label of 'usury'. Further light is thereby shed on the interplay of sex and money in the tale.

The Prioress's piety comes under scrutiny once again this year, notably in two articles by Richard Rex. The work prompts us to consider the nature of true charity, which the Prioress lacks. Not all Christian thinkers were anti-Semitic and there is thus a contemporary cultural framework within which criticism of the Prioress would be possible. Specific encouragement to criticize is found in the nature of the Jews' punishment, which Rex describes as outside the due process of law in 'Wild Horses, Justice, and Charity in the Prioress's Tale' (*PLL* 22.339–51), and in the qualities of pastiche which are evident throughout, revealing – amongst other more arguable ironies – that the Prioress is culpably childish. These are treated in 'Pastiche as Irony in The Prioress's Prologue and Tale' (*SSF* 23.1–8). Douglas Wurtele also looks at 'Prejudice and Chaucer's Prioress' (*UOQ* 55 (1985).33–43), arguing that, though the Prioress imitates the Blessed Virgin in her manners, she naïvely opts to end her tale with martyrdom and persecution when a 'resurrection and conversion' model was at hand – a fact which may prompt the reader to ponder her unwitting hypocrisy.

Lloyd J. Matthews's conclusions on 'The Date of Chaucer's *Melibee* and the Stages of the Tale's Incorporation in the *Canterbury Tales*' (*ChauR* 20.221–34) depend upon a decision of literary criticism: that if Chaucer had had Dante's iconography of Prudence available to him when he wrote Melibee he would have used it in some way, as he did later in *Troilus*. Since he does not use it in Melibee, the work must have antedated his knowledge of the *Divine Comedy*, and Matthews proposes the early date of 1373, some fifteen years before Chaucer decided to include it in the *Tales* and twenty before it was put in Fragment B^2.

The possibility that the sight of Rochester Cathedral impelled the Host to turn to the Monk, remembering the Benedictines there, excites Glending Olson in 'Chaucer's Monk: The Rochester Connection' (*ChauR* 21.246–56) into connecting the Monk's Tale with the Cathedral's 'Wheel of Fortune' painting and with the advocacy of memorial contemplation by its Bishop, Thomas Brinton, who - significantly - was also an outspoken critic of clerical laxness. Richard P. Horvath engages in 'A Critical Interpretation of *Canterbury Tales* B^2 3981' (*ELN* 24:1.8–12) but, as a critic, would prefer not to choose between the usually adopted reading ('For therinne is ther no desport ne game') and the alternative ('Youre tales don us no desport ne game') because, taken together, they reveal Chaucer's awareness of the difference between the meaning of a tale and the audience's perception of its meaning. Vincent DiMarco takes 'Another Look at Chaucer's "Trophee" ' (*Names* 34.275–83) in the Monk's Tale 2117–8, refining Kittredge's 1909 location of its source in *Epistola Alexandri ad Aristotelam* from a different passage in that work in which the word *tropaeum* could be 'misconstrued while still pointing to the oriental pillar or pillars' of the Monk's reference.

No interpretative mode can be called current among medievalists until it has provided a 'solution' for the Nun's Priest's Tale. Derridean poststructuralism suffers this unhappy fate in Britton J. Harwood's 'Signs and/as Origin: Chaucer's *Nun's Priest's Tale*' (*Style* 20.189–202), in which the tale is seen ambivalently as an allegory of the ideas and also, in a quasi-historical way, as hinting at their future currency. By this approach, Chaucer has modified his sources to demonstrate the displacement of things by supplementation and to emphasize the tensions between the stable sign in a transcendent world and the synthetic heterogeneity of sign in a mutually determining sign-system. Words like 'may' and 'threaten to' grease the allegorical wheels, (e.g. 'the *Tale* threatens to show that supplementation has, in the phrase Derrida owes to Heidegger, always already begun').

In his F. W. Bateson Memorial Lecture, 'Chaucer's Canterbury Pilgrimage' (*EIC* 36.97–119), J. A. Burrow reconsiders the Manciple's Prologue as an example of Chaucer's art. After looking at 'realistic' elements, he characterizes in turn the Manciple, Cook, and Host, stressing that Harry Bailly occupies the guide-role usually allocated to an allegorical or mythological figure. William Blake's high estimation of the Host is supported against his latter-day critics.

3. Troilus and Criseyde

In '"Making Strange": The Narrator (?), the Ending (?), and Chaucer's "Troilus" ' (*NM* 87.218–28), Murray J. Evans finds an interesting convergence of medieval rhetorical and modern structuralist approaches which helps to explain the effect of the ending of *Troilus*. The dispersal of ending into a multiplicity of endings, and of final audience-apostrophe into apostrophes to different groups of readers, together with the recurrence of a poet-persona without the traditional authority in love, all serve to defamiliarize the material and compel the reader to recognize the openness of interpretation. The narrator is also the touchstone of E. F. Dyck's discussion of Aristotelean 'Ethos, Pathos, and Logos in *Troilus and Criseyde*' (*ChauR* 20.169–82). He is humanized (pathos) in proportion as he loses rhetorical control (ethos) and, in his final appeals to rational judgement (logos), not only fails to convince but becomes part of Chaucer's appeal to logos. The poem confronts by rhetoric the question 'What, for the poet, is rhetoric?'. A sympathetic but ironic distance initially distinguishes for James F. Maybury 'The Character of the Narrator in *Troilus and Criseyde*' (*NNER* 8 (1983).32–41) from that in Boccaccio. By Book

III his sympathies have reached such uncritical hyperbole that the reader is led to question them and, in the last stanzas of Book V, the religion of love is rejected in a voice that is at once the narrator's and Chaucer's.

Linda Tarte Holley's thesis in 'Medieval Optics and the Framed Narrative in Chaucer's *Troilus and Criseyde*' (*ChauR* 21.26–44) is that the framed narrative expresses a way of seeing that was encouraged by medieval visual theory, a discussion of which lies at the centre of the essay. She begins by examining the frames through which the lovers get their respective initial views of each other, and the microcosmic patterning of the vision-frame in Criseyde's dream. She concludes by emphasizing the importance of perspective in the various frames employed by the characters and by the narrator.

The collapse of feudal systems of dominance informs Chaucer's account of joy and loss, and the failure of aristocratic love becomes 'the ideal paradigm for examining the inadequacy of all dreams for a fruitful and happy life on this earth'. Developing this view in '*Troilus and Criseyde*: The Politics of Love'[9] Arlyn Diamond suggests that, though the social self is excluded in aristocratic love, the social consequences are uneven – Troilus's public honour is enhanced but Criseyde remains socially vulnerable in a world where men control women and treat them as commodities of exchange. Neither Chaucer nor his protagonists can escape from this system, but they cannot fully endorse it.

In 'The "Joie and Tene" of Dreams in *Troilus and Criseyde*'[8] Allen J. Frantzen sees Criseyde encouraged to a falsely optimistic surrender of her independence by her two dreams, while Troilus's corresponding paired dreams lead him to diagnose and then heroically to resist his destiny – first accepting, then actively embracing, the idea of death. Sally K. Slocum asks us to put ourselves in the situation of 'Criseyde among the Greeks' (*NM* 87.365–74) and to give our pity to a homesick, friendless Trojan lady unjustly exiled by her country and misread by her critics. Comparing 'Boccaccio's Criseida and Chaucer's Criseyde' (*Spectrum* 27 (1985).25–32), Lisa Abshear-Seals claims that Chaucer affirms Criseyde's right to her own feelings and understanding, in contrast to Boccaccio's Criseida, by presenting love as the height of human experience and Criseyde as the height of womanhood. George Sanderlin, writing 'In Defense of Criseyde: A Modern "Scientific" Heroine' (*USFLQ* 24:3–4. 47–8), comments briefly on three occasions when Criseyde analyses her problem 'scientifically' and makes her own decision, in contrast to the 'archaic' ideas of honour by which Troilus lives and to which he pays lip service.

A quick survey of the medical tradition of *amor hereos* provides the context for Mary F. Wack's account of 'Lovesickness in *Troilus*' (*PCP*19 (1984).55–61). Augmenting his source with references to lovesickness and its cures enables Chaucer to present Troilus and Pandarus as eluding 'the moral complexities of the situation by an appeal to medical necessity which carries with it no clearcut assessment of the morality of the cure', intercourse with the object of desire. Troilus ultimately transcends this materialistic and deterministic view of love as his memory transfers his love to a realm beyond time and space. Charlotte F. Otten identifies 'The Love-Sickness of Troilus'[18] as erotomania, attested by his continuing egocentricity but curable only by the self-knowledge that follows his release by death – for in life he actively, if unwittingly, conspires with the disease.

Chaucer's minor characters in *Troilus*, such as Hector and Cassandra, serve to widen the narrative perspective and increase its moral richness. It is to this group that John V. Fleming, in his perceptive article 'Deiphoebus Betrayed: Virgilian Decorum, Chaucerian Feminism' (*ChauR* 21.182–99), assimilates Deiphoebus, as a touchstone of the poem's empirical attitude towards feminine stereotyping. Chaucer's Deiphoebus trails resonances of the mutilated victim betrayed by Helen, but is here designated the honest idealist betrayed by a man who is in the process of deceiving a woman. It is, ironically, Deiphoebus who finally bears Diomede's armour and brooch into Troy – the sign of Troilus's own betrayal – and it is Troilus's body that is mutilated. Two articles in *HUSL* begin from the knowledge assumed of his audience by Chaucer – specifically, knowledge of the Theban background. In 'Cassandra's Analogy: Troilus V. 1450–1521' (*HUSL* 13 (1985).1–17), David Anderson shows how Chaucer develops the analogies of Trojan and Theban history, of Troy's and Troilus's fortunes, and Trojan disbelief of Cassandra in the latter's interpretation of Troilus's dream. The ostensibly irrelevant historical preamble to her 'boar-account' has thematically wider resonances which Troilus will not hear. And Paul M. Clogan claims that 'Criseyde's Book of the Romance of Thebes' (*HUSL* 13 (1985).18–28) is the French *Roman de Thebes*, a claim substantiated from the circumstances of Criseyde's reading-party and the details of her summary of the story. Though this is Chaucer's primary source of Theban material in Books II and V, he also relies upon knowledge of Statius's *Thebaid* in those books to underline the ironic link of Thebes and Troy. 'When Chaucer invokes Thesiphone, . . . he sets in motion resonances of a discordant, perverse, sterile, potentially demonic sexuality', claims Robert Levine, who extends the 'Restraining Ambiguities in Chaucer's *Troilus and Criseyde*' (*NM* 87.558–64) to interpretations of Criseyde's possible childlessness and sexual relationship with Pandarus; in both instances, the ambiguity is the message.

In 'Smoky Reyn: From Jean de Meun to Geoffrey Chaucer'[18] John V. Fleming argues that Jean and Chaucer, both translators, looked to a shared corpus of texts. Jean offered Chaucer a model of how to apply Boethian philosophy to Ovidian eroticism that he could not find in Boccaccio and Fleming illustrates his thesis by comparing the accounts of Troilus's lovesickness offered by the narrator and by Pandarus. At the centre of this bold but entertaining essay is an investigation of the literary resonances of *smoky reyn* (Book III, 628) which reverberate to a Virgilian thunderstorm and draw together Genius's torch and Pandarus's candle, with startling displacement of the accompanying smoke!

Margaret Jennings C.S.J. offers a personal, responsive account of scribal variation among the sixteen *Troilus* manuscripts at the love-scene of Book III in 'To *Pryke* or to *Prye*: Scribal Delights in the *Troilus*, Book III'[9], and R. E. Kaske airs some views about the meaning of *Troilus* II, 1732–78, 'Pandarus's "Vertue of Corones Tweyne"' (*ChauR* 21.226–33) in its context of mercy. In 'Educating Reader: Chaucer's Use of Proverbs in "Troilus and Criseyde"' (*Proverbium* 3.47–58) Ann C. Hall argues from the usages of Pandarus and more particularly of the narrator that Chaucer assigns specific functions to proverbs in *Troilus* but also exposes their limitations. Chaucer's twenty-one other usages of *hood* serve Leger Brosnahan as prologue and context for his claim, in '"And Don Thyn Hood" and Other Hoods in Chaucer' (*ChauR* 21.45–52), that *don thyn hood* in *Troilus*, Book II, 954, means 'put on your hood' and is Pandarus's way of telling Troilus not to humble himself.

Mary L. Hurst compares Chaucer's and Shakespeare's heroines in

'Shakespeare, Chaucer, and "False Cressida"': A Reinterpretation' (*SPWVSRA* 8 (1983).1-8), paying particular attention to the changing image of Criseyde in literature, the different male-female stereotypes available in the different periods, and the consequent circumstances in which the two Criseydes are realized.

4. Other Works

Battle is this year joined over whether Thynne ignobly contributed part of the *Book of the Duchess*. Helen Phillips, in '*The Book of the Duchess*, ll. 31-96: Are They a Forgery?' (*ES* 67.113-21), uses a range of textual, linguistic, and literary considerations to argue that Thynne's edition, which contains the lines, may well be an independent witness to what Chaucer wrote. N. F. Blake, in '*The Book of the Duchess* Again' (*ES* 67.122-5), argues against Thynne's use of another (lost) manuscript and then partially shifts to the *via negativa*, claiming that 'there is no reliable evidence which proves that this passage was written by Chaucer'; rather, Chaucer left a gap in the work when he finished it. David Burnley concentrates on ll. 779-804 and 990-1012 (in which he recommends a change from the usual editorial punctuation) to discuss 'Some Terminology of Perception in the *Book of the Duchess*' (*ELN* 23:3.15-22). Chaucer shows his ambition by employing technical terms from perception and cognition and developing his French sources in this respect. Among the main topics dealt with are the superior receptivity of youth, the possibly damaging effect of experience, and the synonymity in context of *passioun*, *wit*, and *suffraunce*.

Two essays of a more general critical character are Sandra Pierson Prior's '*Routhe* and *Hert-Huntyng* in the *Book of the Duchess*' (*JEGP* 85.3-19) and Andrew Lynch's '"Taking Keep" of the "Book of the Duchess"'[17]. Prior uses hunting manuals to define more closely the terminology of Chaucer's hunt, and outlines how the literal and metaphorical hunts are related, with the outcome of the former deliberately left vague so that any explicit reference to the death of the hart is avoided. She emphasizes pity as the key to the poem's various parts - as climax of both hunts, and as the best gift that the poet can make. Lynch rejects any readings which harmonize the poem by assigning it to a particular genre. Assurance and harmony are precisely what the poem suggests are unavailable in life. Instead, the poem thematizes the incapacity of language, failures to observe or attend, and difficulties in reading. It works by abrupt transitions, and it denies us a full assurance that the love of the Man in Black and his Lady was a realized ideal because loss has made verification impossible. All those features assert the Gothic form of the work in which juxtaposition rather than synthesis is most evident. Carol Falvo Heffernan takes hold of 'That Dog Again: *Melancholia Canina* and Chaucer's *Book of the Duchess*' (*MP* 84.185-90). The whelp, which brings one melancholic into the presence of another, is associated with medical treatises on melancholy - the dog gave its name to a severe form of the disease (*melancholia canina*) which became associated with love melancholy. The writer seems on less secure ground when she argues that the dog is not itself suffering from the disease because Chaucer wishes to look to a final easing of melancholy and that although the narrator does not literally exhibit one of the main symptoms (breaking into tombs), he does so figuratively when he brings the dream out of 'his own anguished mind'. The last chapter of Mary Dove's book deals with 'The *ryght yong* man and

Lady Perfect Age in the *Book of the Duchess*' in the context of her general discussion of *The Perfect Age of Man's Life*[22]. Rejecting the Black Knight and
White as representatives of the historical ages of John of Gaunt and Blanche,
she stresses the process whereby the young Knight, having progressed in his
immaturity from domination by Youth to the constant service of White, is now
led to abandon his affectation of a 'winter age' and to be restored to himself, his
May-setting, the present, and his social home by the recollection of White's
completed, ageless perfection.

Robert W. Hanning has produced an important essay on the dream-visions,
'Chaucer's First Ovid: Metamorphosis and Poetic Tradition in *The Book of the
Duchess* and *The House of Fame*'[18], showing how Chaucer 'turned to the
Metamorphoses for help in articulating his relationship to the multiple literary
traditions in which he wrote'. The nature of poetry and the problem of grief
interact in the *Book of the Duchess* where poetry serves to distance a personal
crisis and dialogue is a means to structuring Chaucer's artistic self-consciousness. The 'Ceyx and Alcyone' story, from Ovid and Machaut, is here further
metamorphosed to become for Alcyone and the narrator a vehicle for misreading, and to serve as a source for transformation in the dream as the Black
Knight is compelled to an explicit account of his loss. Against the positive view
of poetic transformation, the *House of Fame* suggests that poetry and *fama*
converge as language, divorced from experience, feeds upon itself, perpetuating a mixture of truth and falsehood in its literary metamorphosis.
Chaucer's debt to the description of Fama's dwelling in *Metamorphoses* is
emphasized in a discussion of the hierarchy of houses, from Venus's
temple – the public face of poetry – to the essentially similar homes of Fame
and Rumour; and reference is made to resonant mythological figures in the
claim that the Eagle 'converts (and subverts) the traditional resonances of the
philosophical flight'. Ovid here serves Chaucer's questioning of the value of
poetry.

Larry D. Benson believes that 'The "Love-Tydynges" in Chaucer's *House of
Fame*'[9] were omitted because the audience already knew them. He proposes
that the poem was completed as it stands and publicly read round about 10
December, 1379, when the news of the termination of marriage negotiations
between Richard II and Caterina Viscontia would provide a suitably comic and
anticlimactic allusion in keeping with the tone of the poem's ending.

Two articles which find a rationale for the three-book structure of the poem
are Elizabeth Buckmaster's 'Meditation and Memory in Chaucer's *House of
Fame*' (*MLS* 16.279–87) and John Finlayson's 'Seeing, Hearing and Knowing
in *The House of Fame*' (*SN* 58.47–57). Both recognize the personal nature of
the work: Buckmaster writes that 'Alone of all of Chaucer's poems, *The House
of Fame* is inner-directed', and Finlayson shows how this, above the other
dream-poems, is mediated to the reader by frequently signalled narratorial
perceptions. While Buckmaster sees the three-part structure as given point in a
progressive attention to memory, intelligence, and foresight (and also past,
present, and future), Finlayson finds that Book I stresses vision, especially
indirect vision, in a descriptive mode with special attention to literature; Book
II emphasizes speaking and hearing by a narrator who participates more in a
scientific context; and in Book III one is aware of the narrator enjoying more

22. *The Perfect Age of Man's Life*, by Mary Dove. CUP. pp. xiii + 175. £34.50.

'direct revelation' but in a confusion of visual and aural perception which expresses the real disorder of experience that Chaucer faithfully records by his refusal to finish the poem. While Finlayson makes several comparisons with *Pearl*, Buckmaster looks beyond the poem to find in the meditative tradition analogous features of internalized writing, the three-part structure, and the poem's technique of artificial memory. While she regards the poem as 'a journey through the author's memory of his knowledge and culture', Finlayson prefers a more synchronic relationship of perception and knowledge.

Jacqueline T. Miller makes a timely contribution to an important topic in current Chaucer criticism with the first two chapters of her book on *Poetic License: Authority and Authorship in Medieval and Renaissance Contexts*[23]. In part this study is intended to correct any mistaken prejudice that earlier periods were not interested in the ambivalences which lie at the heart of notions of literary authority but other medievalists will find its clear exposition of these ambivalences in the *House of Fame* more valuable. Spenser, Sidney, and Herbert provide the other literary contex's for discussion.

In 'Chaucer's *House of Fame*, the Apocalypse, and Bede' (*ABR* 36 (1985).263–77) Robert Boenig seeks to demonstrate that Chaucer adapted numerous details from St John's Apocalypse in a way that inverts or negates Bede's commentary on it, and that the *House of Fame* is consequently a deliberately unfinished work that proclaims itself to be a failed apocalypse of uncertain revelatory value. The eagle is discussed by James Simpson in 'Dante's "Astripetam Aquilam" and the Theme of Poetic Discretion in the "House of Fame" ' (*E&S* 39.1–18). Though Chaucer may not have known the *De Vulgari Eloquentia*, Geoffrey's refusal to learn about the stars from his eagle-guide may be better understood in the light of Dante's warning there to poets that the goose should not try to emulate the eagle which makes for the stars. Chaucer shows discretion in his choice of subject by writing on worldly matters that are not easily susceptible of authoritative pronouncement. His own relationship to other poetic masters, though not competitive, can involve criticism – the eagle that soars may itself be incautious.

In '"'Cloude, – and Al That Y of Spak": "The House of Fame," v. 978' (*NM* 87.565–8) John M. Fyler argues that the cloud perceived after a thought has soared heavenwards with the feathers of Philosophy alludes to Macrobius's definition of the phantasm and may refer to a failing in perception as well as a meteorological phenomenon. Whichever, it emphasizes the doubt and limitation to which Chaucer's vision is subject, unlike the vision of Boethius to whom the passage explicitly refers. This could indicate Chaucer's knowledge of Macrobius earlier than the *Parliament of Fowls*. A. S. G. Edwards supports the deflationary *say* of MSS Fairfax 16 and Bodley 638 against the usually preferred *singen* in l. 143 of 'Chaucer's *House of Fame*' (*Expl* 44:2.4–5).

James Dean's crisply written piece on 'Artistic Conclusiveness in Chaucer's *Parliament of Fowls*' (*ChauR* 21.16–25) suggests that Chaucer invites us to consider a range of differences both within art and between art and life. The specific invitation is provided by the final roundel, which we perceive to be at once an 'image of perfect resolution' and yet also no conclusion at all for a poem given over to dualistic statements and unresolved ethical questions. We

23. *Poetic License: Authority and Authorship in Medieval and Renaissance Contexts*, by Jacqueline T. Miller. OUP. pp. x + 223. £22.50.

recognize in it the capacity of the artist to 'force a conclusion where there can be no true closure'. The article valuably directs us away from any idea that inconclusiveness was an aesthetic goal for Chaucer.

In 'Rewriting Woman Good: Gender and the Anxiety of Influence in Two Late-Medieval Texts'[9] Sheila Delany exemplifies what it means to write as a man and as a woman by comparing Chaucer's *Legend of Good Women* and Christine de Pisan's *Le Livre de la Cité des Dames*. For Chaucer, the contradictions inherent in the experience of Nature mock the God of Love's demand for uncontradicted praise, though Alceste is accepted as living evidence of possible goodness in woman. As a woman, Christine's role as author is less secure, and she is therefore led to propagandize rather than accept the antifeminist tradition, and to appeal to Reason as well as to experience. While Chaucer's Alceste is exterior to the narrator, Christine's Lady Reason is an extension of the self. The two works share considerable ideological solidarity but display individual gender-distinctive features, even though Christine's view has precedents in the writings of men. Ruth M. Ames's account of 'The Feminist Connections of Chaucer's *Legend of Good Women*'[9] surveys the arguments of supporters and opponents of the *Roman de la Rose*. Chaucer invests his ladies with an unromantic and explicit desire for marriage, but makes them also pitiable in their innocence and trust when exploited by innate male badness. Though no supporter of the *Rose*, Chaucer shares its sense of the disastrous idolatry of sex-worship, but while the *Rose* presents that as a trap for men, Chaucer presents it as a trap for women.

'Mediation' is the obsessive key term of Russell A. Peck's discussion of 'Chaucerian Poetics and the Prologue to the *Legend of Good Women*'[9]. The daisy, which so obsessively engages the narrator, emblematizes the poetic imagination celebrated in the poem. From the start, the narrator is a selfless mediator under the governance of the God of Love, and Alceste, mediating between the God and Geoffrey, offers for his emulation her exemplary self-sacrifice in order that he may become creative. The poem juxtaposes three modes of cognition − empirical, bookish, and inspirational − but it is the last that enables the narrator to invest his vision with the force of a religious experience and to mediate it to his audience. Marilynn Desmond's subject in 'Chaucer's *Æneid*: "The Naked Text in English" ' (*PCP* 19 (1984).62−7) is Chaucer's use of the *Æneid* as pre-text for the legend of Dido in the *Legend of Good Women*. Explicitly evoking the *Æneid*, the narrator paraphrases it, 'sensitively misreads' it, and finally turns to Ovid as last resort. Throughout, he assumes an audience familiar with Virgil and Ovid.

In a note more substantial than some articles, M. C. Seymour addresses himself to 'Chaucer's *Legend of Good Women*: Two Fallacies' (*RES* 37.528−34). He proposes that the *Legend* is incomplete not because Chaucer failed to finish it but because its final quires were lost, and that this occurred early in the work's transmission, perhaps during the author's lifetime. He also finds no reason to suggest that Chaucer rather than a fifteenth-century reviser was responsible for the revised Prologue. Constance S. Wright examines 'Lines 880−886 in Chaucer's "Legend of Thisbe" in the *Legend of Good Women*' (*AN&Q* 24.68−9) and, because of source and manuscript evidence, would change the sentence division and correct the tradition in all editions since Thynne so that it is the head of Pyramus, not of Thisbe, that is lifted up in l. 882. In 'Chaucer's Last Dream Vision: The *Prologue* to the *Legend of Good*

Women' (*ChauR* 20.183–99) Michael D. Cherniss takes us through a detailed account of the Prologue in its two versions to reveal a self-confident Chaucer deliberately 'making something of a travesty of the sort of visionary process of enlightenment that the Boethian vision traditionally purports to offer the visionary'. Cherniss finds the narrator of the Prologue to be too clearly identifiable with Chaucer to function in the Boethian way as a representative of the reader, and the vision itself proves not to have offered any new illumination which has changed the visionary's opinions. George Sanderlin looks at the changes which Chaucer makes to Virgil in 'Chaucer's *Legend of Dido* – A Feminist Exemplum' (*ChauR* 20.331–40). Chaucer's focus on Dido, his stereotyping of Æneas as an amatory betrayer, his minimizing of any divine contribution to the tragedy, and his emphasis on Dido's suffering and insecurity rather than on her regal self-judgement, all make the legend into a 'negative exemplum of "equal rights"'.

Jane Chance's article, 'Chaucerian Irony in the Boethian Short Poems: The Dramatic Tension between Classical and Christian' (*ChauR* 20.235–45), offers readings of Chaucer's five Boethian short poems in order to demonstrate a development from secular condemnation (*The Former Age*) to an Augustinian viewpoint that involves a more complex use of Boethian ideas and a more sophisticated manipulation of image and voice (culminating in *Truth*). Lines 47–8 are the focus of Jay Ruud's article, 'Chaucer's *Envoy to Scogan*: "Tullius Kyndenesse" and the Law of Kynde' (*ChauR* 20.323–30). Regarding *frend* here not as Chaucer but as the amorous *frend* of the rest of the poem, the author suggests that Scogan's choice of love has regard neither to natural appropriateness nor to prudence, qualities stressed in Cicero's *De Amicitia*. He has defied the law of Kynde – the love that binds the universe and which is emphasized in the *Somnium Scipionis*. Read in that light the poem assumes a stronger coherence.

The Sixteenth Century: Excluding Drama After 1550

R. E. PRITCHARD and RENÉ J. A. WEIS

The chapter has three sections: 1. General; 2. The Earlier Sixteenth Century: (a) Prose, (b) Poetry and Drama; 3. The Later Sixteenth Century: (a) Prose, (b) Poetry, (c) Sidney, (d) Spenser. Sections 1, 2, and 3(d) are by R. E. Pritchard. Sections 3(a), (b), and (c) are by René Weis.

1. General

The 'new historicism', poststructuralism, mythology, and feminism seem to have dominated the more general discussions of the period. *ELR* No. 1 constitutes an important special number on 'Studies in Renaissance Historicism'. Louis Montrose contributes a brief introductory essay, 'Renaissance Literary Studies and the Subject of History', on the setting of canonical literary texts among non-literary texts and social practices, and the particular suitability of Tudor–Stuart literature to this activity. A fuller discussion is then provided by Jean E. Howard on changed perceptions of the Renaissance, and on Renaissance literature as participating in that culture's re-presentation of the real, as did history and criticism; she also reviews the criticism of Montrose and Stephen Greenblatt, and concludes with an outline of theoretical problems. Jonathan Crewe discusses 'the hegemonic theatre of George Puttenham'; and Annabel Patterson, 'Re-opening the Green Cabinet', considers the connections between *The Shepheardes Calender* and the *Eglogue au roy* (1538) of Clement Marot, Lutheran, nationalist, and Virgilian, a model for the 'pastoral of state and church' and its politically subversive subtexts. The bulk of the rest of the volume deals with drama and seventeenth-century writing. Peter Lindenbaum's study[1] of what might be called 'anti-pastoral pastoral' distinguishes itself from the Montrose–Greenblatt approach by dwelling more on its three authors' general ethical concerns than on their more immediate political situations and motives. He regards Sidney, Shakespeare, and Milton as committed to a conscious misrepresentation of previous pastoralism as negative and escapist, in order to present an ethic of the active life of engagement and well-doing in a real, fallen world. Thus, Sidney (both the *Arcadias* are discussed) and Milton represent a conscious expression of the humanist-

---

1. *Changing Landscapes: Anti-Pastoral Sentiment in the English Renaissance*, by Peter Lindenbaum. UGeo. pp. xiv + 234. £27.25.

Protestant ethos; for example, Belial's counselling of ignoble ease is linked with Pyrocles's advocacy of the contemplative life. Arcadia is a land like any other, requiring good government by a responsible ruler; Milton's non-mythic Eden is indeed a version of pastoral, in providing an image of our normal, complex life in simplified form, continuous with (and illuminative of) our fallen existence. Spenser and Marvell are excluded, as apparently they 'did not feel the influence of English Christian Humanism or Protestantism as strongly or directly', but Shakespeare (*As You Like It*, *The Winter's Tale*, *The Tempest*) is in, as 'a type of control', who also rejects pastoral, educating and directing his characters into social activity.

Jonathan Crewe's *ELR* essay appears also in his own *Hidden Designs*[2], an intriguing collection of essays, set in a narrative frame, concerned with the relation between criticism and theory, especially the 'new historicism'. After the Puttenham piece comes a post-Foucauldian account of 'sympathy' in the Renaissance, and its ambiguities in Spenser's *View of the Present State of Ireland* (which has been getting a lot of attention recently) and *Mother Hubberds Tale*; next Crewe extends Arthur Marotti's view of sonnet-sequences as 'politically' encoded, proposing Sidney's Stella as a 'screen' for not merely Penelope Rich, but Elizabeth, or his sister, or his mother (or himself . . .). Theatricality being a dominant motif, he then suggests the theatricality of Spenser's writing, in its deployment of multiple voices, roles, and personae, before analysing some of Jan van der Noot's *The Theatre for Worldlings*; the last chapters identify (a detective-story conceit operates) Spenser as a possible origin of Puttenham's *Arte*, and then as related to Shakespeare's Oberon.

Less quaint is Patricia Parker and David Quint's *Literary Theory/Renaissance Texts*[3], comprising sixteen essays dealing with 'canonical' Renaissance humanist texts – continental and English – in the light of modern theory. Among essays on Petrarch, Montaigne, Rabelais, and Cervantes the volume contains in its 'Foucauldian' part Stephen Greenblatt on Renaissance selfhood in Elizabethan theatre as the product of legal and cultural practices; and Mary Nyquist reveals Milton's struggle against a corrupted misogynistic tradition of the Fall. Derrida hovers over other sections: textual excess, deferral, and apocalyptic closures are the concerns of Derek Attridge on Puttenham and Patricia Parker on Shakespeare, Jonson, and Cervantes. Richard Halpern argues for Skelton's resistance to the new Tudor ideological organization, as manifested in the structure of *Phyllyp Sparowe*, Louis Montrose considers individuals' manipulation and extension of Elizabethan cultural codes, René Girard examines Hamlet's – and Shakespeare's – resistance to the revenge code, and Victoria Kahn concludes with a consideration of the relation between humanism and 'theory' in the Renaissance and now. In short, a most valuable collection. I cannot say the same of the collections, *Renaissance Genres* by Barbara Lewalski (Harvard) and *Rewriting the Renaissance* edited by Margaret Ferguson *et al.* (UChic), as they were not available for review.

Very much in the new fashion is Jonathan Goldberg's latest, *Voice Terminal*

Echo[4], discussing origin and loss in (in chronological order) the October eclogue of *The Shepheardes Calender*, Milton (with Spenser and Shakespeare in mind), Herbert's *The Temple*, and Marvell's 'The Nymph Complaining'. His concerns are, as he says, with 'the status of representation within the book, the nature of characters as voices for the poet and representation of the act of authoring', and with Renaissance uses of Ovid (especially perhaps the Narcissus and Orpheus myths), providing 'demonstrations of techniques of reading consequent upon the work of writers like [*sic*] Maurice Blanchot or Jacques Derrida' in 'a style assaultive in its refusal of the tactics of making sense'. He has some intriguing things to say, but, combining as he does American poststructuralese with his own elliptical, figurative, perverse style, his meaning is not as clear as it could be. Very different in style is Thomas M. Greene's *The Vulnerable Text*[5], a collection of essays ranging over Erasmus's *Adagia*, Petrarch, Castiglione, Machiavelli, Scève, Montaigne, Shakespeare, and Jonson; the volume is admirably humane, learned, illuminating, the tone almost wistfully elegiac in its overriding theme and sense of how 'the old order changeth, giving place to new'. Against 'post-structuralist synchronicity' and 'hermeneutic narcissism' is set, in sympathetic opposition, a traditional humanist stance, of a response to past literature as to people of another, related culture, requiring (and rewarding with) a sense of recognition of their own mystery and validity, and shared vulnerability to the processes of time.

It was Maurice Evans, back in 1955, who provided the last overview of *English Poetry in the Sixteenth Century* (*YW* 36.94–5), presented in the traditional, humanist New-Critical mode; but now Gary Waller is here, with his *English Poetry of the Sixteenth Century*[6], to teach students the current critical language and preoccupations, profusely scattering all the right names, from Michel Foucault and Stephen Greenblatt (eighteen index citations each) to Roland Barthes and Terry Eagleton (sixteen each). There is an air of excitement as Waller tells us how his students read Wyatt in the light of Barthes, and makes play with ideological conflicts, rhetorical dislocations, and decentred subjects; nevertheless, the essays are clear and helpful, and, apart from there being more Sidneys than of old, and some feminist inscription, the map does not seem so very different (C. S. Lewis, twenty-seven citations, several favourable). Waller urges the importance of feminist readings, and feminism is producing more and more interesting accounts of the period. Mary Beth Rose has edited and introduced a valuable multidisciplinary collection of essays[7] on medieval and Renaissance women's involvement in the cultures of their times. Some essays deal with male–female anxieties and classic male texts, others with women's writing. Of the first, we may single out Carole Levin's account of Foxe's *Actes and Monuments* as perpetuating earlier anxieties about and

4. *Voice Terminal Echo: Postmodernism and English Renaissance Texts*, by Jonathan Goldberg. Methuen. pp. x + 194. hb £16/$26, pb £7.95/$13.95.

5. *The Vulnerable Text: Essays on Renaissance Literature*, by Thomas M. Greene. ColU. pp. xx + 254. $32.50.

6. *English Poetry of the Sixteenth Century*, by Gary Waller. Longman. pp. xvi + 315. hb £15.95/$29.95, pb £6.95/$12.95. (Hereafter Waller.)

7. *Women in the Middle Ages and the Renaissance: Literary and Historical Perspectives*, ed. and intro. by Mary Beth Rose. Syracuse. pp. xxx + 288. hb $29.95, pb $12.50. (Hereafter Rose.)

guidance for female rule, Leah Marcus's discussion of the androgyne cult, as embodying unification and harmony, in relation to Elizabeth and to Shakespeare's comic heroines, and Madelon Sprengnether's psychoanalytic account of *Coriolanus*. From the second group, we may go from the effects of an ideology of self-effacement, that left for female self-assertion only the art of dying well, in Mary Ellen Lamb's examination of Mary Sidney's translations, to Janel M. Mueller's discussion of Margery Kempe's autobiography, with its struggle to relate sexuality, spirituality, and selfhood, concluding with the editor's essay on seventeenth-century female autobiographies, suggesting how 'social chaos can generate female creativity' (cf. Sprengnether?). Stevie Davies, in her *The Idea of Woman in Renaissance Literature*[8], declines the aggressive tone and poststructuralist vocabulary of some feminist writing in favour of eloquent mythography, kindly absorbing or marginalizing the male (apparently essentially uncreative, and even unable to procreate!). She emphasizes the centrality of bisexual and female deities in Renaissance Orphic Platonism, suggesting that at Eleusis, the sacred temple of Ceres/Demeter, Spenser, Shakespeare, and Milton 'found a spiritual home'. Her account of Spenser concentrates, of course, on Book III, 'the book of the womb', celebrating female fecundity, culminating in Book IV in the Jung-Frau herself, Gloriana-Isis. Simon Shepherd's welcome collection, *The Women's Sharp Revenge*[9] (not seen last year), contains five sixteenth- and seventeenth-century protofeminist pamphlets in modernized and annotated texts. The publishers imply that the authors are women, but, as the editor indicates, at least three are men, with perhaps only Jane Anger (1589) and Rachel Speght (1617) actually women, though Shepherd's own ardently feminist introduction and commentaries tend to treat them (except the author of the title pamphlet) as women.

Of three books dealing with classical mythology, the most important is Leonard Barkan's *The Gods Made Flesh*[10], a rich and important study, learned, wide-ranging, acute, and fluently written. The founding chapter analyses how Ovid's metamorphoses manifest psychic transformations – transgressions, self-erasures, self-definitions, and creations; next Barkan discusses the medieval struggle to Christianize Ovid by demystification and allegory; the penultimate, major chapter ranges easily over the Renaissance – Correggio, Titian, Michelangelo, Petrarch, Ronsard, Spenser (especially, of course, Book III and the *Cantoes*) – exploring how Renaissance artists make metamorphosis an explicitly psychological condition, while developing a metamorphic aesthetics; the last chapter presents searching accounts of Shakespeare and his exploration and redefinition of gender, identity, and art. Covering a little of the same ground is James M. Saslow's (necessarily) much slighter *Ganymede in the Renaissance*[11]; while touching on the use of the Ganymede story for Platonist and alchemical allegories, Saslow's

8. *The Idea of Woman in Renaissance Literature: The Feminine Reclaimed*, by Stevie Davies. Harvester/UKen. pp. xii + 273. £32.50/$25.

9. *The Women's Sharp Revenge: Five Women's Pamphlets from the Renaissance*, ed. by Simon Shepherd. FE (1985). pp. 208. £12.95.

10. *The Gods Made Flesh: Metamorphosis and the Pursuit of Paganism*, by Leonard Barkan. Yale. pp. xvi + 398. £30/$30.

11. *Ganymede in the Renaissance: Homosexuality in Art and Society*, by James M. Saslow. Yale. pp. xvi + 265. £25.

well-illustrated study is more concerned to show how changing treatments, from Michelangelo to the Counter-Reformation and the dwindling and neutering of the theme in the seventeenth century, reveal changing attitudes to homosexuality. More spiritually minded is Thomas Hyde's study of Cupid[12], which traces developments in the treatment of Cupid from Andreas Capellanus via Dante, Petrarch, and Ficino, to Spenser's minor poems and *The Faerie Queene*; the complexities of the subject, linking carnality and Platonic love, are explored clearly enough, as Hyde tackles the issue of how Cupid – or, rather, his divinity – could be taken seriously, and harmonized with a Christian, and especially a Protestant, God, as in Spenser. This seems to make a suitable transition to notice Ernest B. Gilman's valuable and illuminating study of true and false images (whether mental or physical) in the Renaissance, *Iconoclasm and Poetry in the English Reformation*[13], that sets image-making (a central activity for any artist) against a logocentric Reformation theology deeply suspicious of images, and alert to the deceptiveness of imagery, the visual, and the pictorial: writers and readers must constantly struggle against creating mental idols. Gilman provides valuable accounts of Sidney's theory; of Spenser's struggles, in Books I and VI of *The Faerie Queene* particularly, against the power of his creation (here Gilman's theme overlaps with that of Kenneth Gross – see section 3(d) below; of Quarles's exploitation of the gap between the pictorial and the verbal elements of his emblems; of Donne's sense of the necessity and deceptiveness of mental images; and of Milton's development of a revolutionary aesthetic. Finally, John Morgan's *Godly Learning*[14] has little to say on literary texts, but will be essential reading for students of the period, for understanding the puritan *mentalité*, and the Puritans' contribution to 'the final flowering of a tradition of attempting to blend faith and reason, enthusiasm and learning into a *Christian* balance'.

2. The Earlier Sixteenth Century

(a) Prose

The most ambitious discussion of Tudor prose recently is Arthur F. Kinney's hefty volume, *Humanist Poetics*[15], which argues the case for the major importance of sixteenth-century prose, as derived from classical and continental humanist texts and concerned with rhetoric and with the relationship between social and individual improvement. The first section proposes an early Tudor 'poetics of wordplay', running from accounts of Erasmus's *Praise of Folly* and More's *Utopia* to Gascoigne's *The Adventures of Master F.J.*; after a mid-century break comes a 'poetics of eloquence', with Castiglione, *Euphues*, Greene, and the *Arcadia*; the latter, twilight days of humanism produce the

12. *The Poetic Theology of Love: Cupid in Renaissance Literature*, by Thomas Hyde. UDel/AUP. pp. 212. $29.50.

13. *Iconoclasm and Poetry in the English Reformation: Down Went Dagon*, by Ernest B. Gilman. UChic. pp. xi + 227. £16.95/$19.

14. *Godly Learning: Puritan Attitudes towards Reason, Learning, and Education, 1560-1640*, by John Morgan. CUP. pp. x + 366. £35/$49.50.

15. *Humanist Poetics: Thought, Rhetoric and Fiction in Sixteenth-Century England*, by Arthur F. Kinney. UMass. pp. xiv + 529. £33.95/$35.

'poetics of doubt and despair' (Nashe, Lodge, etc.). It is a useful book, rather sound-textbook-scholarly in effect, with good readings emphasizing classical models and origins; a final, uneasy chapter opens out into contemplating a posthumanistic poetics (Montaigne, Bacon, and recent criticism – Montrose, Greenblatt, and Annabel Patterson – now appear). Ranging equally widely, but far less effectively, is Peter Ruppert's *Reader in a Strange Land*[16], a rather slight and simplistic application of reader-response theory to utopian writing from More to this century, useful chiefly in summarizing earlier criticism, i.e. other readers: Ruppert's main point is that utopian 'open-ended' writing provides a defamiliarizing critique of the established, provoking the (apparently exclusively female) readers into liberating fantasy and speculations.

Various important editions should be noted: in the Yale edition of More, *The Answer to a Poisoned Book*[17], the 'Letter to Martin Dorp' and the Latin text of *Richard III* with translations[18], and additions to the Toronto Erasmus[19], as well as to Peter G. Bietenholz and Thomas Deutscher's register of early Renaissance figures[20]. It was interesting to see John Rastell's *Pastyme of People* reproduced in facsimile by Albert J. Geritz[21], with its extraordinary and innovative typographical layout, whereby different nations' histories figure in synchronous parallel bands on the same page. Geritz provides a critical introduction, outlines Rastell's remarkable career, and discusses sources and concerns; there is also a reprint of Rastell's intervention in the Simon Fish–Thomas More controversy over church income.

Among discussions of More's own work, of most interest was Elizabeth McCutcheon's 'Mendacium Dicere and Mentiri' in I. D. McFarlane's collection of papers from the recent Neo-Latin conference[22], exploring More's distinction in *Utopia* between 'to tell a lie' and 'to lie', considering the 'style and aesthetic of honest deception' in writing whose equivocations provoke the reader and protect the author. In the same volume Germain Marc'hadour considers that More was not really, as Erasmus had it, 'dragged' into royal service, and K. J. Wilson analyses Thomas Elyot's claim to Cromwell that he had been More's friend only 'usque ad aras' – to the limits of public virtue. In *Moreana* we may note Charles Clay Doyle 'Looking behind Two Proverbs of

16. *Reader in a Strange Land: The Activity of Reading Literary Utopias*, by Peter Ruppert. UGeo. pp. xiv + 193. $19.

17. *The Yale Edition of the Complete Works of St Thomas More*. Vol. XI: *The Answer to a Poisoned Book*, ed. by Stephen Merriam Foley and Clarence H. Miller. Yale (1985). pp. xciv + 424. $60.

18. *The Yale Edition of the Complete Works of St Thomas More*. Vol. XV: *'In Defence of Humanism'* . . . *with a New Text and Translation of 'Historia Richardi Tertii'*, ed. by Daniel Kinney. Yale. pp. cliv + 815. $55.

19. *Collected Works of Erasmus*. Vols. XXV and XXVI: *Literary and Educational Writing, 3 and 4*, ed. by J. K. Sowards. UTor (1985). pp. lx + 678. $95 the set.

20. *Contemporaries of Erasmus: A Biographical Register of the Renaissance and Reformation*, ed. by Peter G. Bietenholz and Thomas B. Deutscher. UTor. Vol. I: *A–E* (1985). pp. 480. $80; Vol. II: *F–M*. pp. 490. $80.

21. *'The Pastyme of People' and 'A New Boke of Purgatory'* by J. *Rastell*, ed. by Albert J. Geritz. Garland (1985). pp. vii + 507. $28.

22. *Acta Conventus Neo-Latini Sanctandreani. Proceedings of the Fifth International Congress of Neo-Latin Studies*, ed. by I. D. McFarlane. CMERS. pp. x + 645. $50.

More', Paul Sawada wondering whether More was 'a Utopian or a Real-
politiker' (neither, but *homo viator*, directed towards the life to come), and
Angele Samaan outlining the treatment of 'Death and the Death-Penalty' in
Utopia and some later utopian/dystopian works from William Morris to
George Orwell. More interesting were discussions of More's contemporaries,
particularly Ward S. Allen on 'The Testing of Tyndale's Bible', a sensitive
analysis of the Authorized Version's use of Tyndale, together with some
modern versions; Richard J. Schoeck considers the differences between More
and Erasmus, whether personal (less than Richard Marius suggested in his biography) or in matters religious, scholarly, or stylistic (Erasmus the more
flexible, scholarly, and graceful); Dale B. Billingsley discusses 'The Editorial
Design of the 1557 *English Works*' of More, considering how Rastell's editorial
method works to make the volume a reliquary, presenting More initially as a
confessor and then as a martyr; Vittorio Gabrieli discusses 'the sources,
characters and ideas of the play of *Sir Thomas More*', and Richard Maber prints
complete 'Pierre Le Moyne's Encomium of Margaret Roper Translated by John
Paulet'. The late C. A. Patrides (*KR*) discusses the Lucianic 'lusory sense of
reality' in 'Erasmus and More', exploring the subtly serious playfulness of *The
Praise of Folly* and *Utopia*, noting the 'darker', more unsettling qualities of the
latter that perhaps make it the greater work. Mark Eccles (*SP*) provides a brief
account of 'Claudius Hollyband [Claude Desainliens] and the Earliest
French – English Dictionaries' of 1570/1.

(b) Poetry and Drama

Skelton did rather well this year. In *PMLA* Susan Schibanoff takes '*Phyllyp
Sparowe* as a Primer for Women Readers' in a lively piece arguing that most
readings of the poem depend on not reading parts of it (the so-called 'transition'
and 'addition'): all reading depends on not-reading, misreading, and rewriting,
as the poem demonstrates through the various voices and writings that
(dis)compose it. Less deconstructionist but equally fashionable is Bernard
Sharratt's application, in 'John Skelton: Finding a Voice'[23], of Bakhtin to an
otherwise s‾ aightforward introduction to Skelton's verse, where finally the
plain-speaking criticism of 'Why Come Ye Nat to Courte?' is preferred as a
model for those confronting a modern Wolsey; straightforwardly scholarly is
John Scattergood on 'Ware the Hauke' (*MÆ*), as a satire traditional in conventions and motifs used earlier in medieval satires on hunting clerics.

Wyatt and Surrey both got book-length treatment. H. A. Mason produced
an unusual volume[24], a careful modern-spelling edition of twenty-four poems,
with textual notes, extensive (though sometimes diffuse) commentaries, and a
critical introduction. The main concern of the study, the fruit of years of
reading and scholarship, is to bring out the unity and essential virtues of
Wyatt's writings, the circumstances of court life and, most of all, the
importance of Wyatt's reading. It is hard to identify the intended readership as,
while relatively familiar words are glossed, much knowledge is assumed that is
hardly to be found among undergraduates. In *N&Q* Mason takes up Wyatt's

23. In *Medieval Literature: Criticism, Ideology and History*, ed. by David Aers.
Harvester/St Martin's. pp. viii + 228. £28.50.

24. *Sir Thomas Wyatt: A Literary Portrait*, by H. A. Mason. BCP. pp. 343. hb £21,
pb £9.95.

reference to being retired to Kent 'emong the muses', a European commonplace dating back to Cicero, and familiar from Boethius and Plutarch. Joost Daalder discusses textual and editorial problems (R. A. Rebholz's edition the target) *à propos* of Wyatt's 'Defamed Guiltiness' (*Expl*) and 'Like as the Byrde' (*ELN*). William A. Sessions provides a thorough study of *Henry Howard, Earl of Surrey*[25], presenting him as a Renaissance humanist primarily concerned with the social function of poetry and the definition of self, and with the principles of *imitatio*, looking to Virgil, Petrarch, and Chaucer. Every poem Surrey wrote is discussed separately, on rather traditional lines, emphasizing rhetorical devices and structure; somehow, Sessions makes Surrey's work and life seem worthy and unexciting. On the other hand, O. B. Hardison's consideration of 'Tudor Humanism and Surrey's Translation of the *Aeneid*' (*SP*) argues that, while Wyatt's versification is essentially traditional, Surrey's verse in the *Aeneid* translation is innovative in its adaptation of Latin technique: Tottel's edition has suppressed the rhythmical subtleties apparent in the 1554 John Day/William Owen version.

Other early Tudor versifiers receive attention: James P. Carley discusses 'John Leland in Paris' (*SP*) and the Latin poems of the 1520s – in one (shades of *Henry V*!), he records the sending of French tennis racquets and balls to friends in England; and A. S. G. Edwards (*N&Q*) suggests echoes of Stephen Hawes's *Pastime of Pleasure* in William Walter's antifeminist poem *The Spectacle of Louers* (1533?) and interest in Hawes in the Wynkyn de Worde circle.

Two significant publications on the drama of the early sixteenth century this year are Peter Happé's edition of the *Complete Plays* of John Bale (Brewer) and J. D. White's reference guide, *Early English Drama: 'Everyman' to 1580* (Hall), neither of which was seen.

3. The Later Sixteenth Century

(a) Prose

The quadricentennial of Sidney's death was a good year for studies of the minor prose of the period. In 'Francis Bacon and the Style of Politics' (*ELR*) F. J. Levy focuses on the original *Essayes* of 1597 which he reads as a 'response to a crisis in English politics which, amidst a more general reorientation of thought, caused Bacon to engage in an examination of his political role'. After an impressive review of Elizabethan court politics and Bacon's advancements and setbacks in it, Levy concludes that through his literary use of aphorisms Bacon intended to 'refashion political thinking'.

Interest in George Buchanan continues unabated in five essays of varying length and merit in *Acta Conventus Neo-Latini Sanctandreani*[22]. Another figure of comparatively minor importance is given prominent if uncritical treatment. In *John Dee: Essential Readings*[26] Gerald Suster offers an anthology (in English translations) of Dr Dee's various letters, diary extracts, and

25. *Henry Howard, Earl of Surrey*, by William A. Sessions. TEAS. Hall. pp. 172. $19.95.

26. *John Dee: Essential Readings*, ed. and intro. by Gerald Suster. Crucible: Aquarian. pp. 157. pb £6.99.

philosophical treatises. The author claims that Dee is a much maligned figure in need of rehabilitation, a kind of misunderstood da Vinci of Elizabethan England. Notwithstanding such hyperboles Suster's anthology provides a good read even if it is unlikely to make many converts to the cause of sixteenth-century English hermeticism and astrology. In *The Heptarchia Mystica of John Dee* edited by Robert Turner [27] we are presented with an English translation of a text by Dee which 'holds together as a unique system of practical occultism'. The reproduced text reads like a scholarly early draft of annotated Jungian animadversions not wholly devoid of interest. A short but stimulating essay by Robin E. Cousins on Dee's residence in Mortlake and a discussion by Turner of Dee's religious magic conclude the volume.

Two searching and timely essays on Deloney appeared in *NM*. In 'Some Notes on Thomas Deloney's Indebtedness to Shakespeare' O. R. Reuter demonstrates with ample illustrations that no fewer than twenty-six passages in Deloney's works are derived almost verbatim from Shakespeare, particularly *Venus and Adonis*. If this theory gains further support, Reuter may come to be seen as pioneering new areas of Renaissance intertextuality. In 'Unity and Meaning in Thomas Deloney's *Thomas of Reading*' Paul Devine argues that Deloney's work anticipates the development of the English novel as well as 'the political underpinnings of the English Civil War'. In spite of its somewhat grand claims, this is a sensitive and well-informed piece of scholarship.

In '*The Strife of Love in a Dreame*, an Elizabethan Translation of Part of the First Book of Francesco Colonna's *Hypnerotomachia*' (*BSRS*) Dudley Wilson analyses the anonymous translation of 1592 of this novel. In this limited but thorough essay the author locates the primarily rhetorical interest of his study in the way in which the 'often strange and esoteric linguistic usages of the original' translate into late Elizabethan English.

Amintas Dale (1592) was the last work of the Sidney protégé Abraham Fraunce. In 'Abraham Fraunce's Debts to Arthur Golding in *Amintas Dale*' (*N&Q*) Anthony Brian Taylor argues that in this work Fraunce deliberately reverts to the earlier and earthier idiom of Golding's 1567 Ovid rather than being in tune with the revival of the slick new 'Ovidianism' of Marlowe and Shakespeare.

Two articles look at the writings of Mary Sidney. In 'The Countess of Pembroke and the Art of Dying' in Rose [7] Mary Ellen Lamb focuses on *The Discourse of Life and Death* (1590), *Antonie* (*c.* 1590), and *The Triumph of Death* (*c.* 1599). All three texts engage the topics of death and dying, and they are read here as jointly constellating 'a female literary strategy through which women could be represented as heroic without challenging the beliefs of the patriarchal culture of Elizabethan England'. If at times Lamb's arguments seem too intent on accommodating the texts to contemporary readings, the author legitimately directs our attention to the links between stoicism and the gradual emergence of a feminist perspective in the late sixteenth century. Margaret P. Hannay's article 'Unpublished Letters by Mary Sidney, Countess of Pembroke' (*SSt*, 1985) studies four holograph letters by Mary Sidney, over-looked originally by Frances Young in her 1912 listing of the Countess's correspondence. The first letter is addressed to Essex and dates from the mid 1590s,

27. *The Heptarchia Mystica of John Dee*, ed. by Robert Turner. Aquarian. pp. 126. pb £6.99.

the other three, all about the infamous Edmund Mathew (*sic*), are dated in 1603 and 1604. They are written to Sir Julius Caesar, 'Knight of His Majesty's Requests', and record the Countess's frustration with the allegations of her former employee. As documents of economic struggles in the period, centred on the Countess's holdings aròund Cardiff, these are fascinating pieces of writing. The letters are usefully transcribed for us by the author.

All students of the period, and of the Sidney circle in particular, will welcome John Gouws' elegant and intelligent edition of Greville's *A Dedication to Sir Philip Sidney* and the Senecan *consolatio*, *A Letter to an Honourable Lady* in *The Prose Works of Fulke Greville, Lord Brooke*[28]. A perceptive general introduction is followed by a detailed textual commentary and a useful chronological table. These are complemented by eighty pages of exegetic endnotes, as well as by a short glossary. There can be little doubt that this sensitively judged edition will establish itself as a standard text for scholars and students.

In a curious article 'The Maidstone Burghmote and John Hall's *Courte of Vertue* (1565)' (*N&Q*) Rivkah Zim investigates the encyclopaedic Tudor miscellany by this respectable burgher of Maidstone and intelligently traces the link between the elder Thomas Wyatt's and Hall's literary practice. The essay's subject matter may be limited, but the execution of it is stylish and suggestive.

Mark Breitenberg's article '". . . the hole matter opened": Iconic Representation and Interpretation in "The Queenes Majesties Passage"' (*Criticism*) studies Richard Mulcaster's iconic and emblematic account of Elizabeth I's entry into London for the coronation. The essay evolves against the background of 'new historicism', particularly as explored by Greenblatt. Breitenberg intelligently matches rhetorical systems, such as Wilson's *The Arte of Rhetoric*, to the spectacle of Elizabethan pageantry and argues that they mutually and meaningfully comment on each other. In pursuing these binary patterns Breitenberg displays a nimble and well-informed mind and offers a valuable commentary on Mulcaster and on current approaches to early modern English literature.

The posthumous writings on Thomas Nashe by Antoine Demadre, the founder of *CahiersE*, are now published in two volumes under the title *Essais sur Thomas Nashe*[29]. The work was originally intended as a major survey of all of Nashe's writings but the author's premature death prevented its completion. The present collection intelligently and methodically deals with early Nashe and *The Unfortunate Traveller*. The projected chapters on Nashe's language and his pamphlets are missing. As a synoptic assessment of Nashe's works, Demadre's book rates as an impressive achievement. Stephen S. Hilliard's *The Singularity of Thomas Nashe*[30] is an important and elegantly written essay on the works of this Elizabethan maverick and university wit. The model preferred here is that of literary history, and the works are treated chronologically and comprehensively. Nashe's attitudes to the Puritans and his controversial attack on Richard Harvey are stimulatingly discussed, and the

28. *The Prose Works of Fulke Greville, Lord Brooke*, ed. by John Gouws. Clarendon. pp. lxvii + 279. £40.

29. *Essais sur Thomas Nashe*, by Antoine Demadre. 2 vols. SSELER. USalz. pp. ii + 507. £30.

30. *The Singularity of Thomas Nashe*, by Stephen S. Hilliard. UNeb. pp. x + 260. £22.50.

reader is left with a picture of an uneasily dissenting ironist who responded to the scepticism of his period and contributed to it. Brief mention ought to be made of J. J. M. Tobin's 'Nashe and *Measure for Measure*' (*N&Q*), in which it is proposed that Shakespeare incorporated Nashean language drawn from *Pierce Penilesse* into his play.

Robert H. West's *Reginald Scot and Renaissance Writings on Witchcraft*[31] (overlooked in the year of its publication) is a perceptive and wide-ranging study of one of the great and often neglected rationalist voices from among Shakespeare's contemporaries. West's study, like Scot's *Discoverie of Witchcraft* (1584), pleads for tolerance and common sense. The author displays a sound acquaintance with the period and particularly the underlying psychological and historical causes of the hysteria which repeatedly swept through Renaissance Europe.

Two substantial essays on Puttenham should be noted. In 'The Hegemonic Theater of George Puttenham' (*ELR*) Jonathan V. Crewe argues that in *The Arte of English Poesie* Puttenham offers 'a view of theater as a major hegemonic institution of the state; as one more important, in a sense, than the state's formal apparatus of legal, educational and bureaucratic institutions'. Crewe's case is weakened, as he recognizes, by the fact that Puttenham did not witness the great Elizabethan drama of the 1590s, but his argument for an intelligent re-appraisal of *The Arte* is convincingly put. In Parker and Quint[3] Derek Attridge writes on 'Puttenham's Perplexity: Nature, Art, and the Supplement in Renaissance Poetic Theory'. The drift of Attridge's argument is that Puttenham's extensive treatise, which lacks the insulatory elegance of Sidney's *Defence*, 'may be read as an attempt to articulate certain crucial problems having to do with the status of poetic language . . . offering a clearer view than a more recent text might do of the tacit assumptions and conceptual parameters that both make possible and set boundaries to our confrontation with the same issues'. Attridge's study is influenced by the deconstructionist polarities of Derrida which he skilfully transposes to the 'nature' and 'art' dichotomies explored by Puttenham in relation to the rhetoric of poetry and drama.

Richard Reynoldes's *A Chronicle of All the Noble Emperours of the Romaines* (1571) and George Whetstone's *A Mirour for Magestrates of Cyties* (1584) are the subject of a thought-provoking study by Paul Dean in 'Contemporary English History in Elizabethan Roman Histories' (*N&Q*).

(b) Poetry

Emblems are closer to poetry and the pictorial arts than to prose. In 'Recent Studies in the English Emblem' (*ELR*) Jerome S. Dees provides a useful short-title list of English emblem books in the Renaissance and then proceeds to offer a well-judged and welcome survey of new writing on emblems arranged under the subject headings of 'General Studies', 'Individual Emblem Writers', 'The Emblem and English Literature', and 'The State of Criticism'. In 'Andrew Willet, England's First Religious Emblem Writer' (*Ren&R*) Peter M. Daly and Paola Valéri-Tomaszuk trace the place in the development of the emblem genre of Willet's *Sacra Emblemata* (*c.* 1592) and argue that Willet, not Geffrey

---

31. *Reginald Scot and Renaissance Writings on Witchcraft*, by Robert H. West. TEAS. Hall (1984). pp. x + 142. $18.50.

Whitney (*A Choice of Emblemes*, 1586), is the first writer in England of an original emblem book. This is a scrupulously observed essay, replete with shrewd and refreshing comments, and it benefits greatly from the authors' grasp of classical languages and literature.

In 'The Case for the 1593 Edition of Thomas Combe's *Theater of Fine Devices*' (*JWCI*) Peter M. Daly argues intelligently for an early publication date in the 1590s of this collection on the basis that it is mentioned in Francis Meres's *Palladis Tamia* (1598) and particularly because it seems to be echoed if not quoted in the 'Four Seasons' tapestries at Hatfield House, which provide a *terminus ad quem* of 1611.

Norman Ault's *Elizabethan Lyrics*[32], first issued over sixty years ago, is reprinted in a revised and corrected version. It contains some 640 poems, ranging from 1533 to 1620 and presented in that order. Ault's splendid anthology retains its pristine attraction and remains unrivalled for its usefulness. The contemporary reader might have been better served though if the selection had been brought into line with modern scholarship. There is little need now in a collection of this nature for long excerpts from Shakespeare, Spenser, and Sidney – instead one wishes for the recovery of the hundreds of minor and sometimes anonymous lyrics which Ault reputedly discarded.

Winifred Maynard's *Elizabethan Lyric Poetry and its Music*[33] offers a very thorough and engaging survey of early songbooks and miscellanies, from Richard Tottel's inspired collection of 1557 to the use of ballad, songs, and masque in Shakespeare's plays. From early lyrical anthologies without music, Maynard proceeds to William Byrd and a discussion of Thomas Morley and English madrigals. Thomas Campion and particularly John Dowland, the outstanding composer of lutesongs in the period, figure prominently here, as do Sidney, Jonson, and Shakespeare. This excellent study of a fruitful area of Elizabethan culture should be recommended reading for any student of the period.

In 'Foxes and Wolves in Elizabethan Episcopal Propaganda' (*CahiersE*) Michael G. Brennan briefly studies a fragment of a sixteenth-century Robin Hood ballad in a British Library manuscript, Harleian MS 367, and relates its animal imagery to the contemporary Puritan attack on episcopacy.

Editing Samuel Daniel is the subject of an interesting essay by John Pitcher[34] whose *Samuel Daniel: The Brotherton Manuscript* (*YW* 62.158–9) remains a model of investigative textual scholarship.

In 'The Eight Parts of a Theme in "Gascoigne's Memories: III"' (*SP*) Nancy Williams argues that in the poem Gascoigne 'discovered a structure which enabled him . . . to analyze the moral implications of debt'. Williams proceeds through a close analysis of Gascoigne's rhetorical techniques and offers interesting reflections on the neglected poet-debtor. John Stephens's essay 'George Gascoigne's *Poesies* and the Persona in Sixteenth Century Poetry' (*Neophil*) was not seen.

In 'Meaning in Context: Fulke Greville's Sonnet LXXX' (*ELR*) Jeffrey A. Goodman advances the thesis that Sonnet 80 is not about poetry at all, 'but is a

---

32. *Elizabethan Lyrics*, ed. by Norman Ault. Faber. pp. xvii + 560. pb £6.95.

33. *Elizabethan Lyric Poetry and its Music*, by Winifred Maynard. Clarendon. pp. xiv + 246. £27.50.

34. In *The 1985 Forum of the Renaissance English Text Society*. RETS. pp. i + 38.

political poem'. This is a hard-hitting and at times overly assertive essay which concedes that Greville's poem is full of pedantic writing, exhibiting little real 'gift for language and rhythm', while maintaining at the same time that Greville's poetry repays detailed study.

R. C. Horne's 'Voices of Alienation: The Moral Significance of Marston's Satiric Strategy' (*MLR*) proposes a thorough, almost congested re-appraisal of Marston. Taking Marston's *The Metamorphosis of Pigmalion's Image* (1598) as his starting point, Horne deduces that the initial expression of Marston's satire is summed up in the myth of man as Pygmalion. He concludes that Marston's man, as he emerges in his poetry, is a 'humanist creature of indeterminate nature', which descends to the level of the beasts while attempting to reach up to the gods.

Chapter 4 of Waller[6] contains ten sound pages on Sir Walter Ralegh. Waller suggests in conclusion that 'Ralegh's poems, then, are haunted by what they try to exorcize'. Jerry Leath Mills's *Sir Walter Ralegh: A Reference Guide* (Hall) was not seen.

In his detailed essay 'The Works of Chidiock Tichborne' (*ELR*) Richard S. M. Hirsch proposes a critical edition of Tichborne's 'Lament' and of his two other poems, 'To his Friend' and 'The Housedove'. He also includes Tichborne's memorable last letter to his wife and his authenticated speech from the scaffold. By his succinct and scholarly edition of the 'Works' of one of the most gifted and tragic figures of Elizabethan England, Hirsch has rendered students of the period an invaluable service, particularly at a time when a vigorous new critical epistemology is refocusing attention on the extent to which we all inhabit history.

(c) Sidney

Chapter 5 of Waller[6] concerns itself with three Sidneys: Philip, Mary, and Robert. The pages on Sir Philip are lucid and excel particularly in the discussion of particular poems. Waller has a sure grasp of the wider philosophical implications of Sidney's poetry and usefully draws on his knowledge of the period in general to elucidate the works. Some fifteen pages deal with Mary Sidney, the Countess of Pembroke, and with Robert Sidney whose poetry, Waller writes, evinces a deep commitment 'to the craft of poetry as well as to its inspiring or calculated consolations of erotic or political favour'.

The most important book on Sidney to appear is *Sir Philip Sidney: 1586 and the Creation of a Legend*[35]. The thirteen essays by different hands in this volume commemorate the four-hundredth anniversary of Sidney's death at Zutphen. The contributions range from an authoritative general introduction by William A. Ringler and a shrewd and knowledgeable essay on Sidney's final year by the late Jan van Dorsten to a suggestive checklist of Sidney allusions in print before 1640 by Jackson Boswell and H. R. Woudhuysen. This elegant symposium ranks as the foremost publication on Sidney for some time, including as it does fresh research by some of the world's leading Sidney scholars. John Gouws' essay on Fulke Greville's account of the poet-courtier's last days, Dominic Baker-Smith's scrutiny of the reception and transmutation of Sidney's death in poetry, and particularly Katherine Duncan-Jones's

35. *Sir Philip Sidney: 1586 and the Creation of a Legend*, ed. by Jan van Dorsten, Dominic Baker-Smith, and Arthur F. Kinney. LeidenU. pp. x + 246. $84.

informed and fluent reflections on *Astrophil and Stella* and the Sidney 'romantic' biography, stand out as masterly and original essays about their chosen topics.

Of a different order is a second collection of essays, *Essential Articles for the Study of Sir Philip Sidney*, edited by Arthur F. Kinney[36]. This selection of twenty-four articles and lectures on Sidney deemed seminal by the editor, a leading expert on Sidney, is divided into seven subject-headings to encompass not only the entire *œuvre*, but also various aspects of the Sidney biography. Edwin A. Greenlaw's important essay on Sidney's *Arcadia* and Elizabethan allegory (1913) is the earliest entry, the latest being Alan Sinfield's discussion of power and ideology in the *Arcadia* (1985). The editor's choices may at times appear idiosyncratic and unadventurous, but they are never injudicious and reflect some of the diversity of scholarly opinion on Sidney, including the current elegiac mood. In Chapter 7 of *Humanist Poetics*[15] Arthur Kinney writes again about the *Arcadia* and the poetic uses of philosophy and suggests that Sidney's prose work constitutes a wilful act 'of humanist poetics that comes in the waning days of Tudor humanism'.

In *The Chivalric Tradition in Renaissance England*[37] Arthur B. Ferguson, after a thorough survey of the literature of chivalry in Elizabethan England in general, concludes that 'it is not surprising that Sidney should have attempted in *Arcadia* to exemplify a code of behaviour that required the traditional values of chivalry to be adapted to the interests of the state'. For Ferguson Sidney embodies the synthesis of chivalric and humanist values in his writings and in his life.

Another major contribution to Sidney research is Robert E. Stillman's full-length study, *Sidney's Poetic Justice: 'The Old Arcadia', its Eclogues, and Renaissance Pastoral Traditions*[38]. Stillman argues that in the *Arcadia* Sidney set out 'to create a new version of pastoral that merges the emphasis upon contentment in the Italianate tradition with the ethical concern of the Christian bucolic' and that the *Arcadia* proposes an analysis of poetic acts as Sidney's most 'powerful and persuasive defense of poetry'. Taking it for granted that the sophisticated structures of Sidney's eclogues signpost his rhetorical intentions, Stillman subtly argues for the thematic coherence of these eclogues and the way they tie in with the major topical concerns of the various books of the *Old Arcadia*. After two preliminary chapters on genre and pastoral the author addresses the *Old Arcadia* book by book and concludes with a study of Sidney's poetic presentation of the natural world and the manner in which a redefined pastoral is used 'to obtain justice and contentment for himself [Sidney] and his readers'.

Two essays on *Arcadia* ought to be noted. In 'Sidney's *Old Arcadia*: In Praise of Folly' (*SCJ*) Elliott M. Simon studies the uses of an Erasmian folly in Sidney's works which, he notes, form an integral part of 'Sidney's Protestant vision of human nature and his use of the Fall as a model for the dramatic action

36. *Essential Articles for the Study of Sir Philip Sidney*, ed. by Arthur F. Kinney. Archon. pp. xvii + 458. £30.45.

37. *The Chivalric Tradition in Renaissance England*, by Arthur B. Ferguson. Folger. pp. 184. $26.50/£16.95.

38. *Sidney's Poetic Justice: 'The Old Arcadia', its Eclogues, and Renaissance Pastoral Traditions*, by Robert E. Stillman. AUP/BuckU. pp. 277. £24.50.

of his story'. Sidney's vision of humanity is fundamentally ironic, Simon argues in this wide-ranging and scholarly contribution, which, if its thesis itself is rather slight, delights with its sheer bulk of supporting information. In 'Devices and their Narrative Function in Sidney's *Arcadia*' (*Emblematica*) Victor Skretkowicz argues that in the short time between completing the *Old Arcadia* and embarking on revisions Sidney 'gained a remarkable insight into current theory and practice of the device. He achieved this through his parti- cipation in the neo-Burgundian allegorical tournaments performed at court.' Skretkowicz writes with sensitivity and elegance on Argalus' shield, Parthenia's devices, and the extent to which their integration into the plot of the romance links up with the reader's need to be entertained. The author's command of his material is superb and his conclusions, far-fetched though they may seem at times, are persuasive.

In '*Astrophel and Stella* 75: A "New Text"' (*RES*) H. R. Woudhuysen offers an intelligently researched piece on Sonnet 75 in the sequence as extant in Archbishop Tobie Matthew's unique manuscript of Sir John Harington's *A Tract on the Succession to the Crown*, now in the York Minster Library. Woudhuysen raises the possibility that the variants between this text and others of the same poem may derive from Sidney himself, and hopes that Harington's part in the transmission of Sidney's texts may be studied in greater depth.

In *Rewriting the Renaissance: The Discourse of Sexual Difference in Early Modern Europe*[39] Clark Hulse addresses the issue of 'Stella's Wit: Penelope Rich as Reader of Sidney's Sonnets'. His main thesis is that Sidney's ori- ginal audience, 'the ideal reader' and the 'principal reader' as described in the poems, are 'all one person, Penelope Devereux Rich'. In a sometimes inspired and sometimes overwritten argument Hulse shrewdly detects the emergence from this act of reading poetry of a political message 'significantly at variance with the overt political ideology of Elizabethan England'. The extent to which Sidney distanced himself from the official party-lines of the Court has been the subject of much critical literature on the *Arcadia*. It appears from this essay that similar patterns of troubled dissent underlie *Astrophil and Stella*.

In *Poems in their Place: The Intertextuality and Order of Poetic Collections*[40] S. K. Heninger Jr argues, in an essay entitled 'Sequences, Systems, Models: Sidney and the Secularization of Sonnets', that sonnet sequences of the period are a 'non-classical genre'. Rather they originate within an aesthetics in which 'art reflects the patterns of cosmos, and the basic form of art . . . is the paradox of multeity in unity'. Heninger ranges widely, and with great authority, through the history of European 'romantic' and erotic medi- tational poetry, including Dante and Petrarch as well as Sidney's con- temporaries. According to the author Sidney assimilated from Petrarch an 'equivocal attitude towards *Madonna*'. Sidney is credited here with providing English sonneteering with 'a poetics of liberated language'. In fact Heninger has provided a masterly survey of a period context from which too many critics

39. *Rewriting the Renaissance: The Discourse of Sexual Difference in Early Modern Europe*, ed. by Margaret W. Ferguson, Maureen Quilligan, and Nancy J. Vickers. UChic. pp. xxxi + 426. $50.
40. *Poems in their Place: The Intertextuality and Order of Poetic Collections*, ed. by Neil Fraistat. UNC. pp. vii + 344. $32.50.

of Sidney in the recent past have preferred to break away for the sake of more attractive and radical readings of Sidney's verse.

Mention should be made of William R. Drennan's short note on Sidney's 'Ister Banke' poem and its treatment of rebellion (*N&Q*) and of a discussion of 'A Historical Source for the Rebellion of the Commons in Sidney's *Arcadia*' by John L. Sutton Jr (*ELN*). There is a short but perceptive appraisal of some recent work on Sidney in a review-article, 'Recent Studies in the English Renaissance', by Richard Helgerson in *SEL*. *SNew* was not seen.

(d) Spenser

Only one book solely on Spenser came my way, but that was a good one, Kenneth Gross's learned, subtle, and suggestive *Spenserian Poetics: Idolatry, Iconoclasm, and Magic*[41]: here 'idolatry' indicates the impulse towards not only the creation of images but, variously, to mystification, reification, definition, or closure, whether in creation or interpretation; 'iconoclasm' may liberate through demystification or clarification, or involve destruction and incoherence, as opposites turn into each other. Spenser is presented as 'a skeptical visionary, a demythologizing mythmaker, an iconoclastic iconographer' working through a polyvalent 'magic' art, in a study ranging from the *View of Ireland*, via analyses of Orgoglio, Britomart's mirror and dream in Isis church, the Garden of Adonis, Mount Acidale, the Blatant Beast, to the *Cantoes'* attempt 'to win back, if only in parable, some measure of reconciliation between Spenser's poem and his world'. Two articles in *PMLA* also had Spenser's poetics particularly in mind: David Lee Miller's 'Spenser's Poetics: The Poem's Two Bodies' is a suggestive and lucid post-Derridean review, deploying Ernst Kantorowicz's account of *The King's Two Bodies*, of the relation between the poem's literal body and the ideal body, that, imaged by the veiled hermaphrodite, confounds sexual difference, and anticipates apocalypse; Gordon Teskey moves 'From Allegory to Dialectic', considering Error in Spenser and Milton – whereas Spenser seeks to make narrative and truth coincide, and to teach by entangling, engaging the reader in an interpretive game, Milton renounces allegory, polarizes error and truth, and presents his epic as an extension of the original Word.

Lillian S. Robinson's study of female knights in Renaissance epics[42] proved unexpectedly interesting. The epics of Ariosto, Tasso, and Spenser are presented as contributions to the development of social thought in the period between chivalric feudalism (evoked to suggest continuities of values between the old and the new) and the development of a market (bourgeois) state, wherein the monarch is required to deploy 'feminine' qualities of flexibility and harmonization: the fictional female knights and Elizabeth's practice had a common ideological origin. Robinson provides introductory chapters on Virgil and sixteenth-century socio-political change, and extended accounts of Ariosto, Tasso, and Spenser, where, of course, she concentrates on the Britomart–Arthegall relationship and its political implications, particularly interestingly on Book V.

41. *Spenserian Poetics: Idolatry, Iconoclasm, and Magic*, by Kenneth Gross. CornU (1985). pp. 271. $24.95.

42. *Monstrous Regiment: The Lady Knight in Sixteenth-Century Epic*, by Lillian S. Robinson. Garland (1985). pp. viii + 412. $55.

There are two collections of essays, one new, the other old. The first is the latest volume of *SSt* (1985): here John N. King argues that Spenser's language, as in the ecclesiastical eclogues of *The Shepheardes Calender*, should be read as marking him not as puritan but as Protestant; in 'The Thirsty Deer and the Lord of Life' Anne Lake Prescott develops the associations between the *Amoretti* and the Church calendar – the hind that surrenders herself in Sonnet 67 has relatives in the liturgy, biblical commentary, Psalm 41/2, and Marguerite de Navarre; Deborah Cartmell argues that *The Ruines of Time* derives not from Du Bellay but from Psalm 137, the song of the exiles who refused to sing in Babylonian captivity; Pamela J. Benson proposes, in 'Florimell at Sea', that the attempted rape and seduction of Florimell demonstrate how chastity, like the other virtues, depends on the gift of grace; Harold L. Weatherby discusses, in '*Axiochus* and the Bower of Bliss', the close relationship between *FQ* II.xii and the 1592 edition of *Axiochus* which, he suggests, Spenser probably translated; David O. Frantz distinguishes between the operations of sight and sound in the Marinell–Florimell relationship, relating them to the Neoplatonic debate on the relative superiority of the senses; in 'Spenser and Sidney on the *Vaticinium*' Louise Schleiner notes how Spenser and E.K. allow a wider scope than does Sidney for the prophetic poet, as distinct from the 'maker'; and David J. Baker argues that Spenser's *View of Ireland* reveals the vulnerability of English law to subversion and manipulation, and was a plea for the direct imposition of Elizabeth's transcendent authority. Somehow it seems a less stimulating collection than some previous volumes.

Major discussions of Spenser, however, fill Harold Bloom's selection of *Modern Critical Views*[43] from the 1960s to 1986; t.:e editor's introductory essay, apparently originally intended for a students' selective edition (waste not, want not) relates Spenser to Bloom's favourite Protestant-mythological tradition of Milton, Blake, and the Romantics, and the last, written for the volume by Donald Cheney, is an interesting if somewhat rambling account of *The Faerie Queene*'s structure and the manipulation of Chaucerian material (especially the Squire), focusing on Spenser's developing sense of Envy, understood to mean all that militates against cohesive creation. In between, Northrop Frye, A. C. Hamilton, and Thomas Greene in the early 1960s discuss the larger structural patterns of the poem, before Thomas P. Roche Jr, Donald Cheney, Bartlett Giamatti, and Harry Berger explore four major mythic centres, and Isabel MacCaffrey, Angus Fletcher, and Patricia Parker consider allegory and romance; and from the 1980s there are Lawrence Manley, Kenneth Gross, Peter Sachs, and John Hollander, concerned with various Spenserian beginnings. The collection is an invaluable introductory volume.

Taking the books of *The Faerie Queene* and minor works in turn: Jacqueline T. Miller notes 'The Omission in Red Cross Knight's Story' (*ELH*) in his failing to tell Una's parents of his involvement with Duessa, despite the narrator's claim that he had been frank, and suggests that the reader is expected to note this, and be provoked into suspicion of the narrative medium. Gerald Morgan provides an impressive and carefully discriminating account of 'The Idea of Temperance in the Second Book' (*RES*) in the light of Aquinas, demonstrating

43. *Edmund Spenser: Modern Critical Views*, ed. and intro. by Harold Bloom. ChelseaH. pp. x + 301. $27.50.

Spenser's skilful analysis of moral qualities, his integration of moral argument with narrative, and the unambiguousness of his poetry (so there!). Books III and IV were favourites for discussion again. L. Woodbridge discusses 'Amoret and Belphoebe: Fairytale and Myth' (*N&Q*), deriving the story of their conception from a medieval version of Sleeping Beauty, where a sleeping rape victim conceives twins, the Sun and Moon (the story being a variant of the myth of Latona, mother of Apollo and Diana by Zeus). Patricia Fumerton provided one of the more intriguing historicist essays in 'Exchanging Gifts: The Elizabethan Currency of Children and Poetry' (*ELH*): here Malinowskian anthropology initiates analysis of Elizabethan (and Irish) practices of child wardship and fostering – child exchange as a means of social cohesion, which she relates not only to the fostering of Amoret and Belphoebe, and the children in the Garden of Adonis, but also to Spenser's offering of his offspring poem to his benefactors, in a cycle of exchange. This seems an appropriate point to note Barbara L. Estrin's *The Raven and the Lark* [44], a study of the Lost Child plot in Malory, Spenser (*FQ* Books I, III–VI), Sidney, and Shakespeare, a romance that explores – and re-assures – anxieties about ancestry and identity, and sublimates anxieties about profiteering from wardship into fantasies of social reform (as Lillian Robinson might note). Theresa M. Krier has to work rather hard with her study of four incidents of 'Abashedness in *The Faerie Queene* [Book III]' (*MP*), presented as moments of psychological drama, when the external world challenges the self's inward privacy and identity, while Reed Way Dasenbrock, in 'Escaping the Squires' Double Bind in Books III and IV' (*SEL*) elaborates complexities equal to Spenser's in connection with the contradictions of Petrarchan love and of inequalities in power and desire, as revealed by the various squires and the main-group lovers: Spenser rejects destructive Petrarchist love, celebrating equality, reciprocity, and complementariness. This rejection is part of Joseph Loewenstein's theme in 'Echo's Ring' (*ELR*), discussing *Epithalamion*, where Spenser models his persona on Orpheus, the poet whose song embodies cosmic sympathies, as the refrain suggests harmony between the song and the created world; but as Orpheus could not wrest *his* bride from death, so echo undermines the power of human utterance; the poem (with the *Amoretti*) interrupts *The Faerie Queene*, operating as a critique of a degenerate Petrarchism, while the cost of marriage threatens to be the loss of lyric voice. The *View of Ireland* and Book V provoked conflicting responses: Paul Gaston offers a shocked modern liberal's view of 'Spenser's Order, Spenser's Ireland' [45], seeing both works in terms of 'fantasy as propaganda', where Spenser's 'imperialistic bigotry' produces fantasies of dehumanized rebels and beneficial authoritarian rule; in contrast, Sheila T. Cavanagh's 'Such was Irena's Countenance' (*TSLL*) defends Spenser against C. S. Lewis's charge of 'wickedness' and 'corrupt imagination' regarding Ireland, suggesting that Spenser's *View* is more informed and benevolent than that of his contemporaries, or has since been recognized, while Book V presents the difficulties of achieving justice in any real world.

44. *The Raven and the Lark: Lost Children in Literature of the English Renaissance*, by Barbara L. Estrin. BuckU/AUP (1985). pp. 228. $29.50.

45. In *Forms of the Fantastic: Selected Essays from the Third International Conference on the Fantastic in Literature and Film*, ed. by Jan Hokensen and Howard Pearce. Greenwood. pp. xiv + 262. $45.

Finally, on Spenser's early verse, we may note Steven Marx's discussion of pastoral[46] as a rejection of middle-age and social responsibility, a liberty claimed by youth and by age: their dialectical struggle provided the essential pattern of Elizabethan pastoral, and Spenser's *Calender* uses it to trace Immerito's progress in his assimilation and harmonization of the debate. In two articles (*N&Q*) Anthony Brian Taylor usefully traces Spenser's debts to Arthur Golding's translation of *Metamorphoses*, both in *The Faerie Queene* and in the minor poems respectively.

46. *Youth Against Age: Generational Strife in Renaissance Poetry*, by Steven Marx. Lang (1985). pp. xiii + 252. $27.70.

Shakespeare

A. N. PARR, RUSSELL JACKSON, JONATHAN BATE, and PAUL DEAN

This chapter has the following sections: 1. Editions and Textual Matters; 2. Biography and Background; 3 Shakespeare in the Theatre; 4. Criticism: (a) General, (b) Comedies and Romances, (c) Histories, (d) Tragedies, (e) Poems. Sections 1 and 2 are by A.N. Parr, section 3 is by Russell Jackson, sections 4(a), (b), and (e) are by Jonathan Bate, and sections 4(c) and (d) are by Paul Dean.

SQ's comprehensive annual bibliography remains well organized and indexed, and has useful brief annotation; this year it includes 3,871 items. *ShS*'s 'The Year's Contributions to Shakespearian Study' takes the form of a narrative; unfortunately its section on 'Critical Studies' is at the moment a year behind those on 'Shakespeare's Life, Times, and Stage', and 'Editions and Textual Studies'. There are review-essays in the appropriate journals, such as *ELR* and *SEL*. *ShJE* has an extensive but unannotated annual listing. Garland continue to produce invaluable annotated bibliographies on individual plays of work published between about 1940 and 1980; recent additions include volumes on *The Merchant of Venice*, *Timon of Athens*, *Richard III*, and *A Midsummer Night's Dream*[1]. All are lucid in their summaries of the material; the massive volume on *Dream* is comprehensive almost to excess, that on *Merchant* thorough enough, and that on *Timon* circumscribed by the limits of criticism on the play. I have not seen the volume on *Richard III*. Larry S. Champion's *The Essential Shakespeare: An Annotated Bibliography of Major Modern Studies*[2], while inevitably selective, is extremely helpful – its aim is to annotate 'the most significant items of Shakespeare scholarship from 1900 through 1984'.

What may in future come to be seen as a key aid, the *Bibliotheca*

1. All Garland. *'The Merchant of Venice': An Annotated Bibliography*, by Thomas Wheeler. (1985). pp. xxii + 386. $36. *'Timon of Athens': An Annotated Bibliography*, by John J. Ruszkiewicz. pp. xxvii + 274. $42. *'Richard III': An Annotated Bibliography*, by James A. Moore. pp. liv + 867. $100. *'A Midsummer Night's Dream': An Annotated Bibliography*, by D. Allen Carroll and Gary Jay Williams. pp. xxxvii + 641. $75.
2. *The Essential Shakespeare: An Annotated Bibliography of Major Modern Studies*, by Larry S. Champion. Hall. pp. xiv + 463. $55.

Shakespeariana[3] on microfiche, has begun to appear. The scale of this project is vast: it will eventually comprise 'the largest body of material on William Shakespeare and his world ever assembled in a single published collection . . . now being made available in convenient and economical microfiche' ('economical' presumably refers to space, not price – the six 'Subject Units' available to date would cost a total of $12,885). The first six collections are: *Shakespeare's Editors Since Rowe*, overseen by the ubiquitous Stanley Wells and Gary Taylor, including such editions as Johnson's, Boswell Jr's twenty-one-volume *Variorum*, and the old Arden; *Printing and the Book Trade*; *The Theatre and its Players in Shakespeare's Time*; *Adaptations and Acting Versions 1660–1980*, an especially valuable collection, with selections all the way from Nahum Tate to Charles Marowitz; *Shakespeare Bibliographies and Periodicals*, from the expert hands of Philip Brockbank and Susan Brock at the Shakespeare Institute, including complete runs of *ShJE* and *ShJW* up to 1980, *SQ* to 1985, *ShS* to 1984, and so on; and *Shakespeare's Life: Facts, Fictions and Speculations (including Anti-Stratfordian Theories)*, edited by Samuel Schoenbaum, embracing everything from facsimiles of original documents to the William Ireland forgeries. So all one needs is a microfiche reader and a very great deal of money, and one can set up a personal Shakespeare research institute [J.B.].

1. Editions and Textual Matters

The year 1986 was a thin one for editions of individual plays: NCaS has temporarily dried up, and the Oxford texts of *Hamlet*, *1 Henry IV*, and *The Tempest* are not published until 1987, although they have a bearing on this review and I shall refer to some of them in passing. Not seen are *Macbeth*, edited by Linda Cookson, *The Merchant of Venice*, edited by Gāmini and Fenella Salgādo, and *Romeo and Juliet*, edited by Patrick Colton (Longman), which have appeared in LST, a series aimed particularly at GCSE candidates and presenting each play with facing commentary, boxed questions, and an introductory essay. The NPS has gained a splendid edition by John Kerrigan of the *Sonnets* and *A Lover's Complaint*[4]. The editor argues persuasively that the neglected *Complaint* is an integral part of Shakespeare's design, which was modelled (as Edmond Malone originally pointed out) on the tradition established by Daniel's *Delia* (1592), whereby a sonnet sequence is followed by a lyric interlude (here, Sonnets 153–4) and a long poem. Trenchant – and occasionally over-dismissive – in its judgements, the introduction is particularly good on the question of homoerotic feeling in the Young Man sonnets; and the commentary

3. *Bibliotheca Shakespeariana*. MI: Pergamon. *Shakespeare's Editors Since Rowe*, ed. by S. Wells and G. Taylor. 770 fiche. $3,100. *Printing and the Book Trade*, ed. by A. Yamada. 419 fiche. $1,300. *The Theatre and its Players in Shakespeare's Time*, ed. by A. Gurr. 284 fiche. $1,150. *Adaptations and Acting Versions 1660–1980*, ed. by M. Dobson. 342 fiche. $1,000. *Shakespeare Bibliographies and Periodicals*, ed. by J. P. Brockbank and S. Brock. 1,172 fiche. $4,140. *Shakespeare's Life: Facts, Fictions and Speculations (including Anti-Stratfordian Theories)*, ed. by S. Schoenbaum. 548 fiche. $2,195. Individual titles available at $4.50 per microfiche.
4. *'The Sonnets' and 'A Lover's Complaint'*, ed. by John Kerrigan. NPS. Penguin. pp. 458. pb £4.95.

is full and illuminating whilst avoiding the excessive ingenuity of certain glosses in Stephen Booth's edition (*YW* 58.167–8).

The major textual event of the year was the publication of the Oxford *Complete Works*, in separate modernized and old-spelling editions[5]. This project is to be completed by a *Textual Companion*, but until that arrives we are reliant on earlier published statements by Stanley Wells and Gary Taylor (*YW* 65.189–90; 66.206–9) for explanation of a text that contains many surprises. The chronology of the works has been revised, and so have the titles of several plays, not to mention characters' names; there are two texts of *King Lear*, and in general the practice of conflating the Quarto and Folio editions of a work in pursuit of a Shakespearean 'original' has been replaced by an attempt to distinguish the playwright's first thoughts from revision, his own or someone else's (Middleton as adapter of Shakespeare looms large in this edition). Not all recent discoveries have found their way in: for instance, in *The Tempest* IV.i.123, Ferdinand still declares 'So rare a wondered father and a wise', although the proven correct reading 'wife' is adopted by Stephen Orgel in his 1987 Oxford edition. But nearly everything has been rethought, and in the modern-spelling volume at least, the results are challenging and accessible, as well as being attractively priced. It deserves a wide audience.

The old-spelling edition raises more doubts. Scholars who at present quote Renaissance texts in 'original' spelling but feel compelled to use a modernized Shakespeare will be able to adopt a more consistent practice; on the other hand, the arrival of this long-wished-for volume may well have the effect of exposing the arguments for old spelling to critical re-examination. The tensions inherent in such editions are far more apparent with Shakespeare than, say, Dekker or Massinger, partly because the editor of the former has an eye on the wider readership and is moved to add stage directions (the resulting pastiche descriptions of stage action, such as 'Musicke plaies', cause me some uneasiness); partly because the text which has evolved over 250 years of modern-spelling editing, with emendations and other rationalizations, is required to be translated back into something like an Elizabethan/Jacobean form. The result, as Frank Kermode pointed out in *LRB*, is to give an appearance of false authenticity to relatively modern adjustments, such as 'An *Automne* 'twas/That grew the more by reaping', or Sir Toby's 'diuers colour'd stocke'.

Yet it may be our expectations of old-spelling texts that are at fault. Modern bibliography has done much to foster the idea that conservative (and virtually unusable) editions like those of Fredson Bowers are good for us, and that their reliability and authority consist in making the achievement of an accurate text separate from the pursuit of that text's meaning. A comment by Gary Taylor in a stimulating article on emendation, 'Inventing Shakespeare' (*ShJW*), is relevant here: 'Insofar as modern textual criticism is . . . ambitious to raise itself to the dignity of a science, to that very degree it inhibits its own imaginative capacity to solve the problems whose existence first brought it into being.' Taylor stresses the primary editorial task of 'the solution of cruces'; that the point needs making today is an indication of how the formidable labours of bibliographers have often failed to connect with wider needs. The Oxford project

5. Both OUP. *William Shakespeare: The Complete Works*, ed. by Stanley Wells and Gary Taylor. Original-Spelling Edition. pp. lxiii + 1456. £75. [Modern-spelling edn.] pp. xlvii + 1432. £19.95.

builds upon the methods but breaks decisively with the spirit of that kind of
textual scholarship; and it has had the courage of its convictions, unlike some of
the recent Cambridge volumes, in printing texts which are the logical outcome
of editorial theories about them. (Thus, both the *Complete Works* and G. R.
Hibbard's separate edition of *Hamlet* give us a text based on the Folio,
believing this to be Shakespeare's revision of the play, and consequently
relegating a number of passages – including most of IV.iv – to an appendix.)
But the imaginative boldness of the enterprise seems oddly compromised in the
old-spelling volume. Here the editors have been slower to emend and embellish,
and yet the extent of their intervention is still such as to jeopardize the claims of
this volume to be in some sense more authentic than its modernized counterpart. An introductory essay by Vivian Salmon claims that it will allow us 'to
study the texts as they appeared to [our] predecessors nearly four centuries
ago'; but anyone in pursuit of this impossible goal is more likely to be consoled
by the plain virtues of the Norton Facsimile of the Folio (*YW* 49.134).

The old-spelling edition is perhaps the clearest indication of the Oxford
editors' lingering belief that the Shakespearean text can be redeemed from
history, that there are indeed originals to be recovered. In separate articles in
SQ Jonathan Goldberg ('Textual Properties') and Marion Trousdale ('A Trip
through Divided Kingdoms') argue that the theoretical implications of the new
textual criticism have not been faced by those practising it – that the sovereign
author and the timeless work of art are concepts at odds with what recent work
has disclosed about the constant remaking of Shakespeare's plays. Goldberg
favours an approach 'more responsive to the radical historicity of the texts that
we miscall Shakespeare's but which are and always have been the product of
textual and critical interventions'. There are the makings of an important
debate here, but unfortunately Goldberg's rejection of the 'rationale of copy-
text' leads him into a strained and pretentious reading of Malvolio's letter scene
(disclosing 'a textuality that is radically unstable') which scarcely illustrates the
fruitful alliance between poststructuralism and textual criticism that both
writers see as the basis of new work.

In '"This Son of Yorke": Textual and Literary Criticism Again' (*SQ*) James
P. Hammersmith tackles the sort of problem which Goldberg's perspective is
unlikely to admit but which remains stubbornly there for the working editor:
namely, how to represent in a modern-spelling edition of *Richard III* the
numerous puns on *sun/son* so that their ironic import is properly registered. He
is surely right to argue that the solution lies in critical judgement as much as in
textual logic, but his case would be less vulnerable to avant-gardist objections if
it did not turn upon establishing Shakespeare's intentions at the moment of
writing. Those intentions are under scrutiny from another angle, for Steven
Urkowitz, 'Reconsidering the Relationship of Quarto and Folio Texts of
Richard III' (*ELR*), has found a new candidate for authorial revision.
Countering D. L. Patrick's argument (*YW* 17.126), accepted by nearly all
modern editors, that the Quarto is a memorial reconstruction of the text found
in F, he emphasizes 'the purposeful variations between [Q] and F' which are
apparent if the two are compared in critical and theatrical terms. Like Gary
Taylor in 'Inventing Shakespeare', Urkowitz demonstrates the need for
creative interplay between textual criticism and other lines of enquiry. And if
the heart sinks a little at his conclusion that 'we need editions of *Richard III*
"texts" rather than of an unknowable *Richard III* "text"', it is nonetheless
one that is logically and forcefully arrived at.

In 'The Relevance of Cast-Off Copy in Determining the Nature of Omissions' (*SB*) Eric Rasmussen contributes to the revision debate by suggesting that where a play was set and printed by formes (and the copy therefore 'cast off') it may be possible to determine whether the omission of lines is the result of a deliberate cut or an oversight on the part of the compositor. He cites *Hamlet* I.ii.58–61, lines which are found in Q2 but whose heavy pruning in F appears to leave the compositor short at the end of his page (sig. nn5v), which he fills by expanding three lines into six. This suggests that the omission of two and a half of the four lines may have been accidental rather than a cut marked in the copy-text. Since the passage is one of those where we might suspect that Q2 has been trimmed to tighten up the action, this line of enquiry is worth extending.

Barbara Everett (*RES*) sets out to solve 'Two Damned Cruces': the 'dam'd colour'd stocke' in *Twelfth Night* I.iii.126, and Cassio 'almost damn'd in a faire Wife', in *Othello* I.i.23. On the latter she is brilliantly suggestive both about the way 'damned' has, 'like all such words of power, exerted a kind of hypnotic force on all the play's editors', inhibiting the effort to make good sense of it; and about the relationship between this verbal puzzle and Iago's art of furtive implication. Her proposed solutions will not convince everyone, but the whole argument deserves attention.

Two pieces in *N&Q* are of interest. In 'Armado's "Fadge Not" in *Love's Labour's Lost*' R. J. C. Watt argues convincingly against Stanley Wells's proposal to emend V.i.141, 'fadge [succeed] not' to 'fadge now', on the grounds that Armado means 'Even if this fails we'll have a show'; and MacD. P. Jackson demonstrates that 'The Manuscript Copy for the Quarto (1598) of *1 Henry IV*' was probably set from a scribal transcript rather than Shakespeare's autograph. Jackson also contributes a lucid and informative chapter on 'The Transmission of Shakespeare's Text' to the new *Cambridge Companion to Shakespeare Studies*[6]. R. L. Horn (*AN&Q*) argues that the Q/F reading 'stayers' in *The Merchant of Venice* III.ii.84 ('whose harts are all as false/As stayers of sand') should be retained in modernized editions, instead of the F4 reading 'stairs'. In '"My father; poorly led?"' (*ELN*) Gilian West has an attractive solution to the supposed crux in *King Lear* IV.i.10, Edgar's first response to the blinded Gloucester. This is a crux only because of the corrected Q reading 'parti,eyd', which has given rise to speculation that the compositor, realizing that his first shot 'poorlie,leed' did not represent what he found in the (perhaps illegible) script, tried to recover the correct reading but failed to make adequate sense of it. The Oxford editors prefer 'partie-eyd' to F's 'poorely led' in *The Tragedie of King Lear*, but oddly retain corrected Q's punctuation 'partie,eyd' in *The Historie*, manifestly defective though it is. West suggests that Shakespeare wrote 'purblid-eied', which is graphically plausible and introduces a word that occurs in other plays. But the argument seems incomplete as long as it remains purely textual.

Two manuscripts which have a rathr oblique relationship to the Shakespearean canon have come under fresh scrutiny in *SQ*. Laetitia Yeandle musters new evidence for 'The Dating of Sir Edward Dering's Copy of "The

6. *The Cambridge Companion to Shakespeare Studies*, ed. by Stanley Wells. CUP. pp. xii + 329. hb £27.50, pb £8.95.

History of King Henry the Fourth"', showing that this conflation of the two parts of Shakespeare's *Henry IV* was made not later than February 1622/3 (thus antedating the First Folio by nearly a year). And Giorgio Melchiori has subjected the manuscript of *Sir Thomas More* to careful analysis and concludes that the additions (including Shakespeare's) and other alterations to the original text were made not later than 1593–4.

Finally, I have not been able to see *One Touch of Shakespeare* edited by John Velz and Frances N. Teague (Folger/AUP), which collects the letters written to J. P. Norris by Joseph Crosby, a nineteenth-century businessman and bibliophile living in America, on numerous problems in Shakespeare's text; it was noticed by Terence Hawkes (*TLS*, 10 April 1987) in a wide-ranging and provocative review of current work.

2. Biography and Background

On the biographical front, the disintegrators and A. L. Rowse have had a year off, and in their absence things have been fairly quiet. John Boe (*SQ*) has found a new candidate for Mr. W.H. in the shape of William Hall, not the publisher nominated by some other critics but the father of Shakespeare's son-in-law John Hall. He constructs a pleasant hypothesis around evidence that in most marriages the two sets of parents 'were at least acquainted', that in Hall's will only his professional books were explicitly bequeathed, and that his other, somewhat irresponsible son Dive was his executor and quite capable, if he found a manuscript of poems by a famous author amongst his father's papers, of selling it to the nearest publisher for ready cash. All of this is pure speculation, as Boe readily admits, but it keeps the pot bubbling.

In an absorbing and well-researched article entitled '"Willm Shakespeare 1609": The Flower Portrait Revisited' Paul Bertram and Frank Cossa (*SQ*) reassess the claims of the painting, now in the Royal Shakespeare Theatre Gallery and recently restored, to be 'the only surviving portrait of Shakespeare made during his lifetime'. The painting is commonly regarded as an eighteenth-century forgery, a view heavily influenced by M. H. Spielmann's contention in the early years of this century that it derives from the Droeshout engraving on the Folio title-page. Bertram and Cossa expose the flaws in Spielmann's reasoning, and use the evidence of the 1979 restoration to reconsider the portrait's claim to be instead the original of the engraving – an argument which has had few supporters since the last century. There is clearly more work to be done on this, and the authors make some useful suggestions about the directions this might take.

In 'Robert Keysar, Playhouse Speculator' (*SQ*) William Ingram enters the litigious world of Jacobean theatrical investment, and traces part of the career of Robert Keysar, who was one of a syndicate managing the children at Blackfriars in 1608 when the Burbages reclaimed the lease on their playhouse. Ingram suggests that such men are unduly neglected, and there is apparently a mass of evidence of their dealings, much of it in lawsuits, waiting to be investigated. In 'Two Notes on *Hamlet*' (*MLR*) G. Blakemore Evans offers support from a contemporary elegy on the death of Richard Burbage for the contention that the reference in *Hamlet* (II.ii.357–8) to 'Hercules and his load' is to the sign of the Globe playhouse (and perhaps also to its flag).

The *Hutchinson Shakespeare Dictionary*[7] shows signs of having been rushed out by its publisher to cash in on the current vogue for guidebooks to the Bard, with a misprint on the cover, a promised set of illustrations that fails to appear, and a contents page made useless by misnumbering. The introductory essay, however, is readable and informative: following a biographical sketch, there is an account of the circumstances of play production in Shakespeare's day, and, rather unexpectedly, a fairly full discussion of the non-dramatic verse. It is a pity in view of the latter that names like Stephen Booth and John Padel are not mentioned or included in the bibliography, but then the whole enterprise, particularly in its A–Z listings, takes little notice of current controversy and debate, offering no help, for instance, to anyone interested in the two-text theory of *King Lear*. On the other hand, the assurance that Lear dies of a broken heart is offered twice, as a result of the odd policy of listing and discussing both play and eponymous hero, and recapitulating plot summary with character sketch. Many of the synopses are similarly old-fashioned and seem to be aimed at a popular audience; yet we are given specialized information like the nicknames of Nashe and Dekker. Are either students or tourists helped by the information that Cleopatra is 'part whore, part queen, and quintessential woman'? Too many statements in the *Dictionary* are similarly obsolescent. Nonetheless, the general reader will find much that is useful, and although the historical entries are occasionally startling (like the reference to Queen Elizabeth's 'affair' with Essex on p. 134), they provide a convenient guide to the contexts of Shakespeare's work. Finally, an unreserved welcome for the new edition of C. T. Onions's *Shakespeare Glossary*[8], enlarged and revised by Robert D. Eagleson: an indispensable reference work brought thoroughly up to date.

3. Shakespeare in the Theatre

(a) Elizabethan and Jacobean Performance

Articles by Peter Thomson and Alan C. Dessen in the *Cambridge Companion*[6] deal respectively with the playhouses and playgoers of Shakespeare's time and the dramatist's use of his theatre's conventions. Two articles in *SEL* address the interpretive significance of Elizabethan staging methods: W. B. Worthen's 'The Weight of Antony: Staging "Character" in *Antony and Cleopatra*' and James L. Hill's '"What, are they children?" Shakespeare's Tragic Women and the Boy Actors'. Worthen considers the relationship between 'character' constituted by the actor's performance and that created in a quasi-novelistic manner by what is said about the person represented; he connects this with the play's metatheatrical strategies. Hill argues that in representing mature women through the medium of boy performers Shakespeare 'has carefully avoided complex motivational and emotional development'. Ways of seeing and signifying are also considered by J.–M. Maguin in 'Strategies for the Page and Strategies for the Stage' (*CahiersE*): the relationship between emblems and stage images should remind us that

7. *Hutchinson Shakespeare Dictionary: An A–Z Guide to Shakespeare's Plays, Characters, and Contemporaries*, ed. by Sandra Clark. Hutchinson. pp. 291. pb £4.95.

8. *A Shakespeare Glossary*, by C. T. Onions, enlarged and rev. by Robert D. Eagleson. Clarendon. pp. xviii + 326. hb £17.50, pb £5.95.

'interpictoriality' (to use Maguin's term) exists as a counterpart to intertextuality. *ShakB* has brief articles on stage convention by Alan C. Dessen ('What's in an Ending?') and Maurice Charney (on soliloquies and asides in *Hamlet*).

(b) Performance Since 1660

The *Cambridge Companion*[6] includes a brief history of British Shakespearean staging from 1660 to 1900 by Russell Jackson. *ThS* has an interesting discussion by Leigh Woods of the treatment of madness in 'Garrick's *King Lear* and the English Malady'.

Shakespeare and the Victorian Stage[9], edited by Richard Foulkes, is a stimulating collection of papers on aspects of theatrical interpretation, which derive from a conference held at the University of Leicester. Peter Thomson contributes a paper on 'The Secret Self of Henry Irving', relating the 'gloom and glory' of the actor's public persona to 'his century's image'. It is interesting to set this beside an essay in Nina Auerbach's *Romantic Imprisonment*[10], which offers a specifically feminist interpretation of Ellen Terry's relationship with Irving and the Lyceum, described in somewhat lurid fashion as home, husband, and prison to the beleaguered spirit of the actress. 'Ellen Terry's laughter', Auerbach claims, 'was her secret from her mythmaking audiences', a statement which may surprise those familiar with the many glowing accounts of her comic talents. The subject matter of the essay resembles that of Elaine Showalter's piece on Ophelia in *Shakespeare and the Question of Theory* (*YW* 66.213), but the strategy is Auerbach's characteristic one of surprising juxtapositions and assertions, producing a feminist melodrama out of seemingly 'innocent' materials. Far more decorous, and much less stimulating, is Mary Hamer's 'Shakespeare's Rosalind and her Public Image' (*ThR*), which cites enough reviews to give a sense of the popular Victorian sentimentalization of this character and some more recent modifications of it. In *ThHS* Daniel J. Watermeier writes on 'Edwin Booth's Iago'. Contemporary reviews and illustrations are cited together with a contemporary manuscript analysis now in the Harvard Theatre Collection. Watermeier draws attention to the quasi-Mephistophelian interpretation of Iago and the ways in which Booth tailored the play to make his character's development the principal focus. In an account of 'Charles Kean's Antiquarianism: The Designs for *Richard II*, 1857' (*TD*) Dennis J. Sporre reproduces illustrations of the designs in question, relates them to Victorian landscape painting and scenography, and raises (in a footnote) the problem of distinguishing between renderings of the designs and 'artists' impressions' of the staged scenes. The phenomenon of the international star is illuminated by Marvin Carlson's *The Italian Shakespearians: Performances by Ristori, Salvini and Rossi in England and America*[11]. Carlson's lively, well-documented book brings together material from Italian, British, and American sources.

Roger Warren, in the *Cambridge Companion*[6], briskly surveys productions 'on the twentieth century stage', with particular emphasis on work at Stratford-

9. *Shakespeare and the Victorian Stage*, ed. by Richard Foulkes. CUP. pp. xviii + 311. £30.

10. *Romantic Imprisonment: Women and Other Glorified Outcasts*, by Nina Auerbach. ColU. pp. xxiv + 316. pb £9.20.

11. *The Italian Shakespearians: Performances by Ristori, Salvini and Rossi in England and America*, by Marvin Carlson. Folger/AUP. pp. 224. £19.95.

upon-Avon and Stratford, Ontario. The work of 'fringe' companies, studio staging at Stratford and elsewhere, and productions outside the English-speaking theatre are not included in his account, which stops with John Barton's 1978 *Love's Labour's Lost*. An uninitiated reader might infer from this that the RSC's proscenium-arch productions represented the *ne plus ultra* of modern Shakespeare. More characteristic of Warren's informed and incisive criticism is his account of the 'John Hirsch Years' (1981–5) at Stratford, Ontario (*ShS*). William P. Shaw (*ThS*) surveys 'Meager Lead and Joyous Consequences: RSC Triumphs among Shakespeare's Minor Plays', proposing bravely to see whether the productions under discussion have anything in common or just happen to be happy accidents of the right show in the right hands at the right time. In this amiable spirit he quotes extensively from reviews of Peter Brook's *Love's Labour's Lost* and *Titus*, the Hall/Barton *Troilus*, and Terry Hands's *Henry VI*. The conclusion is that the ability to give first-class treatment to what may seem second-class scripts is a benefit of having an institution like the RSC. The same company's productions of *Merry Wives* are among those considered in Peter Evans's enjoyable survey '"To the Oak, to the Oak!" The Finale of *The Merry Wives of Windsor*' (*TN*).

In a fascinating account of Margaret Webster's 1943 *Othello* (*ThHS*) Susan Spector draws on unpublished correspondence to show the director's troubled relationship with her cast: in one exasperated letter Webster characterized Paul Robeson, José Ferrer, and Uta Hagen as 'that big, black jelly-fish and those two conceited little asses'. *ThR* has articles by Linda McJ. Micheli, who discusses 'Margaret Webster's *Henry VIII*' (1946), relating it to the grand scenic tradition of Beerbohm Tree and comparing it with Tyrone Guthrie's production, and by Felicia Hardison Londré on the political capital made out of *Coriolanus* in Paris in 1934 at the time of the Stavisky affair. In *Assaph*, a new journal from Tel Aviv, Darko Suvin compares Brecht's *Coriolan* with the reworking of it used in the famous Berliner Ensemble production. Suvin's prose manages to be both terse and opaque, but the comparison yields interesting evidence of divergences between the Ensemble's and Brecht's uses of the play. Ekkehard Schall's discussion of 'Acting with the Berliner Ensemble' (*NTQ*) has a bearing on this production. Ann Fridén's *'Macbeth' in the Swedish Theatre, 1838–1986*[12] is meticulous and ambitious, and includes detailed accounts of important productions by Knut Ström (1928), Olof Molander (1931), and Ingmar Bergman (1940, 1944, and 1948).

In his volume on *Measure for Measure* in the Text and Performance series[13] Graham Nicholls has a workmanlike and perceptive account of the BBC TV version and three stage productions (by John Barton 1970, Charles Marowitz 1975, Barry Kyle 1978). The series format still seems, by dividing into 'text' and 'performance' sections, to imply that plays have a determinable meaning which productions mediate more or less successfully. In Nicholls's case the 'text' section is unremarkably A-levelish but the 'performance' quite well done. Unfortunately there seems to be no space left for a conclusion in which the two might have been married.

12. *'Macbeth' in the Swedish Theatre, 1838–1986*, by Ann Fridén. LF. pp. x + 318. Skr 114.

13. *'Measure for Measure': Text and Performance*, by Graham Nicholls. Macmillan. pp. 94. pb £4.95.

UCrow, more of a gallimaufry than most journals in its field, has a usefully detailed description by Bernice W. Kliman of 'Opportunities Seized and Occasions Created: The Boston Shakespeare Company *Hamlet*' and a curiously redundant article, 'Fortinbras: The Unkindest Cut' in which Robert F. Willson Jr argues against the 'time-honored' theatrical custom of omitting Fortinbras from the same play. Since the 1890s this custom has been more breached than observed (Olivier's and Tony Richardson's films are notable exceptions) and it is hard to see who Willson might need to convince of the usefulness of the figure he calls 'the fabled Norwegian fighter'.

Current and recent productions continue to receive expert attention in *SQ* and *ShS*. In the former the reviews seem as wide-ranging as ever and the reviewers more uniformly expert than has always seemed the case: particularly interesting are the articles by Thomas Clayton, who puts a Minneapolis *Dream* in the context of theatrical and critical history, and Charles Frey, who scrutinizes the aims and achievements of the Ashland, Oregon Shakespearean Festival on its fiftieth anniversary. In *ShS* Nicholas Shrimpton's survey of British productions includes the Orange Tree Theatre, Richmond, staging of the First Quarto *Hamlet* as well as the usual account of National and RSC productions. Peter Holland, in 'Style at the Swan' (*EIC*), reviews the new theatre and its opening productions – including *The Two Noble Kinsmen* – and hopes that the Swan's influence will be felt in the RSC's other work. *CahiersE* continues to be an invaluable source of comment and information on performances – particularly in France – and the two *Jahrbücher* give accounts of German performances. *ShakB* reviews current productions at home (i.e. New York) and away. In *NTQ* Wilfred Harrison describes his experiences directing '*Othello* in Poland', shedding light on differences in British and Polish theatre practice, and Geraldine Cousin compares two 1985 touring productions of *The Taming of the Shrew*: that by the Medieval Players and Di Trevis's RSC staging.

The thirty-ninth issue of *ShS* takes 'Shakespeare on Film and Television' as its theme, offering eight articles and a filmography. The level of writing and scholarship is high, and the publication is a notable event in the study of Shakespeare and the modern media. Anthony Davies opens the volume with an authoritative retrospect of writing on the subject; other articles deal with Orson Welles's treatment of the second tetralogy ('*Chimes at Midnight* from Stage to Screen' by Robert Hapgood), 'Orson Welles's *Othello*: A Study of Time in Shakespeare's Tragedy' (by Lorne M. Buchman), the three modern *Macbeth* films ('*Macbeth* on Film: Politics' by E. Pearlman), 'Representing *King Lear* on Screen' (by Kenneth S. Rothwell), considering adaptations from Edwin Thanhouser (1916) to Laurence Olivier (1983), two studies on aspects of TV Shakespeare ('Verbal–Visual, Verbal–Pictorial or Textual–Televisual: Reflections on the BBC Shakespeare Series' by Michèle Willems and 'Two Types of Television Shakespeare' by Neil Taylor), and a producer's nuts-and-bolts account of 'Shakespeare on the Radio' (by Stuart Evans). This neglected but significant area of Shakespearean performance is also documented in Janet Clare's 'Theatre of the Air: A Checklist of Radio Productions of Renaissance Drama, 1922–1986', published as a supplement to *RDN*.

In the *Cambridge Companion*[6] Robert Hapgood essays a summary of 'Shakespeare on Film and Television' in a dozen pages, but manages to raise important points of discussion on the plays' suitability for performance in the new media. Peter Brook's film of *King Lear* is the principal subject of an article by Laurilyn J. Harris, 'Peter Brook's *King Lear*: Aesthetic Achievement or Far Side of the Moon?' (*ThR*), which compares it with the same director's stage production. *SFNL* celebrates its tenth anniversary with the second issue of 1986. The year's more substantial articles include Alan C. Dessen on 'The Supernatural on Television' and Maurice Charney's thoughtful 'Is Shakespeare Suitable for Television?' *SFNL* is unpretentious and serviceable, and has proved an indispensable forum for the noting and reviewing of film and TV Shakespeare productions.

Jonathan Miller's *Subsequent Performances*[14] is characteristically learned, forceful, stylish, and free from false modesty. Miller considers the principles of performing old texts, offering the notion of 'afterlife' as a means of under-standing what interpreters are doing: 'By submitting itself to the possibility of successive re-creation . . . the play passes through the development that is its birthright, and its meaning begins to be fully appreciated only when it enters a period that I shall call its *afterlife*.' He pursues the arguments for and against the director's place in the theatre, making (as might be expected) a forceful case for his own craft. His various stage and TV productions of Shakespeare's plays are recalled, with frequent reference to their sources in the visual arts and the study of psychology. The book is a fascinating compound of memoir, apologia, and argument by a remarkable director.

4. Criticism

(a) General

Three general introductory books on Shakespeare appeared at around the same time this year. None of them can be recommended particularly warmly. The approach of each is determined by the series in which it appears: OPUS, Rereading Literature, and Past Masters. OUP's OPUS books aim to pro-vide 'concise, original, and authoritative introductions to a wide range of subjects', written by experts for both general readers and students. Few could be more expert on the subject of Shakespeare than Philip Edwards; in *Shake-speare: A Writer's Progress*[15], he concisely and authoritatively surveys the entire canon. But this introduction cannot be said to be 'original': it adopts a traditional humanist approach which sees 'Relationship' as the essence of Shakespeare's plays. Edwards is best when, for example, he considers the role of male friendship in *The Two Noble Kinsmen*, *The Two Gentlemen of Verona*, and the *Sonnets*; he is not, however, willing to problematize questions of human identity – revealingly, he says of Stephen Greenblatt's *Renaissance Self-Fashioning* (*YW* 62.143): 'I can't respond with any enthusiasm to his view of the malleable self cringing under the power-structures and ideologies of the time.'

Terry Eagleton's *William Shakespeare*[16] opposes all that Edwards stands for. Eagleton's brief (conceived by himself, for he is the general editor of

14. *Subsequent Performances*, by Jonathan Miller. Faber. pp. 253. £15.

15. *Shakespeare: A Writer's Progress*, by Philip Edwards. OPUS. OUP. pp. viii + 204. £12.50.

16. *William Shakespeare*, by Terry Eagleton. RL. Blackwell. pp. x + 114. hb £12.50, pb £3.95.

Blackwell's RL) is to show that 'it is difficult to read Shakespeare without feeling that he was almost certainly familiar with the writings of Hegel, Marx, Nietzsche, Freud, Wittgenstein and Derrida'. This he does with considerable panache and frivolity, as befits his central contention that Shakespeare is all about anarchic desire and linguistic 'surplus'. Students will need to be taught to read Eagleton in a spirit as combative as his own, not to swallow him wholesale. My two principal reservations about the book are that it sometimes seems to pursue an argument merely in order to go against the grain of received opinion ('it is surely clear that positive value in *Macbeth* lies with the three witches'), and that the author appears never to have been to the theatre or have attended to the fact that Shakespeare wrote for the theatre.

Refreshingly, given that her brief is to consider her subject's place in the history of ideas, Germaine Greer has much to say about actors and audiences in her Past Master *Shakespeare*[17]. Indeed, her argument turns on the role of the audience in bringing to life Shakespeare's dramatizations of intellectual issues. So far, so good – but which audience? Greer distinguishes too sharply between an Elizabethan public theatre dominated by 'noisy groundlings' and a Jacobean coterie theatre forced to gratify the vanity of its powerful patrons (she seems to have forgotten that the public theatres had patrons too, and that Shakespeare's last plays were written for both the Globe and the Blackfriars). This is a local but symptomatic deficiency; more generally, the book suffers from Greer's *failure* to make proper distinctions, above all between historical reconstruction and personal response: Shakespeare's audience today may, like Greer, value him above all for his espousal of 'tolerance, pluralism, the talent for viable compromise, and a profound commitment to that most wasteful form of social organization, democracy', but I do not think that his original audiences, public or private, would have done so. The outdated bibliography reveals that Greer is unaware of recent research on Shakespeare and Renaissance politics.

Just how rapidly Shakespearean criticism does become outdated nowadays may be seen from the successive versions of CUP's *Companion to Shakespeare Studies*: thirty-seven years passed between the original *Companion* (1934) and the *New Companion* (1971), only fifteen between the *New Companion* and its successor[6]. In tune with the spirit of his editorial work on Shakespeare, Stanley Wells offers here a complete revision, though traces of the old *New Companion* remain visible in Samuel Schoenbaum's essay on the life and W. R. Elton's on 'Shakespeare and the Thought of his Age'. The whole collection is informative and up to date; as one would also expect of a volume edited by Stanley Wells, there is plenty of emphasis on Shakespeare in the theatre – in his own time, down the centuries, and in our own age (film and television also get a chapter). Invidious as it is to pick out individual contributors to a collection of a uniformly high standard, I was particularly impressed by MacD. P. Jackson on 'The Transmission of Shakespeare's Text' and Terence Hawkes on 'Shakespeare and New Critical Approaches', not least for the lucidity with which they introduce readers to such difficult areas as the *ductus litterarum* and the semiotics of deixis.

17. *Shakespeare*, by Germaine Greer. PastM. OUP. pp. viii + 136. hb £9.95, pb £2.95.

Shakespeare's Poetics[18] are the object of a study by Ekbert Faas. This is a thoroughly documented compendium of Shakespeare's implied views on his own art. Its first part traces the well-trodden ground of acting technique, theatrical self-consciousness, and the purposes of drama; its second tries to take on much more, as may be seen from the bold title 'Language, Creativity, Myth, Art, and Nature'. The result is somewhat patchy, moving from genuinely illuminating comparisons with Montaigne and Bacon to a disappointingly thin account of Elizabethan mythopoesis. The book's conclusion is that Shakespeare conceived of himself as above all else 'the poet of nature': a highly questionable hypostatization, for are not ideas of 'nature' always constructed by culture?

Despite what might be described as the 'essentialism' of his treatment of 'nature', Faas takes 'the dismantling of essentialist discourse' to be an effect of Shakespeare's linguistic scepticism. A very different book, Malcolm Evans's *Signifying Nothing*[19], makes much of the same idea. This is second-division Eagleton, full of subsections with titles like 'Jacques Derrida Meets the Sledded Pollax'. At times it deliberately deconstructs itself: we are given extracts from the journal of a schoolmaster in British Honduras guiltily comparing his work with that of the arch-imperialist Prospero, then told in a footnote that the whole edifice is a fiction. (A far richer account of Caliban and the discourse of colonialism is provided by Chantal Zabus in a fascinating article (*CanL*, 1985), 'A Calibanic *Tempest* in Anglophone and Francophone New World Writing'.) At other times, *Signifying Nothing* really does end up signifying nothing as it *unintentionally* deconstructs itself by means of its own misprints and elementary errors of fact: Jacques Derrida becomes Jaques, as if he has entered the text of *As You Like It*; Garrick's Jubilee is made to happen five years early, as if to remind us that facts are fictions, and so on. Evans has taken on an important subject, the inscription of Shakespeare in our national culture, but his treatment of it is glib, ill written, and ill informed. Poststructuralist cultural analysis of a similar sort is undertaken more effectively by Terence Hawkes in *That Shakespeherian Rag*[20], a stylish exposé of the unspoken ideological premises of those British Worthies, Andrew Cecil Bradley, Sir Walter Raleigh, Thomas Stearns Eliot, and John Dover Wilson – an amusing little pasquinade with a crisp political punch.

To turn from self-conscious novelty to established canons: there have been some valuable collections and re-issues. Yale are to be congratulated for making available in paperback an ample selection from the two volumes of their definitive *Johnson on Shakespeare*[21] (*YW* 49.247-8). CUP have put together Sir William Empson's *Essays on Shakespeare*[22]. Apart from a somewhat tendentious account of the Globe theatre, this material will be familiar to Empsonians: included are revised versions of his well-known essays on

18. *Shakespeare's Poetics*, by Ekbert Faas. CUP. pp. xxiv + 263. £25.

19. *Signifying Nothing: Truth's True Contents in Shakespeare's Text*, by Malcolm Evans. Harvester. pp. x + 291. £35.

20. *That Shakespeherian Rag: Essays on a Critical Process*, by Terence Hawkes. Methuen. pp. x + 131. hb £10.95, pb £4.95.

21. *Selections from Johnson on Shakespeare*, ed. by Bertrand H. Bronson with Jean M. O'Meara. Yale. pp. xl + 373. hb £35, pb £9.95.

22. *Essays on Shakespeare*, by William Empson, ed. by David B. Pirie. CUP. pp. x + 246. hb £25, pb £7.95.

Falstaff, *Hamlet*, and *Macbeth*, a characteristically trenchant attack on critics who hunt for religious symbols in the last plays, the notorious *LRB* piece of 1979 in which Puck is compared to Yuri Gagarin, and an introduction to the narrative poems which first appeared in the 1968 Signet Classic edition. The latter includes an intuition about *A Lover's Complaint* that is now borne out by John Kerrigan's work (see p. 214 above): 'I think the poem is evidently by Shakespeare on psychological grounds, and a kind of echo of the sonnets (this of course is why they were kept together, and eventually pirated together).' This way of proving criticism upon his pulses is Empson's hallmark: it is good to have his later Shakespearean essays collected in a single volume, even though they do not reveal the vintage Empson of such essays as 'Fool in Lear' and 'Honest in Othello'. The essays of another, more scrupulous if less dazzling Cambridge Shakespearean, Leo Salingar, are collected in *Dramatic Form in Shakespeare and the Jacobeans*[23]: this includes a wide-ranging piece on Shakespeare's uses of the word 'art', as well as a number of essays on individual plays, noted below.

I had hoped that *Northrop Frye on Shakespeare*[24] would have brought together between a single pair of covers such very short but richly suggestive books as *A Natural Perspective* (*YW* 46.139) and *Fools of Time* (*YW* 48.139–40). Alas, it does not: it is merely a set of undergraduate lectures on a cross-section of plays. The style is annoyingly chatty, quite unlike the Frye one is used to (I was left longing for the elegance and economy of 'The Argument of Comedy'). There are of course local insights, but all in all this is by far the least stimulating work Frye has ever published. Frye, the anatomist of archetypal structures, has never had much time for history. At a time when Shakespeare is being historicized in exciting new ways, publication oi these lectures as a *vade mecum* for college students is distinctly untimely.

So what would be a good introduction to 'the new historicism'? Perhaps an article by Thomas Cartelli, 'Ideology and Subversion in the Shakespearean Set Speech' (*ELH*). This is a helpful starting point because it re-reads and turns upside-down three speeches that have traditionally been seen as expounding 'the Elizabethan world-picture' or exemplifying Shakespeare's conservatism (Henry V on ceremony, Ulysses on degree, Portia on mercy). Cartelli, leaning on Pierre Macherey, neatly sums up the way in which 'new historical' readings subvert received ideologies: 'By "formalizing" ideology, the text begins to highlight its absences, expose its essential incompleteness, articulate the ghostly penumbra of absent signs that lurk within its pronouncements.' Another possible starting point, with an emphasis less on the construction of the body-politic and more on the fashioning of the self, would be Stephen Greenblatt's 'Psychoanalysis and Renaissance Culture' in *Literary Theory/Renaissance Texts*[25]. This account of why a Renaissance text often 'seems to invite, even to demand, a psychoanalytic approach and yet turns out to baffle or elude that approach' is mainly about the strange life of Martin Guerre in sixteenth-century

23. *Dramatic Form in Shakespeare and the Jacobeans: Essays*, by Leo Salingar. CUP. pp. x + 292. £27.50.

24. *Northrop Frye on Shakespeare*, ed. by Robert Sandler. Yale. pp. vi + 186. £12.95.

25. *Literary Theory/Renaissance Texts*, ed. by Patricia Parker and David Quint. JHU. pp. viii + 399. hb $30, pb $12.95. (Hereafter Parker and Quint.)

France, but it offers much incidental illumination of Shakespearean identities. By comparison, I found the directly Shakespearean essay in this volume, Patricia Parker's 'Deferral, Dilation, Différance: Shakespeare, Cervantes, Jonson', to be deconstruction at its most self-indulgently ludic. Another broadly 'new historical' collection, though this time with a feminist slant, is *Rewriting the Renaissance*[26], which includes '*A Midsummer Night's Dream* and the Shaping Fantasies of Elizabethan Culture: Gender, Power, Form', an essay by Louis Adrian Montrose, who in America is seen as second only to Greenblatt, and perhaps Jonathan Goldberg, as a practitioner of this kind of criticism. Montrose uses the standard new historical technique of beginning with a representative anecdote – in this instance, a dream of Simon Forman which, like Bottom's, combines grotesquery with the pleasure of kissing the queen – and ending with the subversiveness of the text under discussion: *Dream* 'discloses – perhaps, in a sense, despite itself – that patriarchal norms are compensatory for the vulnerability of men to the powers of women'. The defensive parenthesis is revealing.

Gender, power, and form are precisely the concerns of Leonard Tennenhouse in his full-length 'new historicist' study, *Power on Display*[27]. As his title suggests, Tennenhouse begins from the Orgel–Greenblatt–Goldberg premise that public display was the basis of the maintenance of Elizabethan monarchical power, that politics were theatrical and theatre was political. For Tennenhouse, the plays are especially concerned with 'representing the aristocratic body'. Under Elizabeth there was a particular interest in the female body, so female characters are placed in traditionally patriarchal positions of power; there was also the question of 'the queen's two bodies', the relationship between person and office, and it was this that led Shakespeare to write his history plays. The tragedies, however, are 'Jacobean formations of power that detach the body of the aristocratic woman from the display of male patriarchal power'. Tennenhouse is quick to point out that he is not reading the heroines of the comedies written in the 1590s as allegorical representations of Elizabeth, but that the drama is addressing issues of gender and power which played a formative role in the political discourse of the time. At times the book's 'strategies' are wilful, but Shakespeare's variety is such that any book like this which treats all the plays in the same way will inevitably succeed with some and fail with others.

One consequence of Tennenhouse's argument is that it explains Shakespeare's generic development, and in particular the break from comedy and history soon after 1600, on political instead of personal grounds. C. L. Barber's posthumous *The Whole Journey: Shakespeare's Power of Development*[28] (worked up for publication by his former student Richard P. Wheeler) is in this sense a much more traditional book: it uses 'power' to mean individual genius, and sets out to explain the development of Shakespeare's art in terms of

26. *Rewriting the Renaissance: The Discourse of Sexual Difference in Early Modern Europe*, ed. by Margaret W. Ferguson, Maureen Quilligan, and Nancy J. Vickers. UChic. pp. xxxi + 426. hb $50, pb $15.95. (Hereafter Ferguson.)

27. *Power on Display: The Politics of Shakespeare's Genres*, by Leonard Tennenhouse. Methuen. pp. x + 206. hb £20, pb £7.95.

28. *The Whole Journey: Shakespeare's Power of Development*, by C. L. Barber and Richard P. Wheeler. UCal. pp. xxx + 354. £33.25.

his life and personality. This may sound like a nineteenth-century approach, but it is not precisely that, for Freud presides as autocratically as Foucault does over the 'new historicists'. The book explores the role of the family and familial relationships in the gamut of Shakespeare's plays; the chapter on the late romances is especially rewarding, which is to be expected, since it is developed from Barber's germinal essay '"Thou that beget'st him that did thee beget": Transformation in *Pericles* and *The Winter's Tale*' (*YW* 50.182). Many of the readings are extremely sensitive, particularly when connections are made between texts – Lear's cell and Prospero's, the triangle in the *Sonnets* and analogous groupings in a variety of plays. But in the end *The Whole Journey* is vitiated by the way it insists on reading and (psycho)analysing Shakespeare in his plays – a marvellous account of doubling and the family in *The Comedy of Errors* ends in the bathos of 'When Shakespeare wrote *The Comedy of Errors*, he had left a wife in Stratford'. And when we are treated to a Freudian reading of the playwright's childhood one begins to wonder if we are not after all being given 'the mythical sorrows of Shakespeare' in another guise.

The title of Diane Elizabeth Dreher's *Domination and Defiance: Fathers and Daughters in Shakespeare*[29] is self-explanatory. I found this book crude in its historical generalizations ('The Puritans regarded life as a pilgrimage, emphasising its developmental quality' – 'all the Puritans?', one wishes to ask), unthinking in its application to Shakespeare of 'developmental psychology', and distinctly questionable in some of its assumptions about the plays (can Lear really be having a 'mid-life crisis' in his eighties?). If one believes that the 'upper tower' in which Silvia is confined by her father in *Two Gentlemen of Verona* is 'obviously phallic', one is likely to be on the same wavelength as Ms Dreher. I am not.

Leonard Barkan's *The Gods Made Flesh: Metamorphosis and the Pursuit of Paganism*[30] is an ambitious book that takes on both Ovid's book of changes and its influence. It ends with one of the best accounts yet written of Ovid's role in shaping the early Shakespeare, and in particular *Titus Andronicus* and *A Midsummer Night's Dream*. Barkan demonstrates wonderfully how reading, communicating, and interpreting are central activities in *Titus* that are derived from Shakespeare's own reading of the Philomel myth. *The Gods Made Flesh* begins with a long and immensely subtle reading of the *Metamorphoses* themselves; it is a pity that a book which starts and finishes so well overstretches itself in the middle, the general account of the Renaissance Ovid, which is altogether too thin.

Shakespeare's Dramatic Structures[31] by Anthony Brennan is a thin book in several senses: just over 150 pages of text, no references, an arbitrary selection of plays, and a limited repertory of arguments. Brennan is interested in patterns of repetition, echo, and variation in Shakespeare's scenic structure; he thus compares the scene where Lear kneels to Regan with that where he kneels to Cordelia, and works with such laborious chapter titles as '"Thrice three times

29. *Domination and Defiance: Fathers and Daughters in Shakespeare*, by Diane Elizabeth Dreher. UKen. pp. x + 204. £18.95.

30. *The Gods Made Flesh: Metamorphosis and the Pursuit of Paganism*, by Leonard Barkan. Yale. pp. xvi + 398. £30.

31. *Shakespeare's Dramatic Structures*, by Anthony Brennan. RKP. pp. viii + 163. £22.50.

the value of this bond'': The Three Trials in *The Merchant of Venice*' and 'The Journey from ''wherefore art thou Romeo?'' to ''Where is my Romeo?'': The Structure of *Romeo and Juliet*'. Brennan has quite a sharp director's eye for the shape of a play, but spends far too much time counting lines and drawing up lists. The book has an outdated feel: one section considers the long absence of Cordelia from the stage, but Brennan's apparent ignorance of the two-text theory means that he misses the opportunity to ask how this is affected by the omission of IV.iii from the Folio version.

Shakespeare's theatrical self-consciousness has been much studied over the past twenty-five years: in *CompD* Richard Fly surveys 'The Evolution of Shakespearean Metadrama: Abel, Burkhardt, and Calderwood' (Ann Righter is oddly absent from this list). Theatre, politics, reception, and influence seem to be the areas favoured by the German contributors to the *Jahrbücher*. *ShJE* includes in the latter categories: Walter Cohen, 'Shakespeares Realität und Shakespeares Realismus: Neue politische Interpretationen' (a review-essay on recent feminist and 'new historical' work); Hans Henning, 'Schillers Shake-speare-Rezeption' (a consideration of both Schiller's prose and his plays); Hartmut Marhold, 'Shakespeare im ''Konsequenten Naturalismus'' [of Arno Holz and Johannes Schlaf]'. *ShJW* has, for politics, Ina Schabert, 'Shakespeare als politischer Philosoph: Sein Werk und die Schule von Leo Strauss', and for influence on other arts, Hildegard Hammerschmidt-Hummel, 'Shakespeare in der Bildkunst – Arbeiten an einem Projekt'. *ShJW* also includes an article in English by Brian Vickers which rather uneasily attempts to relate Shakespeare's shifts between verse and prose to Arnold van Gennep's model of 'Rites of Passage'.

Tetsuo Anzai's *Shakespeare and Montaigne Reconsidered*[32] can be recom-mended. Anzai is not interested in cataloguing local parallels so much as exploring broader affinities. He points out quite properly that the most Montaigne-influenced moments in *Hamlet*, *Lear*, and *The Tempest* are espe-cially important ones for the respective plays' visions. He also suggests that these three plays show Shakespeare moving from stoicism to radical scepticism to a benevolent view of nature, and that this progression corresponds closely to Montaigne's own tripartite intellectual development. This is among the best Japanese Shakespearean criticism I have encountered. Meanwhile, the growth of Chinese interest in the plays is discussed by Qi-Xin He (*SQ*). And from France, a brisk and wide-ranging essay by Jean-Marie Maguin offers a tour through 'Shakespeare et les terreurs de la nuit'[33].

Shakespeare's *Nachleben* is no longer the exclusive preserve of German scholars. Donald W. Rude's 'Two Echoes of Shakespeare in Popular Seventeenth-Century Literature' (*N&Q*) reveals that the popular writers Richard Flecknoe and William Winstanley knew some of the plays. One thinks of Shakespearean allusion in popular writing as an eighteenth- and nineteenth-century phenomenon: it would be interesting to know more of its extent in the mid/later seventeenth century. In *CLS* Nancy Carolyn Michael considers the (albeit indirect) relationship between *A Midsummer Night's Dream* and Andreas Gryphius's *Peter Squentz*. James Gibbs meditates on 'The Living

32. *Shakespeare and Montaigne Reconsidered*, by Tetsuo Anzai. Ren1. pp. iv + 96. Y 1,600.

33. In *La peur*, ed. by Alain Morvan. ULille (1985). pp. 165. Ffr 70.

Dramatist and Shakespeare: A Study of Shakespeare's Influence on Wole Soyinka' (*ShS*). In *The Birth of Shakespeare Studies*[34] Arthur Sherbo surveys that quintessentially eighteenth-century activity, the elucidation of minutiae in Shakespeare's text. He introduces us to a whole gallery of gentleman scholars: Sir John Hawkins explaining what a 'passy-measure pavin' is, a Mr Elderton of Salisbury worrying about a gross anachronism in *3 Henry VI*, Henry John Todd explicating 'Tu-whit, tu-who' in *Love's Labour's Lost*. Small wonder that George Steevens began creating personae and contributing learned notes under their names on such matters as Thersites' 'potato-finger' and Lear's 'plackets'. Moving to the end of the eighteenth century Jonathan Bate has produced an impressively detailed and painstaking book on the relationship between *Shakespeare and the English Romantic Imagination*[35]. This is, remarkably, the first full study of the creative transformation of Shakespeare in the minds and works of Coleridge, Wordsworth, Blake, Keats, Shelley, and Byron. Bate has read everything and missed, apparently, nothing; he has certainly seen what many have previously overlooked, identifying dozens of half-submerged allusions and rhythmical as well as verbal echoes (the chapter on Keats is particularly fascinating in this respect), and is able to show that these poets were far more delicately successful when subconsciously remembering Shakespeare than when consciously trying to emulate him. However, this is far from being a collection of textual notes; it is a re-interpretation of the Romantics' remaking of Shakespeare in their own image, and also a triumphant justification of their beliefs about the alchemical power of the imagination. [P.D.] Bate supplements his book with 'Shakespearean Allusion in English Caricature in the Age of Gillray' (*JWCI*). Also in the Romantic period, Fritz Mende writes on 'Eine unbekannte Quelle Heines zu Shakespeares Mädchen und Frauen' (*HeineJ*), a brief but useful addition to Heine's interesting and original Shakespearean criticism, and, for late Romanticism, Michael Hays in *MD* throws light 'On Maeterlinck Reading Shakespeare'.

Shakespeare's American afterlife is discussed by Sanford E. Marovitz in 'Shakespeare vs. America: From the Monroe Doctrine to the Civil War' (*ZAA*), and in a collection of essays entitled *Shakespeare and Southern Writers: A Study in Influence*[36]. For me, the most interesting contribution to this was Timothy Kevin Conley's 'Resounding Fury: Faulkner's Shakespeare, Shakespeare's Faulkner', which was especially illuminating on the unlikely subject of allusions to *As You Like It* in *Soldiers' Pay*.

Finally, for readers bewildered by the variety of all this material, the Horace Howard Furness Memorial Lectures provide a useful survey of *Shakespeare Study Today*[37]. This collection includes a pedestrian tour by Ann Jennalie Cook of 'Detours and Directions in Fifty Years of Shakespeare Scholarship' and a far better, because much more polemical, essay by Jean E. Howard

34. *The Birth of Shakespeare Studies: Commentators from Rowe (1709) to Boswell Malone (1821)*, by Arthur Sherbo. Colleagues. pp. xvi + 203. $22.

35. *Shakespeare and the English Romantic Imagination*, by Jonathan Bate. Clarendon. pp. xvi + 276. £22.50.

36. *Shakespeare and Southern Writers: A Study in Influence*, ed. by Philip C. Kolin. UMissip (1985). pp. x + 177. $17.50.

37. *Shakespeare Study Today: The Horace Howard Furness Memorial Lectures*, ed. by Georgianna Ziegler. AMS. pp. x + 200. $29.50.

on 'Scholarship, Theory, and More New Readings: Shakespeare for the 1990s' – as good an account of the state of the art as one will find. But then in '"Put Money in thy Purse": Supporting Shakespeare' O. B. Hardison Jr, reflecting on his experiences fund-raising for the Folger Shakespeare Library, reminds us of the painful economic constraints faced by scholarship and the arts in the 1980s.

(b) Comedies and Romances

Marilyn L. Williamson's *The Patriarchy of Shakespeare's Comedies*[38] is among the best of the many feminist books on the plays published in the last decade. Williamson steers a steady course between the Scylla of accusing Shakespeare of uncritically accepting the patriarchy of his day and the Charybdis of lauding him as a proto-feminist; she adopts the new historicist technique of moving between texts and contexts, reading moments in the plays against representative historical material. At times, especially in the first of the three main sections, that on *Much Ado, Merchant, As You Like It*, and *Twelfth Night*, this results in slightly thin treatment of the plays themselves. But then in the chapter on *All's Well* and *Measure*, the method works extremely well: the plays are read in the context of the 'sub-genres' of, respectively, the drama of enforced marriage and the disguised-ruler play, which are in turn related to pressing social issues of the early years of King James's reign. The final chapter offers a feminist perspective on the now familiar area of 'art using nature to mythologize power' in the last plays. Throughout, the style is clear and free from jargon; Williamson's command of recent scholarship is impressive.

Stevie Davies's *The Idea of Woman in Renaissance Literature*[39] is most unlike the run-of-the-mill feminist account of Shakespeare. 'Idea' is the operative word here: instead of reading female characters in the context of woman's status in Renaissance society, Davies relates them to images and Ideas (in the Platonic sense) of women in mythographic, Neoplatonic, and hermetic traditions. The book has chapters on Spenser, Shakespeare, and Milton, but refers in passing to many other writers. Davies is at her very best on Britomart in *The Faerie Queene*, but she casts much new light on Shakespearean comedy. Boy–girl twins are approached without psychoanalytic heavy-handedness, while the moon of *A Midsummer Night's Dream* is convincingly related to the figure of Isis in Apuleius's *Golden Asse*, and Hermione in *The Winter's Tale* to Demeter. I am slightly sceptical about some of the more arcane associations – *Pericles* and the Eleusinian mysteries, Hermione and Hermeticism – but the book as a whole strongly vindicates the principle that the best Shakespearean criticism is true both to its own time and Shakespeare's, for Davies engages at one and the same time with modern feminism and the Renaissance mind.

I think slightly more highly of Kristian Smidt's *Unconformities in Shakespeare's Early Comedies*[40] than my predecessor in these pages did of the

---

38. *The Patriarchy of Shakespeare's Comedies*, by Marilyn L. Williamson. WSU. pp. 208. $24.95.

39. *The Idea of Woman in Renaissance Literature: The Feminine Reclaimed*, by Stevie Davies. Harvester/UKen. pp. xii + 273. £32.50/$25.

40. *Unconformities in Shakespeare's Early Comedies*, by Kristian Smidt. Macmillan. pp. xvi + 235. £27.50.

same author's *Unconformities in Shakespeare's History Plays* (*YW* 64.206–7). I feel that the book offers something more than a rude detection of faults in the eighteenth-century manner, for Smidt's scrupulous eye for inconsistencies tells us a lot about the problems of the working dramatist, especially in the plotting of the earliest comedies. But it is all very microscopic: I doubt if any reader's patience would run to sequels on *Unconformities* in the poems, mature comedies, tragedies, romances . . ..

Going through Richard A. Levin's *Love and Society in Shakespearean Comedy*[41] is a very odd experience. It is a book that harks back to the hoary old method of producing 'readings' of Renaissance plays (in this case *The Merchant of Venice, Much Ado about Nothing*, and *Twelfth Night*) that explain their 'themes': 'The subject matter of Shakespearean comedy is society or, more precisely, man and woman in their social relationships', 'the main theme of which they are a variation – namely, the conflict of love and fortune', and so forth. The oddity lies in that the person who has done most to discredit this critical procedure is Richard Levin, in his fine *New Readings vs. Old Plays* (see *YW* 66.222). Not surprisingly, Richard A. Levin is sheepish about his namesake – he quotes him in the text but only names him in the endnotes. Gail Kern Paster's wide-ranging *The Idea of the City in the Age of Shakespeare*[42] includes a chapter entitled 'The Nature of our People: Shakespeare's City Comedies' on *The Comedy of Errors, The Merchant of Venice*, and *Measure for Measure*, which is interesting on Ephesus, Venice, and Vienna, but dull when it turns to 'readings' of the comedies.

In a pleasant article, 'The Rise and Fall of an Elizabethan Fashion' (*CahiersE*), R. S. White pursues the connections between Shakespearean comedy and Elizabethan prose romance by examining the shared motif of the love-letter. The same author has a more substantial essay in *The Art of Listening*[43], which considers dialogue, and in particular the act of listening, in a range of the comedies. White also contributes a paragraph to *N&Q* linking 'Muscovites in *Love's Labour's Lost*' to the 'slave-born Muscovite' in *Astrophil and Stella*, Sonnet 2.

In 'Shakespeare's Comic Heroines, Elizabeth I, and the Political Uses of Androgyny'[44] Leah S. Marcus shows a strong command of historical material in considering some of the 'remarkable correlations between the sexual multi-valence of Shakespeare's heroines and an important strain in the political rhetoric of Queen Elizabeth I'. The Queen's double representation of her own gender is related to cross-dressing in *As You Like It, The Merchant of Venice*, and *Twelfth Night*. Such an account of the implied politics of representation, convincing as it may be as an intellectual argument, inevitably begs the question of whether an Elizabethan theatre audience would have made the kinds of connection proposed.

41. *Love and Society in Shakespearean Comedy: A Study in Dramatic Form and Content*, by Richard A. Levin. AUP/UDel (1985). pp. 203. £18.50.

42. *The Idea of the City in the Age of Shakespeare*, by Gail Kern Paster. UGeo (1985). pp. xiv + 249. $24.

43. *The Art of Listening*, ed. by Graham McGregor and R. S. White. CH. pp. 220. £19.95.

44. In *Women in the Middle Ages and the Renaissance: Literary and Historical Perspectives*, ed. and intro. by Mary Beth Rose. Syracuse. pp. xxx + 288. hb $29.95, pb $12.50. (Hereafter Rose.)

In 'Renaissance Family Politics and Shakespeare's *The Taming of the Shrew*' (*ELR*) Karen Newman also shows a nice historical and linguistic sense before coming to the predictable 'new historical' conclusion that '*The Shrew* both demonstrated and produced the social facts of the patriarchal ideology which characterized Elizabethan England, but representation gives us a perspective on that patriarchal system which subverts its status as natural'. Lawrence Danson's 'Continuity and Character in Shakespeare and Marlowe' (*SEL*) is concerned with transformation of character and instability of identity in *The Taming of the Shrew* and Marlowe's *Edward II*. It is something of a balancing act: 'because we yearn for the very transformation we fearfully resist, the transformation of Kate gives cause both for hope and for fear'.

In *ELN* Camille Wells Slights glosses 'season' at *Comedy of Errors* IV.ii.58. R. V. Holdsworth (*N&Q*) finds a host of 'Sexual Allusions in *Love's Labour's Lost, The Merry Wives of Windsor, Othello, The Winter's Tale,* and *The Two Noble Kinsmen*' relating to the connection between the word 'squire' and 'apple-squire', 'a harlot's attendant, a pimp'. The revision of Berowne's speech at *Love's Labour's Lost* IV.iii.292–358, is discussed rather ploddingly by Janis Lull in 'Past Texts: Shakespeare, Herbert, and the Revising Process' (*Style*, 1985). A more interesting discussion of a local revision is provided by Barbara Hodgdon in 'Gaining a Father: The Role of Egeus in the Quarto and Folio' (*RES*). Hodgdon shows how the presence of Egeus during V.i in the Folio text of *A Midsummer Night's Dream* (he is absent in the Quarto) strengthens the sense of familial and communal harmony at the end of the play. This way of thinking through the dramatic and critical consequences of Shakespeare's revisions will become increasingly common as the new textual orthodoxy gains ground. Michiru Sasaki's 'The Metamorphoses of the Moon: Folk Belief in Lunar Influence on Life and the Symbolic Scheme of *A Midsummer Night's Dream*' (*ShStud*, 1984–5) is over-schematic. *SN* has an oddly attenuated piece of little more than two pages by R. L. Horn on the undercutting of Theseus' positions in *Dream*.

In 'M. Marcadé and the Dance of Death: *Love's Labour's Lost*, V.ii.705–11' (*RES*) René Graziani comes up with the intriguing suggestion that Monsieur Marcade (who needs the acute accent for the sake of the rhythm) may owe his name to the fact that the Dance of Macabré was corrupted to the Dance of Marcadé in Noël du Fail's *Contes d'Eutrapel* (Rennes, 1585). Had he shown more conclusively that the Dance of Death was known under this name in England as well as France, Graziani would have solved a problem that has long vexed the scholars. The association certainly makes critical sense in view of Marcade's role.

In '"The Sign and Semblance of Her Honor": Reading Gender Difference in *Much Ado about Nothing*' (*PMLA*) Carol Cook plays with word, sword, and phallus, and comes to the alarming conclusion that 'To read others in this play is an act of aggression; to be read is to be emasculated'. Heinz Zimmermann's 'Prinzipien des dramatischen Rhythmus in *Much Ado about Nothing*' (*ShJW*) attends mainly to the dialogue of Beatrice and Benedick. Shyamal Kumar Sarkar (*ShStud*, 1984–5) surveys in workmanlike fashion 'The Structure of *Much Ado about Nothing*'.

The Merchant of Venice has been the object of much interest in recent years. The proceedings of a colloquium at the University of Rouen in 1985 are now published under the title '*Le Marchand de Venise*' et '*Le Juif de*

Malte'[45]. This is a stimulating collection which begins with Leo Salingar asking 'Is *The Merchant of Venice* a Problem Play?' – he decides that the tragi-comic elements are eventually outweighed by the romance motifs (this essay is reprinted in *Dramatic Form in Shakespeare and the Jacobeans*[23]). The rest of the collection is in French, and includes rather more on *The Merchant* than *The Jew*, though at several points considers the interplay between them; an attractive feature is the inclusion of discussion provoked by some of the papers (among which I would single out François Laroque's informative 'Fête, folklore et mythe dans *Le Marchand de Venise*'). Elsewhere, Ronald A. Sharp offers a positive reading of the play via an account of 'Gift Exchange and the Economies of the Spirit in *The Merchant of Venice*' (*MP*); by juxtaposing Shylock's usury with the many gifts that are given and received by other characters, Sharp comes to the heart of the matter. This essay seemed to me more open and generous than Lars Engle's '"Thrift is Blessing": Exchange and Explanation in *The Merchant of Venice*' (*SQ*). Two other essays seem to mirror their authors' own positions more than the play: A. A. Ansari's '*The Merchant of Venice*: An Existential Comedy' (*AJES*) and Carl Goldberg's '"What Ails Antonio?" The Nature of Evil in Psychiatric Disorders' (*JPJ*, 1985). More minutely, Norman Nathan in *AN&Q* considers 'Bassanio's Name', Robert McMahon (*SQ*) offers '"Some there be that shadows kiss": A Note on *The Merchant of Venice*, II.ix.65', and Eric Rasmussen (*Expl*) discusses the song in 'Shakespeare's *The Merchant of Venice*, III.ii.63–8'.

Carl Goldberg's article is just one of a spate of studies that are likely to interest psychoanalysts more than readers and viewers of Shakespeare. Several are focused on the last plays: Bernard J. Paris, under the influence of Karen Horney, '*The Tempest*': *Shakespeare's Ideal Solution*[46]; Joseph Westlund, under that of Melanie Klein, 'Omnipotence and Reparation in Prospero's Epilogue'[47]; and Maydee G. Lande, on Leontes' paranoid delusions, '*The Winter's Tale*: A Question of Motive' (*AI*). *AI* also has Carolyn E. Brown on '*Measure for Measure*: Isabella's Beating Fantasies', which covers much the same ground as her even more alluringly titled article noted below.

In *ELN* (1985) A. Stuart Daley stresses the differences between the topographies of Thomas Lodge's Arden in *Rosalynde* and Shakespeare's in *As You Like It*. The same author undertakes a rather long-winded account of II.i of the same play in 'To Moralize a Spectacle' (*PQ*). He adduces some interesting material about venery. Barbara J. Bono's 'Mixed Gender, Mixed Genre in Shakespeare's *As You Like It*'[48] is a pot-pourri of deconstruction, feminism, psychoanalysis, and new historicism focused on 'Rosalind's deconstructive efforts within her own text'. George Sand's adaptation of the play is discussed

45. '*Le Marchand de Venise*' et '*Le Juif de Malte*': *Texte et représentations*, ed. by Michèle Willems, Jean-Pierre Maquerlot, Raymond Willems. URouen (1985). pp. 176. pb Ffr 71.

46. '*The Tempest*': *Shakespeare's Ideal Solution*, by Bernard J. Paris. UFlor (1985). pp. 35.

47. In *Narcissism and the Text: Studies in Literature and the Psychology of the Self*, ed. by William Coyle. NYU. pp. xvi + 295. $42.50.

48. In *Renaissance Genres: Essays on Theory, History, and Interpretation*, ed. by Barbara Kiefer Lewalski. Harvard. pp. viii + 498. hb £21.95, pb £7.95. (Hereafter Lewalski.)

by Adeline R. Tintner (*RLC*). R. D. Parsons (*N&Q*) supports the conjecture that 'Touchstone's Butterwomen' at III.ii.96 may be pregnant.

Leo Salingar's exemplary 1958 essay on 'The Design of *Twelfth Night*' (*YW* 39.122) in relation to the play's sources is included in *Dramatic Form in Shakespeare and the Jacobeans*[23]. Matthew H. Wikander's 'As Secret as Maidenhead: The Profession of Boy-Actress in *Twelfth Night*' (*CompD*) is a competent essay in the well-trodden field of potentiality, sexuality, cross-dressing, and the passage from adolescence to adulthood. Cynthia Lewis's '"A Fustian Riddle"?: Anagrammatic Names in *Twelfth Night*' (*ELN*, 1985) notes the verbal proximity of the names Orsino and Cesario, and Viola, Malvolio, and Olivia, but argues that to seek meaning in these near anagrams is to over-interpret foolishly in the manner of Malvolio reading 'M.O.A.I.'. A similar argument is pursued in more general terms by Elizabeth Freund in '*Twelfth Night* and the Tyranny of Interpretation' (*ELH*): 'The powerful waywardness of interpretive operations certainly propels the plot . . . Malvolio's despotic way with a text digs his own hermeneutic grave and should stand as a warning to all interpreters who practice the self-deception of believing in the text's penetrability . . .'. J. H. P. Pafford (*N&Q*) derives 'Pigrogromitus: *Twelfth Night*, II.iii.23' from Latin *pigro* + *gromettus*, 'idle servant'.

Twelfth Night: Critical Essays[49], in Garland's new series of Shakespearean Criticism, is a beautifully produced volume containing many of the best essays on the play – Charles Lamb on the tragic Malvolio, John Russell Brown's 'Directions for *Twelfth Night*', C. L. Barber's 'Testing Courtesy and Humanity in *Twelfth Night*', Anne Barton on the ending, and so on. It also represents the theatrical tradition effectively. But the major respect in which it advances on other readily available Casebooks is in the price: should students and librarians really be asked to part with $54 for such a collection?

In a more unusual collection edited by E. A. J. Honigmann, *Shakespeare and his Contemporaries: Essays in Comparison*[50], G. K. Hunter's 'Bourgeois Comedy: Shakespeare and Dekker' carefully reads *The Merry Wives of Windsor* as citizen comedy, making particular comparisons with *The Shoemaker's Holiday*.

Eileen Z. Cohen argues attractively (*PQ*) that in *All's Well that Ends Well* and *Measure for Measure* Shakespeare 'deconventionalizes' the bed-trick in order to subvert our expectations of the virgin bride and the would-be nun, thus portraying unstereotyped women who are both virtuous and assertive, both chaste and outspoken. David V. Harrington contends in 'Shakespeare's Generosity' (*ShJE*) that Shakespeare demands that we forgive Bertram. I am not so sure that Shakespeare makes demands of us. In 'The Argument of *Measure for Measure*' (*ELR*) Paul Hammond approaches the argument of the play via a careful examination of the role of argument in the play. Also in *ELR*, Carolyn E. Brown flogs to death the subject of 'Erotic Religious Flagellation and Shakespeare's *Measure for Measure*'. Catharine F. Seigel's 'Hands off the Hothouses: Shakespeare's Advice to the King' (*JPC*) argues on the basis of very

---

49. *Twelfth Night: Critical Essays*, ed. by Stanley Wells. Garland. pp. xiv + 312. $54.

50. *Shakespeare and his Contemporaries: Essays in Comparison*, ed. by E. A. J. Honigmann. ManU. pp. xii + 143. £25. (Hereafter Honigmann.)

slender evidence that *Measure* is instructing King James not to close down the brothels in the London suburbs. The MMG on the play[51] cannot make up its mind whether 'Many of Vincentio's characteristics are almost certainly based on King James I' or whether 'The most we can say is that certain aspects of Vincentio echo, in varying degrees of directness, some aspects of James's own life and thought'. J. J. M. Tobin's 'Nashe and *Measure for Measure*' (*N&Q*) adduces borrowings from *Pierce Penilesse* (1592). Dieter Mehl's 'Corruption, Retribution and Justice in *Measure for Measure* and *The Revenger's Tragedy*' in Honigmann[50] is a thoughtful consideration not of borrowings but of shared techniques and two dramatists' handlings of similar problems.

In 'Moral Order in Shakespeare's *Troilus and Cressida:* The Case of the Trojans' (*Anglia*) Elaine Eldridge looks at characters who do not act according to their stated beliefs: Hector violates honour, Cressida love, and Troilus both honour and love. John W. Velz claims (*N&Q*) that he has found 'An Early Allusion to *Troilus and Cressida*' that would date the play prior to August 1602 and suggest that it was performed on the public stage; I think it more likely that the text in the public eye at this time which provoked a reference to Hector's death in *Thomas Lord Cromwell* was Chapman's Homer rather than Shakespeare's *Troilus*. Linda LaBranche writes solidly about 'Visual Patterns and Linking Analogues in *Troilus and Cressida*' (*SQ*).

Turning to the romances, David M. Bergeron undertakes a full-scale reading according to the Greenblatt–Goldberg axis. *Shakespeare's Romances and the Royal Family*[52] argues that the last plays constitute Shakespeare's 'reading', or rather 're-presentation', of the 'text' of King James's family. The problem with this book is that it cannot do more than suggest that there are royal families in the plays and there was a royal family when they were written and all royal families get involved in marriage negotiations, without moving towards the kind of overt topical identification (the province of Frances Yates and Glynne Wickham) which it claims to eschew. Thus Bergeron is properly sceptical about one of Wickham's identifications – 'If Perdita, the daughter of Leontes/James, marries Florizel/Henry, don't we encounter incest?' – yet he cannot resist the speculation that the death of Mamillius might have reminded the court audience of the death of Prince Henry (this although *The Winter's Tale* was written before Henry died). The quantity of verbiage reveals the limitations of Bergeron's approach: 'I have opened the text of the Stuart royal family, the book of kings, have read from it, and have interpreted it.'

Bergeron's book includes a not very relevant chapter on representations of the family, sex, and marriage in Jacobean city comedy. More illuminating comparisons between Shakespeare's last plays and the work of other dramatists is provided by Philip Edwards's convincing set of parallels between *The Winter's Tale* and Peele's *The Old Wives Tale* (in '"Seeing is believing": Action and Narration in *The Old Wives Tale* and *The Winter's Tale*') and H. Neville Davies's comparison of '*Pericles* and the Sherley Brothers', the latter from *The Travailes of the Three English Brothers* (1607) by John Day, William Rowley, and George Wilkins; both these essays are in Honigmann[50].

'The Dismemberment of Orpheus: Mythic Elements in Shakespeare's

---

51. *'Measure for Measure'*, by Mark Lilly. MMG. Macmillan. pp. x + 86. pb £1.25.
52. *Shakespeare's Romances and the Royal Family*, by David M. Bergeron. pp. xiv + 257. UKan (1985). $25.

Romances' by David Armitage (*ShS*) perhaps tries to take on too much for a brief article, but is genuinely illuminating on the way that several of the key myths alluded to in the last plays are associated with the Orphic part of Ovid's *Metamorphoses*. *ShS* also has a more focused essay on a classical presence in late Shakespeare, Robert Wiltenburg's 'The *Aeneid* in *The Tempest*', a very suggestive piece which argues (perhaps overstating its case) that the play is a creative reworking of *The Aeneid*. Virgilian connections are pursued in more wide-ranging fashion by Robert S. Miola in 'Vergil in Shakespeare: From Allusion to Imitation'[53]. Stephen Dickey's 'Language and Role in *Pericles*' (*ELR*) plays off Gower and Pericles against each other. David L. Frost in '"Mouldy Tales": The Context of Shakespeare's *Cymbeline*' (*E&S*) argues, as others have before, that the play is self-parodic. Darryll Grantley finds common patterns in '*The Winter's Tale* and Early Religious Drama' (*CompD*). Julia Gasper and Carolyn Williams (*N&Q*) relate 'The Meaning of the Name Hermione' to 'herma', a word which could refer to the statue of a saint.

In perhaps this year's finest article on any of the last plays, 'Shakespeare's Virginian Masque' (*ELH*), John Gillies reconstructs the Virginian context of *The Tempest*. He is interesting on Chapman's *Memorable Masque*, then brilliant on the simultaneously Virginian and Ovidian status of the key motifs of temperance and fruitfulness. There could be no better whetting of the appetite for Stephen Orgel's 1987 Oxford Shakespeare edition of the play – apart, that is, from a fine extract from Orgel's introduction published in *Rewriting the Renaissance*[26] under the eye-catching title 'Prospero's Wife'. Meanwhile, Gary Schmidgall in 'The Discovery at Chess in *The Tempest*' (*ELN*) suggests that Miranda and Ferdinand are discovered at chess because that game was related to political skill, but he fails to consider the implications for his argument of the line 'Sweet lord, you play me false'. Also in *ELN*, Anthony Brian Taylor's '" O brave new world": Abraham Fraunce and *The Tempest*' not wholly convincingly finds a source for Miranda's 'brave new world' in Fraunce's *The Third Part of the Countesse of Pembrokes Yvychurche*. Valentina P. Komorowa usefully considers utopian matters in 'Das Problem der Gesellschaftsform in Montaignes *Essays* und Shakespeares *Sturm*' (*ShJE*). In the same journal James Schevill's 'The Scientist on the Stage: Shakespeare's *Tempest* and Brecht's *Galileo*' is a comparison, not a study in influence. Malcolm Pittock (*N&Q*) writes excellently about the 'Widow Dido' knot: he argues convincingly that Gonzalo is alluding to the medieval tradition of a virtuous Dido remaining loyal to her dead first husband, whereas Antonio and Sebastian know only the baser figure of the Virgilian and Ovidian tradition.

UTQ publishes two somewhat conventional articles back to back: Ellen R. Belton, '"When No Man Was His Own": Magic and Self-Discovery in *The Tempest*' and Richard Hillman, '*The Tempest* as Romance and Anti-Romance'. The latter is the more interesting because it acknowledges more complexity and multiplicity. *SQ* also carries two essays: A. Lynne Magnusson's 'Interruption in *The Tempest*' is an unexceptionable account of a recurring process in the play, while Gary Schmidgall's '*The Tempest* and *Primaleon*: A New Source' demands fuller consideration. Schmidgall proposes that the third

---

53. In *Vergil at 2000: Commemorative Essays on the Poet and his Influence*, ed. by John D. Bernard and Paul D. Alessi. AMS. pp. xiv + 342. $39.50. (Hereafter Bernard).

book of *Primaleon, Prince of Greece*, by an anonymous Spanish author, translated into English by Anthony Munday from an intervening French version, is the major romance source for *The Tempest*. The linchpin of his argument is a splendid-sounding Prospero-like character called 'the Knight of the Enclosed Isle'; a large number of striking parallels are listed though, since Schmidgall juggles their order and underplays dissimilarities between the texts, to judge whether we really do have a source rather than an analogue one would need to read a copy of the now scarce *Primaleon*. The book's scarcity reveals a major difficulty facing Schmidgall's contention: there is no evidence that any of it was published before 1619, though single surviving copies of Books I and II seem to date from the 1590s. That Shakespeare had in his hands when he wrote *The Tempest* a copy of a putative early edition of Book III will have to remain highly conjectural.

The simultaneous appearance of a Macmillan Master Guide and a Penguin Masterstudy on *The Tempest*[54] allows for comparison of the two series. The Penguin wins hands down. Treatment of Prospero's 'Ye elves of hills . . .' provides a good example: where the MMG has one sentence informing us that the speech is derived from Ovid and a second making the bare assertion that Shakespeare's audience would not have objected to the borrowing, the PM thinks through the consequences of the allusion and includes both Arthur Golding's and a modern translation of the Ovidian original in an appendix, together with other 'source' material (relevant passages from Montaigne, Jonson's *Hymenaei*, and so on). 'A' level students should not be allowed near the MMG; they would learn much from the PM.

Take it for all in all, the periodical criticism – especially on individual plays – has not made for exciting reading this year. There are of course notable exceptions, and one can usually guess in which journals they will be found: there is always good scholarship in *ShS*, Gillies on *The Tempest* is typical of the strength of *ELH*, while the articles in *SQ* often seem aimless (though *SQ* remains strong in theatre coverage and is much improved, because more up to date, in book reviews). What is depressing is how so much material in the learned journals conforms to generic conventions with wearisome predictability. A Touchstonian anatomy will perhaps give a sense of the state of the art. The Exposition Courteous is dull but unexceptionable: appearing in a respected journal which has been going for more than half a century, it aims not to coerce us but to elucidate some feature of a play, thus returning us to Shakespeare with an enriched sense of his 'meanings' and 'structures' (examples: Eldridge on *Troilus and Cressida*, Zimmermann on *Much Ado*). The reviewer does not take violent exception, but does not feel inclined to exhort others to read such material. The Note Modest appears in such journals as *N&Q*, *AN&Q*, *Expl*, and *ELN*, and near the back of such as *SQ* and *RES*. It addresses local detail in ways that are sometimes illuminating (Pittock on 'Widow Dido'), sometimes obfuscating (Schmidgall on chess), but often trivial (Nathan, McMahon, and Rasmussen on details in *Merchant*). At the other extreme, there are two categories made of stronger stuff; these tend to appear in newer journals, journals devoted to the discourse in question, and older journals that wish to seem new (pre-eminently *PMLA*). The Appropriation Cir-

54. *'The Tempest'*, by Kenneth Pickering. MMG. Macmillan. pp. x + 86. pb £1.25. *'The Tempest'*, by Sandra Clark. PM. Penguin. pp. 95. pb £1.50.

cumstantial uses some feature of the text as a lever with which to prise the entire play off the ground of a normative reading and into the ether of a particular 'radical' or 'subversive' reading (Freund on *Twelfth Night*). The Appropriation Direct unashamedly wrenches the play into the discourse of psychoanalysis, existentialism, feminism, or whatever (Goldberg and Ansari on *Merchant*, Cook on *Much Ado*). There are intermediate categories, as there are for Touchstone, but strong essays which cut across the categories are few and far between in the periodicals. Their province is more frequently the consciously shaped multi-author collection of essays, such as *Literary Theory/Renaissance Texts*[25] and *Rewriting the Renaissance*[26], which seems to have taken over as the critical medium for our time.

(c) Histories

The intellectual background of the histories and tragedies is illuminated by Robin Headlam Wells's *Shakespeare, Politics and the State*[55], which assembles passages from a wide variety of Renaissance writings on human nature, forms of government, the just ruler, rebellion, providence and history, and natural law, linking them with a commentary which demonstrates the complexity of Shakespeare's engagement with ideas he is still too often assumed to have accepted unquestioningly. Something of the complexity of those ideas themselves also emerges: for instance, recognition of the inadequacy of medieval king-worship in the world of Reformation *Realpolitik* paradoxically co-existed with a monarchical absolutism which was virtually invented by Tudor ideologues. Wells's chapter 'Providence and History' draws on the writings of Calvin and John Ponet alongside the standard chronicle historians in analysing the dramatic capital ('a dialectic in which opposing views are contrasted') which Shakespeare makes out of belief in providential government. We are well reminded that the 'Tudor myth' is in fact 'a composite theory consisting of a number of disparate elements', and that the chronicles themselves were becoming outdated by Shakespeare's time, as historians increasingly located the meaning of events in human character rather than the Divine will – the very issue debated by Henry IV and Warwick in *2 Henry IV* III.i. Wells's skilful and telling juxtapositions of Shakespearean passages and the work of less familiar writers will make this book a handy resource for undergraduates, but it is also, in an unpretentious way, a work of scholarship.

A more extreme interpretation comes from David Scott Kastan's 'Proud Majesty Made a Subject: Shakespeare and the Spectacle of Rule' (*SQ*), which sees the histories as helping to subvert royal authority by exposing its hollowness and promoting recognition of the audience/commoners as 'the ultimate source of authority in its willingness to credit and approve the representation of rule'. In diametrical opposition, Leonard Tennenhouse's chapter 'Rituals of State' in his *Power on Display*[27] presents the histories as reflecting a gradual political emasculation of subversion, expressed in stage terms by carnival or anarchy, these tendencies being eventually incorporated into the monarchy itself in the person of Hal/Henry V. R. L. Smallwood's chapter in the *Cambridge Companion*[6] on 'Shakespeare's Use of History' is curiously

55. *Shakespeare, Politics and the State*, ed. by Robin Headlam Wells. Macmillan. pp. xi + 174. hb £20, pb £6.95. (Hereafter Wells.)

half-hearted and bitty, presenting little sense of the histories as *developing* ideas; his best section deals with discussions of the meaning of history within the plays themselves, although he surprisingly omits *2 Henry IV* III.i, referred to by Wells[55]. Edward Berry, later in the volume, reviews twentieth-century criticism of the histories, concluding that they have 'been relatively untouched by the more venturesome critical theories of the past forty years': he might not have sounded so regretful about this had he read some of the following items.

Critical theorizing of a fruitful kind appears in two outstanding, and coincidentally overlapping, general discussions. Marjorie Garber's '"What's Past is Prologue": Temporality and Prophecy in Shakespeare's History Plays', in Lewalski[48], apart from discussing the multiple ironies issuing from the fulfilment or frustration of prophecies, has two penetrating observations: that the audience is often placed in the Cassandra-like position of possessing knowledge about the events which it cannot use, and that the history play as a genre inhabits the strange realm of 'what will have occurred', since it shows us our past, but as an action that is in the future when the play begins. This is very good, but Phyllis Rackin's 'Temporality, Anachronism, and Presence in Shakespeare's English Histories' (*RenD*) is even better. Studying Shakespeare's 'manipulation of the temporal relationship between past events and present audience' to 'dramatize the distance and the intersection between past and present, eternity and time', she argues that his choosing to include anachronism allies him with poets against historiographers in contemporary Renaissance debate, discusses 'invasions of the time frame of the audience' by characters, outlines the problem of reconciling our passive historical knowledge of the events presented with our active theatrical experience of them, and finishes with extended discussion of the second tetralogy. The argument is conducted on a high level: I eagerly await her promised related book, and regret not having seen her 'Anti-Historians: Women's Roles in Shakespeare's Histories' (*TJ*, 1985).

An aspect of Shakespeare's medieval inheritance in the histories is discussed by Alan C. Dessen[56]. He challenges our received view of *Mankind* or *Everyman* as the paradigmatic morality plays by demonstrating that Elizabethan writers allude most frequently to the Vice, a character absent from those earnest pieces. He then examines *Richard III*, *1* and *2 Henry IV*, and *All's Well* in the light of a number of 'two-phased' moral plays of the 1560s and 1570s – the popular drama of Shakespeare's youth, which he probably saw rather than read – which gratify the audience's superficially incompatible desires for amoral entertainment and moral justice by presenting the Vice, first as a jester running riot, then as a threat to be finally vanquished by an opposing figure of authority. There are interesting similarities between this view and Leonard Tennenhouse's (p. 227). Dessen concedes that his argument is not startlingly original – the duality of our response to Richard III and Falstaff has long been an established critical fact – but his book is valuable for the thoroughness of its discussion, based on extremely wide reading, and its independent synthesis of recent criticism. It overturns some glib modern assumptions about how the Elizabethans regarded dramatic genres, arguing for a more balanced historical approach. That this is still in need of advocacy is shown by such articles as Richard Wilson's '"A Mingled Yarn": Shakespeare and the Cloth Workers'

---

56. *Shakespeare and the Late Moral Plays*, by Alan C. Dessen. UNeb. pp. ix + 196. $19.95.

(*L&H*) in which Jack Cade, in *2 Henry VI*, figures as 'a projection of the sexual and cannibalistic terrors of the Renaissance rich', and Shakespeare is berated for rigging the evidence against the traditions Cade embodies. Comparison with Dessen points up how naïve and anachronistic a view of Elizabethan popular culture this is.

Moving on through the first tetralogy: convincing parallels between 'Richard III and Herod' of medieval drama, art, and biblical exegesis are drawn by Scott Colley (*SQ*). The Book of Revelation is singled out as a key influence by R. Chris Hassel Jr in 'Last Words and Last Things: St John, Apocalypse, and Eschatology in *Richard III*' (*ShakS*); obviously there are connections, but Hassel's arguments for specific debts are thin. His 'Providence and the Text of *Richard III*' (*UCrow*) attributes differences between Q and F to a wish to place increased emphasis on providentialism. A chapter in Robert Jones's *Engagement with Knavery*[57], complementary to Alan Dessen's book, lucidly traces Shakespeare's use of Richard to control our point of view, relating this to Vice-figures as well as to Barabas, Volpone, and Vindice. Pierre Sahel in 'The *Coup d'état* of Shakespeare's *Richard III*: Politics and Dramatics' (*AJES*, 1985) examines III.v and vii as plays within the play. Peggy Endel's 'Profane Love: The Throne Scene of Shakespeare's *Richard III*' (*CompD*) focuses on IV.ii and explores metaphorical connections between excretory functions and diabolical personality, with some surprisingly convincing points amid the frequent (unintentional?) comic touches. There are two relevant essays in *ShJW*; Wolfgang Baumgart's 'Die Krone' and Werner Habicht's 'Rhythmen der Szenenfolge in *Richard III*' – the latter a subject also discussed in Bernard Beckerman's contribution to Honigmann[50]. Comparing 'Scene Patterns in *Doctor Faustus* and *Richard III*', Beckerman finds Shakespeare rejecting Marlovian simplicity in quest of a richer orchestration of dialogue, and hence a greater dramatic immediacy.

Another essay in the same volume, Alexander Leggatt's 'A Double Reign: *Richard II* and *Perkin Warbeck*', shows how John Ford reverses the structure of the Shakespearean play by dividing attention equally between the two claimants and setting a practical king against an imaginative rebel. The second tetralogy is generally better served than the first this year, although there are some exceptions, for instance Georges Lamoine's '*Richard II* and the Myth of the Fisher King' (*CahiersE*) which begins confidently enough (England = the Waste Land, Richard = the sick king) but quickly exposes its own improbability (the crown = the Holy Grail? Exton's sword = the lance?). On a higher level altogether, Clayton G. MacKenzie's learned essay 'Paradise and Paradise Lost in *Richard II*' (*SQ*) examines conflicts in the presentation of England as a prelapsarian and postlapsarian Eden. Nationalism is also the culminating point of Leo Salingar's essay on the *Henry IV* plays, reprinted in his superb collection[23]: this is a fine and loving study of Falstaff, the kinds of blessedly non-Jonsonian humour he embodies and exemplifies, and his place in giving imaginative life to Shakespeare's concept of England. Another vintage Falstaff essay, William Empson's of 1953, appears, substantially revised, in his posthumous collection[22]. These two pieces make others look tepid. Robin

57. *Engagement with Knavery: Point of View in 'Richard III', 'The Jew of Malta', 'Volpone', and 'The Revenger's Tragedy'*, by Robert C. Jones. DukeU. pp. xii + 177. £21.40.

Headlam Wells and Alison Birkinshaw, in 'Falstaff, Prince Hal and the New Song' (*ShakS*), analyse musical allusions to and by Falstaff to support his assimilation to St Paul's type of the Unregenerate Man. If this were the whole truth Hal would have had no difficulty casting him off in the struggle to remain above close relationships commended by Derick R. C. Marsh in 'Lords and Owners of their Faces: A Study of Octavius Caesar and Prince Hal' (*SSEng*, 1985). Ian Donaldson (*SQ*) explains 'Falstaff's Buff Jerkin' (*1 Henry IV* I.ii.41) as a sexual reference to Mistress Quickly. In a wholly superfluous background study, 'When Lord Cobham and Edmund Tilney "were att odds": Oldcastle, Falstaff, and the Date of *1 Henry IV*' (*ShakS*), Robert J. Fehrenbach claims to identify Sir William Brooke as the objector to the use of Oldcastle's name and to narrow the date of composition to late 1596, with performances at Court in the Christmas season of 1596/7 – mentioning in passing that A. R. Humphreys made similar points in his New Arden edition in 1960 (*YW* 41.96). Richard Abrams writes on rumour as a character and a theme in 'Rumour's Reign in *2 Henry IV*: The Scope of a Personification' (*ELR*).

There are several pieces on *Henry V*, two in *ShJE*: Günter Walch's 'Tudor-Legende und Geschichtsbewegung in *The Life of King Henry V*' and Thomas Sorge's 'Der Widerspruch in *Heinrich V*'. Keith Brown's 'Historical Context and *Henry V*' (*CahiersE*) argues for production at the Globe and composition by August 1599, not June as is often thought, and sees parallels between Henry's wooing of Katherine and James VI's of Anne of Denmark. Michael Cameron Andrews, in 'Fluellen: or Speedwell' (*N&Q*), notes that the character's name is Welsh for the herb, whose purgative properties help to explain Fluellen's humiliation of Pistol. Those who find Henry less than admirable are currently in the ascendant, it seems: in a study of 'Katherine of France as Victim and Bride' (*ShakS*, 1985) Lance Wilcox attributes the increasing refinement and sophistication of the character of Katherine to Shakespeare's anxiety to transform Henry from a predator to a monarch of courtesy, a ploy which Wilcox frankly judges a 'near miss'. Roy Battenhouse, reading '*Henry V* in the Light of Erasmus' (*ShakS*, 1985), uses passages on sham piety from *The Praise of Folly* to provide ironic commentary on Henry's behaviour. In 'Mockery and Mangling in Shakespeare's *Henry V*' (*TD*) Richard W. Bovard restates, without adding to, the familiar argument that the comic scenes denigrate Henry: his reductive conclusion ('Henry is Pistol') shows a lack of balance, unlike the play itself, in my view. William Whallon's miniscule note 'Bilingual Word Play on "Neck" and "Chin"' (*ShN*) wonders inconclusively whether the language lesson in III.iv contains even more naughty puns than we may think.

To turn, finally, to the odd plays out: a dispute over whether or not the redundant sheriff directed to enter in I.i of *King John* is a fossil from *The Troublesome Raigne* is initiated by Sidney Thomas (*SQ*) who is opposed by E. A. J. Honigmann and supported by further arguments from Paul Werstine and himself (*SQ*, 1987). Paul Dean discusses the relationship between 'Dramatic Mode and Historical Vision in *Henry VIII*' (*SQ*), while Rick Bowers (*Expl*) studies the character of Buckingham in II.i of the play. Richard Proudfoot's '*The Reign of King Edward the Third* (1596) and Shakespeare' (*PBA*, 1985), which adumbrates views to be developed in his forthcoming edition of *Edward III*, is a conscientious survey of the theatrical auspices, sources, and dramaturgical techniques of this play, which he considers, somewhat tamely, to be 'arguably the work of Shakespeare'. He unfortunately omits to mention the valuable article by Inna Koskenniemi (*NM*, 1964).

(d) Tragedies

Dieter Mehl's *Shakespeare's Tragedies: An Introduction*[58] is adapted from an earlier work in German intended for German students. It is no more and no less than its title suggests: balanced, thorough, keeping to central questions of characterization and theme, unobtrusively aware of previous scholarship, and elegantly written. G. K. Hunter's chapter on 'Shakespeare and the Traditions of Tragedy' in the *Cambridge Companion*[6], which, like Mehl's book, also covers the Roman plays, is, equally characteristically, lucid and probing, arguing for Shakespeare's ability throughout to 'turn round and around the value-systems he works with' and incidentally viewing *Hamlet*, *Lear*, and *Macbeth* interestingly as 'chronicle-tragedies'. Hunter's contribution is complemented by Kenneth Muir's review, in the same volume, of twentieth-century criticism of the tragedies. Maqbool H. Khan, in 'E. E. Stoll and the Bradleian Tragedies' (*AJES*) discusses in some detail the work of a now-neglected critic, who diverged sharply both from Bradley's broadly mimetic theory of drama and from the schematic image-and-symbol-pattern approach of L. C. Knights and Derek Traversi in favour of a stress on the self-sufficiency of artifice in Shakespeare. It is less easy to see the merit of Werner Brönnimann's article 'Shakespeare's Tragic Practice' (*ES*), which seems to be a review-essay of Bertrand Evans's book of that title (published in 1979! *YW* 60.148–50) with special attention to what Evans might or might not have meant by the 'awareness' of the characters and ourselves. An unusual and valuable perspective is offered by Charles R. Forker in 'The Green Underworld of Early Shakespearean Tragedy' (*ShakS*, 1985). The concept of the green world is a familiar one in criticism of the comedies: Forker convincingly traces it in unexpected places elsewhere (Capulet's and Brutus's orchards, Friar Lawrence's herb-garden, Ophelia's willow-bank), showing that in early plays it symbolizes underlying order, in later ones moral decay, before being replaced by landscapes composed of cliffs, deserts, and caves.

It is always hard to know how to organize the bafflingly diverse output on the tragedies: so many 'angles', acute and obtuse, are exploited. I propose to look first at some general, and ominous, critical trends, before discussing individual plays, following the generally accepted chronological order of composition.

Religious interpretations of the tragedies are coming back into fashion, bringing with them the dangers of oversimplification and reductive stereo-typing. Roy Battenhouse in 'Augustinian Roots in Shakespeare's Sense of Tragedy' (*UCrow*) finds, in *Antony and Cleopatra* especially, echoes of the Saint's doctrine that all sins arise from misdirected love, and O. B. Hardison Jr, in 'Shakespearean Tragedy: The Mind in Search of the World' (*UCrow*), exposes some inadequacies in an affective view of the plays, which he interprets as a series of Fortunate Falls. The villainy of Aaron, Shylock, Iago, Caliban, and Edmund derives from their infidelity, according to Earl Dachslager's '"The Stock of Barabas": Shakespeare's Unfaithful Villains' (*UCrow*). A small group of studies reminds us of the violations of innocence entailed in a

58. *Shakespeare's Tragedies: An Introduction*, by Dieter Mehl. CUP. pp. x + 272. hb £27.50, pb £9.95.

tragic universe: Cherrell Guilfoyle sees the mystery plays on the slaughter of the innocents behind the treatment of Desdemona in 'Mactacio Desdemonae' (*CompD*); vaguer connections between the treatment of suffering in the Mysteries and in *King Lear* are proposed by Clifford Davidson in 'La Phénoménologie de la souffrance, le drame médiéval, et *King Lear*' (*RHT*, 1985). Stephen J. Lynch's 'Sin, Suffering, and Redemption in *Leir* and *Lear*' (*ShakS*) traces Shakespeare's transformation of a demonstrative Christian morality into a more probing agnostic exploration. In a revised re-issue[59] of a book originally published in 1982 but not then noticed here R. S. White takes the interesting line that, while we are used to extensive analysis of the emotional turmoil undergone by the central male figures in the tragedies, we less often notice the roles of children and of female characters (e.g. Lavinia, Ophelia, Desdemona, and Cordelia) whose undeserved suffering transforms them into models of goodness by which we judge the flaws of the society presented, including the tragic protagonists. White makes his case by keeping close to the texts, but ranges beyond them in a brief final chapter, suggesting that critics have neglected these victims partly because their presence turns justice into a matter of our emotional identification with them rather than of any neat theoretical scheme of the type beloved by critics: indeed, he stresses that injustice is built into the plays by Shakespeare.

Countering R. M. Frye's argument in *The Renaissance Hamlet* (*YW* 65.225-6), Michael MacDonald in 'Ophelia's Maimed Rites' (*SQ*) sees the treatment of Ophelia's suicide and burial as reflecting Renaissance ethical indecision about such behaviour. A large book on an important subject by Harry Morris[60] sadly does not match the standard of his earlier related essay (*YW* 65.221). His theme – Shakespeare's debt to medieval eschatology and the *ars moriendi* – is handled with insensitive oversimplification which turns even Desdemona into a Christ-figure, and sees Hamlet as a priest-king hearing the confessions of Gertrude and Ophelia, Lady Macbeth as a 'counterpart to the disciples' at Pentecost, and Lear as saved from damnation by Cordelia. The excellent illustrations are often only marginally related to Shakespeare's words. The book represents a lost opportunity. A particularly absurd example of Christianizing is G. R. Wilson's 'The Poisoned Chalice and the Blasphemed Babe: Macbeth's Black Mass' (*AJES*), which tortures Acts I and II on the liturgical rack ('memorize another Golgotha' perverts the making of the sign of the cross, Lady Macbeth's greeting to her husband is an Alleluia, etc.).

Those who cannot find religious consolation in the tragedies sometimes go to the opposite extreme and deny them any coherent meaning at all, even asserting that this was Shakespeare's intention, or that, better still, he intended a *philosophy* of meaninglessness. James L. Calderwood takes this line in his article 'Creative Uncreation in *King Lear*' (*SQ*), while his book[61], incorporating another article, '*Macbeth*: Counter-*Hamlet*' (*ShakS*, 1985), seems to have at its base a fairly conventional view of *Macbeth* as the tragedy of a weak man about whom our feelings are deeply divided, but such a comprehensible, if

59. *Innocent Victims: Poetic Injustice in Shakespearean Tragedy*, by R. S. White. Athlone. pp. x + 149. £20.

60. *Last Things in Shakespeare*, by Harry Morris. FlorSU. pp. xii + 348. $30.

61. *'If it were done': 'Macbeth' and Tragic Action*, by James L. Calderwood. UMass. pp. xvii + 156. £16.65.

unexciting, response is quickly buried beneath discussions of 'parallels' between Macbeth's and Shakespeare's reactions to the horror of tragedy, Oedipal interpretations, mock-metaphysics, and I wot not what. A welter of profitless abstractions also submerges Jacqueline Rose's 'Hamlet – the *Mona Lisa* of Literature' (*CritQ*), which, disagreeing with T. S. Eliot whose phrase the title quotes, sees the weaknesses of the characterization of Gertrude as a source of dramatic strength. A whole book on *Hamlet* by Robert W. Luyster [62] adopts a pseudo-philosophical approach to the theme of *Weltschmertz*, along with the obscure style currently thought proper for such an undertaking. Phenomenology also underpins Joseph Natoli's 'Dimensions of Consciousness in *Hamlet*' (*Mosaic*).

It is a short step from phenomenology to psychoanalysis, and there is as long a queue for the couch as ever. David Willbern's 'Phantasmagoric *Macbeth*' (*ELR*) equates regicide with matricide and infanticide and has diagrams to prove it. David Simpson in '"Great Things of us Forgot": Seeing *Lear* Better' (*CritQ*) detects a 'Lear syndrome', instinctively antipathetic to sexuality, behind much in the play besides Lear himself, whom he agrees with Freud in seeing as wicked throughout. *Hamlet* predictably receives most attention from this viewpoint. In *HSt* 1985, now to hand, we have Craig A. Bernthal's '"Self" Examination and Readiness in *Hamlet*' (Hamlet achieves inner calm by passing through inner turmoil), Vernon Garth Miles's 'Hamlet's Search for Philosophic Integration: A Twentieth-Century View' ('Classical humanistic optimism' versus 'evangelical Protestant determinism'), and Marguerite M. Vey-Miller and Ronald J. Miller's 'Degrees of Psychopathology in *Hamlet*' (when is a mad person not a mad person?). Conclusions so platitudinous are poor reward for the effort of reading this stuff. Michael Srigley claims psychic powers for 'Hamlet's Prophetic Soul' (*SN*) because some Renaissance thinkers associated these with madness and melancholy, but perhaps not even Hamlet could have foreseen what would happen to *Hamlet* criticism.

Gender criticism is well to the fore this year with Lisa Lowe's '"Say I play the man I am": Gender and Politics in *Coriolanus*' (*KR*), Madelon Sprengnether's 'Annihilating Intimacy in *Coriolanus*' in Rose [44], and Coppélia Kahn's 'The Absent Mother in *King Lear*' in Ferguson [26]. The lack of historical awareness in many of these studies makes their assumptions and conclusions very hard to accept. Shakespeare was neither a chauvinist nor a feminist: his understanding of gender and the roles of men and women was fundamentally different from ours, and I cannot honestly see much profit in trying to read the plays as if it were not. To speak of Lear's 'repression of maternal imprinting', for instance, as Coppélia Kahn does, is simply to fail to make sense. Sometimes there is a horrid conjunction of gender criticism and psychoanalysis: Lisa Lowe's article, for instance, features a staggering footnote on Coriolanus's name as a phallic symbol. Surprisingly she makes nothing of the last four letters.

Beneath these perversities lies a modernist suspicion of the whole notion of coherent character and a refusal to believe that Shakespeare could ever have been unironical or unambiguous. So R. W. Desai exposes 'Duncan's Duplicity' (*UCrow*) in, as he thinks, deliberately plotting against poor,

62. *Hamlet and Man's Being: The Phenomenology of Nausea*, by Robert W. Luyster. UPA (1984). pp. viii + 172. hb $26.25, pb $12.25.

ill-treated Macbeth; and Donald W. Foster in 'Macbeth's War on Time' (ELR) denies that Scotland under Duncan was 'anything but bloody and chaotic' and doubts whether critics are right to expect a return to order at the end of the play. It is quite another thing to admit that characterization in Shakespeare is often full of gaps, a fact which receives much examination this year, for example by James L. Hill ('"What, are they children?"': Shakespeare's Tragic Women and the Boy Actors', SEL) in relation to the emotional range of the great female roles, by W. B. Worthen ('The Weight of Antony: Staging "Character" in Antony and Cleopatra', SEL) in relation to disparities between the images of Antony presented to our imaginations and our eyes, by S. Nagarajan ('The Nature of the Tragic Self in Hamlet', ESDEJU), by Michael Orange ('Hamlet: A Cry of Players', SSEng, 1985), by Maqbool H. Khan ('The Fare in Hamlet', AJES), and by A. A. Ansari ('Marcus Brutus: The Divided Self', AJES, 1985). Edward Pechter's essay, 'Julius Caesar and Sejanus: Roman Politics, Inner Selves and the Power of the Theatre' in Honigmann[50] compares Shakespearean and Jonsonian treatments of the dilemma of the politician yearning in vain for the privacy of an inner self (he also has some good remarks about Leonard Digges's commemorative poem in the 1640 Folio). But again it is L. G. Salingar[23] who writes with most insight on this topic; in 'Shakespeare and the Ventriloquists' he subtly examines Shakespeare's explorations of his characters' awareness of their own divided natures. A collection edited by Clifford Davidson, C. J. Gianakaris, and John H. Stroupe[63] reprints essays from CompD, some on the tragedies, including Hamlet, King Lear, and Coriolanus, but without any note of when they were originally published.

We move now from general categories to individual plays. The early tragedies receive scant attention. Rudolf Stamm delicately analyses 'The First Meeting of the Lovers' in Romeo and Juliet (ES) as a pivotal moment simultaneously marking Romeo's emergence from morbid introspection and initiating the lovers' tragedy. Jill Colaco in 'The Window Scenes in Romeo and Juliet' (SP) sees influence from the folk-song motif of the Night Visit, possibly via Antony Munday's Fidele and Fortunio (1584) and The Jew of Malta. Shigeki Takada's 'Calls and Silence: Style of Distance in Julius Caesar' (ShStud, 1984–5) applauds the often-noted coldness of this play as the best medium for the lesson that too much emotionalism is a bad thing for the politician. David Elloway writes on Julius Caesar in the MMG series[64], ably expounding the political and ethical neutrality of the play, although his survey of critical approaches stops short in the mid 1960s.

I have mentioned Hamlet many times already, but there is far more to come. I did not expect to be glad to see the MMG on this play, but it is by Jean Brooks[65], who profits from, without being parasitical upon, Harold Jenkins's great edition, and whose deeply pondered commentary will enlighten scholars as much as schoolchildren. R. S. White brightens the pages of HSt (1985) with a piece on 'The Spirit of Yorick, Or the Tragic Sense of Humour in Hamlet', which examines Hamlet's use of wit as a means of evasion, camouflage, expression of his hidden fears, and a protective mechanism for coping with

63. Drama in the Renaissance: Comparative and Critical Essays, ed. by Clifford Davidson, C. J. Gianakaris, and John H. Stroupe. AMS. pp. viii + 342. $34.50.

64. 'Julius Caesar', by David Elloway. MMG. Macmillan. pp. viii + 88. pb £1.25.

65. 'Hamlet', by Jean Brooks. MMG. Macmillan. pp. viii + 88. pb £1.25.

tragic awareness, as well as a source of genuine *bonhomie*. White's Hamlet is no 'lugubrious neurotic'; on the contrary, he has 'a sublimely healthy psyche in dealing with appalling circumstances'. This refreshing view is something to be grateful for. So is Jonathan Baldo's '"His form and cause conjoin'd": Reflections on "Cause" in *Hamlet*' (*RenD*, 1985), an examination of the way verbal ambiguity ('both a willful or deliberate course of action and a causal logic that suggests that our actions are never free or unconditioned') reflects ambiguity of theme. Too often elsewhere we are back with the weary, stale, flat, or unprofitable. There is some mild interest in Edward Pechter's 'Remembering *Hamlet*; or, How It Feels to Go Like a Crab Backwards' (*ShS*) on the tension between the forward movement of plot and the regressiveness of delay. René Girard's essay 'Hamlet's Dull Revenge' in Parker and Quint [25] sees the play as deliberately guying the absurdity of its own genre, a view better expressed by William Empson in 1953 in an essay now revised for inclusion in his *Essays* [22], without anything corresponding to Girard's ponderous musing on the relevance of *Hamlet* to a world terrified by the threat of nuclear revenge. John S. Wilks in 'The Discourse of Reason: Justice and the Erroneous Conscience in *Hamlet*' (*ShakS*) sees Hamlet, in terms borrowed by Renaissance philosophers from the scholastics, as unable to recognize when he is misapplying to particular circumstances ethical principles which in theory are valid. Ralph Berry's 'Hamlet's Doubles' (*SQ*) over-elaborately discusses both functional doubling (a matter of economic necessity) and doubling to make a thematic point (e.g. the same actor as the Ghost/Fortinbras).

There are several notes on miscellaneous points. William T. Betken offers a line-by-line commentary on 'The "Recorder" Episode of *Hamlet*' (III.ii) (*HSt*, 1985). John Doebler in 'When Troy Fell' (*CompD*) considers passages in *Julius Caesar* and *Hamlet* among others against the background of Renaissance iconographical treatments of Anchises and Aeneas. The latter also features in W. R. Johnson's comparative essay, 'The Figure of Laertes: Reflections on the Character of Aeneas', in Bernard [53]. Robert F. Fleissner sees an alchemical allusion in 'Hamlet's Flesh Revisited' (*HSt*, 1985) and in the same volume Paul Gaudet ('"He is justly served": The Ordering of Experience in *Hamlet*') traces the development of our reaction to Claudius so that we agree with Laertes' judgement. Anthony Miller's 'A Reminiscence of Erasmus in *Hamlet* III.ii.92–5' (*ELN*) sees a reference to the *Colloquies*; Clifford J. Ronan in 'Sallust, Beasts that "Sleep and Feed"', and *Hamlet* 5.2' (*HSt*, 1985) relates IV.iv.33–5 to Sallust's *Bellum Catilinae* II.8–9 and considers other echoes of Sallust in the play; James Taylor explores '*Hamlet*'s Debt to Sixteenth-Century Satire' (*FMLS*), especially as practised by John Marston; J. J. M. Tobin's 'Gabriel Harvey: "Excellent Matter of Emulation"' (*HSt*, 1985), supplementing his earlier article (*AN&Q*, 1980), finds borrowings from Harvey's *A New Letter of Notable Contents* and *Pierce's Supererogation* (both of 1593); Margaret Weedon, in 'Hawk, Handsaw and Ganza?' (*N&Q*), hears an echo of a lost rhyming jingle behind the notoriously cryptic remark; Robert F. Willson Jr, in 'Hamlet's Bellerophontic Letters' (*HSt*, 1985), finds a source for the device in Greek myth, via François de Belleforest.

This has not been a boom year for *Othello* studies. Mary Laughlin Fawcett in 'Chastity and Speech in *Othello* and *Comus*' (*RenD*, 1985) points out that in both plays the heroine can meet attacks on her chastity only with a dignified silence. R. A. Foakes's 'The Descent of Iago: Satire, Ben Jonson, and Shakespeare's *Othello*', in Honigmann[50], locates the play in the context of the poetic and dramatic satire of the 1590s, examining Iago's role as a satiric commentator counting for success upon our guilty complicity. A classical comic heritage concerns Frances Teague in '*Othello* and New Comedy' (*CompD*); she discusses Shakespeare's use of time, place, and character-type, devices which in comedy make for enjoyable chaos but here for frightening anarchy. A. P. Riemer in 'The *Othello* Music' (*SSEng*, 1985) seeks to throw light on Shakespeare's play through Verdi's opera, which he astonishingly prefers. A rather different, more profitable musical angle is adopted by Rosalind King in '"Then murder's out of tune": The Music and Structure of *Othello*' (*ShS*): she examines musical effects and images in the play (e.g. Iago as would-be agent of harmony, Desdemona's song as lyrical expression of her inner conflict).

Salingar's collection[23] contains his essays on 'Romance in *King Lear*' and '*King Lear*, Montaigne and Harsnett': the former is supplemented probably by Guy Butler's 'King Lear and Ancient Britain' (*Theoria*, 1985), which I have not seen, and certainly by Richard Dutton's discussion (*L&H*) of resemblances between the role of mythical British history in *Lear* and in Anthony Munday's pageant *The Triumphs of Reunited Britannia* (1605), a work also discussed by H. Neville Davies in relation to *Antony and Cleopatra* (see below). A welcome contribution comes from René J. A. Weis, whose 'Dissent and Moral Primitivism in *King Lear*' (*English*) sturdily opposes any Christian allegorizing, reminding us that morality is explored, not asserted, in the play, which, far from being nihilistic, gains positive emphasis precisely from that freedom of exploration. This conflict between nihilism and affirmation is also noted by Z. A. Usmani in '*King Lear*: Nothing and the Thing Itself' (*AJES*). Character-studies are popular, and on the whole helpful. Y. B. Olsen, taking 'Edmund and Lear' (*DUJ*) rather than Gloucester and Lear as the axes in the play's structure, sees them both disturbing the equilibrium of the play-world and both finally educated into the meaning of love, whilst Edgar's role as therapist for Gloucester is charted by John Coates's '"Poor Tom" and the Spiritual Journey in *King Lear*' in the same journal. Marian D. Perret, in '*Lear*'s Good Old Man' (*ShakS*, 1985), sees Gloucester as more empathetic than Lear in his humility, absence of isolating negation, and stoical faith. The contrast between Lear's growing wisdom and the Fool's persistent escapism is noted by Gottlieb Gaiser in 'The Fool's Prophecy [in III.ii] as a Key to his Function' (*Anglia*). I found Frederick T. Flahiff's 'Lear's Map' (*CahiersE*) intensely irritating. His subject is a promising one – the play's geographical symbolism – but he insists on interlarding his argument with pretentious 'epigrams', e.g. 'Where Lear's map provides a cloth – and bill of fare – for his heirs' table, Shakespeare had first to dine upon time'. I've read better Christmas cracker mottoes. There are two aids to learning; the MMG by Francis Casey[66], and, for hard-pressed pedagogues, *Approaches to Teaching Shakespeare's 'King Lear'*[67], which contains, first a survey of editions and critical work by the editor, and then sixteen brief essays by other hands on various ways of presenting the play in the

---

66. '*King Lear*', by Francis Casey. MMG. Macmillan. pp. viii + 96. pb £1.25.

67. *Approaches to Teaching Shakespeare's 'King Lear'*, ed. by Robert H. Ray. MLA. pp. ix + 162. hb $30, pb $16.50.

classroom. The general impression of the craving for a marketable 'line' on the play, by students and teachers alike, is depressing. Finally a clutch of notes. Debts to Erasmus's *Apophthegmes* are seen in III.iv by F. G. Butler's 'Who are King Lear's Philosophers?' (*ES*); he thinks they are Diogenes the Cynic and Crates. An allusion to the euphoniously named Cebes of Thebes is also seen by S. Viswanathan in '"This Same Learned Theban": *King Lear*, III.iv.161' (*N&Q*). Joseph Candido argues for Matthew 5 rather than 2 Corinthians or James as the source of 'Lear's "Yeas" and "Nays"' in IV.vi.99-101 (*ELN*); Joseph A. Porter finds 'More Echoes from Eliot's *Ortho-epia Gallica* [1593] in *King Lear* [IV.vi] and *Henry V*' (*SQ*); Clifford J. Ronan proposes connections between '*Selimus* and the Blinding of Gloucester' (*N&Q*), supplementing Inga-Stina Ekeblad (Ewbank)'s note of yesteryear (*YW* 38.144).

It is getting hard to say anything new and useful about *Macbeth*. Even Empson's 1952 essay (revised and reprinted in *Essays on Shakespeare*[22]) is not one of his best, so what hope for the rest of us? Alan Sinfield in '*Macbeth*: History, Ideology and Intellectuals' (*CritQ*) manages to make interesting connections between the antimonarchist ideas of George Buchanan's *History of Scotland* (1582), which reposes sovereignty in the people, and some strands of political thought in *Macbeth*, which he finds less reflective of Jacobean absolutism than is usually assumed. William O. Scott ('Macbeth's – and Our – Self-Equivocations', *SQ*) struggles to be clear about truth, lies, and the gap between intended and conveyed meanings. The modest efforts, which don't try to be too ingenious, often succeed surprisingly well: for instance Christine Mangala Frost's '"Who Dares Do More?": *Macbeth* and Metaphysical Dread' (*SSEng*, 1985) on the nature of moral evil; Susanna Hamilton's '"The Charm's Wound Up"' (*English*) on the relationship between structural/verbal parallelism and ethical ambiguity; or K. Tetzeli von Rosador's essay in Honigmann[50] on the function of temptation in *Macbeth* and *Doctor Faustus* as a means of trapping the protagonists in their own fantasies. This is a convenient place to mention Jean MacIntyre's 'Doctor Faustus and the Later Shakespeare' (*CahiersE*), a modest but successful reminder of Shakespeare's use, in *Macbeth* and, more extensively, Edmund in *Lear*, of the episode in which Faustus stabs himself to write his contract with Mephostophilis (*sic*) in his own blood – the common theme being the individuals' knowing rejection of goodness. I am less happy about Luisa Guj's '*Macbeth* and the Seeds of Time' (*ShakS*), which does contain interesting details of the Renaissance iconography of Time with reference to Petrarch and Titian, but the glide from this to the 'tricephalous hieroglyph of time around which *Macbeth* is shaped' is a bit too slick. Michael Vickers finds 'A Source in Plutarch's *Life of Pelopidas* for Lady Macbeth' (*N&Q*), while one of Whitney's *Emblems* is pressed into service to explain 'Hellkite' by Donald W. Rude in 'A Possible Source for Shakespeare's *Macbeth* V.i.217-9' (*AN&Q*).

Rajiva Verma's 'Winners and Losers: A Study of *Macbeth* and *Antony and Cleopatra*' (*MLR*) ranges more widely than the title suggests in a discussion of these plays as polar opposites aesthetically and psychologically. Rodney Simard studies 'Source and *Antony and Cleopatra*: Shakespeare's Adaptation of Plutarch's Octavia' (*ShJE*), noting that Octavia's role is reduced but not her importance: she intensifies, by contrast, the lovers' relation, throws into relief Antony's impetuousness and Cleopatra's nobility, and exposes Caesar's political ruthlessness. Iconography concerns C. W. R. D. Moseley in

'Cleopatra's Prudence: Three Notes on the Use of Emblems in *Antony and Cleopatra*' (*ShJW*). Drawing for visual analogues on the emblem books of Geoffrey Whitney (1586) and George Wither (1635), he deals with Antony as Colossus, Antony as having to make a 'choice of Hercules' between Cleopatra and Octavia, and the use, in Cleopatra's death scene, of the symbolizing of royal prudence by a snake. Errol Durbach's '*Antony and Cleopatra* and *Rosmersholm*: "Third Empire" Love Tragedies' (*CompD*) claims these plays share a dialectical structure whose synthesis is posited in a more transcendent type of love than their protagonists achieve. In her Leeds inaugural lecture 'Transmigrations of Cleopatra' (*ULR*) the newly transmigrated Inga-Stina Ewbank offers an elegant study of the character of Cleopatra as interpreted before, by, and after Shakespeare. She observes that, in comparison with his sources and analogues, Shakespeare evolves a Cleopatra who is a unique 'combination of contraries . . . both flesh and spirit, both sex and neo-platonic ideal', a duality subsequently split into its separate components. The unusually comprehensive discussion takes in theatre history as well as the writings of Dryden, half-forgotten eighteenth- and nineteenth-century Germans, Théophile Gautier, Charlotte Brontë in *Villette*, and George Eliot in *Middlemarch*. The width of Professor Ewbank's scholarly interests is always exhilarating, but even she, for once, is not a lass unparallel'd, for in H. Neville Davies's 'Jacobean *Antony and Cleopatra*' (*ShakS*, 1985) we have a major contribution to knowledge, comparable to Emrys Jones's 'Stuart *Cymbeline*' (*EIC*, 1961; *YW* 42.124) which the title echoes, and taking its point of departure from Jones's hypothesis, in his New Penguin edition of *Antony*, that the play might have been performed at Court. Davies provides extensive, documented discussion of James's efforts to portray himself as a new Augustus and to discourage the nostalgia for the reign of Elizabeth I. He sets the play in the context of the state visit to England in 1606 of Christian IV of Denmark, James's brother-in-law (as Antony was Octavius's), and known as a bluff, soldierly character, fond of his drink: the pageantry of the visit may have coalesced in Shakespeare's mind with his reading of some (but not all) of the same details in Plutarch. Davies is far too tactful to spoil his case by claiming a reductive historical allegory, but his view that the play makes use of these events, sometimes poetically, sometimes mischievously, is to me wholly convincing.

As for the other late classical tragedies, A. A. Ansari's 'The Protagonist's Dilemma in *Timon of Athens*' (*AJES*) is a sensible study of Timon's unconscious self-destruction, concluding, surely rightly, that the play sacrifices depth of characterization to 'conceptual schematism': while John M. Wallace's '*Timon of Athens* and the Three Graces: Shakespeare's Senecan Study' (*MP*) argues strongly for Seneca's *De beneficiis* as the source for ideas about bounty and generosity in *Timon*, which he sees as ultimately rejecting as hopelessly idealistic the classical model of a just society. Guy Butler's 'William Fulbecke: A New Shakespeare Source?' (*N&Q*) relates *Lear* and *Coriolanus* respectively to Fulbecke's *Book of Christian Ethicks* (1587) and *A Directive or Preparative to the Study of Law* (1600). Stanley D. McKenzie's '"Unshout the noise that banish'd Martius": Structural Paradox and Dissembling in *Coriolanus*' (*ShakS*) unravels paradoxes and ironies of plot, characterization, and language, ending in bafflement before a play which apparently 'leaves us in a moral vacuum', a judgement for which there is perhaps more warrant here than with any other of the tragedies.

(e) Poems

There has been good work on *Lucrece* this year. Katharine Eisaman Maus under the title 'Taking Tropes Seriously: Language and Violence in Shakespeare's *Rape of Lucrece*' (*SQ*) attends closely to the role of metaphor in the poem and the disastrous consequences of the characters' treating poetic figures literally. 'The Rape of Clio: Attitudes to History in Shakespeare's *Lucrece*' by Heather Dubrow (*ELR*) begins with Lucrece looking at the picture of Troy and proceeds to the ways in which the reading and writing of history are among the poem's central preoccupations. This is a fine, scholarly article, which is especially helpful on the differences between Livy's and Ovid's inter- pretations of the story, and between the argument and the body of the poem. A related essay by the same author, 'A Mirror for Complaints', published in Lewalski[48], sets *Lucrece* in the context of the complaint tradition and in par- ticular a group of poems published in the 1590s, such as Drayton's *Matilda* and Daniel's *Complaint of Rosamond*, which concern heroines whose chastity is tested by monarchs. Nancy Lindheim's 'The Shakespearean *Venus and Adonis*' (*SQ*), on the other hand, offers barely anything new.

There are two new candidates for Mr W.H., both hailing from Stratford: John Boe (*SQ*) proposes William Hall, father of the John Hall who married Shakespeare's daughter Susanna, and Barbara Everett – tongue-in-cheek, one hopes – suggests William Hathaway, Anne's brother. Everett's eccentric piece, 'Mrs Shakespeare' (*LRB*), purports to be a review of John Kerrigan's edition of *The Sonnets* and *A Lover's Complaint* (see pp. 214–15) but makes virtually no contact with his fascinating suggestion that the two works are intimately related to each other. Whether or not they agree with Kerrigan's sense of the unity and authority of the 1609 volume, all future readers of the *Sonnets* will have to take into account his rehabilitation of the vastly underrated *Lover's Complaint*.

Antony Easthope's 'Same Text, Different Readings: Shakespeare's Sonnet 94' (*CritQ*) is a useful introduction to how various forms of modern critical theory may be brought to bear on a specific Shakespearean text, but I know a good many non-professional lovers of the sonnets who would contest his claim that these poems live 'almost exclusively within academic institutions, in higher education and some GCE examinations'. Hugh Richmond (*KR*) introduces the reader to a gallery of Renaissance brunettes in support of his intelligent reading of 'The Dark Lady as Reformation Mistress'.

Joel Fineman's *Shakespeare's Perjured Eye: The Invention of Poetic Subjectivity in the Sonnets*[68] is a substantial study. At first I thought it was a brilliant one, but after working through its interminable repetitions, self- definitions, and self-qualifications, I decided it was a self-indulgent and pretentious one. It is a dense, difficult, one-idea book. As far as I can under- stand it, the idea is essentially that Shakespeare inherited a bankrupted Petrarchan tradition of praise and re-invented it, in so doing creating a new

---

68. *Shakespeare's Perjured Eye: The Invention of Poetic Subjectivity in the Sonnets*, by Joel Fineman. UCal. pp. x + 365. $35.

conception of the self, divided between the 'I' and the 'eye', speaking and seeing, metaphor and mimesis, subjectivity and erotic desire. But there is a complete lack of contextualization; Fineman never explores how others in the 1590s engaged with problems of the self while working within the sonnet form – the absence of Fulke Greville's *Caelica* from the index is symptomatic and debilitating. What is more, Fineman claims that Shakespeare invented 'the only kind of subjectivity that survives in the literature successive to the poetry of praise', but makes no reference to that literature. In the end, the most I can say for *Shakespeare's Perjured Eye* is that the slow, careful reading which it demands sends one back to a slow, careful re-reading of the sonnets themselves.

Renaissance Drama: Excluding Shakespeare

MICHAEL SMITH

This chapter has four sections: 1. Editions and Textual Scholarship; 2. Theatre History; 3. Criticism: (a) General, (b) Marlowe, (c) Jonson, (d) Other Playwrights and Plays; 4. Masque and Pageant. A selective review of books may be found in the spring number of *SEL*.

1. Editions, and Textual Scholarship

Let's begin with the bishop and the actress. James Shirley's city comedy *The Lady of Pleasure* has been edited for the Revels Plays by Ronald Huebert [1], and his belated revenge tragedy *The Cardinal* keeps it company, in an edition by E. M. Yearling [2]. Both texts have been carefully prepared. Huebert's commentary is the more widely informative, Yearling's tauter and more consistently to the point. Neither editor sees reason to challenge the prevailing critical estimate of Shirley. They ask us to admire his professional craftsmanship and his sensitive readjustment of dramatic stereotypes; his narrowness of stylistic range is conceded, as is a timidity or complacency which limits his effectiveness as a satirist. The keynote of Yearling's introduction to *The Cardinal* is a cautious scepticism: about the nature of the Caroline audience, about the play's possible political significance, about whether any one work should be identified as the play's main source. Huebert offers an interpretation of *The Lady of Pleasure* as a satirical portrait of fashionable Caroline society and, in particular, of its worship of conspicuous consumption. The play's title may refer to either of two ladies: the profligate, adulterous, and unambiguously named Aretina or the profligate, chaste, and ambiguously named Celestina. Huebert finds the former much more interesting than the latter, impatiently dismissing Celestina's polite duels of manners with the unnamed, not-so-Platonic nobleman that take up much of the last two acts as mere toadying to the fads of Henrietta Maria, and rebuking Shirley for not following through Aretina's career to a thoroughly impolite showdown with her undeceived husband. If Martin Butler is right about the play's point (*Theatre and Crisis*, *YW* 65.253–4), we must conclude that Huebert has not quite got it. Neither of these editions is perfect, but both are welcome extensions to the

1. *The Lady of Pleasure*, by James Shirley, ed. by Ronald Huebert. ManU. pp. xii + 208. £29.95.

2. *The Cardinal*, by James Shirley, ed. by E. M. Yearling. ManU. pp. x + 166. £29.95.

Revels series, all the more so in the continued absence of a reliable collected edition of Shirley's plays.

A world away from the civilities of Caroline London are the events of *A Yorkshire Tragedy*: nasty, brutish – and remarkably short, one can't help thinking, to be granted a Revels edition all to itself[3]. This is, however, a very good edition: Barry Gaines has prepared the text, A. C. Cawley the remarkably detailed and scholarly commentary, and the introduction is shared between them. Besides full accounts of the play's stage and textual history, it contains careful and authoritative discussions of the authorship controversy, of the real-life incidents which lie behind the play, and of the shaping which the playwright has imposed upon them. The contemporary news pamphlet which popularized the sensational story of the Calverley murders, Walter Calverley's own deposition at his trial, and a collection of local legends which have grown up around his name, are reprinted as appendixes.

There is one further Revels volume to report, a collection of three 'witchcraft' plays, edited by Peter Corbin and Douglas Sedge[4], the first such anthology to be published in the recently inaugurated Companion Library series. The texts are edited to the high standard of accuracy characteristic of the parent series, but both introductions and commentaries are scaled down considerably, the latter being relegated from the foot of the page to the back of the book, a bother if you want to consult it regularly but less intrusive if you don't. The volume's thematic design announces itself in the slightly disproportionate amount of space given to the elucidation of references to witchcraft, and in the editors' introductory emphasis on the importance of the witch scenes to the design of their chosen plays. These are: Marston's Carthaginian tragedy *Sophonisba*, Middleton's tragicomedy *The Witch*, and, the only one of the three to have enjoyed a limited recent currency in the theatre, *The Witch of Edmonton*, by Dekker, Ford, and Rowley. Whereas Mother Sawyer and her faithful Dog are undeniably central to *The Witch of Edmonton*, it is possible that the editors exaggerate the importance of Marston's Erictho and even of Middleton's Hecate in the other two plays: a danger of the thematic approach. Nevertheless, this is a largely successful volume, which serves a useful purpose in making more easily available three plays which deserve to be better known.

As luck would have it, Corbin and Sedge are not the only anthologists to have had the bright idea of resuscitating *Sophonisba*. It is also included in the generous selection of Marston's plays edited for CUP's Plays by Renaissance and Restoration Dramatists series by MacDonald P. Jackson and Michael Neill[5]. Their text of *Sophonisba* is in fact slightly preferable to that of the Revels editors, and their annotation more balanced and helpful; the four more famous plays – *Antonio and Mellida*, *Antonio's Revenge*, *The Malcontent*, and *The Dutch Courtesan* – are equally skilfully handled. Confident that Webster's additions to *The Malcontent* can be clearly identified, Jackson and Neill have the courage to take these scenes out of their text and put them into an

3. *A Yorkshire Tragedy*, ed. by A. C. Cawley and Barry Gaines. ManU. pp. xii + 123. hb £25, pb £7.50.

4. *Three Jacobean Witchcraft Plays*, ed. by Peter Corbin and Douglas Sedge. ManU. pp. xii + 259. £29.50.

5. *The Selected Plays of John Marston*, ed. by MacDonald P. Jackson and Michael Neill. CUP. pp. xxxvi + 535. hb £37.50, pb £12.95.

appendix: a contentious decision, perhaps, but the supporting arguments are strong. The plays are prefaced by an account of Marston's life and a full, vigorously annotated bibliography of Marston criticism. The tall, narrow page format standard to the series is no more appealing to the eye than it has ever been, and the paperback cannot be opened flat without breaking the binding. But in every other respect this is a desirable book, meeting a real need.

Colin Gibson's *Selected Plays of John Ford* in the same series does not seem so necessary an addition to the catalogue[6]. In choosing the obvious three (*The Broken Heart*, *'Tis Pity She's a Whore*, and *Perkin Warbeck*), Gibson follows exactly in the footsteps of Keith Sturgess and his Penguin. Although Gibson's annotation is a little more detailed than his competitor's, and his bibliography more up to date, Sturgess's handy edition stands up pretty well to the comparison, and sells at not much more than a third of the new selection's price. While the Penguin remains in print, I doubt whether Gibson's book will make much headway in the student market.

The editions next to be noticed aim at a much more specialized readership. It is unimaginable that John Bale's polemical anti-Roman interludes will ever again hold the stage; even in the sixteenth century their moment was soon over, the drama rapidly turning away (not entirely of its own accord) from the paths down which Bale wished to drive it. Nevertheless, the plays occupy an important place in dramatic history, and a reliable collected edition has long been needed. Peter Happé's[7] fits the bill admirably. His succinct but comprehensive introduction is packed with helpful information about Bale's life, works, aims, sources, and dramaturgy; his commentary deals knowledgeably with the many scriptural references and points of doctrine that pepper the texts, while remaining alert at the same time to practical questions of staging; the whole edition is marked by an energetic and scrupulous attention to detail. It fully lives up to the high standards set by previous volumes in the generally excellent Tudor Interludes series.

Edward Sharpham 'of the Middle Temple, Gentleman' wrote two uneven, rather risqué comedies for the Children of the Revels in the early years of James I's reign. These plays, *The Fleire* and *Cupid's Whirligig*, together with a prose pamphlet probably from Sharpham's pen, *The Discoverie of the Knights of the Poste*, make up 'the works of Edward Sharpham', as edited by Christopher Gordon Petter[8]. A painstaking, bulky doctoral thesis, which might have benefited from severer pruning before it became a book, Petter's edition of Sharpham is useful if time-consuming. Textual analysis and commentary are unexceptionable; a biography of Sharpham is included; and the critical introductions do as much as can possibly be done for the plays, if not indeed rather more.

No comic genius, Sharpham could at least turn out amusing and stageable scenes in his burlesque vein. That is more than can be said for the Oxford man,

6. *The Selected Plays of John Ford*, ed. by Colin Gibson. CUP. pp. xviii + 356. hb £30, pb £12.95.

7. *The Complete Plays of John Bale*, ed. by Peter Happé. 2 vols. Brewer. Vol. I (1985). pp. x + 167. £27.50; Vol. II. pp. xii + 193. £25.

8. *A Critical Old Spelling Edition of the Works of Edward Sharpham, together with Critical Introductions Comprising a Study of the Relationship of his Works to the Tradition of their Age*, by Christopher Gordon Petter. Garland. pp. x + 593. $90.

Samuel Harding, whose sow's ear of a revenge tragedy, *Sicily and Naples*, has been indifferently edited by Joan Warthling Roberts[9]. Her introduction enumerates the revenge-play conventions employed by Harding, and gives some biographical information about the author and his circle. Her footnotes are not always reliable, and contain at least two very bad errors. In an appendix she follows up Fredson Bowers's suggestion that Harding's play was a source for Shirley's *The Cardinal*, adducing some further parallel passages. Caroline specialists may also be interested in the facsimile and transcription of the manuscript of Thomas Randolph's *Praeludium*, published by Georges Borias in *CahiersE*. Borias accepts G. E. Bentley's theory that the piece was written to serve as an induction to Randolph's play *The Muses' Looking Glass*, and suggests that it offers a valuable glimpse into the life of the players in the early 1630s.

Brief mention, finally, for two ongoing series, one old, one new. Webster's *The White Devil*[10] and Jonson's *Bartholomew Fair*[11], both with lively introductions by Simon Trussler, are recent arrivals in Methuen Student Editions. Each volume follows a standard format, the introduction including a scene-by-scene synopsis of the play; a complete set of character sketches; sections on structure, staging, language, and themes; and suggestions for further reading (the list given for *Bartholomew Fair* is, incidentally, somewhat eccentric). The notes give straightforward explanations of difficult words and phrases, and are pitched so as to be of assistance to students who do not speak English as their first language. Photographs of recent productions brighten things up. These are competent, neatly packaged editions which will see many readers through their exams. That was the old series. The new series, again with 'commentaries' by the ubiquitous Simon Trussler and published by Methuen (this time in association with the RSC), is the Swan Theatre Plays. Programmes for productions in the RSC's exciting new auditorium take the form of play-texts (with the company's cuts and alterations marked), prefaced by brief informative introductions that can be read during the interval or after the show. Productions during the first season included Jonson's *Every Man in his Humour*[12] and Trevor Nunn's adaptation of Thomas Heywood's *The Fair Maid of the West*[13]. The only drawback of this excellent innovation is the sight of play-goers straining their eyes to follow the play word by word, a habit which it is to be hoped dies out when the novelty wears off.

From among the year's bibliographical studies, two essays stand out as of major importance, Antony Hammond's meticulous investigation into the printing of '*The White Devil* in Nicholas Okes's Shop' (*SB*) and Giorgio Melchiori's latest contribution to the Thomas More controversy, '*The Booke of Sir Thomas Moore*: A Chronology of Revision' (*SQ*). Hammond demon-

9. *Sicily and Naples; or, The Fatall Union, a Tragedy*, by Samuel Harding, ed. by Joan Warthling Roberts. Garland. pp. viii + 134. $41.

10. *The White Devil*, by John Webster, commentary by Simon Trussler, and notes by Jacqui Russell. Methuen. pp. xlvi + 146. pb £2.50.

11. *Bartholomew Fair*, by Ben Jonson, commentary and notes by Simon Trussler. Methuen. pp. xlii + 164. pb £2.95.

12. *Every Man in his Humour*, by Ben Jonson, commentary by Simon Trussler. Methuen/RSC. pp. 76. pb £2.95.

13. *The Fair Maid of the West*, by Thomas Heywood, adapted by Trevor Nunn, commentary by Simon Trussler. Methuen/RSC. pp. 75. pb £2.95.

strates the likelihood that three, rather than two, compositors were engaged in the setting of *The White Devil*, and reports that his exhaustive analysis of the recurrence of damaged types in the text reveals no out-of-the-way Okesian practices. He manages to be philosophical about this, though must have hoped initially that he would have more to show for his labour. Future editors of the play will find this article indispensable. The same is true of Melchiori's article on *Sir Thomas More*. His close scrutiny of this much-examined manuscript reveals, amazingly enough, some previously unnoticed clues to the order in which the several layers of revision were carried out: the reasoning is too intricate to be summarized here. No less scholarly, but on subjects of less significance, are Paul Mulholland's detailed bibliographical account of Thomas Middleton's prose pamphlet, *The Two Gates of Salvation*, which he finds 'An Instance of Running-Title Rotation at Press' (*Lib*); and another of Gerald D. Johnson's helpful surveys of the careers of members of the Stationers' Company, 'John Trundle and the Book-Trade 1603-1626' (*SB*). A publisher of topical ephemera, Trundle also had a hand in half a dozen play quartos, including *Hamlet* Q1.

2. Theatre History

Yoshiko Kawachi's *Calendar of English Renaissance Drama*[14] closely resembles Alfred Harbage and Samuel Schoenbaum's *Annals of English Drama* (*YW* 45.12–13) in its columnar layout, but is rather different in purpose and scope. Whereas *Annals* is essentially a list of plays, and covers a period of seven hundred years, Kawachi's *Calendar* is a list of recorded (or deducible) performances, and covers only the period from the accession of Elizabeth to the outbreak of the Civil War. Thus, to take a convenient example, there is not only an entry for Marlowe's *Doctor Faustus* against the year 1592 (conjectural first performance), but also twenty-eight further entries, covering performances at Henslowe's Rose and other venues, and concluding with a staging by Prince Charles's Men at the Fortune in 1641. It can be seen that Kawachi offers a much fuller picture of dramatic activity during the period than can be got from Harbage and Schoenbaum. His book certainly appears to be a careful and thorough digest of the information available in published sources, though only prolonged use can properly test the accuracy and exhaustiveness of this heroic feat of compilation. One area in which the *Calendar* already needs updating is provincial drama, to our knowledge of which the REED project is adding all the time. As if to underline the point, David George has unearthed evidence in 'The Walmesley of Dunkenhalgh Accounts' (*REEDN*, 1985) of regular and frequent visits by touring players to a Lancashire manor house; while, across the Pennines, Christopher Dean makes some corrections to the previously published account of 'The Simpson Players' Tour of North Yorkshire in 1616' (*N&Q*).

Work on the London theatres is dominated by Herbert Berry's admirable history of the Boar's Head playhouse[15], which completely displaces C. J.

14. *A Calendar of English Renaissance Drama, 1558-1642*, by Yoshiko Kawachi. Garland. pp. xviii + 351. $79.

15. *The Boar's Head Playhouse*, by Herbert Berry, illus. by C. Walter Hodges. Folger/AUP. pp. 238. £21.

Sisson's book (*YW* 53.197) as the standard work on the subject, and indeed discredits many of Sisson's findings. Berry's expert untangling of the complicated lawsuits to which the building of the playhouse gave rise enables us to gain valuable insights into the way the enterprise was managed and its profits distributed. The exact site of the playhouse is identified, its dimensions deduced, and, with the aid of drawings by C. Walter Hodges, its probable structure clearly explained. By analysing the handful of plays which may reasonably be assigned to the Boar's Head, Berry comes to some tentative conclusions about the nature of the stage fittings. In one of his battery of appendixes he attempts to reduce to order the rampant confusion that has grown up around the two Robert Brownes, one of whom was leader of the Boar's Head company. The fruit of many years' research, Berry's book is throughout scrupulous in its handling of evidence, and lucid and precise in its reasoning: a distinguished piece of scholarship.

These virtues can't, alas, be claimed for Willem Schrickx's *Foreign Envoys and Travelling Players in the Age of Shakespeare and Jonson*[16], a collection of gleanings from the archives of the Spanish Netherlands of material that has some bearing on 'Jacobean intellectual life'. The parts of the book dealing with English players on the continent have been previously published in *ShS* (*YW* 61.125–6; 65.248). The most striking new material is an account of Cyril Tourneur's military and naval career, spectacularly unconvincing in its readiness to conflate several surely separate Turners into one figure, and creating thereby a tangle which makes the Robert Browne confusion look like a simple granny-knot.

This year's crop of articles ranges in style from the speculative to the nitpicking. Laurie E. Maguire has two interesting pieces in *N&Q*, one to do with doubling in *John of Bordeaux*, and the inferences that may be drawn from it about the size of the company and the career of the actor John Holland; the other, 'A Stage Property in *A Larum for London*', suggesting a reason for identifying Henslowe's *The Sege of London* with the extant *A Larum*. John H. Astington's investigations of 'Staging at St James's Palace in the Seventeenth Century' (*ThR*) enable him to hazard a guess about where in the palace performances took place, and the nature of the stage facilities to be found there. Eric Rasmussen points out that 'The Implication of Past Tense Verbs in Early Elizabethan Dumb Shows' (*ES*), such as the dumbshow in *Gorboduc*, is that the texts describe what was actually done in performance. And Robert E. Burkhart has checked 'The Dimensions of Middle Temple Hall' (*SQ*) with a measuring tape, and thinks it worth reporting that the measurements given by Richard Hosley (40′ × 100′) are each a foot or so out.

To conclude this section, a book and an article on modern productions. Ejner J. Jensen's *Ben Jonson's Comedies on the Modern Stage*[17] is disappointing. He has assiduously collated the judgements of newspaper reviewers on productions of Jonson between 1899 and 1972, his aim 'to create the most accurate and comprehensive possible view of what actually happened on stage'. The aim and the method are not perhaps entirely compatible: the buzz of the critics can be

16. *Foreign Envoys and Travelling Players in the Age of Shakespeare and Jonson*, by Willem Schrickx. Universa. pp. 369 + 13 pl. BFr 1750.

17. *Ben Jonson's Comedies on the Modern Stage*, by Ejner J. Jensen. UMIRes (1985). pp. viii + 158. £45.50.

distracting, and on odd occasions one feels transported into a foyer variant of the vapours game, with each man bound to oppose the last that spoke, whether it concern him or no. Part of the problem, as Jensen himself points out, is that professional reviewers are much less familiar with Jonson's plays than they are with Shakespeare's, and tend to fall back on truisms and generalities more readily.

It is to be hoped that the commitment of the RSC's Swan Theatre to the non-Shakespearean repertoire will do something to remedy this situation: indeed, a good start has been made already with a strong production of *Every Man in his Humour*, directed by John Caird. It, and Barry Kyle's samurai production of *The Two Noble Kinsmen*, are subjected to thoughtful criticism by Peter Holland in 'Style at the Swan' (*EIC*), an interesting analysis of the new theatre's potential as an acting space and of the ways in which the company are responding (and failing to respond) to its challenge.

3. Criticism

(a) General

Three collections of essays were published this year, and it will be convenient to mention them first. E. A. J. Honigmann has persuaded a set of distinguished contributors that comparisons are odorous, the result being a set of nine essays, each of which balances a play by Shakespeare against a play by one of his contemporaries [18]. They will be reviewed individually in subsequent sections of the chapter. General impressions of the volume are that Shakespeare is usually made to weigh more heavily than his contemporaries, and that the 'comparison' format, although it gives rise to some fine essays, can at times be constricting. More anon.

The other two collections gather previously published work, fourteen essays by Leo Salingar on dramatic form in Shakespeare and the Jacobeans [19], and twenty essays on various aspects of Renaissance drama culled from the files of *CompD* [20]. Salingar's finely serious collection includes three important essays on Ben Jonson, one on *The Changeling*, and his well-known *Scrutiny* piece, '*The Revenger's Tragedy* and the Morality Tradition', nearly half a century old now but wearing its years lightly. All these essays have been reviewed in earlier volumes of *YWES* (19.142; 48.185; 58.5; 60.175; 62.211–12). Unfortunately, the articles which make up *Drama in the Renaissance* have *not* been noticed in *YWES*, which seems to have suffered from a blind spot for several years when it came to *CompD*. Space does not permit the redress of this oversight: a general notice must serve. The essays, mostly dating from the 1970s, and not confined to English drama, deal with a wide range of subjects from an equally wide variety of standpoints. Ritual, iconography, mannerism, theology, and the 'economics of love' are among the topics discussed; Lyly, Marlowe, Jonson, Tourneur,

18. *Shakespeare and his Contemporaries: Essays in Comparison*, ed. by E. A. J. Honigmann. ManU. pp. xii + 143. £25.

19. *Dramatic Form in Shakespeare and the Jacobeans: Essays*, by Leo Salingar. CUP. pp. x + 292. £27.50.

20. *Drama in the Renaissance: Comparative and Critical Essays*, ed. by Clifford Davidson, C. J. Gianakaris, and John H. Stroupe. AMS. pp. viii + 342. $34.50.

Webster, Middleton, and Ford are among the individual playwrights given sustained attention. It is difficult to spy any overall guiding principles in the selection, beyond the desire to give as broadly representative a sample of the parent journal's contents as possible. Few if any of the essays could be called essential reading, but all are scholarly and worth serious attention.

American 'new historicism', particularly as practised by Stephen Greenblatt and Louis Adrian Montrose, has exerted a growing influence on the study of Renaissance drama over the last decade. Jean E. Howard's helpful analysis of the current state of play, 'The New Historicism in Renaissance Studies' (*ELR*), explains for the benefit of the uninitiated how new historicism differs from old, praises many of its achievements, and isolates what she believes to be its short-comings – a reticence about theory, and a tendency to generalize from insufficient evidence (the remedy proposed is that old nostrum, 'coverage'). In *ELR*'s 'The Hegemonic Theater of George Puttenham' Jonathan Crewe finds in Puttenham a prophet of the new orthodoxy, a theorist who would deny the capacity of theatre to subvert or contest dominant ideologies, much as Green-blatt does today (although in 'Loudun and London' (*CritI*) there may be a softening in his position). That Crewe himself is unhappy with this institutionalized conception of theatre is suggested by his strange, ludic interrogation of the premises of the new historicism, *Hidden Designs*[21], leading as it does to the 'unmasking' of the arch-criminal Spenser as the perpetrator, for reasons of professional advancement, of Puttenham's fraudulent *Arte of English Poesie*. The strategy of Crewe's earnest game is hard to interpret at this distance from Baltimore, and it often seems tiresomely oblique in consequence; but many of the tactics are brilliant.

The next two books are more confident in envisaging theatre as a subversive force in history, both authors crediting it with the power to stage and expose ideology, or, as an earlier critic more approximately put it, to show the very age and body of the time his form and pressure. The more complex and ambitious of the two is Jean-Christophe Agnew's *Worlds Apart*[22], a history of the change of consciousness brought about in the period 1550–1750 by the development of 'free market' economics. Theatre, itself heavily implicated in this change, offered itself as the ideal 'laboratory' in which the conditions of this new, shifting, unstable world of unrestricted exchange could be explored. The generalized medieval 'theatrum mundi' *topos* took on a fresh urgency and particularity of significance during the period, says Agnew, as a way of representing the elations and terrors of participating in a society cut loose from its traditional moorings and pitched into a sea of shifting appearances and endlessly negotiable values. This is far from a new seam of argument, but it is by no means an exhausted one, and Agnew follows its intricate twistings skilfully. He is especially interesting on the mutual recognition of inauthenticity which he contends underlay the hostility between the Puritans and the theatre: the mirror persisted in reflecting an uncomfortable image, and had eventually to be shattered. An article by Laura Levine, 'Men in Women's Clothing: Anti-theatricality and Effeminization from 1579 to 1642' (*Criticism*), sees the matter

---

21. *Hidden Designs: The Critical Profession and Renaissance Literature*, by Jonathan Crewe. Methuen. pp. viii + 181. £25.

22. *Worlds Apart: The Market and the Theater in Anglo-American Thought, 1550–1750*, by Jean-Christophe Agnew. CUP. pp. xvi + 262. £25.

more in terms of projection, the theatre's opponents throwing their own buried fears about the instability of the self and of gender onto a, by implication, largely innocent stage.

Theodore Leinwand's *The City Staged*[23] is more modest in scope than Agnew's book, and focuses more specifically on individual plays, being concerned entirely with a tightly knit group of city comedies produced during the first decade of James's reign. These plays, Leinwand maintains, dramatize the stereotypes Jacobean Londoners made of each other, and, by holding them up to critical scrutiny, force their audiences to question their own complacent prejudices. He concentrates on the representation of merchants, gallants, and women, devoting a lengthy chapter to each. City comedy is a highly parodic, self-conscious genre, full of traps for its audience, who are likely to find egg on their faces before the end of the play: so Leinwand's case is a good one. But there is a kind of inverse complacency towards which these plays can tempt a modern sceptical critic, the unexamined assumption that all their stereotypes are interrogatively inflected (or, more precisely, that this is the case in any play worth serious attention). Leinwand's most interesting chapter, on the portrayal of women, is the one in which he shows himself most conscious of this possible danger, alerted to it perhaps by the pressure of contemporary feminism; in earlier discussions of citizens and gentlemen it is not altogether avoided.

The interaction between drama and society also concerns David Atkinson, who contributes a study of 'Marriage under Compulsion in English Renaissance Drama' to *ES*. He suspects, reasonably enough, that forced marriage was not nearly so widespread a social problem as its recurrence in the drama might lead one naïvely to think; but it does not perhaps follow that the theme is developed purely because of its suitability for dramatic treatment. For instance, the playwrights' shared tendency to displace some of the guilt onto the innocent victims, well brought out by Atkinson, might be thought to enact a social problem of which 'marriage under compulsion' was only a symptom. Problems arising from gender certainly got more stage exposure than problems arising from economic deprivation, as Anat Feinberg seeks to demonstrate in 'The Representation of the Poor in Elizabethan and Stuart Drama' (*L&H*), an essay which is in fact about non-, mis-, and under-representation.

Whether and how covert political meaning can be recovered with any certainty from sixteenth- and seventeenth-century plays is a vexed question which Jerzy Limon attempts to address in his book *Dangerous Matter*[24]. He conducts painstaking analyses of four plays and one masque presented during the 1623/24 season, in order to retrieve the political significance they would have had for their first audiences. The methodological problem is to know what counts as reliable evidence: divergence from sources, offers Limon, and failures of artistic unity (but who is to be the judge of that?). His practical interpretations of individual texts are more successful than the disquisitions on method, which grasp at an objectivity that continually dissolves in the seizing. The works discussed are Ben Jonson's *Neptune's Triumph*, Thomas Drue's *The Life of the Duchess of Suffolk*, Massinger's *The Bondman*, Middleton's

---

23. *The City Staged: Jacobean Comedy 1603–1613*, by Theodore B. Leinwand. UWisc. pp. viii + 233. £23.75.

24. *Dangerous Matter: English Drama and Politics in 1623/24*, by Jerzy Limon. CUP. pp. viii + 174. £22.50.

A Game at Chess, and *The Sun's Darling*, thought to be the outcome of a collaboration between Thomas Dekker and John Ford.

It would help Limon greatly if some members of the plays' first audiences had committed their reactions to paper. But evidence of this kind is rare indeed, and, when it does survive, is often not very helpful, despite scholars' understandable endeavours to milk it for the last drop of significance. A case in point is the copy of the 1625 quarto of Chapman's *Byron* with marginal annotations by Philip, fourth Earl of Pembroke, the existence of which is celebrated by A. H. Tricomi in his 'Philip, Earl of Pembroke and the Analogical Way of Reading Political Tragedy' (*JEGP*). The marginalia have been heavily cropped, which makes it difficult to be certain about their nature. It is possible that they are, as Tricomi claims, musings on parallels between the play and contemporary life, and that they indicate a 'way of reading'; it is possible, too, that they are no more than the doodles of an obsessive list-maker. The whole matter is shrouded in doubt. As is – though it is often taken for granted by scholars – the efficiency and extent of censorship. Philip J. Finkelpearl, in '"The Comedians' Liberty": Censorship of the Jacobean Stage Reconsidered' (*ELR*), puts forward some good reasons for doubting that efficiency, at least during James's reign. He suggests that division of responsibility in the Revels Office, faction at court, and the players' ability to improvise additions to an allowed text must all have severely impeded attempts to bring the drama under central control. Finkelpearl is swimming against the tide here; but it is a worthwhile act of resistance.

Few of the items reviewed so far in this section will have much appeal for undergraduates. T. McAlindon's *English Renaissance Tragedy*[25], however, will be more to their liking. There are substantial chapters on Kyd, Marlowe, Tourneur, Webster, and Middleton, and these are prefaced by fifty pages on the 'common elements' in Elizabethan and Jacobean tragedies. Fall and redemption provide for McAlindon the basic shape of tragic action: the protagonist, lapsing from right reason through the exercise of impassioned will, enters a world of 'contrariety', of strife and loss, from the 'amazement' of which the only escape is through the re-integrating experience of 'the noble death'. This all sounds rather too cut-and-dried, running the risk of collapsing the tragedies back into the morality plays; and, indeed, a severe and simplifying moralism does intrude itself from time to time into McAlindon's book. But his interpretations of individual plays are much more strongly responsive to contrariety than the schematizing of the first chapter might lead the reader to expect. In particular, he is sharply perceptive in his analysis of the 'semantic uncertainty and confusion' that besets the fallen world of tragedy and gathers around certain words and word-pairs: 'resolution' and 'dissolution' in *Doctor Faustus*, for instance, or 'providence' and 'provide', 'good' and 'ill' in *Women Beware Women*. The question is: just how corrosive of the orthodoxies of right reason *are* these mazy ambiguities? But McAlindon's opening chapter has foreclosed the debate.

Since Rowland Wymer's *Suicide and Despair in Jacobean Drama* (Harvester) was not available for review, the only other general consideration of tragedy to be noted is Peter Hyland's 'Disguise and Renaissance Tragedy' (*UTQ*), which finds that the chief functions of tragic disguise are to arouse pathos or to introduce a note of 'bizarre farce' into the proceedings.

25. *English Renaissance Tragedy*, by T. McAlindon. Macmillan. pp. xiv + 269. £25.

Matthew H. Wikander's survey of historical drama from Shakespeare to Brecht, *The Play of Truth and State*[26], contains a chapter devoted to the historical plays of Jonson, Chapman, Massinger, and Ford. While Jonson and Chapman hold sturdily to a humanist faith in the moral usefulness of history, Massinger and Ford, following Shakespeare's lead, 'emphasize the unverifiability of fact and the mysteriousness of identity'. This seems reasonable enough, although Jonson's *Sejanus* is perhaps more problematic in its stance towards history than Wikander allows, while his thoroughgoing interpretation of it as a commentary on the Essex rebellion definitely seems questionable.

Richard Levin bounces back into the ring with another hammer-fisted onslaught on modern critical heresy. His main targets in 'Performance-Critics *vs* Close Readers in the Study of English Drama' (*MLR*) are those who assert the absolute primacy of text over performance, or of performance over text. Levin is surely right to protest that they ought to be interdependent, but he does his cause no service by trying to demonstrate, surely in the teeth of much of the evidence, that the antagonism between page and stage is a creation of the modern academy undreamt of by the sensible Elizabethans.

A calmer and more convincing case for the mutual supportiveness of text and performance is implicitly made by Robert C. Jones in his deceptively simple-looking little book on four celebrated comic villains: Shakespeare's Richard III, Marlowe's Barabas, Jonson's Volpone, and Vindice, the protagonist of *The Revenger's Tragedy*[27]. It is easy to assume casually that these familiar roles are all in some way 'descended from the Vice', and establish similar Vice-like grips on their audiences' attention. Jones gets in behind this stereotypical response, demonstrating by close and theatrically informed analysis of the villains' roles how different all four are from.Vices, and indeed from each other, in the ways they work on an audience. Invoking the audience is of course a ready way to confer an illusion of objectivity on a purely subjective critical response. But Jones is conscious of this danger, does his best to minimize it, and it is a tribute to his steady sense of theatre that one rarely, if ever, finds oneself protesting that the imaginary audience are a most peculiar set of coves. This is a good and highly readable book.

(b) Marlowe

The major event of the Marlovian year was the long-delayed publication of the late Clifford Leech's book, *Christopher Marlowe: Poet for the Stage*[28]. Some of the material is familiar: the chapters on *Edward II*, Hero and Leander, and the structure of *Tamburlaine* are revised versions of articles originally published in the late fifties and early sixties. Much is new, notably two fine chapters on *Doctor Faustus*. Although Leech writes deftly and appreciatively of Marlowe's lightness of comic touch in *Hero and Leander* ('his words frisk

26. *The Play of Truth and State: Historical Drama from Shakespeare to Brecht*, by Matthew H. Wikander. JHU. pp. xii + 287. £20.35.

27. *Engagement with Knavery: Point of View in 'Richard III', 'The Jew of Malta', 'Volpone', and 'The Revenger's Tragedy'*, by Robert C. Jones. DukeU. pp. xii + 177. £21.40.

28. *Christopher Marlowe: Poet for the Stage*, by Clifford Leech, ed. by Anne Lancashire. AMS. pp. x + 250. £37.25.

and prance as his gods and his lovers do'), it is Marlowe's lonely tragic victims, Edward and Faustus, who elicit his most eloquent and imaginative response. A comment on Faustus's Good and Evil Angels is a typical example of Leech's ability to breathe life into dead conventions, and to show you the plays afresh: Faustus 'can hardly, except at the end of the play, utter more than a few words before an angel or a devil is with him to exhort or rebuke. . . . Thus Marlowe dramatizes the grim busy-ness of a solitary man's thoughts, giving a new edge to the proverbial notion that a man may never be less alone than when alone.' As this quotation suggests, Leech's commentary on the plays is always reaching out towards larger concerns: the nature of tragedy, or of solitude, or of power; the idea of damnation; the distinctiveness of the history play as a dramatic genre. This is a learned, beautifully written, and deeply humane book, and an apt remembrance of a great scholar and critic.

I would have liked to review Simon Shepherd's *Marlowe and the Politics of Elizabethan Theatre* (Harvester) in conjunction with Leech's book, but repeated requests failed to elicit a copy from the publisher. Let's turn, then, to essays and periodical articles on Marlowe, of which there are quite a number this year.

The majority, as usual, concern *Doctor Faustus*. Rowland Wymer, in '"When I Behold the Heavens": A Reading of *Doctor Faustus*' (*ES*), finds the play's ironies brought to sharp focus in the expressive gesture of 'looking up', an action which can convey defiant aspiration, obedient trust, repentant beseeching, or the agony of crushing defeat. The 'gestic' nature of Marlowe's plays, and those of his contemporaries, has been insisted on by Michael Hattaway in his valuable book, *Elizabethan Popular Theatre* (*YW* 63.183–5). Wymer's essay is a fresh indication of how fruitful this approach may turn out to be, and improves on Hattaway's rather crude opposition of the spectacular to the ethical by demonstrating that spectacle in *Faustus* can itself be a source of complex moral meaning.

K. Tetzeli von Rosador traverses more well-trodden paths in his analysis of the depiction of '"Supernatural Soliciting": Temptation and Imagination in *Doctor Faustus* and *Macbeth*' [18]. As Elizabethan theories of perception lead von Rosador to expect, it is through their corrupted imaginations that he finds the devil gaining entry to the protagonists' minds. Giving new teeth to the old saw that Faustus and Macbeth are both 'poets', von Rosador goes on to argue that, through their characters' tragic experiences of the delusive power of fantasy, Marlowe and Shakespeare are able to express their own profoundest anxieties about the nature of the artistic imagination.

Three scholars consider the play's structure, and come to widely differing conclusions. Sr Francis Dolores Covella cannot believe that any of the conjurer's jolly japes were part of Marlowe's original conception, and argues, in 'The Choral Nexus in *Doctor Faustus*' (*SEL*), that, before the hacks got to work on it, the play was 'a short play in two parts – a kind of Tudor moral interlude – in which the unifying nexus was a chorus which linked the two main actions: Faustus's making of the covenant with the devil and the final reckoning'. This drastic solution to a notorious problem seems to raise more difficulties than it irons out. At the other extreme, Roy T. Eriksen, in '"What resting place is this?": Aspects of Time and Place in *Doctor Faustus* (1616)' (*RenD*, 1985), defends the integrity of the B-text by displaying symmetries in its treatment of time and location. In 'Scene Patterns in *Doctor Faustus* and *Richard III*' Bernard Beckerman, although conceding Marlowe's adeptness in traditional patterns of scene construction, thinks that Shakespeare's play is much the more 'dramaturgically adventuresome' [18].

Sixth and lastly, Mark Thornton Burnett contributes 'Two Notes on Metre and Rhyme in *Doctor Faustus*' to *N&Q*: one of these concerns an ambiguity which possibly arises from the elision of 'me' and 'im' when Faustus asks Helen to 'make me (im)mortal with a kiss'.

A couple of essays on *Edward II*, omitted last year, deserve mention. Sharon Tyler, in 'Bedfellows Make Strange Politics: Christopher Marlowe's *Edward II*' (*TD*, 1985), insists that the play is a fully political tragedy, not 'domestic tragedy writ large'. Susan McCloskey, in 'The Worlds of *Edward II*' (*RenD*, 1985), claims that the first two acts of the play are governed by causality but the last three by chance, a distinction central to the play's meaning, and communicated in the theatre by changes in costuming, sound effects, indicators of time and place, and use of the playing-space. Whether or not McCloskey's claims about the play's larger conceptual structure are found acceptable, her perceptive analysis of the fine details of Marlowe's stagecraft is worth consulting.

Notes about Marlowe's sources come from Susan E. Joy, who, in 'The Kyd/Marlowe Connection' (*N&Q*), tracks down two minor debts to *The Spanish Tragedy* in *The Jew of Malta*; from Anthony Brian Taylor, who forges rather tenuous links between 'Marlowe and *The Mirror for Magistrates*' (*N&Q*); and from Roy T. Eriksen, who recovers some putative borrowings from and allusions to Petrarch in 'Marlowe's Petrarch: *In Morte di Madonna Laura*' (*CahiersE*).

This leaves only Lawrence Danson's 'Continuity and Character in Shakespeare and Marlowe' (*SEL*) to be considered. He compares Edward II with Kate in *The Taming of the Shrew* as instances of a 'general fact': 'while Shakespeare was experimenting with the phenomenon of apparent change in characters, Marlowe was subjecting his major characters to various tests of their ability to remain always exactly themselves'. If that is what he is up to in the Berkeley dungeons, then these scenes are even more hideously unpleasant than I had thought. But one could ask: has Marlowe conferred on Edward in the first place the sort of 'singular identity' that might tempt a dramatist to see if he could break it down?

(c) Jonson

Rosalind Miles's new life of Jonson [29] meets the by now urgent need for an up-to-date and reliable biography. It is a thoroughly professional piece of work, as close to an 'objective account' (the author's avowed goal) as anyone is likely to get – which, in the case of such an inveterate and skilful self-mythologizer as Jonson, is perhaps not very close at all! Miles doesn't try to edit or explain away the inconsistencies and contradictions in Jonson's career and personality, nor does she push them into the foreground: they are simply allowed to appear as the story unfolds and as different witnesses come forward with their evidence. Narrative rather than analysis is very much the dominant mode. Jonson's privacy is respected, and his works are not raided in search of 'secret' psychodramas. The ideal biography of Jonson would be a more exhilarating read, but Miles's plain, full, and sensible retelling will do very nicely to be going on with.

---

29. *Ben Jonson: His Life and Work*, by Rosalind Miles. RKP. pp. xiv + 306. £19.95.

'When we speak . . . about Jonson's "authorial discourse", what we mean is not in the least the spontaneous expression of his personal feelings, but a complex stylistic construction, the overdetermined hypostasization of several productive relationships.' Thus Peter Womack, subtle doctor, 're-reading' Jonson[30], and bringing out the Surly, no doubt, in a few of his customers. But this is not mere alchemical cant. Womack, by analysing various aspects of Jonsonian theatre – dramatic language, theory of character, the interaction of author, actor, and audience – in terms of a Bakhtinian opposition between the rival energies of absolutist order and carnival licence, does helpfully manage to suggest how intricately implicated the plays are in the cultural struggles of their time. Though Womack is not content to let the matter rest there: his Bakhtinian categories are always pressing to transcend history, to pull then and now into conjunction. Indeed, his own 'discourse', perpetually slipping between demotic and mandarin registers, quite closely replicates the kind of division he detects in Jonson's – prompting one to wonder whether the relation of the poststructuralist critic to his or her readership might not be as problematic as that of the classicist playwright to his audience.

Among this year's harvest of essays and articles, the one I most enjoyed was Ian Donaldson's 'Jonson's Magic Houses' (*E&S*), a witty exploration of the rich significance of the house – as building, as concept, as family – in Jonson's work. All these meanings come to a dramatic focus in *The Alchemist*, Donaldson's fine account of which is the high point of his essay. Rarely has the ironical relationship of the two houses of illusion in the Blackfriars – Lovewit's and the Burbages' – been more deftly explained. Yet Donaldson resists ironical conclusions, and finds an unusually precise way of defining the celebratory quality many sense in the play's ending. But despite the value Jonson places on dwelling, permanence, he himself was, both literally and imaginatively, a contented lodger in other men's houses – a paradox Donaldson considers in his excellent final pages.

Jonson's Roman plays attracted more attention than usual this year. Both Philip J. Ayres, in 'The Nature of Jonson's Roman History' (*ELR*) and Edward Pechter, in his essay comparing '*Julius Caesar* and *Sejanus*'[18], defend the honour of Jonson's Germanicans, and deny that the playwright intended any irony in their presentation. Ayres argues that Jonson consistently simplifies his historical sources to yield stark and instructive moral contrasts. Pechter is more concerned with the ways Jonson finds to make this instruction dramatically effective, that is, to negotiate the problems posed by the inherent untheatricality of Stoic virtue. Thomas F. Scanlon closely examines *Catiline*'s relation to its classical sources in '*Historia quasi fabula*: The Catiline Theme in Sallust and Jonson' (*TD*): Sallust, too, is a moralist and something of a dramatist. A fourth article on matters Roman comes from Richard Finkelstein, who, in 'The Roman Background of Ben Jonson's Audience' (*ISJR*), enters a sensible caution against taking Jonson's descriptions of his audience as empirical observation. Several features of these descriptions, Finkelstein points out, derive from metadramatic exchanges in Roman New Comedy: 'Jonson's awareness of prior audiences to comedies in part creates his own audience.'

Questions of genre engage Geraldo U. de Sousa, who argues in 'Boundaries of Genre in Ben Jonson's *Volpone* and *The Alchemist*' (*EiT*) that the two plays

---

30. *Ben Jonson*, by Peter Womack. Blackwell. pp. x + 181. pb £4.95.

employ the formal devices of deferral and interlacement and are therefore in some shadowy sense romances as well as satires. A rejoinder might be that deferral and interlacement are not exclusive to romance. *Volpone* is understood by Frances Dolan as a dramatized debate between fluid and immutable conceptions of the self. Her essay, entitled ' "We Must Here Be Fixed": Discovering a Self behind the Mask in *Volpone*' (*ISJR*), takes us over some familiar ground. It is often pointed out (not by Dolan) that Volpone shares most of the vices and follies of his clients. It is not so often claimed that Truewit, Clerimont, and Dauphine, the gallants of *Epicoene*, share the flaws and vanities they deride in Daw and La Foole: this is the burden of Diana Benet's ' "The Master-Wit is the master-fool": Jonson, *Epicoene*, and the Moralists' (*RenD*, 1985), an interesting attempt to discredit recent readings of the play which assume the gallants to be Jonson's spokesmen.

Finally, mention should be made of Peter Hyland's ' "The Wild Anarchie of Drinke": Ben Jonson and Alcohol' (*Mosaic*), an interpretation of Jonson's poetic career as a struggle against imaginative intoxication; and of R. A. Foakes's 'The Descent of Iago' [18] in which Jonson's Macilente is put forward as a direct ancestor of Shakespeare's honest ancient.

(d) Other Playwrights and Plays

The arrangement of this section is, as usual, roughly chronological, and we begin with a small scattering of articles on the earlier Elizabethan theatre. Howard B. Norland writes on '*Roister Doister* and the "Regularizing" of English Comedy' (*Genre*, 1985), suggesting that the play is more Aristophanic than Terentian in spirit. Hanna Scolnicov, in ' "To Understand a Parable": The Mimetic Mode of *The Marriage of Wit and Wisdom*' (*CahiersE*), oddly praises this late interlude for its allegorical coherence, ignores its farcical scenes, and helpfully discovers a possible source in the Book of Proverbs. Francis Guinle contributes two notes to *CahiersE*, one 'Concerning a Source of Richard Edwards' *Damon and Pithias*' (Plutarch's life of Aratus), the other, ' "The Boy in Pieces": A Musical Problem?', to do with the music for John Lyly's *Gallathea*.

Kyd, Greene, and Peele all receive attention, some of it rather dubious. James P. Hammersmith tries to prove that 'The Death of Castile in *The Spanish Tragedy*' (*RenD*, 1985) is 'thematically necessary' to the fulfilment of Hieronimo's revenge; but fails to cope convincingly with the objections that Castile's murder results from the last-minute thwarting of Hieronimo's planned suicide, could never have been part of his design, and must appear to the unsuspecting audience as a crazy afterthought. Joost Daalder also seems on shaky ground in arguing that the Senex of III.xiii is in fact Seneca himself, and that 'The Role of "Senex" in Kyd's *The Spanish Tragedy*' (*CompD*) is to reinforce Hieronimo's decision to become a Senecan revenger. Robert S. Miola's 'Another Senecan Echo in Kyd's *The Spanish Tragedy*' (*N&Q*) points out a recollection of Seneca's *Oedipus* independently identified last year by Gordon Braden in his book on the Senecan tradition (*YW* 66.250–1).

Charles W. Crupi has written a good compact study of Robert Greene[31], including a full discussion of the legends surrounding his life, a comprehensive survey of his literary output, detailed analyses of six representative prose works

31. *Robert Greene*, by Charles W. Crupi. TEAS. Hall. pp. xvi + 182. £19.95.

and of each of his plays, a brief account of his reputation, and an annotated bibliography of criticism. The chapter on the plays stresses their serious moral design, though Crupi is not afraid to point out inconsistencies, and among his most interesting pages are those dealing with the uncomfortable, bodged reconciliation of Margaret and Lacy in *Friar Bacon and Friar Bungay*. This is a useful book, and may be confidently recommended to students who ask about Greene and his work. Another study of Greene's comedy is Charles W. Hieatt's 'Multiple Plotting in *Friar Bacon and Friar Bungay*' (*RenD*, 1985), which seeks to refine on William Empson's account of the articulation of the plot, and criticizes Greene for moral confusion, and for employing techniques of construction more suitable to the prose romance than to the drama.

George Peele, who doesn't figure in this section as often as his intrinsic interest warrants, attracts three essays this year. In '"Seeing is Believing": Action and Narration in *The Old Wives Tale* and *The Winter's Tale*' [18] Philip Edwards writes sympathetically about Peele's play, praising the playwright's ability to take a light-hearted attitude toward folk-tale without 'betraying or ridiculing those deeper things which folk-tale may be held to represent and incorporate'. The play is comparable in this respect to *The Winter's Tale*. Edwards also has a good idea about the pages Antic, Frolic, and Fantastic, whom he interprets allegorically as 'qualities which the "young master" has discarded now he is dedicated to serving his lady and which are withering away, deprived of their life-support. They are the qualities Mercutio was sorry to lose in Romeo, the high spirits of unattached young men out to enjoy themselves.' Madge's tale is designed to reconcile them to their master's falling in love. The other two essays on Peele are less memorable. William Tydeman, writing on 'Peele's *Edward I* and the Elizabethan View of Wales' [32], interestingly demonstrates that Peele takes an uncommonly sympathetic view of Wales for an Englishman of his time, but can't seem to find a way to incorporate the Welsh scenes into his reading of the play as a whole. They 'must be admitted to impair the play's consistency of attitude towards disloyalty and insurrection'. Wouldn't it be worth trying out the idea that they set up a debate? Judith Weil takes another underrated play as her subject in 'George Peele's Singing School: *David and Bethsabe* and the Elizabethan History Play' (*TD*), but her complex discussion of its patterns of imagery and relationships is rather elusive.

Still on the history play, Vittorio Gabrieli writes in *Moreana* on '*Sir Thomas More*: Sources, Characters, Ideas', usefully reviewing the play's indebtedness to prior accounts of More's life, defending its overall integrity of design, commenting in detail on its presentation of More's personality, and finding its 'ideological core' in 'the strife between the binding covenant of "conscience", statute law and "frailer life"'.

Dekker gets two articles and a note. In 'Bourgeois Comedy: Shakespeare and Dekker' [18] G. K. Hunter looks at *The Shoemaker's Holiday* and *The Merry Wives of Windsor* in the context of the developing genre. Explaining Shakespeare's anomalous comedy is the essay's main goal, but *en route* Hunter has clarifying things to say about the way class conflict in Dekker's play is

---

32. In *The Welsh Connection: Essays by Past and Present Members of the Department of English Language and Literature, University College of North Wales, Bangor*, ed. by William Tydeman. Gomer. pp. 211. £9.50.

'absorbed but not concealed by the assertions of good fellowship and sexual solidarity', and some telling contrasts to make between Falstaff's holiday rhetoric and Simon Eyre's. Robert C. Evans, in 'Jonson, *Satiromastix*, and the Poetomachia: A Patronage Perspective' (*ISJR*), defends the coherence of the play's two-plot structure, and argues that the special barb of Dekker's satirical portrait of Jonson as Horace is that it shows the poet as unworthy of the patronage he was at the time so desperately seeking. 'The Ring Story in *Northward Ho*, I.i' has its source, says Elizabeth Schafer (*N&Q*), in an English jestbook, *A Hundred Merry Tales*.

A Woman Killed with Kindness continues as the only play of Heywood's that critics want to write about. This year *SEL* carries two articles on the play, Laura G. Bromley's 'Domestic Conduct in *A Woman Killed with Kindness*' and Diana E. Henderson's 'Many Mansions: Reconstructing *A Woman Killed with Kindness*'. Citing contemporary conduct books as evidence, Bromley maintains that Heywood was holding up not only Frankford but also Sir Charles Mountford (the one who pawns his sister to redeem a debt of honour) as exemplars of the 'gentlemanly virtue of moderation', and applauds the playwright as a 'skillful and effective advocate' of the morality of his time. The play is taken to provide guidance for the audience in 'how to deal with' duplicitous adulterers such as Wendoll. But, I object, dealing with Wendoll is precisely what Frankford hasn't a clue how to do, and his coolly collected treatment of his hapless wife demands to be seen in the context of that bewilderment. Henderson agrees with Bromley that Frankford *is* kind according to the standards of the day, but her reading of the play is not so uncompromisingly didactic, and allows for an element of conflict in the audience's response. She sees the play as built upon the basic Christian 'narrative paradigm' of fall, repentance, and spiritual homecoming, and locates the source of the tragic feeling in the last scene as the misfit between paradigm and action. Anne is 'going home' in two senses, to heaven because she is dying, to Frankford because he has taken her back; but we know that she will only return to the marital home in her coffin, and there is pathos in the counterpointing of the transience of earthly reconciliation against the cold eternity of spiritual homecoming, more cruel in this context than consoling: a reading rather in the spirit of Milton's 'Methought I saw my late espoused saint'.

A more challenging approach to 'Drama and Sexual Politics' is that of Kathleen McLuskie, in her essay of that title (*TD*, 1985) – which deals not with Heywood but with 'The Case of Webster's Duchess'. McLuskie will have no truck with the idea that the play labels the Duchess's second marriage sinful, and that therefore there is a degree of justice in her punishment. She argues cogently that the play exposes this kind of masculine judgement as 'commonplace and limiting'. McLuskie objects to modern productions which, like the one at the Royal Exchange, Manchester in 1981, play up the individual sadism of Ferdinand and his brother, and thereby blur the sexual politics. It's a challenging view; though I remember the production in question as one of quite shattering power.

Charles Forker's massive study of Webster, *Skull beneath the Skin* (SIU), I must hold over till next year. So it is time now to turn to articles on Middleton, a smaller than usual cluster. All but one of the essays deal with Middleton's tragedies. The exception is 'Heirs and Identity: The Bases of Social Order in *Michaelmas Term*', by A. L. and M. K. Kistner (*MLS*), a moralized and rather humourless reading of the play as 'a satiric comedy advocating a reinstatement of the values of an older society'.

Two articles concern *Women Beware Women*. A. A. Bromham has published some thoughtful studies of the political bearings of Middleton's plays in recent years: but his construing of *Woman Beware Women* as an intervention in the debate over James's pacific foreign policy seems rather improbable. It is one thing to say that the play suggests the need for 'engagement with the world of action and responsibility', but quite another to translate this moral point into political terms and find in Leantio's misguided attempts to lock Bianca from the world, for instance, a covert warning about the dangers of peaceful isolationism. Bromham's article, 'The Tragedy of Peace: Political Meaning in *Women Beware Women*', can be found in *SEL*; as can Leslie Thomson's '"Enter Above": The Staging of *Women Beware Women*', a detailed analysis of the use of the upper stage in the play's last scene.

Mohammad Kowsar writes on 'Middleton and Rowley's *The Changeling*: The Besieged Temple' (*Criticism*), interpreting it, with much assistance from Julia Kristeva, as a challenge to patriarchal hegemony by the marginalized 'demonic alliance' of Beatrice and De Flores. Beatrice's final confession may appear to be an act of repentance, but Kowsar prefers to hear it as a hostile act of Kristevan 'abjection', 'a militant rhetoric of debasement . . . that remains remorseless to the end'. Such terrorist readings of the play are becoming more common. Dieter Mehl's exploration of possible links between *Measure for Measure* and *The Revenger's Tragedy*, 'Corruption, Retribution and Justice'[18], is analysis of an altogether more traditional kind. Despite their obvious formal differences, these nearly contemporaneous plays show, according to Mehl, 'a very similar concern with the disruption of society, the poisoning effects of lust and the collapse of punitive justice', prompting him towards, if not quite to, the assertion of the imaginative influence of the one on the other.

Finally, four notes about plays in the Middleton canon appear in *N&Q*. R. V. Holdsworth and Marion Lomax suggest sources for *The Second Maiden's Tragedy*, Holdsworth going for Lady Elizabeth Cary's *The Tragedy of Mariam*, Lomax for the Book of Revelation and Spenser's *Faerie Queene*, Book III. Jerzy Limon finds 'The "Missing Source" for Middleton's *A Game at Chess* (V.iii. 141–7)' in Samuel Hieron's sermons. And Paul Yachnin interprets 'The Significance of Two Allusions in Middleton's *Phoenix*' as evidence that the play was written not for the court but for the private theatre.

John Fletcher's skills, says Charles L. Squier firmly, were those of an entertainer, and he does not need to be 'rescued and made important through his incipient neoclassicism, his royalist or antiroyalist political concerns, or his representation of shifting social currents and thoughts'. What matters is his skill at plotting, and his witty exploitation of theatrical conventions. So Squier, in his TEAS volume on the playwright[33], forswears the gravity of themes, and treats us to a series of zestfully appreciative plot summaries. He has a talent for this, able to make even *The Faithful Shepherdess* sound riotous, fun, and a hearty relish for Fletcherian absurdities ('cannibalism is always, under the right conditions, good for a laugh'). The book may even persuade some undergraduates to read Fletcher. Of course, it doesn't do Fletcher full justice, but imagine the kind of tedious brief solemn book we might have got instead!

Barbara K. Degyansky sustains the jolly philistine mood in 'A Reconsideration: George and Nell of *The Knight of the Burning Pestle*' (*ELN*), an enthusiastic appreciation of these two 'ingenuous, delightful, and slightly zany people' whose values she believes the play unambiguously to celebrate. A better and much more subtly developed version of this argument can be found in Sheldon Zitner's introduction to his Revels edition of the play (*YW* 65.239).

John Ford's *Perkin Warbeck* continues to divide its critics. Who is the most admirable, the king or the pretender? In 'A Double Reign: *Richard II* and *Perkin Warbeck*'[18] Alexander Leggatt sees the balance tilting towards Perkin. Ford's Henry VII shares the practical skills of Shakespeare's Bolingbroke, but it is Perkin who possesses Richard's kingly imagination, and, unlike Richard, Perkin reigns calm and secure in the inner world of the mind, a regality no outward misfortune can shake. Verna Ann Foster takes a different view. In '*Perkin* without the Pretender: Reexamining the Dramatic Center of Ford's Play' (*RenD*. 1985) she maintains that Perkin, a wishy-washy player king, all mask, pales into dramatic insignificance beside the complex, theatrically dynamic figure of the real king, Henry, whose public image of virtue we suspect but can never quite prove to be a Machiavellian impersonation. Dale B. J. Randall seems to agree more with Foster than Leggatt, but the main thrust of his monograph on the play[34] is different again. He believes that *Perkin* was written a decade earlier than is usually assumed, in 1622/3. The proofs are the many ways in which Ford has shaped the action of his play to reflect current political events, and to gratify King James by making possible flattering parallels between him and his great-great-grandfather, parallels that Randall argues were very important to James, 'not merely a matter of public image, of royal stance, but also a private, personal matter that lay in his heart's deepest core'. It is a resourcefully argued case, but hardly conclusive. One further article on Ford comes from Phoebe S. Spinrad, who in 'Ceremonies of Complement: The Symbolic Marriage in Ford's *The Broken Heart*' (*PQ*) describes the play as a Caroline version of *Sense and Sensibility*, its moral that the two qualities must be united in a good Christian life. The conjunction of Ford and Jane Austen seems more than a little bizarre.

Mention of two more contributions to *N&Q* concludes this section. Writing 'On the Date of Massinger's *The Maid of Honour*' Donald S. Lawless would place its composition in 1629/30, some eight years later than Massinger's Oxford editors. In 'Original Music for Two Caroline Plays' John Cutts reprints from MS Drexel 4257 the music for a song in Richard Brome's *The English Moore*, and reports that the manuscript also contains songs from other plays.

4. Masque and Pageant

Elizabeth's coronation pageant is analysed by Mark Breitenberg in his '". . . the hole matter opened": Iconic Representation and Interpretation in "The Quenes Majesties Passage" ' (*Criticism*). He sees it as instrumental in forming the 'political vocabulary' of the reign, and identifies its strategies of

---

34. *'Theatres of Greatness': A Revisionary View of Ford's 'Perkin Warbeck'*, by Dale B. J. Randall. UVict. pp. 80. pb $7.

enforcing meaning as repetition and similitude. What appears to be the text of the anti-Catholic masque which so offended Elizabeth when it was presented to her at Hinchingbrooke in 1564 has been discovered by Marion Colthorpe, who reprints and briefly discusses it in 'Anti-Catholic Masques Performed before Queen Elizabeth I' (*N&Q*). Other Colthorpe discoveries are the text of 'Lord Compton's Accession Day Speech to Queen Elizabeth I in 1600' (*N&Q*) and the relevance of two letters to 'Sir John Davies and an Elizabethan Court Entertainment' on Shrove Tuesday 1601/2 (*N&Q*). Christopher Martin reductively argues, in 'Impeding the Progress: Sidney's *The Lady of May*' (*ISJR*), that the chief purpose of Sidney's 'tedious brief comedy' is to bore the queen into taking 'some sort of decision' and thereby 'cut through the verbose disputation'.

Stephen Kogan's *The Hieroglyphic King*[35] is a substantial study of the Jacobean and Caroline masque. Kogan subscribes to the view that after the death of James the masque went into terminal decline, trivialized to flatter Charles I in his absolutist posturing. Thomas Carew's *Coelum Britannicum* is an honourable exception. Other masques discussed at length include Samuel Daniel's *Vision of the Twelve Goddesses*, Thomas Campion's *Lord Hay's Masque*, George Chapman's *Masque of the Middle Temple*, Jonson's *Pleasure Reconcil'd to Virtue*, Aurelian Townshend's *Tempe Restored*, William Davenant's *Salmacida Spolia*, and Milton's *Comus*. Unlike many recent commentators on the masque, Kogan is not terribly interested in political significances, and indeed sees the Caroline 'descent' into partisan royalism as a betrayal of the form's aesthetic independence. Another general study which deals with the masque, Joanne Altieri's *The Theatre of Praise* (UDel), was unavailable for review.

David Lindley's fine book on Thomas Campion[36] includes a substantial sixty-page discussion of Campion's masques. Lindley shows how delicately the masques are attuned to their political occasions, helps the reader to appreciate their skilful formal design, and suggests some interesting differences between Campion's view of the masque and Jonson's. Like Daniel, Campion has 'an attitude to the masque much more provisional than that of the pugnaciously assertive Jonson', a principled uncertainty about its transformative powers. Lindley considers *The Lord's Masque* Campion's 'major achievement as a court poet'; *The Somerset Masque*, on the other hand, finds Campion rendered uneasy in his handling of masque conventions by the awkwardness of the occasion.

Even Jonson found himself embarrassed by the Somerset marriage; though it also found him at his most embarrassing. So claims Lindley in his *ELR* article, 'Embarrassing Ben: The Masques for Frances Howard'. Several of the invited lords boycotted the tilt for which Jonson had penned the challenge, while his *Irish Masque* is judged by Lindley one of his worst productions: morally complacent, trivializing serious issues, and concealing 'the true nature of political power'. Another masque of Jonson's is judged 'utterly irresponsible' by Paul R. Sellin, though he admires its 'clever' design. Sellin's very well-informed analysis of 'The Politics of Ben Jonson's *Newes from the New World Discovered in the Moone*' (*Viator*) demonstrates that the antimasque attack on

35. *The Hieroglyphic King: Wisdom and Idolatry in the Seventeenth Century Masque*, by Stephen Kogan. FDU/AUP. pp. 311. £27.95.

36. *Thomas Campion*, by David Lindley. Brill. pp. xii + 242. Fl 85.

the 'news-market' was a flattering confirmation of the rightness of James's foreign policy (considered 'impractical folly' by Sellin), and a clear warning to the court to stop chivvying him on behalf of the Elector Palatine. This message was so much what James wanted to hear that Sellin wonders whether he didn't have a half-share in its design.

Roy Strong's *Henry, Prince of Wales and England's Lost Renaissance*[37] has an important chapter on 'The Prince's Festivals'. Early Jacobean festivals were not so homogeneous as they may at first sight appear, says Strong. *Oberon, Love Restored, Prince Henry's Barriers*, and, to a degree, *Tethys' Festival* are works which express the Prince's and the Queen's courts, and therefore espouse policies which run counter to those of the King. Strong writes interestingly about the ways conflicts between son and father, particularly between Henry's cult of militarism and James's iconography of peace, created formal difficulties in the masque. A second part of his argument is to demonstrate the artistic innovativeness of masques which Henry commissioned or inspired. If the Prince had lived (a recurrent speculation), 'the art of festival in Stuart England would have taken a very different course from that which ended in the sterility of the self-adulatory masques of the Caroline age'.

One of these, thinks Lawrence Venuti, was James Shirley's *The Triumph of Peace*. Although its sponsors seem to have intended to make some modest criticism of the court, Venuti understands 'the entire thrust of the antimasque' as being 'to discredit the gentry as a political force and ratify the King's autocracy', much as Sellin says of *Newes from the New World* and Lindley of *The Irish Masque*. Venuti's article, 'The Politics of Allusion: The Gentry and Shirley's *The Triumph of Peace*', appears in *ELR*.

Finally, some work on civic pageantry. David M. Bergeron has published a critical edition of Thomas Heywood's pageants[38], a companion volume to his edition of Anthony Munday's pageants, reviewed last year (*YW* 66.267–8). This, is, once again, a valuable book, making more widely available texts hitherto difficult of access. The useful introduction stresses Heywood's unusual reliance on religious themes and imagery in his pageants. This is a subject pursued further in Bergeron's article, 'The Bible in English Renaissance Pageants' (*CompD*), in which he argues that biblical references in Lord Mayors' Shows and royal entry pageants 'serve political purposes, offering in various ways support for the state'.

37. *Henry, Prince of Wales and England's Lost Renaissance*, by Roy Strong. T&H. pp. 264. £12.95.

38. *Thomas Heywood's Pageants: A Critical Edition*, by David M. Bergeron. Garland. pp. viii + 147. $45.

The Earlier Seventeenth Century: Excluding Drama

HELEN WILCOX

Material in this chapter is discussed under three headings: 1. General; 2. Poetry; 3. Prose.

1. General

This year's output is notable for the large amount of conscious re-interpretation of early seventeenth-century texts: critical works are not only rereading and re-assessing writers and their works, but *announce* that they are doing so. The Blackwell Rereading Literature series has reached Ben Jonson, with a volume[1] in which Peter Womack uses Mikhail Bakhtin's theories to assist him in understanding the contradiction of the earthy neoclassicist. It is a pity that Womack largely excludes the non-dramatic poetry from his study, since he goes some way towards 'delivering us', as the general editor Terry Eagleton puts it, 'a Jonson who is not only readable, but usable, for our own times'. But how compatible are 'the postmodern' and 'the Renaissance'? Jonathan Goldberg has the confidence to declare that during the time he was working on his *Voice Terminal Echo*[2], these two terms moved from a state of virtual incompatibility to a position in which they are, 'at least in some quarters, so comfortable as to open upon the prospect of a post-poststructuralism'. He does add, however, that the threat of poststructuralism to 'so-called humanistic criticism' is 'still regarded with horror' in some quarters. Readers from the humanist tradition will, indeed, be bemused (if not horrified) by Goldberg's radical work, whose title probably requires some explanation. A 'voice terminal' is a computerized telephone, and Goldberg's project is 'to show in the Renaissance text voice-as-text, and to show it through a practice of voice terminated'. The results of this re-interpretation of Herbert and Marvell will be discussed later in this chapter, but in general terms (if such are possible) Goldberg's fragmented yet lyrical work is positively disorienting: exciting, annoying, stimulating, and much simpler to participate in than to sum up. That, surely, was his performative intent.

Another flourishing strain of critical re-assessment is the generic approach, found in many an individual article but also gathered together in a volume of

---

1. *Ben Jonson*, by Peter Womack. RL. Blackwell. pp. x + 181. pb £4.95.
2. *Voice Terminal Echo: Postmodernism and English Renaissance Texts*, by Jonathan Goldberg. Methuen. pp. x + 194. hb £16, pb £7.95.

essays edited by Barbara Kiefer Lewalski[3]. In addition to contributions on particular authors (for example, two on Donne, considered below), a number raise relevant general issues. Earl Miner considers the nature of 'genre' itself; Morton W. Bloomfield distinguishes genre (in this case the elegy) from mode (the elegiac); Alastair Fowler, writing on the English georgic, and Annabel Patterson on Virgil's first *Eclogue* re-used, both address questions of direct and loose imitation. Although Milton wrote prose with his left hand, Ann E. Imbrie asserts that Renaissance prose should not be beneath the gaze of genre critics and attempts to define some prose genres; Claudio Guillén identifies several epistolary genres in Renaissance letters.

Historicism, new and old, continues to inform some of the best criticism of this period. Leah S. Marcus has produced a fascinating book[4] on the writings which emerged in response to the *Book of Sports*; entitled *The Politics of Mirth*, her work stresses that there was nothing frivolous in the so-called 'trifles' of Jonson, Herrick, Marvell, and Lovelace (see below) which explored and extended the boundaries of social order. Achsah Guibbory, on the other hand, takes a thorough look at the idea of history itself as it is reflected in seventeenth-century literature, taking her title, *The Map of Time*[5], from Thomas Browne's account of history's transcendent perspective. Guibbory suggests that three views of the pattern of history may be perceived in the literature of the century: degenerative history, as witnessed in Donne's prevailing metaphors of decay; cyclical history, shown in Jonson (for whom cycles still spelt degeneration) and Herrick (to whom the seasons implied renewal); and history as progress, demonstrated in the earlier part of the century in the works of Bacon. Christopher Hill (*SCent*) asks a related but more practical question: how far can literature help us to understand mid seventeenth-century English history? He finds it ironic that while literary critics such as David Norbrook (*YW* 65.165,275) and Margot Heinemann (*YW* 61.178) are re-invigorating historical readings of poets and dramatists, historians still 'ignore' the literature. As if to demonstrate Hill's point, Pamela Tudor-Craig's essay on 'Charles I and Little Gidding' in a Festschrift for C. V. Wedgwood[6], suffers from embarrassingly ill-informed reference to Herbert; it is usefully countered by a more down-to-earth (and accurate) essay in which Robert Van der Weyer re-appraises the Ferrars as less than saintly individuals. Hill also contributed to the Festschrift, with an examination of the word 'revolution', which, he claims, acquired its modern sense well before 1688. Hill's own collected essays continue to appear[7]; Volume II includes his 1981 Clark lecture in which he gave a historian's answer to John Crowe Ransom with a contextualized reading of the opening lines of Marvell's 'To his Coy Mistress'. The other main item of

3. *Renaissance Genres: Essays on Theory, History, and Interpretation*, ed. by Barbara Kiefer Lewalski. Harvard. pp. viii + 498. hb £21.95, pb £7.95. (Hereafter Lewalski.)

4. *The Politics of Mirth: Jonson, Herrick, Milton, Marvell and the Defense of Old Holiday Pastimes*, by Leah S. Marcus. UChic. pp. ix + 319. £23.25.

5. *The Map of Time: Seventeenth-Century English Literature and Ideas of Pattern in History*, by Achsah Guibbory. UIll. pp. 284. £22.50.

6. *For Veronica Wedgwood These: Studies in Seventeenth-Century History*, ed. by Richard Ollard and Pamela Tudor-Craig. Collins. pp. 251. £15.

7. *Collected Essays*, by Christopher Hill. Vol. II: *Religion and Politics in Seventeenth-Century England*. Harvester. pp. xi + 356. £28.50.

literary interest is an essay on the sermons of Dr Tobias Crisp, the Antinomian who apparently not only influenced the Ranters, posthumously, but also anticipated Winstanley and Milton.

This has been a lively year for studies of literature and the visual arts, seeing the publication of Roy Strong's biography of Prince Henry[8], patron of culture in the early years of the century, as well as a special double issue of the *JDJ* devoted to the interrelation of literature and art in the period. Among the general items is John Dixon Hunt's fascinating study of the enigmatic portrait of William Style of Langley by an unknown artist (1636) now in the Tate Gallery; he elucidates the symbolism of the depicted garden and investigates the significance of emblems and inscriptions in the painting. The emblem of the labyrinth is the starting point for an intriguing speculative article by Huston Diehl, 'Into the Maze of Self' (*JMRS*), in which he points out that while medieval mazes tended to have one path from the outside to a heavenly centre, Renaissance equivalents, as in Quarles's *Emblemes*, depict the pilgrim at the centre needing divine guidance to find his way out to reach a distant tower of redemption. Diehl suggests that this subjective viewpoint highlights the Protestant preoccupation with the 'maze of self' and anticipates modern mazes which are of similar construction to Quarles's, disorienting and isolating – the difference being that we are given no guide.

In 'Bodley's Bookcases' (*JDJ*) David Sturdy offers a 'reading' of Duke Humphrey's Library in the Bodleian, not in terms of the contents of its catalogue but by means of an architect's survey of the construction of the shelves and desks which are still in use there today. Samuel Daniel referred to the library, aptly, as Bodley's 'goodly Magazine of witte'. Bodley's own wit in his *Life of Himself* (1609) is considered by Warren W. Wooden (*SP*) in a discussion of the epideictic strategies of encomia. Meanwhile the libraries of Sir Thomas Browne and his son Dr Edward Browne have been catalogued by J. S. Finch for the Sir Thomas Browne Institute (Brill; see p. 15). As an era of great collectors, our period could not be better framed than by Sir Thomas Bodley and Sir Thomas Browne, knights who, as Daniel said of Bodley, created 'most rare monuments', material and literary, to preserve 'the glorious reliques of the best of men'.

2. Poetry

Harold Toliver's *Lyric Provinces in the English Renaissance*[9] is a relaxed and entertaining amble through the imaginary topography of seventeenth-century lyricists, whose work so radically departed from the courtly poetics of the preceding generation. Toliver's contexts are plausible but unsurprising: Jonson's poet-centred group is contrasted with Donne's provinces of the mind defined by opposition or enclosure; while Herbert locates God in words and places, Vaughan's work is characterized by topographical juxtapositions and 'gaps between realms'; and where performance articulates context in Herrick, Marvell is shown to control the relations between specific and metaphoric landscape. Toliver is modest in his purposes, claiming no major initiative in

8. *Henry, Prince of Wales and England's Lost Renaissance*, by Roy Strong. T&H. pp. 264. £12.95.

9. *Lyric Provinces in the English Renaissance*, by Harold Toliver. OhioU (1985). pp. xii + 247. $25.

reading the seventeenth-century poets, offering no conclusion, and even admitting that he is avoiding the 'clogged-up' main critical routes, whether post structuralist or historical.

Meanwhile, traditional studies of lines of poetic influence continue to appear. Geoffrey G. Hiller (*N&Q*) tidies up some 'Allusions to Spenser ...' in the work of 'John Davies', pointing out that this is not Sir John Davies but a hack translator, John Davies of Kidwelly. Anthony Brian Taylor (*N&Q*) illustrates the nature and extent of George Sandys's debt to his predecessor, Arthur Golding (1567), in his translation of Ovid's *Metamorphoses* (1626). Ovid is also the starting point for Gordon Braden's 'Beyond Frustration: Petrarchan Laurels in the Seventeenth Century' (*SEL*), a study of the 'master trope' of compensatory laurels in the love poetry of the seventeenth century, particularly Carew, Cowley, and Marvell.

Jonson's poetry has received an increasing amount of attention in the journals this year. Margarita Stocker (*PEAN*) takes a refreshingly direct approach to his well-known epitaphs on his first son and daughter, asking what we require to appreciate the short Renaissance poem. Her intelligent readings, referring beyond the texts only to the Bible and the *OED*, reveal how limiting a non-contextual approach would be. Don W. Der (*Expl*) examines the first line of Jonson's 'On My First Sonne' to discover the art which conceals art; in the same journal, Robert C. Evans contrasts a humorous pun at the opening of the 'Epitaph on the Countess of Shrewsbury' with a serious and hopeful pun in its conclusion.

Contrasts and polarities continue to fascinate Jonson's readers. Though concentrating mainly on the drama, Ian Donaldson (*E&S*) writes in general terms of the opposition in Jonson's creativity, between building (poetic brick-laying, as it were) and making 'magic houses' whose spirit is more significant than their shape. In 'Who Is Cecilia, What Was She?' the two contradictory poems written by Jonson on Cecilia Bulstrode are shown by Jongsook Lee (*JEGP*) to be more dependent on their context than on either flattery or misogyny on Jonson's part; in the community of his poems, it is argued, Jonson's epideictics transform her from Cynthia to Pucelle, and vice versa. Jonson's own persona is, according to Alan J. Peacock (*EA*), itself divided and transformed in the ironic 'Celebration of Charis'; Jonson the lover is set against Jonson the poetic practitioner whose classical skill creates the lover's scenario. That same classical subtlety is highlighted in a second article by Peacock, 'Ben Jonson, Celia, and Ovid' (*N&Q*), in which Jonson's 'Celia' lyric is shown to assimilate Catullus to a lighter Ovidian mode. Richard Finkelstein (*JMRS*) examines 'Ben Jonson's Ciceronian Rhetoric of Friendship' and though he finds another Jonsonian contradiction – the 'counterpoint' of praise and blame – he argues that there is a unified ethos here in which Jonson dramatizes himself as a friend. Michael McCanles (*Lang&S*) offers a detailed study of 'Punctuation, Contrastive Emphasis, and New Information in the Prosody of Jonson's Poetry' in the light of recent linguistic work on intonation, arguing that contrastive emphasis is fundamental to Jonson's meanings. James A. Riddell (*Expl*) resolves a crux in l. 14 of the ninety-seventh *Epigramme*. And, finally, in a most ingenious and entertaining article, 'The Jonsonian Corpulence; or, The Poet as Mouthpiece' (*ELH*), Joseph Loewenstein works his way as a 'peckish' critic through the interrelation of physical to mental nourishment in 'Inviting a Friend to Supper'.

A useful selection of Donne's poetry and prose[10] for teaching purposes has been published as part of the new Methuen English Texts series. It includes a wide range of Donne's work in different poetic genres, including satires, elegies, and verse epistles as well as most of the devotional sonnets and all but nine of the *Songs and Sonnets*. The editorial decision to include prose was an excellent one, and portions of the *Devotions* will be a bonus for most students; but what a pity it is that the sermon extracts are so short and unadventurous. There is a paucity of information of a textual and critical kind, but the modernized text itself is clear and the glossary helpful. A student could do worse than study this text with the help of Thomas Docherty's radical rereading of Donne[11], in which he aims to deconstruct Donne so that, in the words of John Ashbery, 'understanding/May begin, and in doing so be undone'. Docherty will certainly assist new readers by suggesting that Donne's texts are events rather than objects, and by 'opening up' the poems rather than offering closed or definitive readings. His own readings are vigorous, if occasionally rash, and set Donne firmly in his scientific, socio-cultural, and aesthetic context. At the end of the book one has a dynamic sense of Donne, but isn't there a little more to his work than religion and sex?

The general issue of the relation of Donne's lyrics to their audience is considered in Arthur F. Marotti's study[12] of Donne as a 'coterie poet', which raises intriguing possibilities regarding Donne's cultural position and our socio-historical assumptions about seventeenth-century reading. The book consists of brief analyses of a large number of poems across their traditional groupings, which is always a promising feature in Donne criticism, but there are two major drawbacks to this study. First, the religious works, though claimed as 'coterie' products, get short shrift; more fundamentally, the approach depends upon accurate datings of individual texts, for which in so many cases there is little solid evidence. The basis of Marotti's work, therefore, is a conjectural chronology. A surer historical foundation underpins Ernest B. Gilman's investigation (*JDJ*) of Donne's relation to the iconoclastic controversy, entitled ' "To Adore, or Scorne an Image" '. He argues forcefully that the poems as well as the sermons may be seen in the context of the debate between 'makers and breakers' of images, and shows how Donne's 'tensely self-conscious and agonistic pictorialism' can be better understood in this light. David Evett (*JDJ*) breaks new ground in re-assessing 'Donne's Poems and Five Styles of Renascence Art' - High Renaissance, Mannerism, Baroque, Realism, and the Grotesque - and in testing their usefulness with reference to Donne's poetry.

The debate over the significance of the eagle and the dove in 'The Canonization' continues this year with the discovery by John Manning (*N&Q*) of a possible source in George Chapman's *Ovids Banquet of Sense* (1595). Julia M. Walker (*RES*) suggests as an earlier sixteenth-century source for the cosmographical glass in 'The Good Morrow' a cordiform map in William Cunningham's *The Cosmographical Glass* (1559), while J. Philip Anthony

---

10. *John Donne: Selected Poetry and Prose*, ed. by T. W. and R. J. Craik. Methuen. pp. xi + 299. pb £4.95.
11. *John Donne, Undone*, by Thomas Docherty. Methuen. pp. xiv + 253. hb £25, pb £8.95.
12. *John Donne, Coterie Poet*, by Arthur F. Marotti. UWisc. pp. xviii + 369. £35.

(*Expl*) posits a reading of 'seals' in 'The Relique' as the means of preserving a mystery, the image of God maintained unbroken in the lovers' Platonic relationship. Beyond these studies of specific details in the secular poetry, Donne's treatment of genres is the subject of two essays in Lewalski[3]: John Klause surveys the variety of genres undercut in *Metempsychosis*, and Horation critique in 'Satyre I' is discussed by James S. Baumlin. Dennis Kay (*RES*) has turned up manuscript evidence to date the Donne/Goodyer verse epistle 'Alternis Vicibus' in early spring of 1613. The discovery of this evidence was, it seems, incidental to research on Sir Walter Aston as author of a manuscript elegy of Prince Henry.

An impressive article by Roman Dubinski (*Ren&R*) looks at the influence of the seven penitential Psalms on Donne's Holy Sonnets; this leads not only to new insights into the poems, but also to a possible devotional context for them. The four angels at the 'imagined corners' of 'Holy Sonnet VII' are identified by R. E. Pritchard (*N&Q*) as the four from Revelation 7.1 who are also to be associated with four principles and humours, and thereby with the range of causes of death listed in the poem. The same sonnet is discussed by Beverly Olson Flanigan (*Lang&S*) who seeks to remove difficulties in appreciating the poem by examining it in structural terms as a speech act. Rosemarie Potz McGerr (*N&Q*) finds a source for Donne's phrase 'blest hermaphrodite' from his poem for the newly ordained Mr Tilman, in the early thirteenth-century rhetorical treatise, Geoffrey de Vinsauf's *Poetria Nova*. While this article and several other source studies attest to the range of Donne's literary reading, his legal knowledge and experience are shown in 'The Dean of St Paul's at Court' (*N&Q*) by S. P. Cerasano to have been used in a dispute over a lease during the first year of his appointment. Interesting discoveries about the life of an author are always valuable, but it is a shame that this evidence of Donne's involvement in a legal dispute is put to rather crude use to support John Carey's view of the poet's alleged 'callousness' (*YW* 62.223).

Several recent articles consider Donne's posthumous influence – one, by Robert H. Ray (*N&Q*), revealing hitherto unrecorded allusions to Donne in two mid-seventeenth-century secular works, *Death in a New Dress; or, Sportive Funeral Elegies* by S. F. and Nicholas Hookes's *Amanda*. No fewer than five articles in a special issue of *JDJ* (1985) on the metaphysical poets and the nineteenth century, examine Donne's poetry as seen through the vehicle of his Victorian readers and followers. Two consider Donne and Coleridge: John A. Hodgson insists upon the seriousness of puns in relation to Coleridge's 'On Donne's First Poem', whereas John T. Shawcross, in 'Opulence and Iron Pokers', centres his discussion of the poets on the two versions of Coleridge's epigram, 'On Donne's Poetry'. Browning is the focus for John Maynard's essay on Donne and the Victorians. The attitudes of the ordinary nineteenth-century reader of Donne to his poetry and his life are examined by Dayton Haskin in 'Reading Donne's *Songs and Sonnets* in the Nineteenth Century', and Raoul Granqvist studies the reception of Donne's works into 'fashionable' New England in the 1890s.

After the great rush of publishing on Herbert in recent years, Stanley Stewart modestly asks in the preface to his new study of the poet [13], why do we need yet another book on Herbert? His answer is clear and forthright: to make the new

13. *George Herbert*, by Stanley Stewart. TEAS. Twayne. pp. x + 182. £22.

scholarship on Herbert available to non-specialist readers, and to re-assert the readings of Rosemond Tuve and Joseph Summers which he considers to have been ignored but not superseded by recent criticism. His approach is moderate and historical, and he uses the contemporary evidence of Herbert's biographers and readers, the liturgy, and the Little Gidding *Harmonies* to address the divide between Protestantism and Catholicism in the historical criticism of Herbert. He presents a portrait of the poet as non-Puritan (but also non-Catholic), and argues for the influence of the Ferrars' community on the careful structuring of the three parts of *The Temple*. Stewart concludes by suggesting, quite rightly, that there existed in the seventeenth century a 'school of Herbert' just as widespread as the 'school of Donne' (or the 'tribe of Ben'). This view is upheld by the evidence, also published this year, contained in Robert H. Ray's 'Herbert Allusion Book' (*SP*, Texts and Studies), which lists seventeenth-century allusions to Herbert from an enormous range of texts and authors of widely differing allegiances. This is thorough and scholarly work; it gives no commentary or context for the allusions cited (though Ray's article in this year's *GHJ* sketches in some background) but the book will be an excellent tool for future research into Herbert's early popularity. As Ray modestly notes, no allusion collection will ever be or remain complete; a further seventeenth-century reference to Herbert has already been discovered by John T. Shawcross (*GHJ*).

In a different mode altogether is Jonathan Goldberg's chapter on Herbert in his *Voice Terminal Echo*[2] – an exciting exploration of 'voices' in *The Temple* through questioning of the status of the printed page, the biblical echo, and the self-denying author. Joost Daalder (*GHJ*) uses more conventional critical methods to depict the shifting poetic theories articulated in *The Temple*, while in '"Delight into Sacrifice"' (*SEL*) Douglas Thorpe advances a theory of his own that Herbert's poems are outward signs or metaphors of inward spiritual transformation. The function of Herbert's lyrics as definitions (and of definition as poetry) is examined by Roy E. Aycock (*Lang&S*) in an analysis of the poet's metaphorical use of example, synonym, and negation as rhetorical tools for clarification. The most famous of Herbert's definition poems, 'Prayer' (I), is considered by William Bonnell (*GHJ*) in terms of its eucharistic flavour.

Continuing the great debate on Herbert's spiritual allegiance, John Bienz (*SEL*) has written a convincing essay on the poet's response to images and ceremonial, which Bienz sees as 'less a doctrinal than a pedagogical problem' to Herbert – and thus the solution found in *The Temple* is a rhetorical one. In 'Herbert and Mannerism' (*JDJ*) Murray Roston considers the puzzle of Herbert's rhetoric – structural unity and yet unpredicted reversals, security and yet restlessness – and, while not offering a 'magic formula' to resolve these discrepancies, he compares it in detail to the 'contrived illusionism' of contemporary Mannerist art. The meaning of the title 'The Pulley' is explored by Raymond B. Waddington (*GHJ*), particularly in its implications of spiritual torment. Complexities of different kinds are explicated by Martin Spence and Leonard Mustazza (*Expl*): Spence demonstrates the metaphysical conceit at work in 'Employment' (II), and Mustazza finds in 'The Forerunners' the clearest synthesis of Herbert's invention and plainness. Critics continue to investigate the response of more recent writers to this peculiarly Herbertian mixture of artistry and simplicity. In a fine and timely article Diane D'Amico

(*JDJ*, 1985) painstakingly discovers the basis of those frequently alleged (but rarely explored) similarities between Herbert and Christina Rossetti. In a briefer note, Sidney Gottlieb (*GHJ*) demonstrates how the young T. S. Eliot recalled Herbert's 'Affliction' (I) when drafting 'The Death of Saint Narcissus'.

The precise nature of Herbert's importance to Vaughan is further investigated this year. In '"Poor dust should lie still low"' Gerald Hammond (*English*) claims that Vaughan was no 'magpie' but, echoing Vaughan's poem 'The Match', sees him as a 'match' for Herbert, overcoming the 'tyranny of Herbert's words' by the end of *Silex Scintillans*. In an important and scholarly article Graeme J. Watson (*MP*) looks at the way in which Herbert's Temple symbol becomes politicized in Vaughan's usage, even in so 'purely' devotional a poem as 'The Night'. The work of 'master' and disciple have been published together this year in the Oxford Authors series [14], a very shrewd decision which will be popular among those wishing to teach these two devotional poets side by side. Edited with an elegant and informative introduction by Louis Martz, including exemplary readings of 'The Holdfast' and 'I walked the other day', this reasonably priced and clearly printed volume will help to highlight the contrasts between, for example, Vaughan's expansive mode and Herbert's precision – as well as allowing Vaughan's debt to Herbert to remain clearly in view. The selection is usefully comprehensive (all of Vaughan's religious lyrics and some of his secular work; *The Temple* and *The Country Parson*) and the modernization of the text is discreet – though the thinness of the annotation and the absence of textual innovation are to be lamented.

A new short study of Crashaw by Thomas F. Healy [15] is defended by its author on the grounds that Crashaw's own qualities continue to be underrated, and that as a result we also miss out on artistic and intellectual concepts which would enrich our sense of seventeenth-century English poetry. Healy's book will help on both counts, by means of its lively interpretations of individual poems (particularly 'To the Name of Jesus') and its historical/cultural grasp, especially enlightened in its rejection of conventional categorizations of Crashaw in favour of giving him a native intellectual context. Two of those traditional categories, 'metaphysical' and 'baroque', are the subject of an article, '"Concupiscence of Witt"', by J. W. Van Hook (*MP*) in which he points out that to baroque theorists, the metaphor on which a poem is based was distinct from the conceit which communicated that insight to the reader. Gregory T. Dime (*SEL*) contends that it is an error to assume a close correspondence between 'strong lines' and 'metaphysical poetry', the first being primarily a reference to syntax and accent, the second referring more directly to figurative language. The relationship between the 'metaphysicals' as a group and their nineteenth-century admirers is considered in three articles in *JDJ* (1985): Antony H. Harrison sets the Victorian rereadings, as an exercise in reception theory, in the critical context of the new historicism; John Griffin confronts the surprising 'failure' of influence in the poetry of the Tractarians who, as preachers and thinkers, found so much inspiration in the early seventeenth-century divines; Hopkins's process of 'metalepsis', his response

14. *George Herbert and Henry Vaughan*, ed. by Louis L. Martz. OA. OUP. pp. xxxii + 569. hb £17.50, pb £6.95.

15. *Richard Crashaw*, by Thomas F. Healy. Brill. pp. x + 161. Fl 70.

to the metaphysical poets which expressed itself in identifying with their own precursors, is subtly analysed by Jerome Bump.

This has been a good year for Marvell studies, marked by the publication of an excellent teaching text and a most significant critical book. The edition, prepared by Robert Wilcher[16], consists of a good range of poems and substantial extracts from *The Rehearsal Transpros'd* and other prose including four letters. The texts, modernized and modestly annotated, are prefaced by a brief biographical introduction but followed by the major feature of this edition, an extended commentary on critical approaches to Marvell. This proceeds by looking at critical issues raised by recent readings of clusters of poems, under the headings 'Lyric Voices', 'Social Voices', and 'Public Voices'. This discussion, seen in terms of 'the competing claims of a number of reading strategies' but also confronting 'the nature and function of the study of literature itself', will be of considerable benefit to students of Marvell. Margarita Stocker's study of Marvell[17], on the other hand, is aimed more at the specialist reader, not only of Marvell but of seventeenth-century religious and literary history. Her argument powerfully asserts that central to Marvell's language and thought was the pattern of apocalypse, and that his work, whether secular or sacred, participates in and articulates the eschatological process in history. This new and convincing thesis makes it impossible ever again to see Marvell as a poet of deliberate indecision, and Stocker's approach leads to some splendid readings, most especially of 'Upon Appleton House' (that critical test for any study of Marvell) and 'Bermudas'.

Moving to the study of detail in Marvell's verse, Robert Cummings (*ELN*) suggests that the 'mose' of dust in 'Appleton House' should be emended not to 'mote' but 'mese', an appropriately legalist term for land on which a house might be built. The numerological significance of the fact that there are forty lines to 'On a Drop of Dew' is investigated by George M. Muldrow (*ELN*) who finds the poem to be a statement, in several dimensions, of divine providence. Peter Davidson (*N&Q*) discerns Marvellian vocabulary in an epitaph in a Norfolk church, written by Daniel Scargill in 1680/1 in memory of his wife. In 'Marvell and Milton on Cromwell' another echo is discovered by David Crane (*N&Q*) in a more likely place, perhaps – Milton's sonnet 'To the Lord General Cromwell' – where he suggests that Milton is 'correcting' Marvell's ambivalent image of Cromwell in the 'Horatian Ode'. Margarita Stocker (*N&Q*) corrects the standard translation of a line in Marvell's Latin poem 'A Letter to Dr. Ingelo' (chaplain to the embassy in Sweden); the new translation asserts Cromwell's resolute pursuit of the 'true' Protestant religion in England.

Two of this year's most impressive general critical studies have important points to make about Marvell. Jonathan Goldberg begins his book[2] with a consideration of the poet's creative strategies which, paradoxically, 'annihilate all that's made'. In particular he reads 'The Nymph complaining' as being 'about its own deeply problematized voice' and in a probing, shifting chapter concludes, 'Where is Marvell's voice in this text?'. Leah Marcus's correlation of literary activity and the defence of 'old holiday pastimes'[4] concludes with a

16. *Andrew Marvell: Selected Poetry and Prose*, ed. by Robert Wilcher. Methuen. pp. ix + 292. pb £3.50.

17. *Apocalyptic Marvell: The Second Coming in Seventeenth-Century Poetry*, by Margarita Stocker. Harvester. pp. xvi + 381. £32.50.

chapter in which Lovelace's *Lucasta* is seen as a treasury of motifs for the new country rituals, which Marvell then reworked; while Lovelace was attempting to perpetuate the past, Marvell was coming to terms with and working himself out of the past.

Marcus also offers one of only two accounts this year of Herrick's work, with a chapter on the poet-priest who both celebrated (in his strikingly erotic verse) and regularized country festivals. She cites the parallel of an Oxford priest who preached in favour of sports and then joined in the maypole dance; such intervention upheld holiday mirth but avoided its more radical possibilities. The other discussion of Herrick occurs in Achsah Guibbory's book[5] on patterns of historical thought in the seventeenth century. Herrick appears, she confesses, as a writer who might seem ahistorical – and so to find the cyclical view of history expressed in his verse is an indication of how far the ideas of history permeated in this period.

Two articles in *SEL* this year consider Carew's poetic self-enactment: Renée Hannaford examines 'Self-Presentation in Carew's "To A. L. Perswasions to Love"', and Joanne Altieri analyses 'Responses to a Waning Mythology in Carew's Political Poetry'. And finally, two further essays are the culmination of work on two minor poets of the era. James A. Riddell (*HLQ*) puts us right on the few certain facts about 'The Life of William Bosworth', author of *The Chast and Lost Lovers* (1651). John Eames (*ES*) presents a biographical and critical account of Sir William Kingsmill, a poet of the Civil War period whose work – a typical poetic spectrum of the age, including satires, love poetry, accounts of the country life, religious and critical verse – is to be found in a manuscript in Lichfield Cathedral Library.

3. Prose

'The most comprehensive, the most practical, and the most readable of the many books of instruction written for women in the early seventeenth century' – that is how its 1986 editor, Michael R. Best, describes Gervase Markham's *The English Housewife*[18]. This fine volume, thoroughly introduced and beautifully printed, reveals that Markham was himself as much an editor as an original writer: 'I am but only a public notary who record[s] the most true and infallible experience.' His purpose was to encompass 'the inward and outward vertues which ought to be in a compleat woman'. And though this was originally the second part of a two-volume work in which, after depicting the pastimes of the 'master', Markham 'descends' to consider the mistress of the family, Best rightly points out that Markham's housewife is shown to be vital to the economic as well as social partnership of husband and wife.

In addition to Bacon's role in Achsah Guibbory's *Map of Time*[5] as figurehead of those who held a progressive view of history, his influence on linguistic practice has also been examined this year, in an essay by L. G. Kelly (*Lang&S*) on 'Medicine, Learned Ignorance, and Style in Seventeenth-Century Translation'. Kelly maintains that whether translators began from a Baconian premise (taking language to be an invariant code) or from a Puritan paradigm

---

18. *The English Housewife*, by Gervase Markham, ed. by Michael R. Best. McG–Q. pp. lviii + 321. $35.

(language dominating things), both schools of thought led to literal translation, rejecting the 'humanity of language' in favour of things (Bacon) or God. Our knowledge of seventeenth-century English continues to grow, as two *N&Q* articles demonstrate: R. D. Dunn supplies extensive additions to *OED* from three editions of William Camden's *Remains*, and R. W. McConchie gives further *OED* additions from John Cotta's *Ignorant Practisers of Physicke* (1612).

Jonathan Haynes has published the first full-length study[19] of George Sandys's travel book, *Relation of a Journey begun An. Dom. 1610*, in an attempt to bring this 'minor classic' to the attention of modern readers. In fact Haynes's book serves at least two other purposes as well: it surveys the rise of English travel literature from Richard Hakluyt onwards (incidentally demonstrating that Sandys's is among the more literary of these works), and analyses the historical and cultural awareness of the early seventeenth-century traveller. Haynes argues that, as the humanist Sandys discovered the roots of our tradition in past cultures, and confronted the phenomenon of Islam, he developed a number of different concepts of history – not a uniform view but a 'series of pasts'.

While Sandys understood our civilization through travel, Robert Burton came to similar knowledge, Michael O'Connell maintains, through a world of books. O'Connell's study[20] of Burton, steady and accessible though it is, builds a powerful cumulative sense of Burton's melancholic intertwining of a life and a book. This is, genuinely, a 'biographical and critical' work, introducing the man through the *Anatomy* and vice versa. Even in his consideration of the style of Burton's enormous project, O'Connell suggests that 'English prose' was 'his primary antidote to melancholy'. One of the distinctive features of Burton as subject is that the 'Chronology' at the start of O'Connell's study can begin with the date and hour of his conception. Nicolas Kiessling (*RES*, 1985) has discovered Burton's horoscope in a notebook in the Bodleian, and has also recorded an early fragment of copy of the *Anatomy* in one of Burton's books in Christ Church library in 'Two Notes on Robert Burton's Annotations'.

James Dorrill (*JDJ*, 1985) discerns the influence of the bell-tolling meditation from Donne's *Devotions* in Thomas Hardy's poem 'Drawing Details in an Old Church' (1922). The variety of personae used dramatically in Donne's sermons – as a deliberate spiritual method, indicating the growth and range of acceptable responses to God – is explored in an article by Paul W. Harland (*ELH*). And at last we have a book-length study of the English metaphysical preachers[21], in which Horton Davies sets Donne and Lancelot Andrewes in their rightful context alongside at least forty other preachers. The account of preaching style is a little over-schematic, but the work is immensely valuable, for two features in particular. First, it shatters the Arminian stereotype of the metaphysical preachers, looking at the sermons of, among others, the Calvinist bishops John Hacket and Ralph Brownrig. Second, Davies

19. *The Humanist as Traveler: George Sandys's 'Relation of a Journey begun An. Dom. 1610'*, by Jonathan Haynes. AUP/FDU. pp. 159. £19.95.

20. *Robert Burton*, by Michael O'Connell. TEAS. Twayne. pp. xi + 130. $18.95.

21. *Like Angels from a Cloud: The English Metaphysical Preachers 1588–1645*, by Horton Davies. Huntington. pp. xii + 503. $38.

commendably spreads his investigations to include the expectations, and influence, of the preachers' audiences.

Winifred Crombie (*Lang&S*) has produced a thorough stylistic study of the 'Two Faces of Seneca' in early seventeenth-century English prose, identifying the differences between Lancelot Andrewes's 'metaphysical' style and Sir Thomas Browne's 'baroque'. In addition to the publication of details of Browne's library (see p. 15), two items in *N&Q* this year focus on his biography: G. C. R. Morris traces the family tree of Browne's daughters, and in 'Sir Thomas Browne and *Vox Norwici*' Kitty Scoular Datta argues that the 'Thomas Browne' signing a tract of 1646 in defence of pro-Presbyterian clergy in Norwich was not the author of *Religio Medici* but probably Thomas Browne the worsted weaver.

Charles Cantalupo (*Lang&S*) moves into the open field of Hobbes's eclectic style, and limits himself to answering three (rather large) questions: what were its classical origins, how did the style develop during his career, and what was its relation to the prose of his contemporaries?

The Puritan theory of discourse put forward by Alexander Richardson in his *Logicians School-Master* (1629) is the subject of an impressive article by John C. Adams (*Rhetorica*). He shows that this Ramist treatise, in examining speech as the conveyor of rationality, distinguishes between grammar as a help to understanding and rhetoric as a help to belief. N. I. Matar (*N&Q*) continues his work on the prose of Peter Sterry, this time demonstrating how Sterry was a devoted but not uncritical reader of the German mystic Jacob Boehme; this fact is additionally significant since it would tend to reflect the official Cromwellian view of Boehme. Thomas Killigrew's response to an incident in Europe in 1635 – the so-called possessed nuns of Loudon – is established by J. Lough and D. E. L. Crane (*DUJ*) who have printed the Bodleian manuscript version of Killigrew's letter as closest to the original autograph.

Eamon Duffy (*SCent*) has looked at the evidence of chap-books, the 'penny godlies', to show that Puritanism did indeed penetrate popular culture. Tim Raylor (*N&Q*) doubts whether the proverb, 'He that fights and runs away/May live to fight another day' actually existed in the seventeenth century in that form, as F. P. Wilson's *Oxford Dictionary of English Proverbs* states. Lastly, the plurality of seventeenth-century views of history noted earlier (pp. 275 and 284) is matched by the plurality of worlds to be found in early science fiction, as David Knight (*SCent*) finds, particularly in the work of Francis Godwin and John Wilkins to whom the moon was the 'new world'.

Milton

ARCHIE BURNETT

This chapter has six sections: 1. General; 2. Minor Poems; 3. Paradise Lost; 4. Paradise Regained and Samson Agonistes; 5. Prose; 6. Influence.

1. General

Lois Potter's popular introductory book on Milton has been revised[1]. Some corrections have been made, two new extracts from the poetry are now discussed, and the annotated bibliography has been expanded. In his review of the first edition (*YW* 52.235) C. A. Patrides censured its eclecticism, its over-simplifications, and the procedures followed in its critical analyses. In view of the limitations of the format and the range and complexity of the subject matter, this seems rather severe: it is unlikely that any book of this size could prove wholly adequate on scientific, political, religious, and literary back-grounds, and manage to communicate something of the textures of the texts as well. Given its demanding agenda, the book performs a useful function.

Louis L. Martz's *Poet of Exile* has been issued as an attractive paperback under a slightly different title and with a new introduction[2]. In 1981 C. A. Patrides hailed the book as 'a major critic's major achievement' and as 'one of our time's most thoughtful accounts of Milton's poetry as a whole' (*YW* 61.208,209). There is no need to disagree, even though Martz's study of Ovidian influence has recently been supplemented by others by Richard J. DuRocher (*YW* 66.291–2) and Charles Martindale (below, pp. 289–90).

Most Miltonists will know the nine-volume *A Milton Encyclopedia* (1978–83), and most will also have lamented that it is too expensive for them to buy for themselves. It is therefore good news that the entries on the poems and John T. Shawcross's excellent short entry on Milton's life have now been reprinted in one volume[3]. It will prove very useful to those, students and teachers alike, who wish to find out quickly what has concerned Miltonists in each poem. Its coverage of the scholarship is not up to date, however. There is no discussion of Mary Ann Radzinowicz's 1978 book, *Toward 'Samson Agonistes'* (*YW* 59.213–4), for instance; indeed, nothing after the early seventies is mentioned. An appended bibliography by John T. Shawcross

1. *A Preface to Milton*, by Lois Potter. Rev. edn. Longman. pp. x + 182. pb £6.95.
2. *Milton: Poet of Exile*, by Louis L. Martz. Second edn. Yale. pp. xxvii + 356. pb £10.95.
3. *Milton's English Poetry: Being Entries from 'A Milton Encyclopedia'*, ed. by William B. Hunter. BuckU. pp. 248. £20.95.

provides some redress, but the real problem remains. Given the potential usefulness of the volume, the only other criticism to be made is that it is too expensive: a cheaper paperback would be more likely to meet student requirements. (In *MiltonQ* Maurice Kelley points out some errors and omissions in the original complete set.)

In *Milton and the Sons of God*[4] Hugh MacCallum explores the poetry in terms of Milton's conception of sonship in human and divine relations. In his introduction he outlines his theme in the minor poems and in *Samson Agonistes*, and devotes most of the book to the two epics. He focuses on the mediatory role of the 'son', and discusses the Son of God, the angels, Adam, and, to a lesser extent, Eve as examples of the filial relationship. Extensive use is made of Reformed dogmatics and of *De Doctrina Christiana*, but the difference between formal theology and literary experience is carefully observed. The large central theme is expounded patiently and soundly throughout; and although sometimes – in the chapters on Adam and Eve, for instance – the treatment tends to lose direction and point, the chapter on the identity of the Son in *Paradise Regained* is sharply focused and lively. Overall the book somehow lacks intellectual excitement, due perhaps to its familiar theme or to the predictability of its approach.

Only two general articles have appeared during the year, one biographical and one theological. John Peter Rumrich (*MiltonQ*) considers the possible influence on Milton of Joseph Mead of Christ's College. In the absence of documentary evidence, he indicates instances of intellectual resemblance that at least suggest that Mead's works offer a source for Milton's early encounter with some fundamental themes of the Christian tradition. He also cautions against construing Mead's pusillanimity in the face of Laud's regime as identification with it. Michael E. Bauman (*WTJ*) argues strenuously against William B. Hunter's view that Milton was a subordinationist who advocated the two-stage *Logos* theory.

2. Minor Poems

In '"L'Allegro" and "Il Penseroso": Classical Tradition and Renaissance Mythography' Stella P. Revard (*PMLA*) clearly and convincingly relates Milton's treatment of Mirth and Melancholy in these poems to the conventions of classical hymn or ode and to the myth books of the Renaissance. She stresses the identity of Mirth as the Grace Euphrosyne, identifies Melancholy as the Muse Urania, and interprets the poems as 'two different accounts of the genesis and development of poetical inspiration'. Herbert J. Phelan's article, 'What Is the Persona Doing in *L'Allegro* and *Il Penseroso*?' (*MiltonS*), is good in itself, but either he or an editor of the journal should have read the first chapter of Archie Burnett's *Milton's Style* (*YW* 62.234–5) before publishing it.

In 'Milton's "Three and Twentieth Year" Again' (*N&Q*) Jeremy Maule discredits John Gouws's suggestion (*N&Q*, 1984) about the significance of the age of the Marchioness of Winchester at her death, and, in connection with the mention of the 'three-and-twentieth year' in Sonnet VII, notes that Milton's nephew Edward Phillips records in *Theatrum Poetarum* (1675) that the Scottish

4. *Milton and the Sons of God: The Divine Image in Milton's Epic Poetry*, by Hugh MacCallum. UTor. pp. x + 325. \$35.

neo-Latin poet Arthur Johnston was laureated at Paris before he was twenty-three. He fails to establish any relevance for this information, however. Margo Swiss, in 'Crisis of Conscience: A Theological Context for Milton's "How Soon Hath Time"' (*MiltonQ*), sets Sonnet VII in the context of the letter 'To A Friend', stressing the importance of 'conscience' and 'vocation' in the seventeenth century, and interpreting the poem as 'at once an expression of conscientious anguish and of Christian reconciliation'. In the Italian sonnet 'Donna leggiadra' Ray Fleming (*MiltonQ*) detects a Dantean influence, and David Crane (*N&Q*) considers 'Marvell and Milton on Cromwell', comparing lines from the openings of 'To The Lord General Cromwell', and Marvell's 'Horatian Ode'.

Mindele Anne Treip, in '*Comus* as "Progress"' (*MiltonQ*), offers an imaginative study of problems of dramatic form or genre in *Comus*. She proposes 'a *Comus* presented out of doors ... in the late afternoon, reaching into twilight and evening' and 'a *Comus* framed along the lines of the Elizabethan or Jacobean "progress"'. She duly acknowledges the problems her reconstructions cannot completely solve, and admits of the possibility that the masque could have been designed around the alternatives of outdoor or indoor performance. (The article was accepted by *MiltonQ* early in 1984, and so predates the important studies by John Creaser (*YW* 65.306) and Cedric C. Brown (*YW* 66.289–90).) Martin Butler, in 'A Provincial Masque of *Comus*, 1636' (*RenD*), sheds light on the conditions of performance of provincial theatrical entertainments by examining the accounts kept by the Clifford family for a performance of a private masque at Skipton in 1636. James Obertino in 'Milton's Use of Aquinas in *Comus*' (*MiltonS*) argues that *Comus* presents 'the continuity of nature and grace, with chastity important as a virtue in its own right, as well as a pervasive metonymy for charity, which binds Creator and creature, grace and nature together'. By adducing parallels he identifies Aquinas, rather than Luther or Calvin, as Milton's primary theological source. A different source for ideas in the masque is indicated by Marc Beckwith in '*Comus* and the *Zodiacus Vitae*' (*MiltonQ*): on the basis of the opening and closing speeches of the Attendant Spirit, he alleges that Milton read and remembered Marcellus Palingenius' didactic poem. Cedric C. Brown in 'The *Kōmos* in Milton' (*JDJ*) learnedly traces the literary and iconographical ancestry of Comus, and highlights key aspects of Milton's conception of the figure. The article draws substantially on the third chapter of his book, *John Milton's Aristocratic Entertainments* (*YW* 66.289–90). The same writer, in 'Milton's "Arcades" in the Trinity Manuscript' (*RES*), substantiates his claim that the manuscript 'tells a story of development from a time before performance to a time of preparation for publication', noting that 'there is no "performance" or presentation text' of the entertainment. Finally, in a penetrating comparative study, '"Such Noise as I can Make": Chastity and Speech in *Othello* and *Comus*' (*RenD*, 1985), Mary Laughlin Fawcett explores the intertwined themes of chastity, speech, and silence in the two works.

As its title indicates, R. P. Draper's *Lyric Tragedy*[5] is a study of tragic modes not in drama but in lyric. It covers a wide range from Henryson to Larkin, encompassing Wordsworth, Shelley, Tennyson, Arnold, Hardy, D. H. Lawrence, Wilfred Owen, Edward Thomas, and Sylvia Plath. In his second

5. *Lyric Tragedy*, by R. P. Draper. St Martin's (1985). pp. viii + 231. $31.25.

chapter, on '"Lycidas" and the Pastoral Elegy', Draper draws the unstartling conclusion that '*Lycidas*, despite its tragic material, is not a tragic poem', though he asserts that it nevertheless influenced the shape of later tragic lyrics. The chapter benefits noticeably from Clay Hunt's '*Lycidas' and the Italian Critics* (*YW* 60.212-13), contains virtually nothing original, and, like much of the book, is sensible and rather dull. Expansively indulgent commentary on familiar aspects of the poem soon eclipses an interest in 'tragic satire'. Like the book as a whole, the chapter needs a more sophisticated and better defined ideology of tragedy, as well as a more rigorous argument.

Robert Leigh Davis (*MiltonQ*) employs considerable lexical ingenuity to contend that the 'two-handed engine' 'may be re-interpreted to suggest a cross ... as well as a broadsword', and thus to argue that the image conflates connotations of redemptive mercy with those of wrath. His explanation of 'two-handed' in relation to the cross remains weak, however. Karl P. Wentersdorf (*MP*) explains that the 'Allusion and Theme in the Third Movement of Milton's *Lycidas*' are designed to distinguish virtuous love from lust. And in a posthumously published article, 'Milton's Blind Mouths' (*BC*), Michael Serpell detects echoes in the attack on the false pastors (and possibly also in *Paradise Lost*, IV.183-7, 191-3) of sermons by Frances Rollenson published in 1611.

3. Paradise Lost

Louis L. Martz's well-known 1966 anthology of essays on *Paradise Lost*[6] (*YW* 47.204-5) has been re-issued. Nothing, not even the bibliography, has been changed, and the whole collection looks heavily dated. Do we need again, some fifty years on, to witness T. S. Eliot's vagueness and shiftiness on Milton? Instead of plodding through C. S. Lewis on 'The Style of Secondary Epic', would it not be more productive for students to be taught how to undertake detailed analysis of Milton's poetic language themselves? This is the sort of volume that in Britain supports the tyrannical conservatism of the study of English at 'A' Level, which in turn unfits students for much of further education. Surely criticism naturally moves on, even though some publishers would seem to want it to move back or stand still?

Charles Martindale's book[7] is a classicist's study of Milton's handling of Homer, Virgil, Ovid, and Lucan. On the face of it, that might seem to justify the author's modest claim to 're-assert old truths that are in danger of neglect'; those who have read his article on Ovidian influence in Milton (*YW* 66.293) will know to expect more than that. The author possesses several qualifications for tackling his subject well: he is careful to filter his view of the classics through Renaissance responses; he does not attribute conventional topoi to over-specific sources; he is judicious, as, say, the formidably learned Claes Schaar in his study, 'The Full Voic'd Quire Below' (*YW* 63.218-19), often failed to be, about the meanings an allusion does *not* invoke; and he is able to broaden out his discussion from lexically supported parallels to similarities of poetic strategy and style. There are a number of good sections on specific topics such

6. *Milton: 'Paradise Lost': A Collection of Critical Essays*, ed. by Louis L. Martz. PHI. pp. v + 212. pb £4.95.
7. *John Milton and the Transformation of Ancient Epic*, by Charles Martindale. CH. pp. xiv + 239. £22.50.

as Virgilian simile, Lucan's Caesar and Milton's Satan, and on Homeric and Miltonic treatments of blindness, war, and time. The accounts of style are often subjective and piecemeal, however, and a certain lack of intellectual rigour threatens to take over the author's relaxed, discursive manner; but his urbanity and enthusiasm still make the book recommendable, particularly to English Literature specialists whose knowledge of the classics is not deep. An index of passages in *Paradise Lost* discussed in the book is helpfully appended.

Christopher Kendrick's book[8] is a Marxist assessment of the impact of the Puritan Revolution on Milton's writing, or rather on *Areopagitica* and *Paradise Lost*. He focuses on the oratorical argument in the prose tract for limited deregulation of books, and argues that *Paradise Lost* 'modifies and transgresses against the form of classical epic in the very attempt at re-embodying its spirit'. What is distinctive about all this is the inference drawn from rhetorical and generic analysis that Milton's individualistic ethos both affirms the success of the revolution and exposes the contradictions between freedom and necessity under emergent capitalism. In order to make the political interpretation stick, the central importance of religious or theological concerns is played down – Alastair Fowler's annotated edition of *Paradise Lost* (*YW* 49.208-9) is blamed for apparently being directed at 'poetasting divinity students' – and the range and complexity of the determinants of style are seriously underestimated or misrepresented. Much is asserted – indeed, the author has an irritating habit of drawing attention to what he is proposing, assuming, emphasizing, claiming, or trying to do – but clear demonstration is usually lacking. The reason for this is that the book is appallingly written. Here are two sentences about 'the social significance of the generic process' from the conclusion (p. 216):

> . . . the psychology of transgression projected by the utopian inter-section of the subgenres of romance and pastoral, in which romance desire strives for what it is forbidden, for what is constitutively absent from the pastoral world, is the final symbolic form taken by the counter-plot. Predestination is thus figured as an ethical psychology at work in creation, and this logic provides the dominant generic explanation of the fall, hence of the failure of political desire in the revolution.

If the book finds a fit audience, they will be few.

It is salutary, after reading such a book, to read the collection of essays[9] edited by Galbraith M. Crump on teaching *Paradise Lost*. Though some of the contributors seem to have entered their pedagogical anecdotage, and though some of the students they teach come across as being unctuously enthusiastic, unrealistically demanding, or naïve, it is good for ivory-tower researchers to be reminded that to try teaching Milton to an unfit and very large audience is very much to attempt the art of the possible. The editor's bibliographical guide (pp. 11-23) should nevertheless ensure that students continue to be daunted by Milton, or at any rate by Milton studies, while their teachers are too busy ploughing through a ten-page list of 'essential reference materials that an

8. *Milton: A Study in Ideology and Form*, by Christopher Kendrick. Methuen. pp. x + 240. £25.

9. *Approaches to Teaching Milton's 'Paradise Lost'*, ed. by Galbraith M. Crump. MLA. pp. x + 201. hb $30, pb $16.50.

instructor should consult in preparation for teaching *Paradise Lost*' to pay much attention to them. The volume is not concerned primarily to provide new insights on the poem, though Joan E. Hartman's account of its sexual relations (pp. 126-34) and Herman Rapaport's chapter on its novelistic qualities (pp. 135-44) offer refreshing challenges. What emerges powerfully from the book is how remote the poem seems to be from the experiences of so many students all over the United States, and, accordingly, how self-indulgent so much Milton scholarship begins to look. Any Miltonist must feel compelled to think long and hard about the cultural implications of teaching *Paradise Lost* at the United States Naval Academy, 'an institution', as the instructor himself puts it, 'that is training students to organize and potentially execute violence on an unprecedented scale'.

A number of articles from 1986 deal with verbal texture and detail in *Paradise Lost*. In 'Milton's Poetic Inversion' (*JSaga*) Masahiko Agari conducts a full-scale investigation of word-order, concentrating on subject–verb–object–adverb categories. He provides the most complete account to date, supported by copious examples and by statistical tables of the book-by-book distribution of the types of inversion. Admirable though the whole enterprise is, and welcome though the information it provides may be, it does nevertheless pay only the slightest attention to the normality or abnormality of Milton's inversions, and it says virtually nothing about the poetic functions word-order serves. Leonard Mustazzi (*CLAJ*) relates the language of Adam and Eve to their innocence, sinfulness, and regeneration, but lacks the linguistic cutting edge to penetrate beyond the general surface. At a more detailed level, John E. Gorecki (*N&Q*) acutely catches 'An Echo of *Julius Caesar* in *Paradise Lost*' of the shout of Shakespeare's Roman mob for Pompey (I.i.43-7) in the shout of the demons for Satan (I.541-3), commenting that 'Milton may be underscoring the fickleness and instability of the rebel angels'; Frances Teague (*MiltonQ*) points out associations of the pygmies, twice mentioned in Book I, with over-weening pride punished by divine wrath; and Clay Daniel (*MiltonQ*) discusses 'Astraea, the Golden Scales, and the Scorpion', elucidating the symbolism in IV.996-1004 of Virgo–Libra–Scorpio as an explication of the relationship of Eve, Gabriel, and Satan. Patricia Elizabeth Davis, in 'Covenant and the "Crowne of Life"' (*MiltonS*), offers typological interpretations of floral imagery in the poem, paying particular attention to the crown-garland motif. Thus, in several postlapsarian descriptions she perceives types of Christ's crown of thorns, itself a type of the 'crown of life' that symbolizes heavenly joy and immortality. Another typological reading is suggested by Mary Ruth Brown (*MiltonQ*), who highlights the link between 'the mystical union of Adam and Eve in its typological connection to Christ and the Church, and the vine imagery throughout *Paradise Lost* with its parallels to the vine metaphor in the Bible, especially that of Christ's message to his followers in the Gospel of John, Chapter 15'. Though thoughtfully elaborated, the evidence does not wholly convince: only two of the seven references to the vine in the poem are other than naturalistic, and the elm/vine image is blatantly sexual. Altogether more plausible, mainly because it accommodates the sexual connotations more comfortably, is Todd H. Sammons's '"As the Vine Curls her Tendrils"' (*MiltonQ*), a discussion of the vine/elm and ivy/tree topoi, the one associated with prelapsarian union, the other with postlapsarian eroticism.

The presentation of Eve in the poem continues to attract attention. Diane

McColley (*MiltonQ*) shows how Eve 'can be regarded as an interpretive center for *Paradise Lost* partly because she embodies and performs a great many properties and processes that Milton elsewhere attributes to poetry itself, or to himself as poet'. Though her article observes the routinely bland decorum that afflicts so much Milton criticism, it does go some way to explaining the remarkable sympathy with which Eve is portrayed. Jean Gagen (*MiltonQ*), asking 'Did Milton Nod?', highlights his failure to give a consistent account of the circumstances under which Eve was informed of Satan's malignant design on her and Adam, and attributes the failure to divisions over Eve in his mind. In 'Wrestling with the Angel' William Shullenberger (*MiltonQ*) examines larger feminist questions about Milton's God, Eve's subordination, and Satan, arguing boldly that the subtext of *Paradise Lost* actually encourages and supports feminist readings. His is one of the more searching accounts of the poem in the light of current issues, and should do much to advance his hope for alteration of what he sees as 'the present caricature of Milton'. Edward Le Comte's 'Comments' (*MiltonQ*) picks up errors in previous articles in the same journal by Raymond B. Waddington (*YW* 66.295) and Jane M. Petty (*YW* 66.294). While he is right to insist that Satan's words, not Adam's, precipitate Eve's dream, Jane Petty's point about the confusion between the two, cleverly dramatized by the verbal echoes she pointed out, remains a valid one.

The relation of *Paradise Lost* to other texts is explored in a number of articles. Kenneth J. Knoespel, in 'The Limits of Allegory' (*MiltonS*), broadens out the scope of influence of the Narcissus myth from Milton's account of Eve at the pool to his use of it psychologically to animate Satan and Adam as well as Eve. He argues that Milton transcends the original setting of love psychology to use the fable as a means of indicating qualities of perception and comprehension. Willard McCarty, in 'The Catabatic Structure of Satan's Quest' (*UTQ*), examines the classical heroic patterns of *katabasis*, or descent to, and return from, the lower world, and of *anabasis*, or 'rapacious ascent from a lower world and return there with the spoils of the upper regions'. He considers Milton's use of these generic patterns in the presentation of Satan's journeys. Two articles explore the familiar relation of Milton to Spenser: John N. King (*Ren&R*) shows how the account of the 'blissful Bower' wl.ere Adam and Eve make love before the Fall 'restored to full vitality the doctrine of chaste love that Spenser parodies in the seductive arbors and groves of Acrasia'; and in a well-written and penetrating piece, 'From Allegory to Dialectic: Imagining Error in Spenser and Milton' (*PMLA*), Gordon Teskey contrasts Spenser's association of error with the complex meanderings of narrative with Milton's unambiguous polarization of error and truth. In 'Milton's Coy Eve' (*ELH*) William Kerrigan and Gordon Braden view *Paradise Lost* in relation to Petrarchist and Ovidian traditions within Renaissance love poetry. They argue that Milton's epic 'provides a moral and psychological etiology for the manifold postures and dispositions' of such poetry, and conclude that 'Milton's may be the most reflective, even philosophical account of sexual consummation in all of Renaissance literature'. Given that their subject is love and sex, it is unlikely that all of their hypotheses will command assent. However, the article covers a wide range, is entertainingly written, and unfailingly provokes thought. Alvin Snider, in 'The Self-Mirroring Mind in Milton and Traherne' (*UTQ*), illuminatingly contrasts Traherne's 'Shadows in the Water' and the episode in which Eve contemplates her reflection; he has useful things to say about mirrors in seventeenth-century epistemology, religion, and literature. Sidney Gottlieb (*MP*) compares Milton's reference to Chinese land-ships at III.437-9 with the account of the vehicles in John Wilkins's *Mathematicall Magick* (1648), suggesting that Milton's image provides a wittily ironic contrast to Wilkins's praise of human ingenuity. In 'John Abbot's 1647 "Paradise Lost"' (*MiltonQ*) Richard D. Jordan compares Milton's treatment of the Fall and of the war in heaven with that by Abbot, a Roman Catholic priest, in his *Devout Rhapsodies* (1647).

Predictably enough, there have been a number of studies of the poem's theology. Michael Lieb, in '"Hate in Heav'n"' (*ELH*), faces up to the idea of a God who hates as well as loves, tracing its Old Testament sources and New Testament manifestations, and encouraging us to admire the *odium Dei* as 'a perfect hate'. In 'Heavenly Joy at the Torments of the Damned in Restoration Writings' (*N&Q*) N. I. Matar views the derisive laugh in heaven (XII.59-61) in the context of the joy of the blessed as they witness the suffering of the damned, an uplifting doctrine which he shows to be current in the seventeenth century. Golda Werman stresses Milton's audacious emphasis on Adam's and Eve's freewill 'Repentance in *Paradise Lost*' (*MiltonS*), and argues that his individualistic theodicy often led him to scriptural interpretations which were not Protestant but were 'similar to those found in midrashic literature'. In 'Satan, Sin, and Death: A Mosaic Trio in *Paradise Lost*' Samuel S. Stollman (*MiltonS*) argues that Sin and Death and their encounters with Satan act out Milton's antinomian doctrine of the Mosaic law's impediment to the attainment of Christian liberty. Michael E. Bauman (*CLAJ*) amasses evidence to show that Milton's theology in *Paradise Lost* was regarded as heretical before the publication of *De Doctrina Christiana* in 1825, whilst insisting that questions concerning Milton's orthodoxy are to be settled by appealing not to Milton's past readers but to Milton himself.

A few articles explore the implications of Milton's religious position. Julia M. Walker, in '"For each seem'd either"' (*Milton Q*), argues that though he wished to accept the absolute truth of the images and events in *Paradise Lost*, the problem of free will made this realistically and artistically impossible. She has some good observations on the significance of the word 'seems' in the poem. Looking at 'Milton's Choice of Subject in the Context of Renaissance Critical Theory' (*ELH*) Gordon Teskey relates the choice of epic subject to Renaissance speculations on the idea of the heroic poem, and is particularly enlightening on the conflict between a Protestant totalizing conception of history and neo-Aristotelean formalism. Sharing Christopher Hill's approach, but disagreeing with his equation of the innocent Adam's fall with the ignorant revolutionary leaders' failure, Jun Harada's 'Toward *Paradise Lost*' (*MiltonS*) relates the temptation theme in the epic to Milton's internalized experiences during the revolution. He concludes that the poem 'conjoins experience and theology in a mature presentation and judgment of man's inconstant nature'. His account of the temptation remains generalized - perhaps necessarily so in order to support the analogy with Milton's experience of historical events.

The remaining studies suggest the richness of the poem by their very variety. In 'Unfallen Marriage and the Fallen Imagination in *Paradise Lost*' (*SEL*) Douglas Anderson contends that the process of accommodation results in a treatment of Paradise and of prelapsarian marriage that places particularly high demands upon the reader's imagination. The clarity of his exposition does itself tend to weaken the force of his contention, however, and he also over-simplifies the modes of accommodation by which Heaven and Hell are represented. William Alexander McClung (*VIA*) considers, in 'The Architectonics of *Paradise Lost*', the significance of the architectures of Hell, Heaven, and Paradise. Unfortunately, his fondness for the higher jargon (Pandaemonium is 'a dystopia of the indoors', etc.) consistently clouds his commentary in vagueness and preciousness. More clear-sightedly, in 'Pandaemonium and Babel' (*MiltonQ*), Steven Blakemore views Pandaemonium as 'the original model not only for Babel but for all future postlapsarian architecture', and in so doing draws attention to some aspects of the poem's 'architecture'. Thomas Ramey Watson, in 'Milton's Pyramids' (*AN&Q*), comments upon Milton's employment of pyramidic motifs in the epic, though his tendency to see pyramids in any vertical elevation weakens his assertions. Eve Keller (*MiltonQ*) looks at 'Tetragrammic Numbers' and finds significance in the fact that in 1674 *Paradise Lost* became a poem of 10,565 lines: according to the Cabbalistic *gematria*, the number corresponds to the most holy name of God.

4. Paradise Regained and Samson Agonistes

William Kerrigan, in 'The Irrational Coherence of *Samson Agonistes*' (*MiltonS*), argues that Milton in his last two works replaced 'the conventional alliance between conscience and reason with an alliance, at extraordinary moments in sacred history, between God and will', and launches an attack on the rational-humanistic positions taken up by Douglas Bush, Louis L. Martz, and Mary Ann Radzinowicz. In the only other article of the year to deal with *Paradise Regained*, 'Apollonius of Rhodes and the Resourceless Hero of *Paradise Regained*', James Tatum (*MiltonS*) addresses the problem of the poem's generic frame of reference. He points out the limitations of Anthony Low's view of the poem as georgic (*YW* 64.267), and argues that it evokes instead the classical literary form of narrative poems written as sequels to full-scale epic. In particular, he cites the *Argonautica* of Apollonius of Rhodes, supplying telling parallels between the troubled heroics of Jason and of Satan.

A substantial study of *Samson Agonistes* by Joseph Wittreich [10] deserves to be regarded as the best Milton book of the year, and one of the best of any year. The author proves to be superbly knowledgeable, whether he is dealing with seventeenth-century typological exegesis or with twentieth-century criticism, and the knowledge is brilliantly deployed. It would be altogether misleading simply to record that the book contains discussions of Milton's attitudes to Samson, of the autobiographical element in the poem, or of the poem's relation to *Paradise Regained*, the Book of Judges narrative, or seventeenth-century history: the sheer penetration of the discussion of such familiar topics transforms them to a degree that must effect a radical adjustment of critical opinion. For the first time, the unsettling uncertainties, dissonances, and complexities of perspective in the poem receive due acknowledgement in a way that renders most other readings trite and false. Wittreich, like the poem, 'opposes

10. *Interpreting 'Samson Agonistes'*, by Joseph Wittreich. Princeton. pp. xxxii + 394. $21.80.

automatism in perception', and he has written a mature, revelatory, truly liberating book.

Darryl Tippens, in 'The Kenotic Experience of *Samson Agonistes*' (*MiltonS*), develops a view of the poem which she substantially outlined in last year's *MiltonQ* (*YW* 66.297). Burton J. Weber (*MiltonS*) offers a revised regenerationist version of the poem's 'middle'. And in '"If there be aught of presage"' Daniel T. Lochman (*MiltonS*) traces Samson's 'spiraling progress from a destructive obsession with past promise and present suffering to a unity of present action and providence', concentrating on the change from his being 'a speaker of riddles to a prophet of verbal insight and prophetic act'. Here, even 'spiraling' threatens the neat formulation that follows it, just as the tragic vagueness and uncertainty of Samson's 'prophecies' raise doubts about the reliability of his insights. The question of his alleged baseness continues to be debated: David S. Berkeley and Salwa Khoddam (*MiltonQ*) issue yet another instalment. Last, Howard Jacobson in 'Milton's Harapha' (*AN&Q*) explains from Hebrew word-formation how 'haraphah', meaning 'the giant', could be taken as a proper noun.

5. Prose

Austin Woolrych [11] regards 'The Date of the Digression in Milton's *History of Britain*' as 'an afterthought, composed later than Books III and IV with the object of pointing the moral of certain parallels between the Britons' calamities and some particularly black phase through which Milton was living, but suppressed [in 1670] when its aptness as a tract for the times diminished'. After judiciously weighing up the evidence, he suggests 1660 as a more plausible composition-date than the usual 1643. In '"Shrewd books, with dangerous Frontispices"' David Davies and Paul Dowling (*MiltonQ*) argue that in the frontispiece to *Areopagitica* Milton playfully mistranslates four lines from Euripides' *Suppliant Women* 'in order to establish a kind of Greek/English dialectic which previews important arguments' in the main tract. Thomas Kranidas looks at 'Milton on Teachers and Teaching' (*MiltonQ*) and discerns from those very tracts in which Milton attacks the teaching profession a growing regard for it as being honourable. Leo Miller has been characteristically productive and informative: by referring to Anthony à Wood and Dr Johnson, he explains Milton's reference in *An Apology against a Pamphlet* ... to humming in church as being a conventional signal of approval (*Expl*); he reveals that Gerard Schaep, Dutch envoy to the English Commonwealth, ordered twenty-five copies of *Pro Populo Anglicano Defensio* within a few weeks of its appearance in order to distribute them to members of his government (*N&Q*); and for the first time he provides correct dates for 'Two Milton State Letters' (Columbia Edition, nos. 41 and 42) from the manuscript Order Books of the Council of State at the Public Record Office (*N&Q*).

6. Influence

In '"Many *Miltons* in this one Man"' (*MiltonS*) Carol Gilbertson examines in admirable detail the transposition of images, scenes, and phrases from

---

11. In *For Veronica Wedgwood These: Studies in Seventeenth-Century History*, ed. by Richard Ollard and Pamela Tudor-Craig. Collins. pp. 251. £15.

Paradise Lost in Marvell's Mower poems. Thus, for instance, she illumin-atingly relates the postlapsarian delusion in 'The Mower to the Glo-worms' to Milton's temptation simile of the *ignis fatuus* (IX.633–45). John T. Shawcross (*MiltonQ*) notes various forms and degrees of Miltonic influence in Shelley and G. B. Shaw. And in 'The Portrait in the Spoon' Francis C. Blessington (*MiltonQ*) most convincingly adds Milton to Mark Pattison and others as a model for George Eliot's Casaubon. Last, a different kind of influence: Alan Osler (*MiltonQ*) names John Marchant as the first person to offer a course of lectures on *Paradise Lost* (in November 1758), explaining that lectures on non-scientific subjects were comparatively rare in the eighteenth century. Did Marchant know what he was *doing*?

The Later Seventeenth Century

JAMES OGDEN and STUART SILLARS

This chapter has its usual four sections: 1. General: (a) Poetry, (b) Drama, (c) Prose; 2. Dryden: (a) Poetry, (b) Plays, (c) Prose; 3. Other Authors: (a) Poets, (b) Dramatists, (c) Prose; 4. Background. The treatment of background studies is highly selective, depending heavily on what was sent for review, and the supply of review copies may have affected the balance of other sections. Sections 1(b) and 3(b) are mainly by Stuart Sillars, and the rest is mainly by James Ogden.

1. General

Work published in or before 1982 was noted and assessed in the latest volume of *ECCB*. A gap of four years between the work and the bibliography seems excessive; in a foreword the editor surveys perennial problems, including the occasional inability or unwillingness of publishers to supply review copies. The computerized index combines what *YWES* divides into authors and critics, so some amusing muddles occur: see Fletcher, Dennis, for Joseph Beaumont's collaborator, John Wesley's friend, and *BJECS*'s editor. The bibliography's familiar six-part arrangement (bibliography, history, philosophy, fine arts, literature, individual authors) is borrowed by Paul Korshin for his 'Recent Studies in the Restoration and Eighteenth Century' (*SEL*). Excellent reviews and abstracts appeared in *SCN* and *Scriblerian*. The most current of the current bibliographies remain those in *Restoration*, compiled this year by Homer B. Pettey and Brian A. Connery.

Ladies first. A standard source of information on learned Englishwomen of the sixteenth and seventeenth centuries, George Ballard's *Memoirs of Several Ladies* (1752), has been edited by Ruth Perry[1]. The text is that of the first edition, with the spelling and punctuation modernized, and the work has a substantial introduction, explanatory notes, a useful bibliography, and an index. Among the learned ladies of our period are Katherine Philips, Margaret Cavendish, Lady Dorothy Pakington, Anne Killigrew, Lady Damaris Masham, and Mary Astell. Ballard especially liked respectable pious ladies, and he wrote at length about Lady Pakington, arguing that she was the author of one of the most influential books of our period, *The Whole Duty of Man* (1658). Dr Perry's introduction gives a memoir of Ballard and an account of his methods of research and composition. Two small complaints: her attempt to make the phrase 'vital statistics' mean 'important information' (p. 29) strikes

---

1. *Memoirs of Several Ladies of Great Britain Who Have Been Celebrated for their Writings* ..., by George Ballard, ed. by Ruth Perry. WSU (1985). pp. 486. $35.

me as premature; and room might have been found in the bibliography for Patrick Thomas's Ph.D. thesis, 'An Edition of the Poems and Letters of Katherine Philips' (Aberystwyth, 1982). But in making Ballard's work widely available in a handsome edition Dr Perry has advanced both women's studies and literary history.

Some of Ballard's ladies – Philips, Cavendish, Astell, and Lady Chudleigh – re-appear in *First Feminists*[2], an anthology of excerpts from twenty-eight British women writers of the early modern period. But this collection is especially concerned with feminist polemic, and includes later seventeenth-century ladies – Margaret Fox, Bathsua Makin, Aphra Behn, Sarah Fyge, Jane Barker, and Judith Drake – whom Ballard did not like or did not know. It has a comprehensive introduction, brief biographical and biblio-graphical notes on individual writers, and a longish list of 'Works Not Excerpted'. In the introduction Moira Ferguson relates the writers to their unhappy historical and social circumstances, sketches the development of feminism through the period, and distinguishes four categories of feminist polemic: reactive, sustained, intermittent, and personal. Her account of the social background is fine, but her categorization of the polemical writings seems pointless. Still, these women writers obviously had special insights; their work should be better known; and this anthology is a valuable guide.

An excellent new learned journal, *The Seventeenth Century* (*SCent*), is to concern itself with 'all aspects of the century'. Articles which are likely to be interesting to students of our period are Eamon Duffy's 'The Godly and the Multitude in Stuart England', Odette de Mourgues's 'Love in Molière and in Restoration Comedy', J. M. Armistead's 'The Occultism of Dryden's "American" Plays in Context', and W. R. Owens's 'The Date of Bunyan's Treatise *Of Antichrist*'. Duffy queries the view of some influential historians that in the seventeenth century the poor were resistant to Protestantism. The popularity of religious chap-books shows that the godly made some impression on the multitude, so we should not be too surprised that on 14 July 1667 Samuel Pepys saw a shepherd on the Downs reading the Bible to his little boy. The articles by de Mourgues, Armistead, and Owens are noted in sections 1(b), 2(b), and 3(c) below.

Two very different general studies attracted my attention. N. I. Matar's 'Heavenly Joy at the Torments of the Damned in Restoration Writings' (*N&Q*) shows that versions of this doctrine prevailed with both Anglicans and Dissenters. It was mentioned approvingly by Richard Baxter, Roger Sharrock ('an Oxonian preacher'), Peter Sterry, Thomas Traherne, and Milton; and dis-approvingly by Samuel Butler. Hence Matar disagrees with the late C. A. Patrides, who has argued that Milton's approval of the doctrine in *Paradise Lost* XII.56–61 was contrary to Christian tradition (*YW* 47.201). It could be added that the idea of God's laughter at his enemies remains well known, through the Psalms and Handel's *Messiah*. Kevin L. Cope's 'The Conquest of Truth: Wycherley, Rochester, Butler, and Dryden and the Restoration Critique of Satire' (*Restoration*) makes a long, strenuous, and boring effort to relate *Hudibras*, *The Plain Dealer*, Rochester's longer satires, and *Absalom and Achitophel* to a conception of satire as more iconoclastic than optimistic.

2. *First Feminists: British Women Writers 1578–1799*, ed. by Moira Ferguson. IndU/Feminist (1985). pp. xiv + 461; 7 illus. hb $25, pb $12.95.

(a) Poetry

In *Roman Satirists in Seventeenth-Century England*[3] William Kupersmith aims at discussing 'every published adaptation of classical Roman verse satire to appear in English during the seventeenth century'. For the Restoration period he discusses some twenty authors, including Rochester, Oldham, and Dryden, but excluding some of Dryden's collaborators. Among the minor poets Thomas Wood is found to be 'a major innovator in the development of the Imitation', as in his *Juvenalis Redivivus* (1683) he was the first to combine literary and political satire. Kupersmith's critical procedure is to choose from each poet passages he considers interesting ('after all, the author has to stay awake too', he remarks) and representative. He quotes first the Latin originals, with his own prose paraphrases, and then the adaptations, with his own critical commentaries. Sources, knotty points, and disagreements with other critics are reserved for the notes at the end of the book. This is a very old-fashioned appreciative survey, nicely written, beautifully printed, and a pleasure to read.

In 'Four New English Broadsides' (*YULG*) Frank H. Ellis describes late seventeenth-century broadsides recently acquired by Yale University Library. They are of bibliographical and historical interest.

(b) Drama

The year has been particularly fruitful in studies which link theatre history and textual reading with close enquiry into the changing social and intellectual life of the period. All are brought together most effectively in Rose A. Zimbardo's *A Mirror to Nature*[4]. This argues that dramatic evolution during the period was the result of a shift in the idea of the role of literature from presenting ideal relationships between the seen and unseen worlds to showing the tangible world as it is experienced by mankind. In particular, this facilitates the move to 'affective' drama, as it concentrates increasingly on the psychology of characters, which it invites the audience to share. Zimbardo sees this change as having four stages, and examines the workings of each in representative plays. This is a fine and sensitive study, rewriting the theory of generic change within a much larger context of the history of ideas and including much thoughtful discussion of lesser-known plays as well as readings of more popular works. Its intellectual depth as well as its title suggests that it should be read before, if not placed alongside, M. H. Abrams's *The Mirror and the Lamp* as a piece of aesthetic history and analysis.

Harold Weber's *The Restoration Rake-Hero*[5] is similarly vigorous. It argues that the rake is the first literary character to be impelled wholly by the sexual act and examines how the socially destructive, yet in some ways magnetically attractive, energies of varieties of rakes are directed and controlled in different kinds of plays. The equation between woman, sexuality, and the devil in Jacobean drama is examined with reference to Marston's *The Dutch Courtesan*, and the 'tensions between sensual and aggressive pleasure' in the

---

3. *Roman Satirists in Seventeenth-Century England*, by William Kupersmith. UNeb (1985). pp. xii + 193. £17.95.

4. *A Mirror to Nature: Transformations in Drama and Aesthetics 1660–1732*, by Rose A. Zimbardo. UKen. pp. viii + 248. $25.

5. *The Restoration Rake-Hero: Transformations in Sexual Understanding in Seventeenth-Century England*, by Harold Weber. UWisc. pp. x + 253. $27.50.

Hobbesian libertine-rake are studied in various characters, including Nemours in Lee's *Princess of Cleve* and Dorimant in Etherege's *Man of Mode*. Sexual boredom in marriage in Cibber's *Careless Husband* is the opposite of sexual fulfillment in marriage in Congreve's *Love for Love*. The female rake is also examined, in a chronicle of change from Dekker's *Honest Whore* through Killigrew's Angellica in *Thomaso* to Southerne's attempt to show a woman acting with the freedom of a man in Lucy, the hero of *Sir Anthony Love*. There is much insight, too, into the 'banquet of sense' scene in *The Country-Wife*, which develops an earlier article of Weber's (*YW* 64.285). Other passages of the book have appeared before too (*YW* 63.238; 65.323,337), but this is far more than an assemblage of earlier arguments. It is a cogent, invigorating study of the way in which drama reflects changing sexual *mores* carried out with Weber's habitual scholarship, style, and good sense.

Judith Milhous and Robert D. Hume have collaborated in *Producible Interpretation*[6]. This takes as its premise that a playscript is a 'vehicle to be completed in performance' rather than 'an aesthetic object complete in itself' and defines a 'producible interpretation' as 'a critical reading that a director could communicate to an audience in performance'. The ultimate question for every critic is thus 'does it work?'. As bases of interpretation, critics should consider the text; original cast, scenery, and audience reception; historical context; stage history; and modern critical opinion. There will be no single 'right' reading, but rather a variety of interpretations which make sense for both the study and the stage. The eight plays are examined in terms of textual cruxes, and the other bases of interpretation, to give 'directorial choices' which suggest valid but conflicting readings. All of this is extremely valuable, sensible material. The book grew out of the authors' dissatisfaction at criticism which seeks to find one single key to a play, in terms of imagery, theme, or context. In its practicality and breadth this book should do much to oust such approaches – something which Hume and Milhous have already done much to achieve.

It is a pity that J. L. Styan's *Restoration Comedy in Performance*[7] lacks the breadth and weightiness of any of the books discussed so far, since its price and format will probably ensure it a much wider readership. Its aim is to discover what made Restoration comedy successful in its day and why we find it difficult to recapture those qualities now. There are laudable accounts of the theatres and audiences, the London setting, style in acting in comparison with style in courtly behaviour, costume, movement, speech, and 'the spirit of the performance'. Throughout, etiquette books are quoted alongside passages from texts and records of contemporary and more recent performances to attempt to define the qualities of the plays. Yet the book has many inadequacies, particularly the underlying assumption that Restoration comedy is an unchanging monolith, from which examples of all kinds may be cited from diverse works to show a limited number of basic characteristics. The great diversity beneath the apparent similarity of numbers of rakes and fops, to say nothing of the changing roles of women both on and off stage and the idea of generic change

6. *Producible Interpretation: Eight English Plays 1675-1707*, by Judith Milhous and Robert D. Hume. SIU (1985). pp. xvi + 336. $24.50.

7. *Restoration Comedy in Performance*, by J. L. Styan. CUP. pp. xiv + 271. hb £25, pb £7.95.

within the period are not accommodated. Overall one is left wondering about the intended audience of this book. As a general introduction to Restoration theatre Jocelyn Powell's *Restoration Theatre Production* (*YW* 66.303) is clearly preferable.

The 'Providentialist' theory of Restoration comedy as propounded by Aubrey L. Williams (*YW* 60.235) and others receives short shrift in two articles. Arthur H. Scouten rejects it with wonderful vigour and scholarly directness in 'Recent Interpretations of Restoration Comedy of Manners'[8]. He shows that Williams ignores the thinking of major Protestant figures of the Commonwealth in favour of George Hickes, a relatively minor writer; overlooks that 'providential' has a secular as well as a sacred meaning, and is used largely ironically in the Restoration; places undue and unfair stress on Congreve's ownership of John Tillotson's sermons; ignores much previous scholarship on Restoration drama and has nothing to say on the response of the original audience. Its nine pages not only demolish the Providentialist theory but also offer dire warnings about undigested 'new readings': all graduate students and aspiring critics should read this article. Derek Hughes, in 'Providential Justice and English Comedy 1660–1700: A Review of the External Evidence' (*MLR*) attacks the theory from a different angle. He carefully reviews the evidence of sermons and other sources to conclude that, in general, we should see neither the comedy nor the society of the period as unanimously Christian; and in particular we should not suppose that there was a widespread belief in the doctrine of Providential rewards and punishments in this life.

Scouten also offers 'A Reconsideration of the King's Company's Casts in John Downes' *Roscius Anglicanus*' (*TN*). This takes a fresh look at the 'mixed blessing' of Downes's lists, suggesting that those for Killigrew's King's Company, in which the major inaccuracies exist, were produced not by Downes but by another prompter, probably Charles Booth, between 1660 and 1679. This prompter wrote not the casts of the first performances but simply casts which he had seen perform the plays. This argument is supported by analysis of fourteen cast-lists which are given new dates on the evidence of the period when all the actors named were in the company, to provide what may well be the answer to a conundrum which has puzzled editors and readers for some generations. It continues, and convincingly justifies, the re-assessment of Downes as a reliable source when read correctly which has recently developed (see *YW* 66.302). The concern with Downes is shared by Robert D. Hume, in 'Elizabeth Barry's First Roles and the Cast of *The Man of Mode*' (*THStud*, 1985). This looks again at the claim that Elizabeth Barry played Mrs Loveit when Etherege's play was first produced in 1676. John Harold Wilson's suggestion that Mary Lee created the role and that Barry took it over when she retired in 1685, although widely credited, is discounted by Hume after examining the evidence – including that of Barry's liaison with Rochester – afresh. He concludes that while Barry's creation of a role so demanding so early in her career is surprising, 'there is no reason to doubt it', and surmises that the illness of another actress was in part responsible for her debut.

Stage and theatre history were covered in three articles. John Orrell, in 'Scenes and Machines at the Cockpit, Drury Lane' (*ThS*, 1985), prints the

8. In *Du Verbe au geste: Mélanges en l'honneur de Pierre Danchin*. UNancy. pp. 401; illus. pb Ffr 320.

libretto of *The Loves of Diana and Endimion*, an English translation of a French play by Gabriel Gilbert at the Bodleian (Malone 161,8) performed, most likely, by 'les comediens de Mademoiselle d'Orléans' in 1661. The text calls for many chariot descents and ascents, suggesting that in the time of Davenant and John Webb the Cockpit could present movable scenery with shutters and relieves, cloud borders, and an 'engine' to control the descents. Perhaps more important, Orrell shows that the difference between the Cockpit and theatres in France and the Low Countries was far less than has been supposed. This is an invaluable article, not only for the new text it presents but also because it shows that links between the European spectacular theatre and the English commercial playhouse were just as clear, if not quite as close, as those binding it to the court masque. 'The Afterpiece: Origins and Early Development' (*RECTR*) by Philip K. Jason sees the afterpiece's origins in the introduction of 'after-money', a reduced admission charge for late-comers, and in the rivalry between Drury Lane and Lincoln's Inn Fields. Jason discusses in brief the staging of early afterpieces, most interestingly the career of Congreve's *The Old Bachelor*, various parts of which were used as either afterpiece or first piece between 1703 and 1747. David Bond's 'On Playing Musidors' (*N&Q*) identifies a reference to 'playing musidors' in the accounts of Sir Daniel Fleming at Rydal Hall for Boxing Day 1666. These were not arcane musical instruments; rather, the reference is to a performance of *Mucedorus and Amadine*, an anonymous play dating from about 1590. Bond places this within a context of Christmas-tide revels at Rydal and elsewhere, to suggest that this 'slapstick romance' was only one of many Elizabethan plays revived as festive village drama in the Restoration – a suggestion which offers invaluable hints about rural life and tastes of the time.

William J. Burling writes of 'Four More "Lost" Restoration Plays "Found"' in Musical Scores' (*M&L*, 1984). This lists four plays with music by John Eccles mentioned in *Grove's Dictionary of Music and Musicians* or the *British Union-Catalogue of Early Music*. They are *The Match at Bedlam*, performed with the singer Ann Perrin, at Lincoln's Inn Fields around 1696–8; *The Self-conceit, or, The Mother Made a Property*, probably from 1700–1705; *The Surpriz'd Lovers*, with a song sung by John Boman, dating from anywhere between 1695 and 1706; and *The Midnight Mistakes*, from about 1704. David Ritchey offers 'An Index to the Theatrical Materials in Five Eighteenth-Century American Theatre Journals' (*RECTR*). This lists materials in journals held in the Auburn University Libraries in Alabama. The entries mainly concern later playwrights, but there are references to Dryden, Drury Lane, Otway, Covent Garden, and other topics of interest for those researching the fortunes of Restoration drama in the New World.

(c) Prose

Restoration and Revolution[9] is the title of the volume on our period in the World and Word series. Although the aim of the series, according to its general editor Isobel Armstrong, is to give students an idea of the 'context' (good thing) of English literature, the aim of this volume, according to its editor William Myers, is not to give them access to the 'background' (bad thing) of Restoration

9. *Restoration and Revolution*, ed. by William Myers. CH. pp. viii + 248. hb £19.95, pb £11.95.

literature; it is an anthology of extracts from works which are themselves part of that literature, and which cover all shades of political opinion from Jacobitism to Dissent. Among authors represented are obvious ones such as Clarendon, Marvell, and Halifax, and less familiar ones such as Edward Chamberlayne, Agnes Beaumont, and Richard Baxter. There are useful explanatory notes, a substantial bibliography of secondary sources, and a helpful index of both individuals and topics. In his introduction Myers argues that the revolution of 1688 established the somewhat deplorable 'ethos of Halifax' as the orthodoxy in England, to the exclusion of the more attractive ethos of Baxter. The anthology is meant to be 'provocative', though it seems unlikely that many students of English will be in a position to disagree with its editor.

Two general works on prose fiction moved in and out of the period. Paul Salzman's *English Prose Fiction 1558-1700*[10] surveys all sorts of novellas, romances, picaresque narratives, imaginary voyages, and 'Restoration novels'. Both familiar and neglected works from the later seventeenth century are discussed in some detail: not only Bunyan's allegories, Aphra Behn's novels, and Congreve's *Incognita*, but also Richard Head and Francis Kirkman's *The English Rogue*, Margaret Cavendish's *The Blazing World*, John Dunton's *A Voyage round the World*, and the novels of Alexander Oldys and Richard Blackbourn. It could be complained that the Bunyan chapter does not quite answer the obvious question, 'Que diable allait-il faire dans cette galère?' and the Restoration novels chapter devotes as much space to *Incognita* as to the whole of Mrs Behn. But Salzman has done well to impose order on a sprawling subject, and to arouse interest in some neglected works. Jane Spencer's *The Rise of the Woman Novelist*[11] necessarily concentrates on the eighteenth century, but she sees the acceptance of women novelists at that time as originating in the response to women writers earlier, so she considers the work of Katherine Philips, Margaret Cavendish, Aphra Behn, and others. They were in some ways more adventurous, or at least less restricted, than their successors. Mrs Behn emerges as a remarkably self-confident writer, especially in *Oroonoko*.

The new enthusiasm for old periodicals has inspired two useful studies this year. C. Nelson and M. Seccombe's *Periodical Publications 1641-1700: A Survey with Illustrations*[12] is a sort of preface to their forthcoming short-title catalogue of British serials in this period. Their survey is mainly about bibliographical problems, but it includes an outline history. During the seventeenth century periodical publication increased tenfold, and accounted for a quarter of all publication; in total, over seven hundred titles and 31,000 issues. Despite the efforts of various Governments to control the press, by 1700 periodical publication was well established and rapidly expanding. James Sutherland's *The Restoration Newspaper and its Development*[13] more or less describes part

10. *English Prose Fiction 1558-1700: A Critical History*, by Paul Salzman. Clarendon (1985). pp. xiv + 391. hb £34.50, pb £12.50.

11. *The Rise of the Woman Novelist: From Aphra Behn to Jane Austen*, by Jane Spencer. Blackwell. pp. xii + 225. hb £25, pb £7.95.

12. *Periodical Publications 1641-1700: A Survey with Illustrations*, by C. Nelson and M. Seccombe. OPBS. BibS. pp. (x) + 113; 45 illus. £10.

13. *The Restoration Newspaper and its Development*, by James Sutherland. CUP. pp. x + 262. £25.

of this expansion: it concentrates on the London press, surveys the years 1660 to 1735, and focuses on the years 1679 to 1682. Under the headings 'London News', 'Country News', 'Foreign News', and 'Politics', Sutherland summarizes the contents of the London papers in these 'formative years', especially Benjamin Harris's *Domestick Intelligence*, Nathaniel Thompson's *True Domestick Intelligence*, and John Smith's *Currant Intelligence*. These summaries will be of interest to historians; rare examples of the book review (on works by Evelyn in *True Domestick Intelligence*, 1679), the obituary notice (on Hobbes in *Mercurius Anglicus*, 1679), and the leading article (on the threatened French invasion in the *Flying Post*, 1696) will be noted by literary specialists. Sutherland shows that newspaper publishing was a hazardous business – the Whiggish Harris and Smith were often in jail, and even the Tory Thompson was constantly in trouble – but has difficulty in showing exactly how it was organized, and has to look for evidence in the next century. If this book is not quite the major comprehensive account of its subject that its publishers claim, it is certainly a useful work of reference.

In 'The Royal Society and English Prose Style: A Reassessment'[14] Brian Vickers shows how historical imagination and careful research can demolish received opinion. He argues that R. F. Jones and others have been mistaken in thinking that the New Scientists and the Latitudinarians were against language, rhetoric, and the imagination: 'They were against their opponents' misuse of them – or, perhaps more simply, they were against their opponents.' That is to say, attacks on rhetoric were themselves a rhetorical strategy in the establishment's successful campaign against alchemy, astrology, and fanaticism.

2. Dryden

First, four articles on Dryden's life and ideas. James A. Winn's 'Dryden and Anne Reeves: Some Facts and Questions' (*Restoration*) investigates the relationship of the poet and the actress. Probably their affair lasted from 1671 to 1675; speculation about it is intriguing but inconclusive. Phillip Harth's 'Dryden in 1678–1681: The Literary and Historical Perspective'[15] queries the view of recent biographers that *Absalom and Achitophel* was the culmination of a series of attacks by Dryden on the Whigs during the Exclusion crisis. Harth believes that Dryden at this time was 'faithful to his own political principles but slow to enlist as an active Tory partisan', being busy writing plays. He only enlisted when the publication early in 1681 of *The Spanish Friar*, with its dedication to a Whig nobleman, gave rise to the idea that he himself had Whiggish leanings. The first sign of partisanship was the prologue to John Banks's *The Unhappy Favourite* in the spring of 1681, and other propagandist pieces followed; but as these were not publicly attributed to him, Dryden was not known as a Tory spokesman before the appearance of *Absalom and*

---

14. In *Rhetoric and the Pursuit of Truth: Language Change in the Seventeenth and Eighteenth Centuries*, by Brian Vickers and Nancy S. Struever. CML (1985). pp. vi + 121. $12.50.

15. In *The Golden and the Brazen World: Papers in Literature and History, 1650–1800*, ed. by John M. Wallace. UCal (1985). pp. xiv + 213. $35.

Achitophel and the associated rumours about its authorship. Maximillian E. Novak's 'Shaping the Augustan Myth: John Dryden and the Politics of Restoration Augustanism'[16] maintains that, although there may be little point in calling the period from 1660 to 1800 Augustan, 'some of Dryden's attitudes were ... consciously Augustan': he tried to impose a new mythology based on the ideals of the court, advocated a civilization perfected through conversation, and wrote a poetry of hidden allusions. But the late Thomas H. Fujimura's 'Dryden's Changing Political Views' (*Restoration*) is aimed at dispelling the 'myth' that Dryden always held the same essentially moderate opinions. In James II's reign Dryden asserted the primacy of the King, criticized Parliament for encroaching on the royal prerogatives, endorsed the doctrines of divine right and passive obedience, and supported hereditary monarchy; in William III's reign he asserted the primacy of Parliament, abandoned the doctrine of passive obedience, and seemed less opposed to elective monarchy. I will miss Fujimura, who was an independent and forceful writer. These four articles will have to be considered by anyone who contemplates a new biography of Dryden.

(a) Poetry

Three books were mainly though not wholly devoted to Dryden as a poet. They exemplify criticism as it is now written for the common reader, the fellow specialist, and the examination candidate.

David Hopkins's *John Dryden*[17] is primarily an introduction to Dryden for the common reader: it offers a good account of his versification, and an overall view of his development as a poet. But it is also a challenge to the received opinion of Dryden as above all a satirical commentator on the ideas, events, and personalities of his age. Hopkins argues that Dryden's translations of the Classical poets, Chaucer, and Boccaccio entitle him to be revalued as a philosophical poet, with as much to tell us 'of Man, and Nature, and human life' as ever Wordsworth had. The argument does less than justice to Dryden as a dramatist, satirist, and critic; but it is strongly supported by quotation and analysis. For readers who cannot take Hopkins's advice to ponder the writings on Dryden of Dr Johnson, this book is certainly the next best thing. And Johnson had the advantage of knowing his readers better.

Judith Sloman's *Dryden: The Poetics of Translation*[18] claims that the various collections of verse translations – Ovid's *Epistles*, *Miscellany Poems*, *Sylvae*, *Examen Poeticum*, and *Fables* – are not just miscellanies but unified works. In *Sylvae* and *Fables* especially, Dryden so deliberately selected, juxtaposed, and reworked his originals as to express his personal philosophy of life, and to create major works in this new genre. *Fables* is the mature expression of his contempt for 'conventional figures of power, kings and men of action', and of his admiration for 'philosopher-kings and poet-priests'; indeed it is 'a propaganda statement on behalf of the Catholic's essential humanity and benevolence'. Dr Sloman makes some valid points, and allowances can be made

---

16. In *Greene Centennial Studies: Essays Presented to Donald Greene in the Centennial Year of the University of Southern California*, ed. by Paul J. Korshin and Robert R. Allen. UVirginia (1984). pp. xviii + 489. $27.50.

17. *John Dryden*, by David Hopkins. CUP. pp. viii + 216. hb £25, pb £7.50.

18. *Dryden: The Poetics of Translation*, by Judith Sloman, prepared for publication by Anne McWhir; preface by Patricia Brückmann. UTor (1985). pp. xii + 265. £22.

for a posthumous work, but it must be said that this book is open to all sorts of objections. There are signs of cheerful ignorance of relevant scholarship, for instance on the first page, where she says Homer 'made up his own stories, so far as we know'. Compared with Hopkins (and Kupersmith[3]) she seems poorly acquainted with Dryden's originals, and hence scarcely interested in the quality of his translations. Except in the case of *Fables* she offers little evidence that Dryden himself was aware of making the effects she describes; and if he was aware of them, his readers for three centuries have been strangely unappreciative. Such books would get English specialists a bad name, if anyone else read them.

Raman Selden's *John Dryden: 'Absalom and Achitophel'*[19] helped to promote the Penguin Masterstudies, which the publishers see as 'suitable for literary study at sixth-form and undergraduate level'. Selden makes his contribution in the belief that *Absalom and Achitophel* is 'a poem which yields great aesthetic and intellectual pleasure, but only when the reader is given friendly guidance over the unfamiliar ground of seventeenth-century culture and history'. So he supplies a deal of more or less useful information; but he still has little faith in the ability of the poem and its readers to get on together, so his friendly guidance also includes comments like this: 'Dryden neatly proceeds to throw in some satire on the priesthood ("In pious times, e'er Priest-craft did begin" – as if priests go with impiety!)'. Sixth-formers and students who cannot appreciate such points for themselves will need this book, or something like it, to get them through their examinations, though they would be better advised to study set texts more suited to their abilities.

A number of articles on Dryden's poetry seem worth noting. Cedric D. Reverand II's 'Double, Double Dryden' (*ECent*) is a review-essay on Ruth Salvaggio's *Dryden's Dualities*, a book which gave me toil and trouble too (*YW* 64.278). He finds it 'thought-provoking', but the thought it provokes from him is that Salvaggio, while meaning to save Dryden from academic respectability, actually reduces him to shifty impotence. Ian Donaldson's 'Fathers and Sons: Jonson, Dryden, and *Mac Flecknoe*' (*SoRA*, 1985) demonstrates that Dryden alludes to Ben Jonson more than has been realized; despite Shadwell's pretensions, Dryden was Jonson's true successor. In *Mac Flecknoe* Jonson not only sets the standard by which judgement on Shadwell is reached, but also influences the manner in which it is delivered. Philip W. Martin's 'Lucid Intervals: Dryden, Carkesse, and Wordsworth' (*N&Q*) remarks the use of this medical term in *Mac Flecknoe*, James Carkesse's *Lucida Intervalla*, and Wordsworth's *Evening Voluntaries*. Martin believes that the relationship between Dryden's poem, which he dates 1678, and Carkesse's book, which was published in 1679, has not been noted before; in fact, the poem was probably written in 1676, its link with the book has been noted, and the book has been reprinted (*YW* 60.231). Ann Messenger's 'A Problem of Praise'[20] maintains that the Anne Killigrew ode should not be read as an ironic exercise, but as a thoughtful tribute; Dryden appreciated Mrs Killigrew's artistry, which Messenger illustrates from several poems (see section 3(a) below). Arthur

19. *John Dryden: 'Absalom and Achitophel'*, by Raman Selden. PM. Penguin. pp. 112. pb £1.95.

20. In *His and Hers: Essays in Restoration and Eighteenth-Century Literature*, by Ann Messenger. UKen/Harper. pp. xii + 271. £23.50.

Sherbo's 'Dryden and the Fourth Earl of Lauderdale' (*SB*) shows that, in his translations of Virgil, Dryden is more deeply indebted to Lauderdale and other translators than scholars have appreciated or admitted. Anne Barbeau Gardiner's 'A Jacobite Song by John Dryden' (*YULG*) describes an apparently unique early version of 'The Lady's Song', found in the Yale manuscript volume 'A Collection of Loyal Poems, Satyrs and Lampoons'. She suggests that a stanza was later omitted because it prompted a Williamite reply. Richard Bates's 'Dryden, Boccaccio, and Montaigne' (*N&Q*) relates 'Sigismonda and Guiscardo', ll. 417–20 to the *Decameron* and the *Essays*.

(b) Plays
All for Love, Oedipus, and *Troilus and Cressida* have appeared in the California *Dryden*[21]. As usual in this edition, the texts are beautifully printed and highly accurate, while the scholarship is comprehensive and erudite. The textual apparatus lists early variants and records emendations; the commentary covers the plays' stage history, critical reputation, sources, general character, and particular difficulties. Both Maximillian Novak, writing on *All for Love* and *Troilus and Cressida*, and Alan Roper, writing on *Oedipus*, offer interesting accounts of the theory and practice of adaptation, and do their best to see these plays as 'imitations' rather than travesties of their famous originals; hence they seem at times uncritical of the more vulgar elements in *Troilus and Cressida* and *Oedipus*.

Critical essays varied in character and quality. J. M. Armistead's 'The Occultism of Dryden's "American" Plays in Context' (*SCent*) argues that in *The Indian Queen* and *The Indian Emperor* Dryden 'devised a distinctly Restoration contribution to the tradition of dramatic occultism that had come down to him from the Renaissance', and suggests that he was not alone in seeing a connection between the Restoration and the discovery of the New World. John A. Vance's '"Antony Bound": Fragmentation and Insecurity in *All for Love*' (*SEL*) investigates the imagery of the play and finds that Antony seeks security through bondage. In his extensive footnotes Vance mentions some twenty commentators on the play, mostly men, who have helped him to reach this conclusion. David Bywaters's 'Dryden and the Revolution of 1688: Political Parallel in *Don Sebastian*' (*JEGP*) discerns a series of 'complex parallels' between the *dramatis personae* and actual people; for example, the resemblances between Muley-Moloch and Almeyda and William and Mary set up a comparison, while the differences both save Dryden from prosecution and make the point that Muley-Moloch's fate could prefigure William's. This is a more than usually subtle and persuasive essay of its kind. Judith Sloman's book[18] mainly concerns Dryden as a poet, but has a section on *Don Sebastian*, *Amphitryon*, *Cleomenes*, and *Love Triumphant* as examples of his interest in 'the theme of split identity'. Sloman concludes that 'in the last of his plays he seems to have accepted inner multiplicity as a fact of life'.

Evidence of the manner and extent of Dryden's survival in the Restoration and eighteenth-century theatre is given in Leo Hughes and A. H. Scouten's 'Dryden with Variations: Three Prompt Books' (*ThR*), a careful study of

21. *The Works of John Dryden*. Vol. XIII: *Plays: 'All for Love', 'Oedipus', 'Troilus and Cressida'*, ed. by Maximillian E. Novak; textual ed. George R. Guffey; associate ed. Alan Roper. UCal (1984). pp. (x) + 651; 7 illus. £41.95.

prompt-books for *Oedipus, King of Thebes, The Comical Lovers* (a pastiche of *Secret Love* and *Marriage à la Mode*), and *Don Sebastian*.

(c) Prose

In 'Dryden's Definition of a Play in *An Essay of Dramatic Poesy*: A Structuralist Approach' (*SECC*) Charles H. Hinnant tells us that when Dryden says 'a play ought to be a just and lively image of human nature, representing its passions and humours, and the changes of fortune to which it is subject, for the delight and instruction of mankind', he is using 'a series of binary oppositions' and 'proposing a paradigmatic rather than a syntagmatic system of representation'. Hence Dryden is not a neo-Aristotelean but a respectable theoretician. In 'Dryden and Denham' (*N&Q*) Peter A. Tasch points out that Dryden's joke about Luke Milbourne – 'while he and I live together, I shall not be thought the worst poet of the age' – echoes Sir John Denham's similar joke about George Wither.

3. Other Authors

(a) Poets

The more substantial contributions under this heading concern Traherne, Butler, Rochester, and women poets.

Traherne can stand comparison with Milton, as Alvin Snider's 'The Self-Mirroring Mind in Milton and Traherne' (*UTQ*) sufficiently indicates. Snider compares the episode in *Paradise Lost* Book IV when Eve sees herself mirrored in a lake with Traherne's 'Shadows in the Water', and remarks that both poets made use of the extraordinarily suggestive image of the mirror, associated with medieval philosophy, Baconian science, and Lacanian psychology. He concludes that 'despite their conventional distrust of the senses' Milton and Traherne 'shared a fundamentally optimistic view of the pursuit of knowledge'. Two other articles on Traherne were remarkably different. Marie-Dominique Garnier's 'The Mythematics of Infinity in the *Poems* and *Centuries* of T. Traherne: A Study of its Thematic Archetypes' (*CahiersE*, 1985) explains that 'Traherne's world reads like a yes/no clause written in chiastic signs by a present/absent God', and that 'the same presence/absence, immaterial materiality, can be traced in Newton's mysterious paradigm of a spiritual force motivating matter'. Julia J. Smith's 'Thomas and Philip Traherne' (*N&Q*) considerably amplifies what is known about the poet's younger brother.

Samuel Butler and the Earl of Rochester: A Reference Guide, by George Wasserman[22], offers annotated bibliographies of work on these two authors, from 1692 to 1984 for Butler, and from 1680 to 1985 for Rochester. To have them both in one volume is obviously inconvenient: where does it go on the library shelf? Wasserman does his best to justify the arrangement on the ground that modern criticism 'has begun to draw Butler and Rochester together in relations of mutual significance'. This claim seems exaggerated, though in the introduction Wasserman shows that they have both been drawn into debates

22. *Samuel Butler and the Earl of Rochester: A Reference Guide*, by George Wasserman. Hall. pp. xx + 176. $49.

about the use of the terms 'Restoration' and 'Augustan'. Hence perhaps Rachel Trickett's 'Samuel Butler and the Minor Restoration Poets' (in the *Sphere History*; *YW* 51.202) and Howard Erskine-Hill's 'Augustans on Augustanism' (*YW* 61.220-1) should have been included. Wasserman's bibliography of Butler is undoubtedly the best available, especially for coverage of recent work. His bibliography of Rochester challenges comparison with David Vieth's *Rochester Studies, 1925-1982*[23]. Wasserman covers a longer period, Vieth has better notes – for example Wasserman describes (pp. 133-4) whereas Vieth denounces (p. 37) J. W. Johnson's speculations – and both include a few items omitted by the other. In his introduction Vieth surveys Rochester's reputation as a poet 'from idolatrous over-praise during his lifetime to near-oblivion in the nineteenth century to the current consensus that despite his very small *oeuvre*, he is a major poet'. These attitudes are said to have been a function of two conflicting forces, the genuine appeal of the poems and public morality, but surely a third force should be mentioned: academic industry. Vieth does remark that Rochester studies have reached 'the point where scholars unknowingly duplicate one another's discoveries', but does not say whether he knows about Wasserman's work. The bibliography itself covers editions, bibliography, criticism, biography, and dissertations; it is comprehensive, copiously annotated, and well indexed. Vieth promises 'descriptive rather than evaluative' notes, but happily, as his views are worth having, he often makes them quite clear.

This year's studies of Butler and Rochester do nothing to substantiate Wasserman's claim that modern criticism has begun to draw them together. David Carlson's 'Arthur's Round Table in *Hudibras*' (*JWCI*) discerns the source for Butler's satirical description of Arthur (Canto I, ll. 325-44) in the frontispiece to Jacob Blome's edition of Malory's *Morte Darthur* (1634). The woodcut itself makes Arthur look rather ridiculous. Irène Simon's 'General and Particular in Rochester's *A Satyr against Reason and Mankind*'[8] suggests that in this poem the argument 'shifts from the general to the particular and as such may be faulted', though the poet's particular examples do show why he is generally against mankind and rationality. Gillian Manning's 'Some Quotations from Rochester in Charles Blount's *Philostratus*' (*N&Q*) notes that Blount's quotations from this satire and from the translations of Lucretius and Seneca derive from manuscripts, and so help to establish Rochester's text. Blount shared the ideas expressed in these poems, and it may be that his remarks on the unreliability of death-bed conversions refer to the poet. Manning's 'Rochester and "Much A-Do About Nothing"' (also *N&Q*) maintains that 'Upon Nothing' echoes this early Restoration ballad, not vice versa as Rochester's recent editors have supposed. In the same journal Jessica Munns's 'Does Otway Praise Rochester in *The Poet's Complaint*?' mentions the earlier notes by John D. Patterson and Ken Robinson (*YW* 61.230; 63.236-7) and argues that they have both missed a favourable allusion to Rochester.

A survey of work on women poets can appropriately begin with Lucy Brashear's 'The "Matchless Orinda's" Missing Sister: Mrs C.P.' (*Restoration*). This interesting essay discusses the context and meaning of Katherine Philips's 'To my dear Sister Mrs. C.P. on her Marriage', and

23. *Rochester Studies, 1925-1982: An Annotated Bibliography*, by David Vieth. Garland (1984). pp. xx + 174. $36.

identifies the missing sister as Catherine Phillipps, the wife of the poetess's step-brother Erasmus. Ann Messenger's *His and Hers*[20], a study of literary relationships between men and women, includes three relevant essays. In 'A Problem of Praise' she discusses a number of Anne Killigrew's poems, particularly 'The Discontent', the first 'Pastoral Dialogue', 'Cloris Charmes Dissolved by Eudora', and 'Upon a Little Lady under the Discipline of an Excellent Person', and suggests that Dryden associated her with John Oldham, as poets who had gone a surprisingly long way in a pitifully short time. In 'Selected Nightingales' Messenger compares Lady Winchilsea's 'To the Nightingale' with Crashaw's 'Musick's Duell' and Ambrose Phillips's 'Fifth Pastoral'. In the ancient tradition of contests between nightingales and human voices, Lady Winchilsea's fine poem is apparently the only one in which the nightingale wins, and the only one written by a woman. In 'Novel into Play' Messenger discusses Aphra Behn and Thomas Southerne (see section 3(b) below). Rosemary Foxton's 'Delariviere Manley and "Astrea's Vacant Throne"' (*N&Q*) attributes the anonymous *Elegy upon the Death of Mrs. A Behn* to Mrs Manley, who evidently saw herself as Mrs Behn's successor.

I noted only two Oldham items. A. D. Cousins's 'Oldham in Defence of the Restoration: *Satires upon the Jesuits*' (*NM*) maintains that Oldham saw the Jesuits as plotting the death of Charles II and the restoration of England to the papal empire. To make his argument persuasive, Oldham transferred the rhetoric of heroic villainy from the theatrical to the everyday world. Harold F. Brooks's 'Nathaniel Hodges, *Terrae Filius*' (*BLR*) speculates on possible links between this eminent physician and Oldham.

Finally some work on minor poets. Michael Lieb's 'S.B.'s "In Paradisum Amissam": Sublime Commentary' (*MiltonQ*, 1985) is probably the first extended essay on this Latin poem prefixed to the second edition of *Paradise Lost* and attributed to Samuel Barrow. Lieb closely analyses the poem, compares it with Marvell's 'On Paradise Lost', and notes its 'critical insights' and 'eloquence of expression'. N. I. Matar's 'Peter Sterry and Jacob Boehme' (*N&Q*) examines Sterry's enthusiastic but not uncritical response to Boehme's ideas. Ken Robinson's 'The Authorship of *Ovidius Exulans* (1673)' (also *N&Q*) gives reasons for and against attributing this burlesque of Ovid to Alexander Radcliffe. Peter Davidson's 'An Early Echo of Poems by Marvell' (*N&Q* again) can be heard in an epitaph written in 1680 or 1681 by Daniel Scargill, Rector of Mulbarton, Norfolk.

(b) Dramatists

Sophia B. Blaydes and Philip Bordinat's bibliography of *Sir William Davenant*[24] covers works by Davenant, works about him, and previous bibliographies. Most items are briefly annotated. The lists of editions and reprints, and of works about Davenant, cover his time to ours, with the twentieth-century subsection of the latter divided by decades. An introduction surveys Davenant's achievements and reputation: broadly, as respect for his work's intrinsic quality has declined, awareness of its historical importance has increased. The platoon of Davenant specialists will find this bibliography indispensable, and the army of theatre historians may find it useful, especially if

24. *Sir William Davenant: An Annotated Bibliography 1629-1985*, by Sophia B. Blaydes and Philip Bordinat. Garland. pp. x + 370; 6 illus. $53.

they consult its excellent index. I noted one possible addition and one serious error: there is an allusion to Davenant in Joseph Arrowsmith's *The Reformation* (1673) IV.i, and Isaac D'Israeli was not responsible for the nonsense attributed to him on p. 106, though he did say that Davenant had 'the dignity and the powers of a great genius'. [J.O.]

Several articles looked at lesser-known material from the earlier years of the period. J. P. Vander Motten's 'An Unnoticed Restoration Epilogue' (*ES*) is an eight-line passage of rhymed couplets 'in a hand definitely not Killigrew's' in the copy of his *Three Playes* in the Victoria and Albert Museum which may or may not be an epilogue for *Selindra*, opposite whose final page they appear. If so, there is as yet no answer to the question of how they are related to the play's other epilogue recently discovered in the Philadelphia *Four New Playes*. Whatever the answer, Vander Motten asserts, the lines deserve a place in the canon of surviving Restoration epilogues.

In 'An Interesting Benlowes Allusion' (*N&Q*) Gerald W. Morton discusses a reference to Edward Benlowes in Mildmay Fane's unpublished play *Vertues Triumph* (1644). This suggests that Fane and Benlowes were 'friends who could share a laugh at one another', and probably exchanged writings at gatherings such as that at which the play was performed, to modify the conclusion of Harold Jenkins (*YW* 33.171–2) that they might have exchanged works. David Bond establishes 'The Date of Richard Rhodes' *Flora's Vagaries*' (*PQ*). From evidence in Pepys, Anthony Wood's *Athenae Oxonienses*, and the cast list of the first (1670) edition, he concludes that the play was first performed at Christ Church, Oxford on 8 January 1663/4 and repeated at the King's Theatre 'shortly afterwards, quite possibly on March 7th'. This is of interest largely because it makes more probable the cast-list's suggestion that Nell Gwyn played Flora, her first major role with the company. This chimes well with the claim of Milhous and Hume that Nell Gwyn had appeared in a walk-on part in Shirley's *The Court Secret* between 1661 and 1664 (*YW* 66.301). Richard C. Taylor asserts that 'The Originality of John Caryll's *Sir Salomon*' (*CompD*) lies in the modification of its source, Molière's *L'École des femmes*, to create a quite English play well suited to contemporary taste. The addition of the comic subplot, the comic character of Sir Arthur Addell, and the presence of action such as the brick-throwing incident – described, not represented, in Molière – all testify to the play's originality and Caryll's sensitivity to his audience. The play's value also lies in its combination of knockabout action with an avoidance of what Taylor rather paradoxically calls 'overt innuendo' to make the play 'remarkably chaste without being moralistic'.

The Reformation, a comedy attributed to Joseph Arrowsmith, has been reprinted in facsimile, with an introduction by Deborah C. Payne[25]. As she points out, 'it would be difficult to imagine even academics enjoying this play in performance', but it remains interesting for its satire on Dryden in general and *Marriage-à-la-Mode* in particular. It might have been noted that if Arrowsmith was the author he was evidently forgiven, to the extent that he became a contributor to Dryden's edition of Plutarch's *Lives* (see *YW* 60.226). [J.O.] James Fowler's 'Catiline Quoted in *The Chances*' (*N&Q*) discusses lines quoted verbatim from Jonson's *Catiline's Conspiracy* in the Duke of Buckingham's

25. *The Reformation: A Comedy (1673)*, by Joseph Arrowsmith, intro. by Deborah C. Payne. ARS. CML. pp. xii + (iv) + 80. By subscription.

play based on John Fletcher's earlier *Chances*. The purpose of the quotation is to provide comedy by the incongruous context in which the lines appear, an incongruity increased because they were spoken by Charles Hart, who played Catiline in the King's Company revival of Jonson's play in 1668.

The physical and moral landscapes of Etherege's plays were examined in three articles. N. J. Rigaud considered 'Londres dans les comédies d'Etherege: Un Carrefour à grande circulation' (*Annales du Gerb*, 1984). This provides a tour, geographical and human, of the London of the Restoration as it is presented and modified in Etherege's plays. It explores such places as Whitehall, the Mall, Hyde Park, and the Exchange, along with their significance to the *beau monde* from whose members the plays' characters are drawn. Rigaud concludes that Etherege's London is highly selective, 'un Londres presque cliniquement pur', in which we are allowed to forget 'l'impureté et la menace'. Jean Gagen is concerned with 'The Design of the High Plot in Etherege's *The Comical Revenge*' (*RECTR*). The article suggests that, rather than offering a serious antidote to the comedy of the low plot, the 'high plot' is in itself a comically ironic comment on the 'elegant muddle over honour' which the courtly codes governing behaviour of rivals in love inevitably created. The interpretation rests on close textual reading and concludes with references to Evelyn's account of the play as a 'facecious Comedy' and Pepys's as 'very merry'. This is the kind of interpretation which demands to be tested in production, in the manner that Hume and Milhous[6] suggest. In 'Utopian Rhetoric in *The Man of Mode*' (*ECent*) Robert Wess argues that 'it's time to reconsider the courtship of Dorimant and Harriet ... as a "Utopia of gallantry"'. This he does in terms of Frederic Jameson's conception of Utopia and other modifications of Marxist theories of literature and social change. The relationship achieves a state of 'pure persuasion' in the failure to resolve the question of whether Dorimant demonstrates the triumph of the rake or that of residual romantic ideals. Thus it is 'a parodic rewrite of a residual ideal in the throes of historical development'. There is much quotation from earlier critical writing on the play and general literary theory to support this view; yet one wonders, in the end, whether much has been achieved.

Mary Ann O'Donnell's *Aphra Behn: An Annotated Bibliography*[26] covers both primary and secondary sources. The primary bibliography is a labour of love; it has sections on works by Mrs Behn, works edited or translated by her, works with contributions from her, attributions of some validity, and other attributions. Bibliographical descriptions of all the more important works are very thorough: O'Donnell has solved many problems, defined the Behn canon, and supplied details to delight the bibliophile. The secondary bibliography, an annotated chronological list of 661 items from 1666 to 1985, is admirably done too, though, as O'Donnell admits, J. M. Armistead's reference guide[27] includes some additional items. In her introduction she draws attention to unsolved problems of biography and interpretation. [J.O.] Cheri Davis Langdell's 'Aphra Behn and Sexual Politics: A Dramatist's Discourse with her

---

26. *Aphra Behn: An Annotated Bibliography of Primary and Secondary Sources*, by Mary Ann O'Donnell. Garland. pp. xx + 557. $77.

27. *Four Restoration Playwrights: A Reference Guide to Thomas Shadwell, Aphra Behn, Nathaniel Lee, and Thomas Otway*, by J. M. Armistead. Hall (1984). pp. xxxvii + 448. $65.

Audience' (*TD*, 1985) is a lengthy, general study of Behn's work. It stresses her anger at the role of women in Restoration society, in particular her outrage at arranged marriages and championing of freely arranged contracts, and her constant assertion of the right to write for women in the face of 'sexist taunts and petty jibes by literary and social critics'. There is little new here, and the idea of Behn as a forerunner of twentieth-century feminism needs to be read with as much caution as any other assertion of such historical pairing, yet what it has to say needs to be said. In all, a valuable short introduction for those without access to the longer studies. 'An adapted text, as established halfway through rehearsals' is how John Barton describes the new treatment of *The Rover* produced by the Royal Shakespeare Company[28]. Changes including the cutting of 550 lines and the addition of 350 new ones (many from Killigrew's *Thomaso*) were made, 'to streamline our version and help to clarify a confusing plot'. There are several short sections of introductory material on biographical, textual, and contextual topics, amongst which passages from more recent critical judgements of Behn's work are placed. The whole publication is really more of an extended programme than a text, and clearly the alterations make it something to be read with this production solely in mind – and, no doubt, a fair degree of caution. In 'The Gypsy, *The Rover* and the Wanderer: Aphra Behn's Revision of Thomas Killigrew' (*Restoration*) Jones DeRitter examines the ways in which Behn's play freely adapts Killigrew's *Thomaso*. The male play-wright is concerned with a free, semi-autobiographical fantasy woven around the central hero, whose behaviour is depicted uncritically and is too easily forgiven: Behn is concerned with 'the social consequences of rakish behaviour', most especially those upon women. Killigrew's Serulina accepts Thomaso's infidelities without question: Behn's Hellena uses 'the rake's tools' against Willmore, the character taken from the better aspects of Thomaso. This shift is seen as a reflection of the movement away from the irresponsible mood of the Cavaliers to the greater desire for stability of the Restoration; but it might equally well be an index of the difference in social and sexual outlook between Killigrew and Behn. This is, though, a highly readable article, not least so in its disentangling of lines of influence and resemblance to reveal the striking originality of Behn's text. Adaptation of a different kind is the subject of Ann Messenger's 'Novel into Play'[20], which discusses Thomas Southerne's adaptations of Aphra Behn's novels for the stage. In the case of *Oroonoko*, Messenger wonders why Mrs Behn did not herself use the story for a play; she concludes that she was deeply moved by it, and felt that in the context of Restoration heroic tragedy her hero would not be taken seriously. It is interesting to place this assertion alongside the explanation offered by Weber[5] for the superiority of Behn's novel over Southerne's play.

Otway's work was also the subject of much critical attention. Robert D. Hume's 'The Unconventional Tragedies of Thomas Otway'[8] draws together the plays to show that all are united by Otway's 'bitter pessimism' which makes him unique in the ideology of the Restoration theatre. His political plays, more anti-Whig than pro-Tory, show man's failure to govern the state: those concerned with the affections show his failure to honour his obligations to individuals. Both demonstrate 'the failure of man's self-control'. Despite this,

28. *An Adaptation of 'The Rover' ('The Banished Cavaliers') by Aphra Behn: A Programme/Text*, with Commentary by Simon Trussler. Methuen. pp. 72. pb £3.95.

though, Otway's plays are positive, stressing the value of friendship and honour. He wanted to believe in the heroic virtues, but his plays show their failure, and it is this which unites the political plays and those wrongly seen to be forerunners of the 'pathetic' plays of Banks and Rowe. The political and the personal are again drawn together by Jessica Munns in '"The Dark Disorders of a Divided State": Otway and Shakespeare's *Romeo and Juliet*' (*CompD*). This suggests that in *The History and Fall of Caius Marius* the combination of Plutarch and Shakespeare often seen as a 'clumsy patchwork' is instead a valid response to the political uncertainties of 1679. The relationship of Marius Jr and Lavinia is a reflection of public disunity, in which the trials of the lovers are an index of the disintegration of the state, to show 'the fearful absence of the authoritative father and the fearful presence of the powerful father' in Caius Marius's anarchic rule as both *pater familias* and *pater patriae*. The essay has much to say about the contemporary relevance of the play, and reveals Otway's role as a social commentator of considerable insight and compassion. Harry M. Solomon discusses 'The Rhetoric of "Redressing Grievances": Court Propaganda as the Hermeneutical Key to *Venice Preserv'd*' (*ELH*). He argues that the best way to understand the play is to approach it with the viewpoint of the original audience and see it 'in a white hot political context'. In this way, both conspirators and senators are seen as corrupt Whigs to stress the benevolent Toryism of Charles II. Yet to avoid alienating audience Whigs who might be tempted to conversion, Otway presents his characters as misguided and heroic rather than simply evil, at the same time offering a pattern of Tory continuity in the character of the Duke of Venice. It is a reading supported by analysis of text, epilogue, and context, another valid 'producible interpretation' which deserves to be tested in the theatre.

A further link between stage and state is offered by Richard E. Brown. In 'Nathaniel Lee's Political Dramas, 1679–1683' (*Restoration*) he attempts to tease out the contemporary significance of Lee's plays, dealing first and most extensively with *Lucius Junius Brutus*. Brutus and his sons, Titus and Tiberius, are seen to represent Charles II and his illegitimate son the Duke of Monmouth, Titus showing Monmouth's attractiveness and Tiberius his dangerous ambition. The third son, Sextus, illuminates Monmouth still further, as 'a self-indulgent, criminal son', while Brutus, at the same time, may be seen as Cromwell. Overall the play uses the father–son, monarch–subject equation later popularized by Sir Robert Filmer to explore the state of the nation in a manner whose ambiguity is seen in various forms throughout Lee's political theatre despite his supposed conversion to Toryism in 1682. Where Brown finds Lee's constant combination of conservatism and experimentalism a remarkable achievement for the time, many might rather think of it as prudent, ambivalent pragmatics along the lines of Marvell, but Brown's article has the merit of showing the complexity of the plays and their richness of allusion in the contemporary theatre, and the comparison with Otway's political theatre is intriguing.

Only one article discussed Southerne: N. J. Rigaud's 'Femmes de rebellion et d'intrigue dans les comédies de Thomas Southerne'[8]. This contends that Southerne addresses the question of what happens to a woman who refuses to accept the state of subjection which society has decreed for her. Thus the heroine of *Sir Anthony Love* places herself in positions of authority through male disguise; Mrs Witwoud uses language in *The Wives' Excuse* to exercise her revenge on man; Mrs Wishwell and Lady Trickitt in *The Maid's Last Prayer* exploit a mercantilist society through its own greed. All show the desire to become the *agent moteur* in subtle ways which circumvent the restrictions on female power of a repressive, male culture.

Eugene Nelson James's *George Farquhar: A Reference Guide*[29] lists and briefly comments upon editions, critical studies, biographies, and earlier bibliographies from Farquhar's lifetime to 1979 – a disappointingly early finishing date. Much has been done to bring to light earlier material, and 'any significant mention, however short' has been included. James points out that translations of the plays and their appearance in eighteenth- and nineteenth-century collections are not exclusively recorded; it is a pity, too, that other items have been missed, particularly reviews of more recent performances. There is, for example, no mention of G. C. D. Odell's *Annals of the New York Stage*, which describes the first performance in the United States of *The Recruiting Officer* in 1732. The index of *The Times* would also have provided many more reviews of revivals of the plays in Britain. Overall, though, this book will be a useful first reference, if not quite so useful as the other two bibliographies noted in these pages. Peter Dixon has produced an excellent edition of *The Recruiting Officer*[30]. The text is substantially that of Q1, with the two major authorial changes in Q2 incorporated but not other emendations which Dixon argues are the result of pressure from 'outside forces' – the audience or the printer. The introduction makes clear the relationship between the two quartos, and the third of 1706, and significant variants are given in one appendix while others give the music and theatrical variants introduced on stage and recorded in the 1728 *Works*. As well as explaining the provenance of the text, the introduction has passages on 'the recruiting trade', including a passage from the 1704 'Pressing Act', and the parallels between martial and marital recruiting. A stage history describes the earliest performances and records many others, quoting succinctly from contemporary responses. Overall the approach is sensible and professional, and the account of the text is more detailed and more plausible than those of Michael Shugrue's Regents edition (*YW* 47.219–20) or John Ross's New Mermaid (*YW* 58.226–7). But, at £27.50, it will be simply unattainable to most readers, so that the other two will remain the more popular alternatives.

(c) Prose

The major contributions were on Clarendon and Bunyan.

In *Clarendon and the Rhetoric of Historical Form*[31] Martine Watson Brownley emphasizes the literary value of the *History of the Rebellion*. She sets Clarendon's work in the contexts of his life, his literary *milieu*, and early historiography. She argues that he was able to integrate autobiography with history, to relate his brilliant character sketches to his broad narrative structure, and to achieve the thematic coherence required for great historiography, essentially

29. *George Farquhar: A Reference Guide*, by Eugene Nelson James. Hall. pp. xxiii + 112. $35.

30. *The Recruiting Officer*, by George Farquhar, ed. by Peter Dixon. Revels. ManU. pp. xiii + 207. £27.50.

31. *Clarendon and the Rhetoric of Historical Form*, by Martine Watson Brownley. UPenn (1985). pp. xvi + 239. $24.95.

because he was an imaginative writer relating his knowledge of what had been to his vision of what might have been. I admired Professor Brownley's earlier essay on Clarendon's style (*YW* 63.245) but found her book disappointing. It is enthusiastic, highly informative, and in parts well argued; but it is also long-winded, rather repetitive, and in other parts merely assertive. Some of the thirty-five pages devoted to the largely vain endeavour to find 'The Man behind the Historian' might have been better used to support, by quotation and analysis, interesting and no doubt justifiable claims that Clarendon 'was a master at imitating the styles of others', or that his comparison of Lord George Goring and the Earl of Rochester is 'a comic masterpiece'. From its title onwards *Clarendon and the Rhetoric of Historical Form* tries too hard to impress fellow specialists in historiography and not hard enough to win new readers for the *History*.

Additional studies of Clarendon by Brownley appeared in the learned journals. In 'Clarendon, Gibbon, and the Art of Historical Portraiture' (*ELN*) she notes that the character sketches in the later books of the *Decline and Fall* are more subtle than those in the earlier books, and suggests that 'it is quite likely' that this improvement resulted from Gibbon's rereading of Clarendon. Gibbon perhaps appreciated that while Clarendon shared the interest of earlier historians in the 'ruling passions' of his characters, he was also aware that circumstances modify behaviour. In 'Some Notes on Clarendon, Other Edward Hydes, and Various Literary Pursuits' (*Restoration*) she throws new light on Clarendon's early literary interests and associated problems of attribution and dating.

The latest volume of Bunyan's *Miscellaneous Works*[32] brings us *Good News for the Vilest of Men* and *The Advocateship of Jesus Christ*, edited with an introduction and textual and explanatory notes by Richard L. Greaves. In the introduction Greaves emphasizes that these discourses were composed near the end of Bunyan's life, when he took advantage of James II's relaxed policy towards Dissenters and expanded his preaching in London. *Good News* is addressed to sinners, and *The Advocateship* to saints; together they show how Bunyan would risk driving his congregations to despair at human depravity, with the aim of arousing them to hope for divine grace. His message was funda-mentally optimistic: 'free grace for the vilest of sinners and divine intercession in the celestial court for the saints'. Greaves also considers Bunyan's concern with the unpardonable sin, and his relationship with the Fifth Monarchists. A small point of some interest is that in *The Advocateship* a reference to the *Vita di S. Bruno* was deleted in the second edition; Greaves's explanation of this temporary concession to popery is conjectural.

Bunyan was also the subject of the best critical essay I have read for some time: Margaret Olofson Thickstun's 'From Christiana to Stand-fast: Subsuming the Feminine in *The Pilgrim's Progress*' (*SEL*). Thickstun suggests that Bunyan thought men's spiritual experience superior to women's, and saw Christian as a representative believer, and Christiana only as a representative female believer. Her relationship to God is initially that of the Bride to the Bridegroom, but her encounter with the two 'ill-favoured ones', even though she is not actually raped and proceeds to the Bath of Sanctification, prevents

32. *The Miscellaneous Works of John Bunyan*. Vol. XI: *'Good News for the Vilest of Men'; 'The Advocateship of Jesus Christ'*, ed. by Richard L. Greaves. Clarendon (1985). pp. xliv + 231; 4 illus. £25.

her from retaining this role, which finally passes to Mr Stand-fast because he resisted Madam Bubble. This summary does less than justice to an argument of some subtlety which illuminates *Pilgrim's Progress* in many ways. Dayton Haskin's '*The Pilgrim's Progress* in the Context of Bunyan's Dialogue with the Radicals' (*HTR*, 1984) argues that 'Bunyan was attracted to the radicals' means for correlating ancient biblical truths with more recent religious experience, but his book finally offers a model for reconciling past and present that he inherited from Luther'. Indeed Bunyan concluded that the theology of the radicals was more dangerous than the persecution by the Establishment. W. R. Owens's 'The Date of Bunyan's Treatise *Of Antichrist*' (*SCent*) draws attention to more or less obvious attacks on Roman Catholicism in this posthumous work, which suggest that it was written in the early 1680s but not published once it became clear that James II would succeed to the throne.

Two studies of Restoration prose appeared in a special issue of *PSt* on 'The Literature of Controversy'. Jennifer Chibnall's 'Something to the Purpose: Marvell's Rhetorical Strategy in *The Rehearsal Transpros'd* (1672)' eventually reaches the conclusion that Marvell shows that it is better to be cheerful and tolerant like himself than fearful and intolerant like Samuel Parker; his book both advocates and exemplifies 'the "noble generosity" with which politics might be conducted'. Chibnall's own rhetorical strategy is to demonstrate awareness of advanced critical theory, to relate *The Rehearsal Transpros'd* to its historical context, and to offer a running commentary on its first book. Her essay seems very long. N. H. Keeble's 'The Autobiographer as Apologist: *Reliquiae Baxterianae* (1696)' shows how Richard Baxter deploys 'the moderate persona, the generalising of personal experience, the marshalling of evidence' to serve a contentious view of history: that the Puritans and their successors were the true representatives of the Anglican middle way.

Also well within the perimeters, or what *PSt* would perhaps call the parameters, of the literature of controversy comes *Swift, Temple, and the Du Cros Affair*[33], which reprints four pamphlets published in 1693; it is in two parts, of which the first comprises *An Answer to a Scurrilous Pamphlet* and *Lettre de Monsieur Du Cros*, with an introduction by David L. T. Woolley, and the second the English translation of Du Cros's letter and *Reflections upon Two Pamphlets*, with an introduction by J. A. Downie. Of the two introductions, Downie's is much the more informative. Du Cros was a French double agent about whom Sir William Temple made supercilious remarks in his memoirs. Not surprisingly Du Cros took umbrage, and turned on Temple in the *Lettre*, which prompted the *Answer* and the *Reflections*. Both of these have been claimed as the first published work of Swift, but Woolley and Downie would give this distinction to the *Answer*, which is the more aggressive and professional work.

Finally some miscellaneous contributions from the learned journals, of which the most interesting is Richard A. McCabe's 'Meditation, Pilgrimage, and Paradise: The Literary Career of Henry Hare, Second Lord Coleraine' (*Lib*). This essay introduces a new Restoration author, Henry Hare (1636–1708), whose publications have been mistakenly attributed to his father.

33. *Swift, Temple, and the Du Cros Affair*, Part 1, intro. by David L. T. Woolley; Part 2, intro. by J. A. Downie. ARS. CML (1986-7). pp. xvii + 48 + (xxxiii); xii + 37 + (ii) + 40. By subscription.

These are *The Ascents of the Soul* (1681), a translation of an Italian meditation on Psalms 120–34; *La Scala Santa* (1681), an English version of these Psalms; and *The Situation of Paradise Found Out* (1683), an aristocratic pilgrim's progress. The most remarkable of these works is the last, in which Hare often alludes to contemporary literature, including *Paradise Lost*, but not *Pilgrim's Progress*, perhaps because he did not want to be associated with Bunyan. John Henry's 'A Cambridge Platonist's Materialism: Henry More and the Concept of Soul' (*JWCI*) argues that in trying to clarify pneumatology and refute atheism, More became confused and self-contradictory. His assertion of the reality of the spiritual world made him sound like a materialist; hence he was with some justice attacked by Baxter, and with some irony applauded by Hobbes. Oliver Nicholson's 'Iamblichus in John Aubrey's *Miscellanies*' (*N&Q*) suggests that an odd reference to the fourth-century Neoplatonist may have come from Aubrey's friend Dr Thomas Gale.

4. Background

Students of literature should at least dip into Fr Gerard Reedy's *The Bible and Reason*[34], a learned and elegant study of later seventeenth-century Anglican attitudes to Scripture, especially as exemplified by John Tillotson, Edward Stillingfleet, Isaac Barrow, and Robert South. These divines agreed with the Puritans in thinking that faith should be based on the Bible, but insisted that biblical interpretation should be reasonable, not intuitive. However, their ideas of what was reasonable – of what was plainly taught and necessary for salvation – differed from those of Lord Herbert of Cherbury, John Toland, the Socinians, and Locke, and should not be considered as leading to deism. And of course they were far from accepting the separation of faith and reason found in Hobbes and Spinoza. Their position still commands respect; but not being textual scholars they were unable to refute Fr Richard Simon, whose works showed that the Scriptures were not wholly reliable, and so supported the Roman Catholic emphasis on extrascriptural tradition. Locke's unpublished notebooks, and Dryden's *Religio Laici*, reflect this weakness in the Anglican position, though they deserve credit for tackling Simon at all. Reedy's 'Barrow, Stillingfleet, and Tillotson on the Truth of Scripture'[16] also seeks to distinguish Anglican from secular rationalism, and summarizes some of the arguments of his book.

LockeN this year comprises four essays on *An Essay Concerning Human Understanding*. Michael Ayers reconsiders what Locke meant by 'ideas', Roland Hall discusses his concept of 'spirit', and Ruth Mattern elucidates his theory of 'natural kinds'. S. H. Clark's 'The Philosophical Rhetoric of Locke's *Essay*' comes nearer the normal interests of literary students, and helps to explain the work's extraordinary influence. A rather different explanation is offered by Sascha Talmor's 'Locke's *Essay* and the Rule of Truth' (*DUJ*), namely that it was read both by his contemporaries and some later scholars not as a work of epistemology but as 'a *Logic* or an Art of Reasoning'. It replaced the Aristotelean or Scholastic Rule of Truth with what Locke called 'my new

34. *The Bible and Reason: Anglicans and Scripture in Late Seventeenth-Century England*, by Gerard Reedy, S.J. UPenn (1985). pp. (viii) + 184. $20.

way of knowing *by way of ideas*', and so superseded Aristotle in the universities.

The Bodleian Library in the Seventeenth and Eighteenth Centuries[35] by Ian Philip, first published in 1983 and now reprinted, is based on his Lyell Lectures of 1980-1. Among the chief events of our period were the publications of Thomas Hyde's catalogue of printed books and the 1697 catalogue of manuscripts, and the acquisitions which rapidly made the Bodleian famous as a repository of Anglo-Saxon and early English philology and history. Philip's narrative is succinct, informative, and lively enough, but occasionally I wished his lectures had been expanded, as the sources are entertaining. When I am told that Hyde tried to get Anthony Wood to catalogue manuscripts in return for being allowed to consult them, but according to Wood in this matter 'Mr Hide did not carry himselfe like a gent', I find myself wanting to know the whole story.

Two articles provide comment on musical issues. Margaret Mabbett provides a survey of 'Italian Musicians in Restoration England (1660-1690)' (*M&L*), referring to performers and composers recruited by Killigrew in Italy and Bulstrode Whitelock at the court of Queen Christina in Sweden such as the castrato Hilario Suarez, the violinist Nicola Matteis, and Pepys's household musician Cesare Morelli. This is an important corrective to the view that English music-making was dominated by the French at this time. Curtis Price and Irena Cholij examine a copy of Charles Gildon's version of *Measure for Measure* in the Folger Shakespeare Library in 'Dido's Bass Sorceress' (*MT*). This they assert is the prompt copy for the first professional performance of *Dido and Aeneas*. It suggests that the part of the Sorceress was first sung by a man – a Mr Wilshire or Whiltshire known to have been active as a stage singer in the 1690s. Not only does this restore balance to the opera after the disappearance of Aeneas, it also slots well into the contemporary practice of using male actors to play witches. [S.S.]

35. *The Bodleian Library in the Seventeenth and Eighteenth Centuries*, by Ian Philip. Clarendon (1985). pp. x + 139; 17 plates. £19.50.

The Eighteenth Century

STEPHEN COPLEY and ALAN BOWER

This chapter is arranged as follows: 1. General; 2. Poetry; 3. Drama; 4. Prose; 5. The Novel. Sections 1, 3, and 4 are by Stephen Copley, and sections 2 and 5 are by Alan Bower.

1. General

There is no new volume of *ECCB* to report this year, but the usual listings and reviews are carried in *SEL* (this year by Paul J. Korshin) and in *Scriblerian*. A volume of the *Index of English Literary Manuscripts* covering 1700–1800, A–F, has appeared from Mansell[1], while Harvester Microform has published microfilm collections of British literary manuscripts from the British Library[2] and of popular chap-books from the Robert White collection in the University Library, Newcastle upon Tyne[3].

In *Liberty and Poetics*[4] Michael Meehan traces some of the eighteenth-century developments of 'that simple idea from Longinus, that true sublimity will only be achieved in a free society'. He attempts to counter the assumption that critical discussions of the effects of liberty produced in the period necessarily take the form of Whig panegyrics, insisting instead that the century saw the appearance of investigative writings of considerable interest on the subject of 'freedom's benefits and the proper character of art in a free society'. He offers his study as a 'protest' against 'the decontextualisation of eighteenth-century literary theory, and the consequent simplification of the whole classic-to-romantic question'. The writers he covers include Shaftesbury, Blackwell, Akenside, Hume, John Brown, Thomas Sheridan, Adam Ferguson, Johnson, and Wordsworth. He is at his most interesting when summarizing the arguments of the less well-known writers, or commenting on the less well-known work of the major ones. The least substantial chapter of the book is the penul-

1. *Index of English Literary Manuscripts*. Vol. III: *1700–1800*. Part 1: *A–F*, comp. by Margaret M. Smith and Penny Boumelha. Mansell. pp. 380. £120.

2. *British Literary Manuscripts from the British Library, London*. Series 2: *The Eighteenth Century, c. 1700–c. 1800*. Harvester Microform. Part 1: *Eighteenth-century Manuscripts from the Sloane and Additional Manuscripts*. £1,250. Part 2: *Eighteenth-century Manuscripts from the Sloane and Additional, Burney, Egerton, Harleian, King's, Lansdowne and Stowe Collections*. £700.

3. *Popular Literature in Eighteenth- and Nineteenth-Century Britain*. Part 1: *The Robert White Collection of Chapbooks from the University Library, Newcastle-upon-Tyne*, ed. by Paul Smith and Steve Roud. Harvester Microform. £800.

4. *Liberty and Poetics in Eighteenth Century England*, by Michael Meehan. CH. pp. 190. £17.95.

timate one, on Wordsworth, which moves rather blandly between *The Convention of Cintra*, *The Prelude*, and *The Excursion*, without pursuing its arguments to any particularly challenging ends. Nonetheless this is a worthwhile study which draws welcome attention to some unduly neglected aesthetic writings and throws an interesting new light on others which are already familiar. In a related area, Debra Morris Smith (*SAQ*) considers the idea of inspiration in eighteenth-century literary theory.

In *Intricate Laughter in the Satire of Swift and Pope*[5] Allan Ingram examines the nature of satirical laughter in the work of the two writers via the theories of Darwin, Freud, Bergson, and Laing. Working initially from Steele's rather troubled comments on laughter, in *The Guardian*, he identifies a series of pointed oppositions to be found in seventeenth- and eighteenth-century commentaries on the subject, in particular setting Shaftesbury's attempts to treat the laugh as a humane, socially and morally beneficial force against a tradition stemming from Hobbes in which it 'measures the amount of pain inflicted, imposing as it does so a spurious impression of jovial unity' on those who indulge it. He then explores the implications of these rival interpretations in the difficult area of satire, in which laughter is claimed to have a morally judgemental effect, but may be simply and indulgently malicious. The study is organized thematically, with separate sections devoted to the effects of satire on its victims and on its audiences, the problematic relation between laughter and judgement in satiric writing, and the kinds of partial and ideal readers that seem to be postulated in the satirical text. Ingram's general explorations of his eighteenth-century sources can be interesting and suggestive, and his eclectic trawl of the theoretical resources of zoology, psychology, and behavioural science can have illuminating results. However, his readings of the Pope and Swift texts that he examines are unsurprising, given the elaboration of the route taken to produce them; and at times they can verge on the sentimental.

Lance Bertelsen's study of the Nonsense Club[6] surveys the literary and social activities of writers associated more or less directly with the Club in the 1750s and 1760s – George Colman, Robert Lloyd, Cowper, Charles Churchill – and traces their relations with contemporaries such as Hogarth and John Wilkes. Bertelsen treats the Club as an index of the literary climate of the period and sees the interests of its members as being representative of the milieu of 'middling culture' to which they belong. He provides a series of interesting analytical essays on Lloyd and *The Connoisseur*, Colman and the contemporary theatre, the Club's exhibition of inn signs (described as 'a squib on taste'), and the libertine circles of Wilkes and Churchill. He is more convincing as a cultural historian cast in a fairly traditional mould than he is when he tries to provide psychologizing links between, for instance, the forms of 'rebellion' of Churchill and Lloyd and the suicidal mania of Cowper, or when he makes gestures towards the new and more ambitious forms of cultural/historical analysis that have developed in the wake of Foucault. On his own strong ground, however, he makes telling and suggestive use of his evidence in his investigation of the relation between the development of taste, the local

5. *Intricate Laughter in the Satire of Swift and Pope*, by Allan Ingram. Macmillan. pp. x + 206. £25.

6. *The Nonsense Club: Literature and Popular Culture, 1749-1764*, by Lance Bertelsen. Clarendon. pp. xi + 322. £27.50.

circumstances of literary and cultural production, and the larger social and economic context in which it occurs. Bruce Redford's *The Converse of the Pen* (UChic) and Carey McIntosh's *Common and Courtly Language: The Stylistics of Social Class in Eighteenth-Century English Literature* (UPenn) were not available for review.

Peter Hulme's *Colonial Encounters*[7] (see also pp. 572-3) is a theoretically rigorous and historically convincing study of the discursive confrontation of Europe with the native Caribbean from 1492 to 1797. Organized round a series of textual moments in this confrontation, from sources as widely separated as Columbus's notebook, *The Tempest*, *The Spectator*, and the *Handbook of American Indians*, its argument is dense and its pursuit of the ramifications of the problems it tackles relentless, yet it remains economical and lucid throughout. It is a most impressive contribution to the current debates in poststructuralism on the relation of textual analysis and history. The eighteenth-century material analysed includes *Robinson Crusoe* (in which the battle with the cannibals is seen as the climax of a series of such encounters within the discourse of colonialism), and the many rewrites of the tale of Inkle and Yarico which follow on from Steele's version in *The Spectator*, and which Hulme sees as having 'a fraught and highly mediated relationship' with the extirpation of the island Caribs from the Caribbean.

Jean-Christophe Agnew's *Worlds Apart*[8] presents an ambitious challenge to some of the discursive distinctions that are usually preserved between cultural affairs and market economics. Agnew offers to study the 'aesthetics' of market relations, and to outline the terms of a possible 'phenomenology' of market transactions. To this end, he discusses the relation between conceptualizations of the apparently disparate areas of the market and the theatre in a wide range of texts from the Renaissance to the eighteenth century, and finds much material to support his sometimes outrageous, but often stimulating and convincing theses. He examines the ways in which sixteenth- and seventeenth-century texts suggest that the theatre enacts and reproduces the new social relations of a market economy and, in the eighteenth-century section, examines theatrical metaphors in the new context of commercially printed literature, noticing a movement within these metaphors away from the earlier preoccupation with the place of the actor in the theatre, and towards a new stress on the spectator – apparent in Shaftesbury's 'dramatic' self-examinations, the figure of Mr Spectator, and the 'impartial spectator in the breast' constructed in Adam Smith's *Theory of the Moral Sentiments*. Similar terrain is covered in David Marshall's *The Figure of Theater*[9], which examines theatrical metaphors as they appear in fictional and non-fictional texts from Shaftesbury to George Eliot. The book includes interesting analysis of Shaftesbury's concern about the public or private nature of texts, and capacities of his audiences, as well as discussion of Adam Smith's account of the role of the sympathetic audience in the formation of the moral sentiments. However, Marshall's general argument is not particularly convincing, and his announced intention of treating all the

7. *Colonial Encounters: Europe and the Native Caribbean 1492-1797*, by Peter Hulme. Methuen. pp. xi + 348. £25.

8. *Worlds Apart: The Market and the Theater in Anglo-American Thought, 1550-1750*, by Jean-Christophe Agnew. CUP. pp. xvi + 262. £25.

9. *The Figure of Theater: Shaftesbury, Defoe, Adam Smith, and George Eliot*, by David Marshall. ColU. pp. x + 269. $27.

texts he examines as 'philosophical novels' begs questions which he never addresses.

In *Masquerade and Civilization*[10] Terry Castle outlines the history of the masquerade in eighteenth-century England, and discusses its importance in the fiction of the period by way of a detailed commentary on the masquerade episodes in four novels. Her analysis draws heavily – and rewardingly – on the work of Bakhtin. In the historical section of the book she suggests that the licensed transgressions and displacements of social, political, and gender norms permissible in masquerade provide a unique opportunity for carnivalesque release in the period, reflecting the utopian 'dream of a perfected human community, free of the ravages of difference and alienation', and retaining a latently disruptive political potential. In the fiction, masquerade episodes are seen as exerting considerable narrative fascination, and as often effecting crucial transformations of theme and character. The masquerade episode in Part 2 of *Pamela* is seen as the only part of the narrative in which the heroine regains something of the fluidity of identity that marked her in the 'charismatic original' of Part 1. Fielding's *Amelia*, Burney's *Cecilia*, and Inchbald's *A Simple Story* are also discussed. If at times Castle perhaps overstates her case, in general her argument is developed with subtlety and intelligence in a study which combines an extensive and scholarly grasp of historical detail with an impressive critical rigour.

The Politics and Poetics of Transgression[11] opens with a survey of the strengths and limitations of recent Bakhtinian criticism. Peter Stallybrass and Allon White then offer to move beyond the usual terms of this criticism, and 'to treat the carnivalesque as an instance of a wider phenomenon of transgression'. In this context they argue that 'the underlying structural features of carnival ... are intrinsic to the dialectics of social classification as such', and so, that 'it is no accident ... that transgressions and the attempts to control them obsessively return to somatic symbols, for these are ultimate elements of social classification itself'. In the eighteenth-century section of the book they pursue the argument that 'patterns of discourse are regulated through the forms of corporate assembly in which they are produced', by tracing the emergence of the coffee house as 'a radically new kind of social space, free from the grotesque bodies of the alehouse and yet (initially at least) democratically accessible to all kinds of men – though not, significantly, to women'; and by analysing the position of Augustan literary writers, who, in the name of rationality and culture, repeatedly dissociate themselves from the domain of the popular, the market, and the body but who simultaneously depend on, exploit, and are victims of the proximity of the excluded Other. I find the authors' discussion of the eighteenth century less challenging and less convincing than their treatment of earlier and later material, and am left wanting to question some of the historical generalizations which inform their arguments. However, as a whole, this is a densely argued, stimulating, and valuable study. *Popular Fictions*[12] includes reprints of pieces by Kathy MacDermott on literature and the Grub

10. *Masquerade and Civilization: The Carnivalesque in Eighteenth-Century English Culture and Fiction*, by Terry Castle. Methuen. pp. x + 395. £25.

11. *The Politics and Poetics of Transgression*, by Peter Stallybrass and Allon White. Methuen. pp. xi + 228. hb £16, pb £7.50.

12. *Popular Fictions: Essays in Literature and History*, ed. by Peter Humm, Paul Stigant, and Peter Widdowson. Methuen. pp. xiv + 265. hb £15, pb £6.95.

Street myth, and by Michael Denning on *The Beggar's Opera*. *Literature Politics and Theory*[13] includes a reprint of David Musselwhite's analysis of the 'institutional and discursive location' of the trial of Warren Hastings.

In *Sensibility*[14] Janet Todd has written a concise and lucid introduction to the cult of sensibility and to the literature of the sentimental movement. She begins with an account of the historical and ideological roots of sentimentalism, before providing a well-informed and economical critical survey of late eighteenth-century sentimental literature. As might be expected, she concentrates mainly on fiction, but she also provides interesting chapters on drama and poetry, in the latter case clarifying a number of critical points and definitions in sharp illustrative analyses of poems by Helen Maria Williams and Wordsworth. Acknowledging the notorious problems involved in establishing the historical and stylistic boundaries of her subject and in defining the meanings of its key terms, she does not entirely avoid confusion herself: there are times in her argument when 'sentiment' and 'sensibility' seem to be used interchangeably. In general, however, this is a clear and informative introduction to the subject.

Ann Messenger's *His and Hers*[15] is presented as a contribution to the feminist 'task of revising the history of English literature', which is here conceived of straightforwardly in terms of extending the literary canon. The book includes essays on the work of eight Restoration and eighteenth-century women writers, discussed in relation to that produced by contemporary men. It is difficult to see any cumulative thesis informing the author's choice of subjects. The eighteenth century is represented by commentary on the poems of the Countess of Winchilsea and on the versions of *The Toilette* claimed by Lady Mary Wortley Montagu and Gay; analysis of *The Female Spectator*, which is presented as a handbook of strategies for female survival in contemporary society; comparison of Pope's Arabella Fermor and a character of the same name in a novel by Frances Moore Brooke; and discussion of Anna Barbauld's use of the mock heroic as a 'protective cloak' in her verse, and Ellis Cornelia Knight's reply to *Rasselas* in her *Dinarbas*. The book establishes some worthwhile intertextual connections. However, it employs a strangely dated and self-limiting critical vocabulary, and at times – as in the opening essay on Dryden and Anne Killigrew – its argument amounts to little more than naïve special pleading. The volume reprints some of the poems discussed in an appendix.

Fidelis Morgan's *A Woman of No Character*[16] is an odd and frustrating book, consisting of a selection of extracts from the published works of Mrs Manley, interspersed with a narrative of the facts of her life as it is known. On the grounds that the fictional extracts are 'widely acknowledged to be auto-

13. *Literature Politics and Theory: Papers from the Essex Conference 1976–84*, ed. by Francis Barker, Peter Hulme, Margaret Iversen, and Diana Loxley. Methuen. pp. xix + 259. hb £15, pb £6.95.

14. *Sensibility: An Introduction*, by Janet Todd. Methuen. pp. vi + 169. hb £16.50, pb £5.95.

15. *His and Hers: Essays in Restoration and Eighteenth-Century Literature*, by Ann Messenger. UKen. pp. ix + 271. £23.50.

16. *A Woman of No Character: An Autobiography of Mrs Manley*, by Fidelis Morgan. Faber. pp. 176. £9.95.

biographical', names of characters are changed to their 'real' equivalents and the text is pruned of irrelevant (i.e. non-autobiographical) detail. This obviously begs all the questions that could have been dealt with in a critical study or biography, while minimizing the usefulness of the printed extracts themselves. Bridget Hill has edited a selection of writings by Mary Astell[17], consisting of the complete text of *Reflections on Marriage*, most of *A Serious Proposal to the Ladies* Part 1 (and some of Part 2) and extracts from other pamphlets, poems, and prefaces. The introduction to the volume includes useful critical discussion of the range of concerns encompassed in Astell's feminist polemics, and in particular compares her position on education with that of Defoe. Ruth Perry's *The Celebrated Mary Astell* (UChic) was not available for review. *Gender and Reading*[18] includes a stimulating essay by Kathryn Shevelow on the rhetorical construction of women as readers of the *Tatler*. *Fetter'd or Free?*[19] includes useful essays by Catherine E. Moore on Mrs Barbauld's criticism of contemporary women novelists, and by Mitzi Myers on Hannah More's tracts. These last are also discussed by Susan Pedersen in *JBS*. In 'Fatal Marriages? Restoration Plays Embedded in Eighteenth-Century Novels'[20] Susan Staves argues that 'the embedding of Restoration play texts in ... eighteenth-century novels reveals an appropriation by bourgeois women of sentiments and entitlements that had formerly been the property of aristocratic men'. Penelope Wilson's 'Feminism and the Augustans' (*CritQ*) outlines some of the problems faced by feminist criticism in confronting Augustan satirical writing which 'is perhaps uniquely adept at constructing the terms of its own criticism and at pre-emptive disablement of the opposition'. In 'Learning, Virtue, and the Term "Bluestocking"' Sylvia H. Myers (*SECC*) traces the history of the term 'bluestocking' from its original general sense to its later pejorative application to intellectual women and sees the development as a sign of a 'taboo against learning for women'. Beth Kowaleski-Wallace also discusses women and education in 'Milton's Daughters: The Education of Eighteenth-Century Women Writers' (*FSt*). Laurie Yager Lieb's '"The Works of Women are Symbolical"' (*ECLife*) outlines the 'symbolical' values associated with needlework in the period. Karen E. Davis discusses 'Martha Fowke: "A Lady Once Too Well Known"' (*ELN*), and Moira Ferguson's 'Resistance and Power in the Life and Writings of Ann Yearsley' (*ECent*) marks the literary and personal achievements of Ann Yearsley in the face of the social stigma that attached to her position as a milkwoman.

The eighteenth-century volume of the *Sphere History of Literature*[21] has been re-issued in a revised and updated edition. It remains the most reliable volume of its kind currently available, and includes intelligently written survey-essays and useful bibliographies and chronological tables. In *The Eighteenth*

17. *The First English Feminist: 'Reflections on Marriage' and Other Writings by Mary Astell*, ed. by Bridget Hill. Gower/Temple Smith. pp. vii + 235. £15.

18. *Gender and Reading: Essays on Readers, Texts, and Contexts*, ed. by Elizabeth A. Flynn and Patrocinio P. Schweickart. JHU. pp. xxx + 306. hb $27.50, pb $10.95.

19. *Fetter'd or Free? British Women Novelists, 1670–1815*, ed. by Mary Anne Schofield and Cecilia Macheski. OhioU. pp. xvii + 441. $38.50.

20. In *Augustan Studies: Essays in Honor of Irvin Ehrenpreis*, ed. by Douglas Lane Patey and Timothy Keegan. UDel/AUP. pp. 270. £24.50.

21. *Sphere History of Literature*. Vol. 4: *Dryden to Johnson*, ed. by Roger Lonsdale. Second rev. edn. Sphere. pp. 450. £12.95.

Century[22] James Sambrook provides a straightforward guide to the 'intellectual and cultural context of English literature' in the period. He surveys science, religion, philosophy, politics and history, and aesthetics and the visual arts, and concludes with sections in which he challenges the well-worn denomination of the eighteenth century as 'the age of reason' and discusses the importance of Greek and Roman models for the Augustans. His reading of the period is thoroughly conventional: Newton and Locke are seen as the main influences on intellectual activity in most of spheres covered; the view of history offered is Whiggish. The book contains chronological tables, notes on authors, and subject bibliographies which will be particularly useful for students.

Le Corps et L'Âme en Grande-Bretagne au XVIIIe Siècle[23] includes essays on eighteenth-century medicine and punishment, and on literary topics as noted below. *Languages of Nature*[24] treats eighteenth- and nineteenth-century scientific and literary texts. Ludmilla Jordanova's editorial introduction offers a lucid survey of the general problems raised in subjecting the discourses of science to critical examination. The focus of her essay on eighteenth-century presentation of the family is largely on French texts, as it is in A. C. Pilkington's essay on 'nature' as an ethical norm in the period, but both are relevant to contemporary writings in English. The volume also includes interesting essays on Sterne (by James Rogers) and Erasmus Darwin (by Maureen McNeil), and, in the second half, covers Charles Darwin, George Eliot, and Michelet. In 'Eighteenth-Century Science and Radical Social Theory: The Case of Joseph Priestley's Scientific Liberalism' (*JBS*) Isaac Kramnick discusses the relation between Priestley's scientific interests and his radical social theories. In *ECLife* Lucy B. Maddox discusses 'Gilbert White and the Politics of Natural History'.

Volume IV of *A New History of Ireland*, from 1691 to 1800, edited by T. W. Moody and W. E. Vaughan (Clarendon), was not available, but contains essays on language and literature, art, and music. Seamus Deane's *Short History of Irish Literature* (Hutchinson), covering the same period, was also unavailable. Norman Vance writes on 'Irish Literary Traditions and the Act of Union'(*CJIS*). In *Irish Booksellers and English Writers*[25] Richard Cargill Cole provides a useful account of the Irish book trade and reprint industry from 1740 to 1800. Having discussed production, circulation, and pirating in general introductory chapters, he concentrates on the reprinting histories of eight English authors: Richardson, Fielding, Smollett, Sterne, Johnson, Boswell, Goldsmith, and Gibbon; and he also includes discussion of Irish publishing links with America. John Feather surveys 'British Publishing in the Eighteenth Century' (*Lib*).

22. *The Eighteenth Century: The Intellectual and Cultural Context of English Literature, 1700-1789*, by James Sambrook. Longman. pp. xiii + 290. hb £15.95, pb £7.95.

23. *Le Corps et L'Âme en Grande-Bretagne au XVIIIe Siècle*, ed. by Paul-Gabriel Boucé and Suzy Halimi. Sorbonne. pp. 179.

24. *Languages of Nature: Critical Essays on Science and Literature*, ed. by Ludmilla Jordanova. FAB. pp. 351. hb £25, pb £8.95.

25. *Irish Booksellers and English Writers 1740-1800*, by Richard Cargill Cole. Mansell. pp. xv + 266. £27.

David McKitterick has written an enormously detailed study of *Cambridge University Library*[26] in the eighteenth and nineteenth centuries, taking over where John Oates left off in the first volume of CUP's history of the institution, with the Copyright Act of 1710. In the section concerned with the eighteenth century he details the library's acquisitions; starting with George I's gift of John Moore's collection to it, he follows the gradual emergence of serious attempts to arrange and catalogue the books and house them adequately, traces the internal academic politics of the period, and sets the developments in their larger local and national context. Although he admits that 'the minutiae of a library's organization do not always make the most stimulating reading on a cursory inspection', the book is surprisingly readable, and full of intriguing information, even for the non-specialist. Volume V of *The History of Oxford University* (Clarendon), covering the eighteenth century, edited by L. S. Sutherland and L. G. Mitchell, was not available for review.

I have not seen Stephen K. Land's *The Philosophy of Language in Britain: Major Theories from Hobbes to Thomas Reid* (AMS). A. C. Grayling[27] sets out 'to treat Berkeley's central arguments as having live philosophical interest and to show that some of them are less indefensible than has generally been supposed'. He mounts an interesting and persuasively argued case, and the volume provides a usefully clear introductory survey of the main lines of Berkeley's thought. The articles in 'George Berkeley: Essays and Replies' (*Hermathena*) cover the main philosophical problems in Berkeley's work, and more general topics such as the particular features of the Irish economic situation that facilitated the 'conceptual breakthroughs' of *The Querist*, interestingly discussed by Patrick Kelly. The replies are often sharp and stimulating. *HEI* contains an impressive array of papers from a 1985 Oxford colloquium on Berkeley. G. R. Wall writes on his treatment of God's omniscience in 'Is God Really Omniscient?' (*SECC*), and *JHI* includes an article by David Berman on the possible Jacobitism of *Passive Obedience*.

Antony Flew[28] justifies his decision to write 'another general book on Hume' by claiming that many of the available studies are potboilers, or do not have a sufficiently broad perspective on the full range of Hume's interests. His acknowledgement of this range is welcome. His main claim to originality of emphasis lies in his suggestion that 'almost all' of Hume's conclusions 'are, for better or for worse, conditioned and sometimes determined by an interlocking set of Cartesian assumptions', an argument which has been vigorously contested in some reviews of the book. He presents his case emphatically and at times rather ponderously. ChuoUL has produced a catalogue of its recently purchased collection of editions and letters of Hume and his contemporaries from the library of John Vladimir Price[29]. In *ECS* Ralph S. Pomeroy discusses 'Hume's Proposed League of the Learned and Conversible Worlds'. In

26. *Cambridge University Library: A History: The Eighteenth and Nineteenth Centuries*, by David McKitterick. CUP. pp. xviii + 812. £75.

27. *Berkeley: The Central Arguments*, by A. C. Grayling. Duckworth. pp. xii + 218. £19.50.

28. *David Hume: Philosopher of Moral Science*, by Antony Flew. Blackwell. pp. ix + 189. hb £22.50, pb £7.95.

29. *David Hume and the Eighteenth Century British Thought* [sic]: *An Annotated Catalogue*, comp. by Sadao Ikeda and Michihiro Otonashi. ChuoUL. Unpaginated.

'Hume's Key and Aesthetic Rationality' (*JAAC*) Steven Sverdlik analyses 'aesthetic rationality' in 'Of the Standard of Taste'; in 'Hume and the Standard of Taste' (*HumeS*) Christopher MacLachlan suggests that the essay may be ironic.

Missed in last year's trawl was John Robertson's important historical study, *The Scottish Enlightenment and the Militia Issue* (Donald, 1985). Anand C. Chitnis outlines the work of Scottish university teachers and their students in *The Scottish Enlightenment and Early Victorian English Society* (CH); *A Hotbed of Genius*, edited by David Daiches and John Jones (EdinU) provides a general introduction to the Scottish Enlightenment; Duncan MacMillan's *Painting in Scotland: The Golden Age* (Phaidon) celebrates the painting of the period, and R. D. S. Jack's short survey of *Scottish Literature's Debt to Italy*[30] includes commentary on Ramsay, Thomson, and Smollett. Among journal articles, Franklin E. Court writes on 'Adam Smith and the Teaching of English Literature' (*HEdQ*, 1985), and R. L. Emerson surveys Scottish writings on natural philosophy in 'Natural Philosophy and the Problem of the Scottish Enlightenment' (*SVEC*).

Two studies of Capability Brown are intelligently written and well illustrated. Roger Turner[31] includes general chapters on the historical context of the landscaping movement and on the development of taste in the period, before discussing the landscapes of William Kent, Brown, and some of their successors. The volume includes a useful gazetteer of Brown's work. Thomas Hinde's biographical study[32] includes more detailed critical discussion of the major landscapes, of Brown's social position and status, and of controversies such as the one provoked by the appearance of William Chambers's *Dissertation on Oriental Gardening*. One small point: although Hinde claims that the best impression of the effects made by eighteenth-century landscapes is gained from contemporary prints he does not himself draw on them as he might have done. M. F. Schulz devotes a chapter of *Paradise Preserved: Recreations of Eden in Eighteenth- and Nineteenth-Century England* (CUP, 1985) to eighteenth-century landscape gardens.

Seven volumes of reproductions of British satirical cartoons dating from 1600 to 1832, from Chadwyck–Healey, are an offshoot of the company's 1978 microfilm edition of 17,000 cartoons from BL. Editors of individual volumes have apparently been left to follow their own ways in selection and arrangement of material and commentary. John Brewer prefaces his volume on *The Common People and Politics*[33] with an essay on the problems of interpreting and using the cartoons for historians without visual expertise. He makes some good and useful points, and comments convincingly on the development of available representational stereotypes in the period. However, his arrangement of the cartoons in a non-chronological order dictated by references to them in his argument is unhelpful, particularly as the volume has no index. Other

30. *Scottish Literature's Debt to Italy*, by R. D. S. Jack. EdinU. pp. vii + 86. pb £7.50.

31. *Capability Brown and the Eighteenth-Century English Landscape*, by Roger Turner. W&N (1985). pp. 204. £16.95.

32. *Capability Brown: The Story of a Master Gardener*, by Thomas Hinde. Hutchinson. pp. 224. £15.95.

33. *The Common People and Politics 1750–1790s*, by John Brewer. ESP. C–H. pp. 291. £40.

editors make less elaborate attempts at formal analysis of the designs of their prints, concentrating instead on describing the historical circumstances in which they were produced, and arranging their selections in (more or less) chronological order. Three cover the whole period: Michael Duffy surveys the representation of *The Englishman and the Foreigner*[34], and suggests reasons for the changing popularity of different satirical targets at different times; John Miller's *Religion in the Popular Prints*[35] outlines important religious developments and controversies and considers how far and how accurately the prints reflect them; and J. A. Sharpe, in *Crime and the Law in English Satirical Prints*[36], discusses the relation between convention and circumstantial specificity in the treatment of criminal life, policing, and the law. Other volumes are more particular: H. T. Dickinson[37] considers the treatment of constitutional affairs in prints produced from 1760 to 1832 and outlines some of the strengths and weaknesses of the form as a tool of political commentary; Paul Langford[38] discusses the evolution of the political cartoon and the relation between emblem and caricature, as an introduction to his selection of prints of Walpole and his circle; and Peter D. G. Thomas covers some of the same ground in his introductory comments to a volume of prints concerned with *The American Revolution*[39]. Inevitably, perhaps, Hogarth looms large in the selection of eighteenth-century prints (although some editors announce their intention of avoiding his work as much as possible), and some already familiar cartoons crop up several times in different volumes. I noticed a number of annoying mistakes and discrepancies in the notes to the prints, and sometimes wished that they could have included editorial transcriptions of captions that were unclear in the reproduced originals. However, the series as a whole is handsomely produced and provides a welcome means of making available a range of important material.

In *Hogarth's Blacks*[40] David Dabydeen discusses the remarkable dearth of modern critical commentary on the place of blacks in eighteenth-century art. He argues that the blacks in Hogarth's paintings and prints in particular are not merely caricatured stereotypes, but that they have a complex role as 'satirical signposts' to the artist's designs. In this way, he claims, 'the black' is often 'a detail pregnant with meaning, although a peripheral figure' in his work. I find myself wanting to qualify some of Dabydeen's claims for the uncompromising radicalism of Hogarth. Nevertheless, his commentary is fascinating and valuable, and provides a strikingly new perspective on some familiar images. In related areas, Michel Jouve discusses eighteenth-century caricature in 'Corps difformes et âmes perverses'[23] and R. L. S. Cowley has 'A Revised Date for Hogarth's *The Denunciation*' (*N&Q*).

34. *The Englishman and the Foreigner*, by Michael Duffy. ESP. C–H. pp. 403. £40.
35. *Religion in the Popular Prints 1600–1832*, by John Miller. ESP. C–H. pp. 369. £40.
36. *Crime and the Law in English Satirical Prints 1600–1832*, by J. A. Sharpe. ESP. C–H. pp. 318. £38.
37. *Caricatures and the Constitution 1760–1832*, by H. T. Dickinson. ESP. C–H. pp. 345. £38.
38. *Walpole and the Robinocracy*, by Paul Langford. ESP. C–H. pp. 259. £35.
39. *The American Revolution*, by P. D. G. Thomas. ESP. C–H. pp. 279. £38.
40. *Hogarth's Blacks: Images of Blacks in Eighteenth Century English Art*, by David Dabydeen. Dangaroo (1985). pp. 158. hb £12.95, pb £6.95.

In his highly important, densely argued, and impressively well-documented *The Political Theory of Painting from Reynolds to Hazlitt*[41] John Barrell claims that the criticism of painting in the eighteenth and early nineteenth centuries 'had no language to employ but a political language, and had no ambition to develop an approach to painting which was not political'. In a wide-ranging opening chapter he identifies the terms of a discourse of civic humanism in which the 'republic of fine arts' is conceived and its 'public' constructed and addressed in the work of early eighteenth-century writers such as Shaftesbury; and traces the later modification and attenuation of that discourse in the context of developing commercial society. In subsequent chapters he argues that Reynolds's peculiar adaptation of the vocabulary of humanism involves an attempt to 'ground public spirit not on virtue but on a particular kind of social knowledge'; that James Barry (and Blake) provide the means of extending the 'public' of art to include all the (male) members of the state; and that the writings of Fuseli and B. R. Haydon, and attacks of Hazlitt, mark the end of the discursive tradition he has traced. Morton D. Paley's *The Apocalyptic Sublime*[42] begins with Burke's discussion of the sublime and includes discussion of the work of Joseph Wright, Stubbs, Fuseli, and Benjamin West. Both books are reviewed in later sections of *YWES*.

Rachel Trickett traces 'Some Aspects of Visual Description in Eighteenth-Century Literature'[20]. In his brief volume on the eighteenth century in the *Cambridge Introduction to the History of Art*[43] Stephen Jones provides a general sketch of the main developments in British and European art, architecture, and landscape in the period. The volume includes a short glossary of technical terms and a section of notes on artists. John Summerson's survey of eighteenth-century architecture[44] is elegant and economical in its arguments and very well illustrated. Barry Cunliffe presents his history of Bath[45] as 'a pure self indulgence'. In fact, it is an intelligently written, well-informed, and attractively illustrated volume for the general reader, which offers a useful bibliography and a fair amount of analytical commentary in the course of its narrative. The eighteenth-century section, for example, includes a sharp discussion of the relation between aesthetics and the economic realities of speculative building.

OUP have re-issued Roger Lonsdale's exemplary 'literary biography' of Dr Charles Burney[46]. As the title suggests, Lonsdale treats his subject as an author and man of letters rather than as 'a mere musician': the study contains interesting discussion of that distinction, of the formation of the polite audience for music and literature, and of Burney's relations with the Johnsonian circle. Elsewhere, Betty Rizzo describes 'A New Letter from Charles Burney in Norfolk' (*N&Q*) and Claudia L. Johnson discusses the 1784

41. *The Political Theory of Painting from Reynolds to Hazlitt: 'The Body of the Public'*, by John Barrell. Yale. pp. xi + 366. £16.95.

42. *The Apocalyptic Sublime*, by Morton D. Paley. Yale. xi + 196. £30.

43. *Cambridge Introduction to the History of Art: The Eighteenth Century*, by Stephen Jones. CUP (1985). pp. vi + 90. hb £8.95, pb £4.50.

44. *The Architecture of the Eighteenth Century*, by John Summerson. T&H. pp. 176. pb £4.95.

45. *The City of Bath*, by Barry Cunliffe. Sutton. pp. 186. hb £12.95, pb £6.95.

46. *Dr. Charles Burney: A Literary Biography*, by Roger Lonsdale. Clarendon. pp. xvi + 527. pb £12.50.

commemoration of Handel, and the nature of the musical sublime in '"Giant HANDEL" and the Musical Sublime' (*ECS*).

Among historical studies, J. C. D. Clark supplements his account of English society in the eighteenth century (*YW* 66.321) with an 'iconoclastic and satirical' survey of the schools of interpretation of Stuart and Hanoverian history that have emerged in the last decades[47]. He musters his cast of 'Old Guard', 'Old Hat', 'Class of '68', and 'revisionist' historians wittily, and summarizes their positions sharply (if often unfairly). His determination to maintain his own uncommitted distance from the fray, and simultaneous attempts to score polemical points in all directions, leave the reader puzzling over the purpose of the exercise. Longman have re-issued Charles Wilson's economic history of the period[48] in a substantially revised second edition, which includes a new section on population levels and material improvement in the Industrial Revolution. John Rule's study of the state of the labouring classes from 1750 to 1850[49] is a useful digest of information, clearly laid out and offering some speculations on the feelings of the poor as well as facts about them. The period is also covered in Pamela Horn's *Life and Labour in Rural England 1760–1850* (Macmillan). In a related area, Steven Wallech (*JHI*) writes interestingly about the changing terminology of class and rank in the century in '"Class versus Rank": The Transformation of Eighteenth-Century English Social Terms and Theories of Production'.

Religious life is surveyed in Gordon Rupp's *Religion in England, 1688–1791* (Clarendon, 1985), and in Geoffrey Holmes's *Politics, Religion and Society in England, 1672–1742* (Hambledon). Richard Sharp contributes an article on 'New Perspectives on the High Church Tradition: Historical Background 1730–1780' to *Tradition Renewed: The Oxford Movement*, edited by G. Rowell (Pickwick), while John Gascoigne (*History*) looks at the neglected topic of links between eighteenth-century Anglican latitudinarianism and political radicalism. Frederick Dreyer writes about 'A "Religious Society under Heaven": John Wesley and the Identity of Methodism' (*JBS*), and Heimo Ertl discusses (in German) eighteenth-century Methodist 'Lives' in '"The Manner Wherein God Has Dealt with My Soul"' (*Anglia*). Whitney R. D. Jones has written an interesting biography of David Williams[50], providing a broad survey of his participation in the religious and political controversies of his day, of his writings on politics and education, and of his involvement in the establishment of the Literary Fund.

The Jacobites continue to fascinate. Bruce Lenman's brief and well-illustrated account of the risings, produced in association with the National Trust for Scotland[51], is aimed at the general reader. A. J. Youngson's *The*

---

47. *Revolution and Rebellion: State and Society in England in the Seventeenth and Eighteenth Centuries*, by J. C. D. Clark. CUP. pp. x + 182. hb £20, pb £6.95.

48. *England's Apprenticeship 1603–1763*, by Charles Wilson. Second edn. Longman. pp. xviii + 433. pb £8.95.

49. *The Labouring Classes in Early Industrial England 1750–1850*, by John Rule. Longman. pp x + 408. pb £8.95.

50. *David Williams: The Anvil and the Hammer*, by Whitney R. D. Jones. UWales. pp. xviii + 266. £25.95.

51. *The Jacobite Cause*, by Bruce Lenman. Drew/National Trust for Scotland. pp. 128. pb £4.95.

Prince and the Pretender[52] is a strange book. It consists of two narratives of the '45, one from the Hanoverian perspective and one from the Jacobite, with an introduction in which Youngson considers 'the manufacture of history' by historians. Unfortunately this potentially interesting project is scuppered by the *naïveté* of the introductory discussion, which never really progresses beyond the point of establishing that even true historians will be selective in their accounts of historical events, and will be influenced by a variety of personal interests and motivations.

2. Poetry

Regaining Paradise by Dustin Griffin[53] is a well-argued presentation of his thesis that eighteenth-century poets (and others) grew to maturity in the benevolent shadow of Milton. Johnson's surly Republican was also, unquestionably, the great 'British Muse' who had not only exorcized the fear that there could never be a sublime native epic but released imitators into self-confident experiment with many other genres which took firmer hold in British writing. Dryden, Pope, Thomson, and Cowper, most notably (let alone the Watts or Akensides of the eighteenth-century poetic tradition) owed what Griffin persuasively reveals was a deep and varied debt to their great predecessor even when they honoured him by subverting his secure beliefs or re-interpreting the great myth that Paradise might yet be regained. Griffin's afterword, in which he questions 'the so-called "burden" that a rich literary tradition, or a great individual writer, placed on the shoulders of all literary latecomers', follows easily from his preceding analyses and amply justifies his contention that it is time to question the recent wisdom on the anxiety of influence. As for the other (if very different) book on the century's poetry, Michael Meehan's *Liberty and Poetics*[4], enough has been said in the first section of this chapter to make further comment otiose.

Another monograph with a substantial amount on Pope, Allan Ingram's *Intricate Laughter in the Satire of Swift and Pope*[5] has already been reviewed in that same first section. Three others which promise the whole spectrum from feminism through deconstruction to older-style revision, Ellen Pollak's *The Poetics of Sexual Myth: Gender and Ideology in the Verse of Swift and Pope* (UChic), G. Douglas Atkins's *Quests of Difference: Reading Pope's Poems* (UKen), and Rebecca Ferguson's *The Unbalanced Mind: Pope and the Rule of Passion* (Harvester), were all, frustratingly, unavailable for review. At least Frank Stack's *Pope and Horace: Studies in Imitation*[54] was seen. Stack places the Latin against the Englished versions in a way which builds sensibly on the findings of recent scholarship (Howard Erskine-Hill particularly) into a 'state of the art' monograph which appears to have considerable authority to a reviewer not so comfortable with the Horatian originals as Stack clearly is. The last two book-length studies of 1986 did come my way. The first, Brean S.

52. *The Prince and the Pretender: A Study in the Writing of History*, by A. J. Youngson. CH (1985). pp. vii + 270. £19.95.

53. *Regaining Paradise: Milton and the Eighteenth Century*, by Dustin Griffin. CUP. pp. 299. £25.

54. *Pope and Horace: Studies in Imitation*, by Frank Stack. CUP (1985). pp. 316. £25.

Hammond's *Pope*[55], is energetic in its search for the strands of ideology which contextualize the poet and divides these into various manifestations – the old Whig/new Tory stance (*Windsor Forest, An Essay on Man, Burlington, Imitations*, Chapter Two), unconscious ideology, *pace* Pierre Macherey (*Arbuthnot*, Chapter Three), and so on – with a coda on the limited applicability of feminism. The result is overly schematic even in its own terms. For example, analysis of *Arbuthnot* excludes from Hammond's narrower interest in the poem a possible buttressing of religious ideology. Yet this is also a lucid Marxist account and it avoids too much of the specialist, theoretical vocabulary which might puzzle those students for whom Hammond's conformist selection of 'essential poems' seems consciously (or unconsciously) designed.

All of this is a world away from Rosemary Cowler's editing of Vol. II of *The Prose Works of Alexander Pope*[56] a full half century after the publication of Norman Ault's first volume. Here are all the major prose works of the later years, the Preface to Shakespeare, the Postscript to *The Odyssey*, and the complete *Peri Bathous*. Even so, one doubts it will appear on the reading lists of those who will be Brean Hammond's audience. More's the pity. This is, as Maynard Mack says in his foreword, a collection of texts 'scrupulously collated, fully annotated, and thoughtfully introduced'. 'What more could one ask?' he concludes. Well, perhaps something of the synoptic learning combined with graceful acuteness of Mack's own commentary on texts; but Cowler can hardly be condemned for lacking gifts denied to all but a handful of editor-critics, and even Homer can nod as Graham Cartwright (*N&Q*) demonstrates when he amends Mack's list of Pope's books in the Bishop Hurd library at Hartlebury Castle. Elise F. Knapp is even more daring in her spirited defence of William Warburton as an unjustly denigrated editor in the eighteenth-century meaning of the title which assumed active, welcome collaboration in the communal effort with the poet himself: her 'Community Property: The Case for Warburton's 1751 Edition of Pope' (*SEL*) becomes an interesting if too-brief sally against the author-centred editorial dogma of scholarship dominated by Fredson Bowers, and it thus provides an interesting companion piece to the similarly modest 'theory of literary imitation' on which Dustin Griffin puts down his marker[53].

In the other journal publications, pride of place goes to belated notice of Douglas Oliver's 'Voicing Patterns as One Key to the Pace of Poetry' (*JPhon*, 1984). Few people without linguistic training could follow all his evidence, but his central argument that 'perceptions of cadence and movement in verse are partly dependent upon the inter-involvement of the voice's intonation with the voicing pattern' will emerge well enough for anyone with an interest in metrics. Readers of this chapter in *YWES* have good reason to make the effort since the first four lines of the *Essay on Man* provide one of Oliver's test cases. Still off the track of the familiar, although from this year's crop of shorter pieces, Stephen Szilagyi (*Expl*) takes issue with *OED* on verbal associations in the early 'Two or Three' epigram which show 'young Pope's precision, vigorous economy, and insouciant wit' – and also his ear for an innuendo. More predictable is the regularity of papers on 'Eloisa', although one of these, by John F.

55. *Pope*, by Brean S. Hammond. Harvester. pp. 218. £16.95.
56. *The Prose Works of Alexander Pope*. Vol. II: *The Major Works, 1725-1744*, ed. by Rosemary Cowler. Blackwell. pp. xv + 529. £35.

Sena on 'Melancholy as Despair' (*HTR*, 1983) has escaped the net even longer than Oliver's investigation of voicing. Sena's is a scholarly, theological justification for the sudden transformation of *acedia* through Grace. In 'Woman in a Trap: Pope and Ovid in "Eloisa to Abelard"' (*CollL*) Karen Alkalay-Gut finds a different explanation – in the transforming power of poetic art – prefigured in Ovid's *Heroides*. On the *Rape*, the old argument about interpretative emphasis continues as Robert W. Williams ('Fate and the Narrative of *The Rape of the Lock*', *SSEng*) puts his well-constructed case for the primacy of generic good humour and discriminating value against interest in the forensic details of the Petre/Fermor dispute, whereas Douglas Lane Patey in '"Love Deny'd": Pope and the Allegory of Despair' (*ECS*), like Sena on 'Eloisa', alludes to the theological significance of *acedia* as he suggests an altogether bleaker cast to the poem's balances between delight and instruction. Three other commentators investigate aspects of the *Dunciad*: Dennis Todd (*N&Q*) hears in Cibber's bathetic blasphemy a mock-heroic echo of the atheistical defiance of Mezentius transmitted via the declamations of Celius in *The British Enchanters* by George Granville; William E. Rivers (*PLL*) offers the opinion – without much hard evidence on show – that the attack on University education in Book 4 may owe something to the assault on High Tory Oxford in Nicholas Amhurst's *Terrae Filius*; and, in the most substantial *Dunciad* paper this year, Robert Ness (*ECS*) explores why Opera is the harbinger of dullness in a poem written long after it had waned as a *cause célèbre*. In similar vein, Peter A. Tasch (*N&Q*) mines a wryly sophisticated allusion to Dryden's *Essay of Dramatic Poesy* from the low-key opening of *Arbuthnot*, P. J. Gabriner (also *N&Q*) lists 'Antedatings, Postdatings and Additions' for *OED* from the *Iliad* (some of them quite surprising, as, for example, 'apostrophize' used by Pope in 1718 though first recorded by *OED* only in 1824). Finally, the relationship between Pope and Bolingbroke is the subject of two further items from *N&Q*: G. J. Clingham describes some features of the two-volume quarto copy of the *Works, 1717–1735* (inscribed by the author to Bolingbroke) in Tonbridge School library, and Jeremy Black reprints two letters by Nathaniel Cole (a city lawyer not normally given to literary comment of any kind) which bear witness to the sensation caused by the attack on Pope in the *Advertisement* which accompanied the 1749 edition of *The Patriot King*.

Pope's fellow Scriblerians have a thin time of it this year with the exception of 'poor Matt' Prior who is the subject of a full-scale monograph by Frances Mayhew Rippy[57]. She makes an informative job of it too. There are hints of special pleading, of course: it could hardly be otherwise in a book which has to begin and end with the question 'in what sense may a minor poet have a major significance?' Nevertheless, this is the sort of commonsense portrait of the artist which has become the hallmark of TEAS volumes. The life and works are steadily documented and there may be cold comfort for a few modern poets in that Prior was too sociable, too affable, too easily competent in too many modes to aspire to more than a footnote in the history of the many friends he made and influenced.

Few as they may be, contributions on the poetry of one of those friends, Jonathan Swift, are of consistently high quality this year. Arthur Sherbo

57. *Matthew Prior*, by Frances Mayhew Rippy. TEAS. Twayne. pp. 170. £21.95.

('Swift's Abuse of Poetic Diction', *CollL*) takes the laurel with his delightful exegesis of the many and varied parodies Swift paraded in his verse – parodies which, if recognized, may have spared many a tortured apology by critics embarrassed by apparently wilful scatology – for Sherbo is as alert as Swift himself to the pomposities of mechanical diction in bad poets and the odd sloppiness in their betters. John Irwin Fischer in 'The Government's Response to Swift's *An Epistle to a Lady*' (*PQ*) gives Sherbo a run for his money, though, in a fascinating piece of historical detection which provides solid evidence for dating the *Epistle* in late November 1733 and documentation of the process by which 'Over a twenty day period [early in 1734] ... first Wilford named Aris, then Aris fingered Gilliver, Gilliver implicated Pilkington and Motte, and Pilkington pointed to [Mary] Barber who ended in gaol' as Walpole pursued the perpetrators of the attack. Clearly the legend of heroic printers and friends suffering in silence to protect embattled satirists needs some revision. It is also worthy of note that Walpole did not pursue celebrated *authors* too hard: he knew that when Swift wrote 'In a Jest I spent my rage' he told no more or less than the political truth. In a very different mode but equally refreshing is Timothy Keegan's essay on 'Swift's Self-Portraits in Verse'[20]. Keegan analyses the best with uncomplicated common sense but he refuses to explain away the worst as irony. Those indefatigable annotators Hermann J. Real and Heinz J. Vienken offer two pieces of Swiftiana: first, in 'Swift's *Verses Wrote in a Lady's Ivory Table-Book*' (*BJECS*), a subverted analogue in the poem akin (or so they boldly claim) to the later, more sustained parodies; second (*N&Q*), an explanation of the insulting allusion to Kennel-rakers in 'A Description of the Morning'. John F. Sena's advertised monograph on the Whig rival to the Scriblerians' Arbuthnot, *The Best-Natured Man; Sir Samuel Garth, Physician and Poet* (AMS) was yet another of the volumes which failed to appear for review.

Essays on Fielding's ventures into poetry are rare. All the more welcome then is Hugh Amory's lengthy piece of scholarship, 'The Evidence of Things Not Seen: Concealed Proofs of Fielding's Juvenal' (*PBSA*), which tracks 'Part of Juvenal's Sixth-Satire Modernized in Burlesque Verse' through versions from the first 'sketch' (1726) when Fielding was smarting under amatory disappointment, through adaptation into political satire (1731), into self-censorship (1733). From an unexpected source Amory thus provides engrossing evidence for the way Fielding 'fictionalised' his experience. More predictable are this year's additions to the critical arguments about Thomson. Oscar Kenshur, in *Open Form and the Shape of Ideas*[58], has theoretical vistas in view which stretch far beyond the eighteenth century, but he does usefully take to task Ralph Cohen's view that 'discontinuities point to fragmentation' in *The Seasons*. On the same poem Robert Inglesfield patiently charts the growth of 'Shaftesbury's Influence on Thomson's "Seasons"' (*BJECS*) as he worked and reworked the drafts. Michael Cohen (*ELN*) exercised less care, at least during proof-reading of his paper on 'The Whig Sublime and James Thompson [*sic*]'. Despite initial appearances he *is* talking about the same writer and he works busily with the allegory of Northern Gothic chiefly in Thomson's plays

---

58. *Open Form and the Shape of Ideas: Literary Structures as Representations of Philosophical Concepts in the Seventeenth and Eighteenth Centuries*, by Oscar Kenshur. AUP/BuckU. pp. 140. £16.95.

but also, by way of occasional allusion, in *The Seasons*. That other 'transitional' poet, Thomas Gray, is very well served by close readings this year: Wallace Jackson's knotty argument in 'Thomas Gray: Drowning in Human Voices' (*Criticism*) refuses tired variations on the theme of public v. private, Augustan v. Pre-Romantic in favour of a range of voices; R. S. Edgecombe (*DUJ*) offers an equally spirited defence of the early *Odes* against those other ancient and occasionally modern charges that the poetry chokes on allusion or poetic diction, and he is particularly good on the way Gray manipulates registers. Less celebrated contemporaries have their reputations further dented in other journals. Christina le Prevost's report on her research into the Trinity College Warton papers, 'More Unacknowledged Verse by Joseph Warton' (*RES*), builds carefully on David Fairer's whistle-blowing work to prove that yet more (in fact at least two-thirds) of the *Poems on Several Occasions* published under the name of Thomas Warton the Elder were assemblages by Joseph. She also reveals a fascinating tension in the latter's working practice between the Longinian theories (acquired from Pope of all people!) and his habit of cannibalizing older bits and pieces from his own work in a singularly unsublime fashion to make up 'new poems' supposedly by Thomas the Elder. Poetic justice in every sense then that Hugh Reid (*N&Q*) finds James Grainger plagiarizing Joseph's second edition of the 'Ode to Fancy' for his own 'Ode on Solitude'. Revision of not unrelated simplifications is needed after Robin Dix (also *N&Q*) finds Akenside's unfinished attempt at a quite new *Pleasures of the Imagination* in 1772 looking back to a solidly early eighteenth-century tradition of neoclassical narrative rather than forward to a revolutionary future.

Akenside's emendations are also the subject of Harriet Jump (*N&Q*) in the first of two pieces which are eloquent on the vicissitudes of party versifying in mid century. His *Epistle to Curio*, 1744, with its fulmination against William Pulteney for accepting the Earldom of Bath (and thus betraying the anti-Walpole cause), contains many weakly ironic echoes of his earlier adulatory *Epistle to ... Pulteney*, which, to Akenside's acute embarrassment, was published within days of Pulteney's elevation in 1742. James Sterling had comparable problems as Christine Gerrard demonstrates (*N&Q*) when she follows his *Ode to the Times* from 1734 to 1738. The apparently saving devices which reversed its first political affiliation proved of no material benefit to Sterling for he was forced to emigrate seven years later. Such demonstrations of the vanity of human wishes make this the obvious place to notice writers on Johnson. Niall Rudd, for example, who in 'Cicero's *De Senectute* and *The Vanity of Human Wishes*' (*N&Q*) itemizes some additional 'reminiscences' which should have appeared in his *Johnson's Juvenal* (*YW* 63.260), and Thomas Jemielity who deftly marshals counter-evidence from Johnson's life and opinions to undermine arguments that, since charity was so important to the Great Cham, his *Vanity* cannot be a satire ('Samuel Johnson, *The Vanity of Human Wishes*, and Biographical Criticism', *SECC*). In 'Why are Human Wishes Vain?' (*PEAN*) Gavin Edwards works closely with the text itself, particularly its syntax, to question the notion that its progress is as serenely ordered as commonly supposed. His deliberate omission of any consideration of the poem's relationship to the Latin predecessor is immediately made good by Bill Hutchings and Bill Ruddick's 'Johnson's *London* and *The Vanity of Human Wishes*: Classical and Eighteenth-Century Contexts' (also *PEAN*). Their presentation of this busy paper is a semiotician's delight: in the first half

Ruddick contends that the simultaneous co-existence of Roman and eighteenth-century accounts of human vanity allows both tragic/nihilist and satiric/Christian import; it is therefore almost tangibly appropriate that Hutchings's second half should trace the intertextuality which knits Pope and Crabbe together with Johnson and Goldsmith. Goldsmith too has his supporters this year: Cai Zong Qi does a serviceable job extending the multiple forms of 'Structural Antithesis in Goldsmith's *The Deserted Village*' (*PLL*), while Peter Dixon (*N&Q*) floats the intriguing possibility that 'On Torno's Cliffs' may unite its author's memory of a story in Jean-François Regnard (about the carving of a Latin motto, on the edge of the Arctic) with the explorations of later French geographers. G. J. Clingham in '"The inequalities of Memory": Johnson's Epitaphs on Hogarth' (*English*) also breaks new ground as he speculates stimulatingly on the critical/creative gestation responsible for the modulation from sonorous public lament in Johnson's epitaph on Hogarth into his more intimate memory of those lines. Finally, B. S. Lee (*ESA*, 1985) achieves what he attempts, a thumbnail sketch of Johnson's whole poetic output.

Two of those writers who became celebrities in the second half of the century, Cowper and Churchill, appear with their fellow 'Nonsense Club' members, Bonnell Thornton, Robert Lloyd, and George Colman plus a host of occasional contacts – Goldsmith and Hogarth again, Fielding, Gray, Smollett, Sterne, and the ubiquitous Wilkes – in Lance Bertelsen's *The Nonsense Club*[6]. There are assorted and notable discoveries here (*The Crab*, for example, a poem by Churchill which has lain, unknown, in the BL for three centuries) alongside Bertelsen's graphic portrait of coterie London in the 1750s; and if his homage to Bakhtin is less vigorously persuasive than in, say, the recent writings of Terry Castle on 'carnivalisation', Bertelsen certainly grasps and communicates the feel of Nonsense Club performances. For example, Churchill's hijacking of Georgian proprieties is very well handled even if Wilkes emerges as a disappointingly two-dimensional presence. Publication of James King's *William Cowper: A Biography*[59] is another signal event to be noted this year. Like Arthur H. Cash on Sterne, King eschews interpretation of the works as self-sufficient explanation of the life (or vice versa); rather he records the poems as signposts through the life. That might be expected from the biographer who is also the editor of Cowper's *Letters*. It must be said too that it remains a useful, even necessary corrective: we are not, after all, too far removed in time from superficial use of Cowper's life and works as mutually sentimental or denigratory evidence. The tact and sympathy James King everywhere displays is therefore the more appropriate, though he does not fudge the young Cowper's Nonsense Club activities, the ambiguous sexuality or the long psychological agonies of his castaway subject in what has already, and deservedly, become the standard biography. Modest and tentative by comparison but nonetheless demanding of note are pieces by Arthur Sherbo (*N&Q*) on circumstantial evidence which might link Cowper with some verses from *The Satirist*, 1809, and by Eleanor Ty (also *N&Q*) on a possible echo from the *Rambler* in a *Connoisseur* essay. Christopher Smart, that other 'stricken deer' of eighteenth-century poetry, was certainly linked with Cowper by way of their mutual friendship with Bonnell Thornton in the early days of the Nonsense Club, and it is

59. *William Cowper: A Biography*, by James King. DukeU. pp. 340. £29.75.

tempting to spin suggestions of further associations out of the papers published this year. Betty Rizzo in '"The Bite" – Kitty Smart to Henry Fox' (RES) reports on the manuscript of a witty epigram in praise of Fox written in 1753; in 'Smart's Pillars and the Hutchinsonians' (N&Q) Marcus Walsh investigates Smart's imagery and argues persuasively that it owes much to John Hutchinson mediated through others who also used his philosophy as an assertion of Scripture's literal truth against the encroachment of Newtonians; Mark W. Booth writes sympathetically on 'Song Form and the Mind in Christopher Smart's Later Poetry' (SECC), and in particular on 'the appositional rather than the linear propositional mode of the mind'. Any strained coincidence is just that of course. E. W. Pitcher (AN&Q) brings things down to earth with his additions to Robert Mahoney and Betty Rizzo's Christopher Smart: An Annotated Bibliography, 1743–1983 (1984), and 1987 rather than 1986 promises to be the year in which Smart once more receives his individual due with the publication of more volumes in the Poetical Works by Marcus Walsh and Karina Williamson.

'Towards a Rehabilitation' is the keynote subtitle of one of the essays on Macpherson this year. If it is unusual to find two pieces of any kind published on Ossian in any single year, it is quite remarkable that they should be major and sympathetic re-assessments of such high quality. First, simply because I have already alluded to its subtitle, is Howard Gaskill's work in CCrit. He begins with a combative analysis of the way the long-delayed then longer-savoured discovery of Macpherson's 'forgeries' has betrayed even the most eminent into academic sloppiness (Hugh Trevor-Roper gets a rough ride here); he then turns to the texts in proof of his contention that if Macpherson was not entirely trustworthy, 'Some of the aesthetic defects and more than the occasional incoherence ... can clearly be attributed to the fact that he was not entirely dishonest' either. The truest poetry is the most feigning? Peter T. Murphy's 'Fool's Gold' (ELH) is equally incisive, though it differs from Gaskill's discussion by more consistently linking economic and social analysis with the 'Ossianic phenomenon'. His conclusion, that whatever level of fraud was perpetrated, its destructive power was infinitely disproportionate, picks up one of Gaskill's points too. Certainly there is a bias towards Gaelic culture in both; both are also justified in their insistence that the casual disregard of his work which Macpherson made ironically respectable helped put the icing on the cake of ideological suppression. It is therefore doubly ironic that the minor imprint on history conventionally allowed Macpherson, his Ossianic names, is taken away from him by Torben Kisbye (Nomina, 1985). This too is a useful article so long as one sticks to the onomastics but passes quickly over the decorative linkages as, for example, his view that Ossian 'apotheosized all the new currents ... already ... closing in on Augustan literature'. Burns's reputation is perhaps less in need of rehabilitation. Even so there is a not unfamiliar hint of paranoia combined with righteous indignation in the speculation of Raymond Lamont-Brown (BurnsC) that Robert Heron's hatchet job in his Memoir of 1797 was honed by his jealousy and oiled by the hypocrisy of Henry Mackenzie. Burns was, of course, far too generous with ammunition for use against himself. The Merry Muses of Caledonia was one such hostage to fortune and G. Ross Roy (also BurnsC) does his best to sort out the tangle of mystifications and embarrassed evasions in nineteenth-century editions. Edwina Burness (SSL) has the last word if only because she brings the focus down to our century in a sensible essay on 'The Influence of Burns and Fergusson on the War Poetry of Robert Service'.

3. Drama

Three theatrical biographies have come my way. Inevitably, perhaps, Paul Sawyer's account of Christopher Rich[60] and Helene Koon's study of Colley Cibber[61] both take the form of partisan defences of their subjects. Both have unenviable historical reputations, based, according to their biographers, not so much on fact as on the effectiveness of the literary character assassinations performed on them, in the case of Cibber by Pope, and in the case of Rich by Cibber himself. Setting the record straight, Sawyer provides a thoroughly researched narrative of Rich's career, concentrating on his management of Drury Lane from 1695 to 1709, and offering a detailed account of the internal intrigues and theatrical rivalries of the period. He cannot summon up overwhelming enthusiasm for Rich himself, concluding that 'he hardly seems to have been an admirable man', but he defends him against the more libellous contemporary attacks on his reputation, and presents him as a generally shrewd businessman, whose business 'happened to be the theatre'. Helene Koon follows the course of Cibber's career, discusses his reputation as an actor, weighs the merits of his literary output and writes at some length about the peculiar virulence of the abuse that he attracted throughout his life. Her account of the cumulative political and personal animosities that shaped contemporary attacks on him, from the controversy over *The Non-Juror* to Pope's enthronement of him in *The Dunciad*, is detailed and convincing. About his own writings she reveals mixed feelings. She makes no claims for his 'wretched' and much reviled royal birthday odes, but considers why they should have attracted such extreme odium, when the equally dreadful effusions of his predecessor and successor as laureate largely escaped comment. She is warmer about parts of his dramatic output, but reserves her most favourable comments for the *Apology*, which she presents as 'perhaps the most honest portrait of an actor ever drawn'. Appendixes to the study include a list of Cibber's acting roles and a reprint of his second letter to Pope of 1743. In *CompD* Derek Hughes compares 'Cibber and Vanbrugh: Language, Place, and Social Order in *Love's Last Shift*'.

Alan Kendall's biography of Garrick[62] is an intelligently written and generously illustrated narrative aimed at the general reader. Kendall makes good use of contemporary documentary writings and prints, and allows himself time for asides on a range of topics such as the members of Garrick's circle or the architecture of the Adelphi terrace. Leigh Woods (*ThS*, 1985) discusses Garrick's theatrical roles at Ipswich in 1741.

In *A Mirror to Nature*[63] Rose A. Zimbardo traces the changing relations between art and nature envisaged in Restoration and early eighteenth-century

60. *Christopher Rich of Drury Lane: The Biography of a Theatre Manager*, by Paul Sawyer. UPA. pp. vi + 136. £14.65.

61. *Colley Cibber: A Biography*, by Helene Koon. UKen. pp. xi + 242. £22.50.

62. *David Garrick: A Biography*, by Alan Kendall. Harrap (1985). pp. 224. £12.95.

63. *A Mirror to Nature: Transformations in Drama and Aesthetics 1660–1732*, by Rose A. Zimbardo. UKen. pp. viii + 248. £22.50.

dramatic criticism and realized in contemporary plays. The bulk of the book is taken up in tracing the successive stages of a change of conception from imitation as idea to a new vocabulary of internal psychology as manifested in the late seventeenth century. The final section discusses the new basis on which eighteenth-century sentimental drama claims to be exemplary, encouraging the imitation in life of the virtuous people represented on stage. Over-mechanical construction and disconcerting movement between dramatic and critical texts suggest too readily that contemporary critical discussion can explain dramatic practice. However, the book offers full and convincing documentation and a satisfying sense of the complexity of the issues involved.

OUP have issued a revised second edition of Roger Fiske's marvellously comprehensive survey of English theatre music in the period[64]. When it first appeared in 1973 the book was deservedly lauded for its combination of scholarly erudition and readability. Fiske concentrates mainly on playhouse music, digesting a tremendous amount of information, and providing spirited critical accounts of many operas, masques, pantomimes, ballad operas, burlesques, and pastorals. He is never afraid to take a strong line: of *Arsinoe* he remarks that 'it is tragic that playhouse audiences were taken in by this nonsense', while a little later he congratulates them on realizing 'that Clayton's music in *Rosamond* was cretinous'. The text is generously supplied with illustrations and musical examples and includes a series of full and invaluable appendixes: it will remain the standard book on the subject for the forseeable future.

Wolfgang Zach's lucid and ambitious *Poetic Justice*[65] traces how the idea of 'a just apportioning of reward and punishment' gradually became axiomatic in literary theory and practice after 1660. Concentrating on English comedy from 1660 to 1780, the book's focal point is *The Beggar's Opera*, which according to Zach crystallizes the significance and decline of poetic justice as a literary doctrine. The treatment of literature after 1780 is necessarily abbreviated, but throughout three aspects of poetic justice (the religious/philosophical, the moral–didactic and the aesthetic) are scrutinized. While 'watershed' may exaggerate the significance of this rewarding piece of literary criticism, Zach at least successfully explains one aspect of comedy's ossification between 1700 and 1750, despite the occasional over-categorization. [E.A.M.] A new edition of *The Beggar's Opera* is available from Penguin: John Walker discusses Hogarth's painting of the first night of the play in *Essays in Honor of Paul Mellon*[66]. In *ELN* Michael Cohen discusses 'The Whig Sublime and James Thomson['s plays]'. In *Lessing and the Enlightenment*[67] Thomas A. Kovach discusses 'Lessing, Oliver Goldsmith, and the Tradition of Sentimental Comedy'. I have not seen Constance Clark's *Three Augustan Women Playwrights* (Lang).

64. *English Theatre Music in the Eighteenth Century*, by Roger Fiske. Second edn. OUP. pp. xvi + 684. £55.

65. *Poetic Justice: Theorie und Geschichte einer literarischen Doktrin*, by Wolfgang Zach. Niemeyer. pp. xii + 559. DM 178.

66. *Essays in Honor of Paul Mellon: Collector and Benefactor*, ed. by John Wilmerding. National Gallery of Art, Washington, D.C./UPNE. pp. xii + 427 + illus. pb $22.95.

67. *Lessing and the Enlightenment*, ed. by Alexej Ugrinsky. Greenwood. pp. vi + 188. £22.95.

Peter Davison's Casebook on Sheridan[68] contains the usual mixture of historical and modern material, in this case covering the dramatist's various careers and his critical reputation, as well as the individual plays. The critical essays are well selected and the volume includes a helpful bibliography. I have not seen Bruce Redford's *The Origins of 'The School for Scandal': 'The Slanderers' and 'Sir Peter Teazle'* (PrincetonUL). *Comedy from Shakespeare to Sheridan*[69] includes an essay by Robert Hogan on plot, character, and language in Sheridan's plays, as well as a piece by Rose Zimbardo on the reception of Shakespearean comedy in the seventeenth and eighteenth centuries. Harvester Microform have announced the availability of microfilm collections of playscripts and managerial correspondence from the period of Sheridan's proprietorship of Drury Lane[70], and of archives from the eighteenth- and nineteenth-century British Theatres Royal[71]. Elsewhere, Josette Hérou[23] discusses the place of the body in eighteenth-century comedy and Denise Bulckaen-Messina[23] considers the physical descriptions of actors in *The Rosciad*. In the journals J. M. Armistead's 'Calista and the "Equal Empire" of her "Sacred Sex"' (*SECC*) relates the treatment of Calista in *The Fair Penitent* to the social status of women, Richard C. Frushell discusses the treatment of 'Marriage and Marrying in Susanna Centlivre's Plays' (*PLL*), Richard C. Taylor comments on 'The Originality of John Caryll's *Sir Salomon*' (*CompD*), and William Burling and Robert D. Hume discuss the 'Theatrical Companies at the Little Haymarket, 1720–1737' (*EiT*).

4. Prose

ARS reprints two pamphlets of 1693 under the title *Swift, Temple and the Du Cros Affair*[72]; *See and Seem Blind*, a review of cultural events in London in 1732, possibly by Aaron Hill[73]; and *Bath-Intrigues*, probably by Eliza Haywood[74]. SF&R reprints *The History of our Own Times* (1741), attributed to Fielding[75].

68. *Sheridan: Comedies: A Casebook*, ed. by Peter Davison. Macmillan. pp. 223. hb £20, pb £6.95.

69. *Comedy from Shakespeare to Sheridan: Change and Continuity in the English and European Dramatic Tradition. Essays in Honor of Eugene M. Waith*, ed. by A. R. Braunmuller and J. C. Bulman. UDel/AUP. pp. 290. £26.50.

70. *Drury Lane under Sheridan, 1776–1812: Manuscript Plays and Managerial Correspondence from the British Library, London*. Harvester Microform. £800.

71. *The English Stage After the Restoration: Archives of the Eighteenth and Nineteenth Century British Theatres Royal from the British Library, London*. Part 1: *Additional Manuscripts*. £820; Part 2: *Egerton Manuscripts*. Harvester Microform. £950.

72. *Swift, Temple and the Du Cros Affair*. Part 1: *An Answer to a Scurrilous Pamphlet [1693]*, and, *Lettre de Monsieur du Cros a mylord * * * * [1693]*, intro. by David L. T. Woolley. ARS. CML. pp. xvii + 48 + (xxxiii). By subscription.

73. *See and Seem Blind: or, A Critical Dissertation on the Publick Diversions, etc., [1732]*, intro. by Robert D. Hume. ARS. CML. pp. xii + 30. By subscription.

74. *Bath-Intrigues: In Four Letters to a Friend in London [1725]*, intro. by Simon Varey. ARS. CML. pp. x + 51. By subscription.

75. *The History of our Own Times [1741]*, ed. by Thomas Lockwood. SF&R (1985). pp. 122. $50.

Oxford WC provides texts of *Gulliver's Travels*[76] and *A Tale of a Tub*[77]. The former adopts the text of Herbert Davis's edition and includes an introduction and full notes clearly aimed at the student. The latter reprints the contents of the 1704 volume in which the *Tale* appeared, in a modernized text, with a helpful introduction, notes, a glossary, and an appendix including extracts from works which form the literary context of the publication.

In his 'new reading' of Swift for Harvester[78] Nigel Wood announces, sometimes rather laboriously, the differences between the historical/biographical and New Critical schools of Swift interpretation, and his own deconstructive methods. Having outlined the limitations of author-based and 'coherence model' approaches, he organizes his study as 'an attempt to locate the functions that the first-person serves in the texts that bear [Swift's] name', considering in turn Dean, Bickerstaff, Gulliver, and Drapier. His openness to plural readings of the texts he considers is very welcome, and yields some worthwhile results. However his critical vocabulary sometimes seems top-heavy, and his argumentative position is not sustained with complete consistency. For example, having identified various pairs of opposite '"Characters"' that 'pulsate under the same authorial skin' in Swift's prose, he claims that 'by "decentring" the creative subject (the author), it is possible to affix the paired opposites above to rhetorical effects traversed by ideological and trans-individual discourses'. However, in his discussion, he sometimes falls back rather surprisingly into traditionalist habits of naïve extrapolation of authorial design. His account of the Irish pamphlets, for instance, is grounded in the oddly unproblematized assertion that 'Swift felt that Irish poverty was manufactured by English mercantilism'.

A new journal, *Swift Studies (SStud)*, is a haven for the kinds of criticism eschewed by Wood. It includes articles by J. A. Downie on 'Swift and the Oxford Ministry', John Irwin Fischer on the Remission of First Fruits, F. L. Harrison on Charles Coffey and Swift's '"Description of an Irish Feast"', William Kupersmith on the tone of 'Harley, the Nation's Great Support', Frank H. Ellis with 'Notes on *A Tale of a Tub*', Dirk F. Passmann on 'Degeneration in *Gulliver's Travels*', Sidney Gottlieb on 'The Emblematic Background of Swift's Flying Island' in the third voyage, and David Woolley on 'The Stemma of *Gulliver's Travels*', as well as a number of shorter notes mentioned below. A volume of the *Proceedings of the First Münster Symposium on Jonathan Swift*[79] contains a long list of articles including pieces by H. J. Real and H. J. Vienken on 'The Structure of *Gulliver's Travels*', Eric Rothstein on Part 3 of the book, Michael Treadwell on its editors, Robert Halsband on 'Eighteenth-Century Illustrations of *Gulliver's Travels*', and Heinz Kosok on German translations of it for children. Swift's reputation in eighteenth-century Germany is described by Marie-Luise Spieckermann, and Real and Vienken discuss his relation to libraries. Angus Ross writes on the

76. *Gulliver's Travels*, by Jonathan Swift, ed. by Paul Turner. OUP. pp. xli + 379. pb £1.50.

77. *'A Tale of a Tub' and Other Works*, by Jonathan Swift, ed. by Angus Ross and David Woolley. OUP. pp. xxviii + 237. pb £2.95.

78. *Swift*, by Nigel Wood. Harvester. pp. xiv + 153. hb £16.95, pb £5.95.

79. *Proceedings of the First Münster Symposium on Jonathan Swift*, ed. by H. J. Real and H. J. Vienken. Fink (1985). pp. 396.

treatment of books and reading in *A Tale of a Tub*, and Irvin Ehrenpreis considers 'The Doctrine of *A Tale of a Tub*'. Other articles are by J. N. Schmidt on 'Swift's Uses of Facts and Fiction: *The Drapier's Letters*', Frank H. Ellis on *The Examiner* and James Woolley on *The Intelligencer*, Phillip Harth on 'Swift's Self-Image as a Satirist', Clive T. Probyn on his use of parody, J. A. Downie on 'Swift's Politics', and W. A. Speck on 'Swift and the Historian'.

Elsewhere, Charles Peake[80] defines raillery as 'a mode of irony used not to satirize but to praise', and discusses the importance of the device in Swift's work. His pamphlet includes notes on the writer's Irish literary contemporaries. W. B. Piper in 'The Scope of Discourse in Berkeley and Swift' (*Lang&S*, 1985) compares Swift's ideas about discourse with those of Berkeley and Locke. Margaret Anne Doody[20] examines 'Insects, Vermin, and Horses: *Gulliver's Travels* and Virgil's *Georgics*', Christopher Fox (*ECS*) links the insistent punning on the name of Master Bates at the opening of the book with the 'narcissistic isolation' of Gulliver at the end, and sees his position as being a prototype of the position of the modern author, Ian Higgins (*N&Q*) and Dirk Passmann (*N&Q*) discuss sources for the book, Beth S. Neman (*ELN*) considers the nature of dramatic irony in Part 4, and Uwe Pauschert in '"It Should Be Only *Rationis Capax*"' (*SStud*) remarks briefly on the strength of contemporary philosophical teachings about the rationality of man, which it sets out to subvert. Passmann (*N&Q*), W. B. Carnochan (*SStud*), and Helen O'Brien (*N&Q*) comment on *A Tale of a Tub*, Leslie Moore (*ECS*) discusses the *Meditation on a Broomstick*, Margarette Smith (*PSt*) writes on *The Drapier's Letters*, Dan Doll considers the relation between 'The Word and the Thing in Swift's Prose' (*SECC*), particularly in the *Argument against Abolishing Christianity*, Timothy Keegan[20] looks at Swift's self-portraits in verse, and John Irwin Fischer (*PQ*) surveys the government's response to 'An Epistle to a Lady'. In *SStud* Real and Vienken discuss 'Swift's Knowledge of Filmer' and the contents of Stella's library; in *BJECS* his 'Verses Wrote in a Lady's Ivory Table-Book'; and in *N&Q* his distinctions between Aristotle and Homer and his treatment of infanticide in the *Modest Proposal*, which is also discussed by Ian Campbell Ross in *SStud*. In addition, the journal contains notes by C. C. Thorson on Swift and Fielding, and by J. L. Thorson on Swift and Butler. In *MLN* N. Rand remarks on the first French translations of Swift and Young.

In a study previously overlooked[81] Paula R. Backscheider traces the roots of the eighteenth-century novel in the prose writings of Bunyan, Swift, and Defoe, examining the fictional and narrative strategies that they employ and outlining the assumptions that they make about character and society, which she claims prefigure those of the later form. In *SECC* Manuel Schonhorn suggests that Defoe's political language distances him from Revolutionary and Hanoverian Whiggism, and in *PSt* J. A. Downie discusses problems of authorial intention and reader response in *The Shortest Way with the Dissenters*. *ELN* contains an article by R. Braverman on 'Locke, Defoe, and the Politics of Childhood'. In *RES* W. R. Owens and P. N. Furbank discuss the attribution to Defoe of three pamphlets on imprisonment for debt. In *ES* Owens and Furbank suggest that

80. *Jonathan Swift and the Art of Raillery*, by Charles Peake. Smythe. pp. 31. pb £3.50.

81. *A Being More Intense: A Study of the Prose Works of Bunyan, Swift, and Defoe*, by Paula R. Backscheider. AMS (1984). pp. xxi + 222. $32.50.

critical accounts of his prose are usually askew because they look for 'periodic' sentences rather than the 'improvisatory' ones that he actually writes; in *BJECS* they consider the attribution to him of pamphlets on the Dutch Alliance, and in *PBSA* they wonder 'What If Defoe Did Not Write the *History of Charles XII*?'. Also in *ES* P. N. Hartle considers the place of Charles Cotton's *Wonders of the Peake* in the *Tour*, while in *N&Q* Takau Shimada proposes 'A Possible Source for *The Consolidator*' and F. Bastian suggests that Defoe was in France in 1725.

In *PoeticaJ* Hiroyuki Ito sees the language of *The Spectator* as a transitional factor in the rise of the novel. In *BJA* Robin Dix discusses Addison's treatment of 'novelty' as an aesthetic category, while in *RLC* Thomas Lockwood notes 'An Addison Borrowing from Molière'. J. D. Alsop discusses his income from the *London Gazette* in *N&Q*, and outlines Steele's role in the reform of the journal in *PBSA*. Letters by Steele are published by Jeremy Black in *N&Q* and by P. B. J. Hyland in *Scriblerian*, and the latter also includes an article by R. D. Hume on 'Steele's Petition to the Lords Commissioners of the Treasury'. In *CLAJ* David M. Wheeler discusses John Dennis's treatment of the religious sublime: in *SVEC* Alain Bony considers Arbuthnot's *John Bull*, Aristophanes, and Tory satire. In *JHI* S. H. Daniel discusses 'Myth and Rationality in Mandeville', while E. J. Hundert approaches the writer via Hegel and Diderot, as a 'theorist of civil society'. Jeremy Black comments on Hanbury-Williams's treatment of Bolingbroke (*Scriblerian*) and on 'Bolingbroke's Attack on Pope' (*N&Q*).

The most important text to appear this year for Johnson scholars is Thomas M. Curley's edition of the Vinerian Law Lectures of 1767–1773[82], written by Sir Robert Chambers, in secret collaboration with Johnson. Curley has edited the lectures from the manuscripts drafted for George III, and presents the text in modernized form (an odd editorial decision, given the likely readership of the volumes and the uses to which they will be put). In a substantial introduction he surveys what is known of the relations between Johnson and the dilatory Chambers during the composition of the lectures, analyses the tenor of their presentation of the law, and notes the similarities and differences between the views of legal and constitutional affairs that they sustain and those expressed elsewhere by Johnson. However he does not attempt to resolve the question of how directly and to what extent Johnson was involved in the writing of the finished text. The appendixes include an extensive bibliography of sources, and indexes of cases, laws, and statutes cited.

Bertrand H. Bronson and Jean O'Meara have edited a generous selection of Johnson's comments on Shakespeare from the Yale edition of the *Works*[83]. As Bronson points out in the introduction, these comments can be read as parts of a 'running colloquy', in which they are provoked by the remarks of other editors and commentators; and the edition helpfully includes substantial extracts from the commentaries of Warburton, Theobald, and Pope, in their appropriate places before Johnson's replies.

Two critical studies trace the cumulative effects of recurrent patterns of asso-

82. *A Course of Lectures on the English Law 1767–1773*, by Sir Robert Chambers, ed. by Thomas M. Curley. 2 vols. Clarendon. Vol. I. pp. xix + 483; Vol. II. pp. xv + 445. £70 the set.

83. *Selections from Johnson on Shakespeare*, ed by Bertrand H. Bronson and Jean O'Meara. Yale. pp. xxxvii + 373. hb £35, pb £9.95.

ciation of particular words and concepts in Johnson's work. In *Samuel Johnson and the Scale of Greatness*[84] Isobel Grundy argues that although Johnson is rightly regarded as a Christian moralist, he is unusual in 'his whole complex of attitudes to greatness – in Christian moralist terms, to "worldly greatness"'. She sees his treatment of this theme summed up in 'the question "How important is this?"'. Her study moves from theme to theme rather than dwelling exhaustively on particular texts, beginning with his remarks on literal comparison, scale, and measurement, before examining the metaphorical connotations of littleness, pettiness, and greatness in his writing. The book is well informed, fluently argued, and thorough. Its thesis is generally convincing: doubts only creep in when the categories under which Johnson's dispersed remarks are collected look unduly like authorial homogenizations of recalcitrant material, in the definition of 'competition' in Chapter 6, for example. Typically, however, reservations about the procedures involved here are largely compensated for by the intelligent and complex readings of Johnson's prose offered in the rest of the chapter.

Robert DeMaria[85] presents his new study as an elaboration of Umberto Eco's claim that dictionaries can be regarded as 'disguised encyclopaedias'. He suggests that a study of the 'encyclopaedic' content of Johnson's *Dictionary* is particularly rewarding, helping to 'assimilate' the book to the rest of his work and revealing the strong legacy of humanist educative principle that informs its construction. Concentrating on terms associated with learning, he provides a detailed analysis of Johnson's use of illustrative quotations in his definitions, claiming that although his selection of these quotations is usually justifiable in philological terms alone, other factors also help to determine his choice, the most important being the contribution they can make to useful knowledge and morality. If DeMaria's initial discussion of the genre of the dictionary is rather inconclusive, his analysis of the sometimes conflicting preoccupations that inform the definitions and quotations that he examines is closely and lucidly argued.

Johnson After Two Hundred Years[86] consists largely of papers from a bicentennial conference held at Pembroke College, Oxford in 1984. It is divided into sections on Johnson's life, intellectual development, and works. In the first two sections, Robert Folkenflik surveys modern biographies of the writer; Bertram H. Davis discusses 'Johnson's 1764 Visit to [Thomas] Percy'; Frank Brady assesses his fame among his contemporaries; Paul J. Korshin considers the extant accounts of his last days; James Gray argues that he was a gifted translator from French; Martine Watson Brownley claims that, contrary to reputation, he was keenly interested in history and concerned about stylistic problems in historical narrative; and Elizabeth R. Lambert compares his writings about friendship with his actual friendship for Burke. Among the critical essays, John L. Abbott argues that the Johnsonian canon will continue to expand; William H. Epstein offers a suggestive analysis of *The Life of Mr Richard Savage*, in the

---

84. *Samuel Johnson and the Scale of Greatness*, by Isobel Grundy. LeicU. pp. viii + 278. £27.

85. *Johnson's 'Dictionary' and the Language of Learning*, by Robert DeMaria Jr. Clarendon. pp. xiii + 303. £20.

86. *Johnson After Two Hundred Years*, ed. by Paul J. Korshin. UPenn. pp. vii + 253. £33.25.

course of which he proposes that eighteenth-century biographical writing be seen as an 'individualizing tactic' in the process of secularization of 'pastoral power' described by Foucault; Brian Corman identifies a mixture of adverse judgement and appreciation of 'profane' writing in the *Lives* of Otway and Congreve; Robert DeMaria discusses 'The Theory of Language in Johnson's *Dictionary*'; Peter Seary comments on Johnson's attitudes to earlier editors of Shakespeare; Thomas M. Curley assesses the consequences of the discovery of his contribution to Chambers's law lectures; and Isobel Grundy provides an interesting analysis of the changes in his epistolary style in the course of his life, by comparing the formal sententiousness of his early letters with the 'conversational' familiarity he cultivated later. I have not seen R. L. Harp's edition of *Dr. Johnson's Critical Vocabulary: A Selection from his Dictionary* (UPA), or Magdi Wahba's *Samuel Johnson: Commemorative Lectures Delivered at Pembroke College, Oxford* (Libraire de Liban/Longman).

In *Augustan Studies*[20] Leopold Damrosch argues that 'the ultimate lesson of *Rasselas* . . . is not an aphorism or argument or doctrine, but a recognition of the radical disjuncture between fiction and truth, time and eternity', and J. D. Fleeman provides a list of publishing prospectuses and proposals with which Johnson was probably associated. In 'Johnson and Hume: Of Like Historical Minds' (*SECC*) John A. Vance argues – in terms similar to those of Brownley, above – that Johnson's historical perceptions were acute, and comparable to those of Hume. In *ECS*, A. T. McKenzie considers the treatment of the passions in *The Rambler*, and Steven Lynn argues that the style of the journal is aligned with traditional Aristotelean and Ciceronian rhetoric, but influenced by new Lockean theories of language and knowledge. In *SEL* Adam Potkay discusses the significance of the indeterminacy that he finds in Johnson's use of terms associated with succession, and Donald T. Siebert considers the place of 'low bad' words in the *Dictionary*. In *JHI* James McLaverty traces the influence of Locke in *Dictionary* definitions; in 'Samuel Johnson and Lessing's Lexicographical Work' (*NGS*, 1985) Emma Hawari compares Johnson's attitude to lexicography with that of Lessing. Elsewhere, Owen Chadwick discusses 'The Religion of Samuel Johnson' (*YULG*) and G. M. Ditchfield comments on 'Dr. Johnson and the Dissenters' (*BJRL*). James Gray (*ESC*) examines his views on the authority of authorship, Ian Donaldson (*ELH*) considers his accounts of the art of observation, G. J. Clingham (*English*) compares his epitaphs on Hogarth, and O. M. Brack Jr looks at 'Samuel Johnson and the Epitaph on a Duckling' (*BI*). Jocelyn Harris (*BJECS*) comments on his relations with Richardson; R. C. Reynolds (*CollL*) considers his remarks on Fielding; H. N. Levinson (*EA*) examines his appraisal of Swift; Irwin Primer (*YULG*) traces a source for his *Life of Pope*; D. L. Patey (*JHI*) looks again at his refutation of Berkeley; J. H. Smith (*Thought*) surveys his interest in stories of childhood; and Betty Rizzo (*Lib*) discusses the 'innocent frauds' he produced. *N&Q* includes notes by Niall Rudd on Cicero and *The Vanity of Human Wishes*, J. F. Bartolomeo on Johnson's comments on the readership of Richardson's novels, Eleanor Ty on his connection with *The Connoisseur*, C. S. Lim on his repeated quotation from *Macbeth* in the *Dictionary*, John Muirhead on the model for Polyphilus (in *Rambler* 19), and J. D. Fleeman on the identity of 'Miss Fordice'. In *ABC* Charlotte Stewart describes A. G. Rippey's Johnson collection. I have not seen *Dr. Samuel Johnson and James Boswell* (ChelseaH), edited by Harold Bloom, which includes a selection of critical essays.

Elsewhere, R. L. Chibka (*ELH*) insists that Young's *Conjectures* is a fascinating text in its own right, and not merely an indicator of the state of contemporary taste; Peter A. Tasch comments on 'The First Edition of Young's *Vindication of Providence*' (*N&Q*). Martin C. Battestin surveys 'Fielding's Contributions to the *Universal Spectator* (1736–7)' (*SP*) and reveals that he contributed to *The Craftsman*, W. J. Burling (*N&Q*) suggests that he probably wrote a letter from 'William Hint' to the *Daily Post*, Hélène Desfond[23] compares his discussion of Tyburn in the *Enquiry* with that of Mandeville, and Suzanne Dutruch[23] considers his work as a magistrate. In *PBSA* E. W. Pitcher both comments on the arbitrary signatures in Smollett's *British Magazine*, and identifies some problems in looking at *The Monthly Miscellany*. Samuel H. Woods Jr (*SECC*) outlines Goldsmith's debts to and departures from the image of the Orient developed by the *Philosophes*, and Roger Lonsdale (*RES*) discusses his involvement with *The Weekly Magazine*. Gordon Turnbull (*SEL*) writes about Boswell's personal and professional interests in the criminal biography of Margaret Caroline Rudd; M. W. Brownley (*ELN*) comments on Gibbon's techniques of historical portraiture; William H. Epstein (*ECent*) plays with the idea of 'professing' the text of his *Memoirs*; James E. Crimmins (*SVEC*) looks at John Brown's writings on politics and manners; D. W. Lindsay (*PSt*) discusses Junius and Grafton; F. S. Tray (*MR*, 1985) considers Burke's debts to Aristotle; and G. A. Wells (*BJECS*) surveys his discussion of ideas, words, and imagination in *The Sublime and Beautiful*. I have not seen *Junius and his Works* by Francesco Cordasco and Gustave Simonson, or Cordasco's *Junius: A Bibliography of the Letters of Junius* (both Junius–Vaughan). The major political writings of the 1790s – the later parts of Burke, Paine, Godwin, Wollstonecraft *et al.* – are now covered in the Romantic Prose section of *YWES* (Ch. 14).

5. The Novel

Belated mention of the useful and sensibly selective bibliography of *The Eighteenth-Century British Novel and its Background* by H. George Hahn and Carl Behm III[87] provides a coincidental parallel for our decision to remove *Rasselas* from its usual, if uneasy, place in this section and to link it with *Gulliver's Travels* under 'Prose'. That too is an unsatisfactory solution, of course. Frederick Karl coined the term 'near novels' for the two texts; Hahn and Behm use the same expedient in their final section; we have followed suit. Familiar categories are more honoured in a second general work on the novel which escaped the net last year, *Narrative Technique in the English Novel: Defoe to Austen* by Ira Konigsberg[88], who is quick to declare that his 'general thrust is traditional and practical'. Konigsberg has shrewd things to say on each of the novels to which he gives chronological attention in the pantheon of male writers, *Moll Flanders*, *Clarissa*, *Tom Jones*, *Tristram Shandy*, *Humphry Clinker*, plus the solitary female, *Pride and Prejudice*, and these will no doubt be

---

87. *The Eighteenth-Century British Novel and its Background: An Annotated Bibliography and Guide to Topics*, by H. George Hahn and Carl Behm III. Scarecrow (1985). pp. 392. $29.50.

88. *Narrative Technique in the English Novel: Defoe to Austen*, by Ira Konigsberg. Archon (1985). pp. 315. £21.90.

welcome to students of the novel more comfortable with narrative than narratology, text than intertextuality.

Yet it is precisely Hahn's notion of a gender-specific great tradition (with its token, notable female bringing up the rear) which Jane Spencer rejects in her spirited *Rise of the Woman Novelist*[89], a deliberate and consistently intelligent challenge to the omissions of Ian Watt and his followers. Her thesis, that the history of the female novel is quite as rich, and itself one of strategies to cope with male stereotypes – whether in overt protest, or subversive 'conformity', or oblique Gothic – will not be new to readers of this chapter of *YWES*, but it is unusually well argued and catholic in its scope. Spencer is particularly acute on Fanny Burney, and *Cecilia* appears in a Virago paperback this year with an introduction by Judith Simons[90] whose approach to the novel accords with that of Spencer. Kristina Straub (*ECent*) makes a third on a Burney whose 'creative energy [in Evelina] did not run to criticizing the informing assumptions of female life, but to revealing, without resolving, basic contradictions within ideology'. Jane Spencer also introduces another new Virago, Sarah Scott's *Millenium Hall*[91], while Sandra Shulman argues the case for a comparable consideration of neglected value in a Pandora reprint of Charlotte Lennox's *The Female Quixote*[92], one of the founding publications in a new series, Mothers of the Novel. That is also the title of the 'companion volume' by Dale Spender which introduces the series but was unavailable for review, as indeed was her second involvement, a reprint of Eliza Haywood's *History of Miss Betsy Thoughtless*. Perhaps the sheer numbers of the boom in books by and on female novelists has overwhelmed the publicists, for a number of other relevant items have failed to appear for review. Among them are two SF&R productions, Sarah Fielding's *The Cry* and *Masquerade Novels of Eliza Haywood*, both edited by Mary Anne Schofield. It is therefore some relief to report that I have seen two other contributions to the rewriting of the novel's history. Susan Staves in her paper on 'Restoration Plays Embedded in Eighteenth-Century Novels'[20] finds sexual and ideological tensions in the use of such intertextuality from convenient heroic and sentimental drama, if, curiously, little from the more sexually challenging comedy of the Restoration. Finally, bobbing in the wake of all this feminist enterprise, like Mrs Farrinder's husband, comes Roy Roussel with *The Conversation of the Sexes*[93]. He *does* tackle Restoration comedy, in the shape of Congreve, if only after a reading of *Fanny Hill*, back to Donne, and forward again to both *Pamela* and *Les Liaisons dangereuses*. This anti-chronological design is rhetorically justified by Roussel's argument but it also seems an appropriate correlative for the theoretical nervousness he admits throughout his attempt to read feminocentric works by male authors androgynously. Anyone who assays such a task by starting with *Fanny Hill* cannot be

89. *The Rise of the Woman Novelist*, by Jane Spencer. Blackwell. pp. 225. pb £7.95.

90. *Cecilia, or, Memoirs of an Heiress*, by Fanny Burney, intro. by Judith Simons. Virago. pp. xiii + 99. pb. £6.95.

91. *A Description of Millenium Hall ...*, by Sarah Scott, intro. by Jane Spencer. Virago. pp. xv + 207. pb £4.95.

92. *The Female Quixote, or, The Adventures of Arabella*, by Charlotte Lennox, intro. by Sandra Shulman. Pandora. pp. xv + 423. pb £4.95.

93. *The Conversation of the Sexes: Seduction and Equality in Selected Seventeenth- and Eighteenth-Century Texts*, by Roy Roussel. OUP. pp. 173. £15.

accused of ducking the challenge. Nevertheless, his sinuous and closely woven criticism can also be deflected as he ponders the fact that male appropriation of feminism may be quite as offensive as blithe chauvinism.

Still, male novelists have not been totally eclipsed this year, although even Defoe – the archetypal 'father of the novel' – is scrutinized in some refreshingly new ways, most notably by David Marshall in *The Figure of Theater: Shaftesbury, Defoe, Adam Smith, and George Eliot*[9]. His main thesis on Defoe is that whereas Richardson and Fielding embraced drama by presenting their characters as if in a play, Defoe drew forth his characters as actors of their own self-projections and as parallels to his own problems with the writing of fiction. This produces a lively contribution to the endless jar between critics on Defoe the self-aware sophisticate as opposed to Daniel the oblivious hack, particularly in Marshall's reading of *Roxana* as a metonymic portrait of the actor-artist who dreads exposure of the naked self. Robert James Merrett (*ESC*) finds another sort of model for the novels' rhetorical artistry taken from 'The Traditional and Progressive Aspects of Daniel Defoe's Ideas about Sex, Family and Marriage' dramatized (or at least animated) by dialogue form in earlier tracts such as *Religious Courtship*. Not to be outdone, Maximillian E. Novak, who has fought such a long and learned battle for Defoe the alert ironist, writes persuasively[20] on the Bangorian controversy as a contextual stimulant to Defoe's fictional explorations of the workings of conscience and on the slipperiness of 'sincerity' as a measure or justification of individual judgement. In 'Crusoe's Legacy' (*SNNTS*) Richard Braverman switches the focus of contemporaneity to the power struggle of party politics in his obviously valid if sometimes heavy-handed insistence on *Crusoe* as 'a myth legitimating the men of property ... in the events of 1688–89, vindicating their claim to power by reifying its origin'. Yet other writers on Defoe turn their attention to sources. Takau Shimada (*RES*) finds reports of Christian missionaries the origin for 'the Idols of *China* and *Japan*' in parts of *Serious Reflections of Robinson Crusoe*; and Virgil Nemoianu, in a wide-ranging essay, 'Picaresque Retreat' (*CLS*), takes *Singleton* as a particularly illuminating text for those who wish to trace the progress from Xenophon into picaresque. Two others pursue the origins of poetical snatches in the novels. Manuel Schonhorn (*N&Q*) reveals that Crusoe's one verse of poetic ecstasy (when he first feels dry ground under his feet) is a cannibalization – no pun intended – from *Jure Divino* on mankind's fall from innocence. Another piece of evidence to support Marshall's thesis about metonymy? Perhaps not, for Paul Hartle (also *N&Q*) finds Roxana's teasing couplet on the joys of single life to be not Defoe's invention – as Jane Jack postulated in the Oxford edition – but from Charles Cotton's satirical *The Joys of Marriage* published posthumously in 1689.

In the preface to *Henry Fielding*[94] Simon Varey reveals that a 'substantial portion of my manuscript, all my notes, and even some of my copies of Fielding' were stolen as he prepared the manuscript. After such a horror story one could forgive him almost anything, certainly the odd imbalance. Yet these seem to emerge not from deadline-induced desperation, rather from defensiveness about Fielding's loss of general esteem in a critical climate hostile to neoclassicism. 'Fielding indulges [a revealing verb] almost nowhere in classical

94. *Henry Fielding*, by Simon Varey. CUP. pp. 153. pb £6.95.

epic imitation' he says of *Tom Jones* as he introduces his contention that the novel's structure is 'characteristic of romance, not epic'. True in some respects, wholly misleading in others. Yet everything is here from the early dramatic burlesque to the *Journal of a Voyage to Lisbon*, and Varey does indeed achieve his declared intent, a readable introductory study for those 'who would like some orientation as they come to Henry Fielding's novels'. Sadly, the book which might have provided a different perspective on the same basic issues, James J. Lynch's *Henry Fielding and the Heliodoran Novel: Romance, Epic, and Fielding's New Province of Writing* (FDU) was unavailable for review. However, if the number and variety of items published on individual novelists is any yardstick, Varey's defensive posture is justified, for I could find only one further separate publication devoted to Fielding, a modest piece by Valerie Grosvenor Myer (*N&Q*) which posits analogical connections between Locke's use of 'square' (as a complimentary description connoting good-natured virtue) and the hypocrite who pretends to be as Square as his name. Fielding is there again (*PLL*), with Richardson, in Morris Golden's latest assemblage of contemporary materials as 'Public Context' for 'Imagining Self' in the works of both men (Golden is honest enough to admit that 'we have no way of checking' the validity of his more speculative linkages) but the elevation of *Clarissa* rises to new heights this year. *Samuel Richardson: Passion and Prudence*[95] has one essay on *Pamela* by J. W. Fisher, another piece on *Grandison* by R. T. Jones, a characteristic cameo on 'Richardson and the Bluestockings' from Pat Rogers, and a coda by Park Honan which tracks Richardson through Jane Austen; but the rest of this inevitably uneven volume is taken up by *Clarissa*. Of these shortish chapters the best is by Margaret Anne Doody on the warp and woof of eighteenth-century manufacture in the novel. This, like Rogers' contribution, combines acuteness with learning. The other new contributions, by Keiko Izubuchi, Rosemary Bechler, Lesley Barry, and Valerie Grosvenor Myer (overall editor) range briefly and unremarkably over Anne Howe, Christian dialectic, the dynamic of interpretation, and Shakespearean allusion. A reprint of Angus Wilson's critique completes the collection. Of course, the animated debate between William Warner on the one hand and the two Terrys (Castle and Eagleton) on the other, takes up a deal of the introduction by Myers and it naturally crops up from time to time in the other pieces; but the most animated recruits to the rival standards are to be found in the journals this year. Raymond F. Hilliard's '*Pamela*: Autonomy, Subordination, and the "State of Childhood"' (*SP*) extends Castle's Freudian reading of Richardson into *Pamela* as a covert polemic which predates but bears out Wollstonecraft's rejection of hierarchy and subordination; Katherine Cummings in 'Clarissa's "Life with Father"' (*L&P*) disagrees, for her Richardson 'Though explicitly critical of patriarchal abuses of power ... never questions phallocentric assumptions [and therefore] his message of ideology has tended ... to sustain sexual hierarchies'; while Katharine M. Rogers (*CL*), comparing Clarissa with *Les Liaisons dangereuses* (almost *de rigueur* these days) finds him rather of the Angels' party if a male writer whose 'radical critic-isms of social attitudes were camouflaged'. All three papers are notable more for their energetic conviction than their originality. Tassie Gwilliam's essay (*Novel*) is altogether more interesting as she explores the non-partisan inter-

95. *Samuel Richardson: Passion and Prudence*, ed. by Valerie Grosvenor Myer. Vision. pp. 184. £14.95.

pretative possibilities of metamorphosis in the novel's physical and psychological movements, and John Allen Stevenson (*SEL*) points to Richardson's refusal to contemplate a marriage *ending* to his novels as a sign that 'his most profound dismay is provoked, not by the politics of sexual differences, but by the fact of human sexuality itself'. Fighting talk indeed. At arm's length from the battle, four other commentators deal with historical influences and responses. Robert H. Tener (*ELN*) identifies Richard Holt Hutton as the author of a perceptive piece on *Clarissa* in the *Spectator*, 9 September 1865; Murray G. H. Pittock (*N&Q*) notes that Richardson not only seems to have taken the Cavalier Richard's name in vain but also to have used lines from Marvell's congratulatory 'To his Noble Friend, Mr. Richard Lovelace' in order to reverse their intent; Janet E. Aikins offers a packed and absorbing essay, 'A Plot Discover'd; Or, The Uses of *Venice Preserv'd* within *Clarissa*' (*UTQ*), which traces the text and subtext of allusions to Otway's *Venice Preserv'd* as a schema of rhetorical subtlety which educates the reader of *Clarissa* in the processes of interpretation, 'a curious interpretative struggle that is anything but indeterminate'; and Joseph F. Bartolomeo (*N&Q*) discovers what he believes a contradiction in Johnson's remarks on the same novel (though an alternative reading of these judgements as two levels of approbation seems not only possible but more sensible).

Richardson is also the subject of two studies in German. His original conception of *Pamela* (Vols. I and II) and the 1762 (duodecimo) version reveal, according to Hans-Peter Mai[96], how the inner contradictions of a 'benevolent patriarchalism' result in an 'opportunist' deployment of two strands of commentary, the 'official' and the 'alternative'. This opportunism is also revealed in a surface action which conceals the irrationality of a primarily 'reactive' heroine. Focusing on the rhetorical devices, Mai contends that the text provokes critical readers into awareness of Pamela's shortcomings, but admits that the novel's contradictions cannot be reconciled. [E.A.M.]

Dimiter Daphinoff[97] examines Richardson's narrative procedure in *Clarissa* with particular reference to its English reception 1744–54 and to popular critical notions about the author's naïvety and allegedly inadequate dramatic qualities. *Clarissa* is viewed, in its original form, as a remarkably 'open' text provoking reader-participation, but some aspects of this openness were unintended and became apparent only when *Clarissa* was on the market, so that in order to maintain authorial prerogative and textual autonomy Richardson undertook a massive steering of, and intervention in, the novel's reception. This unforeseeable 'threat', speculates Daphinoff, helped to bring about the demise of the epistolary novel in English. [E.A.M.]

The major publication on Sterne this year is the second and concluding volume of the now standard biography by Arthur H. Cash[98]. Nearly four hundred pages trace the last eight years of Yorick's life, the years of his fame, most of them spent on his European journeys. Johnson might have approved the method here, for though Cash constantly establishes a relationship between life and works, there is no hint of biographical fallacy, let alone psychoanalytic

96. *Samuel Richardsons 'Pamela': Charakter, Rhetorik und Erzählstruktur*, by Hans-Peter Mai. Steiner. pp. x + 216. pb.

97. *Samuel Richardsons 'Clarissa': Text, Rezeption und Interpretation*, by Dimiter Daphinoff. Francke. pp. 324. pb SFr 76/DM 92.

98. *Laurence Sterne: The Later Years*, by Arthur H. Cash. Methuen. pp. 390. £49.95.

speculation. Sterne himself might have approved of the book too, with its handsome typesetting, footnotes where footnotes should be, and not a blank page in sight. What emerges is a splendid portrait of an urbane man equally at ease with his orthodox theology and at aristocratic or artistic dinner-tables. Certainly the shadow of death stalked him on the long journey south, but the Sterne women were a much more unpleasant reality whenever he paused; and Sterne's God, it appears, had made Parson Adams in His own image. Even the ironic indignity which attended the snatching of his corpse by Cambridge students and its dissection by 'a dull lecturer', third-rate anatomist, and worse versifier, turned into tragi-comedy when the sleuths of the Sterne Trust hunted out his bones and reburied the remains at Coxwold in 1969. Coincidentally, a rite of passage reading of *Tristram Shandy* by Valeria Tinkler-Villani, 'The Life of Tristram: Sterne's Sacred Bawdy' (*DQR*), finds a 'Shandean trinity' in the book's three males and strains very hard to make Sterne a follower of Thomas à Kempis but she is undermined by linkages of the 'Sterne may have worked with Christian archetypes instinctively' variety. Elsewhere, Peter Steele assays a highly rhetorical extrapolation on 'performing the script' of *Tristram Shandy*[20], but Patricia Bruckmann (*AN&Q*) strikes a more appropriate chord when she points out that Widow Wadman's interest in Uncle Toby's wound has as much to do with anxieties about her first husband's sciatica and therefore her second love's longevity – interpret that as we will.

Reports on Smollett must be restricted to three notes – one by E. W. Pitcher (*N&Q*) which supports the case for Smollett as author of *The Unfortunate Lovers*, and two by Takau Shimada (*ELN* and *N&Q*) on Japanese sources for *The History and Adventures of an Atom* – because the monograph by Susan Bourgeois, *Nervous Juyces and the Feeling Heart: The Growth of Sensibility in the Novels of Tobias Smollett* (Lang), failed to arrive in time for review. Better luck attended work on the Gothicists. Two volumes of the Gothic *Miscellany*[99] were received this year, one on the canonical texts, another on 'Collateral Gothic', generously interpreted to include everything from Fielding's *A Caution against the Supernatural* to Scott's prefatory memoir on Clara Reeve. Though everything here is reprinted, these two volumes represent a handy assemblage of secondary materials, particularly since they contain a sampling from the French critics who have been so busy on the English Gothic recently. In the new Anglo-Saxon contributions this year, April London writes thoughtfully on *The Mysteries of Udolpho* (*ECLife*) as an uneasy transitional fiction between earlier eighteenth-century confidence in the commerce between reason, propriety, and property and the Romantic Will of later Gothic. Matthew Lewis commands most attention, however, none of it too flattering. George H. Haggerty (*SNNTS*) takes his lead from Eve Kosofsky Sedgwick as he finds various degrees of sublimated homosexuality in Walpole, William Beckford, and Lewis; Daniel P. Watkins (also *SNNTS*) identifies Lewis's desperation for popularity as his literary dynamic; and R. J. Schork (*Expl*) brings together obsessions with prominent bosoms, schoolboy humour, and hagiography in the 'Gothic grotesquery' of the mutilated St Agatha 'carrying double' as the backdrop to a sermon by Abbot Ambrosio. Such murky misogyny takes us back full circle to the arguments of Jane Spencer and the feminist critics.

99. *The English Gothic Novel: A Miscellany in Four Volumes*, ed. by Thomas Meade Harwell. SSELRR. USalz. Vol. II: *Texts*. pp. 353; Vol. III: *Collateral Gothic 1*. pp. 241. pb £60 (4 vols.).

The Nineteenth Century: Romantic Period

J. DRUMMOND BONE, BRYAN BURNS, and JOHN WHALE

This chapter has three sections: 1. Verse and Drama; 2. Prose Fiction; 3. Prose. section 1 is by J. Drummond Bone, section 2 by Bryan Burns, and section 3 by John Whale.

1. Verse and Drama

By far the most useful of the instant bibliographies is *MLAIB*. Other sources are as in previous years. I must again register a protest at the increasing failure of our major libraries to keep up with American publications. And I have to apologize that *Blake* and *WC* have not been available to me in time for consultation, but they will of course be included next year. The successor to *KSMB* has not yet appeared, it would seem. I begin with the more difficult to classify.

One of my favourite out-of-the-normal-run articles was David Bromwich's highly intelligent defence of Lord Francis Jeffrey in 'Romantic Poetry and the *Edinburgh* Ordinances' (*YES*). One feels that Jeffrey would have liked the slightly new-conservative tone of this article. Essentially it distinguishes the critic as the servant of a contemporary cultural dialogue from the artist's perhaps necessary iconoclasm. Jeffrey emerges too as a man concerned to hold all of culture – both what was to become the arts and the sciences – together in literature. An elegantly lucid article. Roger Simpson in *N&Q* gives us a useful reminder of the bibliographic position on Romantic epics, and a scattering of new ones. The titles alone are enough to sink a battleship.

The fall issue of *CL* is dedicated to Paul de Man. In 'Monumental De-Facement: On Paul de Man's *The Rhetoric of Romanticism*' Peggy Kamuf reminds us that de Man saw this journal as fundamental not only to the Comparative Literary project in the U.S., but that that project itself was predicated on Romantic studies. She investigates not only his own attempts to deconstruct Romanticism from idea to figure, but his process of deconstructing his own text. Jean-Pierre Mileur's thesis in 'Allegory and Irony: "The Rhetoric of Temporality" Re-examined' is that de Man's privileging of allegory in Romantic discourse works in the opposite direction from that suspected. This is itself a recognizable de Manian device. It is only proper that this re-examination of 'The Rhetoric of Temporality' should be based on the master's foundation.

Two books deal with Shakespeare and the Romantic period. Martin Greenberg's study[1] is not modern in its critical approach, and really uses

---

1. *The Hamlet Vocation of Coleridge and Wordsworth*, by Martin Greenberg. UIowa. pp. xiv + 209. $22.50.

Hamlet only as a peg on which to hang two fairly general discussions on 'the dangers of the reflective mind split apart from the effective will'. His subjects are Wordsworth and Coleridge. Jonathan Bate's study[2] is altogether more stimulating, and retains balance and poise even though clearly dealing with a subject with obsessive possibilities. There are chapters on all the major poets, and the documentation is notably helpful. This is not a naïve source study, but investigates Shakespeare as part of his new context, without however provoking us to feel that he has really disappeared as a recognizable 'something else'. It does not claim to be, perhaps one should add 'of course', an exhaustive study.

In 'Solomon and Pharaoh's Daughter: Blake's Response to Wordsworth's Prospectus to *The Recluse*' (*JEGP*) Martin Bidney has a most illuminating comparative study, slanted towards Blake, starting from the image of Solomon's temptation ('Prospectus' ll. 31–41) and Blake's 1826 annotation to it. Both poets are rewriting Milton, and Blake of course through Wordsworth in this case. Anyone interested in Romantic attitudes to the Fall and division, and to its varying scenarios for a Paradise Regained, should read this rich piece – all the better for its intertextuality (or historicism, whichever it is) being founded on a real and not too obscure connection. In *PQ* Elizabeth Davis writes on revelation in Blake's *Job*, linking the illustrations with the marginal texts, in particular the exact choice of the latter, to the 'progressive typological thrust ... [in which] Blake strategically arranges eschatological and Christocentric passages'. This to stress that the drama can be re-enacted in every reader's consciousness, somewhat in the manner of nineteenth-century evangelical commentators. I find the contexts interesting, but the analyses of the plates a little pedestrian.

Robert F. Gleckner's scholarly study *Blake and Spenser*[3] arrived too late for inclusion last year. This is an extended essay in intertextuality, and as such has to be accepted on its own terms, if at all. By which I mean it constitutes part of the texture of professional discussion, but cannot have much claim on the attention of anyone simply interested in Blake – if indeed such a naïve reader exists. This is not entirely a flippant remark, for it is characteristic of the American school in Romantic studies that the primary work is seen very easily as an entity existing solely within the discourse of the profession. I am not for a moment saying that this is 'wrong', or that it has not in the past characterized scholarship in the humanities on this side of the Atlantic. Only that at the moment the assimilation of the object of study to the discourse of study in the Romantic field seems by and large an unquestioned given in the U.S. Gleckner's is very much a case in point. Granted its own terms it seems to me to be very fecund indeed. The annotation is particularly rich in suggestion. A must for the Blake specialist. Another absolute must, and without any scruple whatsoever, is Robert Essick's catalogue of Blake works in the Huntington Collections[4], also from 1985. Beautifully produced, and very reasonably priced too (in the U.S. at least). Yet another 'must' is Jerome J. McGann's article on *Urizen* and biblical

2. *Shakespeare and the English Romantic Imagination*, by Jonathan Bate. Clarendon. pp. xiv + 276. £22.50.

3. *Blake and Spenser*, by Robert F. Gleckner. JHU (1985). pp. x + 403. $29.50.

4. *The Works of William Blake in the Huntington Collections: A Complete Catalogue*, by Robert N. Essick. Huntington (1985). pp. xviii + 256. $20.

scholarship, 'The Idea of an Indeterminate Text: Blake's Bible of Hell and Dr. Alexander Geddes', in *SIR*. The claim here is that 'Geddes' investigations licensed Blake to deal with his own works quite freely, and they gave him a model for making a parody Bible which would expose and explain the deceptive transparencies and stabilities of the received Bible of Heaven'. McGann at his best, adroitly erudite.

About Joanne Witke's analysis of Blake's *Jerusalem*[5] I am less sanguine. It sees Blake's philosophical support coming essentially from Berkeley, and from *Siris* in particular. But in this esoteric area one hesitates to commit oneself.

Lucy Newlyn[6] uses Wordsworth's and Coleridge's allusions to each other to chart the nature of their relationship and incompatibility, pointing up how this relationship was often a matter of self-definition, and certainly by no means naïvely expressed by either poet. There are interesting general issues on poetic relationship involved. The readings of the poems are close and unforced, and the book is neither strangled by its thesis nor dominated by its methodology. Another good example of the native tradition from the Clarendon Press, who had a good year in our field. I would have to say that Stephen Bygrave's study[7] of Coleridge's Romantic egotism is not as sympathetically lucid as Newlyn's, but then that is probably in the nature of its subject. Some of his formulations are striking – 'If [self] is activity, [then egotism] is the only word for the "pure" activity of the self: an intransitive noun, as it were.' Or again – 'He will detach himself from his own construction, be a spectator of his own mooted community; and yet those very acts of detachment provide us with a language antagonistic to the closure this suggests ... exemplary but not ideal....' It is, as he says in his preface, a book about concepts – rather than, I would add, about the poems around which it is structured. Worth persevering, I think.

Oddly enough, David Jasper's fine collection of essays[8] on 'the business of interpretation between two realms' in British and German Romanticism, more specifically but not wholly in Coleridge and Schleiermacher, does not come under the umbrella of Macmillan's Studies in Romanticism series, to which it would add considerable weight. It does have some of the problems associated with the publication of conference papers, but equally it avoids the problems of spinning book-length studies out of one idea. If I single out Stephen Prickett's piece on Coleridge's 'language of nature', provocative and wittily terse, and T. H. Curran's on Schleiermacher and translation, it is rather because their subjects interest me personally, than to imply criticism of other contributors, who include Ulrich Simon on utopianism, Kathleen Wheeler on Hegel and Kant in Coleridge's theory of imagination, John Beer on Coleridge's religious thought, and Werner G. Jeanrond on Schleiermacher and today's hermeneutics.

The articles I most enjoyed on Coleridge were scholarly rather than critical.

5. *William Blake's Epic: Imagination Unbound*, by Joanne Witke. CH. pp. viii + 231. £18.50.

6. *Coleridge, Wordsworth, and the Language of Allusion*, by Lucy Newlyn. Clarendon. pp. xvii + 214. £22.50.

7. *Coleridge and the Self: Romantic Egotism*, by Stephen Bygrave. Macmillan. pp. xiii + 235. £25.

8. *The Interpretation of Belief: Coleridge, Schleiermacher and Romanticism*, ed. by David Jasper. Macmillan. pp. xii + 237. £27.50.

Jonathan Bate's on '"Kubla Khan" and "At a Solemn Music"' (*ELN*) is more than a Miltonic source for 'Could I revive within me', but has considerable resonance for our reading of the poem – a fine example of compact plenitude. There is much fun to be had with debate and detective-story suspense in articles by John Beer, J. C. C. Mays, and Jonathan Wordsworth on the 'Barberry Tree', as well as two versions of the text reprinted in *RES*. It seems a shame to spoil the fun, so I shall simply warn the reader not to pass by R. E. Alton's editorial preface.... See also Newlyn's book referred to on p. 355 above. John Beer, earlier in the year in *RES* ('Coleridge, Hazlitt, and "Christabel"'), looks at an authorially annotated copy of 'Christabel', now in St John's College, Cambridge, once the property of Derwent Coleridge, to investigate not only Coleridge's paranoia at Hazlitt's 'hatred', but also the difficulties of establishing the nature, evil or otherwise, of Geraldine – perhaps for Coleridge as well as the reader. As a bonus to an interesting discussion there are two wholly 'new' lines.

There are two articles on *The Ancient Mariner* in *PEAN*. Vincent Newey analyses the relationship of gloss to text, and in that the opposition of impulse to define meaning and the energy of its indeterminacy. Some of the vocabulary of deconstruction is usefully deployed, but this is more of an exercise in reading than methodology. Bill Hughes writes on the quasi-genre of the long poem, but his article is for once too short for real penetration.

Turning to Wordsworth and *SEL* I found that, having praised this journal last year for being free of the article-upon-articles syndrome, William Galperin's piece on 'Authority and Deconstruction in Book V of *The Prelude*' is nearly half taken up with an account of the 'tradition' – broadly, the de Manian. In 'Wordsworth's Images of Language' (*PMLA*) J. Douglas Kneale suggests that there is no stable hierarchy of spoken and written in *The Prelude*, and that the instability of figures of voice and letter in nature is part of Wordsworth's conception of and interaction with nature. Nevertheless 'natural phenomenon tend to the image of the voice'. Except that it flirts with the inevitable notion that instead of narrating a life *The Prelude* narrates the problem of narration, this is not an extreme piece, and some of the close reading is illuminating. Also in *PMLA* Joseph Sitterson has a nicely judged article on 'The Genre and Place of the Intimations Ode', that is, its place at the end of the 1807 *Poems*. If the conclusions are not startling, there is nevertheless a lot of lightly handled cultural context on the way – particularly Milton and Gray. This is in the recent tradition of Neil Fraistat and Stuart Curran, and speaks well of it – as long as it is understood that it is a constitutive act of a (very) literary culture. Again on the Ode, and returning to *SEL*, Anya Taylor, in 'Religious Readings of the Immortality Ode', attacks those who, assuming that religious references are figurative, do not consider them as 'contributing to meaning'. This is an extraordinary notion, and seems to me to reflect more on her than on those she attacks. The best part of this essay is once more contextual, but I always have the feeling that I am being persuaded to swallow a recuperation of Wordsworth to a very particular ideology here, a feeling I have had before with Professor Taylor's work.

ELH has two essays with female themes. Alan J. Bewell's is a well-documented, interesting essay, though it probably goes too far, on the relationship of contemporary theories of hysteria to Wordsworth's choice of women for his poems in this period. The 'witch' figure transformed into the 'type' of the hysteric is both ill but also conceivably open to positive imaginative influence. Whether this helps us with the reading of the poems or not, it is certainly a possible matrix for various structures in their composition. *Yet* again, if this is new historicism, it is interesting. The characterization of Hartman as 'an aggressive male reader' implied in the opening of Marlon B. Ross's essay ('Naturalizing Gender: Woman's Place in Wordsworth's Ideological Landscape') does not, I fear, endear it to me. The idea of Wordsworth transforming the 'socio-historical experience of woman's subordinate position ... that culturally fabricated status ... into a natural and essential place (a transcendent idea)' in the course of his general project for transcendency, is perhaps reasonable, but this essay falls into the trap of transforming its own culturally fabricated discourse into an equally transcendent idea. It forms an interesting pair with the previous article, however, and I have to hope that my judgement is not gender-conditioned.

SIR has various Wordsworthiana. In 'Placing Poor Susan' Peter Manning traces interpretations of 'Poor Susan' as a warning to himself as a new-historicist – the warning is however more heuristic than real. In 'Shades of Milton: Wordsworth at Vallombrosa' Robin Jarvis writes interestingly on Wordsworth and Milton, starting from 'At Vallombrosa', the 'disarticulation of place-name into place and name', and the questionability therefore of continuity and survival. There are two articles on 'Tintern Abbey'. Mark Foster's '"Tintern Abbey" and Wordsworth's Scene of Writing' I find somewhat predictable in its Derridean way, though it is commendably free of an excess of jargon. Much more provocative is Richard E. Matlak's 'Classical Argument and Romantic Persuasion in "Tintern Abbey"' on the use of the classical model of argumentation in Romantic conversation poems. So long as it does not become *the* answer, there is a lot here to ponder. Finally there is Kenneth R. Johnston's judicious inquiry into Wordsworth's politics, 'Philanthropy or Treason? Wordsworth as "Active Partisan"' though he gives less space than he promises to their 'shaping influence' on the poetry. This is perhaps the moment to mention that *SIR* produced an issue in honour of Carl Woodring – and that it has taken my advice of last year of its own accord and will allow musical illustration in comparative articles.

John Turner's book on *Play and Politics* in Wordsworth[9] should have nettled my twin sensitivities to psychology and books constructed on the first-one-poem-then-the-next principle, but it handsomely failed to do so. It deals with the poetry from 1787 to 1800 and the nature of Wordsworth's developing radicalism over this time, and with the importance of the concept of play as it grew into the idea of poetry as an area of the mind where self and other play together. It is distinguished by care both for the poet's word and for its own.

Paul Hamilton on Wordsworth[10] in the Harvester New Readings series is as intelligent and balanced as I would expect. This is very moderate usage of recent critical theory, of whatever camp, and one finds it hard to understand the objections apparently raised during the course of the book's publication (see Hamilton's prefatory note). If anything the problem is one of audience – treated as a series of essays the book prompts the specialist to feel short-changed, and yet it is surely too allusive to the state of Wordsworth studies to be wholly satisfactory as an introduction. But maybe not.

9. *Wordsworth: Play and Politics: A Study of Wordsworth's Poetry, 1787–1800*, by John Turner. Macmillan. pp. xiii + 230. £25.

10. *Wordsworth*, by Paul Hamilton. Harvester. pp. xii + 159. pb £6.95.

I am not sure yet what to think of the MLA's Approaches to Teaching series, being of the school whose instinct is to feel beware of the teacher and beware twice as much of the teacher of teachers. Still, the intention is to stimulate, rather than prescribe, or worse still, provide short cuts. I think. The first part of the Wordsworth volume[11] provides check-lists of materials, and the second some thirty very short pieces on a wide variety of teaching problems - overall approaches, individual texts, and so on. These are *very* short, and come from a disparate teaching experience on both sides of the Atlantic. Perhaps useful to dip into, but not surely for through-reading.

I should like the space and time to take issue with Marjorie Levinson's *Wordsworth's Great Period Poems*[12], since it addresses four-square the great debate of last year's review, that between the historicists and the deconstructionists. In many ways its thirteen-page introduction is as good an account of the discussion in a Wordsworthian context as I have read. The readings attempt a way of bearing the burden of both methodologies - and ideologies - though the weighting is predominantly historical. Our alienation from these poems is what 'enables' our intellectual response. Try the chapter on 'Tintern Abbey' as a sample - sensitive to the word as well as the context, sensitive too to its own discourse. Until at least the concluding five paragraphs in which 'Romantic transcendence is a bit of a white elephant. One wants to find a use for it. I believe that the way we do this today ... is to refuse [it] ... until such time as we can trace its source.' Whatever one's own sensitivities, this is a study which should be read, and read carefully.

John Beer has added a short afterword to the new edition of his *Wordsworth and the Human Heart*[13], reminding the reader that he is not trying to justify Wordsworth, but to show the logic of his development.

The Byron year is the year of Volumes IV and V of Jerome J. McGann's edition, from *The Prisoner of Chillon* to *Marino Faliero* in Volume IV, and *Don Juan* complete in Volume V[14]. Of course it is possible to find fault, but the overall effect is unquestionably magisterial. I can think of two studies already published which have been prompted by these volumes; there are no doubt more, and there *will* certainly be many more. It is also the year of the one-volume selection from the new edition[15], which includes prose extracts, and immediately becomes the standard teaching text. It is a pity though that in this the resetting - done I can only imagine because of a decision to normalize some features of spelling and punctuation - has introduced a rather unseemly number of typos. McGann is also the author of the best essay - both textual and contextual - in the latest volume of that monument to extravagantly bad book design, *Shelley and his Circle*[16] - full of things as ever that one really

11. *Approaches to Teaching Wordsworth's Poetry*, ed. by Spencer Hall with Jonathan Ramsey. MLA. pp. x + 182. pb $14.50.

12. *Wordsworth's Great Period Poems: Four Essays*, by Marjorie Levinson. CUP. pp. x + 170. £22.50.

13. *Wordsworth and the Human Heart*, by John Beer. Macmillan. pp. xxii + 277. pb £9.95.

14. *Lord Byron: The Complete Poetical Works*, ed. by Jerome J. McGann. Clarendon. Vol. IV. pp. xxi + 568. £50; Vol. V. pp. xxiv + 771. £60.

15. *Byron*, ed. by Jerome J. McGann. OUP. pp. xxviii + 1081. pb £7.95.

16. *Shelley and his Circle*, Vol. VII, ed. by Donald Reiman and Doucet Devin Fischer. Pforzheimer Library series. Harvard. pp. xlvii + 1228. $90 for Vols. VII and VIII.

should know, if only one could find them. McGann is dealing with the Pforzheimer *Beppo*.

Peter Vassallo has edited a conference collection on *Byron and the Mediterranean*[17], from which I will single out David Pirie's paper on Byron and Tasso, which also uses quite a lot of Milton and Shelley to enrich our reading. Another example of pleasantly mild contextuality. I might also have mentioned essays by Susan Bassnet and Malcolm Kelsall, but for the fact that they have also appeared elsewhere, at least in large measure, for which neither of the authors nor the editor is really to blame. There are however too many misprints here.

Two worthy full-length studies: Malcolm Kelsall's on Byron's politics, and Mark Storey's on Byron's passion for the material, and its accommodation in his verse. Kelsall's shrewd book[18] has already upset those who believe in a radical Byron, where 'radical' means decidedly more radical than David Owen. Unless involved in the debate, it is hard to see from this reasonable book, which again uses historical context to illuminate the poems, but also the words of the poems to create the historical context, what all the fuss was about. Byron and his verse are placed firmly in the Whig tradition. It is difficult to see how they can be moved, but explosives are, it is known, in preparation. Storey's study[19] has not, so far as I am aware, raised the same kind of stir, but then its concerns, for all their physicality, have a more spiritual dimension. He is concerned mainly with *Childe Harold* and *Don Juan*, and with the way in which Byron's passion for the material, visible universe is transformed – though that is not quite the right word – into intellectual value. His conclusion is oddly reminiscent of Bernard Beatty's recent book on *Don Juan* (*YW* 66.351), and not just in the surface fact of its emphasis on Aurora. Two studies moving in the same direction is an encouraging sign of community.

James L. Hill, in 'Experiments in the Narrative of Consciousness' (*ELH*), gives a somewhat pedestrian account of Byron's debt to Wordsworth in *Childe Harold* Cantos 3 and 4, and of the tensions involved between the desire for the narrative poem of epic scope, and the 'new' lyric impulse. A little old-fashioned too is Leonard S. Goldberg's essay on 'Center and Circumference in Byron's *Lara*' in *SEL*, which apart from last paragraph gestures towards hermeneutic ironies, deals with images and thematic dialectics. It over-schematizes, but it *is* interesting to see *Lara* under the microscope, with serious claims being made for it at least in terms of Byron's development. The documentation however rather disturbingly reflects the conservative tendency. W. Paul Elledge, a Byron critic of distinction, has written on 'Talented Equivocation: Byron's "Fare Thee Well"' (*KSJ*), which is concerned, as he puts it, with 'the dynamics of the relationship between poet-husband and audience-wife as Byron represents them'. A lot to interest in passing, for me notably the contrast 'between the vocabulary of timelessness (forever, never ... still)' and the 'division and ending the poem commemorates'. Peter Graham writes interestingly on Venetian elements in the poetry for *ByronJ*, notably the 'is-and-yet-is-not' of the masquerade. In the same journal is a rich piece of close reading, propped on some Shakespearean intertextuality, in which Anne Barton investigates the subtle modulations of the Haidée episode, concerning herself

17. *Byron and the Mediterranean*, ed. by Peter Vassallo. UMalta. pp. vii + 102.
18. *Byron's Politics*, by Malcolm Kelsall. Harvester. pp. viii + 211. £28.50.
19. *Byron and the Eye of Appetite*, by Mark Storey. Macmillan. pp. ix + 229. £25.

particularly with silence and speech. A very good example of Anglophile straightforwardness. Walter Bernhart (*ByronJ*) writes on Byron and Austrian music informatively rather than excitingly. Eleanor Gates in *KSJ* writes on the 'Leigh Hunt, Byron, and Mary Shelley' nexus, with appropriate sallies at D. L. Moore.

Megan Boyes has written a short biography of Mary Chaworth[20], which adds richness to another Byronic corner.

Shelley has been lucky with his articles this year. There are exceptions. Douglas Thorpe's in *JEGP* only rates a mention because it is one of a group trying to rehabilitate *The Revolt of Islam*, this time by seeing it as Shelley's retreat, if that is the correct word, from history to 'an imaginative trans-formation made possible through poetry.... What endures, the poem suggests, *is* this frame, which is a synechdoche for the poem itself as container'. Where have we seen this gambit before, or rather where have we not? Much more interesting is Robert A. Brinkley's *ELN* essay 'On the Composition of "Mont Blanc": Staging a Wordsworthian Scene'. This dense little article involves not only the question of date and order of composition of the parts of 'Mont Blanc', and their relation to Shelley's experience, but asks questions about the poem's relations to earlier Romantic poems which turned 'loco-descriptive meditations into crisis lyrics'. It pushes the Wordsworthianism a little hard, perhaps, but is never less than involving. There is surely much more here yet. Deborah A. Gutschera's attempt in 'The Drama of Reenactment in Shelley's *The Revolt of Islam*' (*KSJ*) to revive *The Revolt* argues that the poem re-enacts a move from the personal to the communal, and that that re-enactment is a structural principle, a series of 'approximations', both an accumulation and a way of approaching that which cannot be directly expressed. Interesting mainly on the Preface and Dedication, and their relationship to the text of the poem. Also in *KSJ* William Crisman has a well-documented piece, 'Psychological Realism and Narrative Manner in Shelley's "Alastor" and "The Witch of Atlas"', which suggests that this journal has changed places with *SEL* and now arranges discussion of previous critics as appropriate in text or footnote. It starts from the difficulties critics have with the lines in *Alastor* on the poet's early youth, and links these to Shelley's (and one might add later Mary Shelley's) preoccupation with the importance of education, but moves from there to argue for a more 'human' reading of both this and 'The Witch of Atlas'. The readings are close and tactful. Charles Robinson prints a new Shelley to Byron letter from 1814 in *KSJ*, providing evidence of personal contact two years all but a month earlier than previous hard evidence. The content is negligible, but the circumstantial account spun by Robinson is elegant. In *ELN* Robert B. Ogle has some convincing new sources for 'Shelley's Whirlwind Imagery in *Prometheus Unbound*'.

There are two notable articles in *SIR*. Stuart M. Sperry's is a traditional thematic account of *The Cenci* in search of its 'ethical politics', but one which refuses to lose sight of the distinction between abstract moral clarity and the real effect of the play as drama, and which ends with an unusually moving account of Beatrice's failure. In 'Shelleyan Drama' Stuart Curran investigates the political context for the figure of Prometheus, and reminds us that the

20. *Queen of a Fantastic Realm: A Biography of Mary Chaworth*, by Megan Boyes. Boyes. pp. x + 117. pb £3.95.

choice of an author's sources is culturally as well as personally determined, and is therefore valuable for studies across a period, and not merely within one author or one work. As usual, Curran's learning is lightly worn, and the conclusions tactful rather than apocalyptic.

Power and Self-Consciousness in the Poetry of Shelley[21] eschews the temptations of fashionable debate, and brings knowl .dge of a variety of religious traditions to help understand the 'imaginative energies which give form to Shelley's greater poems'. Perhaps the central chapter is that on 'Wisdom and Love', seen as two axes whose polarities of power and mind, reality and humanity, respectively recur throughout Shelley's poetry. This is a modest book however, for all its attempts at schematizations, but it may fall between a variety of stools in not being quite erudite enough about its exotic sources and parallels, and not quite revealing enough in its close reading to startle. I hope not, for it is quietly worth reading.

The attempt in *Shelley's Venomed Melody*[22] to explain Shelley's 'habitual disorder' as venereal suffers from the monomania of those who believe they have found *the* answer. It is not surprising that even 'when Shelley uses illness as a metaphor for a state of mind, the starting point is likely to be some physical pain or illness of his own'; indeed it would be surprising if it were not so. But to try and label the illness at such length seems a curious business – there is a certain irony in the authors' actually apologizing for their relative inconclusiveness.

An issue of *SIR* is largely given over to articles on Keats's politics. There are essays by William Keach, David Bromwich, Paul H. Fry, and Alan J. Bewell, and a reprise of Morris Dickstein's provocative 1983 MLA paper, 'Keats and Politics'. This is a genuine forum, with interaction between the papers, and a concern too for the theoretical issues raised. It is perhaps rather sour in the face of such obvious good intentions to feel slightly disappointed in the result.

Two loosely deconstructive essays on Keats are to be found in *KSJ*. Stuart Peterfreund's 'The Truth about "Beauty" and "Truth"' is the more suggestive, though it is somewhat unnecessarily contorted. It takes up the 'Truth and Beauty' problem in a discussion with Helen Vendler and Philip Fisher. Its world is that of Saussure and Mukařrovský, but though not quoted, the absent presence is Derrida's. Milton and Shakespeare inform the letters which inform the poem. We deal with ekphrasis and the boundary of mortal and immortal. In 'Speech, Silence, and the Self-Doubting Interpreter in Keats's Poetry' Anthony John Harding recognizes a Keatsian topos in the portrayal of 'a moment of recognition', connected with either a taboo against premature speech, or some other species of aphasia. 'Figurative language may only be able to express absence, never presence.' This sentiment places the ideology, but it is a very 'soft' version of it, and in this case that is not a recommendation. It is however in the case of Nigel Wood's *PEAN* essay on what might be called the tactics of *Isabella* and *Eve of St Agnes*. He suggestively argues that various perceived 'problems' may be caused by the critical reader's insistence on Romantic

21. *Power and Self-Consciousness in the Poetry of Shelley*, by Andrew J. Welburn. Macmillan. pp. xiv + 234. £25.

22. *Shelley's Venomed Melody*, by Nora Crook and Derek Guiton. CUP. pp. xii + 273. £25.

transcendency, at the expense of being insensitive to pragmatic, local effectiveness.

Jeffrey Baker's book on the development of Keats's symbolism[23] belongs to a British rather than an American tradition in both style and method, but I am not sure how good an advocate it is for this cause. Its documentation often looks decidedly dated, and there can be an embarrassing literalism about its criticism of sound effect. I doubt that what is new here about the oxymoronic nature of Keats's symbolism is new enough to change things.

Of the 'general' books on my desk I found the debate on literary theory edited by Eaves and Fischer[24] the most enlivening. There are essays by Frye, W. J. T. Mitchell, Hillis Miller, Abrams, and Stanley Cavell, and questions and answers to boot – not to forget Miller's more extended response to Abrams. However it has to be said that the critical balance has shifted fairly dramatically since this project was conceived in 1982–3, and one misses an essay from a Simpson or a McGann. But this is a splendid read, and Abrams is magnificently tetchy. It does not much matter which side you are on as reader.

Geoffrey Harvey's study of Wordsworth and Hardy, Betjeman and Larkin[25] is somewhat overtitled, and its scope is modest to a fault. One wonders a little too at the scholarship of the undertaking. It is ungracious I know to cite particular omissions, but the absence say of Robert Rehder's study from the list of works consulted is peculiarly strange.

Desmond King-Hele has written a study of Erasmus Darwin's influence on the Romantic poets[26], arranged poet by poet, and including the less remembered, notably Eleanor Porden. This is probably best treated as a source book, but unfortunately it is not well arranged for that purpose. A slightly eccentric offering.

There is more than a need for a study of Fichte and British Romantic poetry, and for all that it has upset the Kantian philosophers, Mark Kipperman's book[27] at least identifies the need, and does, as he says, wrestle with the difficulties of finding a vocabulary in which to deal with both formal philosophy and the philosophic structures of art. The Fichtean moment is especially important for Romantic studies in the 1980s too, given its connection with the deconstructivists. If Kipperman's study is in the end disappointingly thin to both philosophers and literary critics, this is partly a measure of the difficult task he has set himself.

Two selections to close – Merryn and Raymond Williams's Methuen English Texts of John Clare's poetry and prose[28], and David Groves's of Hogg's poems and songs[29]. The first is a useful teaching selection, the second somewhat more

23. *John Keats and Symbolism*, by Jeffrey Baker. Harvester. pp. vii + 211. £25.

24. *Romanticism and Contemporary Criticism*, ed. by Morris Eaves and Michael Fischer. CornU. pp. 247. pb $8.95.

25. *The Romantic Tradition in Modern English Poetry: Rhetoric and Experience*, by Geoffrey Harvey. Macmillan. pp. xi + 134. £25.

26. *Erasmus Darwin and the Romantic Poets*, by Desmond King-Hele. Macmillan. pp. vii + 294. £27.50.

27. *Beyond Enchantment: German Idealism and English Romantic Poetry*, by Mark Kipperman. UPenn. pp. xii + 242. £23.75.

28. *John Clare: Selected Poetry and Prose*, by Merryn and Raymond Williams. Methuen. pp. viii + 252. pb £3.50.

29. *James Hogg: Selected Poems and Songs*, ed. by David Groves. SAP. pp. xxxiii + 232. £9.50.

than that, printing some unknown poems and several musical accompaniments; unfortunately the actual mechanics of the printing are less than a model. The same author has a note in *N&Q* which prints fresh from the manuscript versions of 'Robin's Awa' and 'Ode for Music', showing Hogg stressing Burns's sexuality and Byron's Scottishness, and another in the same journal with a new Ettrick Shepherd poem.

2. Prose Fiction

No major work of criticism on the Romantic novel was published in 1986, but the standard of periodical essays has been high, and the new adventurousness as to minor authors which I noted last year seems encouragingly maintained. This is particularly the case with female writers, a number of whom are receiving academic attention for the first time, and whose novels are – sometimes valuably – being reprinted after decades of oblivion.

Thomas Meade Harwell's two volumes[30] attempt a worthwhile task: to collect together, in an organized way, the best critical writing on the Gothic novel. But Harwell is quixotically fond of early, outmoded Gothicists such as Devendra Varma and Eino Railo and of lumbering scholarship of an influence-tracing kind. It is really not good enough to be served up with long excerpts from Varma's *The Gothic Flame* (*YW* 38.197), or moribund controversies as to the cross-fertilization between English and German Romanticism, when excellent books such as Robert Kiely's (1972) and David Punter's (*YW* 61.277), and some brilliant recent periodical work, are neglected. One harmful effect of this is to dilute the interest of Harwell's anthologizing, and to call into doubt the ability of his volumes to support the ambition of their concept. Another is to imbalance one's impressions, at a time when criticism of Gothic fiction is at its liveliest and most inventive. In addition, it is hard to know for whom these volumes are intended: their compendiousness and format, as well as their inclusion of essays in French and German, suggest that they are aimed at an academic audience, yet anyone professionally interested in the Gothic novel will know almost all of Harwell's choices already, and will give few thanks for their re-assembly here. On the other hand, students for whom this material might be fresh will be bemused by its bulk and the often byzantine nature of its concerns.

For years, Maria Edgeworth has unfairly seemed the authoress only of *Castle Rackrent*, so it is good to welcome, on the crest of the feminist wave, the republication of *Belinda* and *Patronage* in Pandora's Mothers of the Novel series, each with a very brief introduction by Eva Figes[31]. Isabelle Bour has a crisp short essay in *EA*, 'Une autre écriture: Les contes moraux de Maria Edgeworth', taking issue with the realist framework within which Maria Edgeworth's novels are usually discussed, and arguing instead for their acceptance as moral fables (though with distinct elements of realism as well). Much less substantially, Twila Yates Papay[32] considers *Harrington* as a Jewish novel and also as a novel of education.

30. *The English Gothic Novel: A Miscellany in Four Volumes*, ed. by Thomas Meade Harwell. SSELRR. USalz. Vol. I: *Contexts*. pp. 341; Vol. IV: *Collateral Gothic 2*. pp. 317. pb £60 (4 vols.).

31. *Belinda*, by Maria Edgeworth, intro. by Eva Figes. Pandora. pp. 434. pb £7.95. *Patronage*, by Maria Edgeworth, intro. by Eva Figes. Pandora. pp. 631. pb £8.95.

32. In *Fetter'd or Free? British Women Novelists, 1670–1815*, ed. by Mary Anne Schofield and Cecilia Macheski. OhioU. pp. xvii + 441. £38.50.

Writing on Scott this year has been rather slight, especially by comparison with the richness and variety of previous years. But Donald Sultana's book on Scott's voyage to Malta in 1831[33] is lively, interesting, and minutely researched. Sultana uses his fine knowledge both of Maltese life and history and of Scott's œuvre illuminatingly to recreate the sad circumstances of this journey in search of health and to cast light on the little-known novel, The Siege of Malta, which was its literary issue. Sultana's book has a more than antiquarian value, then: it is a genuine contribution to Scott's biography and to the understanding of his years of decline.

In SNNTS James Kerr's 'Scott's Dreams of the Past' is a sound, orthodox essay which perceives a disguised political element in The Bride of Lammermoor and treats the novel as a fantasy rather than a work of realism. In 'Historical Ambivalence in Goethe and Scott' (NGS, 1985) Alan Menhennet shows how well Scott learned the value of ambivalence from Goethe's Götz von Berlichingen, which he also translated. W. J. Overton, discussing Scott's excellence as a short-story writer in 'Scott, the Short Story and History' (SSL) and taking 'The Two Drovers' as a well-analysed example, finds that it is the rich contradictoriness of Scott's approach and feelings which mainly contributes to his success in this genre. Louise Z. Smith's 'Dialectic, Rhetoric, and Anthropology in Scott's Waverley' (SSL) takes Waverley as demonstrating Scott's invention of the historical novel, and interestingly shows how this new form combines dialectics and anthropological historicism with other, more familiar elements drawn from the established repertoire of eighteenth-century fiction. In the same periodical, Graham Tulloch tidily charts the way in which 'Imagery in "The Highland Widow"' seems to resist easy harmonization with other elements of the fiction, and thus forbids any too easy view of the theme of the relationship of past and present with which the story is concerned. Joseph Valente's sophisticated study, 'Upon the Braes: History and Hermeneutics in Waverley' (SIR), proceeds, by way of excellent analyses of Flora and Rose in Waverley, to investigate the ambiguous concept of 'the border' underlying the apparently neat patterns of Scott's fiction. In SP Daniel Whitmore's 'Bibliolatry and the Rule of the Word' lucidly points to Scott's unease with literalism in his fiction and shows how antagonistically this life-denying 'bibliolatry' is viewed in Old Mortality.

Work on Jane Austen has been lively and prolific this year, though more in the journals than in full-length books. However, Jane Austen's witty and charming juvenilia, which often point suggestively towards the qualities of her mature fiction, have been collected, together with those of Charlotte Brontë, and well edited by Frances Beer[34].

J. David Grey has edited an extremely thorough and well-executed handbook[35] which offers short essays, written by experts, on a wide variety of Jane Austen topics that might be of interest both to general readers and to specialists. Some of these essays are concerned with matters of fact, such as the details of Jane Austen's life or the publication of her books, or with the gardens and

---

33. The Journey of Sir Walter Scott to Malta, by Donald Sultana. Sutton. pp. xvi + 190. £17.95.

34. The Juvenilia of Jane Austen and Charlotte Brontë, ed. by Frances Beer. Penguin. pp. 389. pb £2.95.

35. The Jane Austen Handbook, ed. by J. David Grey. Athlone. pp. 511. £25.

houses around which they often revolve. Even the most apparently descriptive of these pieces usually has some interpretative point as well. There are also articles assessing questions of scholarship or controversy such as the excellent account of Jane Austen and Romanticism by Susan Morgan. Finally, there are studies of a more purely critical kind, such as John Bayley's on Jane Austen's characterization and David Lodge's on the form and structure of her books; both of these are first-class. In general, everyone will find something new and stimulating in this handbook, which is also commendably well written.

Maggie Lane's is not a scholarly book[36], but an interesting, very nicely produced, and accurate survey of the various towns and country houses which Jane Austen knew, with some indications as to how this familiarity was put to use in the novels. The illustrations are excellent, and there are many new and pleasing quotations from works of the time. The book can be highly recommended both to Jane Austen enthusiasts and to the curious general reader.

Tony Tanner has written brilliantly about Jane Austen in the past, so that any work of his about the novelist must raise high expectations. Unfortunately, these expectations are not quite fulfilled. Tanner's book[37] collects together, in amended form, his well-known introductions to the Penguin editions of *Sense and Sensibility*, *Pride and Prejudice*, and *Mansfield Park*, and adds to them accounts of the other novels writte. at a much later date. From the start, therefore, the work lacks cohesion, and this problem is compounded by Tanner's habit of interpolating brief, highly suggestive references (to Foucault, among many others) which he then does nothing to develop or integrate. But, these caveats entered, the compensations are many. Tanner is one of the subtlest readers of Jane Austen that we possess, and although some of his early perceptions have now passed into common currency, he can still startle and refresh. His interpretation of the novels is generally in terms of their engagement with the difficulties of communication, and he gives an exceptionally fine reading of *Pride and Prejudice*, *Mansfield Park* (seen in the light of the notion of 'guardianship'), and *Emma*. He is much less interesting on *Northanger Abbey* and his account of *Sense and Sensibility* is too convoluted. But he writes well on *Persuasion*, and his account of the scepticism, disillusion, and modernity of *Sanditon* is by far the best that we have. With only a little more effort, this book might have been outstanding; even as it is, no serious student of Jane Austen will be able to pass it by.

Although not quite assured, Michael Williams's book[38] is one of the most helpful studies of Jane Austen's novels to have appeared in recent years. Its central insight is that Jane Austen is much more of a piece with her Romantic period than is often realized, and that this shows itself in the instability and perceptual precariousness of her work. This notion is now fashionable, but Williams gives lucid and substantial analyses of the techniques of the fiction to back up his views. However, while he is adroit in revealing the unease that lies behind the apparent certainty in Jane Austen's writing, and successful in indicating the ways in which she skilfully handles the problem of expression her dilemma poses, Williams does not really explain the roots of Jane Austen's

36. *Jane Austen's England*, by Maggie Lane. Hale. pp. 224. £12.95.

37. *Jane Austen*, by Tony Tanner. Macmillan. pp. 291. £20.

38. *Jane Austen: Six Novels and their Methods*, by Michael Williams. Macmillan. pp. 214. £25.

difficulty, nor situate it in a larger framework. But his account of individual books is acute. There are excellent accounts of the complexity and shiftingness of *Pride and Prejudice* and *Mansfield Park*, but Williams is at his best on *Emma*, where he shows the readers themselves to be implicated in, and put at risk by, the relations between imagination and judgement with which the book is concerned.

In 'New Light Thrown on Jane Austen's Refusal of Harris Bigg-Wither' (*Persuasions*) Joan Austen-Leigh prints an illuminating letter from Caroline Austen to her niece Emma Austen-Leigh, adducing Harris Bigg-Wither's plainness and awkwardness as reasons why Jane Austen could not go through with her proposed marriage to him. In the same periodical, Donald Greene's 'The Curtain Lifts' shows that Jane Austen, as he has suspected, did spend five weeks at Hamstall Ridware, in Staffordshire, in 1806.

In *MLQ* (1984) Lance Bertelsen has a well-researched essay entitled 'Jane Austen's Miniatures: Painting, Drawing and the Novels' on Jane Austen's characterization and its relationship to the conventions of pictorial representation in her day and finds in both a combination of high 'finish' with essential indeterminacy. Patricia Beer is much slighter[39], but points out usefully the ways in which Jane Austen employs indirection and euphemism to convey notions that she cannot frankly express. In *Persuasions* Christine Gibbs's 'Absent Fathers' is a too descriptive and biographical study of the provocative topic of the absent or inadequate fathers in Jane Austen's novels. In 'Jane Austen and the *Athenaeum*' (*Persuasions*) David Groves discusses a fine critical article on Jane Austen which appeared anonymously in the *Athenaeum* in the summer of 1831 and which particularly values the realism and unity of her fiction. Linda C. Hunt[32] considers Jane Austen rather conventionally in the context of other writers about womanhood, and finds in the first three of her novels a portrayal of defiantly unconventional heroines and in the latter three a grappling with the reconciliation of 'the feminine ideal' with a commitment to realism in literature. Gary Kelly[32] gives a rather stolid general survey of Romantic fiction and presents Jane Austen, perhaps too narrowly, as a conservative writer drawing largely upon the anti-Jacobin elements in the fiction of her time; however, his insistence on the serious political concern of her novels is undoubtedly valuable.

James Heldman asks 'Where Is Jane Austen in *The Watsons*?' (*Persuasions*). He goes on to give an interesting account of Jane Austen's only minimal presence in *The Watsons* as narrator and commentator, and suggests that the reason why the work remains unfinished is because of the dangerously revealing affinity between Emma Watson and her creator. In the same periodical Juliet McMaster has an easygoing essay ('"God Gave Us Our Relations"') on the richness and sophistication of Jane Austen's sense of the family in *The Watsons*, and more generally on the use of family life in her novels. Again in *Persuasions*, 'The Watsons as Pretext' by Joseph Wiesenfarth argues that *The Watsons* remains a fragment because almost everything in it could be better used or developed in Jane Austen's other books.

Only Patricia Meyer Spacks has anything on *Sense and Sensibility* this year[32]. She thoughtfully considers the use of the sisters in this novel, as well as in the

---

39. In *Fair of Speech: The Uses of Euphemism*, ed. by D. J. Enright. OUP (1985). pp. vi + 222. £15.95.

work of earlier writers, and shows how Jane Austen not only achieves greater density and realism, but is alone able freshly to present and investigate ambivalences and contrarieties in the sisterly relationship.

Nicely and briefly, Juliet McMaster (*Persuasions*) points out how Jane Austen uses Lady Catherine's weak grammar, in *Pride and Prejudice*, both to characterize and to place this character. Also in *Persuasions*, Kenneth L. Moler's '"Truth Universally Acknowledged"' shows how ironic is Jane Austen's comic use of the language of eighteenth-century philosophical discourse in the first sentence of the same novel. In 'Characterization and Comment in *Pride and Prejudice*' Anne Waldron Neumann (*Style*) gives a highly systematic and analytical account of Jane Austen's subtle use of free indirect discourse in *Pride and Prejudice* both to indicate authorial co-operation (as, often, in the case of Elizabeth) and also satirically to indicate authorial non-co-operation (as in the case of presumptuous minor characters). Stein Haugom Olsen[40], through a rigorous, old-fashioned study of the language of *Pride and Prejudice*, comes to interpret the novel as a moral work successfully dedicated to the fictional reconciliation of apparently antithetical personal and social values.

Katrin R. Burlin[32] learnedly investigates the way Jane Austen, especially in *Mansfield Park*, uses the 'Choice of Hercules' topos to help formulate her own moral and generic choice of Comedy as against 'guilt and misery'. In 'Closure in *Mansfield Park* and the Sanctity of the Family' (*PQ*) David Kaufmann examines the ending of the novel, and also its handling of generations, to show how Jane Austen sets family relationships and duties in some ways against those involved in contractual links such as marriage, and insists on the hegemony of the former over the latter. Joseph Litvak develops a subtle and substantial study in 'The Infection of Acting: Theatricals and Theatricality in *Mansfield Park*' (*ELH*), interpreting the book convincingly as a conservative work, but more uneasy and contradictory, and more responsive to progressive pressures, than has often been supposed. In *PLL* Kate Beaird Meyers considers 'Jane Austen's Use of Literary Allusion in the Sotherton Episode of *Mansfield Park*', discussing the iron gate at Sotherton, rather forcedly, as alluding not just to Sterne, but also to the Bible and Milton. James Thompson has an acute and historically well-grounded essay, 'Jane Austen and the Limits of Language' (*JEGP*), in which he traces the notion of the inexpressible through to the novels of Jane Austen, especially to *Mansfield Park*, in which he finds 'a full human presence beyond the limits of language'.

In 'Austen's *Emma*' (*Expl*) Richard Creese has a tidy short piece on Jane Austen's control of our moral responses in *Emma* by her modulation of the distance between her characters' thoughts and her narrator. J. M. Q. Davies's '*Emma* as Charade and the Education of the Reader' (*PQ*) gives a rather modish and over-extended account of the various riddling elements in *Emma* as hints that we should beware the dangers of trusting to appearances in the novel as a whole. In 'Female Family Romances and the "Old Dream of Symmetry"' (*L&P*) Marianne Hirsch, using Freudianism as a tool, considers *Emma* as an instance of a specifically female 'family romance', and finds that the feminist quality of such a romance remains bound by 'a fundamentally male economy of

40. In *The Nineteenth-Century British Novel*, ed. by Jeremy Hawthorn. Arnold pp. vii + 175. pb £9.95.

desire in which woman is other but cannot be different'. Finally, Irene Taylor[32] has a brief treatment of *Sanditon* as a work of cultural change, bravely paradigmatic of the upheavals that Jane Austen's society was facing.

James Mulvihill, in 'A Tookean Presence in Peacock's *Melincourt*' (*ES*), presents a good case for arguing that the character of Mr Sarcastic owes a good deal to the eccentric John Horne Tooke, with whose work Peacock was well acquainted. In *N&Q* Roger Simpson, similarly, shows that Joseph Ritson's *The Life of King Arthur* was probably 'A Source for Peacock's *The Misfortunes of Elphin*', notably the Melvas episode.

David Groves has been prolific this year. In 'Stepping Back to an Early Age' (*SSL*) he gives a very thorough account of Hogg's *The Three Perils of Woman*, paying particular attention to its derivation from the *Ion* of Euripides and the contrasts between true and false belief around which it is organized. In *N&Q* he has two notes. 'James Hogg: Verses for Burns and Byron' prints two celebratory poems by Hogg, on Burns and Byron respectively, and indicates the numerous changes and bowdlerizations introduced into them by the printers. '"A Vision" by James Hogg' reproduces a pleasing poem by Hogg, not printed again since its original appearance in the *Family Magazine*.

In a rather populist work[41], Ray Hammond treats *Frankenstein* as a harbinger of some of the great controversies of the present day, especially those aroused by the idea of creating new life, or materially interfering with the genetic makeup of the individual. Hammond's approach has the advantage that it properly points to the acumen and gravity of Mary Shelley's awareness of the implications of her story, but in general his book will appeal more to the general reader than to the student of literature.

Samuel Holmes Vasbinder's slight but provocative brief monograph on *Frankenstein*[42] is rather poorly written and organized, but makes points which I have not seen elsewhere. Vasbinder usefully surveys the criticism of the novel, and shows that in general its scientific quality has been neglected in the interests of its treatment as a moral fable. In addition, when he studies the novel, Vasbinder does not find that magical and alchemical elements play nearly as large a role as is often supposed. Instead, with a wealth of documentation, he uncovers many echoes and allusions which prove that Mary Shelley was in fact deliberately making use of the established science of her day in the creation of her monster.

William Veeder's book[43] is meticulous and substantial, but suffers from a certain relentlessness in its eager analysis of the rich biographical and psychosexual circumstances from which *Frankenstein* derived its impetus. Veeder examines the novel in the light of the androgynous model which both Mary Shelley and her husband looked on as the ideal, and reads it thoughtfully as a study in 'psychic bifurcation', pointing particularly to its unease as to the Father and its concern over the uncontrollable nature of male power. This is the most interesting part of Veeder's book, though it is not as new as he seems to

41. *The Modern Frankenstein: Fiction Becomes Fact*, by Ray Hammond. Blandford. pp. 192. £9.95.

42. *Scientific Attitudes in Mary Shelley's 'Frankenstein'*, by Samuel Holmes Vasbinder. UMIRes (1984). pp. 110. £29.60.

43. *Mary Shelley and Frankenstein: The Fate of Androgyny*, by William Veeder. UChic. pp. 277. £22.50.

think. Problems come, however, with the close keying of *Frankenstein* to the lives of Mary and Shelley; this is unconvincingly minute and, although Veeder has a real mastery of his material (revealed to the full in lengthy notes), soon acquires an air of special pleading. In general, then, this is a work of real perception, but one which has outgrown its strength.

In 'Narratives of Seduction and the Seductions of Narrative' (*ELH*) Beth Newman has an elegant and sophisticated essay on the use of framing in *Frankenstein*, and points out the teasing way in which frames do not produce harmony or unity, but instead enclose an irresolvable disjunctiveness from which much of the novel's power is derived. Veeder's psychoanalytical essay on 'The Negative Oedipus: Father, *Frankenstein*, and the Shelleys' in *CritI* is drawn from his book. In 'Hume and Mary Shelley' David Womersley (*N&Q*) argues that the phrase 'as a true history' in *Frankenstein* was taken by Mary Shelley from Hume's *Treatise of Human Nature*.

At last Percy Bysshe Shelley's adolescent Gothic tales, *Zastrozzi* and *St Irvyne* have been republished in the World's Classics[44], with an especially good introduction, emphasizing the author's youthful seriousness of purpose, by Stephen C. Behrendt.

Kathleen Fowler's 'Hieroglyphics in Fire' (*SIR*) is a highly interesting essay which, while it accepts and carefully details the unifying elements in C. R. Maturin's *Melmoth the Wanderer*, also finds the novel deliberately dislocated so as teasingly to resist and question our desire to make complete sense of it.

The most obscure lady novelists of the Romantic period are now being exhumed, and may hope for new readers after long years of neglect. So Susan Ferrier's *Marriage*[45], well introduced by Rosemary Ashton, Lady Morgan's *The Wild Irish Girl*[46], and Mrs Opie's *Adeline Mowbray*[47] are finally retrieved from the tiny niches they have hitherto occupied in literary history. And an even less-known figure, Mary Brunton, is the subject of a useful essay by Sarah W. R. Smith[32] which shows Brunton's commitment to realism and the assured independence of her heroines, and generally casts her in a quietly feminist light.

3. Prose

'Romantic prose' is still significantly defined by limiting notions of literariness and it has not altogether disengaged itself from the idea of the familiar essayist. Work in the field this year ranges from traditional estimates of essayists to analyses of ideological formations in the prose. This range is especially apparent since a majority of work focuses on the related topics of audience, the reader, the public, and popularization.

In his brief and professedly modest study of Romantic prose John R.

44. *'Zastrozzi' and 'St Irvyne'*, by Percy Bysshe Shelley, ed. by Stephen C. Behrendt. OUP. pp. xxxi + 206. pb £2.95.

45. *Marriage*, by Susan Ferrier, intro. by Rosemary Ashton. Virago. pp. xvi + 513. pb £4.50.

46. *The Wild Irish Girl*, by Lady Morgan, intro. by Brigid Brophy. Pandora. pp. xi + 255. pb £4.95.

47. *Adeline Mowbray*, by Mrs Opie, intro. by Jeanette Winterson. Pandora. pp. viii + 275. pb £4.95.

Nabholtz[48] concentrates on the creative use of the reader made by Lamb, Hazlitt, Wordsworth, and Coleridge. His most interesting argument, which is underplayed and understated, is that these various writers and their texts share an assumption about the poetic creativity of their different projected readers. Such 'genial criticism', he argues, finds its 'authenticity in the same inner source as the artistic products [it] describes, the creative capacity of the artist-reader'. As a result of such 'cooperating power' (a phrase he borrows from Coleridge) such works 'challenge the conventional separations between author and text and reader, between paraphrasable argument and affective experience, and – perhaps most significantly – between prose criticism and the artistic process itself'. He offers a detailed account of how Lamb liberates the reader from the confines of a utilitarian viewpoint and involves her/him in the fullness of imaginative vision and supplies an interesting explanation of Hazlitt's use of poetic quotation. In both these chapters he gives a traditional impression of the essayists by focusing on articles which are well known for their familiar geniality. The chapters on Wordsworth and Coleridge deal with the more expressly political material of the *Cintra* pamphlet, *Consciones ad Populem*, and *The Friend* (as well as the Preface to the *Lyrical Ballads*), but even here there is a lack of informing context. At its best Nabholtz's book offers sympathetic and suggestive readings of passages taken from a very selective range of texts and authors.

After a flood of recent publications work on De Quincey is restricted to two related but distinct articles. Both Jonathan Wordsworth and Robert Lance Snyder in their different ways explore the meaning and function of De Quincey's 'Dark Interpreter'. In 'De Quincey's Literature of Power: A Mythic Paradigm' (*SEL*) Snyder sets out to prove the coherence of De Quincey's aesthetic by linking the famous distinction between the literature of knowledge and the literature of power with the 'Dark Interpreter' of *Suspiria de Profundis*. Faced with loss, fall, and incoherence De Quincey attains the knowledge and position of an alternative subjectivity to be found in the act of writing. Out of disconnection comes unity and a revealed identity through 'the hermeneutics of art'. Indeed, Snyder goes as far as to suggest that this attempt to reclaim the Dark Interpreter 'as his own self-projection' 'governs the narrative strategy of all his major imaginative works'. Jonathan Wordsworth in 'Two Dark Interpreters: Wordsworth and De Quincey' (*WC*) approaches the subject of De Quincey's attainment of the power of vision out of sin and loss through more obvious and traditional territory. According to his less sophisticated argument, salvation or solution comes about through acceptance of God's awful power, rather than through purely textual representation and organization. 'The chief problem for the reader in the *Suspiria*', Wordsworth claims, 'is to see how De Quincey's perception of suffering reconciles the Interpreter's association with both the darkness as horror, and darkness as wisdom.' The article draws freely on analogies with Wordsworth and *Paradise Lost* in terms of innocence and fall, and distinguishes De Quincey from the poet by drawing attention to his apocalyptic and prophetic vision.

A backward glance at the achievements of recent Hazlitt criticism can be

---

48. *'My Reader My Fellow-Labourer': A Study of English Romantic Prose*, by John R. Nabholtz. UMiss. pp. ix + 134. $22.

obtained with the publication of *William Hazlitt*[49] which reprints in chronological order articles from Stuart M. Tave to David Bromwich. Harold Bloom's introduction is extremely contentious as he invests heavily in Hazlitt's empiricism at the expense of modern critical theory. Hazlitt criticism is clearly as fraught with a clash between literary and political power as the essayist's own work. In 'Hazlitt on Burke: The Ambivalent Position of a Radical Essayist' (*SIR*) John Whale explores this conflict by examining in detail Hazlitt's appreciation of Burke. 'Under pressure of political argument,' he claims, Hazlitt's 'notion of imagination is subject to a severe inquiry.' John Barrell[50] comes to Hazlitt only at the end of an impressive study of the relationship between the discourse of civic humanism and the theory of painting, but his chapter on Haydon and Hazlitt is richly suggestive. Barrell argues powerfully and intensively that his chosen discourse breaks down from within faced with an antithetical idea of commerce. Though Haydon maintains a strand of it well into the nineteenth century with his valiant efforts in the genre of history painting, even he has problems accommodating his ideas on genius. Rather than representing a problem from within, like Fuseli and Haydon, Hazlitt's challenge is external. He is credited with launching 'the first fundamental attack on the civic humanist theory of art' in his *Encyclopaedia Britannica* article 'Fine Arts'. Hazlitt is taken to task for his obvious elitism – his 'aristocracy of taste', but despite this attack and the specialist limits within which it works, the chapter opens up a number of interesting topics for the whole of Hazlitt's work – in particular his ideas on 'character', 'taste', and 'public opinion'.

Work on Lamb is mainly restricted to *ChLB* where J. R. Watson considers Lamb on food in relation to character, moral philosophy, religious behaviour, anthropology, poverty, and community; John Beer explores the extent to which Lamb understood Coleridge; and, most noteworthy, Kathryn Sutherland in 'The Coming of Age of the Man of Sentiment' compares the way in which Dickens and Lamb use sentiment by looking at the essays of Elia and *The Old Curiosity Shop*. At the same time as considering Lamb's transitional position she assesses the reaction of both writers to realism and the morality of their interest in the city and the crowd, before concluding that 'style is a feeling response to the instability of the crowd; in each case, it is a further variation on the notorious instability of the eighteenth-century ethic'. David Simpson's 'What Bothered Charles Lamb About Poor Susan?' (*SEL*) uses the essayist's misgivings about the last verse of Wordsworth's poem as a springboard for a fascinating article which not only provides it with a disturbing context, but at the same time raises important issues about acceptance of the canon and the relationship of sociological and historical knowledge to the practice of criticism.

Two significant scholarly articles carefully redefine relationships between Romantic essayists and poets. In 'Leigh Hunt, Lord Byron and Mary Shelley: The Long Goodbye' (*KSJ*) Eleanor M. Gates points to the inability of Leigh Hunt's twentieth-century scholars to appreciate *Lord Byron and Some of his*

---

49. *William Hazlitt*, ed. by Harold Bloom. ChelseaH. pp. viii + 184. $19.95.

50. *The Political Theory of Painting from Reynolds to Hazlitt: 'The Body of the Public'*, by John Barrell. Yale. pp. xi + 366. £16.95.

Contemporaries because they are blinded by the supposed immorality of his financial difficulties. Drawing on a number of letters Gates joins forces with Hunt enthusiasts to conclude that he was, despite pecuniary embarrassments, 'a man of undoubted honesty' and that, contrary to some scholarly opinion, Mary Shelley 'maintained a high regard' for him even in the years after their Italian sojourn. John Beer's 'Coleridge, Hazlitt, and "Christabel"' (*RES*) focuses on a much more interesting difficulty in literary relationships. Starting from the poet's annotations on Derwent Coleridge's copy of *Christabel*, he moves through a complex tangle of material (ranging from personal abuse to genuine misunderstanding between the two men) involving sexuality and 'the ambiguity of Geraldine's daemonic powers'.

The 'Literary Periodicals Special Number' of *YES* contains two valuable essays on the relatively neglected pages of the *Edinburgh Review* and *Blackwood's Magazine*. In an eclectic and sometimes oblique article entitled 'Romantic Poetry and the *Edinburgh* Ordinances' David Bromwich qualifies Bagehot's dismissive summary of Jeffrey's life as amounting to no more than a shrewd, practical wisdom. By analysing the complex interrelationship between Jeffrey's own ideas and those of his reviewers (including Hazlitt) on contentious topics such as the poetry of Byron, Shelley, and Keats, Bromwich presents a case for the *Edinburgh*'s and consequently for Jeffrey's common-sense liberalism. By revealing the intricacy of such relationships (which accounts in part for the complex progression of his own argument), Bromwich is able to claim that: 'the possibilities of debate that the *Edinburgh* opened up were more generous than its style on any occasion. Jeffrey's opinions, in particular, are apt to *sound* exclusive: sampled in quantity they display a surprising liberality of taste.' His role as a popularizer – someone in the position to make 'imperceptible infusions' into 'the daily intercourse of society' (to use Jeffrey's own words) can thus be revalued. 'Literary Criticism and the Later "Noctes Ambrosianae"' form the subject of J. H. Alexander's astute contribution. He argues for some originality in John Wilson's commentaries on imagination, explores the Shepherd as one of the most attractive features of the *Noctes*, and assesses the pervasive influence of Wordsworth over the whole series. Though there is a pioneering spirit in evidence here and a justification for further exploration – 'There is a strong place for a purely aesthetic study of the "Noctes" form' – his interest is always wisely tempered: he admits to the unpalatable aspects of the *Noctes* and qualifies his respect for Wilson's achievement by reminding us that he worked in one of the 'dullest decades in British literary history'.

Mark Philp[51] defends the consistency of Godwin's thinking in the different versions of *Political Justice*. This, he claims, is to be found in a fundamental belief in the right to private judgement. He is at pains to stress Godwin's debt to the tradition of Dissent and later to the 'sociable community' he frequented in the 1790s. Worthy in its endeavour to rescue Godwin from being misread as an extreme rationalist and in its attempt to account for the apparent absurdity of his philosophy in the eyes of the modern reader, Philp's study unfortunately suffers from repetition and a rather dogged progression of its argument.

There is also only one piece of work on Wollstonecraft's prose, but it is

---

51. *Godwin's Political Justice*, by Mark Philp. Duckworth. pp. x + 278. £28.

fascinating. Wollstonecraft provides not only the subject of a chapter of Cora Kaplan's *Sea Changes*[52], but figures as an integral part of her argument. *A Vindication* is, Kaplan argues, symptomatic of left-wing feminist thought in its rationalism and rejection of sexual pleasure. The abiding significance of Wollstonecraft's example is to be found in the claim that 'Female sexuality is still the suppressed text of those liberal and left programmes that are silent on the issue of women's subordination'. Kaplan's large-scale thesis is a fascinating and colourful attempt to suggest a politically and sexually enabling reading of fantasy in conjunction with psychoanalytical theory. Kaplan is particularly good on the reaction against feeling, arguing that it is 'seen as reactionary and regressive, almost counter-revolutionary', and on Wollstonecraft's puritanical suppression of pleasure. With characteristic energy she claims that 'woman's reason may be the psychic heroine of *A Vindication*, but its gothic villain, a polymorphous perverse sexuality, creeping out of every paragraph and worming its way into every warm corner of the text, seems in the end to win out'. Side by side with such raciness and freedom is a sound attention to the class basis of Wollstonecraft's writing and its projection to a specific audience.

Two articles on Burke suggest that he can reward the rhetorical critic as much as the traditional historian. Regina Janes's 'In Florid Impotence He Spoke: Edmund Burke and the Nawab of Arcot' (*SECC*) is clearly fascinated by the imagery of Burke's rhetorical prose in his *Speech on the Nawab of Arcot's Debts*. She explores the relationship between such images and political power, concluding that in this neglected speech it is their peculiar separation which is important: 'the vehemence of Burke's imagery erupts from the certainty that there was nothing to be done'. In contrast, James Conniff in 'Edmund Burke's Reflections on the Coming Revolution in Ireland' (*JHI*) is content to deal in the explicit content of Burke's thinking. He challenges the assumption that Burke is 'an unregenerate defender of political reaction' by arguing straightforwardly for the consistently reformist nature of his position on Irish politics.

The year's only two items on Cobbett prove that his prose is more resistant to explication. Roger Sale[53] admits to the peculiar combination of radical and reactionary in Cobbett before concentrating on the relationship between particular observation and general statement in *Rural Rides*. His view of Cobbett is ultimately sentimental and historically vague. In 'William Cobbett: Radical, Reactionary and Poor Man's Grammarian' (*Neophil*) F. G. A. M. Aarts feels the same need to present a supposedly unknown Cobbett to his audience before offering a thorough documentary discussion of Cobbett's work on grammar. Such an introductory piece has much less to offer than would an answer to his own plea that the *Grammar* 'deserves far more attention than it has hitherto received'. Unfortunately, Cobbett studies clearly have some way to go before they can progress beyond such apologetic preliminaries.

52. *Sea Changes: Culture and Feminism*, by Cora Kaplan. Verso. pp. x + 232. pb £6.95.

53. *Closer to Home: Writers and Places in England 1780–1830*, by Roger Sale. Harvard. pp. 153. $15.95.

The Nineteenth Century:
Victorian Period

STEPHEN REGAN, LYN PYKETT, PETER KITSON,
LAUREL BRAKE, and JAMES FOWLER

This chapter is arranged as follows: 1. Verse, by Stephen Regan; 2. The Novel, by Lyn Pykett; 3. Prose: (a) Bibliography and General Works, (b) Individual Authors, (c) Periodicals and the History of Publishing, (d) Visual Art, (e) Social History; sections (a), (b) (except Pater), (d), and (e) are by Peter Kitson, and section (c) and Pater in section (b) are by Laurel Brake; 4. Drama, by James Fowler. A review of a book in Italian in Section 1 is by Steve Ellis and attributed [S.E.]. A comprehensive bibliography appears in *VS*, annotated guides in *VP* and *SEL*, and specialist lists in *VPR*, *BIS*, *PSt*, *JNPH*, and *NCTR*.

1. Verse

It has been a good year for Victorian poetry, with the long-awaited appearance of new books on Elizabeth Barrett Browning and Christina Rossetti, the continuing publication of the poems of Robert Browning and Christina Rossetti in new editions, two excellent collections of essays on Hopkins and the Pre-Raphaelites, an important rereading of Tennyson, and a host of interesting articles on Victorian Romanticism. Even so, the experience of reviewing an entire year's work can be daunting. It is with immense relief and gratitude, therefore, that the reviewer occasionally finds a work like *The Beauty of Inflections: Literary Investigations in Historical Method and Theory*[1]. Jerome J. McGann has established himself as a guiding light in nineteenth-century studies, as readers of his earlier work, *The Romantic Ideology* (*YW* 64.327–8), will appreciate. He is concerned above all with the displacement of orthodox historical methods from the centre of critical debate and with the need to recover and re-assess a broad range of sociological and philological procedures. Scholars of Victorian poetry are well advised to consult his readings of Tennyson and Christina Rossetti, in which he reveals how historical information, including 'reception history', can create new dimensions for a more comprehensive and precise critical approach.

A valuable contribution towards the kind of historical methodology which McGann is seeking is the publication of a four-part catalogue to the extensive Davis collection of nineteenth-century poetry[2]. Over 5,000 titles are listed in

1. *The Beauty of Inflections: Literary Investigations in Historical Method and Theory*, by Jerome J. McGann. Clarendon (1985). pp. x + 352. £22.50.
2. *Minor British Poets 1789–1918*. Part 2: *The Early Victorian Period 1840–1869*, intro. by G. B. Tennyson. UCal, Davis (1985). pp. 170. Part 3: *The Later Victorian Period 1870–1899*, intro. by Peter Allan Dale. UCal, Davis. pp. 315.

Parts 2 and 3, including some rare and unusual imprints and examples of printing and binding, with many books coming from provincial publishers (over half the titles in Part 2 were produced outside of London). As G. B. Tennyson comments in his introduction to Part 2, the variety is startling: there are

> narratives factual and fictional, nature poems, sentimental effusions, patriotic and public verse, hymns of praise and penance, volumes of instruction, collections of games, puns, puzzles – in short, the poetic outpourings of an age.

Titles like *Songs, by Jingo! Sometime a Public-school Boy* sit alongside *Lays from the Poorhouse*. Such diversity calls for a sustained study of the sociology of authorship and literary production, as Peter Allan Dale recognizes in Part 3. His closing remark that there might be 'among all these poets some mute inglorious Hopkins' seems, unfortunately, to miss the point and diminish the significance of these 'minor' works. If, as McGann asserts, each poem is a social event with a specific human history, then this is indeed a rich and valuable collection.

Notwithstanding the multifarious forms in which Victorian poetry appeared, Peter M. Sacks concentrates impressively on a single genre. His study of the English elegy[3] is neither narrowly nor naïvely preoccupied with questions of genre; in fact, it proves itself to be fully alert to the complicating notions of 'presence' and 'absence' that any study of the elegy is likely to encounter in the current critical forum. 'Thyrsis' doesn't quite earn a place here, but there are substantial chapters on Swinburne and Hardy which will be discussed later in this section. Sacks's interpretation of *In Memoriam* has a central role in his book and will surely take its place alongside some of the more influential and suggestive readings of the poem. Although Sacks presents us with a familiar portrait of Tennyson bereft of Romantic idealist assurances, his critique of *In Memoriam* clearly benefits from his earlier informative accounts of *Adonais* and *Lycidas*.

Common ground on which to combine the ideas of McGann and Sacks can be found in Avrom Fleishman's 'Notes for a History of Poetic Genres' (*Genre*, 1985). Some of his assertions are rather shaky, but his argument that genre belongs to 'a thoroughly historical process rather than a fixed system of ideal categories' seems well worth pursuing. Antony H. Harrison writes optimistically of 'the current movement to reconstitute historical studies of literature' in his introduction to a special issue of *JDJ* (4:2) titled 'The Metaphysical Poets in the Nineteenth Century'. What Harrison argues for, and what most of his fellow contributors exemplify in one way or another, is a broad alliance of reception theory and what is referred to (a little prematurely perhaps) as 'the new historicism'. Among those essays which focus on the Victorian interpretation or appropriation of works by seventeenth-century authors, three pieces deserve particular attention: John Maynard writes splendidly in 'Browning, Donne, and the Triangulation of the Dramatic Monologue' about Browning's idiosyncratic redeployment of some of John Donne's strengths as a writer; in 'Reading and Rereading: George Herbert and Christina Rossetti' Diane D'Amico argues that changes in poetic taste have directly affected the comparative positions of Christina Rossetti and George Herbert in literary

3. *The English Elegy: Studies in the Genre from Spenser to Yeats*, by Peter M. Sacks. JHU (1985). pp. xv + 375. hb $27.50, pb $7.95.

history, and Jerome Bump's 'Hopkins, Metalepsis, and the Metaphysicals' shows how Herbert and Rossetti together were influential in shaping the poetry of Hopkins.

A variety of theoretical approaches are brought into play in a special issue of *VP* (No. 4), titled 'Wordsworth among the Victorian Poets'. While the division of nineteenth-century English literature into Romantic and Victorian has long been a bone of contention, there now seems to be a greater determination by critics to confront and rethink the matter, especially through contemporary theories of discourse. William H. Galperin's 'Anti-Romanticism, Victorianism, and the Case of Wordsworth' points to the principal concerns of this special issue and identifies possible misreadings and misapprehensions in the course of literary history. His point that our modern failure to appreciate *The Excursion* has less to do with the poem itself than with the fashions of literary criticism is a fair one, but his further claim that 'the Victorians' read Wordsworth ironically is not really substantiated by his article.

Lawrence Kramer is also concerned, in the same issue of *VP*, with Victorian readings of Wordsworth, though his approach is decidedly psychoanalytic. He claims in 'Victorian Sexuality and "Tintern Abbey"' that a later generation of writers responded to the poem not just as a model of human development and recuperation but as a model of human desire, so giving their own versions of 'restorative encounter' an obvious erotic content. Although Kramer perhaps overstresses the impact of 'Tintern Abbey', he provides a particularly interesting account of the desolate landscapes of Victorian poetry, especially in Arnold's 'The Terrace at Berne'. Wendell Harris carefully points out that Victorian readers responded to Wordsworth in a number of different ways, according to contemporary systems of value and judgement. His slightly teasing article, 'Romantic Bard and Victorian Commentators: The Meaning and Significance of Meaning and Significance' argues that 'Those who gave the highest priority to the moral improvement of the individual lauded Wordsworth; those for whom the improvement of the social structure held pre-eminence were likely to think his poetry naïve'.

The Romantic legacy is also the subject of '"Worlds Not Realised": Wordsworthian Poetry in the 1830s' (*TSLL*), in which Lawrence Poston looks at evidence of 'a hitherto neglected continuity between Lake poetry and the lyric and devotional strains of the mid-Victorian generation'. In a closely related article, 'Poetry as Pure Act: A Coleridgean Ideal in Early Victorian England' (*MP*), Poston claims that a further continuity between two generations of poets lay in a shared endeavour to achieve a perfect fusion of moral and aesthetic issues. There is another essay on the critical ideals of the 1830s in *VP*, in which Patrick Creevy claims that John Stuart Mill's thinking about poetry was deeply influenced by James Martineau's essay 'On the Life, Character and Writings of Dr Priestley'.

Still on the subject of Victorian poetic theory, Michael Bright's 'Metaphors of Revivalism' (*VP*) claims that those poets who dealt with classical and medieval subjects elicited very different responses from contemporary critics, and that these can, in turn, help us to understand the dominant theoretical constructs of the time. Lawrence J. Starzyk, however, argues very cogently in 'The Non-Poietic Foundations of Victorian Aesthetics' (*BJA*) that the crucial determining feature of Victorian poetic theory was its loss of faith in earlier mimetic models of artistic creation. He goes on to explore the frustrations and confusions which attended this breakdown in theory in 'The Reflex of the Living Image in the Poet's Mind: Victorian Mirror Poetry' (*JPRS*). Part Three of Starzyk's thesis can be found in '"The Worthies Begin a Revolution": Browning, Mill, Arnold and the Poetics of Self-Acquaintance' (*Arnoldian*). His concern here is with the growing dissatisfaction shown by Victorian poets towards those ideas of union and reconciliation which were central to Romantic aesthetics. He contrasts the Romantic faith in a genuine self or epipsyche with the diseased self-consciousness and morbid introspection of much Victorian poetry.

One of the most interesting articles on Arnold this year is David H. Covington's 'Aristotelian Rhetorical Appeals in the Poetry of Matthew Arnold' (*VP*). Although Covington adopts an uncritical stance towards the idea of poetry as a medium for universal truths about 'the human condition', he effectively reveals how such poems as 'The Buried Life' and 'To A Republican Friend, 1848' depend largely on rhetorical techniques shaped by Arnold's exposure to Aristotle during his education at Rugby and Oxford. Richard Lessa makes large claims for Arnold the poet in 'Arnold's "Thyrsis": The Pastoral Elegy and the True Poet' (*DUJ*), but his article shows little appreciation or even understanding of Clough's poetry and gives unquestioning assent to Arnold's 'superior insights'. Darrel Mansell argues convincingly in 'Matthew Arnold's "The Study of Poetry" in its Original Context' (*MP*) that what is now regarded as an essay ought properly to be read as the general introduction to T. H. Ward's anthology, *The English Poets*.

The Brownings' Correspondence, now in its fourth volume[4], finds Elizabeth 'condemned to two applications of leeches' for her 'miserable pulse', shortly before the move to Wimpole Street, while Robert puts the finishing touches to *Sordello* before sailing to Venice on his first Italian journey. As the excellent collection of reviews and supporting documents in this volume confirms, the contemporary response to *Sordello* was less than encouraging (the *Dublin Review* called it 'a mass of perplexity and obscurity'), so Browning has reason to be grateful to one of his correspondents: 'You say roses and lilies and lilac-bunches and lemon-flowers about it while every body else pelts cabbage stump after potato-paring'. EBB's letters (a good number of them are to John Kenyon and Hugh Stuart Boyd) allude to the Coronation of the young Victoria and the Royal Wedding of 1840, but the voice of Daniel O'Connell testifies to the actual 'condition of England' in these years. There is much talk of 'animal magnetism' (mesmerism); pots of clotted cream are dispatched to Mary Russell Mitford, and the dog Flush arrives on the scene, but the pleasantries in EBB's life are suddenly and tragically interrupted by the dreadful news of the death, by drowning, of her brother Edward ('Bro') in July 1840. A long silence from July to October is eventually broken by a heart-wrenching letter: 'These walls – & the sound of what is very fearful a few yards from them – that perpetual dashing sound, have preyed on me. I have been crushed trodden down. God's will is terrible.'

An unusual biographical perspective is provided by Michael Meredith's *Meeting the Brownings*[5], originally compiled as a catalogue for an exhibition of

---

4. *The Brownings' Correspondence*, Vol. IV, ed. by Philip Kelley and Ronald Hudson. Wedgestone. pp. xiv + 451. $47.50.

5. *Meeting the Brownings*, by Michael Meredith. ABL. pp. 128. pb $17.50.

books, letters, manuscripts, and other possessions of the Brownings. The catalogue draws extensively on resources in Italy, England, and the United States,
and includes the earliest known photograph of Robert Browning, along with
thirty colour plates. Of special interest here is the account of how visitors to the
Browning household remembered their hosts. Julian Hawthorne remarked
disappointingly that 'Mrs Browning seemed to me a sort of miniature mon-
strosity; there was no body to her, only a mass of dark curls and queer, dark
eyes', while George Stillman confessed, 'I have never seen a human frame
which seemed so nearly a transparent veil for a celestial and immortal
spirit'. The individual catalogue entries are very well produced and helpfully
informative.

'To free Barrett Browning's name from the web of pious legend and sweet
romance that has entangled it for so long must be the first task of any new
critical evaluation.' So writes Angela Leighton at the outset of an excellent new
title in Harvester's commendable Key Women Writers series[6]. There is no room
for simple adulation in this clear-sighted and well-balanced study, and we are
not allowed to overlook the poet's occasional pompousness, her flawed
political ideals, or her derivative Romanticism. The opening chapter of the
book discusses EBB's shifting critical reputation and at the same time establishes its own feminist perspective, one which is perhaps closer to Mary
Wollstonecraft than to Jacques Lacan: what is of primary concern here is a
woman's assertion of her right to speak. The strong biographical import of this
study makes for a consistent and comprehensive analysis of the poems,
informed at every stage by the theme of the disinherited daughter. There are
some perceptive and original comments on the early poems and their signalling
of a contradiction in EBB's attitude to her father. There is none of the usual
embarrassment in the book's treatment of *Sonnets from the Portuguese*, and
the two chapters on *Aurora Leigh*'s private quest and public manifesto are
exemplary. In the current climate of re-appraisal there will be few books on
EBB to equal this one.

Two very good articles concentrate on EBB's problematic inheritance of
Romantic ideals. Kathleen Blake compares *Aurora Leigh* and *The Prelude* in
'Elizabeth Barrett Browning and Wordsworth: The Romantic Poet as Woman'
(*VP*), and reveals how concepts of self and nature are complicated by sexual
difference. In 'Elizabeth Barrett Browning through 1844: Becoming a Woman
Poet' (*SEL*) Dorothy Mermin argues that the essential lack of congruence
between the imaginative worlds created by male poets and the experience of the
female poet led to EBB's sense of exclusion from much of the Romantic
tradition. She develops this thesis in 'Genre and Gender in *Aurora Leigh*' (*VN*)
to consider how EBB remade the structures inherited from male predecessors.
Also by Dorothy Mermin is 'The Damsel, the Knight, and the Victorian
Woman Poet' (*CritI*), in which selected poems by EBB and Christina Rossetti
are seen to explore and protest against the male suppression of the woman as
speaking subject.

Susan S. Friedman is concerned with the implicit maleness of the epic
tradition in 'Gender and Genre Anxiety: Elizabeth Barrett Browning and H.D.
as Epic Poets' (*TSWL*). Comparing the genesis and structure of *Aurora Leigh*

6. *Elizabeth Barrett Browning*, by Angela Leighton. Harvester. pp. xiii + 179.
hb £16.95, pb £5.95.

and *Helen in Egypt*, she argues that both EBB and H.D. 'self-consciously reformulated epic conventions to suit their female vision and voice'. Bina Freiwald adds to the continuing re-appraisal of EBB's work with '"The world of books is still with the world": Elizabeth Barrett Browning's Critical Prose 1842–1844' (*NVSA WC*). This is one of the few articles in recent years to have given serious critical attention to EBB's survey of English poetry in *The Book of the Poets* (1842) and her contribution to *A New Spirit of the Age* (1844).

In an unusual article, 'Taste, Totems, and Taboos: The Female Breast in Victorian Poetry' (*DR*, 1984), Marjorie Stone claims that Victorian poets 'name' the female breast 'more frankly, more variously and more daringly than we do today'. EBB is seen to make particularly frequent and striking metaphoric use of this 'powerful female image', while male poets, in contrast, tend to focus on the breast as an erotic and demonic, rather than heroic and maternal, image. The immediate subject of Judy Rudoe's 'Elizabeth Barrett Browning and the Taste for Archaeological-Style Jewelry' (*BPMA*) is the mosaic brooch worn by EBB in the 1858 portrait by Michele Gordigiani, but there is much in the article to interest future biographers of the poet.

The Ohio-Baylor edition of *The Complete Works of Robert Browning*[7] has now reached its mid-way point and Volume VII, containing the first four books of *The Ring and the Book*, is appearing on library shelves. Acknowledging Browning's remark to his publisher – 'I attach importance to the mere stops' – the editors have taken 'accidentals' in the most literal sense and ambitiously (some might say over-ambitiously) decided to record the minutest details of punctuation. While this might result in a high incidence of error in early print runs it should, ideally, allow the discerning reader to reconstruct a work through the various stages of its textual history. The attempt to record *all* variants attributed to Browning is to be applauded, as is the neat presentation of textual notes at the foot of each page and editorial notes at the end of each volume. The absence of running-heads is presumably a further measure towards the presentation of a clean text, though this can lead to some disorientation in a work consisting of several books. Roma A. King's seventy pages of editorial notes certainly help to elucidate Browning's 'copious literary, historical, and mythological allusions', and include a detailed description of *The Old Yellow Book* and other accounts of the Franceschini trial, along with information on the composition and publication of the text.

As usual, Robert Browning gets the lion's share of critical attention in periodicals. In 'The Diorama "Showman" in *Sordello*' (*SBHC*) David E. Latané Jr offers interesting historical evidence to contradict the view that Browning's narrator in the poem is modelled on the diorama or panorama showman. Michael L. Burduck examines the Gothic features of an early poem in 'Browning's Use of Vampirism in "Porphyria's Lover"' (*SBHC*), while Sidney Coulling calls attention to Browning's thematic linking of certain poems in 'The Duchess of Ferrara and the Countess Gismond: Two Sides of the Andromeda Myth' (*SBHC*).

Stephen H. Ford adds to the familiar discussion about analogies between music and human mortality in 'The Musical Form of Robert Browning's "A Toccata of Galuppi's"' (*SBHC*), while David Parkinson invokes the

---

7. *The Complete Works of Robert Browning*, Vol. VII, ed. by Roma A. King. OhioU (1985). pp. xxiv + 322. $48/£40.80.

formidable company of Saussure, Derrida, and Lacan to give a much more up-
market view of things in '"A Toccata of Galuppi's": Even the Title's an
Octave' (*BSNotes*). Also in *BSNotes*, M. B. M. Calcraft's '"A Place to Stand
and Love In": By the Refubbri Chapel with the Brownings' offers a reading of
'By the Fireside' against a clear account of the Brownings' visits to the Bagni di
Lucca.

John Allen Quintus provides 'A Note on Browning's "Master Hugues"'
(*CP*), claiming that the poem is neither a satire nor an exemplary monologue
but 'a fairly straightforward statement of Browning's beliefs'. Don Perkins,
however, insists in '"Master Hugues of Saxe-Gotha": Robert Browning's
Other "Avison" Poem' (*NVSAWC*) that the poem ought to be read in the light
of Charles Avison's remarks on the roles of composers and performers in his
Essay on Musical Expression (1752).

One of the most impressive articles this year is Sarah Gilead's '"Read the text
right": Textual Strategies in "Bishop Blougram's Apology"' (*VP*). Gilead is
principally concerned with 'the game that hides and seeks the signifier', but
manages to ground this deconstructive approach in a cultural context where
exchanges of speech have a profoundly political significance. The affinity
between Browning's early poems and contemporary visual art is the subject of
an interesting article by Suzanne Edwards: 'Browning's "Saul": Pre-
Raphaelite Painting in Verse' (*JPRS*). Particular attention is given here to the
shared use of biblical subjects, pictorial images from nature, dramatic settings,
and the portrayal of intimate psychological conflict. Ernest Fontana (*SBHC*)
claims that Browning's 'Protus' anticipates 'Orophernis' (1916) and
'Kaisarion' (1918) by Cavafy. In all three poems, 'a modern speaker meditates
upon the failure of a beautiful young ruler from antiquity, articulating a desire
that is explicitly sexual in Cavafy and vague and undefined in Browning'. Clyde
de L. Ryals contributes 'Browning's *Christmas-Eve* and Schleiermacher's *Die
Wechnachtsfeier*: A German Source for the English Poem' to *SBHC*.

Certain Browning poems lend themselves well to the kind of devious interpretive strategy displayed by Joseph A. Dupras in 'The Tempest of Intertext in
"Caliban Upon Setebos"' (*CP*). As if embarking upon a game of 'Dungeons
and Dragons' we are offered a shrill warning that 'The process of reading the
poem, like the process of writing it, involves boldly resisting dominance and
anxiously daring authority to assert itself in order to compose a text that is never
fully composed'. This is clever stuff but it raises doubts about critical methods
that deal in such narrowly textual terms with concepts of power and
dominance. It is reassuring, however, to turn to Robert Alan Donovan's socio-
historical approach in 'The Browning Version: A Case Study in Victorian
Hellenism' (*Greyfriar*, 1985). Donovan compares the idiosyncratic understanding of Greek among the self-taught or privately taught, such as Browning,
with the classical education available to the most privileged segments of English
society, the sons of aristocratic or upper-middle class Anglican families. He
admires the 'roughness and eccentricity' of Browning's translations of
Euripides and credits the poet with re-invigorating Greek studies in England.
Donovan perhaps overstates the social significance of the later development of
Greek studies, but his article is useful and illuminating.

In a rather brief and breezy essay, 'Touches of *Aurora Leigh* in *The Ring and
the Book*' (*SBHC*), James McNally claims that the greatest influence of EBB's
poem on the later 'novel in verse' appears to lie in characterization and chiaro-
scuro. Lee C. R. Baker argues against the grain in 'The Diamond Necklace and

the Golden Ring: Historical Imagination in Carlyle and Browning' (*VP*). Taking *The Ring and the Book* as his main reference, Baker claims that Browning is not the romantic ironist he is often thought to be, and that unlike Carlyle he doesn't openly acknowledge the fictitiousness of his own historical re-creations. 'Deconstruction and Literary Biography: An Interview with Park Honan' (*SBHC*) has little to do with deconstruction but it does offer some interesting insights into Honan's shared endeavours with William Irvine in the composition of *The Book, the Ring, and the Poet: A Biography of Robert Browning* (*YW* 56.307).

'Browning and Women' by Ashby Bland Crowder (*SBHC*) is a disappointing article, partly because of its mechanical organization of materials under headings like 'Qualities in Women Attractive to Browning' or 'What Browning Objected to in Women'. Readers won't be surprised to learn that in his relation-ships with women Browning was 'sometimes drawn to their sexuality' and sometimes to their 'mental and spiritual qualities'. A much better biographical project is 'John Kenyon, the Magnificent Dilettante' (*SBHC*), in which Meredith B. Raymond offers a substantial and informative study of the mutual friend and intermediary of the Brownings.

The Collected Poems of Thomas and Jane Welsh Carlyle, edited by Rodger L. Tarr and Fleming McClelland (Penkevill), was not available for review, but space will be reserved here next year. There is, however, some good news for Clough devotees in the form of a paperback issue of the 1968 Oxford Standard Authors edition of the poems [8]. While not being as comprehensive as the 1951 Lowry, Mulhauser, and Norrington edition on which it is based, this selection does include Clough's best-known works, *The Bothie of Tober-Na-Vuolich*, *Amours De Voyage*, and *Dipsychus*, along with the shorter poems, in chrono-logical arrangement. It omits *Dipsychus Continued*, *Mari Magno*, and a group of 'unfinished and miscellaneous' poems. This is a welcome and sure step towards the greater accessibility of Clough's work. A selection of the poems, edited by Shirley Chew (Carcanet), will be reviewed next year. Michael Timko writes well on Victorian anti-idealism in 'Wordsworth and Clough' (*VP*). Concentrating on Clough's rejection of 'mere pastoral sweet piping from the country', he shows how the poet campaigned for a literature that would deal with 'general wants, ordinary feelings, the obvious rather than the rare facts of human nature'.

The second edition of Tom Paulin's *Thomas Hardy: The Poetry of Perception* [9] (*YW* 56.313–14), is now available in paperback. In a new, pro-vocative introduction Paulin insists that Hardy and Hopkins alike are poets of a Gothic tradition which is 'northern and consonantal' and quite distinct from the 'melodic, vowel-based tradition to which Tennyson belonged'. In his own lively, syncopated style Paulin argues for the priority of a 'fricative, spiky, spoken texture' over the Tennysonian species of 'Virgilian kitsch, all silvery angst and trim melody'. He has some good things to say about the importance of dialect as a language of passion and kinship, and effectively relates the acoustic texture of Hardy's verse to the concepts of vision and perception which

8. *The Poems of Arthur Hugh Clough*, ed. by A. L. P. Norrington. OUP. pp. xix + 320. pb £9.95.

9. *Thomas Hardy: The Poetry of Perception*, by Tom Paulin. Second edn. Macmillan. pp. x + 225. hb £25, pb £8.95.

inform his study. Paulin seems undecided at times about the nature and extent of Shelley's influence and finally leaves us in some doubt about Hardy's 'poetic vision', but his readings of such poems as 'During Wind and Rain' are exceptionally fine, and this book remains one of the few indispensable studies of Hardy's poetry.

While Tom Paulin has Hardy sitting on a rustic fence between romantic idealism and pessimistic empiricism, other critics have gone much further in emphasizing the differences between Romantic and Victorian concepts of imagination. Charles Lock, in '"The Darkling Thrush" and the Habit of Singing' (*EIC*), argues persuasively that Hardy distances himself from the Romantic lyric and shows a decidedly 'post-Romantic awareness of the fallaciousness of metaphor'. On a similar tack, Dennis Taylor claims in 'Hardy and Wordsworth' (*VP*) that Hardy is extremely responsive to his Romantic predecessor but also extremely critical of him, and that his characteristic medium is a fractured Romantic lyricism.

Robert Cirasa notes very shrewdly in 'Thomas Hardy's "Poems of 1912-13"': The Engagement of Loss' (*CP*) that Hardy's sequence is conspicuously lacking in the re-assuring forms of consolation usually associated with the elegy. He detects in the sequence what seems like 'a pathological pessimism', but ends his article admiring Hardy's 'courage to confront personal catastrophe without the solace of the gods'. Cirasa's article ought to be read alongside Peter Sacks's excellent chapter on Hardy in *The English Elegy*[3]. Sacks agrees that Hardy's 'Poems of 1912-13' appear to deny 'the borrowed comforts of the genre', but he also demonstrates how thoroughly the poems draw on well-established elegiac features, and he insists on the importance of reading the entire sequence within a broad elegiac context.

William W. Morgan discusses Hardy's decisions about genre in 'The Novel as Risk and Compromise, Poetry as Safe Haven: Hardy and the Victorian Reading Public, 1863-1901' (*VN*). Hardy's remark that 'Public opinion is of the nature of a woman' leads Morgan to speculate upon the ways in which Hardy's choice of genre was complicated by questions of gender. In 'Hardy, Donne, and the Tolling Bell' (*JDJ*, 1985) James Dorrill claims that 'Drawing Details in an Old Church' is 'one of the few Hardy poems directly traceable to a literary source and dependent on familiarity with that source for full emotional effect'.

Michael L. Johnson is much too anxious about the influence of Thomas Hardy on William Empson. 'From Hardy to Empson: The Swerve of the Modern' (*SoAR*, 1985) makes heavy weather of *clinamen* and *tessera* (and their respective precursors) and invokes some rather large and specious claims about the differences between modern British and American poetry. Much more useful is Samuel Hynes's 1980 essay 'The Hardy Tradition in Modern English Poetry' reprinted in *THJ*. Also of particular interest in this 'modern' context is a fine chapter on Hardy in a new book from John Lucas[10]. In a sympathetic and illuminating reading of the poems, Lucas explores the characteristic sights and sounds of Hardy's work and suggests how certain recurring images reveal a deep-seated communal instinct.

It has been a very productive year for Hopkins criticism, beginning with the

---

10. *Modern English Poetry from Hardy to Hughes: A Critical Survey*, by John Lucas. Batsford. pp. 218. pb £6.95.

welcome publication of Catherine Phillips's edition of the poems in the OA series[11]. What makes this a particularly useful work is that it discards the familiar subsections of previous editions and presents the entire collection of poems in chronological order together with a judicious selection of the prose. In addition, it offers a substantial bio-critical introduction and some ninety pages of editorial notes with an informative commentary on Hopkins's metrical marks. The volume has been prepared from manuscripts, with the last version committed to paper by Hopkins being adopted as the copy text. Accordingly, the layout and punctuation of some poems vary slightly from earlier printed versions, but an appendix conveniently records alterations made to the fourth edition of *The Poems of Gerard Manley Hopkins*, edited by W. H. Gardner and N. H. MacKenzie. It would be wrong, however, to labour the differences between this new edition and its predecessor; it clearly acknowledges its debts to the earlier work and also to the more elaborate textual apparatus currently being prepared by MacKenzie in his OET edition of the poems. Essentially, this new paperback text has much to recommend it and should continue to be a helpful and reliable source for students.

Harold Bloom has edited a volume of essays on Hopkins[12] and can justifiably claim to have gathered 'a representative selection of the best criticism available'. Bloom sees Hopkins as an incurable Romantic and in his introduction is concerned to 'correct anachronistic views of Hopkins as a modernist poet, rather than as the High Victorian ephebe of Keats, and pupil of Walter Pater, that he actually was'. Austin Warren's opening essay from the 1944 Kenyon Critics Collection still provides an excellent introduction to Hopkins, despite the New Critical chiding of poems which 'fail to be organisms'. Geoffrey H. Hartman contributes his impressive account of the dialogue between created senses and created beauty, including a wonderfully animated reading of 'The Windhover'. The essays are well chosen for the variety of perspectives and approaches which they afford, with Elisabeth Schneider's analysis of *The Wreck of the Deutschland* being nicely complemented by Paul A. Mariani's commentary on the late sonnets. Similarly, an extract from James Milroy's pioneering study, *The Language of Gerard Manley Hopkins* (*YW* 58.290), is followed by the less familiar work of Ellen Eve Frank (from *Literary Architecture* (1979)) on Hopkins's 'literary architecture'. Marylou Motto's admirable reading of 'Spring and Fall' from *Mined with a Motion* (*YW* 65.443) is included here, along with J. Hillis Miller's 'distinguished instance of Deconstructive criticism' in which Hopkins is seen to confront the ultimate failure of poetic language.

At first sight, *Hopkins, the Self, and God*[13] appears overtly traditionalist in its insistence on the poet's 'uniqueness' and 'relevance', but this book provides a remarkably penetrating account of what Hopkins called 'the selfless self of self, most strange, most still'. Where it succeeds convincingly is in its claim that the Victorian fascination with external particulars of all sorts was accompanied

11. *Gerard Manley Hopkins*, ed. by Catherine Phillips. OUP. pp. xlii + 429. hb £17.50, pb £7.95.

12. *Gerard Manley Hopkins*, ed. and intro. by Harold Bloom. ChelseaH. pp. viii + 179. $19.95.

13. *Hopkins, the Self, and God*, by Walter J. Ong S.J. UTor. pp. viii + 180. C$23/£14.

by an equally intense fascination with the interior self. The study embarks upon an ambitious account of the history of consciousness and the related demise of the old rhetorical tradition, and moves towards a closer examination of 'the consciousness of self' fostered by Jesuit asceticism. Ong deliberately avoids 'the complex interbreeding of Saussurian linguistics and Freudian psycho-analysis', though he makes a spirited and repeated criticism of Roland Barthes's *Sade, Fourier, Loyola*. Ultimately, however, the book seems to evade some crucial questions about the social and historical positioning of the self. An odd reference to the 'self-consciousness which Hopkins first *picked up* [my italics] from the Victorian milieu' is perhaps an indication of its reluctance to peer too deeply into the workings of ideology.

Hilary Fraser's chapter on Hopkins in *Beauty and Belief*[14] places the poet in a carefully defined post-Romantic, post-Kantian tradition and offers a detailed study of the theory of inscape in terms of its attempted unification of percep-tion and belief. While she credits Hopkins with solving 'long-standing problems of perception in Romantic aesthetics' through a 'brilliant and flawless' theory, she nevertheless feels that inscape failed to meet Hopkins's 'deepest needs' and that it remained 'merely an intellectual solution'. In '"God's Better Beauty": Language and the Poetry of Gerard Manley Hopkins' (*C&L*, 1985) David Jasper offers a lucidly written account of the shifts and stresses in Hopkins's career, from his early celebrations of the inscapes of nature to his final breaking point when 'language was at its very limit and despair most profound'. Jasper ends more optimistically than Fraser by claiming that 'a sharper and more enduring beauty is glimpsed in the surrender of all'. In 'Modes of Religious Response in Hopkins's Poetry' (*HQ*) Donald Walhout attempts to give a more comprehensive and balanced picture of Hopkins's religious verse than was first suggested in *Send My Roots Rain* (*YW* 62.311). In a rather awkward catalogue, he illustrates a variety of 'responses' under the headings of 'self', 'God', and 'community'.

Rosemary Nielsen and Robert Solomon have prepared an interesting commentary on one of the poems (a translation from Horace) which survived Hopkins's burning of his work. In 'Horace and Hopkins: The Point of Balance in Odes 3.1' (*Ramus*, 1985) they argue that Hopkins's translation, apart from indicating a subtle understanding of Horace, constitutes the poet's 'most revealing *cri de cœur*'. What they demonstrate impressively is the extent to which the contemporary language of business and commerce records 'the psychological struggle that exists in a sensitive observer during times of political and economic expansion'.

Adopting a phrase from Canadian critic George Whalley, Norman H. MacKenzie comes to terms with the special difficulties and attractions of Hopkins's 'acts of vision'. His lecture 'Vision and Obscurity in Hopkins' (*ESC*, 1985) demonstrates those skills of analysis which clearly commend him as an excellent editor of the poems. In 'Hopkins's "Spring and Fall" and Modes of Knowing' (*VP*) Gerard A. Pilecki claims that the poem's subtle scriptural allusions evoke intimations of both mortality and immortality. Also in *VP* is James Finn Cotter's 'Apocalyptic Imagery in Hopkins's "That Nature is a Heraclitean Fire and of the Comfort of the Resurrection"', which emphasizes

---

14. *Beauty and Belief: Aesthetics and Religion in Victorian Literature*, by Hilary Fraser. CUP. pp. xii + 287. £25.

Old and New Testament sources over the usual references to pre-Socratic philosophy. Both articles make convincing use of scriptural references. Rachel Salmon (*HQ*) chooses to emphasize the mediating role of the poem between the earlier 'nature' sonnets and the later sonnets of desolation. She argues that this synchronic approach is preferable to the usual sequential interpretation of the poems, but it appears to impose its own restrictions by concentrating rather narrowly on the informing presence of Loyola's *Spiritual Exercises*. Marie Nevill offers a brief account of the poet's ideas of rhythm and musical composition in 'Hopkins' Theories on Music and Poetry' (*Month*).

Robert Boyle's 'Hopkins, Brutus, and Dante' (*VP*) comments on the rich verbal associations of 'The Windhover' and offers some unusual insights into the 'oriflamme' of the Dauphin, Hopkins's studies of the Welsh language, and the influence of Dante. In 'Perspectives of Symbol and Allegory in "The Windhover"' (*HQ*) James Walter very astutely draws our attention to the speaker's reaching for deeper knowledge and effectively relates this to the poem's progression from literal fact to visionary awareness. R. A. Jayantha surveys the field of Hopkins criticism and comments on divergent interpretations in 'Some Responses to "The Windhover"' (*LCrit*). L. E. McDermott emphasizes Hopkins's own notion of poetry as 'current language heightened' and offers a detailed analysis of his use of spoken discourse in a brief but useful article, '"Pied Beauty": Hopkins's Poetic Art' (*CRUX*). In 'A World of Difference(s): Images of Instress in Hopkins' Poetry' (*HQ*) Leonard Cochran makes some observant remarks about the function of 'dappling' in such poems as 'Pied Beauty'. Thomas J. Steele also concentrates, though rather narrowly, on the structure of imagery or 'unitary root pattern' of Hopkins's work in 'The Foundational Pattern of "God's Grandeur"' (*HQ*). Norman White offers a stimulating biographical reading of the later poems in 'Hopkins' Sonnet "No Worst, There is None" and the Storm Scenes in King Lear' (*VP*). He points to the familiar parallel between the sonnet and the opening of *King Lear*, IV.i, but claims that there are 'deeper conceptual and thematic resemblances' which underline the mental anguish suffered by Hopkins during his time of exile.

There has been little discussion of Hopkins and gender in recent criticism, but Jeffrey B. Loomis is concerned to show how Hopkins transcends 'his own dominantly sexist Victorian culture'. His article, 'Birth Pangs in Darkness: Hopkins's Archetypal Christian Biography' (*TSLL*), is essentially a response to the claims of Gilbert and Gubar (in *The Madwoman in the Attic*, 1979) that Hopkins espouses 'the patriarchal notion that the writer "fathers" his text just as God fathered the world'. Donna Moder keeps this particular debate well and truly alive with an explosive psychoanalytic reading in her 'Aspects of Androgyny, Oedipal Struggle, and Religious Defence in the Poetry of Gerard Manley Hopkins' (*L&P*). Though in some ways narrowly Freudian, this article ranges across all phases of Hopkins's career and discovers a progressive psychological conflict which manifests itself in fragmentation of gender, regressive search for the mother, and fantasies of omnipotent control.

By far the most unusual and provocative article on Hopkins this year is 'The Blissful Agony of Hopkins: Notes of a Neo-Reactionary' (*HQ*) by Trevor McNeely. Sharing some of the assumptions of an earlier article by Charles Lock, 'Hopkins as a Decadent Poet' (*YW* 65.445), McNeely claims that critics have chosen to ignore the principal sources of tension in the poet's work, including 'the strange but inescapable contradiction between beauty and grotesquery, purity and perversity'. He is on less sure ground in trying to argue that Hopkins's style is both a strategy of evasion ('an elaborate ruse') and an index of pain, but he certainly throws down a strong challenge to convention.

There is not a great deal of information to record on Housman this year, though a lively dispute has gripped the pages of the normally uncontroversial *HSJ*. P. G. Naiditch argues that claims by Richard Perceval Graves of Housman having met with male prostitutes in Paris are unsubstantiated. Naiditch also contributes 'Notes on the Life of M. J. Jackson' and 'Some Echoes and Allusions in A. E. Housman's Prose Writings' to *HSJ*. Also of interest are T. A. Hoagwood's 'Poetic Design in *More Poems*: Laurence and A. E. Housman' and J. Lary Wilson's 'The Relevance of Housman's "The Name and Nature of Poetry"'. Ghussan R. Greene's 'Housman Since 1936: Popular Responses and Professional Revaluations in America' contains some illuminating remarks on the Armed Services Edition of *The Selected Poems of A. E. Housman*. No doubt the stoical philosophy behind the poems served a useful ideological function, but the edition carefully omitted poems with such lines as 'soldiers marching, all to die' and 'take the bullet in your brain'. John W. Stevenson comments upon 'the small drama of the lyric' in 'The Durability of Housman's Poetry' (*SR*).

An interest in the poetry of John Keble and John Henry Newman is slowly reviving. John Griffin argues soundly in 'Tractarians and Metaphysicals: The Failure of Influence' (*JDJ*, 1985) that the silence of Keble and Newman on the subject of John Donne's poetry was 'neither accidental nor a lapse in taste'. In '"Hail Gladdening Light": A Note on John Keble's Verse Translations' (*VP*) John K. Hale claims that Keble's translation from the Greek foreshadows the future of the Oxford Movement and the parting of the ways between Keble and Newman. *The Dream of Gerontius* can now be obtained in a nicely produced and inexpensive paperback edition [15]. Gregory Winterton's foreword explains the widespread popularity of the poem among Victorian Christians and suggests why it achieved for its author a 'general approbation forgetful of the denominational rivalries of the period'. In addition, we are given a brief introduction to the ideas and beliefs which the poem shares with Newman's *Apologia* and also acquainted with the circumstances of its original production in *The Month*. The reception history of the poem is, in itself, a fascinating subject: at the taking of Khartoum in 1884, General Gordon spent his final moments marking such lines as 'Use well the interval' and 'Now that the hour is come, my fear is fled'.

The fiftieth anniversary of Kipling's death has been the occasion for a massive re-issue of his works. Among the more respectable items to appear on the market is Andrew Rutherford's edition of Kipling's early verse [16], covering Kipling's formative teenage years and including some three hundred previously uncollected poems or fragments. The early Kipling shifts through embarrassing lyrics like 'Parting' ('Hot kisses on red lips that burn') to exuberant parodies of Swinburne ('Foam flakes fly farther than faint eyes can follow'). Rutherford believes that the India period from 1882 to 1889 initiated a crucial transition

15. *The Dream of Gerontius*, ed. with foreword by The Very Revd Gregory Winterton. Mowbray. pp. xx + 55. pb £1.95.
16. *Early Verse by Rudyard Kipling 1879–1889: Unpublished, Uncollected, and Rarely Collected Poems*, ed. by Andrew Rutherford. OUP. pp. xix + 503. pb £5.95.

from a private to a public mode of expression in Kipling's career, and conveniently divides his edition of the poems into 'School Years' and 'India and After'. In a generally forthright and informative introduction, Rutherford describes Kipling's political outlook as 'believing that good government was demonstrably better than self-government for India, and that good government was best provided by a dedicated élite of Britons'. His reference to such a view of government as 'Platonist' seems appropriate and yet doesn't altogether convey the intense hostility which the Bard of Anglo-India occasionally shows towards emergent Indian nationalism.

Rutherford shows in this edition how a number of topical poems excluded from Kipling's self-styled 'Definitive Edition' drew upon the Anglo-Indian newspapers in which they themselves appeared. He provides a further commentary on this journalistic context in 'News and the Muse: Press Sources for Some of Kipling's Early Verse' (*ELT*). Also in *ELT*'s special Kipling issues (Nos. 1 & 2), Nora Foster Stavel seeks to understand Kipling's 'peculiar personality' by reference to an unpublished Christmas poem beginning 'Peace Upon Earth to people of good will'. There are two particularly interesting items in *KJ*. K. M. Wilson comments upon the manuscript of 'The English Flag', which is clearly 'a very fine specimen of the English patriotic genre', and J. J. Ross contributes 'An English History: Kipling's Joint Authorship, with C. R. L. Fletcher, of *A School History of England* (1911)'. The work in question was ostensibly a book for children, but 'in reality the authors sustained a powerful political polemic throughout'.

The epithet 'Pre-Raphaelite' is almost meaningless as a literary term, as Harold Bloom points out in his introduction to a new collection of essays[17], and yet it seems to persist as a convenient label. Bloom doesn't explain what 'deep affinities' he thinks Meredith has with Rossetti, and it is difficult to follow his assertion that 'Pre-Raphaelite painting failed (with a few brilliant exceptions) but the poetry associated with it did not, because the poetry was the legitimate continuation of a central Romantic current'. In what sense 'failed' and why 'legitimate'? Nevertheless, he presents us with a rich and various collection of essays, certainly one of the best in the vast ChelseaH series. There are some familiar and worthy pieces here: John Lucas's finely discriminating study of Meredith's poetry, still unequalled for its insights into the curiously uneven texture of *Modern Love*; Jerome McGann's instructive historical reading of Christina Rossetti's poetry; Sandra Gilbert and Susan Gubar's influential feminist critique of *Goblin Market*; Ian Fletcher's guiding comments on Swinburne; Peter Sacks's generic approach to 'Ave Atque Vale', and Mario Praz's eclectic approach to 'The Angel in the House'. Several of the essays here are 'revisionary' in that they contend with earlier, adverse criticism: George Trail claims that these poets have been read as escapists when, in fact, 'they grind our faces in reality', and Joseph Gardner is concerned to show Rossetti's competence as a wordsmith. Some pieces, like John Hollander's revealing study of musical iconography, are printed here for the first time. Two essays, in particular, should continue to provoke disturbing questions about Victorian sexuality: G. L. Hersey compares the remote beauty of Rossetti's women to that of 'gorgeous corpses lying in open coffins', and Camille A. Paglia

17. *Pre-Raphaelite Poets*, ed. and intro. by Harold Bloom. ChelseaH. pp. x + 309. $29.95.

contributes a powerfully suggestive study of Swinburne's lesbian poems in 'Nature, Sex, and Decadence'.

Along with Carol L. Bernstein's helpful essay on Meredith in the above Pre-Raphaelite collection, readers might wish to consult Renate Muendel's analysis of the poetry in a new addition to TEAS[18]. Muendel emphasizes the agnostic and evolutionist aspects of Meredith's work, and offers a restrained but competent reading of *Modern Love* as a poem which shares some of the essential concerns of Victorian fiction.

William Morris is represented in Bloom's volume by Carole Silver's pertinent study of 'The Defence of Guenevere' and by two pleasingly complementary essays on 'The Earthly Paradise' from Blue Calhoun and Charlotte Oberg. Also on Morris is Ellen W. Sternberg's 'Verbal and Visual Seduction in "The Defence of Guenevere"' (*JPRS*) which sees the poem primarily as a drama about the power of verbal bravura. A rather idiosyncratic approach to the poems is made by Frederick Kirchhoff in 'William Morris's Body: Schematizations of the Self' (*VIJ*). Adopting Paul Schilder's notion of 'body schema', Kirchhoff ventures to explain the curiously disembodied figures of the narrator or protagonist in Morris's early writing and also considers the images of self in the later work. Dinah Birch has a good short essay, 'Morris and Myth: A Romantic Heritage', in *JWMS*. Her point about the attractive 'ahistoricism' of myth might well be challenged, but what is particularly useful here is the comparative study of myth in the works of Ruskin and Keats, and the discerning claim that for Morris, 'the myths of the North had none of the elitist implications that had come to attach themselves to the more familiar myths of Greece'.

One of this year's major publications is Volume II of *The Complete Poems of Christina Rossetti*[19], which means that all of her published collections are now available in a revised and scholarly edition. Volume III will contain uncollected and unpublished poems, along with the privately printed *Verses: Dedicated to Her Mother* (1847). The poems in Volumes I and II are arranged as they were in their respective first editions and are followed by poems which appeared in subsequent editions. The copy text in each case is the first English edition. What we have here, though, is not a projected single definitive version of the poems but a kind of 'variorum' or eclectic text based on the extant manuscripts, letters, editions, and individual printings of the poems in journals and anthologies. The textual notes and variant readings are confined to the end of each volume (leaving a good, clear reading text) and very usefully include listings of manuscript sources, early publication of individual poems, and all English and American editions up to and including William Michael Rossetti's 1904 text. As Laurel Brake pointed out in her review of Volume I (*YW* 60.302), there are no interpretive notes, but such a scrupulous work of editing is, in itself, an indispensable aid to our understanding of the poems.

This complete edition of the poems will eventually contain 1,100 items, a reminder of just how few poems by Christina Rossetti are publicly known. Familiar choices tend to appear in the anthologies or in slim selections like the recent Oxford Illustrated Poets edition[20]. Peter Porter's choice of twenty-six

18. *George Meredith*, by Renate Muendel. TEAS. Twayne. pp. 149. £18.

19. *The Complete Poems of Christina Rossetti*, Vol. II, ed. by R. W. Crump. LSU. pp. xxi + 525. $35/£29.75.

20. *Christina Rossetti*, ed. by Peter Porter. OUP. pp. 59. pb £4.95.

poems is attractively presented with prints from Walter Crane, Arthur Rackham, and others, but his introduction is disappointingly conventional and slight, especially from one who claims to be 'a firm believer in the doctrine that poets make the best critics of poetry'.

Christina Rossetti: The Poetry of Endurance[21] is to be welcomed, along with Angela Leighton's study of Elizabeth Barrett Browning, as a significant contribution to the re-appraisal of nineteenth-century women's poetry. Happily, a good deal has already been achieved and Dolores Rosenblum's opening remarks are replete with the vocabulary of successive feminist labours. In fact the book appears at first to be struggling under a multiplicity of feminist ideals and commitments, and its sense of direction is not immediately clear. What it actually concerns, and eventually demonstrates to good effect, is Christina Rossetti's sheer persistence as a poet, and her creation of female figures or female voices which assert their own endurance. Although some of the commentary (e.g. on *Goblin Market*) seems to drift and never establishes a convincing argument, there is nevertheless some vitally original material in this study, including an incisive account of Dante Gabriel's portraits of his sister and of the process through which resistance to modelling becomes an exploration of ways of seeing and being seen.

Jeanie Watson writes well on Christina Rossetti and Alfred Tennyson in '"Eat Me, Drink Me, Love Me": The Dilemma of Sisterly Self-Sacrifice' (*JPRS*). Focusing on *Goblin Market* and *The Princess*, she shows how both authors deal with the restricted personal and professional roles open to women, and how both use subversive techniques, invoking the fairy tale, to uphold the legitimacy of female self-exploration. U. C. Knoepflmacher also attaches great significance to the fairy tale in a brilliant piece of biographical investigation: 'Avenging Alice: Christina Rossetti and Lewis Carroll' (*NCL*). He argues wonderfully that the poem 'In an Artist's Studio' foreshadows a later creative resistance to the female idealizations of Lewis Carroll, and that *Speaking Likenesses* is an act of retaliation against Carroll's dubious worship of the female child. Readers interested in Lewis Carroll and Victorian fantasy should also consult Knoepflmacher's 'Revisiting Wordsworth: Lewis Carroll's "The White Knight's Song"' in *VIJ*.

Dante Gabriel Rossetti: vita, arte, poesia[22] is a competent biographical-cum-critical survey of Rossetti's career, consisting of eighteen short chapters covering topics like Rossetti and Blake, the quarrel with Buchanan, and the influence of Dante, none of which does more than provide a preliminary overview of its subject. Presumably the book is aimed at Italian students and intended as an introductory guide to Rossetti's work. As such, it is unobjectionable and reasonably comprehensive, and shows an up-to-date acquaintance with Rossetti criticism. It also contains a generous selection of good quality black-and-white reproductions. [S.E.].

One of the most interesting articles on D. G. Rossetti this year is Michael Cohen's exemplary piece of reader-response criticism, 'The Reader as Whoremonger: A Phenomenological Approach to Rossetti's "Jenny"' (*VN*). The argument here is that the poem's readers, including female readers, are made to

21. *Christina Rossetti: The Poetry of Endurance*, by Dolores Rosenblum. SIU. pp. xvii + 247. $23.95.

22. *Dante Gabriel Rossetti: vita, arte, poesia*, by Edvige Schulte. Liguori. pp. 162 + 49 illus. L 15,500.

share the guilt of Jenny's sexual exploitation. Also of challenging import is 'D. G. Rossetti's *The House of Life*: Allegory, Symbolism and Courtly Love' (*JPRS*, 1985), in which Scott J. Mitchell rejects the idea of Rossetti's love sonnets constituting a unified sequence and sees, instead, a fitful but sustained attempt to achieve contradictory goals. In the same issue of *JPRS*, Christopher S. Nassaar's 'Flesh Versus Spirit: D. G. R.'s "The Portrait"' claims that a work traditionally interpreted as Rossetti's glorification of ideal beauty is more convincingly read as the dramatization of an age-old conflict. Two articles in *VP* deal with the pairing of visual and verbal works. In 'Rossetti's Sonnet on "A Virgin and Child By Hans Memmeling"': Considering a Counterpart' Gail Lynn Goldberg makes a well-illustrated claim that the graphic source of Rossetti's poem is actually a work by the Belgian painter, Gerard David. In 'Dante Gabriel Rossetti, Frederic Shields, and the Spirit of William Blake' Robert N. Essick argues impressively that the compositional history of the poem 'William Blake' acquaints us with Victorian perceptions of Blake and offers us insights into the role of pictorial documents as inspiration for literary works. James F. Doubleday writes on the imagery of Rossetti's 'A Birthday' in *Expl*, and Samira Husni gives a detailed account of a lesser-known Pre-Raphaelite poet in 'William Allingham: Cold Words Hiding Life in their Veins' (*JPRS*).

Swinburne, not surprisingly, has a central role in *Baudelaire and the English Tradition*[23]. In fact, Patricia Clements dedicates the opening seventy pages or so to Swinburne's introduction of the French poet to English readers in the 1860s. What is pleasing about this study is its insistence on treating seriously Swinburne's interest in Baudelaire, as well as his intention of confounding 'tradition and the taste of the greater number of readers'. Whether Swinburne really 'changed the course of the main current of the English tradition' is difficult to tell (the English tradition here is something rather vague which culminates in modernism); what is more convincing is the account of how Baudelaire was successfully transmuted by each generation, from the Victorian 'Mephistopheles' to T. S. Eliot's 'Poet and Saint'. The book offers a sustained analysis of Swinburne's critical precepts in such works as *Under the Microscope* and records the public response to *Poems and Ballads*, but it doesn't, unfortunately, have much to say about the poems themselves. There is a good chapter on Arthur Symons, whose poems *are* given extensive treatment, though, once again, the notion of an 'English tradition' only serves to confuse matters: Symons is seen to suffer 'decisive defeat' in his poetic endeavours but nevertheless 'clears the way' for Eliot and Joyce. If a tradition ever existed, was it really an *English* tradition?

Swinburne's response to the 'sweet strange elder singer' is also the concern of Peter M. Sacks who offers a fine reading of 'Ave Atque Vale' in *The English Elegy*[3] (reprinted in Bloom[17]). Sacks regards the poem for Baudelaire as 'one of the finest and least understood elegies in the language', and shows how Swinburne revised the conventions of the genre to escape 'the Victorian obsession with personality' which confined such elegiac works as *In Memoriam* and 'Thyrsis'. While Clements and Sacks read the poem as a careful and personal tribute to the French poet, Melissa Zeiger detects an ironic sense of elegy and

23. *Baudelaire and the English Tradition*, by Patricia Clements. Princeton (1985). pp. x + 442. $33.50.

argues vigorously that Swinburne is concerned to disrupt rather than revise the typical conventions of the genre. In '"A Muse Funereal": The Critique of Elegy in Swinburne's "Ave Atque Vale"' (*VP*) she insists that true consolation is made impossible by a collapse of belief.

'Rereading Nature: Wordsworth Between Swinburne and Arnold' (*VP*) draws impressively on the notion of intertextuality, which Thaïs E. Morgan defines as 'the verbal and ideological relationships among texts'. Her article admits that both Swinburne and Arnold reacted against Romantic modes of representing 'nature', but claims that while Swinburne showed a consistent aversion to Wordsworth's nature philosophy and religious humanism, Arnold eventually compromised his own critical stance. David G. Riede's 'Bard and Lady Novelist: Swinburne and the Novel of (Mrs) Manners' (*VN*) tries to explain why Swinburne chose to write novels in unconventional forms, and finds that the answer has much to do with the Victorian distinction between 'the manly and authoritative art of poetry and the effeminate, gossipy domain of the novel of manners'.

This year sees the publication of *Tennyson's 'Maud': A Definitive Edition*[24] by Susan Shatto. This is the first complete collation of all the known manuscripts of *Maud*, the surviving proofs, the privately printed Trial issue, and the editions of the poem up to and including that of 1889. By carefully examining manuscript evidence in the light of Tennyson's own statements and the letters and reminiscences of his contemporaries, this new edition reconstructs the genesis and development of the poem from the lyric 'Oh! that 'twere possible' to an extended dramatic sequence. The text is neatly laid out to avoid inconvenient breaks and to maintain a close page-by-page collation of the poem and its variant readings. The real value of this work lies in the wealth of biographical and historical research which informs the reconstruction of the poem and the supporting commentary. It is now clear, for instance, that *Maud* occupies a crucially significant position in the contemporary debate about the moral superiority of war over peace, and that Tennyson's revisions to the poem were made not just in response to hostile criticism but in a continuing attempt to clarify his attitudes to the war.

The importance of reading a work like *Maud* in relation to complex social processes is of deep concern to Alan Sinfield in his rousing polemical introduction to *Alfred Tennyson*[25]. In contemplating the 'relevance' of Tennyson, Sinfield shows how well-established literary procedures have effectively ruled out consideration of the historical conditions which govern the activities of writing and reading, so inhibiting political awareness and change. A chapter titled 'The Politics of Poetry' begins with a concise and much-needed account of the utilitarian context which shaped the early Tennyson lyrics, and goes on to describe the poet's development from a Shelleyan exaltation of liberty to a conservative anxiety about civil disturbance. The middle chapters of the book lose some of this precise historical focus as they turn towards a broader theoretical view of language and subjectivity prompted by Tennyson's attempt to 'name the Nameless'. Sinfield nevertheless provides what is perhaps the best example to date of a materialist deconstruction which maintains that 'meaning

24. *Tennyson's 'Maud': A Definitive Edition*, ed. by Susan Shatto. Athlone. pp. xxi + 295. £28.
25. *Alfred Tennyson*, by. Alan Sinfield. Blackwell. pp. x + 202. hb £15, pb £4.95.

is always negotiated in reception, in particular discourses and historical conditions'. Nineteenth-century ideas of sexuality are of central importance here, and Sinfield's discussion of the unconventional handling of gender in *In Memoriam* is brilliantly provocative and revealing.

In sharp contrast, Alastair W. Thomson's *The Poetry of Tennyson*[26] is 'not, in any sense, a radical revision of generally accepted opinions about Tennyson'. This is a pity, since Thomson is clearly well qualified to write on Tennyson and has already produced a useful and informative student guide to the poems[27]. He writes impressively on matters of style, but where Sinfield and McGann are alert to historical determinants he seems reluctant to enquire: 'The age too late of nineteenth-century England and post-Revolutionary Europe undoubtedly had something to do with his avoidance of high themes, as did his tendency to retreat from ideas about the final authority of poetry.' Unfortunately, Thomson seems to share Tennyson's 'tendency to retreat'; that elusive 'something' is never explained and the commentary resorts instead to a rather low-key conventionality. Occasionally the book shifts into a more adventurous mode and we learn of Tennyson's apprehension of 'a world which gives neither metaphors nor reasons'. Such insights leave one wishing that this particular study had been more confidently assertive and challenging.

Daniel Albright[28] adopts a novel approach by emphasizing the conflict that Tennyson faced between 'the urge to the sublime, or the nameless, and the urge to the commonplace'. He argues, with some awkwardness at times, that the incompatibility of the heavenly muse and the earthly muse was both a productive tension and a cause of irresolution, but ultimately it is the narrowly restrictive polarities of his approach which let him down. The discussion of the Victorian sublime is fascinating and the book is well written, if sometimes excessively adjectival and given to odd coinages like 'mythiness', 'overemoting', and 'personalness'. Early and late poems are considered together, with *Idylls of the King* being dispersed throughout the study, so that 'The Lady of Shalott' and 'Lancelot and Elaine', for example, are juxtaposed to good effect. The final section dealing with Tennyson's 'major' poems eventually reveals the shortcomings of the thesis. The analysis of *Maud* is unsatisfactory, largely because of its exclusive preoccupation with the speaker's psychic state, and *In Memoriam* is read in a narrowly reductive context as a tussle between the earthly Melpomene and the celestial Urania. Jerome McGann's remark that 'the study of Tennyson's poetry must begin and conclude in a field of historical particulars' is here undoubtedly vindicated.

Daniel A. Harris[29] gives extensive and exhaustive treatment to a single poem, 'Tithonus', which he believes is 'a central document in Victorian culture' and 'a signal vantage point from which to consider revisionist thinking about personification in the mid-Victorian period'. The linking of 'Tithon' (1831) and 'Tithonus' (1866) gives a broad perspective to the study, as does the concern

26. *The Poetry of Tennyson*, by Alastair W. Thomson. RKP. pp. x + 278. £24.

27. *Alfred, Lord Tennyson: Selected Poems*, by Alastair W. Thomson. Longman (1984). pp. 88. pb £1.25.

28. *Tennyson: The Muses' Tug-of-War*, by Daniel Albright. UVirginia. pp. vii + 256. $24.95.

29. *Tennyson and Personification: The Rhetoric of 'Tithonus'*, by Daniel A. Harris. UMI. pp. xvi + 142. $39.95.

with earlier, Keatsian techniques of 'fluid personification' in 'To Autumn'. The importance of the book, however, is in its successful delineation of the poem's contemporaneity and its revealing account of how 'Tithonus' might be aligned with both Tractarian debates about the Eucharistic presence and the emergence of mythography as a modern discipline. In a nutshell, 'the poem links anthropological and theological perspectives by examining, with great psychological acuity, the system of signification which results from Tithonus' need to spiritualize matter'.

Readers interested in the pictorial representation of Tennyson's poems ought to be delighted with *Ladies of Shalott: A Victorian Masterpiece and its Contexts*[30]. This splendid catalogue was produced by Brown University Department of Art for a recent exhibition and consists of eight substantial essays, sixty-six well-illustrated entries, and a useful bibliography. Much of the emphasis falls on Holman Hunt's *The Lady of Shalott*, as 'the most famous version of its subject', possibly because its provenance in the United States, whereas British spectators are likely to be more familiar with the Waterhouse painting in the Tate Gallery. As its title suggests, however, the catalogue is principally concerned with Victorian methods of interpretation and representation. George P. Landow sets the note in his preface by claiming that Hunt reversed Tennyson's intentions and read the poem as 'a symbolic statement that artistic irresponsibility or lack of commitment brings with it dreadful punishment'. Elizabeth Nelson's opening essay reflects upon the sheer potency of the poem and the ways in which meanings were duplicated and produced by onlookers, while Peggy Fogelman concentrates on the Moxon Tennyson and Pre-Raphaelite illustration. The actual catalogue is excellent, and while the Romantic iconography of the embowered woman is seen to proliferate in familiar works by Rossetti, Morris, and Beardsley, it also provides the occasion for Richard Redgrave's little-known work of social protest, *The Sempstress*.

One of the most impressive articles on Tennyson this year is concerned with the particular nineteenth-century aesthetic and sexual problems which his early 'medieval' poem confronts. In 'A Blessing and a Curse: The Poetics of Privacy in Tennyson's "The Lady of Shalott"' (*VP*) Joseph Chadwick argues forcefully that the allegory is 'not primarily an epistemological one, built on an opposition between illusion and truth, but fundamentally a social one, built on oppositions between feminine and masculine, private and public'. A thoroughgoing Jungian approach is adopted by G. O. Gunter in 'The Inflated Ego in "The Palace of Art"' (*VIJ*). Granted that the poem may be 'a work of remarkable psychological accuracy', the actual analysis yields a familiar conclusion based on Tennyson's fears about the potentially destructive effects of aestheticism. Joanna E. Rapf claims in '"Visionaries of Dereliction": Wordsworth and Tennyson' (*VP*) that Victorian images of ruin and desolation reveal a critical awareness of the Romantic imagination. Traci Gardner comments on Tennyson's star-gazing in 'Locksley Hall' (*Expl*), and K. G. Srivastava offers some brief observations on the closing stanza of 'Break, Break, Break' (*AJES*, 1985).

In 'Tennyson's "Tears, Idle Tears": The Case for Violet' (*VP*), Henry Kozicki contrasts the nineteenth-century emotive or impressionistic approach

30. *Ladies of Shalott: A Victorian Masterpiece and its Contexts.* BrownU (1985). pp. ix + 184. $14.

to the lyric with the modern objective approach, but his explanation of the apparent shift in criticism is not altogether convincing. Ashton Nichols rejects the use of 'mysticism' as an appropriate term in Tennyson criticism and prefers to talk of the literary epiphany. 'The Epiphanic Trance Poem: Why Tennyson is not a Mystic' (*VP*) offers a lively and discriminating account of Tennyson's moments of revelation. Beverly Taylor argues plausibly in 'Tennyson Ludens' (*VIJ*) that a comic, affirmative spirit runs beneath Tennyson's deepest melancholy and finds expression in playful, paradoxical language, delusions, riddles, and puzzling symbols. Even *In Memoriam*, she claims, is really 'a kind of *Divina Commedia*'.

A substantial contribution to research on *In Memoriam* is made by Donald Hair in 'Tennyson's Faith: A Re-examination' (*UTQ*). Emphasizing that Tennyson's faith is not so much a system based on creeds as a way of life, Hair argues that Locke and Coleridge together illuminate two major aspects of Tennyson's thinking: the distinction between faith and knowledge and the affirmation that faith is the expression of a human need from which it gains its authority. In 'Morte d'Arthur: The Death of Arthur Henry Hallam' (*Biography*) Jack Kolb offers a detailed account of Hallam's death in Vienna at the age of twenty-two and surveys 'the troubles, uncertainties, and unresolved questions then and now surrounding it'. According to Kolb, Tennyson himself didn't know where in Clevedon Church his friend was buried, or even from which English port he had been brought home. Simone Lavabre offers French readers a checklist of critical items on *In Memoriam* in 'Bibliographie de Tennyson' (*CVE*).

The significance of what Jerome McGann calls 'reception history' is clearly evident in 'Realism Versus Romance: The War of Cultural Codes in Tennyson's *Maud*' (*VP*) by Chris R. Vanden Bossche. This article assumes that divergent readings of *Maud* reveal something inherent in the poem itself, and that the familiar realism–romance dichotomy can be attributed to a clash between middle-class practicality and aristocratic chivalry. The determination to relate literary practices and social practices effectively removes *Maud* from the stifling conventional terms in which it is frequently discussed and places it in the larger and more fruitful context of Victorian culture. Patricia Elizabeth Davis constructs a plausible and comprehensive thesis in 'Challenging Complacency: The "discords dear to the musician" in Tennyson's "Sea Dreams: An Idyll"' (*VIJ*). Her main argument is that the discordant structure and awkward prosody of 'Sea Dreams' reflect the moral and spiritual confusion of bourgeois individualism, but she also cleverly implies that the poem is an oblique rejoinder to Samuel Smiles's *Self-Help* and not a little to do with Tennyson's loss of £3,000 in Matthew Allen's fraudulent wood-carving scheme. Geoffrey Ward's compelling approach in 'Dying to Write: Maurice Blanchot and Tennyson's "Tithonus"' (*CritI*) is perhaps best described as 'phenomenological'. Reading Tennyson's poems alongside Blanchot's meditations on dying, Ward detects the powerfully subversive presence of death, even in those poems which espouse public conformity.

Idylls of the King continues to stimulate a wide range of critical responses. Howard W. Fulweiler constructs an impressive thesis on the nature of spiritual discernment in 'Tennyson's "The Holy Grail": The Representation of Representation' (*Renascence*). Taking his cue from Owen Barfield, Fulweiler argues that 'The Holy Grail' dramatizes the process of human society undergoing the painful loss of 'participation' or spiritual awareness and calls for a renewal of 'sacramental vision' through its image of the Eucharist. The argument about problems of perception in the later nineteenth century is well presented, if only tenuously linked to the larger sense of social collapse and fragmentation which the poem embodies. John R. Reed offers substantial evidence in 'Tennyson's Narrative on Narration' (*VP*) that the poet 'self-consciously associated the subtleties of narration with the moral function of historical parable', and in a wilfully verbose article, '"To-Day Unsolders All": Tropology and History in *Idylls of the King*' (*VIJ*), William W. Bonney suggests that metaphors of vertical extension are consonant with the poem's depiction of historical process.

A few assorted items are worth mentioning in conclusion. Max Keith Sutton has a good article on the Manx poet T. E. Brown (1830–97) in *JNT*. Concentrating on the role of the implied audience in Brown's *Fo'c's'le Yarns*, he provides a useful model of how readers produce or 'actualize' a text. Ellen Shannon-Mangan, writing in *Éire*, presents a selection of new materials on James Mangan and calls for a thorough revision of the poet's life and work. Murray G. H. Pittock (*ELT*) comments on a strangely evasive letter which Lionel Johnson sent to Victor Plarr in December 1897, and John Leigh (*Paideuma*) shows how Ezra Pound's aesthetic ideas evolved in response to Arthur Symons's views on contemporary music.

2. The Novel

(a) General

> 'The Victorian novel' is not readily grasped as an entity.... It is hard to find a definition that will encompass all the different fictional modes and formal changes occurring between the first numbers of *Pickwick Papers* in 1836 and the publication of *The Wings of the Dove* in 1902.

Thus writes Robin Gilmour in his 'Modern Introduction' to the Victorian novel, reviewed below. Like Gilmour, most of the current writers on Victorian fiction seem less concerned with problems of precise definition than with the multifarious tasks of exploration and explication of the great variety of 'fictional modes and formal changes' in the period. A significant number – perhaps a majority – of these studies are concerned to situate particular Victorian fictions or groups of fictional works in specific historical and cultural locations. Some are actively engaged in the important work of rethinking the relations between texts and contexts.

The re-assessment of the Victorian novel continues apace as the map of the territory is redrawn to accommodate new landmarks, and as the familiar landmarks are viewed from fresh perspectives. The process of re-assessment is particularly evident in a number of this year's books on individual authors, which belong to series self-consciously addressed to the tasks of producing 'New Readings', or rereadings, or of reading women's writing. However, as always, the 'fresh perspectives' of some of this year's studies are no more than tours around a critical maze, whose journey's end is an extremely complicated way of saying 'What oft was thought', and what has frequently been better expressed.

The replotting of the field is central to some of the more general studies. The most widely used of these is likely to be Robin Gilmour's *The Novel in the Victorian Age*[31], which offers a critical and contextual introduction to 'the major and some minor Victorian novelists'. Gilmour is particularly interested in the ways in which the novelists 'responded to, and were in turn influenced by, the social and cultural pressures of the age', and consequently he organizes his study both thematically and chronologically. He begins with an admirably concise and judicious survey of the age and of the novel, its readers, its characteristic forms of publication, and the critical discourse in which it was discussed in fiction reviews. Gilmour goes on to explore such topics as 'the novel and the aristocracy' in the earlier novelists of the period, 'the sense of the present' in the Condition-of-England novelists, and the 'sense of the self' in the autobiographical fictions of the Brontës, treating Dickens as a pivotal figure, and concluding with intimations of the 'Ache of Modernism' in Hardy, Moore, Gissing, Butler, and Mary Ward. In Gilmour's account the Victorian novel is a central aspect of the Victorian compromise, a 'mixed form' which combines the re-assurance of closure with the disturbing subversiveness of indeterminacy. Gilmour's own story shares something of this mixed form, and has a somewhat familiar plot. It is ultimately the story of the novelists' varying attempts to 'interpret their changing world', and to hold on to a hopeful vision of the future until the 'pressure of pessimistic insights' could no longer be contained within the 'reconciling mixed form'. However, other aspects of Gilmour's account have a more challenging indeterminacy, particularly his emphasis on the variousness of the novel and the age.

Despite his inclusion of R. L. Stevenson, George Moore, and Henry James, Gilmour's subject is the *English* Victorian novel, and he is at pains to argue that a history of *British* fiction of the period would be quite a different kind of exercise. Jeremy Hawthorn, on the other hand, has edited a collection of essays entitled *The Nineteenth-Century British Novel*[32] which not only eschews all discussion of the nature of the project, but also fails to discuss any non-English novelists, apart from Scott. However, most of its contributors address themselves seriously to the task of re-assessing the nineteenth century in the light of recent literary theories. Most of the essays are concerned with a particular novel or novelist and will be dealt with in the next section, but two writers attempt more general themes. Angus Easson makes the case for the influence of Wordsworth's poetry on the formation of Victorian narrative technique, in a comparison of Scott's *The Black Dwarf* with *Silas Marner*, which accounts for the changes in narrating practices by reference to the techniques of a poem like 'Michael'. In a more wide-ranging and interesting essay Kate Flint reviews the attitudes to female reading found in articles in the periodicals, and also locates the prevailing view – that fiction was a dangerous drug for female readers – in contemporary ideologies of the civilizing and nurturing role of women, and in nineteenth-century medical theories about the nature of the female brain and nervous system. Flint also challenges these views by analysing the ways in which three well-known sensation novels written by women make demands on their female readers, and create a 'sense of community of knowledge, of shared competence in which [women] could exchange cultural capital'.

31. *The Novel in the Victorian Age: A Modern Introduction*, by Robin Gilmour. Arnold. pp. xiii + 221. hb £22.50, pb £7.95.
32. *The Nineteenth-Century British Novel*, ed. by Jeremy Hawthorn. SUAS. Arnold. pp. vii + 175. pb £9.95. (Hereafter Hawthorn.)

Flint's essay provides further evidence of both an increasing attentiveness to non-canonical texts, and a concern to relate fiction to other forms of discourse, in this case the medical and psychological, as well as the critical. Feminist criticism and Michel Foucault have perhaps been two of the most important factors in these methodological shifts, and both are much in evidence in one of the most interesting and challenging of this year's general books, *Sex, Politics, and Science in the Nineteenth-Century Novel*[33]. Most of the essays in this volume focus on particular novels or authors, and are more appropriately discussed in the following section. However, taken together, the various perspectives they offer on individual novels add up to a fresh view of the Victorian novel in general. Ruth Bernard Yeazell's pithy introduction sums up the shared project, and also serves as a description of an important strand of current scholarship:

> These essays take the nineteenth-century novel seriously by not treating it as privileged – by directing attention ... to the language and systems of representation that it shared with the wider culture, and to the more or less open ways in which it participated in that culture. If the authors are not as obviously concerned with the poetics of fiction as they might have been a decade ago, they are perhaps more alert to the fictiveness of discourse generally, and to the anxieties that any fiction may manipulate and conceal.

As will be seen in the following pages, a growing number of (in my view) the more serious and interesting studies of the nineteenth-century novel share these concerns. In the present volume Gillian Beer's 'Origins and Oblivion in Victorian Narrative' provides a model example of this kind of work, with its subtle examination of a specific cultural moment, which considers how and why some Victorian narratives 'resist or dwell upon the dissolution of record'. The Victorian multi-plot novel (particularly as practised by Dickens and Hardy), serves as one model for the divided impulses of the age, but as in her important book *Darwin's Plots* (*YW* 64.388-9), Gillian Beer reads novelistic narratives alongside other 'creative narratives' such as those of the scientists Charles Lyell, Darwin, and Max Müller.

In the other general essay in the volume, Elaine Showalter explores a different cultural phenomenon: the 'dread of sexual contamination during a period of gender crisis', suggested by the iconography of syphilis which pervades *fin de siècle* English fiction. Showalter's wide-ranging study explores this iconography in the culture generally, as well as investigating its differing functions in the novels of a group of female (and, broadly speaking, feminist) novelists, and a group of misogynistic novels by male writers.

The cultural production of gender and gendered cultural forms are also considered in Carla L. Peterson's Derridean *The Determined Reader*[34], which *inter alia* compares the differing responses to their reading experience of male and female protagonists, and explores the ways in which they rewrite (or fail to rewrite) the stories available to them. *Jane Eyre* and *David Copperfield*, and *The Mill on the Floss* and *Jude the Obscure* are the English texts compared in

33. *Sex, Politics, and Science in the Nineteenth-Century Novel*, ed. by Ruth Bernard Yeazell. JHU. pp. 224. $10. (Hereafter Yeazell.)

34. *The Determined Reader: Gender and Culture in the Novel from Napoleon to Victoria*, by Carla L. Peterson. Rutgers. pp. x + 264. £23.95.

this study. Jane Miller shares Peterson's interest in the ways in which women, in particular, rewrite existing stories. George Eliot and the Brontës figure quite prominently in her general study *Women Writing About Men*[35], which concentrates on the novel 'as a form which women writers have used to question and challenge men's appropriation of women's experience'. Laura Hapke ('She Stoops to Conquer', *VN*) and Mary Burgan ('Heroines at the Piano', *VS*), on the other hand, turn their attention to fictional representations of women, in essays on the portrayal of fallen women and musical women respectively.

'Manliness', specifically the ideal of Christian manliness of Victorian muscular Christianity, is the subject of Norman Vance's interesting and wide-ranging *The Sinews of the Spirit*[36]. The novels of Charles Kingsley and Thomas Hughes in their social, religious, and intellectual contexts, are at the centre of Vance's scholarly study, which traces the origins of this ideal in English traditions of sporting prowess, ideas of chivalry and gentlemanliness, and the preaching of 'vigorous virtue' from St Paul to the Victorian evangelists. The male (according to Victorian ideology) sphere of commerce is the focus of Norman Russell's *The Novelist and Mammon*[37], which offers to examine some of the ways in which Victorian novelists 'reacted to the development of capitalism and its institutions'. However, despite his wide reading in Victorian fiction, and his extensive documenting of the history of commercial and financial institutions, and contemporary economic theories, Russell fails to do justice to this important subject. The book's main shortcoming derives from its author's rather naïve notions about the nature of literary representation and of the nature of the relationship between literature and 'reality'.

Quite a different perspective on the interrelationship of capitalism, commerce, and fiction can be found in N. N. Feltes's *Modes of Production in Victorian Fiction*[38]. Whereas Russell deals with fictional 'responses' to the development of capitalism, Feltes is concerned with specific fiction texts as part of the development of capitalism. In his studies of the initial production of *Pickwick Papers*, *Henry Esmond*, *Middlemarch*, *Tess*, and *Howards End*, Feltes traces a transition from 'commodity-book' production to 'commodity-text' production, which corresponds to the transformation in the England of this period from a pre-capitalist, petty commodity mode to a fully capitalist mode of production. The various Marxisms of Pierre Macherey, Louis Althusser, Nikos Poulantzas, and Terry Eagleton provide the theoretical framework for this regrettably jargon-laden, but otherwise interesting attempt to focus on the text as production rather than as the object of consumption. Harold Orel's *The Victorian Short Story*[39] also, in part at least, attempts to locate the development of a genre in the conditions of production of the publishing industry, in this case in the growth of general-interest magazines and

35. *Women Writing About Men*, by Jane Miller. Virago. pp. viii + 311. pb £5.50.

36. *The Sinews of the Spirit: The Ideal of Christian Manliness in Victorian Literature*, by Norman Vance. CUP (1985). pp. x + 244. £25.

37. *The Novelist and Mammon: Literary Responses to the World of Commerce in the Nineteenth Century*, by Norman Russell. Clarendon. pp. x + 225. £22.50.

38. *Modes of Production in Victorian Novels*, by N. N. Feltes. UChic. pp. xiii + 125. £15.25.

39. *The Victorian Short Story: Development and Triumph of a Literary Genre*, by Harold Orel. CUP. pp. x + 213. £25.

periodicals. However, Orel's approach is quite different from Feltes's, and his book is mainly a history of the careers of individual short story writers.

Also worth noting are Thomas Vargish's exploration of the various modulations of a providential world-view in the novels of Dickens, Charlotte Brontë, and George Eliot[40], and T. R. Wright's consideration of the impact of Comtean thought on Victorian Britain[41], which includes a section on the positivistic aspects of some novelists.

A number of essayists address themselves to particular subgenres of Victorian fiction. J. S. Bratton examines the treatment of nationalism, adventure, history, and chivalry in fiction for children in 'Of England, Home, and Duty'[42], and in 'Les Héros des Cimitières Souterrains ou le Mythe Victorien des Catacombes' (*CVE*) M. Durand explores the cultural, religious, psychological, and literary reasons for the popularity of Catacomb fiction. In *Rep* Jonathan Loesberg and D. A. Miller discuss different aspects of ideology and narrative form in Sensation fiction (see also p. 408). Joanne Porter and Steve Ellis (*JES*) focus on 'Some Uses of Florence in the Victorian Novel'. They identify the 'Florentine novel' as a subgenre of a subgenre – the Italian novel – and show how the depiction of Florence became an 'arena in which battles between various Victorian "ways of seeing" were fought'.

The literary methods adopted by nineteenth-century writers of historical novels are, according to Ewald Mengel[43], a function of their particular views of history and of reality. Three models of history are examined, which correspond in a loose general sense to the epochs, pre-1860, post-1860, and twentieth century. History as progress is revealed by Scott (*Waverley* and *The Heart of Midlothian*), history as cyclical by Dickens (*A Tale of Two Cities*), and history as contingency by Conrad (*Nostromo*). Possible variations are analysed more briefly in a final chapter which ranges from Kingsley's *Hereward the Wake* to John Berger's *G. A. Novel*, but the general failure to qualify key concepts sufficiently renders Mengel's book somewhat inconclusive. [E.A.M.]

A number of miscellaneous essays are also worth mention. Michael Lund's 'Literary Pieces and Whole Audiences' (*Criticism*) surveys attitudes, in the literary periodicals, to the unfinished novels of Dickens, Thackeray, and Trollope, and uses the theories of Wolfgang Iser in an attempt to identify those aspects of plot which are especially effective in unfinished novels. L. M. Findlay (*ESC*) compares the kinds and degrees of reflexivity in a range of novels from *Waverley* to *Daniel Deronda*. In an occasionally impenetrable essay entitled 'Liminality, Anti-Liminality and the Victorian Novel' (*ELH*) Sarah Gilead analyses the function of liminal figures in Victorian fiction, and suggests that these apparent outsiders (orphans, martyrs, scapegoats, bohemians, and non-conformist women) are usually, in fact, the moral representatives and

40. *The Providential Aesthetic in Victorian Fiction*, by Thomas Vargish. UVirginia (1985). pp. xi + 250. $22.

41. *The Religion of Humanity: The Impact of Comtean Positivism on Victorian Britain*, by T. R. Wright. CUP. pp. xiii + 306. £27.50.

42. In *Imperialism and Popular Culture*, ed. by John M. MacKenzie. ManU. pp. vii + 264. £25.

43. *Gesellschaftsbild und Romankonzeption: Drei Typen des Geschichtsverstehens im Reflex der Form des englischen historischen Romans*, by Ewald Mengel. AF. CWU. pp. 317. DM 112.

ultimate renewers, or redeemers of the group or society from which they are separated.

Finally, Ian Small considers the problems involved in 'Annotating "Hard" Nineteenth-Century Novels' (*EIC*), and in the process raises important questions about the various definitions of, and interrelationships between, the writer, the novel, and the audience.

(b) Individual Novelists

The novels of Edward Bulwer Lytton have been restored to a wider audience in recent years, for example in E. Engel and Margaret King's *The Victorian Novel Before Victoria* (*YW* 65.450). Now James L. Campbell Jr[44] has provided a serviceable if pedestrian introduction to Bulwer's writings, which surveys virtually the entire output of this prolific author. In an account which is descriptive rather than critical or analytic, Campbell identifies the main phases of Bulwer's career, summarizes each of the novels, and situates it in its wider Victorian literary context. In 'Bulwer's *Godolphin*' (*SEL*), William Cragg shows Bulwer adapting the genre of the fashionable novel for the treatment of social problems in his early work, *Godolphin*.

Unfortunately I have failed to obtain Valerie Sanders's *Reason over Passion: Harriet Martineau and Women's Writing* (Harvester).

Disraeli receives little but varied attention this year. Norman Russell discusses *The Voyage of Captain Popanilla* in his chapter on financial crisis and mania in *The Novelist and Mammon*[37], and Michael McCully (*CLAJ*) and Nils Clausson (*VN*) offer reconsiderations of *Sybil* and *Coningsby* respectively. I have not seen McCully's essay, but can report that Clausson's 'Disraeli and Carlyle's "Aristocracy of Talent"' makes an interesting attempt to challenge the traditional view of Millbank as Disraeli's version of a new Carlylean aristocracy of talent, by suggesting that the self-made industrialist is subjected to a critique which anticipates Arnold's attack on the middle classes in *Culture and Anarchy*.

This year's Thackeray studies seem to suggest a decisive shift of attention to the post-*Vanity Fair* novels. In '"A sort of confidential talk between writer and reader"' Gunther Klotz (*ZAA*) undertakes a Marxist analysis of Thackeray's approach to history in *Pendennis*, while in '*Pendennis* and the Controversy on the "Dignity of Literature"' (*NCL*) Craig Howes re-treads some familiar ground, but reads the novel closely in relation to the wider contemporary literary context of the early 1850s. The most thought-provoking work is found in two essays on *Henry Esmond*. J. M. Rignall (Hawthorn[32]) offers a perceptive examination of the way in which this novel's 'ironic subversion of pattern and meaning through time' functions as a means of resisting the incipient nihilism of the nineteenth-century realist novel, and indeed of the historical sense in nineteenth-century culture generally. Most interestingly Rignall challenges J. Hillis Miller's deconstructive reading of *Esmond* in *Fiction and Repetition* (*YW* 63.532–3); he argues instead that Thackeray's ironic procedures do not simply negate meanings and certainties, but rather interrogate them, thus producing an open and questioning rather than a negatively indeterminate narrative form. Karen Chase's subtle and lucid essay, 'The

44. *Edward Bulwer-Lytton*, by James L. Campbell Jr. TEAS. Twayne. pp. 156. £17.95.

Kindness of Consanguinity' in *MLS*, argues that the form of the 'memoir', and its treatment of heroism, worldly success, politics, the family, and history are the products of the 'genealogical imagination', whose 'greatest hope is to cheat time by extending the family into perpetuity'. *Denis Duval* emerges from the shadows this year in Michael Lund's previously noted study (see p. 399), and in John Sutherland's further investigation of Thackeray's working methods entitled 'The Genesis of *Denis Duval*' (*RES*).

Kingsley's novels are read in the context of the 'ideal of Christian manliness' in Norman Vance's *The Sinews of the Spirit*, reviewed above (see p. 398). Elsewhere, attention focuses on textual matters, and in particular on the relation between the serial and volume forms of his works. In 'Kingsley's *Hypatia*' (*NCL*) Larry Uffelman shows how Kingsley's revisions of the novel served both to emphasize its linking of family and national life, and to heighten its anti-Catholicism, while in 'Kingsley's *Hereward the Wake*' (*VIJ*) he charts the muting of anti-Catholicism and anti-monasticism as the novel was transformed from a serial in a Protestant magazine to a book published by the theologically liberal Macmillan's.

In one of the numerous works on Dickens reviewed below Badri Raina notes disarmingly: 'Dickens scholarship today is a copious industry, and one need have a good reason to add to it.' While it is true that some of the current work has been produced for no better reason than the furtherance of an academic career, or the pursuit of a private obsession, the continuing boom in the Dickens industry is also producing interesting and varied versions of this author and his works. In particular, as Edwin Eigner notes in his review of recent Dickens studies in *DSA*, Dickens is benefiting from the current questioning of 'classic realism' as the dominant mode of the nineteenth-century novel. Explorations of Dickens's use of romance conventions, and his sometimes fantastical inclination toward the 'romantic side of familiar things' continue to yield interesting results. A number of writers read various aspects of the novels (particularly questions of narrative point of view) through Foucault's work on the surveillance society, and Jonathan Arac's *Commissioned Spirits* (Rutgers, 1979) has clearly stimulated and influenced some of this year's studies. Others have found Mikhail Bakhtin's concept of dialogic form a useful way into Dickens's multiplicity and polyvocality.

A number of these approaches consort promiscuously together in Kate Flint's volume on Dickens[45] for the Harvester New Readings series, a self-conscious attempt to read Dickens for these times of *ours*, and, in the light of recent literary theories, to 'recognise some of the premises on which [Dickens's work] is based, to point to its affinities with its own time'. While asserting the importance of history, Flint eschews chronology for a broadly thematic approach, emphasizing varieties of conflict and contradiction in Dickens's novels, and drawing variously on Bakhtinian concepts of dialogic and polyphonic form, Derridean perspectives (multivocality), Victor Shklovsky's views on the detective novel (plotting), Foucault on the surveillance society (narrative point of view) and, more unusually, A. J. Greimas's theory of actants, which is used to further a feminist analysis of Dickens's 'Disruptive Angels'. Flint seems well versed in critical theory and in recent Dickens criticism, but this is ultimately an unsatisfying little book, whose limpid application of a variety of

45. *Dickens*, by Kate Flint. Harvester. pp. xi + 159. hb £16.95, pb £5.95.

reading strategies fails to engage with the challenge, energy, or excitement of Dickens's novels.

Perhaps the most important event in the Dickens industry this year is the appearance of the first two volumes in the Dickens Companions series [46]. These are the fulfilment of an annotator's dreams: not just a dozen or so pages of notes following the text in decent and deferential obscurity, but the whole of an ample and handsome volume. Nineteen volumes are projected, and the series claims to provide the most comprehensive annotation of Dickens's work ever undertaken. The notes seek to identify and explain allusions to current events, intellectual and religious issues, literary works, and the Bible, etc. The influence of other writers, and autobiographical references and influences are also noted, and information is given on social customs and topography. Ian Small raises some theoretical questions about the nature of such an enterprise in the *EIC* article already noted (p. 400), but within its own terms of reference, and on the evidence of the first two volumes, this series is to be welcomed.

The most ambitious, and I think almost certainly the most important, of the other books is Janet L. Larson's *Dickens and the Broken Scripture* [47]. This is a densely argued and learned, but also fertile and suggestive study of the ways in which Dickens's novels make use of the Bible, liturgical language, and iconography. Larson's view of Dickens's use of the Bible derives from her Bakhtinian view of the novel as a form which is produced by a 'contradictory and multi-languaged world'. She argues that in the late novels in particular, the Bible 'becomes a paradoxical code that provides [Dickens] with contradictory interpretations of experience; it is drawn upon as though it were still a source of stable values ... but it is also becoming a locus of hermeneutical instability'. Larson's study explores the fictional effects of this paradox, and examines the ways in which Dickens 'replays and revises' biblical texts in five novels. Ultimately this is not simply a study of Dickens's 'use' of the Bible, but rather a study of intertextuality, of the way in which his use of biblical patterns and references is mediated through other forms of representation, particularly the forms of melodrama.

The two remaining critical books seek less to explore Dickens's novels than to demonstrate a general (and, in both cases, rather dubious) view of them. Badri Raina [48] tries to read the whole *œuvre* 'as one composite *Bildungsroman* that builds progressively superior insights as each succeeding novel deconstructs its predecessor(s) into a mounting historical graph'. Raina's view of Dickens's career as a constant adjustment of a 'composite self-image', which is expressed in representative figures in the novels, is echoed in some aspects of Graham Daldry's more ambitious attempt [49] to put Dickens criticism on the right track. Daldry argues that 'criticism' has generally failed to meet the challenge of the

46. *The Companion to 'Our Mutual Friend'*, by Michael Cotsell. *The Companion to 'The Mystery of Edwin Drood'*, by Wendy S. Jacobson. DC. A&U. pp. xvi + 316. £27.50; pp. 209. £22.50.

47. *Dickens and the Broken Scripture*, by Janet L. Larson. UGeo. (1985). pp. xvi + 364. $20.

48. *Dickens and the Dialectic of Growth*, by Badri Raina. UWisc. pp. xiii + 172. £27.50.

49. *Charles Dickens and the Form of the Novel: Form and Narrative in Dickens's Work*, by Graham Daldry. CH. pp. 208. £19.95.

novel as practised by Dickens and has, as a consequence, divided Dickens into two writers, one 'concerned with language and the internal concerns of linguistic structure', and the other a writer of social conscience. Daldry seeks to integrate these two approaches by means of a rather idiosyncratic use of the concepts of 'Fiction' and 'Narrative', which he elaborates in a rather tendentious introduction. In fact the book is a narrowly focused, sometimes overingenious, but generally lively formal analysis of seven novels.

My final general book dealing with Dickens is, as its author proclaims, 'unashamedly' an influence study. Edward Stokes[50] seeks to demonstrate that the influence of Hawthorne was one of the most important reasons why English novelists from 1850 onwards did not commit themselves more fully to documentary realism and the treatment of the ordinary. In the case of Dickens, Stokes detects Hawthorne's influence in the development of a more disciplined form, the use of symbolism, and the preoccupation with solitude and alienation in *Bleak House* and subsequent novels. Eloise Knapp Hay takes a more general and contextual approach to the relationship between these two writers in 'Oberon and Prospero' (*DSA*), which attributes their distinctive forms of 'psychomoral melodrama' to the different national traditions in which they wrote. In 'Dickens, Ruskin and the City' (*Dickensian*) Charles Swann is also interested in literary parallels and influences in his comparison of Dickensian and Ruskinian ways of seeing the city and its materials.

The remaining general articles offer a variety of reading strategies (to use Kate Flint's phrase), which produce rather different versions of Dickens's work. In an essay already mentioned (p. 398) Laura Hapke (*VN*) compares Dickens's portrayal of fallen women and their redemption with that in other contemporary novels. 'Dickens's Streetwalkers' also concern Laurie Langbauer in an interesting, if self-consciously modish essay in *ELH*, which reads some of his central female characters as emblems of that 'teasing principle' of romance which disorders plot and diverts it from the straight and narrow.

Gillian Beer's notion of the connections between Dickensian and Darwinian plots is taken up (though with less subtlety) by George Levine's 'Dickens, Darwin, Science, and Narrative Form' (*TSLL*). Levine documents the evidence of Dickens's interest in contemporary science, and compares a number of aspects of his art with Darwin's ideas, concluding that despite his continual 'straining' towards the comfort of design, Dickens – like Darwin – used 'inherited idealist and design-permeated conventions to build almost mythic structures of crossings and recrossings appropriate to the sense of modern urban life'. Michael S. Kearns, on the other hand, sees Dickens as the reviser of an older science in 'Associationism, the Heart, and the Life of the Mind in Dickens's Novels' (*DSA*), which links his idea of the 'reformation of the heart' to his use of Associationist psychology.

Thomas M. Leitch intervenes in the debate about Dickens's endings with 'Closure and Teleology in Dickens' (*SNNTS*), which distinguishes between those novels which simply 'come to rest as the sheer cessation of motion', and those (usually later) narratives, which 'display' their endings as teleological devices which can incorporate 'the binary and irreconcilable endings his fictions seem to predicate'. Conversely, George H. Ford (*Mosaic*) offers an

50. *Hawthorne's Influence on Dickens and George Eliot*, by Edward Stokes. UQP. pp. x + 238. £25.

appreciation of Dickens's skill at beginnings in 'Openers and Overtures in Dickens's Novels'.

Brief mention should also be made of a couple of essays on the shorter fiction in *DQu*. 'In the Meantime' by Deborah A. Thomas explores the stylistic experimentation involved in Dickens's concern with doubling and secret guilt in the short fiction of the late 1850s, while Michael Cotsell's piece entitled 'The Uncommercial Traveller on the Commercial Road' discusses political and formal aspects of his attitude to the East End in the *Uncommercial Traveller* essays.

All of Dickens's novels, with the exception of *Nicholas Nickleby* have been the subject of essays. As usual the later fiction has been the main focus of attention, although *Martin Chuzzlewit* is also widely discussed this year. The 150th anniversary of the publication of its first instalment has occasioned a number of essays on *Pickwick Papers*, and *DQu* celebrates the occasion with a complete number on this novel. Some of its celebrations are a little lacklustre, for example Elliot Engel and Margaret King's review of *Pickwick*'s critical history, and Joseph Rosenblum's discussion of the novel's constant allusions to *Paradise Lost*. On the other hand, Michael Cotsell offers an energetic, if slightly inconsequential, 'Critical Diversion' on *Pickwick* as a travel novel, and Mark M. Hennelly Jr uses Dickens's own attitudes to play, and the ideas of Johan Huizinga, in a lively piece on 'Dickens's Praise of Folly' and the 'primary power of play'. In '"I thought of Mr. Pickwick, and wrote the first number"' Robert L. Patten raises a number of important issues, including the vexed question of whether this work *is* a novel. The essay examines the evolution of Pickwick's character, which shows Dickens 'writing his way out' of the fixities of character dictated by the conventions of 'the graphic evocation of a taxonomy of types', and moving to a 'system of language-as-sign'.

David Paroissien has produced an annotated bibliography on *Oliver Twist* (Garland), which I have not yet seen. New work includes Paul Davis's 'Imaging *Oliver Twist*' (*Dickensian*), an interesting and illuminating comparison of Dickens's novel and Harrison Ainsworth's *Jack Sheppard* as similar experiments in adapting Hogarth to narrative form. Davis uses Eisenstein's concepts of montage and the ideogram to illustrate the way in which Dickens moves away from Hogarth's linear moral dramas, towards a dialectical pattern which 'transforms the novel from a progress into a novel of consciousness'. On the other hand, in 'Structure, Myth and Rite in *Oliver Twist*' (*SNNTS*) Roland F. Anderson attempts to account for what he regards as the 'ramshackle' nature of the plot by relating it to fairy tales, myths, and rites.

Little Nell appears as one of the restless women discussed in Laurie Langbauer's essay (p. 403). In *Novel*, Audrey Jaffe's interest in the conflict between the narrator's 'assertions of omniscient knowledge' and the 'intrinsically "invisible" demands of omniscient narration' leads her to focus on the relationship between omniscience and curiosity in *The Old Curiosity Shop*. This rather difficult and theoretically eclectic (one might even say confused) essay entitled '"Never Safe but in Hiding"' reads Master Humphrey's narrative by reference to the Lacanian concept of the mirror phase, but more generally draws on Jonathan Arac's Foucauldian reading of Dickens's narrative point of view in *Commissioned Spirits*. The single essay on *Barnaby Rudge*, '*Jack Sheppard* and *Barnaby Rudge*' by Natalie Schroeder (*SNNTS*), reads it as a deglamourizing parody of Ainsworth's novel.

Three essays in *DSA* seek to throw further light on Dickens's attitude to America. The most substantial contribution is David Parker's 'Dickens and America: The Unflattering Glass', which explores the ways in which *American Notes* and *Martin Chuzzlewit* 'reflected potential selves' which Dickens had difficulty in coming to terms with. This piece might valuably be read in conjunction with Jerome Meckier's 1984 essay on this subject in *MLR* (*YW* 65.458). John Hildebidle considers the wider structural and thematic function of the American section of *Martin Chuzzlewit* in 'Hail Columbia' and, in the slightest piece, Sylvère Monod examines Mr Bevan as Dickens's complex but half-hearted attempt to portray his idea of a good American. Also in *DSA*, but in quite a different vein, is 'The Labyrinth and the Library', Gerhard Joseph's attempt to read Dickens's novel alongside Umberto Eco's *The Name of the Rose*. The trope of the world as labyrinthine library lies at the centre of a tortuous argument, which strains the reader's credulity and patience, but which also raises some important questions about the nature of Victorian representational realism. More modestly, in '*Martin Chuzzlewit*: Language as Disguise' (*Dickensian*) Barrie Saywood examines the word-play which he sees as the central cohesive principle of the novel.

Dombey and Son receives little attention this year. In 'Dickens and the New Historicism: The Polyvocal Audience and Discourse of *Dombey and Son*' (Hawthorn[32]), Roger D. Sell offers a rather routine reading of the novel in an otherwise interesting review of the current state of Dickens criticism. Particularly interesting is Sell's use of Bakhtin's concept of heteroglossia in a general re-examination of Dickens's depiction of, and relationship to, the middle class. Anna Maria Stuby (*ZAA*) employs the perspective of the older historicism in her Marxist analysis of the novel's allegorizing of time ('Die Allegoreisung der Zeit als Kapitalismuskritik in Dickens' Roman *Dombey and Son*').

Two essays on *David Copperfield* explore its negotiation of various (sometimes conflicting) discourses of the family, class, the home, work, and sexuality. In 'Cookery, Not Rookery', Chris Vanden Bossche (*DSA*) traces how the treatment of David's quest for social legitimacy through the discovery of a true family, both endorses and disrupts dominant ideologies of work, family, and the home. In 'Sex and Seriousness in *David Copperfield*', Ian Crawford (*JNT*) returns to the much-discussed question of David's struggle to discipline his heart, and explores the gap between David's conscious narrative and its subtext of sublimated sexuality. Phillip D. Atteberry's 'The Fictions of *David Copperfield*' (*VIJ*) is also concerned with the tensions between various narrative impulses, in this case between the narrator's preoccupation with 'the exact truth', his desire to demonstrate the operation of a divine Providence, and the narrative's undermining of the narrator's conscious and unconscious strategies. Robert Tracy (*DSA*) takes a less subtle view of David's narrative in 'Stranger Than Truth', a comparison of the novel with Dickens's autobiographical fragment and Trollope's autobiography, which concludes that the fiction is more true than the autobiographies because fictions 'tell' while autobiographies 'explain'.

The double narrative of *Bleak House* receives its annual re-examination in two above-average essays. In 'Fit to Survive' (*SNNTS*) Karen Jahn makes interesting use of recent work on Dickens's Christianity, and his attitude to science and Spencerian social science, and reads the novel's structure, plot, and imagery as a 'lopsided dialectic', which dramatizes the conflict between progressive evolutionary theory and Christian ethics. Graham Hough[51] uses the novel as a yardstick with which to beat back Barthes-inspired attacks on 'classic realism', in a spirited defence of the humanism of Dickens's realist art. Hough examines the nature and interrelationship of the descriptive techniques and rhetorical strategies of the two narratives, in order to demonstrate that it is via the psychology of individual character, revealed in distinctive utterance, 'that both the constitutive role of language and its relation to a non-linguistic reality is guaranteed'. On quite a different tack, Nina Auerbach's 'Alluring Vacancies in Victorian Character' (*KR*) compares the theatricality of Esther's character with those of Gwendolen Harleth and Isabel Archer, and Patricia Eldredge, in an essay which I have not seen, applies the psychological theories of Karen Horney to Esther's self-effacement (in *Third Force Psychology and the Study of Literature*, ed. by Bernard J. Paris for FDU).

Hard Times has always disturbed its 'progressive' readers because it seems to be, as Robert Coles suggests in 'The Politics of *Hard Times*' (*DSA*), 'as much a novel against social reform as it is a novel of social reform'. Coles offers an interesting way into the ambivalence of the novel's politics by examining it in the context of contemporary discourses of social reform, in particular the discourse of *Household Words*, the journal in which it was first published. Robert L. Caserio (*Novel*) explores Dickens's 'liberal politics' by means of semiotics in an essay which makes hard work of *Hard Times*. Caserio has been caught up in the current vogue for Umberto Eco's *The Name of the Rose*, as his title ('The Name of the Horse') indicates, and in his enthusiasm suggests that we reread Dickens's novel 'as a theoretical novel that is aware already of what Eco's semiotics would say about it'. Thus read the novel becomes a 'drama about language, whereby Dickens makes linguistic and semantic structures slip their boundaries'. Patricia Ingham (*RES*), on the other hand, is concerned with the literary representation of spoken language, and in particular the use of dialect. In 'Dialect as "Realism"' she examines two documentary sources for Dickens's use of dialect in this novel, and seeks to explain the failure of Stephen Blackpool in terms of the discrepancy between what the narrator *says* about the character, and what he *hears* him say. Finally, in a brief essay in *DQu* Joan E. Klingel reads the novel as a gloss of St Paul's First Epistle to the Corinthians.

Little Dorrit seems to have retreated into the critical shadows for the moment, but Michael Cotsell may tempt others to explore further some of the welter of detail he casts up in 'Politics and Peeling Frescoes' in *DSA*. Victorian art criticism, Sir Austen Layard, radicalism, the Crimean war, middle-class aping of gentility, and Dickens's own dislike of connoisseurship are some of the issues discussed in this knowledgeable but disparate essay on Dickens's 'European novel'. Alison Booth (*NCL*) is also interested in the approach to contemporary history in this novel, which she sees as Dickens's response to Carlyle's 'On History'. In the interesting 'Little Dorrit and Dorothea Brooke' Booth argues that instead of 'eulogising supermen', Dickens (as well as George Eliot) created in his heroine a figure 'neither pre-eminent nor manly who yet redeem[s] the common experience of a burdensome past'. In *Dickensian* Adela Stczynska focuses somewhat minutely on 'The Shifting Point of View in the Narrative Design of *Little Dorrit*'.

51. In *Realism in European Literature: Essays in Honour of J. P. Stern*, ed. by Nicholas Boyce and Martin Swales. CUP. pp. ix + 206. £25.

If critics have ceased to be as interested as they previously were in 'prison symbolism' in *Little Dorrit*, then Foucault's work on the birth of the prison in *Discipline and Punish* (*YW* 58.232) has turned their attention to Dickens's participation in, and questioning of, a specific cultural discourse of 'disciplinary technology'. In a thought-provoking essay on *Great Expectations* entitled 'Prison-bound: Dickens and Foucault' (*EIC*) Jeremy Tambling is concerned less with physical incarceration in Little Britain than with the novel's depiction of the oppressiveness of the language and mores of British society at large. He is particularly interesting on the way in which the form of this novel both foregrounds autobiography's tendency to define the subject confessionally and privilege individuality, and at the same time explores the social and psychic consequences of this process. On the other hand, in 'Stories Present and Absent in *Great Expectations*' (*ELH*), Eiichi Hara uses the theories of Gérard Genette, Tzvetan Todorov, and, most importantly, Bakhtin's work on carnival and polyphonic form, to show how the novel undermines the view of 'authorship' implied by the autobiographical mode.

DSA devotes three essays to this novel. Hana Wirth-Nester compares 'The Literary Orphan as National Hero' in *Great Expectations* and *Huckleberry Finn* in relation to their respective national cultures and literary traditions; Stanley Friedman explores 'The Complex Origins of Pip and Magwitch' in James Byron's burletta *The Maid and the Magpie*, and Susan Schoenbauer Thurin's 'The Seven Deadly Sins in *Great Expectations*' reads the novel allegorically. Elsewhere in 'The Economic Background of *Great Expectations*' W. J. Lohman Jr (*VIJ*) makes a modest but interesting attempt to situate the novel in the specific economic conditions of the period 1850–70, and Naomi Lightman (*Dickensian*) compares 'The "Vulcanic Dialect" of *Great Expectations*' with similar imagery in Carlyle and Ruskin.

Our Mutual Friend is the subject of one of the first volumes to be issued in the Dickens Companions series noted above[46]. Michael Cotsell has produced a full introduction on the circumstances of the novel's composition, which gives useful details of the two plays from which Dickens borrowed plot elements. Thereafter each chapter is minutely annotated, for example, the phrase 'filthy water', in Bk. 1, Ch. 1, produces the note: 'in London the water was badly polluted by sewage and industrial effluent'. Some notes, however, are considerably less elementary; for example, the two and a half pages on 'highly certificated schoolmaster' (Bk. 2, Ch. 2), which constitutes a succinct essay on aspects of Victorian education. In the only other work on *Our Mutual Friend*, 'From Nightmare to Reverie' (*DUJ*), Mary Ann Kelly discusses its treatment of the power of creative reverie in transforming nightmare conditions.

Some of the mysteries of *Edwin Drood* are clarified by Wendy Jacobson's volume in the Dickens Companions series[46]. Before proceeding to detailed annotation, Jacobson provides a very useful introduction which summarizes the experiences, writing, and reading which resonate in the novel. She also considers some of the mysteries of this perfect mystery novel, and surveys a range of possible endings based on internal clues, and reference to other works by Dickens, or known to him. Charles Forsyte's *Dickensian* piece, 'The Sapsea Fragment – Fragment of What?' also seeks to illuminate the mystery of Dickens's unfinished novel by reference to the 'Sapsea Fragment' found by Forster.

This year's only noteworthy essay on Wilkie Collins (indeed the only essay I have discovered) is D. A. Miller's lively 'Cage aux Folles: Sensation and Gender in Wilkie Collins's *The Woman in White*', which appears in both *Rep* and Hawthorn[32]. Despite Miller's tendency towards a self-indulgent, self-referentiality this is an intelligent and suggestive reading of Collins's novel and its 'revision' in *Lady Audley's Secret*. Miller is particularly interesting on the precise nature and significance of the sensations in 'sensation fiction', and on the ways in which the genre inscribes gender.

Despite their apparently continuing popularity with readers, the novels of the Brontë sisters remain a somewhat minority interest to critics. There are two general books which are both rather narrow in focus. Edward Chitham's *The Brontës' Irish Background*[52] uncovers a great deal of information about Patrick Brontë's Irish ancestors, and considers the influence of this particular heritage on his daughters' novels. His detective work yields its best results in the account of *Wuthering Heights* as a mythologized version of the Irish Brontës' family history. Considerably less successful, despite her evident enthusiasm for the Brontë novels, is Enid L. Duthie's *The Brontës and Nature*[53] which covers rather familiar ground before coming to the rather unsurprising conclusion that 'the relationship of the Brontës to nature was a close one'.

In '*Jane Eyre*: The Apocalypse of the Body' (*ELH*) Paul Pickrel re-examines the now familiar view that *Jane Eyre* is a reply to *Paradise Lost*, by focusing on Rochester as both Richardsonian hero (he has Lovelace in mind) and Satanic figure. Pickrel makes much of the novel's complex perspective on Jane's choice between Rochester's body and St John's deathlike spirituality, whereas Karen Ann Butery views her 'Flight from Decision' from the perspective of *Third Force Psychology* (see p. 406). The most interesting work on Charlotte Brontë is Rosemary Clark-Beattie's essay on *Villette*, 'Fables of Rebellion' (*ELH*), which is particularly illuminating on its relation to prevailing ideologies of class and gender. Clark-Beattie suggests that *Villette*'s anti-Catholicism, like the anti-Catholic novels of Kingsley, Elizabeth Sewell, and Catherine Sinclair, is structured by a 'colonialist impulse': thus, though Lucy escapes to Belgium from her marginalized position in English society, her adherence to the values of the culture she has fled endows her with a sense of superior apartness in her host culture.

One of the more improbable of this year's titles is Robert K. Wallace's *Emily Brontë and Beethoven*[54], and indeed the book is a curious mixture of biographical scholarship, musical history, and a kind of musicological practical criticism. However parts of Wallace's exploration of the extent to which 'the meaning of [the] art' of the writer and the composer is comparable, offers some new perspectives on *Wuthering Heights*, and on Emily Brontë's Romanticism. Marjorie Burns (Hawthorn[32]) takes issue with the recent critical orthodoxy, deriving from Gilbert and Gubar's *The Madwoman in the Attic* (Yale, 1979) that *Wuthering Heights* is simply a reversal of Blake's *The Marriage of Heaven and Hell*, and argues instead that we should see the novel as offering various, often conflicting, versions of Eden. The most interesting discussion of Emily

52. *The Brontës' Irish Background*, by Edward Chitham. Macmillan. pp. ix + 168. £25.

53. *The Brontës and Nature*, by Enid L. Duthie. Macmillan. pp. ix + 273. £27.50.

54. *Emily Brontë and Beethoven: Romantic Equilibrium in Fiction and Music*, by Robert K. Wallace. UGeo. pp. ix + 237. $30.

Brontë's novel is 'Gendered and Layered Narrative' (*JNT*), N. M. Jacobs's comparison of the way in which the 'layered' narratives of *Wuthering Heights* and *The Tenant of Wildfell Hall* are modified from the familiar Gothic frame-tale to serve several gender-related functions.

The current interest in women writers has, rather surprisingly, failed to generate much work on Elizabeth Gaskell this year. Tessa Brodetsky's extremely bland volume in the Berg Women's series[55] adds nothing to our knowledge or understanding of this writer and her work. More illuminating is Robyn R. Warhol's attempt – in 'Letters and Novels "One Woman Wrote to Another"' (*VN*) and 'Towards a Theory of the Engaging Narrator' (*PMLA*) – to develop a theory of the 'engaging' or 'talkative' narrator as a distinctively female rhetorical strategy. It is interesting to note, however, that despite the feminist inflection and the theoretical framework provided by the narratology of Genette, Warhol seems to be returning to something very like the view of the narrator developed in W. J. Harvey's 1958 essay on 'George Eliot and the Omniscient Author Convention' (*YW* 39.257).

Feminist criticism, narratology, the developing interest in the relationships between the literary and other forms of discourse, particularly the scientific, underlie the many and various rereadings of George Eliot's novels. Gillian Beer incorporates many of these approaches in her study of the author as a 'Key Woman Writer'[56], which reads the novels not only in the light of recent critical and theoretical developments, but also in relation to other Victorian writing, especially that concerned with the 'nature' of women and their social position. The attempt to 'historicise' the novels is an important part of Beer's project, and is much in evidence in one of the most interesting chapters which examines George Eliot's reading and revision of novels by other women writers, notably Geraldine Jewsbury, Frederika Bremer, and Elizabeth Gaskell. Discussion of the early fictions focuses on the relationship between gender and narrative voice, while *The Mill on the Floss* is used to explore the recurring problematic of the relationship between heroism and martyrdom in the stories of women's lives. Subsequent chapters focus on the complex treatment of causality, sequence, and Natural Law in the middle novels, ironic perspectives on 'The Woman Question' in *Middlemarch*, and the exceptional woman in *Daniel Deronda*.

George Eliot is also the subject of a volume in Harvester's other new series, New Readings, which offers its (largely undergraduate) audience a novel tour around the existing monuments of English Literature, guided by an eclectic range of the latest critical techniques. Simon Dentith[57] has served his author and the series well with a lucid and well-informed re-assessment of her work. He deftly provides his readers with the means of understanding, in broad terms, the intellectual, social, and historical contexts of the novels, and repeatedly directs our attention to the reasons why we should find George Eliot's efforts and achievements important both in her own age and in ours. Like Gillian Beer, Dentith has organized his study both thematically and chronologically. He explicates George Eliot's doctrine of sympathy in the early fictions, and explores what he perceives to be the breakdown of that fragile synthesis of 'an

55. *Elizabeth Gaskell*, by Tessa Brodetsky. Berg. pp. viii + 113. hb £8.95, pb £3.95.
56. *George Eliot*, by Gillian Beer. Harvester. pp. xii + 206. hb £15.95, pb £4.95.
57. *George Eliot*, by Simon Dentith. Harvester. pp. x + 150. hb £16.95, pb £5.95.

aesthetic of realism linked to a faith in human progress' by the 1860s. His consideration of the later novels focuses on Eliot's view of history, her realism and narrative method, and issues of gender. Although Simon Dentith and Gillian Beer both undertake a historical reading of George Eliot's novels, the effects of this shared project are interestingly different. Beer reads George Eliot 'in history'. That is to say, she situates the novels in a specific socio-historical context, with a proper emphasis on the radical discontinuities between that culture and her own, but she also reminds us of continuities, and in particular of our own implication and participation in the cultural narratives of which she writes. Dentith, on the other hand, reads the novels symptomatically 'as history', a strategy which casts the author in the role of a patient, bearing the symptoms of history, beyond cure, but awaiting diagnosis.

Mary Wilson Carpenter[58] reads the novels neither 'in' history, nor 'as' history, but rather as the consequence of their author's 'fall' from history when she abandoned the Church and its traditions of apocalyptic 'continuous historical' interpretation. Carpenter attempts to show how the resulting sense of 'the diversity and plurality of history' led George Eliot to produce in her novels, 'constructions and deconstructions of illusions of coherence', which revise the discredited apocalyptic modes of interpretation. This dense and difficult book gives a deconstructive turn to Frank Kermode's work on narrative theory and apocalyptic thought in *Sense of an Ending* (1967), but despite its formidable erudition its focus is extremely narrow, and there is little sense of how George Eliot's revised Protestant apocalypse relates to other nineteenth-century discourses of history.

George Eliot also appears in two comparative studies. Edward Stokes pairs her with Dickens in his examination of the influence of Hawthorne on the forms of English realism[50]. More polemically, Richard Freadman[59] undertakes an extended comparison of her novels and theories of fiction with those of Henry James. Freadman concentrates on the conception of character held by these two writers, and its relation to other aspects of their narrative form. Freadman is fired by a missionary zeal to overturn the anti-humanism and anti-realism of poststructuralism, and attempts to recuperate George Eliot's (and James's) fictional practice as 'fictional humanism'. The organizing principle of this book is its author's belief in a concept of 'the substantial, essentialist individual and his [*sic*] fulfilments', and consequently its main emphasis is on George Eliot's treatment of agency, choice, and the identity of subjects.

Most of the essays offer readings of individual novels, but there are a few of more general import. Sheldon Rothblatt focuses on the author's intellectual context in his examination of George Eliot as a 'Type of European Intellectual' (*HEI*), and Michael Bell discusses her treatment of feeling and her attitude to sentimentalism (*GEFR*). More interestingly in 'George Eliot and the Pharmakon' Kathleen McCormack (*VIJ*) offers a Derridean view of 'this strange disease of modern life' in her analysis of George Eliot's development of the Platonic metaphor of the Pharmakon to express her 'wariness of the written word', particularly its power either to aggravate or cure the condition of England.

58. *George Eliot and the Landscape of Time: Narrative Form and Protestant Apocalyptic History*, by Mary Wilson Carpenter. UNC. pp. xiii + 246. £21.50.

59. *Eliot, James and the Fictional Self: A Study in Character and Narration*, by Richard Freadman. Macmillan. pp. x + 285. £27.50.

Unfortunately I have not seen Timothy Pace's discussion of 'Displaced Religious Confession' in 'Amos Barton' (*Style*), which appears to be the only essay on *Scenes of Clerical Life*. However I can report on his closely argued semiotic reading of the trial scene in *Adam Bede* entitled 'Silence in the Courtroom' (*ELWIU*). Pace sees this scene as the climax of George Eliot's attempt, in this novel, to reconcile two opposing views of language, morality, and fictional realism: on the one hand, the view that the deep communal truths of spiritual and moral experience are essentially beyond the reach of language, and on the other the commitment to precise description as the ground of the moral potency of her realist text. Pace's description of the 'semiotics of multiplicity', which he sees as George Eliot's means of resolving this conflict, seems (to this reader at least) remarkably similar to her doctrine of sympathy.

Kerry McSweeney sees the conflict in terms of 'the realistic' and 'the visionary', or 'the truth of experience' and 'the truth of aspiration', in an above-average performance in the annual reconsideration of 'The Ending of *The Mill on the Floss*' (*ESC*). He argues that far from being a *Deus ex Machina*, the ending proceeds from the novel's elaboration of two distinct but complementary modes of memory.

Sally Shuttleworth[60] also discovers a double perspective on memory in *Silas Marner*. Nineteenth-century debates about social and psychological development provide the context for her examination of the paradox of this novel's insistence on both the moral function of memory and the radical discontinuities of the psychic life.

The Clarendon edition of *Middlemarch*[61] makes its weighty appearance this year. David Carroll has based his text on the one-volume cheap edition of 1874 which the author herself corrected, and he has incorporated or recorded the many deletions in the manuscript. Although we have long been familiar with the notebooks and journals in which George Eliot collected and shaped the material for her novel, Carroll adds to our knowledge with a fascinating account of the history of its composition, publication, and revision, which pays particularly close attention to the complexities of George Eliot's adaptation to the demands of part publication. As in the other volumes in this series the textual apparatus and editorial procedures are clearly set out, and brief explanatory notes provide the sources of literary allusions, identify historical figures, and explain obscure words or phrases. The editor – on his own admission – makes no attempt to 'annotate all references to the complex social and political background of the Reform period' of the novel's setting. Perhaps we need a George Eliot Companion, along the lines of the Unwin Dickens Companions, to perform this task.

'One Round of a Long Ladder' (*ESC*) is N. N. Feltes's Marxist analysis of this novel's apparently 'exotic' new publishing format, which he sees as a formal consequence of its female author's 'overdetermined' relation to the structure of literary production. Patricia Lorimer Lundberg also approaches the novel as a gendered text in 'George Eliot: Mary Ann Evans's Subversive Tool in *Middlemarch*' (*SNNTS*). Lundberg seeks (rather unconvincingly) to release the madwoman from George Eliot's attic by uncovering a hidden

60. In *Languages of Nature: Critical Essays on Science and Literature*, ed. by Ludmilla Jordanova. FAB. pp. 351. hb £25, pb £7.95.

61. *Middlemarch*, by George Eliot, ed. by David Carroll. Clarendon. pp. lxxxv + 825. £65.

feminist rage, which subverts the novel's doctrine of renunciation and submission by presenting the main male characters as moral weaklings, and by manipulating the plot to exact vengeance on them. 'St Theresa, St Dorothea, and Miss Brooke in *Middlemarch*' by Hilary Fraser (*NCF*) offers a more complex view of renunciation by exploring George Eliot's use of the 'peculiar blend of sensuality and mysticism' in the St Theresa myth. Alison Booth (*NCL*) compares 'Little Dorrit and Dorothea Brooke' and relates the narrative patterns of *Middlemarch* and *Little Dorrit* to nineteenth-century history and historiography. Finally, Elizabeth Ermarth (Hawthorn[32]) invokes Shakespeare's audience and Feuerbach's I/Thou consciousness in her discussion of the self-conscious humanity of the *Middlemarch* narrator.

Daniel Deronda appears as three rather different novels in the current crop of essays. Jacqueline Rose[62] approaches the novel via Gwendolen's moments of horror, which the narrative 'stages' as 'spectacle'. Rose's main concern is to explore the connections between George Eliot's narrative representation of female experience, and a range of social and medical discourses which constituted 'the Woman' (and particularly female sexuality) as 'the privileged object of investigation and control'. Elsewhere 'The Jewish Question' produces two quite different answers. In 'Awakened Perceptions in *Daniel Deronda*' Rivkah Zim (*EIC*) considers the 'artistic risks' of a novel whose experimental form requires the reader to participate in its hero's cultural and emotional awakening to the force of Judaism. Or, as Catherine Gallagher (Yeazell[33]) puts it: 'a young man who thinks he has a mission to save wayward women turns out to have a mission to save a nation of usurers'. Gallagher's extremely convoluted essay on 'The Prostitute and the Jewish Question' in *Daniel Deronda* sees the novel as the locus of a contest between George Eliot's displaced guilt at having escaped the specifically patriarchal authority of her literary forefathers, by entering the literary marketplace (i.e. prostituting herself), and her subsequent efforts to construct a superseding 'moral economy'.

Gallagher's contention that women who entered the career of authorship 'did not enter an inappropriately male territory, but a degradingly female one', provides a useful perspective in which to view the career and critical history of Margaret Oliphant. A historical study which attempted to read her novels in the context of the literary marketplace, the sorority of writing women, and contemporary discourses of fiction would be a worthwhile undertaking. Merryn Williams's *Margaret Oliphant: A Critical Biography*[63], however, is content to rehearse the circumstances of the author's life, and provide rather uninspiring plot and thematic summaries of the handful of fictional works on which she bases her claims for Oliphant's status as a 'great writer'. Williams has also written a useful introduction to a new edition of Oliphant's short stories[64].

As Margaret Oliphant's career testifies, women were not merely prolific producers of fiction, but they were also prodigious readers and reviewers. Geraldine Jewsbury, who as novelist, publisher's reader, and reviewer had an important mediating role in the production and reception of Victorian fiction,

62. *Sexuality and the Field of Vision*, by Jacqueline Rose. Verso. pp. 256. pb £7.95.

63. *Margaret Oliphant: A Critical Biography*, by Merryn Williams. Macmillan. pp. xv + 217. £27.50.

64. *'The Doctor's Family' and Other Stories*, by Margaret Oliphant, ed. and intro. by Merryn Williams. OUP. pp. xviii + 209. pb £2.95.

is the subject of an informative study by Monica Correa Fryckstedt[65]. Fryckstedt analyses Jewsbury's *Athenaeum* reviews (1849–80) in the context of the general climate of mid-Victorian fiction reviewing, and in the process raises a number of interesting questions about contemporary ideas of fiction and the reading public. Unfortunately a rather simple descriptive approach prevents her from engaging seriously with these questions.

Trollope, another prodigious toiler in the literary marketplace, has received a number of rereadings from a variety of theoretical perceptives. However, R. D. McMaster's *Trollope and the Law*[66] avoids theory, and offers an investigation of the centrality of the Law to Trollope's conservative view of society. In this well-organized study McMaster shows how Trollope's 'philosophical view of English Law' coexists with a great deal of satire on the viciousness of actual lawyers and certain legal procedures. Whereas Coral Lansbury's *The Reasonable Man: Trollope's Legal Fiction* (*YW* 62.327) examines the influence on Trollope's style and structure of particular techniques of legal pleading, McMaster focuses on the representation, in a range of novels, of lawyers, the professional organization of the Law, and the legal system. '"Spontaneous Order" and the Politics of Anthony Trollope' by Robert Hughes (*NCL*) also finds Trollope's attitude to the Law an index of his attitudes towards politics and English life. Hughes relates the 'models of social interaction' in the novels to Friedrich Hayek's notion of 'spontaneous order', and to the body of conservative social thought deriving from Adam Smith, David Hume, and Edmund Burke. Richard C. Burke's 'Accommodation and Transcendence' (*DSA*) examines Trollope's use of wills in his fictional elaboration of this conservative tradition. Elsewhere, David Skilton (Hawthorn[32]) pursues his continuing interest in 'The Trollope Reader'. He investigates Trollope's actual readers and their representatives in the novels of the 1860s, and explores the modern reader's relationship with these actual and implied readers.

The most innovative attempts at rereading Trollope are found in the studies of individual novels. In 'Trollope's Ground of Meaning' (*VN*) Sarah Gilead contrasts the 'paradoxical' Trollope produced by recent criticism, with her own reading of *The Macdermots of Ballycloran* as a 'resolutely monolithic' text which represents human experience 'reduced to an awful hypostasis'. T. Bareham's 'First and Last' (*DUJ*) also re-examines Trollope's first novel, this time in conjunction with his last, in an attempt to establish their continuity of ideology and structure as novels about duty and independence.

D. A. Miller, author of *Narrative and its Discontents* (*YW* 62.318), is certainly discontented with the Trollopian narrative. In 'The Novel as Usual: Trollope's *Barchester Towers*' (Yeazell[33]) Miller sinuously resists what he sees as the novel's cultural strategy of boring its readers into submission to the *status quo*. Miller explores the 'moderate schism' of Barchester's religious and sexual politics, and of Trollope's plotting (or absence of it) in a complex essay which is never boring, but whose delight in its own cleverness may irritate some readers. The formal aspects of Trollope's conservative sexual politics are also explored by Jane Nardin in 'Conservative Comedy and the Women of *Barchester Towers*' (*SNNTS*). Nardin's re-examination of 'Comic Convention in

65. *Geraldine Jewsbury's 'Athenaeum' Reviews: A Mirror of Mid-Victorian Attitudes to Fiction*, by Monica Correa Fryckstedt. Uppsala. pp. 163. Skr 110.
66. *Trollope and the Law*, by R. D. McMaster. Macmillan. pp. xi + 179. £25.

Trollope's *Rachel Ray' (PLL)*, however, produces a more ambivalent Trollope, with its suggestion that the comic plot is merely a disguise for an attack on 'the idea that comic form can appropriately depict a society that does not allow authority and responsibility to women'.

Finally John Sutherland (*NCF*) adds to our knowledge of the publishing history and 'The Commercial Success of *The Way We Live Now*' in some work on the Chatto and Windus Archive. Also worth noting is the appearance of two new editions: *Ayala's Angel*[67] and *'Malachi's Cove' and Other Stories and Essays*[68].

Rather surprisingly, perhaps, recent critical theories seem to have made remarkably little impact on this year's handful of Meredith studies. Renate Muendel[69] has produced a modest but proficient introduction to the novelist's life and work, paying close attention to his 'radically new concept of realism'. James S. Stone[70] focuses on Meredith's politics in a largely biographical study, which is more concerned with the politics of Meredith the historical individual than with the politics of his writings. However, Stone's attempt to suggest Meredith's relationship to contemporary political ideas provides a useful context in which to read the fiction. Meredith's politics are linked to his fictional form in Nikki Lee Manos's essay, *'The Ordeal of Richard Feverel*: Bildungsroman or anti-Bildungsroman?' (*VN*). Manos argues that the failure of Meredith's experiment in rewriting the Carlylean apprentice novel as a Goethean *Bildungsroman* is the result of his sense of the deadly power of *antibildung* forces in nineteenth-century England. Finally, 'The Friend of an Engaged Couple', a previously unpublished story from the early 1860s, appears in *VIJ*'s new 'Texts' section.

Seen through the looking-glass of modern criticism Lewis Carroll's Alice books grow curiouser and curiouser. Alice's 'ethnocentricity' is the main subject of an ingenious article entitled 'Alice the Child-Imperialist and the Games of Wonderland', in which Daniel Bivona (*NCL*) reads *Alice's Adventures in Wonderland* as symptomatic of a fascination with the 'imaginative possibilities latent in a "confrontation of cultures"', which resulted from the nineteenth-century experience of imperialism. In *ESC*, Michael Steig's 'Alice as Self and Other' uses reader-response theories to examine his own, and two of his students' 'stories of reading' *Alice*, while William A. Madden's 'Framing the Alices' (*PMLA*) looks again at the nature and function of the frame poems which Carroll provided for his Alice books. In 'Revisiting Wordsworth' (*VIJ*) U. C. Knoepflmacher offers a wide-ranging examination of Carroll's rewritings of Wordsworth.

There are fewer Hardy studies than of late, but the current works offer considerable range, variety, and interest. There are two new books: the first, elegant, authoritative, and illuminating; the second, wilfully difficult, but suggestive. J. B. Bullen's *The Expressive Eye: Fiction and Perception in the*

67. *Ayala's Angel*, by Anthony Trollope, ed. and intro. by Julian Thompson-Furnivall. WC. OUP. pp. xxxv + 655. pb £4.95.

68. *'Malachi's Cove' and Other Stories and Essays*, by Anthony Trollope, ed. and intro. by Richard Mullen. Tabb (1985). pp. xxi + 145. pb £3.50.

69. *George Meredith*, by Renate Muendel. TEAS. Twayne. pp. 149.

70. *George Meredith's Politics: As Seen in his Life, Friendships and Works*, by James S. Stone. Meany. pp. 199. $45.

Work of Thomas Hardy[71] is, almost certainly, the most important work to date on Hardy's relation to the visual arts, and on the role of the visual generally in his novels. It is, for example, both more detailed and more speculative than Joan Grundy's *Hardy and the Sister Arts* (*YW* 60.318). Bullen seeks to illuminate Hardy's visual symbolism and his fictional structures by exploring, *inter alia*, the artistic milieu in which he wrote, his taste in painting, his reading of Ruskin, and his attitude to contemporary theories of perception. Bullen's detailed readings of Hardy's novels amply demonstrate his contention that, for Hardy, fiction did not merely 'involve the literal transcription of scenes or characters, but was, instead, an expressive medium for communicating ideas and emotions through the selection and manipulation of the constituent elements of the physical world'.

George Wotton's *Thomas Hardy: Towards a Materialist Criticism*[72] reminds us that there are many more contexts in which to read Hardy, than the exclusively high art context explored by Bullen. Wotton aims to 'historicize' Hardy's writing, by viewing it as a 'social event rather than an ideal object'. He seeks to locate the work in a specific process of 'cultural/ideological production', and to explicate its role in 'reproducing the actual relations of production in class society'. In addition to establishing the social, historical, aesthetic, and ideological conditions of production of Hardy's novels, and exploring the relations between ideology and writing elaborated in their 'structure of perceptions', Wotton also examines 'the ways in which "Thomas Hardy" has been produced as literature', and attempts to analyse the social and ideological function of that production.

Various aspects of Wotton's threefold project are espoused by Fred Reid and Peter Widdowson in *THA*. Reid examines the conditions of production, and the relationship between 'Art and Ideology in *Far From the Madding Crowd*'. In this densely historical study, Reid compares the novel's various versions of pastoral with a specific nineteenth-century revival of a conservative pastoral by agrarian and ecclesiastical elites, and with the actual conditions of rural life in nineteenth-century Dorset. In 'Hardy, "Wessex", and the Making of an English National Culture' Widdowson offers a 'critiography', which examines the ways in which 'Thomas Hardy' has been constructed as the 'poet' of an English national culture. He also attempts to disrupt this process by re-instating those Hardyean texts (and aspects of texts), which have been erased by the construction of Hardy as the timeless novelist of character and environment, and poet of the Wessex landscape.

Simon Gattrell (*THA*) is also concerned with the critical institution's erasure of certain aspects of Hardy, and he directs our attention to a reconsideration of the 'Middling Hardy' (*Under the Greenwood Tree*, *The Trumpet Major*, *Far from the Madding Crowd*, and *Two on a Tower*). Also in *THA* Brian Maidment has an extremely interesting and well-informed piece on 'Hardy's Fiction and English Traditional Music'. Harold Orel (*THA*), on the other hand, gives details of 'Hardy and the Developing Science of Archeology' as the context for Hardy's sense of the past, and in 'Hardy, Darwin and Nature' Roy

71. *The Expressive Eye: Fiction and Perception in the Work of Thomas Hardy*, by J. B. Bullen. Clarendon. pp. xvii + 279. £27.50.

72. *Thomas Hardy: Towards a Materialist Criticism*, by George Wotton. G&M (1985). pp. 233. £25.

Morrell (*THJ*) compares his treatment of nature with that of evolutionary science. Elsewhere, 'The Novel as Risk and Compromise, Poetry as Safe Haven' by William W. Morgan (*VN*) focuses on Hardy's narrators, in an examination of the tensions and choices involved in his movement from the novel to poetry, while in 'Hardy's Experimental Fiction' (*English*) David Ball attempts to read *Desperate Remedies*, *The Hand of Ethelberta*, and *A Laodicean* as 'deviously subversive fantasies' like *A Picture of Dorian Gray* and *Orlando*.

Two essays on *Far from the Madding Crowd* fuse the recent interest in Hardy's representation of women, with the continuing interest in visual perception and point of view in his novels. Judith Bryant Wittenberg links 'Angles of Vision and Questions of Gender' (*CentR*) in an interesting examination of various formal and thematic aspects of the novel, viewed in the context of Hardy's concept of the individual eye as 'the inlet of sense knowledge and as a sexual force', and the collective eye as 'the locus of moral judgement'. Wittenberg's interest in the way Hardy repeatedly depicts Bathsheba as the object of the 'male gaze', is approached from a different angle in E. M. Nollen's (*THY*) examination of the different varieties of 'The Loving Look in *Far From the Madding Crowd*'.

Robert Squillace (*NCL*) offers an interesting perspective on the distinctions between Modernist and late-Victorian ideas on the nature of time in 'Hardy's Mummers', a comparison of Hardy's use of the mummers' play in *The Return of the Native*, with Modernist uses of mythological and folk materials. Eustacia Vye is the subject of Charles May's over-complicated essay (*CLQ*), which uses the concept of 'The Magic of Metaphor in *The Return of the Native*' to show how a fictional figure in a modern romance can be at once a 'psychological character' and a 'psychological archetype'.

In the only essay on *The Woodlanders*, 'Hardy's Novel Impression-Pictures' (*CLQ*), Norman Arkans analyses its oft-noted impressionism, and compares Hardy's techniques with those of Impressionist painters whose work Hardy knew.

Ironically the two most illuminating essays on *Tess of the d'Urbervilles* have titles which suggest either narrow specialization or hackneyed subject matter. The first, Glen Wickens on 'Victorian Theories of Language' (*Mosaic*), throws fresh light on many of the novel's broader concerns by relating the contours of Hardy's eclectic style to nineteenth-century changes in language, and to Victorian philologists' views of the evolution of the language. In the second entitled 'Tess and Alec', Kristin Brady (*THA*) returns yet again to the question of Tess's rape/seduction, and uses an interesting emblematic reading of the scene in the Chase as the basis for a wider discussion of Hardy's representation of Tess's sexuality. Elsewhere, attention focuses on narrative method. Jakob Lothe (Hawthorn[32]) uses the narratology of Genette and Franz Stanzel to consider questions of the authorial narrator's knowledge, perspective, and distance, whereas Michael Ponsford (*MQ*) sees Hardy's 'control of sympathy' as a dramatic technique. Laura Claridge explores what she sees as a failure of narrative control in 'Tess: A Less than Pure Woman Ambivalently Presented' (*TSLL*).

Jude is left in relative obscurity this year. F. B. Pinion (*THA*) examines some of its autobiographical and literary sources, while in '*Jude the Obscure* and the Fall of Phaeton' Paul Pickrel (*HudR*) – reading 'as a man' – explores the novel's 'special significance for male readers', by comparing Jude's story with the Phaethon myth, and relating the depiction of Arabella and Sue to the image of the twofold Venus.

Gissing is the subject of an important new book by David Grylls[73], who explores the self-divisions of this complex writer, and seeks to explain their origins in his life and trace their effects in the work. Grylls is not only a well-informed and able explicator of this author and his works, but also an enthusiastic advocate. He endeavours to rescue Gissing from charges of enervating tedium, by demonstrating that although they are pessimistic in tone and structure, and produced by a 'pessimist by temperament and conviction', Gissing's novels have, nevertheless, a 'despondent verve'. In his detailed discussion of the novels, Grylls shows Gissing returning constantly to a core of ideas which he approached from shifting, and often conflicting points of view. He also traces Gissing's recurring attempts to reconcile the demands of romance and realism.

Grylls returns to the relationship between 'Realism and Romantic Convention' (*CVE*) in an essay in which he tries to show how the love plot detracts from, or subverts, the social realism of the earlier novels, but in the later novels, serves to enhance the social analysis. Elsewhere in *CVE*'s special number on realism, Jakob Korg's 'Realism as Discovery in the Novels of George Gissing' investigates the relationship between Gissing's earlier indebtedness to the subjective truthfulness of the mid-Victorian realists, and his later espousal of the techniques of Flaubert and Zola. Pierre Coustillas offers 'Some Personal Observations on Realism and Idealism in *New Grub Street*'. His attempt to set Gissing's 'idiosyncratic' realism in the context of contemporary English realism is marred by an insufficiently subtle awareness of the 'idealism' of 'realist' writers such as Elizabeth Gaskell and George Eliot.

In *GissingN*, the in-house journal of Gissing scholars, Coustillas throws some 'sidelights' on Gissing's publishing career, and Angela Whitehead locates the account of popular radicalism in *Workers in the Dawn* in some contemporary journalistic sources. In the most substantial critical contribution to *GissingN*, entitled 'Prisoners of Illusion', John Sloan unravels (and occasionally ravels up) the ideological contradictions of *Isabel Clarendon*, in particular, its problematic treatment of mid-Victorian ideals of culture and refinement.

The fiftieth anniversary of Kipling's death has occasioned a great number of publications on his work. Much of the work on this author continues to be rather anecdotal, and some has the clubbable tone of enthusiasts writing for fellow-enthusiasts. There are, however, a number of items on Kipling's nineteenth-century works that are of more general interest. In *Kipling's India*[74] Thomas Pinney has gathered together a selection of previously unidentified and uncollected newspaper articles written by the youthful Kipling. A useful introduction outlines Kipling's early journalistic career in the context of the British India he inhabited, and in relation to his later development as a writer. In *CVE* E. Hanquart analyses the social meaning of heroism in three of the early stories. John Bayley does not entirely avoid the clubbable tone in his appreciation of the

73. *The Paradox of Gissing*, by David Grylls. A&U. pp. xiii + 226. £20.

74. *Kipling's India: Uncollected Sketches 1884–8*, ed. and intro. by Thomas Pinney. Macmillan. pp. xiii + 302. £25.

'false structure' of the stories in *ELT*. Other *ELT* essays in this special issue on Kipling include William Scheick's attempt to apply Todorov's idea of the fantastic to 'The Phantom Rickshaw', and Pierre Coustillas on the treatment of artistic bohemia in *The Light that Failed*. Kipling's first novel is also the subject of a psychological study by J. E. Monro (*KJ*). More interestingly, Robert H. MacDonald (*SSF*) focuses on the treatment of race and sexuality in his analysis of 'Discourse and Ideology in Kipling's "Beyond The Pale"', and in *KJ* Ann Parry explores the relationship between narrative form and imperialist ideology in 'The Bridge Builders'.

A handful of other later Victorian novelists receive sporadic attention. Jean-Claud Noël (*CVE*) detects intimations of the 'musical consciousness' of George Moore's later fiction in the narrative techniques of his early short stories. Judith Mitchell examines the modulations of naturalism in *A Mummer's Wife* in *ES*, and again – this time focusing on the treatment of the heroine – in *ESC*. Mary Ward's novels continue to preoccupy Peter Collister, whose essay 'Alpine Retreats and Arnoldian Reveries' examines the Swiss episode in *Lady Rose's Journal* (*DUJ*). And Swinburne appears in his less familiar guise of novelist in David G. Reid's 'Bard and Lady Novelists', an examination of *A Year's Letters* (*VN*). Reid explores issues of gender and authority in his attempt to answer the question of why the poet should have chosen to write an epistolary novel.

Samuel Butler's apparent obsession with symmetry has provided Ralph Norrman with a subject for an extraordinarily obsessive and, in my view, inordinately tedious book[75]. Norrman tries to show how all Butler's scientific theories, his linguistic structures, the structures of his writing, and even his problems with personal relationships derive from his domination by chiastic thinking.

The post-Foucauldian interest in nineteenth-century discourses of sexuality has produced some absorbing new readings of R. L. Stevenson's *Dr Jekyll and Mr Hyde*. Both Elaine Showalter (Yeazell[33]) and Stephen Heath (*CQ*) read this tale as a representation of male sexuality, and both relate it to a specific historical moment of representation. Heath's 'Psychopathia Sexualis' sees *Jekyll*'s representation of male sexuality as either negation or perversion, as analogous to late nineteenth-century sexology, which studied the pathology of the sexual, and the criminal – sexual. He attributes the popularity of the story to its 'inscription of double being', which reproduces the contradictions of Victorian ideology. Ronald R. Thomas, on the other hand, sees Stevenson's use of doubling as an elaborate assault on nineteenth-century ideals of the individual personality, and the cult of character. This extremely thought-provoking essay, 'In the Company of Strangers' (*MFS*), reads *Dr Jekyll and Mr Hyde* alongside Samuel Beckett's *Company* as an example of a 'schizo-text', whose ultimate concern is with the authority of texts and the power of language to represent human life.

3. Prose

(a) Bibliography and General Works
Two annotated bibliographies of working-class autobiography have

75. *Samuel Butler and the Meaning of Chiasmus*, by Ralph Norrman. Macmillan. pp. ix + 315. £27.50.

appeared. *The Autobiography of the Working Class*. Vol. I: *1790–1900*[76] provides entries on the works, family life, occupation, and activities of its subjects, as well as brief, evaluative comment. It contains abstracts of 804 autobiographers and is creditably comprehensive. Its various indexes – general, place, occupation, education, and date – which allow the reader to assess fully the geographic, social, and political context of the autobiographers will be particularly valuable to social historians and students of working-class autobiography. A fine introduction locates its subjects in the area of Puritan spiritual autobiography and tackles the problem of representativeness, in particular, the small number of female autobiographers (less than one in ten, about seventy overall) when the difference between male and female literacy was negligible.

Nan Hackett[77] deplores the abandoning of working-class autobiographies by literary critics to the realm of social history, claiming instead they deserve serious attention as literary documents. Her own bibliography deals with only sixty-four subjects, some of which she finds to have a degree of rhetorical complexity. Unlike the editors of the previous work, Hackett argues that autobiography in the nineteenth century owes little to the traditions of Puritan spiritual autobiography but is instead an attempt to create representative narratives of how a class actually lived. Hackett is also intrigued by the few female autobiographers present but believes that this is explained by the tyranny of their domestic chores. This bibliography covers the area not by author or subject but by period (1800–48; 1848–80; and after 1880), in the belief that both the social attitudes and the style of the writers changed significantly within them. Hackett's bibliography is less easy to use as a source of reference than Burnett, Vincent, and Mayall and cross-referencing is almost impossible; yet as an evaluative survey of this area it is of some use.

A further relevant bibliographical study is Margaret Hambrick's catalogue[78] of part of the library of the leading Chartist George Julian Harney, which lists books presented by James Métivier, Harney's son-in-law, to the library of Vanderbilt University. This catalogue records a collection strong in titles from the English radical publishers in the political history of the French Revolution, covered from what is clearly not a partisan viewpoint. This is perhaps not very surprising, although the catalogue does record a sustained, if latterly, disillusioned preoccupation with American politics and society. One particularly notable facet of Harney's library is its large collection of the works of Byron and of Byromania; Coleridge is represented by only three volumes (all poetry). It is interesting to speculate whether from being an inspiring voice for the Chartist Harney, Byron became a figure of fully historical significance, as the twenty-nine entries in the catalogue might suggest.

Cynthia Huff[79] describes the work of fifty-nine nineteenth-century diarists in an attempt to help reconstruct the lives of ordinary women for use in interdisciplinary, historical, and literary studies. Like Hackett, she lists entries

76. *The Autobiography of the Working Class*. Vol. I: *1790–1900*, ed. by John Burnett, David Vincent, and David Mayall. Harvester (1984). pp. x + 463. £80.

77. *Nineteenth Century British Working-Class Autobiography: An Annotated Bibliography*, by Nan Hackett. AMS (1985). pp. 241. $34.50.

78. *A Chartist's Library*, by Margaret Hambrick. Mansell. pp. 266. £30.

79. *British Women's Diaries: A Descriptive Bibliography of Selected Nineteenth-Century Women's Manuscript Diaries*, by Cynthia Huff. AMS (1985). pp. xxxvi + 139. $32.50.

chronologically rather than by author and provides extensive commentary emphasizing the diarists' biographies and their important moments. Huff arranges her subjects rather hazily according to their social class (aristocracy, gentry, professional–commercial, intelligentsia, and religious) and provides quite basic comment on the stylistic features of the diaries. However, her selections and method are not sufficiently justified to avoid concluding that much is arbitrary here. Finally, Garland have published the third volume (L–P) of Robert Lee Wolff's bibliographical catalogue[80] of nineteenth-century fiction based upon his own collection.

Several anthologies of Victorian prose writings have appeared in line with a general trend. The aim of Cambridge English Prose Texts is to provide students with the opportunity of reading important essays and extracts from larger works which have been generally unavailable in suitable editions. Certainly this seems true of Edwin M. Eigner and George J. Worth's selection *Victorian Criticism of the Novel*[81]. This collection covers the period from Bulwer-Lytton's 'On Art in Fiction' (1838) to Conrad's Preface to *The Nigger of the 'Narcissus'* (1897) and includes pieces by novelists such as George Eliot, Henry James, Vernon Lee, and Robert Louis Stevenson as well as significant criticism by George Moir, Archibald Allison, James Fitzjames Stephen, William Caldwell Roscoe, David Masson, and G. H. Lewes. It can be criticized for excluding selections from Carlyle, R. H. Hutton, and Trollope and for including more of those who argued for romance in the novel than those who stressed realism (as the editors themselves admit). Yet the book has an excellent introductory survey which provides a comprehensive discussion of the major areas of debate. A second volume from the CUP series, *Critics of Capitalism*[82], is a collection of mostly familiar Victorian reactions to 'Political Economy'. The publishers claim to make 'more accessible the socio-economic writings of … authors now better known for their imaginative work'. This is surely not still true of Carlyle, Ruskin, Morris, Arnold, and Shaw who have always been well known for their social work and it seems wholly inapplicable to the Owenite John Bray, J. S. Mill, T. H. Green, Karl Marx, and Friedrich Engels. The inclusion of Marx is itself unusual in a series of English prose texts but the editors do sufficiently justify this. These criticisms apart, this book is a useful and accessible collection of significant writing showing the development of argument from the Owenite socialism of Bray to the collectivism of Green and Shaw and one which offers a wide range of individual response. The vexed question of Marx's influence on English socialist thought is raised but not dealt with in any authoritative manner. Like its partner, this work boasts an excellent introduction and an equally impressive system of notation and an up-to-date select booklist.

Two volumes of the Macmillan series Context and Commentary are of interest to readers of Victorian literature. The aim of this series, we are told, is to provide students of literature with 'a fuller knowledge of the relevant back-

80. *Nineteenth-Century Fiction: A Bibliographical Catalogue Based on the Collection Formed by Robert Lee Wolff*. Vol. III: *L–P*, by Robert Lee Wolff. Garland (1984). pp. viii + 299. $100.

81. *Victorian Criticism of the Novel*, ed. by Edwin M. Eigner and George J. Worth. CUP (1985). pp. vi + 258. hb £27.50, pb £9.95.

82. *Critics of Capitalism*, ed. by Elisabeth Jay and Richard Jay. CUP. pp. vii + 268. hb £27.50, pb £9.95.

ground material behind the topics they study'. J. A. V. Chapple's *Science and Literature in the Nineteenth Century*[83], however, falls uncomfortably into this format. Chapple, in the space of 160 or so pages heavily packed with large quotation, provides a very wide-ranging, erudite, and elegant overview of the area which is both interesting and urbane. He deftly weaves an almost conversational narrative out of a mass of primary scientific and literary texts: dividing his area into specific scientific disciplines of Astronomy, Physics, Chemistry, Meteorology; Palaentology, Geology, Zoology, Biology; and general areas such as Science in Culture. The range of allusion in so economic and compact a work is surprising: for instance, in the space of six pages Chapple moves from Ann Wilkinson to Carlyle, Tyndall, Huxley, Dickens, Kelvin, Maxwell, H. G. Wells, and A. H. Clough, finishing with Dylan Thomas. This book will not provide a basic introduction to the area but it should certainly stimulate readers to further study or to reconsider their opinions. The subject of Elisabeth Jay's *Faith and Doubt in Victorian Britain*[84] allows her selection to fall more easily into the format devised by Macmillan as Victorian writers tended to address the subject of their religion head-on and not so often by the use of symbolic allusion and borrowed metaphor which partially accounts for the mercurial nature of Chapple's study. Only one of Jay's five chapters does in fact consider a variety of expressions of Victorian religious doubt, yet, as Jay points out, the distinction between Broad Church faith and agnostic scepticism was after all merely one of degree. Jay concentrates on the varieties of religious expression to provide both familiar and unusual statements of belief which illustrate evangelicism, the Oxford Movement, Catholic, Broad Church, and Dissenting belief. As one would expect, the ubiquitous Mr Brocklehurst puts in an appearance along with Newman's caricatures from *Loss and Gain*, but so does the evangelical poetess Frances Ridley Havergal and the obscure Tractarian William John Conybeare. Jay's selection forms an accessible and useful introduction without sacrificing subtlety to simplicity.

The final anthology of primary material is *Culture and Society in Britain 1850–1890*[85], edited by J. M. Golby and obviously designed for specific debates and issues covered by the Open University Arts Foundation course. The extracts chosen are from a wide range of sources including poetry, letters, diaries, government reports, and should provide a valuable quarry of relevant material. The deliberate lack of an introduction and explanatory headnotes will render this volume of less use to the general reader than those of the Cambridge and Macmillan series.

Richard D. Altick[86] makes an outstanding contribution to the study of the relationship between visual art and literature. Of especial interest to Victorian scholars, the book charts 140 years in which English literature and art slowly came into conjunction, reaching their maximum contact in the early and mid Victorian periods and then drifting apart to almost total separation by the close

83. *Science and Literature in the Nineteenth Century*, by J. A. V. Chapple. Macmillan. pp. xi + 192. hb £20, pb £6.95.

84. *Faith and Doubt in Victorian Britain*, by Elisabeth Jay. Macmillan. pp. xi + 136. hb £20, pb £6.95.

85. *Culture and Society in Britain 1850–1890: A Source Book of Contemporary Writings*, ed. by J. M. Golby. OUP/OpenU. pp. xiii + 342. hb £12.95, pb £3.95.

86. *Paintings from Books: Art and Literature in Britain, 1760–1900*, by Richard D. Altick. OSU. pp. xxvi + 527. $60.

of the nineteenth century. Altick's study breaks new ground in comparative criticism of this kind, exploring the interaction of middle-class literary culture and popular tastes and arguing that there was a shift around the 1830s to a predominantly middle-class market for art. The scope of this study is wide, dealing with such subjects as the development of the market and tastes for oil paintings of literary subjects; the use of literary quotation in exhibition catalogues (interesting comment on Turner's practice here); the use of theatricality in literary painting and the controversy over 'realism' in Pre-Raphaelite painting; and visual representations of Shakespeare's work. Perhaps the most interesting part of Altick's study is his section describing representations in art of the work of some thirty English writers (including Tennyson, the Brownings, Bulwer-Lytton, Dickens, Thackeray, George Eliot, Rossetti, Morris, and Swinburne). This pioneering study is lavishly illustrated with monochrome representations and is certainly required reading for scholars of Victorian literary and visual culture.

Hilary Fraser[14] attempts to reconcile the claims of Christianity, ethics, and art in a number of writers, and her book is perhaps more controversial than it first appears. Newman, Hopkins, Ruskin, Matthew Arnold, Pater, and Wilde are discussed in terms of their attempts to grapple with the long-standing problems inherited from Romantic aesthetics. Her conclusions will probably not find general acceptance: she argues for instance that Kantian problems of epistemology and perception were 'arguably confronted more honestly and pursued with more resourcefulness and intellectual rigour by Newman and Hopkins than by any of the non-Catholic writers'. In particular, Arnold and Ruskin (unsuitably lumped together in Chapter 3) are harshly treated; their moral aesthetic is 'confused and dogmatic', while Hopkins's idea of a Christocentric universe reflected in his theory of inscape is 'so brilliant and flawless, so complete'. Fraser's study is vigorous but her argument that there are two traditions in Victorian aesthetics (one emphasizing the interrelationship between aesthetics and morality and the other investing art with religious status) imposes a distortion on the writers she chooses to discuss and on the period as a whole. The exclusion of Carlyle from such a discussion must also be seen as a weakness.

The selection of subjects is also a problem in John P. McGowan's *Representation and Revelation*[87] which covers a similar area to that of Fraser: the Victorian attempt to grapple with the aesthetic, epistemological, and moral problems bequeathed to the age by Romantic theories of mind and nature, most notably the conflicting theories of knowledge, arising from the empiricism of Locke and the idealism of Coleridge. This enterprise is linked with the dominance of 'realism', as the characteristic literary mode of the period, but also as an attempt to identify 'the essential nature of a reality whose identity remains elusive', which would make realism the dominant literary mode of most ages. Despite its subtitle the book begins evasively with a chapter on Rossetti and then works its way through Carlyle, Ruskin, Dickens, George Eliot, and Browning, concluding with Yeats (arguably a transitional writer who clarifies Victorian assumptions). The failure to justify choice of subject detracts from the volume's unity, yet McGowan lucidly discusses the writers'

87. *Representation and Revelation: Victorian Realism from Carlyle to Yeats*, by John P. McGowan. UMiss. pp. vi + 206. £23.50.

shared concerns with language, knowledge, and reality, and he provides several good treatments of Victorian writers, with a particularly fine chapter on Ruskin.

W. J. McCormack[88] deals with Anglo-Irish literary history from the time of Edmund Burke to that of Yeats and Joyce. This original and interesting study links the Anglo-Irish literary tradition closely with European Romanticism and demonstrates how the demise of Romantic assumptions led to the origins of Modernism. The book has coverage of such nineteenth-century figures and writers as T. D. Gregg, W. E. Gladstone, J. Sheridan Le Fanu, Standish James O'Grady, Charles Lever, and Matthew Arnold. McCormack's conclusions are challenging and incisive: he interprets Le Fanu's *Uncle Silas*, for instance, as a presentation of an intensified version of the isolated Anglo-Irish ascendancy for whom the local affairs and religious life of the community were closed. The book also contains an interesting discussion of Arnold's *On the Study of Celtic Literature* which sees Arnold's Celticism as an element in his assault on the philistine attitudes of middle-class Saxons.

Max F. Schulz's *Paradise Preserved*[89] is a wide-ranging discussion of humanity's fascination with the paradise myth and with its attempts to recapture Eden. Schulz identifies three shifts in perspective in this infatuation, from the eighteenth-century personal attempt to reclaim one's own Eden out of a country seat, to the Romantic venture of redefining the world in organic terms as the scene of uninterrupted paradisial bliss, achieved through imagination, concluding with the Victorian attempts to recreate Eden both through technological change and in the fantasies of a mythic past. Schulz's discussion of the Victorian manifestations of this idea is interesting if diffuse: too wide a range of reference dissipates the force of his argument and the discussion of the social history of the period is also rather basic, familiar, and not up to date. This study ranges from Joseph Paxton's Crystal Palace, through Turner, Tennyson, Dickens, Patmore, Rossetti and the Pre-Raphaelites, Beardsley, and concludes with Whistler, whose decorations of Frederick R. Leyland's dining-room represent the nineteenth-century's growing disillusionment with the garden and their concomitant placing of paradise in stylized interior decorations. Despite its occasional laboriousness Schulz's study is full of interesting discussion and penetrating insights: it is also an extremely handsome presentation and CUP should be congratulated on this production.

Schulz's discussion of Victorian versions of the 'heavenly city' will no doubt be of interest to F. S. Schwarzbach whose 'Victorian Literature and the City: A Review Essay' (*DSA*) reviews significant recent contributions to this area. In this tough-minded and searching piece Schwarzbach examines general works on the city and literature, specific work relating to Victorian literature, and specific studies on Dickens and the city. Schwarzbach argues that underlying the general narrowness and simplicity of recent work is a failure to grasp the complex interrelations between literary activity and production, and social activity and production as a whole.

Lawrence J. Starzyk has contributed articles roughly in the same area of

88. *Ascendancy and Tradition in Anglo-Irish Literature from 1789 to 1939*, by W. J. McCormack. Clarendon. pp. x + 423. £27.50.

89. *Paradise Preserved: Recreations of Eden in Eighteenth- and Nineteenth-Century England*, by Max F. Schulz. CUP. pp. xv + 368. £30.

Victorian aesthetics. His 'The Non-Poietic Foundations of Victorian Aesthetics' (*BJA*) describes how 'original, eternal forms' which inhered within Plato's aesthetic legacy lost their validity, forcing the nineteenth-century artist to confront evolving, transient concepts. The problems created by the loss of this ideal of perfection which Victorian artists had to face is discussed by Starzyk in 'Imperfection as a Victorian Critical Norm' (*NVSAWC*) where the dialectical tendency of Victorian thought necessitates an endless tension seeking an equipoise that can only be imperfectly allowed at any given historical moment. This leads to imperfection itself becoming the sign of artistic success in Carlyle and Ruskin among others. The antithetical style of nineteenth-century writers is also the subject of Claus Uhlig's obscure 'Conceptual Architecture in Nineteenth-Century Writing' (*CLS*). Uhlig relates this tendency in Carlyle, Arnold, Nietzsche, and Pater to the uncertainty of rapid social change, epistemological instability, and the absence of a knowable God.

Four studies involving nineteenth-century autobiography have come to my attention. Jonathan Loesberg[90] attempts to fashion a methodology with which to read Victorian prose writing. Focusing on Mill's *Autobiography* and Newman's *Apologia Pro Vita Sua*, Loesberg tries to reconstruct the intellectual context which motivated the two men to write autobiography. Loesberg argues that this awareness of the philosophical context is necessary because of the problematic status of nineteenth-century theories of consciousness which led Mill and Newman to make an empirical defence of their philosophies using the narrative as a kind of exemplary tale. Loesberg's method obliges him to foreground Mill and Newman's theories of consciousness in a way that could be seen as distorting, yet his detailed and intelligent discussion of the overlap between literary narrative and philosophical argument makes this an important study, despite a difficult and, at times, convoluted style. I look forward to subsequent discussion of the prose of Carlyle and Arnold which the third section of his work promises.

Linda H. Peterson eschews Loesberg's lateral approach for a more orthodox literary and historical reading of autobiography[91]. Significantly only Newman's *Apologia* receives sustained treatment by both writers. Peterson discusses self-interpretative works such as Carlyle's *Sartor Resartus*, Ruskin's *Praeterita*, and Gosse's *Father and Son*. She maintains that the genre of spiritual autobiography, exemplified by John Bunyan's *Grace Abounding*, was grounded on a tradition of scriptural hermeneutics so that autobiographers attempted more to understand and interpret events rather than simply to present them. Peterson's argument inevitably emphasizes certain elements of autobiography at the expense of others. She argues that the interpretative act was habitual to the thought of her subjects, which is certainly true, but so is it true that Newman's *Apologia* was a defence of his recent conduct as well as a work of theological hermeneutics. Nevertheless, Peterson's method also enables her to look at her subjects in a fresh manner (notably *Sartor Resartus* and *Praeterita*), and she makes some brilliant speculations about why female autobiography is so sparse in the period, arguing that Harriet Martineau was

90. *Fictions of Consciousness: Mill, Newman, and the Reading of Victorian Prose*, by Jonathan Loesberg. Rutgers. pp. ix + 280. hb £35, pb $18.

91. *Victorian Autobiography: The Tradition of Self-Interpretation*, by Linda H. Peterson. Yale. pp. ix + 228. £20.

exceptional in her understanding of the theological and generic traditions of spiritual autobiography which enabled her to write within the
predominantly masculine mode of self-expressive discourse. Peterson's study
concludes by arguing that late-Victorian autobiographers eschewed any system
of biblical hermeneutics for the 'scientific' autobiography typified by Gosse's
easy alternations between biological and literary metaphors in *Father and
Son*.

Julia Swindells covers autobiography from yet another angle[92]. She is mainly
interested in working-class female autobiography which she contrasts with
representations of womanhood in Dickens and Eliot. Among these autobiographies Swindells finds some opposition to the dominant forms of representation in nineteenth-century fiction, although it is not always clear how
these class-conscious autobiographies show that 'something missing' which
Swindells believes is lacking in Victorian fiction. Her study is both wide-ranging
yet at the same time oddly compartmentalized and while she provides much
interesting comment on the relationship between class, gender, and literary
professionalism, her methodology is crude and lacks the subtlety of Loesberg
and Peterson. Surprisingly Swindells hardly mentions Harriet Martineau
whose mediation between the worlds of the lived experience of autobiography
and the professional writer would make her an interesting subject for
discussion.

Two studies of the *fin de siècle* have appeared. Linda Dowling[93] maintains
that late-Victorian Decadence should be seen in a linguistic context. In her
elegant and persuasive study she argues that Decadence emerged from the
disintegration of the high Victorian ideal of English civilization inherited from
the Romantic philological equation of language with civilization so that
language and literature marked the eternal manifestation of the inner spirit of a
nation or people. This ideal was undermined by the linguistic science of Franz
Bopp and Jacob Grimm which gave language an independence from men and
representation, divorcing it from literature and identifying it with living speech,
so that it seemed an autonomous system working blindly towards ends
answerable only to impersonal phonetic laws. Thus the era of Wilde, Beardsley,
and Pater is not one of cultural decline but of linguistic demoralization.
Dowling persuasively shows how this concept of an autonomous language
influenced writers such as Beardsley, Wilde, Arthur Machen, Ernest Dowson,
Lionel Johnson, and the young Yeats, with whom her study concludes. The
main drawback of Dowling's sophisticated analysis is that by concentrating on
the linguistic and literary she downgrades the visual representations of
Decadence but her work is well written and significant.

John R. Reed[94] sees Decadence as a style which permeates a large area of
culture beyond the purely literary. His scope is wider than Dowling's and he
does not see the movement purely in linguistic and literary terms but in the
context of social, economic, and technological change. Reed delineates a particular artistic form which he typifies as Decadent: this elaborates a pre-existing

92. *Victorian Writing and Working Women: The Other Side of Silence*, by Julia
Swindells. Polity. pp. x + 236. hb £19.50, pb £6.95.
93. *Language and Decadence in the Victorian Fin de Siècle*, by Linda Dowling.
Princeton. pp. xvi + 294. £21.70.
94. *Decadent Style*, by John R. Reed. OhioU. pp. xiv + 274. $30.

artistic form to the point of apparent dissolution from which a new artistic order arises. This model Reed perceives in a large collection of late nineteenth-century European artists, literary, visual, and musical. It is somewhat surprising, however, to learn that those poets whom we have generally thought to be Decadent are not so: Wilde's fiction is genuinely Decadent but not his poetry, nor is that of Dowson, Johnson, or Symons. This anomalous position leads Reed to postulate an unconvincing distinction between 'Decadent poetry' (Baudelaire and Swinburne) and 'the poetry of decadence' (Wilde, Dowson, etc.). Despite this, Reed's work is challenging and provocative and should lead to much debate. Of related interest is R. B. Kershner's 'Degeneration: The Explanatory Nightmare' (*GaR*) which demonstrates how the myth of degeneration lent itself to late-Victorian theories of racism, class bias, jingoism, misogyny, and social conservatism.

Andreas Höfele[95] considers the contribution of parody to literary change during the transition from the Victorian to the modern age, concentrating on *Punch*, Swinburne, Wilde, and Beerbohm. Without attempting a taxonomy of parody, Höfele examines its relationship to Romanticism and its analysis in recent literary history, and accepts a loose, popular understanding of parody as comprising invitation, modification, and play. He suggests that a more creative interpretation of parody helps us to understand the genesis of modern literature. Joyce's *Ulysses* and T. S. Eliot's *The Waste Land* represent for Höfele the first high-point in modern literature, in which parody is successfully integrated into artistic creativity. [E.A.M.]

Victorian views of history and historians have once again occupied a number of writers. Raymond Chapman eschews the task of analysing Victorian historical thinking in favour of a discussion of the way certain Victorian writers derived judgemental and constructive comment on their own times from the past[96]. Chapman's book is a work of synthesis and one which proclaims an eclectic method. His discussion of the medieval revival is pedestrian and is insufficiently distinguished from previous work; however, his treatment of some of the less obvious historical periods which influenced Victorian thinking is interesting, particularly his stimulating discussion of the use made by Charles Kingsley, J. A. Froude, and others, of the Elizabethan age, which became a model for a nation confronting papal and Russian 'aggression'. Chapman's treatment of the uses made of the seventeenth century is particularly disappointing, consisting mainly of an extended commentary on John Henry Shorthouse's *John Inglesant: A Romance* (1881): some awareness of the less direct treatments of this period might have been rewarding, for instance, Dorothea Brooke's Puritan ancestry, which is not uncommon for Victorian heroes and heroines. Chapman also covers the eighteenth century and the recent past in this highly readable but fairly general and traditional work.

The Victorian historiography which Chapman refuses to discuss is the subject of Rosemary Jann's eminently scholarly *The Art and Science of*

95. *Parodie und literarischer Wandel: Studien zur Funktion einer Schreibweise in der englischen Literatur des ausgehenden 19. Jahrhunderts*, by Andreas Höfele. AF. CWU. pp. 245. DM 108.

96. *The Sense of the Past in Victorian Literature*, by Raymond Chapman. CH. pp. 212. £22.50.

Victorian History[97]. Jann's title is significant, for the six historians she chooses to discuss are primarily literary historians: Thomas Arnold, Carlyle, T. B. Macaulay, J. R. Green, E. A. Freeman, and J. A. Fróude. There was a strong imaginative dimension to the didactic readings of history in their work; they had a firm sense of their vocation; they had an important awareness of their relationship to a large audience; and each saw the task of the historian to be the propagation of a view of the past which would make sense of the present, whether it was Arnold's view of cyclical time and Christian history, Froude's Protestantism, Macaulay's Whiggism, or Carlyle's apocalyptic visions of truth. Jann provides a conceptual framework for each of her six chapters by asking relevant questions about her subjects' conceptions of history and their need to be both 'scientific' and yet also to recreate the past as art. She courageously and justifiably argues for the historical importance of these literary historians who sometimes held a rather cavalier regard for factual accuracy and archival research, and her chapter on Froude, 'one of the last great Victorian amateurs', is particularly fine. Students of Victorian historical writing will find this scholarly and elegant study invaluable.

Philippa Levine accords with Jann's rejection of the Whig view of nineteenth-century historians in her exploration of the related historical communities of antiquarianism, archaeology, and history[98]. Like Jann, Levine is interested in the increasing sense of professionalism which invades historical research during this period, although in opposition to Jann she banishes the pre-eminently literary historians, Carlyle and Macaulay, from the historical community to the fellowship of essayists and reviewers. Levine's study discusses the social location of 'historical practitioners' and the organizations and institutions within which they worked. There is little that is amateur about Levine's work, which is commendably well researched, with copious reference to manuscript sources. Her style is also lively and attractive, especially when commenting on the less than professional personal exchanges among historians. Ironically Levine points out that the first, true professional historians were in fact not to be found among academics but in the new PRO in Fetter Lane: the descendants of the amateur antiquarians (a view which complements that of Jann). Of related interest to this question is Sir David Wilson's enthusiastic and well-researched study of Augustus Wollaston Franks of the British Museum[99]. Franks, 'one of the least-known English collectors', was a President of the Society of Antiquarians, the Keeper of British and Medieval Antiquaries and Ethnology of the British Museum, and in both the opinions of Wilson and Levine, one of the few professionals at the time. He obtained many outstanding pieces for the Museum and his generosity to the Museum was considerable. This study is well illustrated and produced as we have come to expect from T&H.

This year's number of *CVE* contains conference papers on the subject of 'Héros et héroisme'. Paul Veyriras's 'Sainte Elisabeth de Hongrie héroïne

97. *The Art and Science of Victorian History*, by Rosemary Jann. OSU. pp. xviii + 272. $27.50.

98. *The Amateur and the Professional: Antiquarians, Historians and Archaeologists in Victorian England, 1838–1886*, by Philippa Levine. CUP. pp. x + 210. £25.

99. *The Forgotten Collector: Augustus Wollaston Franks of the British Museum*, by Sir David Wilson. T&H (1984). pp. 63. £4.50.

victorienne?' provides an interesting discussion of the impact of Monta-
lambert's biography of St Elisabeth (1836) on thinkers and artists in England
and France. Veyriras makes the unusual claim that Kingsley's *The Saint's
Tragedy* is an attempt to lay the foundations of 'woman worship' in opposition
to Carlyle's masculine variety, although in Gaskell and Ruskin St Elisabeth's
attraction rests on her blending of piety with efficiency. Michel Durand's 'Les
Héros des cimetières souterrains, ou le mythe victorien des Catacombes' is a
noteworthy exploration of the Victorian fondness for Catacomb fiction and its
early Christian heroes. Christian Comanzo's 'Mythe solaire, héros solaire' is an
original, if speculative, discussion of the fascination of Christina Rossetti,
Tennyson, and Dickens with 'the solar myth'. Kipling's early ideas about
heroism are plausibly discussed in the context of Carlyle's beliefs in Evelyne
Hanquart's '"For the Pride of their Race and the Peace of the Land": Les
Héros anglo-indiens du jeune Kipling', and Jean-Claude Amalric's 'Du réaliste
au surhomme: Les Métamorphoses du héros shavien' provides a subtle account
of the various incarnations of the Shavian hero.

A number of general studies on Victorian thought and culture have
appeared. T&H have reprinted Asa Briggs's *The Nineteenth Century*[100]: a
valuable and lavishly illustrated introductory text, first published in 1970, with
contributions by Briggs himself (art and society), John Roberts (politics and
society), James Joll (protest movements), F. Bédarida (cities), F. M. L.
Thompson (countryside), and Brian Bond (warfare). Although some of these
contributions will now seem a little dated this is certainly still an attractive and
interesting general introduction to the area.

Marriage and Morals among the Victorians[101] is a collection of eleven essays
by the conservative historian Gertrude Himmelfarb written between 1975 and
the present. These essays are exercises in the history of ideas and are pre-
eminently concerned with 'morals' and 'morality' which Himmelfarb identifies
as 'the morality that dignifies and civilizes human beings, removing us from our
natural brutish state'. Himmelfarb writes subtly, intelligently, and sharply
about Victorian marriage (in particular, the un-Victorian examples of the
Ruskins, the Carlyles, the Dickenses, George Eliot and G. H. Lewes, and the
Mills); the relativist ethics of Bloomsbury; the interrelationship between
religion, science, and morality; social Darwinism and sociobiology; Macaulay
and Victorian history; Disraeli; and the Webbs. Throughout these essays
Himmelfarb returns to the belief that the Victorians' obsession with morality
was due to their guilt over their loss of religious faith which led them to make
morality as interpreted by law and social custom a substitute for religion. These
essays are predominantly Whiggish in tone and constitute a defence of the
humanist position.

Diana Postlethwaite[102] discusses nine Victorian figures: Mill, Auguste
Comte, George Combe, Robert Chambers, Charles Bray, Harriet Martineau,
G. H. Lewes, Herbert Spencer, and George Eliot. The reason these figures are

100. *The Nineteenth Century: The Contradictions of Progress*, ed. by Asa Briggs.
T&H. pp. 239. £18.
101. *'Marriage and Morals among the Victorians' and Other Essays*, by Gertrude
Himmelfarb. Faber. pp. xiv + 253. £15.95.
102. *Making It Whole: A Victorian Circle and the Shape of their World*, by Diana
Postlethwaite. OSU. pp. xx + 282. pb $12.50.

chosen is not made specific and one wonders why others are excluded. Postle-thwaite is attempting, like others before her, to delineate 'a Victorian frame of mind'. The key theme in the circle she chooses to discuss is the attempt to synthesize the empirical and the intuitive: a quest she sees as originating from the work of Coleridge. This study is best regarded as a synthesis of received opinion which does not greatly increase our knowledge of the figures discussed but which is very useful in clarifying and elucidating central Victorian concerns. Rutgers have reprinted the excellent collection of fourteen essays *Victorian Science and Victorian Values: Literary Perspectives*[103]. Mostly concerned with the literary and philosophical perceptions of science, those pieces of particular interest are: Robert O. Preyer's discussion of Romantic influences on the natural philosophers at Cambridge; Jeffrey L. Spears's study of the biological analogy in Carlyle's histories; James Paradis's analysis of Darwin's percep-tions of landscape; Paul Sawyer's account of the conflict between Ruskin and Tyndall over theories of glacial movement; Thomas Zaniella's description of the merging of science, art, and philosophy in the depictions of altered English sunsets following the eruption of Krakatoa in 1883; Sally Shuttleworth's analysis of Eliot's *Daniel Deronda* and organic physiology; and Thomas Postlewait's account of G. B. Shaw's hostility to Darwinian evolution and science in general.

The more prosaic and intricate applications of science is the subject of Alan Sutton's *A Victorian World of Science*[104] which is a descriptive commentary on extracts from the popular nineteenth-century periodical, the *English Mechanic and the World of Science*. Sutton presents a rather straightforward descriptive narrative of the industrial, domestic, educational, entertaining, medical, and velocipedial and aviationary uses of science which tends towards the whimsical, but his little book is fascinating for the ingenuity of its subjects. What is revealed by these selections is the apparent popular optimism for scientific and technological advance despite Ruskinian prophecies of doom.

VS has three pieces concerning Victorian educational theory and practice. Alan Bacon's 'English Literature Becomes a University Subject' demonstrates how King's College pre-empted Matthew Arnold by pioneering the teaching of English literature in the 1830s. Bacon gives an interesting account of the contri-bution of the London colleges to the study of English, although he does not fully account for the lack of opposition to English studies at this time which precluded any real pre-Arnoldian debate. J. P. Ward's thorough and detailed '"Came from Yon Fountain"' elegantly argues for the importance of Words-worth's legacy to Victorian educational theory: his chief bequest being the opinion that feeling and suffering are necessary for the cultivation of the intellect. Bernarr Rainbow's 'The Rise of Popular Music Education in Nineteenth-Century England' tells the interesting tale of the restoration of music teaching to the curriculum of nineteenth-century popular education. A fourth contribution to *VS* also deals with Victorian music. Nicholas

103. *Victorian Science and Victorian Values: Literary Perspectives*, ed. by James Paradis and Thomas Postlewait. N.Y. Academy of Sciences/Rutgers (1985). pp. xiii + 362. hb $30, pb $14.

104. *A Victorian World of Science: A Collection of Unusual Items and Anecdotes Connected with Ideas about Science and its Applications in Victorian Times*, by Alan Sutton. Hilger. pp. xi + 227. £12.50.

Temperley's 'The Lost Chord' is an informed and articulate account of the twentieth-century neglect of nineteenth-century English music which constitutes 'The Lost Chord' of music scholarship.

I have not seen a number of general studies of Victorian culture. These are J. E. Chamberlin and S. L. Gilman's *Degeneration: The Dark Side of Progress* (ColU); Anand C. Chitnis's *The Scottish Enlightenment and Early Victorian English Society* (CH); Robert Colls and Philip Dodd's *Englishness: Politics and Culture 1880-1920* (CH); Peter Gay's *The Tender Passion* (OUP); David Knight's *The Age of Science* (Blackwell); David Skilton's *Reform and Intellectual Debate in Victorian England* (CH); T. R. Wright's *The Religion of Humanity: The Impact of Comtean Positivism on Victorian Britain* (CUP); and A. G. L. Haig's 'The Church, the Universities, and Learning in Later Victorian England' (*HistJ*).

(b) Individual Authors

The new OA edition of the poetry and prose of Matthew Arnold[105] has appeared with Robert H. Super editing the prose. Super's selection of the prose intends to show the range of Arnold's interests and the interrelatedness of his treatments of these subjects. Strangely, however, Super does not include any of Arnold's religious criticism, nor, in his introduction, explain its absence, professing instead to concentrate on the more literary productions of Arnold's pen. Scholars will be grateful for this easily accessible edition of Arnold's prose but will be disappointed at the exclusion of some of the more familiar pieces: Super does not print Arnold's Preface to his *Poems* (1853). 'Some Unpublished Letters of Matthew Arnold to Richard D'Oyly Carte' (13 July–14 October, 1883), who acted as his agent during the forthcoming lecture tour of America, are presented by Jane W. Stedman in *Arnoldian*.

A selection of essays unoriginally titled *Matthew Arnold: Between Two Worlds*[106] has been edited by Robert Giddings whose introductory piece places Arnold's thought foursquare in the context of modern times. Giddings's essay is vigorous although it contains some rather bland generalizations, and Giddings's reference to Max Beerbohm as 'that little prick' is not one which is in sympathy with Arnold's love of sweetness and light. The contributions to this volume are uneven but interesting. Alan Chedzoy writes of Arnold's 'real work' as an HMI, opening his piece with an imaginative recreation of Arnold's inspectorial visit to the class of Mr McCheerumchild in the Coketown of 1864. The practical attempts of Arnold to ennoble the working-class offspring and the drawbacks of his methods are well illustrated in Chedzoy's piece. Charles Swann's rather literal 'Reading the Signs of the Times: Some Functions of Criticism – Arnold and Ruskin' argues that Ruskin's ideas were wider and deeper than Arnold's, as Ruskin was always aware of the social context of his work whereas Arnold was prone to a nostalgic, selective amnesia. David Amigoni describes the root cause of Arnold's disagreement with Bishop Colenso as that Colenso wished to retain God at the Bible's expense, whereas Arnold wished to salvage the Bible to the detriment of the concept of a bene-

105. *Matthew Arnold: Selected Works*, ed. by Miriam Allott and Robert H. Super. OA. OUP. pp. xxxi + 616. hb £19.50, pb £7.95.
106. *Matthew Arnold: Between Two Worlds*, ed. by Robert Giddings. B&N. pp. 207. £15.95.

volent God. John Woolford analyses Arnold's recurring fascination with illness and obscurity which grows out of his general notion that his culture is itself ill, his suspicion that the anxiety of influence created by the great Romantics inevitably leads to illness, and his obscure sense that suffering is somehow linked with sublimity. William Kaufman places the grimness of Arnold's work and his antagonism towards comedy in the perspective of his commitment to social reform and his fear of anarchy, and finally Owen Dudley Edwards contributes a full and solid piece detailing Arnold's attempts to convince the British mind of its identity with Ireland and of the reality of the Union.

Several articles have also appeared. Darrel Mansell's 'Matthew Arnold's "The Study of Poetry" in its Original Context' (*MP*) perhaps over-emphasizes the critical misrepresentations of 'The Study of Poetry' which result from the failure to recognize that Arnold's essay was originally written as an introduction to T. H. Ward's anthology of English poetry. *Arnoldian* carries two pieces: Fraser Neiman provides a useful round-up of recent Arnold scholarship and Ruth apRoberts provides a sane and perceptive review of two recent books on Arnold. One of these, James C. Livingston's *Matthew Arnold and Christianity* (USC), I have not seen. The other is Nathan A. Scott's *The Poetics of Belief*[107], which is a series of studies of writers who regard the role of the poetic imagination to be fundamental in the formation of religious belief. In addition to his chapter on Arnold, Scott begins with a fairly familiar account of Coleridge's intellectual career, maintaining that his doctrine of the poetic imagination is more important for his theology than for his aesthetics: a claim which I thought the context of Coleridge's work would make unnecessary. Scott's chapter on Arnold (a reprint of his essay 'Arnold's Vision of Transcendence – the *Via Poetica*' in *JR*, 1979) is more impressive, arguing that Arnold assigns to the poetic imagination the Virgilian function of bringing us into the presence of the numinous. Scott demonstrates how Arnold followed David Friedrich Strauss and Ludwig Feuerbach in naturalizing the Christian myth but diverging from them in attempting to provide a method for understanding the spiritual importance of those biblical ideas and events whose literal truth was no longer tenable. Scott's criticism of Arnold's failure to restate Christian faith seems to me to be an illustration of Arnold's desire to avoid dogma: Scott's overall perspective may be too evangelical for many.

John and Sarah Austin are the subjects of Lotte Hamburger and Joseph Hamburger's biographical study, *Troubled Lives*[108]. John Austin (1790–1857) will probably be more widely known to students of legal history, being a major figure in English legal thought and the propounder of the Austinian theory of jurisprudence, with its central idea that the law is the command of the sovereign. Austin's wife Sarah, who emerges from this account as the more forceful personality, was chiefly known for her work as a writer in literary and political journals and as a translator of German works. John Austin appears as a man who failed to live up to his early promise: his most important work *Lectures on Jurisprudence* (1863) was published posthumously and edited by

107. *The Poetics of Belief: Studies in Coleridge, Arnold, Pater, Santayana, Stevens, and Heidegger*, by Nathan A. Scott Jr. UNC (1985). pp. 198. £22.80.

108. *Troubled Lives: John and Sarah Austin*, by Lotte Hamburger and Joseph Hamburger. UTor (1985). pp. xv + 261. $27.50.

his wife. The Hamburgers suggest that his failure to publish resulted from his growing dissatisfaction with his own ideas. This study is a useful re-assessment of the two people; however, the division of labour on the part of the authors leads to some repetition and discontinuity in and between their several chapters.

Norman St John-Stevas has edited the concluding four volumes (*Letters* and *Miscellany*) of Walter Bagehot's *Collected Works* (Economist Pubns: OUP), which I have not seen. In 'E. Bulwer-Lytton: A Misattributed Article Identified' (*N&Q*) John Russell Stephens denies Edward Bulwer-Lytton's authorship of 'The State of Drama' (*New Monthly Magazine*), attributing the essay to Thomas James Serle.

A number of important studies of Carlyle have come to my attention. The most notable publication is that of Vols. X, XI, and XII of *The Collected Letters of Thomas and Jane Welsh Carlyle*[109]. The volumes cover the years 1838, 1839, and 1840 respectively. Each volume contains a list of letters known to have been received by the Carlyles, a chronology of the important events of that year, and full and sensible footnotes which do not hamper the narrative flow of the letters themselves. Despite some criticism of the slow progress of the enterprise the editors claim (in *CNew*) that the number of Carlyle letters published so far exceeds that of any other Victorian writer and at least one-third of these have not been published elsewhere. A small proportion of the letters published so far belong to Jane Welsh Carlyle but this imbalance will become much less in future volumes. During the three years covered by these volumes, Carlyle was negotiating with Ralph Waldo Emerson about an American edition of *The French Revolution*, giving his course of lectures 'On the History of Literature', and publishing his essay 'Sir Walter Scott' and his 'Varnhagen Von Ense's Memoirs' in the *London and Westminster Review*. We also see the germination and publication of *Chartism* and *On Heroes and Hero Worship*, and the range of Carlyle's emotions is on show, from the tenderness of the letters to his mother, the wry and amicable tone of those to Emerson, to the choleric and denunciatory. Of related interest to Carlyle's correspondence is K. J. Fielding's 'Carlyle and the Speddings: New Letters', a discussion of the relationship between Carlyle and Thomas and James Spedding based on Thomas's unpublished letters to Carlyle (*CNew*).

Chris R. Vanden Bossche argues in 'Carlyle, Career and Genre' (*Arnoldian*) that a literary career was to Carlyle a vocation with the same integrity and authority as the ministerial career which he was intended for. This vocation necessitated the finding of an adequate form or genre through which Carlyle could express himself: Vanden Bossche argues that this was the historical epic. Carlyle's interest in the epic is also the subject of Mark Cumming's 'Carlyle, Whitman, and the Disimprisonment of Epic' (*VS*). This useful piece of comparative criticism maintains that Carlyle attempted to liberate the epic by presenting the 'Romance of Life' in a highly wrought and continuous form. Cumming believes that both Carlyle's *The French Revolution* and Walt Whitman's *Leaves of Grass* attempt to release the Romantic notion of the epic from stale literary conventions, although his discussion of the former is perhaps more convincing.

---

109. *The Collected Letters of Thomas and Jane Welsh Carlyle*. Vol. X: *1838*; Vol. XI: *1839*; Vol. XII: *1840*; ed. by Charles Richard Sanders, Kenneth J. Fielding, and Clyde de L. Ryals. DukeU (1985). pp. xvi + 258; pp. xiv + 236; pp. xiv + 426. £33.25 each.

Two studies of Carlyle as a historian have appeared. Lee C. R. Baker compares Carlyle's theories about art and history with those of Browning in *The Ring and the Book* in 'The Diamond Necklace and the Golden Ring: Historical Imagination in Carlyle and Browning' (*VP*). Baker plausibly argues that both writers attempted to fuse objective facts with their subjective bases of interpretation, Carlyle following Friedrich Schlegel in his use of romantic irony, Browning differing in that he does not wish his reader to be aware that the historical revelation may not be the whole truth. Elizabeth Wheeler's 'Great Burke and Poor Boswell: Carlyle and the Historian's Task' (*VN*) concisely and economically outlines how Carlyle learnt from both Edmund Burke and James Boswell in his *French Revolution*: he avoids Burke's commitment to political theory in an attempt, like Boswell, to present the facts, confident that the truth might emerge from them. Wheeler could, however, have made much more of the influence on *The French Revolution* of Burke's ideas about man, history, and society.

Two useful studies concern *Sartor Resartus*. Lee C. R. Baker discusses 'The Open Secret of *Sartor Resartus*: Carlyle's Method of Converting his Reader' (*SP*). Baker argues that Carlyle's method in *Sartor* is best seen as maieutic rather than rhetorical, for he is acting not as a simple propagandist but as a kind of midwife bringing his reader to a realization which he or she must partly accomplish. The Editor of *Sartor* is aware of Teufelsdröckh's method and makes it his own, playing with the ironic nature of Teufelsdröckh's appearance as Teufelsdröckh had played with the appearance of things. Chris R. Vanden Bossche in 'Desire and Deferral of Closure in Carlyle's *Sartor Resartus* and *The French Revolution*' (*JNT*) sees the Editor of *Sartor* in a much more rigid manner. Both *Sartor* and *The French Revolution*, he argues, dramatize the quest for closure and subvert the closure itself by representing the two conflicting desires in Teufelsdröckh and his Editor (*Sartor*) and the French people and the cautious Girondist faction (*The French Revolution*).

J. D. Rabb examines Carlyle's influence on Herbert L. Stewart and Canadian idealism in *CanL*. *CNew* has appeared once this year. K. J. Fielding gives a brief but sensitive description of a watercolour sketch by Frank Jewsbury of the interior of Cheyne Row (1856) showing a solitary Jane Welsh Carlyle. Ian Campbell notices a previously unknown appreciation of Carlyle's life and work for the short-lived *Border Magazine* of 1842. Margaret Harris argues that George Meredith's character of Nevil Beauchamp in *Beauchamp's Career* is a partially satirical reflection of Frederick Maxse's admiration for Carlyle. Thomas C. Richardson analyses several unpublished letters of John Gibson Lockhart which give evidence of his admiration for Carlyle but also shows his fear of the possible deleterious effects his writings might have on lesser intellects. Anne M. Skarbarnicki reports on new Canadian approaches to Carlyle. Phyllis Harrick discusses Carlyle's unpublished article, 'English Talent for Governing', which details England's maladministration of Ireland. In this piece Carlyle is responding to criticisms of his earlier article 'Repeal of the Union' (*Examiner*, 1848) made by Mill. Finally Rodger L. Tarr describes Carlyle's admiration for Frederick the Great's Scottish Field Marshal, James Keith.

I have not seen Robert L. Oakman's 'Computers and Surface Structure in Prose Style: The Case for Carlyle' in Jacqueline Harnesse's *Computers in Literary and Linguistic Computing* (Champion, 1985) or D. J. Trela's

Cromwell in Context: The Conception, Writing, and Reception of Carlyle's Second History (Carlyle Pamphlets, *CNew*).

Pamela Law contributes a rather straightforward account of the Paris salons of Mary Clarke, an Englishwoman who became a major figure in the Parisian literary and political world (*SSEng*).

Darwin scholarship continues to be a growth industry. With the first volume of Darwin's *Correspondence, 1821–1836* already published (*YW* 66.421) and the second volume to be published next year, Darwin scholars are beginning to recognize the wider affinities of their specialized fields of research. The publication of *A Calendar of the Correspondence of Charles Darwin, 1821–1882*[110] will be of great help to scholars who wish to gain some overview of the central position that Darwin and his work held in the Victorian period. The *Calendar* concisely summarizes 13,925 numbered items of which the editors have located only 2,845 which have been previously published or partially published. The correspondence in the *Calendar* consists of annotated lists of original letters, copies of letters, published letters, drafts, letters in which Darwin was the third party, memoranda sent to Darwin by his correspondents, letters listed in sales catalogues, and empty covers and envelopes. The *Calendar* also contains a list of 321 provenances, including sixty-two private collections. Three appendixes describe the short titles of Darwin's books and papers; a bibliography of works containing printed Darwin correspondence (listing some 320 titles); and a Biographical Register and Index to Correspondents. The *Calendar* makes fascinating reading: a whole host of important Victorian figures appear, including Karl Marx (Darwin thanks him for his gift of the second German edition of *Das Kapital* and wishes he understood more of 'the deep & important subject of political Economy'), Gladstone, Lewis Carroll, Matthew Arnold, Charles Kingsley, Leslie Stephen, Herbert Spencer, G. H. Lewes, and P. H. Gosse. This is a substantial and invaluable work of scholarship which will be of enormous interest to students of Victorian culture generally.

Ronald W. Clark presents a readable chronological account of Darwin's life and work and a history of the idea of evolution into the 1880s[111], tactfully handling such delicate questions as Darwin's debts to Thomas Malthus and A. R. Wallace. Clark is weakest when trying to place Darwin's work in a cultural framework: he sees the publication of *The Origin of Species* as widening the gulf between science and religion whereas most authorities now concur in the belief that the debate which Darwin's work produced was largely contained within the limitations of natural and revealed religion. Despite this weakness Clark's study is sympathetic and for the most part balanced.

The Darwinian Heritage[112] is a substantial collection of essays which gives firm evidence of the richness of the historical debate which surrounds Darwin. David Kohn's collection is divided into three parts which he hopes will reflect the goal of bridge-building between the study of the man and of his place in scientific culture: Part 1 explores Darwin's growth as a scientific thinker from

110. *A Calendar of the Correspondence of Charles Darwin, 1821–1882*, ed. by Frederick Burkhardt and Sydney Smith. Garland (1984). pp. 690. $100.

111. *The Survival of Charles Darwin: A Biography of a Man and an Idea*, by Ronald W. Clark. W&N (1985). pp. x + 449. £14.95.

112. *The Darwinian Heritage*, ed. by David Kohn. Princeton (1985). pp. xii + 1138. £63.40.

his student days to the writing of *The Origin*, Part 2 Darwin's place in the Victorian cultural context, Part 3 the development of the evolutionary communities in Europe and America, and Part 4 philosophical and historical studies. Readers of *YWES* will be most interested in the essays of the second section but they may also wish to consult 'The Immediate Context of Natural Selection' (M. J. S. Hodge and David Kohn) and 'The Ascent of Nature in Darwin's *Descent of Man*' (John R. Durant) from the first section. Part 2 of this collection includes an essay by James R. Moore who provides a detailed and readable account of Darwin's religious life set against the background of the transitional social and intellectual environment he inhabited, with its changing patterns of subordination within an industrializing social order. The growing professionalization of the sciences is a theme of several contributions: Sandra Herbert vigorously outlines the young Darwin's contributions to the field of geology in the 1830s and argues that the Whiggish narrative of historians of science have distorted this, and Martin J. S. Rudwick substantially agrees with Herbert's conclusion that Darwin's concern for the species problem grew out of his geological work in his short and reasonable reply. James A. Secord in a difficult but impressive piece describes social and scientific links with the plant and animal breeders of Victorian Britain. Darwin's immersion in his literary culture is the subject of Gillian Beer's important contribution to the volume. Although Beer's ideas about Darwin are now becoming familiar from her other published work, this essay provides a useful and highly accessible summary of the ways in which she believes Darwin's literary reading conditioned his insights into the problems of creation, succession, and development. I. Bernard Cohen provides a full and scholarly account of the reception of Darwin's theory of natural selection with especial reference to Henry Baker Tristram, Alfred Newton, and Samuel Wilberforce, and, finally, Robert Young vigorously maintains that the intellectual origins of the theory of natural selection are inseparable from social, economic, and ideological issues of nineteenth-century Britain. Kohn's collection shows the variety and the richness of Darwinian studies, yet, paradoxically, its very size and diversity suggest that while there is agreement that Darwin can no longer be contained within the history of science, there is still no real consensus as to how we should regard Darwinism in the future. This belief that the division between traditionalist history of science and other historical disciplines is no longer tenable is also the conclusion of Peter Kitson's review-essay 'Darwin and Darwinism: Recent Studies of the Nineteenth-Century Debate on Man and Nature' in the *Newsletter of the British Society for the History of Philosophy*.

Ralph Colp Jr's 'Confessing a Murder: Darwin's First Revelations about Transmutation' (*Isis*) reconstructs the history of Darwin's communications about the theory of natural selection (1838–48) and suggests some of the personal and strategic factors shaping those communications. Margaret Norris[113] argues that Darwin was the founder of what she calls a 'biocentric tradition' which includes Nietzsche, Kafka, Max Ernst, and Lawrence. Norris's postulation of such a tradition is problematic and, although he is a convenient starting point, to claim Darwin as the founder of the 'deanthropomorphized universe' is to ignore the complexity of the Victorian debate. Norris, however,

113. *Beasts of the Modern Imagination: Darwin, Nietzsche, Ernst and Lawrence*, by Margaret Norris. JHU (1985). pp. xii + 265. $28.

is justified in maintaining that Darwin's unusual awareness of the difficulties inherent in the use of language suggests that his work is important in the foundation of a tradition involving the animality of man. Darwin's language is also the subject of two pieces. Anny Sadrin's 'Langage des origine, origines du langage dans *The Origin of Species*' in *CVE* describes how Darwin's own language is pre-Darwinian, in that Darwin, in his efforts to avoid sensationalism and complexity, does not redefine key terms like 'species' which his own theory demanded that he should. Darwin thus writes in the language of writers who believed in God's creation, and Darwin's personification of nature and his use of war imagery are Hobbesian and Malthusian. This issue is also discussed in R. Keefe's 'Literati, Language, and Darwinism' in *Lang&S*. I have not seen Gillian Beer's 'The Face of Nature: Anthropomorphic Elements in the Language of *The Origin of Species*' in *Languages of Nature: Critical Essays in Science and Literature*, ed. by L. J. Jordanova (Rutgers) or James A. Secord's *Controversy in Victorian Geology* (Princeton).

'Lucie Duff Gordon's Letters from Egypt' are the subject of an informative piece by Charisse Gendron in *ArielE*. Gendron gives a sympathetic and readable account of the life of Duff Gordon and the letters she wrote from Egypt when forced by ill health to emigrate to the sun.

Several relevant studies of Gladstone have appeared. Most important of these is Volume IX of *The Gladstone Diaries*[114] which covers the period from January 1875 to December 1880. As in previous volumes, relevant Cabinet Minutes are included in addition to the complete daily diary text. This volume records one of the most eventful periods in Gladstone's life, opening with his formal retirement from politics in 1875 and recording his return to take the lead in the campaign centring on the Bulgarian atrocities of 1876, his continued attack on Disraeli's foreign and imperial policies, and his own return to power in 1880 when the problems of Ireland and the Transvaal beset him. The *Diaries* also show Gladstone's connections with the literary and artistic world, such as his meetings with Tennyson and Ruskin. The *Diaries* are superbly edited and graced with an excellent introduction by H. C. G. Matthew which places Gladstone's career in the context of his theological and personal convictions.

The *Gladstone Diaries* are the subject of an essay by M. R. D. Foot in *Gladstone, Politics and Religion*[115]. Disappointingly, this piece is merely culled from Foot's much longer and more substantial introduction to the first volume of *The Diaries* (1969). Most of the other ten Gladstone Memorial Lectures have also been printed elsewhere.

H. C. G. Matthew puts his own editorial knowledge of Gladstone's Diaries to good use in an 'extended biographical essay'[116]. Matthew's study is an impressive piece of scholarship which places the major achievements of Gladstone's first career in a personal context. The events of Gladstone's political career will be familiar but Matthew gives a more rounded picture of the

114. *The Gladstone Diaries with Cabinet Minutes and Prime-Ministerial Correspondence*. Vol. IX: *January 1875–December 1880*, ed. by H. C. G. Matthew. Clarendon. pp. xcvii + 714. £55.

115. *Gladstone, Politics and Religion: A Collection of Founder's Day Lectures Delivered at St. Deiniol's Library, Hawarden, 1967–83*, ed. by Peter J. Jagger. Macmillan/St Martin's (1985). pp. xxiv + 183. £16.45.

116. *Gladstone 1809–1874*, by H. C. G. Matthew. Clarendon. pp. xi + 275. £15.

man and what motivated him. We see how Gladstone's changing religious views reflected his sense of political vocation. Matthew's study also lays bare the intimate, personal life of the man: we are confronted with a frank view of Gladstone's sexual psychology, his predilection for pornography, his scourging of himself, and his work in reclaiming prostitutes. This latter activity Matthew views as a charitable enterprise which would no doubt have taken other forms but for that sexual tension which was at the centre of Victorian religious and family life.

Two studies of Edmund Gosse's work have come my way, both by Raoul Granqvist and concerning Gosse's criticism of Donne. The first in *ES* describes the reception of Gosse's *Life of John Donne* (1899) with particular reference to the reviews of H. M. Sanders, Arthur Symons, and Leslie Stephen: the latter two critics tending to give their own expositions of Donne under cover of their reviews of Gosse. Granqvist's other piece is 'Edmund Gosse – The Reluctant Critic of John Donne' in *NM*.

CUP have reprinted T. H. Green's *Lectures on the Principles of Political Obligation*[117] which is chiefly concerned with Green's political philosophy; it also contains in complete form his 'Liberal Legislation and the Freedom of Contract' and 'On the Different Senses of Freedom as Applied to the Will and the Moral Progress of Man', selections from lectures on the English Revolution and the *Prolegomena to Ethics*, and unpublished undergraduate essays and fragments on moral and political philosophy. An excellent introduction to Green's work prefaces this edition, arguing strongly for his place as a political philosopher and the leading exponent of British Idealism.

Malcolm Woodfield's study of *R. H. Hutton: Critic and Theologian*[118] is the first biography of this Victorian critic. Woodfield cogently demonstrates the wide range of Hutton's work but is chiefly concerned with Hutton's thirty-six year stint as editor of the *Spectator*. Throughout Hutton's work, Woodfield discovers a religious bias which reveals itself most notably in his literary criticism. Woodfield argues that Hutton charts his own spiritual progress in his criticism of Newman, and that his interest in Arnold illustrates his concern with the state of religious and imaginative assent. Hutton's view of Wordsworth was of one who opposed the materialistic trends of the age, trends with which he believed Tennyson had colluded. Hutton's readings of George Eliot are particularly interesting: her work became the focus for the realization of his ideals for fiction. Woodfield's elegant little study is scholarly and well researched and is useful in drawing together the ideas and concerns of its fragmentary subject. Also on the subject of Hutton: Robert H. Tener argues strongly for an appraisal of Richardson's *Clarissa* in the *Spectator* (1867) to be attributed to him (*ELN*).

The year's single contribution to studies of T. H. Huxley which I have seen is Ed Block Jr's 'T. H. Huxley's Rhetoric and the Popularization of Victorian Scientific Ideas: 1854–74' (*VS*), which deals with Huxley's development of a rhetorical strategy designed to accommodate the views and prejudices of his different audiences. Block shows how Huxley employed his rhetorical skill in

117. *Lectures on the Principles of Political Obligation and Other Writings*, by T. H. Green, ed. by Paul Harris and John Morrow. CUP. pp. ix + 383. hb £27.50, pb £9.95.

118. *R. H. Hutton: Critic and Theologian: The Writings of R. H. Hutton on Newman, Arnold, Tennyson, Wordsworth, and George Eliot*, by Malcolm Woodfield. Clarendon. pp. x + 227. £25.

the 'mind–matter' debate following his 1868 Edinburgh address, 'On the Physical Basis of Life'.

Geraldine Jewsbury's reviews of fiction published anonymously in *The Athenaeum* (1849–80) are the subject of a study by Monica Correa Fryckstedt[65]. Fryckstedt regards Jewsbury's judgements as the epitome of conventional middlebrow Victorian taste in fiction, although this thesis is not comprehensively demonstrated. Her work is a readable but at times basic account of Jewsbury's reviews for, and her relationship with, the *Athenaeum*. Her analysis of Jewsbury's actual reviews is quite probing: she demonstrates Jewsbury's attitudes to morality, plot, escapism, characterization, and subject matter. Nonetheless, this study claims to but does not actually delineate Jewsbury's real position in the Victorian fiction industry. Also included is a checklist of some 2,300 reviews which Jewsbury contributed to the *Athenaeum*.

Murray G. H. Pittock prints a brief unpublished letter from Lionel Johnson to Victor Plarr in *ELT*. P. Hinchcliff discusses the ethical, evolutionary, and religious thought of Benjamin Jowett and Bishop Colenso in *JEH*. J. Holland Gill argues in *SoAR* that G. H. Lewes and his German source, Gustav Theodor Feckner, have not been given their deserved credit in the confused parentage of the term 'stream of consciousness'. In the year's single contribution to Macaulay studies, Stephen Prickett (*E&S*) wryly details Macaulay's criticism of Southey's pessimism and its connotations for the fate of uncultivated landscape. Macaulay's view of a flower garden atop Mount Helvellyn contrasts with Wordsworth's awareness that progress would lead to the fight to preserve the distinction between London and the wilderness.

A full-length biography of Cardinal Manning has been written by Robert Gray[119]. This readable account of Manning's life and work defends its subject against his many detractors who saw him as ambitious and uncompromising in his Ultramontanism. Gray believes Manning to be a much maligned figure who did a great deal to revive Catholicism in Britain by convincing many of the working classes. Although Gray's book is partial, it is honest in its portrayal of the less attractive sides of the Cardinal's personality: even Gray refers to Manning as 'the tyrannous old man'. Ultimately Gray sees his subject as a pragmatist who defended papal infallibility on the grounds that the more aggressively it was preached the more widespread would be the authority of the Church. To many readers lacking Gray's sympathy with Manning, Coventry Patmore's claim that Manning was 'the meanest soul that ever buzzed in so high a place' may still stand.

Two studies of Harriet Martineau have appeared. The first, a collection of Martineau's writings on women's issues edited by Gayle Graham Yates[120] is problematic because Martineau's feminism was itself problematic; as Yates points out it was part and parcel of her whole political philosophy. Whether we can agree that Martineau's political philosophy was that of a progressive enlightened reformer is debatable given the narrow moral and class perspective which she held. Even if the reader cannot accept some of the large claims which

119. *Cardinal Manning: A Biography*, by Robert Gray. W&N (1985). pp. x + 366. £16.95.

120. *Harriet Martineau on Women*, ed. by Gayle Graham Yates. Rutgers (1985). pp. xvi + 283. hb $29, pb $12.

Yates makes for Martineau as 'a wide-ranging, progressive, and thorough-going feminist in nearly every sense in which that word is used today', he or she will be grateful for this collection.

Valerie Sanders's *Reason Over Passion: Harriet Martineau and the Victorian Novel*[121] is much more aware of the problematic nature of Martineau's work and place in the Victorian intellectual context. Discussing Martineau's role in the development of Victorian fiction, Sanders sees Martineau as innovatory in her attempts to balance realism and romance in a way that pre-empts George Eliot's theories of fiction. Martineau's didacticism, which Sanders carefully delineates, prevents her from fully achieving the scope of Eliot's ideas. Unlike Linda Peterson[91], Sanders believes that Martineau's *Autobiography* should be judged in terms of the fictional strategies involved. This is an informed and attractive study.

Two new letters from George Meredith to F. M. Evans and to James Thomson are printed by Mohammed Shaheen in *ELN*.

No full-length work on Mill has come to my attention this year but several shorter studies have appeared. Patrick Creevy's persuasive and interesting 'J. S. Mill and James Martineau: Possibilities of an Associationist Aesthetic' (*VP*) demonstrates how Mill argued for kinship between poetic thought and the basic perception of objects while remaining within the limits allowed by his belief in associationist psychology, and aided by his reading of James Martineau's associationist explanation of the poet's 'strong concentrative emotion'. Another important piece is Sue Lonoff's 'Cultivated Feminism: Mill and *The Subjection of Women*' (*PQ*) which takes issue with Susan Hardy Aiken (*YW* 64.399) who maintains that Mill is not a liberal thinker but an angry prophet and political deconstructionist. Lonoff sanely and clearly places Mill's *Subjection of Women* where it belongs, in the context of classical rhetoric: Mill, arguing for virtue and culture, is an apostle rather than a prophet.

A substantial number of further discussions of Mill have appeared, few of which will interest readers of literature. Chief of those deserving mention is Martin Warner's searching examination of Mill's *An Autobiography*[121a], which compares this work with St Augustine's *Confessions* and attempts to describe how literary criticism may provide an analogical method for those investigating the consistency and veracity of philosophical systems. Warner deftly shows how Mill's lack of self-awareness in the *Autobiography* detracts from his associationist beliefs which serve to hide his own deficiencies from himself. Worth noting are Brand Blanshard's tribute to Mill in *Four Reasonable Men*[122], and M. Sandbach's 'August Strindberg and John Stuart Mill' (*Scan*), the latter of which I have not seen.

Two interesting works about Jane Morris have appeared. Peter Faulkner has edited Jane's letters of 1883–1913 to Wilfrid Scawen Blunt[123]. Blunt, successor to Rossetti as Jane's lover, was also a man of strong political opinions, not a

121. *Reason Over Passion: Harriet Martineau and the Victorian Novel*, by Valerie Sanders. Harvester. pp. xv + 236. £32.50.

121a. In *Philosophy and Literature*, ed. by A. Phillips Griffiths. CUP (1984). pp. v + 233. pb £9.95.

122. *Four Reasonable Men: Marcus Aurelius, John Stuart Mill, Ernest Renan and Henry Sidgwick*, by Brand Blanshard. Wesleyan (1984). pp. ix + 308. pb $9.95.

123. *Letters of J. Morris to W. S. Blunt*, ed. by Peter Faulkner. UExe. pp. xi + 140. £15.

socialist but a supporter of Egyptian and Irish nationalism. Sadly his letters to Jane are lost and Faulkner prints extracts from Blunt's papers and diaries which help provide commentary on the correspondence. Jane emerges from the letters as a sensitive and predominantly melancholic person, showing interest in her immediate circle of friends and an awareness of current political events. The letters are characteristically brief and do not contain strong expressions of emotion, but a feeling of despondency infuses them and invests the collection with a deep and lasting sense of poignancy. As one would expect, this volume is carefully and neatly edited by Faulkner.

Jane Morris's letters are used to good effect by Jan Marsh[124] who tells the story of Jane and of her daughter May in a simple, straightforward way without any 'theoretical discussion of the place of women' in the period as a whole. Jane's story is that of an intelligent and skilful woman of humble stock raised by marriage to the middle-class artistic lifestyle of Morris's circle. Marsh is tactful and sensitive when discussing those uncertain areas of Jane's personal life. She accepts Jane's statement to Blunt that she never loved Morris, although in later life (due especially to her daughter Jenny's epilepsy) she became concerned and affectionate toward her husband. Marsh's sensitive and informative study gives us a fuller picture of this important Pre-Raphaelite figure and of her daughter May. Sadly, perhaps because the book is so reasonably priced, it is less than carefully printed.

Not a great deal has appeared this year about William Morris but a few worthy articles have surfaced. F. W. Boos discusses the utopian communism of Morris (*HPT*). Frederick Kirchhoff in 'Getting to Know William Morris a Little Better' (*MLR*) perceptively reviews the first volume of *The Collected Letters of William Morris* (*YW* 65.480) and Carole Silver's *The Romance of William Morris* (*YW* 63.315). Deborah Nevins in an interesting piece describes the influence of Morris and Ruskin on the English flower garden (*Antiques*). Morris's dislike of the bedding-out of plants ('an aberration of the human mind') is well illustrated. Jan Marsh contributes a useful and timely piece to *BurlM* on Morris's painting and drawing, describing his pictorial ambitions which, despite common belief to the contrary, he only gradually and partially relinquished. Susan Fisher Miller rather opaquely considers W. B. Yeats's debt to Morris for his personal and poetic symbol Thoor Ballylee (*Éire*).

Ray Watkinson relinquished his editorship of *JWMS* this year and Morris scholars will be grateful to him for his meticulous and scholarly contribution to Morris studies over the years. His last journal is substantial, obviously intended as a double-issue but not marked as such. This issue contains several noteworthy pieces. Dinah Birch offers an analysis of 'Morris and Myth: A Romantic Heritage', and Helen A. Timo discusses the origins of 'William Morris's *The Sundering Flood*', arguing for Jón Thoroddsen's *Pilter og Stúlka* (1850) as a source. A. L. Morton contributes a pugnacious discussion of 'Morris, Marx, and Engels', arguing for Morris's perceptive understanding of Marxist theory, unusual among British socialists. Two contributions are responses to the work of other Morris scholars: Ray Watkinson provides a detailed and well-illustrated review-article about Geoffrey Rubens's *William Richard Lethaby: His Life and Work, 1857–1931* (ArchP), which I have not yet

---

124. *Jane and May Morris: A Biographical Story 1839–1938*, by Jan Marsh. Pandora. pp. xvi + 328. pb £4.95.

seen, and Stephen Coleman takes issue with Barbara Gribble (*YW* 66.424), who sees *News from Nowhere* as an enquiry into self-deception and stasis, whereas he argues that it shows a utopia which is not problem-free but both desirable and attainable. Gudrun Jonsdottir recounts her personal memories of May Morris's and the indomitable Mrs Lobb's visits to Iceland, and finally Margaret Horton describes Morris's influence on the calligrapher Alfred Fairbank. I have not seen Gary L. Aho's *William Morris: A Reference Guide* (Hall, 1985) or Frederick Kirchhoff's 'William Morris's Anti-Books: The Kelmscott Press and the Late Prose Romances' in *Forms of the Fantastic*, edited by Jan Hokenson and Howard Pearce (Greenwood).

In the year that has seen moves towards the beatification of Cardinal Newman a healthy number of predominantly dull works have appeared. Most important is the publication of the first critical edition of Newman's *An Essay in Aid of A Grammar of Assent* (1870)[125]. The editor, I. T. Ker, provides an excellent introduction to this difficult work which elucidates Newman's sinewy arguments and traces the development of his thought. This volume contains an appendix listing all textual variants between the first and last editions of the work published during the Cardinal's lifetime. Newman's novel *Loss and Gain: The Story of a Convert*[126] (1848) has been re-issued by OUP for their WC series. The appearance of this work in a well-produced and inexpensive form is welcome.

A number of articles have appeared which are chiefly concerned with Newman's theology. The April number of *DownR* carries four pieces. Allen Brent's 'Newman's Moral Conversion' contrasts his first visit to Rome (as an Anglican) with subsequent visits (as a Catholic), demonstrating Newman's belief that the strength of the Roman Catholic Church lay in its status as a vision of spiritual power rather than of temporal might. David Hopkins discusses 'Some Anglican Friends of Cardinal Newman', including Matthew Arnold, Froude, and Gladstone. 'In Cardinal Newman Humanly Speaking' Rachel Leach provides an interesting analysis of the stylistic ways in which Newman dealt with the conflict between his religious and his human loyalties, and Terence Merrigan considers 'Newman's Progress towards Rome' in the light of Jung's theories of psychological types.

Leslie Armour's 'Newman, Anselm, and Proof of God's Existence' (*IJPR*) maintains that Newman adapted an idea of Anselm's for his arguments for the existence of God. John R. Griffin provides an explanation for Newman's unexpected praise of William Palmer (*ELN*). *Moreana* contains a comparison of Newman with Sir Thomas More by Germain Marc'hadour. I have not seen J. D. Earnest and Gerard Tracey's *John Henry Newman: An Annotated Bibliography* (Garland, 1985), Andrew Louth's 'The Nature of Theological Understanding: Some Parallels Between Newman and Gadamer' in *Tradition Renewed*, edited by Geoffrey Rowell (Pickwick), or Julia Smith's 'Newman's Idea of a University in 1982 and 1986' (*TCE*).

Four texts by Pater edited by scholars are reviewed this year, as well as two books which include chapters on Pater and religion, a monograph on Pater and

---

125. *An Essay in Aid of A Grammar of Assent*, by John Henry Newman, ed. by I. T. Ker. Clarendon (1985). pp. lxx + 409. £40.

126. *Loss and Gain: The Story of a Convert*, by John Henry Newman, ed. by Alan G. Hill. OUP. pp. xxv + 317. pb £3.95.

modernism, a reception study of Baudelaire in which Pater's work receives detailed attention, and a healthy number of periodical articles.

William E. Buckler edits and introduces *The Renaissance*, *Appreciations*, and *Imaginary Portraits* in one volume[127] which claims in its title a centrality for these works that no reader of Pater would challenge; yet are they more 'major' than the other titles implicitly denied this accolade? Bibliographically the texts are eclectic and bear a fudged relation to the historical existence of volumes which appeared with these titles: the text of *The Renaissance* is that of 1893 'as edited by Donald Hill . . . in 1980'; *Appreciations* appears in the 1910 New Library Edition with the 'restoration' of 'Aesthetic Poetry' (from the 1887 edition) which *replaces* 'Feuillet's "La Morte"' added in 1889; the *Imaginary Portraits* category includes eight rather than the original four, including 'The Child in the House', 'Emerald Uthwart', and 'Apollo in Picardy' (which were collected in *Miscellaneous Studies*, also by implication a 'major text'?), and 'Hippolytus Veiled' (collected in *Greek Studies*), all in the 1910 text. As there is no annotation, the basis for the selection of this hodgepodge is not revealed, and the breathtaking claim that this project 'partial[ly] fulfill[s] . . . a critical need' of undergraduate *and postgraduate* students for 'dependable editions' should not fool scholars and librarians. The seventy-page introduction, 'a critical statement' which 'sacrifice[s] the usual advantages of footnoting', keeps this college textbook notion to the fore, with sections on each of the 'volumes', on 'Pater's Goal', and 'Pater's Method', with perhaps the most telling, 'A Caution about Chronology' which, implicitly defending the ahistorical principles behind this volume, claims that 'Pater's writing agenda was fairly complete before his first book was published'. Despite this, 'A Pater Chronology' and a basic if annotated 'Suggestions for Further Study' are included.

By contrast, Ian Small's *Marius*[128], which is annotated and scholarly, uses the third 1892 edition as copy text and *does* meet the need for a dependable student text and edition. The Explanatory Notes are fuller than Michael Levey's Penguin edition (*YW* 66.426), which prints the 1910 text, and Small's critical and learned introduction on the intertextuality of *Marius* is worth seeking out in its own right. *Marius the Epicurean* serves as the prime illustration of the non-homogenous nature of the audience of some Victorian fiction in 'Annotating "Hard" Nineteenth-Century Novels', Small's thoughtful and provocative contribution to Critical Opinion in *EIC*. Here it is shown convincingly that the intent of twentieth-century editors to annotate texts in order to restore to our contemporaries the clarity of understanding of the original audience is beset with problems; it assumes mistakenly the homogeneity of the audience and 'ignores the possibility that obscurity may be an authorial ploy to distinguish between audiences' that is found in *Marius* and other late nineteenth-century writing. Giving instances of variously mediated allusions or quotation, Small asks when the exercise of the editor's judgement becomes criticism rather than annotation.

127. *Walter Pater: Three Major Texts ('The Renaissance', 'Appreciations', and* • *'Imaginary Portraits')*, ed. by William E. Buckler. NYU (distr. ColU). pp. viii + 550. hb $50, pb $23.50.

128. *Marius the Epicurean*, by Walter Pater, ed. by Ian Small. WC. OUP. pp. xxx + 292. pb £3.95.

Nathan A. Scott Jr's essays on Coleridge, Arnold, Pater, Santayana, Stevens, and Heidegger in *The Poetics of Belief*[107] appear in a series of Studies in Religion, and Scott presents them as defenders of the imagination against its enemies, empiricism, rationalism, and now structuralism. Wresting from the work of Victor Turner an optimistic view of marginality as a seedbed of future vitality, Scott's chatty review of material long familiar to Paterians attempts to acclaim Pater's anti-secularism, to detail his dissatisfaction with materialism and *sensualité*, and to reclaim, in a scurry through *The Renaissance* and close reading of *Marius*, the centrality of the diaphanous man and '*the religious possibility*' in Pater's work.

Hilary Fraser's project in *Beauty and Belief*[14] confines itself to Victorian writing, but the link between aesthetics and religion, the survey of various authors, the attention to *Marius*, and the similar prominence of that old chestnut of Eliot's distaste for aestheticized Christianity invite comparison with Scott. However, Fraser's book is more coherent and historical, with chapters on authors who are associated explicitly with particular subjects such as Theology (Keble, Newman and the Oxford Movement), Epistemology and Perception (Hopkins), Criticism (Ruskin and Arnold), and Aestheticism (Pater and Wilde). Though originating in a thesis, Fraser's book contains a more sophisticated level of discourse on Pater than Scott's, and Fraser knowledgeably distinguishes the positions of Pater and Wilde, while concluding that both turn the Tractarian emphasis on the aesthetic qualities of Christianity on its head and endorse a religion of art which, for Pater, involves the identification of Christ as the perfect merger of content and form.

Two books treat the nature and degree of Paterian influence on his contemporaries and ours, yet both claim to be new versions of the territory that studies of sources or influence formerly covered. F. C. McGrath[129] employs Thomas Kuhn's general definition of *paradigm* in an attempt to formalize the link between Pater and Modernism. McGrath's emphasis on synthesis seems apposite, his belief that 'Pater's strength was his ability to synthesize the best that was thought and said into a reasonably coherent aesthetic program, a program that had a profound appeal to the Modernists', though McGrath's project and method are baldly positivist: 'to construct from Pater's texts an intellectual paradigm that accounts for many of the distinctive features of Modernist literature'. To that end he examines in eleven interesting if stylistically dense chapters 'eleven cardinal principles' common to Pater and Modernism, such as subjectivity, scepticism, idealism, and ends with an analysis of the Paterian–Modernist paradigm in a Modernist text, *A Portrait of the Artist as a Young Man*.

In Pat Clemnts' formidable *Baudelaire and the English Tradition*[23], the uncertainty about Peter's knowledge of Baudelaire seen recently in John J. Conlon's *Walter Pater and the French Tradition* (*YW* 64.400) is dispelled by Clements' demonstration that Pater was heavily influeneced by Baudelaire early on, and that unlike Swinburne who exposed his indebtedness, Pater carefully suppressed his. Clements' revelations of Pater's allusions and borrowings in *Gaston du Latour*, *Plato and Platonism*, 'Aucassin and Nicolette', 'Poems by William Morris', the 'Conclusion', 'The School of Giorgione', and 'Proper

129. *The Sensible Spirit: Walter Pater and the Modernist Paradigm*, by F. C. McGrath. UFlor. pp. xii + 299. $25.

Merimée' are required reading for Paterians. The critical matrix of this absorbing and well-written book accommodates the complexity of reading and writing, and the chapters on Swinburne and Wilde appear as fresh, learned, and provocative as the section on Pater which suggests that 'Pater set Baudelaire at the center, not only of his own work, but also of the current of English literature in the late nineteenth and early twentieth centuries'.

Gerald Monsman and Robert Keefe are among the myriad who acclaim Pater the protomodernist. In 'Pater's "Child in the House" and the Renovation of the Self' (*TSLL*) Monsman treats the essay as autobiography rather than as an imaginary portrait and considers the way in which the mirrored image would 'react upon and refine its "original"'. Linking the essay with that on Charles Lamb which appeared in print two months after, Monsman follows the trail of various images through *Marius* and *The Renaissance* to discern their hidden logic. Robert Keefe in 'Walter Pater: The Critic and the Irrational' (*VN*) alleges that Pater, a 'timid but profound revolutionary', initiated 'a revolt in English letters' which modernists built upon rather than outgrew. Selecting three essays in the 1873 edition of *The Renaissance* and the mid-seventies essays on classical myths, Keefe attempts to make good his claim that, with Nietzsche, Pater in the 1870s elicited cultural renewal out of the coupling of Hebraism and Hellenism first by replacing Apollo, privileged by a Victorian rage for order, with Venus, and then by debowdlerizing Greek myths. This identification of both Pater and modernism with the irrational explains, but does not require, Keefe's construction of Pater's alleged defeat of Venus in the 1880s and 1890s by a 'strangely militant Apollonianism' and the 'embarrassment' of Pater's Sparta. Readers will however remember the Paterian riches of the 1880s, notably *Marius* and the *Imaginary Portraits*, as well as other significant motifs in Pater's essays and reject this narrow model which disallows so much writing of import. Keefe has another piece on an aspect of the irrational in Pater in *ELT*: '"Apollo in Picardy": Pater's Monk and Ruskin's Madness'. Here it is alleged that Pater's last imaginary portrait takes as a subject Ruskin's madness and, insofar as Keefe suggests that Pater's portraits of an irrational Apollo and a mad monk represent 'a stunning recantation' of his own thought which had grown 'too orderly', that this 'tale of the confrontation of a monk named John and a vision of divine anarchy is a satire with a strangely elegiac undercurrent', comprising sardonic comment on Ruskin's moralism and Pater's recognition of Ruskin as his *semblable*. I am not convinced of the 1880s order nor the 1890s anarchy, nor of the Bloomian premise that 'Ruskin was a nearly overwhelming psychological presence for Pater throughout his career' on which this tendentious argument is based.

Bloom and 'Apollo in Picardy' re-appear in another *ELT* article, Jay B. Losey's 'Epiphany in Pater's Portraits', the first of two this year on Pater's portraits. Suggesting that as a genre the imaginary portrait is dependent on epiphany for its success, Losey treats rather mechanically Pater's reliance on epiphany to signify meaning and to develop character. Successive close readings are accorded to epiphanies in 'Emerald Uthwart', 'Sebastian van Storck', 'Duke Carl of Rosenmold', 'Apollo in Picardy', 'Hippolytus Veiled', 'A Prince of Court Painters', and 'The Child in the House', amidst which there is a pinched analysis of the types of epiphanies employed by Pater. Ed Block Jr writes very effectively on the portrait essay in the late nineteenth century in 'Walter Pater, Arthur Symons, W. B. Yeats, and the Fortunes of the Literary

Portrait' in *SEL*. Principally about Paterian examples of the genre ('Diaphaneite', 'Winckelmann', 'Amiel', and 'Prosper Mérimée' in particular), Block usefully identifies their characteristic qualities, properly noting that 'Pater's sensitivity to the conventions of the Victorian periodical prose essay forms the fundamental "theme" upon which he practiced significant variations'. To substantiate his case that these essays served as models for Symons and Yeats, Block goes on to discuss Symons's essay on Paul Verlaine and Yeats's 'The Happiest of the Poets' and *The Cutting of an Agate*.

A second printing of the Brasenose College Pater Society's *Articles to Celebrate the Society's Having Reached its 750th Meeting*[130] has appeared; beside Bernard Richards's 'Walter Pater at Oxford' (*YW* 66.426), the issue contains a piece on 'The Minute Books of the Pater Society [BNC]' by Michael Woods, a report of a minute book of the Queen's College Pater Society (1924–37?) and a list of the members of the BNC Society from 1907, both by Gregory McGrath. While the Society was an essay society, wider in its remit than Paterian essays, its history offers insight into the course of the Pater tradition of writing at Oxford in this century.

PaterN continues to appear semi-annually and to publish news, notes, reviews, and a useful annotated bibliography.

The Letter Book of Charles Reade, the popular Victorian novelist and playwright is the subject of a piece by Thomas D. Clareson (*PULC*). Reade's Letter Book shows him to have been a close friend of Dickens and Bulwer-Lytton and clarifies some of the details of Reade's private life.

Two studies involving William Michael Rossetti's prose have appeared. In 'William Michael Rossetti and *The Germ*' S. W. Propas cogently maintains that Rossetti's account of the PRB is coloured by his loyalty to Dante Gabriel Rossetti and that his own calmness and fairness flatten the youthful enthusiasm of the Brotherhood (*JPRS*). *AL* contains 'Whitman, Charles Aldrich and W. M. Rossetti in 1885' by Roger W. Peattie detailing Rossetti's part in the Whitman subscription of 1885.

Less has appeared on Ruskin than last year but there is still a significant amount of worthwhile material. I have seen no new editions of Ruskin's prose, but Roger W. Peattie reprints an interesting letter of Ruskin's to D. G. Rossetti of 9 August 1870 (*N&Q*). This contains Ruskin's thanks for the copy of Rossetti's *Poems* forwarded to him by the publishers at the poet's request.

Only one full-length study of Ruskin has come to my attention. Malcolm Hardman presents an unusual study of Ruskin's relationship with that great nineteenth-century industrial and cultural phenomenon, the city of Bradford[131]. I was slightly disappointed by this diffuse and, at times, difficult work which attempts to delineate Ruskin's audience of a small, coherent, and 'liberal' establishment which included radicals and Tories. Hardman is evasive about what forms the character of this audience which sometimes expands in time and place to include the strong Pennine tradition of passionate conviction and empiricism (David Hartley is important here: educated at Bradford Grammar School but born in Halifax) as well as Barbara Castle and Lord Vic

---

130. *Articles to Celebrate the Society's Having Reached its 750th Meeting*, ed. by Gregory McGrath. Pater Society, Brasenose College (1985). pp. 50.

131. *Ruskin and Bradford: An Experiment in Victorian Cultural History*, by Malcolm Hardman. ManU. pp. viii + 408. £27.50.

Feather. Hardman's study does, however, contain a fascinating analysis of Bradford's pre-eminence and its distinctive character which places Ruskin's lectures in the intellectual and social context within which they were delivered. This study is very well researched, but overlong and repetitious: we should all know that the proprietor of the *Bradford Observer* founded the first publicly maintained secondary school, but it is not necessary to tell us this at least three times. Several irritating printing errors mar this work which could also have been better illustrated.

Three studies of single works by Ruskin have attracted my attention. Robert Casillo, in a fine piece entitled 'Parasitism and Capital Punishment in *Fors Clavigera*' (*VS*), shows how Ruskin not only advocated capital punishment (along with prominent liberals like Gladstone and Mill) but also desired such executions to be public (public hangings were abolished in 1868). Ruskin's attitudes were strongly influenced by biblical imperatives and by his fear of the murderer's violation of the organic community. Ina Rae Hark pays timely tribute to Ruskin's skill as a satirist in '*Unto This Last* and the Satiric Tradition' (*Arnoldian*), although her placing of Ruskin in the tradition of Pope, Dryden, and Swift is unconvincing. Linda M. Austin contributes a perceptive and sensitive piece, 'The Art of Absence in *The Stones of Venice*' to *JPRS*. Austin argues that the idea of absence and loss motivates Ruskin's narrative: the missing objects in Ruskin's Venice signify a vanished and broken mythos. Austin also provides a sensitive discussion of Ruskin's relationship with Rose La Touche in 'Ruskin and Rose at Play with Words' (*Criticism*). She surveys Rose's diaries and her letter to Ruskin of March 1861, explaining that these documents are evidence of Rose's struggle with her parents, with her illness, with Ruskin, and with her own strivings to attain the authority promised by Scripture. Chris Brooks provides an enthusiastic and knowing review of recent works of Ruskin criticism in *JWMS*.

The conscientiously prolific Robert Casillo has published two more substantial pieces of Ruskin criticism both dealing with the sage's influence on twentieth-century writers. In 'The Stones Alive' (*JPRS*) he discusses Ruskin's problematic influence upon the art critic Adrian Stokes. This piece is detailed but it is not always clear whether Casillo is arguing for the anticipations of Freud in Ruskin or pleading for the validity of a Freudian interpretation of Ruskin's work. I am not so sure that Stokes's psychological method is as close to Ruskin's intuitions concerning self-expression as Casillo thinks. Casillo also has a piece in *UTQ* about 'The Meaning of Venetian History in Ruskin and Pound'. Casillo does not postulate a direct influence but argues that Pound's *Cantos* and Ruskin's *Stones of Venice* share similar values, concepts, and conclusions. Casillo adequately makes his point: for both writers Venice was a constant source of aesthetic, economic, social, and political speculation mostly centring on the loss of medieval spirituality and hierarchy, and its replacement by economic individualism. In a careful and detailed essay entitled 'John Ruskin's Lectionary' Meridel Holland deals with Ruskin's annotations of an eleventh- or twelfth-century Gospel Lectionary which he purchased in 1871 (*DUJ*). These annotations form a kind of journal of 1873–5 and give a detailed analysis of the text of the Lectionary as well as indicating Ruskin's religious doubts, his sense of personal emptiness, his political despair, and his virtual obsession with scriptural texts upon personal riches. It is to be hoped that one day Ruskin's annotations of such pieces will be published in full.

Several lesser but noteworthy pieces deserve comment. William J. Gatens's 'John Ruskin and Music' (*VS*) provides an informative, if pedestrian, account of Ruskin's music criticism: not surprisingly, Ruskin exhibits a later preoccupation with the moral, social, religious, and educational aspects of the art. Robert Keefe's 'Apollo in Picardy: Pater's Monk and Ruskin's Madness' (*ELT*) plausibly relates Pater's imaginary portrait of the Prior St Jean to Ruskin's characteristic moralism when confronted with a vision of divine anarchy. Charles Swann's 'Dickens, Ruskin and the City' (*Dickensian*) examines the shared community of concern of both Ruskin and Dickens for the city. Swann makes a fair case for the view that Dickens's influence was much more far-reaching than Ruskin's comments in 'Fiction, Fair and Foul' might seem to indicate. Regrettably I have not seen *RuskN* which contains J. S. Dearden's 'Ruskin and the Blue Coat School', nor A. Aron's 'Daguerreotypes from the Ruskin Collection' (*Domus*).

The veteran Shavian scholar Stanley Weintraub has edited *Bernard Shaw: The Diaries, 1885–97*[132], which cover the years of Shaw's life from the obscurity of his twenty-ninth year to the fame of his forty-second. Weintraub provides a complete transliteration of Shaw's original Pitman shorthand using Stanley Rypins's pioneering but bowdlerized and incomplete efforts as a starting point. The *Diaries* show in minute detail the concerns of Shaw's personal and everyday life: in particular we are fed seemingly endless details of even the most trivial expenditure. These volumes also give a fair idea of the 'radical' intellectual life of late-Victorian London: near the close of the *Diaries* we see Shaw campaigning in East Bradford on Keir Hardie's behalf in the general election of 1896. Weintraub's edition includes fragments of earlier and later diaries which Shaw had attempted to keep up but soon discontinued. The editorial intrusions into the text are kept to a minimum as Weintraub sensibly adopts a system of running annotations providing necessary clarification without interrupting the narrative flow. Without doubt this edition is a necessary and substantial contribution to our understanding of Shaw's life and work.

Anne Lohri clarifies the identity of the pseudonymous journalist Joachim Hayward Stocqueler as Joachim Heyward (*sic*) Siddons in *N&Q*. I suppose it was only a matter of time before Samuel Smiles's *Self-Help*[133] was given a fresh reprint. This year sees its publication in the Penguin Business Library with an introduction by Keith Joseph which is next to useless for the cultural historian: not surprisingly Joseph stresses the congruence of Smiles's axioms with contemporary market-based economics and the newly re-affirmed faith in the entrepreneur. Surely Smiles deserves better than this. The status of the volume as what Penguin call a 'Management Classic' is problematic, even in its abridged form. Students of Victorian thought and literature will no doubt prefer Asa Briggs's unabridged centenary edition of this work (*YW* 39.260). It is to be hoped that Smiles's stress on the insufficiency of purely financial success, his continued radical faith in public education, and his concluding ideal of the 'true gentleman' who does not 'shuffle or prevaricate, dodge or skulk; but is honest, upright and straightforward' will not be forgotten by his

132. *Bernard Shaw: The Diaries, 1885–97*, ed. by Stanley Weintraub. 2 vols. PSU. pp. vi + vi + 1241. £71.25.

133. *Self-Help with Illustrations of Conduct and Perseverance*, by Samuel Smiles, intro. by Keith Joseph. Penguin. pp. 251. pb £3.95.

latter-day readership. Some awareness in this edition of the status of this text as a social document, and of the critique of Smiles's attitudes by those such as Arnold would have been welcome.

I have not seen the year's single contribution to Spencer studies, H. J. Dahme's 'Sex and Gender in the Work of Herbert Spencer' (*Kolner Zeitschrift für Soziologie und Sozial Psychologie*), *The Farringford Journal of Emily Tennyson* (IOWP), or Alon Kadish's *Apostle Arnold: The Life and Death of Arnold Toynbee, 1852–83* (DukeU).

John Sutherland draws our attention to 'Thackeray and France, 1842' in the form of two unpublished and incomplete articles by Thackeray (*N&Q*), and N. John Hall discusses the posthumous publication of Trollope's autobiography by his elder son Henry Merivale Trollope and the publisher William Blackwood (*PULC*). Barbara Caine's 'Family History as Women's History: The Sisters of Beatrice Webb' (*FSt*) is a detailed and sympathetic account of the tensions and pressures existing within the family group of the Webb sisters. Finally, I have not seen M. MacDonald and J. Newton's 'Letters from the Whistler Collection' which details Whistler's correspondence with French painters (*Gazette Des Beaux Arts*).

(c) Periodicals and the History of Publishing

Phase 2 of *The Waterloo Directory* has appeared; entitled *The Waterloo Directory of Irish Newspapers and Periodicals, 1800–1900*[134], it represents the attempt to check and to refine the 29,000 entries appearing in Phase 1 of *The Waterloo Directory*, which was a compilation from other sources, by a shelf-check of one category of titles in a limited number of libraries. In the event Irish newspapers and periodicals were chosen, and 3,932 titles emerged, over a third more than expected. The *Directory* consists of main entries of varying degrees of fullness, including one location for each periodical (with some entries still repeated) and three other indexes – subject, personal names, and place of publication. The twenty-five descriptive categories for the main entry are perhaps impossibly ambitious and clumsy for directory form, including as they do such items as subtitle, numbering, place of publication, editor, proprietor, printer, price, colour, and circulation which change all the time, sometimes invisibly; with only one copy of a run checked, much information is necessarily absent. However, as perfection belongs to God, this imperfect but invaluable human product has considerable scope for the scholar, with its subject index's lists of almanacs and weeklies, and its twenty-seven entries under John Falconer in the names index. Moreover, it is the closest yet we have come to the exercise of bibliographical control over periodicals on this scale, not one periodical or the double figures in *Wellesley*, but nearly 4,000. In *JNPH* Geraldine Beare, editor of the *Index to the 'Strand Magazine'* (*YW* 64.403–4) describes in detail the pre-computer labour process employed in 1980 in 'Indexing the *Strand Magazine*'; it appears that time and will failed in the subject index which is 'really based on the main subject in each article' as 'there was simply not time to go through them all'. The spring issue of *JNPH* contains a useful rundown on newspapers and periodicals in microform, and 'Sources for Newspapers and

---

134. *The Waterloo Directory of Irish Newspapers and Periodicals, 1800–1900. Phase 2*, Vol. I, by John S. North. NWAP. pp. 838. C\$400.

Periodical History', a department for readers to note for future reference, even though the items in this number pertain to the eighteenth century.

Margaret Beetham, in '"Healthy Reading": The Periodical Press in Late Victorian Manchester' [135], probes the political, class, and gender implications of the received notion of good reading for the populace in Manchester between 1860 and 1900, and decides that healthy-reading magazines aimed at cultural integration through strategies of self-improvement and interest in local dialect. In this important article she surveys the relationship between metropolitan and provincial culture as exemplified in Manchester periodicals, and discusses in more detail locally produced non-political magazines which aimed to provide healthy reading, especially fiction (such as *Ben Brierley's Journal of Literature, Science and Art for the Promotion of Good Will and Good Fellowship Everywhere*). Offering provocative perspectives on nineteenth-century periodicals of all kinds, Beetham straddles theoretical and historical aspects of journalism superbly and should not be missed by anyone seriously interested in the press.

Literary periodicals are the subject of *YES* this year, and six of the fourteen essays are on Victorian topics. In a piece called 'Politics and Literature' Joanne Shattock examines the *Edinburgh Review* from 1829 to 1847 under the activist editor Macvey Napier, and focuses on competition between Henry Brougham and Macaulay, both eminent contributors on political and literary subjects, and the short-lived association of Carlyle with the *Review*. Drawing principally on the correspondence of the men to delineate personal and editorial tensions, this informative article eventually turns to the journal's contents – the balance and nature of its essays and reviews, the transformation of the 'ephemeral' into 'literature' through republication of *Edinburgh Review* articles in book form, and the feuds among journals and critics with which the quarterly was associated in these years. Moving from the beginning to the end of the period, Linda Dowling contributes the sophisticated, informative, and well-written 'Letterpress and Picture in the Literary Periodicals of the 1890s'. 'Letterpress and Picture' takes in the relationship of verbal contents to pictorial and the contest between them for balance or dominance in the periodicals of the 1890s, but also the visual aspects of type, the use of words to illustrate pictures, and the relation of these innovations to commercial and anticommercial postures of the press. The *Yellow Book* is the pivot around which the other periodicals here move, but along with Beardsley and Whistler, a number of them are discussed in this splendid article, including the *Century Guild Hobby Horse*, the *Savoy*, the *Albemarle*, and the *Butterfly*.

Laurel Brake's 'Literary Criticism and the Victorian Periodicals' (*YES*) is a knowledgeable discussion of the growth and development of Victorian literary criticism as it was conditioned by the genre of the periodical and the particular traits and styles of individual periodicals in which it appeared. Building on recent scholarship, Brake elegantly delineates how the growth of professionalism among journalists, the different styles and policies of the periodicals, the practice of individual editors, and the inducements to puffing affected the literary criticism of journalistic writers such as Leslie Stephen, Walter Bagehot,

---

135. In *City, Class and Culture: Studies of Cultural Production and Social Policy in Victorian Manchester*, ed. by Alan Kidd and Ken Roberts. ManU (1985). pp. 228. £25.

R. H. Hutton, G. H. Lewes, and W. M. Rossetti, as well as the more disinterested Matthew Arnold, Pater, and Swinburne. This contribution is a valuable aid in the understanding of the restraints and pressures which shaped Victorian literary criticism. [P.K.]

Three critics in *YES* treat weeklies, James A. Davies the *Examiner* and Robert Tener and Malcolm Woodfield the *Spectator*. Davies's 'The Effects of Context: Carlyle and the *Examiner* in 1848' is ambitious in its conception but, in the event, falls short of its promise. Beginning with a laudable intent to examine Carlyle's three contributions to a periodical in terms of 'the holistic character, the total effect, of each issue', Davies goes on to 'formal literary analysis' of each issue in which the Carlyle pieces appeared. While what he finds – that 'Forster as editor trapped each essay by Carlyle in a powerful tangle of contrasting ideas' – is extremely valuable, the process of reading this series of laboured and detailed descriptions of the contents of each issue is not: the conclusion must be that theoreticians who advocate this methodology (and I concur with James Davies in this) must find more readable and palatable ways of presenting it. Robert Tener in 'Breaking the Code of Anonymity: The Case of the *Spectator*, 1861–1897' continues the longstanding discussion of the functions and foundering of anonymity in the Victorian press and the more recently initiated debate about sources of attributions without, oddly, referring to the work in and about the *Wellesley Index*. However, for those concerned specifically with Hutton and the *Spectator*, Tener provides useful detail. Using internal evidence, Tener makes a case in *ELN* for the possibility and probability that a review of *Clarissa* in the *Spectator* in Sept. 1865 was written by Hutton.

Malcolm Woodfield's study (*YES*) of the same partnership between editor and journal, 'Victorian Weekly Reviews and Reviewing After 1860', is far more contextual and, to a degree, theoretical; a distillation of his book on Hutton[118], this article analyses the flexibility of Hutton's criticism revealingly, through close reading and through extensive juxtaposition with the work of named contemporaries (notably Newman, Arnold, and George Eliot) and periodicals. Perhaps of most interest are Woodfield's remarks on Hutton's positive valuation of the novel, 'a symptom and product of [secularisation] but also . . . a means of *resisting* specific results of [it]', and his yoking of Hutton with George Eliot in their commitment to 'anti-utilitarian realism'. The book does not accommodate the periodical press *per se* very adequately; while surfacing repeatedly in the narrative, it is structurally contained in a short if pithy appendix at the back, in the detailed bibliography, and all too briefly in Chapter One. The focus here is rather on the persona of the editor, his critical temperament, attitudes, and ideas, which Woodfield suggests are relatively static over the thirty-five years of his editorship of the *Spectator*. What the book does is bring to its reader's attention a selection from Hutton 7,000 periodical articles of named articles on five authors which send the reader with interest to the originals. In that sense the range and topics of articles cited here are fascinating, and the book is well documented and indexed.

In 'William Michael Rossetti and *The Germ*' (*JPRS*) the account of the journal by Rossetti, its editor and historian, is assessed by Sharon W. Propas who claims that Rossetti's writings culpably 'present an interpretation rather than a factual catalogue of events'. Since that is the position of all discourse including history, the motivation for her comparison of Rossetti's narrative of the founding and publishing of *The Germ* in his 1901 Introduction to a facsimile edition with his 1849–50 diary and correspondence (published in 1975) seems predicated on a false premise of total disinterestedness and objectivity, but the resulting article is a welcome gathering and critical juxtaposition of mainly published sources on the day-to-day circumstances in which the four issues appeared between January and April 1850. It is fuller than the entry in Sullivan's *British Literary Magazines, 1837–1913* (*YW* 65.485), and is suitable for rapid reference. More information about Rossetti's writing and traffic with the periodicals is found in Roger W. Peattie's 'W. M. Rossetti's Contributions to the *Edinburgh Weekly Review*' in *VPR*. In the first eleven numbers of the journal (which existed Feb.–Oct. 1857) Rossetti's thirteen contributions consisted of ten weekly summaries of art news and three theoretical articles, one on Pre-Raffaelitism not previously identified; these are listed by Peattie who notes briefly the most interesting aspects of their contents. William Sharpe has a speculative and absorbing piece in *VN* on the effect of mass dissemination of art through print. Of interest to cultural as well as art historians, 'J. E. Millais' *Bubbles*: A Work of Art in the Age of Mechanical Reproduction' probes Walter Benjamin's theory that a work of art loses authority when it is reproduced, and concludes that in this case *its* reputation was enhanced, although Millais's suffered.

VPR (1986) is not typographically easy to read, but changes are in train, and many of its articles and reviews make the effort worthwhile; especially of interest is its winter special issue on Kingsley and *Macmillan's Magazine*. I shall divide the *VPR* articles into two groups, those on periodicals and those on persons (authors, editors, proprietors) because to my mind the articles are often of different kinds, with the orientation of the latter group frequently to the individual rather than to the collective periodical. An extreme instance of this second group is Elizabeth R. Epperly's 'Trollope and the Young Austin Dobson' where the emphasis falls on Trollope's role as mentor to the young poet, on the tone of the individual as author in his correspondence with the poet Dobson whose manuscript changes are detailed and occupy the greater part of the article, with very little on Trollope as editor or *per se* on Dobson as contributor. The parameters of this article imply that it is only incidentally about the periodical press, and it remains innocent of the terms of the discourse it purports to be part of; its origins lie rather in the new criticism where comparison of texts and questions of influence have long been germane.

Other articles in *VPR* on persons fare better. Patricia Marks has a splendid piece called 'Harriet Martineau: *Fraser's* "Maid of [Dis]Honour"' which starts with William Maginn's antifeminist commentary on Daniel Maclise's unflattering caricature of Martineau in *Fraser's* in 1833 but moves quickly to a consideration of the treatment of the eight other women who appeared as 'Regina's Maids of Honour' among the eighty-one drawings in the 'Gallery of Illustrious Literary Characters' published 1830–8. This well-informed, entertaining, and lively article undertakes criticism of the verbal and iconographic elements of the series, and the cultural and political underpinnings of the journal and its editor. 'George Eliot's Earliest Prose: The Coventry *Herald* and the Coventry Fiction' is an interesting study of sources by Kathleen McCormack who devotes the first half of her article to correspondences between George Eliot's reading of the Coventry *Herald*, edited by her close friend Charles Bray, and *Felix Holt* and *Middlemarch*, and the second half to parallels between her own contributions to the *Herald* and these novels. In particular, medical advertisements for products and pamphlets, editorial treatment of medical matters, and the tension between these two components of the newspaper are fruitfully examined.

Jane W. Stedman gives an overview of the periodical writings of a medical man (father of W. S. Gilbert), Dr William Gilbert who 'habitually thought, and published, in episodes'. A frequent contributor to Alexander Strahan's periodicals, Gilbert wrote prodigiously in two areas on which Stedman reports, realistic prose on socio-economic themes and psychological and fantastic work, treating of monomania and/or magic.

The *VPR* special number contains five articles on aspects of Kingsley's connection with *Macmillan's Magazine*. Larry Uffelman and Patrick Scott's illuminating treatment of the *Macmillan's* and book versions of *The Water Babies* in 'Kingsley's Serial Novels, II' uses the same comparison-of-texts method as Epperly with the difference that the periodical framework is established and consistently returned to. Kingsley's rewriting for book publication which involves the introduction of a new character who is systematically worked into the story leads the authors to argue that 'Kingsley's revisions show the serial text . . . to be not finished copy . . . but a refined working draft with which he was not completely satisfied'.

Two of the pieces in the special issue of *VPR* ignore *Macmillan's Magazine* despite the issue's title: John C. Hawley, S.J. offers a well-written analysis of the various directions of the hostile 'Responses to Charles Kingsley's Attack on Political Economy', Kingsley being charged by the right (Croker in the *Quarterly*) with 'seditious' politics, by the liberals (W. R. Greg in the *Edinburgh* and *National* reviews) with ignorant and archaic economics, and more generally with an alleged association with Carlyle; Jerold Savory writes informatively if briefly on visual and verbal caricatures of Kingsley in 1872 in 'Charles Kingsley in *Vanity Fair* and *Once A Week*'.

The nature and role of *Macmillan's Magazine* is foregrounded in Alan Hertz's thorough essay on 'The Broad Church Militant and Newman's Humiliation of Charles Kingsley'. Noting that Kingsley's sneering tone if not his criticism of the Roman Church was out of keeping with the broad-minded moderation and critical seriousness of *Macmillan's* in which it appeared in Jan. 1864, Hertz interestingly sets out to assess 'the private influence Kingsley's associates [mainly Alexander Macmillan, proprietor, and David Masson, editor, of *Macmillan's*, and Froude] had on his public behaviour or the effect his public chastisement had on the intellectual circle for which he spoke'. While Newman appears to Hertz to have won the battle through his publication of his *Apologia* soon after, Froude's virulent rejoinder in *Fraser's* remained unchallenged. Still, Hertz concludes, the liberal Mauriceans were split and Newman's reputation rehabilitated by the controversy. Ann Parry moves on to 'The Grove Years 1868–1883: A "new look" for *Macmillan's Magazine*?', which proves the most substantial article in the special number. Through a variety of methods, posited on a statistical sampling, Parry identifies and discusses changes in subject matter, geographical and educational distribution of contributors, and degree and kind of editorial direction which distinguished George Grove's stint as editor from David Masson's. Detailed and documented, and employing manuscript sources, 'The Grove Years' assures this number of *VPR* a long life.

Turning now to contributions to *VPR* whose subjects are periodicals themselves, Monica Fryckstedt provides a mini-monograph and a listing of contents and authorship on a *Wellesley* model for a radical monthly sponsored by *Punch*, 'Douglas Jerrold's Shilling Magazine' (1845-8). This detailed, slightly ungainly piece has six parts – a short introduction, followed by sections of varying fullness on Jerrold, the *Shilling Magazine*, its failure (these being quite short), contributors, contents (these seem distended and attempt to exhaust inexhaustible topics), and a useful comparative section on contemporary monthlies and weeklies. There is an immense amount of information here which scholars will refer to for years to come, and much of the writing is lively and analytical, but it lacks the shapeliness and concentration one has come to expect from an article, even in a quarterly! Diana Dixon surveys journals for children in 'From Instruction to Amusement: Attitudes of Authority in Children's Periodicals Before 1914'. While the sheer proliferation of periodicals for young people by the end of the century shows increasing consciousness of a period of childhood distinct from the notion of little adults, Dixon also notes the shift in editorial columns from authoritarian addresses to the admission of humour, entertainment, and even friendliness. Periodicals for boys are singled out for particular examination in this competent piece. Josef L. Altholz, long interested in another specialist sector of the Victorian press, looks at the 'pre-history' of the four-year controversy over *Essays and Reviews* by identifying and examining the 'Early Periodical Responses', those between 28 March 1860 when the book appeared and October 1860 when Frederic Harrison initiated the public furore in the *Westminster Review*. Altholz's main interest in this illuminating article is the Anglican press, but he briefly notes responses of the non-religious and the non-Anglican religious press. He finds that all the main arguments to be raised by the great reviews appear earlier in the Anglican press which uniformly condemns the essays and essayists, but that since the readers of that press are specialized (sectarian) groups it remained for the quarterlies to make the debate visible to the general public.

The special number of *VPR* also includes Larry K. Uffelman's annual 'Checklist of Scholarship and Criticism' on Victorian periodicals for 1985 which is lightly annotated. It still does not include this section of *YWES*! However, as the only comprehensive and continuous list of this material it is valuable, but its usefulness would be greatly enhanced if the type were larger. Ditto for Christopher Kent's informative listing with introduction of 'More Critics of Drama, Music and Art' (*VPR*) which adds eighty-six new names to the 317 already gathered. Where possible Kent provides biographical information about each critic, and standard categories of the listing are the journal in which the criticism was found, the dates, and references. Still with *VPR* and statistics, John Sutherland writes a brief but fascinating account of '*Cornhill's* Sales and Payments: The First Decade'. It is based on George Smith's notebooks, recently deposited in the National Library of Scotland; these detail 'contributors, payments to contributors, numbers printed, delivered and sold'. Sutherland's lengthy introduction to 'Henry Colburn Publisher' (*PubH*) assembles with gusto the catalogue of denunciation attracted by Colburn's publishing activities, and proposes that Colburn may be located more usefully in the history of publicity, on which this Prince of Puffers expended considerable monies and ingenuity. Other of Colburn's strengths are revealed by Sutherland who glosses positively Michael Sadleir's negative observation that Colburn, book publisher, architect of the silver fork vogue, and enemy if one-time partner of Richard Bentley, 'revolutionised publishing in its every aspect'. Working from book catalogues and the *English Catalogue*, Sutherland chronicles Colburn's various activities from 1806 to 1853 and evaluates his achievements, thus adding much to published accounts.

The letters of 1849 which appear in J. H. Goldstrom's 'The Correspondence between Lord John Russell and the Publishing Trade' (*PubH*) pertain to the trade's dissatisfaction with the British Government's plan to monopolize the publication of schoolbooks by compiling, publishing, and distributing Readers based on Irish models at a low price for the more than two million children in day schools by 1850. In addition to three letters from Longman & Co. and John Murray, Goldstrom reprints two replies from the Government, one from the Irish Commissioners of Education and the other from Lord John Russell, and ensuing correspondence and reports. Appended to this interesting debate defending the private sector's entrepreneurial rights are two appendixes on the circulation and cost of Irish National School books in Britain and Ireland.

John Dempster's 'Aspects of [Plymouth] Brethren Publishing Enterprise in Late Nineteenth-Century Scotland' in *PubH* consists of historically descriptive sections with subsections on topics which include the publishing activities of Donald Ross, the partnership of Henry Pickering with William Inglis, and John Ritchie Ltd. In a second part of the article entitled 'Analytical' headed paragraphs treat stated subjects. While excessively organized, this useful article documents the ways in which periodicals functioned as an important communication network to rally and preserve a religious denomination, and its preachers diversified into writing, editorship, and publishing to cater to the Brethren, who were clearly a reading people.

Joel H. Wiener has collected fifteen articles on the role of the editor in Victorian England in *Innovators and Preachers*[136], a theme on which most of the authors assembled here had lectured at the annual conference of the Research Society for Victorian Periodicals (RSVP). In a succinct, stylish, and characteristically modest introduction the editor of this book on editors assesses the field ('As yet . . . no history of the Victorian editor has been written'), describes the plan, strengths, and deficiencies of the volume, and interrogates the subject. The first section, 'Editor and Audience', includes Anne Humphreys's 'G. W. M. Reynolds: Popular Literature and Popular Politics', a spikey, informed, theoretical, and provocative piece (reviewed in *YW* 64.406 when it appeared in *VPR*). In an essay on a similar topic, 'Editors and Social Change', Stephen Elwell makes a revealing case study of *Once a Week*, 1859–80, looking at the succession of its editors and proprietors, none of whom responded adequately to maintain circulation by the shift of reader from the middle class to a more diverse group (unlike Dickens's *All the Year Round* with its unwavering commitment to serial function and a broader audience). Interestingly, although this article is structured to distinguish in *Once a Week* the reigns of individual editors, it concludes that what united them and characterized the magazine was its adherence to class journalism. Hartley S. Spatt adopts a similar plan in 'The Aesthetics of Editorship: Creating Taste in the Victorian Art World' in which a group of editors and their art periodicals – principally *The Graphic*, *The Portfolio*, and *The Art-Journal* – are

136. *Innovators and Preachers: The Role of the Editor in Victorian England*, ed. by Joel H. Wiener. Greenwood (distr. Eurospan) (1985). pp. x + 335. £35.

compared. However, instead of assessing their 'success' by circulation figures and staying power, he attempts to make 'taste' (i.e. good taste) the arbiter. With his definition clearly implying the purveying of high culture and good art in accessible language, he concludes unsurprisingly by slighting *The Graphic*, the magazine of 'less educated taste' and opting for *The Art-Journal* 'the fullest expression of taste in the world of Victorian art periodicals'. 'Taste' is still a term imprisoned in class and ideology as is clear from this article. Sheila R. Herstein's piece on 'The *English Woman's Journal* and the Langham Place Circle: A Feminist Forum' is serviceably descriptive of the build-up to the founding of the *Journal* and to a degree, of its process of editing and decline, but its emphasis on the group which produced the magazine and the groups the magazine produced does implicitly state a problem raised by a focus on editors: while newspapers and periodicals are collective endeavours, focus on the editor tends to reinforce our own culture's ideology of individualism and to render invisible the collective process of press production. Barbara Quinn Schmidt's 'In the Shadow of Thackeray: Leslie Stephen as the Editor of the *Cornhill Magazine*', the last of this first section, ably portrays Stephen in his capacity as editor of *Cornhill* as lacking the quality of individualism, as neither innovator nor preacher. Content in most respects to sustain existing policy, and beset by expenditure cuts due to George Smith's indulgence of Thackeray before him, Stephen's impress on the journal is manifest in the strengthening of its essay content, and the mediocrity on the whole of its fiction.

Christopher Kent launches the second section, 'The Context of Editing', with his splendid 'The Editor and the Law'. Noting that 'the editor, both in title and function, is essentially a nineteenth-century creation', he goes on to show that the law throughout the period failed to define adequately the editor's rights and responsibilities. In this absorbing essay, Kent considers parliamentary and legal reporting, libel law, definitions, and prosecutions, the legal implications of anonymity, and the contents and extension of what made up the 'public sphere', an area 'largely defined by the periodical press and by the editor in particular'. Pausing to consider the connection between shorthand and 'the whole social construct of reality with which the [Victorian] novel was so intimately connected', the article is seasoned and resonant, and exemplary cultural history.

In 'The Editor as Activist: Editors and Urban Politics in Early Victorian England' Derek Fraser describes the links between editors of provincial newspapers in the 1840s – James Thompson of the *Leicester Chronicle*, John F. Sutton of the *Nottingham Review*, John Jaffray of the *Birmingham Journal*, and William Byles of the *Bradford Observer* – and the politics of local government. The second part of this informative article consists of brief studies of these four cases, while the first part examines more generally the status in the locale and the nation of the provincial editor. The significant differences which emerge between their position and that of editors of the national press are instructive. In the first sentence of 'The Redaction of Catholic Periodicals' – 'We speak of "The Victorian editor"; but in fact the editorship of most developed Victorian periodicals involved a complex of individuals of varying status, titles, and functions' – Josef L. Altholz makes explicit what is implicit in Fraser's description of the matrix of power of the provincial editor. Altholz learnedly attempts to look at so wide a range of the Catholic press, including the *Dublin Review*, the *Tablet*, the *Home and Foreign Review*, the

Lamp, the *Month*, and the *Catholic Herald*, that inevitably this short piece lapses in places into genealogy. What he reveals about the variety of editorial responsibility and procedures is fascinating and provokes the question, when will Altholz give us a longer study of this material from this perspective?

Two further articles complete this section on the context of editing: in 'Editing a "Class Journal"': Four Decades of the *Queen*' Charlotte C. Watkins provides a standard write-up of the *Queen* (1861–), a weekly for 'educated women', in which she examines the impact of the long tenure (1862–94) of its editor, Helen Lowe, and recommends its well-written obituaries, leaders, and articles to cultural historians. Joanne Shattock's lively piece 'Showman, Lion Hunter, or Hack: The Quarterly Editor at Midcentury' was reviewed in *YW* 64.405–6 when it appeared in *VPR*.

The final part of the Wiener volume, 'Some Leading Practitioners', contains five essays which primarily treat at length named editors. Robert A. Colby's splendid piece on the novelist editors, 'Goose Quill and Blue Pencil: The Victorian Novelist as Editor', examines the regimens of Harrison Ainsworth, Charles Lever, Thackeray, and Trollope as editors of *Ainsworth's Magazine*, *Dublin University Magazine*, *Cornhill*, and *Saint Paul's Magazine* respectively. Colby reaps a great deal from his agile comparison of these four in comparatively small space, and the interrelatedness detailed here between the writing of different genres and the periodical form of production is well worth reading. Ann P. Robson and John M. Robson continue their Mill studies in 'Private and Public Goals: John Stuart Mill and the *London and Westminster*' which reviews the psychological underpinnings of Mill's association with the review as well as his conduct of it. The Robsons suggest that Mill's major success here was as author rather than editor.

Joel Wiener writes an engaging and informative piece on the career of 'Edmund Yates: The Gossip as Editor' in which he examines Yates's creation – 'society' or 'personal' journalism – as the prototype of the 'new journalism' which broke in the 1880s and 1890s. Beside *The World* edited by Yates for twenty years (1874–94), Wiener considers material from some of the six other journals edited by Yates, in particular his conduct of his gossip column 'The Lounger at the Clubs' which appeared in the *Illustrated Times* between 1855 and 1863. In *JNPH* Frederick Greenwood's unsuccessful attempts between 1896 and 1908 to secure a government pension on the basis of the primacy of his role in the sale of the Suez canal shares, as well as his part in the affair, are pieced together by J. O. Baylen and B. I. Diamond in 'A Journalist's Quest for Recognition: Frederick Greenwood and the Purchase of the Suez Canal Company Shares, 1875–1909'. Noting the great achievement of Greenwood's journalism as editor of the *Pall Mall Gazette* and other papers, the article ironically observes that Greenwood himself regarded his role in the purchase of the shares (for which he received only posthumous recognition by the government) rather than his journalism as the high point in his career.

Mary Bostetter competently looks at investigative journalism of a different sort in her piece on the reformist medical journal *The Lancet* and its founder editor in 'The Journalism of Thomas Wakley' which covers the period between 1823 and 1846. Readers of Victorian fiction in which so many medical men appear might well consult this piece and the periodical. Lastly, George Spater contributes an intriguing note on 'Cobbett, Hazlitt, and the *Edinburgh Review*' in an effort to remove a slur on Cobbett's character made by Hazlitt concerning Cobbett's weak response to an attack on him by the *Edinburgh*. A useful bibliographical essay of material on the editing of periodicals completes this volume which inaugurates in book form this type of comparative consideration of one aspect of the structure of Victorian journalism. It is a development and a volume to be applauded, and publication in paperback would ensure its use in the classroom for the new generations of journalists and scholars.

Patricia Thomas Srebrnik has written an impressive life of Alexander Strahan[137], the Victorian publisher who often founded and conducted his journals which included *Good Words*, the *Contemporary Review*, and *Saint Paul's*. Well researched and documented, this readable biography includes detailed chapters on *Good Words* and the *Contemporary*. The combination of Strahan's evangelical, Liberal, and populist design for his publications and Srebrnik's interest in his entrepreneurial and eventually disastrous financial arrangements result in an interesting book that is as much concerned with literary production and the economics of the press as the history of its great figures.

James Coover has gathered passages from music journals between 1881 and 1906 on the subject of *Music Publishing, Copyright and Piracy in Victorian England*[138]. This self-styled and interesting book begins with a description of the dramatis personae which is followed by a chronological succession of annotated excerpts, mostly from *Musical Opinion and Music Trade Review*. The acute problem with piracy of the music trade emerges clearly as does the process of litigation and agitation for the act relating to musical copyright which was finally passed in 1906.

The work of a periodicals reviewer is critically assessed and listed in Monica Correa Fryckstedt's monograph on the novelist and publisher's reader Geraldine Jewsbury[65]. Her 2,300 reviews of fiction which appeared anonymously in the *Athenaeum* between 1849 and 1880 are painstakingly identified and listed in the checklist which comprises the last third of this monograph, the first part of which consists of seven chapters concerning the substance of Jewsbury's reviews by subject and period, a chapter on the nature of the mid-century Victorian novel and another fairly short one on reviewing. Fryckstedt has extrapolated a considerable amount of detail from these reviews concerning Jewsbury's understanding of their function for both the circulating libraries and their readers, her views on the morality of fiction, and on specific authors, but it is clear by its exclusive focus on her reviews of fiction rather than those of memoirs, biography, history, cookery books, children's books, and books on household management that the main interest here is Jewsbury on the novel rather than Jewsbury the periodical reviewer or Jewsbury and the *Athenaeum*.

(d) Visual Art

Shelley M. Bennett's *British Narrative Drawings and Watercolours 1660–1880*[139] selects twenty-two examples of narrative art from the thirteen

---

137. *Alexander Strahan: Victorian Publisher*, by Patricia Thomas Srebrnik. UMich. pp. x + 269. $20.

138. *Music Publishing, Copyright and Piracy in Victorian England*, ed. by James Coover. Mansell (1985). pp. 169. £30.

139. *British Narrative Drawings and Watercolours 1660–1880: Twenty-Two Examples from the Huntington Collection*, by Shelley M. Bennett. Huntington (1985). pp. vi + 53. pb $5.

thousand or so British drawings in the Huntington Collection. Among the Victorian artists whose work is featured are David Wilkes, John Martin, Richard Dadd, William Holman Hunt, Richard Doyle, Millais, and Walter Crane. Bennett provides a concise commentary explaining the general trends of narrative art and the special features of each drawing. Victorian artists also feature heavily in Pratapaditya Pal and Vidya Dehejia's handsome volume *From Merchants to Emperors*[140]. This work provides a collection of drawings, watercolours, prints, and photographs which give an impression of the British way of life in India. The authors provide a rather basic narrative account of the British stay in India and a much more sensitive and acute account of the artwork produced by India's guests. Artists such as Charles D'Oyly, William Simpson, Edward Lear, Mortimer Mempes, Ernest S. Lumsden, and John Griffith are discussed as well as the work of 'the Company School' (paintings by Indians for their British patrons), and photographic studies of the country. The other side of the Anglo-Indian coin is shown in Timothy Wilcox's 'High Victoriana in Hyderabad: The Paintings in the Salar Jung Museum' (*Apollo*) which describes the avid collection of Victorian art by Salar Jung III chiefly during the 1930s.

Bernard Denvir has assembled an extraordinarily wide-ranging anthology[141] of material documenting the changes in taste in art and design which constitutes the fourth volume of his Documentary History of Taste in Britain. A scholarly, astute, and lucid introduction adequately recreates the social and historical milieu of his documentation. Not only are the central figures of the Victorian art world represented here (Morris, Wilde, Burne-Jones, etc.) but also the journals and newspapers. Denvir wisely gives a full and interesting selection of pieces reflecting the art market itself which by the Victorian period had reached massive dimensions. The chief drawback of Denvir's work is that the variety of the collection leaves the reader a touch bewildered, shifting quickly from decade to decade and back again with little guidance from the editor.

A small selection of Victorian wallpaper samples[142] taken from the pattern books of Jeffrey & Co. (1837–52) has been published. Attractively presented, it consists of numerous examples from the pattern books but no scholarly apparatus which explains their artistic or technical origin. The introduction by Gill Saunders is slight. The production values of this book are superb, its organization chaotic.

A number of lesser general works deserve noting. Malcolm Warner informs us of recent important acquisitions of Victorian paintings by the Tate Gallery (*Apollo*); J. Faganking describes the influence of photography on the paintings of G. F. Watts and D. G. Rossetti (*History of Photography*); T. Fawcett considers the question of 'Graphic Versus Photographic in Nineteenth-Century Reproductions' (*AH*); G. F. Fyfe discusses the functions of art exhibitions and their importance in the nineteenth century (*Sociological Review Monograph*); and finally, K. McConkey discusses naturalist images of the late nineteenth century (*Arts Magazine*).

140. *From Merchants to Emperors: British Artists, and India, 1757–1930*, by Pratapaditya Pal and Vidya Dehejia. CornU. pp. 231. hb $76.45, pb $32.95.

141. *The Late Victorians: Art, Design and Society 1852–1910*, by Bernard Denvir. Longman. pp. ix + 269. pb £7.95.

142. *Ornate Wallpapers*, intro. by Gill Saunders. Webb&Bower, for Victoria and Albert Museum. pp. 36. £4.95.

Two general articles about the Pre-Raphaelite movement have appeared. Julie F. Codell's 'Expression Over Beauty: Facial Expression, Body Language, and Circumstantiality in the Paintings of the Pre-Raphaelite Brotherhood' (*VS*) analyses the nature of facial expressions in the work of the PRB. Codell persuasively argues that the artists substituted a vernacular idiom for the conventional idealized language of popular Victorian painting in line with their general appeal to nature; thus, the splayed feet and bony toes of Ford Madox Brown's Wickliffe reveal the transitory and unheroic plainness of historical events and personages. Elaine Shefer contributes an interesting piece on the recurrent use of the nun and the convent as symbols in Pre-Raphaelite art (*JPRS*). Dealing primarily with Millais's *St Agnes* and *The Vale of Rest*, Shefer argues that these paintings stress the negative, conventional Victorian attitude to the secluded life.

Several studies of individual artists and their works have appeared. Mary Bennett discusses Ford Madox Brown's *Waiting* (1854–5) (*BurlM*). Christine Poulson describes the process of turning costume designs by Burne-Jones for a production of J. Comyns Carr's *King Arthur* (1895) into a reality (*BurlM*). Burne-Jones's four-picture series *The Legend of the Briar Rose* is the subject of an acute piece by Kirsten Powell in *JPRS* which analyses the series in terms of the political, sexual, and temporal meanings it may contain. Powell also unusually identifies the androgynous sleeping knights of a preparatory sketch with the figures of Maria Zambaco, Jane Morris, and Georgiana Burne-Jones: the sleeping knights have been unsuccessful in their storming of the Castle of Love. John Pfordresher contributes two pieces concerning Burne-Jones's writings. The first in *Mosaic* discusses Burne-Jones's first story, 'The Cousins', which he convincingly argues should not be seen as a Ruskinian conversion to social responsibility but rather as a tale of sexual humiliation and failure, feelings which are closer to the artist's late work. I have not seen Pfordresher's second piece 'Edward Burne-Jones's Gothic Romance "A Story of the North"' (*Archiv*). Rebecca A. Jeffrey provides some biographical information on Walter H. Deverell and a checklist of his works in *JPRS*. Deverell was associated with, but not a member of, the PRB.

The growing interest in the work of the sculptor and goldsmith Alfred Gilbert is reflected by two full-length works. *Sir Alfred Gilbert, R. A.: Sculptor and Goldsmith* [143] is a catalogue of the 1986 exhibition of his work at the Royal Academy of Arts. The catalogue contains useful short studies of Gilbert's life, patrons, and his relationship with the Royal Academy by Richard Dorment; his founding techniques (Duncan James); his skill as a jeweller and goldsmith (Charlotte Gere); the background to the *Shaftesbury Memorial* (Mark Girouard); and the recent restoration of *Eros* (Timothy Bidwell). Giving the relevant information about the exhibits concisely and informatively, it is beautifully illustrated in monochrome with several sumptuous colour photographs: anyone interested in Gilbert's work will wish to possess a copy. Dorment's biography of Gilbert [144] is a full, sharp, and humane account of the life and work of its subject. Narrated with sympathy and wit, Gilbert's relationship with his family and patrons is well evoked in this study which seems to place his

143. *Sir Alfred Gilbert, R. A.: Sculptor and Goldsmith*, ed. by Richard Dorment. W&N/RA. pp. 224. hb £16.95, pb £8.95.
144. *Alfred Gilbert*, by Richard Dorment. Yale. pp. vii + 350. hb £19.95, pb £9.95.

work in the transitional phase between the Gothic Revival and Art Nouveau. Dorment's discussions of Gilbert's individual works such as *Icarus*, the *Shaftesbury Memorial*, and the *Memorial to the Duke of Clarence* are knowledgeable, incisive, and detailed. The book is copiously and beautifully illustrated.

Three studies of the work of William Holman Hunt have appeared. In 'The True Pre-Raphaelite (W. H. H.)' (*JPRS*) Jack T. Harris examines Hunt's claim to have been the only true Pre-Raphaelite. Harris points out that if we accept Hunt's own very narrow definition of the aims of the movement his claim is probably accurate. D. Mansell discusses the connection between Hunt's *Awakening Conscience* and James Joyce's 'The Dead' in *JJQ*. I have not seen James H. Coombs's *A Pre-Raphaelite Friendship: The Correspondence of William Holman Hunt and John Lucas Tupper* (UMIRes).

Rudyard Kipling's father, Lockwood Kipling, is the subject of a short piece by Mildred Archer in *Apollo* which details Kipling's interest in the skills of Indian craftsmen. Two brief works have appeared on Millais. W. Sharpe discusses Millais's *Bubbles* as a work of art in an age of mechanical reproduction (*VN*), and R. Cooper deals with *The Rescue* (*AH*). Not a great deal has appeared about Rossetti's art either. Edvige Schulte's full-length study of Rossetti's life and work[22] is the first Italian biography which attempts to give an integrated account of Rossetti's work. The coverage of Rossetti's visual art is good as Schulte presents a balanced account of the arguments for and against Rossetti's primacy in the PRB. Schulte examines Rossetti's artwork in chronological order and defends his importance as an artist. The book is not well presented but it does contain a sizeable number of illustrations of Rossetti's work.

Dianne Sachko Macleod has contributed two pieces to *BurlM* concerning Frederic George Stephens, one of the seven founder-members of the PRB. The first describes Stephens's halting attempts to become an artist and his subsequent discovery of his flair for art criticism. This is a useful introduction to Stephens's work and his inconsistent appraisals of the work of the PRB. The inclusion of a bibliography of Stephens's published writings will be of great use to scholars of the PRB. The second discusses Stephens's series of articles for the *Athenaeum*, 'The Private Collections of England', which Macleod believes to be important because of the attention it gives to middle-class Victorian art collections. *JPRS* prints two works about John Lucas Tupper, an early member of the Pre-Raphaelite circle and later the influential master of geometrical and scientific drawing at Rugby School. Sushma Kapoor outlines Tupper's biography and his views on art, and George Landow provides an annotated bibliography of Tupper's writings incorporating passages from his unpublished correspondence.

Michael Hancher pays tribute to the work of the illustrator John Tenniel in *The Tenniel Illustrations to the 'Alice' Books*[145] focusing on Tenniel's illustration of Carroll's text and on the conditions and context which produced them. Hancher avoids the temptation to be sentimental and shrewdly shows how Tenniel's work as a staff-cartoonist for *Punch* influenced his illustrations. The technical side of Tenniel's work is well documented by Hancher in his chapters on woodblock engraving and printing which constitute a good

145. *The Tenniel Illustrations to the 'Alice' Books*, by Michael Hancher. OSU (1985). pp. ix + 152. hb $45, pb $17.50.

overview of the relationship between writer and illustrator. The similarity of Carroll's own rather spidery sketches to those of Tenniel imply that he was working from the author's suggestions. This is a detailed and well-researched study of interest to students of the nineteenth-century process of book illustration as well as to admirers of the *Alice* books.

George Frederic Watts's *The Minotaur* is the subject of a piece by Patricia Matthews in *Apollo*. She argues that this famous painting owes something to the scandal created by W. T. Stead's series of sensational articles 'The Maiden Tribute of Modern Babylon' (*Pall Mall Gazette*, 1885) which exposed the horrors of white slavery and child prostitution. James McNeill Whistler interests two scholars. Ronald Anderson discusses the painter's friendship with the Irish nationalist John O'Leary (*Apollo*). He speculates that the paucity of evidence for this firm friendship is due to the laundering of Whistler's correspondence by his sister-in-law and executrix Rosalind Bernie Philips. Toshio Watanabe discusses the importance of certain Japanese prints in Whistler's studio in *BurlM*. Maria Zambaco, Rossetti's model and Burne-Jones's lover, is rescued as a skilful artist by Philip Attwood in *Apollo*. Attwood shows her to have been a versatile painter and sculptor. Finally, I have not seen Barbara Morris's *Inspiration For Design: The Influence of the Victoria and Albert Museum* (V&A).

(e) Social History

This year has seen the publication of two important studies of the English aristocracy as well as important work on popular discontent and on urban, medical, and social history. Rosemary Ashton's lucid and elegant study[146] attempts to tell the story of several German exiles who escaped to Britain in 1848 from reactionary Prussian politics. The obvious exiles are discussed, although Marx does not get very sympathetic treatment (Ashton much prefers Engels), but this study covers the broad range of refugees: Gottfried Kinkel and Friedrich Althaus (bourgeois), and Karl Schapper and J. G. Eccarius (proletariat). Ashton also focuses on women like Joanna Kinkel, an outstanding person limited to teaching piano and singing lessons. The chief value of this study must lie in the cultural assessment of Victorian England by this heterogenous group. They seemed to be perplexed by the paradox of a high degree of civic freedom contrasted with a rigid class system and an ingrained set of religious and sexual prejudices.

Lady Florence Bell's *At the Works: A Study of a Manufacturing Town*[147] has been republished by Virago with an introduction by Angela V. John. Bell's study of nineteenth-century Middlesborough describes the ways in which the more humble men and women than herself managed their daily lives. Bell details the conditions of the town, the work of ironmaking, leisure activities, and expenditure. This is an interesting and useful example of early attempts at social investigation in the tradition of Charles Booth. It is also written from the perspective of the wife of a manufacturer and is not sanguine about working-class attempts to improve their conditions.

146. *Little Germany: Exile and Asylum in Victorian England*, by Rosemary Ashton. OUP. pp. xiv + 304. £17.50.

147. *At the Works: A Study of a Manufacturing Town*, by Florence Bell, ed. by Angela V. John. Virago (1985). pp. xxxii + 272. pb £4.50.

Two excellent studies of the English aristocracy have appeared, both presenting a somewhat revisionist view of that order. J. V. Beckett's *The Aristocracy in England, 1660–1914*[148] is a thorough and scholarly study which reverses the conventional view of the embourgeoisement of the English aristocracy, suggesting instead that it was this order which persuaded the middle class to accept its cultural values. After the Great Exhibition there was, Beckett argues, a gradual loss of confidence in the concepts of technological progress and the idea of the entrepreneur which led to a re-establishment of aristocratic ideology which was, in any case, always pragmatic. Beckett's work carefully corrects many established myths about the aristocracy: its much vaunted openness, its opposition to business interests and the principle of utility, and its tendency to bankruptcy. Rather, Beckett argues how the aristocracy received its power from three main sources: its readiness to take a lead in social and political affairs; its continued acceptance of its inherited role as political governor; and the lack of any sustained ideological challenge to its role. Although a gradual loss of control is perceptible after 1850, it is not until 1918 that aristocratic hegemony was lost. Beckett's challenging study represents this order as pragmatic, flexible, and prepared to take on the major trends of nineteenth-century English society. Certainly, Sir Leicester Dedlock can no longer be considered as in any way typical of the nineteenth-century English aristocracy.

A complementary study to Beckett's is John M. Bourne's *Patronage and Society in Nineteenth-Century England*[149]. This work again challenges received opinion by stressing the social importance and utility of patronage in the period long after it was ceased to be used in the formation of parliamentary majorities. Bourne, like Beckett, views the aristocracy as a relatively tiny but flexible and tenacious group which saw patronage not just as a reward and an obligation but also as an important buttress to its status. Bourne believes that patronage rather than be seen as a political evil should instead be viewed, in its salaried form, as an important factor in the gradual improvement of nineteenth-century administration. Bourne's study is detailed, accessible, and wide-ranging: he also discusses those non-aristocratic sources of patronage, chief among these being the East India Company. Bourne helps to fill in useful background for readers of nineteenth-century literature and manages to demolish many Dickensian myths about the functions of government and administration of the period.

A fine collection of essays by Norman Gash[150] concerning the relations between state and society is another exciting contribution to historical studies. Eight of the fifteen essays have not been previously published and of the other seven, only one is easily available and that ('Bonham and the Conservative Party, 1830–57') has been substantially revised and expanded. The essays deal with such subjects as cheap government, the passing of the three Reform Acts, and nineteenth-century elections and electioneering; and with such personalities as Henry Brougham, Peel, and Lord George Bentinck. Gash is a knowledgeable, scholarly, humanist historian whose insights are presented with a style not always present in the writings of historians.

148. *The Aristocracy in England, 1660–1914*, by J. V. Beckett. Blackwell. pp. xiv + 512. £22.50.
149. *Patronage and Society in Nineteenth-Century England*, by John M. Bourne. Arnold. pp. ix + 198. £28.
150. *'Pillars of Government' and Other Essays on State and Society c. 1770–c. 1880*, by Norman Gash. Arnold. pp. xii + 202. £25.

Three full-length studies of popular discontent have appeared. David J. V. Jones[151] examines the insurrection of the Newport Chartists of 1839 which led to the shooting of some twenty or so insurgents. Jones tells the story of the seven thousand South Wales miners who set out to march on Newport, and analyses the community which formed them. Jones's thorough and detailed study casts doubt on the conventional view which sees the rising as a peaceful show of strength which went badly wrong. Instead he argues that the insurrection must be seen in the context of the violence and terrorism endemic in the South Wales community (a community beyond the pale of the Anglican Church). In terms of its consequences in the last mass treason trial in British history, Jones argues that the rising was instrumental in discrediting the revolutionary tradition in Chartism. This is an important contribution to the study of Chartism and Welsh social history.

John Knott's *Popular Opposition to the 1834 Poor Law*[152] scrutinizes the storm of popular protest which greeted attempts to implement the notorious legislation. Knott takes issue with the view that this opposition was irrationally motivated by fear and anger with no coherent plan or organization. He believes that the wave of popular reaction which followed the passing of the Act was a self-conscious process guided by a rational and coherent system of beliefs and shared assumptions. Knott also argues that the Old Poor Law was generally considered to be humane by the poor and Chartism did not swallow up the anti-Poor Law movement but was an extension of it. Knott's study is thorough and clear, although it often appears too much like the doctoral dissertation that was its original form with its frequently stated conclusions and its overconscious stress on its own method of procedure.

Phillip Thurmond Smith studies the other side of the public order question by tackling the history of Peel's Metropolitan Police force (1830–60)[153]. Smith's work is not as scholarly or astute as the two previous contributions although he gleans much interesting material from his study of the Metropolitan Police Records and the Home Office Records. The discussion of the police surveillance of the Great Exhibition is particularly interesting. Smith is safest when discussing police policy, tactics, and history and less sure when generalizing about nineteenth-century society as a whole. His treatment of the Sunday Trading Riots of 1855, the Garibaldi Riots of 1865, and the Hyde Park Riots of 1866–7 is informative. Of related interest is Carolyn A. Conley's 'Rape and Justice in Victorian England' (*VS*) which should have been more accurately titled 'Rape and Justice in Victorian Kent' as it deals with records for trials for rape of Kent County (1859–80). The cases Conley highlights make predictably sad reading and her conclusion that the law had more concern for male attitudes than for justice is probably accurate. Her study is direct and informative but the lack of a more conclusive treatment of the problems of representativeness and of social prejudice leaves this study limited and imbalanced.

With the re-issue of Eric J. Hobsbawin's seminal 1964 social history

---

151. *The Last Rising: The Newport Insurrection of 1839*, by David J. V. Jones. Clarendon. pp. xii + 273. pb £7.95.

152. *Popular Opposition to the 1834 Poor Law*, by John Knott. CH. pp. 284. £19.95.

153. *Policing Victorian London: Political Policing, Public Order and the London Metropolitan Police Force*, by Phillip Thurmond Smith. Greenwood (1985). pp. x + 229. £32.50.

Labouring Men [154] the debate over the role of the working class in the nineteenth century continues. Logie Barrow's *Independent Spirits* [155] is a contribution from the HWS, and in line with the aims of the series, Barrow's work stresses primary sources and eschews professional and theoretical preparation. His work deals with the intellectual world of plebeian, working-, and lower middle-class spiritualists. He argues that within this period there was a distinctive plebeian spiritualist culture with its own democratic epistemology and doctrinal self-assurance. This culture was nourished by, and partially grew out of, Owenite socialism and was instrumental in disseminating socialist ideas throughout the nineteenth century. Christopher Kent's 'Presence and Absence: History, Theory, and the Working Class' (*VS*) covers the interesting debate over why Victorian England never developed a revolutionary proletariat willing and able to bring about the collapse of capitalism envisioned by Marx. Kent knowingly and sharply covers the arguments from E. P. Thompson's work to that of *HWJ* and Hobsbawm's notion of a labour aristocracy. Kent posits no solution to the dilemma of left-wing historians but, like so many other recent writers, he hopes that forthcoming work on Engels may provide the glimmerings of an answer.

Still with matters urban: Jonathan Brown's *The English Market Town* [156] is aimed at a more general audience than the previous contributions. It is a useful survey (hardly a history) describing different kinds of markets and fairs. Regrettably Brown makes little use of literature as a social document. His work contains only one reference to Thomas Hardy when his discussion of hiring fairs could well have alluded to *Far from the Madding Crowd*. Probably readers of *YWES* will find his sixth chapter about market-town culture most interesting. Altogether this is a pleasant little book, attractively put together and illustrated.

Class, Power and Social Structure in British Nineteenth-Century Towns [157] is a selection of the work of four urban historians each of whom has presented a concise edition of the core of his or her research. The studies in this selection analyse the ways in which power, status, neighbourhood, religion, ethnicity, and the role of the state affected those class relationships founded upon economic divisions. David Gadian considers the role of popular movements in a number of north-western industrial towns and points out their predominantly middle-class leadership. Gadian also argues for the underlying shared experience of the working classes for, despite their famous sectionalism, most members would have had some taste of factory work. John Field surveys Portsmouth's middle class, finding it no more homogenous than the working class, and Joan Smith looks at the ethnic, political, and religious structures of Glasgow and Liverpool. Perhaps the most interesting contribution to the volume is John Seed's account of Unitarianism as a force in the social, political,

154. *Labouring Men: Studies in the History of Labour*, by Eric. J. Hobsbawm. W&N. pp. viii + 401. pb £8.95.

155. *Independent Spirits: Spiritualism and English Plebeians, 1850–1910*, by Logie Barrow. HWS. RKP. pp. xii + 336. pb £9.95.

156. *The English Market Town: A Social and Economic History, 1750–1914*, by Jonathan Brown. Crowood. pp. 176. £12.95.

157. *Class, Power and Social Structure in British Nineteenth-Century Towns*, ed. by R. J. Morris. LeicU. pp. xiii + 222. £27.50.

and ideological change in Britain. All four contributions bear strong signs of the dissertation format from which they were quarried.

From the urban to the agrarian: K. D. M. Snell's *Annals of the Labouring Poor*[158] is a social history which makes full use of literary evidence. Snell's conclusions result from a study of the English and Welsh counties south of Yorkshire and they generally accord with Mrs Gaskell's judgements about urban and agrarian working conditions in *North and South*. In a series of detailed and readable essays Snell covers such areas as agricultural seasonal unemployment, the decline of service and its influence on social relations, the New Poor Law, enclosure and employment, the decline of apprenticeship, and the apprenticeship of women. Snell also includes a study of the rural Dorset reflected in Thomas Hardy's novels, with a detailed account of the social and economic reality of Hardy's Dorset which shows that the real rustics were less docile and deferential than some of the novelist's 'usual reassuringly comic and bovine stereotypes' would suggest. Snell denies that Hardy enters the mentality of the Dorset labourers for any sustained length of time and accuses him of distortion for artistic purposes: Tess labouring at Flintcomb Ash, for instance, symbolizes the depths to which she has fallen but is completely at odds with patterns of female employment in the 1880s. This is an important social history which is able to grapple with the problematic use of literary sources. Still with agrarian matters RKP have reprinted G. E. Mingay's magnificent two-volume collection of studies, *The Victorian Countryside* (1981)[159]. These volumes contain forty-six chapters grouped under the five main headings of land, agriculture, country towns and country industries, landed society, and labouring life. Although the state of the debate has moved on since its original publication it is unlikely that the reader will find a better synthesis of comment and argument on the subject.

A number of social histories concerned with medical matters have appeared. Judith Schneid Lewis's *In the Family Way*[160] studies the writings and histories of fifty women (1731–1834) whom she believes to typify the female aristocracy: a group composed of the wives and daughters of peers and the female members of the royal family. Although focusing on so small a group must lead to problems of representativeness (fertility was much higher among them than the rest of society) Lewis believes she has enough evidence to argue against the usual feminist view that childbearing was an essentially female experience plundered by nineteenth-century male obstetricians. Rather the incipient gynaecologists appear as neutral and benign, dependent on the patronage of their employers. Nor were these women shamed into hiding by their pregnancies as is often maintained: pregnant aristocratic women maintained a high social profile. This is a sane and valuable social history which deals well with the controversial areas of the demystification of childbirth, the privatization of family life, and the growth of professionalism in the medical occupations. Of related interest is M. Poovey's '"Scenes of an Indelicate Character": The

158. *Annals of the Labouring Poor: Social Change and Agrarian England, 1600–1900*, by K. D. M. Snell. CUP (1985). pp. x + 464. £30.

159. *The Victorian Countryside*, ed. by G. E. Mingay. 2 vols. RKP. pp. xvi + ix + 702. pb £10.95 each.

160. *In the Family Way: Childbearing in the British Aristocracy, 1760–1860*, by Judith Schneid Lewis. Rutgers. pp. xi + 313. $29.

Medical Treatment of Victorian Women' (*Rep*). Poovey contradicts Lewis's findings, describing how the use of chloroform during childbirth led to displays of sexual excitation among women, creating a discourse in which the female body became politicized by male obstetricians.

S. E. D. Shortt examines the career of Richard M. Bucke whose fearsome photograph graces the cover of *Victorian Lunacy*[161]. Bucke, who was in charge of the London Asylum in Canada, was involved in some of the major issues and changes in late nineteenth-century psychiatry, including the growing tendency to professionalism and the disputes about the physiological origins of mental disease. Readers of Charlotte Perkins Gilman's *The Yellow Wallpaper* will recognize the name of S. Weir Mitchell who shared Bucke's opinions about the physiological origins of much mental illness. Shortt's study makes the point that psychological medicine was built upon theories of the mind in total congruence with the class relationships of the Victorian period where the inhabitants of public lunatic asylums were known to come from the ranks of the working poor and the paupers. M. Jeanne Peterson's 'Dr Acton's Enemy: Medicine, Sex and Society in Victorian England' (*VS*) challenges the view that the Victorians were repressed about sex and obsessed with such matters as masturbation (Bucke's own opinions lend support to this view) by examining the works of a representative, professional physician Sir James Paget. Paget offers a much more liberal view of sexual habits than the prominent but unrepresentative moralist 'Dr' William Acton whom historians usually accept as typical.

VS contains three other pieces of social history. Edna Bradlow discusses the culture of Cape Colony in the 1850s, arguing that the colony was not mainly an extension of British society but possessed a rigid caste system built on theories of racial difference. John D. Fair provides a quantitative analysis of the House of Commons division lists (1868–1918) which he believes demonstrate that there is no evidence for the contention that Liberal Unionist defections to the Tory Party were motivated by any other factor than support for the Union. Harriet Ritvo discusses the development of the middle-class recreational mode of dog-fancying. In particular she shows how the history of the bulldog epitomized the way in which pedigreed dogs could represent the aspirations of their compulsively respectable owners. Finally, W. Findlay in *CVE* discusses the Admiralty Archives as a source for the study of pre-1914 British social history.

4. Drama

The British and American Playwrights series gains three important editions of leading Victorian dramatists. Donald Roy provides a sure-footed survey of Planché's life and prodigious output which includes around 180 plays as well as verse, translations, travel and costume books in *Plays by James Robinson Planché*[162]. Despite his wide-ranging outside interests, Planché emerges as a

---

161. *Victorian Lunacy: Richard M. Bucke and the Practice of Late Nineteenth-Century Psychiatry*, by S. E. D. Shortt. CUP. pp. xvi + 207. £25.

162. *Plays by James Robinson Planché: 'The Vampire', 'The Garrick Fever', 'Beauty and the Beast', 'Fortunio and his Seven Gifted Servants', 'The Golden Fleece', 'The Camp at the Olympic', 'The Discreet Princess'*, ed. by Donald Roy. CUP. pp. xii + 241; 5 illus. hb £27.50, pb £11.95.

thorough-going theatre professional who was a master of stage effects yet ultimately became sceptical of the value of spectacle. Roy identifies various types of extravaganza Planché popularized, and supplies a full biographical record, list of plays, and bibliography in accordance with the best traditions of the series. Michael Hammett's edition of *Plays by Charles Reade*[163] offers a similarly substantial account of Reade's life and theatrical work. Refusing to view him as a novelist who turned out occasional plays, Hammett demonstrates his considerable involvement with the stage through his relationship with the actress Mrs Seymour and his forays into management. The critique of the plays, which are considered closely in terms of Reade's non-dramatic work and paradoxical personality, is both thoughtful and stimulating. George Rowell lays less emphasis on biography in his introduction to *Plays by A. W. Pinero*[164] and concentrates his astute criticism of the plays represented in the volume into less than one-third of the space taken by his fellow editors. This allows the bonus of four full-length plays to be included as well as some interesting appendixes such as an alternative ending to *The Second Mrs Tanqueray*. Joel H. Kaplan observes structural and thematic parallels between *The Second Mrs Tanqueray* and *Trelawney of the 'Wells'* in a sensitive article, '"Have We No Chairs?": Pinero's *Trelawney* and the Myth of Tom Robertson' (*EiT*). He shows how skilfully Pinero recreates the old theatrical conventions so as to heighten the reality of Robertson's reforms. Despite his romantic admiration for Robertson, Pinero's ultimate concern seems to be with the theatre's capacity for self-renewal and its periodic discovery of fresh methods to galvanize its audiences. Harvester Microform bring out a second useful instalment of manuscripts and typescripts of plays in the Frank Pettingell Collection in the University of Kent[165]. The twenty-six reels of microfilm include Victorian prompt-books for London and provincial productions, particularly for the Britannia Theatre, Hoxton. They are accompanied by a handy guide that gives a detailed listing of the plays and indexes to persons and theatres.

The George Bernard Shaw industry produces a blockbuster with Stanley Weintraub's definitive edition of *The Diaries 1885–1897*[132]. Freshly transcribed and reproduced in their entirety for the first time, these document in amazing detail Shaw's rise from a nobody in his twenty-ninth year to a celebrity aged forty-two. This makes it possible to see precisely when he worked on early plays, what theatres and opera houses he visited and with whom and when, in the context of all his other activities. Though drab from a literary point of view, the diaries are a mine of information sensitively annotated and meticulously indexed, aptly described by the editor as a 'Shavian Baedecker to vanished late-Victorian London'. In a long and thoughtful discussion of 'The Mystery of

163. *Plays by Charles Reade: 'Masks and Faces', 'The Courier of Lyons', 'It Is Never Too Late to Mend'*, ed. by Michael Hammett. CUP. pp. xii + 170; 10 illus. hb £27.50, pb £9.95.

164. *Plays by A. W. Pinero: 'The Schoolmistress', 'The Second Mrs Tanqueray', 'Trelawney of the "Wells"', 'The Thunderbolt'*, ed. by George Rowell. CUP. pp. xii + 291; 4 illus. hb £30, pb £9.95.

165. *The Popular Stage: Drama in Nineteenth Century England: The Frank Pettingell Collection of Plays in the Library of the University of Kent at Canterbury*. Series 1: *Manuscript and Typescript Plays*, Part 2. Harvester Microform. 26 reels + printed inventory.

Candida' (*ShawR*), Bert Cardullo shows how Shaw's 'balanced, humanitarian' viewpoint allows very different values to be emphasized simultaneously in the play. A similarly benign comic vision is also ably explored at length by J. Scott Lee in 'Comic Unity in *Arms and The Man*' (*ShawR*) which examines the play in the light of William Archer's objection that it is not a 'whole romantic comedy unified in its parts'. Paul Sawyer usefully draws attention to Shaw's tinkering with the final reference to Bluntschli which he altered from 'What a man!' to 'Is he a man?' in 1930–32 in 'The Last Line of *Arms and the Man*' (*ShawR*). This revision still appears in many student texts for copyright reasons although just before his death G. B. S. introduced a third reading 'Is he a man!', which is more akin to the sense of the original reading than the second one. It is refreshing to see how far Shaw's politics bear scrutiny. Martha Vogeler offers an informative and provocative account of what he does *not* say in '*Widowers' Houses* and the London County Council' (*ISh*). She shows how far he detached the play from the economic and political circumstances of its day and how it shrinks from Progressive preaching, which makes his defeat as a Progressive candidate in the 1904 London County Council elections look like 'poetic justice'. John R. Pfeiffer maintains his highly detailed annual bibliography of Shaw in 'A Continuing Checklist of Shaviana' (*ShawR*). In '"Heirs of the Great Generation": Yeats's Friendship with Charles Ricketts and Charles Shannon' (*YeA*) J. G. P. Delaney gives an illuminating account of Yeats's relationship with Ricketts and Shannon from its real beginnings in 1899 and the theatrical collaboration it led to.

   Studies of individual plays by other Victorian dramatists include Jim Davis's 'The Importance of Being Caleb: The Influence of Boucicault's *Dot* on the Comic Styles of J. L. Toole and Joseph Jefferson' (*Dickensian*). He ably discusses the character of Caleb Plummer in Dion Boucicault's 1859 stage version of *The Cricket on the Hearth*, showing how it enabled both actors to discover their outstanding talent for combining comedy and pathos. C. Alex Pinkston Jr illuminates 'The Stage Premiere of *Dr. Jekyll and Mr. Hyde*' (*NCTR*). Using a newly discovered prompt book to reconstruct the first stage production of 1887, he analyses why critics on both sides of the Atlantic praised Richard Mansfield's performance as Edward Hyde but were divided over the dramatic interpretation of Dr Jekyll. Tennyson's play of *Becket* and Henry Irving's 1893 production of it is discussed and copiously illustrated in 'The Becket Phenomenon' (*Thph*), D. F. Cheshire's survey of plays about Becket staged 1829–1975.

   Shakespeare and the Victorian Stage[166], edited by Richard Foulkes, contains essays on actors, acting, and staging of relevance to Victorian theatre in general which require notice here. Marion Jones sensitively explores how far historical verisimilitude was actually achieved in the theatre in 'Stage Costume: Historical Verisimilitude and Stage Convention'. She finds that, despite the prodigious research that went into lavish productions, 'much had to be imagined', as one critic candidly observed in 1881. Costumes were modified out of sheer whimsy or to suit current notions of propriety, and performers habitually retained their own undergarments and hairstyles, or had their dresses designed to show off their best attributes. In 'Pictorial Acting and Ellen Terry' Michael Booth

   166. *Shakespeare and the Victorian Stage*, ed. by Richard Foulkes. CUP. pp. xviii + 311; 30 illus. £30.

observes how actors adopted a pictorial style of performing in response to production methods which became increasingly elaborate during the nineteenth century. A prime example was Ellen Terry, who, besides being the subject of many oil paintings, was frequently seen as 'a picture in herself' or even as 'a work of art' on stage. In a brilliant essay, Peter Thomson probes the respectability of Henry Irving and his capacity to endorse decency and threaten it at the same time in '"Weirdness that lifts and colours all": The Secret Self of Henry Irving'. He argues that Irving's best interpretations were based on the idea of the divided self, which enabled his audiences to gain unique and dangerous access to their darker side. Henry Irving's favourite pastime was to visit the morgue. His son H. B. preferred to study the lives and misdemeanours of criminals, as Cary Mazer shows in his illuminating account of 'The Criminal as Actor: H. B. Irving as Criminologist and Shakespearean'. He regarded actors and criminals as role players who lived double or multiple lives, and his writings on crime provide valuable clues to some of his major roles on stage. In the same book, Kathleen Barker recounts the career of 'Charles Dillon: A Provincial Tragedian', one of a number of actors which includes Barry Sullivan, G. V. Brooke, and George Melville, who made their name in the provinces when the touring of stars from London declined during the 1850s. Minor actors can actually give a more comprehensive insight into the theatre of their day than their peers, as Edward Mullaly shows in 'Charles Freer, 1802–1857: The Life of a "Support" Actor in America' (*NCTR*). A product of the East End theatres of London, Freer played much in North America from 1839 before he fell on hard times and eventually took his own life. A fascinating pioneering account of 'The Employment of Children in The Victorian Theatre' by Tracy C. Davis appears in *NTQ*. She explores the social origins, training, and wages of child performers and how their employment was affected by legislation inspired by social reformers. The article is heavily illustrated and very well documented with a wealth of primary sources, and offers a splendid introduction to the subject.

A new series on the history of musical culture, Popular Music in Britain, contains two important collections of essays which analyse music hall in the light of recent debate in social history and cultural studies. They are *Music Hall: Performance and Style*, edited by J. S. Bratton (OpenU), unavailable as yet for inspection, and its companion volume *Music Hall: The Business of Pleasure*[167], edited by Peter Bailey. The latter book aims largely to show how the particular aesthetic of music hall 'took place within and was determined by the structures of music hall as a business'. John Earl provides an admirable curtain-raiser with a lucid and well-illustrated account of 'Building the Halls' which pays special attention to the crucial architectural developments of *c*. 1840 to 1875. Peter Bailey then investigates the relationship between early proprietors and their artists and audiences in 'A Community of Friends: Business and Good Fellowship in London Music Hall Management *c*. 1860–1885'. Dagmar Höher offers a valuable breakdown of 'The Composition of Music Hall Audiences 1850–1900' according to their class, age, and occupation, and assesses the social and cultural role that music hall played in their lives. The efforts of artists to raise their professional standing and protect themselves from

167. *Music Hall: The Business of Pleasure*, ed. by Peter Bailey. OpenU. pp. xxiv + 166; 26 illus. hb £25, pb £8.95.

their employers are recounted in Lois Rutherford's '"Managers in a small way": The Professionalisation of Variety Artistes, 1860–1914'. In '"It was not what she said but the way in which she said it": The London County Council and the Music Halls' Susan Pennybacker shows how the halls were affected by the policies of the LCC before the Progressives lost control of it in 1907. Moving north of Watford, Jeremy Crump gives a full and balanced account of 'Provincial Music Hall: Promoters and Public in Leicester, 1863–1929' which reveals how precarious provincial music-hall finances could be. Finally, Chris Walters recounts the successful attempts of local pressure groups to sabotage the enormous Manchester Palace of Varieties in 'Manchester Morality and London Capital: The Battle over the Palace of Varieties'.

An equally welcome addition to music-hall studies is Benny Green's highly readable compilation of reviews and reminiscences, *The Last Empires: A Music Hall Companion* [168], which captures some of the infectious vitality of the artists and their turns and songs. Apart from the index which is rather too selective, the book provides a valuable and informative introduction to the history of the halls: one hopes it will be issued in paperback so that students can afford it. In 'The Other Lillie Langtry' (*Thph*) Tony Barker features Miss Lillie Langtry, a namesake of the famous 'Jersey Lily', who began her stage career as a child in the 1880s billed as 'Baby Langtry' before going on to work the halls as 'The Electric Spark' until the 1920s.

Johann N. Schmidt's *Ästhetik des Melodramas* [169] consciously avoids dogmatic definitions of melodrama but approaches its subject historically, aesthetically, socially, and psychologically. Distinguishing melodrama as the main popular theatre in nineteenth-century Britain, Schmidt outlines its eclectic procedures and typifying tendency, but attends closely to its emphatic modes of presentation as responses to, or fulfilment of, the audience's desire to transcend everyday reality. The major melodramatists of the nineteenth century are covered in this balanced work which remains unified despite its multiplicity of 'angles', and persuasively argues for the complexity of this usually ignored genre. [E.A.M.]

Among the articles on theatres in *Thph* is Robert Thorne's informative history of 'The Princess's Theatre Oxford Street' from *c.* 1840 to 1931, and Kevin Stephens's account of the career of 'J. L. Hatton' who directed the band there and wrote music for the productions of Charles Kean from 1853 to 1859. A useful chronicle of the Lyceum Theatre covering the years 1771 to 1985 appears in Frederick Johns's 'Theatre in Films No. 7: The Lyceum in *Give My Regards to Broad Street*', also in *Thph*. The Princess's and Lyceum are among scores of London theatres documented in the Theatre Museum, V&A, whose extensive collection of nineteenth-century playbills and programmes is now available on microfiche [170]. First published in 1984, the fiche were to have been issued with an index but this has not, unfortunately, materialized to date. Nevertheless, the bills, arranged chronologically by theatre, are magnificently

168. *The Last Empires: A Music Hall Companion*, ed. by Benny Green. Pavilion/Joseph. pp. xii + 321. £15.95.

169. *Ästhetik des Melodramas. Studien zu einem Genre des populären Theaters im England des 19. Jahrhunderts*, by Johann N. Schmidt. CWU. pp. 408. DM 160.

170. *Playbills and Programmes from London Theatres 1801–1900 in the Theatre Museum, London*. C-H (1984). £3,600.

reproduced, and represent a vital research tool which no major library will want to be without.

Helen and Richard Leacroft make a model contribution to provincial theatre studies with their survey history of *The Theatre in Leicestershire*[171]. Lavishly documented and illustrated with isometric drawings and photographs, the book includes much information about the buildings and repertoire of the Theatre Royal, the Royal Opera House, and amphitheatres built for Victorian circuses in Leicester. In 'A North of England Marionette Theatre in the 1860s' (*TN*) George Speaight analyses a run of playbills to discover that the repertoire of a Sunderland marionette theatre lagged a full half-century behind that of its human counterpart. Finally, Jim Davis describes 'The Royal Dramatic College Fetes' (*TN*) which revived the traditional eighteenth-century fancy fairs during the 1860s to raise funds for retired actors and actresses. Held at the Crystal Palace, they featured on various occasions, burlesque melodramas starring J. L. Toole and Paul Bedford, a reconstruction of John Richardson's booth theatre, and other novelties such as Wombwell's Menagerie and Signor Logreno's Troupe of Performing Birds and Mice. Despite disapproval from the critics, the fetes proved highly popular and demonstrated the capacity of thespians to be a caring and respectable profession.

171. *The Theatre in Leicestershire: A History of Entertainment in the County from the Fifteenth Century to the 1960s*, by Helen and Richard Leacroft. LeicsCC. pp. vi + 137; 165 illus. pb £6.95.

The Twentieth Century

JUDIE NEWMAN, MAUREEN MORAN, JOHN CHALKER,
TREVOR R. GRIFFITHS, and AUDREY McMULLAN

This chapter has the following sections: 1. The Novel: (a) General Studies, (b) Individual Authors: 1900–45, (c) Individual Authors: Post-1945; 2. Poetry; 3. Drama: (a) General Studies, (b) Collections of Plays, (c) Individual Authors. Sections 1(a) and (c) are by Judie Newman; section 1(b) is by Maureen Moran; section 2 is by John Chalker; section 3 is by Trevor R. Griffiths, with the Beckett material in 3(c) by Audrey McMullan.

1. The Novel

(a) General Studies

The relevant volumes of *BHI* and *BNB* provide useful bibliographical aid. *MFS* contains helpful lists of books received. *Current Contents* is most useful in listing the contents of periodicals as they appear. The annual bibliography of scholarship on modern literature in *JML* is also invaluable. The year has seen an increase in studies of popular fiction, and of fiction written by women, but a comparatively thin harvest in general studies of the contemporary period.

India has had a bad press in British fiction for over a century. David Rubin[1], himself a novelist who has lived in India, scrutinizes British novels of India since 1947 (including some excruciating examples) to explore the frequently delusionary mythology which still dominates British attitudes to India. After an introduction summarizing earlier writers (e.g. Forster, Edward Thompson) Rubin delineates the four major modes of Indian romance (escape into the past, fable of transposed racial identities, India as source of light, India as destroyer), analyses the myth of India as a sexual force, and proceeds to detailed analysis of the fiction of Ruth Prawer Jhabvala, Paul Scott, and Kamala Markandaya. Jhabvala is envisaged not so much as an Indian writer as continuing the traditions of colonial British novelists (a fairly harsh reading, but one which later critics will need to take into account) while Scott is applauded for the depth of his understanding of India, together with his technical resourcefulness. Incidental highlights include a perceptive discussion of *The Siege of Krishnapur* in the context of 'Mutiny' novels, and a percipient account of Iris Murdoch's use of Indian philosophy in *Bruno's Dream*. It makes for one of the best books of the year, and fills a real gap in literary history.

1. *After the Raj: British Novels of India Since 1947*, by David Rubin. UPNE. pp. xi + 197. £15.95.

Michael Seidel[2] examines exile *not* as a metaphor for modern alienation, *nor* in terms of modern exilic politics or *émigré* conditions, but as an enabling fiction, an imaginative construct rather than a literary theme. Chapters on Defoe, Conrad, Joyce, Sterne, James, and Nabokov contribute to the conclusion that (to paraphrase) narrative performs not only as an experiential rival, but as an aesthetic substitute. Exilic imagining is thus the mirror and the 'other' of narrative process; mimesis becomes an alien phenomenon which establishes fictional sovereignty on fictional ground. Readers with more discrete interests will find the chapters on Joyce and Conrad rewarding and fresh, particularly in relation to Conrad's language, and to the importance in *Portrait* of Stephen's evocation of Dumas's *Count of Monte Cristo*, a fable of exile and return which romances the Odyssean epic in bourgeois terms. The whole volume, however, fairly glitters with insights, allusions, intellectual playfulness, and intriguing suggestions.

Nearer home, the period from 1957 to 1964 was marked both by growing conservatism in politics and a renaissance of working-class literature. Stuart Laing's incisive exploration[3] of the paradox devotes most of its space to other media (theatre, cinema, television, education, sociology) but includes a first-rate chapter on fiction, marked by a particularly valuable discussion of the problems and conditions of publication, and centred upon Braine, Storey, Barstow, Sillitoe, and Raymond Williams. The autumn issue of *JSSE* includes H. Gustav Klaus's examination of working-class tales of the 1920s. In the absence of anthologies Klaus's task is first and foremost one of recovery, with the essay recording his findings in the Labour press and little magazines, noting common themes (tramps, the workplace, moments of struggle), and commenting on distribution.

One volume is religious in emphasis. Wesley A. Kort[4] sets out to answer two fundamental questions: How do the characteristics of plot determine the appearance of time in modern fiction? Does this fictional time resemble time as experienced in human life? An initial chapter summarizes the various responses currently on offer (Genette, Propp, Greimas, Kermode, Ricoeur, *et al.*) but subsequent chapters reveal a more modest and traditional approach, essentially tending to argue that loss of faith in time diminishes humanity, and that his chosen authors (Hesse, Mann, Woolf, Lawrence, Hemingway, Faulkner) celebrate the order and meaning of time itself. The discussion of rhythm in Lawrence is not particularly new, and that on Woolf understates the darker implications of her fiction in favour of a 'life-affirming' reading.

The Art of Listening[5] is a volume of essays unified by one idea – that the active and creative abilities of listeners and readers deserve as much attention as the skills of speakers and writers. Essays focus on such disparate topics as psychoanalytic theories of reading, sociolinguistics, translation, popular

2. *Exile and the Narrative Imagination*, by Michael Seidel. Yale. pp. xiv + 234. £18.50.

3. *Representations of Working-Class Life 1957–1964*, by Stuart Laing. Macmillan. pp. 246. hb £25, pb £7.95.

4. *Modern Fiction and Human Time: A Study in Narrative and Belief*, by Wesley A. Kort. UFlor (1985). pp. x + 227. $20.

5. *The Art of Listening*, ed. by Graham McGregor and R. S. White. CH. pp. 220. £19.95.

music, Shakespeare, and Tom Stoppard. Two essays are of special interest, in relation to ways in which gender may affect the relation of reader to text: Linda Anderson's discussion of woman as reader in texts by Katherine Mansfield, Grace Paley, and Doris Lessing among others, and Rebecca Hiscock's exploration of women's diaries, which draws on Lessing and Woolf. Gender considerations are also to the fore in a collection of essays most of which focus upon feminist literary theory[6]. Three writers provide material relevant to readers of the modern novel, Lorna Sage on Doris Lessing's use of space, Linda Anderson on women's autobiography, and Marion Shaw, who takes as her subject the writing of women between the wars, identifying two principal directions: experimentalism (Dorothy Richardson, Rosamond Lehmann) and realism (Naomi Mitchison, Phyllis Bentley, Winifred Holtby). Practising novelists (Sue Roe, Emma Tennant) also contribute to a lively volume, in which the variety of topics and approaches makes for interesting reading.

Several volumes are primarily of a historical nature. For anyone who missed Blake Morrison's history of the 'Movement'[7] when it first appeared in 1980 (*YW* 61.380-1) Methuen have now issued this excellent book in paperback. The second edition of Harry Blamires's *Twentieth-Century English Literature*[8] is much as it first appeared in 1982 (*YW* 63.5). The last chapter has been slightly enlarged to accommodate new writers and rediscoveries of the last six years, but there is still no mention of J. L. Carr or John Berger. Bernard Bergonzi has published a selection of his essays spanning some fifteen years[9], loosely held together by a preoccupation with the effect of modernism on major writers. Only lightly revised, they stand as first published in a variety of periodicals, preceded by a short introduction. Not all are dated, however, which is a pity given that Bergonzi informs the reader that 'their dates of publication remain part of their meaning'. Topics include Woolf, Lawrence, Wyndham Lewis, and the Catholic novel. Also in a modernist mould, Peter Faulkner has edited a selection of key critical documents produced by Modernist writers, from 1910-30[10]. No one could quarrel with the selections (which include Woolf, Joyce, Ford, Wyndham Lewis, T. E. Hulme, Lawrence, and others) each of which is preceded by short explanatory notes. The editor's introduction, a model of clarity, situates the authors within their cultural context, without minimizing their disagreements in favour of any easy generalization. The result is an indispensable handbook for students of the period. Another useful handbook for undergraduates is Randall Stevenson's *The British Novel Since the Thirties*[11] which summarizes the work of British novelists under roughly chronological headings, and in relation to experimentalism. Some one hundred

6. *Women's Writing: A Challenge to Theory*, ed. by Moira Monteith. Harvester. pp. vii + 196. hb £20, pb £5.95.

7. *The Movement: English Poetry and Fiction of the 1950s*, by Blake Morrison. Methuen. pp. x + 326. pb £6.95.

8. *Twentieth-Century English Literature*, by Harry Blamires. Second edn. Macmillan. pp. xi + 324. hb £20, pb £5.95.

9. *The Myth of Modernism and Twentieth Century Literature*, by Bernard Bergonzi. Harvester. pp. xviii + 216. £25.

10. *A Modernist Reader: Modernism in England 1910-1930*, ed. by Peter Faulkner. Batsford. pp. 171. hb £14.95, pb £5.95.

11. *The British Novel Since the Thirties*, by Randall Stevenson. Batsford. pp. 257. hb £19.95, pb £7.95.

novelists figure, including Scottish, Welsh, and Irish, though oddly excluding Barbara Pym. The select bibliography of surveys and directories is helpfully annotated. A general essay also considers contemporary fiction. In *BBN* John Walsh provides an informative survey of some forty first novels published between 1983 and 1985, chosen as either well received or 'typical of their time'. Rather marred by an incipient genealogical tendency, it also excludes genre fiction.

Works with a regional flavour have declined in number. The Scottish Collection continues to flourish, making Scottish fiction available to a wide audience in economical but attractive editions. This year includes Neil Paterson's *The China Run*[12], first published in 1948, the tale of a female skipper of a sailing vessel, and Robin Jenkins's *Dust on the Paw*[13], first published in 1961, a novel of Afghanistan. *Irish Writers and Society At Large*[14] is a collection of essays designed to celebrate the establishment of the International Association for the Study of Anglo-Irish Literature, most of which concern poetry or drama or are of a fairly general nature. Women fiction-writers are a particular focus however – Jennifer Johnston and Julia O'Faolain in a doggedly thematic piece from David Burleigh which runs over their works chronologically, Elizabeth Bowen's short fiction (A. C. Partridge) and 'Five Fierce Ladies' (Maria Edgeworth, Somerville and Ross, Bowen, and Molly Keane), as Frank Tuohy entitles his contribution. The latter is less a scholarly essay than the notations of a lively mind, with Tuohy observing that all their writings are tales of inadequate men and masculine women. The best piece on fiction is Augustine Martin's provocative and fresh essay on the prose fiction of the Irish literary renaissance which includes (with Joyce, Moore, and others) a consideration of the early tales of W. B. Yeats, an unusual topic gracefully handled. *EI* contains an essay by Margaret Scanlan on three contemporary novels with Northern Irish settings (by Maurice Leitch, Benedict Kiely, and Bernard MacLaverty) which are compared with Thomas Kilroy's *The Big Chapel*. Scanlan concludes, with a fair degree of conviction, that realistic fiction has special problems in handling present events, whereas the historical novel offers writers a useful means of establishing perspective. The essay draws interestingly on Feuchtwanger. In *Éire* (1985) Klaus Lubbers finds that most modern Irish fiction is not so much universal as about Ireland, and he notes such recurrent themes as escape, dissections of Irish society, autobiography, and the Big House.

James Dickey has described the interview as one of the great art forms of our time, Saul Bellow as thumbprints on his windpipe, Julio Cortázar as a sonata for two instruments. Diana Cooper-Clark quotes all three in her sprightly introduction to a collection of interviews with contemporary novelists[15], which includes two British writers, Margaret Drabble (a reprint from 1980) and Colin Wilson (undated), and amply justifies Cortázar's favourable definition. If Wilson is verbose (answering questions over two pages of text) Drabble is trenchantly informative.

12. *The China Run*, by Neil Paterson. Drew. pp. 95. hb £6.95, pb £2.95.

13. *Dust on the Paw*, by Robin Jenkins. Drew. pp. 384. hb £9.95, pb £3.95.

14. *Irish Writers and Society At Large*, ed. by Masaru Sekine. Smythe (1985). pp. xi + 251. £14.95.

15. *Interviews with Contemporary Novelists*, by Diana Cooper-Clark. Macmillan. pp. 297. £27.50.

Belated mention should be made here of Joseph M. Flora's volume[16] (in Twayne's Critical History of the Short Story) on the English short story in the first part of the century. An introduction by the editor is followed by a number of chapter-length essays by other contributors and a bibliography. All the contributors are American academics, and the audience envisaged is also clearly transatlantic. Robert Gish kicks off (inevitably) with Kipling and the colonial short story, drawing together various writers of exotic tales in an informed and suggestive fashion. Weldon Thornton constructs an excellent case for Lawrence as a more experimental writer in his short fiction than has generally been allowed. The volume then moves on to Woolf and Katherine Mansfield, somewhat briskly surveyed by Joanne Trautmann Banks, followed by Richard Harter Fogle's equally descriptive account of Saki and Wodehouse. James Gindin's chapter on A. E. Coppard and H. E. Bates is altogether more weighty and the topic (ruralism) makes for a more sharply focused essay. The volume concludes with eight pages from William Peden on V. S. Pritchett. Whatever the virtues of the individual essays, the series format sits ill with the title. It is distinctly odd for a 'Critical History' of this period not to discuss Conan Doyle or Wells, and to prefer extended discussion of Wodehouse to Forster, Conrad, Waugh, and Greene. *Scottish Short Stories*[17], now in its fourteenth year and volume, includes work by George Mackay Brown, Ian Rankin, and Iain Crichton Smith among its eighteen stories selected from 248 submissions. Deirdre Chapman's introduction notes the predominance in the submissions of stories of urban low-life, violence, despair, children, and mid-life crises. In addition to offering good reading, the volume also serves as something of a barometer of the state of Scottish writing. *Stepping Out*[18] is an anthology of stories by women writers celebrating women, including Michelene Wandor and Anna Livia among the authors. *Irish Short Stories*[19] is the new title of a collection originally published in 1980 as *The Bodley Head Book of Irish Short Stories* and now re-issued in paperback. Stories are arranged chronologically by date of author's birth, and have been selected on two principles: brevity and an Irish context. Apart from such obvious writers as Joyce, Moore, and O'Connor the thirty-two writers represented include such contemporary practitioners as Neil Jordan, Maura Treacy, and Desmond Hogan.

Lorna Martens's *The Diary Novel*[20], the first attempt to trace the three-hundred-year history of the form, constitutes a substantial achievement. The range is international with a massive bibliography, and chapters devoted to the problems of first-person narration, eighteenth- and nineteenth-century practitioners, and contemporary examples. Of these only one is relevant to students of contemporary English fiction, a discussion of *The Golden Notebook*, in which Martens elucidates Lessing's intentions and tests the novel against them. The whole volume, however, can be recommended to scholars of the novel, comparative literature, and literary theory. Also worth noting is the special

16. *The English Short Story 1880–1945: A Critical History*, ed. by Joseph M. Flora. Twayne (1985). pp. xx + 215. $17.95.

17. *Scottish Short Stories 1986*, intro. by Deirdre Chapman. Collins. pp. 176. £7.50.

18. *Stepping Out: Short Stories on Friendship between Women*, ed. by Ann Oosthuizen. Pandora. pp. ix + 175. pb £4.95.

19. *Irish Short Stories*, sel. and intro. by David Marcus. NEL. pp. 379. pb £3.50.

20. *The Diary Novel*, by Lorna Martens. CUP (1985). pp. xi + 307. £27.50.

issue of *PSt*, devoted to 'Autobiography' (*YW* 66.458), which has now been republished in book form[21].

YES devotes a special issue to the topic of literary periodicals, including contributions on *TLS*, *The Calendar of Modern Letters*, *PNR*, *NLH*, *NYRB*, and *LRB*. The essays are mostly by writers intimately connected with the journals in question, and are exceptionally well informed, and useful in correcting the impression of literary history as individual and biographical. The first issue of *The Fiction Magazine* was published in 1982, since when it has survived and flourished as an outlet for new writers. Dent have now published an anthology[22], which is splendid value, including among others work by Brian Aldiss, John McGahern, Allan Massie, and Aidan Higgins plus interviews with Anthony Burgess and Alasdair Gray. *LMag* has been going for rather longer, twenty-five years in its current form, and Alan Ross's anthology has more to choose from[23]. Ross therefore jettisons all reviews, all stories widely available elsewhere, most long pieces, and most illustrations. Though the result has little of the flavour of the magazine, it does contain work by Lowry, Laurence Durrell, McGahern, R. K. Narayan, Nadine Gordimer, and Kingsley Amis.

This is clearly a period of renewed interest in all forms of popular culture. Jean Radford[24] has edited a collection of essays on popular romance writing from antiquity to the present, which explore the politics of the genre in various directions. Contributors emphasize ways in which popular culture may embody a subversive resistance to the dominant culture, and mostly undercut the image of the reader as passively escapist. Derrick Price discusses Richard Llewellyn's *How Green Was My Valley* as a romance which constructs a myth of Wales in order to displace class antagonisms with an appeal to national unity, Jean Radford examines *The Well of Loneliness*, revealed as dependent on conflicting theories of homosexuality, and other topics include Mills and Boon romances, the family saga novel, and the detective story. The overall impression emerging here is that popular romances offer plural and contradictory readings, particularly as regards the positioning of female subjectivities. Margery Fisher's *The Bright Face of Danger*[25] sets out to define and describe the literary conventions of the adventure story, and to compare those written for adults with juvenile stories. Individual chapters cover such subvarieties as sea stories, historical fiction, cops and robbers, and Ruritania together with character types, settings, and attitudes. The result is genuinely explorative. Fisher avoids easy generalizations, any over-rigid approach, or any suspicion of jargon, and ranges far and wide in her choice of subjects for critical discussion. To take one example, the chapter on 'desert islands' includes Jules Verne, Captain Marryat, Ballantyne, Swiss Family Robinson, Defoe, Golding, Michel Tournier, and television commercials for chocolate bars. Equally

21. *Modern Selves: Essays on Modern British and American Autobiography*, ed. by Philip Dodd. Cass. pp. vii + 192. £18.50.

22. *The Best of 'The Fiction Magazine'*, ed. by Judy Cooke and Elizabeth Bunster. Dent. pp. 312. pb £4.95.

23. *London Magazine 1961–1985*, ed. by Alan Ross. C&W. pp. x + 307. £10.95.

24. *The Progress of Romance: The Politics of Popular Fiction*, ed. by Jean Radford, RKP. pp. xii + 238. pb £5.95.

25. *The Bright Face of Danger: An Exploration of the Adventure Story*, by Margery Fisher. H&S. pp. 440. £12.95.

entertaining and original, *You're A Brick, Angela!*[26], first published in 1976, has now been issued in paperback, with a postscript updating the study to 1985. In contrast to the emphasis on the anodyne which the authors detected in the earlier fiction, in contemporary girls' stories painful topics (racism, violence, dyslexia, bedwetting) have become *de rigueur*, although periodical fiction appears decidedly more conservative.

Traditional crime and mystery fiction written by women is the focus of a collection of essays[27] edited by Jane S. Bakerman, which is worth brief mention. Of the nine subjects four are British: Daphne du Maurier, Margery Allingham, Anne Morice, and Elizabeth Ferrars. The essays, each preceded by a short biographical chronology, are in the main brisk general outlines, though the editor's own piece interestingly highlights the Cinderella motif in all du Maurier's work, and Susan Baker's analysis of Ferrars makes a good case for her as a grim predecessor of contemporary crime-writers rather than as belonging to the cosy world of the classic puzzler. The 1986 issue of *Caliban* is entirely devoted to 'Le Roman Policier Anglo-Saxon', with most of the essays in French and on American authors. Two pieces are well worth mentioning however. Sandra Pla provides a general discussion of P. D. James, pointing to traditional elements within the fiction (police procedure, institutions, middle-class characters, the country house). Ellen Epstein examines that subspecies of genteel British detection (memorably christened the 'Mayhem Parva' school) which is situated in the groves of academe, a useful microcosm lending itself particularly to 'locked room' puzzles. Readers in the groves of British academe, overpruned at present, are unlikely to raise much enthusiasm, however, for such titles as *Landscape with Dead Dons* and *Death in a Tenured Position*.

Two short accounts of horror fiction have appeared. Darrell Schweitzer's *Discovering Modern Horror Fiction*[28] consists of a series of brief, chatty essays on a variety of postwar writers, including Ramsey Campbell and Roald Dahl. There is a useful bibliography by Marshall B. Tymn. 'Horror fiction' is also the subject of a general essay by Phil Rickman in *Words* (January) which provides a lively overview of the genre. Considerable light is thrown on the mechanics of the market for popular fiction in André Jute's *Writing a Thriller*[29]. The author (also a novelist) runs through such topics as thriller-types, the creation of villains ('credible black hats'), plot, and overall length in a direct and candid fashion, simultaneously revealing a great deal about the genre.

Most criticism of science fiction emphasizes its relevance or meaning in terms of the projection of contemporary hopes or fears. C. N. Manlove[30] takes a different approach, concentrating upon its merits as literature and making a fervent plea for the 'indestructible this-ness' of its imagined worlds. Essentially a personal response, the volume tackles ten writers (including Aldiss and

26. *You're A Brick, Angela!: The Girls' Story 1839–1985*, by Mary Cadogan and Patricia Craig. Gollancz. pp. 405. pb £4.95.

27. *And Then There Were Nine . . . More Women of Mystery*, ed. by Jane S. Bakerman. BGUP (1985). pp. 219. hb $19.95, pb $9.95.

28. *Discovering Modern Horror Fiction*, ed. by Darrell Schweitzer. Starmont (1985). pp. 156. pb $9.95.

29. *Writing a Thriller*, by André Jute. Black. pp. 100. pb £4.95.

30. *Science Fiction: Ten Explorations*, by C. N. Manlove. Macmillan. pp. x + 249. £25.

Clarke), breaking new ground in most cases, and communicating the author's enthusiasm for the topic. Brian Aldiss's history of science fiction[31] is written in a very popular 'Now read on' style, but critics should not be deceived by this. The book is a mine of information, handsomely illustrated, critically acute, and both comprehensive and up to date. In addition it moves towards a conclusion – that science fiction's main preoccupation is with power, hence its themes of empire and conquest, and that it is fast becoming an American genre. The spring issue of *MFS* is a special number devoted to 'Science and Fantasy Fiction'. Most of the essays are concerned with general topics though it is worth remarking Robert Crossley's discussion of generic questions in relation to Olaf Stapledon, and a thoughtful consideration of Plato's influence on C. S. Lewis (co-authored by William G. Johnson and Marcia K. Houtman). The volume is of special interest in its internationalism and the variety of its approaches. A collection of conference papers on the subject of fantasy should also be noted. Though topics range widely (children's literature, film, fairy-tale) and include theoretical approaches, individual authors also feature. In Volume I[32] Douglas A. Burger explicates an image in *Lord of the Rings*, and L. L. Dickson outlines ways in which Golding's *The Inheritors* may be seen as a reaction to H. G. Wells's ideas of evolutionary progress. The second volume[33] includes David Stevens on the topic of *The Hobbit*, concluding engagingly that the book is a work about good manners for children, using fantasy elements to sugar-coat a nineteenth-century moral lesson.

There has been a plethora of guidebooks to the modern period, often rather difficult to distinguish one from another. *Modern British Literature*[34] has been updated by the appearance of a fifth volume which covers for the first time Beryl Bainbridge, D. M. Thomas, Barbara Pym, J. G. Ballard, Benedict Kiely, and Mervyn Peake. Each entry consists of critical excerpts from a variety of sources, and short bibliographies are provided. According to Larry McCaffery's *Postmodern Fiction*[35] only four British novelists qualify as post-moderns – Ballard, Fowles, D. M. Thomas, and Ian McEwan. Indeed the genre seems to be almost entirely American. The 'Guide' however has its points. A first section provides 'overview' essays which attempt to define the characteristics of the fiction, and examine its relationships with feminism, science fiction, realism, criticism, and journalism. The second part of the book is occupied by individual author entries which briefly survey the life, career, and significance. The volume positively bristles with useful bibliographies, and some of the individual authors are actually critics, potted summaries of whose

31. *Trillion Year Spree: The History of Science Fiction*, by Brian Aldiss with David Wingrove. Gollancz. pp. 511. pb £9.95.

32. *The Scope of the Fantastic – Theory, Technique, Major Authors: Selected Essays from the First International Conference on the Fantastic in Literature and Film*, Vol. I, ed. by Robert A. Collins and Howard D. Pearce. Greenwood (1985). pp. xii + 295. £35.

33. *The Scope of the Fantastic – Culture, Biography, Themes, Children's Literature: Selected Essays from the First International Conference on the Fantastic in Literature and Film*, Vol. II, ed. by Robert A. Collins and Howard D. Pearce. Greenwood (1985). pp. xii + 284. £35.

34. *Modern British Literature*. Vol. V: *Second Supplement*, comp. and ed. by Denis Lane and Rita Stein. Ungar (1985). pp. xii + 669. £50.

35. *Postmodern Fiction: A Bio-Bibliographical Guide*, ed. by Larry McCaffery. Greenwood. pp. xxviii + 604. £68.50.

ideas are provided. Despite all the information, however, one feels that this is a book for the naïve undergraduate who needs labels to stick on writers. *Twentieth-Century Literary Criticism*[36] follows its usual format (*YW* 66.461). Volume XIX includes H. G. Wells, Volume XX Woolf, and Volume XXI James Hilton. A new feature is the in-depth treatment of selected single works (*Mrs Dalloway* in Volume XX). Its stablemate, *Contemporary Literary Criticism*[37], includes a Yearbook (Vol. XXXIX) which reviews the fiction, poetry, and drama of 1985, excerpts criticism on eighteen writers whose first books were published in that year, lists annual prizewinners with commentary, and provides obituaries, and reviews of literary biographies and of noteworthy volumes of criticism. The other volumes are much as usual (*YW* 66.461) with entries this year for Ballard, Feinstein, David Lodge, and Fay Weldon (Vol. XXXVI), Greene, Pym, and Duffy (Vol. XXXVII), Tolkien and Martin Amis (Vol. XXXVIII), Aldiss, Kingsley Amis, Burgess, Lessing, and Spark (Vol. XL). *Contemporary Authors Autobiography Series*[38] provides detailed autobiographies of more than twenty writers, including Brigid Brophy and John Wain. *Contemporary Authors*[39] (*YW* 66.461) produces five new volumes which include P. D. James and D. M. Thomas (Vol. XVII), Margaret Drabble (Vol. XVIII), Rebecca West and Len Deighton (Vol. XIX), and in its new series Bernard MacLaverty (Vol. CXVIII). *Contemporary Novelists*[40] (now in its fourth edition) is as up to date and informative as ever and follows its usual format (*YW* 63.368). New British arrivals in its pages include Richard Adams, J. L. Carr, Isabel Colegate, Alice Thomas Ellis, Zoe Fairbairns, P. D. James, and D. M. Thomas among others.

(b) Individual Authors: 1900–45

Most critical work in this period still continues to focus on the Modernists, but re-assessments of secondary figures like Kipling and Beerbohm are beginning to appear, and there are several important collections of letters this year. It is interesting to note an increasing emphasis on the fiction as a product of a particular society; some exciting work is emerging on the historical and cultural contexts of particular authors, but there is still a lively interest in verbal play and internal dislocations in specific texts.

George Moore's mimetic strategies continue to interest a range of critics.

---

36. *Twentieth-Century Literary Criticism: Excerpts from Criticism of the Works of Novelists, Poets, Playwrights, Short Story Writers, and Other Creative Writers Who Died between 1900 and 1960, from the First Critical Appraisals to Current Evaluations*, Vols. XIX, XX, XXI, ed. by Dennis Poupard. Gale. pp. 568; 547; 575. $88 each.

37. *Contemporary Literary Criticism: Excerpts from Criticism of the Works of Today's Novelists, Poets, Playwrights, Short Story Writers, Scriptwriters, and Other Creative Writers*. Vols. XXXVI, XXXVII, XXXVIII, XL, ed. by Daniel G. Marowski, Vol. XXXIX, ed. by Sharon K. Hall. Gale. pp. 683; 688; 696; xii + 723; 739. $88 each.

38. *Contemporary Authors Autobiography Series*. Vols. III, IV, ed. by Adele Sarkissian. Gale. pp. 518; 463. $72 each.

39. *Contemporary Authors: A Bibliographical Guide to Current Writers in Fiction, General Nonfiction, Poetry, Journalism, Drama, Motion Pictures, Television, and Other Fields*. New Revision Series. Vols. XVII, XVIII, ed. by Linda Metzger and Deborah A. Straub; Vol. XIX, ed. by Linda Metzger; Vols. CXVI, CXVIII in the continuing series, ed. by Hal May. Gale. pp. 500; 502; 501; 825; 844. $88 each.

40. *Contemporary Novelists*. Fourth edn, ed. by D. L. Kirkpatrick. St James. pp. xix + 1003. £39.50.

CVE devotes a special issue to 'Studies in Realism', singling out George Moore, George Gissing, and Arnold Bennett for detailed study. Two articles are on Moore. Jean-Claude Noël comments usefully (in French) on the ways in which Moore's techniques in his early short stories anticipate his later narrative methods, particularly in his ability to move from 'major' to 'minor' keys through skilful 'modulations'. Judith Mitchell also strikes a musical note in 'Formal Considerations in *Esther Waters*: Early Intimations of George Moore's "Melodic Line"'. She argues clearly that this nineteenth-century novel also anticipates Moore's later technical experiments; Mitchell's discussion of dialogue and anecdote supports her case. The same author also reflects on 'Fictional Worlds in George Moore's *A Mummer's Wife*' in *ES*. This is an altogether more interesting piece which shows how formulaic naturalism (dreary, dismal, and based on scientific observation) is modified and enlivened by Moore. Also in *ES* can be found Elizabeth Grubgeld's 'George Moore's *The Lake* and the Geography of Consciousness', a workmanlike article focusing on the strategies used by Moore to explore the subconscious in his 1905 novel. Not surprisingly, the primary method is through psychescape or 'psychic geography', though Grubgeld adds interest by noting that landscape has its meaning from Father Gogarty's perception of it, not from the narrator's commentary. Those keen to track down the whereabouts of Moore manuscript material will need to consult Edwin Gilcher's 'A Note on Arizona State University's George Moore Collection' in *ELT*.

'It is a fool's business to write fiction for a living', wrote Conrad to Ted Sanderson in 1899; 'the unreality of it seems to enter one's real life, penetrate into the bones, make the very heart beats pulsate illusions through the arteries'. This deliciously provoking comment helps to set the tone for the second volume of *The Collected Letters of Joseph Conrad*[41], fastidiously edited by Frederick R. Karl and Laurence Davies, and covering the period 1898–1902. As Davies points out in his crisp introduction, this is a rich and fascinating period for Conrad scholars for it witnessed important developments in Conrad's personal life (birth of Borys), in his artistic endeavours ('Youth', *Heart of Darkness*, *Lord Jim* among other works), and in his relationship with the critical community. But what now looks to us as a time of increasing purpose and maturity seemed to Conrad a period of insecurity and uncertainty – in matters ranging from his personal finance to his own craftsmanship ('I am finishing the Falk story but with me such a statement may mean anything'). His correspondents of this period – Ford, Galsworthy, Wells, Garnett, Bennett – elicit a variety of moods from their friend – depression, lack of confidence, and a wobbly sense of identity; but a shrewd and determined man is also revealed in the letters Conrad wrote to his agent, J. B. Pinker, and to his publisher, William Blackwood. Davies's able introduction places the correspondence of this period in the context of Conrad's own fears and ambitions at the time, and gives a sense of the distinctive Conradian flavour emerging in the fiction and in the letters. The scholarly apparatus is superb. This is undoubtedly a volume all Conrad scholars will need to consult.

There have also been further discoveries of unpublished letters recorded in various journals, all of which cast some light on aspects of Conrad's attitudes

41. *The Collected Letters of Joseph Conrad*. Vol. II: *1898–1902*, ed. by Frederick R. Karl and Laurence Davies. CUP. pp. xxxviii + 483. £27.50/$44.50.

and art. A number of these appear in *Conradiana*. Peter J. Lowens's 'The Conrad–Pinker Relationship: An Unpublished Letter' reveals that bonds of affection (not just professionalism) united the novelist and his agent. In 'Conrad to Clifford: Some Unpublished Letters' Allan G. Hunter examines Conrad's friendship with Sir Hugh Charles Clifford, a colonial administrator and novelist; and, in the course of this article, he demonstrates the anecdotal nature of certain sections of *Lord Jim*. Wit Tarnawski's 'Conrad and Religion' sheds some modest light on the subject by printing a letter from the Catholic priest who conducted Conrad's burial and a letter from a Conrad scholar recounting an interview with Borys Conrad on just this matter.

Elsewhere Owen Knowles has an interesting piece concerning the correspondence. In 'Conrad and David Bone: Some Unpublished Letters' (*Conradian*) he charts the developing 'sincere, affectionate and resilient' friendship between Conrad and the commander of the ship on which Conrad sailed to America in 1923. Knowles's unobtrusive contextualizing commentary neatly suggests the significance of both the friendship and the letters from Conrad, and helpfully reminds us that Bone's reminiscences (*Landfall at Sunset: The Life of a Contented Sailor*, 1955) provide a good account of Conrad's final years. Also in *Conradian* Donald W. Rude and L. Layne Neeper write briefly on the publishing history of Conrad's translation of Bruno Winaver's play, *The Book of Job*.

This year has also seen the publication of a number of paperback editions of key Conrad texts. The most interesting of these is Allan Ingram's edition of *Selected Literary Criticism and 'The Shadow-Line*[42]. Teachers and students of Conrad will welcome this collection of criticism which ranges handily over major statements by Conrad in his prefaces and notes to his fiction (such as *The Nigger of the 'Narcissus'* preface) and includes some interesting selections from the correspondence (such as his insistence to Richard Curle that his art is 'fluid'). Ingram's introduction is a direct, uncomplicated effort which picks up suggestions by recent Conrad critics that the novelist was in fact a 'double man' who produced work characterized by 'evasive lucidity'. Ingram helpfully points out the ways in which Conrad's critical pronouncements show his awareness of an older tradition of fiction-writing which he rejected or, perhaps, subverted to his new ends. The commentary on *The Shadow-Line* is more predictable but still manages to give a sense of Conrad's complex imaginative re-creation of 'a more innocent time' and view of life. Students will also find the reading list, notes, and glossary of nautical and eastern terms helpful, and the volume concludes with an analytical commentary on the criticism and *The Shadow-Line*, with sharp things to say about the narrative structure of the latter.

The Shadow-Line[43] has also been edited by Jacques Berthoud, this time for Penguin. This edition must really be commended as exemplary for its meticulous editing standards and challenging introduction. Berthoud approaches the novel from a neglected angle, arguing persuasively – and accessibly – that it has an important relationship to its contemporary World War I context: it is 'an oblique meditation on the significance of war' and 'an act of solidarity with

42. *Selected Literary Criticism and 'The Shadow-Line'*, by Joseph Conrad, ed. by Allan Ingram. Methuen. pp. x + 273. pb £3.50.

43. *The Shadow-Line: A Confession*, by Joseph Conrad, ed. with intro. and notes by Jacques Berthoud. Penguin. pp. 157. pb £1.95.

the youthful combatants with whom he could no longer serve'. Although this might seem provocative (and a connection Ingram for one skirts over in his introduction) Berthoud does seem to make his case and illuminate the novel's treatment of heroism in the face of trial. There is a well-annotated bibliography and intelligent explanatory notes which connect the events of the story to Conrad's first command in 1888.

Other new editions are more run-of-the-mill, though it is good to see a range of Conrad texts in print at reasonable prices. Cedric Watts has edited 'Typhoon' and Other Tales[44] ('Falk', 'Amy Foster', 'The Secret Sharer') and provides the introduction, highlighting the (largely thematic) similarities between the tales and suggesting how and at what points readers must 'make' the text to evaluate tone. Watts is lively on those narrative techniques used to promote sympathy for Falk and on the symmetries in 'The Secret Sharer', and there is the usual apparatus of notes, chronology, select bibliography, and glossary.

Cedric Watts and Robert Hampson have edited Lord Jim[45] for Penguin, with Watts again supplying the introduction which puts the novel in its biographical context as well as surveying its publication history and reception. Watts reads the novel rather perfunctorily as a major statement in the old romance–realism debate, with Conrad sceptically inverting romance material and conventions to 'probe the realities of his day'. Those new to the novel will find the discussion of source material interesting, and it is good to see Watts drawing attention to characteristic Conradian narrative techniques and 'defamiliarizing' strategies. There are some suggestions for further reading (not annotated) and Robert Hampson offers interesting bibliographical detail. The notes and glossary are for the most part helpful.

Jocelyn Baines's standard biography[46], first published in 1960, has been re-issued by Penguin. Although serious students of Conrad will also wish to turn to more recent studies for increased scholarly detail, revised judgements, and more searching interpretive analyses (such as Ian Watt's Conrad in the Nineteenth Century, YW 61.350), this is essential reading for all who are interested in the novelist. It is comprehensive in scope, evidencing research and scholarship of a very high standard indeed in its delineation of a man burdened by 'a fundamental pessimism' and 'sense of inevitability' but also one who embraced the ideals of 'professional competence', 'solidarity', 'fidelity', and devotion to duty to create at least an 'illusion of triumph' against the impersonal forces that would control and destroy. Further biographical material is to be found in Zdzislaw Najder's Conradiana piece entitled 'Conrad's Polish Background, or, From Biography to a Study of Culture'. This essay provides a useful counterpart to Baines's approach, for Najder argues that Conrad's personal codes are actually part of 'a cultural [i.e. Polish] language'. Owen Knowles approaches the life 'aslant' in his note on the effect of Conrad's death on Dorothy Richardson and T. W. H. Crosland

44. 'Typhoon' and Other Tales, by Joseph Conrad, ed. with an intro. by Cedric Watts. OUP. pp. xxxii + 324. pb £1.95.

45. Lord Jim, by Joseph Conrad, ed. by Cedric Watts and Robert Hampson, with intro. by Cedric Watts. Penguin. pp. 377. pb £2.50.

46. Joseph Conrad: A Critical Biography, by Jocelyn Baines. Penguin. pp. 606. pb £5.95.

(*Conradian*). Some ironic connections to central Conradian preoccupations are sketched with a deftly light touch.

Critical and interpretive interest in Conrad also continues apace. Suresh Raval's pluralistic and eclectic critical approach in *The Art of Failure: Conrad's Fiction*[47] is designed to mark out a middle ground in Conrad criticism, but is ultimately disappointingly unprovocative and rather meandering. Raval investigates the major works from *Heart of Darkness* to *Victory* as texts which focus on 'the contradictions in human affairs' and their impact on 'social and personal life', 'on actual human conduct'. This socio-political approach embraces a consideration of issues such as personal identity, self-justification, discord, and the 'problematical relation between action and intention, language and experience' to reveal a 'fundamental critique of the central concepts and institutions of Western culture': 'a skepticism concretized in language, action, and character', with an individual's identity presented as 'a social construction' intimately connected to 'the political nature of his community'. Conrad's principal artistic strategy for promoting this is the inversion and subversion of romance paradigms to question cultural assumptions while eschewing prescription. In an effort to modify conventional readings Raval sometimes engages in some rather delicate hair-splitting (Kurtz's cry, for instance) and one generally feels that much of this has been said before – and less repetitively. Still it is helpful to be reminded of Conrad's social and cultural interests at a time when much textual analysis is given over to issues of verbal play and linguistic ambiguities.

Norman Page's *A Conrad Companion*[48] purports to be a guide to the novelist's 'life, background and writings' and includes a chronology, 'A Conrad's Who's Who', brief accounts of the writer's sojourns in Poland, France, England, Africa, the East, and sketchy discussion of his appearance, manner, and grasp of languages. This preliminary material is followed by sections devoted to the fiction, collaborations, plays, and non-fiction writings. The emphasis is generally quite biographical, with a factual account of the genesis, publication, and reception of the texts and some elementary comments on themes, characterization, and other aspects of narrative method. Although there is some interesting material dotted throughout, the readership expected for this 'Companion' is unclear. Its format works against its use as a quick-reference, factual guidebook; and its simplicity and biographical orientation might be rather misleading for students since it gives little sense of other directions which have proved fruitful for Conrad critics (such as psycho-analytic, deconstructive, and mythic approaches).

Some very lively and provocative work appears in the periodicals this year, with continuing emphasis on Conrad's ambiguity and contradictoriness. As usual *Heart of Darkness* is a major focal point. In '*An Inquiry into Some Points of Seamanship*: Narration as Preservation in *Heart of Darkness*' (*Conradiana*) Barbara DeMille provides an excellent discussion of the storyteller's 'restraint' when 'constructing an account of a primary experience'. While the novel can be read as a survival story, it is also about the process of constructing and using 'fictional forms'; and DeMille neatly demonstrates that narrative handled with

47. *The Art of Failure: Conrad's Fiction*, by Suresh Raval. A&U. pp. xiv + 187. £20.
48. *A Conrad Companion*, by Norman Page. Macmillan. pp. xvi + 185. £25.

responsibility is itself a survival strategy by which 'we translate and attempt to order an essentially unfollowable world'. In *JML* Patrick A. McCarthy writes on '*Heart of Darkness* and the Early Novels of H. G. Wells: Evolution, Anarchy, Entropy'. This is a splendid treatment of the nineteenth-century inheritance shared by both novelists, with particular attention to the relation between evolution and morality (in personal and national terms) 'and the relevance of the processes of entropy and atavistic regression to human affairs'. McCarthy ably shows how both writers reacted against Victorian optimism with a pessimistic 'deterministic' stance, though Wells chose a satirical and Conrad a more subtly ironic treatment of such ideals as 'empire' and 'progress'. Further exploration of Conrad's inheritance can be found in *Conradian* where Peter Caracciolo has a piece on 'Buddhist Teaching Stories and their Influence on Conrad, Wells, and Kipling'. Caracciolo is concerned less with Buddhist doctrine than with Conrad's use of 'the literary genres of Buddhism', and in highlighting the Western reception of these stories he comments suggestively on links between their narrative strategies and those of *Heart of Darkness*. This is important groundwork for further examination of possible sources for Conrad's 'oblique narratives' and 'delayed decoding' as Caracciolo himself suggests.

Michael Levenson finds himself 'On the Edge of the Heart of Darkness' when he examines the dialectic between opposing images of edge and centre in the novel (*SSF*). Truth lies only in the margins and beyond the boundaries for Levenson who sharply sees a historical connection here: 'In the age of anthropology the European mind can only discover truths about its origins by going outside the limits of its culture.' Somewhat predictably George Cheatham (*SNNTS*) examines Conrad's manipulation of conventional light/dark, ascent/descent imagery to shed light on Marlow's version of Kurtz's death and his interview with the Intended. 'The Absence of God in *Heart of Darkness*' thus concludes that the visit to the Intended enacts the journey to Kurtz, both becoming a descent into darkness and a re-affirmation of evil. In 'Conrad's Mortal Word' (*CritI*) Henry Staten uses a psychoanalytic approach to draw forceful links between Marlow and Kurtz based on their fear of death (forestalled by Kurtz through his 'sadistic project of mastery' and by Marlow through his feminizing of the jungle). Staten argues this fear permeates all motivation in the novel; even the Intended's cry signifies 'the sentiment of death and at the same time the passionate response of the other who fills the place of the absent mother . . . the response that Marlow/Kurtz had desired all along'. More briefly in *Conradiana* Robert G. Hampson writes on 'Conrad, Guthrie, and '"The Arabian Nights"'', tracing in particular connections between *Heart of Darkness* and 'The Tale of the Fisherman and the Jinn'. In *Conradian* Jeremy Hawthorn examines 'The Incoherences of *The Nigger of the "Narcissus"*', building helpfully on previous work done on the novella's ambiguities and Conrad's ideological tensions and uncertainties. The chief interest of this article lies in its focus on the novelist's inability to deal 'with the schizophrenia of Victorian England with regard to the Negro'. David Manicom does some solid work on the same novel in 'True Lies/False Truths' (*Conradiana*), where he finds the handling of point of view related to Conrad's central thematic conflict of sympathy and egoism. In the same journal Giles Mitchell takes a psychoanalytic approach to Lord Jim who emerges as a troubled neurotic rather than a flawed romantic; the title, 'Lord Jim's Death

Fear, Narcissism, and Suicide', suggests the basic argument. Sea symbolism in the novel interests Joseph Dobrinsky (*CVE*), but little new light is shed on the text by his essay.

Some lively work has been done on *The Secret Agent*. In 'Conrad's Irony: "An Outpost of Progress" and *The Secret Agent*' (*Conradian*) Gail Fraser intelligently demonstrates how the rhetorical devices used in the short story to evoke the reader's moral evaluation of 'an inhumane and materialistic society' foreshadow the ironic techniques used by Conrad to present 'his vision of social and moral disorder' in the novel. *MLR* has a robust article by Martin Ray entitled 'Conrad, Wells, and *The Secret Agent*'. Ray sees Conrad's novel as a coded attack on Wells's scientific optimism and sociological ideas (despite the dedication); such a view accounts for the breakdown of the writers' friendship and the vicious attack on Conrad in *Tono-Bungay*. More Wellsian connections are supplied by the same critic's piece on 'Conrad's Invisible Professor', linking *The Invisible Man* to *The Secret Agent* (*Conradian*) in a speculative fashion.

Coded meanings and enigmas also interest Graham Holderness and Graham McMaster who look at the novel from different but valuable perspectives. Holderness's '"Life Doesn't Stand Much Looking Into": The Secret of *The Secret Agent*' (*DUJ*) explores the connection between anarchy, terrorism, and personal relationships in the novel. Perceptive close textual reading supports the provocative view that the novel 'rejects all ideology' as incapable of providing for or expressing human values; thus, Conrad's only 'imaginative commitment . . . is to the Professor's dream of total annihilation'. In *L&H* Graham McMaster puts the novel in a wider contemporary political context. He discloses 'Some Other Secrets in *The Secret Agent*', namely that the novel serves as xenophobic propaganda with its deftly coded intimations that Germans are 'ferocious if technological savages'. Only 'the British version of empire [is] pure'.

The neglected later works are also coming in now for serious scholarly attention and their reputation is correspondingly enhanced. Gene M. Moore (*Conradiana*) writes on 'Chronotopes and Voices in *Under Western Eyes*', in an effort to apply Mikhail Bakhtin's theory on 'modes of time – space' to the problems of the '"double authority" of the text'. This is a dense and difficult piece which rewards careful reading. Not only does it develop the novel's connection to the East/West debate; it does this by shedding important light on the suspect authority of both Razumov and the narrator which curiously signals 'their mutual dialogic interdependence' and the relation of their discourse to the chronotopes of East (Petersburg) and West (Geneva). In the same journal can be found 'The Ambiguity of Razumov's Confession in *Under Western Eyes*', a neatly complementary essay by Thomas J. Cousineau. This piece is also concerned with centres of authority, though from a more psychoanalytic perspective, since Cousineau's reading shows how the text indicts 'paternal authority' and proposes alternatives 'in the feminine and the maternal'. This essay should be read in conjunction with yet another *Conradiana* article, 'The Name-of-the-Father in Conrad's *Under Western Eyes*', by Josiane Paccaud who adopts a Lacanian approach to issues of parentage, identity, and naming in the novel. Although not all readers will welcome such a perspective, this essay is quite suggestive in the way in which it isolates Razumov's tragedy as 'nameless', 'lawless hero' and also reads the 'socio-historic context as a metaphor for . . . the conflict between an individual's imaginary world and the symbolic order at the root of human culture'. The same critic writes in *EA* (in French) on 'Trahison, parole et verité dans *Under Western Eyes* de Joseph Conrad' in an attempt to foreground structural and thematic links between political treason and language. Adam Gillon takes a more traditional, but useful, approach in 'Conrad's Satirical Stance in *Under Western Eyes*', tracing thematic and textual connections and dissimilarities between Conrad's only Polish story ('Prince Roman') and the novel. Setting off Peter Ivanovitch with a truly heroic Prince is a way of easing a patriotic dilemma. This article is in *Conradiana*, as is David Leon Higdon's bibliographical study of variants in '"Word for Word": The Collected Editions of Conrad's *Under Western Eyes*'. Higdon convincingly suggests that Conrad avoided careful revision of this text as it caused him emotional pain. 'Conrad's Feminine Grotesques' in *Under Western Eyes*, *Chance*, and *The Arrow of Gold* interest Anne Luyat (*Conradian*) in an essay which contains some fascinating material put forward in a somewhat disjointed and undeveloped form. Luyat does not venture much beyond showing basic effects of the juxtapositioning of grotesque and idealized female characters. The essay is useful, though, in indicating where further work can be done on Conrad's women, and on his handling of fantasy and the comic.

Tony Tanner's 'Joseph Conrad and the Last Gentleman' in *CritQ* is a vibrant and wide-ranging essay which surveys the history and uses of the word 'gentleman' in the nineteenth century, the ideological baggage the term carries, and Conrad's use of the term in *Victory* (particularly with reference to Heyst). What is revealed is the 'decorous impotence' of the gentleman caught between the body and language, neither of which he can in the end control. Tanner also includes valuable material on connections between Darwin and the novel. In a minor vein Jeffrey Meyers notes connections between 'The Ranee of Sarawak and Conrad's *Victory*', and Anne Luyat-Moore tentatively suggests some strained parallels between Strindberg and Conrad in 'The Swedish Connection to *Victory* and *Chance*' (both in *Conradiana*).

A range of other works by Conrad also comes in for scrutiny. In 'Untyrannical Copy-Texts for the Prefatory Essays to Joseph Conrad's *A Personal Record*' Jean M. Szczypien conscientiously applies bibliographical principles of Fredson Bowers and W. W. Greg to the Preface and Author's Note; but the conclusion – Conrad is a difficult author to edit – is somewhat flat (*Conradian*). J. H. Stape writes briefly in the same journal on 'Conrad's "The Duel"', suggesting that its flaws actually show Conrad's interest 'in fictional modes and narrative strategies' developed more successfully in later work. The same author writes straightforwardly in *N&Q* on 'The Date and Writing of Conrad's "Stephen Crane: A Note Without Dates"'. Juliet McLauchlan re-assesses 'Conrad's Heart of Emptiness: "The Planter of Malta"' in a valuable piece which connects the novelist's non-naturalistic narrative techniques to his thematic interest in the 'destructive power of illusion' (*Conradiana*). Also in *Conradiana* Michael Murphy chats about the unreliable narrator in '"The Secret Sharer": Conrad's Turn of the Winch', and Mary Ann Dazey offers a brief note on some titular ambiguities in 'Shared Secret or Secret Sharing in Joseph Conrad's "The Secret Sharer"'. The significance of the sea in 'The End of the Tether' is the focus of François Lombard's essay (in French) in *CVE*.

Bibliographical matters include Donald W. Rude's description of aspects of the 'Joseph Conrad Letters, Typescripts, and Proofs in the Texas Tech Conrad

Collection' (*Conradian*) and the same critic's 'Three Bibliographical Notes on Conrad' (on 'Typhoon', 'Legends', and 'Geography and Some Explorers') in *Conradiana*. In *Conradian* Owen Knowles offers two important contributions for all Conrad scholars: his annotated checklist of material relevant to Conrad in 'Recent General Studies and Collections' and his bibliographical essay, 'The Year's Work in Conrad Studies, 1985: A Survey of Periodical Literature'. Jan Verleun and Jetty de Vries choose to focus on eight books on Conrad from the early 1980s in the *ELT* article, 'Conrad Criticism Today: An Evaluation of Recent Conrad Scholarship'. The assessment, however, is rather stiff and prescriptive, and clearly is based on a dislike of current trends and approaches in Conrad criticism. Both *Conradiana* and *Conradian* continue to offer a range of enlightening reviews and notices. Patricia Ann Carlson's collection of essays, *Literature and Lore of the Sea* (Rodopi), was not available for review but according to reports contains an essay by Robert Foulke on elegiac conventions in *The Mirror of the Sea*. Harold Bloom has edited a collection of modern critical views, *Joseph Conrad* (ChelseaH), but this was also unavailable.

Material on Conan Doyle has been quite limited this year. *Aficionados* might find room on their shelves for *Sherlock Holmes: A Centenary Celebration*[49]. This lavishly illustrated coffee-table book traces Conan Doyle's creation of the Holmes–Watson team and goes on to survey the Holmes 'phenomenon', including the various stage adaptations and film versions, as well as parodies, other detective-types modelled on Holmes, and television productions. While Allen Eyles does manage to convey a sense of Conan Doyle's own imprisonment by his creation and his failing inspiration (he was driven to purchasing 'readers' suggestions'), he does little more in his analysis of the stories than recount plots and comment simply on characters and new departures. The bibliography offers a useful list of 'Sherlock Holmes in Performance'. Graham Nown also anticipates the centenary in 1987 with a popular study[50], again surveying familiar ground with copious illustrations from book jackets, engravings, and photographs. He does ring the changes a bit, though, with a section devoted to crime and London street-life in the late Victorian period, the rise of detection and policing as professions, and a glossary of Victorian underworld slang. Both these books, however, are clearly designed for the enthusiastic amateur or general reader, rather than for those with a more scholarly interest in Conan Doyle's most popular character.

M. R. James is a rather neglected figure whose ghost stories may well prove of critical interest with the increase of theoretical work on fantasy literature and the Gothic. Such a revival of interest might be partly stimulated at any rate by two books. Michael Cox's well-written and readable biography of 1983 has appeared in paperback[51]. Cox gives some sense of James's background, antiquarian interests, and significant involvement in British education in the early part of the twentieth century (as Provost of King's College, Cambridge, Vice-

49. *Sherlock Holmes: A Centenary Celebration*, comp. by Allen Eyles. Murray. pp. 144. £10.95.

50. *Elementary My Dear Watson: Sherlock Holmes Centenary: His Life and Times*, by Graham Nown. WL. pp. 143. £12.95.

51. *M. R. James: An Informal Portrait*, by Michael Cox. OUP. pp. xviii + 268. pb £5.95.

Chancellor of that University, and Provost of Eton). Cox clearly highlights major themes in the fiction, but literary analysis is subordinate to his interest in providing an 'informal' study of the life. While James emerges as a formidable scholar and likeable person, there is an unfortunate Mr Chips-ish air to the completed portrait. Michael Cox has also selected and introduced some of James's ghost stories[52], including 'The Mezzotint', 'A Warning to the Curious', and the posthumous 'A Vignette'. His introduction draws attention to James's curious ability to unite the fantastic and the 'real', and he carefully focuses on James's use of scholarly conventions and documentation to give his diabolical tales a haunting plausibility. Cox also gives a lead to future critics when he suggests some further avenues of exploration, not least James's presentation of 'a bleak and anarchic' world. There is a helpful select bibliography.

1986 saw the fiftieth anniversary of Kipling's death, and some interesting critical offerings emerged by way of commemoration. B. J. Moore-Gilbert has done important groundwork in his study of Kipling and the 'characteristic discourses of Anglo-Indian culture'[53]. Parting company with Edward Said's view in *Orientalism*, Moore-Gilbert argues that there were actually two versions of the Western 'Oriental' discourse used to dominate and restructure Eastern experience: the metropolitan version emanating from the mother-country, and the Anglo-Indian version employed by those in the colony who saw themselves as an autonomous 'ideological, social and cultural group'. Moore-Gilbert surveys the discourses used by the British and Anglo-Indian communities to express their views on such issues as empire management, the social life of the community, the Mutiny and its aftermath, and demoralization, earnestly and comprehensively including an impressive range of somewhat obscure, second-rate journalism, fiction, and the like; and the wide scope of material consulted adds weight to Moore-Gilbert's contention that Kipling shared a cultural identity with the Anglo-Indian community, expressing their lack of confidence in imperial rule, unlike the metropolitan view from Britain. He too was anxious about the devaluation and destruction of Indian culture, and this book is thought-provoking in its concern with the narrative means used by Kipling to express his anxieties. But Moore-Gilbert also forthrightly concedes that the Anglo-Indian version of 'Orientalism' could offer no alternatives to the relationship between its own culture and that of India; Kipling, among other writers of the Anglo-Indian view, were 'trapped by the political realities out of which "Orientalism" emerged'. This book has provided Kipling scholars with a wealth of source material which will undoubtedly play a part in any re-assessments of the writer's ideological stance.

KJ should also be consulted by those with a scholarly interest in the writer. In addition to notes, reviews, letters, and memoirs, some valuable articles appeared this year. The most significant of these include Ann Parry's two-part piece on 'Imperialism in "The Bridge-Builders"' which offers a close textual reading of the story and sets it in the context of imperialist attitudes in the Britain of 1893. K. M. Wilson prints a rediscovered manuscript version of the poem, 'The English Flag', Tom Pinney introduces and annotates a reprint of an

---

52. *The Ghost Stories of M. R. James*, sel. by Michael Cox, illus. by Rosalind Caldecott. OUP. pp. 224. £12.95.

53. *Kipling and 'Orientalism'*, by B. J. Moore-Gilbert. CH. pp. viii + 228. £18.95.

anonymous Kipling dialogue, 'Premiers at Play', and a pseudonymous 1912 letter to the *Morning Post*, 'Furor Teutonicus' (on the German menace to the Empire). Nora Crook finds echoes of Dante's *Inferno* in 'The Strange Ride of Morrowbie Jukes' (though these seem quite forced), Elizabeth M. Knowles tracks down some obscure allusions in 'Fairy-Kist', and E. N. Houlton attempts to connect 'Dayspring Mishandled' to Kipling's own life. Links between Kipling and R. S. Surtees interest Frank Brightman, and, perhaps more centrally, Paul Beale comments on rare or arcane words (many from Sussex speech) in Kipling's vocabulary. Christopher Redmond's piece on Conan Doyle's visit to the Kiplings in Vermont in 1894 does not really advance understanding of either author, but J. E. Monro and J. J. Ross provide more substantial fare in their articles. Monro considers *The Light that Failed* 'a study in defective personality' and explores the importance of childhood psychological trauma and delayed sexual development for the novel as a whole. Ross's piece, a workmanlike and crisp essay entitled 'An English History: Kipling's Joint Authorship, with C. R. L. Fletcher, of *A School History of England* (1911)', treats the collaboration between Kipling and Fletcher and assesses the textbook's optimistic Victorian attitude to history and empire in relation to Kipling's other works.

ELT devotes two complete issues to Kipling; these contain varied work, but some very stimulating criticism does emerge, much of it serving to revive Kipling's reputation as a writer of some subtlety and interest. The best general article is Elliot L. Gilbert's 'Silence and Survival in Rudyard Kipling's Art and Life' which connects Kipling's own silence about personal traumas and grief to his artistic penchant for '*aposiopesis*, the rhetorical tactic whose purpose is to withhold some final revelation'. Gilbert imaginatively suggests that Kipling's silences reveal truth best, and offers a re-assessment of the author as part Victorian and part Modernist from this perspective. John Bayley also writes informatively on a wide span of Kipling's fiction in 'The False Structure', which argues that the increasing unreality of Kipling's stories enables the writer to reveal truths often ignored or repressed. Truth most readily appears under the comforting and paradoxical guise of 'different modes of falsity'. More specifically Harry Ricketts offers 'Kipling and the War: A Reading of *Debits and Credits*' which is largely successful in persuading us that the text should be read *as a whole*, since there is a complex 'multiple layering' technique between the stories. John Coates also considers a collection in 'Thor and Tyr: Sacrifice, Necessary Suffering, and the Battle Against Disorder in *Rewards and Fairies*'; Coates defends this unjustly neglected text, suggesting quite cogently that it marks a watershed in the fiction since in it Kipling uses myth and legend to mediate a darker view of life as a place of sacrifice and suffering. Andrew Rutherford provides a scholarly piece on the poetry. He illustrates in 'News and the Muse: Press Sources for Some of Kipling's Early Verse' that many of the topics and allusions in the poems were drawn from Anglo-Indian newspapers for which Kipling worked from 1882–9. Nora Foster Stovel makes quite a lot of a fairly conventional little Christmas poem in 'The "Inky *Gamin*" and the "Egotistical Tongue": Viewing Kipling the Person and the Poet through an Unpublished Poem'.

Individual texts also receive close attention in *ELT*. 'Mary Postgate' fascinates two critics: Norman Page argues enthusiastically for the 'ambiguity' of the story, suggesting that Mary is the victim of a hallucination. Another story, 'Swept and Garnished', shows how to answer the question Page poses in the title: 'What Happens in "Mary Postgate"?'. Lisa A. F. Lewis is much less convincing in her discovery of 'Kipling's Jane: Some Echoes of Austen', which focuses primarily on 'Mary Postgate' and 'The Gardener'. One of the richest articles is by William J. Scheick who, by examining 'Hesitation in Kipling's "The Phantom 'Rickshaw"' in the light of Todorov's concept of the fantastic with its patterns of hesitation, clearly establishes the artistic dexterity and importance of this early story. Also arguing for a neglected early text is Pierre Coustillas in '*The Light that Failed* or Artistic Bohemia as Self-Revelation'. The case for the novel is made through an appreciation of its presentation of Bohemia and a comparison of it to other works on the subject. Kipling, it is suggested a bit limply, reveals his 'fragile emotional stability as a young man' despite the work's obvious imperfections. 'Suppression, Textuality, Entanglement, and Revenge in Kipling's "Dayspring Mishandled"' is a deconstruction of the text by Terry Caesar. Finding 'Dayspring Mishandled' 'divided against itself', Caesar demonstrates what it represses through its omission, silences, and 'incomplete disclosures', thus showing how Kipling's work responds in fruitful ways to poststructuralist approaches. Thomas Pinney offers a preliminary survey of Kipling collections in libraries, and Thomas B. Bagle introduces and prints the late Howard Rice Jr's introduction to a proposed book entitled 'Kipling's Vermont Period'.

Robert H. MacDonald also applies new critical approaches to Kipling (*SSF*) in a heavy-handed essay, 'Discourse and Ideology in Kipling's "Beyond the Pale"', which looks at the tale's evasions, equivocations, and disjunctions between what is promised and what is delivered. He concludes that Kipling shows how the values of a dominant privileged discourse can sow discord, but can also be subverted. Robert Crawford's 'Rudyard Kipling in *The Waste Land*' (*EIC*) gamely suggests that the influence of certain Kipling texts (e.g. 'The Finest Story in the World') can be seen in Eliot's poem, and that Kipling himself was more in tune with Modernist interests ('the things which are underneath', 'the things which are beyond the frontier') than might be acknowledged. In *N&Q* Allan Hunter offers 'Kipling to Clifford: A Rediscovered Correspondence', printing letters from Kipling to Sir Hugh Clifford, a garrulous colonial administrator, minor author, and friend of Conrad – the interest lying in what they show of Kipling's colonial preoccupations.

Robert Crossley[54] deals with Wells's science fiction and fantasy fiction from *The Time Machine* to *First Men in the Moon* as well as touching on the short fiction. His book is clearly intended as an introductory guide, and it does little to dislodge a commonplace view of Wells as a Darwinist and utopian socialist. However, although the overview assessments offered at times seem rather superficial and sweepingly appreciative of Wells's ability to upset 'mental and moral inertia', the individual chapters devoted to the fiction show some concern with narrative methods as well as central attitudes and themes. The general reader or student will come away with a portrait of Wells as 'the great disillusioner' bent in his fantasy on offering 'exhilaration, reflection, and admonition'.

54. *H. G. Wells*, by Robert Crossley. Starmont. pp. 79. hb $15.95, pb $7.95.

David C. Smith has written his biography of Wells[55] from the perspective of a sympathetic admirer. Finding Wells 'a man for all times', Smith attributes a wide range of achievements to his subject – in fact everything from his mediation of evolutionary and other scientific discoveries to the general populace and his broadening of the possibilities of the didactic novel to his 'marvellous role in the opening out of modern feminism', his encouragement of experimental writers, and his formulation of 'a Universal Declaration of Human Rights'. To some readers of Wells this might seem rather fulsome praise. Smith does provide a wealth of detail (including a precise account of the creatures Wells analysed in his mammal anatomy course); but his discussion of other pertinent aspects of Wells's life such as his relationships with Rebecca Wells and Dorothy Richardson seem rather one-sided in their generosity (to Wells who is depicted as a gracious man who 'fell in love easily'). Wells's relationships with other major literary figures like Conrad and Gissing, his sometimes testy connections with publishers, and his efforts on behalf of socialism are all described, and Smith takes pains to justify his vision of Wells as a major prophet of our century. But in the end this biography does lack a certain grittiness and distance in its approach to its subject.

A varied range of articles have appeared on Wells this year. Michael J. Bugeja writes in *NDQ* on '"Culture and Anarchy" in *The War of the Worlds*', testing, with some originality, Wells's novel as an enactment of Arnold's ideas. John Allett's piece in *QQ* ('*Tono-Bungay*: The Metaphor of Disease in H. G. Wells's Novel') is an attempt to link metaphors of disease to Wells's critique of capitalism. The basic idea seems valid enough but the specific diagnosis (tuberculosis) is somewhat worrying! In terms of essay work on Wells, however, pride of place should go to a collection of articles[56] prepared to accompany an exhibition on Wells mounted by Champaign Public Library. A number of these make for engaging reading. In addition to Michael Mullin's overview of the Wells collection at the University of Illinois, Patrick Parrinder writes succinctly and thoughtfully on Wells as writer-prophet (both 'sage' and 'foreteller'), Frank McConnell comments briskly on Wells's influence on early cinema, and Mark Hillegas offers a valuable generic study in his essay on Wells's contribution to utopian fiction. Richard Hauer Costa covers fairly familiar biographical/social ground in an imaginative way in his attempt to recreate Wells's feelings and attitudes on 4 August, 1914. Also looking at familiar material is Leon Stover who does challenge many critical assumptions by arguing that the Darwinism of Wells was both different from T. H. Huxley's version – and more sinister. Melissa Cain offers an annotated selected bibliography of writings by and about Wells to round out this sparky collection.

Attention is directed again this year to the correspondence of Arnold Bennett with the appearance of a valuable new volume devoted to *Family Letters*[57]. Over four hundred letters have been selected from Bennett's extant correspondence to his brother, sister, two wives, and his adopted son/nephew,

55. *H. G. Wells: Desperately Mortal: A Biography*, by David C. Smith. Yale. pp. xviii + 634. £18.50.

56. *H. G. Wells: Reality and Beyond: A Collection of Critical Essays Prepared in Conjunction with the Exhibition and Symposium on H. G. Wells*, ed. by Michael Mullin. Champaign. pp. 91. pb. $5.

57. *Letters of Arnold Bennett*. Vol. IV: *Family Letters*, ed. by James Hepburn with trans. by Rosamund Howe. OUP. pp. xxxviii + 638. £45.

Richard. Many of these have not been previously published or have appeared with major excisions which are now restored. Insights are provided into Bennett's personal relationships, most notably with respect to his romantic and sexual life, as seen through erotic letters of violation and desire. Bennett also appears as a hearty and generous family man; but as James Hepburn points out in his lively and informed introduction, the letters also provide a counterweight to this picture in their glimpses of a harsh individual dealing 'mean-spiritedly' and often injudiciously with the women in his life. In addition to this pertinent introduction, the correspondence is capably edited and adequate supporting annotation is supplied.

Michael John McDonough (*ELT*) highlights an obscure relationship between a major and a minor writer in 'Arnold Bennett and Archibald Marshall: Two Letters from a Forgotten Literary Friendship'. The letters' main interest really lies in their confirmation of Bennett's focus on the importance of characterization through event and conflict. Three essays on Bennett's realism can be found in *CVE*. A. Denjean writes in French on the realist discourse of the Five-Towns novels, supplying cogent analysis of those narrative techniques used to handle the essential contradiction in the realist's project (to present 'objective' truth by disguising the fictive, illusionary nature of the text). J. Lucas's 'The Marriage Question and *Whom God Hath Joined*' is a sharply perceived discussion of the way in which Bennett draws on contemporary 'scientific' work on sexual types of explore 'the psycho-pathology of marriage', though always in a subtle and oblique way. In '"The Lion's Share": Essais sur le réalisme d'Arnold Bennett' Alain Blayac neatly demonstrates how Bennett's techniques of realism in this story, written before he had much knowledge of Russian fiction, enable him to transform a mimetic text gradually into a moral fable.

Robert Viscusi draws eclectically on poststructural theories to examine Beerbohm's cultivated pose as a dandy[58]. Despite a jargony, convoluted, and, at times, affected style, this is a worthwhile study, for it offers a revision of the tradition of dandyism and a reconsideration of Beerbohm's importance within the developments of literature at the turn of the century. Viscusi argues that the dandy code implies a view of self as constructed or written, and offers a particularly subtle vantage point from which to critique social mores and to 'explore and exploit the unconscious'. Beerbohm, it is suggested, transformed dandyism from the art of self-indulgent narcissism to a self-reflexive commentary on the condition of all moderns: 'in his final transformation, the dandy speaks the word not merely of the other-in-the-mirror but of a more absolute Other, of the mirror itself, the mirror as sign of our divided and irrecoverable condition'. The parodist thus emerges as a kind of Modernist in disguise and, to strengthen his case for Beerbohm's interest today, Viscusi rereads *Zuleika Dobson* with particular emphasis on the arts of 'parallel and paralogy'. This novel, it would seem, is almost postmodernist in its structure, for it ultimately deconstructs both writer/dandy and the reader simultaneously, its parallels and doubling of Homer and Dante offering a complex commentary on love and truth which, like dandy desire, are constantly absent and deferred. More modest but still offering an important repositioning of Beerbohm within the

58. *Max Beerbohm, or The Dandy Dante: Rereading with Mirrors*, by Robert Viscusi. JHU. pp. xvi + 267. £17.75.

Terry Caesar's piece in *ArielE*, 'Betrayal and Theft: Beerbohm, Parody, and Modernism', which makes a case for Beerbohm's parodic art as a modernist attempt to reject '"false orders"' and find new strategies of literary representation.

The Ford Madox Ford Reader[59] is a welcome attempt to create new devotees of this rather neglected writer. Although there is insufficient space for a full novel, there are extracts from a substantial number (though not from *The Good Soldier* or *Parade's End* since these are in print). More significant is the ample selection from Ford's reminiscences, literary criticism (including portraits of Wells, Bennett, Hardy, and Wyndham Lewis), cultural and art criticism, poetry, and letters. This volume succeeds in its aim of giving a sense of the scope of Ford's accomplishments as well as a taste of his own strong personality and decided views, and the introduction provides a straightforward assessment of Ford's strengths and major preoccupations, together with sufficient detail to enable readers to contextualize the various selections biographically and historically. Readers looking for primary material by Ford might also be interested in *YR* this year which reprints certain articles to celebrate its seventy-fifth anniversary. The autumn issue contains Ford's defensive 1929 essay on 'Working with Conrad' which explicates their friendship as much as their methods of collaboration.

In *JNT* Richard Creese compares Ford and Greene without altering critical views of the novelists too much in 'Abstracting and Recording Narration in *The Good Soldier* and *The End of the Affair*'. The emphasis is on a fastidious refinement of terminology in narrative criticism ('telling' and 'scene' are too vague – 'abstracting' and 'recording' narration are better) and a linking of Ford to the Modernists because of his preference for psychological processes and 'mental' reality. Greene, on the other hand, despite his admiration for Ford, uses narrators who purport to record the direct experience of the physical world. 'Ford Madox Ford and the Christina Rossetti Influence' in *ELT* is Grover Smith's plucky attempt to explain why Ford admired Rossetti and how his poetry was affected by this appreciation (with emphasis on 'an artistic engagement with emotions and objects of feeling'). In 'Arcadia and Armageddon: Three English Novelists and the First World War' (*EA*) John Bate thoughtfully compares the treatment of war in Ralph Hale Mottram's *The Spanish Farm Trilogy* (1927), Ford's *Parade's End*, and Woolf's *Jacob's Room* and *To the Lighthouse*. He concludes that Ford's work is the most impressive, encompassing the diverse effects of Mottram's and Woolf's explorations of the Great War. Vincent J. Cheng challenges Ford's pride in his eye for detail by establishing that Dowell is writing his novel some months after its publication on 17 March, 1915 ('A Chronology of *The Good Soldier*', *ELN*). Finally, Martin Ray picks up on 'Ford Madox Ford at Folkestone', offering extracts from letters by one of Ford's teachers there in order to clarify and correct claims made by some biographers (*N&Q*).

Elisabeth Bronfen's *Der literarische Raum*[60] investigates the notion of

59. *The Ford Madox Ford Reader*, ed. by Sondra J. Strang, foreword by Graham Greene. Carcanet. pp. xxviii + 515. £18.95.

60. *Der literarische Raum: Eine Untersuchung am Beispiel von Dorothy M. Richardsons Romanzyklus Pilgrimage*, by Elisabeth Bronfen. Niemeyer. pp. x + 373. pb DM 126.

literary space both generally and with particular reference to Dorothy M. Richardson's *Pilgrimage* cycle. This double focus produces unevenness and much repetition, especially in the theoretical sections, which remain somewhat divorced from the analysis of *Pilgrimage* itself. Bronfen's intention is to reveal the intellectual and formal coherence of Richardson's novel-cycle by analysing how space is used, and thereby also to develop 'a generally valid model for describing literary space' and a 'general theory of reading and space'. Bronfen argues that Miriam's sense of identity develops via 'a process of world-making' and self-definition partly by means of spatial metaphors, and also speculates on the possibility of conceiving the whole text as space: this establishes a possible analogy between reading and the experience and recognition of space so that Richardson's method in *Pilgrimage* is an example of spatial textuality. While disagreeing with Joseph Frank and his followers about the priority of space over time, Bronfen prefers Genette's notion that a narrative *produces* space, and goes on to examine the simultaneity and reversibility of the text, and Richardson's techniques which help the reader to produce the text. *Der literarische Raum* does partly justify its starting point, Dorothy M. Richardson's response to the question, 'What would you most like to do, to know, to be', in 1929 when she claimed she would most like to 'build a cottage on a cliff . . . be perfectly in two places at once', and examine 'the goings-on of metaphors': Bronfen convincingly argues for the centrality of spatial awareness. [E.A.M.]

Michael Ffinch's biography of Chesterton[61] draws on original sources to focus on his subject's gradual move from Liberal Unitarianism to Roman Catholicism as a way of upholding his belief in 'the cause of Liberty'. This is an earnest and diligent account of the man and the writer, and Ffinch is keen to give a sense of Chesterton's many talents. Chesterton's pose as the 'jolly journalist' is certainly an ironically understated one; but Ffinch's corrective – the anguished intellectual – seems to be an overstatement in the other direction. There is interesting material here on Chesterton's literary friendships, on his political beliefs and antisemitism, and on his day-to-day activities and pet-hates. But in the end, no new, distinctive sense of Chesterton's personal presence really emerges, and one is inclined to agree with Malcolm Muggeridge's assessment of the man: 'Though so huge, he seemed to have no substance: more a balloon than an elephant'.

Each issue of *CRev* contains reviews, news, comments, and letters of interest to those working on Chesterton. In addition a number of critical articles are printed, of which the most valuable might be selected. Ian Boyd considers 'Chesterton on Censorship', providing an introduction to and reprinting of Chesterton's evidence in 1909 to a Joint Select Committee on censorship of the stage. D. J. Dooley's pert discussion of *The Ball and the Cross* is entitled 'The Ball With or Without the Cross: How the Great Debate Is Resolved in Chesterton and Orwell'. Dooley ably places the novel in the context of the contemporary debate on Providence versus Chance. John Wren-Lewis has an autobiographically based essay on the same novel. In 'Joy without a Cause' he considers Chesterton's depiction of 'mystic-consciousness'. David L. Derus's clear comparison of 'Gissing and Chesterton as Critics of Dickens' lines the writers up in an historical/realist versus romantic confrontation, with

61. *G. K. Chesterton*, by Michael Ffinch. W&N. pp. xiv + 369. £16.

Chesterton emerging as the more witty, fresh, and original commentator on Dickens. This article might be read in tandem with Peter Hunt's 'A Note on R. C. Churchill's Defence of Chesterton on Dickens' which emphasizes Chesterton's appreciation of Dickens's 'social radicalism and symbolic power'. Also interesting is an essay by Aidan Nichols, O.P. who explores 'G. K. Chesterton's Argument for the Existence of God' based on the phenomenon of joy without a cause. The second issue is devoted to Hilaire Belloc, with articles by Gerard Slevin, John P. McCarthy, Jane Soames Nickerson, James V. Schall, Edward N. Peters, Jay P. Corrin, Ralph J. Coffman, and Michael H. Markel on a variety of literary, political, and philosophical aspects of that writer. In the third issue John Coates ably fills in 'The Philosophy and Religious Background of *The Flying Inn*' to restore interest in that neglected novel. Also deserving of mention is 'Broad Swaths and Deep Cuts', an attempt by James E. Barcus to compare the 'autobiographical impulse' in Chesterton and C. S. Lewis, though the conclusion is disappointingly limp (they have little intellectually in common). Judy A. Kroetsch's comparison of Father Brown and Miss Marple is also disappointing in its somewhat naïve treatment of both characters as detectives. Not all the contributions in the fourth issue are germane to the critical study of Chesterton, but attention can be drawn to Stephen Miller's offering which charts Chesterton's influence on Gonzalo Torrente Ballester, the Spanish writer (who gives an interview in the same number).

Six stories of the colonial, expatriate world in Malaysia by W. Somerset Maugham[62] have been collected and published in paperback. There is no introduction (a pity) but Maugham's own recollection of his 'perfect servant' during a Malaysian journey is reprinted as preface. In *ELT* Alistair McCleery analyses John Buchan's attitude to Scottish identity. 'John Buchan and the Path of the Keen' depicts the novelist as unhappily caught between a determination to reject the image of the caricatured Scot and a refusal to collude with a North British ideology which denies any separate Scottish identity. The way in which this debate is enacted in *Witch Wood* and Buchan's own expatriate life gives the article an original perspective.

Daniel R. Schwarz[63] has spotted a trend in Anglo-American criticism of the novel genre which he calls 'humanistic formalism', and which he vigorously defends (despite its apparent lack of self-consciousness at times) as a definite school with identifiable assumptions and a firm intellectual underpinning. Critics from James through Lubbock, Leavis, Booth, Watt, Frye, Kettle, and J. Hillis Miller are all participants in this tradition, though some favour a more formalistic/aesthetic approach, and others an empirical/humanistic focus. Forster of course is represented by a chapter on the importance of *Aspects of the Novel*. Despite Forster's woolliness as an analyser of novel form and conventions (he has a 'lack of theoretical sophistication' as Schwarz puts it), the chapter insists that Forster had insights which made him important at his moment – his emphasis on 'the rhetorical function of characterization', for example. More suggestive is the connection Schwarz spots between the two parts of *Aspects* and early/late Forster fiction; the literary criticism 'enacts

---

62. *'Ah King' and Other Stories*, by W. Somerset Maugham. OUP. pp. iv + 339. pb £4.95.

63. *The Humanistic Heritage: Critical Theories of the English Novel from James to Hillis Miller*, by Daniel R. Schwarz. Macmillan. pp. viii + 282. £29.50.

Forster's values' even in its style. Schwarz's summation of Forster's particular 'humanistic' achievement – he was primarily concerned with 'how aspects of the novel related to aspects of our lives' – is neat enough, but smacks of that blandness which some poststructuralists deem a failing in liberal-humanist criticism overall.

Hilda D. Spear's introductory study-guide to *A Passage to India*[64] contains the usual simplified summation of life, background, and each chapter of the novel. However, the second section which deals with themes, issues, and their relationship to political concerns is not too reductive for a sixth-form student. It is a shame, though, that there is so little on narrative method and style, especially since a sample close reading of a passage is offered as a hint to examinees.

Much more scholarly is the revised edition of B. J. Kirkpatrick's sound bibliography[65]. As with the first edition, the bibliographical information is admirably comprehensive, and the volume now contains a section on 'Audio-Visual Material' and, most helpfully, 'Manuscripts' (with locations). Evelyne Hanquart's review article in *EA*, 'Forsteriana des années quatre-vingts', is also useful.

In '*The Hill of Devi and Heat and Dust*' (*EIC*) Richard Cronin takes an inter-textual line, focusing on the extent to which Ruth Prawer Jhabvala's novel is bound to other literary predecessors, such as Forster and also Malcolm Darling and J. R. Ackerley. Along the way he suggests that the real meaning of Forster's experience in *The Hill of Devi* was carefully repressed and then subtly displaced in *A Passage to India*. In *ArielE* Shirley Chew considers 'Fictions of Princely States and Empire', using *The Hill of Devi* as a background text for consideration of the Indian prince in works by Mulk Raj Anand, Manohar Malgonkar, and Ruth Prawer Jhabvala. In *SNNTS* Doreen D'Cruz is not satis-fied by old readings of *Passage* as a simple dialectic between Being and Non-being. Instead, by 'Emptying and Filling Along the Existential Coil in *A Passage to India*' she finds two journeys in the novel – one to the void of the Caves, the other to the creative climax in the Temple; both 'constitute the two rungs of an eternal coil', so that all become part of an eternal flow. The essay has a point but seems rather belaboured. Francis A. de Caro neatly investigates the relationship of proverbs to truth in '"A Mystery Is a Muddle": Gnomic Expressions in *A Passage to India*' (*MJLF*). In 'Forster's Friends' Rustom Bharucha re-examines homosexuality in the novel, reviewing Forster's relation-ship to Syed Ross Masood (*Raritan*), but a more searching article on homo-sexuality and Forster is to be found in Tariq Rahman's 'Edward Carpenter and E. M. Forster' (*DUJ*). Carpenter's ideas on homosexual love are transformed into 'private myths' in Forster's fiction, according to Rahman, who makes his case quite delicately and shows also how Forster began to move away from Carpenter's views by the time he wrote *Passage*. The same critic follows up his interest in 'Edward Carpenter's *From Adam's Peak to Elephanta* as a Source for E. M. Forster's *A Passage to India*' (*FMLS*). In *N&Q* Safaa Hegazi corrects earlier views on 'The Date and First Publication of Two Essays by E. M. Forster' ('Shakespeare in Egypt' and 'Eliza in Egypt'). *Narcissism and the*

---

64. '*A Passage to India' by E. M. Forster*, by Hilda D. Spear. Macmillan. pp. xii + 82. £0.99.

65. *A Bibliography of E. M. Forster*, by B. J. Kirkpatrick, with a foreword by E. M. Forster. Second rev. edn. Clarendon (1985). pp. xvi + 327. £40.

Text: Studies in Literature and the Psychology of Self, edited by Lynne Layton and Barbara Ann Schapiro (NYU), was not available for review, but contains a psychoanalytic–biographical essay by Peer Hultberg on maternal betrayal in Forster's fiction.

One of the best works this year has been Cheryl Herr's *Joyce's Anatomy of Culture*[66] which follows Said and Jameson in attempting to re-instate texts in their cultural surroundings. By examining specific allusions and, on a macro-level, 'the process of alluding', Herr sets out to show how Joyce interacted with and reacted against social conventions and ideological assumptions. The specific frame of reference for this study is provided by three cultural institutions: the press (the 'primary shaper of consciousness in modern Dublin'), the stage (popular plays and music hall), and the church (notably sermons). Herr's belief – and her careful research bears her out – is that 'the process of allusion in Joyce points to the cultural dynamics by which these major institutions competed for discursive power over the demotic mind'. For this reason, her book is doubly important: it serves as an excellent model for dissecting a culture, drawing attention to the historical conditions affecting the production of popular forms of communication and to the ideological subtexts beneath these forms. Moreover, it clearly places Joyce – in his parodic use of different styles of institutional discourse – in the position of subverter of such dominating discourses through his focus on places of conflict between ideologies (press versus church) or between everyday experience and ideological assertions (e.g. the reality of economic poverty and the Catholic Church's view of social order). By the end of this fascinating and dynamic account Joyce emerges as nothing less than a pre-Foucauldian writer who sees the ways in which individuals become subjects of 'prevailing institutional attitudes', propelled along 'narratives' generated by the institutions enclosing them.

Joyce's relationship with his contemporaries is also a subject pursued in a variety of ways in the periodicals. In *JML* Stanley Weintraub contemplates 'A Respectful Distance: James Joyce and his Dublin Townsman Bernard Shaw'. Although this article is at times rather speculative, it does shed interesting light on Joyce's hopes that Shaw might promote Lucia's career, and shows the somewhat disrespectful treatment of Shavian characters and resonances in the *Wake*. Breon Mitchell also picks up the Shaw–Joyce connection in *JJQ* by looking at the brief but sarcastic correspondence between 'Ezra Pound and G. B. Shaw' regarding Shaw's refusal to subscribe to *Ulysses*. Equally interesting, but shedding a slightly different light on Joyce's literary connections is 'Who Paid for Modernism?' (*SR*) by Joyce Wexler. She begins by considering editors' letters to J. B. Pinker, the British literary agent whose clients included Joyce, Lawrence, and Conrad. It is Wexler's contention – and it has a certain common-sense appeal – that publishers were quite eager to publish modernist writers and indeed attempted 'to prevent the modernist rendering of subject-ivity from degenerating into solipsism'. Writers like Joyce chose to create a myth of the alienated avant-garde artist exploited and ignored by commercial publishers; Wexler thinks Joyce has only himself to blame for a lack of readers since he was content, with patronage and unfortunate timing, to write 'in hermetic isolation' with no need 'to consider the audience at all'. Eunan O'Halpin (*JJQ*) follows up writer–reader relationships in 'British Patronage

66. *Joyce's Anatomy of Culture*, by Cheryl Herr. UIll. pp. xiv + 314. £19.75.

and an Irish Writer', a note describing the support given to Joyce by the British Government in 1916, and Suzanne Stutman does find an enthusiastic reader in 'Portrait of the Artist: Thomas Wolfe's Encounters with James Joyce'. In *JML* she notes that Wolfe met Joyce in 1926 shortly after beginning *Look Homeward, Angel*. Patrick Parrinder's thoughtful 'Joyce-sur-mer' in *CVE* connects Joyce's treatment of the sea to Yeats and Swinburne.

The other major general work to appear this year on Joyce is a collection of essays emanating from the James Joyce Centennial Symposium held in Dublin in 1982[67]. The aim of the volume is to provide 'a representative cross-section of contemporary theoretical approaches and current research' on Joyce; and in this it amply succeeds, with deconstructionist, psychoanalytic, narratological, and mythic approaches to the fore. William Chace has an ironically timely piece on the way in which *Ulysses* shields itself from academic colonization by 'its way of talking about professors as professors talk about it'. Seamus Deane's premise – Joyce repudiated the 'British liberal tradition' as articulated by Matthew Arnold – seems at first rather unsurprising; but it develops in useful directions when Deane considers Joyce's formal and intellectual ability to embrace those contraries (anarchy and order) which Arnold sought to repress into uniformity by an elitist cultural programme. There is a transcript of a panel discussion on Joyce and Yeats led by Ellen Carol Jones, with A. Walton Litz, Giorgio Melchiori, and Richard Ellmann among the participants. The conclusions though, which range from Joyce's fixation on early Yeats, the authors' obsession with tower imagery, and their shared 'metaphysical' stance, are suggestive but disappointingly undeveloped. Karen Lawrence makes a valuable contribution to work already initiated by such critics as Elizabeth Abel on the female *Bildungsroman* in her comparison of *Jacob's Room* and *A Portrait of the Artist as a Young Man*. A study of the narrative voice in both novels shows that, for all his experimental discontinuities, Joyce is still a part of the patriarchal nineteenth-century *Bildungsroman* tradition with his focus on the male ego, the 'dynastic power of paternity', and narrative authority. Suzette A. Henke also comments briefly on a Joyce–Woolf connection in her synthesis of Woolf's perceptive comments on *Ulysses* in her unpublished notebook on 'Modern Novels'. Richard Pearce also comes back to Joyce after considering another author, this time Thomas Pynchon. A comparison between the two makes him mindful of the radical disjunctions in *Ulysses*, and prompts him to speculate that Molly's monologue might be a parody of an epilogue. David Seed's meaty and scholarly consideration of 'naming' in the work of Joyce and Pynchon illuminates both Joyce's political critique (via realistic and non-realistic modes) and Pynchon's absurdist view of the world caught in 'a general process of decline'.

Derek Attridge heads a section devoted entirely to the 'Sirens' episode in *Ulysses* in a densely written piece on Joyce's syntactically odd use of the speech-organs. The eroticism which results notwithstanding, Attridge suggests that such 'displacement' and 'decentering' helps to subvert any fixity of meaning. André Topia's essay takes up this point about syntactic dislocations and their relationship to synecdochic and metonymic displacements in the episode to account for the peculiar way in which the scene builds and dissolves 'in front of

67. *James Joyce: The Centennial Symposium*, ed. by Morris Beja, Phillip Herring, Maurice Harmon, and David Norris. UIll. pp. xviii + 234. £24.75.

our eyes'. Maud Ellmann writes punningly on Bloom's evacuative 'eeee', and Daniel Ferrer professes himself unhappy with the usual musical analogies to describe the episode's style and theme. Instead he suggests sweepingly that 'the perversion of representation' and the focus on vision and narcissism, 'orality and anality', and death itself need to be explored as key themes in the chapter. Jean-Michel Rabaté is also dissatisfied with those musicalizing metaphors; music is 'pretext' and 'theme', not stylistic base. Instead, he argues rather cryptically, the style is 'a highly *mataplastic* idiom, exploiting the flexibility of signifiers for their evocative power'; what is important is the episode's blend of noise and silence, and other paradoxical contraries. Finally in this section, Robert Young cogently relates sex, writing, and bodily functions in the episode; all involve 'a furtive act of veiled secretions', and as illicit acts demand delay and deferment. Bloom himself 'is covered and uncovered by the secrets which he conceals about his person; he gets written by them'.

The third section of this book contains some surprisingly delicate and accessible work on *Finnegans Wake*. Bernard Benstock offers a particularly astute consideration of the use of self-contained tales in the novel. These 'fables' become a commentary on the art of storytelling and set up a dialogue between audience and tale (with narrator a competitor for attention). Carol Shloss argues persuasively that the novel exposes Joyce's attitude to the book-making process as it affected his own art. Beryl Schlossman outlines the Judaic and Christian significance of Pentecost and finds Joyce's novel redolent with connections to the feast-day. While the essay offers possibilities by accounting for the 'multiple language' or 'tongues' in the novel, the implications for our reading of the work remain rather sketchy and undeveloped. Margot Norris briefly considers the 'Tristan and Iseult' chapter, which helps her see the novel as a dream work concerned with desire. Significantly, though, it enacts the dream of old age with its focus on 'loss and dispossession, and . . . the imperishability of desire'. Jean-Michel Rabaté dares to consider a question posed by almost every first-time reader of this novel: is there a narrative lurking somewhere in it? The answer is predictable – and not meant to console; the only narrativity is 'what we, as readers, make up in order to escape from the impasses of self-cancelling or mutually excluding alternatives'. The text is itself 'like another speaking subject, formidable, inscrutable'.

'Joyce's Consubstantiality' is the title given to the next section which contains two worthwhile essays. Sheldon Brivic tackles the old question of authorial absence in Joyce's work, and argues with crisp assuredness that Joyce does not disappear at all. He projects himself 'as a spiritual undercurrent', like a deity – and a feminine one at that? – holding 'several visions at once' and capable of generating 'for his subjects the mystery and potentiality of actual being' with all its unpredictability and freshness. Elliott B. Gose Jr offers a thought-provoking analysis of female archetypes in *Ulysses*, focusing on woman as goddess and on Joyce's transformations of the virgin – whore dichotomy 'into a more creative balance of feminine energy'. In the biographical section a medical doctor, J. B. Lyons, establishes that Joyce did not have syphilis, Ann McCullough shows how Benjamin W. Huebsch, Joyce's American publisher, did much to establish and maintain Joyce's reputation there, and David Hayman outlines the information on Joyce, his family, and his friends which can be gleaned from the papers of Lucia Joyce.

The volume is rounded out by two challenging and appealing addresses.

Hugh Kenner begins by looking at the importance of *'re-enactment'* and *'renaming'* in *Dubliners* and broadens his concerns to show how, using similar techniques, the *Wake* serves as an enactment of the political confusion and violence of the recent past in Ireland. A. Walton Litz follows Hans Robert Jauss and attempts to reconstruct 'the original audience' for *Ulysses*. Joyce's great Modernist text, simultaneously 'traditional' and 'avant-garde' is perfectly positioned to capture its age – a period of 'accelerated cultural change'. But Litz also calmly shows how the novel 'has set limits or "horizons" for our critical ambition' and theory – indeed a salutary conclusion for this wide-ranging and stimulating volume. In fact some of the more esoteric offerings this year might well have something to gain from Litz's caution. In Stephen Whittaker's *SNNTS* essay on 'Joyce's Umbrella: The Pattern of Created Things', this everyday object is seen to 'evolve' in Joyce's work from 'a sign for the entelechy of the soul in *Dubliners*' to (no surprise) 'a symbol for the spiritual/erotic cosmos of *Finnegans Wake*'. Similarly Joanne E. Rea's note in *JJQ* on comparisons of Joyce, Rabelais, and Plutarch does seem to overstate a slim case.

Donald T. Torchiana's attempt to examine *Dubliners*[68] from an empirical, historical, and sociological point of view focuses on Joyce's complex layering of detail – 'national, mythic, religious, and legendary' – and the ends (often ironic) to which it is put. It is Joyce's ability to combine this attention to accurate detail with mythic, legendary, or archetypal structures at the heart of each story which, in Torchiana's opinion, is responsible for the profound effect of the collection. Dublin becomes a place rooted in a specific historical moment, but also 'ancient' and 'timeless', a place of 'seething' and 'emptiness'. There is a nod, too, in the direction of Joyce's economic handling of conventional narrative elements like character, but Torchiana does make the useful point that the accumulation of detail in the short fiction prepares us for Joyce's encyclopaedic approach in *Ulysses* and *Finnegans Wake*. In the end this critique does not result in radically new readings of the stories, but it is filled with interesting individual insights, such as the Yeats–Rosicrucian connection in 'The Sisters' or the relationship of 'Clay' to Celtic myth and ritual.

Edward Duffy is interested in '"The Sisters" as the Introduction to *Dubliners*' (*PLL*), beginning with an examination of ellipsis in the story and going on to consider the ways in which it dramatizes problems of communal repression and censorship. His conclusion to this rich article is that the story's symbolic dimension, foregrounded by Joyce's revisions, points to a belief in the importance of the artist-priest who can serve as confessor, seer, and interpreter for his people. L. J. Morrissey writes with great effect on 'Joyce's Revision of "The Sisters": From Epicleti to Modern Fiction' in *JJQ*. This is a very careful and scholarly piece of work which traces Joyce's transformation of the story from a 'moral call to action' to a 'modernist text' emphasizing inconclusiveness and uncertainty. 'Ambiguity in the Reading Process: Narrative Mode in "After the Race"' (*JSSE*) is the title Harold F. Mosher Jr gives to his application of George Dillon's theory of language processing and Barthes's reading model from *S/Z*. The significance of narrative mode and point of view for our interpretation of the story is indisputable, but the article seems oppressed rather

68. *Backgrounds for Joyce's 'Dubliners'*, by Donald T. Torchiana. A&U. pp. xiv + 283. £25/$34.95.

than enlivened by its theoretical underpinning. The same might be said of Doris T. Wight's piece in *JJQ*, 'Vladimir Propp and *Dubliners*', which is based on an interesting idea; while there are some sharp revelations about individual tales, the contention that *Dubliners* forms a tight, coherent work as a whole is not really new, and the enterprise seems rather ponderous in the end. Fritz Senn writes perceptively on '"The Boarding House" Seen as a Tale of Misdirection' (*JJQ*), focusing on the stylistic and thematic 'wrong turnings' in the story and the need for constant re-interpretation by the reader (to his/her 'general discomfiture'). Joyce's presentation of Charles Parnell is the subject of Thomas B. O'Grady's sensible *Eire* article, '"Ivy Day in the Committee Room": The Use and Abuse of Parnell'.

'The Dead' continues to attract attention. Vincent P. Pecora writes in *PMLA* on '"The Dead" and the Generosity of the World'. This is an important article insofar as it challenges critical commonplaces about Gabriel's awakening to new self-understanding (and helps to explain why some readers feel uneasy with such an optimistic interpretation). For Pecora that 'awakening' is simply an acceptance of Christian, middle-class ideology which Joyce has criticized throughout the collection of stories. Gabriel ironically 'only reimplicates himself blindly in the cultural conditions he longs to transcend'; Joyce thus readily spots the psychological dilemma of both characters and readers, which is how to avoid the cultural conditions from which we are constructed. In *JJQ* Thomas Dilworth has a belaboured piece on 'Sex and Politics in "The Dead"', which connects the two themes to the two parts of the story, while asserting its structural and thematic unity. His reflections on the etymology of the name Conroy are interesting, though, especially for those looking for mythic and ritual connections in Joyce. Also in *JJQ* Darrel Mansell offers a brief speculation on connections between Holman Hunt's *The Awakening Conscience*, Ruskin's discussion of that painting, and Gabriel's vision of his wife on the stairs.

F. C. McGrath re-opens an old argument about *A Portrait of the Artist as a Young Man* in 'Laughing in his Sleeve: The Sources of Stephen's Aesthetics' (*JJQ*) which suggests that both Stephen and Joyce root their aesthetic philosophy in German Idealism (e.g. Kant and Hegel). In *ELH* 'The Artist as Text: Dialogism and Incremental Repetition in Joyce's *Portrait*' is R. B. Kershner's application of Bakhtin's view of the novel 'as a consciously structured hybrid of languages'. The result is a bit heavy-handed, and for all the weighty theory, the conclusion covers familiar territory: the complex linguistic effects of the novel show Stephen 'learning a language', so that he is 'a product of his listening and reading'. Rather more interesting are two articles in *JJQ* which show how techniques and concerns of the *Portrait* connect with the methodology of *Ulysses*. David Hayman's 'The Joycean Inset' is an astute piece on the function of the 'apparent interpolations' in the text (such as the Christmas dinner scene) which shed light on Stephen's consciousness and also on the context by which he is made; the result includes an interesting commentary on the way Joyce deconstructs the traditional *Bildungsroman* in this novel and a coda extending the discussion to the later fiction where disruption is the norm. Joseph C. Heininger attempts an imaginative reconstruction in 'Stephen Dedalus in Paris: Tracing the Fall of Icarus in *Ulysses*', his purpose being to show there is a link between the Stephens of both works in as much as the Paris experiences 'have formed a pattern of frustrations to his hopes of personal distinction and artistic success'. D. M. E. Gilliam and R. W. McConchie explore a cunning idea rather ponderously in *Expl* when they connect Stephen's decision to follow a worldly vocation with the 'elfin prelude' and the tritone or '*diabolus in musica*' which confirms Stephen's relation to the sensuous world.

Richard Wall[69] has produced a slim but valuable reference work for all Joycean scholars, and with particular application to *Ulysses* and *Finnegans Wake*. In an unpretentious introduction he shows that Joyce's use of Anglo-Irish dialect increased as his style matured, particularly to reflect 'the milieu of the episode, or the personality or class of a character', and that in *Finnegans Wake* the effect of such words depends often on their punning 'sound sense', their Anglo-Irish pronunciation. The use of dialect becomes ultimately a gauge for judging Joyce's movement from classical to romantic style, and is an important way he escaped 'some of the limitations of standard English' and increased textual meanings. The three-column glossary is clear and neatly set out, with page/line references, term (with normal form if disguised), and meaning. There is an index of words cited, and an appendix which supplies cross-references for the 1984 Garland and 1986 Bodley Head and Penguin editions.

The effect of the 1984 Garland edition continues to reverberate through Joycean criticism. Of course, this year sees the publication of Penguin's paperback of the reading version (recto) of the Garland edition[70]. Richard Ellmann's preface succinctly outlines the problems faced by Gabler and his editorial team, touches on Gabler's use of manuscript material, typescripts, and proofs, and discusses the contentious restoration of the mysterious 'word known to all men' (love). Ellmann goes on to offer a concise account of the word's thematic importance, arguing that the novel is concluded, not open-ended 'because Molly Bloom countersigns with the rhythm of finality what Stephen and Bloom have said about the word known to all men'. Gabler's afterword offers a brief description of the extant source material he used, and, despite slating other editions as corrupt, admits that no text can be truly definitive. The greatest pity, though, is that the text provides no further scholarly apparatus for the student-reader, particularly because it offers no way of really knowing why certain editoral decisions have been made, but the essays in the next volume reviewed shed further light on this problem.

A range of views on the Garland edition were formulated at a special conference, and are now published[71]. Anthony Burgess's foreword draws attention both to the collection of Irish literature and folklore in the Princess Grace Irish Library and (rather redundantly) to the importance of an emphasis on the textuality of *Ulysses*. C. George Sandulescu comments on some of the benefits and disappointments of the conference (including the non-response and non-appearance of Gabler who was invited). Bernard Benstock is one of

69. *An Anglo-Irish Dialect Glossary for Joyce's Works*, by Richard Wall. Smythe. pp. 131. £8.95.

70. *Ulysses: The Corrected Text*, by James Joyce, ed. by Hans Walter Gabler with Wolfhard Steppe and Claus Melchior, with a new preface by Richard Ellmann. Penguin/Bodley. pp. xiv + 650. pb £7.50.

71. *Assessing the 1984 'Ulysses'*, ed. by C. George Sandulescu and Clive Hart. Smythe/B&N. pp. xxiv + 247. £15.

many contributors to voice reasoned doubts about some of Gabler's editorial decisions which seem based on a belief that *Ulysses* is 'a monolithic structure' and merely the sum of its parts. Rosa Maria Bollettieri Bosinelli is happy provided she can treat the Garland edition as a 'provisional' text, a 'pre-text' as it were; this is because it is necessary to take account of two Joyces – the careless and hasty scribe and the writer who deliberately altered his work. Manuscripts, typescripts, and proofs do not always make the distinction between these two 'constructors' of the text very clear; the only answer seems to be to accept a plurality of texts. Giovanni Cianci takes a particular episode – 'Aeolus' – as a way of examining Garland's approach to typography about which Joyce was very sensitive. Again Gabler is felt to have been without a firm conceptual base for many of his alterations. Carla de Petris comments on the editorial philosophy and method lying behind the 1983 Italian volume *Ulysses – Telemachia*, edited by George Melchiori; this edition rejected some of Gabler's emendations on the basis of internal evidence. Richard Ellmann writes again on that word known to all men; he too is disappointed by Gabler, since the decision to restore the passage naming 'love' deprives the text of Joyce's subtle suggestiveness. Wilhelm Fuger looks at the same restored passage in the light of speech-act theory, and provocatively reaches exactly the opposite conclusion; for him, the new passage increases the 'implications [and ambiguities] of the love theme'. It is a pity there is no further interaction between these two critics and their seemingly incompatible views. Michael Patrick Gillespie approves of the way the Gabler text does make clear the subjective editorial decisions lying behind its creation since this points up the provisional, ambiguous nature of the text, which Joyce himself accepted (capitalizing as he did on discrepancies between his own idea of the text and 'its typographical manifestation'). In a well-judged piece Clive Hart voices his worries about the establishing of copy-text (Joyce as scribe and writer is again the issue) and goes on to complain about the way in which Gabler's text provides a refined, sanitized falsification. The reading text in particular is a silent 'conflation', and hence an impossible work of art.

In one of the most balanced and thoughtful essays in the collection David Hayman questions the philosophical base and procedure underlying the editorial decisions in the 1984 edition. The particular examples he foregrounds raise some worries about the lack of rationale behind many emendations; Hayman's view that Gabler second-guesses too often is convincing. Suzette Henke offers a more broad-based, defensive critical piece in her view of *Ulysses* as 'a deconstructive, many-layered textual game of dialectical components'; even knowing 'love' is the key word 'opens up a free play of signifiers' so that the word remains 'unknown'. Richard M. Kain provides some chatty and meandering asides while identifying the cultural and literary context of Dublin in 1904. Carla Marengo Vaglio has some interesting interpretive points to make in discussing the function of italics in the novel and the danger of too much 'normalising', while Ira B. Nadel's exemplary article offers a good summary and diagram of Gabler's procedure for establishing the text. Despite the rigour seemingly guaranteed by computer accuracy, the edition is affected by the exercise of too much subjective 'editorial discrimination'. Patrick Parrinder examines Gabler's decision to include episode names (though Joyce did not) and humanely concludes there is a great deal to be said for breaking down any barriers between first-time readers and the text.

Charles Peake uses the Telemachia to provide a very lucid assessment of the contribution the edition makes to scholarship although he does not always agree with every change. C. George Sandulescu finds fault with Gabler's concept of the 'diachronic text' which fails to respect the multi-textual nature of the novel and which muddles Saussure's use of the term (which should only be applied to the *langue* or system, never to the *parole* and its structure). Fritz Senn, writing as a researcher-reader, weighs the advantages (universal system of lineation, stability of wording) against the weaknesses of the edition (diacritical symbols, validity of some restored material) and predicts that further argument and instability will be produced. Francisco Garciá Tortosa calls for a new Spanish translation, and Donald Phillip Verene concludes on yet another negative note by urging respect for a text's 'rhetorical spirit', that 'natural validity' which each version of a text possesses. To experience *Ulysses* 'in its original and flawed form' (i.e. the 1922 edition) is to confront the text 'as Joyce did' and to grasp his own understanding of it. However disruptive *Ulysses* is as a text, there is clearly a firm consensus among critics that any tampering with the existing fluid, disjunctive, and ambiguous mass is by and large a dangerous and unsatisfactory practice!

After this, Jack McCarthy's 'walking guide' to the Dublin of *Ulysses*[72] seems rather tame, but useful enough for students and readers who have not been to Dublin or are preparing a tourist visit. With this guide, complete with some captivating photos and valuable maps, they can retrace the physical movement of the main characters in Dublin on Bloomsday.

Most of the articles on *Ulysses* this year take a particular episode as their focal point. However, among the general essays of some interest are Monika Fludernik's two pieces on the novel. The more substantial of these is in *JJQ*, '*Ulysses* and Joyce's Change of Artistic Aims: External and Internal Evidence' which succinctly shows that Joyce neither imposed an inflexible framework on the novel 'nor abruptly changed direction'; his plan evolved gradually which necessitated 'readjustments in earlier episodes'. In *Style* the same critic's statistical analysis of different forms of dialogue in the novel confirms the established view that the narrative mode moves 'from realistic to mythic presentation'. Textual game-play lies behind 'Covert Riddles in *Ulysses*', Helen Georgi's contribution in *JML*. She plays the game only to discover that 'each riddle is a prototype based on a traditional legend, myth, or on esoteric lore in which a problem has been resolved negatively or not at all', though 'all riddles end in cosmic harmony'. There are useful distinctions made here between motif and riddle and suggestive comments on the progression of riddle-solving in Joyce. Hazard Adams writes with his usual flair on 'Critical Constitution of the Literary Text: The Example of *Ulysses*' (*NLH*); especially good is his discussion of the 'so-called authority of the text' and its accommodation to deconstructive notions of 'anti-authority'. *Ulysses* appears to Adams as the 'antitype' of the *Odyssey*, not just an ironic parody. On the other hand, in a somewhat plodding comparison entitled 'Lapsarian Odysseus' (*JJQ*), Patrick Colm Hogan finds structural parallels between Joyce's novel and *Paradise Lost* which confirm for him Joyce's 'parodic diminution and inversion' of Milton's 'grand, tragic necessities'. A more light-hearted piece comes from Hugh Kenner ('Beaufoy's

72. *Joyce's Dublin: A Walking Guide to 'Ulysses'*, by Jack McCarthy, with maps by Bob Conrad. Wolfhound. pp. 80. hb £8.95, pb £3.95.

Masterplaster') who reprints a prize-winning *Tit-Bit* story by Philip Beaufoy whose tale, 'Matcham's Masterstroke', is 'celebrated' in *Ulysses*. This article is in *JJQ* as are a number of minor notes of a general nature: Erwin R. Steinberg suspects that Ellen Higgins Bloom was a Catholic, Michael H. Begnal finds Stephen's 'Parable of the Plums' a rather vulgar joke, Wilhelm Fuger connects references to eyes with Bloom's self-deception, and Stanley Sultan reveals Joyce's hatred of bigotry (with reference to Bloom's 'ethnic identity').

Monika Fludernik (*JNT*) provides more commentary, this time on 'Narrative and its Development in *Ulysses*', a heavy-handed effort which focuses on the early episodes of the novel to rebut claims about Joyce's 'initial style' (there *is* none in her view, though there is a general continuity in the development of the narrative). In Robert E. Spoo's '"Nestor" and the Nightmare: The Presence of the Great War in *Ulysses*' (*TCL*) there is a lively attempt to track the historical situation of 1917 within Joyce's 1904 timeframe, primarily through thematic analysis. The 'Proteus' episode attracts the attention of Murray McArthur who perceptively comments in '"Signs on a White Field": Semiotics and Forgery in the "Proteus" Chapter of *Ulysses*' (*ELH*) on Joyce's interest in signification, and his anticipation of a postmodernist (Derridean) critique of Saussure. The argument includes interesting findings on the use of onomatopoeic figures in the novel. Timothy P. Martin (*JJQ*) writes briefly on links between the 'Proteus' and 'Aeolus' episodes and the libretto of *The Flying Dutchman* with particular reference to 'Stephen's artistic development'. Also in *JJQ* is Susan Bazargan's note on the connections between 'cinematic "syntax"' and the 'rhetorical devices' in 'Aeolus'. Another note is provided by Bruce Bassoff (*Expl*) who shows how 'Scylla and Charybdis' contains a major philosophical confrontation between Joyce and Plato/Socrates: 'eros and art' does battle with 'eros and philosophy'. Brook Thomas (*JJQ*) neatly locates history in the 'gaps' in the novel through the brief analysis of a short passage from 'Wandering Rocks'.

Steven Helmling (*SR*) offers a thoughtful and illuminating piece, 'Joyce the Irresponsible', which considers Joyce's stylistic development after the Armistice, as seen in the 'Sirens' episode, for example. Stylistic experimentation is part and parcel of the novelist's 'antagonistic and adversarial' response to his audience; but unlike the parodic, 'impersonal' cultural critiques of Pound and Eliot, 'Joyce's practice indicates a more conflicted and personal relation of participation in and animus toward its objects'. *Finnegans Wake* is a culmination of Joyce's strategy and purpose; it is a mediation between solipsism and universality, marked by a sense of 'irresponsible' artistic responsibility 'to the motions of one's own whim, and capacity for error'. Also of particular interest on 'The Substructure of "Sirens"' is Sebastian Knowles's knowledgeable tracing of correspondences between the sirens myth and the episode, focusing primarily on Molly as the 'quintessence' of the novel (*JJQ*). John M. Warner also benefits from adopting a mythic approach (*JJQ*) in 'Myth and History in Joyce's "Nausicaa" Episode' which explores the tension between synchronic and diachronic visions in the episode. Warner identifies 'Nausicaa' as the crucial point where Bloom sees the need 'to mediate between the languages of history and myth'. Also in *JJQ* can be found two notes of interest on 'Oxen of the Sun': Steven Reese establishes connections between the episode and Charles Doughty's 1908 *Adam Cast Forth*, and Robert Janusko reports on the 1985 'Oxen' workshop in Zurich. Robert D. Newman's note

(*JJQ*) on left-handedness in 'Circe' is an inflated attempt to show the episode as 'a kind of collective memory'. For Barbara Stevens Heusel, 'Eumaeus' becomes the climax of the novel – in moral terms and in its enactment of 'the writer's struggle to communicate, superimposing it over the protagonists' struggle to be heard amidst the devitalized language'. This *SNNTS* article, 'Vestiges of Truth: A Study of James Joyce's "Eumaeus"', is a dense and somewhat meandering piece but nonetheless contains a valuable overview of the ways in which Joyce defers and recaptures meaning (through archetype and parody, for instance) paralleling the narrator's insecurity and fear of commitment. Harold D. Baker offers a challenging, packed essay exploring the tension between technique and information in 'Rite of Passage: "Ithaca", Style, and the Structure of *Ulysses*' (*JJQ*) which certainly repays careful reading. According to Baker this is an episode unique to the novel in its mockery of 'the façade of objective description' through parody and stylistic dexterity. Although billed in *JJQ* as a 'note', Sally Abbott has done some worthwhile work on Molly Bloom's relationship to the Penelope archetype and 'the pre-Homeric Artemis' (though there is no evidence Joyce read the appropriate sources to support the thesis advanced here). Robert D. Newman takes a profitable Jungian approach to 'The Transformative Quality of the Feminine in the "Penelope" Episode of *Ulysses*' (*Journal of Analytical Psychology*).

The work on *Finnegans Wake* this year has, for the most part, been difficult but stimulating. Not quite in this category is John Gordon's 'plot summary'[73] which aims, oddly, at being a 'thoroughly reductive' account of the novel. Gordon's effort is based on his belief that the novel is a mimetic text, with the 'objective world' filtered through 'some individual consciousness'. His descriptive summary, therefore, which covers 'Place', 'Time', 'Males', 'Females', 'Dreamer(s)', as well as a chapter-by-chapter summary, thus surveys objects, settings, and characters and 'what the mind in question makes of them'. Beneath all of this lurks Gordon's basic thesis – that the novel is one of reconciliation of father with son, of brother with brother, and its multi-layered nature is formed from 'extended autobiographical myth-making structures'. There is a great deal of question-begging going on here, not least being assumptions about the autobiographical and therapeutic nature of the text and the seemingly oversimplified grasp of mimesis as a concept applied to the novel genre.

On a different level of sophistication altogether is John Bishop's first-class study of the novel[74] which takes as a starting point Joyce's comment that it is a 'work [that] takes place chiefly at night'. Unlike Gordon, Bishop insists on abandoning all hopes that the novel offers literalism, chronology, or objective representation. Instead he sees it as a dream text, and susceptible to the interpretive techniques outlined in Freud's *The Interpretation of Dreams*. But Vico's *New Science* and the Egyptian Book of the Dead are also assimilated by Joyce into the text, and in a really outstanding section Bishop suggests the ways in which Vico gave Joyce insight into the 'language of dreams' and the dynamic of unconsciousness revealed 'in the evolution of language'. The unconscious meaning thus embraced by the text – and indeed by all human language – 'is the "meaning" of the human body'. In this sense Joyce's work becomes an

73. *'Finnegans Wake': A Plot Summary*, by John Gordon. G&M. pp. x + 302. £30.
74. *Joyce's Book of the Dead*, by John Bishop. UWisc. pp. xvi + 480. £23.75.

exercise in the shedding of ego-identities, 'disselving', so that all individuals become 'the freshly reinvested "flesh and flood" of one body'. This is one reading of the *Wake* which illuminates at the same time as it respects the novel's enigma, fluidity, and openness.

Perhaps more predictable, but still filled with lively perceptions, is Grace Eckley's book on children's lore, activities, and knowledge in the novel[75]. This is a way of examining both the irrationality and mischief of the *Wake* and the significance of particular episodes (e.g. the Prankquean riddle), characters (such as HCE and his connection with William Stead), and themes (most obviously courtship, love, and marriage). The relationship of children in the novel to myth and ritual and to the cycle of the Fall provides the most fruitful new material, and the author provides a number of appendixes (such as references to Humpty Dumpty and Lewis Carroll) which create a foundation for further work in this area. Eckley also follows up these matters in *JML* where she writes further on connections between William T. Stead (assistant editor of the *Pall Mall Gazette*) and HCE, linking both to Sir Richard F. Burton's *Thousand and One Nights*. A related article of interest is Suzette Henke's 'James Joyce East and Middle East: Literary Resonances of Judaism, Egyptology, and Indian Myth' (*JML*) which is an excellently clear account of the use and function of the Orient in Joyce's work, including his interest in myths of rebirth and reincarnation, and in archetypes of woman as erotic Other. Claudine Raynaud (*JJQ*) considers the 'dream-characters' in the novel with special reference to 'female narcissism' and the way it 'finds its textual equivalent in women's letterwriting'. This essay, 'Woman, the Letter Writer; Man, the Writing Master', is a difficult but informed piece on gender differences and their significance in the novel and in critical accounts of it. Grace Fredkin's 'S in *Finnegans Wake*' is a rather convoluted attempt in *JJQ* to connect the mysterious S with the 'oedipal father', a repressive authoritarian force situated within the subject. Susan Swartzlander turns her attention quite profitably to 'Multiple Meaning and Misunderstanding: The Mistrial of Festy King' (*JJQ*); the inclusion of much extraneous material in the episode leads her to argue convincingly that the section 'becomes a metaphor for Joyce's "trial"', that is, the complaints leveled against him and his work'. Elsewhere in *JJQ* Radu Lupan notes Joyce's Romanian connections (primarily in the *Wake*), and David Lawson comments on changes in the last line of 'Chamber Music XXXVI' in the light of the theories of psychiatrist Harry Stack Sullivan (Joyce is repressing things once again). Danis Rose comments (critically) on some recent Joyce scholarship, and all students are reminded of Alan M. Cohn's invaluable 'Current JJ Checklist' in each issue of *JJQ*, complementing that journal's excellent collection of relevant reviews, notes, and letters. Work on Joyce not seen for review this year includes two collections of essays: *International Perspectives on James Joyce*, edited by Gottlieb Gaiser (Whitston), and *James Joyce*, edited by Harold Bloom (ChelseaH); and Michael J. O'Shea's *James Joyce and Heraldry* (SUNY) and Joseph Campbell and Henry Morton Robinson's *A Skeleton Key in 'Finnegans Wake'* (Penguin).

Feminist perspectives continue to permeate critical writings on Virginia Woolf which this year include three interesting books. Ellen Bayuk Rosenman

---

75. *Children's Lore in 'Finnegans Wake'*, by Grace Eckley. Syracuse (1985). pp. xxii + 250. £28.

bases her study of the mother–daughter relationship in Woolf's life and writings[76] on the theoretical insights of Nancy Chodorow concerning 'the pre-Oedipal attachment' and its importance for female experience. Seen in these terms the mother becomes an ambivalent figure of conflict as well as sustenance, and, Rosenman argues, every aspect of Woolf's imaginative output is suffused with a desire both to recover and to defeat the mother. This means that previously perceived motifs (such as merging and fusing), themes (the notion of inheritance), and feminist attitudes in the work can be reconciled by linking them to Woolf's mother-fixation. There are suggestive separate chapters on *Mrs Dalloway*, *To the Lighthouse*, and *Between the Acts*, this last providing an excellent account of the way in which ritual and pageant are linked to a cultural need for the wholeness residing in the absent mother. Best of all, perhaps, is the chapter on Woolf's writing on women's writing which sets the novelist's conflict between self-effacement and self-assertion against Harold Bloom's *Anxiety of Influence*. Rosenman deftly substitutes the Demeter – Kore model for Bloom's Oedipal one when discussing the issue of the female literary tradition: 'daughters invite the revision of literary history which reveals not only particular precursors but the sense of female creativity which is continuity itself'. All in all this is a critical study which sheds exciting new light on issues of femininity and identity in Woolf's art while respecting the integrity of the fiction.

Woolf claimed that 'the truth of fact and the truth of fiction are separate and must remain so'. Nonetheless, for Pamela J. Transue[77] much of Woolf's significance as a novelist lies in the way in which she transformed her own criticism 'of the patriarchal social and political system of values in the western world, particularly as it related to women' into art. The result for Transue is a distinctive adaptation of the novel's generic conventions, privileging displacement and indirection (over 'traditional plot progression') and suggestive imagery (which could bring unconscious material to the surface). Again psychoanalytic terminology is useful for describing this process of transformation, and Transue argues quite elegantly, given the complexity of her material, that Woolf's presentation of her political views makes use of the psychological processes of 'sublimation, transference, displacement and condensation'. This metamorphosis of ideology into art is tracked through all the novels in turn, with quite perceptive insights offered on the experimental techniques of *Jacob's Room* and the significance of the point of view in that novel. The handling of *Mrs Dalloway* and *To the Lighthouse* aptly bears out Transue's thesis, though it must be said in the end the reading of the novels offered is fairly conventional. This is, however, a coherent and thoughtful approach to Woolf, and will prove of use not only to those interested in her polemical attitudes and their non-didactic articulation but also in the ways in which women novelists have sought to undermine novel conventions to subvert 'the one-sidedness of the masculine perspective'.

Lucio P. Ruotolo charts what is ultimately well-known territory in his examination of Woolf's use of interruption or 'disorienting moments' in her

76. *The Invisible Presence: Virginia Woolf and the Mother–Daughter Relationship*, by Ellen Bayuk Rosenman. LSU. pp. xiv + 181. £22.50.

77. *Virginia Woolf and the Politics of Style*, by Pamela J. Transue. SUNY. pp. vii + 222. hb $39.50, pb $14.95.

fiction[78]. Inspired by Mikhail Bakhtin's interest in 'openendedness, indecision, indeterminacy', Ruotolo concentrates on Woolf's gradual rejection of existing structures and (patriarchal) artistic strategies in order to represent and embrace the fluidity and incompleteness of life. Ruotolo is most lively when showing how this disruptive aesthetic was not an easy one for Woolf to embrace; she too was seduced by 'the promise of wholeness' signified by artistic closure and stasis. But increasingly, techniques of 'uncertainty' (such as the fragmenting narrative voice) and 'interruption' (suggesting 'change, and the growing expectation that society is on the verge of radical transformation') come to dominate her fiction. The importance of 'anonymity' in *Mrs Dalloway* and *To the Lighthouse* is discussed with some acumen, and there are useful links made to *The Waves*, *The Years*, and *Between the Acts* where the concept of 'centrality' and hierarchical authority is finally vanquished stylistically. The vision of Woolf which emerges – part existentialist, part anarchist – depends on seeing the connection between disruption (of authority, of artistic sequence and closure) and regeneration; but this is not, after all, inviting a fundamental revision of current thinking about Woolf's work.

Once again most interest in Woolf in the periodicals focuses on *To the Lighthouse*, but there are some other useful and stimulating foci. Phyllis McCord considers the self-reflexive element of 'Sketch of the Past' in '"Little Corks That Mark a Sunken Net": Virginia Woolf's "Sketch of the Past" as a Fictional Memoir' (*MLS*), and Thomas C. Beattie (*MFS*) investigates closure in a range of works by Woolf ('Moments of Meaning Dearly Achieved: Virginia Woolf's Sense of an Ending'). Susan J. Leonardi (*Novel*) links Woolf's own interest in masculine and feminine sentences to *Night and Day* in order to approach the novel as a feminist-modernist statement on the relationship of men and women and women and language. In 'Bare Places and Ancient Blemishes' she argues that Woolf's belief in a new language which would reject the false myth of an ordered world, express the feminine consciousness, and encompass the 'hideous and beautiful' can be seen in Woolf's symbolic strategies. Two scholarly bibliographical pieces examine the significance of Woolf's revisions for our understanding of particular novels. In *TCL* E. L. Bishop writes on 'The Shaping of *Jacob's Room*: Woolf's Manuscript Revisions', persuasively showing how Woolf's gradual move to an allusive style in the drafts challenges assumptions about character and motivation. What Woolf achieves is a subtle style better suited to the presentation of Jacob's consciousness and her own artistic beliefs, for the room becomes a definer of 'psychic space and the text itself'. 'The Raverat Proofs of *Mrs Dalloway*' (*SB*) by Glenn P. Wright is rather more down to earth for it shows Woolf's revision to proofs as often less significant than might be imagined; she could be 'haphazard and careless', especially when ill or working under pressure. Herbert Marder's reading of the central character in the same novel, 'Split Perspectives: Types of Incongruity in *Mrs Dalloway*' (*PLL*), is a straightforward but nonetheless crisp attempt to account for the disconcerting mix of snobbery and humaneness in Clarissa. Such dual perspectives universalize the character and can be related to the 'modernist assault on personality' while remaining within the 'boundaries of social realism'. The theories of Julia

78. *The Interrupted Moment: A View of Virginia Woolf's Novels*, by Lucio P. Ruotolo. Stanford. pp. xiv + 262. $29.50.

Kristeva are applied with some dexterity to *Mrs Dalloway* in Jean Wyatt's 'Avoiding Self-Definition: In Defense of Women's Right to Merge' (*WS*), while in the same journal Susan M. Squier ingeniously connects *Orlando* to the mimetic tradition within the novel genre, finding some sources in the work of Defoe ('Tradition and Revision in Woolf's *Orlando*').

A rather surprising overlap can be found in a couple of essays on *To the Lighthouse*. Both Elissa Greenwald and Peter Knox-Shaw choose to examine the novel as prose elegy. The former's essay in *Genre* ('Casting Off From "The Castaway": *To the Lighthouse* as Prose Elegy') is the more sophisticated of the two, tackling the amorphous subject of lyrical elements in the narrative with panache by anchoring discussion on Woolf's transformation of Cowper's poem in order to move her novel away from strict mimesis and towards 'a deeper reality' and a more positive communal vision. In *ESA* Peter Knox-Shaw's '*To the Lighthouse*: The Novel as Elegy' relates the novel's elegiac structure to cultural themes (separation, death) and its location in a historical moment (the First World War). This is ultimately quite predictable, with the three parts of the novel treated as an enactment of the stages of mourning (from stability, to destruction, to the stimulus to creation). Lynda S. Boren (*CentR*) also offers a rather familiar reading of Lily's artistry in 'The Performing Self: Psychodrama in Austen, James and Woolf', though the painter is in somewhat unexpected company (*Persuasion* and *The Turn of the Screw*). Boren's study of dramatic form in the novels shows how Lily creates a unified vision, but the concluding vision of the critic – the three novelists at a celestial tea table – rather undermines the enterprise. Much more valuable is Kate Flint's piece in *EIC* on 'Virginia Woolf and the General Strike'; the connection between Woolf and her social context in specific terms is a much neglected area of study, and Flint offers an excellent model for just such investigation. This piece provides a succinct summary of Woolf's attitudes to the Strike and working-class power, and shows incisively how these can be identified in the novel with 'her desire for reconciliation . . . unity . . . wholeness'. Pride of place among the essays on *Lighthouse*, however, must go to Joan Lidoff's 'Virginia Woolf's Feminine Sentence: The Mother–Daughter World of *To the Lighthouse*', an essay best read in conjunction with Rosenman's book[76]. In this well-controlled and tough-minded *L&P* article Lidoff ranges over Woolf's interest in the feminine sentence, her transformation of the elegiac and novel genres 'into distinctively female modalities', and certain key themes in the novel ('fusion' and 'lack of separation') to show how the novel's 'philosophical, aesthetic and psychological premises' are rooted in 'the sense of the world that derives from the state of fusion with the mother'. Once again the theoretical writing of Nancy Chodorow plays an important part, but Lidoff's essay must be singled out for its clarity, breadth of vision, and concern with both style and theme. Gloria G. Fromm (*JML*) makes a case for 'Re-inscribing *The Years*: Virginia Woolf, Rose Macaulay, and the Critics', a revisionist return to *The Years* as published with 'social, political, and sexual details' removed. Taking issue with feminist critics who prefer draft material, Fromm sees the published version as a triumph partly due to Woolf's rivalry with Rose Macaulay; although Fromm argues that Woolf came closer to Macaulay's viewpoint and could see the nineteenth-century inheritance was not necessarily oppressive psychologically, this article fails to convince. *YR* reprints Woolf's 1934 essay 'A Conversation about Art' which uses Sickert as a springboard for discussion of narrative and non-representational elements in artistic products.

David Thomas and Joyce Thomas's Compton Mackenzie bibliography[79] is a carefully produced tribute to a minor but prodigious writer. The bibliography includes books by Mackenzie as well as his contributions to books, journalism (including literary and record reviews), and broadcasts as well as critical reviews of him. The brevity of these latter certainly show the neglect he has suffered. There are brief annotations for most of the major pieces, and a concise introduction which shows how Mackenzie revised and issued compilations of his works in order to increase 'his earning power'.

The work on D. H. Lawrence has been of very varied quality this year. Daniel Weiss was a critic fascinated by the contributions which Freudian theory could make to literary interpretation, and was adept at showing readers how modern writers absorbed 'a conception of a working unconscious' from Freud and must be considered in this light. After Weiss's untimely death in 1976, Eric Solomon and Stephen Arkin have collected some of his outstanding critical material and published it as readings in psychology, myth, and fiction[80]. The result, which ranges over such authors as Stephen Crane, Sherwood Anderson, Hemingway, Faulkner, and Bellow, includes material on Lawrence which could safely be recommended to undergraduates coming to Freudian interpretations of Lawrence for the first time. Weiss argues that it is Lawrence's mother-fixation and fear of incest which underpins his 'rejection of mental consciousness' and his treatment of sexuality in terms of destruction. Even more interesting, and perhaps less conventional, is his consideration of the messianic theme in Lawrence's writings, which for Weiss connects more logically to myths of Attis and Osiris (with their subsequent mutilations) than to Christ's crucifixion and resurrection.

Lawrence is one of three writers considered by Marianna Torgovnick in her study of the treatment and function of 'the visual arts and pictorial elements' in the emerging Modernist novel[81]. This is a potentially fascinating – and vast – subject, and Torgovnick has done a good job of assembling a wealth of material on James, Lawrence, and Woolf, ranging from their own particular artistic predilections (James for the Impressionists, Woolf for Impressionism and abstract art, and Lawrence for Cézanne and the Futurists) to the 'decorative', 'biographical', 'ideological', and 'interpretive' uses of visual art references in the novel. Indeed it is just this wealth of material which renders the book a disappointment, for there are so many categories of use and allusion and so many different perspectives on the function of the arts engaged and then swiftly abandoned, that no coherent vision of any specificity emerges. A chapter on Virginia Woolf and Vanessa Bell for instance takes a biographical line, focusing on how Woolf's love–envy relationship with her sister surfaces in *To the Lighthouse*; the next chapter, one of the more incisive, switches ground to the way in which the metaphoric use of artistic allusion in Woolf and

79. *Compton Mackenzie: A Bibliography*, by David Thomas and Joyce Thomas. Mansell. pp. x + 309. £40.

80. *The Critic Agonistes: Psychology, Myth, and the Art of Fiction*, by Daniel Weiss, ed. by Eric Solomon and Stephen Arkin. UWash (1985). pp. xii + 270. $25.

81. *The Visual Arts, Pictorialism, and the Novel: James, Lawrence, and Woolf*, by Marianna Torgovnick. Princeton (1985). pp. xii + 268. £17.80.

Lawrence highlights their ideological differences. Whereas Woolf saw ways in which Impressionistic non-representational techniques could be adapted to writing to explore states of mind, Lawrence thought modern art encoded 'the negative and the corrupt' in Western culture and believed his mystical, transcendent states of mind could be represented only by language if at all, certainly not by the 'seen'. Yet another chapter on Lawrence seems to retreat from this position in looking at pictorial images in *Women in Love*; Torgovnick thinks this an economical technique for recalling themes and issues in a subtle way and for stimulating the 'visionary awareness' of the reader. A resounding conclusion might have given these multifarious perspectives a kind of coherence after the fact; instead the book finishes with a rather weak and arbitrary examination of the use of works of art in *A Dance to the Music of Time*. There is much meaty material to be found here, but its deployment is rather shapeless and disappointing.

Geoffrey Harvey has produced the *Sons and Lovers* volume for Macmillan's Critics Debate Series[82], designed to illuminate different critical approaches to key canonical texts. Part 1 is a concise bibliographical overview and assessment of the main critical interpretations of the novel according to such approaches as 'source criticism', 'psychoanalytical criticism', 'historical criticism', 'feminist criticism', 'formalist criticism', and 'genre criticism', though structuralist, linguistic, and deconstructionist perspectives are thought to be 'less helpful'. Part 2, Harvey's own reading of the novel, is a fairly familiar liberal humanist – formalist digest, aimed at proving Lawrence transcended autobiography and produced 'art' through his technical accomplishments, primarily the handling of point of view and the creation of 'organic unity'. While it is a pity that more opportunity was not taken to provide a strikingly revisionist reading of the novel, Harvey is sound and readable on such perennial topics as Paul's Oedipal complex, his 'emotional bond with the mining community', and on the two plots and the unity of the two parts of the novel. Undergraduates coming to Lawrence for the first time will no doubt find this a useful overview, but it is doubtful they will be challenged to employ new theoretical perspectives for themselves by this rather conventional approach. Another handbook to *Sons and Lovers* has been produced by R. P. Draper[83] as a student guide. This contains an undistinguished account of the life and background, reductive chapter summaries, and identification of major themes and issues. Unlike many of such guides, however, the section on techniques is quite good, focusing as it does on Lawrence's relation to the mimetic tradition within the novel genre, and concerned with such matters as plot, structure, language, imagery, and symbolism.

Michael Black's consideration of the early fiction[84] is a curiously old-fashioned Leavisite analysis which seems almost totally disengaged from contemporary critical theory. Black pointedly highlights his debt to 'earlier writers on Lawrence', and opts for a New Criticism 'close reading' of *The White Peacock*, *The Trespasser*, *Sons and Lovers*, and short stories from 'A

82. 'Sons and Lovers', by Geoffrey Harvey. Macmillan. pp. 84. hb £15, pb £3.95.
83. 'Sons and Lovers' by D. H. Lawrence, by R. P. Draper. MMG. Macmillan. pp. viii + 86. pb £1.25.
84. D. H. Lawrence: The Early Fiction, by Michael Black. Macmillan. pp. x + 280. £27.50.

Modern Lover' to 'New Eve and Old Adam'. The works are seen to have a kind of coherent development, partly because of their connection to Lawrence's own life, but also because Black sees in them an organic progression linked to a belief in being as a dynamic process. There is too much descriptive character sketch and synopsis, and the identification of recurrent themes and preoccupations is fairly simplistic. A few bright moments – such as an aside on Paul's predatoriness – remain undeveloped; despite comments on Lawrence's maturing style, his 'personal metaphor-system', and his intuitive understanding of the feelings behind myths and legends of the past, there is little penetrating analysis. The lack of a bibliography points up the rather naïve air of the whole production.

A better model for introductory student guides is Graham Holderness's Open University production on *Women in Love*[85], a kind of distant-learning study pack, which aims to provide a 'tutorial' between writer, text, and reader. The fundamental starting point is that texts are open to a plurality of interpretations, and Holderness sketches in the historical, biographical, and cultural background necessary to enable readers to reach their own interpretation. Each chapter focuses on a particular section of the novel from a particular critical perspective (e.g. 'Character, Narrative', 'Ideas, Language', 'Sexual Politics: Homosexuality, Feminism', 'Biography, History'). Students are guided in their reading and note-taking; and every 'task' is followed by a 'discussion' which gives the reader Holderness's own view of possible responses. There is a relevant collection of additional material (letters, extracts from critical theory essays) and good suggestions for further reading. The overall result, although favouring a 'visionary' rather than 'mimetic' reading, gives ample scope for reader-initiative while encouraging close reading techniques against the background of a wider perspective.

While mythic approaches are rather thin on the ground this year, readers interested in Lawrence's primitivism will be pleased to know *Mornings in Mexico*[86] is now available again in a cheap paperback edition. Important connections between Lawrence's fiction and the primitive rituals of resurrection he encountered among the Indians of Mexico and the southern United States can be supported by many of the travel essays here. Lawrence's concern with the unstable Mexican political situation is further illumined by a letter printed by Keith Cushman in *DHLR* ('D. H. Lawrence in Chapala'). In 'Lawrence and Sicily' Julian Moynahan considers significant connections between Lawrence and 'the place of places' (*Mosaic*).

Elsewhere in *DHLR* two worthwhile essays appear on *The Captain's Doll*. Although he does not escape from a rather jargony presentation, Gerald Doherty profitably explores the comic dimension of the novella in 'A "Very Funny" Story: Figural Play in D. H. Lawrence's *The Captain's Doll*', locating humour in the 'parodic play' and 'incongruence' which signal a debate in the text between the totalization of meaning and the creation of equivocation and ambiguity. More immediately accessible is W. R. Martin's study of Hannele's acceptance of Hepburn's marriage proposal which is seen in 'Hannele's "Surrender": A Misreading of *The Captain's Doll*' to be dynamic 'collaboration', not just capitulation. Rae Rosenthal, Dennis Jackson, and Brad

85. *'Women in Love'*, by Graham Holderness. OpenU. pp. x + 140. hb £13.50, pb £3.95.

86. *Mornings in Mexico*, by D. H. Lawrence. Penguin. pp. 91. pb £2.95.

Howard contribute to the 'Checklist of D. H. Lawrence Criticism and Scholarship, 1979–1983' (*DHLR*).

DHLR combines issues 2 and 3 in a special collection of Centennial Essays presented at a 1985 conference entitled 'D. H. Lawrence: Creativity and Conscience'. These range very widely over general concerns and specific texts. 'Lawrence and Touch' is an ably written essay by James C. Cowan on the relationship between 'human touch' and Lawrence's moral attitudes to 'true relatedness' which he skilfully connects to Lawrence's theory on 'the psychophysiology of the unconscious'. Kingsley Widmer's 'Desire and Denial, Dialectics of Passion in Lawrence' is a more conventional consideration of the way in which Lawrence reverses traditional moral views on passionate desire through a variety of tropes. Carol Sklenicka writes well on *The Rainbow* and other fiction in her exploration of Lawrence's own views about the evolution of consciousness and its effect on his methods of characterization as he revitalized 'the tradition of symbolically innocent child figures'; her essay is entitled 'Lawrence's Vision of the Child: Reimagining Character and Consciousness'. Another quite suggestive line of inquiry is pursued by Kathleen Verduin in 'Lawrence and the Middle Ages' which probes the influence of the nineteenth-century medieval revival on Lawrence (in his treatment of anti-industrialism for instance) and his ultimate rejection of emasculating, effete antiquarianism. Holly Laird considers 'The Poems of "Piano"', arguing fluently that the revision of the poem and its positioning in *New Poems* show Lawrence's firm wish to expose 'his reader to emotion, awakening in him resistance and response'. Murray S. Martin returns to the controversial issue of male bonding and Lawrence's 'homoerotic urges' in '*Kangaroo* Revisited', an account of the novel's sexual tension against the background of 'Australian mateship'.

More gender issues interest Jan Good in the same double issue. The relationship between gender confusion and psychic instability is the subject of her packed article, 'Toward a Resolution of Gender Identity Confusion: The Relationship of Henry and March in *The Fox*'. Michael L. Ross finds surprising similarities in his comparison of *The Fox* and David Garnett's *Lady into Fox*, written in 1922. The conclusion to 'Ladies and Foxes: D. H. Lawrence, David Garnett, and the Female of the Species' is rather bland, though, with Lawrence advocating 'male superiority' simply to restore the balance upset by 'a perverted femininity of will and idealism'. In 'From Thimble to Ladybird: D. H. Lawrence's Widening Vision?' Laurence Steven argues energetically that 'The Thimble' shows a maturity of vision even greater than that of *The Ladybird* which it fostered. Revisions to the short story indicate Lawrence's desire to 'universalize and mythologize'. Peter Balbert rejects Kate Millett's attack on another tale in 'Snake's Eye and Obsidian Knife: Art, Ideology, and "The Woman Who Rode Away"', principally by asserting that Lawrence does regard the 'primitive "darkness"' with some antagonism, recognizing its potential for savagery. This is an appealing interpretation, but the rebuttal of Millett is not ultimately convincing for this reviewer. Thematic and formal connections fascinate Jack F. Stewart in 'Expressionism in "The Prussian Officer"' which is quite perceptive on the hallucinatory imagery of the story and on connections between sexual tensions and prewar German culture as it affected Lawrence. Finally Kathryn Van Spanckeren writes on 'Lawrence and the Uses of Story', a survey of Lawrence's achievement in the short story genre, but a rather general appreciation when all is said and done.

Lively work on Lawrence has appeared in other periodical sources. Paulina

S. Pollack (*L&P*) looks for psychoanalytic explanations for Lawrence's anti-Semitism, and, while every reader might not agree with her findings, she puts up a determined case for Lawrence's fear of the father-figure in 'Anti-Semitism in the Works of D. H. Lawrence: Search for and Rejection of the Father'. Angus Easson provides a very readable reassessment of 'Lawrence's responses to Apocalypse, in terms both of ideas and of technical possibility' (*AJES*, 1985). The treatment of myths and images in *Women in Love* is particularly useful, and there is a deft connection of Lawrence's imagistic 'understanding' to the Romantic tradition.

Paul Eggert reviews the familiar in 'Edward Garnett's *Sons and Lovers*' (*CritQ*), showing how the facsimile manuscript reveals Lawrence's artistic conflicts; Garnett is slated for misunderstanding Lawrence's use of Paul's subconscious life as a structuring principle. Malcolm Pittock (*EIC*) hammers the novel in '*Sons and Lovers*: The Price of Betrayal', putting its 'imaginative slovenliness' down to Lawrence's need to 'sustain his repressions' and hence to 'deform reality' (not least in his treatment of Jessie Chambers). Once again this offers little that is new, but it is an engagingly aggressive piece. Victoria Middleton presents some important background and contextualizing material in 'In the "Woman's Corner": The World of Lydia Lawrence' (*JML*), a detailed examination of Lydia's 'Victorian ethos of self-development' and her 'self-consciousness of one's capacities' against which Lawrence rebelled. Judith Puchner Breen (*WS*) revisits men/women relationships in a war context in 'D. H. Lawrence, World War I, and the Battle between the Sexes: A Reading of "The Blind Man" and "Tickets, Please"'. Peter G. Christensen's breezy *SNNTS* article is on '*Mr Noon*: Some Old Problems in a New Text'; this exploration of Lawrence's attempt to cope with the problem of 'an incomplete differentiation between the narrator's consciousness and the psyches of his characters' picks up a crucial issue but with too light a touch. There is a textual note in *MP* by JoEllyn Clarey on the importance of *Studies in Classic American Literature* (highlighting Lawrence's use of an edition of *Moby-Dick* without the epilogue). Howard Mills (*English*) considers Lawrence's introduction to *Memoirs of the Foreign Legion* by Maurice Magnus; the point made in this pleasantly discursive essay is that this introduction should be read as a piece of narrative writing with intricate and creative 'patterns and strategies'. In *LMag* A. Banerjee looks at Yone Noguchi, his influence on Lawrence's versification, and his reception and significance in England. Cornelia Nixon's *Lawrence's Leadership Politics and the Turn Against Women* (UCal) was not available for review.

Three novels by Ronald Firbank[87], published between 1915 and 1917, have been collected and issued in paperback. Ernest Jones's pert introduction highlights Firbank's strengths, but also suggests his weaknesses (an inadequate 'sense of Evil' and an inability to construct a plot) and hints at some of the reasons for Firbank's neglect by his contemporaries (he did not espouse the 'modified naturalism' of such popular writers as Arnold Bennett). Jones's case for regarding Firbank as part of the tradition of Woolf and Joyce is perhaps a bit overstated, but he does foreground his subject's celebration of the fragmented world of café society with its dandyist interest in ennui and trivia and

87. *Three More Novels: 'Vainglory', 'Inclinations', 'Caprice'*, by Ronald Firbank, intro. by Ernest Jones. ND. pb £7.95/$11.95.

the toughness and ironic humour behind the surface fantasy of the novels. This collection should go some way to reviving interest in an all-but-forgotten novelist.

In *ArielE* Edwin Ernest Christian examines 'Joyce Cary's Major Poems', preferring to concentrate on content rather than form and to suggest connections to the fiction via such themes as 'the injustice of life, the necessity of freedom, and the world's creative character'.

Ida Constance Baker's memories of Katherine Mansfield[88], first published in 1971, have been issued in paperback. These memoirs cut two ways. They purport to be a quiet, unpretentious, and affectionate portrait defending the writer by one who knew her as devoted friend and 'helpmate'. But the treatment of this self-effacing woman by Katherine Mansfield and John Middleton Murry – set up as a housekeeper/servant to them at one point, excluded from their intellectual and literary circles – scarcely puts them in a good light. Mansfield's emotional extravagance, her conflicting demands for supportive companionship and unsmothering solitude, her self-dramatizing scenes (arriving for her marriage to George Bowden dressed in mourning) are all revealed in a series of telling vignettes from the period 1908–12. Baker lavished financial, moral, and emotional support on her friend; Mansfield responded with adoring words (finding Ida 'absolute' and 'the nearest thing to "eternal"') but also with accusations of vicious cruelty (Ida, it appears, was also a devouring 'hysterical ghoul'). The picture of both women which emerges is overwhelmingly pathetic. More literary and analytical is Judith S. Neaman's *TCL* article on 'Allusion, Image, and Associative Pattern: The Answers in Mansfield's "Bliss"'; she argues against lesbian readings of the story as well as noting that love in the story is revealed as imperfect.

John Middleton Murry's first child of his second marriage has written a personal biography[89] of her father's family life. Katherine Middleton Murry does not attempt to disguise her 'partiality' in the case, but even allowing for the subjective colouring of her child's-eye view, there seems to be ample evidence for her claim that Middleton Murry's life was ruined by his 'idealisation' of Katherine Mansfield according to Mansfield's 'own projection of herself'. This is not a sophisticated nor particularly fluent examination of all aspects of Murry's life, but there is a certain ghastly compulsiveness about the details of Murry's appalling domestic situations, Lawrence's 'unrequited passion' for him, and Murry's retreat from his children's needs to his own philosophical and political enterprises.

Lenemaja Friedman is responsible for the TEAS study of Enid Bagnold[90] which takes the usual form of a narrative account of the life and a survey of the works. Unfortunately, this popular novelist is ill served by this guide which is very rudimentary and elementary in its judgements and perceptions. Written in a rather irksome, effusive, and disjointed manner, the study never rises much above the identification of recurrent character types, their linking to Bagnold's own personal development, and some strained comments on technique and

88. *Katherine Mansfield: The Memories of L. M.*, by 'L. M.' [Ida Constance Baker], intro. by A. L. Barker. Virago (1985). pp. xxx + 240. pb £4.50.

89. *Beloved Quixote: The Unknown Life of John Middleton Murry*, by Katherine Middleton Murry. Souvenir. pp. 219. £14.95.

90. *Enid Bagnold*, by Lenemaja Friedman. Twayne. pp. xii + 147. $19.95.

experimentation with impressionistic form. To distinguish between the novels and the plays largely on the basis that there are 'more disagreeable' characters in the drama scarcely supports the conclusion that Bagnold's best work 'can be compared favorably with the best in modern literature'. Some areas which would be worth developing do get a glance (e.g. the issue of sexual emancipation), but the whole discussion requires a more informed and rigorous theoretical and critical base.

The development of interest in Rebecca West is signalled by two works. Harold Orel's assessment of West's literary achievement[91] takes the form of a standard 'introductory' volume, offering biographical background, personal and political preoccupations, and a survey of her critical reception (with *Black Lamb and Grey Falcon* the 'masterwork') and development of an increasingly conservative viewpoint. Given the nature of this book, the amount of descriptive summary is probably understandable, albeit disappointing. But there are useful accounts of West's literary criticism, her political convictions, her interest in theological issues like that of original sin and free will (as seen in her 'psychohistory' of St Augustine), and her concern with gender differences (e.g. masculine and feminine psychologies). However, Orel's stylistic and technical judgements are rather trite and lacking in precision ('she has made the past live again in scene after lustrous scene').

Very different in nature and intention is Fay Weldon's book on West[92] for the Lives of Modern Women series. This opens with a chatty introduction by Weldon outlining her own enthusiasms for West, followed by a series of letters written to the young Rebecca West 'from the Future' exposing at one and the same time the motivations, conflicts, ebbs, and flows of her relationship with Wells and indicating the significance of West's decisions for the women's movement later in the century. This imagined recollection of fictionalized conversations and events contrasted with present 'freedoms' focuses on the plight of the dependent woman. Ultimately this study invites readers to look at West as 'a woman writer'; but it also will be of value to those with an interest in Fay Weldon herself.

A miscellaneous collection of essays by Aldous Huxley[93] has been issued in paperback. Topics range from truth and tragedy in literature, to modern Romanticism and 'the beauty industry'. Whatever the subject, however, Huxley's observations are ironic, witty, and scathingly incisive on some of the foolish pretentions of modern culture. In *DUJ* J. W. Blench considers the important 'Influence of Richard Jefferies upon Henry Williamson', encouraging the latter in his close observation of natural phenomena. Patrick Scott rereads *Goodbye, Mr Chips* (*SAQ*) and challenges views that it is sentimental liberal twaddle in 'James Hilton's *Goodbye, Mr Chips* and the Strange Death of Liberal England'. Since 'the traditionalist interpreter [of British History] himself must die', Hilton can only be suggesting that liberal values and ideas are ineffectual; 'civilizations by which we find humane significance in the world tragically cloister us from the world's reality'. This is a lively and

---

91. *The Literary Achievement of Rebecca West*, by Harold Orel. Macmillan. pp. xii + 235. £29.50.

92. *Rebecca West*, by Fay Weldon. Penguin (1985). pp. 107. pb £2.95.

93. *'Music at Night' and Other Essays including 'Vulgarity in Literature'*, by Aldous Huxley. Triad: Grafton. pp. 236. pb £2.50.

provocative piece. And in *LMag* Stephen Spender identifies the Manichean vision of the unjustly neglected Edward Upward, a Marxist writer of the 1930s.

Patrick Reilly[94] divides his study of George Orwell's 'greatness' rather artificially into two parts – 'The Man' and 'The Works' – and follows other critics in suggesting that Orwell's importance lies less in his artistic achievement (which is uneven and flawed) than in his moral attitudes, the 'pluck and sincerity' with which he spoke against 'the unfashionable, unwelcome truth'. What is unusual about Reilly's treatment, though, is his view that Orwell's concern for the future of mankind lay in his perception of the twentieth century as ethically bankrupt, 'without any need of a faith that exalts love and community above egoism and self-interest'. Given Orwell's attitude to organized religion, it would appear that Reilly has a very difficult case to make; but he does put up good arguments for accepting Orwell as a writer concerned with the loss of religious faith, with the impact on society of 'the death of God and the revocation of eternity'. The first section thus deals with Orwell's attitudes (firmly founded on 'the addiction to truth') and his desire for a new myth 'to evoke belief and motivate conduct'; the second part, on the writings, traces Orwell's indirect and oblique treatment of the consequences of a loss of faith, and includes consideration of his critiques of both liberal humanism and socialism. The culmination of the artistic output, *Nineteen Eighty-Four*, is read as neither a surrender to nor a rebuttal of despair but as a 'conditional prophecy'; ironically the defeat of humanism in the novel is linked to the death of God – a phenomenon humanists are too ready to applaud. Although not all readers would agree with Reilly's conclusions, this is a stylishly written book with a provocatively unconventional thesis.

George Watson has spotted some illuminating connections between *Nineteen Eighty-Four* and the remarks of Hitler reported to Hermann Rauschning (*SR*). These comments reveal Nazi ideology saw totalitarianism as subjectivist, and Watson thus emphasizes his belief that Orwell's writings need to be examined against the political debates of his time and alongside current 'theories of knowledge'. Not available for review were Robert Mulvihill's edition of essays on Orwell entitled *Reflections on America, 1984: An Orwell Symposium* (UGeo) which includes articles by Hugh Kenner and Robert Coles among others and Bernard Oldsey's collection of previously published material, *Critical Essays on George Orwell* (Hall).

In *EIC* John Whitehead makes a rather obvious point when he compares Isherwood's first novel, *All the Conspirators*, and Auden's early poetry. The two men share 'a common intellectual climate coupled with the sexual ingredient in their friendship' and this, he speculates, can be seen in shared themes, allusions, diction, and mood.

Philip Toynbee once asserted that if he were 'cultural dictator of England . . . [he] would make *At Swim-Two-Birds* compulsory reading at all our universities'. He may not have had his way but a new casebook on the novel[95], containing a range of previously published essays, testifies to continuing academic interest in Flann O'Brien's work. In his introduction Rüdiger Imhof

94. *George Orwell: The Age's Adversary*, by Patrick Reilly. Macmillan. pp. xiv + 316. £27.50.

95. *Alive – Alive O! Flann O'Brien's 'At Swim-Two-Birds'*, ed. by Rüdiger Imhof. Wolfhound/B&N (1985). pp. 213. £15.

offers a brief biographical sketch of O'Brien, points to the novel's meta-fictional status, surveys main trends in its critical reception, and hints at the influence of the novel on contemporary experimental fiction. Part 1 contains brief comments and extracts from contemporary reviewers (and from O'Brien himself) both at the time of publication (1939) and of re-issue (1960). Part 2 has essays or extracts which focus in a more detailed and scholarly way on the novel and the novelist. A number of these are quite effective, such as Bernard Benstock's overview of O'Brien's literary achievement, or J. C. C. Mays's discussion of O'Brien's counterpointing methods and the seriousness which lies below the humour. Others, like Anthony Burgess's brief extract on O'Brien's distinctive blend of 'myth, fiction and actuality', give a good indication of further areas needing elucidation. Niall Sheridan offers some personal recollections of the origin of the novel and of Joyce's reaction, Stephen Knight relates the structure of the novel to O'Brien's critique of 'epistemological certainties', and, in a well-judged but difficult examination of the novel's metafictional nature, Miles Orvell looks at the ways in which O'Brien controls reader-response. Anthony Cronin comes ably to O'Brien's defence against critics who see the novel simply as a parody of Joyce (*At Swim* is a typically modernist text according to Cronin), and Anne Clissman sketches in the opposing arguments with her treatment of the novel as a conscious take-off of Joyce's *Portrait* and *Ulysses*. The best essay in the collection is also the most challenging one – Ninian Mellamphy's consideration of O'Brien's theory of fiction as exemplified by his practices in the novel. Again O'Brien is seen to face in what might be called a modernist direction for he rejects previous 'conventions of mimetic fiction' as inadequate for representing the complex nature of human perception. Rüdiger Imhof links O'Brien, quite understandably, to the tradition of 'comic-experimental, or, preferably, meta-novelists' embracing Sterne and B. S. Johnson. There is a helpful select bibliography and what appears to be a 'leg-pull' in true O'Brien fashion – an article from the notorious de Selby. It is good to see interest in O'Brien revived, though the lack of any really up-to-date work on the novel in terms of current theories of fantasy in the bibliography suggests a further potentially fruitful area for investigation.

In *LMag* Jeremy Lewis argues that Roy Fuller's strength as a novelist lies in his ability to 'distil and reflect . . . behaviour and states of mind that are familiar to us all'.

(c) Individual Authors: Post-1945

This section deals with writers who have produced all or part of their work after 1945. Authors have been arranged chronologically. As usual there has been a large amount of published work this year, particularly on women writers (Barbara Pym's meteoric rise continues, and Elizabeth Bowen also benefits) and on popular authors (le Carré, P. D. James, J. G. Ballard). Irish writers are also receiving more attention. Conversely work on such established figures as Anthony Powell, Angus Wilson, and Lawrence Durrell has declined in quantity almost to vanishing point, though the year has been marked by the appearance of the first critical studies of J. G. Farrell and John Berger, both long overdue and excellent.

One's first thought on contemplating Marius Buning's *T. F. Powys: A*

Modern Allegorist[96] is the luxury involved in being able to devote 261 pages to the study of two novels by an obscure author whose works are not readily available or even all in print. Would a British publisher take the risk? In fact, however, the book is more general than first appears, devoting one-third of its space to theories of allegory from Coleridge to Paul de Man, and then two meaty chapters to a close examination of his chosen texts. It reads well and is clearly the product of a sophisticated critical intelligence, but the specialized nature of its subject places it somewhat beyond the evaluative powers of the present reviewer. The nature of Dostoevsky's influence on John Cowper Powys is re-assessed by Charles Lock in 'Polyphonic Powys' (*UTQ*), which emphasizes points of agreement between Powys and Mikhail Bakhtin in their reading of Dostoevsky, and suggests a possible explanation of the shift in Powys's career from the monologic *Wolf Solent* to the polyphonic *A Glastonbury Romance*. Despite the complexity of this subject, Lock handles his arguments with intelligence and lucidity.

PowysR seems to be able to attract interesting material on a regular basis. Together with letters, reviews, photographs, an unpublished poem by J. C. Powys, and the text of *Mordaunt Ap Gryfith*, an incomplete romance written when J. C. Powys was sixteen, No. 18 includes a substantial and wide-ranging essay by Glen Cavaliero on the comic dimension of his novels, entitled 'The Comic Spirit in the Novels and Fantasies of John Cowper Powys'. J. C. Powys is also the focus of four other essays. Ian Hughes's suggestion in 'The Genre of John Cowper Powys's Major Novels' (up to and including *Maiden Castle*) that they are best considered as philosophic romances, influenced by Walter Pater's conception of that genre, indicates a fruitful new approach. Susan Rands discusses '*Rodmoor*: Aspects of its Provenance and Direction', drawing attention to its autobiographical interest, while Meirion Pennar goes 'In Search of the Real Glendower', considering ways in which Powys's eponymous hero differs from the historical Glendower. Jacqueline Peltier's 'American Landscapes in John Cowper Powys's Letters to His Brother Llewelyn' concentrates on the former's experience of America, in an essay which sets out to remedy the lack of attention hitherto paid to his residence in the United States. Only one essay is directly concerned with T. F. Powys, a discussion of 'The Wisht Hound Tradition and T. F. Powys's *Mark Only*'. Angela Blaen's succinct piece is precise, scholarly, and incidentally throws interesting light on *The Hound of the Baskervilles*. No. 19 also concentrates on John Cowper, with the exception of J. Lawrence Mitchell's detailed account of 'The Education of T. F. Powys'. Oliver Marlow Wilkinson reproduces letters between John Cowper and Frances Gregg, with commentary, and Frederick Davies offers 'Recollections of John Cowper Powys and Phyllis Playter'. Michael Ballin's 'John Cowper Powys's *Porius* and the Dialectic of History' considers the dialectical structure of this historical novel, producing a radically new reading of it. Dorothee von Huene Greenberg makes quite an interesting short essay out of the unpromising topic of 'Stone Worship and the Search for Community in John Cowper Powys's *A Glastonbury Romance*'. *PowysR* is, as usual, lavishly produced, and is noteworthy for providing space for extended essays,

---

96. *T. F. Powys: A Modern Allegorist. The Companion Novels 'Mr Weston's Good Wine' and 'Unclay' in the Light of Modern Allegorical Theory*, by Marius Buning. Rodopi. pp. 261. Fl 90.

something of a rarity nowadays. H. W. Fawkner's *The Ecstatic World of John Cowper Powys* (FDU/AUP) was not seen.

Mary S. Wagoner has managed to write a critical study of Agatha Christie[97] without giving away the ending of the stories. It seems a curious accomplishment, and one wonders who would want a critical analysis of a novel which they had not yet read. Wagoner also elects to comment on the bulk of Christie's prolific output and to ignore most of the sociological or psychological theorizing on offer in favour of an emphasis on Christie's story-telling, dividing her works into four types (formula, fairy-tale motifs, supernaturalism, and comedy of manners). The result is better than one might expect, with a persuasive case for Christie's success as based on mastery of a formula which combined predictable resolution with considerable variation but, on the whole, writer and the TEAS series format make for odd bedfellows.

Polygon have now re-issued Neil M. Gunn's *The Atom of Delight*[98], first published in 1956, a form of spiritual autobiography influenced by Zen Buddhism and covering Gunn's first eighteen years. A short introduction by J. B. Pick situates the work in its literary context. *SSL* includes a lengthy account of the sources of *The Silver Darlings* from Alistair M. McCleery. It is a fairly useful essay though the present reviewer was unconvinced by his description of the image of the Highland Clearances as the product of an established Gloomy Memories genre, exacerbated by Celtic Twilight pangs of doom: folk memories in Caithness are keener and less literary than this allows for.

Tolkien enthusiasts will welcome the fourth volume of Christopher Tolkien's History of Middle-Earth[99], which takes the reader up to the 1930s. As well as reproducing Tolkien's writings, each preceded by commentary, the volume also prints diagrams and maps, and provides an index of interrelated place and personal names. Specialists should also be aware of the existence of *Inklings* which continues to flourish with essays this year (in German) on Charles Williams, George MacDonald, and C. S. Lewis (with English summaries) and two essays on Tolkien in English. J. S. Ryan contributes a scholarly discussion of oath-swearing in *The Lord of the Rings*, Andrzej Zgorzelski extols the lyricism of the same work. *Arda* is another scholarly annual devoted to the works of Tolkien, published in Stockholm in Swedish. Essays in the 1982–3 issue include 'Studies in Tolkien's Language' by Nils-Lennart Johannesson, reviews, bibliographical essays, and short notes, followed by summaries in English.

Isobel Murray has edited a volume of Naomi Mitchison's stories[100], ranging from 1932 to 1982, which provides a characteristic selection of her work, including stories of the ancient world, of Scotland, and of Africa. The title story, first published in a slim volume in 1935, was the result of a unique collab-

97. *Agatha Christie*, by Mary S. Wagoner. Twayne. pp. 162. $17.95.

98. *The Atom of Delight*, by Neil M. Gunn, intro. by J. B. Pick. Polygon. pp. 243. pb £4.95.

99. *The Shaping of Middle-Earth: The Quenta, The Ambarkanta, and The Annals together with the earliest 'Silmarillion' and the first Map*, by J. R. R. Tolkien, ed. by Christopher Tolkien. A&U. pp. 380. £14.95.

100. *Beyond This Limit: Selected Shorter Fiction of Naomi Mitchison*, ed. and intro. by Isobel Murray. SAP. pp. xix + 217. pb £4.95.

oration with Wyndham Lewis, whose original illustrations are handsomely reproduced. The year also saw a paperback reprint of Mitchison's memoir, *You May Well Ask*[101], which is a mine of information on the political and literary climate of the interwar years, and exceptionally good value.

Belated mention should be made here of Lee D. Rossi's comparative study of Tolkien and C. S. Lewis[102]. Rossi sets out to contest the easy labels of 'conservative' or 'rightist' in relation to his chosen subjects and makes a case for both as fundamentally apolitical, though he draws a distinction between Tolkien's profound pessimism and Lewis's search for non-materialist values in scholarship, friendship, and religion. It is a modestly successful volume, though perhaps overestimating the authors' intentions and underestimating the political responses of their readership. Lewis's critical stance is the focus for Bruce L. Edwards Jr in 'Deconstruction and Rehabilitation: C. S. Lewis's Defense of Western Textuality' (*JETS*), which juxtaposes Lewis's supposed 'rehabilitative' stance with what the author perceives as the nihilism currently besetting literary criticism. *CSLBull* has the usual conference reports, short notes, letters, and bibliographical information, with contributions on almost every aspect of Lewis's activity. Though no essay on the fiction deserves to be singled out, the bulletin remains useful for the enthusiast.

Hermione Lee has edited a bumper selection of Elizabeth Bowen's nonfiction[103], including essays, reviews, prefaces, letters, broadcasts, and an autobiographical fragment. An essential companion to the fiction, the volume brings out the close relation between Bowen's fictional subjects and her childhood experiences, her feeling for place, and her impatience with the anaesthetized emotions of the modern world. Lee identifies in her writing a consistent paradox, a convergence of sensation and detachment, which is also borne out in the selection. The introduction and commentary are intelligent, balanced (the gush of the letters and the gentleness of the reviews do not go unremarked) and highly informative. French-speaking scholars will also welcome Dominique Gauthier's monumental volume[104] on the subject of Bowen's conception of the real. Despite the cumbersomely exhaustive format of the French thesis, Gauthier manages to keep the ball of argument rolling, with only the odd *longueur*. At the end, however, her speculation that interest in Bowen has decreased since the 1970s seems premature, given the volume of work now appearing. Patricia Craig's biography of Bowen[105], in Penguin's new Lives of Modern Women series, is too short to add more than the odd detail to Victoria Glendinning's 1977 biography (*YW* 58.363–4), but includes some discussion of the works, is generally perceptive, and makes a good read at a low price. *Éire* features a useful essay from Phyllis Lassner which examines the 'Big House' motif in *The Last September*, as representing moral, political, and psychological contradictions which shape the Anglo-Irish. James M. Haule

101. *You May Well Ask: A Memoir 1920–1940*, by Naomi Mitchison. Flamingo: Fontana. pp. 240. pb £3.50.

102. *The Politics of Fantasy: C. S. Lewis and J. R. R. Tolkien*, by Lee D. Rossi. UMIRes (1984). pp. x + 143. £29.60.

103. *The Mulberry Tree: Writings of Elizabeth Bowen*, sel. and intro. by Hermione Lee. Virago. pp. x + 325. £12.95.

104. *L'Image Du Réel Dans Les Romans D'Elizabeth Bowen*, by Dominique Gauthier. Didier. pp. 498. Ffr 335.

105. *Elizabeth Bowen*, by Patricia Craig. Penguin. pp. 143. pb £2.95.

(*CLQ*) notes a different formative influence, Rider Haggard's *She*, persuasively establishing that the image of the female capable of a power beyond moral control recurs in veiled form in many of Bowen's works.

The spring issue of *JSSE* is a special number devoted to the work of V. S. Pritchett. An interview reveals the influence on his writing of his family background, other writers, and sense of place, together with his own views on the aesthetics of short fiction. The issue also reprints a short story ('Oedipus Complex') dating from 1945. Seven critical essays then follow, treating such topics as fantasy ('The Diver'), poetic form ('Many Are Disappointed'), character, narrative ('The Fly in the Ointment'), water imagery, comedy ('The Aristocrat'), and expressionism. The contributions, all from French academics, are invariably interesting, and particularly valuable for their detailed and specific readings of individual stories.

D. S. Savage's 'Richard Hughes, Solipsist' is a substantial essay in *SR* on Hughes, envisaged as haunted by solipsism, painfully aware of the isolation of the ego, the illusory nature of human experience, and the hollowness of all accepted moral standards. A source study is also worth remarking in connection with Richard Hughes. Writing in the June number of *N&Q*, Ian Milligan notes the extent of Hughes's borrowing from the sketches of a Scottish journalist, Michael Scott, in *A High Wind in Jamaica*.

There is the beginning of a revival of interest in the work of Anna Kavan, with a general re-assessment, discussion of the fiction, and biographical sketch from Günther Stuhlmann in 'Anna Kavan Revisited', and a discussion of her relationship with her publishers from Peter Owen, both essays appearing in *Anais* (1985).

Scots may have mixed feelings concerning the new Penguin re-issue of Lewis Grassic Gibbon's *A Scots Quair*[106]. A more scholarly format (e.g. notes) would have been preferable, and the introduction (from David Kerr Cameron) adds little to the reader's understanding. The information that Gibbon was 'laid in his mother's plaid in the shelter of a stook' is of dubious importance, and Cameron's later flights are reminiscent of Waugh's William Boot. ('He knew the poetry of the plough and the blitheness of haytime. His writing imbibed the smell of the soil, the odour of dung.') Nor will those 'sturdy folk' who inhabit the Grampian area be entranced to discover their forebears characterized as 'malicious and foulmouthed'. Penguin could have done better than this.

Michael L. Storey's comparative essay (*CLS*) links Frank O'Connor's 'Guests of the Nation' with Camus's 'The Guest'. While no direct influence of one on the other is discernible, Storey draws out the strong similarities, which appear to spring from their personal experiences of independence-struggles.

Two books have appeared concerning Evelyn Waugh. Martin Stannard's *Evelyn Waugh: The Early Years*[107] is the first biography for eleven years, drawing upon a large amount of disparate material which has recently appeared, and is therefore likely to become the standard work for some time. It is easily the fullest biography to date (at times too full) and (apart from Waugh's admiration for Mussolini which is soft-pedalled) does not pull its

106. *A Scots Quair*, by Lewis Grassic Gibbon, intro. by David Kerr Cameron. Penguin. pp. 496. pb £4.95.

107. *Evelyn Waugh: The Early Years 1903–1939*, by Martin Stannard. Dent. pp. xiv + 537. £14.95.

punches. The Waugh who emerges from it is an unhappy, isolated neurotic, constructing a bold persona as a hard shell over a very soft centre. It has to be said, however, that this shift of emphasis is all that is really *new* to the book. Stannard has interviewed the first Mrs Waugh and is able to make various minor corrections to previous accounts of the period; he has collated the various memoirs and reminiscences of Waugh's contacts; and has done a workmanlike job of writing up the results of his researches. But much of it seems to be going over well-tilled ground with a fine rake. Jacqueline McDonnell's book[108] is certainly redundant. Far from giving a comprehensive view of the women in the novels, its supposed intention, it sets out to seek originals for them, proceeding to hunt for sources in an obsessive fashion. From its opening pages (a checklist of heroines and their admirers) to the four appendixes with which it closes it is methodologically confused, mixing fiction and biography in an unenlightening fashion, drawing up lists of such topics as the heroines' attitudes to money, and subdividing chapters under such headings as 'Blue Eyes' or 'Cat-like'. It is a pity, as the subject itself was a good one.

Interest in Waugh also provokes a number of articles. Kurt Schlueter examines time in *Brideshead Revisited*[109]. Though he makes rather a meal out of the distinction between present and past action, Schlueter does draw attention to an interesting silence in the novel – the time between the end of the remembered action (1939) and that of the present action (1943) is bypassed, even though it contains the most important act of Ryder's life, his religious conversion. In *MFS* James J. Lynch makes sensible and detailed use of biographical data in order to assess how Waugh's own anxieties about money, health, and reputation contributed to the persecution mania of the *Pinfold* breakdown. Waugh's travel writing is the focus for Robert Murray Davis in *Renascence*, who, in 'The Rhetoric of Mexican Travel', compares *Mexico: An Object Lesson* with Greene's *Another Mexico*, examining style, narrative strategies, and techniques. Greene's (the better book) emerges as characteristic of his writing in ways which Waugh's is not. Davis also contributes a short note in *JML* on Waugh's interest in Thomas Merton and his editing of his writings. *EWN* is full of interest in 1986. In the first number Donald Greene explicates various recondite allusions in the fiction. (The account of the detective work involved in the hunt for 'Burton's stucco tent', discovered in a churchyard in Mortlake after a long tramp around the area's cemeteries, makes for fascinating reading.) In the second number D. J. Dooley sheds light on Waugh in Yugoslavia, Kurt Schlueter returns once more to the time-scheme of *Brideshead Revisited*, and Gerhard Wölk provides a supplementary list of criticism. The third number includes Auberon Waugh (on his father's interest in wine), Mark L. Gnerro (explicating echoes of the Anima Christi in *Men at Arms*), and Robert Murray Davis and Thomas Argiro, comparing Waugh and Greene as reviewers in the 1930s. There are the usual reviews and brief notes, and the entire volume bears the mark of serious scholarship worn lightly.

Grahame Smith's study of Greene[110] adopts a fairly traditional critical

108. *Waugh on Women*, by Jacqueline McDonnell. Duckworth. pp. x + 239. £19.95.

109. In *Elizabethan and Modern Studies: Presented To Professor Willem Schrickx on the Occasion of his Retirement*, ed. by J. P. Vander Motten. UGhent (1985). pp. 343. $25.

110. *The Achievement of Graham Greene*, by Grahame Smith. Harvester. pp. 228. £18.95.

approach, blending biography with close study of the works, but is none the worse for that. Smith's strengths lie in his ability to situate Greene in the context of twentieth-century art forms (popular fiction, the cinema) in an accessible style which reaches out to the general reader, and in a pleasantly balanced exploration of the political and religious themes. Weaknesses include the omission of any consideration of *Doctor Fischer of Geneva*, *The Tenth Man*, *Monsignor Quixote*, and *Getting to Know the General*, despite a blurb promising an up-to-date survey of the whole range of Greene's writing. There are also some minor errors (Wormald for Wormold). In a short space, however, Smith has a fair stab at illuminating a prolific and various writer.

A. A. DeVitis's critical volume[111], first published in 1964, has now been comprehensively revised and updated, to include discussion of all Greene's novels, short stories, and dramatic works. In most respects the emphasis remains much as before, on Greene's artistic and imaginative treatment of religious matters, with DeVitis now detecting a movement from a concern with the dogma of Roman Catholicism towards a broader kind of Christian humanism, accompanied in the later novels by a growing awareness of the possibilities of tragicomedy. Constrained by the series format as much as by Greene's own prolific output, DeVitis at times makes his points in rather summary fashion, with interesting ideas (e.g. chess imagery in *The Human Factor*) insufficiently developed. A systematic discussion of Greene's elusive political stance is also lacking. Nonetheless, this is probably the best available general work on Greene, and a good departure-point for students.

In *JNT* Richard Creese compares the narrative strategies of Ford's *The Good Soldier* and *The End of the Affair*, concluding that despite Greene's suggestion that his novel owes much to Ford, in fact the two works use very different patterns of narrative: 'abstracting' (Ford) in which the narrator mentally processes narrated reality, imitating the motions of the human mind rather than the physical world, and 'recording' where the narrator pretends to imitate experiential reality. For all the technical terminology and the modish invocation of Gérard Genette, the essay does not really contribute much to the understanding of either author, though there are occasionally useful incidental observations. One can be more positive about Randall Craig's essay (*Renascence*) on 'Good Places and Promised Lands in *The Comedians*', as a rich example of the complex function of place in Greene's fiction. The exploration of dramatic metaphors and of the function of dreams in the novel also deserves special mention. *CLS* contains an essay by Patrick Henry on Cervantes and Unamuno in connection with *Monsignor Quixote*, reminiscent of his earlier essay on the same topic in *CollL* (1985). A short note from Michael Routh in *NConL* points out that the race gangs in *Brighton Rock* derive from contemporary newspaper reports, particularly the beating of two bookmakers at Lewes race-track in 1936. Penguin have recently republished Greene's *Collected Short Stories*[112] which include the thirty-seven originally published as *May We Borrow Your Husband?*, *A Sense of Reality*, and *Twenty-One Stories*. It is high time, however, for a longer volume to be published to include Greene's many uncollected short stories. Only one writer considers the short fiction – Peter P. Clarke in *ELN* who reads 'The Destructors' as an anarchist parable specficially

111. *Graham Greene*, by A. A. DeVitis. Twayne. pp. 218. $15.95.
112. *Collected Short Stories*, by Graham Greene. Penguin. pp. 367. pb £3.95.

influenced by Bakunin. It makes a great deal of sense. In *Kunapipi* (1985) Mark Williams argues that Greene solved the problem of writing an interesting account of a tedious journey (*Journey without Maps*) by turning the African coast into a moralized landscape, a strategy which draws on Conrad and invites comparison with Lowry, Patrick White, and Wilson Harris. Williams accepts the invitation and spends most of the essay on the last two named.

Oddvar Holmesland's critical introduction[113] to the novels of Henry Green is very much a work for enthusiasts and specialists. Holmesland raises an important problem (the absence of clearly defined moral preoccupations in the fiction), arguing that far from simply portraying the multiplicity and complexity of life Green subtly directs the imaginative participation of the reader, notably by using montage techniques to reveal his attitude to his characters and events. Though Holmesland makes out a good case, the book does not exactly flow smoothly from point to point. There are frequent pauses for close analysis of passages, comparative suggestions, and quotations from Green and others, with the result that the force of a fair argument is attenuated.

There has been less work than usual on the fiction of Samuel Beckett. (*JBeckS* was not available for review). In *MFS* Ronald R. Thomas reads Beckett's *Company* in tandem with *Dr Jekyll and Mr Hyde* as examples of 'schizo-textuality' i.e. accounts of the self's entrapment within the text and within language, and narratives of escape. The present reviewer escaped from Thomas's essay and turned with some relief to Geoffrey Strickland's more accessible *CQ* piece, 'The Seriousness of Samuel Beckett', a consideration of whether or not the reader should take Beckett seriously. Strickland ranges widely over the drama and fiction, drawing attention to the intellectual integrity of Beckett's writing but also to its terrible reductiveness.

Nos. 17 and 18 of *MLNew* form a bumper double-issue which features for the first time some half-tone photographs. The 150 pages are largely taken up with reviews, short notes, announcements, a bibliographical list, reminiscences of Lowry and of Dollarton, plus a poem and a short story about Lowry. Duncan Hadfield contributes two more substantial essays, elucidating the influence of Conrad's *Heart of Darkness* and 'Youth' on *Under the Volcano*, but the overall impression is of a volume whose contributors are overly preoccupied with trivia. It is doubtful whether anyone other than Chris Ackerley (who raises the question among some fifty other queries of a similar nature) burns to uncover the actual model for the 'hell bunker' in *Under the Volcano*, though Ackerley's description of his researches on the course at the Royal Liverpool Links at Hoylake, and his plaintive appeal for clarification of the matter, provided this reviewer with some welcome light relief.

In contrast *MPR* has rather a memorial tone to it, with reminiscences of Peake from Lonnie and Sebastian Peake, John Watney, and Kaye Webb together with illustrations by Peake for the magazine *Lilliput*, a description of foreign illustrations for the *Titus* books, and a brief essay (by Tanya Gardiner-Scott) on 'War Images and Influences in Mervyn Peake's *Titus Alone*'. If there is nothing here of an unusual nature, it is nonetheless all valuable material, unassumingly produced in a modest format.

William Golding has not so far had a journal dedicated to him, despite

---

113. *A Critical Introduction to Henry Green's Novels: The Living Vision*, by Oddvar Holmesland. Macmillan. pp. x + 250. £27.50.

continuing interest in his work. Philip Redpath[114] offers his study as the first book-length discussion of Golding to benefit from structuralist and poststructuralist ideas, disclaiming any attempt at an explanation of the meaning of the novels in favour of exploring ways in which possible meanings are created. While this is an admirably undogmatic and explorative approach, the volume tends over much towards a 'nuts and bolts' analysis of the structures of individual novels (with diagrams, arrows, lists) and a tendency to overstate the obvious. (The new structure discovered in *Lord of the Flies* turns out to be the alternation of trips to the forest with trips to the mountain). In addition, while commending Golding's deliberate artifice and obscurity, Redpath's own preference for a succession of short declarative statements makes for slow reading and inhibits the sense of a developing argument. (A chapter-length digression comparing Golding and Ted Hughes also interrupts the flow.) There are real strengths here, particularly in the comparison of pairs of novels which explore opposed hypotheses, but one wishes that Redpath had not been quite so bashfully even-handed in his interpretations. John Carey's volume[115] is very much a birthday party of a book, affectionately celebrating its subject. Five essays are essentially memoirs (including a fascinating account of Golding's atheist, socialist father) and four are discursive pieces by fellow-writers (Fowles, Craig Raine, Ted Hughes, Ian McEwan) plus a poem by Seamus Heaney, and the text of an interview with John Carey. A quintet of literary critics considers the fiction from various angles. Anthony Storr's psychological approach concentrates on Golding's hatred of rationalism and his concern with sadism and violence. John Bayley ruminates on impersonality, Barbara Everett on pity, Ian Gregor on the religious imagination, and Mark Kinkead-Weekes on the disparity between the visual and the visionary in the works. Though the essays are as interesting as one might expect from such august contributors, there is a curious sense in which Golding evaporates under their gaze, with Bayley finding no intimate sense of the writer's self in the novels and Everett discussing the lack of a personal style.

Other critics, undeterred by any elusiveness, have produced a diverse collection of essays. In *SoRA* B. R. Johnson contests the common view of Golding as an evangelist writing pessimistic sermons, in favour of a more explorative and optimistic novelist. A persuasive reading of *The Inheritors* demonstrates that its current devaluation as parable does serious harm to its larger scope. Philip Redpath's analysis of *Darkness Visible* (*ArielE*) from a structural point of view is admirably clear (time-scheme and diagrams included) whereas John Coates, writing about the same novel in *Renascence* dwells on its 'loaded obscurity' in terms of biblical analogues, acts of invocation, and religious quest. The results could have been expressed more succinctly. Irène Simon, in a speculative essay[109], takes as her subject the supernatural design of *The Paper Men*, teasing out both its ambiguities and its structural flaws. Macmillan have now included *The Spire* in their Master Guides series[116], which provide biographical information, a synopsis, chapter summaries, and a

114. *William Golding: A Structured Reading of his Fiction*, by Philip Redpath. Vision/B&N. pp. 222. £17.95.

115. *William Golding: The Man and his Books. A Tribute on his Seventy-fifth Birthday*, ed. by John Carey. Faber. pp. 191. £12.50.

116. *'The Spire' by William Golding*, by Rosemary Sumner. MMG. Macmillan. pp. ix + 78. pb £1.25.

critical commentary, all aimed at student readers. It looks fairly useful though Sumner's students seem an odd bunch. She covers such topics as psychology, good and evil, and characterization by means of a conversation between imaginary student-readers who bear little resemblance to the real. Their familiar phraseology includes 'purports', and they refer easily to Kakfa, Browning, and Arnold, plus (even less likely) contemporary Golding scholars.

Four essays on Flann O'Brien are well worth reading. In *JIL* Patricia O'Hare argues that it is a mistake to consider *At Swim-Two-Birds* solely in the context of the tradition of the reflexive novel, for throughout it O'Brien worked closely with the conventions of traditional Irish legend and folklore. The figure of Finn MacCool is the major focus in a solidly researched essay. Joseph M. Conte (*RCF*, 1985) explores metaphor and metonymy in the same novel, drawing on the theories of Roman Jakobson. Marilyn Thorne's 'The Provocative Bicycle in Flann O'Brien's *The Third Policeman*' (*Éire*) emphasizes the female gender of the trusty steed, which represents sensuality, kept in the cycles of hell under the lock and key of the law. Thorne handles her learning lightly here in a most engaging essay, which is a tribute to its subject in style as well as content. Sanford Pinsker's general essay (*Éire*, 1985) also makes for lively reading, throwing off suggestions in various directions.

Robin Jenkins has published more than twenty books since 1951, but features very rarely in accounts of the contemporary novel. The autumn issue of *Cencrastus* is therefore particularly welcome, including an excerpt from an unpublished novel, a biographical piece (Bernard Sellin), a general assessment (Glenda Norquay), and a more detailed discussion of the ironies of *Guests of War* (Douglas Gifford). The whole is handsomely illustrated and provides a useful introduction to Jenkins's work.

Hogarth Press have now issued *A Day in Summer*[117], J. L. Carr's first novel, with a new introduction by D. J. Taylor. Although Taylor interestingly highlights the Englishness of the novel, its tragic quality, and its attention to the 'woman question', it is to be hoped that his assertion that J. L. Carr's 'literary tastes were fully formed by 1939' will prompt a fuller study of a writer whose complexity remains underrated.

Robert Liddell's *Elizabeth and Ivy*[118], billed as an affectionate memoir of a three-sided friendship (Liddell, Ivy Compton-Burnett, Elizabeth Taylor) is disappointingly slim. Though Liddell is himself a novelist, the real interest of the volume lies in the light shed on Taylor by excerpts from her letters. Liddell corresponded with both women for years, but unfortunately lost Taylor's early letters, and adopts a somewhat dog-in-the-manger attitude to the rest, suppressing large numbers of them. Though he makes much of his scrupulous observation of Taylor's own wishes in the matter, one cannot help feeling that the decent alternatives in such a case are total silence or total publication, rather than a heavily edited and expensive selection.

Angus Wilson's *Reflections in a Writer's Eye*[119] is a somewhat uneven collection of travel pieces written between 1957 and 1984. Though several places evoke drab reactions (Japan, America, the Channel Islands) Wilson's

117. *A Day in Summer*, by J. L. Carr, intro. by D. J. Taylor. Hogarth. pp. 219. pb £3.95.
118. *Elizabeth and Ivy*, by Robert Liddell. Owen. pp. 126. £10.50.
119. *Reflections in a Writer's Eye*, by Angus Wilson. S&W. pp. 184. £9.95.

accounts of his visits to South Africa (1961) and India (1975) are penetratingly observant and enlightening.

The booming interest in Barbara Pym continues. (Four critical studies are apparently in preparation.) 1986 saw the publication of another posthumous novel, *An Academic Question*[120], prepared for publication by Hazel Holt, who has amalgamated two drafts (first-person, 1971, third-person, 1972) into a coherent whole. Though readers may have their doubts about this type of editing procedure, the resultant novel reads well and is particularly interesting in its anthropological subject matter (inspired by a wrangle in the journal *Africa*) and in the transitional nature of its heroine, an 'excellent woman' updated. Two book-length studies have also appeared. Robert Emmet Long[121] proceeds chronologically novel by novel, in a sensible fashion, if somewhat encumbered by plot summary. Major emphases are Pym's ambivalent attitude to romance, her ironic reversal of courtship norms, and the absence of characters with a strong sense of their own existence. The biographical introduction contains some new material and the author has benefited from consulting the manuscripts. Diana Benet's study[122] is altogether more focused and lively, arguing that Pym develops from the feminine towards more universal concerns, and from comedy to tragedy. For Benet, Pym's whole subject is love; her characters are always in quest of an emotional context or focal point. It makes for some illuminating readings.

The year also saw the first issues of *The Barbara Pym Newsletter* (*BPN*), which carries reviews, letters, information, and a survey of recent scholarship. Four essays are worth noting. Kate Browder Heberlein's discussion of 'Pym's Carry-Over Characters' suggests the various effects achieved by this device, and Merritt Moseley's short article on the 'darker' novels (*Quartet in Autumn* and *The Sweet Dove Died*) underlines their distinctive qualities. In the second issue, J. M. Geddes's 'Boiled Chicken and All That' discusses food and drink in Pym's fiction, while Louise Flavin, concentrating upon '*A Few Green Leaves*: Separating Novelist from Anthropologist', relates 'carry-over' characters to Pym's desire to forge a new kind of realism by exploiting the similarities between novelist and anthropologist. Carefully produced, the *Newsletter* is unpretentious, succinct, and well worth consulting.

TCL contains two essays on Pym. In '*The Sweet Dove Died*: The Sexual Politics of Narcissism' Mason Cooley sees Leonora as a narcissist. The point is well substantiated though Cooley goes about it in too leisurely a fashion. In addition to her novels Pym wrote more than thirty pieces of short fiction. In 'The Short Fiction of Barbara Pym' Anthony Kaufman investigates ways in which her preoccupation with failure permeates the stories, which he recognizes as of varying quality. In *MFS* Jill Rubenstein uses the theory of speech acts as developed by J. L. Austin and John Searle, among others, as a conceptual tool to examine failed communication as the primary source of Pym's comedy. *Less Than Angels* is the major focus in a short but broadly suggestive essay. *UWR* (1985) carries an article by Mary Anne Schofield on 'Patterns of Cooking and Eating in the Novels of Barbara Pym', which draws usefully on Levi-Strauss to

120. *An Academic Question*, by Barbara Pym. Macmillan. pp. 182. £9.95.

121. *Barbara Pym*, by Robert Emmet Long. Ungar. pp. xi + 256. $16.95.

122. *Something to Love: Barbara Pym's Novels*, by Diana Benet. UMiss. pp. 164. pb £8.95.

underline the way in which culinary processes, undertaken by female protagonists, are attempts to civilize and socialize the male. In *SDR* Patricia Kane divides Pym's female characters into three types (observers, manipulators, typists) and runs through them, fitting them into their categories. Lorna Peterson's 1984 checklist has now been updated (*BB*) by Judy Berndt who supplies a supplementary list of secondary sources, including reviews, essays, and dissertations on Pym.

In contrast to Pym, the Colin MacInnes revival limps on rather haltingly. *The Colin MacInnes Omnibus*[123] contains his three London novels, *City of Spades*, *Absolute Beginners*, and *Mr Love and Justice*. The recent rediscovery of Denton Welch has prompted Penguin to re-issue *Maiden Voyage*[124], an autobiographical travelogue first published in 1943, and the first book in the author's brief career. Michael De-la-Noy's biography[125], first published to critical acclaim in 1984, and now re-issued in paperback, deserves to be widely known. Working from original source material from the archives of the University of Texas, and hundreds of letters, De-la-Noy provides a comprehensive, well-written, and entertaining account of the life of a writer who has been neglected by historians of the 1940s.

Geoffrey Aggeler has edited a selection of critical essays on Anthony Burgess[126], to which he contributes an excellent introduction, outlining critical reactions to Burgess's works and briefly surveying the works themselves. He ends with the claim that 'there is plenty of room for more articles and additional book length studies and it is to be hoped that this collection will encourage future Burgess scholarship'. This pious hope might better have been realized, however, had the volume itself contained more original work. Only two of the sixteen essays are new. The others, though important, are all readily available elsewhere in periodicals or in their authors' books. (The editor himself contributes two of them.) Both new pieces are worth reading (Michael Rudick on the Enderby novels, and François Camoins's brief review of *Tremor of Intent*) but $38 seems rather a lot to pay for them. *NConL* (1985) includes a short note from Ellen McDaniel on *The End of the World News*, noting the inappropriateness of medium (lightweight genres) to message, and concluding that the work is designed to highlight the dangers of forgetting our cultural heritage and adulterating our art.

Muriel Spark is the subject of Alan Bold's brief study[127], which covers all the major works. Though Bold notes that her works are 'haunted by the spectre of a theological eternity' he emphasizes that nothing is sacred as far as Spark's satirical wit is concerned, whether in religious or literary terms (e.g. the deconstruction of realism in the fiction). One senses that Bold is somewhat cramped by the series format, advancing at times in summary fashion, via the catalogue, but on the whole he provides a useful introduction to Spark.

Both the general reader and the specialist will find many meaty bones of

123. *The Colin MacInnes Omnibus*, by Colin MacInnes. A&B (1985). pp. 176. hb £12, pb £6.95.

124. *Maiden Voyage*, by Denton Welch. Penguin. pp. 256. pb £3.95.

125. *Denton Welch: The Making of a Writer*, by Michael De-la-Noy. Penguin. pp. 303. pb £4.95.

126. *Critical Essays on Anthony Burgess*, ed. by Geoffrey Aggeler. Hall. pp. vii + 231. $38.

127. *Muriel Spark*, by Alan Bold. Methuen. pp. 128. pb £3.50.

contention in Peter J. Conradi's study[128] of Iris Murdoch. Sympathetic without proselytizing, Conradi supports his contention that Murdoch is (in Isaiah Berlin's famous phrase) more of a fox than a hedgehog, one who knows many things rather than one. Comedy, the understanding of power, the limits of rationalism, are just some of the matters tackled, and Conradi also sweeps aside several critical concerns (existentialism, George Eliot) as red herrings, in a solidly researched study which is also an exceptionally good read. One minor cavil – the use of asterisks to interrupt the argument in the conclusion is a tiresome mannerism. Despite its title *A Character Index and Guide to the Fiction of Iris Murdoch*[129] also includes plays. Otherwise it is entirely what it says it is, citing and annotating some 2,000 characters, places, animals, and organizations appearing in the works. A short introduction provides a cogent discussion of the interaction between Murdoch's characterization and moral philosophy, but otherwise the book is essentially one very long list.

Four periodical essays have also appeared. Lindsey Tucker contributes an intelligent essay to *ConL* on *The Sea, The Sea*, noting that *The Tempest* is used in a number of ways to reinforce meaning and structure, and that the novel also reveals a special emphasis on Tibetan Buddhism. The two apparently disparate elements are mutually supportive, in that each deals with the nature of dreams and reality, and the surrendering of magic in preparation for death. *Nuns and Soldiers* is the focus of Margaret Scanlan's excellent essay (*Renascence*) which explores the problem of the past in the novel, concluding that Murdoch's characters, enmeshed in the permanent crisis of an uncommunicable past, lack access or connection to a shared world of public history. Murdoch's pessimism emerges strongly from this thought-provoking essay. Howard Moss's general discussion of the novels, which appears in *GrandS*, is noteworthy for its attention to recent works, including *The Philosopher's Pupil* and *The Good Apprentice*, and for its stylish clarity ('Obsession is Iris Murdoch's meat and drink'). *DUJ* includes an essay by Ray Snape on *Henry and Cato* which sets out to analyse the topic of Murdoch's intelligence, arguing that the novel reveals a distinct lack of curiosity about the larger world outside the novelist's own specialized interests, and a disconcerting slickness in her realization of the latter. Though *Henry and Cato* may have its faults, Snape's conclusion that Murdoch's art is unintelligent seems somewhat sweeping, to put it politely. Amin Malak (*IFR*) contributes a short note on patterns of power in Orwell (*Nineteen Eighty-Four*) and Murdoch (*The Flight from the Enchanter*).

Benedict Kiely is the subject of an essay in *JSSE*, in which Frank Kersnowski examines the mixture of the sacred and profane in *A Ball of Malt and Madame Butterfly*, drawing usefully upon an interview with the author.

The year saw the first book-length study of Doris Lessing's science fiction[130], a distinguished work of criticism from Katherine Fishburn. The central thesis, that Lessing found in science fiction a new vehicle for the philosophical principles and social conscience of her earlier work, is richly supported with highly sophisticated discussions of the influence of Marxism, Sufi thought, and

128. *Iris Murdoch: The Saint and the Artist*, by Peter J. Conradi. Macmillan. pp. xvi + 304. £27.50.

129. *A Character Index and Guide to the Fiction of Iris Murdoch*, by Cheryl Browning Bove. Garland. pp. xiii + 272. $47.

130. *The Unexpected Universe of Doris Lessing: A Study in Narrative Technique*, by Katherine Fishburn. Greenwood. pp. ix + 184. £27.95.

modern physics to boot. Devoting one chapter to each of Lessing's science fiction novels, Fishburn highlights the steady rise to prominence of the narrator as guide-leader (reminiscent of Sufi teaching-stories), developing the various ways in which Lessing employs science fiction to challenge anthropocentric views of the universe and to modify definitions of reality. The volume concludes with an excellent bibliographical essay. Eve Bertelsen[131] has edited a fine collection of pieces relating to Lessing, in a volume which aims to make available basic information (chronology, bibliography) together with a variety of literary opinions (press reviews, reprints of published critical essays, the editor's own 1984 interview with Lessing). Four essays are new to print, Anne Hedin's discussion of the mandala as an organizing pattern in the later fiction, Jenny Taylor's study of Lessing's alienation, Margaret Daymond's account of the methodological connections between the African stories and *The Memoirs of a Survivor*, and Roswell Spafford's consideration of the changing nature of the collectivity in the fiction. The selection of published essays covers such topics as feminism, Rhodesia, and postmodernism, with a pleasantly eclectic range of approaches. The whole is altogether a splendidly useful volume, with a model introduction by the editor, almost an essay in its own right, which sketches the broad contours of the work and the surrounding debate, identifies central stylistic features, and addresses the question of Lessing as an African writer. *JCL* reprints a somewhat fuller version of the above interview, in which Lessing is fairly forthcoming. Interviewed in *RAL* by Stephen Gray, however, she is tetchy about academic attempts to label her as feminist, African, mystic, or realist. Gray does manage, none the less, to elicit some interesting comments on the African nature of *Shikasta*, on her interest in theatre, and her early years in Rhodesia.

There has been a good crop of periodical essays too. M. J. Daymond's discussion (*ArielE*) of *The Memoirs of a Survivor* and the African stories deserves extended mention. Essentially Daymond argues that the spatial dimensions into which experience is organized in the novel can be seen to have evolved from the recorded divisions of experience in the white-settler lives of the stories. New capacities of the mind are therefore registered as spatial areas. Paraphrase is inadequate to convey the virtues of this essay, which is highly original. In *CentR* Ellen G. Friedman explores Lessing's transcendence of the conventions of women's writing, in a sensible, lucid fashion. Cécile Oumhani (*RLC*) notes that Lessing has introduced several elements which belong to Persian miniatures into *The Marriages between Zones Three, Four and Five* where they illuminate the progress of the central character. The essay (in French) argues that Lessing is moving farther away from realism and into mysticism. Belated mention should be made here of Jan Verleun's general consideration of *The Summer before the Dark* (*Neophil*, 1985), marred by a somewhat Lawrentian style (Kate Brown is described as struggling against the cynicism 'which seems about to smother the very flame of life in her'). Another late arrival to these pages was well worth waiting for: Claire Sprague's discussion of the politics of sibling incest in 'Each Other' (*SJS*), which draws upon Thomas Mann's 'The Blood of the Walsungs'. Sprague provides a trenchant analysis of the central issues (subversion, its cost, its relation to the patterns which it claims to overthrow).

131. *Doris Lessing*, ed. by Eve Bertelsen. McGraw–Hill (1985). pp. vii + 217. pb £20.95.

DLN continues to flourish with reviews, announcements, and short pieces. In the spring issue Lessing herself discusses the Jane Somers hoax. Mona Knapp considers her publishing history in West Germany, and Rebecca Kelly contributes a personal account of her reaction to *The Summer before the Dark*. The fall issue is noteworthy for two essays, Elizabeth Maslen's account of the versatility Lessing displays in manipulating the relationship between narrator and reader (excellent) and Sue Matheson's exploration of theatrical and architectural metaphors in *The Memoirs of a Survivor*. The lengthy reviews of other critical works are a distinctive feature of *DLN*, as, unfortunately, is the irritating practice of splitting essays into pieces, so that the reader has to pursue them through the journal.

Dale Salwak's interview with P. D. James (*Clues*) was not available for review when it appeared in 1985. James reveals her influences, notably Waugh and Greene, describes the writing of crime fiction as a means of sublimating the fear of violence and death and indicates her preference for 'malice domestic' in a memorable phrase: 'Stands the church clock at ten to three, and is there arsenic still for tea?'

Though subtitled 'Essays', *My Appointment with the Muse* is actually a selection of Paul Scott's lectures[132], given during the 1960s and 70s to a variety of audiences. It is an absolute mine of information for readers of Scott. Apart from pieces on the mechanics of the novel and on its relation to society, the volume includes autobiographical material, a strong attack on Enoch Powell's racism, and discussion of *The Birds of Paradise* and *The Raj Quartet*. The editor adds the odd footnote or minor correction, but wisely leaves most of the talking to Scott. It makes for one of the more necessary books of the year. Perhaps someone might do the same for Scott's reviews? Two essays have also appeared. In *WHR* (1985) Janis Tedesco envisages Scott as torn, in *The Raj Quartet*, between two interpretations of history, whereas in *Staying On*, to which most of the essay is devoted, a space – time continuum is firmly established in style and structure. Christopher Hitchens's discussion of *The Raj Quartet* in *GrandS* (1985) is more general, but provides a political context for the tetralogy and demolishes Salman Rushdie's preceding strictures. Also in *GrandS* (1985) is 'Kingsley Amis' by D. A. N. Jones who considers the charges of sexism, racism, ageism, and classism against Kingsley Amis's *Stanley and the Women*, finding them for the most part proven.

J. P. Donleavy's Ireland[133], despite presenting the appearance of a coffee-table book, lavishly illustrated and spaciously typeset, is actually a meandering literary memoir of postwar Dublin, shedding incidental light on the author's own works.

It was high time that somebody wrote a critical study of John Berger, and it is a pleasure to discover that in Geoff Dyer's volume[134] Berger is in capable hands. Dyer makes an excellent case for Berger's importance, without the slightest

---

132. *My Appointment with the Muse: Essays, 1961–75*, by Paul Scott, ed. and intro. by Shelley C. Reece. Heinemann. pp. vii + 175. £14.95.

133. *J. P. Donleavy's Ireland: In All her Sins and in Some of her Graces*, by J. P. Donleavy. Joseph. pp. 223. £12.95.

134. *Ways of Telling: The Work of John Berger*, by Geoff Dyer. Pluto. pp. vi + 186. pb £4.95.

tinge of hagiography (the early novels are dismissed as failures). An appendix covers the films Berger wrote with Alain Tanner, and there is a full and useful bibliography. It makes a very welcome book.

James R. Baker has interviewed John Fowles in *MQR*, drawing him out concerning his interest in history, in particular. The interview also includes some stylish sideswipes from Fowles at contemporary critics of his works. It is not likely to deter them, however, judging from the quantity of work available. In *ConL* John Haegert focuses upon *Mantissa* to argue that it represents a development in Fowles's treatment of women. Whereas the heroines of his previous novels have a catalytic role in transforming the male protagonist, in *Mantissa* Fowles is not content to celebrate the role of woman as mysterious Other, or as functionary in the spectacle of male discovery, but instead seeks to internalize the authority of women. This is a thought-provoking and suggestive essay. As its title suggests ('Realism and Metafiction in John Fowles's Novels') Günther Klotz's essay (*ZAA*) is general in intention, providing a sensible résumé of the topic. The conclusion, that Fowles's realism has absorbed new devices and developed old ones which have long been part of the realist tradition, is worth noting as a contrast to the more usual emphasis on Fowles's experimentation. *PoT* features K. R. Ireland who provides an analysis of *The French Lieutenant's Woman* as a repertoire of narrative sequence, embracing over twenty different types. Though the essay aims to promote a syntagmatics of fiction by encouraging more precise terminology the general reader is liable to stumble at the first hurdle, a text which swarms with symbols, diagrams of quite horrendous complexity, and such headings as 'Narratorial Internal Analeptic Overlap'. Narrative concerns are also to the fore in Silvio Gaggi's study of Pirandellian and Brechtian aspects of Fowles's fiction (*CLS*) in an accessible essay which draws genuinely illuminating comparisons, particularly in relation to Conchis's 'godgame' in *The Magus* and modern theatrical theory. In *ESC* (1985) K. A. Chittick argues that Fowles now sees narrative as a way of thinking, distinct from systematic propositional reasoning, as *Daniel Martin* demonstrates. The epigraph to *The Collector* attracts the attention of David Leon Higdon (*MFS*) who discovers that it is drawn from the thirteenth-century romance of courtly love, *La Chatelaine de Vergi*, and has ironic reverberations throughout the novel, since it is part of the process whereby Fowles invites his readers to read the tale in terms of other literary texts.

In *SHR* Joyce Rothschild interviews Alan Sillitoe. Salient points include the influence of Yiddish stories upon him, his political stance, his reading (largely American) and his latest novel, an excerpt from which concludes the interview. In *SovL* (1985) Valentina Ivasheva provides an account of a meeting in Moscow with Stan Barstow whose novels are popular in the Soviet Union, where he is not considered to be 'saturated with the poison of anti-Sovietism' (to quote from the author's opinion of other popular writers).

Writing in *Éire*, Joseph Connelly explicates allusions to popular culture, lyrics, and legends in three novels by Jennifer Johnston. To readers of Rüdiger Imhof's evaluation of Johnston, however, in *EI* (1985), this effort must seem of doubtful value. Imhof points to glaring deficiencies in the novels, which are overschematic, in his view, and overdependent on two structural patterns (either a combination of diary entries and third-person narrator, or a circular narrative utilizing a framing device). Imhof does a superb hatchet-job here, wondering idly at one point 'why, if anyone in Johnston's fictional world plays, or listens to, a piece of music, it has, without fail, to be something by Chopin'. Peter Brigg's short study of J. G. Ballard[135] is no. 26 in The Starmont Readers' Guides to Contemporary Science Fiction and Fantasy Authors series, which can be recommended to those with special interests in this field. In addition to a comprehensive discussion of the works, including short fiction, there is an excellent bibliography and a pleasant blend throughout of information, enthusiasm, and evaluation.

The recent flowering of Marxist and structuralist literary theorizing has produced a concern to analyse the transmission of ideology in literature and hence a growing interest in popular writers. John le Carré has benefited from the trend, with two critical studies appearing this year, both excellent. Tony Barley's volume[136] centres upon the espionage novels in order to establish the complexity of le Carré's political insights, contextualizing him within the spy-thriller genre, but also delineating ways in which he diverges from generic conventions, using thriller patterns selectively and subverting the ideological assumptions of the genre. Neither defensive nor over-inflated, Barley's subtle analysis also avoids being reductive, asking and answering some excellent questions. Thus, while demonstrating a firm grasp on the various ideological readings on offer, Barley also traces literary continuities (Greene, Hoffman), delves into recent history, and considers such topics as nostalgia, games-metaphors, and the liberal dilemma in succinct and provocative terms. This is one of the best books of the year, and certainly the best to date on le Carré. Eric Homberger's shorter study[137] is inevitably more modest and the discussions of individual novels cannot rival Barley's essay-length chapters. On the other hand Homberger's scope is wider, including non-espionage fiction, and *A Perfect Spy* (1986), and also supplying biographical information and an outline history of the spy-thriller. Homberger sees layers of political implication in the fiction which undertakes a searching investigation of post-imperial Britain, placing moral values in conflict with policies and institutions. This moral emphasis, however, is not in the least dull. Like his subject, Homberger succeeds in being serious and entertaining at the same time.

Ann Weekes contributes a sparkling essay to *Éire* on Julia O'Faolain's *No Country for Young Men*, arguing that the novel provides a creative revision of the myth of Grainne, in order to demonstrate that male history is a record of the consequences of following principle at the expense of community.

In an essay in *PSt* Andrew Hassam ponders, Polonius-fashion, on the genre of B. S. Johnson's *Trawl*. Is it an autobiography, a novel, a fictionalized autobiography, an autobiographical novel, a dramatized autobiography, or some intermediate species? Hassam constructs a closely argued case for each option, incidentally shedding some light on the distinction between fiction and autobiography.

Even if Ronald Binns's study of J. G. Farrell[138] were not the first monograph to appear it would still be exceptionally useful. While touching lightly on the early novels and the unfinished *The Hill Station*, Binns wisely devotes most of

135. *J. G. Ballard*, by Peter Brigg. Starmont (1985). pp. 138. pb $7.95.
136. *Taking Sides: The Fiction of John le Carré*, by Tony Barley. OpenU. pp. vii + 175. hb £20, pb £5.95.
137. *John le Carré*, by Eric Homberger. Methuen. pp. 112. pb £3.50.
138. *J. G. Farrell*, by Ronald Binns. Methuen. pp. 109. pb £3.50.

his space to the Empire trilogy, emphasizing Farrell's ironic treatment of genre (fairy story, adventure tale, blockbuster) and subtle use of symbolism. The fresh biographical material is especially valuable, as is the discussion of *The Singapore Grip*. The politics of the trilogy are notoriously elusive and ambiguous, as Binns admits, but his remarks on the last-named novel highlight percipiently Farrell's debt to J. A. Hobson's Liberal critique of imperialism, and his satire on scientific and Marxist explanations of human behaviour. More attention could have been paid to narrative structure, and one wishes that the bibliography were longer, but these are minor points which should not detract from an excellent short study.

D. M. Thomas's *The White Hotel* is the subject of three essays. For David Cowart (*Novel*) Thomas converts the psychological life of his heroine into a symbolic treatment of human consciousness in the modern era. The novel thus becomes a *speculum mundi* reflecting the individual and collective life of the age. John Burt Foster Jr (*SHR*) has doubts about the full artistic success of the novel but none the less writes at some length about its connection with the response of the magic realists to the extremities of history. In *MLS* Ronald Granofsky finds similarities in the treatment of holocaust (nuclear or genocidal) between the novel and Russell Hoban's *Ridley Walker*, particularly in fire symbolism. This seems a fairly obvious point.

John Hannay's short, sharp study of Margaret Drabble[139] advertises itself as a contribution to the study of intertextuality. Be that as it may, it certainly contributes to an understanding of Drabble. Essentially focusing on three novels representative of stages in the author's development, Hannay elucidates allusions to literary works and traditions, examining Drabble's self-reflexive play with the concept of fate, and with the notion that real life structures itself according to patterns familiar from literary tradition. Three paradigms associated with fate emerge: erotic passion in the tragic romance (*The Waterfall*), family as destiny in the return to origins (*The Needle's Eye*), and the longing for justice in the Providential model (*The Ice Age*). In a remarkably short space the volume highlights Drabble's textual irony, undermines the traditionalist thesis, and develops a sophisticated awareness of her relation to realism. Jean Wyatt works along rather similar lines in *PCL* (1985), where she analyses the politics of reading and writing in *The Waterfall*, in which the heroine sees her own experiences in structures borrowed from fiction.

Lynn Veach Sadler has received an award for 'Extraordinary Undergraduate Teaching' from an American college. Her study of Drabble[140] is eminently suitable for undergraduates, whether extraordinary or otherwise, providing biographical details and a discussion of all the fiction in thematic terms. The sense of an argument rarely emerges, however, from its amorphous pages, and is not assisted by thematic subheadings (e.g. 'More Drabbleanism', 'Males in Drabble's Novels') which truncate the argument further. Sadler's headlong prose dashes across the terrain, scattering points as it goes. While some are worth making (a sensible emphasis on the social conscience, imagery, and allusion) others are not (Drabble wears a floppy hat, her living room is red, she is a 'remarkable person'). This is a pity as the author has clearly done her

---

139. *The Intertextuality of Fate: A Study of Margaret Drabble*, by John Hannay. UMiss. pp. 112. pb £7.25.
140. *Margaret Drabble*, by Lynn Veach Sadler. Twayne. pp. 152. $14.95.

homework, amassing and digesting information from a variety of sources with evident enthusiasm.

Pamela S. Bromberg's useful if somewhat compressed essay (*JNT*) traces the development of narrative technique in Drabble's novels in relation to her changing understanding of how character, coincidence, and environment converge. Marjorie Hill Goss contributes a short note on bird imagery in *The Ice Age* to *NConL*.

2. Poetry

The most important and engaging book of the year is C. K. Stead's *Pound, Yeats, Eliot and the Modernist Movement*[141]. Stead's *The New Poetic* (1964) is one of the best brief introductions to Modernist poetry: in the present study he develops and very considerably expands the argument of that book, particularly through discussion of Hardy and Pound. But the central thesis remains the same, that Modernism, as developed by Pound and Eliot, was a revolutionary force which, by bringing together the apparently divergent qualities of Symbolist and Imagist poetry, created open-ended works that imposed a new kind of creative responsibility on the reader. From this standpoint Yeats, under Pound's influence, became modern in language and rhythm but not a Modernist. The high point of Eliot's work is *The Waste Land* and in comparison the *Four Quartets* is regressively discursive, the product of the thirties, an age dominated by political and other 'ideas' that lead to closure rather than openness. Only Pound retained into later life the Modernist aesthetic and in the late *Pisan Cantos* produced, in appalling conditions, some of his finest work. Stead is positive, even aggressive, in arguing his case and every reader will be stimulated to opposition on occasion. He seems to me, for example, to impose a structure of meaning on 'Gerontion' in a way that he strenuously resists with 'Prufrock'. But he writes with bravura and the provocation is always refreshing.

Martin Booth's *British Poetry 1964-1984*[142], an angry lament for the present state of affairs, is in two parts. The first is concerned with the conditions of authorship in the early seventies, with the proliferation of small presses and magazines, the interest in poetry by large publishers, the popularity of poetry readings, the success of the Arvon Foundation in promoting poetry courses. Taken together these developments show that poets at that time were able to speak both to and for a large and committed audience. The second part is a survey of the main groups of poets working in that period, with brief but effective characterizations of each writer's work, with particular emphasis on Ted Hughes. Despite some reservations, Booth sees this as a Golden Age, now lost, partly through the poets' own loss of nerve, but also because of a timid academicism which stifles experiment. Much of what Booth says is valid and the tone is often exciting. But ultimately the book suffers from a failure to address the underlying social, political, and economic reasons for the changes that are examined.

141. *Pound, Yeats, Eliot and the Modernist Movement*, by C. K. Stead. Macmillan. pp. vii + 393. £27.50.

142. *British Poetry 1964-1984: Driving Through the Barricades*, by Martin Booth. RKP (1985). pp. vii + 268. £13.95.

Henry Gifford's Clark Lectures for 1985[143], a penetrating study of the public role and function of poetry in the twentieth century, takes its examples mainly from Russian literature but there are important observations also on Yeats and on T. S. Eliot.

A number of brief but stimulating articles in *PoetryR* consider the notion of 'Englishness' in twentieth-century writers. 'English Equivocation' by John Bayley looks freshly at Edward Thomas's 'Adlestrop'; Stan Smith's 'Unnatural Relations' comments on Auden's problematic relation to England; and Philip Hobsbaum's 'Larkin's England' argues that Larkin's work has established 'the first decisive alteration to the poetic landscape since Eliot's cabhorses steam under the gas lamps'.

Edward Thomas continues to attract important work. Michael Kirkham's *The Imagination of Edward Thomas*[144] is a thorough and sensitive evaluation which sees Thomas as a more complex and positive figure than the quiet elegist he has often seemed. Certainly Thomas has an acute sense of the transience of things manifested in his presentation of personal and historical loss, but Kirkham finds a 'characteristic movement of poems outward and away from the originating personal conditions of enervation and isolation' towards imaginatively apprehended values 'from which the poems take their bearings'. Thomas's response to nature (somewhat confusingly termed 'naturalistic') is 'often enthusiastic, sometimes rapturous but rarely sentimental'. The case is argued with subtle analysis of language, the movement of the verse, metaphor, and poetic structure. This is a helpful contribution to the continuing re-evaluation of Thomas's work.

Stan Smith[145] makes excellent use of the extensive prose to build up a full, and again somewhat surprising, account of Thomas's ideas and attitudes. Smith begins by questioning the received view of Thomas's 'Englishness'. The writer thought of himself as an expatriate Welshman of 'accidentally Cockney nativity' and he fretted about deracination despite his undoubted love of the English countryside. These ambiguities are reflected in his attitude to England as a social and political force at a time of acute class conflict and economic deprivation: 'irony and rueful resignation counterbalance . . . revolutionary sentiments'. Smith deals well with these issues and also with the ideas underlying Thomas's sense of the mystery of landscape, his Romantic 'attempts to seize hold of an inapprehensible core of meaning felt to lurk within the endlessly dissolving flux of things'. His attitude to the war was also ambiguous at first but enlistment offered eventually an escape from the contradictions and also from 'the miserable routine of marriage and endless unrewarding writing'. Smith brings an attractive sense of engagement to the presentation of this argument.

Two articles also call for a fresh approach to Thomas. Peter Mitchell's 'Edward Thomas and the Georgians' (*UTQ*) is concerned to define the elusive nature of the poet's art by arguing that, although at times Thomas's work is

143. *Poetry in a Divided World: The Clark Lectures 1985*, by Henry Gifford. CUP. pp. xi + 111. £15.

144. *The Imagination of Edward Thomas*, by Michael Kirkham. CUP. pp. xi + 225. £25.

145. *Edward Thomas*, by Stan Smith. Faber. pp. 221. pb £3.95.

similar to what we find in Georgian anthologies, he goes beyond Georgian celebration and melancholy to an 'emotional complexity and a degree of intellectual comprehensiveness that result in ambivalencies and hesitations that are quite unlike the other Georgians'. This is a helpful discrimination. 'The Childhood of Edward Thomas' (CQ) by Piers Gray is a discussion of Thomas's autobiographical fragment, first published in 1938, and its relation to nostalgic and regressive elements in the verse. Gray finds the key to Thomas's work in the suddenness of his transition from childhood to 'oppressive adulthood' which came through his early marriage and the strains that this imposed.

Amongst war poets Owen has attracted most attention. Dominic Hibberd's *Owen the Poet*[146] is a major study of the writer's development and an assessment of his value. Hibberd gives detailed attention to the literary influences affecting Owen, especially Laurent Tailhade, Harold Monro, and Sassoon, and he provides a valuable commentary on Owen's reading. New evidence is given concerning Owen's early religious crisis, his experiences in France in 1913–14, his treatment by Dr Brock at Craiglockhart, and his homosexuality. There is a full discussion of the long but fragmentary early poem *Perseus* and two final chapters give a detailed analysis of 'Strange Meeting' and 'Spring Offensive'. Owen is seen as a poet who 'holds a transitional place between the nineteenth century and Modernism' who, had he lived, might have bridged the gap between Modernist experiment and the native tradition. Dominic Hibberd also contributes a note on 'A Publisher of First World War Poetry: Galloway Kyle' (N&Q). Kyle was founder of the Poetry Society and editor of its *Poetry Review* for many years. Hibberd shows that he was also a publisher under the alias Erskine Macdonald and that his business practices were dubious.

In 'Wilfred Owen and Abram' (WS) Caryn McTighe Musil considers the rejection of 'patriarchal' values and of the 'male warrior myth' in the statements and imagery of Owen's work and relates this to his fondness for his mother and their shared cultivation of 'feelings, tenderness and sensitivity'. Paul Norgate's '"Dulce et Decorum Est" and Some Amendments to the Dating of Wilfred Owen's Letters' (N&Q) proposes many minor changes in the dating of some ninety letters and argues that the correct date of composition for 'Dulce et Decorum Est' is 8 October 1917. In 'Some Echoes of Barbusse's *Under Fire* in Wilfred Owen's Poems' (N&Q), Simon Wormleighton finds several clear echoes of a book lent to Owen by Siegfried Sassoon in later 1917. G. Cordery's 'Owen's *Futility*' (Expl) is a careful analysis defending the poem against F. W. Bateson's dismissal of it. Finally, Herbert Lomas's 'The Critic as Anti-Hero: War Poetry' (HudR) is a discriminating article, mainly on Owen, with observations on rhetorical and sentimental aspects of his work.

Catherine W. Reilly has produced a comprehensive bibliography of the poetry of the Second World War[147]. She covers 3,072 separate publications, including eighty-seven anthologies issued during the years 1939–80 and she identifies 2,679 poets although some only by pseudonym or initials. Surprisingly this comfortably exceeds the number of poets who published on

146. *Owen the Poet*, by Dominic Hibberd. Macmillan. pp. xii + 244. £25.

147. *English Poetry of the Second World War*, by Catherine W. Reilly. Mansell. pp. xxviii + 393. £35.

the Great War, perhaps because of the greater involvement of the population at large. Succinct biographical details are provided whenever possible. This compilation will be an essential tool for those working in the field.

There has been some excellent work on Yeats. Edward O'Shea's catalogue of Yeats's library[148] is a volume of great interest in itself and an important research tool. Yeats left a library of some 2,500 items and the collection demonstrates vividly what one would expect, 'that he opened up his own mind and therefore English literature to multiple and even heterodox influences: to the oriental, the occult, theosophy, magic, myth, the antiquarian, anthropology, philosophy, archaeology and the visual arts'. As well as providing basic bibliographical information, O'Shea reproduces Yeats's frequent annotations and these give important insights to the direction of his interests. There is an extensive subject index.

The first volume of Yeats's *Collected Letters*[149] has appeared, edited by John Kelly and Eric Domville and very handsomely produced by the Clarendon Press. The complete edition is expected to take twelve volumes. Yeats was a spontaneous correspondent, untroubled by conventions of spelling and punctuation and the general editorial policy has been to reproduce the physiognomy of his letters, 'orthographic warts and all', with only sufficient tidying up to make them easily readable. The result is a volume of great immediacy in which Yeats's day-to-day concerns are brought vividly before us. The letters illuminate Yeats's biography and chart his literary development but they are valuable also, as the editors claim, in helping us to form a sense of period as we see Yeats reacting to passing historical events and to the deeper currents of the time. Extensive footnotes 'attempt not only to identify individuals and to provide information on particular points or references but also to supply wider contextual material' and there is a valuable Biographical and Historical Appendix. This is an edition warmly to be welcomed.

Peter Kuch's *Yeats and A.E.*[150] gives an account of Yeats's friendship with George Russell ('A.E.') from their first meeting in the Art Schools in Kildare St., Dublin, to their quarrels in 1907 over the policies of the Abbey Theatre. Their early reaction against Victorian conformism led to an interest in Theosophy though there were important differences between them. Russell sought a 'whole faith' where Yeats was more interested in the stimulus of a new position and his lack of seriousness was mocked by Russell. They shared for a time a millenial attitude towards the Celtic Revival but as the movement to establish Irish Drama developed there was antagonism between them. Russell wanted a small amateur theatre which would encourage local talent whereas Yeats was more professional and demanding in his standards. Their lives meet, however, at significant points and this book will be welcomed as a clear and detailed account of their relationship.

Writing to Olivia Shakespear in 1928 Yeats said that on rereading 'The Tower' he was astonished 'at its bitterness' but he recognizes that this bitterness gave the book its power and he feels that 'this is the best book I have written'.

148. *A Descriptive Catalogue of W. B. Yeats's Library*, by Edward O'Shea. Garland (1985). pp. xxiii + 390. $56.

149. *The Collected Letters of W. B. Yeats*. Vol. 1: *1865–1895*, ed. by John Kelly, with assoc. ed. Eric Domville. Clarendon. pp. xlii + 548. £22.50.

150. *Yeats and A.E.*, by Peter Kuch. Smythe/B&N. pp. xiii + 291. £17.50.

Joseph M. Hassett's *Yeats and the Poetics of Hate*[151] is about the creative power of hatred and the theme proves a rich one. There are chapters on Yeats's hatred of Lockean rational philosophy and of 'all that Whiggish world' associated with it; on his dislike of realism in art and drama and on the association of realistic attitudes with his father; on the 'prophetic rage' that links Yeats to Swift; on the hatred of abstractions; on Yeats's response to Blake's 'old thought that sexual love is founded upon spiritual hate'; and on the hatred of progressivist views which led Yeats to adopt a cyclical conception of history. In all these areas Hassett's exposition is clear and he uses his material to make sensitive interpretations of the poetry. This is an unpretentious and useful book.

Kathleen Raine's *Yeats the Initiate*[152] should be noted. This is a substantial and impressive collection of papers, mainly on Yeats and the occult, written over a period of twenty years. All have been published elsewhere though some are now extensively revised. There is a wide range of illustrations.

William H. O'Donnell offers an attractively presented and readable introduction to Yeats[153]. After a brief biography and a chapter on the esoteric and metaphysical background of Yeats's work, O'Donnell deals chronologically with each volume, selecting a few poems from each for special commentary, paying particular attention to the occasion of their composition and to technical details. This is a helpful guide for new readers.

YeA no. 4, edited by Warwick Gould, is a formidable compilation which contains much of interest. Donald T. Torchiana's 'Yeats and Croce' examines Yeats's annotations of works by the Italian philosopher and finds that he was particularly impressed by passages where Croce insists that concepts must be concrete and by those which hint at unity of being. Croce often supports beliefs derived by Yeats from a range of earlier idealist thinkers but he also exerts a direct influence of his own. In 'Yeats's Passage to India' Ruth Nevo interprets the very difficult play 'The Herne's Egg' in the light of Indian philosophy, seeing it as a genesis myth which raises fundamental questions about the value of 'fallen' experience. The interpretation, however, is as difficult to come to grips with as the play itself. 'The Secret Society of Modernism: Pound, Yeats, Olivia Shakespear and the Abbé de Montfaucon de Villars' by James Longenbach discusses Pound's attitude towards esoteric knowledge in the period 1913–16 and brings this interestingly to bear on his attitude to symbolism and the function of the image. Elizabeth Cullingford's 'Yeats and Women: "Michael Robartes and the Dancer"' is a long and wide-ranging discussion which argues that 'Yeats's treatment of women reveals a striking split between theory and practice'. Despite his opposition to 'opinionated' women, many of the women he admired and loved, including Maude Gonne, were of a different stamp, emancipated people whose actions ran counter to Yeats's social conservatism.

Two articles have biographical interest. '"Heirs of the Great Generation": Yeats's Friendship with Charles Rickett and Charles Shannon', by J. G. P.

151. *Yeats and the Poetics of Hate*, by Joseph M. Hassett. G&M. pp. ix + 189. £25.

152. *Yeats the Initiate: Essays on Certain Themes in the Work of W. B. Yeats*, by Kathleen Raine. Dolmen/A&U. pp. xii + 449. £35.

153. *The Poetry of William Butler Yeats: An Introduction*, by William H. O'Donnell. Ungar. pp. xvi + 192. $14.95.

Delaney, is an interestingly presented account of a relationship which flourished in spite of some serious disagreement about such matters as the occult and Irish Nationalism. John Harwood's 'Olivia Shakespear and W. B. Yeats' is a detailed account of this unsatisfactory relationship, written from the viewpoint of Mrs Shakespear. It contains new information and makes effective if tentative use of Mrs Shakespear's six novels. In an 'Afterword on *Rupert Armstrong*' Deirdre Toomey argues that one of Olivia's novels is a *roman à clef* based on the life of J. E. Millais.

'Ezra Pound's Versions of Fenollosa's Noh Manuscripts and Yeats's Unpublished "Suggestions and Corrections"', by Yoko Chiba, explains Pound's editorial practice, presents Yeats's comments for the first time, and concludes that 'Pound's Noh translations . . . realized Fenollosa's dreams theatrically, beyond mere translation, by the creation of an image whereby Noh can be used in Western drama'. In 'Coming to Grips with Proteus' A. D. Hope comments on five poems, one previously unpublished, that he has written about Yeats. '"Do We or Do We Not, Know It?": An Unpublished Essay on W. B. Yeats by Thomas Sturge Moore', probably written in 1929–30, has been edited by Warwick Gould.

Continuing the series on 'Significant Research Collections' initiated last year, Pamela M. Baker and Helen M. Young write on 'W. B. Yeats Material in the University of London Library' and Peter G. W. van de Kamp contributes 'Some Notes on the Literary Estate of Pamela Hinkson', the daughter of Katherine Tynan. There are several shorter notes, extensive reviews, a section on 'Recent Postgraduate Research' and a bibliography covering 1983–4. All in all this is an impressive volume.

J. Hillis Miller's *The Linguistic Moment* [154] contains a chapter on Yeats with an important close reading of 'Nineteen Hundred and Nineteen'. The 'linguistic moment' for Miller is 'the moment when a poem, or indeed any text, turns back on itself and puts its own medium in question'. In asking what man should do when he sees that 'no monument of art or intellect can stand' against the violence of the times, Yeats's poem raises the most fundamental doubts about its own validity, yet finally asserts that things are preserved by being turned into emblems.

'Refraining from the Romantic Image: Yeats and the Deformation of Metaphysical Aestheticism' (*SIR*), by Janice Haney-Peritz, is a long, intricate, and challenging essay which modifies the traditional view that Yeats's greatness depends on his 'formal achievement of a unity of being' by arguing that his poetry is more open than is generally recognized to 'loopholes, evasions, displacements and supplements'. In 'Oblique Contexts in Yeats: The Homer of "The Nineteenth Century and After"' (*PQ*) Ian F. A. Bell argues on stylistic grounds that the poem should be read as affirmative rather than simply regretful about the passing of earlier values. Rachel Billigheimer's 'Self and Soul in W. B. Yeats' (*Éire*) is a fairly straightforward exposition of ideas on life and immortality in *The Tower* and *The Winding Stair*.

Donald Pearce's 'Shadows Deep: Change and Continuity in Yeats' (*CLQ*) is a brief article which relates themes and images in 'When you are old and grey' and 'The Lake Isle of Innisfree' to Yeats's later work, suggesting that the

---

154. *The Linguistic Moment: From Wordsworth to Stevens*, by J. Hillis Miller. Princeton (1985). pp. xxii + 445. £31.70.

effectiveness of these lyrics for us depends on these later echoes. 'Yeats's *The Wild Swans at Coole*' (*Expl*), by Martin Puhvel, suggests that the remarkably specific number of the swans (fifty-nine) may owe something to the number of bells worn by the Elfish Queen's horse in the Scottish ballad *Thomas Rhymer*.

Before turning to Eliot a useful Hulme item may be noted. K. E. Csengeri's 'T. E. Hulme: An Annotated Bibliography of Writings About Him' (*ELT*) lists 340 books, articles, broadcasts, dissertations, and published letters about, or containing significant references to, Hulme. Eliot has attracted less attention than in many recent years. A useful descriptive survey of *T. S. Eliot Criticism and Scholarship in German*[155] has been compiled by Armin Paul Frank. This is concerned both 'to trace the vicissitudes of Eliot's fate with German critics and scholars' and also to call attention to the diversity of German contributions in this area. It lists and briefly describes in English fifty-eight books and dissertations and 458 contributions to books, dissertations, and periodicals, and there is a lively preface which surveys the development of German responses to Eliot. It is helpfully indexed.

F. B. Pinion's descriptive survey of Eliot's life and work[156] has a substantial biographical section followed by accounts of the poetry, essays, and plays, all of which combine summary and commentary in a convenient if slightly ponderous fashion. 'All in all, as poet, critic, and dramatist', Pinion concludes, 'Eliot still seems to be the major figure in English literature of the twentieth century . . . How great he is remains a question for the future.' But it is also a question for us and one would like to see it addressed more directly. The book is presumably intended primarily for new readers of Eliot but the lack of conviction here may be found dispiriting.

Four articles discuss poems in Eliot's first two volumes. His general interest in anthropology is well known but studies usually stop short at Sir James Frazer and Jessie M. Weston. 'Dissociation in "Dead Land": The Primitive Mind in the Early Poetry of T. S. Eliot' (*JML*) by Marc Manganaro, examines Eliot's debt to Lucien Lévy-Bruhl, whose book *How Natives Think* (1910) distinguished sharply between the logical thought processes of modern society and the mystical modes of primitive civilization. Manganaro sees Lévy-Bruhl's influence as important in Prufrock and other 'dissociated' figures of Eliot's early work and in the conception of a 'dead land' in 'The Hollow Men'. This article opens up a new line of enquiry. In '"Prufrock" and the Problem of Literary Narcissism' (*ConL*) Robert McNamara uses several poems by Arthur Symons to define a turn-of-the-century 'poetic of mood', characterized by 'sentimental emotion and poetic artifice'. He argues that 'Prufrock' offers a critique of this mode but that it fails to find a satisfactory answer to the problems raised. There is some good discussion of detail, but marred by jargon. In 'Walker Percy and T. S. Eliot: The Lancelot Andrewes Connection' (*SoR*) John Desmond demonstrates some similarities of theme and imagery between 'Gerontion' and Percy's novel *Lancelot* (1977) and discusses the differing debts of the two writers to Lancelot Andrewes' sermons. The comparison seems

155. *T. S. Eliot Criticism and Scholarship in German: A Descriptive Catalogue*, by Armin Paul Frank, ed. by Erika Hulpke. V&R. pp. ix + 215.
156. *A T. S. Eliot Companion. Life and Works*, by F. B. Pinion. Macmillan. pp. xii + 304. £27.50.

somewhat strained. John Coakley compares 'T. S. Eliot's *Mr. Appollinax* and Frost's *The Demiurge's Laugh*' (*Expl*).

In 'Modernism and Empire: Reading *The Waste Land*' (*CQ*) David Trotter adumbrates a new approach to this seemingly inexhaustible poem. He outlines Edwardian and Georgian fears about the dangers facing the British Empire both by attack from outside and from the degeneration of the race at the centre, and suggests that these fears may underlie some of the apocalyptic and sexual references in *The Waste Land*. The fashionable emphasis on the poem's confessional aspect ('a kind of rhythmical grumbling') needs to be modified by awareness that there is indeed a social and political dimension to the work. Giles Mitchell's 'T. S. Eliot's *The Waste Land*: Death, Fear, Apathy and Dehumanization' (*AI*), on the other hand, discusses the poem in terms of a psychological hypothesis, namely that there is a close connection between the fear of death and the fear of life. Many examples are cited of violence against the body in *The Waste Land*: these spring from the emotional apathy of the figures, itself a product of two psychological elements demonstrably present in the work, narcissism and oedipal fixation. Mitchell's approach relates some central elements of the poem interestingly but it is difficult for non-psychologists to apply. 'Legends of Lil: The Repressed Thematic Center of *The Waste Land*' (*WS*) by Eileen Wiznitzer, analyses the pub scene from a feminist perspective and demonstrates that Lil, as presented by the female speaker, is drawn according to patriarchial assumptions concerning her function. Wiznitzer suggests that Lil's rejection of the conventional wifely role can be seen as a refusal to participate in patriarchal definitions of attractive and appropriate female behaviour. In 'Rudyard Kipling in *The Waste Land*' (*EIC*) Robert Crawford makes some general observations on Eliot's debt to Kipling and gives a convincingly detailed analysis of his use of 'The Finest Story in the World'. P. Marudanayagam's 'T. S. Eliot's *The Waste Land*' (*Expl*) finds a source in Indian legend for the line 'Who is the third who walks always beside you'.

In 'T. S. Eliot's *Ariel Poems*' (*Expl*) Richard A. Sylvia calls attention to correspondences between Eliot's sequence and Lancelot Andrewes' 1622 sermon on the nativity.

A small but interesting biographical item may be noted. Stuart Barr's 'A Propos d'Une Lettre Retrouvée d'Alain-Fournier a T. S. Eliot' (*Bulletin de l'Association des Amis de Jacques Rivière et d'Alain Fournier*) prints a letter from the young writer who acted as Eliot's tutor during his stay in Paris in 1910-11. The letter shows that the two were on easy terms and comments on a programme of reading in English literature that Eliot had recommended to Alain-Fournier. Finally, William Harmon's 'Eliot and his Problems' (*SR*) may be recommended as a lively survey of recent criticism.

Crocker Wight has compiled a definitive bibliography of John Masefield[157], designed to 'list in chronological order not only the first editions of the author but also special, limited and other unusual editions'. A full bibliographical description is given of each volume. The work, very handsomely produced, will be of interest to collectors and to those undertaking research on Masefield.

Holly Laird's 'The Poems of "Piano"' (*DHLR*) is a close and careful study

---

157. *John Masefield: A Bibliographical Description of his First, Limited, Signed and Special Editions*, by Crocker Wight. BostonAL. pp. xxxi + 214.

of four versions of D. H. Lawrence's 'Piano' (two so far unpublished), the first written before his mother's death, the last reflecting Lawrence's response to that event.

Some articles on writers mainly active between the wars may be grouped together. Paul Fussell's 'Modernism, Adversary Culture, and Edmund Blunden' (*SR*) is an attack on what are seen as the limitations of Modernism – rigidity and exclusiveness in its rejection of the immediate past – and an appreciation of the humanity of Blunden's work. David Jones sympathised with Germany because of the injustice of the settlement that concluded the Great War and he was critical of postwar democracy, but Thomas Dilworth argues cogently, in 'David Jones and Fascism' (*JML*) that this by no means implies sympathy towards Fascism. Jones's poetry is explicitly anti-Fascist and this is consistent with what we know from biographical sources. Jack F. Stewart gives an interpretation of 'Graves' "The Cool Web"' (*Expl*) which is seen as presenting the necessity for 'a marriage of opposites between language and sensation'. Hamish Whyte's 'MacDiarmid and the Beatniks' (*SLJ*) reproduces and comments on the manuscript of a short poem by MacDiarmid reflecting his dislike of postwar international developments such as Beat poetry.

When Auden revised his charade *Paid on Both Sides* during his visit to Berlin in 1928–9 he introduced whole-hearted use of parody and caricature and a more specifically political frame of reference than in the earlier version. In 'Berlin and the Two Versions of W. H. Auden's "Paid on Both Sides"' (*ArielE*), Sidney Poger suggests that these changes reflect Auden's experience in Berlin and in particular the influence on him of Bertolt Brecht, and that they antedate developments generally thought to occur only with the 1930 *Poems*. John Whitehead's 'Auden and *All the Conspirators*' (*EIC*) examines some verbal and thematic links between Auden's early work and Isherwood's first novel to demonstrate that the two 'shared a common intellectual climate'.

Walford Davies's *Dylan Thomas*[158] adopts the pedagogic formula familiar from much Open University material for literature courses. It raises questions, invites the reader to participate in problem solving, and avoids prescription. The tone can occasionally seem patronising ('Don't worry too much as yet if the poem resists any easy paraphrase') but it is a method attuned to the reader's experience and it is particularly successful in developing an understanding of Thomas's linguistic and syntactic complexities. The opening chapter deals concisely with biographical information and the last speculates interestingly on the fact that Thomas grew up as a non-Welsh speaker in a Welsh-speaking environment and thus 'found in the English language a medium that had to be forced and willed into effects not instinctively natural to it'.

Caitlin: A Warring Absence[159], a moving narrative of Caitlin's life with Dylan Thomas, is the result of a collaboration. It is based on some fifty hours of tape-recorded interviews, edited by George Tremlett to form a continuous story. It is complemented by a series of photographs. Rob Gittins's *The Last Days of Dylan Thomas*[160] is a chronicle account of Thomas's final visit to

158. *Dylan Thomas*, by Walford Davies. OpenU. pp. x + 134. hb £13.50, pb £3.95.
159. *Caitlin: A Warring Absence*, by Caitlin Thomas and George Tremlett. S&W. pp. xvi + 212. £10.95.
160. *The Last Days of Dylan Thomas*, by Rob Gittins. Macdonald. pp. 200. £10.95.

America and the bizarre sequence of events leading to and attending his death. It is a work of purely biographical interest and while fascinatingly detailed it suffers from a frenetic tone and from the complete lack of scholarly apparatus.

'Crafty Dylan and the Altarwise Sonnets: "I build a flying tower and I pull it down"' (*UTQ*), by Don McKay, is an intricate but interesting argument claiming that in Thomas's verbal and rhetorical elaboration 'we can sense a willed grotesquerie . . . a deliberate violation of decorum' whose function is subversive of accepted literary conventions. This produces a carnival atmosphere in the sonnets that is both exciting and disturbing.

There are a number of items on Philip Larkin. In a full-length study Terry Whalen makes a detailed exploration of Larkin's four volumes of verse and attempts a re-assessment of his place in English poetry[161]. He largely avoids the well-covered ground of Larkin's affinities with Hardy and the Movement writers, stressing instead his debt to D. H. Lawrence and the Imagists and his relationship to Ted Hughes, Thom Gunn, and R. S. Thomas. To establish this case he argues persuasively that Larkin is essentially a dramatic poet whose personae 'blend and compete with one another more than the customary generalities about the poet's personality suggest'. The frequent tone of sarcasm and disenchantment should not always be taken as authorial. The book contains much patient and sensitive analysis. Andrew Swarbrick's *'The Whitsun Weddings' and 'The Less Deceived'*[162] is an essentially pedagogic introduction to Larkin's volumes, addressed primarily to 'A' level candidates, but it is a model of its kind, effectively designed to lead pupils to respond more fully to the poems. There is a brief biographical introduction and an attempt to locate Larkin in literary history but most of the space is taken up with analysis of individual poems. These are sensible and straightforward but sufficiently detailed to open up the complexities beneath the bland surface of Larkin's work.

Larkin praised John Betjeman for his 'astonishing command of detail' and the 'imaginative and precise location' of his poetry. Bill Ruddick convincingly analyses the relationship between the two in '"Some ruin-bibber, randy for antique": Philip Larkin's Response to the Poetry of John Betjeman' (*CQ*). He demonstrates that Larkin often used situations and mannerisms from Betjeman but concludes that he remained 'healthily active and independent'. James Harrison's 'Larkin's *Ambulances*' (*Expl*) finds significant 'concessions to the poetic' in this apparently low-key poem. Pat Dale Scrimgeour identifies an allusion in 'Philip Larkin's "Dockery and Son" and Julian Hall's *The Senior Commoner*' (*N&Q*).

Neil Corcoran's *Seamus Heaney*[163] is a straightforward and sensitive exposition of Heaney's work for the general reader. It opens with a biographical chapter, including an account of initial critical responses to Heaney's poetry and then moves chronologically to a commentary on each volume of verse. There is considerable explanatory material on Irish history and politics and on literary allusions but also sharp critical assessments. The

161. *Philip Larkin and English Poetry*, by Terry Whalen. Macmillan. pp. ix + 164. £25.

162. *'The Whitsun Weddings' and 'The Less Deceived' by Philip Larkin*, by Andrew Swarbrick. Macmillan. pp. ix + 86. pb £1.25.

163. *Seamus Heaney*, by Neil Corcoran. Faber. pp. 192. pb £3.95.

Select Bibliography is helpful, especially in its listing of interviews. Nicholas McGuinn has written a stimulating introduction to Heaney for 'A' level students[164]. He provides perceptive analysis of individual poems, together with useful background information about history, politics, and mythology.

'Heaney's Sweeney: The Poet as Version-Maker' (*PQ*), by H. A. Kelly, compares Heaney's *Sweeney Astray* with J. G. O'Keeffe's translation of *Buile Suibhne* and concludes that Heaney introduces more frequent changes than his introduction suggests and that these changes move his work towards burlesque. Here and elsewhere the achievement of a cultural and historical dimension in Heaney's poetry through reference to Ireland's past is generally recognized. In 'Time and History in Seamus Heaney's "In Memoriam Francis Ledwidge"' (*Éire*) Robert Di Nicola studies a specific and neglected instance of this process, showing that Heaney's tribute to Ledwidge, an Irish poet killed in the First World War, combines references to the present, the period of the war itself, and the seventeenth century.

Dannie Abse[165] by Tony Curtis is a descriptive biographical and critical survey which discusses Abse as novelist and dramatist as well as poet. The effect of his medical training, the Jewish element in his work, and the Movement/Maverick controversy are economically discussed and his development clearly plotted. This is an engaging account addressed to the general reader.

Peter Barry's 'Language and the City in Roy Fisher's Poetry' (*ES*) is a substantial discussion of *City* and 'Handsworth Liberties', particularly concerned with changes in Fisher's language and with the relationship between the 'real' and 'fictive' elements in his work. Barry concludes that *City* is a great achievement, a notable Modernist poem in the tradition of *The Waste Land*, David Jones's *Anathemata*, or Basil Bunting's *Briggflatts*, and it is so because, unlike 'Handsworth Liberties', 'it resists the temptation of speaking with a single voice'.

In '"I could have outlived myself there": The Poetry of Andrew Motion' (*CQ*) Michael Hulse calls for a more strenuous critical attitude towards Motion's work. His stylistic strength is as an elegist but he is received, on his own terms, as a narrative poet and here, Hulse argues, he is often flat and mechanical in manner and suspect in his underlying values. Both 'his personal grief and his national nostalgia carry a political charge, since both are predicated upon scrutiny of the past rather than of the present'.

Mike Jenkins writes appreciatively in 'The Inner Exile: The Merthyr Poems of Leslie Norris' (*PoetryW*) of a number of Norris's poems based on memories of childhood and youth, often involving Wordsworthian recollection and epiphany, and he suggests that Norris is at his best 'when writing (like Joyce about Dublin) of what he has rejected'. Mercer Simpson's 'Leslie Norris: Reluctant Exile' (*PoetryW*) explores a related theme and identifies in Norris's work some diverse stylistic and thematic elements from Welsh, Anglo-Welsh, and English poetic traditions.

Peter Reading is interviewed by Alan Jenkins in 'Making Nothing Matter' (*PoetryR*). Discussion centres on the apparent morbidity and pessimism in

164. *Seamus Heaney: A Student's Guide to the Selected Poems 1965–75*, by Nicholas McGuinn. A–W. pp. 126. pb £2.25.
165. *Dannie Abse*, by Tony Curtis. UWales. pp. 123. pb £3.50.

Reading's work. In 'A Dual Heritage' (*PoetryR*) George Szirtes reflects on his early experiences when his family moved from Hungary to England and on the problems facing a writer with two cultures.

Finally, it is to be noted that an issue of *EA* (1985) was devoted to 'British Poetry 1970–1984'. Two articles are particularly worth mention. Damian Grant's 'The Voice of History in British Poetry 1970–1984' discusses the use of the past in work by Seamus Heaney, Derek Mahon, Tony Harrison, and James Fenton. Paul Volsik's 'La Poésie Britannique dans les années 1970: Retour au Principe de *Gentility*?' takes Alvarez's attack on the Movement as its starting point and examines the opposition between 'gentility' and radicalism in the seventies, considering Clive Wilmer and Douglas Dunn as writers limited by 'gentility' and Heaney and Geoffrey Hill as in different ways transcending it.

3. Drama

This section has three categories: (a) General Studies, beginning with reference works and proceeding in broadly chronological order of topic; (b) Collections of Plays; (c) Individual Authors, in alphabetical order. New plays are not listed unless they contain introductions or some kind of critical commentary or have some other claim to be included, such as being based on a previously existing literary work or exciting particular controversy. Coverage of film and television is confined to works by writers with a substantial theatrical reputation. *MD* should be consulted for the annual bibliography by Charles Carpenter, and *LTR* for reprints of reviews of current London productions.

(a) General Studies

An implicit theme of many of this year's publications in modern drama is the forging of canons, through critical works analysing the dramatic output of schools of dramatists, of theatres, of particular periods, through attempts at new generic groupings, or through anthologies of various kinds, some of an individual writer's works, some of the plays of a particular period. Much of this year's review is, therefore, concerned with what Philip Barnes describes in his *Companion to Post-War British Theatre*[166] as 'eccentricities of inclusion and omission'. Barnes's book is serviceable but the selection of entries tends to be biased geographically towards southern England so that there is, for example, no entry for the Citizens' Theatre, Glasgow and its extraordinary managerial triumvirate or for the Belgrade Theatre, Coventry which has its own claims to fame as the first completely new postwar theatre. Other conspicuous absences are the Arts Council, the Roundhouse (and Centre 42, although both appear in the entry on Wesker), the Royal Exchange Manchester, David Aukin, Thelma Holt, Heathcote Williams, and C. P. Taylor. Verse Drama has an entry but Political Theatre does not. Although the book was published in 1986 the entries tail off in mid 1984, with the result that an accomplished performer like Lindsay Duncan whose reputation had been mainly established on the Fringe does not rate inclusion whereas Alan Rickman, her co-star in *Liaisons Dangereuses*, does. The individual entries appear to be factually accurate,

166. *A Companion to Post-War British Theatre*, by Philip Barnes. CH. pp. 277. £18.95.

although critical opinions tend towards the consensual. The most unnecessary feature of the volume is the inclusion of explanations of theatrical terms such as 'bums on seats' and of terms like 'the Scottish play' which are certainly not confined to postwar usage.

Jan McDonald's analysis of *The 'New Drama' 1900–1914*[167] is a crisply economical and perceptive account both of the Barker–Vedrenne managements at the Court and the Savoy, Charles Frohman's 1910 repertory season and the provincial repertory movement and of four of the dramatists who contributed to those enterprises: Granville Barker himself, Galsworthy, St John Hankin, and Masefield. McDonald excels at sketching in major social, theatrical, and dramatic changes and issues in a brief compass, and her analyses of the theatrical virtues of Barker and Galsworthy should help to secure them a higher critical standing than they currently have, even if she can do little to restore the reputations of the others. Her discussion of the status of women in these plays is particularly significant as she stresses the way that the 'liberation' of women in them is associated with their willingness to procreate, so that the new woman in the 'New Drama' is, like Ann Leete, often 'more a symbol of rebirth than an assertion of individual female identity'. Her insistence that the 'New Drama', for all its virtues, was not a popular drama is also a salutary reminder that a political drama and a popular theatre are not necessarily the same thing.

Despite its subtitle, 'Implicating the Audience', David Ian Rabey's *British and Irish Political Drama in the Twentieth Century*[168] is more concerned with rather literary discussions of the work of some thirty-eight dramatists from Shaw to Nigel Williams, than with theatrical interplay between writers and audiences whose likely political views may be at variance. For example, there is no consideration of the practical problems of staging *Man and Superman*, which surely has some bearings on the relationship between theatrical and social convention which is supposed to underlie the whole book; equally the author's reliance on texts rather than productions leads him into error in his references to the unsettling effect on audiences of the prologue of Griffiths' *The Party*, which was not used in the original production or in subsequent revisions of the play. Quite simply, the book is too short at 215 pages of text to deal adequately with its ostensible subject at the rate of, on average, six pages per writer (though this conceals a divergence between twenty-two pages on Shaw and less than one for C. K. Munro), although it does have the not inconsiderable virtue of devoting attention to a number of writers who seldom receive much critical attention.

The documentation of workers' theatres of the thirties and forties receives a further boost (after last year's *Theatres of the Left, 1880–1935*, *YW* 66.522) with another analysis of the Workers' Theatre Movement and the early days of Unity in *Theatre as a Weapon*[169], and with *Agit-Prop to Theatre Workshop*[170],

167. *The 'New Drama' 1900–1914*, by Jan McDonald. Macmillan. pp. viii + 203. hb £15, pb £4.95.

168. *British and Irish Political Drama in the Twentieth Century*, by David Ian Rabey. Macmillan. pp. x + 237. £25.

169. *Theatre as a Weapon*, by Richard Stourac and Kathleen McCreery. RKP. pp. xvi + 336. £30.

170. *Agit-Prop to Theatre Workshop: Political Playscripts 1930–50*, ed. by Howard Goorney and Ewan MacColl. ManU. pp. lvii + 205. £21.50.

a collection of 'political playscripts 1930–50', edited by Howard Goorney and Ewan MacColl. (It would also be appropriate to mention here Goorney's 1981 *The Theatre Workshop Story* (Methuen), an important study by a company member of one of the most significant twentieth-century British theatre companies.) *Theatre as a Weapon* is a comparative study of workers' theatre movements in Germany, the USSR, and Britain and its treatment of the WTM inevitably overlaps somewhat with that of *Theatres of the Left* since it draws on some of the same limited sources. Nevertheless it has independent value, particularly in offering international points of comparison on the WTM's activities and in its attempt to explain the reasons for the decline of the WTM. Goorney and MacColl were themselves participants in the movements described in *Theatre as a Weapon*, so their own collection is doubly valuable, both in rescuing some important texts from oblivion and in offering their own insights which amplify, and sometimes suggest rather different approaches from the essentially metropolitan bases of *Theatres of the Left* and *Theatre as a Weapon*. Indeed, MacColl offers a more concise, integrated, and moving account of the roots of such enterprises than the more eclectic studies. He is both a good writer and a fine self-critic. Goorney's Epilogue makes the important point, which these volumes all bear out, that there is a long history of attempts to create a genuinely popular workers' theatre. The scripts included are *John Bullion* by James H. Miller and Joan Littlewood, *Newsboy*, a WTM piece ultimately from a poem by V. J. Jerome, extracts from *Last Edition* by Littlewood and MacColl, and three plays by MacColl alone: *Johnny Noble, Uranium 235*, and *The Other Animals*.

Another attempt to create a rather different kind of 'alternative' theatre forms the subject of Kenneth Pickering's *Drama in the Cathedral*[171], subtitled 'The Canterbury Festival Plays 1928–1948', which offers far more than a parochial account of Christian verse drama and is of considerable interest to anyone concerned with the history of 'alternative' theatre, although individual chapters on the plays by contemporary writers staged at Canterbury form the bulk of the book. There is certainly some significant material on plays by relatively unconsidered dramatists such as Dorothy L. Sayers, Charles Williams, Laurie Lee, and Christopher Hassall as well as the obvious big names Eliot and Fry; but the book gains much of its considerable value from its desire to resituate these plays in the context of nineteenth- and early twentieth-century secular verse drama and the antagonism between church and stage. Some stimulating points about both didactic drama and innovations in staging techniques suggest tendencies, links, and parallels between these stagings and other, perhaps better-known because secular, innovations. Many significant, and sometimes unexpected, figures in the development of British theatre in the twentieth century find a place in this study, but its usefulness is diminished by its lack of an index, murky illustrations, and lapses in production.

In *Modern Tragicomedy and the British Tradition*[172] Richard Dutton attempts to relocate works by Beckett, Pinter, Stoppard, Albee, and Storey out of the Absurd and into a short-lived manifestation of tragicomedy between 1955 and 1975. There is an introductory essay on the genre, particularly in its

---

171. *Drama in the Cathedral*, by Kenneth Pickering. Churchman (1985). pp. 373. £14.95.

172. *Modern Tragicomedy and the British Tradition*, by Richard Dutton. Harvester. pp. x + 227. hb £18.95, pb £7.95.

Jacobean form, followed by discussions of individual modern plays. I found some of the necessary generalizations problematic; for example, an attempt to distinguish between a political and an absurdist tradition which meant lumping writers as formally different as Bond and Wesker in the same category. Five plays by Pinter, three by Stoppard, two by Beckett, and one each by Storey and Albee receive individual but not particularly insightful treatment. As the author points out himself, he is attempting to draw analogies 'whose sole function is elucidation'. For the most part, I did not find these analogies offered the most interesting points of critical departure in analysing the plays.

D. Keith Peacock's 'Chronicles of Wasted Time' (*TD*) offers the best study so far of the relationship between Angus Calder's *The People's War* and plays by Ian McEwan, David Hare, and Howard Brenton, focusing on the ways in which they use the Second World War as 'a means of questioning the quality of post war change'. The essay is particularly concerned with the dramatists' analysis of the reasons for the unfulfilled prospect of a (leftwards) social realignment. The main thrust of the essay is to sketch in contexts and trace influences, rather than to analyse plays in detail, but there is still some worthwhile analysis of individual plays, particularly in terms of the significance of the central female character in *Licking Hitler*, *The Imitation Game*, and *Plenty*. The author's analysis could also have been profitably extended to cover the changes Hare made for the film version of *Plenty*.

There are still too few studies of the operation of theatre companies and the interaction between financial and organizational pressures on the one hand and artistic imperatives on the other. Philip Roberts's study of the Royal Court under William Gaskill[173] is a fascinating and often illuminating attempt to bridge that gap. The best parts of the book are those in which the author, drawing on official records and on personal reminiscences, tells the story of the turbulent seasons between 1965 and 1972; the accounts of the productions of Bond's *Saved*, Lawrence's *The Daughter-in-Law*, Storey's *The Changing Room*, and Brenton's *Magnificence* could usefully have offered more insight into the actual production processes at the expense of some of the plot narration. Overall, though, the book is still one of the best accounts available of the day-by-day processes which lie behind the creation of theatre. John Haynes's *Taking the Stage*[174] offers an excellent complement to Roberts's study with its reproductions of Haynes's production photographs, many of them from the Court, and Lindsay Anderson's introductory account of some of the changes in stage photography in recent years.

Michelene Wandor's *Understudies* (Methuen, 1981) was a major analysis of theatre and sexual politics, with its main emphasis on the seventies, by a writer with both theatrical and academic credentials. The revised version, *Carry on Understudies*[175], reflects many of the developments of the eighties, pursuing a more analytical approach than was possible in the earlier volume where recording history was paramount. In the revised version, Wandor develops her idea of feminist dynamics (also found in an important issue of *Drama* in 1984

173. *The Royal Court Theatre, 1965–1972*, by Philip Roberts. RKP. pp. x + 192. £18.95.

174. *Taking the Stage*, by John Haynes, intro. by Lindsay Anderson. T&H. pp. 128. pb £8.95.

175. *Carry on Understudies*, by Michelene Wandor. RKP. pp. xxi + 210. pb £5.95.

devoted to 'Women in Theatre') and adds analyses of some important plays by both women and men that have appeared since 1981. Although there has been some criticism of the author by other feminists for not updating the work sufficiently, it remains the best introduction to the study of women in all aspects of their roles in the production of theatre and continues to define the terms of debate.

Carl Tighe, in 'Theatre (or Not) in Wales'[176], offers an informed and polemical overview of developments in the Welsh theatrical scene, primarily over the past fifteen years, but with some consideration of the economic – cultural roots of the current situation. It will be a useful starting point for anyone attempting to engage with the difficult cultural and aesthetic issues in contemporary Welsh theatre.

An actor and a director conclude this section. Joy Leslie Gibson's pedestrian biography of *Ian McKellen*[177] plods through a recital of parts and reviews, with rather too many misprints for comfort. The few attempts to consider institutional issues like touring or the role of the company in modern theatre founder on a patronizing metropolitanism and an apparent ignorance of the existence of organized small-scale touring theatre in Great Britain. Fortunately, Jonathan Miller's *Subsequent Performances*[178] is a very different proposition. It is a beautifully presented extended meditation on the role of the director in theatre, opera, film, and television which draws on Miller's own experiences and the work of theorists from Walter Benjamin to Henri Zirner. The arguments are complex and compelling, the range of reference is very wide, and the book offers an outstanding account of the state of the art of directing.

(b) Collections of Plays

Tribute should be paid to Methuen who continue to play a substantial part in creating canons through their publications of modestly priced anthologies of plays. Howard Brenton and Simon Gray have volumes of their plays in the World Dramatists series, each with an introduction by the author[179]. Gray concentrates on the circumstances of the plays' composition and production whereas Brenton addresses questions of theory. The volumes include plays from throughout the authors' careers and the texts of *The Churchill Play* and *The Common Pursuit* are revised versions, not previously published. From a comparison of the two authors one becomes aware that although both are technically adept, Brenton has a far greater range and is much more inventive theatrically.

A popular dramatist who attracts virtually no critical attention is Willy Russell, a collection of whose plays[180] includes brief introductory material by the author, some of which has previously appeared as the introduction to the Longman edition of *Educating Rita* (*YW* 66.532).

The rather ambitiously titled *Landmarks of Modern British Drama*, divided

176. In *Wales: The Imagined Nation*, ed. by Tony Curtis. PWP. pp. 306. hb £14.95, pb £5.95.

177. *Ian McKellen*, by Joy Leslie Gibson. W&N. pp. 190. £10.95.

178. *Subsequent Performances*, by Jonathan Miller. Faber. pp. 253. £15.

179. *Plays: One*, by Howard Brenton. Methuen. pp. xv + 390. pb £3.95. *Plays: One*, by Simon Gray. Methuen. pp. xiii + 353. pb £3.95.

180. *Educating Rita; Stags and Hens; and Blood Brothers*, by Willy Russell. Methuen. pp. 232. pb £3.95.

into *The Plays of the Sixties* and *The Plays of the Seventies* [181], includes a total of fourteen plays in two volumes, together with quite substantial general introductions, individual essays on the dramatists, and useful bibliographies. The picture of contemporary theatre offered by the anthologizers, Roger Cornish and Violet Ketels, is adequate as an introduction, covering the main developments with due acknowledgement of the standard sources and mentioning those other substantial dramatists who narrowly missed inclusion. Although one might disagree with the assignment of particular dramatists to one decade rather than the other, the actual selection is relatively uncontroversial: Arden, Barnes, Bond, Orton, Osborne, Pinter, and Wesker for the sixties; Ayckbourn, Brenton, Churchill, Gray, Nichols, Shaffer, Stoppard for the seventies. The most obvious omissions are probably those of David Edgar, Pam Gems, Trevor Griffiths, and David Hare, although the compilers also mention Howard Barker, Stephen Poliakoff, Michael Frayn, C. P. Taylor, Christopher Hampton, David Rudkin, David Storey, and David Pownall as near misses. Of the plays chosen, *A Patriot for Me*, *Just Between Ourselves*, and *Quartermaine's Terms* are perhaps surprising choices as landmarks in their respective authors' careers, although *Patriot* is being revalued upwards these days. There is also something irritating about *Roots* and *Serjeant Musgrave's Dance*, both first performed in 1959, representing the sixties and *Passion Play*, *Quartermaine's Terms*, and *Top Girls*, all first performed in the eighties, representing the seventies. There is no bibliographical information on the state of the plays' texts other than a copyright page statement that the text used 'was that currently in print in 1985' and the standard of proof-reading in the editorial matter is not particularly high: Maugham's comment on Jimmy Porter and his ilk was that they were 'scum', not 'slum' as reported here.

Plays by Women [182] has reached its fifth volume, now under the editorship of Mary Remnant, whose selection continues Michelene Wandor's policy of adventurous eclecticism by mixing plays by established authors (Pam Gems's *Queen Christina* and Lorraine Hansberry's *A Raisin in the Sun*) with those by less well-established writers (Rona Munro's *Piper's Cave* and Jacqueline Rudet's *Money to Live*). The living authors offer the usual brief afterwords and Yvonne Brewster contributes a note on her recent production of *A Raisin in the Sun*. The presence of plays by two black writers does a little to remedy an obvious gap in current play publishing.

Michael Wilcox's second selection of *Gay Plays* [183] includes three relatively recent plays, by Timothy Mason (*Bearclaw*), Martin Sherman (*Cracks*), and C. P. Taylor (*Lies about Vietnam*), as well as Roger Gellert's 1958 *Quaint Honour*. Gellert, Mason, and Sherman contribute notes on their own plays and Wilcox writes on Taylor as well as introducing the whole volume.

(c) Individual Authors

James Harding declares in the foreword to his biography of the theatre critic James Agate [184] that 'It is time to decide' whether Agate was, 'as obituaries

181. *Landmarks of Modern British Drama*, intro. by Roger Cornish and Violet Ketels. Vol. I: *The Plays of the Sixties*. Vol. II: *The Plays of the Seventies*. Methuen (1985 and 1986). pp. xxxvi + 732; pp. xxxii + 623. pb £4.95 each.

182. *Plays by Women*, Vol. V, ed. by Mary Remnant. Methuen. pp. 181. pb £4.50.

183. *Gay Plays*, Vol. II, ed. by Michael Wilcox. Methuen. pp. 126. pb £3.95.

184. *Agate*, by James Harding. Methuen. pp. xv + 238. £12.95.

claimed, the Hazlitt of his age'. Unfortunately the issue is never addressed in a systematic way, as Harding contents himself with tracing the exotic path of Agate's increasingly bizzare life and loves. The book is anecdotally valuable for its account of a certain kind of literary life in the twenties and thirties but it lacks any sustained analysis of Agate's criticism to justify the comparison with Hazlitt.

The later plays of John Arden, written with Margaretta D'Arcy, tend not to receive a great deal of critical attention, so Javed Malik's 'The Polarized Universe of "The Island of the Mighty": The Dramaturgy of Arden and D'Arcy' (*NTQ*) is particularly welcome. Economically tracing Arden's development, Malik devotes most of his essay to an essentially textual analysis of *The Island of the Mighty* which draws on Bakhtinian ideas to develop an argument in terms of the binary oppositions in the text. It is a useful reading of the play, but (as the editors point out), unusually for *NTQ*, it does not centre on a production.

Bernard F. Dukore's 'Craft, Character, Comedy: Ayckbourn's *Woman in Mind*' (*TCL*) is the first critical assessment of a challenging play which Dukore saw in its initial production at Scarborough. The essay is mainly devoted to introducing and explicating the play's form and characteristics, with many acute observations en route. As Dukore says, Ayckbourn is still critically undervalued and underdiscussed. From my experience of the London production, I would agree with the majority of Dukore's points, though he does see the play in more purely character-based terms than I would, perhaps underestimating the sexual politics and the importance to the play's initial success of the ways in which the dramatist plays with audience expectations.

Enid Bagnold's claim to critical attention as a dramatist rests mainly on *The Chalk Garden*, once described by Kenneth Tynan as 'the finest artificial comedy to have flowed from an English (as opposed to an Irish) pen since the death of Congreve'. Anne Sebba's well-researched biography[185] recreates the circumstances surrounding the composition and production of that and other plays with considerable skill but makes no great claims for its subject's status as a dramatist. There are many incidental glimpses of the great and famous.

Once again Howard Barker receives no critical attention, so his own views expressed in an interview with Finlay Donesky in *NTQ*, under the title 'Oppression, Resistance and the Writer's Testament', are welcome. Another relatively neglected writer, Peter Barnes, is the subject of Bernard F. Dukore's introductory analysis of *Barnes' People III* in 'Newer Peter Barnes with Links to the Past' (*EiT*). Dukore shows how Barnes is now developing a dramaturgy which responds to the current funding limitations in theatre by modifying his previous epic practices towards a less resource-demanding short play with fewer characters than previously. Dukore's analysis goes some way to proving his contention that, at their best, these short plays offer an 'Ibsenite indictment of audiences, through subversion of their received values; and an organic merger of content, form, and an effort to make audiences become part of the world of the play'.

As Samuel Beckett's eightieth birthday fell in April 1986, the year brought an abundance of Beckett studies, collections of articles, and tributes to the author.

185. *Enid Bagnold: The Authorized Biography*, by Anne Sebba. W&N. pp. xv + 317. £15.95.

Unfortunately his publishers, Faber, spoilt their contribution by offering a *Complete Dramatic Works*[186] which reprints the expurgated 1956 text of *Waiting for Godot* rather than the restored text of 1965. It may be too soon for the kind of variorum edition implicit in the views of James Knowlson (*YW* 66.526) but there can surely be no justification for perpetuating the censor's amendments at the expense of the author's text in a collected works, given that the same publishers had issued the uncensored version in 1965.

Not primarily a critical tool, Eoin O'Brien's elegant and expensive *The Beckett Country*[187], generously illustrated with black and white photographs (mainly by David Davison), invites a reconsideration of both the Irish dimension and the treatment of 'outer reality' in Beckett's work through juxtaposing factual and visual material about Beckett's birthplace, Dublin characters, institutions, cityscapes, and surrounding landscapes with the Beckett texts in which they appear. In the foreword, James Knowlson sees the value of the book not in the neatness of identifications between fact and fiction, but in the revelation of how many of even the most apparently abstract of Beckett's texts have their roots in 'outer reality'; indeed, in a specifically Irish outer reality.

Beckett's birthday presumably also prompted the outpouring of collections of articles which, taken together, form an impromptu survey of the past and present state of Beckett scholarship and offer some possible directions for the future. Beckett's alma mater, Trinity College Dublin, produced a special issue of its review *Hermathena*, under the title 'Beckett at 80: A Trinity Tribute', which included articles by Terence Brown, Brendan Kennelly, Declan Kiberd, Derek Mahon, Vivian Mercier, Alec Reid, and, the most significant, W. J. McCormack. McCormack's 'Seeing Darkly: Notes on T. W. Adorno and Samuel Beckett' places *Endgame* in the specific historical moment of postwar Europe, and sees the contemporary crisis in culture reflected in the play.

The French paid tribute with a glossy, though appallingly bound, special issue of *RE*, which included articles by such theoreticians as Tzvetan Todorov and Anne Ubersfeld. Its principal interest for the (francophone) student of Beckett's drama, however, lies in its coverage of the material aspects of Beckett in performance, with essays on Beckett's production notebooks and his use of music and technology. These essays cover the full range of Beckett's dramatic output for radio and television as well as theatre, paying attention to the latest and the earliest plays – there are even extracts from *Eleuthéria*. There is some valuable bibliographical material, though the number of printing errors diminishes its usefulness somewhat.

As No Other Dare Fail[188], edited by John Calder, is primarily a series of homages to Beckett by 'friends and admirers' including Enoch Brater, Martin Esslin, Sorel Etrog, James Knowlson, Eoin O'Brien, and Billie Whitelaw. Perhaps the most significant essay is a detailed account by the French actor Pierre Chabert of being directed by Beckett in Robert Pinget's *Hypothèse* in 1965. This was Beckett's first experience of directing and also the only occasion on which he has directed a play he did not write. Chabert draws parallels between *Hypothèse* and Beckett's own plays, concentrating on Beckett's development of scenic relationships 'between the actor and a material object

186. *The Complete Dramatic Works*, by Samuel Beckett. Faber. pp. 476. £12.50.
187. *The Beckett Country*, by Eoin O'Brien. Black Cat/Faber. pp. xxvi + 402. £40.
188. *As No Other Dare Fail*, ed. by John Calder. Calder. pp. 135. £10.95.

(the manuscript) and between the actor and technical and scenic media (the film images)'.

Patrick McCarthy's introduction to *Critical Essays on Samuel Beckett*[189] gives a useful potted history of major events in Beckett criticism since Kenner's 1961 *Samuel Beckett: A Critical Study*. The bulk of the essays are devoted to the prose, and the drama section is dominated by the familiar names of Ruby Cohn on *Godot*, Martin Esslin on the visual metaphors, Edith Kern on Beckett's affinities with medieval drama, James Knowlson on *Play*, and Enoch Brater on *Footfalls*. Among the second generation of Beckett critics represented are Robert Zaller, who couples *Godot*, not entirely happily, with Hobbes's *Leviathan*; James Acheson, who demonstrates the inadequacy of various interpretational approaches to *Endgame* from the allegorical to the psychoanalytical without really investigating the mechanisms whereby 'The play is deliberately designed to resist even the most ingenious of explications'; and, finally, Susan Brienza on myth and ritual in Beckett – the only author to deal substantially with the more recent drama.

S. E. Gontarski's collection, *On Beckett: Essays and Criticism*[190], includes among the essays on the prose Georges Bataille's 'Molloy's Silence', Maurice Blanchot's 'Where Now Who Now?', and Wolfgang Iser's 'When is the End not the End? The Idea of Fiction in Beckett'. The drama section is devoted mainly to the plays in the context of performance, including informative interviews with Roger Blin, Jack MacGowran, and Alan Schneider, and accounts of Beckett as director from Ruby Cohn and Walter Asmus, the German director, whose notes on *Godot*, *That Time*, and *Footfalls* are particularly useful. James Knowlson draws on Asmus's notes in his study of *Footfalls*, and Paul Lawley perceptively analyses the counterpoint between stage image and text in *Not I*. Martin Esslin discusses the radio plays and there is some attention given to the later plays in Pierre Astier's interesting, if somewhat fanciful, work on The Isle of Swans (and the Statue of Liberty) in *Ohio Impromptu*, Gontarski's brief essay on *Quad* and *Catastrophe*, and Enoch Brater's somewhat descriptive piece on *Rockaby*.

Brater's own collection *Beckett at 80: Beckett in Context*[191], the only one devoted entirely to the theatre, is, together with *RE*, the most contemporary, offering a synchronic rather than diachronic perspective. In a retrospectives section, Ruby Cohn, John Russell Brown, and Normand Berlin remember the impact of their first encounter with *Godot* and there are attempts to evaluate Beckett's influence on Pinter, Stoppard, and Albee (by Cohn and Russell Brown), Fugard, Soyinka, Shepard, and Mamet (by Thomas Whitaker). In 'Happy Days and Dramatic Convention', Charles Lyons interestingly considers the 'recurrent paradigmatic structure that playwrights have found useful in representing character in a formal process through which they represent acts of self-consciousness'. He emphasizes the characters' attempts to situate themselves both in relation to an external witness who observes and judges them (drawing comparisons with Orestes and Phaedra), and in relation to a narrated past which is unverifiable and inaccessible. Keir Elam brings together a variety of disciplines, including linguistics, psychoanalysis, and

189. *Critical Essays on Samuel Beckett*, ed. by Patrick McCarthy. Hall. pp. 240. £35.
190. *On Beckett: Essays and Criticism*, ed. by S. E. Gontarski. Grove. pp. 384. £10.95.
191. *Beckett at 80: Beckett in Context*, ed. by Enoch Brater. OUP. pp. 238. £17.95.

semiology, in his study of '*Not I*: Beckett's Mouth and the Ars(e) Rhetorica'. Since Elam's own rhetoric is an integral part of his style, the essay is difficult to summarize, but his point of departure is the argument that 'Beckett moves progressively away from a full semantic and expressive investment in the sign'. Elam develops Beckett's negative rhetoric concentrating on the play/audience relationship, on the dramatization of the relation between language and subjectivity, and on the scepticism towards the logos implied in Beckett's comparison of his plays to 'fundamental sounds', in an essay which accounts well for the complexity and dramatic intensity of this minimal piece. Other contributions include Esslin on time and repetition, Bernard Beckerman on 'The Act of Listening' in Beckett's plays, Katharine Worth on listeners within the plays, particularly the later ones, and Knowlson on the English and German versions of *Ghost Trio/Geister Trio*.

MD is, as usual, a reliable source of Beckett articles. Kripa K. Gautam and Manjula Sharma offer a rather laboured consideration of 'Dialogue in *Waiting for Godot* and Grice's Concept of Implicature'. James L. Calderwood uses waiting as a central figure of synecdoche in 'Ways of Waiting in *Waiting for Godot*', examining the relevance of the title to the play as a whole, and meditating on Beckett's 'art grounded in negation'. Martha Fehsenfeld gives an account of a more recent example of Beckett's poetics of negation in '"Everything Out But the Faces": Beckett's Reshaping of *What Where* for Television'. Her study both illuminates this short cryptic piece – the latest of the late plays – and reveals the extent to which Beckett explores and exploits the medium in which he is working. Beckett's minimalism is also considered by William Hutchings in 'Abated Drama: Samuel Beckett's Unbated "Breath"' (*ArielE*). *Criticism* has one of the year's best articles on Beckett: 'The Contentless Passion of an Unfruitful Wind' by Sharon O'Dair who concentrates on the use of the comic in *Endgame*. Referring to Kierkegaard's distinction between an ironic and a humorous relation to the comical, she argues that laughter in *Endgame* is of the hollow, ironical kind, rooted in the 'contentless passion of an unfruitful wind raging over the naked ground'. In 'Beckett's Monologues: The Context and Conditions of Representation' (*MLR*) Patrick O'Donovan deals well with Beckett's self-conscious use of theatricality and the conditions of theatrical production in a number of the later plays, underlining the role of language as the medium of the character's self-representation.

Of the three individual studies of Beckett this year, Linda Ben-Zvi's[192] is the most disappointing. Perhaps limited by the format of the Twayne series which requires her to deal with the entire canon, her sections on the plays, dealt with individually, are seldom more than descriptive. S. E. Gontarski's *The Intent of Undoing in Samuel Beckett's Dramatic Texts*[193] offers a highly scholarly piece of genetic criticism, tracing Beckett's works through the numerous manuscript stages of their composition. In his excellent introduction he examines the contradictions inherent in the Beckettian aesthetic which emerges through 'the pattern of artistic choices', arguing that Beckett's plays are rooted in the very realism he derides. Gontarski focuses on the processes in which that 'outer reality' is transformed and emphasizes Beckett's art of erasure, of 'writing

192. *Samuel Beckett*, by Linda Ben-Zvi. Twayne. pp. 256. $16.95.
193. *The Intent of Undoing in Samuel Beckett's Dramatic Texts*, by S. E. Gontarski. IndU (1985). pp. xvii + 222. £24.50.

himself out' of his texts. This is a well-researched book, which is not only constantly illuminating – on, for example, *Fin de Partie*'s roots in Beckett's experience of war-time and postwar France – but also points towards some areas of critical investigation into Beckett's work which remain largely unexplored.

Peter Gidal's *Understanding Beckett*[194] is certainly the most controversial of this year's offerings. Written from outside the academy, this book deliberately eschews any semblance of conformity to scholarly structure or style. The format is based on the juxtaposition of texts by Beckett, Gertrude Stein, H.D., Wittgenstein, Nietzsche, and Marx (to name but a few) with Gidal's own text. The style is self-consciously elliptical and occasionally unreadable. Nevertheless, this is an important contribution to Beckett studies since it links Beckett's linguistic subversion – his rejection of the authority of the logos – to a politics of representation which focuses on 'the *processes* of contradiction, struggle (of voice, act, subjectivity and the social)' and reveals that Beckett's formal preoccupations are far from apolitical.

Two articles deal with Beckett and other artists. In 'Symbols, Signs and Language: The Brothers Yeats and Samuel Beckett's Art of the Theatre' (*CompD*) Gordon Armstrong argues that 'the medium is the only possibility of a message'. He suggests that the work of Jack Yeats had more influence on Beckett's aesthetics than W. B.'s did, and he emphasizes that the evocative power of the plays lies in their form, pattern, and architectonics, rather than in their content. Estelle Manette Thaler's 'Apocalyptic Vision in *Heartbreak House* and *Endgame*: The Metaphor of Change' (*ZAA*) reads each play individually as examples of twentieth-century apocalyptic drama. Opportunities for comparison are ignored and the reading of Beckett's play is disappointingly unwilling to question the veracity of the characters' vision of the world either in terms of the hints in the text that the world goes on as before or in terms of the role of the audience in validating the characters' vision. Beckett also figures in two more general studies: L. A. C. Dobrez deals with *Godot* and *Endgame* in a philosophical context which takes little account of dramatic form[195] and Richard Dutton examines the same plays in his book on tragicomedy[172]. [A.M.]

Edward Bond's attitude to Shakespeare and his preoccupation with myth drew considerable attention this year. In two articles in *MD* James C. Bulman offers clear readings of 'Bond, Shakespeare, and the Absurd' and '*The Woman* and Greek Myth: Bond's Theatre of History' which show Bond's engagement with our culture's myths in the form of Shakespeare himself, *King Lear*, and the Trojan War. As Bulman suggests in the essay on *The Woman*, the plays 'are so permeated with those myths that he appears, paradoxically, to be half in love with those artifacts of a culture whose ideology he abhors'. There were three useful essays on *Bingo*: Lou Lapin's 'The Artist in Society: Bond, Shakespeare, and *Bingo*'[196] offers a sound introduction to Bond's treatment of the issues referred to in his title; Christy L. Brown's 'Edward Bond's *Bingo*: Shakespeare and the Ideology of Genius' (*ISJR*) covers similar ground but with more of an

---

194. *Understanding Beckett*, by Peter Gidal. Macmillan. pp. xvii + 278. £29.50.

195. *The Existential and its Exits*, by L. A. C. Dobrez. Athlone. pp. 400. £28.

196. In *Before His Eyes: Essays in Honor of Stanley Kauffmann*, ed. by Bert Cardullo. UPA. pp. x + 185. $24.50.

emphasis on the Renaissance historical context. Both these essays complement Jenny Spencer's incisive essay on 'Edward Bond's *Bingo*: History, Politics and Subjectivity' (*TD*). Spencer focuses on the contrasting roles of Shakespeare and the Son as a means of exploring the play's dialectic in terms of the Freudian power of the father and Marxist potential of religion to be a radical force while also paying due attention to the presentation of women as victims in the play. I know of relatively little work on *Summer*, so Pete Mathers's 'Edward Bond Directs "Summer" at the Cottesloe, 1982' (*NTQ*) is a valuable record, particularly as it combines textual and performance analysis with consideration of such issues as the significatory functions of programme and poster.

There is still relatively little critical, as opposed to biographical, writing on Noel Coward, so Robert F. Kiernan's *Noel Coward*[197] is particularly welcome as a sound and illuminating study of his work. It is far more than the basic anecdotal introduction implied by its series title, Literature and Life. The choice of plays for detailed discussion inevitably overlaps with that of John Lahr in the only other substantial critical treatment of Coward (see *YW* 63.413) but Kiernan is a lively and independent critic who gives due weight to non-verbal communication in Coward's plays. He is also perceptive on the relationship between Coward's writing and the generic models within which he worked, as in his observation that 'His impulse was to temper the well-made play into an Art Deco curve'. Between them, Lahr and Kiernan offer complementary insights into the undervalued achievement of a great dramatist. Coward's *Autobiography* (Methuen) was not available for review.

The only essays on T. S. Eliot's plays this year, with the exception of Kenneth Pickering's discussion of *Murder in the Cathedral*[171], were Stephen Wade's 'The Orchestration of Monologues: "The Cocktail Party" and a Developing Genre' (*Agenda*) and Kurt Tetzeli von Rosader's 'Christian Historical Drama: The Exemplariness of *Murder in the Cathedral*'. Wade's is a diffident piece which suggests that 'the confessional monologue is extremely useful for the presentation of religious and philosophical themes' and that the play uses 'such techniques in a way that has pointed out the future of the genre', but then does little to develop the argument before tailing off in a confession of the author's realization that 'there are critics who would not consider the verse plays as Eliot's greatest successes, and one must have some reservations, but I hope I have stimulated some thought on the matter'. Von Rosader's is adequately summed up by its closing statement that

> If the representation of Christian historicity and its complex relationship between the history of salvation, of the world, and of the soul by paradoxical, allegorical, or figural means makes a play qualify as Christian historical drama – and not the mere staging of documented facts and subject-matter with some piously religious tinge – *Murder in the Cathedral* must be considered fully exemplary.

James Gindin's *John Galsworthy's Life and Art*[198] is a worthy biography which pays due attention to the plays without presenting any startling new

---

197. *Noel Coward*, by Robert F. Kiernan. Ungar. pp. xiv + 183. $14.95.

198. *John Galsworthy's Life and Art: An Alien's Fortress*, by James Gindin. Macmillan. pp. xvii + 616. £27.50.

insights; Jan McDonald's account[167] discussed above is more interesting and lively.

Trevor Griffiths' *Judgement over the Dead*[199], which reached the television screen as *The Last Place on Earth*, has a wide-ranging introductory conversation between the author and Misha Glenny in which they discuss both specific points relating to the production of the series and more general issues relating to 'authorship' in theatre and television. Among the many significant points to emerge is the suggestion that the crucially important first episode lacked coherence as a result of having three different directors.

David Hare's battle with critics over the interpretation of his *Plenty*[200] is taken a stage further in the edition published to coincide with the release of the film version (see *YW* 65.582 for an earlier stage in the debate). In his 'note on performance' Hare argues for a sympathetic reading of the character of Susan Traherne in the face of the acknowledged contrary predisposition of large sections of the English audience; an argument that would be more convincing if his own alterations for the film had not further reduced the opportunities for presentation of the socio-political context. In the introduction to *The Asian Plays*[201] (*Fanshen, Saigon, A Map of the World*) Hare discusses the difficulties of working in television in relation to *Saigon*, in similar vein to Griffiths, makes some fairly familiar points about the genesis of *Fanshen*, and talks about the Adelaide premiere of *A Map of the World*. Perhaps the most surprising aspect of the introduction is Hare's statement that 'To claim to see the world through Asian eyes is, to me at least, transparently absurd'; there appears to me to be no small discrepancy between this view and an earlier statement of his that 'Looking at the world through the eyes of women is to see the world more clearly'. Bert Cardullo's 'Brecht and *Fanshen*' (*Gestus*) is a straightforward account of Hare's play in the light of both Brechtian notions of characterization and material from William Hinton's original book, particularly relating to the presentation of Yu-Lai.

Peter Nichols is another dramatist, like Barker and Barnes, who attracts less critical attention than he deserves. This year brought only '"The Cure is Removal of Guilt": Faith, Fidelity and Fertility in the Plays of Peter Nichols' (*MD*) in which the usually illuminating Richard Foulkes struggled valiantly to make something more out of Nichols's contacts with John Layard than they seem capable of bearing.

It was a relatively quiet year for O'Casey studies in which the only substantial new contribution came from Bernice Schrank's two essays on *The Plough and the Stars* and Leslie Thomson's on *Juno and the Paycock*. Inevitably there is some overlap between Schrank's 'Anatomizing an Insurrection: Sean O'Casey's *The Plough and the Stars*' (*MD*), her 'Language and Silence in *The Plough and the Stars*' (*MSpr*), and her 1985 *IUR* essay (see *YW* 66.530–1). The *MD* essay is a more general introduction to the play while the one in *MSpr* is particularly concerned with aspects of silence and non-verbal communication and the detailed analysis amplifies and consolidates that of the *IUR* article, rather than breaking new ground. Leslie Thomson's 'Opening the Eyes of the Audience: Visual and Verbal Imagery in *Juno and the Paycock*' (*MD*) is an

199. *Judgement over the Dead*, by Trevor Griffiths. Verso. pp. xlv + 305. pb £7.95.
200. *Plenty*, by David Hare. Methuen. pp. 88. pb £3.95.
201. *The Asian Plays*, by David Hare. Faber. pp. xiv + 229. pb £4.95.

ultimately somewhat misogynistic reading of the play in which he argues that the critical reception of Juno herself has been too generous, that two mothers are only relatively better than one, that nothing has changed 'because the delusions and their causes remain' and that there will be a chaotic world 'so long as boys refuse to become men and mothers, whether real or symbolic, encourage *by their very existence* [my italics] the worship of fantasies and the avoidance of reality'. Ultimately the reading seems tendentious and to rely on setting up a straw Juno whose faults are never acknowledged by the play or by critics. There is now a *File on O'Casey*[202] compiled conscientiously by Nesta Jones. The selection of brief comments on each play is illuminating and the bibliographies offer a good starting point for further investigation, but I am not convinced that there is an obvious audience for the series. Casebooks are, in general, more substantial and offer the undergraduate lengthier extracts dedicated to individual works; scholars will still want to conduct their own bibliographical searches.

Harold Pinter's *Collected Poems and Prose*[203], an expanded version of *Poems and Prose 1949–1977* with no new material of direct relevance to the plays, includes the short story version of *Tea Party*, the poem 'A View of the Party', and the essay on Anew McMaster. Michael Scott's Casebook[204] on *The Birthday Party*, *The Caretaker*, and *The Homecoming* is a very useful compilation which represents both academic and theatrical perspectives. As well as extracts from established Pinter critics representing such diverse viewpoints as Martin Esslin and Austin Quigley, there are reviews of both original productions and revivals which all contribute to the important sense of the legitimate diversity of interpretation which is at the heart of the Casebook enterprise in general and this volume in particular.

In 'De la Fête au Sacrifice dans le Théâtre de Pinter' (*RHT*) Jeanne Andrée Nelson sees similarities between several of Pinter's plays in the ways that normally happy events turn sour and extends this into a Girardian reading in terms of the genesis of cultural institutions, arguing that such a reading permits us to understand the plays more fully. Ruth in *The Homecoming* thus emerges as a willing sacrificial victim. The general line is, perhaps, not as new as the author thinks but she presents her case with considerable verve, somewhat spoiled by proof reading which, for example, offers us *The Butler's Going Up* in the text as the title of the work correctly called *Butter's Going Up* in the notes. In '*Old Times*: Pinter's Drama of the Invisible'[196] Art Borreca argues that critical frustration with the play's refusal to yield a definitive meaning stems from a failure to recognize Pinter's central concern with the experience of existing in time and with the impossibility of an absolute past. The essay is well aware of the interaction between the Pinteresque tradition and the interpretation of new Pinter plays and offers perceptive comments on the difficulties of finding an appropriate style for this play with detailed reference to the 1984 New York production. Graham Woodroffe's ' "One says yes, the other says no" ' (*L&P*) is a 'psychoanalytic investigation of a slip of the tongue' in *The*

202. *File on O'Casey*, comp. by Nesta Jones. Methuen. pp. 96. hb £7.95, pb £3.50.

203. *Collected Poems and Prose*, by Harold Pinter. Rev. edn. Methuen. pp. viii + 116. pb £3.95.

204. *Harold Pinter: 'The Birthday Party', 'The Caretaker', 'The Homecoming': A Casebook*, ed. by Michael Scott. Macmillan. pp. 208. hb £20, pb £6.95.

Caretaker. The slip in question is Davies's 'coming looking after me' which is analysed in somewhat Lacanian terms so that Aston and Mick are seen as parents with Davies as their child. Even the bag passed between Mick and Aston serves as a metaphor for Davies's infant psyche: it appears to be his but it actually belongs to someone else. There is always a danger that this type of analysis can mistake the critic's virtuosity for analysis of the possibilities of the text but that is not the case here. Of a rather different kind is Daniel Salem's 'The Impact of Pinter's Work' (*ArielE*), a generalized meditation which lacks concrete application of its insights, such as that Pinter's comedy is one of exposed repression, to actual plays or productions. Elin Diamond's *Pinter's Comic Play* (AUP) was not available for review.

B. A. Young's reticent biography of Terence Rattigan[205] covers its subject's life and plays without ever delving very deeply into questions of dramaturgy. Despite the author's apparent access to what the publisher's blurb describes as 'new and unpublished material' there are no major revelations and the issue of the relationship between the author's character, particularly his sexuality, and his work is handled gingerly. The most interesting observations are on Rattigan's belief in the one-act play, in defiance of conventional theatrical wisdom, and on the fact that all his characters tend to be 'united by the thraldom of middle-class behaviour'. Ultimately, however, the biography is a rather old-fashioned work, likely to interest 'Aunt Edna' rather than serious students, who will also regret the lack of an index and footnotes.

After the flood of essays in recent years, 1986 was a relatively quiet year for studies of Peter Shaffer's drama. The best study was undoubtedly Bernard Beckerman's 'The Dynamics of Peter Shaffer's Drama'[206], which offered much good sense in a brief compass. Concentrating on *Equus*, Beckerman reaches the conclusion that the disparity critics have discovered between the dramatic and theatrical actions of the play derives from the fixity of Dysart's own condition, which is manifested in his monologues and in the fact that 'In the course of the play we learn nothing much about the source of or motivation for' his attitudes.

There is the usual crop of Shaviana but little that is particularly illuminating. Indeed two of the three essays on Shaw in the Eric Bentley Festschrift[206] seem to me to offer little to reflect Bentley's own critical acumen: Jacques Barzun's 'Eros, Priapos and Shaw' is a piece of rhetorical casuistry which attempts to rescue Shaw from a series of straw charges against him; Stanley Kauffmann's 'A Paragraph by Shaw', an analysis of a comment by Shaw on how much he was influenced by Dickens, is no more than extempore practical criticism. The third essay, Michael Goldman's 'Shaw and the Marriage in Dionysus' is rather more substantial, offering a reading of *Major Barbara* in terms of a Shavian 'wedding of individual will to a source of higher power' in which props and staging play their part in generating possibilities of meaning.

Many of the essays in the annual *ShawR* are primarily concerned with establishing contexts and making links: Sean Morrow offers material on the unrelated Mabel Shaw who 'was the model for the missionary in the first pages

205. *The Rattigan Version: Sir Terence Rattigan and the Theatre of Character*, by B. A. Young. HH. pp. ix + 228. £12.95.

206. In *The Play and its Critic: Essays for Eric Bentley*, ed. by Michael Bertin. UPA. pp. xxvii + 348. $28.50.

of the *Black Girl*'; Fred D. Crawford compares Shaw's attitude to the First World War with Swift's to the War of the Spanish Succession in 'Swift and Shaw against the War'; Desmond J. McRory's 'Shaw, Einstein and Physics' traces Shaw's relationship with Einstein and the probable effects it had on his attitude to science in his later work; Susan Albertine traces 'Shaw's Interest in Harold Frederic', and Katherine Lyon Mix looks at 'Laurence Housman and Bernard Shaw'. Bridging the gap between the contextual and the critical are Holly Hill's 'Saint Joan's Voices: Actresses on Shaw's Maid', based on interviews with Wendy Hiller, Barbara Jefford, Judi Dench, and Eileen Atkins, which provides a stream of fascinating insights into the ways in which actresses have played the part of Saint Joan; Paul Sawyer's examination of the variants of 'The Last Line of *Arms and the Man*', and Stanley Weintraub's 'A Jennifer from Australia. Edith Adams, her Husband, and *The Doctor's Dilemma*', a discussion of the ways in which Shaw may have based aspects of *The Doctor's Dilemma* on his knowledge of Edith and Francis Adams. There are two purely critical essays: Bert Cardullo's 'The Mystery of *Candida*' interestingly considers the play as a modern equivalent to a medieval mystery play which 'interweaves secular and sacred mystery', and J. Scott Lee takes William Archer's review of the first production as his starting point in an occasionally convoluted attempt to find 'Comic Unity in *Arms and the Man*'. The volume also includes two previously unreprinted pieces by Shaw, the usual reviews and checklist of Shaviana, and a rather splendid account by Alan G. Brunger of the discovery of the resemblance between the profile of Shaw and a peninsula in Quebec which has subsequently been renamed Pointe Bernard Shaw!

Although the scope of Jane Ann Crum's '"I must get out of this into the air": Transfiguration and Ascent in Three Plays by Bernard Shaw'[196] is fairly well conveyed by its title, the essay combines theological, dramaturgical, and theatrical insights to considerable effect in outlining the relationship between stage directions, dialogue, and Shaw's own 'theological' statements. The plays concerned are *Major Barbara*, *Misalliance*, and *Saint Joan*. Bert Cardullo's 'The Artistic Evolvement of *Androcles and the Lion*' (*SN*) shows briefly but effectively how 'the plurality of beliefs in the play is reflected by the plurality of forms of which it is composed'. In *CVE* Jean-Claude Amalric is concerned to trace the Shavian hero 'Du Realiste au Surhomme: les Métamorphoses du Héros Shavien'. The argument is not unfamiliar: the heroes evolve through a series of experiments from Bluntschli to Don Juan/Tanner. In *Éire* Tramble T. Turner examines 'Bernard Shaw's "Eternal Irish Concerns"' in *John Bull's Other Island*, placing the play usefully in its Irish context but also insisting on its wider significance. The majority of Shaw criticism continues to be untroubled by the newer methodologies, so Richard F. Dietrich's 'Deconstruction as Devil's Advocacy: A Shavian Alternative' (*MD*) is particularly welcome, even if it seems unduly defensive at times, since it suggests some new approaches which could help to release Shaw from some critical straitjackets.

Shaw's *Major Critical Essays*[207], 'The Quintessence of Ibsenism', 'The Perfect Wagnerite', and 'The Sanity of Art', have been published in one volume with a sound but basic introduction by Michael Holroyd. In 'What They Really Wrote about G. B. S.: Shaw and Pearson's "Retreat to

207. *Major Critical Essays*, by Bernard Shaw, intro. by Michael Holroyd. Penguin. pp. 373. pb £4.95.

Moscow"' (*JML*) William F. Cash uses unpublished material to show how Shaw rewrote Hesketh Pearson's basically unfavourable account of his trip to Russia in order to present Shaw in a much more acceptable light. The essay offers a fascinating view of Shaw's own construction of his legend.

There is about the usual amount of interest in Stoppard, reflected in another full-length study, a collection of reprinted essays, four interesting articles, and a *File on Stoppard*[208], compiled by Malcolm Page to the series' usual high standards (although my doubts about the potential audience remain).

Tom Stoppard[209] by Susan Rusinko is a conscientious introduction to the dramatist's work in all media including the most recent pieces, *The Real Thing*, *Squaring the Circle*, and *Rough Crossing*. The brevity of the book allows little scope for sustained analysis or critical innovation, which means that, for British readers in particular, it is unlikely to replace any of the previously available accounts of Stoppard's work. The most noteworthy part of the collection of critical essays on *Tom Stoppard* edited by Harold Bloom[210] is the editor's own new introduction in which he worries away in characteristically erudite style at the question of Stoppard's ultimate place in the pantheon. Otherwise the volume is very much in the Casebook tradition, reprinting already published work, mostly from North America.

In 'How Do We Know That We Know What We Know in Tom Stoppard's *Jumpers*?' (*TCL*) Barbara Kreps makes intelligent use of unpublished material relating to the original National Theatre production to clarify the nature of the play as we now have it and to suggest that 'the play talks in a direction that its action contradicts'. Neil Sammells's 'Earning Liberties: *Travesties* and *The Importance of Being Earnest*' suggests that the critical attempt to find a spokesman for Stoppard's views in the play is misconceived, since it is the play's engagement with Wilde's original which offers Stoppard's view of the nature and limits of art. This is a sensible reading which reaches the conclusion that the play 'is a refusal and a criticism of the available alternatives of conformism and delinquency'. The other two essays deal with more minor works. Katherine E. Kelly's 'Tom Stoppard's *Artist Descending a Staircase*: Outdoing the "Dada" Duchamp' (*CompD*) reads Stoppard's play intertextually with Marcel Duchamp's *Nude Descending a Staircase* to show the ways in which both artists use 'repetition with slight variation to spotlight the limits of their respective media', arguing that Stoppard's yearning in this play for a transcendent aesthetic is a 'manifestation of his general yearning for transcendent values'. It is a well-judged and informative example of a genuinely comparative method. The usually reliable Elin Diamond recovers from the rather odd statement that 'Stoppard's political phase proved to be shortlived' to produce an interesting account of 'Stoppard's *Dogg's Hamlet, Cahoot's Macbeth*: The Uses of Shakespeare' (*MD*). She notes that in one play Shakespeare's text supports the oppressor and in the other it is subversive, so that a 'non-canonical Shakespeare, a deinstitutionalized Shakespeare is no longer a monument but a minefield'.

In '"Invisible Events" and the Experience of Sports in David Storey's *The*

208. *File on Stoppard*, comp. by Malcolm Page. Methuen. pp. 96. hb £7.95, pb £3.50.
209. *Tom Stoppard*, by Susan Rusinko. Twayne. pp. [xi] + 164. $14.95.
210. *Tom Stoppard: Modern Critical Views*, ed. by Harold Bloom. ChelseaH. pp. x + 191. $19.95.

Changing Room' (*Proteus*) William Hutchings opens with a survey of the relationship between sports and drama, suggesting that for most authors sport provides a means to an end in which the significance of an athlete's experience *as an athlete* is subordinate to other concerns. He sees the essential action of *The Changing Room* as its formation of the team bond. Although even some of the examples he uses would support a reading along state-of-Britain lines, the essay is both a good general introduction to the play and to the issues raised by the presentation of sport in literature in general.

The solitary essay on Synge, 'La Mer dans le Théâtre de Synge' by Thérèse Vichy (*CVE*), sees the sea as an underlying metaphor throughout Synge's major plays which offers two ways forward, anticipating both Artaudian and Absurdist theatre.

Arnold Wesker is subjected to an exhaustive and erudite analysis by Heinz Zimmermann in *MD*. His title is 'Wesker and Utopia in the Sixties' and he deals with prose and lectures as well as the plays. The argument is too complex to summarize briefly but the focus on Wesker's search for wholeness of vision, his humanism, and the dramaturgical problems these cause is noteworthy: Wesker's concern with causation leads him towards the epic, but his 'didactic aim, as well as his fondness for the great tradition in art, makes him decide for a conventional naturalistic dramaturgy with only occasional expressionistic insets'. Wesker's own thoughts on 'The Nature of Theatre Dialogue' are to be found in *NTQ*.

Jane Goodall's 'Musicality and Meaning in the Dialogue of *Saint's Day*' (*MD*) is a brave attempt to rescue John Whiting's play from critical abuse. She argues that textual analysis can reveal its 'meticulously plotted underlying logic and that logic can be realised on stage, even if it was missed in the original production'.

There is a considerable contrast between the two articles this year on Yeats's drama: Warren Leamon's 'Yeats: Skeptic on Stage' (*Éire*) mentions many of the plays without articulating a thesis; Joseph Chadwick offers a tightly argued account of 'Family Romance as National Allegory in Yeats's *Cathleen ni Houlihan* and *The Dreaming of the Bones*'. Chadwick's essay benefits from its concentration on two works and he is able to develop a sophisticated reading of each play, using Lacanian ideas to show how ultimately *The Dreaming of the Bones* offers a critical revision of the earlier play's allegory.

American Literature to 1900

A. ROBERT LEE

This chapter has the following sections: 1. General; 2. Early and Eighteenth Century; 3. Nineteenth-Century Poetry; 4. Nineteenth-Century Prose. Henry Claridge of the University of Kent has reviewed relevant books and essays by the author of this chapter. These carry the attribution [G.H.C.].

1. General

Current bibliographical listings for the field and period continue to be available quarterly in *AL* and annually in *PMLA* and in the Summer Supplement of *AQ*. *AmLS* for 1984 offers its customary chapter-length, judicious evaluations of the entire span of the year's scholarship on American literature. The nine pre-1900 essays cover Emerson, Thoreau and Transcendentalism (Philip Gura), Hawthorne (Rita K. Gollin), Poe (Kent P. Ljungquist), Melville (Brian Higgins), Whitman and Dickinson (Jerome Loving), Mark Twain (Louis J. Budd), Henry James (Robert L. Gale), 'Literature to 1800' (William J. Scheick), and '19th-Century Literature' (David J. Nordloh). That these, and the volume's other contributions, read comprehensively yet with an individualness of manner which never gives way to undue special pleading, reflects well on J. Albert Robbins whose several stints as General Editor begin to approach the long-standing service logged up by the founding name of James Woodress.

The commissioning powers behind the DLB, principally Matthew J. Bruccoli, Richard Layman, and C. E. Frazer Clark Jr, similarly have shown no slackening of appetite or energy, not, at least, on the evidence of their latest compilations to do with American culture, literary genres, and writers. Perry J. Ashley has edited a volume given over to 'those great pioneers who created the American press', pre-1900 American journalists who if at something of a pinch count among their number William Bradford, William Cullen Bryant, Frederick Douglass, Benjamin Franklin, Horace Greeley, Thomas Paine, and Noah Webster[1]. All of these exert larger historical claims, but to have them located within the one vocational perspective of newspapers, broadsheets, pamphlets, and 'copy', gives a valuable specificity to their lives and reputations. A slightly staider body of reference is to be encountered in Peter Dzwonkoski's two volumes on American literary publishing houses from 1638 to the end of the nineteenth century[2]. Houses long faded, as well as those

1. *American Newspaper Journalists, 1690–1872*, ed. by Perry J. Ashley. DLB. Gale (1985). pp. xiii + 527. $88.
2. *American Literary Publishing Houses, 1638–1899*, ed. by Peter Dzwonkoski. 2 vols. DLB. Gale. pp. xxiv + 715. $176.

familiar and enduring like Beacon Press, Bobbs – Merrill, Dodd Mead, Rand McNally (of map and atlas fame), Riverside, Scribner's, and Wiley, amount to histories in themselves. Inevitably, however, they take on added interest in terms of who they published, when, and to what effect. Hence more in detail might have been made of particular author–publisher business relations and correspondence, especially where key work-in-process was involved as, say, in the cases of Hawthorne with Ticknor and Fields, of Melville with Wiley and Putnam and then with Harper's, and given the eventual turn-of-the-century importance of the New York Edition, of Henry James with Scribner's.

Trudier Harris and Thadious M. Davis contribute a welcome volume on Afro-American writers prior to the Harlem Renaissance, a founding gallery of black literary talent[3]. But why is neither Booker T. Washington nor James Weldon Johnson included when, for instance, W. E. B. DuBois, Paul Dunbar, and Charles Chesnutt are (rightly enough) given full entries? As usual with the DLB, the illustrations and reprints of title-pages and portraits in this volume are excellently done. Glenn E. Estes puts his contributors to the task of assessing pre-1900 American children's writers[4], though with the startling omission of Nathaniel Hawthorne whose *A Wonder Book for Boys and Girls* (1851) and *Tanglewood Tales* (1853) – often subtly puritanized retellings of classical myth – made for vintage reading in New England and beyond. None the less the volume offers scrupulous entries on the likes of Louisa May Alcott, Horatio Alger, Joel Chandler Harris, and Harriet Beecher Stowe, among many (if lesser) others, often with commendable awareness, too, of how children's story-telling helped to set up key markers for the turnings and hierarchies of more general American popular taste.

Richard M. Ludwig and Clifford A. Nault Jr manage a quite different order of reference work[5]. Consciously modelled on *Annals of English Literature 1495–1950*, their American *Annals* does a year-for-year listing of literary titles major and minor from the earliest Puritan and exploration records through to work published during the Reagan presidency. A right-hand column lists contemporaneous political and historical events together with writing by non-American authors. Registers of this kind can look a touch factitious, a production-line 'made' book. But used imaginatively as a cumulative date-line of the literary record, their bibliographical utility is not to be denied. Volume 40 of *SB*, edited as usual by the redoubtable Fredson Bowers, includes one contribution on a nineteenth-century American author, a typically meticulous set of ground rules by G. Thomas Tanselle for a model bibliographical description with Melville's *Redburn* as a case-study. Inexplicably, and culpably in a volume issued under these auspices, no less than sixteen pages in the copy received by *YWES* have been bound blank.

Four sets of European conference proceedings on American themes testify to the lively persistence (and multidisciplinary range and depth) of scholarly interest in the New World by the Old. *The Origins and Originality of American*

3. *Afro-American Writers Before the Harlem Renaissance*, ed. by Trudier Harris and Thadious M. Davis. DLB. Gale. pp. xv + 369. $88.

4. *American Writers for Children Before 1900*, ed. by Glenn E. Estes. DLB. Gale (1985). pp. xiii + 441. $88.

5. *Annals of American Literature, 1602–1983*, ed. by Richard M. Ludwig and Clifford A. Nault Jr. OUPAm. pp. 396. $29.95.

Culture[6], no less than seventy-three papers from the International Conference in American Studies held at the University of Budapest in 1980, yields a quite heady variety of focus and tactics. Under the exemplary editorship of Tibor Frank, it reproduces lectures and analyses which call upon a sweep broad enough to include considerations of Puritanism, the American Renaissance, Southern and modern fiction, drama, modern poetry, American ethnicity and ideology, and two sections on American English and linguistics. Each of these contributions keeps to about 3,000 words, which the editor reprints more or less as given – thereby retaining the freer style of spoken delivery. Of those with a nineteenth-century focus, the following especially stand out: Aladár Sarbu's 'Hawthorne's Portrait of the Artist' which explores the artist-narrator 'type' in the key romances and short fiction; Daniel Hoffman's 'Poe's Obsessive Themes', a kind of coda to the Freudian reveller he depicted in his *Poe, Poe, Poe, Poe, Poe, Poe, Poe* (1972); and Eric Mottram's 'Fears of Invasion in American Culture', which ranges from Puritan heresy-hunting and persecution through the vampirism of Charles Brockden Brown and Poe to the troubled hauntings of Melville and Hawthorne and on eventually to McCarthyist Cold War paranoia. Although the volume has been long in provenance, its contents speak well of Hungarian seriousness and interest in American culture.

American Studies in Transition[7], a Danish collection of fourteen conference papers given at Fåborg in 1984, emphasizes still more a 'studies' approach, though mainly in the direction of modern materials. Hans Hauge begins by considering the utility of a Jacques Derrida/deconstructive input into the very notion of American Studies. Dorothy Skårdal examines the busy 'ethnicity' debate with a lively and informative annotation of Danish-American writing. Robert Baehr engagingly addresses himself to the historic lure and mythologies of manned flight in American culture, with stop-offs at the Wright Brothers, Charles Lindbergh, the *Enola Gay*, NASA, and the moon-landings, a model of associative reference and analysis. John Carlos Rowe has a pugnacious, deconstructive piece on the 'social ideology' of the Vietnam legacy in film, TV, and popular fiction; Christen Kold Thomsen sets the stunning musicianship of Miles Davis in a jazz and general black-cultural context; and in two complementary literary-historical contributions Fredrik Brøgger probes the social and period subtexts within *The Great Gatsby* and Charles Swann the 'detective' format and philosophy of Melville's 'Benito Cereno'. None of these, or the collection's other essays, yields other than a productive 'field' approach, early modern and contemporary American culture viewed as the upshot of greatly diverse interactive energies which call upon and generally achieve a methodology to match.

Both *L'Amérique et L'Europe: Réalités et représentations*[8] and *Amst* set their sights a shade more narrowly. The former, the upshot of a GRENA-sponsored American Studies conference held in March 1986, consists of ten essentially literary and historical essays (six in French, four in English). Of the

6. *The Origins and Originality of American Culture*, ed. by Tibor Frank. AK (1984). pp. xi + 801. £37.50.
7. *American Studies in Transition*, ed. by David Nye and Christen Kold Thomsen. OdenseU. pp. 325. £13/$16.50.
8. *L'Amérique et L'Europe: Réalités et représentations*, Vol. II, preface by Serge Ricard. UProvence. pp. 190. Ffr 80.

nineteenth- and early twentieth-century pieces, Noelle Batte argues assiduously for Washington Irving's *Sketch Book* as a literary-cultural homologue to the founding of the republic; Yves Carlet re-examines the impact of American frontier behaviour upon Frances Trollope and Harriet Martineau as British travel-writers; and Yves Lemeunier develops a lively excavation of vestigial Russian and *stetl* themes in Abraham Cahan's *The Rise of David Levinsky*. Wolfgang Iser leads off the thirteen essays of *Amst* with a further new run of speculations on self-reference in literary texts. Of the essays with a nineteenth-century focus, Heinz Ickstad illuminatingly compares James Fenimore Cooper with his radical younger contemporary George Lippard as popular-culture writers in Jacksonian America; Sacvan Bercovitch sets out the ideological impetus behind Melville's involuted styling of *Pierre*; and Ursula Brumm, the dedicatee of this issue, traces the pastor figure and Horst Kruse the museum motif in selective nineteenth-century American fiction. Viola Sachs, in line with her several past forays into American literary 'cosmology' (see her *The Game of Creation*, 1982) none too enlighteningly juxtaposes the Book of Mormon with *Moby-Dick* as two would-be 'hieroglyphic' or 'scriptural' New World texts.

Nor have native-born Americanists been any the less busy in bringing theory to bear. *Ideology and Classic American Literature*[9], nineteen substantive chapters in all, argues for the fuller recognition of how 'the political categories of race, gender, and class enter into the formal making of American literature'. In other words, with due allusions to Marx, Lukács, the Frankfurt School, Raymond Williams, and American commentators on the canon from Van Wyck Brooks and F. O. Matthiessen to Leslie Fiedler and Richard Chase, they propose returning the literature to 'history'. In an inspired piece of commissioning, the editors have Henry Nash Smith, Leo Marx, and Richard Slotkin take a backward glance at the very ideology of Americanness in their landmark myth-and-symbol studies, respectively *Virgin Land* (1950), *The Machine in the Garden* (1964), and *Regeneration Through Violence* (1973). The returns are illuminating, and set the quality of argument for the essays which follow. Among the best of them are Gerald Graff on the ideology of past and present valuations of American literature; the co-editor Myra Jehlen on the dynamic of class in the classic American canon; Houston Baker on the 'alternative' contribution of slave-narrative; and Alan Trachtenberg on the need for a changed ideology of what American Studies should be, if it is to do justice to the historicity of American culture. Subsequent essays propose 'ideological' readings of Poe's 'The Man in the Crowd', Hawthorne's *The Scarlet Letter*, Stowe's *Uncle Tom's Cabin*, Thoreau's *Walden*, and Melville's *Moby-Dick*, *Pierre*, and 'Benito Cereno', to different reaches of effect. Essentially, the argument throughout centres on a need to challenge the Arnoldian formalism of American canon-formation, to see historical and social process as vital to the tradition.

In *Reconstructing American Literary History*[10] Sacvan Bercovitch again returns to the editorial helm; and again his goal is to subject American literature to the new dispensations of historicism, class and ideological analysis,

9. *Ideology and Classic American Literature*, ed. by Sacvan Bercovitch and Myra Jehlen. CUP. pp. xii + 451. £35/$34.50.
10. *Reconstructing American Literary History*, ed. by Sacvan Bercovitch. Harvard. pp. xii + 351. hb £15.95, pb £7.25. (Hereafter Bercovitch.)

ethnicity, gender-analysis, and a more elastic sense of genre. To this end, for instance, Robert A. Ferguson challengingly looks at the rhetoric of control in the Declaration and other founding documents of the American republic, Sandra M. Gilbert the sexual presentation of self in the poetry of Whitman and Dickinson, Werner Sollors the pitfalls and challenges of a 'melting-pot' theory of American culture, Robert von Hallberg the tradition of American poet-critics, and Robert B. Stepto the necessary *distrust* of the reader in Afro-American writing from Douglass to Wright. As in his other collection, Bercovitch and his fellow-contributors deserve wide recognition for the liveli-ness of their intervention: here are the roots of a new American literary history.

The same impetus lies behind Russell J. Reising's *The Unusable Past*[11], a slightly lower order of polemic but always interesting. Having first dutifully elaborated major past theories of American literature – those taken up with the Puritan shaping of the culture (the tradition of Perry Miller), those seeking a more 'culturist' overview (the tradition of Lionel Trilling), and those committed to the endemic self-reflexiveness of American literary work (names like Charles Feidelson and John Irwin) – he, too, puts the argument for an increased historicization and eclecticizing of the tradition. To this end he excoriates ritual oversights and downgradings like ethnic and women's writing, hitherto assumed non-literary or marginally literary forms, and the plethora of popular and regional literature. Usefully to the point, he develops a specimen analysis of how a supposed 'subliterary' text like Frederick Douglass's *Narative* can (and should) be incorporated into the mainstream.

In *Beyond Ethnicity: Consent and Descent in American Culture*[12] Werner Sollors – himself German-born – also unpacks the myth of a vast, one-standard Americanness. In a virtuoso display of literary and popular sources, Euro-American of every kind, Jewish, Afro-American, Indian, and Hispanic, he shows how 'ethnic' Americans have evolved their own fables of origin and their own 'hyphenated' American identity (Italian-American and the like) and how apt or otherwise has been the theory of the melting-pot. On Sollors's thesis, to which he brings lavish illustration, these ethnicities amount to 'codes of Americanness', the very DNA of American nationhood. Mary V. Dearborn's *Pocahontas's Daughters*[13] similarly refuses what increasingly might be called the 'old' American literary canon, WASP, Eastern Seaboard, and overwhelmingly male. As her subtitle indicates, her focus falls upon a historic non-WASP sisterhood of letters. Her 'ethnic texts' include the recently recovered Harriet E. Wilson's *Our Nig* (1859) and a line of black women's writing from Frances E. Harper during Reconstruction through Harlem Renaissance names like Jessie Fauset, Nella Larsen, and Zora Neale Hurston to contemporaries like Toni Morrison and Gayl Jones; Jewish writing from Mary Antin's *The Promised Land* to Gertrude Stein's *The Making of Americans*; and a diversity of immigrant-European, Indian, Asian-American, and Hispanic texts by women. In these, as Dearborn makes emphatic, the actual historic

11. *The Unusable Past: Theory and the Study of American Literature*, by Russell J. Reising. Methuen. pp. xii + 290. hb £15, pb £6.95.
12. *Beyond Ethnicity: Consent and Descent in American Culture*, by Werner Sollors. OUPAm. pp. xiii + 294. $24.95.
13. *Pocahontas's Daughters: Gender and Ethnicity in American Culture*, by Mary V. Dearborn. OUPAm. pp. 266. £19.50.

silence of Pocahontas – whatever her myths of voice or action – finds a legacy of voice.

And it is this same notion of legacy which supplies an enterprising new feminist journal from the University of Massachusetts with its title. *Legacy: A Journal of Nineteenth-Century Women Writers* graduated in spring 1984 (Vol. 1) from newsletter (essentially a bibliographical listing of the field) to its present magazine format. Vol. 2 contains among other things a revaluation of Hawthorne's famous 'scribbling women' (by Nina Baym), of Lydia Marie Child (by Carolyn L. Kercher), of Fanny Fern (by Joyce M. Warren), and deservedly, once again, of the pioneer black novelist and speaker Frances E. Harper (by Elizabeth Ammons). Vol. 3, No. 1 (spring 1986) takes the form of a Centenary Issue for Emily Dickinson. Contributions include analyses of her as a woman of 'double' identity (by Suzanne Juhasz), of her 'subversion' of an identity founded on domestic labour (by Gertrude Reif Hughes), of her 'invisibility' in the world and repudiation of the 'gospel of silence' regularly thought women's lot (by Joanna Dobson). Two short profiles of Helen Hunt Jackson (by Rosemary Whitaker) and Mabel Loomis Todd (by Polly Longsworth) make helpful adjunct reading. Vol. 3, No. 2 (fall 1986) contains lively revaluations of Constance Fenimore Cooper (by Joan Myers Weimer) and of Elizabeth Stuart Phelps's interesting novel of 1871, *The Silent Partner* (by Judith Fetterley).

Harold Beaver's *The Great American Masquerade*[14], as stylishly turned as it is insightful and spacious in range, deserves any number of plaudits. It exhibits zest, an attractively worn erudition, and above all a solid core of argument. Essentially Beaver sets himself the task of examining how impersonation, the quite extraordinary tradition of concealment or faking of identity, has operated inside American literary culture. Beginning from Elizabethan explorer-buccaneers in motley, he makes his stopping-places West African slaves 'acting out' to save their very lives, a patrician-born Melville 'gone native' in the Marquesas, a Poe even in his shabbiness affecting the role of a Dixie aristocrat and dreaming dreams of Antarctic polar discovery, a Harriet Beecher Stowe on the Hallelujah trail of abolition, a Twain the one-time Hannibal provincial parading down Broadway in his Oxford robes, and a valetudinarian Francis Parkman foregoing Harvard and Boston to play frontier Indian scout in *The Oregon Trail*. Beaver, too, pushes forward to subsequent twentieth-century masqueraders from Hemingway, Fitzgerald, and West to contemporary meta-fictionists like Burroughs and Pynchon, with excursions into the role of 'place' – the South, the Village, and most of all Hollywood – in the transmission of American public and sexual identity. Taking as one of his main conceptual cues Bakhtin on 'mask', he so 'reads' America as having issued virtually a call to proteanism or self-invention in writer and citizen alike. *The Great American Masquerade* reads infectiously and at high pace, a model typology.

In *Colonial Encounters*[15] Peter Hulme's concern is Europe's encounter with the Caribbean, 'the fabulous Indies', be they the islands themselves, the Latin

14. *The Great American Masquerade*, by Harold Beaver. Vision/B&N (1985). pp. 238. £18.95/$28.50.
15. *Colonial Encounters: Europe and the Native Caribbean 1492–1797*, by Peter Hulme. Methuen. pp. xi + 348. £25.

American hinterland, or the Southern coastal regions of the Old Dominion of Virginia. Despite a profession of Marxist credentials, his study really offers an old-fashioned, though nothing less than perfectly useful, account of colonial myths and counter-myths, with reconsiderations of the John Smith/ Pocahontas story, Shakespeare's *The Tempest*, and Defoe's Crusoe/ Friday pairing. David Morse's two volumes on American Romanticism[16] begin from the proposition that 'American literature is born of excessive hopes and excessive claims, burdened from the start by an overblown national rhetoric'. Morse has any number of energetic local insights to offer, but his notion of excess as the gestural essence of American Romanticism leads him too readily on occasion into bossiness and circularity ('Poe's characters cannot but be excessive – and if they were not excessive they could not exist') and reductios of paraphrase ('Whitman, notoriously, celebrated himself . . .'). Inger Christensen's *The Shadow of the Dome: Organicism and Romantic Poetry*[17] betrays the slightly burdensome imprint of doctoral scholarship. Nor can the ground it covers be said to be unfamiliar. On offer, at any rate, is a straight-forward enough delineation of 'organicist philosophy' in the writings of Coleridge, Emerson, Whitman, and Denise Levertov.

Two further volumes in the Cambridge American Literature and Culture series represent altogether more consequential scholarship. Both concern themselves with 'provincialism' as a regional or geo-cultural (and hence unpejorative) designation. Lawrence Buell's *New England Literary Culture: From Revolution through Renaissance*[18], much in the same conscientious manner as his impressive *Literary Transcendentalism* (1973), situates the key period figures – 'Emerson, Thoreau, Hawthorne, Stowe and Dickinson particularly' – within a schema organized more by topic and gender than simple chronology. Tracking New England literature from its essentially 'amateurist' beginnings, be they Puritan or secular, through to the efflor-escence called for symptomatically in Emerson's 'The American Scholar', Buell makes busy and enlightening cross-reference to the region's oratory, its pietistic writing (in his terms 'literary scripturism'), the adaptations and fic-tionalizations of Puritan history, the tireless output of reform, state, local-historical and naturalist tracts, and what he calls 'provincial Gothic', that 'nether' world of Puritan psychology and shadow best exploited by Hawthorne. Buell's exposition of the unremitting bookishness and intellec-tuality of New England, comprehensive both in scope and detail, should make his account a standard work of reference.

On a related tack, Albert J. Von Frank suggests in *The Sacred Game*[19] that for the founding names of American literature provincialism was not only 'quite the ordinary context for artistic expression' but a kind of pro-ductive anxiety. The imaginative working-out of 'provincial' themes led,

16. *American Romanticism*, by David Morse. Vol. I: *From Cooper to Hawthorne*. Vol. II: *From Melville to James*. B&N Imports/Macmillan. pp. 176; 144. £25 the set.

17. *The Shadow of the Dome: Organicism and Romantic Poetry*, by Inger Christensen. UBergen (1985). pp. 170.

18. *New England Literary Culture: From Revolution through Renaissance*, by Lawrence Buell. CUP. pp. xii + 513. £35.

19. *The Sacred Game: Provincialism and Frontier Consciousness in American Literature 1630–1860*, by Albert J. Von Frank. CUP. pp. viii + 188. £20/$24.95.

paradoxically, to deprovincialization, whether Anne Bradstreet's 'domestication of the infinite', the playwright Royall Tyler's application of the satiric techniques of Sheridan to American manners in *The Contrast*, or a foundling democracy mocked in the interests of a better democracy in Hugh Henry Brackenridge's *Modern Chivalry*. Moving into the nineteenth century, Von Frank looks to Irving's 'Rip Van Winkle' as both subverting and respecting American provincial life; to the Hawthorne of 'The Custom House' and *The Scarlet Letter* as transforming (in Hawthorne's own phrase) the locally 'Actual' into the more encompassing 'Imaginary'; to the 'universals' sought by Emerson from his 'culture of the spirit' and Thoreau from his 'home-cosmography'; and to Margaret Fuller's endeavour well before Oscar Wilde to make her own life imitate art. Von Frank offers persuasive and subtly particular argument.

David Simpson's *The Politics of American English, 1776–1850*[20] sets itself the task of annotating how Americans freed themselves not only from British governmental, but also linguistic hegemony. Written in a vigorous and commendably untechnical style, it demonstrates pretty decisively that 'America had, by about 1850, a version of English that was recognizably its own'. Using the late-Augustan English of the Declaration of Independence as his starting point, Simpson deploys as specimen case-studies the lexicography of Noah Webster, early vernacular frontier and dialect usage, Jacksonian locutions, the language of Cooper's novels, native-American idioms, and the impact of Transcendentalist rhetoric – the latter a mode he upbraids for its tendency to abstraction. A great merit of Simpson's study, apart from its reminder that language-study can be freed of the too hermetic grasp of the linguistician, is its location of American English within American political history, the language as fascinatingly both the medium and the message of the New World's emergence into a distinct national identity.

Teresa Toulouse's *The Art of Prophesying*[21], earlier portions of which deservedly won the Davis prize awarded by *EAL*, analyses the impact on American religious belief and practice of four momentous New England preachers, John Cotton, Benjamin Colman, William Ellery Channing, and Ralph Waldo Emerson. Beginning from the great Puritan debates about Election and Covenant, Toulouse pursues the process whereby a founding Calvinism softened into Unitarianism and then Transcendentalism – and the contributing interventions by sermon and doctrinal challenge alike of her four 'prophesiers'. She makes well-chosen reference to the early Jeremiads, to the role of the sermon in New England communal life, and to the eventual supplanting of the cleric by the artist as the 'moral spokesman for his culture' (appropriately she closes with a reference to Dimmesdale's Election sermon in *The Scarlet Letter*, the sermon made over imaginatively from actuality into art). As an account of clericalism's place in the life and mind of New England this marks an investigation to genuine good purpose.

Enikó Bollobás's *Tradition and Innovation in American Free Verse: Whitman to Duncan*[22] again attests to the strength of Hungarian interest in

20. *The Politics of American English, 1776–1850*, by David Simpson. OUPAm. pp. x + 301. £22.

21. *The Art of Prophesying: New England Sermons and the Shaping of Belief*, by Teresa Toulouse. UGeo. pp. xii + 211. $23.

22. *Tradition and Innovation in American Free Verse: Whitman to Duncan*, by Enikó Bollobás. AK. pp. 328. pb £13.50.

American literature, a diligent prosodic study of *vers libre* from Whitman to T. S. Eliot, Ezra Pound, and William Carlos Williams, and on to selected Black Mountain and Beat poets. It offers formalist annotations of Whitman's 'breath line' and supposed 'catalogues', the imagism of Pound and Eliot, and the 'projective' experiments of the Williams–Olson–Duncan cadre. Maria Diedrich's *Ausbruch aus der Knechtschaft*[23] similarly brings a formidable diligence and breadth of reference to its account of Afro-American slave narrative, an analysis of themes, subgenres, historical elements and allusion, and an excellent perception of how such narrative gives a bedrock to latter-day black autobiographical tradition.

Steven E. Kagle's *Early Nineteenth-Century American Diary Literature*[24] takes as its aim 'the canon of American diaries with intrinsic merit'. His coverage includes the 'spiritual journals' of Quakers like Samuel Cole Davis and Charles Osborn, the travel diaries of Merriwether Lewis and William Clark – those stalwarts of American frontierism, Francis Parkman, Washington Irving, and the great naturalist John J. Audubon, 'diaries of situation' like those of President James K. Polk, the 'Life Diaries' of John Quincy Adams, and the Transcendentalist journals of Emerson and Bronson Alcott. Kagle rightly can claim to have opened a key line of American self-expression in the form of this diary literature, not only as a genre hitherto too little attended but also as a revelation of the 'created personality' to hand. *The Labor of Words*[25] by Christopher P. Wilson, spanning the period from the 1880s to the 1920s, sets out a detailed case-history of the American print media and journalistic muckraking in the Progressive Era. Especially informative is the highlighting of Jack London, Upton Sinclair, David Graham Phillips, and Lincoln Steffens as popular newspapermen and of the role of moguls like William Randolph Hearst in creating American press empires.

The poets discussed in *Nineteenth-Century American Poetry*[26] belong, on the whole, to the latter half of the century and the choice is broadly canonical, though David Seed writes intelligently and informatively about the 'minor' New England poets Jones Very and Frederick Goddard Tuckerman. Lee's introduction speaks of the 'double tension in American poetry, its inward and outward inclination', and many of the essays here sensitively illuminate the paradox of self-meditation and confession at the heart of American poetry. Thus Mark Kinkead-Weekes in a careful *explication du texte* dismisses Whitman's attitudes ('sadly flabby') and looks instead at the language and syntax of two of Whitman's more elegiac and contemplative poems, 'When lilacs last in the dooryard bloom'd' and 'Out of the cradle endlessly rocking'. The editor himself makes a bold case for the modernist 'difficulty' of Melville's poetry, mainly by pointing to its kinship with *Moby-Dick* and the major prose works; the discussion of the Civil War poetry here is particularly enlightening. Eric Mottram looks to Whitman as a prophet of political and sexual health;

23. *Ausbruch aus der Knechtschaft: Das Amerikanische Slave Narrative Zwischen Unabhängigkeitserklärung und Burgerkreig*, by Maria Diedrich. Steiner. pp. 310.

24. *Early Nineteenth-Century American Diary Literature*, by Steven E. Kagle. Twayne. pp. 166. $18.95.

25. *The Labor of Words: Literary Professionalism in the Progressive Era*, by Christopher P. Wilson. UGeo. pp. xviii + 239. $24.

26. *Nineteenth-Century American Poetry*, ed. by A. Robert Lee. Vision/B&N. pp. 224. £16.95/$28.50.

Robert von Hallberg writes on the oddly symbiotic relationship between Poe's poetry and his criticism; and Jim Philip and Brian Harding offer challenging new views of, respectively, 'mind' in Emily Dickinson and 'architecture' as an image of the imagination in Ralph Waldo Emerson. Of the two remaining essays, James H. Justus analyses 'The Fireside Poets' (Bryant, Longfellow, Whittier, Holmes, and Lowell) as more critical of the harshly aggressive society that fostered them than has normally been conceded, and Graham Clarke, in a wide-ranging essay, discusses the pictorialism of American landscape poetry from Bryant to Whitman and beyond and its analogues in American painting and photography. [G.H.C.]

'No one approach governs the essays in this collection', A. Robert Lee announces in his introduction to *The Nineteenth-Century American Short Story*[27] and a great deal is gained by allowing each contributor his or her line of critical argument. The result is a body of essays on a range of levels covering the major figures, from Irving through Poe, Hawthorne, Melville, Twain, Crane, Bierce, Chopin, and concluding with James. Andrew Hook writes illuminatingly about the chief weaknesses of Twain's short stories, particularly those that arise from his difficulties in sustaining a coherent narrative voice; Herbie Butterfield makes a persuasive case from the Civil War stories of Ambrose Bierce, though he concedes that the overall achievement is a 'limited' one; A. Robert Lee explores the complex tactics of 'voicing' in Melville's Piazza and other tales; and Michael Wood, in one of the outstanding essays in the volume, shows how the 'very dubious' ideas in Poe's tales actually function as an essential part of the 'thoroughly theoretical nature of his fictional enterprise'. As a whole the volume clearly benefits from its diversity of focus and enterprise, offering 'readings' to interest both student and professional. As to the enduring question of *why* American writers have shown so strong and successful an attachment to 'the brief prose tale' (as Poe described it), that perhaps inevitably is left for the most part unanswered. [G.H.C.]

2. Early and Eighteenth Century

'Each contributor has moved confidently into his or her subject in the secure knowledge that there is intrinsic merit in the poetry of the Puritans.' So, in his preface, Peter White introduces the twenty-two essays of *Puritan Poets and Poetics*[28], a commendably busy and evaluative overview of what the subtitle fairly calls 'Seventeenth-Century American Poetry in Theory and Practice'. The first of the collection's three sections, 'Puritan Aesthetics and Society', includes essays on printing and publishing in the Colonies (Jayne K. Knibbs), Puritan women poets (Pattie Cowell), typology (Karen E. Rowe), Puritan iconography (Lynn M. Haims), and the intriguing issue of 'Alchemy in Early American Poetry' (Cheryl Z. Oreovicz). Section 2 offers re-estimations of a number of the standard names, especially Anne Bradstreet (Rosamond R. Rosenmaier), Edward Taylor (Karl Keller) – this somewhat too synoptic a piece – and the impact of Petrus Ramus on so stark a Puritan visionary as

27. *The Nineteenth-Century American Short Story*, ed. by A. Robert Lee. Vision/B&N. pp. 196. £14.95/$28.50.

28. *Puritan Poets and Poetics: Seventeenth-Century American Poetry in Theory and Practice*, ed. by Peter White. PSU (1985). pp. xvii + 343. £29.75.

Michael Wigglesworth (Alan H. Pope), together with the case for lesser Puritan lights like John Saffin (Kathryn Zabelle Derounian). A third section turns to 'Selected Poetic Forms' – almanac verse (Robert Secor), anagrams and acrostics (Jeffrey Walker), baroque free verse (Harold Jantz), Latin Puritan verse (Lawrence Rosenwald), and a judicious concluding essay on meditative verse by Ursula Brumm ('Edward Taylor's *Preparatory Meditations* are the crowning achievement of American Puritan poetry'). This substantive volume should easily and deservedly become required reading on the literary achievement of the Puritans.

Leon Howard's *Essays on Puritans and Puritanism*[29], a posthumous essay collection intended as homage to a scholar whose best claim to fame rests on his biography of Melville (1951), offers less a literary than a historical and theological perspective on Puritanism. As a guide into the beliefs, wrangles, power-politics, and general culture of the English, Continental, and American Puritans, Howard could not have written a better primer. In a series of linked essays he outlines with remarkable clarity the 'Puritan impulse' from its Lutheran and Calvinist roots through to the different Reformation church communities and politics and the ferrying of that heritage into the New World. Ramus, Shakespeare, and Milton serve as foci for the collection's second half, Puritanism's transformation into the literary word. A bracing companion piece to Howard would be Theodore Dwight Bozeman's 'The Puritans' "Errand into the Wilderness"' (*NEQ*), an argument which suggests that Perry Miller's profoundly influential 1952 'Wilderness' essay with its thesis that 'the founders of Massachusetts were an "organized task force" bent upon a world-saving mission' has far too often been misunderstood. Bozeman plausibly contends that the Puritan concern with 'mission' does not equate with the supposed call for an utterly messianic society, the apocalyptic notion of making the world over into a born-again godly kingdom. He usefully shows that the 'Congregational Protestantism' of the Pilgrims aimed more modestly, that it was a theocracy certainly but one which found its adherents 'speaking with humility, even skepticism, about the exemplary function of their society'. The re-issue of Harrison T. Messerole's *American Poetry of the Seventeenth Century*[30], originally published in 1968, makes available once more a generous anthology of Puritan verse, a New England in good voice.

In 'John Cotton and the Rhetoric of Grace' (*EAL*) Eugenia Delamotte examines Cotton's use of figurative language in key writings like *On the Holiness of Church Members*, *The New Covenant*, and *A Treatise of the Covenant of Grace*, and in a number of his better-known sermons. She ties in Cotton's language and theology to 'the Antinomian Crisis of 1636–1638' and especially its prime incarnation in Anne Hutchinson. The American Indians as descendants of the Old Testament Lost Tribes is re-examined in Richard W. Cosley's 'John Eliot and the Origins of the American Indians' (*EAL*), especially Eliot's personal conjectures based on his missionary activities in New England. Paul R. Sternberg in 'The Publication of Thomas Morton's *New English Canaan* Reconsidered' (*PBSA*) explores the paradox of *Canaan*'s

29. *Essays on Puritans and Puritanism*, by Leon Howard, ed. by James Barbour and Thomas Quirk. UNM. pp. xiii + 221. $19.95.

30. *American Poetry of the Seventeenth Century*, ed. by Harrison T. Messerole. PSU. pp. 576. hb £29.75, pb £16.95.

influence given that only one edition was actually published, a mark of the extraordinary power of the spoken word in Puritan culture. In 'Sewall's *Diary* and the Margins of Puritan Literature' (*AL*) Lawrence Rosenwald, while recognizing that the *Diary* and Sewall's other works, are 'intelligible and appreciable as the products of a Puritan writer', argues that Sewall should be also likened to a 'secular' diary writer of the status of Samuel Pepys. Too automatic an insistence on Sewall as Puritan, suggests Rosenwald, has eclipsed his more writerly claims; he was a man of his wider time and world and not only of Calvinist theology. For Michael Schuldiner in 'The Christian Hero and the Classical Journey in Edward Taylor's "Preparatory Meditations. First Series"' (*HLQ*), Taylor's *Meditations* to be sure enact a Calvinist paradigm, 'the Christian drama of the soul's progress', but at the same time they borrow and adapt the epic formulations of the *Odyssey*.

Norton Critical Editions now include *Benjamin Franklin's Autobiography*[31], an edition which has already run into niggles and cavils about the authority of the text. It follows the usual Norton format of including Notes and Critical Essays. Kenneth Dauber's 'Benjamin Franklin and the Idea of Authorship' (*Criticism*) designates the *Autobiography* not only 'America's primary epic', 'a true original' which proffers 'a vision of ceaseless amelioration', but also a form of writing which bridges high and popular and so makes the very style of the work an aspect of its *ad hominem* message. Eid A. Dahiyat's 'Milton and Franklin' (*EAL*), a brief but scholarly note, links Franklin's writings on education – his *Proposals Relating to the Education of Youth in Pennsylvania* especially – to Milton's *Tractate of Education*, the latter as a call to self-improvement and the moral way. In 'Benjamin Franklin, the Inveterate (and Crafty) Public Instructor: Instruction on Two Levels in "The Way of Wealth"' (*EAL*) Patrick Sullivan argues for a Franklin who is anything but the 'naïve moralist'. Rather 'The Way to Wealth' and his almanac-writing in general rely upon a shared recognition between writer and reader of the likely shortfall between the ideal and the probable in human behaviour.

Phillis Wheatley as pioneer black writer receives a modern Afro-American salute from the poet June Jordon in her 'The Difficult Miracle of Black Poetry in America or Something Like a Sonnet for Phillis Wheatley' (*MR*). More academic in manner is Sandra O'Neale's 'A Slave's Subtle War: Phillis Wheatley's Use of Biblical Myth and Symbol' (*EAL*), a recognition of Wheatley's tactics in allegorizing her own unconscionable slave status by reference to Hebrew enslavement and imagery as taken from the Old Testament.

For Gregg Camfield in 'Joel Barlow's Dialectic of Progress' (*EAL*) Barlow's political pamphlets of the early 1790s embody the contradiction of seeking a revolutionary 'perfect society' in the face of an imperfect citizenry, one for instance not always mindful of Franklin's calls to betterment. A similar issue preoccupied Barlow's contemporary, Hugh Henry Brackenridge. At least so argues Mark R. Patterson in 'Representation in Brackenridge's *Modern Chivalry*' (*TSLL*), a scrutiny of the satiric tactics and devices deployed in Brackenridge's Cervantean novel in the interests of pointing to a better,

31. *Benjamin Franklin's Autobiography*, ed. by J. A. Leo Lemay and P. M. Zall. Norton. pp. 352. £5.95.

corruption-free American political order. In '*Wieland*: Accounting for Appearances' (*NEQ*) Beverly R. Voloshin invokes Locke's *Essay Concerning Human Understanding* to show how Charles Brockden Brown in fact doubted Lockean theories of perception and behaviour. *Wieland*, accordingly, depicts 'a world frighteningly in flux', anything but amenable to harmonious interpretation or 'understanding'. Discontent with 'psycho-symbolic interpretations' of Brown moves Dennis Berthoud in 'Desacralizing the American Gothic: An Iconographic Approach to *Edgar Huntly*' (*SAF*) to discern a far more 'local' impulse in this novel, viewing Brown as, if not exactly the local-colourist, then a writer whose use of American iconography and landscape gives a more 'actual' (and hence non-Gothic) texture to his writing.

Royall Tyler as a juggler of political divisions within the Revolutionary period attracts the attention of Richard S. Pressman in 'Class Positioning and Shays' Rebellion: Resolving the Contradictions of *The Contrast*' (*EAL*). Tyler's pioneer play attempts a timely reconciliation between a 'class-divided America', between on the one side a 'self-satisfied, materialistic, Anglophilic élite' and on the other a truly 'revolutionary' American cadre. Susanna Haswell Rowson has the interesting claim of having written America's first bestseller in *Charlotte Temple* (1794). But she also left behind a fascinating other body of diverse witness to the Birth of the Nation. This Patricia L. Parker takes up in her Twayne study, *Susanna Rowson*[32], a case well argued for this interesting woman, not a major literary figure but a British-born American patriot, witness, and inveterate recorder of her impressions.

3. Nineteenth-Century Poetry

On Steve Olson's account in 'A Perverted Poetics: Bryant's and Emerson's Concern for a Developing American Literature' (*ATQ*), William Cullen Bryant wrote not only American–Wordsworthian romantic verse but a call-to-arms for a national literature. Comparing Bryant's 'On Originality and Imitation' (1825) with Emerson's 'The American Scholar' (1837), he emphasizes how, like Emerson, Bryant advocated a direct, unmediated response to Nature as preferable to a preoccupation with the past as a 'restorative' to the poetic spirit. A life-and-works overview of America's best-known 'fireside' or 'domestic' bard, Longfellow, is to be found in the prolific Edward Wagenknecht's *Henry Wadsworth Longfellow: His Poetry and Prose*[33]. Wagenknecht does his job fully and dutifully, right through to an interesting appendix on Longfellow's translations and anthologies, but he presses for no especially new re-evaluation either of the man or his verse. Helen Carr in 'The Myth of Hiawatha' (*L&H*) reopens the issue of Longfellow's mythologizing of the native American, the Indian as necessarily domesticated stereotype to meet the standard of Victorian American verse. Daniel Royot's 'James Russell Lowell: Un humoriste Yankee face au Sud et à l'esclavage' (*EA*) offers a conscientious account of the vernacular satire of the *Biglow Papers* as an instance of New England abolitionist attitudes, a nicely observant essay.

32. *Susanna Rowson*, by Patricia L. Parker. Twayne. pp. 146. $19.95.
33. *Henry Wadsworth Longfellow: His Poetry and Prose*, by Edward Wagenknecht. Ungar. pp. v + 266. $16.95.

James E. Miller's 'Whitman's *Leaves* and the American "Lyric-epic"'[34] takes as its departure point Poe's celebrated assertion that 'there is no such thing as a long poem', 'true' poetry like beauty being a thing of evanescence and short-lived duration. Tackling first *Leaves of Grass*, then a succession of American long poems through to A. R. Ammons's *Tape for the Turn of the Year* (1965) and *Sphere: The Form of Motion* (1974), Miller steps round Poe, arguing for the 'lyric-epic' as a kind of inevitable American poetic form in which the whole is achieved through a recurring interfoliation of image and motif. Miller applies not only his frequently demonstrated credentials as a Whitman critic but a lively appreciation of Whitman as the principal begetter of this 'lyric-epic' genre, a mode of poem strikingly suited to America's 'largeness' and 'multitude'. Kieran Quinlan attempts a more modest task in 'Sea and Sea-Shore in "Song of Myself", Whitman's Liquid Theme'[35], a study of sea and shoreline as an organizing imagery of boundary and transition.

In 'The Identity of American Free Verse: The Prosodic Study of Whitman's "Lilacs"' (*Lang&S*, 1985) Rosemary L. Gates adopts a closely metrical and even syllabic approach to Whitman's great lyric, a strictly technical enquiry into the poet's use of measure. Jeffrey Steele subjects the poem to psycho-analytic scrutiny in 'Poetic Grief-Work in Whitman's "Lilacs"' (*WWR*, 1985), seeing the poem as both private and national therapy at the death of Lincoln. Also in *WWR* (1985), William White publishes two useful bibliographical contributions: 'Whitman: A Bibliographical Checklist', a list of first-printings and recent reference works, and 'Whitman: A Current Bibliography', critical and scholarly publications on Whitman for 1984–6.

The rest amounts to something of a miscellany. Ian F. A. Bell's 'Lockean Sensationalism and American Literary Language' (*JAmS*) persuasively, if briefly, notes the impact of Lockean 'picturing' theories of language upon Whitman and Emerson. M. Wynn Thomas in 'Walt Whitman's Welsh Connection: Ernest Rhys' (*AWR*) sets out the tie both in life and correspondence between an ageing Whitman and the young Ernest Rhys, the latter still to make his mark as the founder of the Everyman Library. In 'Self-Marriage, Dream Children, and the Poetic Imagination: A New Reading of Whitman's "Twenty-Eight Young Men"' (*ATQ*) Pamela Postma looks to section 11 of 'Song of Myself' as a synechdoche for the very workings of Whitman's imagination. The 'young men' are not literal but 'dream children' birthed by their poet-mother, an argument worth pause if only for its ingenuity. Chanita Goodblatt and Joseph Glickson, with a due nod towards William James, diagram the nature of the 'consciousness' in Whitman's so-called catalogues in their 'Whitman and Cognitive Psychology' (*Mosaic*), a solemnish treatment of Whitman's phenomenological appetite. Of passing bibliographical interest are Arthur Golden's 'Nine Early Letters, 1840–1841' (*AL*), and in the same issue of *AL*, Roger W. Peattie's 'Whitman, Charles Aldrich and W. M. Rossetti in 1885: Background to the Whitman Subscription', among other things a further testimony to William Rossetti's lifelong devotion to his Victorian poet-sage. Lastly, on a more personalized note, the poet Robert

34. In *Poems in their Place: The Intertextuality and Order of Poetic Collections*, ed. by Neil Fraistat. UNC. pp. vi + 342. $32.50.
35. In *Literature and Lore of the Sea*, ed. by Patricia Ann Carlson. Rodopi. pp. ix + 288. $35.

Bly in 'Whitman's Line as a Public Form' (*APR*) argues that Whitman, in common with Kit Smart and William Blake, bequeaths a special resource by their form of utterance to writers like himself interested in addressing issues of political power. Whitman's 'line', specifically his long breath-line, gives drama, energy, what Bly terms a 'forward sweep', to the declamatory mode, a claimed affinity Whitman would surely have appreciated.

The process of consolidating Emily Dickinson's reputation as America's foremost woman poet in no way abates. And understandably: her once too-long eclipsed and enigmatic New England life and poetry almost invite continuous deciphering. Such, precisely, represents the task Cynthia Griffin Wolff sets herself in *Emily Dickinson*[36], a dedicated and informed overview. Matching biography to an unfolding exegesis of the poems, Wolff works steadily across the career, most astutely as to the importance of family and place in Dickinson's sensibility, her *annus mirabilis* of 1862, the play and range of her poetry's first-person voice, and the 'life' behind Dickinson's key pre-occupations with death, love, and belief. As a life-and-works approach, Wolff's study merits high respect. Jerome Loving's *Emily Dickinson: The Poet on the Second Story*[37], in exploring the 'slant' perspective of her poetry – notably Dickinson's teasing use of the 'lie' of imagination to get after truth – also deploys a great deal of biographical material, much of it garnered since Richard Sewall's nonetheless still authoritative *The Life of Emily Dickinson* (*YW* 55.486). In Loving's argument, Dickinson's retreat to the second storey of the Amherst family home led as much to an imaginative self-opening as closure. Acting on this cue, he turns with considerable style to other kinds of paradox in Dickinson: the self so ostensibly distanced from the world yet so engaged by its different behaviours; the unmarried recluse so evidently passionate about modes of human and spiritual union; the 'Nobody' of Amherst as she proclaimed herself whose 'I' could hardly sound more audible or alive.

Helen McNeil's study[38] nails its critical colours to the mast right from the outset. Emily Dickinson signifies 'one of the indispensable poets in English', yet a poet even so, both as a woman and an American still too imperfectly understood. Arguing from feminist and Derridean assumptions she uninhibitedly applies both to a concourse of Dickinson themes: Dickinson's appetite for meeting and decoding her immediate world; the nature of her 'difference'; the Dickinson house as both fact and metaphor; and the singularity of her own poet's kind of knowledge ('What Emily Knew', as McNeil titles the chapter). If the account veers a little at times towards preciousness, the acuity of the readings makes up; they are intelligent, highly particular, and engaging. John Robinson's *Emily Dickinson*[39] offers a sound enough general introduction, commonsensical and sturdily expository in manner. Priyamvada Tripathi Anantharaman, for her part, casts an Eastern eye upon Dickinson in *The Sunset in a Cup*[40], emphasizing the pervasive spirituality of the poetry. Sadly

36. *Emily Dickinson*, by Cynthia Griffin Wolff. Knopf. pp. xii + 641. $25.

37. *Emily Dickinson: The Poet on the Second Story*, by Jerome Loving. CUP. pp. xv + 128. £20/$19.95.

38. *Emily Dickinson*, by Helen McNeil. Virago. pp. xxv + 208. pb £3.50.

39. *Emily Dickinson*, by John Robinson. Faber. pp. 191. pb £3.95.

40. *The Sunset in a Cup: Emily Dickinson and Mythopoeic Imagination*, by Priyamvada Tripathi Anantharaman. Cosmo. pp. xiii + 196.

her study suffers any number of disfiguring misprints and oddities of locution.

Four other full-length studies turn far more upon Dickinson's rhetorical tactics, the 'words themselves' according to E. Miller Budick in his *Emily Dickinson and the Life of Language*[41]. Budick argues for 'the symbolic vitality' of Dickinson's verse, its self-acknowledging, self-aware 'animation'. Despite lapses on his own part into a certain lack of animation, especially in his account of Dickinson and Transcendentalist idiom, Budick exhibits an attentive ear and touch in many of his local readings. Cristanne Miller's *Emily Dickinson: A Poet's Grammar*[42] uses a rather similar approach: the seeming incongruence between 'the elliptically compressed, disjunctive [and] at times ungrammatical' language of the poetry and Dickinson's evident desire to make her reader feel (as she once said as a test of good poetry) 'as if the top of my head were taken off'. Miller, accordingly, sees her as 'writing antagonistically', her voice alive with a repertoire of adversary tropes and metaphors. In *Lunacy of Light*[43] Wendy Barker relatedly concerns herself with a number of 'metaphoric clusters' in Dickinson's poems, especially the recurrent allusions to nature's lights and darks as modes of environmental expression for the lights and darks of her own creative personality. Greg Johnson's *Emily Dickinson: Perception and the Poet's Quest*[44] proposes Dickinson as a 'divided being', a poet of near Blakean opposites who contradictorily found 'life' in the contemplation of death, sureness in the enactment of doubt, and the promise of eternity in the essentially transient. These, and other forms of Dickinson paradox, Johnson responsibly and copiously supports by direct allusion to the language of the poetry.

Paula Bennett's *My Life, A Loaded Gun*[45], before moving on to Sylvia Plath and Adrienne Rich, designates Dickinson a 'Queen of Calvary', a proto-typically martyred and messianic figure of womanly creativity. Recovered she may now be, but Dickinson was punished for her imaginative autonomy by an entrenched patriarchy. Crowd-pulling as this might be – and even allowing it contains a partial truth – it reduces Dickinson to pietistic myth, and leaves the poetry most of all in the role of pared-down 'evidence'.

Periodical scholarship on Dickinson has been just as busy. In 'Renunciation Transformed, Emily Dickinson and Margaret Atwood' (*WS*) Suzanne Juhasz suggests, not altogether convincingly, that where Dickinson transformed the 'renunciation' of her life into a prime ingredient in her poetry, Atwood (however clearly a woman of her and our own time and not subject to any of the life-contraints which Dickinson experienced) has only recently begun to write with due recognition of the renunciations *she* has made as a woman and author. In 'The Poet of the Moment: Emily Dickinson and Søren Kierkegaard' (*DicS*) Niels Pastor Kjaer suggests, albeit in list-like manner, yet another pair of life

41. *Emily Dickinson and the Life of Language*, by E. Miller Budick. LSU. pp. 233. $22.50.

42. *Emily Dickinson: A Poet's Grammar*, by Cristanne Miller. Harvard. pp. 212. $20.

43. *Lunacy of Light: Emily Dickinson and the Experience of Metaphor*, by Wendy Barker. SIU. pp. xi + 214. $19.95.

44. *Emily Dickinson: Perception and the Poet's Quest*, by Greg Johnson. UAla. pp. xii + 231. $25.50.

45. *My Life, A Loaded Gun: Female Creativity and Feminist Poetics*, by Paula Bennett. Beacon. pp. xv + 300. $21.95.

parallels: Dickinson and Kierkegaard as both raised under Puritan patriarchy, as both suffering unrequited loves, as both religious sceptics, and as both ignored by any wider readership in their own lifetimes. Also in *DicS*, William White offers a brief current Dickinson bibliography: books, pamphlets, and articles for 1985-6.

One of the more nicely ironic Dickinson articles of the year has to be Marianne Boruch's 'Dickinson Descending' (*GaR*), a wry, sharp-eyed contemplation of the way Emily Dickinson, characteristically a poet of 'strain and silence', has been drawn, abducted almost, into full public scrutiny by scholarship from within her Amherst retreat, second-storey, or attic. And not least, symptomatically, in an article like Joan Burbick's 'Emily Dickinson and the Economics of Desire' (*AL*), an assiduously gender-centred account of desire (that most Barthesian commodity) in the poetry, Dickinson's response to the alleged male regulation of women. Françoise Delphy, no doubt out of an instinctive Gallic instinct for style, exhibits a lighter touch in her 'La Présence d'Emily Dickinson' (*EA*, 1985). Hers amounts to a playful, phenomenological version of Dickinson as a poet of feminine selfhood faced with the 'other' of maleness and its world. Paul Scott Derrick develops another kind of European connection in 'Emily Dickinson, Martin Heidegger and the Poetry of Dread' (*WHR*), a 'historical conversation' as he expresses it between two writers who 'transcend void' through the life-making process of creative expression. Katherine A. Monteiro's 'Dickinson's "Victory Comes Late"' (*Expl*) aspires to no such heights. Rather it offers a firmly eyes-on-the-text exegesis of Poem 690 in the Thomas Johnson *Complete Poems*; it is modest, for sure old-fashioned, critical labour, but oddly welcome.

4. Nineteenth-Century Prose

Washington Irving's fear that his best-known volume would run foul of the 'piracy' of the publishing houses is interestingly explored in David W. Pancost's 'How Washington Irving Published *The Sketch Book* in England' (*SAF*), which considers his game of bluff and counter-bluff to avoid unauthorized use of his writing. Despite the familiar version of Irving as 'genial' amateur, a version he himself played up to, for Jeffrey Rubin-Dorsky in 'Washington Irving: Sketches of Anxiety' (*AL*), this was obfuscation, a deliberate mask. Irving's 'strategies of indirection' in story after story signal a writer beset by anxiety about his own status as author, his own modes of self-expression, and above all his unsure sense of a sympathetic readership. Such the price of being a literary founder. Rubin-Dorsky takes another kind of aim at *The Sketch Book* in 'Washington Irving and the Genesis of the Fictional Sketch', in *EAL*, an enquiry into Irving's ground-breaking transformation of 'the readily available travel sketch' into an imagined simulation of 'travel', a fantasy. Brigitte Bailey also examines Irving's pictorial imagination in 'Irving's Italian Landscapes: Skepticism and the Picturesque Aesthetic' (*ESQ*), a study of how in his use of the Hudson Valley painters of his native upstate New York through to the Italian painters alluded to in his Italian journal Irving's deployment of landscape was rarely other than ironic, a subtle and often satiric commentary on the foreground of his plots.

'He adapted his literary structures from novels he knew to be popular – novels by Opie, Austen, Scott – but he drew his substance from subliterary narratives, legends, traditions, the gossip of the nation.' Thus, in *Early Cooper and his Audience*[46], James D. Wallace neatly summarizes his view of how Cooper 'created' a novelistic form to meet the expectations of his American readers. Enlighteningly comparing Cooper with Charles Brockden Brown as fellow initiators of American fiction, Wallace looks in particular at the reception of *The Spy* and *The Pioneers*, fictions which steer a middle course between credible 'history' and historical romance. Robert Clark gives his contributors their own critical head in his *James Fenimore Cooper: New Critical Essays*[47]. But they all share an avowed aim, 'to broaden our view of Cooper beyond the Leatherstocking tales' and to address Cooper's 'ideological and historical complexity', an aim on the whole well enough fulfilled. To such an end Heinz Ickstadt shrewdly compares Cooper with his co-Jacksonian George Lippard by reference to *Notions of the Americans*, *The American Democrat*, and his 'three explicitly political novels', *The Bravo* (1831), *The Heidenmauer* (1832), and *The Headsman* (1833); James D. Wallace looks into Cooper's creation of 'a community of readers' in *Precaution* and *The Spy* (some overlap here with Wallace's study); Eric Cheyfitz looks at naming and nomenclature in Cooper, the registers of place, people, and frontierism which encode his world; Charles Swann ingeniously excavates the New York game laws and their implications for 'ownership' in *The Pioneers*; Richard Godden similarly delves into the issues of commodity and property in the same novel, an elegantly turned Marxist–structuralist view of Cooper; John P. McWilliams analyses Cooper's process of mythicizing his Indians; Gordon Brotherston unpacks Cooper as 'the epicist of the United States and its founding days'; and Robert Clark himself tackles Cooper's complex attitude to law-breaking and the American Revolution, external and domestic Toryism compared. These contributions do Cooper new critical service, offering a challenge to too reductive a view of America's first novelist of substance – either as 'the American Scott' or simply the begetter of the Leatherstocking books.

Frank Bergmann's 'The Meaning of the Indians and their Land in Cooper's *The Last of the Mohicans*'[48] suggests that Cooper's novel profitably oscillates, in E. M. Forster's terms, between 'the opposing ranges of Poetry and History', a 'narrative of 1757' transposed into a parable of Indian white 'rightful coexistence'. Penguin have added *The Last of The Mohicans*[49] to their list, with a pertinent introduction by Richard Slotkin. Bryan N. Wyatt's 'Cooper's Leatherstocking: Romance and the Limits of Character' (*CLAJ*) argues that by so mythicizing Leatherstocking Cooper ensured his failure as a fictional character. Rather, he serves as an 'embodied oxymoron', 'a Christian savage, a learned ignoramus, a humble braggart, a girlish *macho*, a sinless killer', in all a type more than an individual. April Selley links Cooper to TV's best-known space adventure in '"I have always Been, and Ever Shall Be, Your Friend": *Star Trek*, *The Deerslayer* and the American Romance' (*JPC*), an enquiry of a superficial sort into literary and pop- cultural presentations of interracial male

46. *Early Cooper and his Audience*, by James D. Wallace. ColU. pp. xi + 230. $35.

47. *James Fenimore Cooper: New Critical Essays*, ed. by Robert Clark. Vision/B&N. pp. 208. £15.95/$28.50.

48. In *Upstate Literature: Essays in Memory of Thomas F. O'Donnell*, ed. by Frank Bergmann. Syracuse. pp. xvi + 222. hb $24, pb $11.95.

49. *The Last of the Mohicans*, by James Fenimore Cooper, ed. by Richard Slotkin. Penguin. pp. xxviii + 352. pb £3.95.

friendships. Steven Blakemore, more terrestrially, analyses the interplay of sublime and vernacular in Cooper's fiction in his 'Language and World in *The Pathfinder*' (*MLS*), an analysis of the stylistic components within his writing. Pictorialism offers Douglas Anderson his focus in 'Cooper's Improbable Pictures in *The Pioneers*' (*SAF*), an enumeration and favouring evaluation of the visual exuberance of Cooper's novel. The idea of Ben Franklin rather than Cooper's own father, Judge Cooper of Cooperstown, as a model for Judge Temple in *The Pioneers*, is given an airing by Michael Clark in 'Benjamin Franklin and Cooper's *The Pioneers*' (*ELN*). Clark returns to the same novel in his 'Caves, Houses, and Temples in James Fenimore Cooper's *The Pioneers*' (*MLS*), a studious annotation of Cooper's use of frontier iconography and architecture as 'ballast' for his story. The source referred to in 'The Source for an Incident in Cooper's *The Redskins*' (*ELN*) by Donald A. Ringe is James Thacher's *Military Journal During the Revolutionary War*, specifically the episode in which Hugh Littlepage forbids the removal of a canopy in St Andrew's Church.

In *Fables of Mind*[50] Joan Dayan starts from the assumption of Poe as 'a philosophical writer' whose fictions enact 'complicated critiques of the law of identity and contradiction, the law of cause and effect, and of any abstract notion of body and soul'. Citing the ideas of *Eureka*, she discerns precisely this 'philosophic' Poe not only in his essays and marginalia but in landscape stories like 'The Domain of Arnheim' and 'Landor's Cottage' (in a chapter appropriately called 'The Poet in the Garden'), in his stories of 'dream-dimmed ladies' – 'Berenice', 'Morella', and 'Ligeia' principally, and in his satires of the notion of 'Spirit', stories like 'Words', 'A Decided Loss', 'Loss of Breath', 'The Bargain Lost', and 'Bon-Bon' in which he depicts the very edge between life and death. If the argument of *Fables of Mind* at times betrays uncertainty, a want of apparent firmness about its own direction, it nevertheless seeks for Poe a better recognition of the method in his 'madness', Poe as a maker not just of 'tales' but of an overall, encompassing philosophy. I. M. Walker's *Edgar Allan Poe: The Critical Heritage*[51] follows the RKP format for this series, a meticulous account of the author's reception from the beginning through to the present day followed by a full selection of reviews written during or near to his own lifetime, in this case from 1827 to 1856. Of especial interest, if only for their duplicity, are the pieces by Poe's ill-chosen executor, the Rev. Rufus Wilmot Griswold, exquisite monuments of bad faith.

'The fascination, for good or ill, that Poe continues to exert' offers the departure point for the ten critical essays commissioned by A. Robert Lee in *Edgar Allan Poe: The Design of Order*[52], and the strength of the collection lies, essentially, in having the contributors address themselves to those works which lie at the centre of Poe's claims to literary importance. Thus Mark Kinkead-Weekes contributes a most attentive and penetrating reading of 'The Fall of the House of Usher' and Harold Beaver a Derridean and Lacanian account of 'MS.

50. *Fables of Mind: An Enquiry into Poe's Fiction*, by Joan Dayan. OUPAm. pp. 273. £22.50.

51. *Edgar Allan Poe: The Critical Heritage*, ed. by I. M. Walker. RKP. pp. xvii + 419. £27.50.

52. *Edgar Allan Poe: The Design of Order*, ed. by A. Robert Lee. Vision/B&N. pp. 224. £15.95/$28.50.

Found in a Bottle'. The comic in Poe (an aspect of his work too often overlooked) is intelligently described in an essay by James H. Justus through the perspective of Southwestern humour. Arnold Goldman treats the stories of premature burial as a kind of literary subspecies, linking for example 'A Decided Loss' and 'Loss of Breath' as trial runs for *The Narrative of Arthur Gordon Pym*. *Pym* is also the subject of the editor's own essay, an account of its virtuoso and endemic self-reflection. To David Murray falls the task of making a case for Poe's poetry. To an extent Murray sidesteps the issue of evaluation and calls his essay an 'approach', one that takes him from Romantic poetic theory as Poe inherited it to John T. Irwin's poststructuralist view of him. The volume concludes with perhaps the most interesting of the essays, John Weightman's 'Poe in France: A Myth Revisited'. Weightman argues that Baudelaire's translations of Poe's 'vividly symbolic prose-writings became a form of self-expression by proxy', and that, as a result of Baudelaire's intercessions, 'Poe was worshipped *a priori*'. Concluding the volume as it does, Weightman's essay strikes a somewhat discordant note, for it is unequivocally dismissive of those who would claim Poe as a writer of the first rank. [G.H.C.]

Judith P. Saunders's '"If this I saw": Optic Dilemmas in Poe's Writings' (*ATQ*) analyses the treatment of 'visual perception' in stories like 'The Sphinx' and 'The Murders in the Rue Morgue', the limits and deformations as Poe perceives them in normal human ways of 'seeing'. In 'The Flights of a Good Man's Mind: Gothic Fantasy in Poe's "The Assignation"' (*MLS*) Benjamin Franklin Fisher suggests that to read this story as simply 'the frothy parody of the Byronic' misses its true aim, namely, the attempt at a first telling of Poe's great theme of 'the death of a beautiful woman' with all that such implies for the author of *Eureka* and the critical essays. Furthermore, as Fisher goes on to suggest, 'The Assignation' depends upon 'a muddleheaded story-teller who . . . misunderstands events transpiring before him', an instance of Poe's use of the untrustworthy and inadequate narrator. For Edward W. R. Pitcher in '"To die laughing": Poe's Allusion to Sir Thomas More in "The Assignation"' (*SSF*), the best clue to the story's meaning lies in the deployment of More as moral touchstone, a figure of rebuke to the narrator's own limitations. T. J. Matheson in 'Poe's "The Black Cat" as a Critique of Temperance Literature' (*Mosaic*) opens with an observation from Increase Mather to the effect that 'Wine is from God, but the Drunkard is from the devil'. He sees 'The Black Cat' as a Poe parody of the then-current Temperance belief that 'redemption' for man's evil can be secured by so simple a gesture as abstinence from alcohol. Not only does this give hope to the heavy drinkers in *YWES*'s readership but it recognizes Poe's humour. Michael Clifton in 'Down Hecate's Chain: Infernal Inspiration in Three of Poe's Tales' (*NCF*) pursues the hell-imagery in 'Usher', 'The Duc de l'Omelette', and 'The Pit and the Pendulum', an analysis intended to show how Poe sought to signal the danger to any artist moved to 'explore the innermost recesses of his mind for his art's sake'. Craig Howes's 'Burke, Poe and "Usher": The Sublime and Rising Woman' (*ESQ*) proposes 'Usher' as Poe's supreme example of his vaunted '*single effect*', seeing the Burkean Sublime as embodied in Madeline Usher who survives the collapsing house and even death. In 'Explanation in "The Fall of the House of Usher"' (*SSF*) Beverly R. Voloshin invokes Locke's notion of the mind's 'representation' of reality to explain 'Usher'. As she sees it the Usher house represents Usher's mind which dissolves only to be reconstituted in the reader's consciousness.

Adeline R. Tintner believes she has spotted a hitherto unnoticed borrowing from Dickens in Poe. In 'A Possible Source in Dickens for Poe's "The Imp of the Perverse"' (*PoeS*) she suggests that Poe may well have read and consciously or otherwise borrowed the words 'imp' and 'perverse' from *Oliver Twist* as spoken by Bill Sykes to Oliver. Joan Tyler also does some source-hunting in her 'Poe's "The Man That Was Used Up": Another Bugaboo Campaign' (*SSF*), alleging that the military celebrity General Smith was the 'man' referred to in the title. But she then goes on to argue that in his bid for self-aggrandizement the narrator himself gets 'used up', consumed by his own bid to be taken as the story's authority. Fresh from the controversies aroused by his *American Hieroglyphics* (*YW* 61.404), John Irwin leaves no one in doubt that they are in for a portmanteau read by the very title of his 'Mysteries We Reread, Mysteries of Rereading: Poe, Borges, and the Analytic Story: Also Lacan, Derrida and Johnson' (*MLN*). Irwin begins with a recapitulation of three previous readings of 'The Purloined Letter' by Lacan, Derrida, and Barbara Johnson, moves on to the other Dupin stories – with frequent allusion to Borges – and suggests that these stories not only offer 'detection' in the usual sense but serve as instances of the subtle 'detective' strategies whereby literature actually constitutes itself as literature. Or so one takes his argument to suggest. But those familiar with *Hieroglyphics* will recognize the terrain and the kind of thesis to hand. Not dissimilar in approach is William Goldhurst's 'Self-Reflective Fiction by Poe: Three Tales' (*MLS*), a study of the 'calculated self-indicators' in 'The Oblong Box', 'The Gold Bug', and 'The Sphinx', each a classic instance of story-telling which 'contains' the author as well as 'representing' him. The manner in which Poe concludes *Pym*, if conclude is the appropriate term, has from the outset been a stimulus to controversy. Jules Zanger returns to the issue in his 'Poe's Endless Voyage: *The Narrative of Arthur Gordon Pym*' (*PLL*), a lively comparison of the efforts in turn of Jules Verne, Charles Drake, and H. P. Lovecraft to complete Poe's only novel in the face of the author's own 'indeterminate' sense of an ending.

John McCardell's 'Poetry and the Practical: William Gilmore Simms'[53] takes on Simms's treatment of Southernness both as myth and historical reality, providing a local-culture study which opens usefully into a larger perspective on Southern culture in general.

The Transcendentalist writing of New England continues to take a central place in scholarly attention, with Emerson as its oracle and presiding presence. In *Emerson and his Legacy: Essays in Honor of Quentin Anderson*[54] the editors do a double service. They provide re-assessments of Emerson as American culture spokesman and they do honour to the exceptional criticism and pedagogy of the Columbia University teacher Quentin Anderson, a mind at its subtlest in *The Imperial Self* (*YW* 52.396–7). The best of the contributions most directly focused on Emerson brim with intelligence: Ormond Seavey's 'Emerson as Itinerant' skilfully delineates Emerson's commitment to 'the

53. In *Intellectual Life in Antebellum Charleston*, ed. by Michael O'Brien and David Moltke-Hansen. UTenn. pp. xiv + 468. $45.

54. *Emerson and his Legacy: Essays in Honor of Quentin Anderson*, ed. by Stephen Donadio, Stephen Railton, and Ormond Seavey. SIU. pp. ix + 250. $24.95.

disruption of the settled life', his deeply felt opposition to 'system' both in social and intellectual behaviour; Denis Donoghue's 'Emerson at First' re-subjects *Nature* to an exhaustive close reading, its significance as a prospectus for Emerson's whole notion of 'Mind'; Stephen Railton's 'Seeing and Saying: The Dialectic of Emerson's Eloquence' pursues the notion of 'eloquence' as the ideal articulation of truth in the Emersonian schema; and Carl Hovde's 'English and American Traits' looks to Emerson's 1857 volume for the acuity of its comparison of the representative and relative merits of American and English culture. Other essays (of the eleven in all), notably Stephen Donadio in a comparison with the Poe of *Eureka* and *Pym* and the late Paul Zweig in a scintillating piece on Whitman as Emersonian bard, concern themselves with Emerson as mentor and visionary.

Less heady though no less substantial is David Van Leer's *Emerson's Epistemology: The Argument of the Essays*[55], which likens Emerson to Kant and Swedenborg as a philosophic mind instead of viewing him as one whose epistemological forays serve as rather hang-dog addenda to his feats of oratory. Van Leer offers tough reading, a carefully weighed assessment of Emerson as thinker. Two critics of longstanding reputation also return to Emerson, the New England brahmin as a source of cultural re-invigoration. In *The American Newness*[56], his 1986 Massey Lectures at Harvard, Irving Howe ponders the rich ambivalence of Emerson's legacy – its easy eclipse as a politics in the face of America's speed of industrialization and citification and yet its great power as a prompting to new reaches of individual selfhood. In this latter respect Howe has stimulating comparisons to make with Hawthorne and Melville. For Richard Poirier too, in *The Renewal of Literature*[57], Emerson continues to serve as an affirmer of the presence of 'self', a smack at the seeming insistence of modernism upon the self as simply a trick of language, a fiction supposedly shown for what it is by those of a deconstructive bent. Poirier's opening chapter in fact first appeared in his own journal *Raritan*, and it is an essay indeed impressive and perfectly free-standing in its own right which argues that Emerson's ostensible opposition to past works of genius, like *Hamlet* no less, expresses not some patrician quirk but the belief 'that on behalf of us he is clearing the way for some forever postponed and unparalleled human performance'. Emerson, in other words, was early to see the perniciousness of bardolatry, the need to find a way through and beyond the 'anxiety of influence'. Poirier writes with brilliance, conviction, and a willingness to engage his reader in debate.

Other journal scholarship, worthy as it may be, can hardly avoid looking procedural by comparison. Michael Strelov's 'Emerson Abroad and at Home: The Making of the Paradigm in *Essays, First Series*' (*ATQ*) argues that Emerson's visit to the Natural Science Exhibition in Paris in 1832 in which Cuvier, Lamarck, and others challenged the taxonomies of Linnaeus, had a profound impact upon his own developing taxonomy for American culture at large. In 'Emerson's Playful Habit of Mind' (*ATQ*) David Shimkin traces out the ludic impulse and idiom in Emerson's writing, his self-avowed 'incapacity

55. *Emerson's Epistemology: The Argument of the Essays*, by David Van Leer. CUP. pp. xviii + 282. £27.50/$29.95.

56. *The American Newness*, by Irving Howe. Harvard. pp. 95. $12.50.

57. *The Renewal of Literature: Emersonian Reflections*, by Richard Poirier. RandomH. pp. 244. $19.95.

for methodical writing' and preference for the more poetic 'fluxional' utterance. The paradox of 'intoxication' as a pivotal metaphor in the expression of one so literally abstentionist is neatly elaborated in Nicholas O. Warner's 'God's Wine and Devil's Wine: The Idea of Intoxication in Emerson' (*Mosaic*), which depicts the voice of Transcendentalism as a bibber of the non-vinous kind. J. Lasley Dameron in 'Emerson's "Each and All" and Goethe's "Eins und Alles"' (*ES*) argues that Goethe's poem may well have lain behind Emerson's crucial change of his original 'Each *in* all' to 'Each *and* All', the self not as separate from but inclusive within the whole. Robert M. Greenberg takes his title-phrase in 'Shooting the Gulf: Emerson's Sense of Experience' (*ESQ*, 1985) from a line in 'Self-Reliance', a revealingly existential figure of speech which he suggests gives the lie to those who charge Emerson with too pronounced a remoteness from life. David Leverenz's 'The Politics of Emerson's Man-Making Words' (*PMLA*) attempts a deconstruction of the pervasive imagery of male power in Emerson, a gender-centred study which suggests Emerson wrote self-compensatingly in order to downplay the feminine side to his nature, as for instance at the early tragic death of his son Waldo in 1842. Emerson's affinities with the English Romantics are examined once more in, respectively, 'Emerson's Chagrin: Benediction and Exhortation in "Nature" and "Tintern Abbey"' (*MLN*) by John Michael, a comparison of his and Wordsworth's treatment of solitude in their two canonical works, and in 'Emerson and Byron' (*ATQ*) by Larry Bielawaski, which endeavours essentially to promote *Childe Harold's Pilgrimage* as an under-acknowledged source in Emerson. Peter Carofiol's 'Reading Emerson: Writing History' (*CentR*), a fairly tame recapitulation of Emerson's meaning and legacy, moves from Emerson himself on to an attempted larger definition of Transcendentalism, with stop-overs at Emerson on 'language' and 'unity'.

Sharon Cameron's *Writing Nature: Henry Thoreau's Journal*[58] undauntedly takes on the forty-seven volumes Thoreau wrote between 1837 and 1861, both as a species of *Grundrisse* for *Walden* and as a massive repository of his ideas and self-shapings in and for themselves. Realistically conceding that this 'great nineteenth-century American meditation on nature' remains 'largely inaccessible to the general reader', Cameron urges its especial freshness of perception, the great contrast between the 'mediated' way *Walden* speaks to its readership and the way the *Journal* 'extends nothing towards us'. In this, for Cameron, inheres the essential Thoreau, the transcriber of an unmoralized, otherly Nature as against the 'literary' sensibility at work in *Walden*. Denis Donoghue, reviewing *Writing Nature* (and the LAm *Thoreau) for the TLS* under the companionable title of 'A Poet of the Self and Weather', sees limitations to Cameron's thesis. 'Unmediated' the *Journal* may be and a quarry of rich, first-hand observation and insight, but that even so should not be allowed to outweigh vintage Thoreau – for Donoghue to be met with in a classic chapter of *Walden* like 'Spring'. Thoreau's evolution as a thinker is also the theme of Robert D. Richardson's *Henry Thoreau: A Life of the Mind*[59], an 'intellectual biography' of Thoreau from the age of twenty through to his death

58. *Writing Nature: Henry Thoreau's Journal*, by Sharon Cameron. OUPAm (1985). pp. x + 173. $17.50.

59. *Henry Thoreau: A Life of the Mind*, by Robert D. Richardson. UCal. pp. x + 455. $25.

in 1862. Chronological, straightforwardly told, Richardson's account lacks the spiritedness of Cameron's. But it faithfully makes good on what it promises, Thoreau as 'a writer, a naturalist, and a reader'.

Ian Marshall's 'Thoreau's Walden Odyssey' (*ATQ*) convincingly shows Thoreau to have taken the figure of Ulysses as his conscious model, his adopting the Homeric voyager as alter ego for the 'traveller' at Walden Pond. In 'The Voices of *Walden*' (*ESQ*) Henry Golemba, invoking the different manuscript drafts of *Walden*, illustrates Thoreau's ventriloquy in his masterwork – 'the witty, clever punster; the intent high-sounding idealist with his exhorting style; the zany clown or the undercutting skeptic'. Thoreau's Eastern interests once again come under review in Barbara Stoler Miller's 'Why Did Henry David Thoreau take the *Bhagavad-Gita* to Walden Pond?' (*Parabola*), the Sanskrit classic as a necessary comfort and source in *Walden*. Michael Fischer's 'Speech and Writing in *The Senses of Walden*' (*Soundings*), a review-essay of Stanley Cavell's 1972 study of Thoreau, sees *Walden* through a Derridean vista, Thoreau's account of his 'private business' deconstructed. On a not dissimilar tack, Thoreau comes under Bakhtinian rules in Malini Schueller's 'Carnival Rhetoric and Extra-Vagance in Thoreau's *Walden*' (*AL*), an argument for the recognition of how Thoreau 'carnivalizes' established language and social hierarchy in order to 'create his own terms of reference'.

Two new analyses of *The Maine Woods* have made an appearance. In '"Ktaadn": Thoreau in the Wilderness of Words' (*ESQ*) John Tallmadge underlines the extraordinary vivacity of the first chapter of *Woods*, unusual for Thoreau in its depiction of a hostile Nature. Donald H. Williams's 'Thoreau looks at "Katadn"' (*TSB*) offers a minor piece of elucidation about whether Thoreau's phrase 'our first sight of Katadn' in fact refers to a *last* sight. Thoreau's sense of the past as a stream or flux into the present gives Daniel H. Peck his focus in '"Further Down the Stream of Time": Memory and Perspective in Thoreau's *A Week on the Concord and Merrimack Rivers*' (*ThoreauQ*), a study in the extensive use of a key Thoreauvian motif. Which, almost to the letter, also represents the interest of Yves Carlet in 'Thoreau et le temps retrouvé: *A Week on the Concord and Merrimack Rivers*' [60]. John Van Driesche delivers himself of a few sobering reflections in 'Thoreau and Self-Government' (*TSB*), which discusses the mind-concentrating experience of teaching 'Civil Disobedience' to prisoners in the Oregon State Penitentiary. Items of bibliographical note are to be found in 'Another Review of Thoreau's *Week*' (*TSB*), a reprint of a generally favourable notice in the *Literary World* for 22 September 1849, and Walter Harding's 'Addition to the Thoreau Bibliography' (*TSB*), a series of up-dates of scholarship and criticism through the four issues of *TSB* for 1986.

Of the other New England Transcendentalists and literati, Kenneth Walter Cameron's *Transcendentalist Curriculum, or Bronson Alcott's Library* [61] offers an annotated catalogue of Alcott's domestic books, as much to indicate the eclectic sources of Transcendentalism itself as to illuminate the reading of this classic Massachusetts reformer. As a kind of preliminary to their

60. In *Age d'or et apocalypse*, ed. by Robert Ellrodt and Bernard Brugière. Sorbonne. pp. 364.
61. *Transcendentalist Curriculum, or Bronson Alcott's Library*, by Kenneth Walter Cameron. Transcendental. pp. 69. $30.

forthcoming *Selected Letters of Louisa May Alcott* Joel Myerson and Daniel Shealey in 'Three Contemporary Accounts of Louisa May Alcott, with Glimpses of Other Concord Notables' (*NEQ*) delineate something of the private woman behind the celebrity associated with *Little Women*. Reproduced are two letters, from Elizabeth Susan Greene who would later illustrate some of Alcott's writings, and from Bessie Holyoke, an old family friend, together with a memoir by Anne B. Adams, daughter of abolitionist John Brown, which recalls not only Bronson Alcott's daughter but gives a picture of Concord figures like Thoreau, and Nathaniel and Sophia Hawthorne. Myerson and Shealey also give their attention to a 'previously unrecorded' skit (which they reprint) written by Louisa May Alcott of Emerson, Hawthorne, Thoreau, and the rest in 'Louisa May Alcott's "A Wail": An Unrecorded Satire of the Concord Authors' (*PBSA*). Margaret Fuller as an under-acknowledged liter-ary theorist and critic – and her debts to late eighteenth-century Scottish writers like Lord Kanes, Hugh Blair, and Archibald Alison – serves as the occa-sion for Sharon George's 'Margaret Fuller's *Dial* Criticism: The Merging of the Scottish Common Sense and Romantic Traditions' (*ATQ*), a timely effort to win another kind of due for the author of *Woman in the Nineteenth Century*.

One of Oliver Wendell Holmes's 'medicated' novels, as he was pleased to have them called, comes under fresh consideration in 'Poisonous Creature: Holmes's *Elsie Venner*' (*SNNTS*), in which Margaret Hallissy sees the 'serpent-woman metaphor' imposed on Elsie as a reworking of the Lamia myth, female sexuality made over into diabolism by a provincial and fearing Puritan New England community. Francis Parkman comes under an even more bracing feminist analysis in Kim Townsend's 'Francis Parkman and the Male Tradition' (*AQ*), a reading sympathetic to Parkman in the illness he mentions in *The Oregon Trail* but interpreting him as a figure who nonetheless found his own 'renewal', his own enmasculinizing, in the ritual of subjugating 'dangerous people of color – and women'. Townsend places Parkman in a line of subsequent male adventurers from Teddy Roosevelt to Ronald Reagan who have acted out the 'familiar stance' of frontiersmen be it in life or celluloid fantasy. Henry Adams, in his turn, comes in for another style of psychoanalysis in two articles, the first by George Moraitis in 'The Two Readings of *The Education of Henry Adams*' and the second by Mark R. Schwehn in 'Reviewing Henry Adams', both in *Psychoanalysis: The Vital Issues*, Vol. I[62]. Essentially Adams as a man of anxiety, a complex and disturbed inwardness, emerges. On more literary terrain, Viola Hopkins Winner in 'Style and Sincerity in the Letters of Henry Adams'[63] sees in Adams the correspondent a writer of near Jamesian indirection and subtlety. Raymond Carney's 'The Imagination in Ascendance: Henry Adams's *Mont Saint Michel and Chartres*' (*SoR*) re-examines Adams's treatment of medieval Christianity and the role of 'imagination' in the making of an organic culture.

The six contributions which make up Eric J. Sundquist's *New Essays On*

62. *Psychoanalysis: The Vital Issues*. Vol. I: *Psychoanalysis as an Intellectual Discipline*, ed. by John E. Gedo and George H. Pollock. IntUP (1984). pp. xiv + 436. $40.

63. *In Essaying Biography: A Celebration for Leon Edel*, ed. by Gloria G. Fromm. UHawaii. pp. vi + 248. $12.95.

'*Uncle Tom's Cabin*'[64] all recognize the massive ambiguity behind the novel's popularity: its exemplary Christian-abolitionist call to arms, yet its creation of one of the most enduring racist stereotypes, that of Uncle Tom himself. Richard Yardborough takes up precisely 'black characterization' in an opening essay which compares *Uncle Tom's Cabin* with black-written fiction by Martin Delany, Frances Ellen Watkins Harper, and Charles Chesnutt. Jean Fagan Yellin sees Stowe's novel as an instance of 'domestic feminism', an attack upon the essentially white patriarchal institution of slave-ownership. To Karen Halttunen this novel of stored fears and memories incorporates all the hell-fired Gothic Calvinism of Stowe's family and father-dominated Connecticut upbringing. Robert B. Stepto compares Stowe with the ex-slave authors Henry Bibb and Frederick Douglass in their depictions both of 'black heroism' and of the possibilities of black revolution. He so calls attention to Stowe as a chronicler of *both* Uncle Tom and Nat Turner. Elizabeth Ammons believes that 'No book matters more to the history of women in America than *Uncle Tom's Cabin*' and goes on to link Stowe with a range of other American literary women black and white, arguing for the novel's 'matrifocal values', its triumphant advocacy of 'maternal' values in the face of slavery and male oppression. Stove again features in two other 'gender' studies. In Mimrose C. Gwin's *Black and White Women of the Old South*[65] she is used as an essential touchstone both in *Uncle Tom's Cabin* and *Dred* (1856) for a comparison with women writers across the racial line in the nineteenth-century South. In 'Slavery and Sentimentalism: The Strange Career of Augustine St. Clare' (*WS*) Amy Schrager Lang argues for an androgynous, feminized St Clare, killed off early in the novel because his 'womanly' sentiments about slavery cannot survive the male world of slave-ownership.

Stowe also offers a reference point in several new studies of Afro-American writing. In 'From Fugitive Slave to Man of Letters: The Conversion of Frederick Douglass' (*JNT*) Lucinda H. MacKethan shows how Douglass's 'portrait of himself as a priest of true Christianity' (as against the Christianity of slavery-supporting Southern Christians) in his *Narrative* parallels his other 'conversion' from illiteracy to literacy, both processes in which 'the word' serves as a metaphor of enlightenment amid an enclosing dark. Harriet Brent Jacobs's slave-narrative *Incidents in the Life of a Slave Girl* takes centre place in two new essays. Minrose C. Gwin, in 'Green-Eyed Monsters of the Slavocracy: Jealous Mistresses in Two Slave Narratives'[66], an engrossing piece of historical excavation, compares Jacobs's *Life* with Elizabeth Keckley's *Behind the Scenes* in their treatment of white mistresses and black slave women and servants. Jean Fagan Yellin's 'Text and Contexts of Harriet Jacobs' *Incidents in the Life of a Slave Girl: Written by Herself*'[67] examines Jacobs's depiction of sexuality and gender as components in her overall account of racial encounter. The Jeremiad as rhetorical model is given attention by Dolan

64. *New Essays on 'Uncle Tom's Cabin'*, ed. by Eric J. Sundquist. CUP. pp. viii + 200. hb £20, pb £6.95.
65. *Black and White Women of the Old South: The Peculiar Sisterhood in American Literature*, by Minrose C. Gwin. UTenn. pp. vii + 238. $19.95.
66. In *Conjuring: Black Women, Fiction, and Literary Tradition*, ed. by Marjorie Pryse and Hortense J. Spillers. IndU. pp. 266. hb $29.95, pb $10.95.
67. In *The Slave's Narrative*, ed. by Charles T. Davis and Henry Louis Gates. OUPAm. pp. xxxiv + 342. $29.95.

Hubbard in his 'David Walker's *Appeal* and the American Puritan Jeremiadic Tradition' (*CentR*), the *Appeal* as deriving from the genre best favoured by the New England founders. Jane Campbell's *Mythic Black Fiction: The Transformation of History*[68] looks into what she terms 'mythic history' as a dominant mode of Afro-American prose narrative, the process whereby 'historical truths' shaped and re-patterned into imaginative form. Her study runs from William Wells Brown through to Toni Morrison, with key nineteenth-century chapters on Frances Harper and Pauline Hopkins, and Sutton Griggs and Charles Chesnutt.

Nathaniel Hawthorne[69], like the others in the ChelseaH series under Harold Bloom's ubiquitous and seigneurial editorship, reprints what for the most part are well-known essays (or chapters) on the romances and principal stories. Among the starring names are Daniel Hoffman, Frederick Crews, Larzer Ziff, and Richard Brodhead. Similarly *Nathaniel Hawthorne's 'The Scarlet Letter'*[70], one of a run of ChelseaH's critical compilations on a single text under Bloom's aegis – seven essays of which six can be found previously issued in journal or chapter form: it would seem that having issued the gospel of literary gnosticism Bloom has moved into literary mogulship. Not that his contributors do not have their own distinct flags to fly. Nina Baym, for instance, who is reprinted in *Nathaniel Hawthorne* and has long been at the forefront of 'gender' interpretations of American fiction, has published her own full-length *'The Scarlet Letter': A Reading*[71], a diligent, keenly alert account which pays especial attention to 'the feminine' throughout Hawthorne's fashioning of his principal romance.

In journals, too, like the emblem itself, *The Scarlet Letter* continues to elicit a cross-ply of interpretation. Paula Banting's 'Miss A and Mrs. B: The Letters of Pleasure in *The Scarlet Letter* and *As for Me and My House*' (*NDQ*) points Hawthorne northwards even of New England, offering a comparison of sexual transgression in *The Scarlet Letter* and Sinclair Ross's lesser-known Canadian novel in an essay heavy with allusions to 'the erotics of space' and the like. Less rhetorical is Lois A. Cuddy's 'Mother–Daughter Identification in *The Scarlet Letter*' (*Mosaic*), a psychoanalytic but unobfuscatory case-study of the 'bonding' of Hester and Pearl. But Hawthorne returns more firmly to the analyst's couch in Daniel Clay's '*The Scarlet Letter*: Hawthorne, Freud and the Transcendentalists' (*ATQ*), Hester's defiance of Puritan writ as expressing nothing less than Hawthorne's own Oedipal rejection of Transcendentalism. Laurie N. Rozakic suggests in 'Another Possible Source for Hawthorne's Hester Prynne' (*ATQ*) that the tombstone of Elizabeth Pain, still to be found in the King's Chapel Burial Ground in Boston, may have provided a stimulus both for the naming and the 'crime' of Hester (Pain was accused but acquitted on a charge of murder). Chester Wolford's 'Intimations of Epic in *The Scarlet*

68. *Mythic Black Fiction: The Transformation of History*, by Jane Campbell. UTenn. pp. xvii + 180. $16.95.

69. *Nathaniel Hawthorne: Modern Critical Views*, ed. by Harold Bloom. ChelseaH. pp. viii + 240. $19.95.

70. *Nathaniel Hawthorne's 'The Scarlet Letter': Modern Critical Interpretations*, ed. by Harold Bloom. ChelseaH. pp. vii + 144. $24.50.

71. *'The Scarlet Letter': A Reading*, by Nina Baym. Hall. pp. xxix + 116. hb $10.50, pb $5.95.

Letter'[72] takes a rather hit-or-miss run at Hawthorne's classic as a species of 'failed epic', with Hester and Pearl cast in the roles of mythic outcasts from a morally oppressive Puritan America.

Cudgels once again get taken up against the narrator of *The Blithedale Romance* in Beverly Hume's 'Restructuring the Case Against Hawthorne's Coverdale' (*NCF*), absolving him of the actual murder of Zenobia but none the less, casting him as a Hawthorneian Unpardonable Sinner, cold in heart and feeling despite his eventually professed love for Priscilla. Coverdale also takes centre place in Thomas Strychacz's 'Coverdale and Women: Feverish Fantasies in *The Blithedale Romance*' (*ATQ*), this time as a woman-hater whose ostensible idealizations of woman mask his implacable hostility to them. George Monteiro's 'Hawthorne's Summer Romance' (*DQR*) slightly lowers the temperature, a return to the argument that *Blithedale* portrays an American world turned upside down, a Brook Farm utopia caught in its own contradictions and so rendered dystopian. For Byron L. Stay in 'Hawthorne's Fallen Puritans: Eliot's Pulpit in *The Blithedale Romance*' (*SNNTS*), Hawthorne's romance 'hinges on the complex relationship between the Blithedalers and the Puritans', the latter typified in the rock-formation known as Eliot's Pulpit and which ironically also comes to serve as an emblem of the failure of the communitarians. Hubert Zapf's 'The Poetological Theme in Hawthorne's *Blithedale Romance*' (*ATQ*) underscores yet again the story's self-reflexive nature, Hawthorne's 'practice of incorporating problems of art into his fictional themes'.

Nathalie Cole Michta considers the pull of the Cenci legend for Hawthorne in her '"Plucked up out of a mystery": Archetypal Resonance in Hawthorne's *The Marble Faun*' (*ESQ*), especially the Shelley version, Beatrice Cenci and her imbroglio as models for the Miriam–Donatello–Hilda–Kenyon quartet, a fresh working-over of otherwise well-known literary parallels. Beatrice Cenci also features in Mary Cappello's '"Rappaccini's Daughter" as Translation' (*PQ*), Hawthorne's 'translation' of a literary archetype as also a trope for the story's 'translations' of one reality into another. It is Dante's Beatrice, too, who features in David L. Cowles's 'A Profane Tragedy: Dante in Hawthorne's "Rappaccini's Daughter"' (*ATQ*); but not only Beatrice, for Cowles suggests that the Comedy's 'three-tiered cosmos' as Hawthorne read it in the Cary translation helped shaped the depiction of the fatal Rappaccini garden. And in an article which deserves some kind of award for the unwinsomeness of its title, 'Hawthorne's Beatrice Rappaccini: Unlocking Her Paradoxical Nature with a Shelleyian Key' (*CLAJ*), Martin F. Kearney returns us to the parallel between Shelley's Beatrice and Beatrice Rappaccini as women 'in whom purity and poison hopelessly are intermingled through no fault of [their] own'.

E. Miller Budick's 'The World as Specter: Hawthorne's Historical Art' (*PMLA*) argues not so much for a rehistoricization of the stories as for a better appreciation of how Hawthorne *imagines* history in them – and in 'Young Goodman Brown' in particular – as forms of 'spectral' or dream history. In 'Hawthorne's Portraits' (*PLL*), a review-article of Rita Gollin's *Portraits of*

---

72. In *Forms of the Fantastic: Selected Essays from the Third International Conference on the Fantastic in Literature and Film*, ed. by Jan Hokenson and Howard Pearce. Greenwood. pp. xiv + 262. $45.

Nathaniel Hawthorne (1983), Joseph Kestner enumerates both the literal portraits available of Hawthorne and those to which he alludes in his fiction. He then moves on, more tellingly, to the issue of portraiture itself as a major ingredient in Hawthorne's story-telling. Dana Brand in 'The Panoramic Spectator in America: A Re-reading of Hawthorne's Sketches' (*ATQ*) begins from 'Sights from a Steeple' and links it and the seemingly minor sketch 'Main Street' to the *flâneur* tradition, that which Walter Benjamin called 'panorama literature'. Brand astutely then extends the implications of this notion to the longer romances, *The Blithedale Romance* most especially. Hawthorne's steeple sketch also engages Jeffrey H. Richards in 'Hawthorne's Posturing Observer: The Case of "Sights from a Steeple"' (*ATQ*), more, however, as an early display of authorial ambiguity and role-playing than as intended panorama.

Allienne R. Becker's '"Alice Doane's Appeal": A Literary Double of Hoffman's *Die Elixiere des Teufels*' (*CLS*) speculates that Hawthorne may well have read the Hoffman story in *Blackwood's* and consciously or otherwise incorporated its themes of murder and incest into his own. Steven Youra in '"The Fatal Hand": A Sign of Confusion in Hawthorne's "The Birthmark"' (*ATQ*) hypothesizes that Hawthorne wittingly or not 'confuses' the hand on Georgiana's face with Aylmer's own hand, angel and devil so rendered inextricable – with all the attendant difficulties of interpretation for the reader. In a half-page note, William V. David in 'Hawthorne's "The Minister's Black Veil": A Note on the Significance of the Subtitle' (*SSF*) sees Mr Hopper not, as often alleged, as 'one of Hawthorne's arch villains' but as a self-appointed 'living parable' of the omnipresence of sin – which rather misses Hawthorne's more fundamental point. Martin K. Doudna interestingly highlights one of the easily overlooked stories in Hawthorne's *Wonder Book for Girls and Boys* – 'The Paradise of Children' – in his 'Hawthorne's Pandora, Milton's Eve, and the Fortunate Fall' (*ESQ*), arguing that it should be read as the author's way of introducing young readers to the Christian notion of the *felix culpa*.

Finally two articles on 'Young Goodman Brown': Bill Christophersen in '"Young Goodman Brown" as Historical Allegory: A Lexical Link' (*SSF*) sees this best-known of Hawthorne stories as a variation of the Pilgrim 'Errand into the Wilderness', taking Brown's forest-journey as emblematic of the Puritan American journey-at-large; and Patrick W. Shaw in 'Checking Out Faith and Lust: Hawthorne's "Young Goodman Brown" and Updike's "A & P"' (*SSF*) compares the eroticism (and New England locale) of the two stories, discerning in Hawthorne's night fantasy a likely analogue for Updike's touching sixties-style tale of adolescent errantry. And Hawthorne's consequential wife Sophia gets a further recognition in Edwin Haviland Miller's 'A Calendar of the Letters of Sophia Peabody Hawthorne' (*SAR*), a listing of her 'almost 1,500 extant letters' with an accompanying brief introduction and index of correspondents.

The Northwestern–Newberry *The Writings of Herman Melville* has now issued Vol. IX, *The Piazza Tales and Other Prose Pieces 1839–1860*[73]. It has

73. *The Writings of Herman Melville*. Vol. IX: *The Piazza Tales and Other Prose Pieces 1839–1860*, ed. by Harrison Hayford and Hershel Parker. Northwestern. pp. 700. $82.95.

been a long time aborning (as Merton Sealts's Historical Note for 1981–2 bears witness), but is necessary and of major import. Not only does this volume make the entire range of the Piazza and other 1850s short fiction available in definitive texts, but also Melville's early reviews, his sequence of spoofs, 'Authentic Anecdotes of '"Old Zack"'', and his reconstructed three lectures delivered a number of times over between 1857 and 1858. A timely scholarly accompaniment to the ongoing Northwestern–Newberry texts has been edited and organized by John Bryant in the form of *A Companion to Melville Studies*[74], a substantive twenty-five critiques and essay-reviews set out in five sections: 'Melville's World' (the latest state of knowledge as to the biography, his travels, his connection to 'the Duyckinck crowd'); 'Melville's Work' (the entire *œuvre* from *Typee* through to *Billy Budd*); 'Melville's Thought' (with an especially distinguished essay by Milton Stern on 'Melville, Society and Language'); 'Melville's Art' (his 'ontological heroics', comedy, and aesthetics); and 'Melville: His Mark' (G. Thomas Tanselle on 'bibliographical' Melville). A number of seasoned Melvilleians contribute, among the best Walter E. Bezanson (on *Moby-Dick*), Vincent Kenney (on *Clarel*), and Kingsley Widmer (on 'Melville and the Myths of Modernism'). The volume overall reflects the state of American Melville studies to date; it amounts to an utterly professional, substantial collaboration. William B. Dillingham's *Melville's Later Novels*[75] completes his trilogy of critical interpretation of Melville – the predecessors being *An Artist in the Rigging* (*YW* 53.423–4) and *Melville's Short Fiction, 1853–1856* (*YW* 58.443–4) – and represents a continuance of his resolve to confirm Melville's 'central subject' to be 'survival through self-knowledge'. Dillingham's thesis is well taken, but he tends at times to allow too insistent an emphasis on theme to get in the way of a sufficiently due or exacting regard for the tactics of Melville's telling, his play of viewpoint, voice, and tone. *Herman Melville*[76], a ChelseaH MCV collection and edited as usual by Harold Bloom, reprints a selection of (by now) fairly vintage Melville criticism – notably by Charles Olson (from *Call Me Ishmael*), Newton Arvin (from *Herman Melville*), R. W. B. Lewis (from *Trials of the Word*), Robert Penn Warren (on Melville's poetry), and Michael Paul Rogin (from *Subversive Genealogy*). Oddly, the essays appear out of order with the chronology of Melville's publications.

Early Melville comes under reconsideration in Stephen de Paul's 'The Documentary Fiction of Melville's *Omoo*: The Crossed Grammars of Acculturation' (*Criticism*), which views *Omoo* as 'a loose and open kind of literary text' that projects its narrator as a *bricoleur* or indeterminate self-in-flux set down in a Tahiti itself neither wholly Tahitian nor wholly European-ized. In 'Spenser and the Structure of *Mardi*' (*SNNTS*) Carole Moses suggests that Melville's borrowings from *The Faerie Queene* extend well beyond mere embellishment: Melville imitated the very structure of Spenser's poem or did so at least as far as can be inferred from *Mardi*'s notoriously circular 'Voyage Thither'. Brian Saunders's 'Facing the Fire at Home: Redburn's

74. *A Companion to Melville Studies*, ed. by John Bryant. Greenwood. pp. xviii + 906. $85.

75. *Melville's Later Novels*, by William B. Dillingham. UGeo. pp. xii + 430. $30.

76. *Herman Melville: Modern Critical Views*, ed. by Harold Bloom. ChelseaH. pp. x + 250. $19.95.

"Inland Imagination"' (*SNNTS*, 1985), an exercise in extrapolation much influenced by Michael Paul Rogin's *Subversive Genealogy* (1983), sees *Redburn* as revealing far more of Melville's own private neuroses and history than previously recognized. For Neal Tolchin, also, in 'The Social Construction of *Redburn*'s "Mourning Pilgrimage"' (*SNNTS*), Melville's fourth novel articulates deeply bruised feelings of loss and anger at his father Allan Melville's death in 1832. To his credit, Tolchin deftly avoids many of the usual reductions of psychobiography, mainly by keeping his eye firmly on the novel's undoubted imagery of lost or unresponsive paternity. Susan Vanzanten Gallagher, in 'Jack Blunt and His Dream Book' (*AL*), suggests that a likely overlooked model for the dream book was *Napoleon's Book of Fate*, popularly available in the 1830s, and a possibility hinted at in Blunt's own reference to his 'Bonaparte Dream Book'.

Maria Ujhazy's *Herman Melville's World of Whaling*[77], a busily annotative Hungarian study of Melville's literal and figurative uses of whaling with *Moby-Dick* at its centre, has been to hand for some time. A perfectly valiant effort, it does not always show itself clear as to its own argument however. Kerry McSweeney's *'Moby-Dick': Ishmael's Mighty Book*[78] does another kind of recapitulatory job; it offers exegesis respectable and busy in kind, but along familiar lines. Richard H. Brodhead's *New Essays on 'Moby-Dick'*[79] offers distinctly more to bite on – notably Brodhead himself on *Moby-Dick*'s resistance to any single official or mastering interpretation, Lawrence Buell on *Moby-Dick* as a species of Protestant scripture or Book of Revelation, Carolyn Porter on the text's purposive, riddling 'double-talk', and Bryan Wolf on pictorialism and the sublime in *Moby-Dick*. Harold Bloom's *Melville's 'Moby-Dick'*[80] offers reprints as usual: Charles Olson, Henry A. Murray, David Simpson, and Bert Bender among them, these being 'the most useful criticism available' in Bloom's estimate. In 'Behind Closed Doors: Ishmael's Dream and Hypnogogic Trances in *Moby-Dick*' (*ATQ*) Harold Hellenbrand explores the analogy between whaling and writing, seeing Ahab as Melville's figure of the would-be articulator of all the world. Gayle L. Smith in '*Moby-Dick* and the Limits of the Language' (*ESQ*) sees Melville's frequent double negations and 'negated verbs and nouns' as evidence of his writerly frustration with words, his determined but inevitably unachievable ambition to make sign and signal always perfectly cohere.

Pierre, unsurprisingly given its love story, comes in for a 'gender' reading in Nicholas Canaday's 'Pierre in the Domestic Circle' (*SNNTS*): the 'arrested sexuality' of the hero prevents his success either as a lover of Isabel or Lucy and his success as a writer; a mother-fixated son unable to achieve adult masculinity. Of the stories 'Benito Cereno' continues to attract most interest. Gloria Horsley-Meacham in 'Melville's Dark Satyr Unmasked' (*ELN*) alleges that the slave-crew are 'disguised Moors' re-assailing an imperial Spain in the

77. *Herman Melville's World of Whaling*, by Maria Ujhazy. AK (1982). pp. 195. £10.50.

78. *'Moby-Dick': Ishmael's Mighty Book*, by Kerry McSweeney. Twayne. pp. xii + 131. hb $10.50, pb $6.95.

79. *New Essays on 'Moby-Dick'*, ed. by Richard H. Brodhead. CUP. pp. viii + 184. hb £20, pb £6.95.

80. *Herman Melville's 'Moby-Dick': Modern Critical Interpretations*, ed. by Harold Bloom. ChelseaH. pp. viii + 159. $24.95.

person of Benito Cereno himself, a notion too close for critical comfort to Bruce Franklin's long-established arguments in *The Wake of the Gods* (1963). Two far more original historicist readings can be met with in Eric Sundquist's 'Benito Cereno and New World Slavery' (in Bercovitch[10]), which sees the Haitian Slave Revolt as a vital implicit analogue in 'this most troubled and explosive tale of America's antebellum destiny'; and in Charles Swann's '*Benito Cereno*: Melville's De(con)struction of the Southern Reader' (*L&H*), a discussion of the blindness of the Southern slave-holder to the humanity of his property as re-enacted in Delano, Cereno, and the larger imperialist cultures from which they emanate.

Thomas Pribek's 'Melville's Copyists: The "Bar-tenders" of Wall Street' (*PLL*) takes up the lawyer's offer to Bartleby to help him become a bartender and expands upon it as a revealing piece of word-play with links to Nippers, Turkey, and Ginger Nut, and also 'tenders' (and so waiters-on) at the 'bar' of the law as much as the tavern or hostelry. Pribek takes another shot at 'Bartleby' in his 'The "Safe" Man of Wall Street: Characterizing Melville's Language' (*SSF*), again an interpretation which rests upon an alleged play of meaning, this time on 'safe', especially as applied to the lawyer. Melville's ex-Master of Chancery, losing much of his vaunted 'safety' in the encounter with Bartleby becomes 'ultimately capable of some self-doubt and sarcasm', which on my reading at least is to understate the case by a mile. In 'A Cock Fight between Melville and Thoreau' (*SSF*) Joseph Rosenblum speculates, plausibly enough, that the vainglorious cockerel Merrymusk could well represent among other things a Melville pastiche of the Thoreau of *A Week on the Concord and Merrimack Rivers*, a volume Melville is reported to have told Hawthorne it was his firm intention to put under the satirical hammer. John Bryant's 'Allegory and Breakdown in *The Confidence-Man*: Melville's Comedy of Doubt' (*PQ*) looks to the dissolution of fixed meanings for 'author', 'text', and 'reader' in Melville's great Mississippi masquerade, his 'willful creation of and negations of norms [pushing] us beyond authority and certitude into a world of perpetual questioning'. Bryant's line begins well; but his essay needs a more fused sense of where his own considerations are leading him.

At a general level of consideration, Frederick Busch looks to the disappointed, increasingly desperate Melville of the post-1850s, in his lively 'Melville's Mail' (*IowaR*), an analysis of the deeply revealing cluster of allusions to 'undelivered incoming mail (the world's attention) and the outgoing mail (his writing)'. Busch rightly cites to advantage Melville's Agatha correspondence with Hawthorne, 'Bartleby', and the Hunilla story in 'Sketch Eighth' of 'The Encantadas'. Sanford E. Marovitz's 'More Chartless Voyaging: Melville and Adler at Sea' (*SAR*) examines the implications of Melville's meeting with George J. Adler, a Professor of German Literature, on his crossing to England aboard the *Southampton* in October 1849, an encounter which gave Melville the opportunity to talk 'German metaphysics' and prompted an alert Adler to comment aptly on his fellow voyager's 'restless mind'.

Forrest G. Robinson's *In Bad Faith: The Dynamics of Deception in Mark Twain's America*[81] first takes aim at 'idyllic' interpretations of Twain's two

---

81. *In Bad Faith: The Dynamics of Deception in Mark Twain's America*, by Forrest G. Robinson. Harvard. pp. viii + 255. $18.50.

Mississippi novels, *Tom Sawyer* and *Huckleberry Finn*. He insists rather that both hold up to scrutiny the historic 'bad faith' of America in the allied forms of racism and slavery. For Robinson, Twain's catalogues of sheer human damage, violence, and white racial abuse of blacks and Indians suggest that no escape-clause about Huck's 'lighting-out' can alleviate the malaise to hand. Injun Joe and Jim as racial butts, Tom's nightmare encavement, Huck's recurrent bouts of shoreline 'sickness' – these and other forms of trauma speak to, and out of, the St Petersburg and river order of things. 'Something is not right in *Huckleberry Finn*,' Robinson avers, 'and we know it.' 'Not right', that is, in the sense that not even Twain's command of vernacular or great eddies of frontier irony and comedy can be thought assuagement. A dark moral current runs through both books, and that 'darkness' Robinson thinks – rightly – needs restoring to our sense of Twain, his best-known fictions as essentially calls to moral conscience and awakening. For Harold Beaver in his '*Huckleberry Finn*' [82] a book-length study in itself, that 'darkness' co-exists with a redeeming energy and hope. His preface sets the tone. *Huck* remains 'as irresistibly fresh and joyous today as anything committed to words since Homer's *Odyssey*', a claim he sets himself to vindicate with all critical guns blazing. At customary pace, he touches off at the following: the context of ante-bellum Missouri and slavery; the Hannibal world which Twain transposed so affectingly into St Petersburg; the Huck–Tom dualism; 'Huck as writer'; Southwestern story-telling and argot; and Jim as for always the book's figure of accusation and witness. As testimony to why *Huckleberry Finn* has so held the world's attention, Beaver's study does excellent service.

Robert Giddings's *Mark Twain: A Sumptuous Variety* [83], nine fairly eclectic essays, clearly reflects the editor's willingness to let his contributors follow their own line. Nor does the introduction make reference to the essays which follow. But that cavil recorded, there is much of serious interest here. John S. Whitley explores the persistence of the boy in Twain's fiction, writing illuminatingly of Tom Sawyer and a little more predictably of Huckleberry Finn. A. Robert Lee redirects our attention to the 'moral resonance' of *The Adventures of Huckleberry Finn* and in so doing reminds us of the moral intelligence that is at the heart of the novel. A variation on the moral theme is picked up in Eric Mottram's 'A Raft Against Washington: Mark Twain's Criticism of America' where the Twain of social satire and ridicule is cogently described. The editor continues in similar vein in his own essay 'Mark Twain and King Leopold of the Belgians' in which he argues, not altogether persuasively, that *King Leopold's Soliloquy* is an expression, albeit covert, of Twain's distaste for contemporary American Indian policy as well as imperialism in general. The essay by Robert Goldman, 'Mark Twain as Playwright', it might be noted, has a number of errors of fact which might be corrected in a second edition. [G.H.C.]

Richard Lederer's 'Mark Twain and the English Language' (*Verbatim*) pays tribute to Twain's rich quarry of *dicta* to do with the English language, typically his gibe at the use of the first-person plural pronoun – 'Only presidents, editors, and people with tapeworms have the right to use the editorial we'. For Tjebbe Westendorp in '"He backed me into a corner and blockaded me with a

82. '*Huckleberry Finn*', by Harold Beaver. A&U. pp. 192. £18.
83. *Mark Twain: A Sumptuous Variety*, ed. by Robert Giddings. Vision/B&N. pp. 225. £18.95/$27.50.

chair": Strategies of Mark Twain's Literary Campaigns' (*DQR*), a well-intended but unexceptional consideration of hoax and tall-tale in Twain, Twain's 'basic strengths' lie in his 'obsessive love of impersonation'.

Thomas A. Maik's contention in 'The Village in *Tom Sawyer*: Myth and Reality' (*ArQ*) much resembles that of Forrest G. Robinson[81]. St Petersburg is far from some idyllic children's-book sense of place. Rather, Twain deliberately strips away 'the mythology of Eden' to reveal a world of 'lies, smugness, hypocrisy, human cruelty, murder, and greed'. Maik so calls attention to a 'dark' Twain well before that usually associated with the later writings. The Penguin American Library has also issued *The Adventures of Tom Sawyer* with an introduction by John Seelye[84]. Douglas Anderson's 'Reading the Pictures in *Huckleberry Finn*' (*ArQ*) offers a detailed account of how E. W. Kemble's illustrations for the first edition of the novel 'extend and enrich the meaning of Mark Twain's text'. Kemble personifies to perfection the role of the illustrator as 'first reader'; his drawings (several of which are reproduced) providing a crucial guide to how the text initially could be 'envisaged'. For James L. Kastely in 'The Ethics of Self-Interest: Narrative Logic in *Huckleberry Finn*' (*NCF*), the novel pits the 'community' or republic of two of Huck and Jim against the 'community' of the shoreline, the former oddly left in suspension once Huck 'lights out' for the territories ahead. Tim William Machan, on the other hand, in 'The Symbolic Narrative of *Huckleberry Finn*' (*ArQ*) presses for a 'non-literal' version of the book, one full of reductions which all too stalely argues the river as a life-metaphor.

Of Twain's other novels, John Daniel Stahl gives a steadfast account of the father–son typology in his 'American Myth in European Disguise: Fathers and Sons in *The Prince and the Pauper*' (*AL*); A. L. Nielson (*Greyfriar*) interestingly compares the depiction of the mulatto in *Pudd'nhead Wilson*, William Wells Brown's *Clotelle*, and Frank T. Webb's *The Garies and their Friends* (though fellow black authors like Charles Chesnutt and Paul Dunbar are left out); and Forrest G. Robinson astutely unpacks the play of division and contradiction in *Innocents Abroad* in 'Patterns of Consciousness in *The Innocents Abroad*' (*AL*). Mark Twain's warm affection for Jewish tradition and writing is the subject of a whole issue of *MTJ*, a respect symptomatically expressed in Twain's reversal of the usual cliché about Shalom Aleichem being the Jewish Mark Twain by his relish of the prospect of being thought the American Shalom Aleichem. A note in the same issue calls attention to Twain's love for, and affinity with, Horace Bixby, the pilot he so praises in *Life on the Mississippi*. In his 'Mark Twain as Pilot and Writer', Edgar M. Branch sees a fundamental analogy between the craft of piloting as Twain recalls it and the craft of authorship as he later practised it.

In *The Black Heart's Truth: The Early Career of W. D. Howells*[85], John W. Crowley offers 'an elaborately contextual study of *A Modern Instance*', an unabashed effort to read out from this 'best' Howells the story of Howells's breakdown and 'the problematic workings of a neurotic writer's imagination; his black heart's truth'. Good as Howells can sometimes be, one wonders

84. *The Adventures of Tom Sawyer*, by Mark Twain, ed. by John Seelye. Penguin. pp. xxiv + 226. pb £2.50.

85. *The Black Heart's Truth: The Early Career of W. D. Howells*, by John W. Crowley. UNC. pp. 192. $19.95.

why – given the extraordinary inner complexity of the man – he was not always better, but this is not a consideration taken up by Crowley, unfortunately. Edwin H. Cady adds to his previous Howells scholarship with *Young Howells and John Brown*[86], a monograph which begins from Howells's poem 'Old Brown' and traces the impact of John Brown on Howells's own radicalism as 'the image of the martyr of liberty'. Sarah B. Daugherty invokes Tolstoy as an influence on Howells in her study of his lifelong agnosticism in 'Howells, Tolstoy and the Limits of Realism: The Case of *Annie Kilburn*' (*ALR*). Howells as an urban writer, and of New York rather than the Midwest where he grew up or Boston where he first made his literary bow, gives Amy Kaplan her theme in ' "The Knowledge of the Line": Realism and the City in Howells's *A Hazard of New Fortunes*' (*PMLA*), the city as at once a site for the clash of capital and labour but also the 'unreal city' of the ailing relationship between Basil and Isabel March. Success and failure and their moral implications interest C. A. Erickson in 'The Tough- and Tender-Minded: W. D. Howells's *The Landlord at Lion's Head*' (*SNNTS*), an essay which makes helpful reference to the impact of William James on Howells. 'The New Age of Narcissism: The Sexual Politics of *A Modern Instance*' (*Mosaic*) by Sam B. Girgus looks to Howells's interest in 'the new sexual freedom' and divorce. On Girgus's well-founded argument, Howells saw the problem that without divorce marriage could become 'a prison'; yet 'he also realized that a loveless society based on the narcissism of perpetual demand would lock each one of us in a prison of the self'. Girgus opens up an important dialectic in not only *A Modern Instance* but Howells's treatment of sexual relationship elsewhere in his fiction. In 'A Sermon without Exegesis: The Achievement of Stasis in *The Rise of Silas Lapham*' (*JNT*) Fleda Brown Jackson traces the imagery of movement and paralysis in Howell's most acclaimed novel, Lapham's evolution from a figure of action to one of reflection.

Bettina L. Knapp's *Stephen Crane*[87], offers a respectable if procedural account of Crane, a run-through of his life and writing which aspires to a certain dash ('Crane's bold and brash metaphors and epithets hit their marks like bullets') but which rarely catches the serious nuance of Crane. It will pass muster, however, as an introduction, if such still be needed. One of the important features of Lee Clark Mitchell's collection, *New Essays on 'The Red Badge of Courage'*[88], lies in its use of the 'reconstructed' *Red Badge*, the text as offered by Henry Binder (see his landmark '*The Red Badge of Courage* Nobody Knows' in *SNNTS*, 1978), in which a more darkly ironic Crane than that of earlier versions of the novella emerges. Hershel Parker tells the history of this text, Binder's part in it especially, and looks again at the implications for the story's ending. Other essays address issues of context and structure: Andrew Delbanco examines Crane and the mythology of the Civil War; Amy Kaplan situates *The Red Badge* as the very 'paradigm of the modern American war novel'; Howard C. Horsford links Henry Fleming to other personae of young manhood; and Christine Brooke-Rose, ever faithful to Paris structuralism, unpicks the play of oppositions in the text, Crane's way as she sees it of

86. *Young Howells and John Brown: Episodes in a Radical Education*, by Edwin H. Cady. OSU (1985). pp. 116. $17.50.
87. *Stephen Crane*, by Bettina L. Knapp. Ungar. pp. ix + 198. $15.95.
88. *New Essays on 'The Red Badge of Courage'*, ed. by Lee Clark Mitchell. CUP. pp. x + 150. hb £20, pb £6.95.

handling what he calls 'the red sickness of battle'. In a striking but non-literary comparison Rosalie Murphy Brown in 'Alcoholism and Family Abuse in *Maggie* and *The Bluest Eye*' (*Mosaic*) invokes Crane and Toni Morrison as warning voices against the impact of parental drinking on the young, seeing their two stories as exemplary calls-to-attention. Crane as a 'Western' writer, a frontier story-teller, is given an airing by Michael J. Collins in 'Realism and Romance in the Western Stories of Stephen Crane'[89], an examination of the Western motif in 'The Bride Comes to Yellow Sky' and 'The Blue Hotel'. Stanley Wertheim's 'Cora Crane's Thwarted Romance' (*CLC*) amounts to Craneiana; it discusses Crane's wife Cora's love affair with the American journalist and historian Poultney Bigelow.

In 'Loss, Habit, Obsession: The Governing Dynamic of *McTeague*' (*SAF*) Barbara Hochman suggests that the structural sense of Frank Norris's novel lies in 'the problem of personal loss and the implication for the self', a version which seeks – against the general run of interpretation – to challenge too easy a reliance on 'determinism' as Norris's major thematic interest. André Poncet in his 'Procédures de Sémantisation dans la Production du Texte de *McTeague*' (*EA*) studiously delineates the verbal texture of the novel, Norris's 'récurrences lexicales, palimpsestes et collages' as they build into a whole throughout the telling of the story. *The Octopus* as epic narrative is given attention in James L. Machor's 'Epic, Romance and Norris's *Octopus*' (*ALR*) and as sexual-agrarian metaphor in Mark Seltzer's 'The Naturalist Machine'[90]. *The Octopus* has also been issued as a Penguin book[91] with an introduction by Kevin Starr. Robert C. Leitz's '"A Christmas in Transvaal": An Addition to the Norris Canon' (*SAF*) reprints Norris's brief reminiscence with a commentary of his stay in the Boer enclave before he was expelled by the government. Linda A. Dover's 'Frank Norris's "A Man's Woman": The Textual Changes' (*RALS*) sets out Norris's changes and revisions in the composition of the story.

Harold Frederic as local-colour author is explored in Stanton Garner's 'The Other Harold Frederic'[48], a timely endeavour to free him from the customary naturalist label. Two new editions of important Frederic novels have been issued: *The Damnation of Theron Ware, or, Illumination*[92] in Penguin with an introduction by Stanton Garner and *Gloria Mundi*[93] edited by Larry Brawley. In his 'Passion, Authority, and Faith in *The Damnation of Theron Ware*' (*AL*) Fritz Oehlschlaeger links *Ware* to *The Scarlet Letter* as a depiction of 'female sexuality', comparing its impact upon the puritanical and increasingly prurient Ware with Hester Prynne's impact upon Arthur Dimmesdale.

Mary Jane Lupton's 'Women Writers and Death by Drowning'[94] compares the treatment of suicide in Kate Chopin with the 'drownings' in George Eliot's

89. In *Under the Sun: Myth and Realism in Western American Literature*, ed. by Barbara Howard Meldrum. Whitston. pp. vi + 230. $22.50.

90. In *Sex, Politics, and Science in the Nineteenth-Century Novel*, ed. by Ruth Bernard Yeazell. JHU. pp. xiv + 195. $10.

91. *The Octopus*, by Frank Norris, ed. by Kevin Starr. Penguin. pp. xxxiv + 656. pb £4.95.

92. *The Damnation of Theron Ware, or, Illumination*, by Harold Frederic, ed. by Stanton Garner. UNeb. pp. x + 506. $25.

93. *Gloria Mundi*, by Harold Frederic, ed. by Larry Brawley. UNeb. pp. 481. $30.

94. In *Amid Visions and Revisions: Poetry and Criticism on Literature and the Arts*, ed. by Burney J. Hollis. MorganS. pp. xiv + 150. $10.

The Mill on the Floss and Sylvia Plath's *The Bell Jar*, offering a strongly feminist critique. In 'The Female Artist in Kate Chopin's *The Awakening*: Birth and Creativity' (*WS*) Carole Stone argues that the novella's impact lies not simply in its recognition of 'sexual pleasures outside marriage' but in its questioning of 'the assumptions that childbirth and child care are a woman's principal vocation'. Charlotte Gilman, too, attracts two strong feminist readings. In 'Monumental Feminism and Literature's Ancestral House: Another Look at "The Yellow Wallpaper"' (*WS*) Janice Haney-Peritz seeks to establish that the story's 'feminist thrust' lies in the narrator's signalling of her own confinement within marriage and patriarchy. Christopher P. Wilson's 'Charlotte Perkins Gilman's Steady Burghers: The Terrain of *Herland*' (*WS*) analyses gender-roles in Gilman's 'Utopian Romance', the interplay of masculine and feminine social styles as constructed in the novel.

The Sarah Orne Jewett holdings at the University of Florida are listed in 'A Descriptive Catalogue of the Sarah Orne Jewett Collection' in *The Parkman Dexter Howe Library*, Part 3[95], of relevance to anyone with a scholarly interest in her manuscripts. *CLQ* devotes a special issue to Jewett which includes essays on violence in 'A White Heron' (Elizabeth Ammons), apple symbolism in *A Country Doctor* (Josephine Donovan), Jewett's correspondence with Lillian M. Munger (Marti Hohmann), Jewett's female characters (Marilyn E. Mobley), the image of the New England garden in Jewett's fiction (Gwen L. Nagel), the source of Mrs Todd in *Pointed Firs* (Sara W. Sherman), and 'initiation' in Jewett and Emily Dickinson (Carol J. Singley) – all papers from a Jewett conference held at Westbrook, Maine. In 'Silence or Capitulation: Prepatriarchal "Mothers' Gardens" in Jewett and Freeman' (*SSF*) Josephine Donovan compares 'A White Heron' with Mary E. Wilkins Freeman's 'Evelina's Garden' as fables of female sanctuary intruded upon by 'patriarchal' outsiders, a self-proclaimed 'gynocritical' reading of the two stories.

The undoubted Henry James highlight of the year has to be the publication of *The Complete Notebooks of Henry James*[96], under the joint editorship of Leon Edel and Lyall H. Powers, which adds to and now supplants the Matthiessen–Murdock edition of the *Notebooks* originally issued in 1947. In all, over 20,000 words of new James notes, jottings, and observations are made available, including his series of so-called Pocket Diaries, a mix of appointments and brief self-reminders for stories. Of especial interest, alongside the projects for plays, full-length novels, and his several deathbed dictations, is the unfinished story 'Hugh Merrow', a piece most likely composed during 1898–1900. If ever a guide to James's own House of Fiction were needed, it would be found here, in material which represents the very engine-room of his creative thinking and achievement. The *Notebooks* in this format stand as a scholarly asset, a model of meticulous and loving custodianship.

Adeline R. Tintner's *The Museum World of Henry James*[97], to which Edel contributes a warmly approving preface, brings a trained art-historian's eye to bear on James's fiction, demonstrating an informed familiarity with the actual

95. *The Parkman Dexter Howe Library*, Part 3, ed. by Sidney Ives. UFlor.

96. *The Complete Notebooks of Henry James*, ed. by Leon Edel and Lyall H. Powers. OUP. pp. xxix + 633. £25.

97. *The Museum World of Henry James*, by Adeline R. Tintner. UMI. pp. xxvii + 390. $49.95.

canvases, sculptures, museums, and galleries which recur as reference points in the story-telling and which give an actuality to his use of visual consciousness. No excursions here into 'the other', or *le regard*, or the competing pheno-menologies of perception. Tintner gives each allusion straight, whether to a Doré, Raphael, Andrea del Sarto, Holbein, or Expressionist, together with reproductions of the plate or painting actually alluded to in the text. Matching, as she says 'James's private museum' to those he relished like the Metropolitan, the British Museum, the Louvre, or the Vatican, and in which his *habitué*'s eye found such essential nourishment, her study imports a rare stratum of specificity into the discussion of his fiction.

John Auchard begins his *Silence in Henry James*[98] by citing a review James wrote of the Carlyle–Emerson correspondence in 1883, in which the novelist's attention was drawn to Carlyle's own summary of his work as 'the gospel of silence, in thirty volumes'. He argues that for James, too, silence – words withheld, feelings unarticulated or inarticulable, equally obtained, as for instance in the case of the dying Milly Theale or of Kate Croy and Merton Densher. Auchard writes with considerable verve, even if at times he edges towards the exquisite. James's 'blest nouvelle' gets fresh scrutiny in *The Nouvelle of Henry James in Theory and Practice*[99], a study which touches all the right bases in the Prefaces and key novellas like 'Daisy Miller' and 'The Birthplace'. But it does so largely without alighting on any notable new insights, or even, it would seem, without great passion for the fiction to hand. Nor do two other full-length James studies exactly set the blood racing. Donna Przybylowicz's *Desire and Repression: The Dialectic of Self and Other in the Late Works of Henry James*[100] subjects James to the full Barthesian–Derridean formulae, treating 'desire' and its workings as a major imaginative fulcrum in late James with critical argot to match. For her part, Marianna Torgovnick in *The Visual Arts, Pictorialism, and the Novel: James, Lawrence and Woolf*[101] compares her three authors' modes of picturing as ways of dramatizing human perception, the 'seeing' consciousness as it were. Nicola Bradbury's *An Annotated Critical Bibliography of Henry James*[102] lives up to its title, providing a selective run of annotations of James studies.

'It is difficult to imagine Henry James in relation to any kind of politics' observes Darshan Singh Maini in 'The Politics of Henry James' (*HJR*). Indeed so, or at least indeed so at first glance; but Maini makes a good case that political consciousness of a sort does play a part in the fiction, sexual politics in the instance of the Olive Chancellor–Basil Ransom tension in *The Bostonians* and the politics of radicalism in *The Princess Casamassima*. Maini rounds out his essay with an approving reference to Irving Howe on James's 'comely Conservatism'. Alfred Habegger in 'Henry James's Rewriting of Minny

98. *Silence in Henry James*, by John Auchard. PSU. pp. 182. $20.

99. *The Nouvelle of Henry James in Theory and Practice*, by Lauren T. Cowdery. UMI. pp. 136. $39.95.

100. *Desire and Repression: The Dialectic of Self and Other in the Late Works of Henry James*, by Donna Przybylowicz. UAla. pp. 358. $36.95.

101. *The Visual Arts, Pictorialism, and the Novel: James, Lawrence and Woolf*, by Marianna Torgovnick. Princeton. pp. 275. $26.50.

102. *An Annotated Critical Bibliography of Henry James*, by Nicola Bradbury. Harvester. pp. viii + 142. £20.

Temple's Letters' (*AL*) uses James's restyling of many of his cousin's letters (Minny who 'had a greater effect on his creative life than any other woman') to probe the implications of his 'elegiac protectiveness' towards her. Habegger gives thirteen pages of the originals with James's versions alongside, examples of how, as he says, James transformed 'female life – into art'; and an indication, too, of how his later fiction would portray Minnie under an array of imaginative disguises. William Veeder's 'Image as Argument: Henry James and the Style of Criticism' (*HJR*) pursues the imagistic textures of James's critical writing, which are as much a feature there as in the fiction itself. The essays, Prefaces, and Notebooks, thereby, become art-forms in their own right, part of an overall Jamesian act of *écriture*.

James as 'conservative humanist' is compared with a line of Catholic writers which includes Evelyn Waugh and Flannery O'Connor in Joseph Hynes's 'The Fading Figure in the Worn Carpet' (*ArQ*), a return to the issue of moral serious-ness as a condition of his fiction. *ArQ* also contains 'Monsters, Bagmen, and Little Old Ladies: Henry James and the Unmaking of America' by Annette Larson Benert, an account of *The American Scene* which surmises that the reason James 'as an artist, as a social being . . . could not live in America' had to do with its sell-out, as he saw it, to a drab, enervating commercial ethic.

The year appears to have seen some slight ebb in the criticism directed at the full-length novels. Christina Light as 'complexity and mystery' elicits the attention of Ronald Emerick in 'The Love Rectangle of *Roderick Hudson*: Another look at Christina Light' (*SNNTS*), a well-taken deciphering of the novel in which Rowland Mallet egotistically never recognizes (and as a consequence never requites) Christina's love for him. Alfred Habegger has a second James piece in which he delineates the assumedly fraught terrain of the older man–younger woman relationship in 'Precocious Incest: First Novels by Louisa May Alcott and Henry James' (*MR*), a comparison of *Watch and Ward* with Alcott's *Moods*. Dorothy Berkson re-opens an old issue in her 'Why Does She Marry Osmond? The Education of Isabel Archer' (*ATQ*), contending that under the terms of the *Bildungsroman*, which she takes James to have been following, Isabel must act true to her initial idealism even at the expense of her deadly marriage to Osmond. Isabel as a commodity, caught up at least in 'the structure of consciousness engendered by monopoly capitalism', constitutes the thesis of Michael L. Gilmore's 'The Commodity World of *The Portrait of a Lady*' (*NEQ*), a heavily programmatic Marxist reading of the text.

Millicent Bell takes up sexuality and the establishing of a self-created social identity by women in her 'The Bostonian Story' (*PR*), a critique which makes productive use of the film version of *The Bostonians*. Warren Johnson looks to the competing characterological and moral claims of Hyacinth and the Princess in '*Hyacinth Robinson* or *The Princess Casamassima*?' (*TSLL*), an attempt to establish just where the imaginative balance of interests in the novel can fairly be said to reside. Christopher Brown's 'The Rhetoric of Closure in *What Maisie Knew*' (*Style*) shows how 'open' a novel James wrote in *Maisie*, not least through the text's indirections and deliberate obliquenesses. David Seed tackles the 'gap between the narrator's artistic consciousness and the awareness of the other guests at Newmarch' in his 'Completing the Picture: Deduction and Creation in Henry James's *The Sacred Fount*' (*EA*), a shrewd, attentive analysis of 'this notoriously puzzling novel'. Seed's way of opening the different and competing forms of consciousness in *The Sacred Fount* makes good sense, especially as he moves out from a concern with plot to James's overall preoccupation with how the human imagination 'edits' and orders reality.

Penguin have added a new edition of *The Wings of the Dove* to their list with a predictably challenging introduction by John Bayley (and notes by Patricia Crick). For Michael Moon in 'Sexuality and Visual Terrorism in *The Wings of the Dove*' (*Criticism*) the novel yields a portrait of 'phallic power', with Kate Croy as male to Merton Densher's female and Millie anything but the 'passive and manipulated' icon – rather as much as anyone an adept in 'the psycho-sexual power games that characterize life in her milieu'. Moon certainly puts a challenge to the received version of the novel. Elissa Greenwald in '"I and the Abyss": Transcendental Romance in *The Wings of the Dove*' (*SNNTS*) proposes a parallel between *Wings* and Hawthorne's *The Marble Faun*, both engaging in 'non-realistic mode(s) of representation' and both using the dove and other allusions in common as organizing imagery. Derridean theory once again comes into play in Julie Rivkin's 'The Logic of Delegation in *The Ambassadors*' (*PMLA*). She links Strether's final renunciation to the Derridean concept of 'supplementation' – as an instrument of another he can continue his 'infinite ambassadorship' to experience indefinitely. Joseph A. Boone's 'Modernist Maneuverings in the Marriage Plot: Breaking Ideologies of Gender and Genre in James's *The Golden Bowl*' (*PMLA*) suggests that in exploding the 'happy marriage' ending of Victorian fiction James does so by at the same time breaking the 'code' of fictional realism, theme and form so deployed to mutually supporting ends.

Of the shorter fiction, Ron Childress offers a brief if inconclusive annotation of the pattern of references to fear in 'James's *Daisy Miller*' (*Expl*). At greater length Leland S. Person ponders the analogy between the narrator's failure to 'possess' the papers of Jeffrey Aspern and his own failure to 'possess' Tina in 'Eroticism and Creativity in *The Aspern Papers*' (*L&P*), a determinedly Freudian interpretation. James W. Gargano's 'Imagery as Action in "The Beast in the Jungle"' (*ArQ*) takes up James's own phrase for the story as 'a great negative adventure' and pursues the imagery of burial, denial, and death which runs throughout. 'The only climactic image' of the story, thereby, becomes 'the beast itself'. 'The beast', however, for Eve Kosofsky Sedgwick in 'The Beast in the Closet: James and the Writing of Homosexual Panic'[90], amounts to that old James familiar, homoeroticism, Marcher as a man fearful of, indeed paralysed by, the prospect of heterosexual love, and a Jamesian surrogate *par excellence*. As with Adeline Tintner's other recent essays on James's pictorial interests, her 'Hogarth's *Marriage à la Mode* and Henry James's "A London Life"' (*JPRS*) is largely incorporated into *The Museum World of Henry James*[97]. 'Refurbishing James's "A Light Man"' (*ArQ*) by W. R. Martin and Warren U. Ober offers as a source for its narrator Maximus Austin none other than St Augustine, the *Confessions* as a departure point both for the imagery and plot-structure of the story.

Gerald E. Myers's *William James: His Life and Thought*[103] may well become one of the standard works on 'the other James'. It offers a rich, splendidly elucidatory study of nearly six hundred pages which sets out both the life and contours of William James's intellectual interests with greatest distinction. As a

103. *William James: His Life and Thought*, by Gerald E. Myers. Yale. pp. 672. $35.

guide to James as thinker, psychologist, and philosophic pragmatist this will take some bettering. For Frank Lentricchia in 'On the Ideologies of Poetic Modernism, 1890–1913: The Example of William James' (Bercovitch[10]), whether William James is a 'maverick thinker' or not he serves precisely in proportion to how he gave the lie to any one defining 'modernism'. Essentially he bequeathed an 'urgent plea for the recognition of irreducible plurality', an insistence that our 'modern' humanness inheres in selves and their creativity unexplained and so unlevelled by any one programme.

American Literature: The Twentieth Century

DAVID SEED and IAN F. A. BELL

This chapter has the following sections: 1. General; 2. Poetry: (a) General, (b) Individual Authors; 3. Fiction; 4. Non-Fictional Prose; 5. Drama: (a) General, (b) Individual Authors. Sections 1, 3, and 4 are by David Seed, and sections 2 and 5 are by Ian Bell.

1. General

J. Albert-Robbins has edited the volume of *AmLS* which covers 1984. This follows the pattern of previous volumes in layout and thoroughness. Three points should be noted here. Firstly the personnel has changed slightly so that Philip F. Gura, Brian Higgins, and Michael S. Reynolds have taken over the respective chapters on Transcendentalism, Melville, and Hemingway and Fitzgerald. Secondly in Jerome Klinkowitz's admirable coverage of contemporary fiction the 1950s have been shifted into the preceding chapter which is a logical change in view of the surge of experimentalism in the 1960s. Finally, in contrast with the 1983 volume, six substantial sections have been included on foreign criticism from Japan, Eastern Europe, etc. The regular bibliographies in *AL*, *SoR*, and other periodicals have also been noted in the compilation of this chapter. Of equally general reference is Jack Salzman's new handbook of American literature[1] which contains seven hundred and fifty concise entries on authors, texts, etc. Salzman stresses that the book's emphasis is firmly literary but he also includes important periodicals, historians (e.g. Jefferson), and utopian communities like Fruitlands. He has covered a considerable number of contemporary writers (such as Maya Angelou) but on the other hand has omitted a number of twentieth-century authors who are currently enjoying a revival. Chronological tables and select bibliographies help to make this handbook a very useful guide to its field.

As usual DLB has issued a number of important new volumes. Priority must be given to a three-part series on American poets from 1880 to 1945 edited by Peter Quartermain, who sees the period as unified by a common perception of a fragmented world. Forty-four poets are covered in the first series[2] where predictably pride of place is given to major figures like Pound, Eliot, and

---

1. *The Cambridge Handbook of American Literature*, by Jack Salzman. CUP. pp. 286. £15.
2. *American Poets, 1880–1945: First Series*, ed. by Peter Quartermain. DLB. Gale. pp. xxii + 490. $88.

Conrad Aiken; but also to writers like H.D. and Charles Reznikoff whose works have been steadily gaining stature since the 1960s. The rest of the volume comprises either minor poets such as John Peale Bishop or Maxwell Bodenheim, or writers more famous in other fields like the critics Van Wyck Brooks and S. Foster Damon. The second series[3] covers roughly the same number of poets among which the main figures are now cummings, Crane, and Berryman. Quartermain has usefully included entries on minor expatriates like Caresse and Harry Crosby, as well as on the novelists Kay Boyle and May Sarton. The current productivity of the latter two writers suggests that Quartermain's dates should not be read as hard and fast limits; and there is also a certain amount of overlap with other volumes in the series so that Kenneth Patchen appears both here and in Ann Charters's *The Beats* (*YW* 64.503). The third series[4] completes this survey and gives prominence to Robert Frost (Donald J. Greiner gives a valuable account of Frost's prosodic experiments), Amy Lowell the promoter and publicist of Imagism, and Wallace Stevens whose debt to the French Symbolists is examined in some detail. The most substantial coverage of all is reserved for William Carlos Williams where an impressively thorough entry discusses the influences of Whitman and contemporary painting, etc. One recurring theme in these volumes is the importance of expatriation and another is the efforts by many poets (Sandburg, Masters, and others) to break away from European models and strengthen a tradition using native American materials. An excellent appendix reproduces the contents pages and – even more valuable – the introductions and forewords from the key anthologies of the period.

Equally important is the continuing series of volumes on Afro-American writers being edited by Trudier Harris. The volume covering the period before the Harlem Renaissance (co-edited by Thadious M. Davis)[5] traces the origins of this tradition in the eighteenth century with Jupiter Hammon's inspirational poems and addresses. But the first real flourishing takes place at the end of the next century, in years which saw the beginning of dialect poetry and independent publishing outlets. One excellence in this volume is that many writers have been rescued from an obscurity sadly underlined even by an uncertainty about their dates. Abolitionist writers like Frederick Douglass are included and a particularly full entry is rightly devoted to the astonishingly productive W. E. B. DuBois who was active from the 1890s right up to his death in 1963. To give the reader a flavour of the raw materials consulted, the appendixes supply excerpts form the Port Royal diaries of Charlotte Forten and documents by the journalist John Edward Bruce. The next volume takes us from the Harlem Renaissance up to 1940[6] and covers a much broader range of known writers such as Claude McKay, Jean Toomer, and Zora Neale Hurston whose works are currently enjoying a revival. Harris is careful not to exaggerate

---

3. *American Poets, 1880–1945: Second Series*, ed. by Peter Quartermain. DLB. Gale. pp. xxi + 510. $88.

4. *American Poets, 1880–1945: Third Series*, ed. by Peter Quartermain. 2 vols. DLB. Gale. pp. xxi + 734. $180.

5. *Afro-American Writers Before the Harlem Renaissance*, ed. by Trudier Harris and Thadious M. Davis. DLB. Gale. pp. xvi + 369. $88.

6. *Afro-American Writers from the Harlem Renaissance to 1940*, ed. by Trudier Harris. DLB. Gale. pp. xvi + 386. $90.

Harlem's importance as a cultural centre, so attention is also drawn to Washington and Chicago. Finally Carl Van Vechten has been included as a tribute to his promotion of Afro-American writing. Two other volumes of DLB should be mentioned. Randall Clark has edited a second series of American screenwriters[7], sixty-three figures ranging from S. N. Behrman (a script-writer for Garbo) to Woody Allen. Also represented are *émigrés* like Walter Reisch and the Hungarian playwright Ernest Vajda, and – even more important in this context – figures known mainly as writers, such as S. J. Perelman and William Faulkner. Also on the margin of American literature is Peter Dzwonkoski's survey of almost two hundred American publishing houses[8]. Naturally the giants are prominent (Viking, Random House, etc.), but it is particularly welcome to have the histories of presses which pioneered experimental literature (New Directions, Grove Press, City Lights) and also to see a selection of small presses represented. Thus we have entries on Upton Sinclair's Sinclair Press as well as more recent concerns like the Ecco and North Point Presses. The entries usefully outline developments within the companies and indicate the main editors; and separate mention is given to the Modern Library imprint and to the Federal Writers' Project from the 1930s. All the above volumes follow the standard DLB format of including bibliographies and copious illustrations where appropriate.

From the same press come two volumes in the Contemporary Authors Bibliographical Series. James J. Martine has edited a collection of entries on ten novelists[9] including Baldwin, Heller, and Mailer. Inevitably questions arise about this severe selectivity. Can Eudora Welty be included and not Thomas Pynchon? A standard pattern is followed in each entry whereby selective primary and secondary bibliographies precede an essay summarizing the criticism on these writers. The second volume on poets edited by Ronald Baughman[10] has the strengths and weaknesses of the first. It covers eleven poets, mostly central figures like Lowell, Berryman, or Roethke; but does not represent the Beats, the New York School, or San Francisco writers. The essays are the most valuable part of this series in giving such clear and concise summaries of the current critical standing of such complex writers as Charles Olson. A different kind of undertaking has been tackled by Larry McCaffery whose 'bio-bibliographical' guide to postmodernism[11] considers Latin America and Europe but concentrates overwhelmingly on the United States. In the first part of this volume a number of survey-articles examine the origins of postmodernism, which McCaffery sees as hostile to mimesis. Nevertheless categories are still admitted which are called 'magical realism' (Lori Chamberlain) or 'experimental realism' (Jerome Klinkowitz). Also of particular note are essays by John Hellman on postmodern journalism (which revolves around a 'direct confrontation of fact with form') and by Ron Silliman

7. *American Screenwriters: Second Series*, ed. by Randall Clark. DLB. Gale. pp. xii + 464. $88.

8. *American Literary Publishing Houses, 1900–1980: Trade and Paperback*, ed. by Peter Dzwonkoski. DLB. Gale. pp. xx + 465. $88.

9. *American Novelists*, ed. by James J. Martine. CABS. Gale. pp. xviii + 431. $48.

10. *American Poets*, ed. by Ronald Baughman. CABS. Gale. pp. xvi + 387. $48.

11. *Postmodern Fiction: A Bio-Bibliographical Guide*, ed. by Larry McCaffery. Greenwood. pp. xxviii + 604. £68.50.

on the new prose poem. The second part of this volume alphabetically lists postmodern authors and critics, giving biographical summaries and brief accounts of their work. This guide supplies an absolutely indispensable overview of contemporary experimental writing in America.

Among the year's other reference works Archibald Hanna has assembled a bibliography of American social fiction from 1901 to 1950[12] which includes collections of short stories and sketches as well as novels. With virtually 4,000 entries Hanna supplies a brief indication of content and a useful thematic index. He also cross-refers most items to citations in the standard bibliographies of modern American fiction. As a matter of editorial policy he excludes westerns and detective stories, the latter because they have 'few social implications'. Recent scholarship in the genre completely refutes this assertion, but Hanna anyway has more than enough material to cope with in his chosen area. A more specialized work is Mary Lee Morris's bibliography of South-western fiction for the years 1960–80[13] which saw the publication of some five hundred works. These are listed according to author and then categorized according to their theme, chronology, and genre. Frances F. Povsic has compiled a bibliography of children's literature in which Eastern Europe figures[14]. Her volume is broken into seven geographical areas (Albania, Bulgaria, Czechoslovakia, Hungary, Poland, Romania, and Yugoslavia). All items listed are American editions with a brief indication of content and, although most works (autobiographies and fiction) deal directly with Europe, an important number concern emigrants to America and their problems with adjusting to the New World. This bibliography then will be particularly useful for studying ethnic areas of American Literature. A. LaVonne Brown Ruoff (*ASInt*) has produced an excellent bibliographical essay on American Indian literature which draws initial distinctions between traditional oral forms and then surveys the written literature. In the latter area the 1960s marked the beginning of a new surge in production. Criticism and biographies are surveyed next and the article concludes with alphabetical lists of primary and secondary material. A. Robert Lee (*DUJ*) has given a useful and thoroughly documented summary of developments in Afro-American writing from its beginnings up to the Harlem Renaissance and the Second World War. Finally Robert A. Baker and Michael T. Nietzel have compiled a survey of American detective fiction[15] which reads rather like a discursive bibliography. They begin with founders of the genre like Chandler and Hammett, and come right up to date with such contemporaries as Stanley Ellin and the humorist Leo Rosten. In each case they give a biographical summary and details of collaborations, film adaptations, pseudonyms, etc. Apart from an interesting introductory essay where Baker and Nietzel note the recoil from fictional gentility, the method of their volume prevents it from being particularly analytical and it is an annoying mannerism

12. *A Mirror for the Nation: An Annotated Bibliography of American Social Fiction, 1901–1950*, by Archibald Hanna. Garland. pp. xiv + 472. $67.

13. *Southwestern Fiction, 1960–1980: A Classified Bibliography*, by Mary Lee Morris. UNM. pp. xiii + 101. pb $9.95.

· 14. *Eastern Europe in Children's Literature*, by Frances F. Povsic. Greenwood. pp. xxvi + 200. £32.50.

15. *Private Eyes: One Hundred and One Knights: A Survey of American Detective Fiction, 1922–1984*, by Robert A. Baker and Michael T. Nietzel. BGUP (1985). pp. 385. hb $29.95, pb $17.95.

repeatedly refer to the private eyes as 'knights' although the chivalric analogy is only occasionally relevant.

The main anthology to be published this year is the second shorter edition of the *Norton Anthology of American Literature*[16]. The selection has been revised in four main areas: early American literature (extra poems have been added), fiction (new stories by Steinbeck, Philip Roth, and others), more works by women, and a more comprehensive sampling of Afro-American writing. This anthology, which is not simply a shortened form of the two-volume edition (*YW* 66.552), has followed an admirable policy of including complete works wherever possible, and also contains updated bibliographies. Richard A. Long and Eugenia W. Collier have revised another anthology, this time of Afro-American writing[17]. They have dropped some minor figures and increased the selections by Frederick Douglass and James Baldwin. The introductions to each section have been revised in the light of recent criticism and a totally new section ('The Seventies and Beyond') has been added where contemporaries such as Ishmael Reed, Maya Angelou, and Alice Walker are represented. This anthology gives an excellent cross-section of this literature and includes a considerable number of essays, pieces of political polemic, and even spirituals.

Where these anthologies are very general a number of other collections have been organized on regional and thematic lines. 1985 was designated the Year of the Pennsylvania Writer by the Pennsylvania Humanities Council, and Lee Gutkind used the occasion to gather together pieces from that state[18]. His collection consists of essays, stories, and excerpts from novels; in all it represents some twenty-two writers, the vast majority of whom are little known. Two of the most famous authors featured here are John Updike with a memoir of growing up in Shillington and W. S. Merwin with an essay on western Pennsylvania. The selections are mostly introduced by a brief personal statement from the author about the state. Of equally specialized interest is *Homewords*, an anthology of Tennessee writings edited by Douglas Paschall and Alice Swanson[19]. Once again most of the contributors are little known and for that reason it is a pity that the contributors' notes were not expanded. However among the famous writers represented are Andrew Lytle, Robert Penn Warren, Lisa Alther, and Nikki Giovanni. The aim of this anthology was to give the reader an idea of the geography, history, and social mores of Tennessee, whereas Jon L. Breen and Rita A. Breen have edited eleven long stories from the periodical *American Magazine*[20]. They have been selected from the period 1934–54 but do not include anything by the magazine's best-known contributor, Rex Stout, because his works are available elsewhere. Apart from demonstrating a variety of generic characteristics these stories

16. *The Norton Anthology of American Literature: Second Edition Shorter*, ed. by Nina Baym *et al.* Norton. pp. xxxii + 2651. hb $21.95, pb $14.95.

17. *Afro-American Writing: An Anthology of Prose and Poetry*, ed. by Richard A. Long and Eugenia W. Collier. Second edn. PSU (1985). pp. xlv + 737. $22.75.

18. *Our Roots Grow Deeper Than We Know*, ed. by Lee Gutkind. UPitt (1985). pp. xv + 290. hb $19.95, pb $9.95.

19. *Homewords: A Book of Tennessee Writers*, ed. by Douglas Paschall and Alice Swanson. UTenn. pp. [v] + 387. pb $12.95.

20. *American Murders*, ed. by Jon L. Breen and Rita A. Breen. Garland. pp. xiv + 452. $18.95.

interestingly incorporate materials from contemporary American life (supermarkets, jet-planes, etc.). The volume concludes with a checklist of the *American Magazine* Mystery Novel Series. A similar underlying social purpose has motivated Barbara Melosh's collection of nine short stories dealing with nurses in the Garland History of American Nursing series[21]. These are designed to show the changing image of the nurse whether of social marginality (Conrad Aiken and Dorothy Parker), under the stress of private duty (Ellen Glasgow), or as a comically talkative figure (Ring Lardner). All the stories focus on the nurse as a woman rather than an official and for Barbara Melosh 'testify to the enduring sense of anomaly with which our culture regards working women'. In 1850 *Harper's* Magazine was founded and Horace Knowles has now edited a 'treasury' of writings from that periodical[22]. He explains that many big names such as Henry James have been ruled out because they are available elsewhere. The majority of writers represented are American but E. M. Forster and Aldous Huxley also figure. John Fischer has supplied an introduction where he outlines the history of *Harper's* and explains that its policy was to act as a forum for ideas as well as new literature. Social and political comment thus features prominently with selections from E. B. White's 'One Man's Meat' series and a particularly interesting essay on desegregation by Faulkner. On more literary topics Carl Van Doren surveys the twenties and Katherine Anne Porter gives a dry 'self-portrait' of Gertrude Stein. Poems and short stories are included in this anthology, but the essays are to be particularly recommended for their fascinating insights into American life.

From the American Poetry and Literature Press has come a brief anthology of writings on the Vietnam War[23]. First is a series of poems by Jack Strahan using a variety of lyrical and meditative forms to capture different areas of the war experience. R. L. Barth has supplied several more classically wrought poems and Peter Hollenbeck both poems and a section from his forthcoming novel *The Lotus and the Night* which interestingly assembles Vietnamese and American perspectives. Three other work-in-progress anthologies have been published this year. *American Made* gathers new short pieces from the Fiction Collective[24]. In his introduction Larry McCaffery points out that these writers share a common perception that 'we live *in* language'. Their ways of responding, however, vary considerably with some writers (Jonathan Baumbach, George Chambers) turning anxiously inwards to examine their means of narration. Raymond Federman transforms the historical crises in literature into a comic battle between Ancients and Moderns; and in several other pieces (by B. H. Friedman, Clarence Major, and Ronald Sukenick) the consumer items of the modern city become importuning signs soliciting protagonists' attention. Where *American Made* testifies to the continuing

21. *American Nurses in Fiction: An Anthology of Short Stories*, ed. by Barbara Melosh. Garland (1984). pp. xi + 165. $25.

22. *A Treasury of American Writers from 'Harper's' Magazine*, ed. by Horace Knowles, intro. by John Fischer. Bonanza: Outlet. pp. xix + 696. $35.

23. *Vietnam Literature Anthology*, by Jack Strahan, Peter Hollenbeck, and R. L. Barth. APL (1984). pp. vii + 67. hb $12.95, pb $7.95.

24. *American Made: New Fiction from the Fiction Collective*, ed. by Mark Leyner, Curtis White, and Thomas Glynn, intro. by Larry McCaffery. FictionColl. pp. 214. $15.95.

vigour of one kind of writing, Mary Dougherty Bartlett has edited excerpts from current novels by American Indian writers[25], the most famous being N. Scott Momaday. Some of these novelists now appear in print for the first time. Purely formal criteria have determined the composition of *Sudden Fiction* edited by Robert Shapard and James Thomas[26]. This enterprising collection of seventy 'short short stories' represents the productions mainly of the last five years. An indication of the subgenre's ancestry has been given by the inclusion of pieces by Hemingway, Langston Hughes, and Fielding Dawson. There is a very broad range of techniques employed from naturalism through monologues, dialogue, and even a questionnaire. In a particularly interesting appendix of Afterwords the authors have commented on the short short story's status, whether in creative writing courses or in using erasure.

Turning from anthologies to criticism, two very different general collections should be noted. Marc Chenetier has edited a volume of essays on modern American literature by European critics[27]. The first group of pieces consists of very broad discussions of postmodernism, the status of the author, the construction of non-representational texts, and related topics. The only essay to consider poetry is Ellman Crasnow's elegantly lucid application of *Gestalt* theory to explain the shifting relation between figure and ground in the works of Frost, Stevens, and Ashbery. Among the more specific topics Claude Richard sustains a detailed close analysis of Walker Percy's *The Moviegoer* which concentrates on the condition of exile and the notion of the real as an absence. In another of the best essays in this book Chenetier examines the stories of Raymond Carver, determined not to reduce them to simple naturalism. This whole collection is marked by a very high theoretical calibre. Nothing could make a sharper contrast than Peter S. Prescott's *Never in Doubt*[28], his collected criticism from 1972 to 1985. Prescott has been *Newsweek*'s main reviewer for some fifteen years and inevitably his pieces suffer from a need to make instant impressive judgements: they are characterized by exaggerated epigrams, overassertiveness, and a rather self-regarding wit. That being said, they are also very intelligent essays, a mine of insights into contemporary American novelists. The list of Prescott's *aperçus* would be very long so the following are only a mere sampling: Vonnegut's plots are a pretext for digressions; Heller's *Good As Gold* has lost satire's traditional implied norms; Burroughs juggles with disparate popular plots in *Cities of the Red Night*. Prescott is clearly the heir to S. J. Perelman's squibs and deploys his irony to telling effect whether he is discussing Vietnam reportage or comparing Theroux to Conrad.

A small series of volumes has concentrated on particular American locations. Anne E. Rowe has investigated the part played in the American imagination by Florida[29]. Initially seen as a paradisal garden, early in the nineteenth century

25. *The New Native American Novel: Works in Progress*, ed. by Mary Dougherty Bartlett. UNM. pp. viii + 132. hb $22.50, pb $9.95.

26. *Sudden Fiction: American Short Short Stories*, ed. by Robert Shapard and James Thomas. Peregrine Smith: GMSmith. pp. xvi + 263. hb $18.95, pb $10.95.

27. *Critical Angles: European Views of Contemporary American Literature*, ed. by Marc Chenetier. SIU. pp. xxv + 251. $21.95.

28. *Never in Doubt: Critical Essays on American Books, 1972–1985*, by Peter S. Prescott. ArborH. pp. x + 302. $18.95.

29. *The Idea of Florida in the American Literary Imagination*, by Anne E. Rowe. LSU. pp. xiv + 159. $25.

Florida became established as a place for convalescence or tourism. Rowe's account is essentially a narrative of visitors – Stephen Crane reporting on the Spanish – American war, Henry James gathering material for *The American Scene*, and Hemingway seeking adventure off the keys. More recently Marjorie Kinnan Rawlings celebrated the pristine back country in such works as *Cross Creek* and James Branch Cabell drew on Florida for his fantasy kingdom of Poictesme. David Wyatt has written a rather more penetrating analysis of reactions to California[30], which starts with early travelogues and surveys. His main emphasis falls on twentieth-century writers and he gives excellent demonstrations of how landscape figures in their works. Thus Frank Norris measures man in vertical space; Steinbeck exploits the garden as a utopian image of elusive happiness; and Chandler uses failed pastoral to reveal civic corruption. This study concludes with discussion of Robinson Jeffers and Gary Snyder. Don Herron has produced a literary guidebook to San Francisco[31], which pays eloquent tribute to the astonishing number of writers who have had links with the city. Herron starts with the city centre and expands outwards towards the suburbs. Although figures like Bierce and Twain are mentioned, most of the writers are twentieth-century, Dashiell Hammett (central) and Jack London (Oakland) receiving sections to themselves. Due attention is paid to North Beach and the establishment of the City Lights Bookshop, but the guide even extends as far as Big Sur, the former home of Henry Miller; and to Monterey and Salinas, crucial to Steinbeck's prewar fiction. A special issue of *MQR* has been devoted to Detroit where Laurence Goldstein surveys its treatment in modern literature. He notes Sinclair Lewis's satire of urban mission in *Dodsworth* and argues that the automobile companies' boosterism 'forms a literary genre of itself'. He then goes on to compare depictions by Céline, Harriette Arnow (*The Dollmaker*, a proletarian novel), and more recent writers such as Joyce Carol Oates.

Once again the relation of journalism to fiction has engaged the critics' attention and Shelley Fisher Fishkin has examined in unusually close detail the ways in which journalism has fed the careers of a number of American writers[32], arguing that they turn from literary formulas to the notation of fact. Whitman's spectatorial stance leads straight into the perspectives of *Leaves of Grass*, and Dreiser's newspaper writings of the 1890s induces in him a scepticism towards the promise of the big city. Fishkin is rather less original on Hemingway, going over familiar ground about his work on the Kansas City *Star* and the design of *In Our Time*. While there is not much theoretical analysis of the division between journalism and fiction it is still a useful survey of some relevant figures. Within the same area Phyllis Frus McCord (*Genre*) sets the non-fiction novel within a nicely broad context, relating it to the 'preposterous reality' theme, i.e. the traditional lament that the novelist cannot keep up with American reality. McCord shrewdly points out that it is *media images*, not reality itself, which novelists cannot rival, and goes on to examine the ontological implications of various narrative forms. In *JNT* Evelyn Cobley

30. *The Fall into Eden: Landscape and Imagination in California*, by David Wyatt. CUP. pp. xviii + 280. £25.

31. *The Literary World of San Francisco and its Environs: A Guidebook*, by Don Herron. CL (1985). pp. viii + 247. pb $9.95.

32. *From Fact to Fiction: Journalism and Imaginative Writing in America*, by Shelley Fisher Fishkin. JHU (1985). pp. xiv + 265. £19.95.

uses World War I fiction as a reference point from which to examine reportage in Michael Herr's *Dispatches*. She considers how Herr coped with the flood of information from official news briefings and relates the work usefully to New Journalism to explain Herr's rejection of the disinterested observer. Vietnam has also figured prominently in a symposium on 'The Writer in Our World' as reported in *TriQ*. Here Ward Just attacks the self-obsession of the fiction dealing with this war and Robert Stone insists on the moral obligation of the novelist to present war as authentically as he can. Related to this issue is the question of naturalism and June Howard[33] has shed new light on this much-discussed topic. She characterizes naturalistic works as ones resting on oppositions (nature versus culture, instinct versus free will, etc.), and she places this proposition within a historical context by relating the mode to the fears of class warfare around the turn of the century. Howard demonstrates considerable insight into the formal implications of this fiction and shows, for instance, that the spectatorial perspectives established in the novels of Dreiser, London, Crane, and others externalize the workers or the poor into a collective Other estranged from the implied reader. This fine study concludes with an account of the incomplete structures produced by naturalism which follow a strategy of documentary accretion.

Turning from mode to theme Laurence Goldstein has surveyed the treatments of flying machines in modern literature[34]. He locates interesting connections between Lindbergh's romanticism and the imagery of fascism; and shows that Lindbergh himself was converted into a figure of myth by Hart Crane, but questioned by Dos Passos. The relation of flight to manifest destiny is next examined in Robert Frost and Thomas Pynchon, and Goldstein finally discusses the tension between myth and scientific reporting from the lunar astronauts. Goldstein's study nicely assembles a very broad range of diverse materials whereas Mimi Reisel Gladstein surveys what she calls the 'indestructible woman' in Faulkner, Hemingway, and Steinbeck[35]. The general negatives of these writers' works are offset by 'a few characters who symbolize or represent the positive possibilities for human survival'. In practice this leads Gladstein to read Faulkner's nature imagery as evidence for a mythic identification of woman with matter, and to infer from an imbalance between Hemingway's male and female characters that he was afraid of women. The conclusions and methods of this study are very limited and so near to conventional wisdom that they resemble clichés.

Leaving questions of reportage and theme behind we must now turn to studies of particular groups of writers – ethnic and otherwise. John Tytell's 1976 study of the Beats, *Naked Angels*[36], has now been re-issued. When it first appeared there was relatively little critical competition but the situation has now changed. Tytell's introductory essay placing the Beats within the Cold War

33. *Form and History in American Literary Naturalism*, by June Howard. UNC (1985). pp. xii + 207. £18.05.

34. *The Flying Machine and Modern Literature*, by Laurence Goldstein. Macmillan. pp. xiv + 253. £27.50.

35. *The Indestructible Woman in Faulkner, Hemingway, and Steinbeck*, by Mimi Reisel Gladstein. UMIRes. pp. xii + 139. £54.

36. *Naked Angels: The Lives and Literature of the Beat Generation*, by John Tytell. Grove. pp. 273. pb $8.95.

era still stands as an excellent indication of their context but his account of Kerouac has been entirely superseded by Gerald Nicosia's splendid biography (*YW* 66.622) and Burroughs criticism is rapidly reaching a sophistication way beyond Tytell's comments. Among other omissions are information on Burroughs's collaborator Brion Gysin, connections between the Beats and San Francisco writers, and for that matter the very identity of the Beat movement. With all these reservations *Naked Angels* still stands as a useful introduction to Burroughs, Kerouac, and Ginsberg. David Bergman (*KR*) takes issue with the opposition between family life and gay values proposed by some psychologists and casts a fresh eye over American gay fiction. He finds an uncertainty and evasiveness in Andrew Halloran's acceptance of this opposition and sees Edmund White as much more typical in his depiction of father-centred families. This broad-ranging article also discusses the works of Robert Ferro and David Plante.

Alan L. Berger has produced a challenging study of reactions to the Holocaust in Jewish-American fiction[37]. He defines the notion of covenant as being central to Judaism and outlines three broad responses. The first is to stay within the Midrashic framework and he cites examples from Cynthia Ozick, Eli Wiesel (who surely does not qualify unambiguously as an *American* author). The second option is to see the covenant as damaged and to secularize Judaism (e.g. Bellow). Finally there remains a vestigial or symbolic Judaism such as that found in Philip Roth or in Edward Wallant's *The Pawnbroker*. As Berger himself admits, there is a problem at the heart of his topic since religious faith has demonstrably weakened in the postwar period, and there is therefore a procrustean danger in applying sharp theological distinctions to these texts. Nevertheless *Crisis and Covenant* is an important contribution to the debate about identity in Jewish-American fiction. Jules Chametzky[38] uses many of the same writers to consider how a culture appropriates writers from a minority, drawing on both Jewish-American and Southern fiction. He gives prominence to Abraham Cahan whose career, he argues, demonstrates a series of compromises with the cultural establishment. Chametzky also considers different phases in this literature, shifts from minority to cosmopolitan stances, and nicely balances close reading against general discussion. His Jewish-American materials receive the best analysis and would have offered Chametzky more than enough to work on without turning to Southern writers like Thomas Wolfe or William Styron. In 1979 the photographer Mark Morrow set out to take a series of portraits of Southern writers and has now published a portfolio of forty-eight writers[39] ranging from Erskine Caldwell to Eudora Welty. Facing each photograph Morrow has supplied thumbnail sketches of the writers' careers and often amusing comments on their reactions to being photographed. Still in the South John Griffith Jones has edited interviews with six Mississippi writers[40], of whom the first, Walker Percy, is by far the best

37. *Crisis and Covenant: The Holocaust in American Jewish Fiction*, by Alan L. Berger. SUNY. pp. viii + 226. hb $39.50, pb $12.95.

38. *Our Decentralized Literature: Cultural Mediations in Selected Jewish and Southern Writers*, by Jules Chametzky. UMass. pp. x + 155. hb £23.75, pb £9.50.

39. *Images of the Southern Writer*, by Mark Morrow. UGeo (1985). pp. 97. $24.95.

40. *Mississippi Writers Talking II*, ed. by John Griffin Jones. UMissip. pp. viii + 227. £14.25.

known. Percy discusses changes in the Southern economy from the plantation system, his early life, and his decision to pursue writing rather than medicine. If Faulkner is a crucial background presence for these writers, Percy stands out as an influence on Ellen Douglas and on the journalist-turned-novelist Willie Morris. Margaret Walker has on the other hand acknowledged an influence from Richard Wright to whom she has dedicated a critical study. Robert H. Brinkmeyer Jr has examined the significance of Catholicism for three Southern writers – Allen Tate, Caroline Gordon, and Walker Percy[41]. He shows that Tate searched throughout his career for a unification of religion, morality, and art long before his reception into the Catholic Church in 1950. Like Tate a prey to spiritual homelessness, Gordon was swayed by a yearning for the Old South and she too converted in 1947. Percy, however, became a Catholic before he embarked on his writing career so that comments on his conversion must remain largely conjectural.

Where Brinkmeyer stresses religion Keith E. Byerman sees black history and folk art as crucially important to Afro-American fiction[42]. Accordingly he examines ten writers who have a common interest in notions of performance, a group which includes Ernest Gaines, Alice Walker (*The Color Purple* incorporates fairy-tale elements), and Ishmael Reed who dissolves conventional literary structures in favour of his alternative Neo-Hoodoo. Byerman convincingly demonstrates a continuity between these writers and the earlier experiments with folk materials by such figures as Jean Toomer or Zora Neale Hurston. Joe Weixlman and Chester J. Fontenot have edited a collection of Afro-American criticism[43] with particularly broad reference. One of the leading figures in this field, Houston A. Baker, has written on the need to draw on the vernacular and on the blues as a cultural matrix. John M. Reilly argues vigorously against approaching Afro-American literature as sociology, insisting that we should pay more attention to language and literary structure. Exceptionally good detailed accounts are given of Nikki Giovanni's career (by Margaret B. McDowell), the Umbra Poets' Workshop (by Michel Oren who does an excellent job of unravelling the factions in this group), and developments in Afro-American theatre in the 1960s (by Amiri Baraka). The general standard of this collection is as high as that of *Conjuring*, a volume of essays on Afro-American women writers edited by Marjorie Pryse and Hortense J. Spillers[44]. These pieces cover the 1970s and 1980s, and, taking *The Color Purple* as a reference text, Pryse and Spillers argue that these authors began writing as 'metaphorical conjure women', producing the sort of texts which draw our attention to origins and ancestry. Essays deserving special mention here are Deborah E. McDowell's skilful account of Jessie Fauset's use of genres to mask her subjects; Bernard W. Bell on Ann Petry's debunking of cultural myths; and Minrose C. Gwin's demonstration of the slow synthesis

---

41. *Three Catholic Writers of the Modern South*, by Robert H. Brinkmeyer Jr. UMissip. pp. xvi + 190. £19.25.

42. *Fingering the Jagged Grain: Tradition and Form in Recent Black Fiction*, by Keith E. Byerman. UGeo. pp. 308. $30.

43. *Belief versus Theory in Black American Literary Criticism*, ed. by Joe Weixlman and Chester J. Fontenot. Penkevill. pp. 262. $25.

44. *Conjuring: Black Women, Fiction, and Literary Tradition*, ed. by Marjorie Pryse and Hortense J. Spillers. IndU. pp. 266. hb $29.95, pb $10.95.

of folk, historical, and biographical materials in Margaret Walker's *Jubilee*. Other novelists to receive comment here are Toni Morrison, Octavia E. Butler, and Toni Bambara. Barbara Christian adds a salutary overview where she points out the enormous problems and prejudices Afro-American novelists had to struggle against. Mari Evans has edited a collection of articles and interviews with Afro-American women writers. For details see the Literary Theory chapter of this volume. In *BALF* Mary Jane Lupton proposes that the Cinderella story is relevant to Jessie Fauset's *Comedy: American Style*, *The Color Purple*, and *Tar Baby*. All three works show a concern with clothes *vis-à-vis* gender identity. Lupton relates this issue nearly to the formal closure of the novels. Leonard Diepeveen (*AL*) takes up a historical topic, namely the importance of Negro folk-tales in the Harlem Renaissance. In a well-informed essay he points out that most of the writers did not accept them, and thus Diepeveen sheds some new light on the attitudes of the Afro-American writers to their folk past. In *AmRev* Victor Hernandez Cruz has written a polemical survey of Chicano literature which, he argues, sets out to 'battle the sterility of Anglo culture'. A writer himself, Cruz sees this literature as engaged in a prolonged effort of ethnic self-expression.

Gender rather than ethnicity is Carol Fairbanks's concern and she has written a very impressive historical account of the presentation of women in prairie literature[45] which should demolish once and for all the notion that the reluctant female emigrant was the predominant image. Starting in the nineteenth century with Fenimore Cooper and Margaret Fuller, Fairbanks extends her scope to include Canadian fiction, painting, guidebooks, and even statuary. Out of this diverse material a number of themes are extrapolated like the trope of the prairie as a garden, the treatment of the Indians, and the debate between the town and the country. *Prairie Women* will make a first-rate background study to the works of Willa Cather or Ole Rolvaag. Catherine Rainwater and William J. Scheick have followed a more conventional critical path in putting together a collection of essays on contemporary women writers[46]. They have included full bibliographies with each essay, although standard and scope vary considerably. Ronald Schleifer gives a good account of Grace Paley's hostility to metaphor and Linda W. Wagner lucidly explores the complex variety of narrative methods used by Toni Morrison. On the other hand the essays on Alice Walker (*The Color Purple* yet again) and Marge Piercy concentrate narrowly on single works. *RFEA* has devoted a special issue to women writers in the U.S.A., mainly concentrating on modern novelists. Diana Collecott analyses narcissistic themes and mirroring in H.D. and a number of poets; Geneviève Fabre offers an unusual analysis of Afro-American women writers by the projection of a genealogy; and Joanne Jacobson fruitfully considers the treatment of myth and the quotidian by Midwestern women writers. Much less convincing is a projection of Erica Jong ('Superwoman Jong') by Rolande Diot as a calculated violator of taboos.

Of the critical works concentrating on formal experiments in American fiction pride of place must go to Jerome Klinkowitz who continues his studies

45. *Prairie Women: Images in American and Canadian Fiction*, by Carol Fairbanks. Yale. pp. xi + 300. $22.

46. *Contemporary American Women Writers: Narrative Strategies*, ed. by Catherine Rainwater and William J. Scheick. UKen. pp. 234. £14.95.

of the contemporary scene with two new volumes. *Literary Subversions*[47] reinforces his view of experimental fiction still being fed by the energies of the 1960s. He discusses Barth's hostility to non-Aristotelean narratives and also John Irving's polemic within his novels against radical experimentalism. So, although at times Klinkowitz proposes a rejection of realism, his specific discussions are rather more pluralistic and actually demonstrate that new realism can incorporate linguistic self-consciousness (Updike), metafictional reference (Grace Paley), or the tradition of manners (Thomas McGuane). McGuane proves to be one of the main figures in Klinkowitz's other volume, *The New American Novel of Manners*[48], which also deals with Richard Yates and Dan Wakefield. He argues that theirs is not an anachronistic enterprise but rather an extension of realism where social codes and patterns are often askew of individuals' fulfilment. The result in the fiction of Yates is 'rejection, alienation, and despair'. Wakefield presents a more complex case, having begun his career as a sociological researcher, and he builds into his novels an unusual sensitivity to media images. By contrast McGuane is more of a regionalist evoking a microcosm of local manners in Michigan or the Florida Keys. Also on a general level John Kuehl (*JNT*) has written a valuable account of the ludic impulse in contemporary American fiction. He considers alphabetic ordering (Walter Abish, Gilbert Sorrentino), typographical games (Raymond Federman, William H. Gass), and the blending together of different genres (Sorrentino again, Alexander Theroux). Narrowing our scope we find that Seong-Kon Kim has written a study of Barth and Pynchon[49]. After a rather overloaded theoretical introduction both writers are considered as trying to come to terms with the ineffectuality of language in the postmodern era. Barth's sceptical temper, we are told, informs his early fiction whereas there is an 'ultimate reconciliation with the absolute' in *Chimera*. Father-figures in Barth and the motif of parentage in Pynchon are both explored. Kim finds repression to be a central factor in the latter's work and surveys efforts by Pynchon's characters to break out of closed systems. This study gives a useful rehearsal of some central preoccupations in both writers. Peter Humm (*L&H*) compares treatments of the Rosenberg spy case by E. L. Doctorow and Robert Coover. The latter parodies the procedures of the historical novelist in *The Public Burning* and Doctorow's *Book of Daniel* also rejects the 'addictions of history'. The last item in this section is one of the most interesting, the first book about Ronald Sukenick and Raymond Federman, written by the Polish scholar Jerzy Kutnik[50]. In spite of their very different backgrounds both novelists have been influenced by jazz and Kutnik argues that they have rejected realism for a narration-as-process, a moment-by-moment performance. Sukenick employs digressions and unpredictability to produce a 'stream of character' which is constantly changing. Where Stevens offered Sukenick one

47. *Literary Subversions: New American Fiction and the Practice of Criticism*, by Jerome Klinkowitz. SIU. pp. xlii + 203. $18.95.

48. *The New American Novel of Manners: The Fiction of Richard Yates, Dan Wakefield, and Thomas McGuane*, by Jerome Klinkowitz. UGeo. pp. x + 176. $19.

49. *Journey into the Past: The Historical and Mythical Imagination of Barth and Pynchon*, by Seong-Kon Kim. ASIS: Knowledge (1985). pp. ix + 194.

50. *The Novel as Performance: The Fiction of Ronald Sukenick and Raymond Federman*, by Jerzy Kutnik. SIU. pp. xxviii + 275. $22.50.

kind of a model, Federman looked to Beckett for a fully developed anti-realistic aesthetic. The latter suggested the possibility of what Federman has called 'surfiction', a kind of narrative which repeatedly draws attention to its own procedures. Kutnik has produced a good original study, one which makes intelligent use of these novelists' own critical writings.

2. Poetry

(a) General

It is a pity that, with one exception, Willard Bohn's *The Aesthetics of Visual Poetry*[51] includes no discussion of American poets (the exception is a brief final chapter on Marius de Zayas, one of the key figures during the early years of the New York avant-garde and claimed as the first to introduce visual poetry to the United States). It would have been useful and interesting to see this well-researched study cast its gaze across the Atlantic. Nevertheless, the material covered by Bohn (Guillaume Apollinaire, the Italian Futurists, and the impact of visual poetry in Spain) constitutes valuable contextual reading for that period in American poetry which witnessed the early experiments of Pound, Williams, and Stevens – those poets who were most sensitive to aspects of the visual.

Tradition and Innovation in American Free Verse[52] is a rather severe study (severity of tone being, perhaps, a residue of its original form as a doctoral thesis) where Enikő Bollobás regards free verse not as 'a breed of literary counter-culture' but as 'a natural child of modern poetry', governed by laws that are available to formulation. To maintain her case, Bollobás examines three prosodic paradigms of innovation: Whitman's 'prosody of grammar related to the sentence level', Eliot's 'prosody of metrical approximation', and the 'prosody of textual contiguity' practised by Pound, Williams, and the post-modernists. Her examination seeks to establish prosodic avantgardism as *the* major achievement of modern poetry, and to acknowledge the techniques of that poetry as indebted to the prosody of lineation in Whitman's grammar-dominated typography: 'the ideogrammic method in his collages; Imagism's visual intensity in his photographic seeing; the performative force of poetry in his oratorical impulse'. There is rigour to this argument, and it is a rigour which, to sustain its case, is not inhibited by an assumption of monolinear development: that is, in establishing the radicalization of Whitman's liberation of poetic forms, Bollobás is not tempted to claim that it was followed by a tendency toward further radicalization. Whitman's achievement is seen more realistically as setting up a 'pluralistic prosodic scene, where diverse formalities and licences are allowed'. In other words, the history of free verse reveals it as an alternative amongst competing alternatives; not as an innovation which, once practised, becomes some further absolute form: 'Prosodic pluralism means that free verse provides an option and not a compulsion for poets.' Bollobás has produced a book that is worthy of its project.

51. *The Aesthetics of Visual Poetry, 1914–1928*, by Willard Bohn. CUP. pp. x + 228. £27.50.

52. *Tradition and Innovation in American Free Verse: Whitman to Duncan*, by Enikő Bollobás. AK. pp. 328. pb £11.25.

Lloyd Davis's *Contemporary American Poetry: A Checklist*[53] is an invaluable listing. It continues the work of the checklist compiled by Davis and Robert Irwin in 1975 by the simple and effective virtue of providing, in alphabetical order, 5,224 poetry publications which appeared between 1973 and 1983. The volume is exhaustive but, sensibly, omits publications by vanity presses, works of joint authorship, anthologies, translations, broadsides, postcards, poemcards, poemcomics, and publications of fewer than ten pages. Davis concludes with an index of titles in an offering that is thoroughly serviceable.

'What is American Modernism?' is the question posed by Margaret Dickie in *On the Modernist Long Poem*[54], a collection of essays on Eliot, Hart Crane, Williams, and Pound. Her discussions of *The Waste Land*, *The Bridge*, *Paterson*, and *The Cantos* prompt the conclusion that 'It is the long writing of the long poem' where the meaning of the genre is shared by the process of composition and the final shape of the poems themselves. Dickie's story is patiently and decently told. As a descriptive reading of the idea of the long poem and of its main exemplars, it introduces its topic to a non-scholarly audience with clarity and tolerance. One is left, however, with a powerful sense of what that reading omits or suppresses. Dickie raises, for example, the questions of 'public' materials and the 'conservative' impulse of the modernist aesthetic, questions which are vital to her project; but they are never analysed, never conceptualized to any degree of sophistication, and never theorized beyond a limited arena of ideas that are simply assumed as given.

By concentrating upon the poetry, R. Barbara Gitenstein's brief study, *Apocalyptic Messianism and Contemporary Jewish-American Poetry*[55], goes a long way towards filling a gap in critical accounts of Jewish-American literature, accounts which, in the main, have tended to focus upon its prose. Her approach depends upon Kabbalistic exegesis and provides a theoretical discussion of apocalyptic historiography and messianic aspiration, an analysis of the allegorical patterns of Hebrew angelology where she stresses poetic concerns with the fearfulness of antinomianism and the struggle for communication with God, and an account of poems where the writer articulates mystical answers to ontological questions. The final section is the most interesting in an interesting book, displaying how poets 'find symbolic structure in Kabbalistic emanation theory and interpretation of the Hebrew alphabet'. Gitenstein, with an informing sense of earlier history, attends illuminatingly to the present scene, taking her examples from Jack Hirschman, Irving Feldman, David Meltzer, Robert Mezey, Harvey Shapiro, Rose Drachler, Susan Mernit, Jerome Rothenberg, and John Hollander. In the course of her argument, she offers an important separation between American-Jewish poets and their European counterparts in the experience of post-Holocaust literature, finding in the former a reversion to the traditional Jewish mode of confronting catastrophe where the Jewish apocalyptic is often given

53. *Contemporary American Poetry: A Checklist. Second Series, 1973–1983*, by Lloyd Davis. Scarecrow (1985). pp. iii + 297. $24.

54. *On the Modernist Long Poem*, by Margaret Dickie. UIowa. pp. xii + 176. $15.95.

55. *Apocalyptic Messianism and Contemporary Jewish-American Poetry*, by R. Barbara Gitenstein. SUNY. pp. xiv + 137. hb $39.30, pb $12.95.

imaginative and epistemological precedence over the Nazi final solution. This is a fascinating account of a neglected and important body of literature.

The eleven essays which comprise Jonathan Holden's combatively interrogative *Style and Authenticity in Postmodern Poetry*[56] spring from questions about why we might have recourse to poetry in the mid 1980s, about what we expect and want from poetry. Holden's concerns move from considerations of poetic convention (where detailed examination is given to the 'most prevalent type', the conversation poem, and to the decline of imagistic poetic convention in favour of more abstract styles) through the theme of poetic discovery (where particular stress is placed on the activity of the reader) to the notion of poetry as a form of moral action (where the 'use' of poetry is seen to embody specific implications about audience, style, content, format, and authority). Holden is agreeably, and refreshingly, overtly partial about the poetry he admires; what he terms the 'vernacular poetry of personal ethos', a 'low mimetic mode' which he finds exemplified in Whitman and Wordsworth, leading through Hardy and Frost to William Stafford, Richard Hugo, and Denise Levertov. At the same time, he is capable of responding positively to the 'ludic, whimsical, lyric weathers of discourse' he discovers in John Ashbery, Paul Valery, and Wallace Stevens. The personality he claims as the greatest achievement of postmodern poetry is not one that is narrowly self-involved but serves, rather, 'serious and worthwhile intentions'. It would be difficult to disagree with such criteria, however widely spread. Nevertheless, one might wish for somewhat less reliance upon a critical engagement which depends upon trust and sincerity, and for a less blunt faith in the belief that the 'revelatory' core of a poem is a 'mystery' which is always liable to be reduced to 'mere "meaning"' by exegetical practices.

R. Baxter Miller's editorship of *Black American Poets Between Worlds*[57] wants to compensate for what he feels, justly, as the lack of sustained critical analysis of black American poetry. His choice of subjects is dictated by those who are taught frequently in universities and colleges, poets whose work tracks the line from the Harlem Renaissance of the 1920s through to the activism of the 1960s and whose reputations had become established by 1940, the starting point for the volume as a whole. Three of the six poets treated here are accorded the attention of two essays each. Mariann B. Russell, in 'Evolution of Style in the Poetry of Melvin B. Tolson', examines Tolson's epic form and his development of the hero figure in order to demonstrate how his evolving style 'concerns the maturation of his thought', while Tolson's dense allusiveness interests Jon Woodson's 'Melvin Tolson and the Art of Being Difficult' which argues that plain deductiveness of reference is insufficient for reading work embedded within the intellectual legacy of the Harlem Renaissance and the influence of Gurdjieff and Jean Toomer. In 'Margaret Walker: Folk Orature and Historical Prophecy' Richard K. Barksdale dissociates Walker from those other writers 'in the shadow of the academy' (Robert Hayden and Melvin Tolson) in order to highlight her prophetic sensitivity to 'problems and dilemmas confounding an unintellectualized, urbanized, and racially

56. *Style and Authenticity in Postmodern Poetry*, by Jonathan Holden. UMiss. pp. v + 190. £18.95.

57. *Black American Poets Between Worlds, 1940–1960*, ed. by R. Baxter Miller. UTenn. pp. xv + 190. $15.95.

pluralistic America', and R. Baxter Miller's 'The Intricate Design of Margaret Walker: Literary and Biblical Re-Creation in Southern History' locates the culture into which Walker was born. The subject of 'Perception of Men in the Early Works of Gwendolyn Brooks' by Harry B. Shaw is Brooks's images of the black man as citizen which display 'the paradoxes that abound in the disparity between the American creed and the American reality', and Brooks's *In the Mecca* is taken to signify the fruition of her 'quest for epic form' in Miller's '"Define . . . the Whirlwind": Gwendolyn Brooks' Epic Sign for a Generation'. Rather greedily (given the conventional politenesses of editorial power), Miller emerges for a third time in '"Endowing the World and Time": The Life and Work of Dudley Randall' by considering Randall as editor and polemicist as well as poet. In 'Portraits and Personae: Characterization in the Poetry of Robert Hayden' Fred Fetrow argues that the characters in the Hayden canon provide 'a composite portrait of its creator', and the evolution of Danner's literary voice is the topic of Erlene Stetson's 'Dialectic Voices in the Poetry of Margaret Esse Danner'.

The main strength of Michael North's well-read and intelligent *The Final Sculpture*[58] lies in its new display of an important subject. He uses the status and imagery of public monuments to reveal a particular struggle within modern poetry, the struggle of a contradiction which he describes as being 'between hermeticism and public ambition, between the poem as self-contained object and as seed of a new culture'. Part of the story has to do with the issue of poetry's audience. Here, Yeats and Pound provide the most apposite examples of the kind of writer who 'hopes to build a culture to receive his own work partly by calling attention to other works of art'. It is in their work, which in general responded so powerfully to the resonances of architectural signification, that the conflict between cultural aspiration and poetic privacy is especially marked and makes particularly ambiguous demands upon the ambiguous roles of monuments. Within the more indigenously American grain, North then examines Stevens, Berryman, and Lowell to show how working with American as opposed to European material demonstrates 'a particularly American queasiness about the idealization characteristic of monuments'. In this latter context, North notes how the nature of monuments conditions what may be the only genuinely public discussion of art itself and, further, displays the ambivalence of a demand to be 'memorialized' whilst simultaneously resisting that demand. North's well-researched and perceptive handling discloses monuments in their mediatory function between writer and audience and between past and future, in their role on behalf of political and social utopianism, and in their status as both didactic and non-referential.

Sherman Paul's deployment of the 'primitive' in *In Search of the Primitive*[59] belongs to the anthropologist Stanley Diamond's wish to 'educate a chaotic and narrowing society to a more spacious view of human possibilities'. It is an integral part of the politics of that strand of post-World War II poetry which this volume confronts, a poetry which 'is of necessity often at war with the state' in its search for a 'fuller' human nature. Paul's approach is meditative:

58. *The Final Sculpture: Public Monuments and Modern Poets*, by Michael North. CornU. pp. 262. $27.45.

59. *In Search of the Primitive: Rereading David Antin, Jerome Rothenberg, and Gary Snyder*, by Sherman Paul. LSU. pp. ix + 301. £26.15.

the volume is given the shape of a diary or day-book in which the author records a specific period of thinking about his three poets (David Antin, Jerome Rothenberg, and Gary Snyder) during the early 1980s. Space is then made available for the poets' responses to his thoughts and for communications with other critics of whom Marjorie Perloff is a notable example. This shape is strongly innovative in mainstream publishing; and it is immensely refreshing to be released from the organized and linear progressions of customary exposition and scholarship. Paul's term for it is 'open', taking a cue from Rothenberg's ambition for 'the thwarting of ends': 'open' in the sense of dialogical, implicitly exploring the boundaries of how criticism is consumed.

Energetically in *The Dance of the Intellect*[60], Marjorie Perloff collects ten essays which extend and revise the preoccupations of *The Poetics of Indeterminacy: Rimbaud to Cage* (*YW* 62.442). The volume begins with the work of Pound, considered against that of Stevens, in order to probe the 'aesthetic dichotomy of the heart of Modernism', the dichotomy of collage and lyric, encyclopaedia and meditation, the jagged fragment and the still moment. Pound's *Memoir* of Gaudier-Brzeska is then discussed as a 'radical decentering, of aesthetics through the form of documentary collage, a blend of manifesto, memoir, autobiography, and art criticism', which is seen to be 're-invented' by the 'lecture poems' of John Cage. Rather too briefly, given the novelty and inventiveness of the topic, Perloff turns to the epistolary exercises of Pound and Joyce which enable her to present the constructivist strains of Modernism in a suggestively fresh light. The next three essays focus upon individual workings within the 'Pound Tradition'. Drawing upon the resources of Dada and Cubism, Williams's 'visualisation of poetry' is expertly dramatized; and then the poetry of George Oppen, so often associated by critics with Williams's, is released from the misconception by a carefully plotted metrical analysis where Williams's field of force is opposed to Oppen's 'discrete series' of lines which are 'disjunctive, discriminating, abrupt – a movement of fits and starts'. Finally here, Samuel Beckett's 'free prose' prompts Perloff, on behalf of recent poetics (particularly those of John Ashbery and Guy Davenport), to begin questioning 'our continuing faith in Romantic and modernist paradigms for poetry', a questioning which demands that we reconstruct our notions of what may constitute poetic discourse. Recent poetics, in the four essays which conclude the volume, are then considered in wider terms. Contemporary poetry's renewed interest in narrative (exemplified by Frank O'Hara, John Ashbery, and Ed Dorn) leads Perloff to conclude that 'the lyric of the solitary self, engaged in the ceaseless longing for disclosure, may well be giving way to a more communal poetry'. Against the complaint that poetry finds currently a shrinking audience, she argues strongly that the Yeatsian 'cry of the heart' is increasingly subjected to the play of the mind in postmodernism as part of an urge to widen poetry's field, to include the political, ethical, historical, and philosophical materials that the Romantic lyric refuses. The new openness of the world that Perloff finds to be characteristic of postmodernism is then more closely discussed through the work of John Cage and of the poets associated with the L=A=N=G=U=A=G=E project.

'Time is male/and in his cups drinks to the fair' wrote Adrienne Rich.

---

60. *The Dance of the Intellect: Studies in the Poetry of the Pound Tradition*, by Marjorie Perloff. CUP. pp. xii + 243. £22.50.

Conversely in the present century, according to Deborah Pope's *A Separate Vision*[61], the sheer volume of women writers expressing a female consciousness outstrips that of any other period and requires that we begin to re-examine the conventional discourses of aesthetic criticism from the perspective of such consciousness. Pope chooses to begin the process by concentrating upon the discourses of isolation in order to 'determine the ways in which contemporary American women's poetry qualifies or extends our understanding of the alienated human sensibility as it has been described by men'. She takes the situation of women artists as 'emblematic' of the marginality and divergence of all women, nominating the discourses of victimization, personalization, split-self, and validation as strategies she exemplifies in the work of Louise Bogan, Maxine Kumin, Denise Levertov, and Adrienne Rich. In all cases, isolation is understood in terms of culture and gender, not as a temporary or idiosyncratic condition of solitude or loneliness (its customary form within the authorizations of male writing), and each is seen to have specific implications for revising matters of imagery, style, tone, and voice. Deborah Pope's intelligent and discriminating monograph provides not only a fine series of readings within refreshed criteria of subject and manner, but also a significant intervention in the necessary debate about what and how we read. Her chosen poets are praised, ultimately, according to their capacity for re-imagining human possibilities at a time when many male poets 'seem mired in rehearsals of disintegration'.

T. S. Eliot, Charles Olson, and John Ashbery provide the poetic and poetical material for *The Failure of Modernism*[62], an exciting and rigorous monograph where Andrew Ross attends to the problem of subjectivity ('the result of a confusion between subjectivism and subjectivity') and to the assumption that it can be solved by reforming language: 'Under modernism, the perception of subjectivity aṣ an unnecessary obstacle could at last be combined with the redeeming perception that language can be acted on at will.' By addressing himself to modernism's attempts for a discourse that might be assumed as 'authentic' to our 'experience of the natural world', Ross shows how poetics functions as 'a set of different and often conflicting discourses that are ideologically produced and therefore irreducible to any particular author's "vision" '. To this end, he claims a correspondence between the philosophical rebuttal of subjectivism and the efforts to pursue similar theoretical goals within poetic discourse, and he describes how language resists these theoretical advances and 'reaffirms its irreducible share of subjectivity'. Additionally, he invokes the 'failure' of his title to refer not only to the confusion over subjectivity but to a consistent feature of modernist writing itself: demonstrating why and how the experience of failure is written into modernist discourse. This is an intelligent and challenging study which draws upon wide and pertinent reading within psychoanalytical and poststructuralist theory to analyse the notion of the human subject in a donative manner.

In *Vietnam Heroes IV*[63], published to mark the tenth anniversary of the

61. *A Separate Vision: Isolation in Contemporary Women's Poetry*, by Deborah Pope. LSU (1984). pp. 174. $20.
62. *The Failure of Modernism: Symptoms of American Poetry*, by Andrew Ross. ColU. pp. xviii + 248. $25.
63. *Vietnam Heroes IV: The Long Ascending Cry*, ed. by J. Topham. APL (1985). pp. vi + 57. $12.95.

ending of the war, J. Topham has collected poems and prose written by the war's veterans (there is one exception – a poem written by the mother of an army nurse). They testify to absence and loss, and their achievement lies simply and persuasively in their avoidance of the sentimentality of complaint.

The starting point and perhaps the governing principle for Lewis Putnam Turco's wonderfully opinionated and direct collection of essays in *Visions and Revisions of American Poetry*[64] is a distinction between the amateur and the professional poet, the 'visionary' and the 'maker, the artificer of language'. For the former (whose spokesman is Emerson and whose main representatives are Whitman and Crane), the poet is 'the sayer, the namer' whose poetry is 'not any kind of performance or entertainment' but a 'revelation of the "truth" transcendentally perceived'. So, without any of the trappings of the academy and with a wit and sensitivity that avoids dogmatism, Turco reads the history of American poetry as a 'warring' between 'Sayers' and 'Makers' where his sympathies are allied ultimately with the latter. He begins with Anne Bradstreet versus Edward Taylor, and continues the story down to the present. It is a story whose narrative, in tone and stance, not infrequently seems reminiscent of the intelligent mischievousness of Yvor Winters, particularly when it takes on the shibboleth of *The Waste Land* (read, properly, as belonging to Pound as much as to Eliot), when it advocates 'The Matriarchy of American Poetry' (which includes a claim for the neglected Phillis Wheatley), or when it offers nicely judged, one-liner observations such as 'when America finally decided that a little entertainment was all right, Cooper read a bad English novel, decided he could do at least as well as that, and did'. This is a fun book that is refreshing amongst all the present seriousness.

In an interesting and well-researched piece of scholarship, '"The Columbian Ode" and *Poetry: A Magazine of Verse*: Harriet Monroe's Entrepreneurial Triumphs' (*JAmS*), Ann Massa tells the tale of Monroe as 'a poetic business-woman' by charting a beginning in the composition and reception of, and subsequent law-suit over, 'The Columbian Ode' she wrote for the 1892 World's Fair in Chicago (an exercise in 'audacious over-kill'), and a summation in the founding of *Poetry* magazine in 1911 (an exercise in 'artful undersell'). It is a good tale, and well worth the telling, sketching as it does some of the determining relations between culture and commerce at the turn of the century.

Sagetrieb, a journal hitherto neglected by *YWES*, is devoted to 'Poets in the Pound–H.D.–Williams Tradition' and originates from the fertile stable of the University of Maine's National Poetry Foundation which is governed by the indefatigable hand of Carroll F. Terrell with the substantial support of Burton Hatlen. The journal began publication in 1982, and the specimen volumes I have before me display the uniformly excellent standards characteristic of its endeavours. In the spring issue of 1985, Basil Bunting receives the attention of Peter Makin whose 'Bunting and Swinburne' is a gritty and combative reading of the two poets' Northumbrian features, and of Alan J. Peacock who, in 'Basil Bunting's Boastful Monuments', discusses the 'verbal promptings', the sounds and shapes of phraseology he derived from Horace. Charles Olson also attracts double service. In 'The Primacy of Source: The Derivative Poetics of Charles Olson's *The Maximus Poems* (Vol. I)' Mark Kalins attends to Olson's

---

64. *Visions and Revisions of American Poetry*, by Lewis Putnam Turco. UArk. pp. viii + 178. pb $9.50.

American orientalism and his emphasis on the local to claim that he presents not a 'singular voice' but the 'heterogeneous and cumulative voice of recorded history', while Gerald Burns, in 'In Medias [Olson's] K', attempts a 'common' reading of the middle-early poem 'The K'. Denise Levertov's essays (collected in *The Poet in the World* and *Light Up the Cave*) and her long poem 'Staying Alive' provide the material for an account of her enquiries into the relationship between poetry and politics in Paul A. Lacey's 'The Poetry of Political Anguish'. Cyrena N. Pondrom, in 'H.D. and the Origins of Imagism', argues that H.D.'s early poems were 'models which enabled the precepts of imagism to be defined' and that they had a catalytic role in the course of modern poetry. Michele Leggott's '"See How the Roses Burn!": The Epigraph of Zukofsky's *80 Flowers*' is an exhaustively researched explication of Zukofsky's epigraph which sees its concern with concealment as a 'meditation . . . on *making*'. Charles Reznikoff's habit of having his work published privately is seen by Robert Franciosi in 'Charles Reznikoff's Privately-Printed Way' as being determinant for his sense of poetic career. The issue concludes with Hayden Carruth's brief reminiscence of a walk with Denise Levertov to ask 'What "Organic" Means?'. The spring 1986 issue begins with '"I See Her Differently": H.D.'s *Trilogy* as Feminist Response to Masculine Modernism' where Melody M. Zajdel examines H.D.'s mythology as a repudiation of the hopelessness and degeneration associated with patriarchal tradition and as a means of recreating and re-vision. Scott Thomas Eastham, thinking mainly of *Paterson*, claims that for Williams 'the way-making of the poetic act is equally a love-making' in '"By defective means – ": Poetic Diction and Divine Apparition in William Carlos Williams' Later Poetry'. Charles Olson's *In Cold Hell, in Thicket* and Clayton Eshleman's *Indiana* are seen by Paul Christensen's 'Postmodern *Bildungsromans*: The Drama of Recent Auto-biography' as marking turns in conceptions of the self, the creation of a persona 'whose morality is suffused with natural sympathies'. In 'Formlessness and Form in Gary Snyder's *Mountains and Rivers Without End*' Woon-Ping Chin Holaday investigates the extent to which the 'anti-teleological' verse of Snyder's volume is based on the anti-teleological strand of Buddhist philosophy where meaning and form are interdependent: there emerges no distinction between 'formlessness' and 'form'. Louis Zukofsky is the subject of three pieces in this issue. Cid Corman's 'Working the Desert' briefly considers him through Pound, while Bruce Comens's 'Soundings: The "An" Song Beginning "A"-22' reads 'An' as exemplifying Zukofsky's habit of suppressing and shifting contexts in order to overcome 'the limitations of rational argument' and D. M. Hooley's 'Tropes of Memory: Zukofsky's *Catullus*' sees his translations as 'a grand experiment with time' whose key is memory. Finally in this issue, and characteristic of the journal's efforts to create space for new primary material, David McAleavey's 'Oppen on Oppen: Extracts from Interviews' presents the results of conversations with George and Mary Oppen during January 1978, usefully catalogued under succinct titles for guidance such as 'Chronology of Poems in *Discrete Series*'.

(b) Individual Authors

John Ashbery's eleven volumes of verse have not been easy of access in Britain. With the publication of his own selection from amongst them in

Selected Poems[65], his status within the postwar romantic line of American poetry will be more clearly recognizable. In 'The Prose of Imposture: Ashbery's "Self-Portrait in a Convex Mirror"' (*TCL*) Lee Edelman's clever and difficult account of a clever and difficult poem attends to the displacements involved in the poem's engagement with 'the representation of (self) representation'. Edelman refuses the deconstructivist tag of 'self-reflexive' as inadequate for the poem's project, arguing instead that the poem shores up its identity (as a self-portrait) precisely by 'thematizing its deconstruction'. He displays the intricate process whereby the text 'reappropriates the knowledge and integrity of its selfhood by acceding to the dispersal of the self', and claims convincingly that it is in the pose of self-exposure where, paradoxically, authenticity may be found.

In the faintly anachronistic *The Stock of Available Reality*[66] James D. Bloom examines the close poetic and critical relationship between R. P. Blackmur and John Berryman, a relationship seen as embodying the questions of the 'burden-of-the-past' and the 'anxiety-of-influence' that for Bloom (I wonder how he feels about the resonance of his surname) 'pervade current literary discourse'. Such pervasion, if indeed it is pervasive, is hardly current. Nevertheless, Bloom gives a substantial description of the critical and poetic worlds engineered by both writers. He concentrates upon their awkward place in New Criticism, their responses in particular to Eliot, Yeats, Stevens, Milton, and Keats, and their ambitions for an 'American Sublime'. He displays how they 'shared (sublimist) aspirations toward the poetry of personality and affect that Yeats stood for, eagerly embraced the worldliness Milton would exact from practitioners of the "poet's trade", and renounced the very difficult self-effacements to which Eliot and Stevens resigned poets'. Bloom thus presents a notable, and rather neglected, chapter in the history of Anglo-American aesthetic practice and, most significantly, recognizes the extent to which the 'deliberate, scrupulous sense of limitation' evinced by both writers should be located in the 'constraints and sacrifices their exacting literariness imposed on them and on the idioms each cultivated'. Poetry such as Berryman's is often too loosely labelled 'confessional' and notoriously attracts too easily those forms of commentary which evade its historical occasions. Luke Spencer, in 'Politics and Imagination in Berryman's *Dream Songs*' (*L&H*), is sensitive to the personal issues of the poems, but he argues sturdily for a claim that the volume 'owes its shape and substance as much to the way Berryman responded to public issues and to the terms in which he viewed his relation to American society as to any more narrowly temperamental factors'. The result is an impressive reading which sees the poems as symptomatic of the widespread failure of postwar American intellectuals in their 'lack of a radical political vision that could simultaneously resist the ravages of private neurosis and the manipulations of public ideology'.

Anne Merrill Greenhalgh's *A Concordance to Elizabeth Bishop's Poetry*[67] is

---

65. *Selected Poems*, by John Ashbery. Carcanet. pp. 348. £16.95.
66. *The Stock of Available Reality: R. P. Blackmur and John Berryman*, by James D. Bloom. BuckU (1984). pp. 216. $24.50.
67. *A Concordance to Elizabeth Bishop's Poetry*, by Anne Merrill Greenhalgh. Garland (1985). pp. xv + 291. $111.

keyed to *The Complete Poems, 1927–1979* (1980). For understandable (although not excusable) reasons, she omits translations from her catalogue of poems and omits articles from her list of words, but she does cross-reference foreign words and handles well the problem of Bishop's extensive use of hyphens. She concludes with an alphabetical listing of word frequencies which, although helpful, is not quite as useful as a listing organized according to frequency itself would have been.

The subject of Paul Giles's clever book on *Hart Crane*[68] is the ambiguity of *The Bridge*, an ambiguity constructed out of an intricate series of puns and paradoxes. Now the pun can tempt the critic into both a narrow etymological literalness and a baroque labyrinth of ingenious speculation, but handled by a mind which combines sophistication and common sense, as it is by Giles, it can provide a dazzling and innovative scheme for reading a difficult and frequently misunderstood text. Giles assumes throughout puns' capacity for disturbance and recognizes the absurdity of any expectation that the pun 'fit in' with a more specific programme. Equally, Giles is alert to the non-puns of the poem as forming 'part of that pre-existent world which the puns themselves are reacting against'. *The Bridge* utilizes the 'relative' pun where 'social decorum is to some extent maintained – although it always hovers on the brink of being overturned'. This procedure enables the pun to be truly subversive, always in opposition to the grammar of the everyday world and registering the 'struggle between the world the right way up and the world upside down that forms the essential dialectic within *The Bridge*'. The contexts Giles proposes for the poem cover surrealism, capitalism, relativity, psychoanalysis, specific history (a city poem of the Prohibition era 'when disguise and deception were all the rage'), and eroticism. They interfere with each other to produce a poem of radical scepticism where words become liberated from 'the moralistic business of sedentary denotation'. Giles has achieved a remarkable feat of critical understanding.

H.D. continues to attract excellent attention. Susan Stanford Friedman's *Psyche Reborn*[69] is a richly documented, polemical, and intelligent study charting H.D.'s 'lifelong revolt against a traditional feminine destiny', a revolt which led to 'a woman-centered mythmaking and radical re-vision of the patriarchal foundations of western culture'. The poet is presented as quester through the frameworks of her experience as an analysand with Freud and her explorations of occult and esoteric thought. For Friedman, these frameworks are integrated: the dialectical compact with Freud enabled the development of an authentic female voice from within patriarchal assumptions, while the Kabbalah continued the lesson by revealing possibilities for transcending polarities. To sustain her case for the woman as quester through the metamorphosis of phallic culture, Friedman offers biography, critical biography, a study of influence, a history of ideas, textual criticism, and feminist criticism. The result, unusually, is a portrait of the female struggle for aesthetic and social integrity from within the very centres of patriarchal thinking, a dialogical process, rather than from an assumed and reductive position outside those

68. *Hart Crane: The Contexts of 'The Bridge'*, by Paul Giles. CUP. pp. xi + 275. £25.
69. *Psyche Reborn: The Emergence of H.D.*, by Susan Stanford Friedman. IndU. pp. xvi + 332. $22.50.

tensions which leads invariably only to monological schematizations. Friedman's is a splendid and rewarding achievement.

Friedman has served H.D. well in a further area this year by guest-editing, with Rachel Blau DuPlessis, the winter issue of *ConL* to mark the centenary of the poet's birth. The issue begins, via an introduction by Raffaella Baccolini, with Pound's previously unpublished fragment on H.D.'s 'Regents of the Night', written when he heard of her death in 1961, and, via a foreword by the editors, with the first four chapters of H.D.'s first extant novel, *Paint It To-Day* (1921) which also remains unpublished. The remainder of the issue is taken up by five scholarly essays. In 'What Do Women (Poets) Want?: H.D. and Marianne Moore' Alicia Ostriker provides a powerful account of their challenge to traditional authority and of their alternative vision; displaying elements of contact which, she argues rightly, have been obscured by readings that stress the contrasts between them. Through pressure and release, nourishment and communion, Moore and H.D. are seen as generative 'mothers' through whom contemporary women poets, by thinking themselves back, can find resources for their future shape. Adalaide Morris, in 'A Relay of Power and of Peace: H.D. and the Spirit of the Gift', similarly reads H.D. as restructuring traditional modes of power ('a capitalistic ethic of having, tending, and augmenting') by displacing the ethos of an individualistic market economy through 'the spirit of the gift'. This most substantial and exciting single essay on H.D. to date takes her handling of three of 'the commonplace relay points of twentieth-century life' (the circulation of money, a name, and a child) to show how it 'opens into a larger spiritual economy that provides a ground for the rituals that center her poems, novels, and autobiographical tributes'. The 'gift' connects the personal to the political and the spiritual, organizing relations which create community and assume responsibility for civic issues. Through Morris's fine explication, the 'gift' emerges as one of the strongest of feminism's alternative strategies. Eileen Gregory attempts to restore the status of H.D.'s early poetry in 'Rose Cut in Rock: Sappho and H.D.'s *Sea Garden*' by insisting on the seriousness of the figure of the 'Poetess' who serves H.D. as a guide. Gregory reverses the customary values associated with the figure (predominantly by male hegemony) to argue that it 'suggests not limitation but scope, not shallowness but depth of erotic experience, not shamefulness and cowardice but deliberate courage'. Her aim recognizes H.D.'s placing of herself within an 'archaic lyric tradition' where the voice of the woman poet has potency. *Palimpsest* receives sophisticated service in Deborah Kelly Kloepfer's 'Fishing the Murex Up: Sense and Resonance in H.D.'s *Palimpsest*' where it is seen as containing two contradictory impulses: creating a text that is both augmented and reduced, and accommodating multiplicity while designing a cryptic and distorted space. The text thus becomes 'both what is sought and the means of seeking it (self)'. In 'H.D.'s "Athenians": Son and Mother in *Hedylus*' Joseph Milicia argues that by the device of devoting sections to the parent's as well as to the youth's point of view, H.D. renders her text as a 'double study' in problems of identity – the most damaging of which is too close an identification between son and mother.

Tandy Sturgeon's 'An Interview With Edward Dorn' (*ConL*), conducted in 1984, stresses Dorn's pragmatism, and the interview's straight talking registers one of contemporary poetry's rarest voices which, when asked about what has been learned about writing, responds 'not to be so full of shit'.

Robert Duncan has always ranged widely across the variousness of poetics and mythopoesis, and collected in *Fictive Certainties*[70] are thirteen essays which form the most comprehensive body of his thoughts on these subjects to date. Characteristically, theology, anthropology, psychoanalysis, and phenomenology provide the informing discourses for exploring the visionary line in contemporary poetry, the line which Duncan exemplifies perhaps more than anyone. Although these essays resist, by their catholicity of concern, most convenient classifications, they tend to focus upon issues of philosophy ('The Truth and Life of Myth', 'Poetry Before Language', 'Towards an Open Universe', 'Kopoltus', and 'Man's Fulfillment in Order and Strife'), poetic theory ('Ideas of the Meaning of Form', 'From a Notebook', 'Notes on Poetics Regarding Olson's *Maximus*', and 'The Self in Postmodern Poetry'), and specific poetic achievements ('The Sweetness and Greatness of Dante's *Divine Comedy*', 'Changing Perspectives in Reading Whitman', 'The Adventure of Whitman's Line', and 'An Introduction: John Taggart's *Dodeka*'). Duncan's intellectual curiosity provides an exciting landscape of discovery which, combined with an almost scholarly scrupulousness, ensures the adventure of an encounter with a richly informed mind. Visionary Duncan certainly is, but he is equally capable of sturdy political denouncement: it is a mixture that renders these essays an especially vibrant occasion.

Duncan was given critical space in 1985 in a special issue of *Sagetrieb*. The issue begins with poems in celebration of Duncan by figures including Robert Creeley, Hayden Carruth, Ted Enslin, and Thom Gunn. It includes a substantial amount of primary material in the forms of a further extract from the *H.D. Book* (Part 2 Chapter 5), a particularly informative interview conducted by Michael Andre Bernstein and Burton Hatlen in 1985, and a selection of Duncan's letters to William Everson, edited by Lee Bartlett. Of the critical essays, three are explicatory: Carl D. Esbjornson's 'Tracking the Soul's Truth: Robert Duncan's Revisioning of the Self in *Caesar's Gate*', George F. Butterick's 'Seraphic Predator: A First Reading of Robert Duncan's *Ground Work*', and Thomas Gardner's '"Where We Are": A Reading of *Passages* 1–12'. Bernstein begins the essays which offer more general excernment with 'Robert Duncan: Talent and the Individual Tradition', a supple case for seeing Duncan as continuing the 'Pound–H.D.–Williams' line while simultaneously challenging that line's premises and boundaries. Joseph G. Kronick, with a more theoretical argument in 'Robert Duncan and the Truth that Lies in Myth', confronts an allied area in claiming that Duncan's denial of originality is fundamental to his understanding of poetry and myth; and that his notion of linguistic communality conceives of myth as a theory of language, not as a body of knowledge or universal truth. R. S. Hamilton continues a similar enquiry in 'After Strange Gods: Robert Duncan Reading Ezra Pound and H.D.' on behalf of Duncan's revisionary tactics in the *H.D. Book*. Norman Finkelstein's '"Princely Manipulations of the Real" or "A Noise in the Head of the Prince": Duncan and Spicer on Poetic Composition' sees the two poets as sharing a return to poetry's vatic role. In '"Crude Mechanical Access" or "Crude Personism": A Chronicle of One San Francisco Bay Area Poetry War' De Villo Sloan recounts the battle in the Bay Area poetry newspaper, *Poetry Flash*, between   the   adherents   of $L=A=N=G=U=A=G=E$ and   the

70. *Fictive Certainties*, by Robert Duncan. ND. pp. 234. hb $21.95, pb $9.95.

mainstream avant-garde (derived from Black Mountain and Beat out of the Whitman–Williams line) of whom Duncan may be taken as representative. As Sloan concludes, rightly, the issues raised by the battle 'involve a definition of what literature is in the late twentieth century and how it will proceed'.

It has been another heavy year for books on T. S. Eliot. What is to be admired most in Angus Calder's sturdy contribution to the Harvester New Readings series, *T. S. Eliot*[71], is its gritty courage. Calder attends to the 'surface' of his texts rather than to their presumed 'profundities', and offers what he calls a 'bifocal' reading (placing the work historically and evaluating the worth of its present meanings) which is strongly encoded by his sense of Eliot's appeal to writers and readers from Third World backgrounds and by the 'shock' of the Falklands War. Calder wants to remind us of the playful Eliot, to encourage us to 'enjoy the language for its own sake' and to engage in readings 'with attention to its pleasurable or disturbing surface, where its special kind of meaning lies'. He has a fine summary of that meaning as it applies to the early poetry. Dividing his discussion into 'Modernism', 'Tradition', and 'Christianity' (where the texts select themselves), Calder provides the cleanest and strongest introduction to Eliot that I know of.

Continuing at the introductory level, but signally less impressively, is F. B. Pinion's urbane and handy *A T. S. Eliot Companion*[72] which begins with a survey of Eliot's life and proceeds to a chronological and essentially descriptive account of the poetry, criticism, and drama. He insists that Eliot's work is 'inextricably related to the main course of cultural tradition', but that relation is asserted rather than explained; a habit which is rather worryingly in tune with the general tenor of the book to be illustrative rather than interrogative. No one should be deceived by the illusions of objectivity or neutrality that are so often associated with introductory volumes of this sort, but it is nevertheless discomforting to find its conclusion ending with the assertion that Eliot's 'greatness cannot be dissociated from the high value he placed on Christian principles in the redemption, preservation, and promotion of civilised democracy'. This is precisely the sort of evaluation which keeps Eliot so unproblematically within the canon, that inhibits a full analysis of modernism and, concomitantly, keeps his politics so sanitized. Pinion knows his subject and presents it through a stylish prose, but his bibliography (an essential part of a guide) is less than adequate: it omits, for example, any notice of one of the two best accounts of Eliot to have appeared in recent years (the other being Ronald Bush's *T. S. Eliot: A Study in Character and Style*, which is noticed) – A. D. Moody's *Thomas Stearns Eliot: Poet*. Pinion remembers that Companions require graceful clarity and clear intelligibility, but forgets that their subservience should not conceal more workaday usefulnesses.

Eliot's ambitions for what he called 'the free play of intellect' are taken as symptomatic of his 'catholicity and generosity' by Agha Shahid Ali in *T. S. Eliot as Editor*[73], and as an excuse for a testimony to Eliot's editorial openness (or the declaration of that openness) rather than an occasion for analysis of the carefully delimited flexibility espoused by his particular form of conservatism. And the criteria of *The Criterion*? They are of course ethical,

71. *T. S. Eliot*, by Angus Calder. Harvester. pp. ix + 182. hb £16.95, pb £5.95.
72. *A T. S. Eliot Companion*, by F. B. Pinion. Macmillan. pp. xii + 304. £27.50.
73. *T. S. Eliot as Editor*, by Agha Shahid Ali. UMIRes. pp. ix + 173. $39.95.

theological, political, and literary: economics seems to be the only branch of the human sciences not encompassed within a spectrum so wide that it hinders any sophisticated investigation. Ali is right to claim that one of the 'significant journals of this century, edited by one of the great writers of this century' deserves the attention it has not yet received in the few essays which have attempted to account for its significance. He is right also to claim that the journal provides an 'index' to, rather than a 'record' of, English and European thought during a crucial period. Nevertheless, while Ali presents a clear and well-documented history of his subject, one cannot help but wish that its ideological moment had been more fully confronted, and that its wider relations during the inter-war years had been more extensively explored. As it stands, Ali's monograph performs a decent but parochial job.

Two books are devoted to *The Waste Land*. In *T. S. Eliot and Hermeneutics*[74] Harriet Davidson invokes the aid of Martin Heidegger, Paul Ricoeur, Jacques Derrida, and Jacques Lacan to confront the 'opacity' of the poem through the agency of what she regards as the major philosophic enterprise of the century, 'the attempt to see the universe in linguistic terms'. Reading the 'Waste' of the title as suggestive of 'excess, of plenitude beyond consumption', Davidson recognizes that not only does any attempt to define a meaning for the poem necessarily waste multiple other meanings but, crucially, that meaning itself here is determined 'not by reference, but by the relation between elements in a system'. The poem emerges as 'full of strategic absences', thematically (of love, for example) and structurally (its system of allusion whose signification depends upon absence), with the most important that of a controlling consciousness. This disappearance of the self as an 'autonomous and unified whole' engenders a multiplicity of hermeneutic activities, located with reference to Heidegger and Ferdinand de Saussure. Davidson demonstrates how common assumptions about the poem (principally assumptions of a governing persona or an ultimately correspondential structure) have failed to acknowledge the play of radicalism. She then devotes two chapters to Eliot's contributions to a critique of consciousness – mainly his dissertation on F. H. Bradley, his opposition to philosophical dualism in 'Tradition and the Individual Talent', and his criticism of Romanticism and the cult of the individual. A final chapter focuses on the absence of self from the world in the poem and the multiplicity of voices which disallows any transcendent subjectivity or objectivity. Davidson handles a complex subject with clarity and persuasiveness, but the reader is left with a firm sense that, despite impressive knowledge and astute alertness to philosophical sophist-ications, she does not perhaps advance much beyond a clever placing of her texts across a grid of, what ought to be by now, familiar precepts. While proper and intelligent, is the placing as novel as claimed? This is not to say, however, that Eliot fails to benefit from the kind of reading Davidson offers.

In a broad sense, *He Do the Police in Different Voices*[75] takes on similar issues but arrives at different, and potentially more fruitful conclusions. Here, Calvin Bedient claims there are two major issues in *The Waste Land* which

74. *T. S. Eliot and Hermeneutics: Absence and Interpretation in 'The Waste Land'*, by Harriet Davidson. LSU (1985). pp. 143. £14.90.

75. *He Do the Police in Different Voices: 'The Waste Land' and its Protagonist*, by Calvin Bedient. UChic. pp. xi + 225. hb £23.85, pb £10.95.

remain unresolved: the emotional, intellectual, and cultural disposition of the poem and the nature of its protagonist. These issues structure his excellently researched and supplely deployed explication which argues that there is a single presiding consciousness in the poem, a poet-protagonist who dramatizes 'the history of his own religious awakening', and that an analysis of this protagonist's performances enables a much closer reading of the poem's disposition, its metaphysics of salvation. The crisis of the poem is presented as a psychoanalytical and historical straying which finds redemption ultimately through a metaphysical reality. Bedient, thankfully, is less interested in metaphysics as such than in the structures and tactics for negotiating a path through metaphysical issues; the poem's 'doing' of the voices which reveals a protagonist who is 'cunningly conscious of the need to get round the hostile skepticism of the age by disguising an extremism of faith with an apparent extremism of ironic disorder'. This is a sophisticated and invigorating work which gives explication a richer and wider arena of play than we customarily expect. It is also a virtuoso reading of *The Waste Land*. *EIC* includes a graceful and intelligent demonstration by Robert Crawford of Eliot's greatest debt to 'Rudyard Kipling in *The Waste Land*', a poet 'whom, as he told the Kipling Society, he felt destined to follow'. Kipling's short story of 1891, 'The Finest Story in the World', is offered as one of the key texts behind the poem.

Eliot's substantial range of intellectual allegiances preoccupies the remaining monographs. Henri Bergson, as Paul Douglass would probably freely admit, has hardly been neglected in commentaries upon twentieth-century literature, but he has never received the sort of attention afforded by Douglass's *Bergson, Eliot, and American Literature*[76]. He seeks to 'reintroduce a Bergsonian vocabulary in discussion of American literary Modernism' by showing how Bergson's ideas of openness, containment, and tension become expressed through particular writers. Douglass begins with a very useful review of Bergson's philosophy and aesthetics; and then examines Eliot's work in relation to his reading of Bergson in order to stress Eliot's importance in the dissemination of Bergsonian ideas in America. This dissemination is tracked through the New Critics, Allen Tate, John Crowe Ransom, and Robert Penn Warren, through William Faulkner, and, briefly, through the 'American Modernism' of Henry Miller, William Carlos Williams, Robert Frost, and Gertrude Stein. What is especially good about this study is its strong sense of how Bergsonian ideas actually work within a text, rather than operating as a conceptual resource which merely clothes its subject.

'Surely some tertium quid is at hand', cries Eugenia M. Gunner, which will navigate between those who reject the issue of Eliot's Romanticism and those who find it latent within his entire aesthetic. Hence the 'Dilemma' of her title, *T. S. Eliot's Romantic Dilemma*[77], which points to the conflict between his critical rejection of Romanticism and his poetic depiction of its effects: or, 'how does a critic who believes in tradition and ideal order in literature reject any part of literary history, and yet how can he explain the inclusion of the

76. *Bergson, Eliot, and American Literature*, by Paul Douglass. UKen. pp. xii + 210. £20.75.

77. *T. S. Eliot's Romantic Dilemma: Tradition's Anti-Traditional Elements*, by Eugenia M. Gunner. Garland (1985). pp. iii + 158. $33.

anti-traditional, the Romantic?' Such schisms herald a study which lacks the suppleness and the subtlety its subject requires, a lack foregrounded syntactically as well as conceptually. Romanticism and tradition receive a catalogue of statements providing the ground for Gunner's 'tertium quid' which, unsurprisingly, notates the integration of the one into the other through the notion of the poet-critic. The struggles of that integration are seen as manifesting themselves most clearly in the project for *The Waste Land* where, in one of this book's few moments of novelty, Coleridge is awarded an unaccustomed role. Readers will find little to excite them here.

Louis Menand's subject in *Discovering Modernism*[78] is the period of literary and cultural change (roughly 1910–22) examined through the ways in which Eliot took advantage of that change and through the consequences of his 'opportunism' understood as an indication of 'the mechanisms by which art adapts itself to circumstance'. The subject involves confronting the difficult question of Eliot's ambivalence – his role as conservator of a certain tradition in literary values while simultaneously analysing their exhaustion. Menand argues that this ambivalence is a deliberate strategy which Eliot used to establish his authority as a cultural figure 'not by an exertion of personal will, but by borrowing strength from the very forces that mitigated against him'. Here, Eliot is not 'formulating a coherent cultural program' but 'exploiting a contemporary cultural condition', the condition in which the value, status, and meaning of literature experienced radical interrogation. Menand, whose interest is thus in the 'how' rather than the 'what' of Eliot's enterprise to 'capture the central ideological ground of an entire literary period', is perhaps too keen on invoking irony at moments of difficulty, and too concerned to avoid schematizing Eliot's thought to the point where his exegesis occasionally lacks clarity; but his wide-ranging and well-researched monograph offers a very full picture of Eliot as cultural tactician.

Eliot's thought, famously, was as eclectic as his writing. The temptation for the critic, of course, is to attempt a synthesis, as William Skaff does in *The Philosophy of T. S. Eliot*[79] where the effort is to 'construct a coherent pattern of mind out of what would otherwise remain isolated pieces of a puzzle'. Readers who prefer pieces of puzzles to coherences might well be advised to use Skaff's study for its impressively detailed documentation of Eliot's intellectual furniture rather than for its design of a pattern in which that furniture may be housed. Skaff attends to the two formative decades of Eliot's life, beginning with his graduate work at Harvard in 1909 and ending with his baptism into the Church of England in 1927, and documents Eliot's early forays into scepticism and mysticism which compound a general philosophy of mind as the unconscious. This is then elaborated into a philosophy of art (primitive experience) and a philosophy of religion (mythic consciousness), finally to become a philosophy of poetry (surrealism). There is much to admire here: a mass of pertinent research, a particularly enlivening account of the surrealist Eliot (not a common topic amongst the commentators), and a wisely cautious approach to developmental chronology which speculates that Eliot's thought

78. *Discovering Modernism: T. S. Eliot in his Context*, by Louis Menand. OUP. pp. 211. £16.50.

79. *The Philosophy of T. S. Eliot: From Skepticism to a Surrealist Poetic, 1909–1927*, by William Skaff. UPenn. pp. viii + 250. £25.

became established in its rudimentary form between 1913 and 1916, and thereafter became subject to elaboration and clarification. Skaff is admirably thorough in telling us what and how Eliot read, and he is good on sources (logical positivism, for example) that have hitherto proved elusive. However, Skaff's urge for order makes for too comfortable a yoking together of diverse elements and, in some cases, a distinct distortion – it is to Pound rather than to Eliot, for example, that we would look for a 'new synthesis' of science and spirituality on behalf of modern consciousness. Nevertheless, the range of documentary evidence and a careful intelligence render this study extremely useful.

Against the search for essence or immanence, the homogenizing process whereby figures of identity construct the discourses of continuity in critical practice, Michael Beehler sets the anarchic nomad of difference, engineered to persuade us of the plurality of proliferation and the discontinuity of displacement. By concentrating upon the question of sign and representation in *T. S. Eliot, Wallace Stevens, and the Discourses of Difference*[80], Beehler advocates the centreless play that characterizes his poets' 'energizing differential process'. It is tough going, even for those who are acclimatized to poststructuralist intolerances; but this study alleviates such intolerances to a considerable extent by confronting its primary texts in a detailed and substantial manner. There is a solidity of engagement here, that may be measured not by a reliance upon its familiar theoreticians (Nietzsche, Derrida, Foucault, and Michel Serres), but upon the grittier speculations of quantum mechanics and thermodynamics. What results is the valuable reading that the world of modern poetry is a world of adventure, 'lateral slidings from one uncertain cognition, one metaphor, one differential siting, to another', a world that is 'dynamic' in its most productive sense of risk and perpetual interference.

In the journals, Eliot is seen comparatively. John Desmond's 'Walker Percy and T. S. Eliot: The Lancelot Andrewes Connection' (*SoR*) compares 'Gerontion' and Percy's *Lancelot* as exemplars of the tradition in prophetic writing whose modern shape is 'inextricably bound up with the problem of human self-consciousness, the self reflecting upon itself as a creature of history who nevertheless longs for authentic transcendence'. In 'T. S. Eliot on Gilbert Murray' (*ELN*) Randel Helms argues convincingly that Eliot's attack on Murray involved unacknowledged literary politics. Eliot's focus is shown to be not so much on Murray as a translator, as on the generation prior to Eliot's own, and his attack is against the Victorian mode of liberal humanism which simultaneously created the modernist space for Eliot's own enterprise. More textually specific is '"Prufrock" and the Problem of Literary Narcissism' (*ConL*) where Robert McNamara reworks Lukács's critique of modernism and Leo Bersani's critique of realism to argue that, in 'Prufrock', Eliot engages the fantasies of coherent selfhood and the representational forms supporting it in order to show Prufrock's paralysis as 'the result, in large part, of his desire for a totalizing image of himself'. Reading the poem as a reaction to the dominant turn-of-the-century lyrical mode, McNamara sets it against a poetic of mood which valorizes moments of intense feeling as bases for the temporary recovery of a unified self. Such moments characterize a 'fundamentally narcissistic

80. *T. S. Eliot, Wallace Stevens, and the Discourses of Difference*, by Michael Beehler. LSU. pp. xi + 182. £26.15.

ethos', the core of Eliot's concern, where analysis (the poem's prevailing mode) reveals sensitivity as a sentimentality which lacks self-awareness. In a tight conclusion, McNamara suggests that Eliotic analysis paradoxically becomes a further form of paralysis (by its inability to posit alternatives) and hence repeats the problem of the Victorian discursivity it seeks to replace.

Robert Crawford's title in *JAmS*, 'Robert Frosts', points the variousness in Frost's presentations of different, 'partly fabricated', selves, and his tight, sinuous essay argues persuasively that 'It was the way his various facets intersected and tugged at each other that enriched his poetry in its ironic and other aspects'. Frost's disguises are often played down by the commentaries' emphasis on the New England farmer, and Crawford's investigations into two of his other major masks, the 'Scotch symbolist' and the 'Indian/archaeologist', cleanly present new instruments for responding to the major works and new reasons for reading the minor works. Less helpful is 'Frost's Synecdochism' (*AL*) where George F. Bagby Jr argues that, from Swedenborg to Emerson, Frost developed his uses of symbol and synecdoche in ways which were both stylistic and ontological. There is little here that will surprise the reader of either Emerson or Frost. The same journal carries 'Diverging and Converging Paths: Horizontal and Vertical Movement in Robert Frost's *Mountain Interval*' in which Robert T. McPhillips's theme is the fluctuation in Frost's volume between poles which incorporate, unsurprisingly, further antinomies of form and chaos, restraint and freedom, reality and imagination. His handling of the theme is, however, more sophisticated than its schismatic form would suggest, and his close, acute reading of the volume has value beyond a confined account of the poems themselves – the value of suggesting the peculiar a-modernist difficulties of Frost's work in its tendency to uproot itself in losing 'the distinction between height and breadth' which McPhillips argues is the 'distinguishing characteristic of the strong poet'. Frost's anticipations of redemptive possibilities and his attraction towards the 'flight from form into the chaos of silence' are seen as major elements in that uprootedness. Again in *AL* appears 'The Poet as Neurotic: The Official Biography of Robert Frost'. Here, Donald G. Sheehy relies upon Lawrance Thompson's unpublished 'Notes from Conversations with Robert Frost' and upon Karen Horney's *Neurosis and Human Growth* (which Thompson has acknowledged as a decisive influence for his biography of Frost) to present a fascinatingly revisionist story of Thompson's portrayal of the poet. The fascination lies not only in its view of its poetic subject and in its correction to the reception afforded to that portrayal, but in its display of the problems besetting biography in general.

Mary Jarrell's edition of *Randall Jarrell's Letters*[81] begins with Robert Penn Warren in 1935, a brisk and business-like letter concerning poems and putative articles for *SoR*, and ends with Adrienne Rich, thirty years later, where the briskness of literary interests is softened by friendship. Allen Tate and John Crowe Ransom figure prominently in the early correspondence, to be superseded by Robert Lowell (Jarrell's advice on the composition of *Lord Weary's Castle* is especially illuminating), Peter Taylor, and, much later, Michael di Capua. Despite the overwhelming literariness of the letters selected

81. *Randall Jarrell's Letters: An Autobiographical and Literary Selection*, by Mary Jarrell. Faber. pp. xvi + 540. £25.

here (some 350 are chosen from the 2,500 recovered), it is noticeable that the range of Jarrell's circle of writer/correspondents was small. The editorial policy of choosing 'the most literary and biographical' letters makes sense, of course, and one cannot help but be moved by Mary Jarrell's wish 'to memorialize the poignant, enduring affection that existed between Jarrell and Taylor and Lowell'. His army letters to his first wife contain invaluable information for readings of *Little Friend, Little Friend* and *Losses*, and those from Princeton to his second wife offer a similar service on behalf of his only novel, *Pictures from an Institution*. Throughout we learn a great deal of what and how Jarrell read, but one always has the sneaking feeling, particularly when the selector happens also to be a wife, that the process of selection may suppress as much as it reveals.

Poems 1968–1972[82] is the third retrospective volume of Denise Levertov's work to be published by New Directions, following on from *Collected Earlier Poems 1940–1960* and *Poems 1960–1967*. It collects *Relearning the Alphabet*, *To Stay Alive*, and *Footprints*, revealing the extent to which, as she noted in her Preface for *To Stay Alive*, Levertov recognizes a collective effort in herself, 'weaving a fabric, building a whole in which each discrete work is a part that functions in some way in relation to all the others'. Political activism may be assumed in substance without too much difficulty, given faith, but in form it presents dilemmas. These dilemmas of form are catalogued on behalf of Levertov by Lorrie Smith in 'Songs of Experience: Denise Levertov's Political Poetry' (*ConL*) where they are summarized as 'an awareness of history as it impinges on the present moment, of reality beyond her direct apprehension, and of unassimilable dualities at odds with her innate impulse to synthesize experience through poetic vision'. Smith charts very well the shifts in Levertov's work (taking her response to the Vietnam war as decisive) from a willingness for 'the interpenetration of inner and outer that sustains psychic equilibrium' to a polarization of good and evil. Politics itself tends to get rather lost in Smith's account (partly as a result of her somewhat unquestioning disjunction between 'political anguish and poetic affirmation'), but she is revealing on the loss of 'the innocent and easy epiphany' in the early poems and on the consequent re-interrogation of poetry's power to change political structures and to offer a systematic programme for social regeneration.

Steven Gould Axelrod and Helen Deese have compiled mainly new essays in *Robert Lowell*[83], a collection that is substantial by any account. In general, it seeks to return critical attention to the text after a lengthy period of attention to the life. This is the particular concern of Axelrod's introductory essay, 'Lowell's Living Name', which examines the present space for the poetry that is left by recent biographical material, and concludes with a discussion of 'George III' to emphasize 'a late poem in which socio-historical awareness is paramount'. Two of the essays adopt a psychoanalytical approach: Jay Martin's 'Grief and Nothingness: Loss and Mourning in Lowell's Poetry' places Lowell generally within 'the great tradition of grief' to read his continued encounters with grief and death, while in 'Freud and the Skunks', Lawrence Kramer focuses upon *Life Studies* by questioning its modes of self-inquisition

82. *Poems 1968–1972*, by Denise Levertov. ND. pp. 259. pb $8.95.

83. *Robert Lowell: Essays on the Poetry*, ed. by Steven Gould Axelrod and Helen Deese. CUP. pp. xii + 269. £27.50.

and its rhetoric in order to reveal the volume's inquiry 'into the nature and possibility of having a self, and into the question of the self's relationship to language and culture'. Sandra M. Gilbert's 'Mephistophilis in Maine' selects 'Skunk Hour' from the same volume to find it 'rich with moiling Modernist and Postmodernist anxieties', and Albert Gelpi's 'The Reign of the Kingfisher' persuades the centrality of Lowell's early work, particularly *Lord Weary's Castle*, in 'measuring his lasting achievement'. For Marjorie Perloff, the *'Poetes Maudits* of the Genteel Tradition' are Lowell and John Berryman, a claim she sustains through exciting readings of *Life Studies* and *For the Union Dead* to argue that Lowell should be seen as 'marking the end of an era rather than ushering in a new one'. Late Lowell receives particularly interesting treatment by Alex Calder in *'Notebook 1967–68*: Writing the Process Poem' and by Calvin Bedient in 'Illegible Lowell'. Calder is convincing in his claim that the 'kinetics' of Lowell's long poems arise not out of the unfolding of a personality or the organic structures of consciousness mapping but out of writing itself ('a process of constant revision'), and Bedient illuminatingly plots a 'competition of discourses' generally through the last works. *Day by Day* provides the material for the remaining contributors. Alan Holder's 'Going Back, Going Down, Breaking' discusses the volume's concern with powerlessness, while in *'Day by Day*: His End Game', A. Kingsley Weatherhead pursues a similar line in seeing Lowell as debating his present style with his earlier styles to find it 'wanting', a debate where the poet recognizes that 'there is no substitute for the glorious fallen powers he has lost through infirmity'. Different conclusions, however, are offered by Helen Deese who, in the nicely illustrated 'Lowell and the Visual Arts', argues for new potencies released through the resources of paintings and photographs, and by George McFadden's '"Prose or This": What Lowell Made of a Diminished Thing' which finds the volume possessing, amongst other things, a humour that reclaims it from debilitating despair. With this collection, Lowell is beginning to be salvaged from the prison of 'self' and returned to the exercises of writing.

It is a particular pleasure to find in *Reflections*[84] Archibald MacLeish's mature thoughts on a wide range of issues that extend beyond poetry into political and social commentary and affairs of state. The volume constitutes what he calls 'the autobiography of my professional life', and is constructed from a series of interviews conducted by Bernard A. Drabeck and Helen E. Ellis during the years immediately prior to his death, between 1976 and 1981. It begins in the Paris of the 1920s and moves chronologically through his journeyings and his editorship of *Fortune* in the 1930s, his governmental roles of the early 1940s, and his life at Harvard in the 1950s to end with the quieter activities of the 1960s and 1970s. As Richard Wilbur's foreword concludes, the story is of 'A generous man, a magnanimous man, whose voice it is good to hear again' – the story of a man who, in a letter to the editors of this volume outlining his sense of what the project should be, wanted 'not "research" into *me* but into certain aspects of human experience over the last fifty years with which I have been involved and which *my* experience might illuminate'. Drabeck and Ellis have accomplished their task tactfully, informatively, and with genuine commitment. The result is a volume which is not only essential for

84. *Reflections*, by Archibald MacLeish, ed. by Bernard A. Drabeck and Helen E. Ellis. UMass. pp. xii + 291. £19.10.

any history of modern poetry in its wider contexts, but a volume which, to use John Berryman's phrase, is 'thick with excellent life'.

MacLeish's talk is in strong contrast to that in Frank Manley and Floyd C. Watkins's *Some Poems and Some Talk About Poetry*[85]. The poems providing the occasion for this collaboration are all reprinted from Manley's *Resultances* of 1980 ('Dead Letters', 'Retardation Center', 'Fig Bush', 'Poor Tom', 'Heliogabalus', 'Erasmus in Love', 'Ghost Story', 'Ghost', and 'Going Out') and the talk between Manley and Watkins that provides its substance is predominantly explicatory. The ordinariness of the former is matched by the unsurprising dialogue of the latter.

It is the signal triumph of Judith Moffett's intelligent and sympathetic *James Merrill*[86] that such seeming opposites as thoughts and things richly inform each other in her account of the poet's twin strategies of evasion and directness. These strategies persuade Merrill's view of art as metaphor, enabling it as both 'a form of flight' and 'a form of healing'. Moffett's introductory chapter (preceding a chronological survey) is titled 'Masking and Passion' – a splendidly economical summary of Merrill's manœuvrings; and here, her comments on one of his most pervasive preoccupations, love, point to the quality of her overall engagement with him: 'Rather than bewail the certainty that love doesn't last, he chooses to be grateful to masks for making intervals of love possible. Far from despised as a snare and a delusion, masks are the "sparkling appearances" to which the brave heart leaps in assent.' It would be difficult to imagine a better introduction to a complex body of work.

Happily, not only is attention to Marianne Moore on the increase, but its developing sophistication is yielding a fuller picture of the dispersive tactics which characterize her writing. Taffy Martin's *Marianne Moore: Subversive Modernist*[87] is sturdily true to the promise of its title. The 'subversive' nature of Moore's poetry is understood as a 'misfit', being 'both at the centre of twentieth-century modernism and at its outer limits', and expressing a 'jagged confusion' that always resists repose. Martin's reading throughout is underpinned by the assumption that Moore's modernism is 'subversive' to the extent that its redefinitions of modernism itself anticipate the preoccupations of postmodernism – the artificial time constraints and found sounds of John Cage, or the startling metaphors of Frank O'Hara, for example. Moore's stance is thus seen as dialectical and, above all, deeply questioning of language's stability. Her preparation for being a poet is carefully tracked, and her idiosyncratic creative process and her editorial work for *The Dial* are examined to display the aesthetics of her radicalism. The poetry is claimed as a discourse of deconstruction, featured by indeterminacy and ambiguity which resist solution and by quotations, her habitual gesture, which 'disfigure rather than preserve speech'.

Moore once wrote of Henry James's 'rapture of observation', and it is in the spirit of such 'rapture' that Grace Schulman's *Marianne Moore: The Poetry of*

85. *Some Poems and Some Talk About Poetry*, by Frank Manley and Floyd C. Watkins. UMissip. pp. xvi + 134. £11.75.

86. *James Merrill: An Introduction to the Poetry*, by Judith Moffett. ColU. pp. xxiv + 247. $22.

87. *Marianne Moore: Subversive Modernist*, by Taffy Martin. UTex. pp. xv + 151. $16.95.

Engagement[88] discusses the processes of Moore's art. These processes incorporate an aesthetic in which art comes to terms with the world as a 'form for engagement with larger issues'. Hence the objects which fill her poems are regarded as being there to enable specific mental activities which yield people and events; and what Schulman celebrates is an act of perception which (in 'The Mind is an Enchanting Thing') 'tears off the veil'. She begins by placing Moore within the 'international American tradition' inaugurated by Pound, and goes on to adumbrate the precision Moore associates with perception, her dialectic of factuality and mystery, her imagery enacting the transformative power of consciousness, her conversational cadences, and her fascination with worldly things where 'her concept of freedom is that liberty which is won despite the laws of restraint'. Schulman's meditation eschews density of scholarship in favour of a congenial flowing of appreciation where she reveals herself as an acute and discriminating reader of poetry.

In *The Savage's Romance*[89], John M. Slatin has produced a fine and timely monograph which considers the poetry of Moore produced between 1915 (the first occasion of going to print) and 1936 (the year after the publication of *Selected Poems* and the beginning of her first serious period of silence). His justification for concentrating upon her early work is, rightly, that it affords 'the basis for Moore's claim to status as a significant poet'. His method is explicatory in order to demonstrate both how the poems attempt to secure autonomy for themselves and how their failures 'create the disruptions upon which explication depends for its clues'. And so in his hands, explication disturbs autonomy by reading Moore within the network of her literary relationships. This in itself is unusual, not least because of the extraordinary obliquity Moore always maintained towards such relationships. Slatin distinguishes three phases in Moore's early work: the syllabic verse of 1915–20, the free verse of 1921–5, and the return to syllabic verse of 1932–6. The battle is fought between conservative and innovative aesthetics and genteel and bohemian personalities, producing a series of resistances which awkwardly structure shapes for a poetic self. Moore's difficult, and often simply baffling, allusiveness is tracked with singular acumen by a critic who traces her affinities not only with Williams, Pound, and Eliot, but with Emerson, Thoreau, Hawthorne, and James. Moore is as 'difficult' a poet as Pound (although for instructively different reasons), and it is to Slatin's credit that he does not shirk her difficulty, nor does he reduce it for the sake of critical comfort. He has written the best single study of Moore I have seen – an acute intelligence and discriminating research display in all its complexity the modernist Moore at a time when so many commentaries on modernism are becoming rather tired.

Material on Lorine Niedecker does not lie thickly on the ground, and a volume which charts substantially her life during her final decade is very welcome. Lisa Pater Faranda's collection of her letters to Cid Corman in *'Between Your House and Mine'*[90] is a fine testimony to Sherman Paul's

---

88. *Marianne Moore: The Poetry of Engagement*, by Grace Schulman. UIll. pp. xi + 136. £16.25.

89. *The Savage's Romance: The Poetry of Marianne Moore*, by John M. Slatin. PSU. pp. viii + 282. $24.50.

90. *'Between Your House and Mine': The Letters of Lorine Niedecker to Cid Corman, 1960 to 1970*, ed. by Lisa Pater Faranda. DukeU. pp. x + 261. $26.95.

comment that 'The new movement in American Letters was to a great extent encouraged by letters' and it presents a splendid history of what poetic activity during the 1960s was all about. Niedecker's letters show us, in Faranda's words, 'how very much being a poet in America is a matter of choice, hard work, and, for someone like Lorine Niedecker, a rugged commitment to the realities of time and place'. The letters are revealing particularly for the story they tell of the experience of being not only on the margins of literary life in general but on the margins of a body of ideas (accumulated as Objectivist) that was felt itself to be marginal. This volume, excellently edited, marks the first substantial academic attention to Niedecker: it will help a continuation of that attention and, with any luck, a new, commercially viable, edition of her poetry.

In *Charles Olson, The Critical Reception 1941–1983*[91] William McPheron presents a dauntingly full (although admittedly 'not exhaustive') compilation of Olson's critical reception: 1,630 items of discussion are assembled, each one accompanied by notes which summarize succinctly its basic argument. McPheron begins with Olson's earliest scholarly essay, 'Lear and Moby-Dick' in 1938, and ends with the definitive edition of *The Maximus Poems* in 1983. His scope extends well beyond books and articles devoted primarily to Olson and includes any discussion which treats him substantially. Entries are listed chronologically by the year of their original publication and, within each year, they are arranged alphabetically by author. Three separate indexes (listing titles of Olson's works, personal names, and periodicals) make it the simplest task to find one's way around. We can be thankful, simply, for the indispensable endeavour MacPheron has undertaken.

Dorothy Parker's interest in the 'other' Iseult, Tristan's wife in the legend, is the subject of 'Parker's "Iseult of Brittany"' (*Expl*) by Ruthmarie H. Mitsch. Richard M. Matovich's *A Concordance to the Collected Poems of Sylvia Plath*[92] is keyed to Ted Hughes's edition of Plath's *Collected Poems* (1981) and analyses all the poems except for the literal, prosaic translation of Rilke's 'A Prophet'. Words are organized alphabetically and their frequency is given in an additional index which lists them in descending order from 'The' (used 3,847 times) to 'Zinging' (used, unsurprisingly, once). This latter tool is especially useful, revealing that the vast majority of Plath's words are used less than three times and of those, most occur just once. I am slightly uneasy about the editorial decision to give only a counted figure for certain words which are used a large number of times and which, Matovich tells us 'would not add to the value of this concordance' (words such as 'A', 'In', and 'To'). At least he provides a further separate listing of such words so that, in a sense, we know where we stand, but such restraints (presumably for financial reasons of space) do blemish the undeniable value of the exercise. Stephen Tabor is the author of *Sylvia Plath: An Analytical Bibliography*[93], the fourth separately published bibliography of Plath to appear since 1970. It has, however, proper claim to many firsts. It is the first to contain analytical physical descriptions of the

91. *Charles Olson, The Critical Reception 1941–1983: A Bibliographic Guide*, by William McPheron. Garland. pp. xxi + 427. $62.

92. *A Concordance to the Collected Poems of Sylvia Plath*, by Richard M. Matovich. Garland. pp. xi + 623. $86.

93. *Sylvia Plath: An Analytical Bibliography*, by Stephen Tabor. Mansell. pp. xvi + 268. £40.

books; the first to organize the poems and the prose works under uniform titles with reference to the definitive editions, *Johnny Panic and the Bible of Dreams* (1977) and *Collected Poems* (1981); the first to point out textual variants in the poems; and the first to benefit from the Plath collections at Indiana University and Smith College. The volume is divided into categories which list Plath's separate works; her contributions to, or editing of, monographs; her contributions to periodicals; and her recordings, broadcasts, and manuscripts. Additionally, Tabor catalogues works about Plath (separate works, articles, reviews, and theses), and translations and adaptations (musical and dramatic) of her works. He has accomplished a marvellously detailed record of Plath and her reception with a scholarly care that is unlikely to be equalled for its thoroughness and completeness. Further work on Plath will be made much more efficient with Tabor at its side. In 'Plath's "Brasilia"' (*Expl*) Lori Walburg reads the poem's concern with 'the emptiness of Catholicism' and with Plath's belief that 'glorification proceeds from annihilation'.

Pound studies are advanced considerably this year by four first-rate books. 'Some of our Best Poets are Fascists' is the title of Martin A. Kayman's introductory chapter to his excellent and innovative *The Modernism of Ezra Pound*[94]. It is a title which points the great strength and originality of Kayman's approach – a willingness to analyse that most complex of aesthetic endeavours: the politics of the reader's pleasure in confronting totalitarian art. I know of no other study which even attempts this most necessary issue that is raised not only by Pound but by the classic line of modernism in general. The most sophisticated of recent works (I am thinking in particular of Peter Nicholls's *Ezra Pound: Politics, Economics and Writing* (*YW* 66.581–2), Christine Froula's *To Write Paradise: Style and Error in Pound's 'Cantos'* (*YW* 66.582–3), and the monographs by Rabaté and Lindberg reviewed below) have recognized the need to desanitize the separation of poetry and politics, but it is Kayman who is the first to relocate that separation in the arena of reading and thus radically to alert us to the political fissures embedded in that arena. Kayman finds the discourses of science which underpin Pound's poetics at every stage to be decisive for Pound's attempt to create a distinctive space for his poetry. The discourses of science are also determinants for Kayman's attempt to articulate a means of talking about Pound which avoids the self-sealing reduplication of Pound's own terminology – that is, the closure practised by so many of the more formalist commentaries after Hugh Kenner. Stridently new histories are thus brought to bear upon the main pillars of the Poundian enterprise, histories which find their most potent resources in the exercises of empirio-criticism and the 'objective' poetics of phenomenalism. These new histories recognize 'Pound's courageous and rigorous confrontation of the aesthetic and the political in the field of poetry and the authoritarian consequences of his historically conditioned options as both the justification of his importance and the starting-point for a reassessment of the modernist crisis'. Kayman's study is 'donative' in Pound's sense of the word; powerfully requestioning the histories within which exemplary modernism is read and radically persuading us to interrogate the politics of such reading itself.

Martin Heidegger and Jacques Lacan provide the basis for the conceptual

94. *The Modernism of Ezra Pound: The Science of Poetry*, by Martin A. Kayman. Macmillan. pp. xv + 199. £27.50.

structure of Jean-Michel Rabaté's quite dazzling foray in *Language, Sexuality and Ideology in Ezra Pound's 'Cantos'*[95] where the issue of language focuses readings that are at once political, economic, and ideological. Any précis will do disservice to the rich and complex sophistication of this monograph but it is probably safe to say that its central project is to voice the main paradox in reading the *Cantos*: the confrontation between 'an urge towards synthesis' (itself immediately problematized by the poem's totalitarian nature) and 'the opening of a new space of writing where anarchy and difference come into play'. Rabaté's economic debate needs challenging, principally on the grounds of its distrust for the materiality of history – inevitable, in one sense, given Rabaté's critical allegiances – and its ignoring of the reconstructions effected by consumer culture, but the important thing is that such a challenge itself generates fresh understandings of the poetry. In company with Kayman, Rabaté does most to probe the deepest assumptions of our reading habits and genuinely alters the equipment we use in responding to the *Cantos*.

Unusually, and refreshingly, the subject of *Reading Pound Reading*[96] is Pound's 'Kulchur'. Kathryne V. Lindberg chooses to concentrate upon his prose, directed towards disrupting ways of thinking about culture. Her rhetorical analysis is advertisedly Nietzschean, a reading of reading procedures, and Nietzsche himself figures in his own right and through the mediations of Herbert Spencer, Wyndham Lewis, Oswald Spengler, Remy de Gourmont, and Leo Frobenius. The palimpsest which emerges of Pound's reading habits thus stresses a deconstructive resistance to genealogy and unity, a preference for metaphor over method, an engagement with language's multiplicity, and a predilection for borrowing, quotation, selection, and cross-reference. Lindberg begins with the polemical sense of modernism discoverable in Nietzsche and then displays the parallels and intersections of Pound's reading programmes with Nietzschean interpretation. The Pound–Eliot relationship of the 1930s is seen to contrast literary and religious orthodoxy with lawless interpretation and authoritarian politics, and the impact of Remy de Gourmont is focused upon strategies of dissociation and a spermatic reading economy. *Guide to Kulchur* is read as a search for method through lenses found in Frobenius and Spengler, serving to introduce an argument for the totalized art of the *Cantos*. The volume concludes with a postscript tracing Pound's notion of an American literary tradition to Henry Adams, Whitman, and Emerson, where Lindberg offers the metaphor of the rhizome to specify thinking that is 'weedlike, asystematic, antihierarchical'. Lindberg has produced a major study both of Pound and modernism, a study that is productively 'after' Nietzsche and is certainly one of the best graphs of the Nietzschean filter we have. It is exciting reading which, if occasionally unnecessarily weighty, requires us, again, to rethink our patterns of reading.

Mediumistic sexuality is the subject of Kevin Oderman's *Ezra Pound and the Erotic Medium*[97]. It is a large and important subject, one that has been

95. *Language, Sexuality, and Ideology in Ezra Pound's 'Cantos'*, by Jean-Michel Rabaté. Macmillan. pp. x + 339. £27.50.

96. *Reading Pound Reading: Modernism After Nietzsche*, by Kathryne V. Lindberg. OUP. pp. xi + 280. £24.

97. *Ezra Pound and the Erotic Medium*, by Kevin Oderman. DukeU. pp. xii + 158. $22.50.

approached, skirted around, alluded to, and received fragmentary attention, but it has never been confronted head on in its own right at book length – Oderman's treatment is thus especially necessary and welcome. A large part of the problem in providing the subject with appropriate exposition lies in the simple facts of its centrality and its extensiveness. So profoundly embedded is it within virtually the whole range of Pound's thinking, that to do it full justice would require, literally, volumes. Oderman wisely recognizes this problem; and by concentrating upon the major prose texts ('Psychology and Troubadours', the Postscript to the translation of Gourmont's *The Natural Philosophy of Love*, 'The New Therapy', and 'Cavalcanti') and upon the bearings of these texts for the early poems and judiciously selected moments in the *Cantos*, he essays (and indeed achieves) the properly modest ambition of establishing the germinal nature of Pound's sexual aesthetic without becoming enmeshed in the full web of its affiliations. Throughout, Oderman insists upon his theme's experiential dimension, which controls firmly any tendency towards the kinds of foolishness that can so often beset literary criticism when dealing with occult matters: it is greatly to Oderman's credit that he never falls prey to the mystique of mysticism. Careful, intelligent exegesis which avoids pedantry is the chief characteristic of this strongly researched and thoroughly recommendable study.

I propose to continue the overtly biased practice of previous years by mentioning only those items in *Paideuma* which seem especially noteworthy. From a good crop, two essays are outstanding, and they both happen to be by authors of this year's monographs: Kathryne V. Lindberg's 'Tradition and Heresy: Pound's Dissociation from Eliot', and Martin A. Kayman's 'Ezra Pound: The Color of His Money'. Lindberg, in an intricate and well-researched argument, attends to Pound's less familiar work of the 1930s in the context of its response to Eliot. This leads her to discriminate between Eliot's canonical orthodoxy and Pound's canonical interruptions, presenting a telling opposition between preservation and propagation. Kayman's essay offers one of the most sophisticated and informed alliances of Pound's aesthetic and economic theories to date. His powerful argument locates the contradictory problem of Pound's notions of 'value' in their site outside the economic circuits of exchange. In 'Birds, Said Hudson, Are Not Automata' Walter Bauman, with characteristically passionate and scrupulous scholarship, finds a fine meaning for the obscure line in Canto 97 through a reading of W. H. Hudson. Hugh Witemeyer tells the fascinating story of 'The Strange Progress of David Hsin-Fu Wand', an instructive history of Poundian discipleship, while John Leigh and Tim Redman in, respectively, '"An Odd Sort of Post-Graduate Course": Ezra Pound's First Course in Modern Poetry Discovered' and 'Pound's Library: A Preliminary Catalog', provide invaluable bibliographical information. Three essays are notable for their critical alertness towards their subjects and their engagements with necessary ideas. Marianne Korn's 'Ezra Pound: The Dance of Words' re-questions the generic nature of the poetry by interrogating the identity of the logopoeic subject, while Francis McKee offers a lively and enlivening 'Commentary on the *Drafts and Fragments*'. In '*Guide to Kulchur*: The Book as Ball of Light' Lionel Kelly gives welcome and rare attention to Pound's last original prose work as 'autonomous text' – a singular essay which encourages us to speculate afresh about the general nature of the Poundian enterprise. Finally, in what is his last coverage for *YWES*, the present reviewer cannot resist suggesting that the gentle reader might find something of interest in Ian F. A. Bell's 'A Mere Surface: Wyndham Lewis, Henry James, and the "Latitude" of *Hugh Selwyn Mauberley*' which proposes that the poem may be read as a refusal to appropriate the freedom of its audience by its resistance to novelistic illusions and its concern to maintain possibilities for imagining alternative worlds.

The spring 1986 issue of *YR* prints papers from the Yale Conference to mark the centenary of Pound's birth. Between 1895 and 1948, Pound wrote over eight hundred letters to his parents, and in 'Pound as Son: Letters Home' Mary de Rachewiltz selects for attention the relationship between son and mother, Isabel Weston Pound, on the understandable grounds of her neglect by the commentators. The friends in Emily Mitchell Wallace's 'Some Friends of Ezra Pound: A Photographic Essay' are, predictably, Ford, Yeats, Joyce, Gaudier-Brzeska, Eliot, Lewis, Hemingway, and Marianne Moore (although less familiarly, she includes 'Tommy' Cochran, a childhood school-friend). Equally predictable are the brief résumés of the friendships. The photographs, however, are always worth seeing again. '"Remember that I have remembered": Traces of the Past in *The Pisan Cantos*' is A. Walton Litz's elegant and eloquent meditation on the importance of memory for Pound, as for so many other writers during the 1940s. Taking his cue from Pound's neglected relation with D. H. Lawrence, Louis L. Martz, in 'Pound: The Prophetic Voice', suggests that their shared admiration for Whitman laid the ground for the prophetic image Pound envisaged for his poetry. Lloyd G. Reynolds is an academic economist. His 'Economics in History: The Poetic Vision of Ezra Pound' finds both virtue and vice in Pound's understandings of money: a determined intolerance (which, instructively, he refuses to sanitize as 'eccentric') and an admirable welfarist instinct. Barry Goldensohn's 'Pound and Antisemitism' is the most substantial essay in this special issue. It is a firm expression of that difficult ground 'between my moral revulsion and my delight in Pound's mastery of language'. Nevertheless, it remains yet a further liberal complaint of discomfort which, although sensitive and intelligent, falls far short of the path mapped by Kayman's *The Modernism of Ezra Pound* (see above) in failing to recognize this ground as the occasion for questioning rigorously the politics of one's own pleasure in such 'mastery': in the end, poetry and antisemitism are left as separate categories. Goldensohn's essay may be compared usefully with Charles Bernstein's 'Pound and the Poetry of Today' in a later issue of *YR*. Bernstein's is a brief and acute claim for returning Pound's poetry to its politics (seeing the *Cantos* as 'a (failed) fascist epic') by realizing the history within which the structures of his poetry emerge. Bernstein finds the relevance of Pound for contemporary poetry to lie predominantly in those works that have confronted the 'politics of Poundian "textualization" and appropriation' and have realized alternatives to it.

A skilfully argued and richly documented essay by Robert Casillo, 'The Meaning of Venetian History in Ruskin and Pound' (*UTQ*), reads the neglected subject of Pound's affiliations with Ruskin through their shared interest in Venice. Casillo eschews textual borrowings and demonstrable lines of influence between the two in favour of adopting what Guy Davenport has called the 'contemporaneity' of discontemporaneous minds to display 'a constant affinity in thought, feeling, temperament and interest'. He demonstrates with remarkable clarity the entangled arena of their responses to Venetian history which 'figures as a constant source of aesthetic, economic, social, and political speculation', and which emblematizes for both the loss of medieval spirituality and hierarchy, the emergence of economic individualism and the acquisitive society, the end of craft and the triumph of luxury and aesthetic formalism, and 'perhaps most important', the 'irresistible self-aggrandizement of the modern state'. This is an excellent piece of scholarship with a fine sense of comparative discrimination. In 'Towers and the Visual Map of Pound's *Cantos*' (*ConL*) Michael North extends some of the concerns of his *The Final Sculpture* (see above) to offer an agile and suggestive discussion of the figure of the tower and of ways of seeing in Pound's work. With the aid of Rudolph Arnheim and Roland Barthes, North claims a new reading for Pound's version of the poet's power, a power that is 'neither purely physical nor entirely abstract, neither practical nor entirely impotent in the world of action'. His conclusion is that Pound's towers indicate the visual sense that is so important to modern poetry, and that this sense need not be historically innocent or rigidly exclusive: 'From certain vantage points the eye can combine scattered elements with a power rivalled only by the mind itself. Eyesight can also, at such moments, encompass time, both collapsing and containing history.' The story told by R. Peter Stoicheff in 'The Composition and Publication History of Ezra Pound's *Drafts and Fragments*' (*TCL*) is an important one. Pound's last volume was rushed into print without the poet's final affirmation; mainly as a response to the pirated edition published by Ed Sanders's 'Fuck You Press' in 1967, and arising from worries over his deteriorating health. Stoicheff establishes that the version published by the Stone Wall Press, Faber and Faber, and New Directions in 1968 is the 'first authorized edition', and he is properly cautious of what the volume can and cannot tell us about the ending of the *Cantos*. It is not a 'finished' volume in any sense, and although Stoicheff feels confident in establishing its chronological sequence, rightly he is sceptical of the possibilities for a complete copy-text. Stoicheff's story is intricate and cleanly handled, displaying *Drafts and Fragments* not as a 'finalized aesthetic object' but as a 'tentative movement toward ending the *Cantos*'. Traci Gardner's 'Pound's *Hugh Selwyn Mauberley*' (*Expl*) is an excellent reading of the line 'Bent resolutely on wringing lilies from the acorn' through Ulysses' experiences on Circe's isle. She itemizes one of the reasons for the 'failure' of the art of 'E.P.' with persuasive simplicity.

Adrienne Rich's theme, according to Claire Keyes in *The Aesthetics of Power*[98], is 'woman in the kingdom of the fathers' where patriarchal power, 'power-as-force', is rejected gradually for the 'power-to-transform'. This new power is a re-invocation of the ancient compact between woman and nature that is understood through womanhood, out of the condition whereby the woman is relegated to the position of the Other. The programme here is not only to re-integrate gender-based dichotomies (what has been named 'the unconscious, the subjective, the emotional' with 'the structural, the rational, the intellectual') but, finally, to 'annihilate' them altogether in the process of creating a 'post-androgynous' society. Keyes plots Rich's progress chronologically, from *A Change of World* (1951) to *A Wild Patience Has Taken Me*

98. *The Aesthetics of Power: The Poetry of Adrienne Rich*, by Claire Keyes. UGeo. pp. xi + 216. $22.50.

This Far (1981), and her perspective does not prevent her from taking Rich to task over those areas where a blanket refusal of male literature is seen to distort the power of her poetry and her politics. Rich is without doubt the most important and influential politicized poet writing about women at the moment. Keyes's strong study does full justice to her politics and to her poetry which is continually prepared to rework the conditions of politics, a poetry where 'truths are not preordained but discovered in the process of making the poem'.

In *Theodore Roethke's Meditative Sequences*[99] Ann T. Foster's intention is to see Roethke's poetry as structured by his mystical reading, predominantly through the practices of contemplation and meditation. At the same time, Foster is alert to the fundamental contradiction of her enterprise; as Roethke commented in an early notebook, 'there is something in the psychology of the mystical precept "he who knows does not speak"'. For Foster, poetry and meditation meet in 'the creative act' and reshape the self and its journey toward 'union with Absolute Reality'. Her study is less a work of critical analysis than a testament of faith which possesses all the virtues and limitations inherent within the perceptions of a true believer. It has the benefit of substantial rummaging amongst Roethke's notebooks, albeit from a less than flexible perspective. *Expl* carries two commentaries on Roethke: Ronald R. Janssen's 'Roethke's "My Papa's Waltz"' attends to the varying tonal and associational shifts of the word 'waltz', while Nancy Ann Smith, in 'Roethke's "Where Knock is Open Wide"', explicates the line 'A real hurt is soft' in terms of the child's perception.

Jerome Rothenberg's new volume, *New Selected Poems 1970–1985*[100], a companion to the earlier *Poems for the Game of Silence 1960–1970* (1971), takes its material from *Poland/1931, A Seneca Journal, Vienna Blood, That Dada Strain, 15 Flower World Variations*, and adds one new and previously uncollected poem 'Visions of Jesus'. In Rothenberg's own words, it is 'an attempt to isolate in the work of the last 15 years (and a little more) the thread of a single long poem or sequence that the individual books published in that time may have tended to obscure'. The thread, loosely, is an encounter with the personal and generational past where figures and voices in his earlier volumes 'here find a location and a shape', and Rothenberg's ambition is to establish a 'report' on that thread which continues still. The present volume testifies to Rothenberg's overriding schema of inclusiveness and of the language for that inclusiveness as part of 'the open invitation of our poetry since Whitman'.

In *Oedipus Anne*[101] Diana Hume George sees Anne Sexton as having 'assimilated the superficially opposing but deeply similar ways of thinking represented by poetry and psychoanalysis'. This reading is important for a study which aims at both an analysis of Sexton's poetry and at a contribution to American 'psychoanalytic feminism'. George argues that although American feminism has engaged sociological, historical, and political inquiry, it has until recently lacked a 'coherent depth psychology' – and so Sexton's poetry

99. *Theodore Roethke's Meditative Sequences*, by Ann T. Foster. Mellen. pp. ix + 197. $49.95.

100. *New Selected Poems 1970–1985*, by Jerome Rothenberg. ND. pp. viii + 149. hb $23.50, pb $8.95.

101. *Oedipus Anne: The Poetry of Anne Sexton*, by Diana Hume George. UIll. pp. xvii + 210. £22.50.

emerges as 'a powerful reminder of the necessity of understanding and dealing with the psychic underworld'. Crucially here, her poetry rethinks the schisms whereby patriarchal authority encodes social living: Sexton makes explicit 'the intimacy of forces persistently treated as opposites by the society she lived in'. I take it that such rethinking constitutes one of the most significant strategies of the gender debate in general. George discusses Sexton's work in psycho-analytical terms (particularly familial) to stress her role as poetic analyst of culture through the figure of an Oedipal truth-seeker, explores Sexton's attitudes towards the dualities of the physical and the spiritual, the functions of her first-person speakers, and concludes with an account of her theories on the death instinct. George has written a moving and committed study of poetry which at the same time extends significantly the psychoanalytical resources of the gender issue.

After what seems like an endless procession of attention to 'metaphor', one wants to shout hurray for 'simile' in coming across Jacqueline Vaught Brogan's *Stevens and Simile*[102]. Her alert study reads Wallace Stevens within the philosophical and literary history (by no means confined to the twentieth century) of what she describes as 'the unavoidable conflict between linguistic mutability and the desire for meaning' – the competition of the logocentric impulse for language's stability and the disjunctive impulse for its deferral. Metaphor does sneak in here as a trope for the former, while fragmentation is advanced on behalf of the latter. It is Brogan's argument that Stevens's practice is to refuse both these linguistic and epistemological poles in their absolutist sense, and that through simile 'he found a way of sustaining the interaction of these competing poles simultaneously'. A signal part of the success of Brogan's reading is that it avoids the temptation of equilibrium, recognizing that Stevens's search is for a mode of writing which 'reveals and sustains both possibilities of language at once while exposing their relation'. The stress here lies on 'possibilities', the 'as if' posited by Hans Vaihinger who provides such a determinant resource for Brogan – the positing of an identity even as that identity is denied which, semantically, proposes a simultaneous unity and fragmentation as workable fictions. Brogan's enquiries into Stevens's similetic notions of representation appear also in 'Wallace Stevens: "The Sound of Right Joining"' (*TSLL*).

George S. Lensing's *Wallace Stevens*[103] proclaims an 'investigation into the lineament and character of Stevens' planet of words'. He draws upon biography and history to read a Stevens poem as a 'cry of its occasion' and he does not want to offer yet another 'paraphrasing' of poetic argument that can constrain even the best commentaries: as Stevens himself once noted, a paraphrase is 'a sort of murder. It makes one say a good many things that are true only when they are not said this way.' Lensing's is an attractive proposition, particularly since it is supported by a substantial use of the previously unpublished material at the Huntington Library (two of the notebooks for example, *Schemata* and *From Pieces of Paper*, are reproduced in full). The first part of this elegant and wise monograph charts the poet's

102. *Stevens and Simile: A Theory of Language*, by Jacqueline Vaught Brogan. Princeton. pp. xii + 214. £19.

103. *Wallace Stevens: A Poet's Growth*, by George S. Lensing. LSU. pp. xii + 313. £33.25.

biography up to *Harmonium*, while the second part displays his compositional practices by means of his notebooks, his correspondence, and his reading. The final part attends to Harriet Monroe's sponsorship of Stevens and to Stevens's own readings of his works.

A tracing of the insufficiently acknowledged sources for the formulation of Stevens's aesthetic during the 1940s and early 1950s is B. J. Leggett's subject in *Wallace Stevens and Poetic Theory*[104]. These sources are found in contemporary works of poetic theory read by Stevens at the time of composing the lectures collected in *The Necessary Angel* and his most intensely theoretical poems, *Notes Toward a Supreme Fiction* and 'The Auroras of Autumn'. Particular attention is paid to I. A. Richards's *Coleridge on Imagination*, H. P. Adams's *The Life and Writings of Giambattista Vico*, Charles Mauron's *Aesthetics and Psychology*, and Henri Focillon's *The Life of Forms in Art*. By Leggett's careful and perceptive argument, these sources provide entry into many of the central issues of Stevens's theorizing. The implications of their presence are richly various for Stevens's notions of abstraction, origination, history, nature, the psychology of creativity, desire, irrationality, and the over-riding notion of the imagination – and that list barely skims the surface. As a result of this splendidly informative monograph, such issues are much more powerfully understood.

For *Wallace Stevens: The Poetics of Modernism*[105], Albert Gelpi has chosen his contributors from amongst those critics outside the 'Stevens critical establishment' – outside, in other words, of the 'consensus' for 'explicating the strategies for fictionalizing the interaction of the imagination and reality into poems'. As an alternative, this collection aims to specify Stevens's wider place within the development of modernist poetics, a place which spans the experimentation at the beginning of the century and contemporary writing. Gelpi himself pairs Stevens with William Carlos Williams to examine the Symbolist and Imagist strands of modernism as a 'dialectic about the nature of poetry itself'. With considerably tough ingenuity and sophistication, Gerald L. Bruns asks 'What happens to our reading of Stevens' poetry when the problem of how the mind links up with reality is no longer of any concern to us?' The answer, schematically, is to approach Stevens across a reading of Martin Heidegger and Mikhail Bakhtin; to ask not how the mind links up with reality but 'what to do about other people?' The problem of Stevens thus emerges most productively as a problem of dialogue, of the speech that presupposes the discourses of others. Marjorie Perloff invigoratingly continues her examination of what she terms the 'impasse of modernist lyric' by locating *Notes Toward a Supreme Fiction* as a 'fearful and evasive' response to the social and political events of 1941–2, the middle of World War II. Stevens's poetic use of the visual arts (a figurative and conceptual borrowing of the associations of the elements and techniques of painting) is refreshingly tracked by Bonnie Costello, while Charles Altieri, within a narrower focus, regards his adaptation of painterly principles as conditional for his imperative towards abstraction. In the two final essays, elements of Stevens's impact are traced;

104. *Wallace Stevens and Poetic Theory: Concerning the Supreme Fiction*, by B. J. Leggett. UNC. pp. x + 224. £19.15.
105. *Wallace Stevens: The Poetics of Modernism*, ed. by Albert Gelpi. CUP. pp. x + 165. £19.50.

first by Alan Golding who, in pointing Louis Zukofsky's attraction to his early style, suggests a generally unrecognized mingling of seemingly opposed modernisms, and then by Michael Davidson who regards Stevens (particularly the Stevens of the *Notes* . . .) as the mediator of a Romantic organicism for the line of contemporary poetics marked principally by John Ashbery and Robert Duncan. By registering a necessary widening of the arena in which he needs to be considered, this collection establishes itself as an important moment in the history of Stevens criticism.

Stevens's letters present, notoriously, similar complexities to those of his poetry and critical prose. *Secretaries of the Moon*[106], edited by Beverly Coyle and Alan Filreis, collects his correspondence between late 1944 and early 1955 with Jose Rodriguez Feo, the young Cuban critic, translator, and editor of *Origenes* whom Stevens described as his 'most exciting correspondent'. There are ninety-eight letters in all, fifty-four of which are from Feo and are published here for the first time. Of Stevens's letters, those published originally in Holly Stevens's edition of the *Letters of Wallace Stevens* are reprinted with all omitted passages restored, and there are ten letters that are previously unpublished. The correspondence from Stevens reveals very forcefully how geographical strangeness operates as more than a paradoxical metaphor on behalf of his own reserve and his topographical limits. His delight in the exoticism of Havana, both real and imagined, constructs a world of otherness that goes beyond what the editors note as Feo's ability to 'draw out' the poet to a degree not achieved by his other interlocutors.

Charles Doyle's contribution to a series that is always useful, *Wallace Stevens: The Critical Heritage*[107], covers not only all of Stevens's verse but also the essays of *The Necessary Angel* and the *Letters*. Reviews of the poetry begin in 1916 with Shaemas O'Sheel's survey of current numbers of *Poetry* where the opening stanza of 'Phases' is chosen to exemplify 'ranting' war poems which are 'untruthful and nauseating to read', and end in 1960 when Elizabeth Jennings finds evidence in *Opus Posthumous* for seeing Stevens as 'a religious man who repudiated dogma, an agnostic who hungered for certainty'. The collection as a whole gives testimony that Stevens has attracted some of the best critical and poetic minds of the century.

Three brief notes conclude a year in which attention to Stevens has proliferated. R. W. Desai's 'Stevens' "Peter Quince at the Clavier" and *Pericles*' (*ELN*) is a tight and convincing explication of the poem via the play, while *Expl* includes commentaries on 'The Idea of Order at Key West' and on 'The Death of a Soldier'. In the first, Kinereth Meyer points the poem's concern with creativity by reference to Genesis, and in the second, Charles D. Hanson reads the elegy not as 'a war poem' but as 'a poem about peace and reconciliation', a 'peaceful poem about a bitter reality of war'.

In *The Poetry Reviews of Allen Tate*[108] Ashley Brown and Frances Neel Cheney have collected fifty-four reviews, devoted in the main to the works of

106. *Secretaries of the Moon: The Letters of Wallace Stevens and Jose Rodriguez Feo*, ed. by Beverly Coyle and Alan Filreis. DukeU. pp. x + 210. $19.95.

107. *Wallace Stevens: The Critical Heritage*, ed. by Charles Doyle. RKP (1985). pp. xv + 503. £20.

108. *The Poetry Reviews of Allen Tate, 1924–1944*, ed. by Ashley Brown and Frances Neel Cheney. LSU. pp. xii + 214. £19.15.

individual poets ranging from the new (Laura Riding and e. e. cummings, for example) through the established (such as Edward Arlington Robinson) to the experimental (Pound and Eliot in particular). Tate's subjects are predominantly American (with exceptions that include Spender, Auden, and Yeats), and they all belong to the present century (with Baudelaire and Whitman thrown in for good measure). As the editors claim, rightly, the volume offers an 'important commentary on one phase of our literary history', a phase which witnessed the fruition of modern verse and the beginnings of serious poetry criticism in America – a seriousness abetted in no small part by Tate himself. This collection is valuable as a 'chronicle' of modern poetry and as a register of how one figure contributed to it. No less valuable is that Tate emerges here as a very sturdy and perceptive critic. The volume lacks an index but, since Tate is not overfond of cross-referencing or comparison and since the reviews are mostly singular to their named subject, an index has not the urgency one might otherwise demand.

The transcript of an interview conducted by Christopher Lydon with Derek Walcott and Seamus Heaney on Robert Penn Warren for 'The Ten O'Clock News', WGBH-TV, Boston, is published as 'Robert Penn Warren' (*PR*). The general focus of the conversation is on the question of America having a poet laureate and issues raised by that question. William Bedford Clark's 'Robert Penn Warren's Love Affair with America' (*SoR*) is a fairly unsurprising essay that is true to its title.

Advertised as the first volume of the William Carlos Williams Archive Series, *Something to Say*[109] is a splendidly useful gathering by James E. B. Breslin of Williams's published and unpublished writings on the present century's 'younger' poets (those born after 1900). Breslin provides a lively and discriminating introductory essay. 'The Presence of Williams in Contemporary Poetry' where Williams's engagements with those poets is seen as a mixture of selfless generosity and personal aggrandizement, and where his stricture that 'the only way to be like Whitman is to write *unlike* Whitman' functions as an accurate diagnosis of that 'Presence'. The range of Williams's observations and advice covers both the familiar (George Oppen, Laura Riding, Kenneth Patchen, Louis Zukofsky, Kenneth Rexroth, David Ignatow, Robert Lowell, Cid Corman, and Allen Ginsberg, for example) and the less familiar (including James McQuail, H. H. Lewis, Sidney Salt, Charles Henri Ford, Muriel Rukeyser, Sol Funaroff, Harry Roskolenko, and Marcia Nardi). Williams's 'Presence' for younger poets is, indeed, direct and oblique, single and various, immediate and distant. To track that 'Presence', the reader has here an excellent starting point.

Bernard Duffey's major analysis of Williams in *A Poetry of Presence*[110] is unusual in two basic respects. It covers the *whole* corpus of his output considered as an 'interrelated and interdependent web', and its epigraph from Wittgenstein offers a direct angle (as opposed to the modishly oblique angle) on its method: 'We are talking about the spatial and temporal phenomenon of language, not about some non-spatial, non-temporal phantasm.' Its title is

109. *Something to Say: William Carlos Williams on Younger Poets*, ed. by James E. B. Breslin. ND (1985). pp. vi + 280. $23.95.

110. *A Poetry of Presence: The Writing of William Carlos Williams*, by Bernard Duffey. UWisc. pp. xiii + 231. £23.75.

equally direct: for Duffey, Williams is an 'open and fluid personality shaped by his scene and his agencies of the moment' who generates a concept of writing as 'linguistically present action' – what Kenneth Burke terms a 'dramatistic presence'. Duffey's interrogation is dependent upon Burke's *A Grammar of Motives* in which the poet is an 'agent' working in relation to a 'scene' that is his subject. Interaction between the two then enables the 'agencies' of writing itself, informed by the last of Burke's terms, 'purpose', a term livened by Duffey's characterization of Williams's 'dramatic sense of himself as literary actor seeking embodiment of a dynamic and altering whole'. Consequently, his works are examined as interactive in general and specifically in the 'lights that seem most immediate to them'. These 'lights' are the pervasiveness of scene in *In the American Grain* and the fiction; of agent or poetic person in *Kora in Hell*, *A Voyage to Pagany*, *Paterson*, and *Pictures from Brueghel*; of poetic agency in the short poems; of poetic purpose in 'The Pink Church', 'Russia', *The Embodiment of Knowledge*, and 'The Desert Music'; and of poetic action as a whole in the two plays, *Many Loves* and *A Dream of Love*. Duffey's use of Burke's categories is pragmatic and productive, picturing a writer who is 'more engaged in expressing literary action than in forging literary objects'. Such a kinetic, 'dramatistic' view of Williams is crucial. An interplay between background and foreground establishes the middle ground of the imagination's realm that is the 'home' of the writing Williams practises, and Duffey's recognition of its manageable and human features points the core of that writing's democratic achievement.

On a less ambitious scale, we have Marilyn Kallet's *Honest Simplicity in William Carlos Williams' 'Asphodel, That Greeny Flower'*[111]. For Kallet, Williams's long late poem discovers the 'lyrical place' by a 'sustained willingness to improvise in a disciplined manner'. Kallet is alert to the idea of the effort which led to that 'lyrical place', hearing 'the echoes of a lifetime of struggle that shuttle through the lines', but the trouble is that this struggle is always subordinated to her sense of the 'poem's music', a music seen as somehow rising above it. She acknowledges that Williams was 'especially gifted at taking risks in his work', but those risks are inevitably sanitized by propositions for his control. Thus, 'reconciliation' is proposed as the poem's keynote; and although 'Asphodel' is claimed to possess 'memory of how hard it was to get there', such memory has all its awkwardness defused through a notion of myth whereby the past is used to create 'a timeless image'. Kallet knows her Williams and is acute on his development of the triadic line. She makes pertinent use of the draft worksheets, but she rests far too content with the shibboleths of a reading which demands resolution and the smoothing out of contradiction and difficulty.

Two essays take *Paterson* as their subject. Margaret Dickie's 'Williams Reading *Paterson*' (*ELH*) is an interesting exercise on behalf of both the poem itself and theories concerning the activity of the reader. Williams's willingness to disrupt his text with his reactions to it as a reader is examined in order to emphasize the struggle between reading and writing that for Dickie provides the 'source' of *Paterson*: 'once it ceased, when Williams learned how to read, the best of the writing was over', she claims, noting further that Williams's double role serves to inhibit *our* role as readers, an inhibition which gives access to the

111. *Honest Simplicity in William Carlos Williams' 'Asphodel, That Greeny Flower'*, by Marilyn Kallet. LSU. pp. xii + 163. £14.90.

poem's curious contradiction whereby 'the display of its openness is closed off'. What emerges is an intriguing 'strategy of unmastery' in the poem which replaces a notion of reading as 'a positive rewarding experience' by a notion that it is 'difficult, destructive, irritating, and contradictory'; a replacement where reading joins writing as 'a lonely and inconsolable act'. Rather less interesting is '"The Radiant Gist": "The Poetry Hidden in the Prose" of Williams' *Paterson*' (*TCL*), a somewhat directionless, although not unintelligent foray where Brian A. Bremen describes Williams's development of the means to 'reconcile the poetry with the prose' in *Paterson*, taking Williams's discovery of Byron Vazakas' *Transfigured Night* as a decisive intervention in the difficulties of composition. Two essays have more general concerns. Taking its material from Bertrand Russell, William James, Ernest Fenollosa, Alfred Sidgewick, John Dewey, and A. N. Whitehead to register the late nineteenth- and early twentieth-century attack on logic as part of the widespread disruption of ideas about reality, Patrick Moore's 'William Carlos Williams and the Modernist Attack on Logical Syntax' (*ELH*) makes a good case for reading Williams's intellectual milieu during his formative years as a poet within contemporary disturbances of syntax and representation. His participation in the breaking of logical structures is not unfamiliar (although discussions of this participation at the syntactical level have been uncommon), but Moore is a firm reader of the poetry and demonstrates clearly how the innovations of Williams's syntax belong to his experimentalism in general. Bernhard Radloff's 'Name and Site: A Heideggerian Approach to the Local in the Poetry of William Carlos Williams' (*TSLL*) is a richly and powerfully intelligent essay which, with the aid of tools from Heidegger's phenomenology, attempts to formulate a 'poetics of the local'. It responds to the question 'If the poetry of the local is defined by the unified expression of work, thing, and locality, then what is the source of this unity?' and, by examining 'The Yachts', 'The Red Wheelbarrow', 'The Locust Tree in Flower', and 'Asphodel, That Greeny Flower', shows that this 'source' (or 'site') is to be located in a particular notion of temporality, the means whereby 'the movement of time – the extended interplay of past and future which bears upon and originates the present – [comes] to word'.

Terry Comito's *In Defense of Winters*[112] is an excellent and informative 'understanding' or 'representation' of Yvor Winters. It is also a powerful phenomenological plea for a restoration of the human in current critical practice. With a persuasive play of poststructuralist sophistication and blunt commonsensical literalism, Comito seeks not to preserve or resurrect Winters but to 'engage him in a dialogue' that will produce 'active reading' rather than 'reproduction' within a renewed hermeneutic tradition. Perhaps the most telling, and certainly the most exciting, thrust of Comito's approach is its release of language from the safety of the page by returning words to the conduct of society. Here, poetry is conceived as one of several kinds of activity we use to make sense of the world within 'the communicative praxis of society'. It is characterized by a rejection of mystique and by an insistence on the continuity of poetic and ordinary language, on the irreducible conceptual content of words, on the importance of paraphrase (as an element of poetic

112. *In Defense of Winters: The Poetry and Prose of Yvor Winters*, by Terry Comito. UWisc. pp. xxix + 329. £27.10.

structure and as an instrument for critical analysis), and on the methodological primacy of taste (understood in moral and social terms) and of 'semantic indices'. In Comito's wise and perceptive handling, Winters's concern with language places knowledge within the 'dense physical particularities of the words themselves'. Comito, with the lessons of Raymond Williams, Frank Lentricchia, and Hans-Georg Gadamer firmly in mind, manages marvellously to show how Winters's notions of tradition and the apparent closures of his verse propose not conformity but critique, not a sealed circle but a horizon. This is a stimulating and enriching study which presents simultaneously an invigorating assessment of Winters and a series of analytical explorings that provoke necessary speculations on our habits of criticism.

In *Expl* Terence Allan Hoagwood reads Elinor Wylie's 'The Crooked Stick' as, characteristically, 'a dialectical interplay of contraries'.

3. Fiction

A number of works by Edith Wharton have been reprinted this year. *The Mother's Recompense*[113] comes with a new afterword by Marilyn French who discusses the various issues raised by the book. She argues that it presents an unconventional heroine who is a divorcee, in her forties, and who has abandoned her child. Marilyn French has also written an afterword to *Hudson River Bracketed*[114], Wharton's portrait of the artist as a young person, whose protagonist is muddled and ambivalent. French puts this down to a split in Edith Wharton's attitude. On the one hand she wanted to investigate the artistic temperament; on the other she did not want to base the artist on herself. She may in fact have used several young writers as models (although the book's jacket confidently declares that Vance was inspired by Thomas Wolfe). A volume of four novels by Wharton has now been issued by LAm[115]. For these the first American edition has been taken as the authoritative text by R. W. B. Lewis. In fact it was the only one established for *The Reef*, but Wharton did revise the periodical versions of *The House of Mirth*, *The Custom of the Country*, and *The Age of Innocence* for publication in book form. In the case of the latter subsequent minor changes were made for the later print runs. Lewis has added helpful notes for this volume which explain contemporary allusions and which demonstrate the extent of Wharton's knowledge of French culture. Jean Gooder (*CQ*) finds a double-edged critical attitude to Wharton which at once praises her technique, but also finds it arid. She argues that this is justified by the nature of her narrative methods, her novellas, for instance, being 'examples of a head determined to solve, unaided, the problems of the heart'. Wharton's strength then lies in her analytical crispness. This is a broad and challenging article which discusses the shorter works, the autobiography, and *The Reef*. The James critic Adeline R. Tintner (*JNT*) sets out to find the structure underlying Wharton's quartet *Old New York*. Her brief article lists a number of devices used (recurring family names, vivid openings, etc.) and also

113. *The Mother's Recompense*, by Edith Wharton, afterword by Marilyn French. Virago. pp. 353. pb £3.95.

114. *Hudson River Bracketed*, by Edith Wharton, afterword by Marilyn French. Virago. pp. 547. pb £4.95.

115. *Novels*, by Edith Wharton, ed. by R. W. B. Lewis. LAm/CUP. pp. 1328. £30.

takes into account the quartet's publishing history. R. B. Hovey (*ALR*) has examined in detail the two main interpretations of *Ethan Frome* by Cynthia Griffin Wolff and Elizabeth Ammons. The former psychological reading wrongly concentrates on Frome at the expense of his mother, while Ammons's interpretation is vitiated by feminist bias. Hovey insists that the power of the novella resides in its central drama between Ethan and Zeena, making a cautionary point against ignoring the obvious in a search for the subtext. Within the same expatriate circle as Edith Wharton was Howard Sturgis whose 1904 novel *Belchamber* has now been re-issued[116]. In his new introduction Noel Annan presents the work as an indictment of an aristocratic class gone decadent. The weakness and ineffectuality of its protagonist Sainty thus carries historical implications in suggesting the deterioration of an inheritance. When the novel was first published Sturgis's friend Henry James declared to A. C. Benson: 'he had his chance and made *nothing* of it', a harsh judgement against which Annan argues with vigour.

One of the best biographies of Edith Wharton's contemporary Gertrude Stein has now been issued in paperback[117]. Janet Hobhouse highlights the latter's divergence from her brother Leo around 1908 when she struck out decisively as a writer and art collector in her own right. A thirst for fame ('*gloire*') fuelled Stein's ambition but it was not until the 1930s that she became established as a celebrity. Hobhouse also gives a very clear outline of the phases in her literary career from a kind of prose cubism in the 1910s to a new accessibility in the 1930s. *Everybody Who Was Anybody* gives an account of Gertrude Stein's life which should help to place her works in context. One of the most famous aspects of Stein's life is the influential part she played in shaping the style of young writers like Hemingway, and Philip Galanes (*ParisR*) has edited a number of letters which she wrote in the 1930s to an aspiring novelist called Wendell Wilcox. These letters are full of helpful suggestions about his style and about getting his works published. One of Gertrude Stein's main correspondents was the novelist Carl Van Vechten and their letters have now been published in an excellent scholarly collection edited by Edward Burns[118]. The letters cover the period from 1913 to 1946 and amply justify Van Vechten's enthusiasm in 1941 when he exclaimed: 'Those letters! . . . It is a marvellous series and gives your entire professional career.' The correspondence contains countless details about each author's productions and about each writer's opinions of the other. Although Van Vechten never really understood Stein's work it is to his great credit that he became her most ardent publicist and was instrumental in negotiating for their publication. The letters begin in formality and astonishingly changed very little during the last war, although in 1940 both writers decided to donate their correspondence to Yale. In the double-length hundredth issue of *ParisR* James Laughlin has edited an early short story by Ezra Pound called 'In the Water-Butt', written under the influence of Browning.

Two further expatriate novelists have also continued to attract critical

116. *Belchamber*, by Howard Sturgis, intro. by Noel Annan. OUP. pp. xii + 334. pb £3.95.
117. *Everybody Who Was Anybody: A Biography of Gertrude Stein*, by Janet Hobhouse. Arena: Arrow. pp. x + 180. pb £4.95.
118. *The Letters of Gertrude Stein and Carl Van Vechten*, ed. by Edward Burns. 2 vols. ColU. pp. xv + 901. $70.

attention. A British edition of Djuna Barnes's collected interviews, full details of which are given in *YW* 65.632, has now appeared [119]. Barnes has also been the subject of a biography by Andrew Field [120] which locates the beginnings of her career in a general climate of sexual revolt. His emphasis on the colourful eccentrics of Greenwich Village curiously effaces Barnes from his account at times and never quite does justice to her literary works. The 1930s marked a low point in her career from which she was rescued by Peggy Guggenheim and by the publication of her most famous novel *Nightwood*. Barnes's last years before her death in 1982 were marked by isolation and neglect as if she were a writer living out of her time. Field has revised and updated this biography from the original hardback edition. H.D. has featured more prominently, partly because her *œuvre* is much more extensive. *Nights*, a novel which she originally published in a small private edition under the pen-name of John Helford, has now been issued [121]. Her daughter Perdita Schaffner explains in her introduction that the novel is a *roman-à-clef* with its characters being thinly disguised versions of H.D.'s Switzerland circle. Rachel Blau DuPlessis has written a first-class study of H.D.'s whole career [122] where she examines her complex relationships with Pound and Richard Aldington. H.D.'s interest in Greek writers like Sappho was strategic because it began her life-long engagement with issues of gender. For DuPlessis her prose fiction attempted 'to unify such female experiences as sexuality and motherhood with creative power'. A fine exposition of H.D.'s 'mythic method' is given with its biographical debts to her Moravian upbringing, her visionary experiences in Corfu, etc. The two world wars had a symbolic importance for her as hinted at in the fire imagery of *Trilogy* which suggests the breaking of fixed moulds; and the period from 1946 was taken up with the narrative and linguistic investigation of female desire. The winter 1986 issue of *ConL* is a special issue devoted to H.D. which contains an interesting variety of contributions. It opens with a brief unpublished tribute by Pound and with four chapters from *Paint It To-Day*, a short unpublished novel which she wrote in 1921. The latter is introduced as the first prose work in which H.D. 'explores the significance of gender for creativity'. Comparisons are drawn with Marianne Moore and Sappho, and Adalaide Morris argues cogently that H.D.'s works are related to a pre-capitalist gift-economy, the gift for her standing in opposition to the market-place. Two of H.D.'s prose works receive especially detailed attention. Deborah Kelly Kloepfer struggles to make sense of the textual confusions of *Palimpsest*, concluding that it is a trilogy of related characters and themes where past and present are firmly distinguished. Joseph Milicia gives a semi-biographical reading of *Hedylus* which he sees as treating parent–child relationships through mythic themes. This special issue offers a particularly rewarding variety of articles.

Turning to novelists who stayed with native American materials, Willa

119. *I Could Never be Lonely Without A Husband: Interviews*, by Djuna Barnes, ed. by Alyce Barry, foreword by Douglas Messerli. Virago. pp. 396. pb £5.50.

120. *Djuna: The Formidable Miss Barnes*, by Andrew Field. Second edn. UTex (1985). pp. 287. pb $8.95.

121. *Nights*, by H.D., intro. by Perdita Schaffner. ND. pp. xvi + 106. pb $19.95.

122. *H.D.: The Career of That Struggle*, by Rachel Blau DuPlessis. Harvester. pp. xxi + 168. hb $16.95, pb £5.95.

Cather's works have also appeared in LAm [123]. The relevant volume opens with her first collection of short stories, *The Troll Garden*, some of which were revised for their first publication in book form (this version is taken as the authoritative one) and for subsequent editions. Sharon O'Brien also uses the first edition as the copy-text for the four novels included here (*O Pioneers!*, *The Song of the Lark*, *My Antonia*, and *One of Ours*) in preference to the heavily revised Autograph Edition where Cather deleted many descriptive passages. O'Brien has, however, helpfully included in her notes the Autograph Preface to *The Song of the Lark* and also the revised Introduction to *My Antonia*. It is particularly pleasing to find the original version of the latter restored along with W. T. Benda's illustrations. Bernice Slote has edited seven uncollected stories [124] which Cather wrote between 1915 and 1929 which will now complement the 1965 *Collected Short Fiction*. All these stories deal with urban life, the first two being set in Pittsburgh, the remainder in New York. Of the latter 'Coming, Eden Bower!', a tale of New York Bohemia at the turn of the century, is an anomaly in being a revised form of the first story in *Youth and the Bright Medusa*. Slote places these stories within Cather's career, noting her relationship with H. L. Mencken as the editor of *The Smart Set*, and discussing the variety of the stories' techniques. Cather's last novel, *Sapphira and the Slave Girl*, has also been re-issued [125] with a new introduction by Hermione Lee who relates the book to Cather's own family background, noting a tension between nostalgia and critical retrospection. The novel presents slavery as a subtly divisive institution which even sets daughter against mother. The different histories of the slaves and the whites, Lee argues, are not reconciled with each other and the novel ends in rather evasive nostalgia. Susan J. Rosowski [126] has acted on Willa Cather's location of herself within a Romantic tradition to examine her whole career in these terms. The result is a fresh analysis which breaks her fiction down into three main periods. Initially Rosowski sees a celebration of the imagination in *Alexander's Bridge* and of idyllic pastoralism in *O Pioneers!* In *One of Ours* there is an unresolved disparity between subject and object; and in *The Professor's House* a romantic version of the Fall. Finally *Lucy Gayheart* and *Sapphira and the Slave Girl* are Gothic novels exploring the 'underside of the romantic imagination'. This study is particularly successful in interpreting symbolism and structure (such as the alternation between separation and union in *My Antonia*), and will make a valuable addition to Cather criticism. Fritz Oehlschlaeger (*MFS*) applies the theories of R. D. Laing and Ernest Becker to *Alexander's Bridge* and the story 'Consequences' which are, he suggests, illuminated by the former's notion of ontological insecurity. This is primarily a psychological approach which is useful for explaining the divided nature and suicide of both protagonists. Alice Hall Petry (*SSF*) attempts to rescue the story 'Coming Aphrodite!' from critical neglect on the grounds that it includes an impressive portrait of a dog

123. *Early Novels and Stories*, by Willa Cather, ed. by Sharon O'Brien. LAm/CUP. pp. 1336. £30.

124. *'Uncle Valentine' and Other Short Stories: Willa Cather's Uncollected Short Fiction, 1915–1929*, ed. by Bernice Slote. UNeb. pp. xxx + 183. pb £6.60.

125. *Sapphira and the Slave Girl*, by Willa Cather, intro. by Hermione Lee. Virago. pp. xxiv + 295. pb £3.95.

126. *The Voyage Perilous: Willa Cather's Romanticism*, by Susan J. Rosowski. UNeb. pp. xvii + 284. £21.80.

and that it is a parable of the betrayal of artistic ideals. Thomas F. Strychacz (*SAF*) is even more impatient with the critics, taking them severely to task for refusing to read *The Professor's House* in the light of Cather's assertion that it was her only ironic work. He demonstrates that ostensibly ideal environments in this novel are undermined and that Cather exposes Tom Outland's vision as being incorrigibly naïve.

There have been three other reprints of novels from the 1920s by women novelists. Of the three the most famous is Ellen Glasgow's *Barren Ground*[127] which comes with a new introduction by Paul Binding in which he claims that the novel marks a turning point in Glasgow's career. Specifically it grew out of a suicide attempt during the First World War and carries a symbolically bleak landscape to reflect her changed outlook on life. Although the novel reacts against Presbyterianism, Binding nevertheless declares that this is a very Protestant novel in its stress on individual self-reliance. Evelyn Scott was the subject of a biography by D. A. Callard in 1985 (*YW* 66.601) and her novel about familial failure and collapse, *The Narrow House*, has now been reprinted[128]. Margaret Leech's *Tin Wedding*[129] is also a novel of flawed domesticity and describes the discovery of a New Yorker that her marriage has been founded on deceit. In view of the fact that neither Evelyn Scott nor Margaret Leech are well known these two reprints suffer from the absence of introductions which would place the novels in a context.

Where the American Naturalists are concerned, two volumes of Jack London reprints have appeared. Three comparatively little-known stories – 'All Gold Canyon' (1905), 'The Night Born' (1911), and 'The Red One' (1918) – have been edited by London's biographer, Earl Labor[130]. *The Cruise of the 'Snark'* has been re-issued with a new introduction by Kaori O'Connor[131] who places the book within the context of London's life. He summarizes the familiar story of London's varied jobs, his experiences in the Yukon, and his interest in socialism. This voyage (1907–9) was partly inspired by London's childhood reading of Stevenson and Melville, and once it had been undertaken it 'renewed his faith in individual effort, courage, and daring'.

Critical interest in Dreiser has produced new interpretative studies rather than reprints, although one exception is a *Sister Carrie* Portfolio which has been published by James L. W. West III[132] who set up the definitive Pennsylvania text of that novel. This gives a documentary history of the novel's composition. Reproducing key passages from manuscripts and typescripts, West shows how Dreiser's wife 'Jug' constantly tinkered with the text, toning down its sexual references, and how errors crept in during copying. Dreiser's friend Arthur Henry also played a part in revising the novel, although Dreiser himself added a philosophical coda which was subsequently changed by Jug

127. *Barren Ground*, by Ellen Glasgow, intro. by Paul Binding. Virago. pp. xii + 409. pb £4.50.

128. *The Narrow House*, by Evelyn Scott. Norton. pp. 221. pb £5.95.

129. *Tin Wedding*, by Margaret Leech. Norton. pp. 279. pb £5.95.

130. *A Trilogy*, by Jack London, ed. by Earl Labor. Kingman: JLRC. pp. 50. pb $8.

131. *The Cruise of the 'Snark'*, by Jack London, intro. by Kaori O'Connor. RKP. pp. 307. pb £6.95.

132. *A 'Sister Carrie' Portfolio*, by James L. W. West III. UVirginia (1985). pp. vii + 87. $25.

when making a fair copy. After the novel's first rejection Dreiser made further extensive revisions, again with the help of Henry. This portfolio is a sad testimony to Dreiser's difficulties in getting his first novel published. Richard Lingeman has written a new biography of Dreiser (Putnam) which was not available for review, and Jeanetta Boswell has compiled a bibliography of writings about Dreiser [133], some of them from as early as 1911. She arranges her 1,708 items alphabetically and includes pieces which only mention Dreiser briefly as well as forewords and afterwords to his works. Some of the pieces listed here have been tracked down in very obscure periodicals and credit must be given for the sheer thoroughness of this bibliography. Where items are substantial an indication of content and often direct quotations are supplied. Sensibly Boswell decided not to include reviews since these have already been covered in Jack Salzman's *The Critical Reception* (1972). This bibliography will be of great interest to readers of Dreiser because it will enable them to check out, for instance, the critical controversy over his pessimism. Arun Mukherjee [134] has breathed new life into a familiar topic – Dreiser's treatment of business in his fiction. He argues that we should not separate the discourse of his novels from that of business publicists, and demonstrates that the latter is based on the figure of the heroic quest and the imagery of knight errantry. He then examines Dreiser's autobiographical works and stresses the presentation of the city as a fairyland and the connection between the theatre and the rags-to-riches myth. In contrast with many previous Dreiser critics Mukherjee presents the Cowperwood Trilogy as a satire on the success pattern and argues that Dreiser's other novels apply the heroic myth ironically (hence the importance, for instance, of military metaphors in *Sister Carrie*). Mukherjee does a very good job of explaining the implications of Dreiser's language, whereas Nathan Glick (*Dialogue*) has written a bland re-appraisal which argues that Dreiser's work is of abiding interest because he opened up new subject areas which had been neglected by earlier American fiction. Carol A. Schwartz (*ALR*) neatly sidesteps the critical emphasis on naturalism by discussing the collision between the Cinderella story and Tolstoyan social criticism in *Jennie Gerhardt*. She denies that a philosophical frame of reference is important for understanding this novel. Stephen C. Brennan (also in *ALR*) uses *An Amateur Laborer* to discuss the sexual reasons for Dreiser's nervous breakdown, taking the protagonist as a partial projection of the author. This year's numbers of *DN* open with an account of the factual unreliability of *Newspaper Days* by T. D. Nostwich, who is preparing a critical edition of this work. He reprints a sketch from 1894, 'The Last Fly of Fly Time', to demonstrate Dreiser's distorting description of it. Thomas P. Riggio has described the Dreiser commemoration held at Los Angeles Public Library in 1946 and Philip L. Gerber examines the significance of acting in *Sister Carrie* as a demonstration of the 'drive to become what one is not'. A checklist of Dreiser criticism in 1985 is also included, as is the important announcement that a definitive Pennsylvania Edition will be produced of all of Dreiser's works.

As usual the three big names of Fitzgerald, Hemingway, and Faulkner

133. *Theodore Dreiser and the Critics, 1911–1982*, by Jeanetta Boswell. Scarecrow. pp. ix + 305. £27.50.

134. *The Gospel of Wealth in the American Novel*, by Arun Mukherjee. CH. pp. 229. £19.95.

dominate the critical scene. Penguin has issued Fitzgerald's collected stories [135] in a volume which puts together *The Diamond as Big as the Ritz*, *The Pat Hobby Stories*, etc. It carries no new introduction and includes none of the uncollected stories subsequently edited by Matthew J. Bruccoli. Nevertheless it is useful to have these stories in one cheap edition. Two memoirs have appeared which relate to Fitzgerald's later years. In the first Sheilah Graham [136] has written an account of the period from 1937 to his death in 1940, which tries to set the record straight on a number of issues including that of Fitzgerald's alcoholism. The first chapters give an outline biography, really an oblique autobiography since they draw so heavily on what Fitzgerald told Sheilah Graham. He receives praise as a father until he tries to involve his daughter Scottie in his deteriorating relationship with Zelda. Fitzgerald's drinking is described rather than analysed, although Graham does show the strange personality changes which drunkenness brought on. A tactful portrait of Fitzgerald as a lover emerges but the most interesting chapters show his difficulties with the Hollywood system. In this period (when writing *The Last Tycoon*) Fitzgerald collaborated with Graham on a play, *Dame Rumor*, which is included in this volume. Liberal quotations from unpublished letters also help to make this memoir of more biographical interest than Sheilah Graham's earlier volume, *Beloved Infidel*. In 1939 Fitzgerald advertised for a secretary and the post was filled by Frances Kroll (as she then was), who has now written her own account of Fitzgerald's last year [137]. It is a frankly partisan account but her excellent recall of details helps to counter the stereotyped image of Fitzgerald the alcoholic. She shows how even small practical details were a problem to him, particularly as he was trying to do some writing every day. Of particular interest is Frances Kroll Ring's description of his work on *The Last Tycoon* (which she helped to have published posthumously). Fitzgerald emerges as a perfectionist, meticulously correcting his drafts. *Against the Current* is an informative memoir which reproduces many of Fitzgerald's notes in the text.

Matthew J. Bruccoli has edited a new collection of essays on *The Great Gatsby* [138] in the first of which Richard Anderson considers the 'shadow' of Gatsby as it falls on other novelists such as Budd Schulberg and John Irving. Roger Lewis then adds a rather bland essay on the disconnection between Gatsby's love for Daisy and his acquisitive drive for money. Susan Parr usefully (though in great detail) demonstrates that paradox is central to the novel, particularly when characters knowingly embrace illusion; and Kenneth Eble takes up the potentially fascinating question of how *The Great Gatsby* relates to the notion of the Great American Novel. In practice, however, this boils down to gestures towards *Moby-Dick* and *Huckleberry Finn* as a preamble to locating the novel's greatness. One of the best pieces in this collection is George Garrett's analysis of the relation of time to language, proposing that the novel excels as an example of the written vernacular. This makes an exception to the

135. *The Collected Stories of F. Scott Fitzgerald*. Penguin. pp. 582. pb £5.95.

136. *The Real Scott Fitzgerald*, by Sheilah Graham. Comet. pp. 259. pb £5.95.

137. *Against the Current: As I Remember F. Scott Fitzgerald*, by Frances Kroll Ring, intro. by A. Scott Berg. CA (1985). hb $14.95, pb $6.95.

138. *New Essays on 'The Great Gatsby'*, ed. by Matthew J. Bruccoli. CUP. pp. viii + 120. hb £20, pb £6.95.

bulk of these essays which tread in familiar paths. Kathleen Parkinson has contributed a study of *Tender is the Night* to the Penguin Masterstudies series [139] in which she relates the novel to a number of contexts (Fitzgerald's biography, World War I as a cultural watershed, expatriation, etc.). She also considers its divergences from linear chronology and the play of one perspective against another. Richard Godden (*L&H*) surveys the broad shifts in the American economy in order to place *Tender is the Night* within fiction of manners. In an interesting application of Marx he argues that the novel's subject is the 'relocation of accumulations' and that Dick Diver becomes a composer of mental interiors. In the same journal Geoff Cox explores the relation between language and ideology in *The Great Gatsby*, considering ways in which the book as commodity affects how we constitute its text. John Skinner (*JNT*) goes back to the familiar topic of Fitzgerald's respect for Conrad, specifically to compare *Heart of Darkness* with *The Great Gatsby*. The result is to show that the latter possesses a far greater variety of narrative modes. Leland S. Person Jr (*SSF*) puts forward Fitzgerald's story 'O Russet Witch!' as epitomizing the dual image of woman in American literature diagnosed by Leslie Fiedler. Caroline, the main female character, is both creative and destructive, an ambivalence established by the repressed Merlin Grainger's perspective on her. Gerald Pike in the same journal acts on Fitzgerald's statement that the story 'Winter Dreams' represented a trial of the idea for *The Great Gatsby*, showing how he varied his narrative voice to straddle cynicism and romantic ideas.

Most of the books on Hemingway this year have been biographical, but a new work by him has appeared. In 1946 he began a novel called *The Garden of Eden*, worked on it for fifteen years, and left it among his papers on his death. It has now been published [140] with minor cuts and corrections. The novel takes up many scenes from his prewar fiction and presents a *ménage à trois* centring on a young American writer living in the South of France. Undoubtedly the main study of Hemingway this year is Jeffrey Meyers's biography [141] which sheds important new light on several areas of his life. Meyers argues that the real Hemingway was a quiet, meditative artist but that his efforts to live up to the self-images of sage and soldier turned him into a bully and a braggart. The parade of women in his life makes a chilling narrative of Hemingway's egotism. He also demonstrates interesting influences from Kipling and Tolstoy. The common factor linking the three writers is war and Meyers shows that Hemingway was at his best in combat. Drawing on the latter's extensive F.B.I. file, he examines Hemingway's private spy network in Cuba, his work for the O.S.S. in 1944–5, and even demonstrates that the F.B.I. dogged him to the Mayo Clinic where he received electrotherapy in 1960–1. Meyers has produced an excellent and scholarly study which makes no attempt to mask the unattractive side of his subject.

By coincidence two accounts of Hemingway's youth have appeared. In *The Young Hemingway* [142] Michael Reynolds excludes Hemingway's famous

139. *F. Scott Fitzgerald: 'Tender is the Night': A Critical Study*, by Kathleen Parkinson. PM. Penguin. pp. 103. pb £1.50.

140. *The Garden of Eden*, by Ernest Hemingway. Scribner. pp. 247. $18.95.

141. *Hemingway: A Biography*, by Jeffrey Meyers. Macmillan. pp. xv + 646. £16.95.

142. *The Young Hemingway*, by Michael Reynolds. Blackwell. pp. 291. £14.95.

wound in Italy from his study. For him the paradoxical combination of conservatism and openness to change in his home town Oak Park reflects a similar combination of qualities in the writer (experimental style, traditional structure). Reynolds is excellent on background, influence (Teddy Roosevelt and Kipling once again come in for particularly substantial discussion), and on Hemingway's 'genetic inheritance' from his parents. It was his mother who played a repressive role in projecting her puritanical mysticism on to her son and so, not surprisingly, it was against her that Hemingway rebelled. Reynolds's account closes with the young Hemingway preparing to set out for the Continent. In *Along With Youth*[143] Peter Griffin has used various new collections of Hemingway materials (letters to his friend Bill Horne, for instance) to give a remarkably detailed narrative of his life up to his marriage with Hadley. He too stresses the complicating influence of his mother and includes five hitherto unpublished short stories which show how quickly Hemingway transmuted his own experiences into fiction. One of the most interesting implications of this book – it is a problem that it seems to deal in implications and not explicit comment – is that Hemingway's high-school course in journalism and subsequent practical experience led him to experiment with prose vignettes long before he went to Paris. Anthony Burgess's brief biography of Hemingway[144], which still remains one of the best summaries of the subject, has been reprinted. Burgess's crisp and ironic style nicely distances us from Hemingway's postures and obsession with death. This work carries a generous selection of photographs. Gerald B. Nelson and Glory Jones have produced a Hemingway volume for the Facts on File Chronology Series[145]. This consists of a year-by-year biographical skeleton which lists publications and then Hemingway's varied activities in sport, writing, etc. The entries relate the life to contemporary world events and make a useful synthesis of factual data which will be worth consulting by anyone with an interest in Hemingway. Finally, the novelist's son Jack has written a cross between a memoir and an autobiography, *Misadventures of a Fly Fisherman*[146]. As a child he witnessed his father's struggles to establish himself as a writer and glimpsed his friendship with other expatriates like Pound and Gertrude Stein. When Hemingway divorced Hadley, Jack ('Bumby') became a commuter between Florida and Europe and during this period developed a passion for the outdoors, for fishing in particular. A large proportion of this volume is thus devoted to his various hunting and fishing expeditions. During the war Jack joined the O.S.S., serving behind enemy lines in France, and subsequently joined the psychological warfare unit of special forces. Although he led an eventful life Jack Hemingway's volume is mainly of interest in connection with his father. He corrects some details of fact (when Hemingway signed his will, for instance), and criticizes the shortcomings of the various Hemingway biographies.

Turning to Hemingway criticism, Earl Rovit and Gerry Brenner have

143. *Along With Youth: Hemingway, The Early Years*, by Peter Griffin. OUP. pp. x + 258. £12.95.

144. *Ernest Hemingway*, by Anthony Burgess. T&H. pp. 128. pb £3.25.

145. *Hemingway: Life and Works*, by Gerald B. Nelson and Glory Jones. FOF. pp. 200. hb £12.95, pb £6.95.

146. *Misadventures of a Fly Fisherman*, by Jack Hemingway. TaylorCo. pp. 326. $17.95.

brought out a new edition of their study for TUSAS [147] which skilfully pinpoints central issues. They stress the relationship between a hero/tutor and a tyro as one underpinning much of his fiction, a pattern which helped to establish a life code, although they admit that no individual work ever quite illustrates that code. A detailed analysis of *The Sun Also Rises* is given to demonstrate general themes and valuable chapters are devoted to time, the Hemingway legend, and posthumous works. In the latter case a cautionary note is struck because other (editorial) hands have assembled these volumes. By taking into account the proliferation of recent Hemingway scholarship Rovit and Brenner have ensured that their book will stay the best critical introduction to his works. Chelsea House has started a major Modern Critical Views series under the general editorship of Harold Bloom which will cover all the main writers in English of this century. Among its first publications is a collection on Hemingway [148] (other volumes were not available for review), in which a miscellany of classic (and, it must be added, now rather dated) pieces by Lionel Trilling, Edmund Wilson, Harry Levin, and others figure. The famous *ParisR* interview is included, as are Malcolm Cowley's reflections on Hemingway *vis-à-vis* the writer's trade. Three essays have particular value here: Mark Spilka's discussion of the death of love in *The Sun Also Rises*, Steven K. Hoffman's exploration of the concept of *nada* (a 'series of significant absences') as a unifying theme in the short fiction, and John Hollander's examination of Hemingway's 'extraordinary reality'. The latter essay was written for this volume and analyses the enigmatic and symbolic dimensions of Hemingway's landscapes. Oddvar Holmesland (*ES*) opposes David Lodge's reading of 'Cat in the Rain' and queries whether structuralism is really of value in approaching texts. He sees the significance of the big cat as problematic but arrives at the conclusion that the story presents a 'spatial opposition between fertility and its contrast'. Jerry A. Herndon (*SAQ*) joins the critical debate over 'The Snows of Kilimanjaro' and agrees that the dream-flight ending is redemptive. He sees this as the resolution of a meditative sequence whereby the protagonist achieves honesty with himself. Kenneth G. Johnstone (*SSF*) relates the story 'A Way You'll Never Be' to Hemingway's own life, but beyond suggesting some approximate correspondence does not add much to our knowledge of the story. George Monteiro (also *SSF*) suggests situational parallels between 'The Battler' and Melville's 'Benito Cereno'. A refreshing change from these slight pieces is Paul Smith's analysis of the stories Hemingway wrote between 1919 and 1921 (*AL*). Drawing on manuscript sketches and drafts he describes the variety of styles tried (the 'Chicago style' coming ready-made from Ring Lardner and others) and considers Hemingway's imitations of E. W. Howe's small-town sketches. This is a valuable critical and bibliographical article. It is a sad comment on the critical neglect of John Dos Passos that a recent number of *RALS* (1983) should consist of general articles surveying treatment of his life (Townsend Ludington) and criticism (Linda W. Wagner). Among the gaps they find to be filled are exact details on Dos Passos's involvement with the Communist Party and his activities as a painter and playwright.

147. *Ernest Hemingway*, by Earl Rovit and Gerry Brenner. Twayne. pp. 214. $15.95.
148. *Ernest Hemingway: Modern Critical Views*, ed. by Harold Bloom. ChelseaH. pp. 233. $24.50.

By contrast the Faulkner industry is at full production. First of all LAm has brought out a volume of novels from the period 1930–5 [149], i.e. *As I Lay Dying*, *Sanctuary*, *Light in August*, and *Pylon*. The editor, Noel Polk, has taken as his copy-texts Faulkner's own corrected typescripts and has discovered that Faulkner's publishers made countless small changes to spelling and punctuation, changes which amounted to 'wholesale revision' in the case of *Pylon*. With *Sanctuary* the situation is even more complex and further confused by Faulkner's notoriously misleading 1932 introduction to that novel. Polk (who has also published the original version of *Sanctuary* in a separate volume) therefore deserves congratulations for having set up authoritative texts of these novels. UMissip has continued to bring out volumes in their guide to the Brodsky collection, but these were not available for review, and Brodsky himself (*SB*) has published the text of a short speech delivered by Faulkner in Caracas in 1961, acknowledging his receipt of the Order of Andres Bello. The speech comes accompanied with a biographical commentary. A rather more important article also by Brodsky has appeared in *SoR*, where he demonstrates Faulkner's consistent view of himself (and writers in general) as ineffectual. In a very well-documented survey Brodsky shows that the heroic figure of the soldier countered this passivity and that, in spite of his obvious success Faulkner's projected self-image (in letters, speeches, etc.) never squared with the facts of his career. In *SAQ* Carl E. Rollyson Jr draws on existing Faulkner biographies to try to understand his relation with his wife Estelle. If she never seemed to represent a complete woman to him, on the other hand he never did her real justice either.

Of this year's Faulkner criticism two books should be mentioned first. James A. Snead's *Figures of Division* [150] offers a fresh look at the novels from 1929 to 1942. This apparently stale undertaking is given new vigour by Snead's assimilation of political and linguistic structures which brings original insights. For instance Benjy's chaos at the beginning of *The Sound and the Fury* collapses racial distinctions together and is expressed gesturally by going through a fence (i.e. a barrier). Or again, in *As I Lay Dying* divisions of language are nicely related to social exclusion. Snead argues forcefully that a critical emphasis on characters' psychology in Faulkner's early works has resulted in a lopsided view of his fiction, one which understates the all-present social issue of racial separation. So *Go Down, Moses* exploits the wilderness as a counter to this division. Snead gives us a very interesting account of presence and absence in Faulkner, whereas Wook-Dong Kim [151] has developed an approach to Faulkner initiated by French critics in the 1940s, namely that he should be read as a consistent existentialist. Accordingly Kim uses Sartre, Kierkegaard, and other theorists to argue that Faulkner sees man as a 'lonely, anguished being in an absurd universe'. He backs this up with a close discussion of Faulkner's obsession with time, the insistent theme of death, use of the prison image, etc. This careful study ranges over the whole of Faulkner's career

149. *Novels 1930–1935*, by William Faulkner, ed. by Noel Polk. LAm/CUP. pp. 1034. £30.

150. *Figures of Division: William Faulkner's Major Novels*, by James A. Snead. Methuen. pp. xvii + 237. £28.

151. *The Edge of Nothing: An Existential Reading of William Faulkner*, by Wook-Dong Kim. ASIS: Knowledge. pp. 243.

and usefully points out his concern with alienation. One reservation must be noted: Kim moves rather too easily from the stated beliefs of characters to those of Faulkner himself.

MissQ has issued a special Faulkner number introduced by a vigorous denunciation of critics' attitudes to Temple Drake in *Sanctuary*. Dianne Luce (in the face of strong textual evidence to the contrary) argues that Temple is initially an innocent and that she seeks sanctuary throughout. Steve Price also concentrates on character, this time on Shreve's fascination with Bon in *Absalom, Absalom!* which leads him to give his story a final closure. Laurie A. Bernhardt tries to rectify the overemphasis on Harry Wilbourne in *The Wild Palms* by showing that the novel is as much the tragedy of Charlotte Rittenmeyer and David Paul Ragan scrutinizes *Absalom, Absalom!* to try to pinpoint what exactly Quentin learned on his visit to Sutpen's Hundred in 1909. These are all very specific, not to say narrow, essays concerned with niceties of fact and character but the journal also includes a previously unpublished version of the story of Flem Snopes and the horse auction at Frenchman's Bend entitled 'As I Lay Dying'. Jerry A. Varsava (*IFR*) briefly considers the complexities of the characters in *Flags in the Dust* as the result of direct and indirect means of depiction. Susan V. Donaldson (*SoR*) puts forward the story of Isaac McCaslin as an exception to Faulkner's usual 'cycle of repetition and entrapment'. McCaslin, she suggests, tries to close the gap between his vision and reality. David Krause (*CentR*) re-examines the importance of Mr Compson's letter to Quentin in *Absalom, Absalom!*, approaching it as a text-within-a-text. He notes among other things Quentin's deference to his father's authority, and a number of other issues. Lothar Hoennighausen (*Amst*) has examined those aspects of the same novel which arrest its forward movement and suggest that it should be read as a modernist poem. This is good rhetorical analysis dealing with repetition, suspended moments, leitmotifs, etc. and is part of a forthcoming book on Faulkner's relation to his context of artistic experiment. David Kleinbard (*SoR*) charts the development of Darl's illness in *As I Lay Dying*. Partly this is a pathological outline; and partly he considers how Darl's symptoms (e.g. his ability to identify with other members of the family) make him an unconscious novelist. Charles Palliser (*AL*) on the other hand relates Darl's barn-burning to Addie's adultery. Both are desperate acts, but while Darl accepts his fate Addie rages against hers. Palliser finds textual invitations to compare the monologues of both characters (for instance in their use of the term 'shape'). Laura Matthews (*JNT*) tackles the monologues of this novel from a more formal viewpoint. She too considers Darl's role specifically, arguing that his insanity gave Faulkner a pretext for inserting 'poetical language' into his story. Her article gives a good discussion of how one narrator corroborates another. Michael Grimwood (*SSF*) approaches Faulkner's story 'Golden Land' as thinly disguised autobiography which expresses his own 'emerging ambivalence about "home"' and which is therefore not just a satire of utopian dreams in California. Dirk Kuyk Jr, Betty M. Kuyk, and James A. Miller (*JAmS*) have used the story 'That Evening Sun' to argue generally that Faulkner virtually always avoids using black stereotypes in his fiction. They consider the publishing history and critical assessments of 'That Evening Sun' as well as giving an analysis of its structure and political themes. Turning to the later works Louise K. Barnett (*CentR*) sees *The Hamlet* as depicting a restricted speech community where characters' speech gives an immediate indication of their status, and John E. Bassett (*SLJ*) sees *The Reivers* as a revision of *Go Down, Moses* in two ways: 'the updating of stories through sequels or reanalysis of motivations' and 'new treatments of a type of conflict or theme'. Bassett uses this example as part of a rather obvious general argument that Faulkner's later works revise his earlier ones. Finally we should mention that in *RALS* (1985) Panthea Reid Broughton has surveyed Faulkner criticism for 1984.

Among work on the contemporaries of these writers Clare Colquitt (*MFS*) surveys critical treatments of Sherwood Anderson's *Death in the Woods* (which has been reprinted by Norton but was not available for review). She relates this work to the death of Anderson's mother and then gives a detailed close reading which concentrates on the aesthetic transformation of the protagonists. Charles E. Bodlin, Hilbert H. Campbell, and Kenichi Takada (*SB*) have assembled a list of additions to Anderson's bibliography including his contributions to *Vanity Fair* and to the little magazines of the period. Aldo P. Magi and Richard Walser have edited twenty-five interviews with Thomas Wolfe [152] which cover the period 1929 to 1938 and which, it must be admitted, are rather repetitive. The interviews constantly put a stress on Wolfe's physical size referring to him as 'prodigious' and the 'weary giant'. The themes covered in these pieces include: writing from experience, the acceptance of *Look Homeward, Angel*, Wolfe's own life, his writing methods, and his reading (he sets his admiration for Whitman firmly on record). The interviews are mostly brief and in many cases summarized to the point where they became portraits. Richard Reed (*SLJ*) points out that the transactions in real estate in *Look Homeward, Angel* closely correspond to the dealings of Wolfe's own family. They are used in the novel to develop character dynamics (e.g. Eliza Grant's ambitions). This year's numbers of the *TWN* carry a reminiscence of the novelist by his cousin Mary Westall and an analysis by Leslie Field of George Webber (the protagonist of *The Web and the Rock*) who is seen as being trapped in a set of oppositions. Rena R. Corey discusses and illustrates Wolfe's brief contacts with the Hudson River aristocracy and James Boyer surveys Wolfe's methods of characterization from early caricature onwards. A. P. Hamilton makes a plea for a more favourable reading of Eliza Grant and a survey is concluded of music in Wolfe's works. Two noteworthy pieces here are Randy W. Oakes's brief discussion of myth in *The Web and the Rock* which he relates to Eliot and Joyce; and James Ray Blackwelder's examination of literary allusions in Chapter 24 of *Look Homeward, Angel* which, he argues, has been much misunderstood by critics. These numbers also carry pieces on the staging of the latter novel and its relation to the manuscripts as well as the usual Wolfe bibliography. Joel Fisher (*JAmS*) sets out to rescue Sinclair Lewis from critical neglect by arguing that he is a 'synthetic' writer blending different modes together as well as history and politics. Fisher concentrates on *Main Street* and *Babbitt* in this judicious article exploring the implications for Lewis's stance as a diagnostician in the symbolism of marriage contracts.

Japanese critics have continued to take a leading part in Steinbeck criticism, but first we must mention two new publications by Steinbeck himself. His journal of *The Grapes of Wrath* has been issued by Viking but was not available for review. To celebrate the eleventh anniversary of the opening of the Steinbeck Research Center a letter from Steinbeck to Dennis Murphy has been printed as a pamphlet[153]. Murphy was the son of a childhood friend of Steinbeck's and in 1957 was working on his first novel, *The Sergeant*. Steinbeck's letter has two main sources of interest. Firstly he was in the middle of a modern rendering of Malory's *Morte D'Arthur* and had become, as he admits, an incorrigible medievalist. Secondly his advice to Murphy is to resist any outside influences while writing his novel. Tetsumaro Hayashi has collected three essays on *The Moon Is Down* into a pamphlet[154]. The first draws on *Macbeth* to highlight the novel's political motifs of determinism, betrayal, etc., all bearing on the ultimate issue of freedom. The parallels and analogies with *Macbeth* persist in the second essay which considers the evocation of a 'hell on earth'. Here the world of the novel is examined under different aspects in turn (physical, psychological, political, and so on). In the third essay Hayashi interestingly describes the dramatic function of Dr Winter as chorus, indicator of the seasons, and prophet. Part I of Hayashi's study of Steinbeck and the Vietnam War[155] has now been published, a vital reminder that he did not only write about California. Hayashi shows that Steinbeck's romantic allegiance to quest-patterns and his disillusionment with the Communists in the 1930s heavily influenced his hawkish attitude to this war. A further important factor was Steinbeck's personal friendship with L. B. Johnson. Steinbeck interpreted his role as war correspondent as requiring praise and support for the American soldiers in the field, although his pessimism increased as the war dragged on. In 1974 the Steinbeck Research Center was founded at San Jose State University and over the subsequent years built up a substantial collection of materials from donations and purchases. Robert H. Woodward has now produced 'A Descriptive Catalogue' of this collection (*SJS*, 1985). He lists editions of Steinbeck's works (mainly American); then follows Steinbeck's contributions to books and periodicals. One of the main sections is, of course, the list of manuscripts which includes the ledger where Steinbeck wrote most of the stories for *The Long Valley*, the original version of *The Forgotten Village*, and the film-script of *The Pearl*. There are also important collections of correspondence, volumes of Steinbeck photographs, several of which are reproduced in this catalogue. John H. Timmerman[156] has set himself a particularly difficult task in attempting to formulate Steinbeck's literary creed from passing comments in letters; nevertheless he has persisted in his attempt, although he sometimes gives an impression of Steinbeck writing in a vacuum. It is valuable to argue that Steinbeck was a symbolist, although the view of him as a simple naturalist is surely now defunct. And it is obviously also important to point out the notion of the 'phalanx' (the human group), but here again Timmerman does not relate it to contemporary sociological or evolutionary

153. *'Your Only Weapon Is Your Work': A Letter by John Steinbeck to Dennis Murphy*, pref. by Robert DeMott. SRC (1985). pp. 20. pb $22.

154. *Steinbeck's World War II Fiction, 'The Moon Is Down': Three Explications*, by Tetsumaro Hayashi. SRI. pp. vi + 43. pb $30.

155. *John Steinbeck and the Vietnam War*, Part I, by Tetsumaro Hayashi. SRI. pp. xii + 23. $#0.

156. *John Steinbeck's Fiction: The Aesthetics of the Road Taken*, by John H. Timmerman. UOkla. pp. xvi + 314. $22.50.

thought. The main body of his study consists of a thematic analysis of Steinbeck's fiction. His discussion of the interchapters in *The Grapes of Wrath* is useful, as is the examination of literary allusions in *East of Eden* which is helpful to show how imagistic patterns are established. With the exception of those chapters, however, the discussion tends to be rather flat and does not do adequate justice to the sophistication of Steinbeck's narrative techniques. Roy S. Simmonds (*MissQ*) has compared Cathy Ames from *East of Eden* with Rhoda Penmark from William March's *The Bad Seed* as two child monsters, bringing out the patina of innocence, their similar family backgrounds, and their symbolic roles in the respective novels. Ray Lewis White (*RALS*, 1983) has assembled an annotated list of the reviews of *The Grapes of Wrath* to assess its reception in 1939. This year's *StQ* carries the rather perfunctory answers which Steinbeck wrote in 1938 to a questionnaire from one of the first researchers on his work. Since 1986 marks the twentieth anniversary of the Steinbeck Society a good deal of space is devoted to tributes. However Richard S. Pressman has taken exception to critical attempts to deny Steinbeck's proletarian sympathies. He argues ingeniously that collectivism is constantly undercut in *The Grapes of Wrath* by a counterforce pulling groups apart, and that the novel itself is riven by two extremes, a 'non-teleological biology and collectivist politics'.

Several less-known writers whose careers began in the 1930s have either had works reprinted or been the subject of criticism. A selection by Tom Kromer, which includes his one published novel *Waiting for Nothing* (1935), has now been edited [157]. Kromer started a second proletarian novel called 'Michael Kohler' and the few chapters which he managed to complete before abandoning his career as a writer appear in this collection along with Kromer's essays, stories, and book reviews. The novelist John Sanford, whose career was initially helped by William Carlos Williams, has started an autobiography which is written in a startlingly unusual style. The first volume [158] assembles a series of short scenes which alternate with fragments from the alternative socialist history of the United States. *The Waters of Darkness* [159] is devoted to his first novel, *The Water Wheel*, and the publication of his second, *The Old Man's Place*, in 1935. These are the years of his friendship with Williams and of his decision to adopt his present pen-name. Naomi Diamant (*ConL*) examines areas of discourse in Henry Roth's *Call It Sleep*. She classifies the work as a *Bildungsroman* revolving around the 'enormous power of metaphor', and analyses with fruitful results the interplay between the authorial, narrative, and experiential universes of this work. Charles Reznikoff is known primarily as a leading member of the Objectivists and *By the Waters of Manhattan* was used by him as a title for a selection of his poems in the 1960s. Much earlier, however, in 1930 he had already used this title for his first novel which has now been re-issued [160]. In his new introduction Milton Hindus draws attention to the

157. *'Waiting for Nothing' and Other Writings*, by Tom Kromer, ed. by Arthur D. Casciato and James L. W. West III. UGeo. pp. vii + 297. hb $24, pb $9.95.

158. *Scenes from the Life of an American Jew*. Vol. I: *The Color of the Air*, by John Sanford. BSP (1985). pp. 301. pb $12.50.

159. *Scenes from the Life of an American Jew*. Vol. II: *The Waters of Darkness*, by John Sanford. BSP. pp. 289. pb $12.50.

160. *By the Waters of Manhattan*, by Charles Reznikoff, intro. by Milton Hindus. Wiener. pp. xx + 264. pb $9.95.

importance of Reznikoff's legal training, the influence of Joyce, and the novel's modernistically open ending. This reprint will make available once again a novel from the early phase of Jewish-American fiction.

That *enfant terrible* of the expatriates Henry Miller has been the subject of four books this year, three of which characteristically are memoirs. The first, *Dear, Dear Brenda*[161], consists of a series of letters which Miller wrote to the actress Brenda Venus, placed within a tactful (and not uncritical) commentary by her. They met in 1976 when she went to hear Miller speak at an acting class and a relationship developed where she played 'muse and nurse', as Lawrence Durrell puts it in his introduction. Only a small proportion of the 1,500 letters Miller wrote have been selected here but they reflect an imaginative gusto in the way he composes erotic reveries about Brenda Venus and himself. These letters also reveal interesting details about Miller's taste in music and about his painting. They run up to 1980, a period when friends like Isaac Singer were proposing Miller for the Nobel prize. A new portion of Anais Nin's legendary diary, which covers 1931–2 when she took Miller as a lover, has been published[162]. Most of the material already available in the diary for 1931–4 has been omitted here, and these excerpts revolve around Anais Nin's exploration of her own sensuality. It is thus a diary of love-making, actual or imagined, where the diary itself is used as a confidant. Recording becomes complicated when portions are shown to Miller, and complicated yet again when she finds another confessional outlet in a psychoanalyst. A later period (1944 to the 1960s) is covered by Kathryn Winslow's memoir[163]. Although she was a friend and adviser of Miller's, she is never carried away by adulation. Instead she gives detailed reports of his friendships while he was living in Big Sur, and about his water-colours which represented a constant interest. In this period Miller was contributing essays to numerous little magazines while working on his own books (*Sunday After the War*, *The Rosy Crucifixion*, etc.); and he also collaborated with the painter Bezalel Schatz on a mixed-media volume, *Into the Night-Life*. In 1949 Winslow took over a studio in Chicago and converted it into a gallery and a means of promoting Miller's writings as well as those of Anais Nin. This cause was furthered by the establishment in 1954 of the Henry Miller Literary Society. *Henry Miller: Full of Life* sheds a lot of new light on Miller's later years. Miller's position as a writer is one where his status is bolstered by such memoirs while criticism of his works lags far behind. It is therefore welcome to see a new assessment of his major works by Leon Lewis[164]. He argues against treating Miller's works as allegories, suggesting instead that Miller was driven by a vision of transcendence. Accordingly he divides Miller's works into two categories. In the first Miller is a spectator or observer as in *Tropic of Cancer*, where he distances himself from the damaged characters of Paris, *The Colossus of Maroussi*, where he is a tourist, and *Black Spring*. The second category shows Miller as a participant and is represented by *Tropic of Capricorn*, *Sexus*, and *Nexus*. Lewis gives good explanations of motif

161. *Dear, Dear Brenda: The Love Letters of Henry Miller to Brenda Venus*, ed. by Gerald Seth Sindell, intro. by Lawrence Durrell. Morrow. pp. 191. $15.95.

162. *Henry and June*, by Anais Nin, ed. by Rupert Pole. HBJ. pp. viii + 274. $14.95.

163. *Henry Miller: Full of Life*, by Kathryn Winslow. Tarcher. pp. xvi + 364. $18.95.

164. *Henry Miller: The Major Writings*, by Leon Lewis. Schocken. pp. vii + 247. $19.95.

and structure but has curiously little to say about Miller's style (the flux of imagery, extended sentences, etc.) or about his possible connection with Surrealism.

The period between the wars saw the rise of the detective story and Dennis Dooley has written a valuable introduction to one of its founding members, Dashiell Hammett[165]. Rather than incorporating much Hammett criticism he has concentrated on close readings which stress irony, perspective, pace, and the treatment of violence; and which will therefore be of value to those coming to Hammett's fiction for the first time. He admits that it is impossible not to be conscious of Hammett's subsequent life, especially his difficulties during the McCarthy era, but insists that we should bear in mind the historical and social context of the novels. In 1947 Raymond Chandler struck a deal with Universal Studios to write single-handed the screenplay for a film to be called *Playback*. He produced two drafts (the later one has only recently been discovered) but a financial recession forced Universal to cancel the project. In line with his usual practice of reworking material, Chandler moulded the screenplay into a narrative and the novel *Playback* was published in 1958. Now the original screenplay has also been published[166], which gives us an excellent opportunity to study Chandler's management of scene and dialogue. Frank MacShane's masterly biography of Chandler has been issued in paperback[167]. Quoting extensively from unpublished material, he presents a complex view of Chandler as an Anglophile whose values were moulded in his years at Dulwich College. MacShane fills out the familiar story of Chandler's beginnings with *Black Mask* magazine noting that his inclination was always towards longer novels and towards burlesque. His work in Hollywood also provoked a complex reaction, a combination of exhilaration, depression, and outrage which pushed him towards drink. Some of these insights are echoed in Keith Newlin's brief study of Chandler's comic style, *Hardboiled Burlesque*[168]. He proposes three phases to Chandler's career. At the beginning he was heavily influenced by Hemingway and Hammett towards an objective style, one based on 'dialogue and concrete detail', as Chandler put it. Even in his early stories, however, Chandler was beginning to burlesque the clichés of the genre (coincidence, the lucky shot device, etc.). In the early 1940s Newlin argues that Chandler achieved a comic poise stylistically distinguished by the self-parodic wisecrack. From *The Little Sister* (1949) onwards Chandler's style declined into sentimentality. Harrap have reprinted James Ross's novel *They Don't Dance Much*[169] which Chandler praised for its authentic treatment of corruption. Two novels by W. L. Heath have been reprinted. *Violent Saturday*[170], his first work, is presented by Edward Gorman as a study of moral failure in a small Southern

165. *Dashiell Hammett*, by Dennis Dooley. Ungar (1985). pp. xv + 174. pb $5.95.

166. *Raymond Chandler's Unknown Thriller: The Screenplay of 'Playback'*, by Raymond Chandler. Harrap. pp. xxi + 168. £8.95.

167. *The Life of Raymond Chandler*, by Frank MacShane. HH. pp. xii + 306. pb £5.95.

168. *Hardboiled Burlesque: Raymond Chandler's Comic Style*, by Keith Newlin. hb Borgo (1984), pb Brownstone (1984). pp. 50. hb $14.95, pb $4.95.

169. *They Don't Dance Much*, by James Ross. Harrap. pp. 296. pb £5.95.

170. *Violent Saturday*, by W. L. Heath, intro. by Edward Gorman. CA. pp. x + 139. pb £2.95.

town; and *Ill Wind*[171] is related by Gorman to suspense fiction whereby a familiar situation is outlined prior to the introduction of a disruptive element. Gorman also gives a useful biographical summary showing Heath's war background and his beginnings in journalism.

A whole series of novelists from the Second World War up to the 1960s, working within a broadly realistic mode have had important works reprinted. A figure whose career begins even earlier, Thornton Wilder, has been the subject of an introductory study by David Castronovo[172]. He presents Wilder as a far more experimental writer than is widely recognized. The early novels deal with issues of isolation; the picaresque novels *Heaven's My Destination* and *Theophilus North* both treat of the dangers of idealism; and large abstract questions such as the nature of choice and freedom come to the forefront in the late novels *The Ides of March* and *The Eighth Day*. According to Castronovo, Wilder was impatient with naturalism in the theatre and his one-act pieces thus tended to question the nature of the well-made play. To complete this otherwise full picture a few comments would have been welcome on Wilder as a scholar of Spanish literature. Another writer whose career has a very broad span is Kay Boyle. Her second novel *Year Before Last* has been re-issued with an afterword by Doris Grumbach[173] who points out that it is clearly based on Boyle's relationship with the Irish-American poet Ernest Walsh. Numerous correspondences exist, some suggested by the memoir she wrote with Robert McAlmon, *Being Geniuses Together*. This novel is interpreted as a tribute to Walsh whereas *My Next Bride*[174], a later work, draws on Boyle's experiences in the colony founded by Raymond Duncan. Grumbach also points out that this novel marks a departure from earlier methods in using impressionistic and even occasional Gothic techniques. Sandra Whipple Spanier[175] has written a critical biography, long overdue, of Kay Boyle. She shows how Boyle came from a highly cultured family, receiving excellent support for becoming a writer from her mother. In the 1920s she lived in France, contributing to *transition* and other expatriate journals. In the 1930s she produced a series of psychological novels which towards the end of the decade showed more and more concern for politics. Boyle was actively involved in reconstruction work in postwar Germany and in the McCarthy hearings; and during the 1960s participated vigorously in the campaign against the Vietnam War. Spanier was fortunate enough to engage in correspondence with Boyle which has clearly helped her explication, but Boyle's life has been so varied that it is virtually impossible to do justice to her career. However one theme does emerge very clearly: that her writings were fuelled by political indignation.

Another writer whose fiction demonstrates political engagement is Martha Gellhorn (see also p. 692). Her first novel, *A Stricken Field*[176], which was

171. *Ill Wind*, by W. L. Heath, intro. by Edward Gorman. CA. pp. x + 189. pb £2.95.

172. *Thornton Wilder*, by David Castronovo. Ungar. pp. xi + 174. $14.95.

173. *Year Before Last*, by Kay Boyle, afterword by Doris Grumbach. Virago. pp. 329. pb £3.95.

174. *My Next Bride*, by Kay Boyle, afterword by Doris Grumbach. Virago. pp. 330. pb £3.95.

175. *Kay Boyle: Artist and Activist*, by Sandra Whipple Spanier. SIU. pp. vi + 261. $22.50.

176. *A Stricken Field*, by Martha Gellhorn. Virago. pp. 313. pb £3.95.

written in 1939 against the background of Hitler's invasion of Czechoslovakia, has been re-issued. John Hersey also started his career in the war and has given an Art of Fiction interview for *ParisR* where he discusses his childhood in China, his job as a manuscript-reader for Sinclair Lewis, his early experiences as a journalist, and his use of limited points of view in *Hiroshima*. A paperback edition of Irwin Shaw's collected short stories has been issued [177], the earliest of which date from the 1930s. The latter are Hemingwayesque exercises in naturalism which repeatedly use boxing as a theme and metaphor. After the war Shaw's subjects broaden geographically and politically, including European settings and themes from the McCarthy years. John O'Hara's stories [178] have also appeared under the editorship of Frank MacShane. In his introduction he discusses the importance of speech for O'Hara, as well as the influences of journalism and Hemingway. According to MacShane, O'Hara virtually invented the *New Yorker* short story single-handed. O'Hara's career is examined in an impressively broad article by Lee Sigelman (*JAmS*). In particular he explores the presentation of social order and sees O'Hara's works as displaying anger at the failure of the egalitarian dream. Sigelman is particularly good at explaining class animosity in the fiction although he declares that O'Hara pulled his political punches, not always following up the implications of his vision. A selection of Damon Runyon's stories [179] has been issued with a new introduction by Tom Clark, who suggests that Runyon has transposed the Wild West code of the outlaw onto the New York scene. He shows how Runyon's early experiences in journalism gave him plenty of material to weave into his stories, and how Runyon's ear for speech-patterns stood him in good stead for *Guys and Dolls*. Many of the Broadway tales turn out to be thinly disguised portraits of actual characters Runyon had observed in New York.

A slightly more miscellaneous series can be introduced by reprints of two women writers currently engaging critical interest. Dorothy Canfield's novel *Her Son's Wife* [180] comes with an excellent new introduction by Dorothy Goldman which draws on unpublished material to place this work in the author's whole career. She argues that Dorothy Canfield's purpose was to investigate roles and relations. Although the novel asserts the primacy of the family, it is not at all conservative about the position of women. *Her Son's Wife* is about education towards independence, thereby reflecting Canfield's active interest in Montessori methods. Further reprints by her are promised from Virago. Elizabeth Hardwick's *The Ghostly Lover* [181], her first novel, has also been reprinted with an afterword by the author which sets the book in a biographical context. Arthur Miller has written a new introduction to his sole novel *Focus* [182] which explains that it draws on his own experiences in the

177. *Short Stories: Five Decades*, by Irwin Shaw. Pan. pp. x + 756. pb £5.95.

178. *The Collected Stories of John O'Hara*, ed. with intro. by Frank MacShane. Pan. pp. xii + 414. pb £4.95.

179. *'Romance in the Roaring Forties' and Other Stories*, by Damon Runyon, intro. by Tom Clark. Beech Tree Bks: Morrow. pp. 394. pb $9.95.

180. *Her Son's Wife*, by Dorothy Canfield, intro. by Dorothy Goldman. Virago. pp. xvi + 288. pb £3.95.

181. *The Ghostly Lover*, by Elizabeth Hardwick. Virago. pp. 282. pb £3.95.

182. *Focus*, by Arthur Miller. Penguin. pp. 235. pb £3.95.

Brooklyn Naval Yard. He also reflects on the rise of Israel and the subsequent persistence of antisemitism in America. John P. Hayes's fine biography of James A. Michener[183] has been brought out in an English edition (see *YW* 65.647). And Edmund Wilson's 1946 novel *Memoirs of Hecate County*[184] has been re-issued, but without any new introduction.

The regional coherence of Southern fiction continues to attract a variety of critical treatments. Darlene Harbour Unrue[185] has located a unity in Katherine Anne Porter's fiction, namely the search for truth. She then considers the stories to test out this proposition, so that 'Maria Concepcion' and the early Mexican stories portray a decaying idealism. In effect Unrue is explicating this fiction along lines suggested by the author herself in statements of purpose with the result that the metaphysical is regularly given priority over other dimensions of meaning. Thus 'Flowering Judas' is about 'inner darkness' rather than revolution although Unrue has plenty to say about the impact which Mexican culture made on Porter. The commentaries on symbolism (on light in 'A Day's Work', for instance) are particularly penetrating and naturally prominence is given to Porter's novel *Ship of Fools* whose composition and structure are interestingly explained. Eudora Welty's novel *Losing Battles*[186] has been reprinted, but the reprint does not carry a new introduction. *MissQ* has devoted a special number to Welty which opens with an interview where she reminisces about her friendship with Elizabeth Bowen (a comparison between the two writers is later drawn by Peggy Whitman Prenshaw) and about the political mood of the 1960s. Harriet Pollack ingeniously bends reader-response theory back on the author to show that Welty's fiction 'repeatedly elicits expectations that it promptly defies', confirming this position with a close analysis of the story 'Powerhouse'. Discussions of specific works (*Delta Wedding, One Time, One Place*, and *One Writer's Beginnings*) are given as well as broader treatments. Danièle Pitavy-Souques tackles the rather neglected side of Welty as a modernist, demonstrating how her style thinly screens the unfamiliar; and Patricia S. Yaeger productively applies Bakhtin to show how Welty 'expropriates and redefines images from the masculine tradition'. This varied and valuable number concludes with a checklist of writings by and about Welty since 1973 which has been compiled by Pearl Amelia McHaney. James Walter (*JSSE*) considers the mythical and chronological implications of Phoenix Jackson's progression in 'A Worn Path', explaining him as a visionary quester; whereas Charles Clerc (*SSF*) pursues a close recording of 'Where is the Voice coming from?' to demonstrate the complex ironies of this monologue. Clerc also takes into account changes Welty made during composition. In the same journal A. R. Coulthard denies that 'Keela, the Outcast Indian Maiden' is a straightforward story of guilt and sees it rather as a depiction of purposelessness. Jill Fritz-Piggott (*SLJ*) pin-points moments of ripeness in Welty's *The Golden Apples*, epiphanies which clarify themes and which demonstrate a dualistic attitude towards experience. In the same number Barbara Wilkie

183. *James A. Michener: A Biography*, by John P. Hayes. Allen. pp. xiv + 276. £10.95.

184. *Memoirs of Hecate County*, by Edmund Wilson. Hogarth. pp. 457. pb £3.95.

185. *Truth and Vision in Katherine Anne Porter's Fiction*, by Darlene Harbour Unrue. UGeo (1985). pp. xiv + 267. $24.

186. *Losing Battles*, by Eudora Welty. Virago. pp. 436. pb £3.95.

Tedford offers a rather inconsequential discussion of references to West Virginia in Welty's work. In *SoR* Suzanne Marrs gives examples of Welty's portrayal of black characters in *Delta Wedding* and *The Golden Apples* where racial separation is metaphorically extended to represent the inevitable isolation of human life. Finally Floyd C. Watkins (also *SoR*) considers Welty as a writer in search of a whole society. *The Robber Bridegroom* is thus seen as dealing with an 'unfallen world' where love-making relationships in general receive a double treatment.

The other major Southern novelists to receive extended treatment are Flannery O'Connor and Walker Percy. Frederick Asals[187] has found a polarizing impulse at the centre of O'Connor's fiction, especially in her later works where extremes move the narratives away from a humanistic centre. The polarities might vary from the racial to a contrast between night and day but Asals asserts that the pattern is fairly constant. He notes influences from West and Poe on *Wise Blood* and engages with O'Connor's use of sacramental symbolism. He puts forward a consistent and plausible case against seeing her as a realist, demonstrating her selective deployment of melodrama, biblical allusion, etc. As if drawing back from the bleak implications of O'Connor's grotesque narratives, Asals tries to find 'inverted affirmations' even in such unlikely characters as Hazel Motes. Harold Fickett and Douglas R. Gilbert[188] have produced a volume on O'Connor which is really two books in one. Fickett gives a lucid account of her life and literary career, stressing the importance of the South and the effects of her illness. Like Asals he too sees O'Connor's sacramental sensibility as one which refused to accept the limitations of naturalism. It is rather a leap from these assertions to the tendentious proposition that O'Connor was writing from the viewpoint of an orthodox Christian, since this would have difficulty in coping with her repeated images of blocked or inverted spirituality. Gilbert concludes this volume with a photographic essay on the South which stresses rural and small-town settings. Shirley Foster (*JAmS*) wisely leaves questions of affirmation aside and examines O'Connor's 'aesthetic of discomposure' whereby distortion and shock tactics are used to assault the reader. Concentrating on a selection of short stories she demonstrates that the two main levels of assault are physical violence and 'intellectual chastisement'. Where this article actually investigates the experience of reading O'Connor, William Rodney Allen (*AL*) turns to imagery surveying the references to animals and closed spaces in *Wise Blood*. These images are then related dutifully to the distorted psychologies of O'Connor's characters. Arthur E. Kenney (*MR*) takes up O'Connor's own assertion that her fiction deals with religious grace. He finds that she presents a warped version of religion but denies that she leaves faith behind. On the contrary her fiction is designed to 'recognize sin for what it is', but Kenney does not spell out the formal consequences of this purpose. Robert H. Brinkmeyer Jr (*SLJ*) also takes up religion, but finds crucial signs of Southern fundamentalism in O'Connor's works in spite of her Catholic beliefs. Evidence for this unusual position includes the revival scene in *The Violent Bear It Away* and

187. *Flannery O'Connor: The Imagination of Extremity*, by Frederick Asals. UGeo. pp. 268. pb $10.

188. *Flannery O'Connor: Images of Grace*, by Harold Fickett and Douglas R. Gilbert. Eerdmans. pp. 151. $18.95.

parallels between her narrative style and the methods of evangelical sermons. Also in *SLJ* Jeffrey J. Folks brings out O'Connor's hostility towards mechanization and her formulation of a creed that 'demanded complete fidelity to the naturalistic facts of the objective world while it sought to express supranaturalistic insights'. And so by another route we come back to sacramental symbolism. Ashley Brown (*SoR*) has edited a small collection of letters between Flannery O'Connor and Susan Jenkins Brown. The two women only met once in 1955, when Brown tried to enlist her help in publishing a novel by Caroline Gordon, but the friendship lasted until 1959.

Jerome Taylor[189] has surveyed the works of Walker Percy through a reading of Kierkegaard, a philosopher whom Percy greatly admires. Accordingly it is not surprising that Percy has given a public endorsement of this study. Taylor's method is to extrapolate a topic from Kierkegaard and then to apply it to Percy's non-fiction and to his characters who are treated as the personifications of philosophical standpoints. Where Kierkegaard resists depersonalization, Taylor argues, Percy correspondingly rejects a purely biological view of man. A perfectly plausible case for Kierkegaard's influence is made out and Taylor also helpfully indicates some of Percy's general preoccupations (with self-abstraction, impersonation in American life, etc.). In the process he reads Percy's novels as parables, even referring to him as a 'modern-day seer'. William Rodney Allen[190] brings us back to earth by insisting that 'it is time to reclaim Percy as an American and, more specifically, a southern writer'. In spite of this brave declaration Allen takes us again through the intellectual issues dealt with by Percy's other critics. The influence of Kierkegaard reappears specifically on *The Moviegoer* and Allen also notes Percy's long-running quarrel with psychoanalysis. Identifying Percy's American characteristics virtually boils down to spotting allusions to earlier writers; so *Huckleberry Finn* has left its traces in *The Last Gentleman*, and *Lancelot* has been influenced by Robert Penn Warren's *All the King's Men*. The value of Allen's study lies more in its attempt than its achievement since he has rightly stated that a philosophical approach is not necessarily the only way to read Percy. John Desmond (*SoR*) also considers Percy's novel *Lancelot*, but draws comparisons with Eliot's 'Gerontion' to place Percy within a tradition of prophetic writers meditating on the shortcomings of contemporary society. Both works, he suggests, show the decline of the spiritual into the secular. In *MissQ* Desmond concludes that *Lancelot*'s protagonist is used to 'expose certain obsessions of the age'. In other words the novel is presented as an investigative or diagnostic narrative.

The historical trilogy of the Tennessee novelist and journalist T. S. Stribling has now been reprinted. Stribling began planning the series in the 1920s but the first volume, *The Forge*[191], did not appear until 1931. In a new introduction Randy K. Cross points out interesting examples of how Stribling changed the historical events of the Civil War in his novel, which revolves around the Vaiden

189. *In Search of Self: Life, Death, and Walker Percy*, by Jerome Taylor. Cowley. pp. 174. pb $7.95.

190. *Walker Percy: A Southern Wayfarer*, by William Rodney Allen. UMissip. pp. xx + 160. £21.95.

191. *The Forge*, by T. S. Stribling, intro. by Randy K. Cross. UAla (1985). pp. xvi + 525. hb $27.50, pb $12.95.

family of Alabama and dramatizes the changes which took place during Reconstruction. In *The Store*[192], according to Cross, Stribling presents the portrait of an age 'through the everyday lives of his characters'. This volume deals with the fate of the freed slaves and also with the economic shift from the big plantations to small-scale holdings. *Unfinished Cathedral*[193] concludes the trilogy with an account of the social changes of the 1920s which affected Southern blacks and Southern women alike. Moving forward to more recent fiction, Constance M. Perry (*SLJ*) uses Carson McCullers's short story 'Wunderkind' to show the importance of sexual initiation in *The Heart Is a Lonely Hunter*. The story prefigures Mick Kelly's characterization. *SoQ* has brought out a special number on the Mississippi novelist Stark Young, in which John Pilkington explores Young's family background to demonstrate his Southern roots. V. F. Gutendorf assesses Young's drama criticism for the *New Republic* and G. Frank Burns broadens the latter topic to explain Young's views on the artist's relation to society (Young, it is worth remembering, was a contributor to the Agrarian anthology *I'll Take My Stand*). Specimens of Young's fiction are discussed and an interesting comparison with Faulkner closes this issue. In the 1960s Richard Yates was commissioned to produce a screenplay of William Styron's novel *Lie Down in Darkness*, but then found it impossible to place with any movie company. The work was subsequently unearthed by DeWitt Henry, the editor of *Ploughshares*, and it has now been published under that imprint[194]. George Bluestone has supplied an introduction which examines Styron's central theme of religious redemption and which evaluates Yates's management of scenes and transitions in this same novel. The former is interpreted as a parodic disruption of community whereas the latter constitutes a 'form of worship binding individual lives to a social community'. Also in *SLJ* Anne Foata argues that Andrew Lytle's novel *The Velvet Horn* possesses a three-layered structure. Lucius Cree's coming of age repeats an earlier action, both of which overlay a mythic theme of a fall into history. She provides an illuminating commentary on the chronological complexities of this novel whereas Thomas M. Carlson (*SoR*) begins to explore its labyrinthine structure, bringing out its riddles and ironic use of myth. This is such a close detailed discussion that it constantly verges on paraphrase. Lewis P. Simpson has edited three works of Southern Gothic in one volume[195], works chosen to confirm the survival of that tradition which revolves around the 'drama of the estrangement of the soul from the tradition of faith'. The first two date from the 1970s: *Beasts of the Southern Wild* by the North Carolina novelist Doris Betts, and *McAfee County* by another Carolina writer, Mark Steadman. The latter demonstrates a debt to Faulkner in assembling a series of interconnected short stories set in a fictitious area of Georgia. The third is

192. *The Store*, by T. S. Stribling, intro. by Randy K. Cross. UAla. pp. xiii + 571. hb $27.50, pb $12.95.

193. *Unfinished Cathedral*, by T. S. Stribling, intro. by Randy K. Cross. UAla. pp. xiii + 383. hb $27.50, pb $12.95.

194. *William Styron's 'Lie Down in Darkness': A Screenplay*, by Richard Yates, intro. by George Bluestone. Ploughshares. pp. 208. pb $8.95.

195. *Three by Three: Masterworks of the Southern Gothic*, by Doris Betts, Mark Steadman, and Shirley Ann Grau, intro. by Lewis P. Simpson. Peachtree. pp. xiv + 568. hb $22.95, pb $14.95.

Shirley Ann Grau's *The Black Prince* (1955). Turning to the Texan novelist Larry McMurty, Ernestine P. Sewell (*WAL*) has examined the protagonist and action of his novel *Lonesome Dove*, drawing comparisons with *Don Quixote* and extrapolating a myth of a Cowboy-God.

Only the leading practitioners of science fiction receive critical attention outside specialist journals. On the death of Philip K. Dick in 1982 Paul Williams became his literary executor. Earlier, in 1974, while assembling a profile of Dick, Williams recorded a number of conversations which he has now edited [196], setting them within a context of well-informed comment on Dick's career. The conversations revolve around a mysterious break-in to Dick's apartment, his nervous breakdowns, and his concern about extremist political organizations in California. Keith N. Hull (*MFS*) identifies an interrogation of humanity as one of the main themes in science fiction and addresses himself to those novels by Ursula K. Le Guin which best exemplify it. We are told that she challenges the reader's sense of human limitations through fiction which 'risks being polemical and sentimental'. One might query the assumption that polemic does not belong in successful novels but the article otherwise offers a lucid and straightforward introduction to this author. Kurt Vonnegut's second novel, *The Sirens of Titan* [197], has been reprinted without a new introduction in the new Gollancz series of Classic Science Fiction.

From writers in the period immediately before the big wave of experimentation in the 1960s Herbert Gold has collected twenty-seven stories [198] together, which were published over some forty years. In his introduction Gold finds a surprisingly strong thematic continuity between these works, a preoccupation with the family and with wanderlust. He views his stories as enquiries into meaning, enquiries which sometimes refuse to limit themselves to a compact story-form and grow into full-blown novels. The Irish-American writer J. P. Donleavy has put on record his memories [199] of the years from 1946 onwards when he began a course of studies at Trinity College. This is part auto-biography, part comic narrative told in the high style of a born raconteur, full of flourish. Donleavy quietly takes his bearings from the time of Joyce, even describing the same pubs. He was variously a student, painter (exhibiting regularly), and an amateur farmer in Kilcoole village where he began *The Ginger Man*. Donleavy's exploration of his origins sours over the implacable Irish hostility to *The Ginger Man*. A. Carl Bredah (*SNNTS*) compares the use of pictures in Wright Morris's *The Home Place* and *In Orbit* to show his concern with the resolving of divisiveness. This article is rather more wide-ranging than such a specific comparison might suggest and Bredah has many interesting points to make about the connotations of motion and fixity. The novelist Peter Matthiessen has published a collection of essays, *Nine-Headed Dragon River* (RandomH), but these were not available for review. Peter Parisi

196. *Only Apparently Real: The World of Philip K. Dick*, by Paul Williams. ArborH. pp. viii + 184. pb $7.95.

197. *The Sirens of Titan*, by Kurt Vonnegut. Gollancz. pp. 224. pb £2.95.

198. *Lovers and Cohorts: Twenty-Seven Stories*, by Herbert Gold. Fine. pp. 331. $17.95.

199. *J. P. Donleavy's Ireland: In All Her Sins and in Some of Her Graces*, by J. P. Donleavy. Joseph. pp. 223. £12.95.

has edited a volume of essays on Paul Goodman, *Artist of the Actual*[200], which does ample justice to the variety of his talents. Parisi demonstrates that Goodman has retained a consistent vision of human estrangement from actuality ('the organism and the environment', as Goodman puts it). George Woodcock places him within the line of anarchist thinkers; Neil Heims considers the theme of the emergent self; and Bernard Vincent relates Goodman's writings to American naturalism. His most famous novel, *Empire City*, has been discussed in two essays. Lewis Fried gives a first-rate account of the different narrative resources used to examine the theme of the individual's relation to alienating or totalitarian systems; Edouard Roditi outlines the stages of the novel's composition. This volume also includes an analysis of Goodman's flouting of decorum in his poetry, an interview with his brother, and a bibliography of his writings.

A particularly exciting development in criticism has been the recent surge of interest in Paul Bowles and this interest should now be consolidated by an excellent bibliography of his works[201] which Jeffrey Miller has compiled. Although he modestly calls this work 'pedantic', it is in fact thorough, clearly arranged, and the result of astonishing labours. The main sections list Bowles's books from his 1931 pamphlet *Two Poems* onwards, and his many articles and reviews. Also listed are translations of and by Bowles (the latter mainly from Moghrebi), his published and unpublished music, and his records. A concluding section of miscellanea gives details of broadsheets, theatre programmes, screenplays, etc. Miller has corrected several ascriptions and done a magnificent job of tracking down Bowles's many contributions to little magazines. The current proliferation of Bowles reprints means that this bibliography will soon have to be updated. *Pages from Cold Point*[202], a volume of stories written between 1950 and 1967, has been re-issued without a new introduction. A particularly interesting collection of translations, *She Woke Me Up So I Killed Her*[203], has been selected mainly from the Surrealist periodical *View*. Bowles's long-standing collaboration with Mohammed Mrabet has resulted in one reprint, *Love with a Few Hairs*[204] (first published in the 1960s) and one new volume, *Marriage with Papers*[205], which consists of two novellas. *TCL* has a special Paul Bowles issue which opens with a collage of personal impressions by friends and interviewers. Among the critical essays attention is given to unusual aspects of Bowles as translator, autobiographer, and poet (Edward Butscher supplying an exceptionally incisive explanation of the different tactics used by Bowles for self-exploration). Marcellette G. Williams discusses time-senses in Bowles's fiction and Wayne Pounds has

200. *Artist of the Actual: Essays on Paul Goodman*, ed. by Peter Parisi. Scarecrow. pp. vii + 194. $20.

201. *Paul Bowles: A Descriptive Bibliography*, by Jeffrey Miller. BSP. pp. 323. $50.

202. *'Pages from Cold Point' and Other Stories*, by Paul Bowles. Arena: Arrow. pp. 156. pb £2.95.

203. *She Woke Me Up So I Killed Her: Translations*, by Paul Bowles. Cadmus. pp. 91. pb $7.95.

204. *Love with a Few Hairs*, by Mohammed Mrabet, transl. by Paul Bowles. Arena: Arrow. pp. 176. pb £2.50.

205. *Marriage with Papers*, by Mohammed Mrabet, transl. by Paul Bowles. Tombouctou. pp. 79. pb $6.

written two outstanding essays on the interaction between character and landscape, and comparing Bowles with Poe on the destruction of the ego.

Two reprints by Bowles's one-time associate William Burroughs have appeared. Penguin has issued an unexpurgated edition of *Junky*[206], one of Burroughs's earliest works. Allen Ginsberg has supplied an introduction which describes the circumstances of the novel's publication. *The Last Words of Dutch Schultz*[207] has also been reprinted, as has *The Process*[208], Brion Gysin's 1969 novel (Gysin has been Burroughs's main collaborator). For years rumours have been circulating of another forthcoming novel by Gysin with such working titles as *The Beat Museum* and *The Fault Line*. Finally it has appeared as *The Last Museum*[209].

From 1959 to 1961 Jack Kerouac wrote a 'Last Word' by-line for *Escapade* and some of these pieces have been collected by Tom Clark[210]. One of the first articles puts on record Kerouac's important contacts with jazz and bop, and demonstrates his use of jazz rhythms in his prose. In the same by-line Kerouac reports on a bull-fight, discusses his interest in Buddhism, and reflects bitterly on the American news media. After an interval of several years Kerouac made one last contribution to this journal, a look at his own techniques of spontaneous composition. These essays, especially the latter, will make suggestive glosses on Kerouac's fiction and Clark has helpfully placed them within the context of his career. From Regina Weinreich[211] comes one of the first substantial critical assessments of Kerouac. She sees in his fiction a prolonged attempt to discover form and takes *The Town and the City* as a preliminary step in this direction, although one overshadowed by the influence of Thomas Wolfe. In three novels, Weinreich argues, Kerouac managed to achieve his Duluoz legend: *On The Road* consists of an elegiac romance alternating images of collapse and rebirth; *Visions of Cody* blends synchronic effects, interviewing tropes, and versatile images; and *Desolation Angels* achieves even more successful visionary effects through a circular narrative structure. One unusual strength in this study is Weinreich's capacity to blend jazz theory with a close analysis of the novels' styles. This is just the sort of approach which Kerouac needs and the results are extremely suggestive. Fred Madden (*MFS*) insists that critical discussion of Ken Kesey's *One Flew over the Cuckoo's Nest* has revolved too much around the protagonist McMurphy, and draws on Kesey's own statements to deny that the former becomes more self-reliant as the novel progresses. In contrast with McMurphy's acquiescence Chief Bromden becomes more able to make choices. More is involved here than character-contrasts because Madden asserts that the 'conflict between individual choice and social pressure' is central to the novel.

206. *Junky*, by William S. Burroughs, intro. by Allen Ginsberg. Penguin (1985). pp. xvi + 158. pb £2.95.

207. *The Last Words of Dutch Schultz: A Fiction in the Form of a Film Script*, by William S. Burroughs. Calder. pp. 115. pb £3.95.

208. *The Process*, by Brion Gysin. Quartet (1985). pp. 353. £8.95.

209. *The Last Museum*, by Brion Gysin. Faber. pp. 186. pb £3.95.

210. *Kerouac's Last Word: Jack Kerouac in 'Escapade'*, ed. by Tom Clark. Water Row. pp. 49. pb $10.

211. *The Spontaneous Poetics of Jack Kerouac*, by Regina Weinreich. SIU. pp. xvi + 180. $16.95.

Another line of experiment by American novelists has been dominated by Nabokov whose early novel *The Defence*[212] had been re-issued with his own foreword explaining the complexities of the narrative parallels to chess moves. One of the major publications of the year has undoubtedly been a new biography of Nabokov by Andrew Field[213]. Already well established as a Nabokov scholar by his previous studies, Field has constantly borne the fiction in mind here, so that his biography repeatedly shades into critical commentary. The early years in Russia were important for establishing Nabokov's stance as a 'professional dandy' and Field clearly demonstrates the persistence of this role throughout Nabokov's life, whether he was coining Wildean epigrams or performing as a scholar virtuoso. By 1924 he was well established in the Russian *émigré* community of Berlin, and one of the most painstakingly researched sections of this biography details the intricacies of this minority culture. Field also describes Nabokov's controversial but charismatic style as a lecturer in America and recounts his friendship with Edmund Wilson which was crucial to getting his works published. Field has done an admirable job of penetrating Nabokov's fictions about himself – that he knew no German, for instance – and his biography should remain the standard study for years. Equally impressive scholarship has been demonstrated in Michael Juliar's bibliography of Nabokov[214]. Undaunted by the appalling difficulties of locating the publications of prewar Russian *émigré* presses, he has managed to list all Nabokov's known works in Russian, French, and English. It is symptomatic of his difficulties that the first item (a poem printed as a pamphlet in 1914) is listed as non-extant and dependent on Nabokov's memory for its citation. Juliar rejects the suggestion that Nabokov's early Russian editions may have been multiple, and in his listing even gives details of dust-jackets, print-runs, etc. Nabokov's scientific publications are included along with his many letters on chess problems. Separate sections are devoted to interviews and translations. In every respect this bibliography deserves the highest praise for its meticulous thoroughness.

Victor Lange (*MQR*), between 1948 and 1957 a colleague of Nabokov's at Cornell, has recorded his memories of these years in an interview. In particular he recalls the controversy over Nabokov's appointment, his techniques as a lecturer, and his insistence on lexical accuracy in translations. J. H. Garrett-Goodyear (*JNT*) sees the relation between the narrator and the protagonist of *Pnin* as a complex means of raising questions about narrative perspective. Belittling *Pnin* aggrandizes the narrator and this shifting relation makes it impossible to locate the narrative centre of the novel. Steven H. Butler (*SNNTS*) complains of critics trying to gloss over the erotic dimensions of *Lolita*. Nympholepsy, he argues, is actually an integral part of Humbert's perception of beauty, a combination of the pure and impure. While this article helps to keep track of Humbert's shifting attitude towards Lolita, Lance Olsen (*MFS*) attributes the novel's mixed reception to the culturally subversive implication of its fantasy-themes. Drawing on Nabokov's interviews (collected

212. *The Defence*, by Vladimir Nabokov. OUP. pp. 201. pb £3.95.

213. *VN: The Life and Art of Vladimir Nabokov*, by Andrew Field. Crown. pp. 417. $19.95.

214. *Vladimir Nabokov: A Descriptive Bibliography*, by Michael Juliar. Garland. pp. xiii + 780. $80.

in *Strong Opinions*) he asserts that the novelist did not accept a communal reality, hence the use of double time-schemes in *Lolita*. Peggy Ward Corn (*JNT*) turns to a more recent work, *Pale Fire*, to consider Nabokov's parodic use of a story-within-a-story by comparing Shade and Kinbote. This comparison brings the rather bland conclusion that Nabokov was indulging in 'combinational delight'. Marianna Torgovnick (*Style*), however, finds in *Pale Fire* anticipations of subsequent developments in literary theory. The formal self-consciousness of this work thus indicates such controversial issues as the status of critical evaluation or the stability of language. Evelyne Keitel (*Amst*) has produced one of the most interesting articles of the year by transposing the notion of the unconscious onto the text of *Ada*. Her Lacanian reading of the novel gives a good account of transference and displacement, and locates two discourses which demand two different responses: intellectual sense-making and the creation of the reader's desire for a text. D. Barton Johnson (*CL*) also plunges into the structural intricacies of *Ada* to explore the incest theme. He suggests that this theme links Nabokov's novel with *Eugene Onegin* and points out that incest is totally lacking in Nabokov's early Russian works. Johnson then places *Ada* against the background of German treatments of incest, probably familiar to Nabokov from his Berlin years, thus balancing a close reading of the novel against a usefully broad context.

William Gaddis's massive novel *The Recognitions* displays a complexity worthy of Nabokov, but is only discussed intermittently. Brian Morton (*PNR*) has taken a fresh look at Gaddis's treatment of forgery, his allusive density, and his treatment of commercialization in art. This essay includes brief mention of his two subsequent novels. Lance Olsen (*SNNTS*) has written a useful article on Thomas Pynchon's use of fantastic strategies in *Gravity's Rainbow*. He demonstrates how Pynchon plays off one kind of discourse against another, multiplies characters astonishingly, collapses his verb-tenses into an extended present, and repeatedly indulges in lexical disruption. Steven Moore (*ConL*), the leading Gaddis critic, has related the fiction of Alexander Theroux to the tradition of learned wit which includes both Gaddis and Pynchon. He finds influences from Proust and Rolfe, and gives a particularly interesting discussion of the incorporation of Elizabethan materials into *Darconville's Cat*. Donald J. Greiner has written a useful introduction to John Hawkes[215] in the new series, Understanding Contemporary American Literature, edited by Matthew J. Bruccoli. Greiner deals skilfully with Hawkes's exploitation of violence, his inversion of sympathy, and his repeated dislocation of the reader. Hawkes's unusual combination of the comic and the repulsive and his use of nightmarish imagery in *The Owl* make that novella a good introduction to his works. Greiner then proceeds to examine each of his main novels to date. Carol A. McCurdy (*ConL*) has also produced a valuable broad study of Hawkes, this time of his landscapes which she sees as suggestive and circumscribing emblems of waste. In 1964, she argues, Hawkes begins to put a new emphasis on man's reactions and on first-person narrators who project landscapes out of a pastoral impulse. In the most recent works she discerns a progressive internalization of landscape.

---

215. *Understanding John Hawkes*, by Donald J. Greiner. USC. pp. x + 177. hb $19.95, pb $7.95.

Among the writers who experimented with fantastic and non-realistic techniques in the 1960s Joseph Heller has of course become a classic. His latest work, *No Laughing Matter*[216], uses comedy to offset what would otherwise have been an appalling experience. In 1982 (while working on *God Knows*) he suffered a disease of the nervous system which totally paralysed him. Against the odds he recovered and together with his friend Speed Vogel has written an account of the experience. In *SAF* Robert Merrill has given us a particularly lucid explanation of the structure of *Catch-22*. In the first sixteen chapters (the most comic), characters are introduced; the middle section suspends plot sequence and totally revises these early episodes; and in the last eight chapters the narrative becomes both more linear and bleaker. This article is an excerpt from a book in progress about Heller which shows signs of being of a high standard. Penguin has issued a new expanded edition of Philip Roth's *Reading Myself and Others*[217] which now includes three interviews from the 1980s. Here Roth discusses his own works in the main, denying that they are autobiographical. He reserves scathing comments for the so-called Jewish-American school of fiction, declaring that resemblances are simply the result of a common background. He also touches on his Zuckerman trilogy, his working methods, and his visit to Prague. Edward P. Walkiewicz has written a very thorough introduction to John Barth[218]. Taking the latter's key essays 'The Literature of Exhaustion' and 'The Literature of Replenishment' as a starting point, he examines the philosophical ironies of the first two novels, Barth's renewal of language through play in *The Sot-Weed Factor*, and his use of Menippean satire in *Giles Goat-Boy*. Walkiewicz does justice to Barth's interest in other literature, noting influences from the *Arabian Nights*, picaresque fiction, and Nabokov. He also emphasizes the persistence of the quest-romance pattern in Barth's fiction, even in the recent *Sabbatical*. Monique Pruvot (*EA*) goes over familiar ground in interpreting *The Floating Opera* as a self-reflexive novel commenting on its own processes where a nihilistic philosophy is offset by linguistic vigour. L. L. Lee (*SSF*) rejects the view that Robert Coover's *Pricksongs and Descants* is wholly metafictional. The argument that Coover is not just playing with language but also engaging with propositions about existence proves quite useful for showing his application of fairy-tale motifs and disruptions of chronology. E. L. Doctorow has given an interview for *ParisR* where he admits his recent interest in oral history especially in connection with *World's Fair*. Reprints of James Purdy's novels have continued with *I Am Elijah Thrush*[219], a bizarre work which moves between theatre, pantomime, and erotic ritual. In his new introduction Paul Binding suggests an influence from Lorca (whom Purdy is known to admire) and underlines a theme running throughout Purdy's works that identity is precarious. The mysterious transformations of self which occur here, Binding argues, demonstrate the importance of homosexuality in Purdy's fiction.

Finally we must note works concerning two women novelists who make extreme contrasts. The one works comfortably within the academic establish-

216. *No Laughing Matter*, by Joseph Heller and Speed Vogel. Cape. pp. 385. £10.95.

217. *Reading Myself and Others*, by Philip Roth. Penguin. pp. x + 326. pb £3.95.

218. *John Barth*, by Edward P. Walkiewicz. Twayne. pp. 170. $18.95.

219. *I Am Elijah Thrush*, by James Purdy, intro. by Paul Binding. GMP. pp. 120. hb £9.95, pb £3.95.

ment using techniques close to realism, and the other delights in breaking through narrative decorum. Francine Lercangee has assembled an annotated bibliography of the former, Joyce Carol Oates[220]. In his preface Bruce F. Michelson surveys her prodigious output as novelist, critic, playwright, and poet; and he too, like Binding above, points to 'problems of identity' as her central theme. Lercangee lists Oates's non-fictional prose in a separate section which has the interest of showing that her quarrel with postmodernism has been consistent and long-standing. The section listing her reviews of other novelists' work usefully supplements her more theoretical criticism. That seven critical assessments of Oates have already appeared only confirms the need for this bibliography. *OH* carries one of the first interviews Kathy Acker has given for a British journal and from it she emerges as an articulate commentator on her own work. She describes, among other things, her early use of fragmented narrative and her turn towards 'copying' under the influence of the New York Metro picture painters. Most details are devoted to her new novel *Don Quixote* which reveals her current interest in African folk-tales, and particularly trenchant attacks are directed against the writing and publishing establishment in the United States.

Turning now to a series of writers who like Joyce Carol Oates have continued to work more or less within the realistic mode, we should first note that three sections of the novel *Unanswered Prayers*[221], which Truman Capote left unfinished on his death in 1984 have now been published. R. G. Collins (*RALS*, 1985) uses an extended review of Susan Cheever's *Home Before Dark* (*YW* 66.628) to speculate on John Cheever's heritage. Dana Gioia (*HudR*) records meeting Cheever while at the Stanford Business School. Cheever spoke of his writing methods, his religious beliefs, and his triumph over alcoholism, and ironically had to take second place to Saul Bellow who visited the college at the same time to give a reading. Martin Bidney (*SSF*) examines Cheever's reworking of Wordsworth's Immortality Ode in his story 'The Common Day' and finds common links through the motifs of sun, prison-house, heart, and nature. Donald J. Greiner has already examined John Updike's poetry and drama (see *YW* 62.440) and now considers the novels[222]. He stolidly refuses to promote a thesis, preferring instead to deal with the works in thematic groupings. Each novel receives a detailed close analysis which stays so factual that it does not extrapolate the critical issues strongly. Greiner gestures towards the relation between running and searching in the novels, and towards the treatment of myth in *The Centaur*, but comparatively little is said about Updike's use of regional locales or the presence of religion in his works. One interesting side to Greiner's study is that he gives an outline of the critical reception of Updike's novels. In *LitR* Emma Gilbey has interviewed Updike mainly in connection with his latest novel *Roger's Version*. Here Updike comments on the calculated unattractiveness of his characters, the role of sex, and the nature of scepticism in the novel. Albert E. Wilhelm (*JSSE*) briefly considers the thematic contrasts and imagistic continuity in the short story

220. *Joyce Carol Oates: An Annotated Bibliography*, by Francine Lercangee, pref. by Bruce F. Michelson. Garland. pp. xxii + 272. $48.

221. *Unanswered Prayers*, by Truman Capote. HH. pp. 181. £9.95.

222. *John Updike's Novels*, by Donald J. Greiner. OhioU. pp. xvi + 223. hb £23.95, pb £9.95.

collection *Too Far To Go*, and Charles Berryman (*SAQ*) attempts to answer the question of how Updike can use witchcraft in his novels and still retain the conventions of realism. In *The Witches of Eastwick* he finds a mixture of the natural and the supernatural, so that the dividing line between the two becomes blurred. He also relates witchcraft to different means of artistic expression. Jeff Henderson has edited a lively collection of essays on John Gardner[223]. In the first section Gardner's beginnings as a writer are surveyed as is his complete fate at the hands of the reviewers. Gregory L. Morris gives a finely tactful account of Gardner's unacknowledged borrowings in his works (spotted by Peter Prescott among others). Essays are also devoted to Gardner as poet, editor, and translator. In the second grouping Kenneth C. Mason argues cogently that *Grendel* should be seen as an existential narrative whereas Robert D. Child takes language as the reason for the protagonist's defeat. Controversy surfaces again when Carol McCurdy asserts that the publication of *On Moral Fiction* in 1978 trapped Gardner into defending a role he could not sustain. In the third section lunacy and the supernatural are considered in Gardner's fiction, to which these essays taken together make a very good introduction.

Of the novelists most strongly influenced by their Jewish heritage Bernard Malamud stands out and a lecture which he delivered at Bennington College in 1984 has now been published as a pamphlet[224]. Malamud describes this lecture as a 'selective short memoir', in other words as an outline of the different phases of his career. Among other things he notes the importance of his visit to Italy and of his contact with other writers such as John Hawkes. Joel Salzberg has helped to consolidate Malamud's standing by producing a guide to the criticism of his works[225]. It arranges the materials in chronological sequence and gives concise summaries of each item, even including short notes. Salzberg's introduction gives a useful overview of Malamud criticism in the last thirty years. Salzberg has also argued (*SSF*) that the story 'Take Pity' (in *The Magic Barrel*) has been unjustifiably neglected by critics and he then proceeds to give a close reading which brings out the importance of the story's interrogation scene. Cynthia Ozick has written a brief obituary tribute to Malamud in *PR* and has also given an interview for *ParisR* where she discusses her writing methods, her memories of being taught by Lionel Trilling, and the importance for her of Judaism. Michael G. Yetman (*PLL*) interprets Saul Bellow's novel *The Dean's December* as a rejection of the 'non-poetic, objectivist biases of contemporary social thought'. This results in a lively and not particularly flattering depiction of Bellow as a neo-Victorian defender of high culture, but, Yetman admits, Bellow is too realistic to be optimistic about the triumph of poetry. Elaine M. Kauver (*ConL*) has interviewed Chaim Potok who declares that he was initially influenced by Joyce and who insists that the 'central problem of our time is how people confront ideas different from her own'. Potok is particularly interesting when he comments on the relation of fiction to Judaism, particularly in connection with his novel *Davita's Harp*.

223. *Thor's Hammer: Essays on John Gardner*, ed. by Jeff Henderson. UCA (1985). pp. iii + 197. pb $12.95.

224. *Long Work, Short Life*, by Bernard Malamud, intro. by Nicholas Delbanco. BennC (1985). pp. 19. pamphlet $3.

225. *Bernard Malamud: A Reference Guide*, by Joel Salzberg. Hall (1985). pp. xxii + 211. $45.

The early phase of Afro-American fiction figures as usual through reprints. Zora Neale Hurston's novel *Their Eyes Were Watching God*[226] has been re-issued with a new introduction by Holly Eley which places the novel within Hurston's career. Sherley Anne Williams has also supplied an afterword which examines the significance of the protagonist Janie's search for fulfilment through a series of marriages. This novel also makes sophisticated use of dialect and natural symbolism. The second Hurston reprint is her autobiography *Dust Tracks on the Road*[227]. Dellita L. Martin contrasts this work with other Afro-American autobiographies in that it reveals Hurston's ambivalence about defining herself in relation to her community. This work is thus elusive about Hurston herself and says little about the Harlem Renaissance, but Martin suggests that the figure of the indomitable black woman is used by Hurston as a mask for her feelings of abandonment and alienation. From the Feminist Press has come an anthology of pieces by Hurston[228] which includes autobiography, journalism, and fiction. In her introduction Mary Helen Washington agrees with Dellita Martin that *Dust Tracks on the Road* is full of strategies for not revealing herself. Alice Walker has given an afterword from her own collection *In Search of Our Mothers' Gardens* (*YW* 66.633). Certainly one of the best biographies of the year has been Robert E. Hemenway's life of Hurston[229] which draws on newly discovered collections of unpublished materials and which penetrates Hurston's evasions about her own life. Hemenway finds that her career centred on an attempt to reconcile two impulses – to write fiction and to record Negro folklore. He declares that she was unique in the Harlem Renaissance in recognizing that folklore depended on performance. Her fascination with these materials was fed by her teacher Franz Boas and led her to undertake collections in Florida, Jamaica, and Haiti (where she planned to write a book on voodoo). The role which Hurston adopted of being one of the folk helps to explain why her writings are quite distinct from the proletarian literature of the 1930s and Hemenway also records her debt to teachers like Alain Locke and her abortive collaboration with Langston Hughes. Her later years were marked by a growing conservatism. Cheryl A. Wall (*BALF*) has written a good general introduction to the novels of Nella Larsen which comment on 'issues of marginality and cultured dualism'. She examines the importance of mulatto characters and also the critical reactions to *Quicksand* and *Passing*. Ann Petry's first novel *The Street*[230] has been re-issued without a new introduction.

Langston Hughes's autobiography, *The Big Sea*[231], has been reprinted this year. Arnold Rampersad has issued the first volume of his biography of Langston Hughes[232] which rapidly disposes of such rumours as Hughes's

226. *Their Eyes Were Watching God*, by Zora Neale Hurston, intro. by Holly Eley, afterword by Sherley Anne Williams. Virago. pp. xv + 297. pb £3.95.

227. *Dust Tracks on a Road*, by Zora Neale Hurston, intro. by Dellita L. Martin. Virago. pp. xviii + 348. pb £4.95.

228. *I Love Myself When I Am Laughing. . . ,* by Zora Neale Hurston, intro. by Mary Helen Washington, afterword by Alice Walker. Feminist. pp. 313. pb £9.95.

229. *Zora Neale Hurston: A Literary Biography*, by Robert E. Hemenway, foreword by Alice Walker. Camden. pp. xxiii + 371. pb £7.95.

230. *The Street*, by Ann Petry. Virago. pp. 312. pb £3.95.

231. *The Big Sea*, by Langston Hughes. Pluto. pp. 335. pb £4.95.

232. *The Life of Langston Hughes*. Vol. 1: *1902–1941: I, Too, Sing America*, by Arnold Rampersad. OUPAm. pp. viii + 468. $22.95.

homosexuality. Rampersad has discovered that a sense of parental abandonment led Hughes to seek approval from his race. His first literary contacts in Harlem during the 1920s led him to experiment with jazz rhythms in his poetry and after forming friendships with Carl Van Vechten and Zora Hurston (whose temperamental patron he shared) Hughes soon established himself as the 'poet of the modern Negro proletariat'. He then gained recognition in Cuba, Russia, and Spain, which he visited during the Civil War, and began to diversify his own writing. As if that was not enough, Hughes started theatre groups, went briefly into publishing, and gave extended lecture tours. He became a leading figure in the radical literature of the 1930s, enlisting the help of Richard Wright and Ralph Ellison in racial causes. This impeccably researched study breaks off with the Second World War.

Richard Wright has been the subject of several articles, most of which concentrate on *Native Son*. Louis Tremaine (*SAF*) accuses his critics of not doing justice to the divided sensibility of Bigger Thomas. Although he rightly points out that Bigger has no adequate way of articulating himself and that the reader is limited to his world, Tremaine brings off a less weighty interpretation than he promises. Tony Magistrale (*CLS*) examines in detail the influence of *Crime and Punishment* on *Native Son* and indicates a common concern in both works with how environment shapes values and the alienating effect of murder. Robert James Butler (*BALF*) takes up the violence in *Native Son*. This promising subject turns disappointingly into yet another character study of Bigger who predictably is described as the victim of environmental factors. In the same journal Yoshinobu Hakutani and Toru Kiuchi have given an annotated bibliography of Richard Wright's critical reception in Japan. John E. Loftis (*SSF*) takes Wright's story 'The Man who Was Almost a Man' as a parody of American hunt narratives by drawing contrasts with Faulkner's 'The Old People', and Yoshinobu Hakutani (*SAF*) puts forward *Lawd Today* as an anomaly in Wright's career. Its resemblances to *Ulysses* and the overloading of its naturalistic descriptions with gratuitous metaphors undermine its success as a satire.

Although Chester Himes is known mainly for his Harlem detective novels it is welcome to see his early novels coming back into print. *If He Hollers Let Him Go*[233] has been re-issued with a new foreword by Graham Hodges who points out similarities between its style and that of contemporary hard-boiled detective fiction. *Lonely Crusade*[234] has never been reprinted until now and Hodges explains this odd situation through the hostile reception of its unflinching portrayal of racism in American life. Himes also for good measure indicts the Communists as duplicitous manipulators. Trudier Harris[235] has responded to a gap in Baldwin criticism by scrutinizing that novelist's depiction of black women. To a large extent the result is a thematic and classificatory study which shows that women are presented as figures of guilt or as sexual outcasts, but very rarely by female narrators. Baldwin uses traditional roles to define his

---

233. *If He Hollers Let Him Go*, by Chester Himes, foreword by Graham Hodges. TMP. pp. ix + 203. pb $7.95.

234. *Lonely Crusade*, by Chester Himes, foreword by Graham Hodges. TMP. pp. x + 398. pb $8.95.

235. *Black Women in the Fiction of James Baldwin*, by Trudier Harris. UTenn (1985). pp. viii + 229. $22.50.

women (sister, wife, etc.) but these are often points of departure, as in *Go Tell It on the Mountain*. Harris does not set out to show progress in Baldwin's portraits, but nevertheless Julia in *Just Above My Head* is put forward as his richest and most complex female character.

Alice Walker's novel *The Color Purple* has by now become firmly established as a classic in contemporary Afro-American fiction and has been issued in a British edition[236] along with her first novel *The Third Life of Grange Copeland*[237], which Walker describes as a study in 'spiritual survival'. M. Teresa Tavormina (*JNT*) explains the implications of clothing in *The Color Purple*. Cloth-working becomes an image of creativity and clothes become a means of placing a character socially or generationally. This fruitful discussion which produces insights like the analogy between quilt-making and narrating, contrasts with Deborah S. Ellis's (*CE*) comparison with Chaucer's Clerk's Tale which is intended to bring out debate elements and each writer's treatment of patient suffering. Gerard Early (*AL*) casts a disapproving eye over the film version of *The Color Purple*, the last in a 'long line of inept Hollywood films about black life'. Having demolished the film he then sets about the novel because it 'lacks any real intellectual or theoretical rigor or coherence'. Early's bold provocation contrasts refreshingly with the monotonous adulation in most of these articles. Trudier Harris (*SAF*) pursues his hobby-horse of assessing women characters and decides that in Walker's early fiction they are incomplete stunted figures. After 1981 (*You Can't Keep a Good Woman Down*) communication becomes a more pressing need for Walker's characters and they cease to be merely passive victims. In *BALF* Harold Hellenbrand reads Walker's first novel as a family chronicle and a narrative of racial confrontation, drawing parallels with Richard Wright. In the same journal Karen F. Stein puts forward an interesting interpretation of *Meridian* as an indictment of the civil rights movement's failure to 'acknowledge women's selfhood' through the frustration of its protagonist's revolutionary ideals. And finally Philip M. Royster (*BALF* again) relates Walker's stance as an outcast to her campaigning on behalf of civil rights and women's liberation. He concludes polemically that instead of mothers' gardens Walker may be seeking 'our fathers' protecting arms'.

Alice Walker's main rival on the contemporary critical scene appears to be Toni Morrison, whose works are examined in a new volume of essays edited by Bessie W. Jones and Audrey L. Vinson[238]. This collection is intended as a teaching text with each chapter being followed by a list of exercises. Nevertheless the essays engage interestingly with metaphors of escape, physical grotesques, the use of fairy-tale motifs in *The Bluest Eye*, and the settings of the fiction. The high point of the volume is a long interview which Morrison gave in 1981, in which she explains autobiographical elements in her works, the connection between irony and ethnicity, and other topics related to her fiction. Cynthia Dubin Edelberg (*AL*) has surveyed Morrison's works only to conclude that there is a repeated opposition beween folk inheritance and institutional education. The latter is held up to ridicule in a 'brutal fictional world' and is

236. *The Color Purple*, by Alice Walker. WP. pp. 245. pb £3.95.
237. *The Third Life of Grange Copeland*, by Alice Walker. WP. pp. 247. pb £3.95.
238. *The World of Toni Morrison*, ed. by Bessie W. Jones and Audrey L. Vinson. K/H. pp. x + 158. pb $12.95.

presented as part of a racially tainted culture. Terry Otten concentrates on a far more specific issue, the necessary fall in *Tar Baby*, which usefully explains the general parallels with the Eden myth as well as Morrison's treatment of self-knowledge. Equally specific is Marco Portales's (*CentR*) comparison of the two little black girls Claudia and Frieda in *The Bluest Eye*, who are treated by the adults as mere objects. Portales here brings out the maturing process and has useful remarks to make on child's-eye perspectives in this novel. Louise Meriwether's portrait of Harlem life in the Depression, *Daddy Was a Numbers Runner*[239], has been re-issued without a new introduction. Two other Afro-American novelists remain to be mentioned. Keith A. Sandiford (*BALF*) gives a detailed commentary on Paule Marshall's use of mythic and folk elements in *Praisesong for the Widow* and Gerard Early (*BALF* again) explains Kristin Hunter's application of the life of Billie Holiday in her first novel *God Bless the Child*.

Finally, a survey of the critical comment which has appeared on other contemporary novelists. Matthias Schubnell has written a full introduction to the work of N. Scott Momaday[240] in which he examines his poetry, his academic career, and his painting as well as his fiction. An initial biography underlines Momaday's debt to Yvor Winters, a crucial personal and intellectual influence. Subsequent chapters demonstrate how Momaday has digested the Indian oral tradition, his interest in the land, and also his decision to investigate his racial past in such works as *The Way to Rocky Mountain*. Schubnell analyses the fiction and poetry in considerable depth, showing influences from the American Transcendentalists and Isak Dinesen, and this fine study concludes with a thorough primary and secondary bibliography. Naomi Jacobs (*SSF*) has interpreted Tillie Olsen's novella *Tell Me a Riddle* as an indictment through the self-examination of its protagonist of the narrow roles projected for women, and Carmen Cramer (*Crit*) locates a struggle between the individual and society at the heart of Marge Piercy's *Woman on the Edge of Time*. Briefly she demonstrates how the protagonist Connie resists pressures to reduce her to a social automaton. Hortense Calisher was interviewed during the Brockport Writers Forum and the result has appeared in *SWR*. She discusses her own writing methods, her preference for the short story form, and her interest in transportation as an American myth. John Irving has also been interviewed for *ParisR* where he sets on record his desire to be an old-fashioned story-teller. He admits influences from Dickens, Grass, and Vonnegut, and also comments on violence and contacts with his fellow-writers. Mark A. R. Facknitz (*SSF*) has also looked at a leading practitioner of the short story to consider briefly how Raymond Carver has evoked hope in his stories since 1980, offering in effect comments on the affirmative implications of character and action. Julian Cowley (*Crit*) surveys the range of Steve Katz's fictional techniques showing that he regards both appearances and the efficacy of language as problematic. His fictional role is thus to challenge 'any rigid, presumptive view of reality'. *HC* has a good feature-length article on Tim O'Brien by Daniel L. Zins which rightly stresses the importance of Vietnam in his career. Zins also notes

239. *Daddy Was a Numbers Runner*, by Louise Meriwether. Methuen. pp. 188. pb £3.50.

240. *N. Scott Momaday: The Cultural and Literary Background*, by Matthias Schubnell. UOkla. pp. viii + 336. £20.75.

O'Brien's structural hallmark of trying to make his chapters self-contained units, but makes little mention of his early journalism. The same journal has also a long essay on the novelist Anne Tylor in whose novels (ten to date) Anne C. Jones finds a recurring theme of psychic growth expressed through metaphors of home and wandering.

In *SLJ* Charmaine Allmon Mosby places Tom Wicker's *Facing the Lions* within the tradition of Southern political fiction, arguing that the novel shows the 'delusive effect of political power', and J. Frank Papovich asks whether the Southern landscape is important in Harry Crews's *A Childhood*. Crews also figures in *Crit* where David K. Jeffrey proposes his eighth novel, *A Feast of Snakes*, as his best because it revolves around powerful clusters of images, most notably that of the snake which suggests male power and spiritual evil. Ronald E. McFarland in the same journal extrapolates a pattern common to David Wagoner's comic Westerns where adolescent protagonists seek self-fulfilment, and Steve Yarborough usefully explains the functions of flashbacks and other devices in the short stories of Andre Dubus. Like McFarland, Jack Branscomb pin-points a pattern in the fiction of Russell Hoban, this time the search for psychic wholeness. Albert E. Wilhelm (still *Crit*), on the other hand, looks at the bleaker stories of Breece Pancake which uniformly dramatize grim struggles against poverty. Pancake has also been the subject of a rather more technical examination by Geoffrey Galt Harpham (*SSF*) who argues that setting in these stories functions as a trap to characters who can only dream of a symbolic outside. Sanford Pinsker (*LitR*) has held one of the first interviews with the novelist Jay McInerney (author of *Big Lights, Big City*) who compares his own treatment of New York with that of Dos Passos and Fitzgerald. He also comments on failure and father–son conflicts which he is weaving into his next novel, *Ransom*. Roger A. MacDonald (*IFR*) looks at another city, Fredericton, which is a constant setting in the fiction of Kent Thompson, and Robert Murray Davis (also *IFR*) uses Alvin Greenberg's stories to underline the postmodern writer's difficulty in creating an audience. In *Crit* there have been valuable discussions of Steven Millhauser's *Edwin Mullhouse* as a comic novel (by Michael Pearson) and of Frank Conroy's *Stop-time* as a mock-autobiography (by Timothy Dow Adams). Two essays in the same journal examine William Kennedy's *Ironweed*, the one (by Peter P. Clarke) bringing out how myth stands behind the characters and action, and the other (by David Black) explaining that memory functions as a refuge from the passage of time in this novel. Larry T. Blades has sketched out the sexual development of the protagonist in Alice Adams's *Rich Rewards* and Jane Bowers Hill relates the redemptive children in Ann Beattie's fiction to a post-romantic tradition of viewing the child as a symbolic figure. The above essays suggest that there has been a shift in *Crit*'s policy towards discussing writers who have not previously been the subject of much criticism.

4. Non-Fictional Prose

Reportage has featured in a number of this year's publications. Robert A. Hohner (*SAQ*) draws on unpublished materials to explain the unlikely friendship between the journalist and critic H. L. Mencken and the Methodist bishop James Cannon Jr, which formed partly on the strength of Mencken's sympathy for Cannon's defiance of politicians when he was accused of sexual and commercial wrong-doing. During the 1930s both figures united in their hostility to Roosevelt. The value of Hohner's article is biographical whereas Mark Allister (*PSt*) considers how seeing, knowing, and being are interrelated in James Agee's *Let Us Now Praise Famous Men*. Allister finds a struggle between the desire to produce a documentary and to retain the particularity of his experience. It was his perfectionism which then led Agee to reject novelistic devices of representation. Virago has issued a new expanded edition of *The Face of War*, dispatches by the novelist Martha Gellhorn [241] (see also p. 673). Between 1979 and 1981 a series of child murders were committed in Atlanta, Georgia. A young man called Wayne Williams was subsequently arrested and charged with two of these crimes. James Baldwin was invited to report on this case and *Evidence of Things Not Seen* [242] (a reversal of the title of Elizabeth Daly's thriller *Evidence of Things Seen*) is the result.

Several memoirs have appeared this year of which predictably two deal with the experiences of Americans in Paris. Journalist and editor of the periodical *transition*, Elliot Paul has set down a record of Paris between the wars in *A Narrow Street* [243] (published in 1942 under the title *The Last Time I Saw Paris*). C. W. Gusewelle is a journalist for the Kansas City *Star* as well as short-story writer and essayist. He has now collected together his impressions of a recent visit to Paris [244] which will be of interest in comparison to prewar descriptions of the city.

In 1974 Greenfield Community College established an Archibald MacLeish Collection and one of their main projects was to undertake a series of interviews with MacLeish from 1976 to 1981 which ultimately constituted what he called the 'autobiography of my professional life'. These have now been published [245] and show MacLeish discussing his early years at Harvard and his period in Paris, as well as offering a running commentary on his own works. He is particularly scathing of the critics Malcolm Cowley and Edmund Wilson, and modestly understates the variety of his own career as lawyer, poet, and Librarian of Congress. MacLeish served in the Office of War Information and then in 1949 began a new phase in his career by taking an academic post. Even in his last years there was no let-up to his activity since he worked equally hard on radio drama and poetry readings. The journals which Edmund Wilson kept during the 1950s were apparently intended to be published but this was not a purpose he realized in his lifetime. Leon Edel has now transcribed and edited them [246], in some cases from a very disorganized state. As we might expect from Wilson, these journals range over a whole series of topics from the personal (inheritance of the family home) to political commentary on the McCarthy years and his struggles with Hebrew to analyse the Dead Sea Scrolls. Visits to Europe also give fascinating glimpses of the British literary scene. Edel has

241. *The Face of War*, by Martha Gellhorn. Virago. pp. xix + 292. £10.95.

242. *Evidence of Things Not Seen*, by James Baldwin. Joseph. pp. xiv + 125. £8.95.

243. *A Narrow Street*, by Elliot Paul, foreword by Sam White. Harrap. pp. xiii + 230. pb £5.95.

244. *A Paris Notebook*, by C. W. Gusewelle. Lowell. pp. xiii + 211. pb $9.95.

245. *Reflections*, by Archibald MacLeish, ed. by Bernard A. Drabeck and Helen E. Ellis, foreword by Richard Wilbur. UMass. pp. xiii + 291. £19.

246. *The Fifties*, by Edmund Wilson, ed. by Leon Edel. Macmillan. pp. xxxii + 663. £19.95.

supplied useful annotations at the end of each section. From the same period *ParisR* has published an autobiographical essay by Mary McCarthy dealing with her schooldays and her discovery of serious literature.

Where MacLeish and Wilson were central figures in the American literary establishment, Herbert Huncke's claim to fame rests on the marginal role he played in the early days of the Beat movement. In his introduction to Huncke's recollections, *The Evening Sun Turned Crimson*[247], Allen Ginsberg notes Huncke's appearances in Beat fiction and proposes him as a minor culture-hero, a member of an underground resisting totalitarianism. Huncke himself is far from self-dramatizing, narrating his experiences in an uneven laconic style which has the value of a historical document in hipster slang. While he never remotely lives up to Kerouac's claim that he was a 'great story-teller', Huncke's narratives make a significant addition to Beat writing. Although Andy Warhol is known primarily in the visual arts he is the author of one novel (*A*, 1968), and his other prose work *From A to B and Back Again* has now been re-issued[248]. It is virtually impossible to categorize since it combines ironic autobiography, reflections on our sense of beauty, and memories of the rise of the counter-culture in the 1960s. Of particular interest here are Warhol's comments on advertising, television, and tape-recording, the latter being used extensively in his novel.

In the area of belles lettres and essays one of the most unusual volumes to appear this year has been the collected sketches of the American expatriate Logan Pearsall Smith[249]. From 1903 onwards he began publishing a series of volumes of 'trivia' – prose vignettes, aphorisms, and miniature *causeries*. Smith was a close friend of Henry James and on the fringes of the Bloomsbury Group; nevertheless he is now almost a forgotten writer. In his new foreword to this collection Gore Vidal argues that Smith should be more appreciated within the Anglo-French essay tradition. This is a tradition which would also include the 'bagatelles' of Delmore Schwartz which have now been published[250]. His literary executor Robert Phillips has collected nineteen such pieces, light personal essays which give Schwartz's intellectual imagination an opportunity to play over his subjects. Phillips hints that there are other works (novels, an autobiography, etc.) which can be salvaged from Schwartz's papers at Yale and it is to be hoped these will be forthcoming soon. Maurice Zolotow (*MQR*) acts on the current surge of interest in Schwartz to point out the discrepancy between the self-images projected in his letters and the way Zolotow actually remembers him when they were both at college in the 1930s. In this important biographical piece Zolotow points out that Schwartz's projection of himself as an intellectual guru was largely fictitious. Sixty essays which Kenneth Rexroth wrote for the *Saturday Review* have now been collected[251]. These comparatively brief pieces all cover classics, from the *Epic of Gilgamesh*

247. *The Evening Sun Turned Crimson*, by Herbert Huncke, intro. by Allen Ginsberg. CV. pp. 224. pb £3.95.

248. *From A to B and Back Again*, by Andy Warhol. Picador: Pan. pp. 223. pb £3.50.

249. *All Trivia*, by Logan Pearsall Smith, foreword by Gore Vidal. Penguin. pp. xxiii + 197. pb £3.95.

250. *The Ego Is Always at the Wheel: Bagatelles*, by Delmore Schwartz, ed. by Robert Phillips. ND. pp. xii + 146. $14.95.

251. *Classics Revisited*, by Kenneth Rexroth, afterword by Bradford Morrow. ND. pp. ix + 214. pb $8.95.

through Greek, Roman, and English literature to *Huckleberry Finn*. As they make clear and as Rexroth himself stresses in his introduction, he is interested in archetypal patterns of myth which 'put man into nature'. Thus he argues that the Communist Manifesto is a classic because it promotes an eschatological myth. These essays too were found among Rexroth's papers on his death by Bradford Morrow who has supplied a brief tribute to this modern polymath.

In the 1950s the novelist James T. Farrell delivered a series of lectures, a selection of which have now been edited by Donald Phelps[252]. The first of these sets a pattern in using Whitman as a point of departure for discussing democratic freedoms. Farrell is particularly concerned with how the writer engages with society, what sort of institutional pressures are exerted on him, and on how to cope with the mass media. As we might expect, he is firmly committed to realism (proposing the novelist's role as an elaboration of the day-to-day) and places his main emphases on such writers as Crane, Hemingway, and Dreiser (the latter being the strongest influence on his career). The lectures now seem rather dated by the comparative absence of formal concerns. A new collection of reviews, essays, and addresses by Ralph Ellison[253] also considers social issues. The main argument running through *Going to the Territory* is that there is an inevitable tension between communal and individual self-images in American culture, and that this clash between images can produce verbal and physical violence. Ellison draws on the theories of Kenneth Burke in seeing language as symbolic action and also offers an extended gloss on his own novel, *Invisible Man*. He has comparatively little to say on the civil rights movement (interestingly he champions L. B. Johnson) or about the new stress on ethnicity in Afro-American writing, partly because he is preoccupied with a nineteenth-century tradition of American classics. For its insights into American culture *Going to the Territory* will importantly supplement Ellison's earlier collection of prose, *Shadow and Act*.

Eliot Weinberger, unlike Ellison, is exclusively an essayist and his first collection, *Works on Paper*[254], has now been published. This book falls into two sections. In the first Weinberger reflects on topics related to the Orient, examining Confucian poetry and Chogyam Trungpa, the guru of Boulder's Naropa Institute. In the second half he considers a number of modern poets in relation to their context. George Oppen, Langston Hughes, Charles Reznikoff, Clayton Eshleman, and, unusually, the former Communist agent Whittaker Chambers are all discussed, the first of these through self-contained paragraphs which mimic Oppen's epigrammatic style. Finally a number of broader issues are considered. The bombing of Hanoi occasions some reflections on war poetry and in one of the most interesting essays in the volume Weinberger examines the relation of modernism to totalitarian politics. Charles Bernstein, a poet in the L=A=N=G=U=A=G=E group, has now shown himself to be a skilled and agile theorist in his collected essays[255]. Approaching language

252. *Hearing Out James T. Farrell: Selected Lectures*, ed. by Donald Phelps. The Smith. pp. 167. pb $8.95.

253. *Going to the Territory*, by Ralph Ellison. RandomH. pp. 338. $19.95.

254. *Works on Paper: Essays*, by Eliot Weinberger. ND. pp. 175. hb $22.95, pb $9.95.

255. *Content's Dream: Essays 1975–1984*, by Charles Bernstein. S&M. pp. 465. $17.95.

as an essential medium of thought and utterance, he is particularly persuasive in pointing out the political implications of poetical forms. Thus he finds Charles Olson's heroic stance limited and male-oriented. Bernstein ranges over film as well as literary topics, creatively varying the format of his own essays. His collection sheds much new light on literary perspective and confessional modes, and shows an enviable ease at incorporating theories of perception into critical discussion.

Before concluding with American humorists, two more works must be considered, the one an autobiography by a leading critic of modern American literature, the other a study of a group of critics. *Out of Egypt*[256] is a volume in which Ihab Hassan describes his childhood in prewar Egypt with all the attendant social divisions and political unrest. On graduating from the University of Cairo he decided to emigrate to America and here his autobiography breaks off. *Out of Egypt* is a work which finely enacts the processes of recall and is in every way different from Alexander Bloom's *Prodigal Sons*[257] which traces the history of the New York intellectuals from their origins on the Lower East Side up to the present. Educational aspiration was stimulated by such role models as Morris Cohen, a teacher at City College, and Edmund Wilson. Bloom identifies an abrasive style as common to these thinkers and demonstrates how important were their journals for the promulgation of their ideas. The founding and subsequent revision of *PR* reflected the intellectuals' shift away from the proletarian literature movement and the immediate postwar period saw them adopting a much less adversarial stance towards the U.S.A. and turning instead to an analysis of their own Jewish identity. A revised radical liberalism was formulated by such figures as Lionel Trilling and a third generation of critics (Stephen Marcus, Irving Howe, etc.) channelled fresh energy into journals like *Dissent*. This is an admirably thorough analysis of a chapter in New York's intellectual history, and one which bears again and again on modern literature.

It is pleasing to note that the humorist S. J. Perelman has been the subject of two important new studies. The first is a biography by Dorothy Herrmann[258] which does more than justice to the variety of his career. The son of Russian-Jewish immigrants, Perelman started drawing cartoons early in life, a skill which secured his first job in New York. One of the most significant friendships in his life was formed with Nathanael West while both were at Brown University, and in fact Perelman himself had ambitions to become a comic novelist. His one attempt in this area, *Parlor, Bedlam, and Bath*, was not successful. Perelman was restless in Hollywood (he called it a 'dreary industrial town') although it occasioned collaborations with the Marx Brothers and Ogden Nash. Herrmann makes it clear that Perelman's true genius was as a parodist, whether of advertisements, success manuals, or pulp detective fiction; and she argues that these parodies reflected a deep-seated pessimism about man's inability to change his lot. Steven H. Gale has assembled an annotated

256. *Out of Egypt: Scenes and Arguments of an Autobiography*, by Ihab Hassan. SIU. pp. xi + 114. $15.95.

257. *Prodigal Sons: The New York Intellectuals and their World*, by Alexander Bloom. OUPAm. pp. xii + 461. $24.95.

258. *S. J. Perelman: A Life*, by Dorothy Herrmann. Putnam. pp. 337. $18.95.

bibliography of Perelman[259], for which he had considered dividing the works into different categories. In the event Gale had to abandon this plan because so many genres overlapped in the same works. He also admits to extraordinary difficulties in tracking down all the editions and shorter pieces of Perelman, and for that reason his bibliography should be seen as a preliminary work. Only selected book, film, and drama reviews are listed, for instance. Nevertheless this work will be an essential bibliographical tool and should help to bolster Perelman's growing critical status. The last work to be noted this year is a new collection of pieces by the *enfant terrible* of stand-up comedy, Lenny Bruce[260]. His daughter Kitty has assembled transcripts of live performances, letters, and *Stamp Help Out*, a concert 'programme' giving facetious views of marijuana smoking. This work, billed by Bruce as a series of short stories, was thought to have disappeared completely after his prosecution for obscenity in San Francisco. The latest pieces in the collection reflect Bruce's preoccupation with the laws of obscenity and the maintenance of double standards in American social decorum.

5. Drama

(a) General

The 'staging standards' of American musical theatre which provide the subject for Carol Lucha-Burns's *Musical Notes*[261] extend the category of those works that have become part of a 'cultural tradition' to include those that 'should be seen more often at schools, regional and community theatres around the globe'. The entries in this 'Guide' are arranged alphabetically, providing information on authorship and original production, a substantial synopsis of the story-line, notes on the production of the show (which include Tony Awards, ideas on technical and costume requirements, possible pitfalls, and budget suggestions), a list of songs of special interest, and details of instrumentation. A supplementary section on 'Concept, Rock, Nostalgia and Others' differs from the main body of entries in providing abbreviated overviews rather than detailed synopses. Appendixes on 'Music Theatre Annual' and 'Chronology of Long-Running Musicals' present, respectively, a chronological listing of productions from 1915 to 1985 and a listing of those productions with the lengthiest tenure both on and off Broadway. The great virtue of the volume is its eye to use, to putting on the shows, and so further appendixes list songs and their performance requirements for use in workshop or class study, and compile addresses of licensing agencies and specialist stores. In addition to a substantial bibliography, the volume concludes with indexes to shows and their years of production, songs and their sources, and professionals and their specialities. It would be difficult to imagine a more thorough or more useful guide to mounting a musical production: this volume ensures that the shows will go on.

259. *S. J. Perelman: An Annotated Bibliography*, by Steven H. Gale. Garland (1985). pp. xxviii + 162. $26.

260. *The Almost Unpublished Lenny Bruce*, ed. by Kitty Bruce. FE. pp. 128. pb £5.95.

261. *Musical Notes: A Practical Guide to Staffing and Staging Standards of the American Musical Theatre*, by Carol Lucha-Burns. Greenwood. pp. xvii + 581. £44.95.

Nearly thirty years and over one hundred issues of *MD*, founded in 1959, are commemorated in *Essays on Modern American Drama*[262]. Dorothy Parker has anthologized from these issues four (and in the case of Albee, five) of the 'best' articles on each of her selected playwrights who are chosen as 'representative of the main stream of American dramatic tradition'. The editorial policy has been to correlate the 'best' articles (first published between 1967 and 1984) with the 'major' plays in each instance. There is nothing very surprising or adventurous in the anthology, but the journal itself, after all, has not been noted for its hospitality towards risk or experimentation. Tennessee Williams is covered by Nancy Baker Traubitz's 'Myth as a Basis of Dramatic Structure in *Orpheus Descending*', Brian Parker's 'The Composition of *The Glass Menagerie*: An Argument for Complexity', Mary Ann Corrigan's 'Realism and Theatricalism in *A Streetcar Named Desire*', and Leland Starnes's 'The Grostesque Children of *The Rose Tattoo*'. Arthur Miller receives the attention of Barry Gross's '*All My Sons* and the Larger Context', C. W. E. Bigsby's 'The Fall and After – Arthur Miller's Confession', Robert A. Martin's 'Arthur Miller's *The Crucible*: Background and Sources', and Lawrence D. Lowenthal's 'Arthur Miller's *Incident at Vichy*: A Sartrean Interpretation'. Edward Albee is accommodated by Robert B. Bennett's 'Tragic Vision in *The Zoo Story*', Jay Flasch's 'Games People Play in *Who's Afraid of Virginia Woolf?*', C. W. E. Bigsby's 'Curiouser and Curiouser: A Study of Edward Albee's *Tiny Alice*', Robbie Odom Moses's 'Death as a Mirror of Life: Edward Albee's *All Over*', and Lucina P. Gabbard's 'Albee's *Seascape*: An Adult Fairy Tale'. Finally, Sam Shepard is considered in Charles R. Bachman's 'Defusion of Menace in the Plays of Sam Shepard', Bruce W. Powe's '*The Truth of Crime*: Sam Shepard's Way with Music', Tucker Orbison's 'Mythic Levels in Shepard's *True West*', and Thomas Nash's 'Sam Shepard's *Buried Child*: The Ironic Use of Folklore'. It would be churlish to deny that this is a serviceable compilation, but one would wish for a little more excitement in its range and approach.

In *Stage Left*[263] R. C. Reynolds is interested in the debate over 'artistry' and 'reality' which has characterized many of the attitudes towards the American theatre of the 1930s, and he probes the evaluative criteria (of social commentary, theatrical technique, and artistic merit) structuring that debate. Predictably, Reynolds finds that the strength of the period's drama lies in an ultimate conjoining of all three criteria in which 'drama was a weapon' through a method of writing 'which would both entertain and inform, which would interpret life rather than merely imitate it'. He selects his material from plays produced in New York between 1929 and 1939, negotiating both the main streams of political theatre and social comedy in chapters of general survey, and devoting individual chapters to Clifford Odets and Lillian Hellman. The author clearly knows a great deal about his subject, but his urge towards synthesis and a largely journalistic tone make for fairly bland reading. This is a capable enough survey at the descriptive level, but what is absent is the grittiness of a more engaged level of analysis and the benefit of an index.

Contemporary reviews of more than 140 New York stage productions

262. *Essays on Modern American Drama: Williams, Miller, Albee, and Shepard*, ed. by Dorothy Parker. UTor. pp. xiii + 218. hb $28.50, pb $13.50.

263. *Stage Left: The Development of the American Social Drama in the Thirties*, by R. C. Reynolds. Whitston. pp. xxx + 175. $22.50.

between 1931 and 1950 are collected by Anthony Slide in a culmination of a valuable series, *Selected Theatre Criticism*, Vol. III[264]. The dramas, comedies, and musicals are selected on the basis of 'their contemporary and historical importance, both in terms of critical and popular regard', and the reviews relate to original productions with the exceptions of those revivals that are 'particularly noteworthy'. In addition to a general name index, there is an index to the critics and a title index to the whole three-volume series which begins with the productions of 1900. Not only does the volume present a fascinating history of critical response but, inevitably, some wonderful quotes – such as the anonymous one-line comment from *Life* in 1931 on Saunders and Charig's *Nikki*: 'It should be gone before you decide not to see it.' Slide has saved us all a lot of leg-work.

The sheer mock-modesty and self-indulgence of Zoltan Szilassy's *American Theater of the 1960s*[265] (which begins 'How dare I – a middle-aged, Eastern European comparativist at a small university in a tiny country with my amateur singer-performer past, with my ESL and International Anguish – write a book concerning American theater in the 1960s?') registers a solemnity and a pretension that, when they are not irritating are simply leaden and frequently result in the impenetrable. His approach, he tells us subjunctively, 'would be that of an interdisciplinary nature, by which the delicate balance of a binary system of paradoxes made the theatrical equilibrium work during the American 1960s'. I am not at all sure what Szilassy means here, and the experience of the text itself (made trebly opaque by a weighty personal pronoun, an impacted style, and the absence of a clear perspective) does nothing to dissolve the haze. The author begins with Edward Albee (as a moment of personal discovery), examines the 'Varieties of the Albee Generation' (in particular, Jack Richardson, Arthur Kopit, and Jack Gelber) and (the title is symptomatic) the 'Dramaturgical Kaleidoscope of the Sixties', and concludes with surveys of 'Happenings and New Performance Theories' and the 'Regional Alternative Theater'. Szilassy's insistent retelling of his plays' stories and his flirtations with critical debates which have long since been superseded suggest that the provincial persona with which he begins is more than a device of rhetoric.

(b) Individual Authors

From the founder of *High Performance* in 1978 (in her own words 'the first magazine ever to be devoted exclusively to performance art, defined then as live performance created by visual artists'), Linda Frye Burnham's '*High Performance*, Performance Art, and Me' (*TDR*) is an indispensable first-hand account of the history and issues of its subject. 'Trisha Brown: All of the Person's Person Arriving' (*TDR*) transcribes an interview with Brown conducted by Marianne Goldberg between August 1983 and October 1985, and is preceded by Goldberg's intelligent assessment of Brown's career to date: one choreographer talks well to another. In 'Walt Disney's EPCOT and the World's Fair Performance Tradition' (*TDR*) Steve Nelson takes the 1893 Columbia Exposition in Chicago and the 1939 World's Fair in New York as his comparative examples to argue that Disney's EPCOT belongs to a lengthy

264. *Selected Theatre Criticism*, Vol. III: *1931–1950*, ed. by Anthony Slide. Scarecrow. pp. viii + 289. $21.50.
265. *American Theater of the 1960s*, by Zoltan Szilassy. SIU. pp. xiii + 113. $12.95.

tradition where performance and theatrical techniques play significant roles in communicating cultural and political messages. His is a well-documented and persuasive argument which sees EPCOT as sharing the principal aim of this tradition: the packaging of culture and technology as entertainment for consumption by a mass American audience.

Plays[266] is the second collection of works by Maria Irene Fornes, one of the most interesting of contemporary writers. It has a characteristically perceptive and gritty preface by Susan Sontag who sees her work as 'both a theatre about utterance (i.e. a meta-theatre) and a theatre about the disfavoured', and the volume includes four of Fornes's most recent plays (first performed between 1982 and 1985): *Mud, The Danube, The Conduct of Life*, and *Sarita.*

Saxe Commins of Liveright and then Random House was one of the century's great editors. He first met Eugene O'Neill in 1915 and correspondence between the two began in 1920, continuing until 1951. In *'Love and Admiration and Respect'*[267], Dorothy Commins has collected those few letters of her husband's to the O'Neills that have survived, all of O'Neill's and approximately half of Carlotta Monterey O'Neill's letters to Commins and herself. Additionally, she provides substantial excerpts from Commins's memoir of O'Neill, and the collection is prefaced by Travis Bogard's brief biographical sketch of 'The Complexities of a Friendship'. Complex, indeed, it was, and the volume is a well-edited contribution to an understanding of O'Neill's life. Its only shortcoming (and this is probably a fault of the material rather than the editing) is that it contains so little on his literary habits. And what little there emerges is confined for the most part to comments such as the following on *Dynamo* from a letter of April 1929: 'I am changing "generator" wherever found to "dynamo" so as not to confuse readers'.

With due solemnity and diligence, Peter Egri's *Chekhov and O'Neill*[268] examines O'Neill's expressionism as a successor to the 'pattern of Chekhovian realism, enhanced by naturalistic, impressionistic and symbolist features'. He focuses his description through his authors' shared preoccupations with theatrical usages of the form of the short story and with the compositional and generic relationships developed between short-story pattern and dramatic structure. The most characteristic elements of these usages are catalogued as the coincidence of culmination in the short story and the short play; the cascade connection of narrative – dramatic units in long plays; the concurrence of narrative and dramatic climaxes in multiple-act plays; and the total fusion of a mosaic design. It is Egri's argument that the parallelism between his two writers is not a matter of direct influence (as it would be in, say, the instances of O'Neill's responses to Ibsen or Strindberg), but rather of a 'typological convergence prompted by a similarity of social, psychological and moral constellations and personal attitudes'. His subject is a necessary one in that the Chekhov–O'Neill connection has not received the degree of attention it might warrant, but too frequently in Egri's earnest hands description serves the office of analytical criticism.

266. *Plays*, by Maria Irene Fornes. PAJ. pp. 147. pb $7.95.

267. 'Love and Admiration and Respect': The O'Neill–Commins Correspondence, ed. by Dorothy Commins, foreword by Travis Bogard. DukeU. pp. xxi + 248. $32.50.

268. *Chekhov and O'Neill: The Uses of the Short Story in Chekhov's and O'Neill's Plays*, by Peter Egri. AK. pp. 183. £12.50.

In 'On the American Line: O'Neill's *Mourning Becomes Electra* and the Principles of the Founding' (*SoR*) John Alvis presents a strong-minded and sinuously argued claim for O'Neill's ability to write himself clear of what the author sees as the 'reductionist' consequences of economic determinism and Freudian psychology, and thereby 'reestablishing a moral meaning for equality and liberty'. Alvis's sense of 'moral' implies little more than an unreconstructed series of possibilities that are essentially individualistic; but this is, nevertheless, a sturdy piece. Equally as sturdy is 'Letting the Dead be Dead: A Re-interpretation of *A Moon for the Misbegotten*' (*MD*) where Stephen A. Black goes against most commentaries on the play to argue that it is organized not around Jim Tyrone but around Josie Hogan, and finds the play's drama to lie in the process by which she 'resists awareness of something well known, but unconsciously known'. The catharsis of mourning confronted by the play reveals, through Josie, the 'point where neurotic misery mostly ceases, and is replaced by ordinary unhappiness, the lot of every life'.

Pamela Cooper's 'David Rabe's *Sticks and Bones*: The Adventures of Ozzie and Harriet' (*MD*) finds the play to have lost a measure of its impact by its temporal distance from the Vietnam War and, more importantly, from the media coverage of the war. She finds also, however, that it retains the dignity of Rabe's commitment, discernible in the power of its symbolic resonances and in the nakedness of the emotions it explores. Cooper claims further that the play's concentration on language signals a 'healthy swing' away from the emphasis on visual effects and spectacle which influenced theatre in the 1960s.

In 'Memories of the Sea in Shepard's Illinois' (*MD*) Johan Callens argues against reading *Buried Child* as one of Shepard's 'realistic family plays', preferring to remind us of its mythic–symbolic dimensions which in turn allow us to see the more positive part played by the female characters. His argument is that the play's engagement with a deterioration from an original Emersonian state of One-ness (figured through water and fertility symbols) recognizes that deterioration as a thwarting of longing which is ultimately feminine. By displaying the feminine role in the safeguarding of 'continuity', Callens hopes to redress the 'one-sided negative view of woman' in the play. 'Sam Shepard and Super-Realism' (*MD*) offers an instructive comparison where Toby Silverman shows a shared world between Shepard and the super-realists to involve a movement 'away from the conceptual toward the perceptual, away from idea toward fact and event'. It is a world of 'cool', pop culture, the mythology of the West, maleness, American-ness, nostalgia for the recent past, and the high gloss of surface. Charles G. Whiting's concern in 'Inverted Chronology in Sam Shepard's *La Turista*' (*MD*) with the question of why the second act of the play chronologically precedes the first is to argue that Shepard's is a theatre not of 'resolutions' but of 'explorations, discoveries, and new beginnings'.

In keeping with the introductory format of the Macmillan Modern Dramatists series, Roger Boxill's *Tennessee Williams*[269] summarizes Williams's life and the major principles of form, theme, and character in his work before paying particular attention, chronologically, to his early one-act plays, *The Glass Menagerie*, *A Streetcar Named Desire*, *Summer and Smoke*, *Cat on a Hot Tin Roof*, the Wanderer plays, and the late plays. A serviceable bibliography completes this cleanly written, intelligent survey. 'The no-nose girl married the

---

269. *Tennessee Williams*, by Roger Boxill. Macmillan. pp. xv + 186. £18.

no-brain man' was Williams's comment on Jane Wyman, late in Albert J. Devlin's collection of interviews, *Conversations with Tennessee Williams*[270], which begins with a journalistic chat for *The Commercial Appeal* (Memphis) in 1940 and ends with the marvellously open and witty response for *ParisR* in 1981. These interviews present an interesting mixture of the practitioner, the honest speaker, and the self-promoter, and it is on behalf of the latter that Devlin wisely advises: 'By dramatizing the artistic self in search of balance and coherence, the interview played a heuristic role that should not be underestimated in studying Tennessee Williams' life records.' This is a rich and diverse volume that in many ways offers a better picture of its subject than any biography. It offers also some very good gossip.

Begun at Harvard and completed in Paris in 1925, *Mannerhouse*[271] is the second of Thomas Wolfe's two plays. Set in the Civil War period, it tells a not unfamiliar story of aristocratic Southern decline. The play was first published in book form in 1948 by Harper, but, as the present editors, Louis D. Rubin Jr and John L. Idol Jr display convincingly, this version differs markedly from the 1925 typescript. It is that early version which is reproduced here. While it goes without saying that an authentic copy of a minor work by a major writer has an obvious value, one would have to agree with Rubin's judgement that its value has less to do with its intrinsic virtues than with its place in the development of Wolfe's creativity.

270. *Conversations with Tennessee Williams*, ed. by Albert J. Devlin. UMissip. pp. xx + 369. hb $24.95, pb $14.95.

271. *Mannerhouse*, by Thomas Wolfe, ed. by Louis D. Rubin Jr and John L. Idol Jr. LSU. pp. ix + 147. £14.90.

African, Caribbean, Indian, Australian, and Canadian Literatures in English

PHYLLIS POLLARD, SUSHEILA NASTA, PRABHU GUPTARA, JOHN THIEME, and KENNETH HOEPPNER

This chapter has the following sections: 1. Africa: (a) General, (b) West Africa, (c) East and Central Africa, (d) Southern Africa, by Phyllis Pollard; 2. The Caribbean: (a) General, (b) The Novel/Prose, (c) Poetry, (d) Drama, by Susheila Nasta; 3. India: (a) General, (b) Poetry, (c) Fiction, by Prabhu Guptara; 4. Australia: (a) General, (b) Individual Authors: 1789–1920, (c) Individual Authors: Post-1920, by John Thieme; 5. Canada: (a) General, (b) Fiction, (c) Poetry, (d) Drama, by Kenneth Hoeppner.

1. Africa

(a) General

In 1986 *JCL* included bibliographies of 'Africa: East and Central' by R. N. Ndegwa, 'Africa: Western' compiled by Daniel Britz and introduced by Ernest Emenyonu, and 'South Africa' by Dorothy Driver, all covering 1985. Richard Bjornson has produced a bibliography of Cameroonian literature (*RAL*) which includes Anglophone writers and Nancy J. Schmidt contributes a preliminary bibliography/filmography 'African Literature on Film' to the same journal. Also in *RAL* is a bibliographical record of undergraduate dissertations produced by the Department of English at the University of Jos, Nigeria.

Invaluable bibliographical information is included in what is undoubtedly the most exciting general study of 1986, Albert S. Gérard's ambitious and comprehensive *European-Language Writing in Sub-Saharan Africa*[1]. Bringing together essays by sixty-two scholars and critics from sixteen countries in Africa, North America, and Europe (West and East), Gérard has attempted 'a survey and a synthesis of the historical development' of all African literatures in European languages. The first three sections are historical: 'Under Western Eyes', 'Black Consciousness', and 'Black Power', while the fourth, 'Comparative Vistas', begins to explore the network of relationships which exist between Africa and other parts of the world. Inevitably, in such a compendious work the essays vary in quality from the incisively analytical to the more routine survey pieces. As the book's preface warns, there are some omissions: recent South

1. *European-Language Writing in Sub-Saharan Africa*, ed. by Albert S. Gérard. 2 vols. AK. pp. 1288. (Hereafter Gérard.)

African drama and poetry, for example, and the comparative section rarely succeeds in being illuminating, but the book as a whole is a remarkable achievement with Gérard's emphasis on 'the scholarly approach, ponderous, élitist, persistent and reliable' evident throughout. His introduction and the final section (entitled 'Birth and Early Growth of a New Branch of Learning') are useful sources of bibliographical information, the first providing a historical survey of European-language literature in Africa, the latter delineating the main trends and identifiable phases in the reception and study of African literature in European languages.

The first chapters offer an introduction to early African writing, including Paul Edwards's lively and informative piece on 'Eighteenth-Century Writing in English' which looks at Phillis Wheatley, Ignatius Sancho, and Olaudah Equiano. Gérard has contributed an essay, 'The Western Mood', to the Negritude chapter in the 'Black Consciousness' section which takes a historical view, arguing that the concept resulted from a slow development of the Western image of the Negro, the starting point being the Comte de Gobineau. Abiola Irele in 'The Negritude Debate' looks at the initial hostility of English-speaking intellectuals like Soyinka to the movement as a whole because of its apparent acquiescence in the stereotype of the black man as a non-rational creature.

In his introduction to the 'Comparative Vistas' section Gérard urges a comparative approach in the plurilingual state of Africa. African literature in progress, he suggests, is moving steadily and fast towards more linguistic differentiation rather than less, against the express wish of many African intellectuals. George M. Lang's 'From National Consciousness to Class Consciousness: A Bilingual Approach' argues that nowhere in African literature does class-consciousness correspond to European philosophical definitions of it, especially those set out by Lukács or other Marxist thinkers. The crucial paradigm for class-consciousness, he suggests, appears to be found in the thought of Frantz Fanon and to take either an Angolan or an East African form. Lang posits a new literary period in African writing, a phase which will redirect social and literary revolt towards analysis of the contradictions within African society. Willfried F. Feuser has contributed two essays to the comparative section: the first, 'The Rise of an Urban Civilisation in African Fiction', is a lengthy and unfocused survey, leaping from country to country and treating a number of themes very superficially; the second, 'Aspects of the Short Story', for which Feuser investigated 497 stories, is a boring formalist catalogue of overlapping themes 'arranged in order of frequency'. More stimulating is Michel Fabre's essay 'Richard Wright, Negritude and African Writing', which raises fascinating questions of cultural kinship between members of the black diaspora. Fabre argues that Wright's view of African culture was that of a Western-educated, Marxist-orientated agnostic, quite conscious of the differences between Afro-American and African social, political, and cultural conditions. His conclusion is that Wright stood at best halfway between integration and Negritude, attempting at times to mediate between the aspirations of two different and often diverging groups. Also illuminating is Jacqueline Leiner's scholarly 'Africa and the West Indies: Two Negritudes', which contrasts the African Negritude of Léopold Senghor with the dislocated West Indian Negritude of Aimé Césaire, 'which cries out for fulfilment'.

The question of language is inevitably in evidence in a work like this. Gérard takes a pragmatic approach to the question of whether literature in non-African languages can be truly 'African'; not so Ngugi wa Thiong'o in *Decolonising the Mind: The Politics of Language in African Literature*[2]. 'From now on it is Gikuyu and Kiswahili all the way' declares Ngugi in this his 'farewell to English' as a vehicle for his writing. The book is a summary of the issues with which Ngugi has been passionately involved for the last twenty years and he relates again the importance in his own development of the Kamiriithu experiment in people's theatre. Readers familiar with these events will be equally familiar with Ngugi's conclusion that English is 'foreign to Africa'. The real language of humankind, says Ngugi, is 'the language of struggle', a judgement which begs many questions and needs to be set alongside Gérard's dismissal of the proposal that Swahili should become *the* Pan-African language as 'ludicrously Utopian'.

A comparative approach to new literatures is advocated in *A Sense of Place in the New Literatures in English*[3], the proceedings of a weekend seminar held by the Macquarie Unit for the Study of New Literatures in English. In the title piece, 'A Sense of Place in the New Literatures in English, but particularly South Africa', Stephen Gray offers a model for comparing literatures that are at different stages of development but warns of the danger of failing to take account of the 'dense and unique specifics of one place'. K. L. Goodwin's theme in 'The Land and its People in African and Australian Fiction' is that, while the literary origins and traditions of both literatures are different, there is a commonalty, though again with important differences, of political and social experience. The main difference is that one comes chiefly from the indigenous people, the other almost exclusively from the settlers. Thus in Australia political independence creates hardly a ripple on the surface of the literature, whereas in Africa hard-won independence has dominated much of the literature of the last two decades.

The remaining full-length study to be noted is devoted to African literary feminism. *Ngambika: Studies of Women in African Literature*[4] is an anthology of eighteen essays, a selection, as the editors say, rather than an overview of critical analyses of literature about the African woman, and very variable in quality. The emphasis is on what they call the 'substance' – social, political, and psychological – of women's presence in the literature. Several of the essays explore men's consciousness of women. The book is divided into three sections, those in the first examining the depiction of women from the male or general social perspective, the second considering woman's self-perception, while in Part 3 emphasis is on thematic analysis of literary presentations of political and social institutions as they influence women. In practice these divisions do not work very well and there is considerable overlap. In spite of being riddled with pretentious jargon the introductory chapter by Carole Boyce Davies provides useful bibliographical material and a scholarly survey of the development of African literary feminism. She bravely attempts a definition of African feminism and a critical methodology with which to approach it. Of the general essays Esther Y. Smith's 'Images of Women in

2. *Decolonising the Mind: The Politics of Language in African Literature*, by Ngugi wa Thiong'o. Currey. pp. xiv + 114. pb £4.95.

3. *A Sense of Place in the New Literatures in English*, ed. by Peggy Nightingale. UQP. pp. viii + 152. £19.95. (Hereafter Nightingale.)

4. *Ngambika: Studies of Women in African Literature*, ed. by Carole Boyce Davies and Anne Adams Graves. AWP. pp. xi + 298. pb $11.95. (Hereafter *Ngambika*.)

African Literature: Some Examples of Inequality in the Colonial Period' is a bland survey which covers too much ground too superficially. Smith examines changing images of women in novels about the colonial period, from the conservers of tradition to those who sought practical approaches to preservation by accommodating themselves to colonialism and finally to those who found themselves changed by the roles they played in the nationalist struggles. In 'The Grandmother in African and African-American Literature: A Survivor of the African Extended Family' Mildred A. Hill-Lubin offers a routine discussion of Frederick Douglass's *My Bondage and My Freedom*, Maya Angelou's *I Know Why the Caged Bird Sings*, Ama Ata Aidoo's *No Sweetness Here*, and Ezekiel Mphahlele's *Down Second Avenue*, all novels in which the grandmother functions as preserver of the African extended family, as the repository of family history and black lore, and as the communicator of values and ideals which support herself and her community. Similar material is covered and a similarly unexciting thematic approach adopted by Ebele Eko in 'Beyond the Myth of Confrontation: A Comparative Study of African and African-American Female Protagonists' (*ArielE*) which looks at black mother/daughter confrontations in Ama Ata Aidoo's *Anowa*, Gloria Naylor's *Women of Brewster Place*, Bessie Head's *Maru*, and Paule Marshall's *Brown Girl, Brownstones*. Rebellion leads, suggests Eko, quoting Mary Washington's 'For black women, the mother is often the key to that unity', to self-knowledge for both generations.

The role of the journal in furthering the production and study of black literature is a recurrent theme in the Gérard collection. Louise Fiber Luce's 'Neo-Colonialism and *Présence Africaine*' (*AfrSR*) is an interesting examination of the origins of the journal and its shifting role as 'an agent of change' in reflecting and informing the values of black nations. Embarking initially on a path to correct colonialism and to question the marginalist position assigned to black writers, one of its key roles has been to legitimize cultural production, thus liberating new literary forms. Luce draws on research carried out by Femi Ojo-Ade in identifying editorial policy from 1947 to 1972 and in the journal's most recent decade finds new prominence given to women's issues, to language, and towards national self-appraisal and self-criticism. Charles R. Larson offers a bleak reminder of the problems faced by African writers in 'The Precarious State of the African Writer' (*WLT*). Economically, argues Larson, the African writer is hardly better off today than during colonial times and what he sees as a decline in African literature in quality and in quantity is the result of the fear of political reprisals. Interestingly, Larson touches on conditions in America and Europe which work to the disadvantage of African writers, instancing the censoring of one of his own articles on Nuruddin Farah because authorities in the State Department feared to offend officials in Somalia. He comments, too, on Heinemann's decision to curtail the scope of its African Writers Series, the major publishing outlet for the continent's writers during the last twenty years. The view that at the moment publishers in the West are interested in publishing only those African writers whose work is already widely known and deemed profitable is made by Wendy Davies (*NewA*) in a discussion of the Heinemann–Longman New Look fiction series. No packaging, she suggests, can disguise that the emphasis in both these launches is on re-publication.

Three essays address the question of aesthetics and ideology. Chidi T. Maduka's 'Aesthetics of Social Criticism: Irony as a Social and Political Act'

(*JAfM*) is a slight and blinkered article, making the obvious point that through a study of ironic situations the reader may gain insight into the author's vision of society. Maduka differentiates between what he calls 'Irony of Inclusion' found in works whose moral universe does not discriminate between good and evil and 'Irony of Exclusion' where the writer presents positive values at the expense of negative ones. The latter, suggests Maduka, could be used by the African writer as a means of revealing and attacking the ambiguities and contradictions in contemporary society. More critically incisive is Dan Izevbaye's 'Reality in the African Novel: Its Theory and Practice' (*PA*). This is a densely argued, provocative, but oddly disjointed piece which examines methods of achieving fictive reality, beginning with the way in which the novel as a form has responded to the African past. African writers, suggest Izevbaye, have found it difficult to create a truly historical novel because of their preoccupation with re-creating contemporary reality, thus reflecting no more than a contemporary consciousness of the past. He then looks at place and characterization, considering contrasting landscapes in works by Achebe, Soyinka, and Armah and exploring some of the means by which a novelist may give a communal character and function to an individual form. Concluding with a discussion of Armah's *Why Are We So Blest*? he suggests that the narrative's true direction is towards 'a non-realistic, non-novelistic genre' like fable or allegory. Ime Ikiddeh's 'Ideology and Revolutionary Action in the Contemporary African Novel' (*PA*) is a predictable study of *Two Thousand Seasons*, *Season of Anomy*, and *Petals of Blood*, torn between an ideological reading and sensible though unadventurous textual explication. The three novels, argues Ikiddeh, reach beyond disillusion and make 'imaginative strides towards recovery' from the present chaos in African society. He praises the 'tough, unsentimental call to action' of *Two Thousand Seasons*, but concludes that Armah's vision fails to combine the historical and revolutionary with the analytical and dialectical, because he fails to establish the economic nature of antagonistic social forces. In *Season of Anomy* Ikiddeh, again predictably, finds a tension between Ofeyi's individualism and the Dentist's revolutionary action, the result of Soyinka's lack of total ideological commitment. *Petals of Blood*, on the other hand, is an overtly political novel with an unequivocal political message, but fails because of its ideological 'obtrusiveness', though Ikiddeh praises its 'largeness and sharpness of vision' in representing the complex relationship between art and life.

The repercussions of Chinweizu's onslaught on literary neo-colonialism continue to be in evidence. James Gibbs's '"Larsony" with a Difference: An Examination of a Paragraph from *Towards the Decolonization of African Literature*' (*RAL*) is an earnestly argued examination of the section in Chinweizu's book describing Soyinka's return to Nigeria in 1960 and his early attack on Negritude in *The Horn* which suggests that Soyinka is a cultural mercenary, a fellow-traveller serving Western imperialist interests. Gibbs concludes by a painstaking analysis that Chinweizu *et al.* use dubious arguments, present facts in emotional terms, slander by association, neglect to examine relevant material, and extend findings quite unjustifiably. It is rather like taking a sledge-hammer to crack a nut. Chinweizu, Onwuchekwa Jemie, and Ihechukwu Madubuike offer a sharply argued, often offensive, but witty reply to Gibbs in 'Gibbs' Gibberish' (*RAL*), re-asserting their claim that the anti–Negritude campaign in *The Horn* and the later Kampala Writers Conference were instances of the 'forces of Eurocentric pseudo-universalism' attempting to check 'the threatening momentum of negritude and of African nationalist consciousness in English-language African literature'. On both occasions, they argue, Soyinka used his powers of ridicule to undermine African nationalism.

Two remaining essays are to be noted. Anthony Kirk-Greene's 'West African Historiography and the Underdevelopment of Biography' (*JCL*) is a scholarly and informative survey of biographical literature on Anglophone West African historiography. The Luo proverb 'Never ask what a chief is like until he is dead' is Kirk-Greene's simple explanation for the dearth of African biographical literature. Martin Seymour-Smith's section on 'African and Caribbean Literature' in his *Guide to Modern World Literature*[5] is a sketchy, uninformative survey.

(b) West Africa

In his preface to Daniel Britz's bibliographical instalment in *JCL*, 'Africa: Western' Ernest Emenyonu writes interestingly on the development of indigenous publishing initiatives, now a major fact to be reckoned with in the West African book industry and in part a response to the foreign-exchange limitations which have restricted importation from Europe. The year 1985, he concludes, however, has not really been a year of celebration for creative writers, literary critics, and the book industry in general in West Africa.

Three essays in the Gérard collection consider the emergence of West African Anglophone writing. In 'The Primacy of Didactic Writing in English and in French' Robert W. July looks at the writings of a group of nineteenth-and early twentieth-century West African intellectuals, Bishop Crowther, James Johnson, Africanus Horton, and Edward Blyden. These constitute a unique phenomenon on the black continent, suggests July, because they elaborated all the basic tenets of Negritude long before this word came into being, providing insight into a period before the relations between Europe and Africa were thoroughly corrupted by racialism and imperialistic exploitation. George Lang's 'Ghana and Nigeria' is a sharply argued survey of literature in the Gold Coast and in Nigeria prior to 1960 inasmuch as this foreshadows later themes in West African literature. Lang traces the comparatively rapid rise of Ghanaian writing in comparison with colonial Nigeria to the early growth of a literate class educated largely on the Gold Coast itself. Although Nigeria assumed literary and cultural leadership after independence, the main themes of West African literature had been sketched out and at rare moments, as in the work of the poet Raphael Armattoe, realized in the works of mid-century Gold Coast writers. In a bleakly informative survey of Liberian writing Femi Ojo-Ade blames the 'exile mentality' of the freed slaves returning from America for the paucity of writing and the mediocrity of quality in Liberia. With no national commitment, no cultural consciousness, and no deep-rooted literacy literature cannot prosper, and his conclusion is that 'the country is not on the literary map of Africa'.

5. *Guide to Modern World Literature*, by Martin Seymour-Smith. Macmillan. pp. xlvi + 1396. pb £14.95.

Robert Fraser's *West African Poetry: A Critical History*[6] is a scholarly and panoramic treatment of West African poetry from its beginnings to the 1980s, examining its relationship with Francophone poetry and demonstrating the oral foundations from which it has drawn much of its richness. Fraser's emphasis is on formal elements. His principal contention is that the inception of written African verse initially marked a sharp break with the tradition of oral verse, after which occurred 'a slow flirtatious reconciliation'.

Gérard devotes an entire chapter to the development of writing in Nigeria. In 'Amos Tutuola: Literary Syncretism and the Yoruba Folk Tradition' Bernth Lindfors takes a fresh look at the influence on Tutuola of *The Pilgrim's Progress* and D. O. Fagunwa. Both Fagunwa and Tutuola, he argues, began as didactic writers combining Christian theology with traditional Yoruba moral wisdom but Tutuola, after initially following Fagunwa's example in Africanizing Bunyan, returned to more indigenous sources of artistic inspiration. Tutuola is thus the missing link between preliterate and literate man, for his creativity is firmly rooted in the cultural heritage of both. More workmanlike is Juliet Okonkwo's 'Popular Urban Fiction and Cyprian Ekwensi', which places Ekwensi historically in the context of the Onitsha chapbooks and provides a useful sociological survey of the development of modern Nigerian writing. There are some inconsistencies in literary judgement here: Okonkwo suggests that Ekwensi's art has not seriously transcended the level of Onitsha chapbooks and at the same time compares his 'naturalistic narrative technique' to that of Zola.

Three essays in Gérard[1], collectively grouped as 'The Ibadan Cluster', consider the stimulus to Anglophone West African writing made by *The Horn*, *Black Orpheus*, and the Mbari Club. W. H. Stevenson examines the changing poetic themes in the student magazine *The Horn* from 1958 to its last issue in May 1964, arguing that its single most important feature was its publication of J. P. Clark. The development and influence of *Black Orpheus*, 'a landmark in African literary history, a monument to black creativity', is Bernth Lindfors' incisive contribution while Jeanne N. Dingome assesses the role of the Mbari Club, like *Black Orpheus* a monument to Ulli Beier, as part of 'the mighty creative impulse' which had started in Nigeria in the mid-fifties.

T. M. Aluko is the most underrated of Nigerian novelists, suggests Patrick Scott in 'The Older Generation: T. M. Aluko and Gabriel Okara' (Gérard[1]), and the aim of his lucidly economical survey is to demonstrate the cultural significance of Aluko's novels in spite of their apparently limited realism. 'His books are neither paeans for progress, nor elegies over a vanished colonial past, but tragi-comedies of change.' Scott praises the symbolic power of Okara's novel, but argues that the privateness and self-absorption of Okara's fictional mode has found few echoes in subsequent Nigerian writing. Still with Gérard[1], Catherine L. Innes covers familiar ground but with a judicious eye in her essay on Chinua Achebe. She conveys elegantly and economically the historical impact of Achebe and establishes him as the founder of a new tradition of novel-writing in Africa. The Igbo novelists of the sixties who immediately followed Achebe are reconsidered by Alain Severac. After raising the initial question about whether the inspiration behind novelists like Onuora Nzekwu

6. *West African Poetry: A Critical History*, by Robert Fraser. CUP. pp. 351. hb £35, pb £12.50.

was Mammon or the Muse, Severac distinguishes two trends in the Igbo novel, one comic and satirical, the other realistic and sociological. The most important development in fiction in the period came not from Eastern Nigeria but from the West with the publication in 1965 of Wole Soyinka's *The Interpreters*, a novel which, as Severac concludes, has clearly outgrown the narrative devices of nineteenth-century realistic fiction.

One full-length study and several essays, including three in Gérard[1], are concerned with Soyinka. James Gibbs, Ketu H. Katrak, and Henry Louis Gates Jr are the compilers of *Wole Soyinka: A Bibliography of Primary and Secondary Sources* (Greenwood) which unfortunately was not seen. In *Wole Soyinka*[7] James Gibbs has produced a workmanlike and comprehensive introduction to Soyinka's drama, beginning with a 'Brief Life', moving to 'Sources and Influences', and offering sections on the various phases of Soyinka's development. If descriptive, bland, and carefully uncontroversial, his study will be useful in presenting a reassuring approach to a writer who is often intimidating to students. Joel 'Yinka Adedeji's 'Wole Soyinka and the Growth of Drama' (Gérard[1]) is a survey of the work of James Ene Henshaw, J. P. Clark, Soyinka, and Duro Ladipo. This is an uneven piece, narrowly focused on the Yoruba elements and marred by an alarming pursuit of portentous meaning. In 'The Unfolding of a Text: Soyinka's *Death and the King's Horseman*' (*RAL*) Jasbir Jain covers familiar ground in seeing the play as the tragedy of Elesin's 'laggard' will. More questionably Jain suggests there is no approval or disapproval in Soyinka's stance, only 'a mere unfolding of the cultural sensibility, of the meaning so firmly and irrefutably embedded within its own world'. Two essays in Gérard[1] consider Soyinka's use of Greek mythology. Danielle Bonneau in 'From Myth to Rite' simply maps out the relationship between Soyinka's adaptation of Euripides' *Bacchae* and the original play, and concludes that Soyinka's interest in the *Bacchae* can probably be accounted for by his personal attitude towards the essential nature of rite as generator of myth. Syncretism is again the main point in André Lefevere's 'Changing the Code: Soyinka's Ironic Aetiology', but treated with more sophistication. Soyinka's mode of ironic aetiology, argues Lefevere, distances and manipulates the original text so that we are invited to share the playwright's interpretation and also prepared for the often striking departures from that material. These reflect Soyinka's vision, not only in terms of ideology, but in the revaluation of gestural, theatrical elements.

Obi Maduakor has contributed two essays on Soyinka. In 'Autobiography as Literature: The Case of Wole Soyinka's Childhood Memories, *Ake*' (*PA*) he finds *Ake* lacking in universality in comparison with Camera Laye's *The African Child* and argues that *Ake* fails to move the reader because it is not the story of a typical African nature but the autobiography of a Westernized African. Maduakor's 'Soyinka as a Literary Critic' (*RAL*) is a routine explication of the essays in *Myth, Literature and the African World* and later ones written in reply to the attacks made on Soyinka by the Ibadan-Ife Leftist critics and Chinweizu. Maduakor covers familiar ground, seeing Soyinka as 'a writer in the mythic mode as distinct from one whose imagination is historical'. More critically incisive is James Booth's 'Myth, Metaphor and Syntax in Soyinka's Poetry' (*RAL*). Booth's essay considers approaches to Soyinka's poetry and

7. *Wole Soyinka*, by James Gibbs. Macmillan. pp. ix + 175. hb £18, pb £5.95.

the poet's own use of language with insight and authority. Soyinka's distinctive style, argues Booth, may be attributed to his mythic Yoruba depths or to his divided postcolonial sensibility. Brilliant and assured in tone as the poetry is, it is also metaphorically irresponsible and syntactically messy, and these are poetic sins of no small order.

One of the areas considered by Ernest Emenyonu (*JCL*) as provoking continued critical interest is the writings inspired by the Nigerian Civil War. Chidi Amuta's 'The Ideological Content of Wole Soyinka's War Writings' (*CE&S*) is a useful addition to the debate about the degree to which Soyinka's metaphysical conception of history affects his treatment of contemporary African experience. The significance of Soyinka's war writings, witnessing as they do the beginnings of a gradual but decisive movement away from myth to a more secular, even radical political inclination, is their transitional nature, argues Amuta. However, if Soyinka's disposition in these works is revolutionary, his revolutionary consciousness is of a basically utopian and moral order. In 'Anomy and Beyond: Nigeria's Civil War in Literature' (*PA*) Willfried F. Feuser gives a survey of the writing produced by the war, beginning with a discussion of Soyinka's *The Man Died* and Elechi Amadi's *Sunset in Biafra* as 'witness literature'. Feuser divides the war fiction into realistic 'chronicles' and mythical novels or moral parables. Although he declares that 'our topic is a literary one', much of this piece is a familiar restatement of the economic, social, and political conditions which gave rise to the war.

In 'After the Civil War' (Gérard[1]) Dieter Riemenschneider extends his coverage of the fiction produced by the war to include a discussion of the 'problematics of the young urban generation', providing a useful discussion of new Nigerian writers like Festus Iyayi, Kole Omotoso, and Buchi Emecheta. By the late seventies, he concludes, a new emphasis on individual experience is becoming evident. Dapo Adelugba's contribution in 'After the Civil War' is on drama. In a lively piece, full of first-hand theatrical knowledge but rudimentary in critical analysis, Adelugba looks at the work of Wale Ogunyemi, 'Zulu Sofola, and Ola Rotimi. A challenging and important survey of the major developments in postwar Nigerian writing is provided by Femi Osofisan, who is both ideologically aware and critically sensitive, in 'The Alternative Tradition: An Insider's Postscript' (Gérard[1]). Despite the 'almost unrelieved lack of distinction' of Nigerian literature which proliferated with oil, immediately postwar, it shows a healthy reaction against the 'negritudinist exotica' of the previous generation. Osofisan finds three trends in postwar writing, that produced by the war itself, popular literature on Onitsha market lines, and 'socialist literature', which constitutes the 'alternative tradition', drawing its stimulus from mass participation but seeking social change, in brief, popular literature *à thèse*. A version of this article appears in *PA*.

Three essays adopt a feminist perspective. In 'Reintegration with the Lost Self: A Study of Buchi Emecheta's *Double Yoke*' (*Ngambika*[4]) Marie Linton Umeh examines the way in which Emecheta creates individuals who are suppressed by patriarchal social organizations. Naana Banyiwa-Horne's 'African Womanhood: The Contrasting Perspectives of Flora Nwapa's *Efuru* and Elechi Amadi's *The Concubine*' (*Ngambika*[4]) predictably argues that Nwapa provides a complex feminine perspective on African womanhood, while Amadi's is male, limiting and reinforcing stereotypical impressions about African women. Another *Ngambika*[4] essay which contains no surprises is

Carole Boyce Davies's 'Motherhood in the Works of Male and Female Igbo Writers: Achebe, Emecheta, Nwapa and Nzekwu'. Boyce Davies has a tendency towards the generalized and the clichéd: 'African women writers in detailing the submerged realities of African women's lives are participating in the struggle to achieve the correct balance.' Her conclusion is that male writers present womanhood and motherhood within the context of larger societal problems, while women deal with the conflicts of motherhood.

In 'Christopher Okigbo and the Growth of Poetry' (Gérard[1]) Romanus N. Egudu provides a useful survey of the development of Nigerian poetry in English from its beginnings to the Civil War, showing that its growth pattern shows movement thematically from the trauma of colonialism to the national disaster of the young republic and stylistically from English to Nigerian aesthetics. Okigbo is established as the most significant poet of this generation but Gabriel Okara, J.P. Clark, and Soyinka are also discussed with economy and critical insight, as instanced by his judgement of Soyinka's poetry as 'turgid exercises in cryptic language and confusing syntax'. John Haynes's 'Okigbo's Techniques in "Distances I"' (*RAL*) is an interesting but disjointed discussion which attempts to counter the charges of obscurity, un-Africanness, and élitism made against the poet. Okigbo's central philosophical idea, argues Haynes, involves modernity and its clash and mesh with his traditions. Modernism, he suggests, is not the monopoly of élitist and capitalist-orientated poets, and in its radical disruptiveness it works to subvert received canons. Okigbo's obscurity is attacked by African critics on the left for the same reason that Joyce and Kafka and the Surrealist poets of the 1920s were attacked by Lukács. A revolutionary poetry, asserts Haynes, must help its audience to think and to perceive in new ways. In what is the most incisive and scholarly contribution to *Ngambika*[4], 'Okigbo's *Labyrinths* and the Context of Igbo Attitudes to the Female Principle', Elaine Savory Fido argues that Okigbo's poetry needs to be seen in the context of a society which has depended on close and relatively balanced relations between male and female. While the feminine is closely intertwined with his idea of traditional religion, the male-dominated Christian ethos shaped Okigbo's public idea of himself as a man in colonial and postcolonial society, thus creating a tension at the heart of his work.

On drama in Nigeria Austin Ovigueraye Asagba's 'Roots of African Drama: Critical Approaches and Elements of Continuity' (*Kunapipi*) advocates the need for studying the historical and social traditions that gave birth to contemporary African drama, in particular, the influence of festival. Also aware of the influence of rite and ritual on Nigerian theatre is Oyekan Owomoyela in 'Creative Historiography and Critical Determinism in Nigerian Theater' (*RAL*). Owomoyela's thesis is the emergence of the *Alarinjo* theatre from the dramatic roots of the *Egungun* and its influence both in terms of content and form on Nigerian (and especially Yoruba) dramatists like Soyinka, Clark, Ladipo, and Ogunyemi.

The development of Anglophone writing in Ghana is also treated in Gérard[1]. Richard Priebe's survey of the novel is especially useful on early Ghanaian fiction, arguing that from its early days the novel in Ghana has been informed by a deep sense of *gravitas*, a serious commitment to the welfare of the people. The ground was thus prepared for the two leading post-Independence writers, Ayi Kwei Armah and Kofi Awoonor. Priebe is a little careless in detail – *Two Thousand Seasons* does not recount the effects of two thousand years of slavery in Africa – but he is enlightening in establishing the main tendencies in Ghanaian writing and on the 'profound eloquence' of the present literary silence in Ghana after the fertile sixties. A routine but useful survey of drama in Ghana, concentrating on Efua Sutherland, Ama Ata Aidoo, and Joe de Graft is provided by Anthony Graham-White. Daniel S. Izevbaye's examination of the beginnings of English-language poetry in Ghana emphasizes the formal and thematic possibilities of oral poetry, the key to the development of a Ghanaian poetic idiom, he argues. Izevbaye shows that poetry was the genre in which Ghanaian writers before Independence chose to express their response to the political issues of their time.

Derek Wright has produced another stimulating and scholarly contribution to Armah studies in 'Flux and Form: The Geography of Time in *The Beautyful Ones Are Not Yet Born*' (*ArielE*). After an initial discussion of traditional African concepts of time, drawing particularly on J. S. Mbiti and Mircea Eliade, Wright's premise is that in Armah's writing a linear and diachronic conception of time is playing against the cyclic structures which shape narrative and theme. A central aspect of traditional time-concepts is that time is measured by what happens, but a key feature of Armah's novel is that nothing is happening, the railway office serving as a microcosm of the state in which repetition is the reality behind an illusion of change. The novel's residue of history requires some strenuous act of removal or re-activation, and Wright concludes that Armah inverts Eliade by turning African history into an archetypal repetition of unexemplary events, of which white imperialism is only one. Lemuel A. Johnson in 'Anti-Politics and its Bourgeois Representation in Cuban and African Literature: Edmundo Desnoes and Ayi Kwei Armah' (Gérard[1]) compares *Why Are We So Blest?* with Desnoes's *No Hay Problema* and *Inconsolable Memories* as examples of 'a literature of narcissistic self-mortification'. The novels are offered as 'bourgeois' points of view, in privileged and alienated forms. Johnson's range of cultural reference is wide, but the essay is marred by too much distracting quotation. A more routine approach is evident in 'Parasites and Prophets: The Use of Women in Ayi Kwei Armah's Novels' (*Ngambika*[4]), in which Abena P.A. Busia argues that Armah shifts between two central perceptions of women, the parasite and the liberating prophet. The parasites are usually Westernized African or European women, the prophets those who are true to the ancient African 'way'. A feminist approach is also taken by Chimalum Nwankwo in 'The Feminist Impulse and Social Realism in Ama Ata Aidoo's *No Sweetness Here* and *Our Sister Killjoy*' (*Ngambika*[4]), a pedestrian essay suggesting that Aidoo's feminism is balanced by an awareness of the realities of African society.

Three West African contributions to Gérard[1] remain to be noted. Stephen Arnold's 'Emergent English Writing in Cameroon' is a useful historical survey of the region. In 'Ironic Stances in Cameroon and Nigeria' Janis A. Mayes provides routine explications of Ferdinand Oyono, Mongo Beti, and Soyinka. Eustace Palmer's 'Sierra Leone and the Gambia', on the other hand, is a judicious and well-illustrated piece tracing the development of Sierra Leonean literature from its Creole beginnings to its move into the mainstream of African and modern literature. The two leading writers from the Gambia, William Conton and Lenrie Peters, are given brief but pertinent treatment.

(c) East and Central Africa

In the introduction to the *JCL* bibliography R. N. Ndegwa comments on the general lack of literary creativity in this region, putting his lament in the context of the harsher financial and political climate of the 1980s in comparison with the 1960s and early 1970s.

Mohamed Bakari and Ali A. Mazrui have contributed two essays to Gérard[1]. The first, on the early phase of East African writing, is a quirky, wide-ranging essay which establishes stimulating intellectual perspectives. The authors begin by examining the general cultural context of African literature in English, then turn attention to the history of that literature in East Africa, before proceeding to consider some of the themes which concerned East African writers in the years before Independence. Particularly valuable is the discussion of Makerere College, the 'cradle of creative writing in English', the journals *Penpoint* and *Transition*, and the Makerere conference of 1962. The extensive treatment of Christianity in East African literature is given judicious attention. 'The Triple Heritage in East African Literature' is a discursive and again provocative essay, examining the three major influences which have shaped literature in East Africa in the twentieth century, the ethno-African, the Afro-European, and the Afro-Islamic.

The development of writing in Kenya is given very comprehensive treatment by Elizabeth Knight in Gérard[1]. Not surprisingly, her scholarly and informative account is dominated by Ngugi, since, as she points out, the history of Kenyan literature since Independence can largely be summarized by reference to his career. Knight looks at the rise of literary journals like *Busara*, developments in literary criticism, and recent developments in local publishing and in popular literature, which she sees as an agent of cultural imperialism, putting forward 'a way of life, a concept of beauty and of love that [is] essentially Western'.

Werner Glinga's '*The River Between* and its Forerunners: A Contribution to the Theory of the Kenyan Novel' (*WLWE*) is a densely argued and at times illuminating study of the 'proto-literary tradition', which existed in Kenya prior to the publication of Ngugi's novel in 1964, exemplified by Jomo Kenyatta's *Facing Mount Kenya* and Mugo Gicaru's *Land of Sunshine*. The attempt to deal with the great historical events made use of by Ngugi in *The River Between*, evangelization, education, and circumcision, form an integral part of these proto-literary narratives and constitute, argues Glinga, the link between literature and historical reality. Glinga questions the notion of the African novel being imported, suggesting that Ngugi's novel takes up the problems where the proto-literary texts leave them and that the Kenyan novel therefore was born out of necessity rather than imitation. Glinga's argument, while persuasive, is not wholly convincing, but this does not invalidate one of the strengths of the essay which is to throw light on some of the contradictions in Ngugi's early writing. A linguistic approach is taken by Stewart Crehan in a perceptive study of textual elements in 'The Politics of the Signifier: Ngugi wa Thiong'o's *Petals of Blood*' (*WLWE*). Crehan argues that the moralistic urgency of the novel and Ngugi's revolutionary status have largely prevented critics from honestly confronting the aesthetics of the novel, in particular its failure to bridge the gulf between the personal and the social or historical. The 'political message' is not something that can be extrapolated but derives from the entire text, and Ngugi's narrative strategies can be evaluated in political as well as in aesthetic terms; they are 'independent signifiers carrying their own signifieds'. Chief of these is the voice of the implied author whose monologic discourse talks down to or speaks for rather than becomes one of the people. Not only does *Petals of Blood* fail to invite us to see the world afresh, its narrative strategies clash with its explicit political message. Crehan's persuasively argued explanation for this is that *Petals of Blood* is a transitional novel, an example of '"bourgeois" literature trying to dissolve itself in the people's struggle'.

In a feminist approach to Ngugi, Charles A. Nama's 'Daughters of Moombi; Ngugi's Heroines and Traditional Gikuyu Aesthetics' (*Ngambika*[4]) argues that Ngugi portrays his heroines, in conformity with the traditional role assigned to them in Gikuyu mythology, as the embodiment of traditional values and as leaders in the liberation struggle. More enlightening is Tobe Levin's scholarly and provocative study 'Women as Scapegoats of Culture and Cult: An Activist's View of Female Circumcision in Ngugi's *The River Between*' (*Ngambika*[4]), which claims that though Ngugi takes a complex approach to the issue, ultimately he is content with compromise. Muthoni is right to defy her father, but wrong to choose clitoridectomy. Also to be noted is an interview with Ngugi for *JCL* by Hansell Nolumbe Eyoh.

Christopher Kamlongera's 'The Growth of Popular Theatre in East and Central Africa' (*NLRev*) is a bitty and discontinuous piece, divided into poorly linked subsections. Kamlongera considers the origin of the dance form known as Malipenga as an example of folk drama and then moves to a discussion of Ngugi's plays as examples of agit-prop theatre, here going over the familiar ground of the Kamiriithu experiment in people's theatre. More originally Kamlongera gives an account of the radio drama Kapalepale, produced weekly by the Malawi Broadcasting Corporation, heavily didactic and originating from radio drama broadcast in the Federations of Rhodesia and Nyasaland from the 1950s to early 1960s.

George Heron's account of Ugandan writing in Gérard[1] is inevitably dominated by the sudden disruption of intellectual life that Uganda suffered in the seventies. Heron gives a workmanlike survey, rather reliant on plot summaries, of Ugandan writing from the late fifties onwards. Central to his discussion is the contrast between the literature produced in the Ganda heartland, which had managed to keep its traditional political systems largely intact during the colonial period, and the uneasy chaos of the northern region, a contrast reflected in the difference in tone between the Acoli poet Okot p'Bitek's impassioned defence of threatened traditions in *Song of Lawino* and Barbara Kimenye's tranquil description of Ganda village life in *Kalasanda*. Writers who responded to the political violence under Obote and Amin tended to come closer together in theme and tone, whatever part of Uganda they came from.

The poet Taban Lo Lyong, observes Heron, remained isolated from these trends, commenting usually on general African ills. Ezenwa-Ohaeto takes a comparative look at Lo Lyong in 'Black Consciousness in East and South African Poetry: Unity and Divergence in the Poetry of Taban Lo Lyong and Sipho Sepamla' (*PA*). This is a ponderous statement of the obvious, full of turgid moments of apparent insight like his remark that in Sepamla's writing 'creativity and the existence of man have a consensus'. The prose writing of Taban Lo Lyong is considered by Frank Schulze in 'Taban Lo Lyong's Short Stories: A Western Form of Art' (*WLWE*), a slight and unfocused look at the comic treatment of Christianity as an agent of colonialism. Schulze relies on long passages of quotation and his critical comment is woolly and generalized. What does it mean, for instance, to say of Leonard Kibera that his 'style' and 'humour' are 'abstract' and 'placeless'?

On Okot p'Bitek, Mark Weinstein's 'The Song of Solomon and *Song of Lawino*' (*WLWE*) is an inconsequential piece, suggesting the Song of Solomon as a source for *Song of Lawino* because of its 'metaphorically sensuous descriptions of physical love'. Inconsequential in a different way is Ogo A. Ofuani's 'The Image of the Prostitute: A Re-Consideration of Okot p'Bitek's Malaya' (*Kunapipi*). The Malaya has suffered in comparison with Lawino, says Ofuani, in part because she has been dismissed as a 'mere prostitute'. Ofuani spends an inordinate amount of time attempting to establish the point that such prejudices arise from preconceived moral positions and deals only sketchily with his interesting point that the Malaya is a 'liberated' woman who is aware of the choices open to her.

Stephen Arnold's brief survey in Gérard[1] of Tanzania brings out its peculiar position in Anglophone African writing. English is no longer a language of great power as it is in Uganda and Kenya and most writers who have proved themselves in English have later switched to Swahili. Arnold quotes John Povey's 1970 prediction that English and Swahili literature would coexist indefinitely in Tanzania and suggests that now the balance has tipped in favour of Swahili. The comparative literary precociousness of Malawi, the least economically developed among the successor states of the Central African Federation, is Gérard's starting point in his informative study[1] of the state of Anglophone writing in that country. While Malawi, for obvious economic and geo-political reasons, has gravitated to the orbit of South Africa, the cultural and literary pull towards East Africa was established by David Rubadiri, who explicitly describes himself as an East African writer. Gérard illuminatingly discusses the effect of the Censorship Board set up in 1968, especially in the proliferation of irony and understatement and the choice of poetry as a favourite means of expression. His austere conclusion is that it is difficult to entertain any high hopes for the immediate future of Anglophone imaginative writing in Malawi. Michael R. Ward contributes a perceptive account of Zambian literature in English, seeing it as a 'composite response' to a composite society and to Kenneth Kaunda's ideal of Zambian humanism. The pursuit of an ideological goal is one of the characteristics peculiar to the budding national literature of Zambia, as is the recognition that human beings are prone to betray that goal.

David F. Beer's essay on Somalia in Gérard[1] makes the point that British cultural influence there has never been very active and the only writer of significance to use English is Nuruddin Farah. Farah is the subject of Ian Adam's stimulating if over-ingenious 'The Murder of Soyaan Keynaan' (*WLWE*), which argues that *Sweet and Sour Milk* has a generic affinity with the detective story or, more precisely, with the thriller. In assuming the role of detective investigator on the death of Soyaan Keynaan, his brother Loyaan begins to participate in the highly political life of Soyaan. The novel, Adam argues, departs radically from the genre in its rejection of closure, not the result of epistemological scepticism but of anti-authoritarianism, preferring plurality and provisionality to finality. Anver Versi has reviewed Farah's *Maps* for *NewA*, suggesting that this is Farah's most philosophical work to date.

In an informative survey of Ethiopia David F. Beer (Gérard[1]) depicts Anglophone writing existing alongside a growing body of Amharic literature. English translations from Amharic and Ge'ez have usually directly preceded significant creative work in English by Ethiopian writers, who in turn have inevitably been influenced by their country's unique history and long-established religion and ancient literary tradition. Their main handicaps, Beer suggests, are in overcoming this centuries-old literary tradition and in having to work without complete freedom of expression. The work of Daniachew Worku, Solomon Deressa, and Tsegaye Gabre-Medhin is the high point of over twelve years of Ethiopian writing in English, but the future is doubtful, because for several reasons English is showing signs of losing ground as a strong second language.

(d) Southern Africa

In the introduction to her bibliographical contribution in *JCL* Dorothy Driver remarks on authors whose work is shifting into 'English literature' from the Afrikaans, generally because they have begun to compose in English or because they translate – and in some sense rewrite – their own work. Not only is the definition of 'English literature' problematical but also that of 'literature' itself in the case of writers like Thomas Mofolo, whose work belongs in the oral tradition but has been taken up by the critical world virtually as an English text. A. J. Coetzee, Tim Couzens, and Stephen Gray have contributed a useful survey to Gérard[1], 'South African Literature to World War II', an insightful and wide-ranging piece which considers Rider Haggard and Wilbur Smith and the magazine and review journalism of the 1930s and 1940s.

A comparative approach to Olive Schreiner is taken by J. M. Coetzee's 'Farm Novel and Plaasroman in South Africa' (*EinA*), a penetrating and ideologically aware examination of the farm in *The Story of an African Farm* and Pauline Smith's *The Beadle*, placing them finally against the Afrikaans *plaasroman*. Schreiner and Smith, Coetzee argues, write with an English literary tradition behind them and, in the case of Smith, with a mythic ideal of the farm. Schreiner's farm is an unnatural and arbitrary imposition on an ahistorical landscape, while Smith's pastoralism, seen in the context of the crisis on the *platteland* in the 1920s, wishfully transplants a model of rural society from England to Africa. Also ideologically incisive is Margaret Lenta's 'Creative Choice in Schreiner and Joubert' (*ArielE*), which considers *The Story of an African Farm* and Elsa Joubert's *The Long Journey of Poppie Nongena* as novels investigating the need of women in particular societies to become economically independent, autonomous decision-makers. Both writers see their heroines as taking heroic, creative roles in their societies, but whereas Poppie succeeds in transforming herself Lyndall fails, Joubert thinking, argues Lenta, that Xhosa society in the 1960s and 1970s possesses the dynamism to change its structures; Schreiner, though she sees settler society desperately needing change, cannot envisage an individual produced by that society who could carry it through. Society's hostility is not the only deterrent for Lyndall, but is the result of Schreiner's recurrent problem of reconciling sexual fulfilment with personal independence.

Elsa Joubert's *Poppie Nongena* is an instance of the process noted by Dorothy Driver whereby a text written originally in Afrikaans 'shifts' into 'English literature'. In 'The Flight from Politics: An Analysis of the South

African Reception of *Poppie Nongena'* (*JSAS*) David Schalkwyk writes perceptively about the relationship between political structures and literary-critical orthodoxy. That the story of a black woman, hounded by the apparatus of apartheid, should catch the imagination of a reading public who are instrumental in keeping those laws on the statute books is the result of the refusal of formalism to admit that politics and literature are in any way connected. If the dissemination of the 'literary sensibility' helps to disengage readers from social existence and at worst legitimizes actions and perceptions which constitute a continuous enactment of tragic disorder, the significance of *Poppie Nongena* lies in its unflinching revelation of that disorder. Also to be noted as instancing the same 'shift' are four essays in *EinA* devoted to Thomas Mofolo's *Chaka* – Albert Gérard's 'Rereading *Chaka*', Daniel P. Kunene's 'Ntsoanatsatsi/Eden: Superimposed Images in Thomas Mofolo's *Moeti oa Bochabela*', Neil Lazarus's 'The Logic of Equivocation in Thomas Mofolo's *Chaka*', and Mbongeni Malaba's 'The Legacy of Thomas Mofolo's *Chaka*'.

Also concerned to understand the relation between art and society is Michael Rice's 'Douglas Blackburn's *A Burgher Quixote*' (*Kunapipi*), which invites re-appraisal of a little-known author and a novel which was hailed as the Boer War novel of its day. Blackburn is a satirist whose strength lies in his ability to focus on the particular and the general at the same time. *A Burgher Quixote* is, however, founded in a particular era, with the central character Sarel's struggle standing as a paradigm of the Boer's struggle to come to terms with the demands of a new century. Blackburn's portrayal of the Boers makes use of the negative stereotypes expected by a readership derived largely from a sophisticated imperial power, but on closer reading, Rice argues, he also directs his satire at the very forces which were exploiting and waging war against the Transvaal in the name of imperialism. Stephen Gray's 'William Plomer's Stories: The South African Origins of New Literature Modes' (*JCL*) is full of insight too. By examining his habit of upsetting a character's securities, his exploration of power, sexuality, and madness in an oppressively patriarchal puritan environment and his departure from realism, Gray argues persuasively that Plomer was an innovator far ahead of his time in terms of the major drift of South African letters.

Michael Wade's 'White South African Literature After World War II' (Gérard[1]) is a routine survey confined to the novel and treating white writers only, but providing a useful historical context for writers like Nadine Gordimer and J. M. Coetzee. Two studies of the former are to be noted. Stephen R. Clingman's *The Novels of Nadine Gordimer: History from the Inside*[8] is an important book not only because of its informed exposition, but because of its critically sensitive handling of the relationship between literature and history. Clingman follows her developing consciousness of history through the novels, showing how they contribute towards a history of consciousness in South Africa. Each novel is related to the social and cultural moment from which it emerges and for which it in turn offers an 'inside' perspective. The final chapter 'Deep History' considers Gordimer's 'split position' in South Africa. Ideologically her work has ranged both within and beyond her 'class' situation; she identifies with the 'disprivileged' in South Africa, yet she does so from a

8. *The Novels of Nadine Gordimer: History from the Inside*, by Stephen R. Clingman. A&U. pp. xi + 276. £25.

position of privilege; 'Gordimer, quite simply, is not "of" the black South African world'. Less ideologically searching is John Cooke's *The Novels of Nadine Gordimer: Private Lives/Public Landscapes*[9], which argues that Gordimer's career has been an attempt to escape the confines of her white South African identity by finding some way to identify with the population of the country as a whole. Her career can thus be seen as a progression from colonial writer to African writer; and in her best work she succeeds. Cooke's analysis is heavily reliant on plot and character summary and rather glib in its conclusions.

Concentrating on the stories, Martin Trump's 'The Short Fiction of Nadine Gordimer' (*RAL*) takes an ideological approach like that of Clingman, but more reductively so. He too notes Gordimer's paradoxical social position: a white person living in privilege in South Africa, fêted by an international readership and yet espousing the causes of the deprived black South African masses. The ideological implications of her works are populist and yet their form and mode of expression are élitist. Trump looks at the special relationship, based on a shared victimization, that develops in the stories between white women and black people. Richard G. Martin's 'Narrative, History, Ideology: A Study of *Waiting for the Barbarians* and *Burger's Daughter*' (*ArielE*), is, as the title promises, ideologically aware and at the same time scholarly and illuminating. Although both novels are about politics, history, and the relations between these and the individual, they differ in almost every formal and literary particular, Coetzee's novel being a symbolic and evocative parable while Gordimer's is a detailed representational history. Martin argues that Gordimer thereby limits her text to its own significance, binding itself irrevocably to its own historical position.

The postmodernism of J. M. Coetzee continues to attract attention. Stephen Watson's 'Colonialism and the Novels of J. M. Coetzee' (*RAL*) is a significant article inviting a revaluation of Coetzee. Like other South African novelists, Coetzee's theme is the human relationship basic to colonialism, that of power and powerlessness, but in his novels the theme is subject to the transfiguration of myth. Coetzee wishes to register the impact of colonialism, not, as is customary in the realist novel, through a series of incidents or events, but at the more basic level of language itself. Barthes's reflections on the frustrations of language in *S/Z* are echoed by Magda in *In the Heart of the Country*. In the same way that human relations are extinguished in the colonial situation, so Coetzee's novel seems to suggest, argues Watson, language itself fails to signify, to mean at all. Robert M. Post in 'Oppression in the Fiction of J. M. Coetzee' (*Crit*) tries unsuccessfully to turn Coetzee into a representational writer by looking at the novels as a series of analogues to the South African situation. Post is engagingly simplistic: when the protagonist in *Life and Times of Michael K* longs for food that comes out of the ground from seeds he has planted, his comment is 'This is the nonwhite South African asking for his own land'. Dick Penner's 'Sight, Blindness and Double-Thought in J. M. Coetzee's *Waiting for the Barbarians*' (*WLWE*) is a formalist approach dependent on close textual reading which looks at Coetzee's use of the *leitmotif* of blindness and sight. Penner is determinedly and somewhat defensively neutral: 'The

9. *The Novels of Nadine Gordimer: Private Lives/Public Landscapes*, by John Cooke. LSU (1985). pp. xii + 236. $27.50.

following analysis of *Waiting for the Barbarians* is not basically political in focus, but connections between Coetzee's fictional world and the present state of affairs in South Africa should be apparent.'

Joyce Johnson's 'Structures of Meaning in the Novels of Bessie Head' (*Kunapipi*) is a thorough, rather laborious examination of imagery and symbolism drawn from the natural elements in Head's work. Head, suggests Johnson, exploits the analogies between the conflict of forces within individuals and within a community and between the behaviour of human agencies and the operation of cosmic forces. This analogical method at the same time mirrors the thought patterns of the society in which the novels are set. Kathryn Geurts's 'Personal Politics in the Novels of Bessie Head' (*PA*) is workmanlike and predictable. She defines personal politics as having to do with using one's power and deciding where to place one's energy and commitment. Her essay treats Head under three headings: male/female relationships, exile and alienation, and the community organization of production. Virginia U. Ola takes a feminist approach in 'Women's Role in Bessie Head's Ideal World' (*ArielE*), a routine survey which explores the familiar issues of power and identity on the personal and social levels. Sadly, two postmortem tributes to Bessie Head are to be noted. Agnes Sam's 'Bessie Head: A Tribute' (*Kunapipi*) is an elegant memorial, suggesting that Head's work is best approached through her non-fictional book, *Serowe, Village of the Rain Wind* and Jane Grant has contributed an obituary in *JCL*.

Es'kia Mphahlele is the subject of an issue of *EinA*. Katherine Skinner and Gareth Cornwell's 'Es'kia Mphahlele: A Checklist of Primary Sources' is a provisional list of Mphahlele's published writing as part of a bibliographical project carried out by the National English Literary Museum, Grahamstown. In 'The Southern African Setting of *Chirundu*' Dorian Haarhoft argues incisively that Mphahlele's choice of a Zambian setting is an attempt at a bridging novel in which traditional themes from north and south of the Zambesi are brought into relationship with each other within the peculiar circumstances of Zambia in the late sixties. Norman Hodge's '"The Way I Looked at Life Then": Es'kia Mphahlele's *Man Must Live and Other Stories*' discusses Mphahlele's first collection of short stories as showing his apprentice-ship as a writer and stemming from a period before the full flowering of black South African literature. The 'quintessentially South African relationship' of master and servant is explored by Damian Ruth in an essay rich in insights, 'Through the Keyhole: Masters and Servants in the Work of Es'kia Mphahlele'. Ruth takes Mphahlele's remark 'We see each other through a keyhole – we blacks and whites in South Africa' to explore the relationships in the short story 'Mrs Plum'. 'Es'kia Mphahlele Remarks on *Chirundu*' is the transcript of a seminar given by the author at the Rand Afrikaans University, Johannesburg in 1981.

Lewis Nkosi's 'South Africa: Black Consciousness' (Gérard[1]) traces the genesis of black 'protest' literature in South Africa beginning with the two Zulu poets, Herbert Dhlomo and Benedict Vilakazi, in the inter-war period. It is to the next generation, beginning with Mphahlele and Peter Abrahams, that we look for the most significant expression of the theme of racial conflict in fiction and autobiography. Nkosi is thoughtful and stimulating throughout this piece, particularly so in his use of Walter Benjamin's notion that 'a work of literature can be politically correct only if it is also correct in the literary sense' as a central evaluative principle. This leads him to a judgement on Bessie Head with which not every reader would agree, that *Maru* is 'as nearly perfect a piece of writing as one is ever likely to find in contemporary African literature' but *A Question of Power* is marred by an 'unassimilated use of religious mysticism and classical symbols'. The nature of 'protest' writing is the subject of Njabulo S. Ndebele's perceptive and clearly argued survey, 'The Rediscovery of the Ordinary: Some New Writing in South Africa' (*JSAS*), in part a history of writing in South Africa, in part a directive for the future. The history of South African literature, says Ndebele, has largely been the history of spectacle as oppressive social conditions have prompted a demonstrative form of literary representation. What has come to be known as 'protest' literature has been largely misunderstood by an audience schooled under a Eurocentric literary tradition and failing therefore to understand its transformation of reality. For a black reader protest writing offers recognition, understanding, historical documentation, and indictment. 'Protest', Ndebele argues, is a misnomer because it reinforces the expositionary intention without establishing its own evaluative literary grounds. Bernth Lindfors' 'Exile and Aesthetic Distance: Geographical Influences on Political Commitment in the Works of Peter Abrahams' (*IFR*) establishes the importance of Abrahams's visit to South Africa as a reporter for the London *Observer*. Abrahams's homecoming, by putting him back in direct contact with his roots, had a beneficial effect on his art, enabling him to rediscover the stark realities of the landscape he had left behind. A tribute to Alex La Guma by Jan Carew (*Wasafiri*) is to be noted.

In 'The Troubadour: The Poet's Persona in the Poetry of Dennis Brutus' (*ArielE*) Tanure Ojaide identifies what he calls 'the poetic mask' of Dennis Brutus. Ojaidi argues in this largely descriptive account that Brutus fulfils the 'troubadour' roles of lover and fighter in his poems. The ideological position of a very different kind of poet, the Afrikaner writer Breyten Breytenbach, is the subject of Neil Lazarus's thoughtful 'Longing, Radicalism, Sentimentality: Reflections on Breyten Breytenbach's *A Season in Paradise*' (*JSAS*). This, he argues, is Breytenbach's 'cahier d'un retour au pays natal' and an exploration of the disjuncture between the idea and the reality of home for the South African writer. Lazarus finds a blend of radicalism and sentimentality in Breytenbach's 'philosophical thought', reflecting his contradictory social position as humanist and as Afrikaner.

A comprehensive and informative survey of theatre production in South Africa is provided by Andrew Horn's 'South African Theater: Ideology and Rebellion' (*RAL*). Horn finds two clearly discernible groups, those which serve to reinforce or to adjust existing social and economic relations and those which are moulded in opposition. Into this latter category Horn places the new black drama born in the turbulence leading up to and following on from the Soweto uprising of 1976 with playwrights like Matsemela Manaka and Maishe Maponya. Albert Wertheim's 'Political Acting and Political Action: Athol Fugard's *The Island*' (*WLWE*) is a rather slight piece, making the point that *The Island* is a play about acting and that the essence of it is Fugard's use of the myth of Sisyphus and the Antigone story as embodiments of the history of protest.

Recent South African writing is treated in three essays. Paul Rich's 'Growing and Grappling, Sipho Sepamla and the Construction of a Black South African Literary Identity' (*Wasafiri*) combines incisive critical comment with a wide-

ranging knowledge of South African politics. As one of the most prominent
South African poets Sepamla was crucial in the re-establishment of a black
literary identity after the near destruction of the earlier 'new renaissance'
writers in the 1950s. Rich traces the development of Sepamla's writings from
poet to his latest novel *A Ride on the Whirlwind*, which takes urban insurgency
as its theme. Different in scope, but useful as a survey of some of the newer
writers in Southern Africa, is Alastair Niven's '"History is Spring Cleaning":
Some Impressions of Recent South African Writing' (*Wasafiri*). Niven's
purpose is to attract attention to writers like Shimmer Chinodya from
Zimbabwe, whose work is unfamiliar in Britain. Kenneth Parker's 'Apartheid
and the Politics of Literature' (*RedL*) is another survey of a collection of
recently published works, literary, autobiographical, cultural, and historical,
which take their inspiration in different ways from the South African liberation
struggle. Parker's comments on individual works are of necessity brief but
incisive and revealing, and the piece is held together by his assertion that South
Africa is a 'construction' which privileges white society and from which blacks
are the 'excluded ever-present'. A short report of an interview with Mbulelo
Mzamane for *NewA* is also to be noted.

John Reed provides a stimulating analysis of Rhodesian, counter-
Rhodesian, and Zimbabwean literature in 'The Emergence of English Writing
in Zimbabwe' (Gérard[1]). Reed's discussion of Lessing is particularly incisive:
while her novels, he argues, constitute a powerful critique of white Rhodesian
society, her link and attachment to the subject matter of her work is a kind of
disdain, conveying a sense of the artist dealing with and despising the subject
matter 'as if writing it out of herself in order to escape from it'. It was not until a
younger generation of black writers emerged that the true novelist's imagination appeared in Zimbabwe, represented in the seventies by Charles
Mungoshi and Dambudzo Marechera. Both use English with mastery, says
Reed, Mungoshi with restraint and decorum, Marechera with 'New York
abandon'.

In 'Tracking Through the Tangles: The Reader's Task in Doris Lessing's *The
Grass Is Singing*' (*Kunapipi*) Eva Hunter applies reader-response theory in a
closely argued and provocative essay. Judgement is elicited from the reader, she
argues, on the central character Mary Turner and also on the white settlers.
While condemnation of the settlers is inescapable, towards Mary there is a
covert ambivalence in the narrator's attitude that makes the reader's final
judgement of her problematic. The novel, she says, is finally 'punitive of its
protagonist', the writer rejecting Mary's character to the point of killing her
off. M. J. Daymond's 'Areas of the Mind: *The Memoirs of a Survivor* and
Doris Lessing's African Stories' (*ArielE*) is a thoughtful essay which examines
the epistemological correspondences between the African stories and *Memoirs*.
The three-fold space of *Memoirs* – 'in here', 'out there', 'through' – reflects
the patterns Lessing observed in the white settler community, in which the
settler ethic is designed to ensure the protection and preservation of the group.
It is this shaping relationship, Daymond argues, which is the point of continuity
in her work. The notion that for the white settler community Southern
Rhodesia was not 'home' but part of a huge 'empty' continent is explored by
Kevin Magarey, in 'The Sense of Place in Doris Lessing and Jeans Rhys'
(Nightingale[3]). Lessing's sense of place, he says, is continental and generalized,
though evoking a vivid sense of landscape and climate, thus reflecting an aspect

of the human geography of Southern Rhodesia during Lessing's time there. Colin Style's 'Doris Lessing's "Zambesia"' (*EinA*) is a chatty and inconsequential piece by, as Style describes himself, 'a native "Zambesian"', which looks at Lessing's depiction of white colonial society. Style's comments on Lessing's parodying the tradition of Rhodesian romantic fiction are interesting, but the essay lacks clear direction. Two interviews with Lessing are finally to be noted. Stephen Gray's 'An Interview with Doris Lessing' (*RAL*) surveys her development as a writer, charting her movement away from realism and her unhappiness with the labels which have been assigned to her at various points in her career. Lessing's comments on the continuing influence of her African past are illuminating: 'I certainly couldn't have written *Shikasta* without it because there are whole sections in *Shikasta* that are straight from Africa.' Less searching is Eve Bertelsen's interview with Lessing (*JCL*).

2. The Caribbean

(a) General

The most worthy bibliographical aid this year is the publication of *Fifty Caribbean Writers: A Bio-Bibliographical Sourcebook*[10]. In the introduction to this extensive work, the editor Daryl Cumber Dance sets the development of the Caribbean critical tradition firmly in a historical context charting the 'movement of Caribbean Literature . . . from the derivative writings of the 18th and 19th centuries [mainly Eurocentric in character] . . . to the strikingly innovative art of a Derek Walcott or a Wilson Harris'. Critical attention in the past has tended only to focus on a select group of Caribbean writers as is often the case with 'colonial literatures'; one of the book's strengths is its attempt to focus on the breadth of talent which has emerged from the Caribbean in recent years. Notables included in the bibliography who have previously suffered neglect are: C. L. R. James, Martin Carter, Mervyn Morris, Michael Anthony, Jan Carew, Austin Clarke, Denis Williams, Jean D'Costa, and Earl Lovelace. Among new, young writers covered are Erna Brodber, Jamaica Kincaid, and Michael Thelwell.

This collection of bio-bibliographical essays provides substantial bibliographical data as well as offering sound critical reviews of major works and themes, listings of honours, and an evaluative survey of selected scholarship. As an updating and supplement to earlier data, this collection is admirable; moreover, the range of interests and different methodologies reflected by the variety of contributors will serve both the advanced scholar and the research student seeking a convenient overview. Whilst there is unevenness in the material on the relatively unknown female poet Dionne Brand, the volume succeeds in the main in achieving the editor's hope that Caribbean writers are 'firmly enshrined in the arena of World Literature', and it reflects the belated recognition of Caribbean literature in North America.

A complementary work has been published jointly by the University of Warwick's Centre for Caribbean Studies and the Dangaroo Press. In the introductory note to *Black British Literature: An Annotated Bibliography*[11],

10. *Fifty Caribbean Writers: A Bio-Bibliographical Sourcebook*, ed. by Daryl Cumber Dance. Greenwood. pp. 530. £65.
11. *Black British Literature: An Annotated Bibliography*, ed. by Prabhu Guptara. Dangaroo. pp. 176. pb £12.95.

Prabhu Guptara discusses the arguments surrounding the definition of this body of writing as 'Black British'. He concludes that 'Black Britons' are those people of 'non-European origin, who are now, or were in the past, entitled to hold a British passport and displayed a substantial commitment to Britain . . . by living a large part of their lives here'. While several counter-arguments could be suggested in answer to Guptara's broad labelling of a whole spectrum of cultural traditions and backgrounds, the bibliography is a practical and much-needed resource. The bibliographical details provided give basic information for locating books and the annotations should be read in conjunction with the introduction which contains additional information on authors. The information on writers of Caribbean origin is sound.

A useful *Checklist of Caribbean Writing*[12] is divided into seven sections which range from general surveys and criticism to notes on individual authors, periodicals, and booksellers. The scholar familiar with this area will not be greatly surprised by the listings; for those seeking fast access to the range of material available in London, the guide will provide an informative starting point for research. The publication of the guide was timed to coincide with the Caribbean Writers Conference held in London during this review period and to celebrate 'Caribbean Focus Year' in Britain.

JCL's annual West Indian bibliography has appeared on time this year. There is good coverage by Victor Ramraj of creative writing in Britain, the Caribbean, and Canada. A similar but briefer survey has also been published in 'The Year That Was' (*Kunapipi*).

Several journals have devoted special issues to the Caribbean. These include *JCSt*, *KompH*, *Wasafiri*, and *Kunapipi*. Mention should also be made of another new journal in the field: *JWIL* first appeared in October of this review period and is published in the Caribbean, drawing on a strong regional editorial board. Attention should also be drawn to the work of small presses such as the Peepal Tree Press in Leeds and Hansib Publishing in London. On the international publishing scene Heinemann and Longman have launched new series of African and Caribbean writers or re-issued or newly published titles which are introduced by leading critics. Reflecting the multicultural needs of the schools' market in Britain and overseas, it also confirms the literature's increasing general readership.

Linguists working in areas connected with language planning and language policy in the Caribbean have tended largely to operate with a supposedly value-free framework. They have seen their role as simply to describe and analyse language problems, recommending solutions within the structures laid down by the existing social, political, and economic order. Hubert Devonish's important book *Language and Liberation: Creole Language Politics in the Caribbean*[13] aims to fill some of the gaps left by such approaches. Devonish begins his study with an in-depth historical analysis of the language question within the double contexts of human society and socialist transformation; he explores these questions from the period of the ancient Egyptians to the contemporary Caribbean. In extending a 'universal language phenomenon' to Creole languages, Devonish presents a fascinating and generally convincing argument

12. *Checklist of Caribbean Writing*, by Roger Hughes. Commonwealth Institute Library Services. pp. 49. pb £1.50.
13. *Language and Liberation: Creole Language Politics in the Caribbean*, by Hubert Devonish. Karia. pp. vi + 149. hb £9.95, pb £5.95.

on bilingualism, disglossia, and the modes by which language debates are inextricably linked to questions of national politics and liberation. As such Creole languages, 'the ordinary everyday languages of millions of people', can and should play an essential role in the process of nationalism.

A special issue of *TSAR* focuses on Indo-Caribbean literature. Edited meticulously by Frank Birbalsingh, the volume contains stories and poems by a number of East Indian writers (old and new) including Samuel Selvon, Ramabai Espinet, John A. Ramsaran, Rajkumarie Singh, Unis Kisson, Ismith Khan, Rooplall Monar, Angus Richmond, Cyril Dabydeen, and Neil Bissoondath. The publication of this collection of essays, articles, and creative writing is striking in its placing of Indo-Caribbean writing within the wider Caribbean tradition. It marks an important milestone in the belated recognition of the Indian diaspora.

There has not been a vast number of general articles this year. However, Laurence A. Breiner's 'Is There Still a West Indian Literature?' (*WLWE*) provides a pertinent revaluation of the concept of its title twenty-five years after its creation. The notion of a 'West Indian Literature' developed originally alongside the political goal of Federation in the period immediately following Independence in the islands. Breiner asserts that there is more concern today with the relationship of 'West Indian Literature' to 'the body of polyglot Caribbean literature'; for the present, it is the '*internal* coherence' that is of paramount significance – whether it is 'feasible to speak of Jamaican, Guyanese, Trinidadian literatures, and . . . whether . . . we are thereby indicating [its] diversity . . . or its dissolution'.

Patricia Ismond has raised pertinent questions concerning the subject of nationalism and regionalism in 'Self-Portrait of an Island: St Lucia Through the Eyes of its Writers' (*JWIL*). While the discovery of a common literary identity has been paramount in the work of Caribbean writers, each artist comes to this 'collective endeavour' from the 'lived experience of his island background'. Ismond focuses her analysis on the work of Derek Walcott and Garth St Omer. It is the scenes of St Lucia's 'small peasant communities and fishing villages' that comprise the 'most seminal presence' in Walcott whereas in St Omer we find a central preoccupation with the 'dilemma of the educated native son, returning home to take his place and make a contribution to [St Lucian] society'.

Unlike his contemporaries – V. S. Naipaul, George Lamming, and Wilson Harris – Samuel Selvon has not published critical pieces on Caribbean culture or theoretical essays regarding the Caribbean novel. In 'Three Into One Can't Go – East Indian, Trinidadian or West Indian' (*Wasafiri*), he explores the question of an East Indian identity. This essay provides illuminating detail both on Selvon's own perspective regarding creolization and cultural identity as well as discussing more general issues concerning the position of East Indians in the Caribbean, a topic of political concern in recent years and one that is increasingly becoming predominant in literary debates.

In 'Creative Writing – What Is Emerging?' (*NewBR*) Janice Shinebourne, the Guyanese novelist, surveys the results of the forum on new writing held during the fifth International Book Fair of Radical Black and Third World Books. The Caribbean discussion was led by the Jamaican critic Carolyn Cooper who examined the questions of form and structure in women's writing particularly in the work of Erna Brodber, Kay Anderson, and Jean Rhys. Anne

Walmsley's 'The Caribbean Artists Movement 1967–72: Its Inauguration and Significance' (*Wasafiri*) illustrates the centrality of CAM in the launching and supporting of a number of major writers and painters during the period 1967–72 in London. Whilst CAM was critical in the careers of many of these figures, there has sadly been little formal documentation to date of its impact and importance.

(b) The Novel/Prose

The Afro-American novel has frequently evinced a concern with the presence of West Indians in the U.S. As Melvin B. Rahming points out in his interesting study of this phenomenon, *The Evolution of the West Indian's Image in the Afro-American Novel*[14], works written between 1859 and the present contain 'several West Indian characters of varying degrees of thematic importance, a fact which testifies to the persistence of the Afro-American attempts to deal with the nature of the West Indian'. Rahming's book explores and assesses the 'nature, role, and psychocultural implications' of these portraits in the Afro-American novel: in addition he examines the stages in the historical evolution of the Afro-American's attitude towards West Indians. In the past the representation of West Indian figures has often been one-dimensional or stereotypical. Rahming's convincing analysis offers an alternative perspective on this seldom-treated subject and includes an examination of a number of Caribbean novels which reflect 'authorial attitudes and objectives that support, contradict or otherwise illumine' those of the Afro-American novelists. His discussion of Paule Marshall's *Brown Girl, Brownstones* (1959) and *The Chosen Place, The Timeless People* (1969) is particularly stimulating.

A comparative approach also forms the basis of *Voices from Under: Black Narrative in Latin America and the Caribbean*[15], edited by Luis William, which represents a noble attempt to fill the vacuum of available comparative discussions on black narrative in the Spanish, English, and French Caribbean. The study of blacks as a basis for such an approach is a relatively recent venture in literary criticism; the breadth of the book's aims allows a full analysis of this literature outside the manifestation of a particular country's national literature and makes possible valuable insights into the lives of people whose destiny was altered and determined by others. It is 'the enslavement, oppression and marginality of Blacks in Africa and in the New World . . . [that] brings their history and literatures together'; moreover it also enables an alternative reading of history to the Eurocentric perspective on the Americas and the Caribbean. The collection comprises a number of essays on this theme ranging from the editor's historical approach in 'History and Fiction: Black Narrative in Latin America and the Caribbean' to Richard L. Jackson's 'Slavery, Racism and Autobiography in Two Early Black Writers: Juan Francisco Manzano and Martin Morna Delgado'. Topics such as the Maroon figure in Francophone Caribbean prose are also explored. Selwyn R. Cudjoe writes on 'V. S. Naipaul and the Question of Identity' and O. R. Dathorne contributes 'Towards Synthesis in the New World: Caribbean Literature in English'. Particularly

14. *The Evolution of the West Indian's Image in the Afro-American Novel*, by Melvin B. Rahming. AFP. pp. ix + 160. £22.35.

15. *Voices from Under: Black Narrative in Latin America and the Caribbean*, ed. by Luis William. Greenwood (1984). pp. xiii + 261. £23.95.

unusual is Lisa E. Davis's coverage of the 'World of the West Indian Black in Central America'. The collection is well edited and contains an informative bibliographical essay which places it in a context of works already published on this subject such as Janheinz Jahn's *A History of Neo-African Literature* (1968) and Richard Jackson's *The Black Image in Latin American Literature* (1976).

In 'The Outsider's Voice: White Creole Women Novelists in the Caribbean Literary Tradition' (*JWIL*) Evelyn O'Callaghan proposes the notion of 'syncretism' as a paradigm for the development of a West Indian literary tradition in its sharing of features with the Creole languages of the region. Examining the critical theories of notable figures such as Derek Walcott, Wilson Harris, and E. K. Brathwaite, O'Callaghan attempts to see whether or not white Creole women novelists form an integral part of this development. Her argument focuses on the works of Eliot Bliss, Jean Rhys, and Phyllis Allfrey and she concludes that while these writers may represent the 'outsider's voice', it is a voice that cannot be denied. The perspective of the white West Indian cannot be provided by the native Afro-Caribbean writer and it was a vision which gave a great deal of impetus to early West Indian writing. Most importantly, it forms an inextricable aspect of what she calls 'syncretic creolization', the amalgamation of several voices which is the ultimate base of Caribbean literature.

It is surprising that more articles like Bruce Woodcock's 'Post-1975 Caribbean Fiction and the Challenge of English Literature' (*CritQ*) have not appeared in recent years. Woodcock's anecdotal starting point is a description of the extraordinary power that the 'great tradition of English literature' has as an institution even when teaching Wordsworth in Jamaica. Woodcock examines and assesses the revaluations that have occurred in the Caribbean and English traditions and those of other world literatures in English. Importantly he asserts that it is the new emergent literatures that are creating 'fissures' in the 'monument' along with a 'plurality of new forms and structures'. The article will be useful to those unfamiliar with these debates; it is also valuable for noting the centrality of new female writers such as Lorna Goodison, Zee Edgell, and Erna Brodber in the post-1975 period.

In '"The African and the Asian Will Not Mix": African–Indian Relations in Caribbean Fiction: A Reply' (*Wasafiri*), Jeremy Poynting provides more detailed evidence in support of Kenneth Ramchand's argument on the same topic in *Wasafiri* (1985). While Poynting supports Ramchand's observation that West Indian novelists tend to write about the ethnic groups they grew up in, he also stresses that there are 'some interesting differences between the role each group plays in the fiction of the other'. Poynting elaborates his discussion of the experiences of Indians in the Caribbean in 'Limbo Consciousness: Between India and the Caribbean' (*TSAR*). Commenting on the period after the end of indenture in 1917 he says 'It was in the gap between losing an old world and gaining a new one that Indians . . . had to construct for themselves a new identity'. The article stresses the work of Indo-Caribbean writers who have explored this state of limbo and concludes that the consciousness of this theme is unlikely to disappear, for 'by virtue of their relationship to the other cultures of the Caribbean, Indo-Caribbeans will never be able to live within a culture that is closed and static'.

In '"In the Cabinet": A Novelistic Rendition of Federation Politics'

(*ArielE*) Elaine Campbell illustrates Phyllis Allfrey's sense of responsibility towards the 'notion of autobiography in art'. Campbell stresses that while Allfrey saw the black nursemaid narrator in *The Orchid House* as 'her hidden self' – a person who expressed her desire to be one of the majority of the society rather than among the rejected white Creoles – it is Joan, the political activist, who mirrors the novelist's own life and career. It is interesting, therefore, that *In the Cabinet* (an unpublished incomplete novel) presents a literary admission of this autobiographical presence thirty years later, for in this fiction it is Joan who returns to the fictional island landscape of Anonica (Dominica). The novel represents Allfrey's 'disillusionment with West Indian politics' and it is through Joan's musings that Allfrey comes through as a 'disillusioned idealist: not a cynic, not a sceptic'.

In recent years the work of the Trinidadian Ralph de Boissière has begun to be revalued by the literary market in Britain and overseas: *Crown Jewel* (1952) reappeared in 1981, and in 1984 A&B republished *Rum and Coca-Cola* (1954). In 'The American Invaders: Ralph de Boissière's *Rum and Coca-Cola*' (*JCL*) Reinhard Sander examines this previously neglected novel by focusing on the correlations between Trinidad's history during the period 'when the island was over-run with American troops' and De Boissière's realistic narrative mode.

'The Fertility of the Gardens of Women' (*NewBR*) by Carolyn Cooper is an important examination of Erna Brodber's first novel, *Jane and Louisa Will Soon Come Home* (1980); Cooper illustrates how the novel's narrative method exemplifies 'an interpretation of scribal and oral literary forms'; it is a narrative in which the oral mode of family history and 'pure gossip' flourishes alongside the world of books. In it 'a modernist, stream-of-consciousness narrative voice' holds easy dialogue 'with the traditional teller of tales, the transmitter of anansi story, proverb, folksong or dance'.

Another female writer whose works deserve more prominence is Jean D'Costa. In 'Finding a Literary Medium: Jean D'Costa's Novels for Children' (*Wasafiri*), Joyce Johnson has provided a range of stimulating ideas on D'Costa's children's books as well as an interesting discussion of the author's use and integration of standard and non-standard varieties of English in her texts. A study of D'Costa's use of language is central to a reading of her novels for in them she presents the complexity of the entire 'linguistic environment of Jamaica'.

In an interview first recorded in 1983 and now published in *WLWE*, Terrence Craig explores a number of central issues in Austin Clarke's fiction including the role of autobiography, the experience of exile, and the political background, as well as distinguishing certain major influences in his writing such as the jazz movement, living in Camden, Saul Bellow, and Samuel Selvon. The interview makes accessible a great deal of previously unknown biographical detail.

The number of substantial critical studies on the work of Wilson Harris continues to expand. In *Wilson Harris and the Modern Tradition: A New Architecture of the World*[16] Sandra E. Drake's aims are ambitious and appropriately so given the complex influences informing Harris's critical and creative output to date. The book's main focus is on the connections between the

---

16. *Wilson Harris and the Modern Tradition: A New Architecture of the World*, by Sandra E. Drake. Greenwood. pp. xi + 169. £27.95.

various cultural traditions affecting Harris's art; in addition his belief in the possibility for 'a meaningful apprehension of truth and knowledge' distinguishes his writing from that of many Western modernists, especially because of his sense of the 'necessity of revising the way the modern world conceives of its own history . . . in terms of centers, origins, and identity'. The book is well organized: the first two chapters are devoted to an analysis of historical relations between the West and the Caribbean in the context of the development of modernism. The following six focus on close textual readings of four of Harris's novels that are particularly pertinent for their exploration of Caribbean society and its relationship with the West. The final chapter examines Harris's theories of language in relation to his critical views on the novel, the structure of the psyche, and historical experience. One of the most exciting features of the book is its placing of modernism within a Third World context; 'Non-Western paradigms' are firmly shown to constitute a 'central part of the Modernist tradition'. Drake refers to Western scholars such as Derrida or Lacan not to make a Derridean or Lacanian analysis of Harris, but to illuminate to Western scholars how Harris has adapted non-Western beliefs and how such paradigms also constitute part of the modernist tradition.

Fred D'Aguiar's interview with Harris in *Wasafiri* offers a stimulating discussion between the young Guyanese poet and the older writer. It deals with the relevance of psychic experience, mythical history, and the notion of community and commitment. The interview was recorded at the ICA in London. In 'Revisioning Allegory: Wilson Harris's *Carnival*' (*Kunapipi*) Stephen Slemon takes as his starting point the notion that Harris's previous novels can be shown to be engaging with a tradition of the author's own making: 'the apparent unity of his . . . output standing as a trope for that seemingly monumental inheritance of history through which Harris seeks gateways into imaginative release' and through which postcolonial societies are able to revaluate and transform 'received modes of perception' into new and liberating patterns of recognition. Slemon suggests that this dialectical process of 'infinite rehearsal' has important new significations in Harris's most recent novel *Carnival*. Although Harris risks certain fictional dependencies for the first time – the novel can be read as an allegory deriving directly from Dante's *The Divine Comedy* – the 'sovereign theatre' of tradition is 'thematised as an external text' enabling a gateway into the ongoing process of 're-reading tradition'.

In 'Wilson Harris: An Interview' (*Kunapipi*) Jane Wilkinson questions the novelist on his critical theories and their relationship to the structure of his fictional works; she also investigates Harris's concern with history in his expression of 'new temporal and spatial dimensions'. The interview was conducted in Turin in 1985 and contains interesting material on the relationship between poetry and prose in Harris's art.

In 'Wilson Harris's Divine Comedy of Existence: Miniaturizations of the Cosmos in *Palace of the Peacock*' (also *Kunapipi*) Gay Wilentz illustrates Harris's concern in his art with the exposure of contradictions to the Western notion of the 'unified ideal' or 'homogeneity', by his movement away from concepts of the absolute – 'rigid distinctions of subject and object, identity and nonidentity' – towards a 'mutuality' and 'heterogeneity' which all authors share. In so doing Harris has created a twentieth-century 'divine comedy of existence', which transforms the sovereign, absolute and homogeneous imperatives implied by the myths inherent in Dante and enables the potential for a meaningful 'dialogue' between oppressed and dominant cultures. In *Palace of the Peacock* Harris reveals a 'mutuality between what is called the "third world" and the dominant world of the former colonialists'.

Rhonda Cobham correctly begins her perceptive essay '*The Jumbie Bird* by Ismith Khan: A New Assessment' (*JCL*) by making the important observation that Khan's novels 'have all too often been neglected to the footnotes of West Indian literature'. She locates a number of reasons for this neglect and suggests that perhaps the major factor has been 'his path of exile', a journey which took him to North America rather than Britain, 'leaving him outside the range of somewhat myopic Caribbean or Commonwealth scholars'. Cobham attempts to redress the balance and illustrates forcefully how Khan's experimentations with a variety of language registers in his fiction add 'an important dimension to the language debate' in the work of other Trinidadian writers such as Samuel Selvon and Earl Lovelace, as well as Jamaican figures including Louise Bennett and V. S. Reid.

Introduced and edited by Kenneth Ramchand, Longman's new collection of previously published short stories by Roger Mais, '*Listen, the Wind' and Other Stories*[17] is a useful work, which will provide the reader interested in Mais's fiction with a variety of material previously difficult to locate. The short stories are not well known because many existed only in typescript form in the Mais Collection in Jamaica and those 'that have been published are in books and magazines now rare, defunct or out of print'. Another publication in the new Longman series in Edgar Mittelholzer's *My Bones and My Flute*[18]. The introduction by Mark A. McWatt is divided into sections on style and characterization in a useful format for students and teachers meeting Mittelholzer for the first time. McWatt stresses that one of the main aspects of Mittelholzer's significance as a Caribbean writer is his sense of a 'psychological division'; it is a division that is one of the most 'salient features of the West Indian personality to emerge in West Indian literature'. It haunts the writer and the characters in his fiction.

In 'The Crisis of the Absurd in Orlando Patterson's *An Absence of Ruins*' (*Kunapipi*) Avis G. McDonald has drawn interesting links between Patterson's second novel and the existentialist writings of Camus and Sartre. While these figures may now be seen, in a postmodernist world, as representative of a dated ideology, the existentialist Absurd is nevertheless a central key in comprehending Patterson's portrayals of a postcolonial world. 'He finds in Existentialism the deepest analysis of the "modern crisis" or the "exilic crisis"' and his fictional works as well as his non-fictional writings exhibit a heavy debt to both Camus and Sartre. The re-publication of Patterson's earlier novel *The Children of Sisyphus*[19] reflects a resurgence of critical interest in his art.

In *Jean Rhys: The West Indian Novels*[20], a remarkably lucid and revealing

17. '*Listen, the Wind' and Other Stories*, by Roger Mais, ed. and intro. by Kenneth Ramchand. Longman. pp. xxxii + 160. pb £2.50.
18. *My Bones and My Flute*, by Edgar Mittelholzer, intro. by Mark A. McWatt. Longman. pp. xxii + 168. pb £2.50.
19. *The Children of Sisyphus*, by Orlando Patterson. Longman. pp. 184. pb £2.95.
20. *Jean Rhys: The West Indian Novels*, by Teresa F. O'Connor. ColU. pp. 247. $35.

study, Teresa F. O'Connor analyses the cultural, historical, and family influences on Rhys in providing the most complete account yet of her art. The book draws on both Rhys's published works and important but unpublished manuscripts and biographical sources. Most significant of these is Rhys's private journal in the 1930s which she called 'The Black Exercise Book'. O'Connor uses this as source material in locating the alienation, despair, and self-destroying sexuality which informs so much of the fiction. In addition, she uncovers a number of biographical and artistic factors underlying Rhys's perpetuation of the myth regarding her homeland, Dominica. It is by an understanding of the peculiar identification Rhys made between her indifferent, rejecting mother and Dominica itself that we can perceive many of Rhys's preoccupations. The study is unique in its presentation of the relationship between Rhys's published and unpublished work; it also succeeds in clearly chronicling the various levels at which Rhys used the facts of her own experience to create her art.

As with the subject of autobiographical relevance, the question of woman as victim has frequently been the concern of Rhysian criticism. Wendy Brandmark's essay in *Kunapipi*, 'The Power of the Victims: A Study of *Quartet*, *After Leaving Mr MacKenzie* and *Voyage in the Dark* by Jean Rhys', illustrates how the passivity of so many of her heroines is also a form of rebellion. The typical Rhys character may negate herself in relation to men, society, and the 'bourgeois-code', but this saying 'no' also enables a freedom of soul and the potential of escape to a 'sensual landscape' and 'the externalization of the female psyche'. Brandmark's essay offers a forceful alternative to previous arguments on this subject and she suggests that Rhys's preoccupation with the victim syndrome is also a preoccupation with an important aspect of the 'female soul'. A similar subject concerns Erika Smilowitz in 'Childlike Women and Paternal Men: Colonialism in Jean Rhys's Fiction' (*ArielE*). Smilowitz's essay sets out to explore further the particularly resonant relationship between Rhys's colonial background, a world divided between the 'natives and the English élite' and her portrayal of 'destructive male/female relationships'. Helen Tiffin noted this parallel in 'Mirror and Mask: Colonial Motifs in the Novels of Jean Rhys' (*WLWE*, 1978), but Smilowitz develops the idea further by focusing her discussion on the recurrent pattern of childlike women and paternal men in Rhys's fiction.

A new edition of Namba Roy's *Black Albino*[21] has appeared, with an informative anonymous introduction providing details on Nathan Roy Atkins (Namba Roy) and his Jamaican background.

In 'Individual Integrity in Selvon's *Turn Again Tiger* and *Those Who Eat the Cascadura*' (*TSAR*) Harold Barratt makes a welcome contribution to Selvon scholarship by comparing two of Selvon's Trinidadian works in the hope that the contrast will 'shed . . . significant light on [his] treatment of individual integrity in the pluralistic society of Trinidad psychologically hobbled by years of colonialism'. Few essays on *Those Who Eat the Cascadura* have appeared before and it is pleasing to see the novel discussed in depth in Barratt's informative article.

The influence and significance of carnival as a literary form has recently been

---

21. *Black Albino*, by Namba Roy. Longman. pp. xiv + 206. pb £2.95.

a central subject for discussion in the writings of two Trindadian authors, Earl Lovelace and Samuel Selvon. However, essays of this type have tended to focus either on Lovelace's *The Dragon Can't Dance* or Selvon's most recent work which employs carnival as its central motif, *Moses Migrating*. In the context of such debates it is interesting that John Thieme in '"The World Turn Upside Down": Carnival Patterns in *The Lonely Londoners*' (*TSAR*) has pinpointed a number of carnivalesque patterns in Selvon's *early* novel of exile. Thieme distinguishes V. S. Naipaul's technique in *Miguel Street* from that of Selvon and draws on Bakhtin to discuss Selvon's innovative narrative method in *The Lonely Londoners*. He makes an important correlation between carnival as a system of discourse employed by major European writers who were taking issue with the 'dominant literary conventions of their day' and its implications in terms of a theory for West Indian culture. Within this frame, Thieme demonstrates how the structure and themes of *The Lonely Londoners* are carnivalesque; it is a 'seminal . . . text in that it subverts the norms of the dominant tradition of Western fiction by instituting the oral in the place of the literary'. While many of the episodes involve what he calls a 'parallel creolization of experience' which allows Selvon's 'boys' a 'modus vivendi', it is ultimately questionable whether carnival values can be 'metamorphosed' to enable them to deal with life in Britain. The article represents a valuable addition to Selvon criticism. Longman have recently republished the novel and Selvon's first work *A Brighter Sun*[22].

Few interviews have been conducted with the new generation of young women writers. In 'Olive Senior: An Interview' (*Kunapipi*) Anna Rutherford questions the Jamaican writer about the predominant concerns of her fiction. The interview discusses the centrality of the child in Olive Senior's stories and also touches on the role of autobiography. Senior's comments on the position of women in Caribbean society offer interesting details on this frequently neglected subject: for instance she says that although 'the myth of the black matriarch projects an image of the Caribbean woman as strong and powerful . . . that role might be forced on her because of an absence of male support'. Furthermore, the myth tends to disguise the 'fact of her powerlessness in the modern society'.

Garth St Omer's *The Lights on the Hill* was first published in 1968 with *Another Place, Another Time* in a volume entitled *Shades of Grey*, which Heinemann have now republished with a helpful introduction[23].

Lionheart Girl[24], in which the stories of twelve Jamaican women are distilled through the dramatic productions of the internationally renowned Sistren Collective, deserves special mention. Since 1977, the women of Sistren have been exploring the lives of Caribbean women from which they create plays, workshops, and screen prints for presentation throughout the world. The stories in *Lionheart Girl* are the accounts of working-class women originally recorded on tape and edited for the purpose of this collection. As such they provide an 'invaluable record of oral history' as well as penetrating the depth and humorous potential of Jamaican 'nation-language' and the oral mode.

22. *A Brighter Sun*, by Samuel Selvon. Longman. pp. 215. pb £2.95.
23. *The Lights on the Hill*, by Garth St Omer. Heinemann. pp. 119. pb £3.50.
24. *Lionheart Girl*, ed. by Honor Ford Smith. WP. pp. ix + 283. pb £5.95.

(c) Poetry

The most impressive publication by far this year is Paula Burnett's *The Penguin Book of Caribbean Verse in English*[25]. Although several collections of Caribbean verse have appeared over the years – such as John Figueroa's seminal *Caribbean Voices* (1966) and O. R. Dathorne's *Caribbean Verse* (1967) – no other anthology achieves the range or depth of this volume. Even very recent publications (with an eye on the 'Black British' market or with different objectives in mind), like James Berry's *News for Babylon* (*YW* 65.712) and Stewart Brown's selection of contemporary Caribbean verse (*YW* 66.681), lack the breadth of perspective offered here. The aims of the editor are large: the book attempts to provide the first historical survey of the complexity of cultural and linguistic forces informing the development of a Caribbean poetic tradition from its beginnings in the eighteenth century to the present day. Moreover, the anthology is divided into two main sections, 'oral' and 'literary', and the parallel *oral tradition* – born originally from the African rhythms and chants of the plantation slave songs before Emancipation – is given thorough representation. We are also provided with extensive biographical details and cultural contexts for the majority of contributors. Given the range of this anthology, it is surprising that the editor does not incorporate or allow a third major section in which the reader could assess the *new directions* and forms which have derived from the interweaving of the various voices of the Caribbean language continuum. A similarly strange omission occurs in the discussion of women poets where certain predictable names are included, but there are several disappointing gaps. However, the anthology does include some little-known verse by the Dominican writers Jean Rhys and Phyllis Allfrey.

Martin Carter's collection *Poems of Succession* was published in 1977. Few critical essays deal with Carter's poetry and it is pleasing therefore to note Jeffrey Robinson's analysis 'The Root and the Stone: The Rhetoric of Martin Carter's *Poems of Succession*' in *JWIL*. Robinson makes the valuable observation that a great deal of Carter's work since *Poems of Resistance* has been explicitly political; however, it may be 'necessary to distinguish between Carter the poet and Carter the political myth', for in the poetry, art and political statement can both be seen as aspects of a unified commitment to truth.

Rhonda Cobham has written an interesting review-article of Merle Collins's collection of poems, *Because the Dawn Breaks*[26]. In 'Making It Through the Night' (*NewBR*) she sees the taut and epigrammatic lines –

> Be quiet
> Words born of pain
> And oozing with hurt
> Are often not worth
> The paper they're on

– as forming the pivot of the book's themes and marking 'the nadir' of the

25. *The Penguin Book of Caribbean Verse in English*, ed. by Paula Burnett. Penguin. pp. xv + 443. pb £4.95.

26. *Because the Dawn Breaks: Poems Dedicated to the Grenadian People*, by Merle Collins, intro. by Ngugi wa Thiong'o. Karia. pp. vi + 92. hb £8.95, pb £3.95.

poet's relationship to Grenada before and after Maurice Bishop's People's Revolutionary Government. Collins develops the political tradition of Martin Carter and has at her command the oral and literary techniques that the 'new generation of poets since Brathwaite (Kwesi Johnson, Keens-Douglas, Grace Nichols, and Michael Smith) have been developing'.

In 'Goodison on the Road to Heartease' (*JWIL*) Edward Baugh traces Lorna Goodison's poetic evolution from her first collection *Tamarind Season* to the forthcoming *Heartease* sequence. He identifies central features of Goodison's poetic technique and illustrates how her voice is becoming what he calls the 'voice of a people'. Baugh stresses Goodison's importance as a figure in Jamaica and illustrates the modes by which she is steadily refining and extending the ventures of linguistic possibility by 'sliding seamlessly between English and Creole' and 'interweaving erudite literary allusion with the earthiness of traditional Jamaican speech'.

In 'Religion and Poetry: A Study of Mervyn Morris's *On Holy Week*' (*JWIL*) Gloria Lyn has explored the religious theme in Morris's second collection; she concludes that the 'chief unifying principle' is biblical imagery and draws parallels with seventeenth-century religious verse. Morris's art is further discussed in Roydon Salick's '"Balanced/in Pain": A Study of the Male/Female Relationship in the Poetry of Mervyn Morris' (*JWIL*). Salick focuses on the variety of linguistic contexts in Morris's published verse, seeing the poet as drawing his material from such divergent sources as 'music, the circus, revolution, the colonial past, university life, liturgy, mythology, chivalry and the Bible'. Morris's work mirrors the 'prismatic reality of quotidian Caribbean experience' and themes such as sex, politics, race, and death are frequently developed within the imagistic matrix of the male/female relationship.

A new collection by the Jamaican-born Elean Thomas *Word Rhythms from the Life of a Woman*[27], a combination of poetry with some short stories, is introduced by Carolyn Cooper. It is also encouraging to see the publication of a third collection by Milton Vishnu Williams, *Years of Fighting Exile: Collected Poems (1955–85)*[28], introduced by Jeremy Poynting. Williams's work is described as that of a visionary, whose art grows out of his response to a distinctly twentieth-century experience: 'migration from a third world country made marginal by world capitalism, to the metropolis which abandoned it'.

There have been a number of articles on Derek Walcott again this year. Elaine Savory Fido has written an interesting piece on Walcott's *œuvre* from a 'feminist' perspective. In 'Value Judgements on Art and the Question of Macho Attitudes: The Case of Derek Walcott' (*JCL*) Fido qualifies her use of 'feminist' at an early stage, preferring to place her analysis in the context of other new criticisms in the 'late twentieth century ferment of debate'. Fido's argument explores the modes by which 'masculinist male writers in Third World Societies . . . often . . . reflect mass male prejudice/myth about women'. Taking Walcott as a case in point, she demonstrates that his work not

27. *Word Rhythms from the Life of a Woman*, by Elean Thomas, intro. by Carolyn Cooper. Karia. pp. xx + 112. hb £8.95, pb £3.95.
28. *Years of Fighting Exile: Collected Poems (1955–85)*, by Milton Vishnu Williams, intro. by Jeremy Poynting. Peepal Tree. pp. 85. pb £2.95.

only reinforces negative sexual stereotypes but illustrates that such biases are often associated with a 'weakening of power in his writing'.

An alternative perspective is provided in Patricia Ismond's 'North and South – A Look at Walcott's *Midsummer*' (*Kunapipi*). Ismond examines Walcott's recent volume for its reflection of the poet's responses to this change of scene since he left Trinidad to reside in the U.S. in 1983. And in 'Re-mapping the World: The Recent Poetry of Derek Walcott' (*ArielE*), James McCorkle employs the notion of the map as metaphor in Walcott's verse, asserting that in both *The Fortunate Traveller* and *Midsummer* Walcott is concerned with 'travelling and mapping' where 'history becomes the knowledge only places can give'. In the first collection, Walcott's central poem 'North and South' reflects the tension and dialectic which exists between these two poles but foresees no 'resulting synthesis' except the holocaustic. In *Midsummer* however, where Walcott moves fully into the 'South', the form of the writing suggests an ambivalence and rupture. Ironically in 'Tropic Zone' Walcott reveals himself to be lost, a resident but a 'displaced person, the radical version of the traveller'.

(d) Drama

The publication of material on Caribbean drama still remains relatively slight although a new collection of plays by Trevor Rhone, *Two Can Play* and *School's Out*[29], is an important addition. Mervyn Morris has introduced the plays in an informative background essay which provides valuable insights into the history of Jamaican theatre and the development of Rhone's career as a dramatist. Morris describes *School's Out* as offering a 'bleak view of human nature' whereas *Two Can Play* is praised for its optimism and promise of new possibilities.

In 'Myth and Reality in Caribbean Narrative: Derek Walcott's *Pantomime*' (*WLWE*) Patrick Taylor explores the notion of two fundamental types of narrative structure, 'mythical and liberating'. Taylor suggests that *Pantomime* takes the old but 'enduring myth of Crusoe and Friday' (Prospero and Caliban) and transforms it to bring 'Caribbean man to a true confrontation with his freedom in history'. He shows how in Walcott's play the mythical (which can ultimately be dependent on a 'closed past-oriented approach to tradition'), is released into the realms of a 'universal history', a history that resists the illusions of simply creating new myths of a 'permanent Golden Age'. The play is powerful in its presentation of an 'authentic openness to reality', an openness that accepts that 'reality is generated and actualized in human social activity'. Thus Walcott is able to liberate and recreate his narrative, and 'the mythical form, the Prospero–Caliban archetype' is transformed by the play's content: 'the reality of man in history'.

3. India

It is surprising that so little attention is paid to Indian literature in English in the West. Has this anything to do, one wonders, with the economics of international publishing and the opportunities that critics have for advancement? Considerable attention is paid to the subject in India, of course, for English-

29. *'Two Can Play' and 'School's Out'*, by Trevor Rhone, intro. by Mervyn Morris. Longman. pp. xxii + 138. pb £2.95.

language academic and literary life in India is relatively self-contained: the debates about whether Indians write for a Western audience (and about how 'Indian' the literature is) are merely academic. However, due to the economics of Indian publishing, it is difficult to obtain many of the books in the West. This section is therefore based, not on a complete acquaintance with what was published during the year, but on material to which I have been able to gain access.

(a) General

Partha Mitter surveys the relationship between various art forms and relates them to the nationalist impulse in 'Art and Nationalism in India' (*LCrit*); this enables one to see the wider cultural context of one phase of Indian English Literature. C. N. Ramachandran's richly suggestive 'In Search of the Text: A Comparative Study of Western and Eastern Concepts' (also *LCrit*) is, for its length, a fairly detailed piece of work.

(b) Poetry

As part of an annual survey of Indian literature in *IndL*, the journal of the Indian Academy of Letters (the Sahitya Akademi), G. S. Amur provides a survey of Indian English literature titled 'The Indo-English Scene: The Year of the Poet'. In it, he points out that the Sahitya Akademi's award in English has gone for the third successive year to a poet (Kamala Das) and argues that this demonstrates the maturity of Indian poetry in English. I should have thought that it demonstrated precisely the opposite: Das burst on to the literary scene some twenty years ago with a volume of poems more remarkable for its unorthodox and uninhibited ideas and emotions than for poetic technique, and she has not produced any new poems of note since then. Amur then goes on to discuss some twenty first-volumes of poems, which do indicate how vigorously poetry is being pursued by Indian English writers; however, that is the sort of quantity that emerges more or less every year. What the award to Das demonstrates is that her quasi-feminist sentiments are now acceptable to India's middle-class literary establishment.

Meena Alexander enquires into the 'complex feminism' of Sarojini Naidu in a piece titled 'Romanticism and Renaissance' (*ArielE*). It can be stimulating deliberately to look at writers from earlier periods of history through the lenses which come with our age, but I wonder how it is then possible to guard against twisting and distorting the original phenomena. Alexander manages this by using the term 'feminism' merely as a peg on which to hang an examination of Naidu's life and work, poetic and political: 'Did the [passionate] female self she discovered in political action successfully subvert the passive if anguished images she picked up from turn-of-the-century English poetry?' Alexander concludes that Naidu's English-language 'confrontation with the sometimes tragic bonds of her own culture empowered her psyche, permitting it to attack the public bonds laid down by a colonising power. If there is regret that her poetry did not keep pace with her life, it is equally possible to sense that her private and at times agonising conflicts, as recorded in poetry, were crucial to the integrity of her living voice.'

Madhusudan Prasad, in 'The Echoes of a Bruised Presence: Images of Woman in the Poetry of Jayanta Mahapatra' (*LHY*), suggests that Mahapatra's exploration of the female psyche is 'cursory' but that his images of women, 'singularised by elegant patterning and subtle interrelatedness as well as continuity, evoke at once the local and the universal, the contemporary and the perennial, and help us comprehend his poetry . . . and his outlook on life'. Niranjan Mohanty's 'Roots' Rapture: The Poetry of Jayanta Mahapatra' (*LitH*) argues that Mahapatra's talent lies in his capacity to transform memory into myth and myth into reality – 'His is a triumph of style. His poetry moves with a certain deftness, an ease, a grace lent by limpid diction and imaginative associations.'

Disappointed, in 'Vikram Seth's *The Golden Gate*: A Quick Look' (*LCrit*), Rowena Hill argues that it is hard to see how Seth can be considered an Indian writer, except by accident of birth: 'there are few Indian references in the text [and it is] in fact a totally Californian novel'. Though she concedes irony and compassion to the work, she resents the 'dose of gloating in his celebration of the Californian way of life . . . which can be irritating to anyone who has been exposed to the Californian claim to represent the vanguard of humanity in awareness and know-how'.

Suresh Chandra Dwivedi's 'Faithful to my Own Temperament: The Poetry of Nissim Ezekiel' (*LitH*) sees Ezekiel's work as the outcome of his attempts to come to terms with himself: 'influences, borrowings and derivations from poets and writers are totally transformed under the weight of his . . . unique temperament . . . [resulting in poetry which] is suggestive and emotive, beginning in delight and ending in wisdom'. Havovi Anklesaria was guest editor of a special issue of *JIWE* on Nissim Ezekiel, which carries an interview with the writer, as well as extracts from Toni Patel's notebook of meetings with Ezekiel. The most valuable of the essays in the volume is N. Prabhaker Acharya's 'Achievement and Failure in Ezekiel's Poetry' which surveys the poems chronologically, analysing some of Ezekiel's poetic qualities: exquisite craftsmanship, a rich and supple rhythm capable of subtle modulation, the wry ironic tone which can change easily and naturally to express passion, and mastery over a variety of styles and poetic modes. He contends that 'judged by his best [work] Nissim Ezekiel remains the most important Indian poet who has written in English'. Much of Ezekiel's work has not had the study it deserves: Havovi Anklesaria's own 'On the Fringes of Journalism' is only the second study of Ezekiel's literary and other reviews to have appeared so far; Santan Rodrigues's examination of 'The Plays' is the first, to my knowledge, to have been published. D. Ramakrishna's 'Ezekiel's Credo' is a wide-ranging examin-ation of the writer's poetry and prose (occasional as well as substantial) which discovers an 'unmistakable sense of Indianness': 'Ezekiel's quest as writer and critic over the years has been for a proper communication of the meaning of life.' Ananya Sankar Guha's 'Nissim Ezekiel's India' finds the writer accepting Indian reality without complaint, the irony remaining effective without being trenchant; however, while 'Whitman had an inner view or vision of America ("I hear America sing"). . . . Ezekiel's view is moulded only by outward perceptions, by what he sees and hears'. P. M. Chacko's 'Ezekiel's Family Poems' finds that 'untrammelled by formality and inhibitions, the true self of the poet has a free-play [*sic*] within his domestic confines. . . . It is here that he confronts his biggest problems, mainly emotional [ones]. . . . No Indian poet has written so much and so well about [the family]. . . . He has virtually created a new type of poetry which may rightly be called family poetry.' Zerin Anklesaria examines four volumes of the poet's work in search of the most significant and extended exercises in 'Wit in the Poetry of Nissim Ezekiel'. M. K. Naik's study of 'Ezekiel and Alienation' finds that the writer has not succeeded 'fully in transmuting his alienational experience into major poetic utterance, except occasionally . . . though he certainly offers us many interesting variations on the theme; . . . by and large, his is a poetry which seems to prefer to dwell on the periphery of the alienational experience without attempting to reach its hard, central core'. A. N. Dwivedi studies 'Modernity in Nissim Ezekiel's Poetry' with particular reference to his attitude to religion. Charu Bhagwat sees 'The Poet–Rascal–Clown of *Hymns in Darkness*' illustrating 'a more general failure – that of the Indo-English poet writing serious poetry in an Indian city'.

André Dommergues's 'Rabindranath Tagore: The Poet of *Gitanjali*' (*CE&S*) argues that, 'in *Gitanjali*, Tagore plays hide and seek with various moods: despair, melancholy, expectation, gratitude, tenderness, enthusiasm, gaiety, severity, etc. But the prevailing emotion is joy. It is the origin and end of the universe.'

(c) Fiction

Meenakshi Mukherjee principally discusses Indian regional language novels in *Realism and Reality: The Novel and Society in India*[30]. She has little to say directly about Indian English literature. Yet her book ends up being a history of the realist novel in colonial India, with implications for Indian English fiction as well. C. N. Srinath's 'Native Roots and Novel Foliage: An Understanding of the Achievement of Indian Fiction in English' (*LCrit*) discusses *Comrade Kirillov* and *The Cat and Shakespeare* by Raja Rao, G. V. Desani's *All About H. Hatterr*, Anantanarayanan's *The Silver Pilgrimage*, Arun Joshi's *The Apprentice*, and R. K. Narayan's *Swami and Friends*. Srinath starts with a bit of a tautology: 'What is relevant is not to grope in search of the native roots of the Indian novel nor even to seek connections between these roots and the Western, but to identify the distinct recognisable manifestations of the Indian vision because of, and in spite of, the possible pervasiveness of the culture of the Western novel.' However, his concern is an interesting though by no means novel one: 'how [has] the Indian novel made departures [from the Western novel] that are essentially Indian'? His answers satisfy him, but may be less satisfactory to other readers.

Shirley Chew's 'Fictions of Princely States and Empire' (*ArielE*) points out that though the Indian princely states ceased to exist soon after India's independence, they continued to tease and draw the literary imagination. However, 'the perspective was altered, and with it the highlights and depths, appearances and relationships'. Chew discusses E. M. Forster's *A Passage to India* and *Hill of Devi*, Mulk Raj Anand's *Private Life of an Indian Prince*, Manohar Malgonkar's *The Princes*, and Ruth Prawer Jhabvala's *Heat and Dust*; and enquires into the ways in which the novelists gained access to the past. She discovers a continuing and vital literary relationship between the writers of the past and the writers of the present; a relationship which led them to ideas and doctrines which were later discarded, but which were actually believed in and lived out by the people of the time.

30. *Realism and Reality: The Novel and Society In India*, by Meenakshi Mukherjee. OUPI (1985). pp. 218. Rs 125.

Raja Rao's wide-ranging, dense, multi-faceted and multi-lingual philosophical peroration ('The Ultimate Word') must have quite overcome his audience at the University of Texas at Austin in the spring of 1984; the printed version (*LCrit*) provides opportunity to study the piece at one's own speed; though it does not enlighten one on how the contradictions between real life and Vedantic philosophy can be resolved, it does reveal the seamless Indian web of thinking behind all of Rao's fictional writings.

Susheela N. Rao's 'England in the Novels of Kamala Markandaya' (*JIWE*) looks at the British–Indian relationship through a business arrangement (in *The Coffer Dams*), through a social situation (in *The Nowhere Man*), through cultural contact (in *Two Virgins*), and in a political context (*The Golden Honeycomb*); in each of these, 'the British are seen as undemocratic, ununderstanding [*sic*] and insensitive'.

H. Summerfield's 'Holy Women and Unholy Men: Ruth Prawer Jhabvala Confronts the Non-Rational' (*ArielE*) points out that the oft-made comparison of Jhabvala with Austen and Chekhov suggests, in fact, the variety of her work. All three writers base their judgements of people and actions on experience and reason; superficially, Jhabvala resembles Austen in her witty portrayal of snobbery and self-deception, and Chekhov in her delicate, humorous evocations of mood and feeling. 'On a deeper level, she shares Austen's and Chekhov's conviction that the dictates of reason and experience should prevail over emotion and provide a guard against irrationality. Jhabvala regards submission to a guru as a form of extreme emotionalism accompanied by indifference to others' suffering and by a failure of the respect due to the uniqueness of each individual'.

Viney Kirpal's 'An Image of India: A Study of Anita Desai's *In Custody*' (*ArielE*) argues that the book's moments of humour, of the comic, and of the mock-heroic 'work to defuse and edit the gravity with which the characters are prone to take events and happenings that do not match their expectations. . . . [Events are] reviewed from a comic perspective, often to suggest that the characters have taken their problems far more seriously than was [appropriate]. . . . The pervading philosophy in the novel [calls for life] to be faced squarely, with courage, integrity and responsibility – . . . the novel ends on a note of optimism. It evokes through creative language, structure and technique, an image of India that belies the impression of a "dead", "stagnant" India . . . an image . . . full of hope . . . transcending the superficial irritants that many Anglo-Indian novelists have referred to – the heat and dust of India.'

4. Australia

(a) General

ALS continues to provide the definitive bibliography for the field. The bibliography for 1985, which appears this year, has been compiled by staff of the Fryer Library at the University of Queensland under the direction of the journal's editor Laurie Hergenhan and acting editor Martin Duwell and follows the usual format: it comes close to being exhaustive in its listings of books and articles and also offers selective coverage of reviews and prefaces. Its 'General' section remains first-rate; its 'Individual Authors' section would be similarly so, were it not for the policy of aiming at comprehensiveness where those authors who have been admitted into its canon are concerned – at the expense of the total exclusion of listings for other writers. *JCL*'s annual primary and secondary bibliography, compiled by Van Ikin, Brenda Walker, and John Maddocks, remains most valuable for its coverage of new creative work, as does Mark MacLeod's useful contribution to *Kunapipi*'s 'The Year That Was' section. *ALS* includes one of its two-yearly checklists of 'Research in Progress in Australian Literature'. Approximately 170 projects being undertaken by staff and postgraduate students in Australian tertiary institutions are listed.

The most important general book to be published this year, Ken Goodwin's *A History of Australian Literature*[31], takes its place beside W. J. Keith's *Canadian Literature in English* (*YW* 66.703) as the second Commonwealth volume in the Macmillan History of Literature series. As a general survey of the field this succinct and well-organized study has not been bettered and, in addition to being a first-rate primer for newcomers to Australian writing, it also contains insights that will be of value to more seasoned readers. Goodwin concentrates on the last fifty years on the grounds that the most significant literature belongs to this period. He does not, however, do so at the expense of neglecting earlier writing entirely: an opening chapter, which establishes the paradigm of a rivalry between land and landscape as crucial in Australian writing, explores the 'nature' of the country's literature and other early sections look at the literature of the first hundred years of colonization, the *Bulletin* school, and the quest for national self-definition in the work of writers like Henry Handel Richardson, Mary Gilmore, Norman Lindsay, Katharine Susannah Prichard, and Vance Palmer. Australian criticism has spoken with many voices in recent years and the writer of a volume such as this is faced with the problem of what kind of discourse to adopt. Goodwin's discriminating approach strikes a happy medium between the traditionalist and contemporary and he is equally catholic in the range of material he covers (from the writing of the first settlers to recent work by Aborigines and migrants). The *History* comes with well-chosen illustrations, an equally well-selected bibliography, and an even more useful forty-page chronology of publication dates and historical and literary 'events'.

Harry Heseltine's *The Uncertain Self*[32], which brings together previously published and new material but justly claims to be a unified volume, is one of two essay collections by important Australian critics to have appeared this year. It includes a number of perceptive essays on Australian poets – Kenneth Slessor, Judith Wright, A. D. Hope, and Robert D. Fitzgerald among them – and two essays on Hal Porter. The title essay sets the tone for the whole collection: it examines the problem faced by the 'creating self' in the 'cultural vacuum' of the 'unfamiliar antipodean land' with reference to a wide range of authors, most of them drawn from earlier periods of Australian writing. Heseltine offers this as a preliminary contribution to a possible re-interpretation of Australian literary history and the subtext seems to be that earlier versions have emphasized social determinants at the expense of individual

31. *A History of Australian Literature*, by Ken Goodwin. Macmillan. pp. xii + 322; 15 illus. hb £27.50, pb £8.95.

32. *The Uncertain Self: Essays in Australian Literature and Criticism*, by Harry Heseltine. OUPAus. pp. viii + 222. A$30.

creativity. The problem for many readers is likely to be that the approach will seem outmoded, a *Scrutiny*-like revaluation in the 1980s. But Heseltine is well aware of the possible danger: he presents himself, in the preface, as a New Critic subsiding into middle age and for those who like his style of criticism he is one of its best practitioners in Australia.

Fay Zwicky's essays in *The Lyre in the Pawnshop*[33] are concerned with essentially the same theme: an early sentence asserts 'The creative consciousness is always probing the interchange between a man's individual powers and the culture to which he belongs'. Apart from a shift in tone, this could be straight out of Heseltine's book, but Zwicky's approach turns out to be markedly different. She interrogates the notion of 'creativity' and that conceptualization which accords it 'virtually angelic powers' while opposing it to the 'negative' and 'destructive' force of the rational critical intellect. Her essays are probing, investigative accounts of the problematic linguistic site occupied by Australian writing and display a particular interest in exploring the difficulties encountered by those writing about the theme of love in an Australian context, where inherited European genres are alien discourses. Zwicky is also particularly good at examining the paradoxical mixture of *bonhomie* and reserve that she identifies in the Australian character and the similar stylistic opposition of large gesture and laconic understatement; in essays such as a piece on Bruce Dawe's 'ambivalent ockerism' she offers incisive commentary on both the specifics of a particular author's work and on the cultural context more generally. In addition to major essays on a range of Australian writers, including Randolph Stow, Christopher Brennan, Henry Handel Richardson, and Patrick White, *The Lyre in the Pawnshop* includes a number of reviews and an interview Zwicky conducted with Denise Levertov.

Dorothy Green's *The Writer, the Reader and the Critic in a Monoculture*[34], the text of her 1985 Colin Roderick lectures, is a wide-ranging analysis of the contemporary situation of literature, a plea for humanist values in an age of scientism and materialism. In the development of her liberal thesis Green moves between Australian and other cultures and some of her commentary is forceful, as when, for example, she refers to attempts to elevate the status of pop culture as 'a sort of Leavisite-process-in-reverse'. However, both her general tone and her unquestioning use of the term 'monoculture' (even though she discusses Aboriginal oral narrative and African drumming in Sydney) are indebted to notions of shared experience and cultural monism that are difficult to sustain.

Reading the Country[35] (previously overlooked) is another award-winning volume from one of the recent success-stories of Australian publishing, Fremantle Arts Centre Press, whose director Ian Templeman outlines its ten-year history in a *Westerly* special issue on 'Literature and Locality' that also includes tributes to the Press from Elizabeth Jolley and Peter Cowan. *Reading the Country* concerns itself with the problems of 'reading' a landscape, here that of the Roebuck Plains (an area near Broome in the northern part of

33. *The Lyre in the Pawnshop: Essays on Literature and Survival 1974-1984*, by Fay Zwicky. UWAP. pp. x + 297.
34. *The Writer, the Reader and the Critic in a Monoculture*, by Dorothy Green. FALS. pp. 72. pb.
35. *Reading the Country*, by Kim Benterrak, Stephen Muecke, and Paddy Roe. FACP (1984). pp. 251; 19 colour 'paintings' + 43 illus. A\$29.50.

Western Australia) and employs a range of narrative and pictorial modes to do so. Its three main contributors (others are acknowledged as well) are Kim Benterrak, a Moroccan-born artist, Stephen Muecke, a white-Australian academic, and Paddy Roe, an Aboriginal 'patriarch' and storyteller. Together they provide a multi-optic, as well as a multi-cultural, response to the 'traces' of landscape and language that the book's journey explores; these include maps, photographs, diagrams, fine colour reproductions of paintings, traditional and contemporary Aboriginal songs and narrative, and 'European' historical and geographical narrative. Framing them all is a series of linking and frequently theorizing essays that provide the journey-structure which is central to the book. In an interview at the end Stephen Muecke, the writer of these pieces, confesses that he is prepared to assume major responsibility for codifying the whole and this foregrounding of the method helps to counteract the possible objection that the apparently egalitarian fusion is in fact controlled by the 'authority' of the academic voice.

Certainly Aboriginal novelist Colin Johnson takes an approving view of Muecke's work when he comments that his editing of Paddy Roe's stories has demonstrated a sensitivity to the *form* of traditional Aboriginal tale-telling which has been markedly absent in the practice of earlier editors, viewed here as having been guilty of forcing the traditional content 'into forms akin to the fairy tale, an oral tradition in itself which has been forced into a nineteenth century written format'. Johnson's comment comes in a useful paper included in *Aboriginal Writing Today*[36], a volume edited by Jack Davis and Bob Hodge, which consists of papers delivered at the First National Conference of Aboriginal Writers, held in Perth in 1983. The papers have been transcribed from recordings and several have clearly been delivered as impromptu pieces – particularly engaging is one delegate's praise for Archie Weller's fine novel *The Day of the Dog*, which, he tells the audience, he *started* to read the night before. Yet this lack of observation of the conventional academic proprieties proves to be as much a strength as a weakness: the volume exudes a sense of occasion and one has the sense of a latter-day equivalent of a corroboree in which the communication between participants has been very direct. From the literary point of view the most valuable pieces are Johnson's 'White Forms, Aboriginal Content', Jack Davis's 'Aboriginal Writing: A Personal View', both of which provide basic information and discuss periods and aesthetic perspectives, and Cliff Watego's rather more academic discussion of the poetry of Kath Walker, which traces parallels between her verse and that of Henry Lawson. Kevin Gilbert and Bruce McGuiness contribute pieces that put their main stress on Aboriginal politics; Faith Bandler discusses the role of research in her work; and, on a very different subject from all the other papers, which are essentially concerned with recent writing by urban Aborigines and part-Aborigines, Catherine Berndt (apart from Ronald M. Berndt the only white speaker) discusses traditional Aboriginal oral literature, curtailing her paper to allow three women from the north to tell stories, an element which seems to have been completely overlooked by the organizers of the conference.

Aboriginal art and literature is the subject of an *Aspect* special issue (not seen) which includes Colin Johnson's 'Guerilla Poetry: Lionel Fogarty's

36. *Aboriginal Writing Today*, ed. by Jack Davis and Bob Hodge. AIAS (1985). pp. viii + 111. pb A$9.95.

Response to Language Genocide' (also published in *Westerly*) and an auto-biographical piece by Kath Walker. Bob Hodge's 'Aboriginal Myths and Australian Culture' (*SoRA*) attacks contemporary attempts to integrate Aboriginal traditional culture into the Australian mainstream through 'popularisation' and argues instead for an approach 'that tries to retain as much as possible of the qualities of the Aboriginal texts, yet confidently situates this literature in the context of Australian culture, including contemporary popular forms'. He exemplifies such an approach with an ingenious structuralist comparison of a Kuniyanti tale and *Mad Max III: Beyond Thunderdome*. Lyndall Ryan's 'Reading Aboriginal Histories' (*Meanjin*) reviews a number of prominent recent histories, including *Reading the Country* which she finds 'fascinating' but 'curiously male', and concludes by identifying four common attributes: a focus on recovering the past and Aboriginal survival; a distinctive Aboriginal style; an equally distinctive humour; and a method in which the storyteller is an integral part of the history. Tony Scanlon's 'Evangelists: The Aborigines in Missionary Literature' (*Westerly*) finds that early missionaries' responses to the tribes they had come to convert provide 'some startling insights into the darker recesses of the European psyche' and offers copious quotation in support of such a thesis.

Candida Baker's *Yacker*[37] is the first in a series of interviews with Australian writers modelled on the *ParisR* 'self-portrait' approach. The writers included in this first collection are all novelists, apart from Tom Shapcott and David Williamson. They include many of the most interesting voices in contemporary Australian fiction – among them Peter Carey, Blanche d'Alpuget, Helen Garner, and Elizabeth Jolley – as well as the late Christina Stead who is the subject of a two-part interview with Robert Drewe. The Stead piece apart, the interviews conform to a common format: they are all conducted by Baker herself and she adopts an informal approach which attempts to lay bare the personal forces that have produced the writing as well as to glean insights into the work itself. In her introduction she notes that her women interviewees tended to make more personal revelations, but given the chance to tidy up the original transcript also made more excisions of the personally revealing. *Yacker* is both informative and lively; it should appeal to the general reader as well as the student of literature. Jennifer Ellison's *Rooms of their Own* (PenguinA), a collection of interviews with contemporary Australian women writers, was not available for review.

Diversity Itself: Essays in Australian Arts and Culture[38], edited by Peter Quartermaine, is the first in a new series produced by the Centre for American and Commonwealth Arts and Studies at the University of Exeter. Literary contributions include Sneja Gunew's 'Constructing Australian Subjects: Critics, Writers, Multicultural Writers', which examines the sign-systems through which migrants have been constructed in Australia, and Delys Bird's 'Writing Women/Reading Women: The Double-Voiced Discourse of Australian Women's Fiction', which is most useful for its comments on Barbara Baynton. Both are pieces which respond to the situation of being

37. *Yacker: Australian Writers Talk about their Work*, by Candida Baker. PanA. pp. 315. pb A$14.95/£3.95.

38. *Diversity Itself: Essays in Australian Arts and Culture*, ed. by Peter Quartermaine. UExe. pp. x + 182; 7 illus. pb £7.95.

defined as 'other' by the mainstream Anglophone, male tradition. Peter Quartermaine writes about the special responsibilities attached to the teaching of Australian (and Commonwealth) studies in British education, Werner Senn offers some practical observations on curriculum development in the field of Australian literature, and Don Grant identifies important recent developments in interdisciplinary Australian studies, as well as commenting on books which have advanced debate on the subject. This useful collection also includes essays on Australian film and the visual arts and Henry Reynolds's 'The Breaking of the Great Australian Silence: Aborigines in Australian Historiography 1955–83', which shows how the scholarship of the last twenty years has transformed white Australia's knowledge of the Aboriginal past.

Anthologies continue to proliferate, many of them reflecting a continuing national concern with self-definition and redefinition. Most of this year's crop are characterized in differing ways by an egalitarian impulse. Pride of place, if only because of its bulk and prestigious imprint, must go to Les Murray's *New Oxford Book of Australian Verse*[39], a fiercely democratic volume which presents itself as an anthology intended for reading not study and omits notes, biographical commentary, and other appendages in the belief that this will avoid the imposition of filters and allow room for more poems to be included. In an endeavour to avoid 'a recent preoccupation with grading and weighting', no author is allowed more than three poems and there is an attempt to break down the distinction between 'vernacular' and 'pukka' verse which, as Murray sees it, was responsible for the comparative neglect of much fine earlier Australian poetry. Aboriginal verse, both traditional (in translation) and modern, is well represented and Murray's selection is reasonably fair to poets who belong to schools with which his own work shows little affinity. Thus the 'generation of '68' are dealt with even-handedly. All of this is no more than what one would expect from the 'peasant mandarin', but a problem exists nonetheless, for, while eschewing value-judgements, Murray says that the acid test for inclusion has been 'how much poetry a text has in it'. Disappointingly, the reader is never told how this has been assessed and can only come to the conclusion that a subjective notion of poetic value is involved, but the overall result is a collection that brings together much of what is generally acknowledged to be best in Australian verse and poems that until now have languished in obscurity.

Murray must have had a busy time of it as an anthologizer in recent years for he is also responsible for another fairly hefty collection, *Anthology of Australian Religious Poetry*[40]. The reader who approaches this apprehensive that the conception may involve special pleading on behalf of the Catholic Mafia that has long cast its shadow over Australian verse is quickly reassured. 'Religious poetry' is constituted in the broadest of ecumenical senses to allow for the inclusion of a wide range of experiences, among them Michael Dransfield on the 'semblance of forever' that comes from a fix administered in the middle of the night, Clive James's 'The Philosophical Phallus' – a playful response to the philosopher Roger Scrutton's assertion that 'Female desire aims to subdue, overcome and pacify the unbridled ambition of the phallus' – and

39. *The New Oxford Book of Australian Verse*, sel. by Les Murray. OUPAus. pp. xxvi + 399. £15.
40. *Anthology of Australian Religious Poetry*, sel. by Les Murray. Collins Dove. pp. xviii + 302. £15.95.

Bruce Dawe's not altogether ironic celebration of the religion of Australian Rules football, 'Life-Cycle'. Once again a fair amount of space is found for Aboriginal poetry and, while, as in *The New Oxford Book*, the volume for the most part avoids ancillary material, in some cases translators' notes have been retained for this verse. This is an interesting collection, but ultimately its supposed eclecticism is as puzzling to the reader as the hidden value-judgements that seem to lie behind the Oxford selection: the poems are ordered neither chronologically nor by author, but some unspecified structuring principle appears to be at work, for thematically similar pieces often appear close together. And another possible problem is that one comes away from the volume with the sense that the writing of religious poetry in Australia has been a primarily male activity.

An egalitarian impulse is also to the fore in anthologies that provide a forum for voices that until recently have been marginalized. *Latitudes: New Writing from the North*[41], edited by Susan Johnson and Mary Roberts, follows Barry O'Donoghue's *Place and Perspective* (*YW* 65.730) in furnishing an outlet for the work of contemporary Queensland writers. This time the emphasis is on the short story not poetry and the material has been chosen from around six hundred stories submitted to or solicited by the editors. The collection includes pieces by the big names of contemporary Queensland writing, Thea Astley, David Malouf, and Tom Shapcott, as well as a story by the Canadian-based Janette Turner Hospital and the work of several less well-known writers, including the two editors themselves. Dimitris Tsaloumas's *Contemporary Australian Poetry*[42] is a bilingual volume, offering Greek translations of the editor's choice of contemporary Australian verse alongside their English originals. The present reviewer is unable to comment on the quality of the translations, but the volume would seem to be more valuable for making Australian verse available to Greek speakers than for its anthologizing practice: Tsaloumas disarmingly confesses that some poems have been chosen for inclusion because of their responsiveness to translation and his introduction offers only a fairly vapid overview of Australian verse from the nineteenth century onwards, even though the anthology's focus is on the contemporary period. Recent years have seen the publication of similar volumes in Italy and France. What is different about this collection is that it is Australian-published (again by the innovative UQP) and would seem to be addressed primarily to Greek-*Australians*.

The Penguin Book of Australian Women Poets[43] can be seen as attempting to remedy another inequality: the gender bias that has underlain the supposedly egalitarian ideal of mateship. Pointing out that in 'fifteen well-known collections of Australian poetry published since 1970, the average of female authors selected was 17 per cent' and that 'the average number of pages of women's poetry was 13 per cent', its editors Susan Hampton and Kate Llewellyn set about redressing this imbalance. While recognizing that 'the-

41. *Latitudes: New Writing from the North*, ed. by Susan Johnson and Mary Roberts. UQP. pp. xii + 223. pb £7.95.

42. *Contemporary Australian Poetry*, sel. and trans. by Dimitris Tsaloumas. UQP. pp. xxviii + 265. £19.95.

43. *The Penguin Book of Australian Women Poets*, ed. by Susan Hampton and Kate Llewellyn. PenguinA. pp. xviii + 293. A$12.95.

feminist-poet has become a stereotype' and that 'there are many feminisms', they write from within feminist discourses and their introduction is characterized by democratic lower-case section-headings and a concern with the part played by language and formal experimentation in reconstructing notions of gender identity. It also includes a section, 'notes for a feminist history', which lists feminist presses, magazines, and editors as basic information for readers. All of this might lead one to expect a choice of verse dominated by recent theoretically inspired women's poetry, but in fact the net is cast much more widely and Aboriginal songs, an anonymous ballad about transportation, and work by important early women poets like Ada Cambridge and Mary Gilmore are included, along with poems by major twentieth-century figures and writers who *are* responding to contemporary debates within feminism. This is an anthology that should be essential reading alongside *The New Oxford Book*, which despite its presentation of itself as open to all traditions, turns out, when the number of women poets included is totted up, to come very close to the average of seventeen per cent that Hampton and Llewellyn have found in their 'fifteen well-known collections'. In *Overland* Terry Harrington also provides a statistical analysis of the percentage of women poets included in a number of prominent anthologies of Australian poetry, but his arithmetic is questioned by Jennifer Strauss in the next issue of the same journal. My own spot-check confirms her doubts about his calculations.

Laurie Hergenhan's *The Australian Short Story*[44] is another anthology, valuable both for the range of fiction it makes available in a single volume and for its introduction, which represents an important contribution to the subject. The stories chosen range from early classics such as Lawson's 'The Union Buries its Dead' and Baynton's 'The Chosen Vessel' (Hergenhan argues that the only important figure in the short story prior to the 1880s was Marcus Clarke) to postmodernist fictions such as Frank Moorhouse's 'The Airport, the Pizzeria, the Motel, the Rented Car, and the Mysteries of Life' and Michael Wilding's 'Sex in Australia from the Man's Point of View'. Hergenhan points out that the only full-length history of the short story in Australia to date is an unpublished Ph.D. thesis (Stephen Torre's 'The Australian Short Story 1940 to 1980', University of Queensland, 1982) and his own introduction, which contextualizes the work of the various writers included and covers a very impressive amount of ground in a short space, is rendered all the more valuable by this absence of a definitive, comprehensive study. He traces the genesis and development of the form from its fostering in the *Bulletin* in the 1880s through to the contemporary period, arguing that the short story has always been particularly open to innovation, because notions of what it should be have been less fixed than with other genres. His account of its development is centred on the movement away from 'bush realism', though he rightly questions whether the Australian short story was ever as 'realistic' as recent rebels against this aspect of the tradition have argued. The collection comes with biographical notes on the authors and a valuable secondary bibliography which offers listings of both general critical material on the short story and on the work of the particular authors included.

44. *The Australian Short Story: An Anthology from the 1890s to the 1980s*, ed. by Laurie Hergenhan. UQP. pp. xxiv + 329. pb £8.95.

Hergenhan's collection is likely to vie with Kerryn Goldsworthy's *Australian Short Stories* (*YW* 65.731-2) for use in tertiary-level courses and Goldsworthy has now produced another prose anthology, *Coast to Coast*[45]. This takes its title from a series of collections of Australian short stories that appeared between 1941 and 1973 and more than lives up to the standards set in its illustrious predecessors. In one respect, however, it is quite different: non-fiction is included as well as fiction and Goldsworthy says she welcomed the opportunity to juxtapose them, since choosing and assembling the pieces served to increase her conviction that the distinction between them is 'a highly unstable one'. Her anthology concentrates on *very* recent Australian writing and conveys a strong sense of contemporaneity as well as offering pieces by many of the best young and not-so-young prose writers in Australia today, among them Tim Winton, David Malouf, Olga Masters, Kate Grenville, John Clanchy, Elizabeth Jolley, and Helen Garner. Another distinctive quality of this collection is the ordering of the constituent parts so that it can be read as a continuous narrative: each selection in some way carries on from the previous one.

Another collection of *very* recent Australian prose, Don Anderson's *Transgressions*[46], is intended as a sequel to Frank Moorhouse's *The State of the Art* (*YW* 65.732) and mainly comprises pieces which appeared in Australian little magazines between April 1983 and April 1985. In his introduction Anderson speaks of the 'very strong sectional interests demanding representation in Australian writing', but says that insofar as his selection has reflected such interests, it has done so not by succumbing to pressure but as a result of his choosing what he perceived to be the 'best'. The collection's title refers both to moral 'transgressions' – attempts to subvert what Moorhouse has called the 'platitudinous humanism' of Australian writing – and, in Barthesian terminology, 'transgressions of language' which contest dominant structural and rhetorical patterns. The first story, Richard Lunn's 'Mirrors', is full of multiple choice instructions that allow readers to reassemble it if they so choose and Anderson invites readers to practise a similar kind of transgression with his thematic divisions of the stories, if they are so minded. The line-up of writers included is similar to Kerryn Goldsworthy's and the overall ethos is once again geared towards an attack on the conservative–realist hegemony that Anderson claims is still uppermost in Australian short fiction. Such a view begins to appear clichéd and no longer carries the same resonance as it did when Wilding and Moorhouse were articulating it a few years ago, but for those who want a companion-piece to *The State of the Art* this is another fine anthology. Don Anderson has also published *Hot Copy*[47], a collection of his book reviews and articles. Just over half the volume is devoted to Australian topics, including longer pieces on Moorhouse, on dinner parties in Stead, and 'anthropophagy and communion' in White (all reprinted from *Southerly*). The shorter pieces are written somewhere between the academy (Anderson lectures in English at the University of Sydney) and Grub Street (they mainly appeared in newspapers)

45. *Coast to Coast: Recent Australian Prose Writing*, sel. by Kerryn Goldsworthy. A&R. pp. xii + 194. pb £4.95.

46. *Transgressions: Australian Writing Now*, ed. by Don Anderson. PenguinA. pp. x + 246. pb A$8.95/£3.95.

47. *Hot Copy: Reading and Writing Now*, by Don Anderson. PenguinA. pp. xxii + 224. pb A$11.95.

and in his introduction Anderson presents himself as the victim of this schizophrenia. However, on the evidence of this volume, his strength lies in his ability to occupy this middle ground, to write sharp instant assessments of new books and trends in a readable journalistic style which only sometimes becomes glib in its quest for the telling phrase or gesture.

Cecil Hadgraft's *The Australian Short Story Before Lawson*[48] does little to contest Laurie Hergenhan's view that Clarke is the only notable Australian short story writer before Lawson. In fact there is a moment in Hadgraft's solid and scholarly introduction when, after having identified Clarke as 'the most important prose writer' before Lawson, he confesses that 'the plain fact is that Clarke's stories do not rank with those of the masters'. So this is an anthology directed primarily towards charting the territory, not towards arguing a case for the undiscovered literary excellence of the early stories. The introduction, which makes up about a fifth of the volume, offers a full historical outline that considers the material in three chronological periods: 1830–60; 1860–80; and 1880–93; it discusses the major short story writers in each of these periods and also identifies prominent genres and themes, including the moral tale, stories about Aborigines, the historical tale, 'lost child' stories, tales of mystery and detection, and stories dealing with the supernatural. The anthology includes work by writers whom Hadgraft has identified as the most significant short story practitioners in this early period, among them John Lang, James Skipp Borlase, Clarke, Rosa Praed, and Price Warung. This is not an exciting volume, but it performs a valuable service by filling in an expanse that has been blank on the literary map of Australia and by making the stories available to a wider readership.

Philip Neilsen's *Penguin Book of Australian Satirical Verse*[49], another collection that makes a body of fairly inaccessible nineteenth-century material available, as well as reprinting a number of well-known late nineteenth-century and twentieth-century poems, does not look at first sight as though it will be the year's most significant anthology – it is less weighty than Les Murray's two collections and does not initially appear to be as radically revisionist as *The Penguin Book of Australian Women Poets* – and yet this is exactly what it turns out to be. The introduction cites A. D. Hope on the 'critical fallacy . . . that humorous, satirical, and polemical verse cannot be poetry of the highest order' and argues that in Australia this 'fallacy' has led to a critical orthodoxy that privileges 'a romantic convention of personal or lyric expression'. This view has been put forward before, by Elizabeth Webby as well as A. D. Hope, but Neilsen's articulation of it is rendered particularly persuasive by the body of evidence constituted by the poems he has chosen. The contemporary selections, ranging from an 'Ern Malley' piece to Peter Porter's 'Phar Lap in the Melbourne Museum', from Tom Shapcott poking fun at Queensland politics to John Tranter parodying a range of his fellow-poets, are predictable enough and serve to confirm the popular notion of Australian humour as irreverential and given to debunking sacred cows. It is the older pieces that, both individually and cumulatively, provide the surprises: on the evidence of the satirical poems by

48. *The Australian Short Story Before Lawson*, ed. by Cecil Hadgraft. OUPAus. pp. viii + 274. A$35.

49. *The Penguin Book of Australian Satirical Verse*, ed. by Philip Neilsen. PenguinA. pp. xii + 298. pb A$14.95.

Charles Harpur and Henry Kendall included here, Neilsen's contention that standard assessments of their work as essentially Romantic involve distortions is convincing; the satirical verse that Lawson wrote for his pre-arranged debate with Paterson on the merits of the bush emerges as among his finest; and, all in all, the reader comes away with the sense that an Augustan strain has been important in Australian poetry from the earliest times right up to the present. Prominent in the collection are a number of poems, including 'Frank the Poet's' (Francis MacNamara's) 'Convict's Tour to Hell', Harpur's 'The Patriot of Australia', Hope's 'Dunciad Minor', and Peter Lawrence's 'Don Juan in Melanesia', which argue that the mock-epic, with its comic inversions of value, has always been important 'down under'. *Meanjin* includes a substantive review of this anthology by Jack Hibberd.

Geoffrey Dutton's *The Australian Collection*[50] is the kind of volume that he excels at. It provides solid, middle-of-the-road commentary which, if it does little to advance knowledge about the subject, will do much to popularize it. Beautifully produced, this coffee-table volume is more than an anthology: it is a compendium of short extracts from just under a hundred Australian prose works, each of which is accompanied by a rather longer discussion by Dutton, a brief biographical sketch, and fine colour illustrations (paintings, photographs, and drawings) that include work by leading Australian artists. The extracts include fiction, explorers' narratives, autobiography, children's books, humorous works, histories, and general books on Australian culture; novels like *The Fortunes of Richard Mahoney* and *Voss* rub shoulders with children's books like *Dot and the Kangaroo* and *The Complete Adventures of Snugglepot and Cuddlepie* and non-fiction classics like Geoffrey Blainey's *The Tyranny of Distance* and A. B. Facey's *A Fortunate Life*. No attempt is made to distinguish between the 'popular' and the 'serious'; all that links the books is their 'Australianness', seen in Dutton's introduction to inhere not in any narrow nationalistic definition, but in 'an acceptance of a common environment, both human and natural, and an Australian use of language' and in the national characteristic of independent-mindedness, a quality that is embodied in this typically demotic volume. Dutton's *The Innovators: The Sydney Alternatives in the Rise of Modern Art, Literature and Ideas* (Macmillan) was unavailable for review, as was Graeme Turner's *National Fictions: Literature, Film and the Construction of Australian Narrative* (A&U).

Westerly has not published too many special issues over the years, but, in addition to its 'Literature and Locality' issue, in 1986 it also published one on the 1930s. This includes four pieces on literary subjects: Peter Cowan's 'The Novel in the Nineteen Thirties – A Western Australian View' surveys the output of fiction from the state during this decade with a particular emphasis on Henrietta Drake Brockman's historical novels and J. M. Harcourt's realistic accounts of life in the Depression years; Robert Darby also focuses on Harcourt, whose *Upsurge* was one of very few Australian novels to be banned by the Book Censorship Board, in his 'The Censor as Literary Critic', a survey of censorship practices between 1933 and 1939; Sharyn Pearce attempts to

---

50. *The Australian Collection: Australia's Greatest Books*, by Geoffrey Dutton. A&R (1985). pp. 405; 270 illus. A$39.95.

supplement the paucity of information available about Australian women's lives during the 1930s in her 'Changing Places: Working-Class Women in the Fiction of the Depression', a piece which is most useful for its comments on Kylie Tennant; Julian Croft's 'Poetry of the Nineteen Thirties' examines the notion that Australian poetry of the decade was characterized by its 'stylistic conservatism' and concludes that this was certainly not the case in three major poems, Bertram Higgins's '"Mordecaius" Overture', R. D. FitzGerald's 'The Hidden Bole', and Kenneth Slessor's 'Five Bells', which are seen as showing 'the triumph of modernism in Australia'. Other pieces in this issue which are likely to be of interest to the literary critic include Bruce Molloy's 'Images of Australia: Feature Films of the 1930s', Dorothy Green and Sandra Burchill's 'Australian Studies: The Untaught Tradition', and Geoffrey Bolton's 'Newspapers for a Depression Child'.

Island offers a forum on literary reviewing in Australia, an area that became contentious when Gerard Windsor delivered a polemic on the subject during an otherwise fairly uncontroversial Writers' Week at the 1986 Adelaide Festival. Windsor's argument, in 'Writers and Reviewers' (reprinted in the *Island* forum), is that Australian reviewing is a fairly incestuous business – the bulk of reviewing is done by people who are themselves writers – and this leads to factionalism and ideological warfare. As examples he cites Susan McKernan's *Meanjin* attack on the fiction of Christopher Koch and Les Murray's defence of his 'mate's' work, and the present adulation of women's writing that inhabits what he calls 'Garner/Farmer territory', that is concentrates on domestic pain. Amanda Lohrey's 'The Dead Hand of Orthodoxy' takes the view that reviewing is accorded far too much importance. Subjective opinions, all too often formed on the basis of a quick flick-through, are passed off as authoritative judgements. As an antidote Lohrey advocates an approach in which critics 'come clean' by eschewing the stance of objectivity and identifying their own ideological positions. Kerryn Goldsworthy's 'Dense Clouds of Language' attacks Windsor's 'feminist mafia in power' suggestion and stresses 'the more positive aspects of operating in a small and tightly knit literary community'. Susan McKernan's 'Reviewers and Readers' draws attention to the value of reviews for the general reader in a piece which makes only passing reference to Windsor's comments on her own critical practice. In 'Windsor Castled?' (reprinted in *Hot Copy*[47]) Don Anderson owns up to being the anonymous reviewer mentioned by Windsor who has championed the supremacy of women, but goes on to cite evidence against the contention that women enjoy favoured status. Only one contribution to the forum, John Hanrahan's 'Reviewing: Generosity, Timidity, Incest and All the Other Virtues', comes out in support of Windsor, taking the view that Australian book reviewing *is* permeated by too much 'tribal self-endorsement'. To the non-Australian reader the symposium reads amusingly with contributor after contributor at pains to associate or dissociate him/herself with Windsor and/or certain factions and thus demonstrating the côterie-like quality of the Australian literary community. This does not, however, necessarily support the thesis that unhealthy inbreeding is rife; instead it gives a sense of passionate debate, of a kind that one seldom finds in Britain and the United States, making for a situation in which the social role of writing is constantly under assessment. Jennifer McDonnell's 'Sydney Writers at Festival Time' (*Southerly*) provides a concise, but informative and entertaining account of a gathering of the literary community that has yet to acquire the status of Adelaide Writers' Week, but is growing all the time.

Brian Matthews's 'Directions in Recent Fiction' (*Island*) discusses a range of recent novels, but is particularly interesting for its remarks on the reception of women's fiction, which place recent writing in a long historical context with reference to the appropriation – and consequent distortion – of Baynton and Franklin as nationalist writers. Matthews takes issue with Gerard Windsor's suggestion that women are currently being given privileged treatment. He also offers some interesting comments on Windsor's *Memories of the Assassination Attempt*, in which he finds the narrative voices, male and female, of the various stories almost uniformly the same. C. J. Koch's 'The New Heresy Hunters' (*Overland*), a response to Susan McKernan's attack on his fiction, argues that a new kind of ideological witch-hunting has begun to permeate Australian criticism in much the same way as right-wing conformity dominated the Menzies era. In the same *Overland* issue Robert Darby's consideration of *The Oxford Companion to Australian Literature* (*YW* 66.685–6) affords him the opportunity for a general discussion of the critical situation in Australia, which follows on where John Docker's *In a Critical Condition* (*YW* 65.723) leaves off, arguing that the publication of the *Companion* and the re-issue of H. M. Green's *History of Australian Literature* (*YW* 65.721–2) have broken down the barricades erected by the Australian New Critical hegemony represented by *The Oxford History of Australian Literature*. There certainly does not seem to be any end in sight with regard to what John Docker has called 'struggles for the control of Australian literature'. Docker himself has contributed an *Overland* piece on the carnivalesque in Australian literature. Using Bakhtinian terminology, he particularly examines inversions in the form of melodrama in Australian writing and argues for a plurality of genres rather than a hierarchy. The material included here gives a foretaste of what to expect from a book on carnival which Docker is currently writing with Ann Curthoys. Docker adopts a similar stance in an *ADS* article, 'In Defence of Melodrama: Towards a Libertarian Aesthetic'.

Three pieces that discuss magazines also demonstrate a concern for the state of Australian letters. John Sendy tells 'The Story of *Overland*' in the pages of the journal itself. This fully documented piece puts the stress on the magazine's anti-élitism and its adherence to the Furphy quote which provides its motto: 'Temper democratic, bias Australian'. Recent issues, such as that in which the Koch and Darby pieces referred to above appear, serve to confirm its reputation as a fair-minded and independent arbiter in matters of cultural debate. Alister Kershaw offers 'A Comment on *A Comment*', a little magazine of the 1940s, in *Quadrant*. Peter Murphy's 'After *925*' discusses a late nineteenth-century little magazine that offered a warts-and-all alternative to the jingoistic celebration of rural Australia by writers like 'Banjo' Paterson.

Among the year's crop of general articles in *ADS* (not seen) are May-Brit Akerholt's 'Translations and the Australian Theatre' and Terry Goldie's 'Indigenous Stages: The Indigene in Canadian, New Zealand and Australian Drama'. *Outrider* continues to make an important contribution in the area of migrant writing, but was unavailable for review. David Carter's 'The Natives Are Getting Restless: Nationalism, Multiculturalism and Migrant Writing' (*Island*) argues that it is possible to reconcile notions of nationalism and multiculturalism in an alliance 'aimed at the absorptive, silencing, centralising power of universalist arguments and of "monoculturalism"'. With particular reference to Peter Skrzynecki's *Joseph's Coat: An Anthology of Multi-Cultural Writing* and *Writing in Multicultural Australia 1984: An Overview*, a collection of papers from the Australia Council's Literature Board's Multicultural Writers' Weekend in 1984, Carter argues that multi-culturalism can be seen as part of the host culture, absorbing and revitalizing itself through the admission of new elements. Reading writers like Silvana Gardner, Antigone Kefala, and their like, he contends, involves a rereading of writers like Hope and White and has the effect of helping to bring about a dismantling of the notion of literary hierarchy.

Meanjin has brought out a special issue on humour, in which pride of place is given to 'A Fugitive Art', an interview with Barry Humphries by Jim Davidson. Humphries talks about the origins and evolution of his best-known characters, Edna Everage, Sir Les Patterson, Sandy Stone, and Bazza McKenzie. He identifies himself as a 'regional monologist' who is always most at home far away from his native Melbourne. Max Gillies talks about Humphries's creations in an interview with Helen Thompson that mainly focuses on political satire and Wendy Harmer attempts a self-interview that is mainly concerned with the problems of the woman comedian, though she denies that gender makes for a distinctively different comedy. Don Watson's 'The Joke After God' laments the demise of an audience for Australian rural humour. Judith Brett, the journal's editor, contributes an essay on 'The Chook in the Australian Unconscious', offering the bird as a symbol of Australian cultural difference. This might seem to be promising ground for a witty article, but her discussion is characterized by a ponderousness that illustrates the problems theoreticians can encounter when they try to analyse humour. The issue also includes an essay by Bob Ellis on the monologue, which points out the variety of guises this form has assumed in Australian discourse from Lawson to Paul Hogan, a welcome reprint of a 1964 piece on the clown Mo by Max Harris, and Tom Thompson on 'Political Satire in Sydney'.

Alan Frost's 'On Finding "Australia": Mirages, Mythic Images, Historical Circumstances' (*ALS*), a review-article which discusses several important recent studies of the construction of Australian national identity, is one of a number of other significant articles published this year. Placing the texts he is considering in the context of other seminal studies published in the period since World War II, Frost argues that they represent a second generation of writing on this subject, but finds them in some ways still very partial in their notions of what constitutes 'Australianness'. Quite apart from its critical commentary, this article offers an excellent general survey of the literature available on this topic. Laurie Hergenhan's 'Texts and Contexts: Problems of the Availability and Editing of Australian Texts' (also *ALS*) provides a discriminating examination of a variety of factors that are retarding Australian textual scholarship and criticism. Thomas E. Tausky takes over the procedures used by Richard N. Coe in a 1981 *Southerly* article entitled 'Portrait of the Artist as a Young Australian' for his *ArielE* essay '"A Passion to Live in this Splendid Past": Canadian and Australian Autobiographies of Childhood', that is to say he uses autobiography as a means of defining the way the minds of young artists are responding to the cultural climate of their nation. His approach is, however, primarily concerned with *Canadian* autobiographies and Australian examples of the genre mainly feature as comparative reference points. Dorothy Jones's

'Mapping and Mythmaking: Women Writers and the Australian Legend' (*ArielE*) charts the struggle of Australian women writers to map 'two territories simultaneously – the new land and the nature of female experience within it'. This very perceptive article is mainly concerned with contemporary writing and includes incisive discussion of Beverley Farmer's *Alone*, Thea Astley's *An Item from the Late News*, and Dorothy Hewett's *The Man from Mukinupin*. K. L. Goodwin's 'The Land and its People in African and Australian Fiction' (Nightingale[3]) cautiously attempts to find parallels between these two 'new literatures' and concludes that, while African writing comes mainly from the indigenous people and Australian mainly from the descendants of settlers, commonality exists in the political novel, the metapolitical novel, and the similarities between the emerging Aboriginal novel and its African counterpart. Cross-cultural connections are also explored in Bruce Bennett's 'Perceptions of Asia in Australian Poetry' (*CE&S*), a thorough and informative survey which places the poetry considered in both a social and a more general literary context. It shows how the racism of the *Bulletin* writers was supplanted by an interest in Asia as a source of spiritual enlightenment in poetry by Victor Daley and Bernard O'Dowd and how this has led on to the interest in Taoism displayed in the work of Randolph Stow and John Tranter. Bennett also briefly discusses Vietnam War poems, 'tourist' poems, work by non-'Anglo-Celtic' writers such as Colin Johnson and Vicki Viidikas, and the poetry of the Malaysian-born Ee Tiang Hong.

(b) Individual Authors: 1789–1920

There were no major studies of early Australian authors this year. PenguinA published selections of Lawson's short stories and Harpur's prose and poetry. John Barnes's *The Penguin Henry Lawson Short Stories*[51] reprints several of the best-known stories and comes with notes, a glossary, and a judicious introduction, which usefully draws attention to differences between contemporary notions of the short story genre and those available in Lawson's own day. Barnes points out that for Lawson the 'sketch' was a form quite discrete from the story and he conceived of many of his best-known pieces as belonging to this genre. Hence, it transpires, 'sketches' like those in *While the Billy Boils* and particularly 'The Union Buries its Dead' have been misread – and criticized – for failing to demonstrate narrative unity and a momentum that are simply not part of their method. Michael Ackland's introduction to *Charles Harpur: Selected Poetry and Prose*[52] is, like Barnes's Lawson introduction, a brief, all-purpose account intended mainly for the general reader. It concentrates on the growth of Harpur's reputation as Australia's most important colonial poet. The selection brings prose and poetry together in a number of thematically arranged sections. Ackland has also contributed 'Plot and Counter-Plot in Charles Harpur's *The Bushrangers*' to *ADS*. Vincent O'Sullivan's extended *Westerly* review of Elizabeth Perkins's *The Poetical Works of Charles Harpur* (*YW* 66.696–7) is a substantive piece in is own right. It provides a general discussion of Harpur's verse centred on the classic colonial

51. *The Penguin Henry Lawson Short Stories*, ed. by John Barnes. PenguinA. pp. viii + 229. pb A$4.95.

52. *Charles Harpur: Selected Poetry and Prose*, ed. by Michael Ackland. PenguinA. pp. x + 169. pb A$8.95.

paradigm of the discrepancy between perceived experience and the poetic voice used to realize it.

It has also been a thin year for articles in this area, though a few important pieces on the major novelists have appeared. Robert Dixon's 'Rolf Boldrewood's *War to the Knife*: Narrative Form and Ideology in the Historical Novel' (*ALS*) contends that *War to the Knife* is 'a formulaic tale of frontier adventure', the structure of which is a reflection of the novelist's conservative response to social change. Dixon draws on Lukács's analysis of Scott as a basis for his argument that Scott's Australian disciple Boldrewood is like his mentor in his ability to lay bare significant forces of social change without under-standing them. The same *ALS* issue includes pieces on Marcus Clarke and Joseph Furphy. Avis G. McDonald's 'Rufus Dawes and Changing Narrative Perspectives in *His Natural Life*' examines a range of exterior and interior narrative perspectives in an attempt to reconcile two seemingly incompatible aspects of Dawes's character, his degradation by the convict system on the one hand and his appearing to remain a suffering, essentially noble innocent on the other. This is a fascinating essay, which concludes by showing how a similarly paradoxical contrast in the novel's vision – between naturalistic and melo-dramatic elements – can also be resolved through an approach that focuses on its narrative flexibility. Ivor Indyk's 'Reading Men Like Signboards: The Egalitarian Semiotic of *Such is Life*' attempts to re-establish the text's lost reputation as an 'egalitarian' classic without denying its complexity and diversity. Indyk argues that Furphy repeatedly stresses 'the most ordinary things' and refuses to 'rank them in a hierarchy of significance' and that a moral pragmatism based on a belief in social equality emerges. Elizabeth Morrison's *ALS* note on 'Newspaper Publication of the Novels of Ada Cambridge' draws attention to material published in papers other than the *Australasian*.

Harpur apart, there is very little on the early poets. R. J. Dingley's 'The Track to Ogygia: A Note on Henry Kendall' (*Southerly*) argues against W. H. Wilde's view that 'Ogyges' is an '"affirmation of life"'. After examining the source on which Kendall drew for the poem's mythology, Lemprière's *Classical Dictionary*, Dingley describes Ogyges as a figure 'left desolate by his senile incapacity'. Kendall's influence on Robert Adamson is discussed by Michael Wilding in another *Southerly* article (see p. 758). Cliff Hanna once again points out the error of simply accepting the commonly received version of 'The Public Image of John Shaw Neilson' (*ALS*). David McKee Wright is the subject of two articles by Michael Sharkey: 'A Lost Satire on the 1890s *Bulletin* Writers and Bohemians' (*ALS*) reprints excerpts from 'Apollo in George Street', a mock-heroic work by Wright which Sharkey has discovered in the Fisher Library of Sydney University; 'Apollo in George Street: A Reappraisal of David McKee Wright' (*Southerly*) takes issue with views of Wright which have seen his main importance as lying in his friendship with and editing of Lawson and have regarded him as a minor Celtic Twilight figure by arguing that he was an eclectic, experimenting poet who offered serious treatments of history and poetry.

(c) Individual Authors: Post-1920

Randolph Stow and Patrick White, writers who have not infrequently been linked as poetic-symbolist novelists exploring interior landscapes as a kind of secularized spiritual questing, are the subjects of major studies. Anthony J. Hassall's *Strange Country*[53] is the first full-length critical study of Stow's work. It offers a thorough, workmanlike account of each of the novels including the little-known early works, *A Haunted Land* and *The Bystander*, taking the view that *The Merry-Go-Round in the Sea* and *Visitants* are the most important to date, and a valuable chapter on Stow's poetry. Hassall's main thesis is that Stow's writing is primarily a response to the alien psychic terrain of the antipodes, the 'strange country' of the title. The two recent East Anglian novels, *The Girl Green as Elderflower* and *The Suburbs of Hell*, are seen as continuing the exploration of psychic division and attempts at reconciliation, albeit in the 'haunted' ancestral landscape to which Stow has returned. Hassall writes particularly interestingly on the critical reception of *Tourmaline* and the mixture of 'thriller' and 'medieval morality' in *The Suburbs of Hell*, and his chapter on the poetry, which suggests affinities with the fiction, is an important contribution on a neglected aspect of Stow's work. If the study has a weakness, it lies in its predictability; the central argument is not new and sometimes one feels a little more knowledge could be taken for granted. Stow talks about the two East Anglian novels in '"The Self-Critical Craftsman"', a *Southerly* interview with Peter Kuch and Paul Kavanagh.

The central theme of Carolyn Bliss's *Patrick White's Fiction*[54] is summed up by its subtitle, 'The Paradox of Fortunate Failure'. Bliss identifies failure as a major motif in the development of Australian society and proceeds to analyse how this archetypal pattern replicates itself in developing forms in a succession of White's novels. Issues of style and technique are segregated off for consideration in an ingenious final chapter which relates aspects of White's work such as conditional syntax and equivocal narrative stance to the central notion of 'necessary failure'. The overall effect of the book is vaguely reminiscent of myth criticism on the *felix culpa* in nineteenth-century American literature and when Bliss finally asserts 'Failure thus becomes felicitous' her indebtedness to this body of writing seems confirmed; she would also seem to be following in the footsteps of W. J. Slatoff's 1960 study of Faulkner, *Quest for Failure*. All in all, this solid and well-written book offers a dated critical approach, which has been better handled elsewhere in relation to White and which seems to represent a universalist response to what has initially been located as an Australian predicament. Veronica Brady's *Westerly* essay on *Memoirs of Many in One*, 'Glabrous Shaman or Centennial Park's Very Own Saint? Patrick White's Apocalypse', offers more insights in a few pages than one finds in the whole of Bliss's book. Brady contends that White's latest novel 'calls into question the presupposition which makes of reading and writing an act of consolation' and finds the unnaming process in which the book engages approximating towards a kind of mysticism. In an *ALS* note Joy Hooton draws attention to a dramatic sketch by White which is not listed in the available bibliographies of his drama.

Elizabeth Jolley, it seems, can do no wrong where critics are concerned. *Westerly*, a magazine that steadily rejected her submissions when she was first trying to get her fiction published, includes a symposium of three articles on her

53. *Strange Country: A Study of Randolph Stow*, by Anthony J. Hassall. UQP. pp. xx + 213. £19.95.
54. *Patrick White's Fiction: The Paradox of Fortunate Failure*, by Carolyn Bliss. Macmillan. pp. xvi + 255. £27.50.

work. Dorothy Jones's '"Which hend you hev?": Elizabeth Jolley's *Milk and Honey*' examines the range of biblical and literary allusion used in this novel about sin and redemption. Among the influences she detects are the first two books of the Bible, Blake, *Jane Eyre, Dr Jekyll and Mr Hyde, The Picture of Dorian Gray*, and *Rasselas*. Helen Daniel provides an excellent survey of Jolley's whole *œuvre* to date in 'Elizabeth Jolley: Variations on a Theme', a piece which focuses particularly on the disruptions of Jolley's postmodernist fictional practices. The 'variations' of Daniel's title refers both to the musical motifs that are important in all Jolley's fiction and her use of a contrapuntal narrative mode. A. P. Riemer's 'Displaced Persons – Some Preoccupations in Elizabeth Jolley's Fiction' shows how being a displaced person becomes a 'complex metaphor' in Jolley's work with particular reference to two stories from *Woman in a Lampshade*, and the novels *Milk and Honey* and *Foxybaby*. Jolley discusses her Western Australian regionalism, her English origins, her use of 'lesbian' themes, and her reading preferences in a *Scripsi* interview with Stephanie Trigg, who also provides a full review of *Palomino* in the same issue. Paul Salzman has contributed a Barthesian analysis, 'Elizabeth Jolley: Fiction and Desire', to *Meridian* (not seen), a journal which has also published a piece by Laurie Clancy on 'The Fiction of Thea Astley'. Kerryn Goldsworthy brings Jolley and Astley together in her *ALS* article 'Voices in Time: *A Kindness Cup* and *Miss Peabody's Inheritance*', an essay which draws on narratological theory to demonstrate how both of these very different novels problematize the act of storytelling. She finds that in *A Kindness Cup* 'what is true cannot be written', whereas in *Miss Peabody's Inheritance* 'what is written becomes true'; the temporal complexities of the former are as problematic as the constant fore-grounding of the process of fiction-making in the latter.

D. R. Burns's 'The Active Passive Inversion' (*Meanjin*) argues that, in Christina Stead's *For Love Alone*, Helen Garner's *Monkey Grip*, and three novels by Elizabeth Harrower, a 'radical depth is discovered within a very tradi-tional, clearly conservative playing of sex roles'. In each case, Burns argues, the situation in which the female appears to act the role of passive Jane Eyre to the male's Mr Rochester is reversed on closer examination, which reveals her to be 'active participant'. Cassandra Pybus's 'Loss and Reassurance' (*Island*) is a welcome discussion of the fiction of Beverley Farmer, a writer who despite her popularity has received little serious critical attention. Pybus identifies the experience of loss as the theme that dominates Farmer's 'distinctive subjective vision'. Joan Kirkby's 'Daisy Miller Down Under: The Old World/New World Paradigm in Barbara Hanrahan' (*Kunapipi*) locates Hanrahan as an Australian Hawthorne, a Gothic writer who at times explores the power of the imagination, the position of women, and the international theme. Dorothy Jones, who has written so many fine pieces on contemporary women's fiction in recent years, contributes 'Digging Deep: Olga Masters, Storyteller' to the same *Kunapipi* issue. She argues that Masters's fiction contains multiple layers of narrative and that the process of story-making is an essential part of her writing. Her remarks on gossip, 'a source of narrative delight' as well as 'a highly repressive means of social control', are particularly interesting. Arlene Sykes's 'Jessica Anderson: Arrivals and Places' (*Southerly*) notes that all five of Anderson's novels to date begin with a visit or arrival and goes on to show how such arrivals and visits are part of a typically Australian longer journey. Roslynn D. Haynes's 'Art as Reflection in Jessica Anderson's *Tirra Lirra by the*

River' finds Nora Porteous, the protagonist of Anderson's novel, a Lady of Shalott figure and suggests that, like Tennyson's Lady, she 'weaves her tapestries, her works of art, not from reality, but from the reflection of that reality'. This process is seen as analogous to the novel's own art of reflection.

UQP have brought out Jean Devanny's hitherto unpublished auto-biography, *Point of Departure*[55]. Carole Ferrier's introduction addresses the question of why it has remained unpublished for thirty-five years, as well as trying to suggest why it is likely to be of 'absorbing interest' to contemporary readers. She argues that its importance lies in the insights it gives into the evolution of a woman committed to socialism and into working-class struggles more generally, and in the information it provides about the development of an undervalued writer. *The Peculiar Honeymoon*[56] is an anthology of the writings of Mary Grant Bruce, which includes examples of her journalism as well as extracts from her highly popular 'Billabong' books. Prue McKay's intro-duction places Bruce as a second-generation bush writer, who provided a 'modernized and domesticated version' of the bush legend, albeit not without a strong colonial bias. *ALS* prints a 1983 letter of Shirley Hazzard's in which she discusses poets who have influenced her.

Patrick Buckridge's 'Colonial Strategies in the Writing of David Malouf' (*Kunapipi*) is a densely argued article which identifies three recurrent motifs in Malouf's fiction: 'gaps', 'substitutes', and 'machines'. Each of these involves a whole complex of associations and functions: thus the concept of the gap refers to distances between fathers and sons, between Europe and Australia, between social classes, and to spaces between writer and reader. They are part of a 'grammar of composition' that helps to define the writer's position in post-colonial Australia. Arguably comments which Malouf makes on Australia's recent reconstructions of its past in a *Southerly* interview with Paul Kavanagh can be related to this approach. Peter Pierce's consideration of 'The Sites of War in the Fiction of Thomas Keneally' (*ALS*) sees Keneally's work as 'an anti-podean *comédie humaine*', in which the major themes (such as 'battle') and the major characters (such as Joan of Arc) were present almost from the start. He relates Keneally's treatment of civil war to the 'major domestic inquiry in his fiction, his exploration of all that divides the ostensibly homogenous [*sic*] fabric of Australian society', before going on to examine how Keneally depicts nations as trying through war to instate themselves in the narrative of history, an attitude towards which Australians have always been ambivalent. Keneally talks about his concern with history and war in an interview in the same *ALS* issue, in which he responds to questions drafted by Laurie Hergenhan. Hena Maes-Jelinek's *Kunapipi* article 'History and the Mythology of Confrontation in *The Year of Living Dangerously*' applies Wilson Harris's notions of the transformational possibilities of myth to C. J. Koch's novel, placing particular emphasis on the mythic patterns suggested by the novel's use of the Javanese *wayang kulit* shadow puppet plays. In the same issue of *Kunapipi* Koch writes about his experiences as an Australian in the London of the 1950s, and talks about 'double' identity and 'other' places, both recurrent themes in his fiction,

55. *Point of Departure: The Autobiography of Jean Devanny*, ed. by Carole Ferrier. UQP. pp. xxx + 332; 11 illus. £25.

56. *'The Peculiar Honeymoon' and Other Writings*, by Mary Grant Bruce, ed. by Prue McKay. McPheeG. pp. viii + 242; 10 illus. A$24.95.

in an interview with John Thieme. *Quadrant* prints a speech Koch gave at the magazine's thirtieth-anniversary dinner, in which he discusses its contribution to the Australian literary scene and offers reminiscences of James McAuley.

Emmanuel S. Nelson's 'Connecting with the Dreamtime: The Novels of Colin Johnson' (*Southerly*) discusses Johnson's exploration of the relationship between the Aboriginal quest for selfhood and the need to reclaim the past. Michael Cotter's '"Perth or the bush?" Sense of Place in the Novels of Colin Johnson' (Nightingale[3]) sees Johnson's protagonists as engaged in a Naipaulian search for accommodation, both metaphorical and literal. Gerald Murnane's work is the subject of a substantive *Meanjin* article, 'On Gerald Murnane' by Imre Salusinszky, which charts some of the relationships between philosophy and literature that occur in Murnane's difficult writing. His Catholic upbringing is seen as a crucial formative influence, but after his first two novels, Salusinszky argues, his work is concerned with attempting 'to rescue a personal metaphysic from the disaster of Christianity'. The same *Meanjin* issue includes Murnane's own 'Why I write what I write'.

In 'Liberating Acts – Frank Moorhouse, his Life, his Narratives' (*Southerly*), one of the fullest essays to have appeared on Moorhouse to date, Graeme Kinross Smith presents him as a latter-day Henry Lawson, 'a country-boy become city writer'. This primarily biographical account locates Moorhouse's fiction in the context of his developing career. Michael Wilding has tended to be grouped with his Sydney contemporaries like Moorhouse, but Bruce Clunies Ross's 'Paradise, Politics and Fiction' (*Meanjin*) chooses to emphasize his distinctiveness from them, which he locates in his indebtedness to pre-realistic narrative models and his early West Midlands background. He sees Moorhouse's fiction as informed by an Old World vision of Australia as an Edenic place and connects this with Arcadian images of the West Midlands, such as one finds in *Piers Plowman*, Milton's *Masque Presented at Ludlow Castle*, Pope's presentation of the Man of Ross, and 'Tintern Abbey'. Wilding is interviewed by Giulia Giuffre in *Southerly*. Graeme Turner's 'American Dreaming: The Fictions of Peter Carey' (*ALS*) examines the charge that Carey's fiction is 'international' by looking at American influences in his work. He says Carey's Americanness appears to inhere in his use of forms which foreground and interrogate the text's fictional status, but argues that his work frequently resists American cultural domination by generating Australian *meanings* and that in fact his formal models are transformed and used in tandem with Australian influences. Thus the metafictiveness of *Illywhacker* is indebted to Furphy's *Such is Life* as well as American 'fabulatory models'. Helen Daniel's '"The Liar's Lump" or "A Salesman's Sense of History": Peter Carey's *Illywhacker*' looks at the multiple narrative perspectives of the novel and argues that it frequently contests Herbert Badgery's account, dislocates notions of linear progression, and lays bare its own artifice. Brian Matthews's 'Burning Bright' (*Meanjin*) discusses the quests for meaning undertaken by the protagonists of Tim Winton's novels. Stephen Knight's 'Real Pulp at Last' (also *Meanjin*) provides a welcome discussion of the crime fiction of Peter Corris, which examines how Corris has adapted classic structures of the genre to an Australian context. Corris is quoted as saying that his detective Cliff Hardy is representative of an older generation of Australians, 'strong and not really silent, tough rather than rough, deeply imbued with a colloquial sense of rectitude'. Knight's essays is valuable for helping to identify aspects of Corris's writing that make him one of the best chroniclers of inner city life writing in Australia today, and also contains some particularly interesting remarks on the postmodernism of Corris's recent novel *Deal Me Out*.

Les Murray and A. D. Hope are the poets in this period who have received most attention this year. Andrew Taylor argues in 'Past Imperfect: The Sense of the Past in Les A. Murray' (*SoRA*) that Murray's pervasive concern with the past does not manifest itself as narrative, but in a meditative and lyrical style. He finds Murray's notion of the past 'an idiosyncratic amalgam of ancient non-Athenian Greek, Christian, Celtic and Australian Aboriginal elements'. These come together in his professed 'Boeotianism', a preference for proletarian rural values, which provides a sense of the past that helps 'to make origin seem accessible'. Bruce Clunies Ross's 'Les Murray's Vernacular Republic' (in *Diversity Itself*[38]) surveys Murray's poetic output to date, arguing that, despite the variety of his subject matter, everything he has written is distinctively of a piece. Clunies Ross also stresses Murray's Boeotianism, but disagrees with Taylor in finding him an accomplished exponent of verse narrative. His essay is an excellent short introduction to Murray's work and one which helps to identify the particularly Australian vision and idiom of his poetry. Murray is interviewed by Laurence Bourke in *JCL*. Noel Macainsh's 'Fine Wine and Triumphant Music – A. D. Hope's Poetic' (*Westerly*) finds analogies between the cultural and natural, as well as the very notion of analogy itself, central to Hope's poetic. He sees Hope as a Mannerist writer who treats classical themes unclassically. In *ALS* Ruth Morse talks about her experiences 'Editing A. D. Hope' for her recently published Carcanet edition, and Hope is interviewed by Peter Kuch and Paul Kavanagh in *Southerly*.

Syd Harrex discusses how the topography, climate, and cultural situation of Tasmania have informed the work of three lyric poets in 'Island Lyrics: Vivian Smith, Gwen Harwood, and James McAuley' (*Island*). He traces correspondences between 'environments of place and mind' and sees as particularly characteristic of Tasmanian writing a response to the sea and a provinciality which, while it may sometimes look to Sydney and Melbourne as the metropolis, may also 'by-pass them to visit a Britain of hereditary fact imaginatively acquired'. Harwood is interviewed by Stephen Edgar in the same issue of *Island* and contributes an autobiographical essay, 'Words and Music', on the growth of her interests in music and poetry to *Southerly*. Vivian Smith's 'Translation: Some Personal Notes' appears in *Outrider* and his work is discussed in Noel Rowe's 'Patience and Surprise' (*Southerly*), a piece which argues that the tight control of Smith's poetry serves an expressive rather than a repressive function. *Quadrant* has published 'The Later James McAuley', a brief extract from Leonie Kramer's forthcoming *The Portable James McAuley*.

Michael Wilding's '"My Name is Rickeybockey": The Poetry of Robert Adamson and the Spirit of Henry Kendall' (*Southerly*) sees Adamson's quest for a poetic persona as analogous to that of Kendall: both find the lack of a public role for poetry gives them freedom, but this freedom is that of 'the freed slave'. Wilding finds Adamson's tone characterized by a mocking self-awareness and a commitment to the demands of art. Dennis Haskell looks at 'Humanism and Sensual Awareness in the Poetry of Robert Gray' (*Southerly*) in the context of Gray's imagistic presentation of perceived objects. Deliberately eschewing an approach that sees language as a self-enclosed structure, Haskell sees Gray's 'great subject' as 'the relationship of the individual voice to the physical world at large' and examines a cross-section of his poetry from this point of view. Gary Catalano's 'The Weight of Things' (*Overland*) examines the recurring images of Kevin Hart's three volumes of poetry – images of stones, hands, shadows, sunlight, water, winds, mirrors, horizons, moons, and clocks. Catalano traces developments in Hart's poetry – a movement from the visual to the tactile and aural and an increasing stress on interaction between images – and examines the way in which the world of common experience is frequently, though not always, presented as an encumbrance. Andrew Taylor's 'John Tranter: Absence in Flight' (*ALS*) discusses Tranter's poetry in the context of his well-known distrust of the notion of poetry as a humanist discourse, as expressed in his anthology *The New Australian Poetry* (1979). He concludes by considering the possibility that Tranter's recent poem 'Lufthansa' may mark 'a rapprochement with Humanism'. Noel Rowe's 'Emotions of a Destiny: The Poetry of Philip Martin' (*Southerly*) sees Martin's verse as engaged in a series of archaeological excavations to discover subconscious presences. Tom Shapcott identifies 'Some Sources of *White Stag in Exile*' in *ALS*. Patricia Excell's 'Francis Webb's *Collected Poems*' (also *ALS*) notes some last-minute changes that Webb made to the 1969 collected edition of his work.

David Williamson remains Australia's most popular dramatist. His work is discussed by Brian Kiernan in 'Comic-Satiric-Realism: David Williamson's Plays since *The Department*' (*Southerly*), an essay which contends that, while all Williamson's plays are 'realistic', there is considerable tonal variety within his work and his use of comedy 'is not what we would most readily associate with naturalism'. This is not, however, an argument that does much to disturb the orthodoxies of Williamson criticism: Kiernan still sees him as a socially engaged dramatist who employs satire to expose transgressions from moral norms. Bruce Williams has contributed 'David Williamson: The Powerless Audience' to *Meridian* (not seen). In a *Southerly* interview with Paul Kavanagh and Peter Kuch, which is most interesting for the comments Williamson offers on *The Perfectionist* and *Sons of Cain*, he says that he does not see his theatre as a catalyst for social change.

Joy Hooton's 'Lawler's Demythologizing of the *Doll*: *Kid Stakes* and *Other Times*' (*ALS*), argues that the two 'anterior' plays of Ray Lawler's trilogy change the perspective that seemed to be uppermost in *The Summer of the Seventeenth Doll*, so that 'a universally relevant study of the effects of time' has been replaced by 'a specific study of a certain kind of infantile, but magnetic psychology'. She suggests the possibility of an Ibsenite production of the *Doll* with Olive cast as the unwitting villain. *ADS* (not seen) includes articles on Ron Blair and Stephen Sewell. Alex Buzo is interviewed by Geoffrey Sirmai in *Southerly*.

D. R. Burns's '*The Watcher on the Cast Iron Balcony*: Hal Porter's Triumph of Creative Contradiction' (*ALS*) argues that Porter's verbal skills enable him to construct an autobiographical narrative which is both completely unremarkable and radiantly revealing in its presentation of the young Hal's growing awareness of time and place. Finally, *Culture and History*[57]

57. *Culture and History: Essays Presented to Jack Lindsay*, ed. by Bernard Smith. H&I (1984). pp. 455; 31 illus. £24.95.

(previously overlooked) is a collection of essays presented to that prodigious all-round man of letters, Jack Lindsay. It includes pieces on Lindsay's early life in Australia and his experiences as a poet and publisher in London, along with discussions of his poetry, his association with the theatre, his fiction, his histories, and his biographical writings. A second section considers cultural issues of a more general kind and has the same kind of Renaissance quality: it includes essays on topics as far apart as 'Athens in the "Dark Age"' and 'Wagnerism and the Visual Arts'. The volume concludes with an essay by Lindsay himself and detailed bibliographical listings of his writing. This is a book which will, of course, be essential reading for anyone interested in Lindsay's work; it is also of considerable interest with regard to Australian culture more generally.

5. Canada

(a) General

W. H. New introduces Moshie Dahms's compilation of a bibliography of Canadian non-critical writing for 1985 (*JCL*). *UTQ* continues its 'Letters in Canada' review of Canadian literature and criticism, and Mary Ann Jameson continues to provide an annotated bibliography of the criticism of poetry in *CanPo*. Several bibliographies and bibliographical essays focus on regions. Eric L. Swanick's bibliographical essay on New Brunswick literature is a useful guide to researchers in the field, its main emphasis being on what needs to be done (*SCL*). *line* published a bibliography of Talonbooks, 1967–86. *Essays on Saskatchewan Writing*[58] contains a list of works by and about Saskatchewan writers.

Research tools for work on individual authors continue to be developed, UCalgary publishing inventories of six authors' papers held in the university library's Special Collections: Joanna Glass, Robert Kroetsch, Hugh MacLennan, W. O. Mitchell, Alice Munro, and Rudy Wiebe[59]. Each volume contains a biocritical essay. UManitoba Libraries published a similar inventory of the papers of Dorothy Livesay[60] and UWaterloo published a preliminary bibliography of Lucy Maud Montgomery[61]. NLC published a guide to theses, Jesse J. Dossick's *Doctoral Research on Canada and Canadians, 1884–1983*[62].

What critics do with these various reference tools continues to receive

58. *Essays on Saskatchewan Writing*, ed. by E. F. Dyck. Saskatchewan Writers Guild. pp. xxi + 268. C$14.95.

59. All UCalgary Library Special Collections Division; compiled by Jean M. Moore, et al. *The Joanna M. Glass Papers*. pp. xxxviii + 278. C$18. *The Robert Kroetsch Papers*. pp. xlviii + 371. C$18. *The Hugh MacLennan Papers*. pp. xxx + 161. C$14. *The W. O. Mitchell Papers*. pp. xxix + 218. C$18. *The Alice Munro Papers: First Accession*. pp. xxxv + 211. C$18. *The Alice Munro Papers: Second Accession*. pp. xxi + 222. C$18. *The Rudy Wiebe Papers: First Accession*. pp. xxxiv + 328. C$21.50. All pb.

60. *The Papers of Dorothy Livesay*. Dept of Archives and Special Collections, UManitoba. pp. xxviii + 419. C$15.

61. *Lucy Maud Montgomery: A Preliminary Bibliography*, by Ruth Russell, Delbert Russell, and Rea Wilmshurst. UWaterloo. pp. xxiii + 175. C$25.

62. *Doctoral Research on Canada and Canadians, 1884–1983*, by Jesse J. Dossick. NLC. pp. xv + 559. C$38.75.

attention, although the number of polemical essays on the theory of criticism seems to have declined. E. D. Blodgett provides a useful overview of Canadian criticism from Frye to the present, placing it in the context of European theory (*ZGKS*). Robert Kroetsch[63] suggests that Canadians' not being able to agree on a 'metanarrative', that narrative structure that allows for great heroes, dangers, voyages, and goals, marks Canada as a postmodern country. Don Precosky's 'Seven Myths about Canadian Literature' wittily addresses issues such as funding for Canadian writers, George Woodcock as critic, and the beginnings of modernism at McGill, although its use of 'myth' is certainly counter to the Frygian concept of myth as 'shaping idea and structure' (*SCL*).

Feminist theory draws upon European theory as it interrogates the myths about women's writing in Canada. In a special number of *CFM* devoted to feminist writing, Barbara Godard, Daphne Marlatt, Kathy Mezei, and Gail Scott use the form of the dialogue as essay to undercut prevailing concepts of the essay as structured, unified, linear discourse, a critical practice also much in evidence in *A Mazing Space* edited by Shirley Neuman and Smaro Kamboureli[64]. The volume brings together thirty-nine important essays on women writing in Canada, which are reviewed in the relevant sections below.

Ira B. Nadel criticizes Canadian biography for too often being unaware of its narrativity, citing recent biographies of Louis Riel (Flanagan), Emily Carr (Tippett), and Hugh MacLennan (Cameron) as evidence that such an awareness results in attention to 'broader themes that organize and, in turn, analyse the life' (*ECW*). He might have advanced the criticism of biography even further had he considered specific narrative patterns biographers employ, consciously or unconsciously. Such an awareness is present in Laura Groening's writing on E. K. Brown's correspondence with Lorne Pierce. She identifies Brown as a 'middle-stander', mediating between the traditionalists and the modernists (*CanL*). On the other hand, John Coldwell Adams's biography of Sir Charles G. D. Roberts seems to lack such awareness in its focus on the individual life almost detached from the larger cultural and political context[65]. Occasionally, the complete lack of awareness results in revelation, as Diana Skala's memoir of C. G. D. Roberts illustrates, her recollections ingenuously confirming the stereotype of the romantic artist (*SCL*).

That readers are interested in writers' lives is evidenced by publication of Gale's volume of biocritical essays on Canadian writers, edited by W. H. New[66], and by the abundance of interviews published. The interviews, instead of romanticizing the role of the writer, personalize that role, the number suggesting the writer is not uncommon. Few 'experimental' writers have been able to 'deconstruct' conversation, as interviews with bill bissett, Barry McKinnon, Brian Fawcett, Norbert Ruebsaat (all *ECW*), Michael Ondaatje (*PrairieF*), Fred Wah (*Brick*), Leonard Cohen (*Matrix* and *MR*), Daphne Marlatt (*CapR*), Dennis Cooley (*line*), or Jim Brown (*line*) show. Conversation

63. In *Canadian Story and History 1885–1985*, ed. by Colin Nicholson and Peter Easingwood. EdinU for CCS. pp. x + 110. pb C$5.50. (Hereafter *Story and History*.)

64. *A Mazing Space*, ed. by Shirley Neuman and Smaro Kamboureli. NeWest. pp. xi + 427. C$12.

65. *Sir Charles God Damn: The Life of Sir Charles G. D. Roberts*, by John Coldwell Adams. UTor. pp. x + 235. C$29.95.

66. *Canadian Writers Since 1960: First Series*, ed. by W. H. New. DLB. Gale. pp. xiii + 445. $92.

among members of hiatus, a Winnipeg writers' group comprising Pamela Banting, Di Brandt, Jane Casey, Kristjana Gunnars, Jan Horner, Smaro Kamboureli, and Kathie Kolybaba (*PrairieF*), differs from most interviews in its focus on the group more than on writing or poetic theory.

Other writers interviewed include F. R. Scott (*CanPo*), Dorothy Livesay (*PrairieF*), A. G. Bailey, Northrop Frye (both *SCL*), D. G. Jones (*Matrix*), Timothy Findley, Austin Clarke (both *WLWE*), Alistair Macleod (*JCL*), Jane Urquhart, and Margaret Atwood (both *CFM*). As we now have theories of biography and autobiography, the quantity of interviews suggests that we will soon have theories of interviews.

Three collections of essays, some autobiographical, some critical, provide insight into the lives and ideas of writers and critics. Eli Mandel in *The Family Romance*[67] brings together a number of previously published essays, theoretical and critical. Malcolm Ross's collection of his previously published essays, *The Impossible Sum of our Traditions*[68], reveals developments in Canadian critical approaches from 1954 to 1982. Birk Sproxton invited statements from a number of contemporary prairie writers, presenting these in the context of essays on western Canadian writing previously published[69].

Literature of exploration and travel was examined for its informing myths, Bruce Greenfield considering the idea of discovery as shaping Samuel Hearne's narrative (*EAL*). Three essays in *A Mazing Space*[64] take a feminist approach to the literature of travel and exploration. Marni L. Stanley classifies travel narratives into four groups, those that 'show', 'tell', 'slam' (criticize), and 'quest', the latter being the true explorers. Bina Freiwald describes Anna Jameson's writing as a 'feminocentric discursive universe in which narrator, narratee and narrated are all significantly female', the essay's terminological overburden occasionally burying the 'narrated', although Freiwald's attention to narrative pattern does yield an understanding of Jameson's process of self-transformation. Heather Murray argues that women's 'wilderness' writing, being close to nature, is marginalized because the dominant English-Canadian critical discourse privileges 'culture', the editing of Susanna Moodie's *Roughing It in the Bush* providing Murray with the evidence supporting her thesis.

While female writing may be 'marginalized', so is popular writing. *CanL*, realizing that the distinctions between 'high art' and popular culture are not as clear as they might once have been, devoted a special number to the subject of popular literature, thereby signifying its understanding that most of its readers would not appreciate articles on Harlequin romance side-by-side with a consideration of *Surfacing* as romance. Audrey Thomas's essay on popular romance makes the interesting observation that the reader of this fiction knows more than the central character, a point which seems inconsistent with her conclusion that she finds the content disturbing. Similarly, Geoff Pevere wants more critical attention to be given to popular culture, not because critic and audience share in their enjoyment of it, but because popular culture is part of the ideological apparatus by which a society ensures the reproduction of the

67. *The Family Romance*, by Eli Mandel. Turnstone. pp. xii + 259. C$12.95.

68. *The Impossible Sum of our Traditions*, by Malcolm Ross. M&S. pp. 211. C$19.95.

69. *Trace: Prairie Writers on Writing*, ed. by Birk Sproxton. Turnstone. pp. xiii + 328. pb C$12.95.

existing relations of production. Lorna Irvine perceptively notes that qualities of the tricksterish confidence man, as exemplified by Pierre Berton's persona, are as much a part of the Canadian character as are the qualities of victim and survivor.

Popular culture as reflected in magazines is Robin W. Winks's subject. Winks compares American and Canadian popular magazines, finding that 'the glossies' in Canada follow their U.S. counterparts, while 'magazines of opinion take their form from British models'. Baseball as postmodernism, almost all signifier and 'very little signified' is George Bowering's contribution to the analysis of sport in popular culture. Peter Narvaez hypothesizes that 'modern technological media fosters expansionist involvement [continuity in space], however, it also encourages immersion in the present, and *discontinuity in time*', demonstrating the validity of his theory by examining Newfoundland folklore. In a chapter of his book on detective fiction and culture[70], Ray B. Browne reads Canadian detective fiction in order to arrive at a fuller understanding of the idea of the 'border' between the United States and Canada.

(b) Fiction

E. D. Blodgett's observation that 'the most impressive change . . . taking place in Canadian criticism . . . is the rise of feminist theory' (*ZGKS*) is borne out by the criticism of Canadian fiction in 1986. *A Mazing Space*[64] marks the changes by focusing attention on writers generally regarded as canonical: from Anna Jameson and Susanna Moodie to Sharon Riis and Nicole Brossard. The equation of the female body with the body of language reflects the book's post-structuralist position. Barbara Godard's 'Voicing Difference: The Literary Production of Native Women' differs by treating oral texts as performance, oral history, and anthropology. While the writers and speakers discussed in *A Mazing Space* are predominantly post-Second World War Canadians, the critics do not concern themselves with differentiating Canadian and non-Canadian feminist writing and reading.

Similarly, Carol Fairbanks's purpose in *Prairie Women: Images in American and Canadian Fiction*[71] is not to distinguish Canadian from American women writers' response to the prairie, but rather to demonstrate that the female response is not that of the reluctant pioneer or the character lost in the land's expanse. Instead, she demonstrates that the prairies are most often seen as a positive force in women's lives. While Fairbanks does mention some pot-boilers and romances, her emphasis is on the works of established writers. Among the thirty-four Canadian women writers discussed, about one quarter are non-contemporary. Fairbanks's work gains credence from its breadth, but in *Sub/Version*[72], Lorna Irvine's close readings of Thomas, Atwood, Munro, and Gallant give credence to her feminist analysis that subversive stories seem to characterize female texts, effecting a fictional breakdown of reified male perspectives. The premise that women writers' works resonate with connections to a body of knowledge lost to Western culture, derived from Annis Pratt's

70. *Heroes and Humanities: Detective Fiction and Culture*, by Ray B. Browne. BGUP. pp. 141. $19.95.
71. *Prairie Women: Images in American and Canadian Fiction*, by Carol Fairbanks. Yale. pp. xi + 300. C$22.
72. *Sub/Version*, by Lorna Irvine. ECW. pp. 193. C$14.

work, is a female re-inscription of the traditional views of mythic, archetypal resonance, a Frygian approach from a female perspective, as Irvine herself notes. But she also links colonial space, in Dennis Lee's terms, and female space, noting secrecy and silence, deceit and disguise, doubling and repression, sisters and mothers, and broken connections as dominant patterns in women's fiction, and by implication in colonial space.

Two works of feminist criticism, Carrie MacMillan's 'Seaward Vision and a Sense of Place: The Maritime Novel, 1880–1920' and Janice Kulyk Keefer's 'Recent Maritime Fiction: Women and Words' (both in *SCL*) consider women writers from a specific place. MacMillan's article is important for two reasons: it identifies successful maritime women writers of the period 1880–1920 other than Lucy Maud Montgomery and Margaret Marshall Saunders, namely Carrie Jenkins Harris, Alice Jones, Maria Amelia Fytche, Grace Dean Rogers, and Susan Carleton Jones; and, it gives serious critical treatment to three kinds of novels usually excluded by critics biased toward realistic fiction – the historical romance, the international novel, and the regional idyll. Keefer's introduction to the works of Nancy Bauer, Susan Kerslake, and Antonine Maillet demonstrates her point that contemporary Maritime women writers have freed themselves from the role of silence traditionally imposed on them by culture and literature.

The somewhat more conventional concern with defining the characteristics of a subgenre informs Dennis Duffy's *Sounding the Iceberg: An Essay on Canadian Historical Novels*[73]. Duffy focuses attention on works which modernists rejected as melodramatic pot-boilers treating of surfaces rather than psychological depths. He places contemporary works by Rudy Wiebe, Timothy Findley, Ann Hébert, and Graeme Gibson in the tradition of historical fiction, tracing the development of the subgenre from popular and revered, to popular, and finally to serious, and linking the diverse works through their development of nationalist themes. Each of the chapters contains a useful bibliography of historical fiction in Canada. While the book contends that historical fiction is a useful opposition to the realist canon, the work traces the movement from romance to realism in the mode of historical fiction. Ronald Hatch (*CanL*) has no such hesitation about earlier historical fiction, dismissing it as romance, while tracing the progress of writers such as Grove, Wiebe, Gallant, and Findley towards the view that history is not a series of events but a construct of language.

Whereas Duffy compares French-Canadian and English-Canadian types of the subgenre, noting that the French reflect a nationalist vision based on fear and exclusion while the English reveal an optimistic, individualistic outlook, Philip Stratford in *All the Polarities*[74] images the writings of the two cultures as parallel lines, each line defined by the presence of the other. Examining pairs of novels by MacLennan and Roy, Ross and Langevin, Laurence and Hébert, Munro and Blais, Kroetsch and Carrier, Atwood and Aquin leads him to the observation that the dramatic, tragic structure dominates in the French-Canadian novels he discusses as opposed to the comic, episodic structure in the

73. *Sounding the Iceberg: An Essay on Canadian Historical Novels*, by Dennis Duffy. ECW. pp. 84. C$15.

74. *All the Polarities: Comparative Studies in Contemporary Novels in French and English*, by Philip Stratford. ECW. pp. 109. C$15.

English-Canadian. His close attention to detail allows him to make subtle distinctions, but he shows his awareness of the larger issues as he asks whether the differences are idiosyncratic or suggestive of major cultural and sexual differences, his conclusion implying that the two main cultures of Canada differ so much in their perceptions of experience that they can hardly be said to have common experience.

Canada is multi-cultural, not bi-cultural, thus multiplying the difficulties of sharing historical and cultural constructs, as Hallvard Dahlie's *Varieties of Exile*[75] reminds us. While recognizing the richness of the writing creating an entirely new reality that has resulted from dislocation, Dahlie sees the new reality as often 'disturbing and chaotic'. While that may be the modernist response, one Grove would share, such need not be the postmodernist reaction, as Reginald Berry (*Landfall*) suggests. He implies that postmodern writers' writing themselves into their novels marks the end of the colonialist, modernist removal of the self, a point he demonstrates in his discussion of Bowering's *Burning Water* and C. K. Stead's *All Visitors Ashore*. The difference can also be read in comparing the two book-length works on individual writers of fiction produced in 1986, *A Stranger to My Time: Essays by and about Frederick Philip Grove*[76], edited by Paul Hjartarson, and Robert Lecker's *Robert Kroetsch*[77]. Hjartarson, providing previously unpublished documentary evidence of Grove's theory of art, demonstrates his belief in the need for artistic, ascetic detachment, but by providing more biographical information, he confirms Grove's need to fictionalize himself, a point illustrated also by J. J. Healy's 'Grove and the Matter of Germany: The Warkentin Letters and the Art of Liminal Disengagement'. Margaret Stobie, writing elsewhere (*CanL*), provides the final chapter in Grove's life, his living his own fiction as a rather pathetic gentleman farmer in the white range-line house in Simcoe. K. P. Stich (*Mosaic*), by reading Grove's *Over Prairie Trails* as a psychological analysis of 'the projections, repressions, defenses and transformations of Frederick Philip Grove alias Felix Paul Greve', helps us understand, if not applaud, Grove's 'contradictory penchants for repetitiveness and sameness, for hubris, self-doubt and morbidity, and for creative lying', simultaneously trying to reveal and hide himself. Kroetsch, the postmodernist, openly writes himself into his fiction, delighting in the border between autobiography and fiction, as Robert Lecker observes. Lecker summarizes Kroetsch's position, supports his summary with reference to other commentators, and incorporates other critical work on Kroetsch in order to support his thesis. In the chapter on *Badlands*, though, Lecker departs from the usual, often feminist interpretation that Anna Dawe is freed at the end, to suggest that Anna speaks the male story so that the male characters can live in the freedom of anti-story, Anna's narrative trick-sterishly, self-consciously parodying traditional narrative forms. Both Lecker and John Thieme (*Kunapipi*) note Kroetsch's increasing emphasis on textual erotics and the erotics of space. While Lecker's work conveys the sense of play which distinguishes Kroetsch's writing from Grove's, it doesn't consider Kroetsch as trickster: Lecker adopts a postmodern stance in writing about a

75. *Varieties of Exile*, by Hallvard Dahlie. UBC. pp. 216. C$22.50.

76. *A Stranger to My Time: Essays by and about Frederick Philip Grove*, ed. by Paul Hjartarson. NeWest. pp. xii + 356. C$9.95.

77. *Robert Kroetsch*, by Robert Lecker. Twayne. pp. 165. $19.95.

writer who defines himself as postmodern.

That interest in the postmodern is further evidenced by Hinchcliffe and Jewinski's collection of essays, *Magic Realism and Canadian Literature*[78] and Nicholson and Easingwood's collection, *Canadian Story and History*[63] both collections demonstrating the contemporary concern about the connections between fiction and history by examining contemporary works. An article useful for its distinction between the modern and postmodern story as the distinction between the development of awareness and the exploration of a developed awareness, as much as for its reading of Gladys Hindmarch's 'boat stories' is Pauline Butling's (*ECW*). The irony of postmodernist critics or humanists generally adopting a progressivist position by virtually ignoring pre-Second World War or pre-twentieth-century texts is also notable again in attention given to individual authors in the academic journals. In addition to Dennis Duffy's and Carrie MacMillan's works mentioned previously, only three essays on pre-twentieth-century works appeared, but all demonstrate the possibilities for re-visioning early Canadian fiction.

Mary Lu MacDonald (*CanL*) closely examines often forgotten texts in order to challenge the idea that the natural world as hostile, the 'Wacousta syndrome' and the 'garrison mentality', accurately represents the images of nature in early Canadian literature. In a thematic interpretation of the novel emphasizing *Emily Montague*'s delineation of the ideal of equality within marriage, Ann Edwards Boutelle (*WS*) interestingly links the absence of violence in the novel with Frances Brooke's 'own disavowal of a heroism that destroys rather than creates'. Lorraine York's '"Sublime Desolation": European Art and Jameson's Perceptions of Canada' (*Mosaic*) argues that Anna Jameson could not make the Canadian landscape fit her concept of the ideal, the picturesque, and the sublime. York's exposition of the resulting aesthetic and psychological tension in Jameson's *Winter Studies and Summer Rambles* reinforces our contemporary awareness of art and aesthetic theory as constitutive of the categories of perception.

Contemporary awareness of binary structures shapes critical perception in two papers on Sara Jeannette Duncan's work. Both papers examine the play of opposites, Misao Dean's 'A Note on *Cousin Cinderella* and *Roderick Hudson*' (*SCL*), maintaining Duncan's view to be that 'the Empire must be held together by sentiment rather than by submission', creates an opposition not entirely present in Duncan's work, while Elizabeth Morton's reading affirms that *The Imperialist* favours the pragmatic and realistic over the ascetic or idealistic, but misses the opportunity of reading the novel as interrogating that view (*SCL*). Stephen Leacock's work is also re-assessed, UOttawa publishing the proceedings of the Leacock Symposium[79]. Ed Jewinski's assessment of *Sunshine Sketches* is the most explicitly poststructuralist reading, Gerald Lynch concentrating on the satire on romance and religion, and Clara Thomas investigating the relationship between narrator and reader. Beverly Rasporich and James Steele are concerned with the 'nationality' of Leacock's humour and voice.

Of twentieth-century fiction, Margaret Atwood's once again receives the

78. *Magic Realism and Canadian Literature: Essays and Stories*, ed. by Peter Hinchcliffe and Ed Jewinski. WLU. pp. 126. C$10.

79. *Stephen Leacock: A Reappraisal*, ed. by David Staines. UOttawa. pp. 172. C$14.95.

most attention, much of it from feminist critics. Sharon R. Wilson (*ARCanS*) examines Atwood's illustrations, noting the resonance of Gothic images from fairy-tales or myths in novels and poems whose treatment of gender relations is 'neither single nor simple'. Frank Davey (*CanL*) develops the idea of alternate stories, also present in Lorna Irvine's work. He reads the short fiction to discover two main kinds of 'alternate stories': Atwood's are marked by characters' secret scripts, while Thomas writes disjunctive narratives containing multiple stories. Instead of constituting a larger unity, these alternate stories suggest 'counter-structures'. As was also the case with Irvine's approach, these 'counter-structures' are known to critics prior to reading the stories: they want the text to be constitutive, but they are the privileged readers who can reconstitute the hidden narratives. In 'Tales within Tales: Margaret Atwood's Folk Narratives' (*CanL*) Barbara Godard continues her investigation of the role of oral narratives in literary narratives by reading Atwood's *Surfacing*, *Lady Oracle*, and *Bluebeard's Egg* as revealing her shift from using folk narratives as marks of difference and distance from literary narratives to privileging oral narratives of local experience, demonstrating Godard's awareness of the political and literary implications of this breaking down of the divisions between high art and popular culture. Emily Jensen, in 'Margaret Atwood's *Lady Oracle*: A Modern Parable' (*ECW*), perceptively analyses the application of three literary parables to Joan Foster's resolution of the 'dilemma of the professional woman who wants both to be loved as a woman and to be respected for her mind': Hans Christian Andersen's 'The Red Shoes' and 'The Little Mermaid', and Tennyson's 'The Lady of Shalott'. Julian Jaynes's theories of the origins of consciousness and the structure of romance provide an interesting frame for Ildikó de Papp Carrington's examination of *Life Before Man*, one that invites further investigation, for Carrington does not fully explore the connection between the breakdown of the bicameral mind and the structure of romance (*ECW*). Exploring more familiar territory are papers by Peter Klovan, Nora Foster Stovel, and Judith McCombs. Klovan enters the controversy about the extent to which the narrator 'surfaces' in *Surfacing* by tracing her family relationships, suggesting that she has only reached a partial understanding of her parents (*ECW*). In the same issue of *ECW* Nora Stovel's reflections on mirrors in Atwood's novels are caught in the doubleness of her own images when she describes Atwood's main characters' being drawn by their anti-selves to the void as a metaphysical affirmation of life, and Judith McCombs (*WS*) applies *Survival's* four attitudes to victimization to Atwood's fictional artists, noting two stages: 'the Closed, divided, Mirroring World', and 'the realistic Open World'.

As already noted, Audrey Thomas's work has been receiving increasing attention from feminist critics as two other papers, Linda Hutcheon's '"Shape Shifters": Canadian Women Novelists and the Challenge to Tradition'[64], reading *Intertidal Life* as linking the sexual and the social, and Colin Nicholson's 'Mother Countries: Audrey Thomas's Writing' (*BJCS*), focusing on female relations, confirm. Coral Ann Howells's 'Marian Engel's *Bear*: Pastoral, Porn, and Myth' (*ArielE*) does not take an overtly feminist approach to Engel's work. Situating Engel's *Bear* in the Canadian tradition of animal stories and wilderness literature, Howells's paper argues that the novel is about 'the inviolability of the natural order and the healing corrective power of nature to save us from ourselves'.

Michael Darling brings together eight perspectives on Mordecai Richler[80]. Essays by Michael Greenstein and Margaret Gail Osachoff examine patterns of imagery in Richler's work, Greenstein seeing Richler's main characters as 'runners' in 'a race with no end in sight', and Osachoff considering the 'urban pastoral'. Laura Groening, Thomas Tausky, Wilfred Cude, Zailig Pollock, and Stephen Bonnycastle employ various critical approaches in elucidating Richler's moral vision, and Robert Cluett and Suzanne Ives use linguistic analysis with a similar result.

Continuing to be critically popular are Alice Munro and Rudy Wiebe, the treatment of Munro's work being especially illustrative of the diversity of contemporary critical practice. In distinguishing Munro's realism from other realisms (*QQ*), George Woodcock observes that the form is akin to that of the super-realist painters while, in contrast to the prairie realists, the content represents 'a decaying established culture rather than a frontier one'. His view that Munro's realistic technique has remained unchanged has been challenged. Philip Stratford notes the polyvalence of Munro's narrative technique[74] as does Smaro Kamboureli[64]. Lorna Irvine's close reading of 'Dulse'[72] sees narration as paradigmatic of women writers' need to give the narrative voice authority while at the same time emphasizing connections and relationships. Thomas Tausky (*SCL*), using the Alice Munro Papers to trace the development of the artist in *Lives of Girls and Women*, convincingly challenges the conventional interpretations of the work's concluding artistic credo rejecting gothic romance for the 'sobriety and artistic responsibility' of the realist's art. In his reading, romance and realism co-exist.

Current criticism of Wiebe's work is more unified, stressing the role of vision in his fiction. Marie Vautier (*CanL*), noting the tension between history as a past to be discovered and history's narrative structure as a construct, lauds Godbout and Wiebe for conflating history and fiction into a new myth-making. Once again, myth is considered to be superior to history, Vautier using Frye's distinction that history is sequence but myth is history in 'participating form' to support her analysis, but her relativizing of history suggests that Wiebe's 'history' is but one version. Yet Gabriel Dumont, for example, hears the voice in the chapel and 'knows', a point made in Kenneth Hoeppner's 'Politics and Religion in Rudy Wiebe's *The Scorched-Wood People*' (*ESC*). Coral Ann Howells's 'Rudy Wiebe's Art and Acts of Narrative in *The Scorched-Wood People*' in *Story and History*[63] also emphasizes that novel's importance in 'revisioning' prairie history.

Two papers on Sinclair Ross revise interpretations of *As for Me and My House*, although not revising prairie history. The literary detectives Evelyn J. Hinz and John J. Teunissen discover Mrs Bentley's 'real' story, analysing the novel as dramatic monologue to reveal that Mrs Bentley used her pregnancy by Percy Glenn to trap Philip into marriage, this analysis demonstrating that Ross, not the postmodernist reader, has controlled the meaning of the novel (*CanL*). A reading completely at odds with that of Hinz and Teunissen, Frances W. Kaye's 'Sinclair Ross's Use of George Sand and Frederic Chopin as Models for the Bentleys' (*ECW*) argues that Mrs Bentley is herself an artist as well as the guardian of Philip's artistry. Perhaps Kaye could have established the case for Ross's knowledge of the Sand–Chopin relationship more fully.

80. *Perspectives on Mordecai Richler*, ed. by Michael Darling. ECW. pp. 183. C$15.

History and myth are the focus of papers on Clark Blaise, Howard O'Hagan, Mavis Gallant, and Timothy Findley. Arguing that for Blaise, everything, including narrative strategy and form, is structured in twos, Robert Lecker (*CanL*) reads himself into the narrative as he explores the dialectics between the primitive and the civilized, the mythical and the historical, depths and surfaces in 'Notes Beyond a History', Margery Fee's poststructuralist reading of O'Hagan as dismantler of monolithic 'Myth' into its constituent, contradictory myths, 'revealing how myth is created to suit a particular need in a particular time and place', convincingly argues its thesis. It invites our wondering about the myths by which we constitute our experience, for our belief in multiplicity and egalitarianism must be as much a belief in myth as another culture's belief in myths being fixed, universal, and authoritative (*CanL*). Arnold Davidson (*CanL*) examines the biblical parallels in *Tay John*, noting that the parallels undo the model on which the novel is based: 'we are denied gospel, authority, transcendence, the final enduring word'.

Janice Kulyk Keefer's and Neil Besner's papers concern themselves more with history than myth in Mavis Gallant's work. Keefer sees Gallant as differing from other Canadian writers in that she consciously deals with history as every day living (*UTQ*). Besner (*ECW*), while observing that Gallant's stories ought not to be read as 'simple slices of life', does not share Keefer's concern with linking history and ordinary experience. Instead, he deals primarily with those elements traditionally considered realistic. As already noted, Lorna Irvine reads the truncated narrative patterns in Gallant's work as being balanced with the alternative narrative stressing creative production, thus emphasizing Gallant's feminist social concerns.

Diana Brydon's two papers on Timothy Findley's *The Wars*, 'A Devotion to Fragility' (*WLWE*) and '"It could not be told"' (*JCL*) pay careful attention to imagery and theme while Sister M. L. McKenzie notes the parallels in the presentation of destructive psychological reactions to war in her 'Memories of the Great War: Graves, Sassoon, and Findley' (*UTQ*).

Dealing with the war that never was, Lawrence Mathews (*CanL*) speculates that critical neglect of Cohen's *The Colours of War* supports Edgar Z. Friedenberg's thesis that Canadians are unwilling 'to recognize the political implications of any given situation', a point hardly supported by the review of criticism for 1986. Anthony Hopkins's account of critical response to Elizabeth Baird's *Waste Heritage* also suggests that critics have neglected the work for political rather than aesthetic reasons. Hopkins's essay (*SCL*) usefully reminds us that it is not only an accurate documentary, but an aesthetically crafted novel, yet he does not demonstrate the latter point.

Two papers, Naomi Jacobs's 'Michael Ondaatje and the New Fiction Biographies' (*SCL*) and G. Lernout's 'Creation-science and Jack Hodgins's *The Invention of the World*' (*RBPH*), attempt new generic definitions. Jacobs distinguishes the new fiction biography from traditional fiction and biography by its movement away from biographical time, its abandonment of the omniscient narrator for multiple narrators or a first person narrator, its use of poetic language, controlling metaphor and literary motif, and its establishment of a factual and fictional basis, illustrating the new genre with reference to Ondaatje's *Coming Through Slaughter*. She does not develop her statement that the new genre makes large claims for the importance of fiction, however. Lernout distinguishes 'traditional post-modernism', the novel of exhaustion, from a new novelistic form, 'the novel of replenishment', the new form characterized by abundance of plots as opposed to minimalist plots, communal, rural as opposed to alienated, urban settings, and oral, earthy as opposed to writerly, intellectual language and tone. The dense theoretical work somewhat upstages Hodgins's *The Invention of the World* in the discussion, but Lernout cogently observes that such novels should be 'approached from another perspective than that of traditional post-modernist criticism . . .', the science of folklore being one such possible approach.

Alice Van Wart's '*By Grand Central Station I Sat Down and Wept*: The Novel as a Poem' (*SCL*) observes that the novel's use of tropes (metalepsis, zeugma, and hyperbole), mythical and literary allusions to love in exile, and images of blood and water, result in a fusion of the two genres, but Van Wart's close reading of the novel needs to be framed by the question of the significance of such fusion.

Minority literatures and regional literatures received only slight attention. Suwanda Sugunasiri (*WLWE*) usefully acquaints us with the names of the writers of South Asian Canadian Short Stories: Stephen Gill, Lino Leitao, Saros Cowasjee, Cyril Dabydeen, Clyde Hosein, Harold Sonny Ladoo, M. G. Vassanji, and the author of the article himself. Identifying realism in place, character, and language to be the predominant mode of these stories, Sugunasiri does not explain why this is so. Also questionable is his implicit assumption that stories employing symbolism and myth are superior to those which do not, a view revealing some confusion about the nature of language itself.

Erika Gottlieb's reading of Joy Kogawa's *Obasan* (*CanL*) attends more closely to the non-literal use of language. Gottlieb reveals the universal, psycho-logical, and political dimensions of the central character's development by explicating the three interconnected circles of symbolism in the novel: the universal-apocalyptic pattern drawn from the Book of Revelation, the psycho-logical pattern of the narrator's soul as wasteland, and the reality of the actual Canadian landscape. The journey through these circles leads the narrator to the centre of meaning. Similarly showing the universality of regional experience, William Connor (*WLWE*) might give greater insight into the fictional characters' entrapment and desire for escape. Such entrapment is not a regional, socio-economic phenomenon, as is evidenced by Connor's being able to appreciate the characters' dilemmas. O. S. Mitchell, however, celebrates the regional as he situates W. O. Mitchell's love of the tall tale in the oral tradition of the prairie (*CanL*).

Some absences in the criticism of twentieth-century Canadian fiction in 1986 are particularly noteworthy. Only one new article on Margaret Laurence's work appeared, Arthur Ravencroft's 'Africa in the Canadian Imagination of Margaret Laurence' (*LCrit*). Similarly, there was only one essay on Ethel Wilson's work, Mary-Ann Stouck's 'Structure in Ethel Wilson's *The Innocent Traveller*' (*CanL*), an essay examining the tension between propriety and individual freedom. Callaghan is treated from the perspective of exile developed in Hallvard Dahlie's book, and Sheila Watson's or Ernest Buckler's work is hardly mentioned.

(c) Poetry

Work on early Canadian poetry consisted primarily of the presentation of new editions. D. M. R. Bentley edited *Abram's Plains: A Poem* by Thomas Cary[81], Mary Lu MacDonald published 'new' poems by Adam Hood Burwell (*CanPo*), and G. M. Story published the anonymous 'The Rocks of Quidi Vidi,' a Newfoundland colonial poem (*NewSt*). Edward Mullaly deals with Thomas Hill's songs and poems written in mid-nineteenth century New Brunswick (*SCL*). Carl Ballstadt focuses on Susanna Moodie's awareness of her readers in her dramatization of events surrounding the uprising of 1837, Moodie's having established a reputation for the loyal or patriotic poem predisposing her readers to accept her narrativization of a historical event (*CanPo*).

Poets of the confederation received somewhat more attention, Archibald Lampman and D. C. Scott receiving most of the attention. D. M. R. Bentley edited Lampman's *The Story of an Affinity*[82], and L. R. Early published *Archibald Lampman* in TWAS[83]. Lampman's devotion to Romantic models approaches literary conservatism, L. R. Early writes. Early identifies the tension between the Romantic idea of poetry and the suspicion that poetry may be of little consequence as Lampman's chief uncertainty, Lampman being more influenced by mood than by system. In his evaluation, Early does not consider James Steele's argument about Lampman as modernist.

Janice C. Simpson (*CanPo*) analyses D. C. Scott's 'A Scene at Lake Manitou' to suggest that Scott's official view of the inevitability of Indian assimilation was more complex than that indicated in his *The Administration of Indian Affairs in Canada*. That debate is not likely to be closed, as L. P. Weis's situating Scott in the nineteenth-century idea of progress leads to the view that Scott saw the 'death of Indian culture as beneficial to *individual* Indians', Indian culture being anachronistic (*CanL*). Similarly, E. Brian Titley examines Scott's record in the administration of Indian Affairs to reach that conclusion[63]. Although Tracy Ware's close reading of 'The Height of Land' (*CanL*) is more concerned with Scott's romanticism, his poem's failure to reconcile subject and object, thought and nature, Ware's comment that Scott distinguishes evolution and progress suggests Ware can also be read as part of the debate.

As with fiction, modern and contemporary poetry received the most critical attention. Dorothy Livesay's work received overdue recognition in *A Public and a Private Voice*[84]. David Arnason revises the history of modernist poetry in Canada by stating that Livesay's *Green Pitcher* and *Signpost* were the first widely available books of modernist poetry by a Canadian poet. Jonathan Peirce observes that images of dancing and singing connect the personal and the social in Livesay's poetry, although he does not examine the relationship in any great detail. Joyce Wayne and Stuart Mackinnon rekindle the cosmopolitan/native distinction and dispute as they document Livesay's involvement in the Communist Party and suggest its resulting in her being excluded from the A. J. M. Smith-defined mainstream of Canadian poetry.

81. *Abram's Plains: A Poem*, by Thomas Cary, ed. by D. M. R. Bentley. CPP. pp. xlviii + 43. pb C$6.50.

82. *The Story of an Affinity*, by Archibald Lampman, ed. by D. M. R. Bentley. CPP. pp. xxxi + 85. pb C$6.50.

83. *Archibald Lampman*, by L. R. Early. Twayne. pp. xiv + 175. $19.95.

84. *A Public and a Private Voice: Essays on the Life and Work of Dorothy Livesay*, ed. by Lindsay Dorney, Gerald Noonan, and Paul Tiessen. UWaterloo. pp. 139. C$17.50.

Livesay's journalism and its connection to her poetry is Lee Thompson's subject. Rota Herzberg Lister traces Livesay's drama to 'agitprop'. Paul Tiessen and Hildegard Froese Tiessen describe Livesay's work in radio drama, noting her use of counterpoint, montage of successive voices, and the mixing of poetic and conversational voices. Paul Denham attends carefully to form and voice in Livesay's poetry as he argues for the unity of lyric and documentary. Dennis Cooley identifies three positions in Livesay's work: inside and outside as female/male in her early work, the sun and wind outside being metaphors of male sexual power to which the lyric voice responds with intense excitement; the identification with sun; and finally, rooted in place – woman as prophet and spirit of earth. Ed Jewinski observes Livesay's use of 'repetends to underscore that "being" is that which always exists one step beyond language'.

Examining Livesay's feminist poetic and practice, Diana Relke sees Livesay's early poetry as presenting an integrated world-view that has been constant in her work since, a view that sees the woman poet as mediator between culture and nature (*ArielE*). Phyllis Webb's poetry is also read from a feminist perspective. Cecelia Frey reads Phyllis Webb's work as revising 'the literary text of male authority' and her own early conventional text of female despair at lack of authority by 'the intertransformation of opposites, of female and male' (*PrairieF*), perhaps imposing greater unity on Webb's themes than the poetry invites. John Hulcoop follows a similar line of argument, but notes that Webb is also 'self-mocking, critical, and sometimes even satirical in writing about her own sex' (*CanL*). Hulcoop also provides useful information on the form of the ghazal. Pauline Butling[64] also reads Webb 'for the quality and quantity of play to be found there', not for the urgency of the message. George Woodcock emphasizes Webb's formal techniques without considering her feminist themes (*QQ*).

James Doyle documents the appearance of Canadian poets in American little magazines of the 1890s, adding to the understanding of the beginnings of modernist poetry in Canada (*CanL*). Patricia Whitney focuses attention on Patrick Anderson's 'attempt to realize that harmony of individual creation and social purpose' in his founding of *Preview* and *En Masse* (*CanPo*). Whitney's preparation of an introduction and index to *En Masse* (also *CanPo*) further emphasizes Anderson's attempt to bring together the arts and social concerns.

In the modernism of A. M. Klein, form and social concerns are interconnected. Susan Gingell's careful attention to metre and rhythm reminds readers that A. M. Klein used prosodic techniques to encode meaning, a kind of study Gingell rightly notes is part of the process of understanding Klein's 'cultural systems of enormous diversity', her analysis of the interplay of British and Jewish literary tradition in 'Ave Atque Vale' being but one illustration of her thesis (*CanPo*). Robin Edwards Davies's numerologically and Kabbalistically based explication of A. M. Klein's 'The Provinces' leads to her conclusion that unity and diversity coexist, 'interpenetrate' (*CanPo*).

Even the 'dandyist' form has social implications. Brian Trehearne places Robert Finch's work in the 'dandy' mode of Sitwell and Betjeman. He notes that the British writers' 'intense formalism' was a response to the hereditary aristocracy's loss of cultural and economic power, inviting an exploration of Finch's adoption of that mode in Canada. A. G. Bailey's verbal dandyism is linked to Finch's in Travis Lane's paper (*CanPo*).

The idea of transcendence is not usually associated with modernism, but A. R. Kizuk's exploration of the metaphysical and transcendent in W. W. E. Ross (*CanPo*) from the perspective of Gaston Bachelard's dialectic of the imaginative and the empirical suggests that poetry acts as an affirmation of the spiritual in the materialistic world, a view not commonly held in the 1980s, but one informing Canadian criticism until the end of the age of Frye. Such ideas of transformation also appear in Lorraine York's reading David Helwig's *Catchpenny Poems* as taking the reader on a journey from 'ignorance to awareness', an awareness of the coexistence of darkness and light, pain and joy (*CanPo*). And Dennis Lee, in his 'Afterword' to Purdy's collected poems, reads attentively, although his emphasis on Purdy as a poet of transcendence derives as much from Lee's poetic as it does from Purdy's poetry. Such a search for transcendence occasionally results in misreading. Suzanne Juhasz, comparing Atwood to Emily Dickinson, creates a false dichotomy between poet and genius, a dichotomy that leads to her looking for transcendence in poetry, looking for Atwood's renunciation of the world in order to repossess it, as she claims Dickinson did. Without really attending to Atwood's poetry, Juhasz claims that Atwood has not used figurative language to transform (*WS*).

Poetry of place is the focus of attention in a number of essays on modern and contemporary writers. Elizabeth Waterston (*CanPo*), arguing that 'place creates poets, poets create place', traces the movement of literary centres in Ontario from Niagara-on-the-Lake to Guelph, Peterborough, Ottawa, Kingston, Toronto, and London, but recognizing that the model of a literary heartland may not apply in the 1980s, she does not consider that shift as one of the effects of transportation and communication. *ECW*'s collection of essays on West-Coast writers illustrates the tendency to combine moral and ethical criticism with the situating of a poet in a region, although Jean Mallinson's essay on Pat Lowther is an exception. Bringing together the text of the poem, its sources in Edmund Carpenter's 'Image Making in Arctic Art' and Paul Riesman's 'The Eskimo Discovery of Man's Place in the Universe', and her own analysis of 'the tropes through which the prose sources are transformed into a poem', Mallinson reads Lowther's 'Woman On/Against Snow' analogically as an image of poetry's power to transform 'suffering into nourishment and form'. Sharon Thesen's and Fred Wah's essays deal as much with poetics as they do with region. Sharon Thesen introduces the work of George Stanley, placing him in the San Francisco, West-Coast tradition of Robert Duncan, Jack Spicer, and Robin Blaser, and Fred Wah carefully reads Sharon Thesen's poetry through Charles Olson's concept of cadence as being lyric poetry's equivalent to individual emotion registered as feelings in the 'stomach, pulse, heart, breath, etc.' While Travis Lane criticizes Kevin Roberts's poetry for its sometimes uncontrolled metaphors, its images that do not work for all parts of the poem, his main criticism is of Roberts's presumably unconscious, unexamined 'racism/male chauvinism'. John Harris's overview of Brian Fawcett's poetry and prose commends Fawcett's work for its social significance, for its 'drawing a myth out of the B.C. interior', but that myth of the conflict between industrial capitalism and nature is hardly what Harris calls 'a new perspective on our world'. Peter Buitenhuis's primarily thematic overview of Dale Zieroth's two volumes of poetry distinguishes 'prairie poet' from 'Pacific-west poet' by the former's regarding the landscape with fear and awe, the latter with 'knowledge, appreciation, and love', a distinction that invites a rereading of poets in both groups. Steve McCaffery[85] writes primarily about West-Coast writers such as Wah, Bowering, and bissett, but he is more concerned with theory than with place.

Dealing with contemporary poetry on the Atlantic coast, Michael Thorpe introduces the work of writers in Newfoundland and Prince Edward Island (*AR*). Fred Cogswell compares Janice Tyrwhitt's biography of Alden Nowlan in *Reader's Digest* with the Nowlan he knew and with the Nowlan that emerges from his poetry. He also questions Michael Brian Oliver's treatment of Nowlan as 'Canadian' rather than 'regionalist' (*SCL*). Present in most criticism but foregrounded in Laurie Ricou's collection of essays on P. K. Page's 'The Permanent Tourists', is the question of the relation between theories of criticism and the practice of reading. He brings together three pedagogical approaches to P. K. Page's 'The Permanent Tourists': Kay Stockholder's psychoanalytical approach, Shirley Neuman's poststructuralist, and D. M. R. Bentley's historical/practical (*CanPo*), an exercise that demonstrates the continuing, necessary emphasis on close reading in the classroom.

OpL devoted a special issue to bp Nichol, the overall effect of which is to make 'readable' a poet whose work has often been considered a deconstruction of readability. Punning on 'train', George Bowering trains readers to read 'train' as symbol in bp Nichol's poetry. Barbara Caruso writes about Nichol's collaboration with visual artists, illuminating his attention to the configuration of letters on a page. Stephen Scobie gives a Derridean reading of the 'paraph' 'bp'. Nichol's 'composition by association of ideas' as the reflection of the 'community's ethos' is the subject of Rafael Barreto-Rivera's examination of Book 5 of *The Martyrology*, a paper defining 'community' rather narrowly. More significant are two articles suggesting Nichol's break with post-modernism. Brian Henderson's reading of *The Martyrology* in the context of other poems, particularly Christopher Smart's *Jubilate Agno*, 'preoccupied with spiritual transformation' surprises the postmodernist reader and critic accustomed to reading poetry as a denial of 'presence'. Frank Davey defines this position as 'courageous' in the face of dominant aesthetic ideologies. Steve McCaffery, demonstrating that *The Martyrology* may be read as a representation of Lacanian or Bakhtinian theory, would not agree with Henderson and Davey, but he seems too determined to read Nichol through the theorists to be fully persuasive.

The question of 'what is poetry' is foregrounded in Robert Billings's paper on 'The Prose Poems of Roo Borson and Robert Priest' (*CFM*).

(d) Drama

Two books on theatre in Quebec appeared, Elaine F. Nardocchio's[86] and Jonathan M. Weiss's[87], both noting the close connections between politics and theatre. Both books agree that the church hindered the development of theatre in Quebec, and that the rising nationalism of the 'Quiet Revolution' of the 1950s and 1960s coincided with the growing importance of the experimental

85. *North of Intention: Critical Writings 1973-1986*, by Steve McCaffery. Nightwood. pp. 240. C$14.95.

86. *Theatre and Politics in Modern Quebec*, by Elaine F. Nardocchio. UAlberta. pp. xii + 157. C$12.95.

87. *French Canadian Theater*, by Jonathan M. Weiss. Twayne. pp. 179. $29.50.

and the revolutionary in Quebec theatre. While both emphasize works written and performed from 1960 to about 1980, they differ somewhat in their treatment of the cultural and political contexts; Nardocchio emphasizes the political and Weiss the literary and theoretical, with Weiss providing closer analysis of individual plays. Elaine Nardocchio (*CanD*) provides a numerical analysis of plays performed in Montreal between 1958 and 1968 to supplement her more general review in her book. Rota Herzberg Lister's edition of 'Whittaker's Montreal: A Theatrical Autobiography, 1910–1949' is a useful companion work providing a perspective on English theatre in Montreal (*CanD*).

Early Canadian drama received scant attention, but David Beasley made a valuable contribution. He introduces Major John Richardson's farce 'The Miser Outwitted', a long-lost play Beasley found in the library of the British Theatre Association (*THIC*). Popular entertainments produced by nineteenth-century Maritime Temperance Societies allowed playwrights to develop their skills, Mark Blagrave argues (*THIC*).

Twentieth-century drama outside Quebec received more extensive treatment. James Hoffman, writing in *THIC* about Carroll Aikins's 1920s Home Theatre in Naramata, B.C., observes that Aikins had toured Europe before going to Naramata; consequently bringing art theatre to B.C. and Canada. Léa V. Usin's history of the Great Canadian Theatre Company in Ottawa, a nationalist, leftist theatre, describes the plays performed and critics' responses to them and notes the theatre's shift from 'public' to 'private' politics as a likely reason for its continuing success (*THIC*). In contrast, her history of Ottawa's Town Theatre appropriately emphasizes the theatre's financial as well as its early artistic success in producing entertainment, but attributes its failure to its lack of a well-defined purpose (*CanD*).

Theatre in Saskatchewan receives Diane Bessai's attention. Her essay argues that drama in Saskatchewan counters the 'myth of embittered individual struggle, alienation, and defeat' which characterizes established Saskatchewan fiction, with its 'explorations of the positive collective values of community', a stimulating perspective that invites examination of the popular tradition in Saskatchewan fiction as well[58]. Richard Paul Knowles adopts a similar perspective in his account of one theatre company, the Mulgrave Road Co-op of Guysborough County, Nova Scotia (*CanD*).

Y. S. Bains's study of popular-priced stock companies in the 1890s argues that 'the term "popular" need not be equated with worthless and cheap', a view with which B. K. Sandwell did not agree. As Anton Wagner makes clear, Sandwell's dramatic aesthetic was based on the concepts of the well-made play and the 'modern classics' of Ibsen and Chekhov (*CanD*), an aesthetic that excluded much of the popular and workers' theatre in Canada.

Malcolm Page, examining the reception of Canadian plays in Britain, observes that 'if a prevailing tone can be found in British reviews of Canadian plays, it comes somewhere between weary resignation and exasperation at wasting time attending the plays at all' (*CanD*), touching on, but not quite addressing the question of the Canadian need to export plays.

Books Received

Chapter I. Reference, Literary History, and Bibliography

Alkon, Paul K., *Origins of Futuristic Fiction*. UGeo, 1987. $30.

Attridge, Derek, *Peculiar Language: Literature as Difference from the Renaissance to James Joyce*. Methuen, 1988. hb £25, pb £8.95.

Badawi, M. M., *Modern Arabic Drama in Egypt*. CUP, 1987. £27.50.

Banks, R. A., and F. D. A. Burns, *Advanced Level English Language*. H&S, 1987. pb £6.95.

Birrell, T. A., *English Monarchs and their Books: From Henry VII to Charles II: The Panizzi Lectures 1986*. BL, 1987. pb £11.50.

Brewer, Derek, *Symbolic Stories: Traditional Narratives of the Family Drama in English Literature*. Longman, 1988. pb £6.95.

Brook, J. M., ed., *Dictionary of Literary Biography Yearbook: 1986*. Gale, 1987. $95.

Cairns, David, and Shaun Richards, *Writing Ireland: Colonialism, Nationalism and Culture*. ManU, 1988. pb £5.95.

Castillo, Debra A., *The Translated World: A Postmodern Tour of Libraries in Literature*. FlorSU, 1985. pb $18.

Castronovo, David, *The English Gentleman: Images and Ideals in Literature and Society*. Ungar, 1987. $17.95.

Cave, Terence, *Recognitions: A Study in Poetics*. Clarendon, 1988. £40.

Cohen, Michael, *Engaging English Art: Entering the Work in Two Centuries of English Painting and Poetry*. UAla, 1987. $28.95.

Commire, Anne, ed., *Something about the Author*. Gale, 1987. Vols. XLVI and XLVIII. $66 each; Vol. XLIX. $68.

Crossley, Ceri, and Ian Small, ed., *Studies in Anglo-French Cultural Relations*. Macmillan, 1988. £29.50.

Dillon, Hans-Jürgen, ed., *Images of Germany*. CWU, 1987. pb DM 50.

Estes, Glenn E., ed., *American Writers for Children Since 1960: Poets, Illustrators, and Nonfiction Authors*. DLB. Gale, 1987. $92.

Goytisolo, Juan, *Landscapes After the Battle*, trans. by Helen Lane. Serpent's Tail, 1987. pb £7.95.

Haefner, Gerhard, *Impulse der englischen Lyrik*. CWU, 1985. DM 56.

Hall, H. W., ed., *Science Fiction and Fantasy Reference Index, 1878–1985: An International Author and Subject Index to History and Criticism*. Two vols. Gale, 1987. $175.

Hall, Sharon K., ed., *Contemporary Literary Criticism: Yearbook 1986*. Gale, 1987. $92.

Hardin, James, ed., *German Fiction Writers, 1885–1913*. Two vols. Gale, 1988.

Hardin, James, ed., *German Fiction Writers, 1914–1945*. Gale, 1987. $90.

Harris, Laurie Lanzen, and Sheila Fitzgerald, ed., *Short Story Criticism: Excerpts from Criticism of the Works of Short Fiction Writers*, Vol. I. Gale, 1988. $70.

Herendeen, Wyman H., *From Landscape to Literature: The River and the Myth of Geography*. Duquesne, 1986. $32.

Homberger, Eric, and John Charmley, ed., *The Troubled Face of Biography*. Macmillan, 1988. hb £27.50, pb £8.95.

Johnston, William M., *In Search of Italy: Foreign Writers in Northern Italy Since 1800*. PSU, 1987. $24.95.

Legat, Michael, *The Illustrated Dictionary of Western Literature*. Continuum, 1987. $29.50.

Marowski, Daniel G., and Roger Matuz, ed., *Contemporary Literary Criticism*. Gale, 1987. Vol. XLII. $90; Vols. XLIII and XLV. $92 each.

Marsh, Nicholas, *How to Begin Studying English Literature*. Macmillan, 1987. pb £4.95.

Martindale, Charles, *Ovid Renewed: Ovidian Influences on Literature and Art from the Middle Ages to the Twentieth Century*. CUP, 1988. £29.50.

May, Hal, ed., *Contemporary Authors*. Gale, 1987. Vols. CXIX and CXX. $90 each; Vol. CXXI. $92.

May, Keith M., *Nietzsche and Modern Literature: Themes in Yeats, Rilke, Mann and Lawrence*. Macmillan, 1988. £27.50.

Nakamura, Joyce, ed., *High-Interest Books for Teens: A Guide to Book Reviews and Biographical Sources*. Gale, 1988. $95.

Patterson, Annabel, *Pastoral and Ideology: Virgil to Valery*. Clarendon, 1988. £35.

Peck, John, *How to Study a Poet*. Macmillan, 1988. pb £4.95.

Person, James E., ed., *Literature Criticism from 1400 to 1800*. Gale, 1987. Vol. V. $88; Vol. VI. $92.

Pine, Richard, *The Dandy and the Herald: Manners, Mind and Morals from Brummell to Durrell*. Macmillan, 1988. £27.50.

Rustin, Margaret, and Michael Rustin, *Narratives of Love and Loss: Studies in Modern Children's Fiction*. Verso, 1987. hb £22.95, pb £7.95.

Salomon, Roger B., *Desperate Storytelling: Post-Romantic Elaborations of the Mock-Heroic Mode*. UGeo, 1987. $32.50.

Sarkissian, Adele, ed., *Contemporary Authors Autobiography Series*, Vol. V. Gale, 1987. $85; Vol. VI. Gale, 1988. $88.

Schatzberg, Walter, Ronald A. Waite, and Jonathan K. Johnson, ed., *The Relations of Literature and Science: An Annotated Bibliography of Scholarship, 1880–1980*. MLA, 1987. hb £40, pb $19.75.

Senick, Gerard J., ed., *Children's Literature Review*, Vols. XII and XIII. Gale, 1987. $80 each.

Storey, Mark, ed., *Poetry and Ireland Since 1800: A Source Book*. RKP, 1988. hb £27.50, pb £8.95.

Turner, Peter, *Issues: A Course Book for Advanced Level English Language*. Arnold, 1987. pb £6.50.

Valenzuela, Luisa, *The Lizard's Tail*. Serpent's Tail, 1987. pb £7.95.

Vickers, Brian, *English Science, Bacon to Newton*. CUP, 1987. hb £27.50, pb £9.95.

Chapter II. Literary Theory

Adorno, Theodor, *Philosophy of Modern Music*. Sheed&Ward, 1987. pb £6.95.

Arac, Jonathan, *Critical Genealogies: Historical Situations for Postmodern Literary Studies*. ColU, 1987. $32.50.

Armstrong, Nancy, and Leonard Tennenhouse, ed., *The Ideology of Conduct: Essays in Literature and the History of Sexuality*. Metheuen, 1987. hb £20, pb £7.95.

Bakhtin, M. M., *'Speech Genres' and Other Late Essays*, ed. by Caryl Emerson and Michael Holquist. UTex, 1986. $25.

Baldick, Chris, *The Social Mission of English Criticism, 1848–1932*. OUP, 1987. pb £8.95.

Barrell, John, *Poetry, Language and Politics*. ManU, 1988. hb £21.50, pb £5.95.

Barry, Kevin, *Language, Music and the Sign: A Study in Aesthetics, Poetics and Poetic Practice from Collins to Coleridge*. CUP, 1987. £25.

Barry, Peter, *Issues in Contemporary Critical Theory*. Macmillan, 1987. hb £20, pb £6.95.

Barthes, Roland, *Michelet*. Blackwell, 1987. pb £8.95.

Baudrillard, Jean, *Forget Foucault*. Semiotext (e), 1987. pb $3.95.

Bennington, Geoffrey, *Lyotard: Writing the Event*. ManU, 1987. £22.50.

Bjørhovde, Gerd, *Rebellious Structures: Women Writers and the Crisis of the Novel 1880–1900*. OUP, 1987. £19.50.

Borgmeier, Ulrich, ed., *Gattungsproblem in der anglo-amerikanischen Literatur: Beiträge für Ulrich Suerbaum zu seinem 60. Geburtstaq*. Niemeyer, 1986. DM 118.

Bowie, Malcolm, *Freud, Proust and Lacan: Theory as Fiction*. CUP, 1987. £25.

Brenkman, John, *Culture and Domination*. CornU, 1987. $24.95.

Brooker, Peter, *Bertolt Brecht: Dialectics, Poetry, Politics*. CH, 1988. £30.

Browne, Alice, *The Eighteenth Century Feminist Mind*. WSU, 1987. $25.

Bull, J. A., *The Framework of Fiction*. Macmillan, 1988. hb £20, pb £6.95.

Butler, Judith P., *Subjects of Desire: Hegelian Reflections in Twentieth-Century France*. ColU, 1987. £17.75.

Cascardi, Anthony J., *Literature and the Question of Philosophy*. JHU, 1987. £20.95.

Clarke, D. S., *Principles of Semiotic*. RKP, 1987. hb £15.95, pb £6.95.

Clément, Catherine, *The Weary Sons of Freud*. Verso, 1987. pb £6.95.

Deleuze, Gilles, *Foucault*. Athlone, 1988. £32.

Deleuze, Gilles, and Félix Guattari, *A Thousand Plateaus: Capitalism and Schizophrenia*, trans. and foreword by Brian Massumi. Athlone, 1988. hb £35, pb £16.

Derrida, Jacques, *The Archeology of the Frivolous: Reading Condillac*. UNeb, 1987. pb £7.55.

Derrida, Jacques, *Glas*. UNeb, 1987. £47.50.

DeSalvo, Louise, *Nathaniel Hawthorne*. Feminist Readings. Harvester, 1987. hb £18.95, pb £5.95.

Dews, Peter, *Logics of Disintegration: Post-Structuralist Thought and the Claims of Critical Theory*. Verso, 1987. pb £7.95.

Doane, Janice, and Devon Hodges, *Nostalgia and Sexual Difference: The Resistance to Contemporary Feminism*. Methuen, 1987. hb £20, pb £6.95.

Docherty, Thomas, *On Modern Authority: The Theory and Condition of Writing, 1500 to the Present Day*. Harvester, 1987. hb £18.95, pb £5.95.

Eagleton, Terry, *Saints and Scholars*. Verso, 1987. £9.95.

Elliott, Gregory, *Althusser: The Detour of Theory*. Verso, 1987. pb £10.95.

Epstein, William H., *Recognizing Biography*. UPenn, 1987. $29.95.

Foster, Dennis A., *Confession and Complicity in Narrative*. CUP, 1987. £20.

Foucault, Michel, *The Care of the Self*. Pantheon, 1986. $18.95.

Gelly, Alexander, *Narrative Crossings: Theory and Pragmatics of Prose Fiction*. JHU, 1987. £15.95.

Genette, Gérard, *Seuil*. Seuil, 1987. Ffr 150.

Greimas, A.-J., *On Meaning: Selected Writings in Semiotic Theory*. Pinter, 1987. £25.

Griffith, Peter, *Literary Theory and English Teaching*. OpenU, 1987. pb £7.95.

Gunn, Giles, *The Culture of Criticism and the Criticism of Culture*. OUP, 1987. £22.50.

Habermas, Jürgen, *The Philosophical Discourse of Modernity*. Polity, 1987. £25.

Harland, Richard, *Superstructuralism: The Philosophy of Structuralism and Post-Structuralism*. Methuen, 1987. pb £5.95.

Harris, Roy, *Reading Saussure*. Duckworth, 1987. pb £9.95.

Hawthorn, Jeremy, *Unlocking the Text: Fundamental Issues in Literary Theory*. Arnold, 1987. pb £4.95.

Holbrook, David, *The Novel and Authenticity*. Vision, 1987. £16.95.

Howells, Coral Ann, *Private and Fictional Words: Canadian Women Novelists of the 1970s and 1980s*. Methuen, 1987. pb £6.95.

Humm, Maggie, *An Annotated Critical Biography of Feminist Criticism*. Harvester, 1987. £45.

Hutcheon, Linda, *A Poetics of Postmodernism: History, Theory, Fiction*. RKP, 1988. £28.

Huyssen, Andreas, *After the Great Divide: Modernism, Mass Culture and Postmodernism*. Macmillan, 1988. hb £29.50, pb £8.95.

Jackson, Bernard S., *Semiotics and Legal Theory*. RKP, 1987. pb £7.95.

Jacobus, Mary, *Reading Woman: Essays in Feminist Criticism* (1986). Methuen, 1987. pb £8.95.

Jardine, Alice, and Paul Smith, ed., *Men in Feminism*. Methuen, 1987. hb £25, pb £7.95.

Jennings, Michael W., *Dialectical Images: Walter Benjamin's Theory of Literary Criticism*. CornU, 1987. $24.95.

Josipovici, Gabriel, *The Lessons of Modernism*. Second edn. Macmillan, 1987. hb £29.50, pb £9.95.

Kearney, Richard, *Modern Movements in European Philosophy*. ManU, 1986. £25.

Knapp, Bettina L., *Women in Twentieth-Century Literature: A Jungian View*. PSU, 1987. $24.95.

Koelb, Clayton, and Virgil Lokke, ed., *The Current in Criticism: Essays on the Present and Future of Literary Theory*. PurdueU, 1987. hb $27.50, pb $12.95.

Krieger, Murray, *The Aims of Representation: Subject/Text/History*. ColU, 1987. $35.

LaCapra, Dominick, *History, Politics, and the Novel*. CornU, 1987. $22.50.

Leavey, John P., *Glassary*. UNeb, 1987. $50.

Lee, Hermione, sel. and intro., *The Secret Self 2: Short Stories by Women*. Dent, 1987. pb £4.95.

Lentricchia, Frank, *Ariel and the Police: Michel Foucault, William James, Wallace Stevens*. Harvester, 1988. £29.95.

MacCabe, Colin, ed., *Futures for English*. ManU, 1988. hb £25, pb £7.50.

McCloskey, Mary A., *Kant's Aesthetic*. Macmillan, 1987. £27.50.

MacHale, Brian, *Postmodernist Fiction*. Methuen, 1987. pb £7.95.

Machin, Richard, and Christopher Norris, ed., *Post-Structuralist Readings of English Poetry*. CUP, 1987. hb £30, pb £10.95.

Mahony, Patrick, *Psychoanalysis and Discourse*. Tavistock, 1987. hb £25, pb £12.95.

Martin, Luther H., Huck Gutman, and Patrick H. Hutton, ed., *Technologies of the Self: A Seminar with Michel Foucault*. Tavistock, 1988. pb £8.95.

Meijis, Willem, *Corpus Linguistics and Beyond*. Rodopi, 1987. pb DM 75.

Merod, Jim, *The Political Responsibility of the Critic*. CornU, 1987. $24.95.

Michael, Ian, *The Teaching of English: From the Sixteenth Century to 1870*. CUP, 1987. £40.

Moi, Toril, ed., *French Feminist Thought: A Reader*. Blackwell, 1987. pb £8.95.

Nagele, Rainer, *Reading After Freud: Essays on Goethe, Hölderlin, Habermas, Nietzsche, Brecht, Celan, and Freud*. ColU, 1987. $29.

Nash, Christopher, *World Games: The Tradition of Anti-Realist Revolt*. Methuen, 1987. £39.50.

Norris, Christopher, *Derrida*. Fontana, 1987. pb £4.95.

Olsen, Stein Haugom, *The End of Literary Theory*. CUP, 1987. £25.

Pagnini, Marcello, *The Pragmatics of Literature*. IndU, 1987. $22.50.

Papadakis, Andreas C., *The New Modernism: Deconstructive Tendencies in Art*. AcademyE, 1988. pb £7.95.

Parker, Patricia, *Literary Fat Ladies: Rhetoric, Gender, Property*. Methuen, 1987. hb £28, pb £9.95.

Parrinder, Patrick, *The Failure of Theory: Essays on Criticism and Contemporary Fiction*. Harvester, 1987. £28.50.

Peterfreund, Stuart, *Culture/Criticism/Ideology*. NorthU, 1986. pb £5.65.

Pusey, Michael, *Jürgen Habermas*. Tavistock, 1987. pb £4.25.

Rabinowitz, Peter J., *Before Reading: Narrative Conventions and the Politics of Interpretation*. CornU, 1987. pb $8.95.

Rayan, Krishna, *Text and Sub-Text: Suggestion in Literature*. Arnold, 1987. £19.50.

Ree, Jonathan, *Philosophical Tales*. Methuen, 1987. pb £5.95.

Rigney, Barbara Hill, *Margaret Atwood*. Macmillan, 1987. hb £16, pb £4.95.

Rimmon-Kenan, Shlomith, *Discourse in Psychoanalysis and Literature*. Methuen, 1987. pb £7.95.

Roberts, Julian, *German Philosophy: An Introduction*. Polity, 1988. £27.50.

Roith, Estelle, *The Riddle of Freud: Jewish Influences on his Theory of Female Sexuality*. Tavistock, 1987. pb £10.95

Rotman, Brian, *Signifying Nothing: The Semiotics of Zero*. Macmillan, 1987. pb £10.95.

Rudnytsky, Peter L., *Freud and Oedipus*. ColU, 1987. $30.

Russell, Charles, *Poets, Prophets, and Revolutionaries: The Literary Avant-Garde from Rimbaud through Postmodernism*. OUP, 1987. pb £8.95.

Rylance, Rick, ed., *Debating Texts: A Reader in Twentieth-Century Literary Theory and Method*. OpenU, 1987. hb £22.50, pb £6.95.

Salusinszky, Imre, *Criticism in Society*. Methuen, 1987. pb £5.95.

Savile, Anthony, *Aesthetic Reconstructions*. Blackwell, 1987. £25.

Schleifer, Ronald, *A. J. Greimas and the Nature of Meaning: Linguistics, Semiotics and Discourse Theory*. CH, 1987. pb £8.95.

Schneiderman, Stuart, ed., *Returning to Freud: Clinical Psychoanalysis in the School of Lacan*. Yale, 1987. pb £8.95.

Schor, Naomi, *Reading in Detail: Aesthetics and the Feminine*. Methuen, 1987. hb £25, pb £8.95.

Scott, Bonnie Kime, *James Joyce*. Feminist Readings. Harvester, 1987. hb £18.95, pb £5.95.

Silverman, Hugh J., *Philosophy and Non-Philosophy Since Merleau-Ponty*. RKP, 1988. pb £9.95.

Sorenson, Dolf, *Theory Formation and the Study of Literature*. Rodopi, 1987. pb DM 70.

Spanos, William V., *Repetitions: The Postmodern Occasion in Literature and Culture*. LSU, 1987. £35.65.

Sprinker, Michael, *Imaginary Relations: Aesthetics and Ideology in the Theory of Historical Materialism*. Verso, 1987. £24.95.

Stratton, Jon, *The Virgin Text: Fiction, Sexuality and Ideology*. Harvester, 1987. hb £28.50, pb £9.95.

Swingewood, Alan, *Sociological Poetics and Aesthetic Theory*. Macmillan, 1987. hb £27.50. pb £8.95.

Szondi, Peter, *Theory of the Modern Drama*. Polity, 1987. pb £6.95.

Tallack, Douglas, ed., *Literary Theory at Work: Three Texts*. Batsford, 1987. hb £14.95, pb £6.95.

Tallis, Raymond, *Not Saussure: A Critique of Post-Saussurean Literary Theory*, Macmillan, 1988. pb £10.95.

Timms, Edward, and Peter Collier, *Visions and Blueprints: Avant-Garde Culture and Radical Politics in Early Twentieth-Century Europe*. ManU, 1988. £29.50.

Todorov, Tzvetan, *Literature and its Theorists: A Personal View of Twentieth-Century Criticism*. RKP, 1988. £19.95.

Udoff, Alan, ed., *Kafka and the Contemporary Critical Performance: Centenary Readings*. IndU, 1987. $27.50.

Valdés, Mario J., *Phenomenological Hermeneutics and the Study of Literature*. UTor, 1987. £17.50.

Warminski, Andrzej, *Readings in Interpretation: Hölderlin, Hegel, Heidegger*. UMinn, 1987. hb $29.50, pb $12.95.

Warnke, Georgia, *Gadamer: Hermeneutics, Tradition and Reason*. Polity, 1987. hb £25, pb £7.95.

Weber, Samuel, ed., *Demarcating the Disciplines: Philosophy, Literature, Art*. UMinn, 1986. hb $25, pb $11.95.

Weedon, Chris, *Feminist Practice and Poststructuralist Theory*. Blackwell, 1987. pb £6.95.

Welsch, Roger L., and Linda K. Welsch, *Cather's Kitchens: Foodways in Literature and Life*. UNeb, 1987. £16.10.

White, Hayden, *The Content of the Form: Narrative Discourse and Historical Representation*. JHU, 1987. £18.80.

Wilson, Katharina M., ed., *Women Writers of the Renaissance and the Reformation*. UGeo, 1987. hb $40, pb $19.95.

Chapter III. English Language

Allen, Harold B., and M. D. Linn, ed., *Dialect and Language Variation*. Academic, 1986. pb $24.95.

Anderson, John, and Jacques Durand, ed., *Explorations in Dependency Phonology*. Foris, 1987. hb Fl 90, pb Fl 54.

Anderson, John M., and N. Macleod, ed., *Edinburgh Studies in the English Language*. Donald, 1988. £18.

Anderson, Peter M., *A Structural Atlas of the English Dialects*. CH, 1987. £37.50.

Arndt, Horst, and Richard Wayne Janney, *InterGrammar: Toward an Integrative Model of Verbal, Prosodic and Kinesic Choices in Speech*. MGruyter, 1987. DM 185.

Asbach-Schnitker, B., and J. Roggenhofer, ed., *Neuere Forschungen Zur Wortbildung und Historiographie der Linguistik: Festschrift für Herbert Ernst Brekle*. Narr, 1987. DM 178.

Banks, R. A., and F. D. A. Burns, *Advanced Level English Language*. H&S, 1987. pb £6.95.

Barron, Dennis, *Language and Gender*. Yale, 1987. £8.95/$13.95.

Bartsch, Renate, *Norms of Language*. Longman, 1987. pb £9.95.

Bettinger, Elfi, and Thomas Meier-Fohrbeck, *Von Shakespeare bis Chomsky: Arbeiten zur Englischen Philologie an der Freien Universität Berlin*. Lang, 1987. Sfr 68.

Brown, Penelope, and S. Levinson, *Politeness: Some Universals in Language Usage*. CUP, 1987. pb £8.95.

Brumfit, Christopher, and Ronald Carter, ed., *Literature and Language Teaching*. OUP, 1986. pb £7.55.

Burke, Peter, and Roy Porter, ed., *The Social History of Language*. CUP, 1987. pb £25/$34.50.

Byrne, Frank, *Grammatical Relations in a Radical Creole*. Benjamins, 1987. $38.

Cook-Gumperz, Jenny, W. A. Corsaro, and J. Streeck, ed., *Children's Worlds and Children's Language*. MGruyter, 1986. DM 178.

Coupland, Nikolas, *Dialect in Use: Sociolinguistic Variation in Cardiff English*. UWales, 1988. £14.95.

Coupland, Nikolas, *Styles of Discourse*. CH, 1988. £35.

Cowan, William, Michael K. Foster, and Konrad Koerner, ed., *New Perspectives in Language, Culture, and Personality: Proceedings of the Edward Sapir Centenary Conference (Ottawa, 1–3 October 1984)*. Benjamins, 1987. Fl 170/$68.

Crombie, Winifred, *Free Verse and Prose Style*. CH, 1987. £25.

Davis, Lawrence M., *English Dialectology: An Introduction*. UAla, 1983. $10.95.

Dirven, René, and Günter Radden, ed., *Concepts of Case*. Narr, 1987. pb DM 56.

Dwyer, John, *Virtuous Discourse: Sensibility and Community in Late Eighteenth-Century Scotland*. Donald, 1987. £20.

Evans, A. Donald, and W. W. Falk, *Learning to be Deaf*. MGruyter, 1986. DM 128.

Fabb, Nigel, Derek Attridge, Alan Durant, and Colin MacCabe, ed., *The Linguistics of Writing*. ManU, 1987. £40.

Fishman, Joshua A., A. Tabouret-Keller, M. Clyne, B. Krishnamurti, and M. Abdulaziz, ed., *The Fergusonian Impact: In Honour of Charles A. Ferguson*. MGruyter, 1986. DM 435.

Freeborn, Dennis, *A Course Book in English Grammar*. Macmillan, 1987. hb £20, pb £6.95.

Gilbert, Glenn, G., ed., *Pidgin and Creole Languages: Essays in Memory of John E. Reinecke*. UHawaii, 1987. £33.25.

Greimas, Algirdas J., *On Meaning: Selected Writings on Semiotic Theory*. Pinter, 1987. £25.

Halliday, M. A. K., and R. P. Fawcett, ed., *New Developments in Systemic Linguistics*. Vol. I: *Theory and Description*. Pinter, 1987. £28.50.

Harris, Martin, and Paolo Ramat, ed., *Historical Development of Auxiliaries*. TiLSM. Gruyter, 1987. DM 145.

Hogg, Richard, and C. B. McCully, *Metrical Phonology: A Coursebook*. CUP, 1987. hb £27.50, pb £9.95.

Hudson, Richard, *Word Grammar* (1984). Blackwell, 1986. hb £27.50, pb £7.95.

Hughes, Arthur, and P. Trudgill, *English Accents and Dialects: An Introduction to Social and Regional Varieties of British English*. Second edn. Arnold, 1987. pb £4.95.

Jakobson, Roman, and Linda R. Waugh, with Martha Taylor, *The Sound Shape of Language*. Second edn. MGruyter, 1987. DM 48/$19.95.

Jones, Malcolm, and P. Dillon, *Dialect in Wiltshire*. Wiltshire County Council Library and Museum Service, 1987. pb £7.95.

Joseph, John E., *Eloquence and Power: The Rise of Language Standards and Standard Languages*. Pinter, 1987. £28.50.

Knowles, Gerald, *Patterns of Spoken English: An Introduction to English Phonetics*. Longman, 1987. pb £6.95.

Kristensson, Gillis, *A Survey of Middle English Dialects 1290–1350: The West Midland Counties*. LundU, 1987.

Laine, Eero J., *Affective Factors in Foreign Language Learning and Teaching: A Study of the 'Filter'*. English Dept, JyväskyläU, 1987. pb.

Lass, Roger, *The Shape of English: Structure and History*. Dent, 1987. £30.

Leech, Geoffrey N., *Meaning and the English Verb* (1971). Second edn. Longman, 1987. pb £5.50.

Logue, Calvin M., and H. Dorgan, ed., *A New Diversity in Contemporary Southern Rhetoric*. LSU, 1987. £30.90.

Macafee, Caroline, and I. Macleod, ed., *The Nuttis Schell Essays on the Scots Language Presented to A. J. Aitken*. AberdeenU, 1987. £19.50.

MacCabe, Colin, ed., *Futures for English*. ManU, 1988. pb £7.50.

Milroy, Lesley, *Language and Social Networks*. Second edn. Blackwell, 1987. pb £8.95.

Milroy, Lesley, *Observing and Analysing Natural Language: A Critical Account of Sociolinguistic Method*. Blackwell, 1987. pb £8.95.

Monaghan, James, ed., *Grammar in the Construction of Texts*. Pinter, 1987. £25.

Montgomery, Michael B., and G. Bailey, ed., *Language Variety in the South: Perspectives in Black and White*. UAla, 1986. $29.95.

Nehls, Dietrich, ed., *Interlanguage Studies*. Groos, 1988. pb DM 66.

Opie, Iona, and P. Opie, *The Lore and Language of Schoolchildren*. OUP, 1987. pb £4.95.

Page, Norman, *Speech in the English Novel* (1973). Second edn. Macmillan, 1988. £25.

Palmer, F. R., *Mood and Modality*. CUP, 1986. hb £25, pb £8.95.

Pateman, Trevor, *Language in Mind and Langauge in Society: Studies in Linguistic Reproduction*. OUP, 1987. £25.

Philips, Susan U., S. Steele, and C. Tanz, ed., *Language, Gender and Sex in Comparative Perspective*. CUP, 1987. pb £9.95.

Postal, Paul M., *Studies of Passive Clauses*. SUNY, 1986. hb $49.50, pb $24.50.

Preisler, Bent, *Linguistic Sex Roles in Conversation*. MGruyter, 1986. DM 128.

Rickford, John R., *Dimensions of a Creole Continuum: History, Texts, and Linguistic Analysis of Guyanese Creole*. Stanford, 1987. $42.50.

Roberts, Peter A., *West Indians and their Language*. CUP, 1988. pb £8.95.

Roberts, Philip Davies, *How Poetry Works*. Penguin, 1986. pb £3.95.

Romaine, Suzanne, *Pidgin and Creole Languages*. Longman, 1988. pb £9.95.

Russom, Geoffrey, *Old English Meter and Linguistic Theory*. CUP, 1987. £22.50.

Ryden, Mats, and Sverker Brorström, *The Be/Have Variation with Intransitives in Engish, with Special Reference to the Late Modern Period*. SSEL. A&W, 1987. pb £17.50.

Sajavaara, Kari, *Application of Cross-Language Analaysis*. English Dept, JyväskyläU, 1987. pb.

Schiffrin, Deborah, *Discourse Markers*. CUP, 1987. £30.

Schogt, Henry G., *Linguistics, Literary Analysis, and Literary Translation*. UTor, 1988. £21.

Sebba, Mark, *The Syntax of Serial Verbs*. Benjamins, 1987. $32.

Sebeok, Thomas, and J. Umiker-Sebeok, ed., *The Semiotic Web 1986*. MGruyter, 1987. DM 248.

Shuman, Amy, *Storytelling Rights: The Uses of Oral and Written Texts by Urban Adolescents*. CUP, 1987. £25.

Siegel, Jeff, *Language Contact in a Plantation Environment: A Sociolinguistic Study of Fiji*. CUP, 1987. £30.

Sneck, Seppo, *Assessment of Chronography in Finnish–English Telephone Conversation: An Attempt at a Computer Analysis*. English Dept, JyväskyläU, 1987. pb.

Sørensen, Knud, *Charles Dickens: Linguistic Innovator*. Arkona, 1985. pb.

Swiggers, Pierre, *Grammaire et Théorie du Langage au 18e siècle: MOT, TEMPS & MODE dans l'Encyclopédie Méthodique*. ULille, 1986. Ffr 90.

Tristram, Hildegard, Brigitte Gulden, Axel Koberne, and Joachim Thurow, ed., *Sound, Sense, and System: Herbert Pilch and Postwar German Studies in English Linguistics (1955–1985)*. CWU, 1987. DM 130.

Trudgill, Peter, *Coping with America*. Second edn. Blackwell, 1985. pb £4.95.

Umiker-Sebeok, Jean, and T. A. Sebeok, ed., *Monastic Sign Languages*. MGruyter, 1987. DM 228.

Upton, Clive, S. Sanderson, and J. Widdowson, *Word Maps: A Dialect Atlas of England*. CH, 1987. pb £11.95.

Urdang, Laurence, and Frank R. Abate, *Loanwords Dictionary*. Gale, 1988. $80.

Ventola, Eija, *The Structure of Social Action: A Systemic Approach to the Semiotics of Service Encounters*. Pinter, 1987. £29.50.

Wardhaugh, Ronald, *Languages in Competition: Dominance, Diversity, and Decline*. Blackwell, 1987. pb £9.50.

Wilson, Kenneth G., *Van Winkle's Return: Change in American English, 1966–1986*. UPNE, 1987. pb £7.95.

Chapter IV. Old English Literature

Arnold, C. J., *An Archaeology of the Early Anglo-Saxon Kingdoms*. RKP, 1988. £27.50.

Bodden, Mary-Catherine, ed. and trans., *The Old English Finding of the True Cross*. Brewer, 1987. £22.50.

Brown, George Hardin, *Bede the Venerable*. Twayne, 1987. $19.95.

Calder, Daniel G., and T. Craig Christy, ed., *Germania: Comparative Studies in the Old Germanic Languages and Literatures*. Brewer, 1988. £35.

Campbell, James, *Essays in Anglo-Saxon History*. Hambledon, 1987. £22.

Heffernan, Carol Falvo, *The Phoenix at the Fountain: Images of Woman and Eternity in Lactantius's 'Carmen de Ave Phonice' and the Old English 'Phoenix'*. UDel/AUP, 1988. £20.

Mandel, Jerome, *Alternative Readings in Old English Poetry*. Lang, 1987. $34.50.

Simon-Vandenbergen, A. M., ed., *Studies in Honour of René Derolez*. Seminarie voor Engelse en Oud-Germaanse Taalkunde. UGhent, 1987. pb Bfr 1500.

Stanley, Eric Gerald, *A Collection of Papers with Emphasis on Old English Literature*. PIMS, 1987. pb $35.

Sturluson, Snorri, *Edda*, trans. and intro. by Anthony Faulkes. Dent, 1987. pb £4.95.

Todd, Malcolm, *The South West to AD 1000*. Longman, 1987. pb £12.

Chapter V. Middle English: Excluding Chaucer

Arn, Mary-Jo, and Hanneke Wirtjes, with Hans Jansen, ed., *Historical and Editorial Studies in Medieval and Early Modern English*. Wo-No, 1985. Fl 62.25.

Arthur, Ross G., *Medieval Sign Theory and 'Sir Gawain and the Green Knight'*. UTor, 1987. $28.50.

Bald, Wolf-Dietrich, and Horst Weinstock, ed., *Medieval Studies Conference Aachen 1983*. Lang, 1983. pb.

Bullock-Davies, Constance, *A Register of Royal and Baronial Domestic Minstrels 1272–1327*. B&B, 1986. £29.50.

Davies, Peter V., and Angus J. Kennedy, ed., *Rewards and Punishments in the Arthurian Romances and Lyric Poetry of Mediaeval France*. Arthurian Studies. Brewer, 1987. £35.

Dean, Christopher, *Arthur of England: English Attitudes to King Arthur and the Knights of the Round Table in the Middle Ages and the Renaissance.* UTor, 1987. £17.50.

Fewster, Carol, *Traditionality and Genre in Middle English Romance.* Brewer, 1987. £29.50.

Rigg, A. G., ed., *Gawain on Marriage: The 'De Coniuge Non Ducenda'.* PIMS, 1986. pb.

Sheingorn, Pamela, *The Easter Sepulchre in England.* MIP, 1987. hb $37.95, pb $17.95.

Smithers, G.V., ed., *Havelok.* Clarendon, 1987. £45.

Spearing, A. C., *Readings in Medieval Poetry.* CUP, 1987. £27.50.

Thompson, John J., *Robert Thornton and the London Thornton Manuscript: British Library MS Additional 31042.* B&B, 1987. £39.50.

Tissier, André, ed., *Recueil de Farces (1450–1550).* Droz, 1987. pb.

Tricomi, Albert H., ed., *Early Drama to 1600.* CMERS, 1987. pb.

Wickham, Glynne, *The Medieval Theatre.* CUP, 1987. pb £7.95.

Chapter VI. Middle English: Chaucer

Bishop, Ian, *The Narrative Art of the 'Canterbury Tales': A Critical Study of the Major Poems.* Dent, 1987. hb £15, pb £5.95.

Bowden, Betsy, *Chaucer Aloud: The Varieties of Textual Interpretation.* UPenn, 1987. $44.95.

Chaucer, Geoffrey, *The Riverside Chaucer.* Third edn, ed. by Larry D. Benson. HoughtonM, 1987. $45.95; OUP, 1988. pb £8.95.

Chaucer, Geoffrey, *Troilus and Criseyde* (1974), ed. by John Warrington. Dent, 1988. pb £3.95.

Chaucer, Geoffrey, *A Variorum Edition of the Works of Geoffrey Chaucer.* Vol. II: *The Canterbury Tales.* Part 20: *The Prioress's Tale,* ed. by Beverly Boyd. UOkla, 1987. $38.50.

Fichte, Joerg O., ed., *Chaucer's Frame Tales: The Physical and the Metaphysical.* Narr/Brewer, 1987. £25.

Howard, Donald R., *Chaucer and the Medieval World.* W&N, 1987. £16.95.

Jordan, Robert M., *Chaucer's Poetics and the Modern Reader.* UCal, 1987. £19.95.

Kratzmann, G., and J. Simpson, ed., *Medieval English Religious and Ethical Literature: Essays in Honour of G. H. Russell.* Brewer, 1986. £27.50.

Lindahl, Carl, *Earnest Games: Folkloric Patterns in the 'Canterbury Tales'.* IndU, 1987. $25.

Stokes, Myra, and T. L. Burton, ed., *Medieval Literature and Antiquities: Studies in Honour of Basil Cottle.* Brewer, 1987. £29.50.

Stone, Brian, *Chaucer: A Critical Study.* PM. Penguin, 1987. pb £2.95.

Chapter VII. The Sixteenth Century: Excluding Drama After 1550

Buxton, John, *Sir Philip Sidney and the English Renaissance.* Macmillan, 1988. hb £29.50, pb £12.95.

Fox, A., and G. Waite, ed., *A Concordance to the Complete English Poems of John Skelton.* CornU, 1987. $49.50.

Heale, Elizabeth, *'The Faerie Queene': A Reader's Guide*. CUP, 1987. hb £22.50, pb £6.95.

Kay, D., ed., *Sir Philip Sidney: An Anthology of Modern Criticism*. Clarendon, 1987. £35.

Sidney, Sir Philip, *The Countess of Pembroke's Arcadia: The New Arcadia*, ed. by V. Skretkowicz. OUP, 1987. £65.

Zim, Rivkah, *English Metrical Psalms: Poetry as Praise and Prayer 1535–1601*. CUP, 1987. £35.

Chapter VIII. Shakespeare

Adamson, Jane, *'Troilus and Cressida'*. Harvester, 1987. hb £22.50, pb £7.95.

Boorman, S. C., *Human Conflict in Shakespeare*. RKP, 1987. £25.

Bradshaw, Graham, *Shakespeare's Scepticism*. Harvester, 1987. £32.50.

Brennan, Anthony, *Shakespeare's Dramatic Structures*. RKP, 1988. pb £6.95.

Cavell, Stanley, *Disowning Knowledge in Six Plays of Shakespeare*. CUP, 1987. hb £25, pb £8.95.

Clemen, Wolfgang, *Shakespeare's Soliloquies*. Methuen, 1987. hb £25, pb £6.95.

Dubrow, Heather, *Captive Victors: Shakespeare's Narrative Poems and Sonnets*. CornU, 1987. $32.95.

Fleissner, Robert F., *The Prince and the Professor: The Wittenberg Connection in Marlowe, Shakespeare, Goethe, and Frost: A Hamlet/Faust (us) Analogy*. CWU, 1986. pb DM 32.

Gallatin, Michael, *Shakespearean Alchemy: Theme and Variations in Literary Criticism*. QED, 1985. hb $16.95, pb $9.95.

Garber, Marjorie, *Shakespeare's Ghost Writers: Literature as Uncanny Causality*. Methuen, 1987. hb £22.50, pb £7.95.

Goy-Blanquet, Dominique, *Le roi mis a nu: l'histoire d'Henri VI de Hall a Shakespeare*. Didier, 1986. pb.

Griswold, Wendy, *Renaissance Revivals: City Comedy and Revenge Tragedy in the London Theatre, 1576–1980*. UChic, 1986. £30.

Hamilton, Charles, *In Search of Shakespeare: A Study of the Poet's Life and Handwriting*. Hale, 1986. £16.95.

Hassel, R. Chris, Jr, *Songs of Death: Performance, Interpretation, and the Text of 'Richard III'*. UNeb, 1987. £20.85.

Hawkins, Harriett, *'Measure for Measure'*. Harvester, 1987. hb £22.50, pb £7.95.

Holderness, Graham, ed., *The Shakespeare Myth*. ManU, 1988. pb £5.95.

Holderness, Graham, Nick Potter, and John Turner, *Shakespeare: The Play of History*. Macmillan, 1988. £27.50.

Howard, Jean E., and Marion F. O'Connor, ed., *Shakespeare Reproduced: The Text in History and Ideology*. Methuen, 1987. hb £28, pb £9.95.

Jones-Davies, M. T., ed., *Le Roman de Chevalerie au Temps de la Renaissance*. Touzot, 1987.

Kott, Jan, *The Bottom Translation*. Northwestern, 1987. hb $32.95, pb $14.95.

Leggatt, Alexander, *Shakespeare's Political Drama: The History Plays and the Roman Plays*. RKP, 1988. £27.50.

Lindenbaum, Peter, *Changing Landscapes: Anti-Pastoral Sentiment in the English Renaissance*. UGeo, 1987. $27.50.

Lomax, Marion, *Stage Images and Traditions: Shakespeare to Ford*. CUP, 1987. £27.50.

McGee, Arthur, *The Elizabethan Hamlet*. Yale, 1987. £14.95.

Mackinnon, Lachlan, *Shakespeare the Aesthete: An Exploration of Literary Theory*. Macmillan, 1988. £27.50.

Mahon, John W., and Thomas A. Pendleton, ed., *'Fanned and Winnowed Opinions': Shakespearean Essays Presented to Harold Jenkins*. Methuen, 1987. £32.

Manley, Lawrence, ed., *London in the Age of Shakespeare: An Anthology*. CH, 1986. £25.

Montano, Rocco, *Shakespeare's Concept of Tragedy: The Bard as Anti-Elizabethan*. Gateway Edns: Contemporary, 1985. pb $12.

Nevo, Ruth, *Shakespeare's Other Language*. Methuen, 1987. £25.

Orkin, Martin, *Shakespeare against Apartheid*. Donker, 1987.

Poole, Adrian, *Tragedy: Shakespeare and the Greek Example*. Blackwell, 1987. £19.50.

Rowse, A. L., *Shakespeare the Man*. Rev. edn. Macmillan, 1988. £18.95.

Sanders, Wilbur, *'The Winter's Tale'*. Harvester, 1987. hb £22.50. pb £7.95.

Schoenbaum, S., *William Shakespeare: A Compact Documentary Life*. Rev. edn. OUPAm, 1987. pb $13.95.

Scott, Mark W., ed., *Shakespearean Criticism: Excerpts from the Criticism of William Shakespeare's Plays and Poetry, from the First Published Appraisals to Current Evaluations*. Gale, 1987. Vols. IV and V. $85 each; Vol. VI. $92.

Scragg, Leah, *Discovering Shakespeare's Meaning*. Macmillan, 1988. £27.50.

Shakespeare, William, *Hamlet*, ed. by G. R. Hibbard. OS. Clarendon, 1987. £19.50.

Shakespeare, William, *Henry IV Part 1*, ed. by David Bevington. OS. Clarendon, 1987. £19.50.

Shakespeare, William, *The Merchant of Venice*, ed. by M. M. Mahood. NCaS. CUP, 1987. hb £15, pb £2.95.

Shakespeare, William, *Much Ado About Nothing*, ed. by F. H. Mares. NCaS. CUP, 1988. hb £15, pb £2.95.

Shakespeare, William, *An Oxford Anthology of Shakespeare*, ed. by Stanley Wells. OUP, 1987. £12.95.

Shakespeare, William, *The Songs and Sonnets of William Shakespeare* (1915), illus. by Charles Robinson. Lamboll, 1987. £9.95.

Shakespeare, William, *The Sonnets*, illus. by Ian Penney. B&J, 1988. £10.95.

Shakespeare, William, *The Tempest*, ed. by Stephen Orgel. OS. Clarendon, 1987. £19.50.

Shakespeare, William, *Troilus and Cressida*, ed. by R. A. Foakes. Penguin, 1987. pb £1.95.

Steiner, George, *A Reading against Shakespeare*. UGlas, 1986. pamphlet £1.

Stockholder, Kay, *Dream Works: Lovers and Families in Shakespeare's Plays*. UTor, 1987. $35.

Sturgess, Keith, *Jacobean Private Theatre*. RKP, 1987. £30.

Weiser, David K., *Mind in Character: Shakespeare's Speaker in the Sonnets*. UMiss, 1987. $24.

Chapter IX. Renaissance Drama: Excluding Shakespeare

Anderson, Donald K., Jr, ed., *'Concord in Discord': The Plays of John Ford, 1586–1986*. AMS, 1986. $34.50.

Barthelemy, Anthony Gerard, *Black Face, Maligned Race: The Representation of Blacks in English Drama from Skakespeare to Southerne*. LSU, 1987. $27.50.

Beaumont, Francis, and John Fletcher, *The Maid's Tragedy*, ed. by T. W. Craik. Revels. ManU, 1988. £29.50.

Berry, Herbert, *Shakespeare's Playhouses*. AMS, 1987. $34.50.

Cave, Richard Allen, *'The White Devil' and 'The Duchess of Malfi': Text and Performance*. Macmillan, 1988. pb £4.95.

Chapman, George, *The Plays of George Chapman: The Tragedies with 'Sir Gyles Goosecappe'*, gen. ed. Allan Holaday. Brewer, 1987. £60.

Clark, Sandra, *John Webster: 'The White Devil' and 'The Duchess of Malfi'*. PM. Penguin, 1987. pb £2.50.

Coles, Chris, *How to Study a Renaissance Play: Marlowe, Jonson, Webster*. Macmillan, 1988. pb £4.95.

Empson, William, *Faustus and the Censor: The English Faust-Book and Marlowe's 'Doctor Faustus'*, ed. by John Henry Jones. Blackwell, 1987. £17.50.

Farley-Hills, David, *Jacobean Drama: A Critical Survey of the Professional Drama, 1600–25*. Macmillan, 1988. £29.50.

Fricker, Robert, *Das ältere englische Schauspiel*. Vol. III: *Ben Jonson bis Richard Brome*. Francke, 1987. Sfr 68/DM 82.

Gurr, Andrew, *Playgoing in Shakespeare's London*. CUP, 1987. £27.50.

Honigmann, E. A. J., *John Weever: A Biography of a Literary Associate of Shakespeare and Jonson, together with a Photographic Facsimile of Weever's 'Epigrammes' (1599)*. RevelsCL. ManU, 1987. £27.50.

Jonson, Ben, *The Alchemist*, ed. by Peter Bement. Methuen, 1987. pb £4.95.

Leggatt, Alexander, *English Drama: Shakespeare to the Restoration, 1590–1650*. Longman, 1988. pb £6.95.

Lever, J. W., *The Tragedy of State: A Study of Jacobean Drama (1971), intro. by Jonathan Dollimore. Methuen, 1987. pb £4.95*.

Lomax, Marion, *Stage Images and Traditions: Shakespeare to Ford*. CUP, 1987. £22.50.

McMillin, Scott, *The Elizabethan Theatre and 'The Book of Sir Thomas More'*. CornU, 1987. $17.95.

Maguire, Nancy Klein, ed., *Renaissance Tragicomedy: Explorations in Genre and Politics*. AMS, 1987. $34.50.

Mangan, Michael, *Christopher Marlowe: 'Doctor Faustus'*. PM. Penguin, 1987. pb £2.50.

Mercer, Peter, *'Hamlet' and the Acting of Revenge*. Macmillan, 1987. £27.50.

Middleton, Thomas, and Thomas Dekker, *The Roaring Girl*, ed. by Paul Mulholland. Revels. ManU, 1987. £35.

Shepherd, Simon, *Marlowe and the Politics of Elizabethan Theatre* (1986). Harvester, 1988. pb £9.95.

Streitberger, W. R., ed., *Jacobean and Caroline Revels Accounts, 1603–1642*. MSR. MS, 1986.

Sturgess, Keith, *Jacobean Private Theatre*. RKP, 1987. £30.
Wharton, T.F., *Moral Experiment in Jacobean Drama*. Macmillan, 1988.
    £27.50.

Chapter X. The Earlier Seventeenth Century: Excluding Drama

Brennan, Michael G., *Literary Patronage in the English Renaissance: The*
    Pembroke Family. RKP, 1988. £25.
Cook, Elizabeth, *Seeing through Words: The Scope of Late Renaissance*
    Poetry. Yale, 1986. $20.
Edmond, Mary, *Rare Sir William Davenant*. ManU, 1987. £27.50.
Quarles, Francis, *Argalus and Parthenia*, ed. by David Freeman. AUP, 1988.
    £12.50.
Ryley, George, *Mr. Herbert's 'Temple' and 'Church Militant' Improved and*
    Explained, ed. by Maureen Boyd and Cedric C. Brown. Garland, 1987.
Singleton, Marion White, *God's Courtier: Configuring a Different Grace in*
    George Herbert's 'Temple'. CUP, 1988. £27.50.
Summers, Claude, and Ted-Larry Pebworth, ed., *The Eagle and the Dove:*
    Reassessing John Donne. UMiss, 1986. $24.
Vickers, Brian, ed., *English Science, Bacon to Newton*. CUP, 1987. hb £27.50,
    pb £9.95.
Wilding, Michael, *Dragons Teeth: Literature in the English Revolution*.
    Clarendon, 1987. £25.

Chapter XI. Milton

Bernard, John D., ed., *Vergil at 2000: Commemorative Essays on the Poet and*
    his Influence. AMS, 1986. £39.50.
Cardwell, Richard A., and Janet Hamilton, ed., *Virgil in a Cultural Tradition:*
    Essays to celebrate the Bimillenium. UNott, 1986. pb £7.50.
Dahiyat, Eid Abdallah, *John Milton and Arab–Islamic Culture*. S&A, 1987.
Griffin, Dustin, *Regaining Paradise: Milton and the Eighteenth Century*.
    CUP, 1986. £27.50.
Grossman, Marshall, *'Authors to Themselves': Milton and the Revelation of*
    History. CUP, 1987. £25.
Hartmann, Geoffrey H., and Sanford Budick, ed., *Midrash and Literature*.
    Yale, 1986. £30.
Macdonald, Ronald R., *The Burial-Places of Memory: Epic Underworlds in*
    Vergil, Dante and Milton. UMass, 1987. £17.50.
Nyquist, Mary, and Margaret W. Ferguson, ed., *Re-membering Milton: Essays*
    on the Texts and Tradition. Methuen, 1987. hb £30, pb £14.95.
Rumrich, John Peter, *Matter of Glory: A New Preface to 'Paradise Lost'*.
    UPitt, 1987.
Sacks, Peter M., *The English Elegy: Studies in the Genre from Spenser to Yeats*
    (1985). JHU, 1987. pb £7.75.
Steadman, John M., *Milton and the Paradoxes of Renaissance Heroism*. LSU,
    1987. £30.90.
Swaim, Katheleen M., *Before and After the Fall: Contrasting Modes in*
    'Paradise Lost'. UMass, 1986. £22.

Wilding, Michael, *Dragons Teeth: Literature in the English Revolution*. Clarendon, 1987. £25.

Chapter XII. The Later Seventeenth Century

Ashcraft, Richard, *Revolutionary Politics and Locke's 'Two Treatises of Government'*. Princeton, 1986. £23.90.

Astell, Mary, *The First English Feminist: 'Reflections upon Marriage' and Other Writings*, ed. by Bridget Hill. Gower, 1986. £24.

Bunyan, John, *Grace Abounding*, ed. by W. R. Owens. Penguin, 1987. pb £2.95.

Bunyan, John, *The Miscellaneous Works*. Vol. III: *'Christian Behaviour'; 'The Holy City'; 'The Resurrection of the Dead'*. ed. by J. Sears McGee. Clarendon, 1987. £40.

Burns, Edward, *Restoration Comedy: Crises of Desire and Identity*. Macmillan, 1987. £27.50.

Collier, Jeremy, *A Short View of the Immorality and Profaneness of the English Stage*, intro. by Arthur Freeman. Garland, 1972. $61.

Danchin, Pierre, ed., *The Prologues and Epilogues of the Restoration 1660-1700*. Part III: *1691-1700*. UNancy, 1987. pb Ffr 650.

Flecknoe, Richard, *The Prose Characters of Richard Flecknoe: A Critical Edition*, ed. by Fred Mayer. Garland, 1987. $95.

Haley, K. H. D., *An English Diplomat in the Low Countries: Sir William Temple and John De Witt, 1665-1672*. Clarendon, 1986. £35.

Jones, Kathleen, *A Glorious Fame: The Life of Margaret Cavendish, Duchess of Newcastle, 1623-1673*. Bloomsbury, 1988. £15.95.

McGugan, Ruth, *Nahum Tate and the Coriolanus Tradition in English Drama. With a Critical Edition of Tate's 'The Ingratitude of a Common-Wealth'*. Garland, 1987.

Mendelson, Sara Heller, *The Mental World of Stuart Women*. Harvester, 1987. £30.

Osborne, Dorothy, *Letters to Sir William Temple*, ed. by Kenneth Parker. Penguin, 1987. pb £5.95.

Sharpe, Kevin, and Steven N. Zwicker, ed., *Politics of Discourse: The Literature and History of Seventeenth-Century England*. UCal, 1987. pb $19.95.

Southerne, Thomas, *The Works of Thomas Southerne*, Vol. II, ed. by Robert Jordan and Harold Love. Clarendon, 1988. £48.

Vanbrugh, John, *The Confederacy*, ed. by Thomas E. Lowderbaugh. Garland, 1987.

Winn, James Anderson, *John Dryden and his World*. Yale, 1987. £19.95.

Chapter XIII. The Eighteenth Century

Allen, Brian, *Francis Hayman*. Yale, 1987. £20.

Atkins, G. Douglas, *Quests of Difference: Reading Pope's Poems*. UKen, 1986. $19.

Battestin, Martin C., and J. Paul Hunter, *Henry Fielding in his Time and Ours*. CML, 1987. pb $8.

Beckford, William, *The Grand Tour of William Beckford: Selections from 'Dreams, Waking Thoughts and Incidents'*, ed. by Elizabeth Mavor Penguin, 1986. pb £3.95.

Bevis, Richard W., *English Drama: Restoration and Eighteenth Century 1660–1789*. Longman, 1988. pb £7.95.

Bloom, Harold, ed., *Jonathan Swift: Modern Critical Views*. ChelseaH, 1986 $19.95.

Brophy, Elizabeth Bergen, *Samuel Richardson*. Twayne, 1987. $18.95.

Browne, Alice, *The Eighteenth Century Feminist Mind*. Harvester, 1987 £28.50.

Burke, Edmund, *A Philosophical Enquiry into the Origin of our Ideas of the Sublime and Beautiful*, ed. by James T. Boulton (1958). Rev. edn. Blackwell, 1987. pb £8.95.

Carnochan, W. B., *Gibbon's Solitude: The Inward World of the Historian* Stanford, 1987. $29.50.

Carter, Jennifer J., and Joan H. Pittock, ed., *Aberdeen and the Enlightenment*. AberdeenU, 1987. pb £14.90.

Christensen, Jerome, *Practicing Enlightenment: Hume and the Formation of a Literary Career*. UWisc, 1987. pb £16.65.

Cibber, Colley, *A Critical Edition of 'An Apology for the Life of Mr Colley Cibber, Comedian'*, ed. by J. M. Evans. Garland, 1987.

Cibber, Colley, *The Double Gallant*, ed. by John Whitley Bruton. Garland 1987.

Clifford, James L., *Hester Lynch Piozzi (Mrs Thrale)* (second edn, 1952), intro. by Margaret Anne Doody. Clarendon, 1987. pb £12.50.

Cohn, Jan, *Romance and the Erotics of Property*. DukeU, 1988. £27.95.

Cowper, William, *The Letters and Prose Writings of William Cowper*. Vol. V: *Prose 1756–c. 1799 and Cumulative Index*, ed. by James King and Charles Ryskamp. Clarendon, 1986. £30.

Cumberland, Richard, *Richard Cumberland's 'The Wheel of Fortune': A Critical Edition*, ed. by T. J. Campbell. Garland, 1987.

Dabydeen, David, *Hogarth, Walpole and Commercial Britain*. Hansib, 1987. £15.95.

Day, Geoffrey, *From Fiction to the Novel*. RKP, 1987. £18.95.

Devlin, D.D., *The Novels and Journals of Fanny Burney*. Macmillan, 1987. £25.

Dijkstra, Bram, *Defoe and Economics: The Fortunes of 'Roxana' in the History of Interpretation*. Macmillan, 1987. £29.50.

Douglas, William, *The Cornutor of Seventy-Five* (1748); and Tobias Smollett, *Don Ricardo Honeywater Vindicated* (1748), intro. by R. A. Day. ARS. CML, 1987. By subscription.

Einberg, Elizabeth, intro., *Manners and Morals Hogarth and British Painting 1700–1760*. Tate, 1987. hb £30, pb £12.95.

Erickson, Robert A., *Mother Midnight: Birth, Sex and Fate in Eighteenth-Century Fiction (Defoe, Richardson, and Sterne)*. AMS, 1987. $39.50.

Faller, Lincoln B., *Turned to Account: The Forms and Functions of Criminal Biography in Late Seventeenth- and Early Eighteenth-Century England*. CUP, 1987. £30.

Ferguson, Rebecca, *The Unbalanced Mind: Pope and the Rule of Passion*. Harvester, 1986. £35.

Fielding, Henry, *'An Enquiry into the Causes of the Late Increase of Robbers' and Related Writings*, ed. by Malvin R. Zirker. Clarendon, 1988. £50.

Fielding, Henry, *Joseph Andrews*, ed. by Stephen Copley. RKP, 1987. pb £5.95.

Fielding, Henry, *'The True Patriot' and Related Writings*, ed. by W. B. Coley. Clarendon, 1987. £55.

Finch, Anne, Countess of Winchilsea, *Selected Poems*, ed. by Denys Thompson. Carcanet, 1987. pb £3.95.

Greene, Donald, and John A. Vance, *A Bibliography of Johnsonian Studies, 1970-1985*. ELS. UVict, 1987.

Guilhamet, Leon, *Satire and the Transformation of Genre*. UPenn, 1987. £28.45.

Hammond, Brean, *'Gulliver's Travels'*. OpenU, 1988. pb £4.95.

Hawthorn, Jeremy, ed., *Propaganda, Persuasion and Polemic*. SUAS. Arnold, 1987. pb £9.95.

Hays, Mary, *Memoirs of Emma Courtney*, intro. by Sally Cline. Pandora, 1987. pb £4.95.

Hind, Charles, ed., *The Rococo in England: A Symposium*. V&A, 1986. pb.

Hinnant, Charles H., *Purity and Defilement in 'Gulliver's Travels'*. Macmillan, 1987. £25.

Hinnant, Charles H., *Samuel Johnson: An Analysis*. Macmillian, 1988. £27.50.

Holcroft, Thomas, *Seduction*, ed. by Joseph J. Latona. Garland, 1987.

Hook, Andrew, ed., *The History of Scottish Literature*. Vol. II: *1660-1800*. AberdeenU, 1987. £16.50.

Hoppit, Julian, *Risk and Failure in English Business, 1700-1800*. CUP, 1987. £22.50.

Hume, Robert D., *Henry Fielding and the London Theatre 1728-1737*. Clarendon, 1988. £27.50.

Hunt, John Dixon, *William Kent: Landscape Garden Designer: An Assessment and Catalogue of his Designs*. Zwemmer, 1987. £29.95.

Janik, Detlev, *Adel und Bürgertum im englischen Roman des 18. Jahrhunderts*. CWU, 1987. DM 72.

Jones, Whitney R. D., *David Williams: The Anvil and the Hammer*. UWales, 1986. £25.95.

Jordanova, Ludmilla, ed., *Languages of Nature: Critical Essays on Science and Literature*. FAB, 1986. pb £8.95.

Kelly, Hugh, *An Old Spelling Edition of Hugh Kelly's Comedy 'The School for Wives'*, ed. by Jean S. Gottlieb. Garland, 1987.

Kelly, Lionel, ed., *Tobias Smollett: The Critical Heritage*. RKP, 1987. £27.95.

Kenrick, William, *Love in the Suds; A Town Eclogue . . .*, intro. by T. J. Campbell. ARS. CML, 1987. By subscription.

Kernan, Alvin, *Printing Technology, Letters and Samuel Johnson*. Princeton, 1987. £19.50.

Kors, A. C., and Paul J. Korshin, ed., *Anticipations of the Englightenment in England, France, and Germany*. UPenn, 1987. £28.45.

Last, B. W., *Politics and Letters in the Age of Walpole*. Avero, 1987. £14.

Lemay, J. A. Leo, ed., *Deism, Masonry, and the Englightenment; Essays Honoring Alfred Owen Aldridge*. AUP/UDel, 1987. £19.95.

Lonsdale, Roger, ed., *Sphere History of Literature*. Vol. IV: *Dryden to Johnson* (1971). Rev. second edn. Sphere, 1987. pb £4.95.

McGugan, Ruth, *Nahum Tate and the Coriolanus Tradition in English Drama: With a Critical Edition of Tate's 'The Ingratitude of a Common Wealth'*. Garland, 1987.

McNeil, Maureen, *Under the Banner of Science: Erasmus Darwin and his Age*. ManU, 1987. £27.50.

Meier, Thomas Keith, *Defoe and the Defence of Commerce*. ELS. UVict, 1987.

Nokes, David, *Raillery and Rage: A Study of Eighteenth Century Satire*. Harvester, 1987. pb £10.95.

Nussbaum, Felicity, and Laura Brown, ed., *The New Eighteenth Century: Theory, Politics, English Literature*. Methuen, 1988. hb £28, pb £9.95.

O'Hara, Kate, *Two Burlettas of Kate O'Hara: 'Midas' and 'The Golden Pippin': An Edition with Commentary*, ed. by Phyllis T. Dircks. Garland, 1987.

Passman, Dirk Friedrich, *'Full of Improbable Lies': 'Gulliver's Travels' und die Reiseliteratur vor 1726*. Lang, 1987 pb Sfr 77.

Peterson, Spiro, *Daniel Defoe: A Reference Guide 1731-1924*. Hall, 1987. £45.

Pope, Alexander, *Selected Poetry and Prose*, ed. by Robin Sowerby. RKP, 1988. pb £4.95.

Pope, Alexander, *Selected Prose of Alexander Pope*, ed. by Paul Hammond. CUP, 1987. £27.50.

Probyn, Clive T., *English Fiction of the Eighteenth Century, 1700-1789*. Longman, 1987. hb £15.95, pb £6.95.

Pugh, Simon, *Garden-Nature-Language*. Cultural Politics. ManU, 1988. hb £25, pb £5.95.

Ramachandran, C. N., *Self-Conscious Structures: A Study of the British Theatre from Buckingham through Fielding and Sheridan*. Ajanta, 1987. Rs 100.

Reitan, Earl, *The Best of the 'Gentleman's Magazine', 1731-1754*. Mellen, 1987. $59.95 (series subscription $39.95).

Rembert, James A. W., *Swift and the Dialectical Tradition*. Macmillan, 1988. £29.50.

Richetti, John J., *Daniel Defoe*. Twayne, 1987. £17.95.

Rossi, Sergio, ed., *Science and Imagination in Eighteenth-Century British Culture/Scienza e Immaginazione Nella Cultura Inglese Del Settecento*. UNICOPLI, 1987. L 50,000.

Rousseau, G.S., and Roy Porter, ed., *Sexual Underworlds of the Enligtenment*. ManU, 1987. £29.50.

Royle, Edward, *Modern Britain: A Social History 1750-1950*. Arnold, 1987. pb £9.95.

Sabor, Peter, ed., *Horace Walpole: The Critical Heritage*. RKP, 1987. £25.

Schweizer, Karl W., *Lord Bute: Essays in Re-interpretation*. ULeic, 1988. £27.50.

Sena, John F., *The Best-Natured Man: Sir Samuel Garth, Physician and Poet*. AMS, 1986. $34.50.

Sharpe, J. A., *Early Modern England: A Social History 1550-1760*. Arnold, 1987. pb £9.95.

Simon, Richard Keller, *The Labyrinth of the Comic: Theory and Practice from Fielding to Freud*. FlorSU, 1985. $27.95

Sloan, Kim, *Alexander and John Robert Cozens: The Poetry of Landscape.* Yale, 1986. hb £20, pb £8.95.

Smart, Christopher, *The Poetical Works of Christopher Smart.* Vol. III: *A Translation of the Psalms of David,* ed. by Marcus Walsh. Vol. IV: *Miscellaneous Poems English and Latin,* ed. by Karina Williamson. Clarendon, 1987. £50 each.

Smith, Adam, *The Correspondence of Adam Smith.* Second edn, ed. by E. C. Mossner and Ian Simpson Ross. Clarendon, 1987. £45.

Smith, R. J., *The Gothic Bequest: Medieval Institutions in British Thought 1688–1863.* CUP, 1987. £22.50.

Smyth, John Vignaux, *A Question of Eros: Irony in Sterne, Kierkegaard, and Barthes.* FlorSU, 1986. pb $29.95.

Summerson, John, *The Architecture of the Eighteenth Century* (1969). T&H, 1986. pb £4.95.

Sutton, Michael, ed., *History of Ideas: Colloquium.* Newcastle upon Tyne Polytechnic, 1987. pb £3.50.

Temmer, Mark, *Samuel Johnson and Three Infidels: Rousseau, Voltaire, Diderot.* UGeo, 1988. $25.

Thomson, James, *'Liberty', 'The Castle of Indolence' and Other Poems,* ed. by James Sambrook. Clarendon, 1986. £65.

Thomson, James, *The Plays of James Thomson 1700–1748: A Critical Edition in Two Volumes,* ed. by J. C. Greene. Garland, 1987.

Tracy, Clarence, *A Portrait of Richard Graves.* Clarke, 1987. £19.50.

Van den berg, J., and G. F. Nuttall, *Philip Doddridge (1702–1751) and the Netherlands.* Brill/LeidenU, 1987. $18.25.

Walpole, Horace, *Historic Doubts on the Life and Reign of Richard the Third,* ed. by P. W. Hammond. Sutton, 1987. pb £5.95.

Watson, E. A., *A Study of Selected English Critical Terms from 1650 to 1800.* Lang, 1987. Sfr 119.

Wesley, John, *The Journal of John Wesley: A Selection,* ed. by Elisabeth Jay. OUP, 1987. pb £4.95.

Chapter XIV. The Nineteenth Century: Romantic Period

Alexander, J. H., *Reading Wordsworth.* RKP, 1987. £14.95.

Bachinger, Katrina, *The Multi-Man Genre and Poe's Byron.* USalz, 1987.

Barry, Kevin, *Language, Music and the Sign: A Study in Aesthetics, Poetics, and Poetic Practice from Collins to Coleridge.* CUP, 1987. £25.

Beatty, Bernard, *Byron: 'Don Juan' and Other Poems: A Critical Study.* PM. Penguin, 1987. pb £2.50.

Blake, William, *'Songs of Innocence and Experience' and Other Works,* ed. by R. B. Kennedy. Northcote, 1988. pb £6.95.

Blank, G. Kim, *Wordsworth's Influence on Shelley.* Macmillan, 1988. £27.50.

Bromwich, David, ed., *Romantic Critical Essays.* CUP, 1987. hb 25, pb £8.95.

Brown, Iain Gordon, ed., *Scott's Interleaved Waverley Novels: The 'Magnum Opus': National Library of Scotland MSS. 23001–41: An Introduction and Commentary.* AberdeenU, 1987. £16.50.

Brunton, Mary, *Discipline,* intro. by Fay Weldon. Pandora, 1987. pb £4.95.

Burke, Edmund, *The Political Philosophy of Edmund Burke*, comp. by Iain Hampsher-Monk. Longman, 1987. pb £5.95.

Butler, Marilyn, *Jane Austen and the War of Ideas*. OUP, 1988. pb £9.95.

Byron, Lord, *Don Juan (1819)* (1969), ed. by Brian Lee. Northcote, 1988. pb £5.95.

Calder, Angus, *Byron*. OpenU, 1987. pb £4.50.

Clayton, Jay, *Romantic Vision and the Novel*. CUP, 1987. £27.50.

Coffman, Ralph J., *Coleridge's Library: A Bibliography of Books Owned or Read by Samuel Taylor Coleridge*. Hall, 1987. $75.

Corbett, Martyn, *Byron and Tragedy*. Macmillan, 1988. £27.50.

Cox, Jeffrey N., *In the Shadows of Romance: Romantic Tragic Drama in Germany, England and France*. OhioU, 1987. $36.95.

Davies, Hugh Sykes, *Wordsworth and the Worth of Words*. CUP, 1987. £30.

Evans, Mary, *Jane Austen and the State*. Tavistock, 1987. pb £4.95.

Fielding, Sarah, *The Governess*, intro. by Mary Cadogan. Pandora, 1987. pb £4.95.

Frank, Frederick S., *The First Gothics: A Critical Guide to the English Gothic Novel*. Garland, 1987. $50.

Fuller, David, *Blake's Heroic Argument*. CH, 1988. £35.

Hamilton, Mary, *Munster Village*, intro. by Sarah Baylis. Pandora, 1987. pb £3.95.

Hartman, Geoffrey H., *The Unremarkable Wordsworth*. Methuen, 1987. pb £8.95.

Honan, Park, *Jane Austen: Her Life*. W&N, 1987. £16.95.

Jones, Ann H., *Ideas and Innovations: Best Sellers of Jane Austen's Age*. AMS, 1986. $42.50.

Keats, John, *Poems of 1820* (1969), ed., by D. G. Gillham. Northcote, 1988. pb £5.95.

Kelley, Theresa M., *Wordsworth's Revisionary Aesthetics*. CUP, 1988. £27.50.

McFarland, Thomas, *Romantic Cruxes: The English Essayists and the Spirit of the Age*. Clarendon, 1987. £15.

Mooneyham, Laura G., *Romance, Language and Education in Jane Austen's Novels*. Macmillan, 1988. £27.50.

Mulvihill, James, *Thomas Love Peacock*. TEAS. Twayne, 1987.

Musselwhite, David E., *Partings Welded Together: Politics and Desire in the Nineteenth-Century English Novel*. Methuen, 1987. hb £28, pb £8.95.

Pagliaro, Harold, *Selfhood and Redemption in Blake's 'Songs'*. PSU, 1987. $20.

Peacock, Thomas Love, *'Headlong Hall'; and 'Gryll Grange'*, ed. by Michael Baron and Michael Slater. WC. OUP, 1987. pb £4.95.

Roe, Nicholas, *Wordsworth and Coleridge: The Radical Years*. Clarendon, 1988. £27.50.

Shelley, Mary, *The Journals of Mary Shelley, 1814–1844*, ed. by Paula R. Feldman and Diana Scott-Kilvert. Clarendon, 1987. Vol. I. £55; Vol. II. £45.

Sheridan, Frances, *Memoirs of Miss Sidney Biddulph*, intro. by Sue Townsend. Pandora, 1987. pb £5.95.

Simpson, David, *Wordsworth's Historical Imagination: The Poetry of Displacement*. Metheuen, 1987. £25.

Spender, Dale, *Mothers of the Novel*. Pandora, 1986. pb £4.95.

Stafford, William, *Socialism, Radicalism, and Nostalgia: Social Criticsm in Britain 1775-1830*. CUP, 1987. pb £10.95.

Swingle, L. J., *The Obstinate Questionings of English Romanticism*. LSU, 1988. £26.60.

Watkins, Daniel, *Social Relations in Byron's Eastern Tales*. FDU, 1987. £16.95.

Wollstonecraft, Mary, *A Vindication of the Rights of Women*, ed. by Carol H. Poston. Norton, 1988. pb £5.95.

Wordsworth, William, and Samuel Taylor Coleridge, *Lyrical Ballads* (1969), ed. by Derek Roper. Northcote, 1988. pb £8.95.

Wordsworth, William, and Dorothy Wordsworth, *The Letters of William and Dorothy Wordsworth*. Vol. VII: *The Later Years*, ed. by Alan G. Hill. Clarendon, 1988. £70.

Chapter XV. The Nineteenth Century: Victorian Period

Abbey, Cherie D., and Janet Mullance, *Nineteenth-Century Literature Criticism*, Vols. XIV, XV, and XVI. Gale, 1987. $109.25 each.

Acton, Lord, *Selected Writings of Lord Acton*, ed. by J. Rufus Fears. Vol. I: *Essays in the History of Liberty*. Vol. II: *Essays in the Study and Writing of History*. Vol. III: *Essays in Religion, Politics and Morality*. Liberty, 1988. pb $7.50 each.

Allen, Michael, *Charles Dickens' Childhood*. Macmillan, 1987. £27.50.

Anderson, Nancy Fix, *Women against Women in Victorian England: A Life of Eliza Lynne Linton*. IndU, 1987. $29.50.

Armstrong, Nancy, *Desire and Domestic Fiction: A Political History of the Novel*. OUP, 1987. £19.50.

Auerbach, Nina, *Ellen Terry: Player in her Time*. Dent, 1987. £17.50.

Baldick, Chris, *In Frankenstein's Shadow: Myth, Montrosity, and Nineteenth-Century Writing*. OUP, 1986. £22.50.

Bennett, Arnold, *The Old Wives' Tale*. GMP, 1987. pb £6.95.

Berg, Maggie, *Jane Eyre: Portrait of a Life*. Twayne, 1987. £17.95.

Bjørhovde, Gerd, *Rebellious Structures: Women Writers and the Crisis of the Novel 1880-1900*. OUP, 1987. £19.50.

Bottigheimer, Ruth, ed., *Fairy Tales and Society: Illusion, Allusion and Paradigm*. UPenn, 1987. £29.70.

Bottigheimer, Ruth, *Grimms' Bad Girls and Bold Boys: The Moral and Social Vision of the 'Tales'*. Yale, 1987. £22.50.

Boucicault, Dion, *Selected Plays of Dion Boucicault*, sel. and intro. by Andrew Parkin. Smythe, 1987. hb £17.50, pb £4.95.

Braddon, Mary Elizabeth, *Lady Audley's Secret*, ed. by David Skilton. WC. OUP, 1987. pb £4.95.

Briggs, Julia, *A Woman of Passion: The Life of E. Nesbit 1858-1924*. Hutchinson, 1987. £16.95.

Bristow, Joseph, ed., *The Victorian Poet: Poetics and Persona*. CH, 1987. hb £27.50, pb £8.95.

Brontë, Charlotte, *An Edition of the Early Writings of Charlotte Brontë*, ed. by

Christine Alexander. Vol. I: *The Glass Town Saga 1826–1832*. Blackwell, 1987. £40.

Brontë, Charlotte, *Jane Eyre*, ed. by Richard J. Dunn. Norton, 1988. pb £5.95/$10.75.

Brontë, Charlotte, *The Professor*, ed. by Margaret Smith and Herbert Rosengarten. OUP, 1987. £40.

Browning, Robert, and Elizabeth Barrett Browning, *The Brownings' Correspondence*, Vol. V, ed. by Philip Kelley and Ronald Hudson. Wedgestone, 1987. $55.

Buckler, William E., *Walter Pater: The Critic as Artist of Ideas*. NYU, 1987.

Bull, J. A., *The Framework of Fiction: Socio-Cultural Approaches to the Novel*. Macmillan, 1987. £27.50.

Burnett, Frances Hodgson, *The Secret Garden*. WC. OUP, 1987. pb £4.95.

Cambridge, Ada, *The Three Miss Kings*. Virago, 1987. pb £4.50.

Carlyle, Thomas, and Jane Welsh Carlyle, *The Collected Letters of Thomas and Jane Welsh Carlyle*, ed. by Clyde de L. Ryals and K. J. Fielding. Vol. XIII: *1841*. Vol. XIV: *January–July 1842*. Vol. XV: *August–December 1842*. DukeU, 1987. £35.65 each.

Chitham, Edward, *A Life of Emily Brontë*. Blackwell, 1987. £24.95.

Clough, Arthur Hugh, *Selected Poems*, ed. by Shirley Chew. Carcanet, 1987. pb 5.95.

Collins, Wilkie, *Blind Love*. Dover, 1986. pb $6.95.

Collins, Wilkie, *'The Yellow Mask' and Other Stories*. Sutton, 1987. pb £2.95.

Colls, Robert, and Philip Dodd, ed., *Englishness: Politics and Culture 1880–1920* (1986). CH, 1987. pb £12.95.

David, Deirdre, *Intellectual Women and Victorian Patriarchy: Harriet Martineau, Elizabeth Barrett Browning, George Eliot*. Macmillan, 1987. hb £29.50, pb £10.95.

Dennis, Barbara, and David Skilton, ed., *Reform and Intellectual Debate in Victorian England*. CH, 1987. hb £27.50, pb £6.95.

Dickens, Charles, *David Copperfield*. OUP, 1987. £4.95/$8.95.

Dickens, Charles, *Great Expectations* (1953). OUP, 1987. £4.95/$8.95.

Dickens, Charles, *Hard Times*, ed. by Terry Eagleton. Methuen, 1987. pb £4.95.

Dickens Charles, *The Pickwick Papers*. OUP, 1987. £4.95/$8.95.

Disraeli, Benjamin, *Letters*. Vol. III: *1838–1841*, ed. by M. G. Wiebe, J. B. Conacher, John Matthews, and Mary S. Millar. UTor, 1987. £40.

Disraeli, Benjamin, *Sybil* (1981). WC. OUP, 1986. pb £2.95.

Draper, R. P., ed., *Thomas Hardy: Three Pastoral Novels: A Casebook*. Macmillan, 1987. hb £20, pb £4.95.

Edgeworth, Maria, *Helen*. Pandora, 1987. pb £5.95.

Ellmann, Richard, *Oscar Wilde*. HH, 1987. £15.

Ellsberg, Margaret R., *Created to Praise: The Language of Gerard Manley Hopkins*. OUP, 1987. £15.

Engelberg, Karsten Klejs, *The Making of the Shelley Myth: An Annotated Bibliography of Criticism of Percy Bysshe Shelley, 1822–1860*. Mansell/Meckler, 1988. £40.

Ermath, Elizabeth Deeds, *Realism and Consensus in the English Novel* (1953). Princeton, 1987. hb £16.60, pb £8.20.

Evans, Ray, *'The Mayor of Casterbridge' by Thomas Hardy*. MMG. Macmillan, 1987. pb £1.95.

Flint, Kate, ed., *The Victorian Novelist: Social Problems and Social Change.* CH, 1987. hb £27.50, pb £9.95.

Gardner, Burdett, *The Lesbian Imagination (Victorian Style): A Psychological and Critical Study of 'Vernon Lee'.* Garland, 1987. $90.

Gaskell, Elizabeth, *Mary Barton*, ed. by Edgar Wright. WC. OUP, 1987. pb £2.50.

Gaskell, Elizabeth, *Wives and Daughters*, ed. by Angus Easson. WC. OUP, 1987. pb £3.95.

Gill, Richard, *'In Memoriam' by Alfred Tennyson.* MMG. Macmillan, 1987. pb £1.95.

Glynn, Jennifer, *Prince of Publishers: A Biography of the Great Victorian Publisher George Smith.* A&B, 1986. £14.95.

Halperin, John, *Gissing: A Life in Books.* OUP, 1987. pb £6.95.

Hamer, Mary, *Writing by Numbers: Trollope's Serial Fiction.* CUP, 1987. £25.

Handley, Graham M., *Anthony Trollope: 'Barchester Towers'.* PM. Penguin, 1987. pb £2.50.

Hardy, Barbara, *The Collected Essays of Barbara Hardy.* Vol. I: *Narrators and Novelists.* Harvester, 1987. £35.

Hardy, Thomas, *The Collected Letters of Thomas Hardy*, ed. by Richard Little Purdy and Michael Millgate. Vol. VI: *1920–25.* OUP, 1987. £27.50.

Hardy, Thomas, *The Mayor of Casterbridge*, ed. by Dale Kramer. WC. OUP, 1987. hb £25, pb £1.75.

Hardy, Thomas, *Tens of the d'Urbervilles*, ed. by Juliet Grindle and Simon Gatrell. OUP, 1988. pb £1.95.

Hardy, Thomas, *The Trumpet-Major.* Penguin, 1987. pb £1.95.

Harrison, Antony H., *Christina Rossetti in Context.* Harvester, 1988. hb £25, pb £8.95.

Harrison, Antony H., *Swinburne's Medievalism: A Study in Victorian Love Poetry.* LSU, 1988. £26.15.

Houghton, Walter, Esther Houghton, and Jean Slingerland, *The Wellesley Index to Victorian Periodicals 1824–1900*, Vol. IV. UTor/RKP, 1988. £95.

Kadish, Doris Y., *The Literature of Images: Narrative Landscape from 'Julie' to 'Jane Eyre'.* Rutgers, 1987. £30.95.

Kalikoff, Beth, *Murder and Moral Decay in Victorian Popular Literature.* UMI, 1987. £40.

Keefe, Robert, and Janice A. Keefe, *Walter Pater and the Gods of Disorder.* OhioU, 1988. £23.70.

Kennedy, Gerald J., *Poe, Death and the Life of Writing.* Yale, 1987. £19.50/$26.50.

Kenny, Anthony, *God and Two Poets: Arthur Hugh Clough and Gerard Manley Hopkins.* S&J, 1988. £16.95.

Kucich, John, *Repression in Victorian Fiction: Charlotte Brontë, George Eliot and Charles Dickens.* UCal, 1987. $32.

LaCapra, Dominick, *History, Politics and the Novel.* CornU, 1987. £22.50.

Laski, Marghanita, *George Eliot.* T&H, 1987. pb £3.95.

Lederer, Wolfgang, *The Kiss of the Snow Queen: Hans Christian Andersen and Man's Redemption by Woman.* UCal, 1987. £18.95.

Lee, Vernon, *Supernatural Tales: Excursions into Fantasy.* Owen, 1987. £10.90.

Linton, David, and Ray Boston, *The Newspaper Press in Britain: An Annotated Bibliography.* Mansell, 1987. £45.

Livingston, James C., *Matthew Arnold and Christianity: His Religious Prose Writings*. USC, 1986. $19.95.

MacDonald, George, *The Princess and Curdie* (1966). Penguin, 1986. pb £1.95.

MacDonald, Susan Peck, *Anthony Trollope*. TEAS. Twayne, 1987. £17.95.

Mackay, Carol Hanbery, *Soliloquy in Nineteenth-Century Fiction*. Macmillan, 1987. £27.50.

Maidment, Brian, ed., *The Poorhouse Fugitives: Self-taught Poets and Poetry in Victorian Britain*. Carcanet, 1987. £14.95.

Martin, Philip, *Mad Women in Romantic Writing*. Harvester, 1987. £29.95.

Maynard, John, *Charlotte Brontë and Sexuality*. CUP, 1987. pb £10.95.

Meckier, Jerome, *Hidden Rivalries in Victorian Fiction: Dickens, Realism and Revaluation*. UKen, 1987. $29.

Michie, Helen, *The Flesh Made Word: Female Figures and Women's Bodies*. OUP, 1987. £15.

Miles, Robert, *'Jane Eyre' by Charlotte Bronte*. MMG. Macmillan, 1987. pb £1.95.

Mill, John Stuart, and Jeremy Bentham, *'Utilitarianism' and Other Essays*, ed. by Alan Ryan. Penguin, 1987. pb £4.50.

Muendel, Renate, *George Meredith*. Macmillan, 1987. £17.95.

Musselwhite, David E., *Partings Welded Together: Politics and Desire in the Nineteenth-Century English Novel*. Methuen, 1987. pb £8.95.

Myer, Valerie Grosvenor, *Charlottë Bronte: Truculent Spirit*. Vision, 1987. £18.95.

Nadel, Ira Bruce, ed., *Victorian Fiction: A Collection of Essays from the Period*. Garland, 1986. $45.

Nelson, Walter W., *Oscar Wilde from 'Ravenna' to 'Salomé': A Survey of Contemporary English Criticism*. DublinU, 1987.

Nesbit, Edith, *Long Ago When I Was Young*. Macdonald, 1987. £6.95.

Newton, Ken, *'Barchester Towers' by Anthony Trollope*. MMG. Macmillan, 1987. pb £1.95.

Oliphant, Margaret, *Chronicles of Carlingford*. Vol. III: *The Perpetual Curate*. Virago, 1987. pb £4.50.

Orel, Harold, *The Unknown Thomas Hardy: Lesser-Known Aspects of Hardy's Life and Career*. Harvester, 1987. £28.50.

Orel, Harold, ed., *Victorian Short Stories: An Anthology*. Dent, 1987. pb £3.95.

Owens, Coilin, ed., *Family Chronicles: Maria Edgeworth's 'Castle Rackrent'*. Wolfhound, 1987. £17.50.

Palmegiano, E. M., *The British Empire in the Victorian Press, 1832–1867: A Bibliography*. Garland, 1987. $40.

Parker, Gilbert, *Gilbert Parker and Herbert Beerbohm Tree Stage 'The Seats of the Mighty' in Washington (1896) and London (1897). The Prompt-books for the Production at Her Majesty's Theatre, London, 28 April 1897*, ed. by John Ripley. S&P, 1986. $29.95.

Pater, Walter, *Appreciations with an Essay on Style*. Northwestern, 1987. pb $11.95.

Peacock, Thomas Love, *'Headlong Hall' and 'Gryll Grange'*. WC. OUP, 1987. pb £4.95.

Pearson, Hesketh, *Conan Doyle*. Unwin, 1987. pb £6.95.

The Popular Stage: Drama in Nineteenth Century England: The Frank Pettingell Collection of Plays in the Library of the University of Kent at Canterbury: An Inventory to Series One: Manuscript and Typescript Plays, Part 3. Harvester Microform, 1986. Refer to publisher for price.

Redmond, Christopher, *In Bed with Sherlock Holmes: Sexual Elements in Conan Doyle's Stories of The Great Detective*. S&P, 1987. £16.50/C$29.95.

Redmond, Christopher, *Welcome to America, Mr Sherlock Holmes: Victorian America Meets Arthur Conan Doyle*. S&P, 1987. C$19.95.

Richards, Bernard, *English Poetry of the Victorian Period 1830–1890*. Longman, 1988. hb £15.95, pb £6.95.

Ricks, Christopher, ed., *The New Oxford Book of Victorian Verse*. OUP, 1987. £15.95.

Riede, David G., *Matthew Arnold and the Betrayal of Language*. Virginia, 1988. $30.

Robb, David S., *George MacDonald*. SAP, 1987. pb £4.95.

Roe, Sue, ed., *Women Reading Women's Writing*. Harvester, 1988. £30.

Ross, Alexander M., *The Imprint of the Picturesque on Nineteenth-Century British Fiction*. WLU, 1987. £27.50/$35.

Ruskin, John, and Charles E. Norton, *The Correspondence of John Ruskin and Charles Eliot Norton*, ed. by John Bradley and Ian Ousby. CUP, 1987. £45/$59.50.

Sabiston, Elizabeth Jean, *The Prison of Womanhood: Four Provincial Heroines in Nineteenth-Century Fiction*. Macmillan, 1987. £27.50.

Schreiner, Olive, *An Olive Schreiner Reader: Writings on Women and South Africa*, ed. by Carol Barash. Pandora, 1987. hb £12.95, pb £5.95.

Schreiner, Olive, *The Story of an African Farm*, ed. by Doris Lessing. Hutchinson, 1987. £15.95.

Sethna, K.D., *The Obscure and the Mysterious: A Research in Mallarmé's Symbolist Poetry*. SriA, 1987. pb.

Shatto, Susan, *The Companion to 'Bleak House'*. Unwin Hyman, 1988. £30.

Shuttleworth, Sally, *George Eliot and Nineteenth-Century Science: The Make-Believe of a Beginning*. OUP, 1987. pb £10.95/14.95.

Stephen, Julia Duckworth, *Stories for Children, Essays for Adults*, ed. by Diane F. Gillespie and Elizabeth Steele. Syracuse, 1987. $24.95.

Stephenson, Edward, *What Sprung Rhythm Really Is*. IHA, 1987. pb £8.

Stevenson, Robert Louis, *'The Strange Case of Doctor Jekyll and Mr Hyde' and Other Stories*. Star, 1987. pb £1.95.

Stevenson, Robert Louis, *'The Strange Case of Doctor Jekyll and Mr Hyde' and 'Weir of Hermiston'*, ed. by Emma Letley. WC. OUP, 1987. pb £2.95.

Stoneman, Patsy, *Elizabeth Gaskell*. Harvester, 1987. hb £18.95, pb £5.95.

Tabachnick, Stephen E., *Explorers in Doughty's 'Arabia Deserta'*. UGeo, 1987. $35.

Tennyson, Lord Alfred, *The Poems of Tennyson*, ed. by Christopher Ricks. Second edn. Three vols. Longman, 1987. £40 each.

Trollope, Anthony, *Barchester Towers*, ed. by Michael Sadleir and Frederick Page. WC. OUP, 1987. pb £2.50.

Trollope, Anthony, *The Bertrams*. Dover, 1987. pb £8.95.

Trollope, Anthony, *Cousin Mary*. WC. OUP, 1987. pb £3.95.

Trollope, Anthony, *Kept in the Dark*. Sutton, 1987. pb £2.95.

Trollope, Anthony, *Trollope: Interviews and Recollections*, ed. by R. C. Terry. Macmillan, 1987. £25.

Uglow, Jennifer, *George Eliot*. Virago, 1987. pb £4.95.

Waddington, Patrick, *Tennyson and Russia*. TennS, 1987. pamphlet £1.50.

Walters, Huw, *The Welsh Periodical Press 1735–1900*. NLW, 1987. pb £1.70.

Watson, J.R., ed., *Everyman's Book of Victorian Verse* (1982). Dent, 1987. pb £4.50.

Weissman, Judith, *Half Savage and Hardy and Free: Women and Rural Radicalism in the Nineteenth-Century Novel*. Wesleyan, 1987. £25.95.

Williams, A. Susan, *The Rich Man and the Diseased Poor in Early Victorian Literature*. Macmillan, 1987. £27.50.

Williams, Meg Harris, *A Strange Way of Killing: The Poetic Structure of 'Wuthering Heights'*. Clunie, 1987.

Williams, Raymond, *Culture and Society: Coleridge to Orwell* (1958). Hogarth, 1987. pb £6.95.

Winnifrith, Tom, *A New Life of Charlotte Brontë*. Macmillan, 1987. £27.

Wotton, George, *Thomas Hardy: Towards a Materialist Criticism*. G&M, 1985. £25.

Chapter XVI. The Twentieth Century

Acheson, James, and Kateryna Arthur, ed., *Beckett's Later Fiction and Drama: Texts for Company*. Macmillan, 1987. £27.50.

Anderson, Linda R., *Bennett, Wells and Conrad: Narrative in Transition*. Macmillan, 1988. £27.50.

Arden, John, and Margaretta D'Arcy, *Whose Is the Kingdom?* Methuen, 1988. pb £6.95.

Armstrong, Paul B., *The Challenge of Bewilderment: Understanding and Representation in James, Conrad and Ford*. CornU, 1987. $29.95.

Bagnold, Enid, *The Happy Foreigner*, ed. by Anne Sebba. Virago, 1987. pb £3.95.

Bagnold, Enid, *The Squire*, ed. by Anne Sebba. Virago, 1987. pb £3.95.

Baldwin, Dean R., *V. S. Pritchett*. Twayne, 1987. $18.95.

Banks, Morwenna, and Amanda Swift, *The Joke's on Us: Women in Comedy from Music Hall to the Present Day*. Pandora, 1987. pb £5.95.

Banta, Martha, ed., *New Essays on 'The American'*. OUP, 1987. hb £20, pb £6.95.

Barale, Michele Aina, *Daughters and Lovers: The Life and Writing of Mary Webb*. Wesleyan, 1986.

Barbara, Jack, William McBrien, and Helen Bajan, *Stevie Smith: A Bibliography*. Mansell/Meckler, 1987. $47.50.

Bayley, John, *The Short Story: Henry James to Elizabeth Bowen*. Harvester, 1988. £35.

Beckson, Karl, *Arthur Symons: A Life*. Clarendon, 1987. £35.

Bedford, Sybille, *Aldous Huxley: A Biography*. Two vols. Paladin, 1987. pb £4.95 each.

Bell, Quentin, Angelica Garnett, Henrietta Garnett, and Richard Shone, *Charleston: Past and Present*. Hogarth, 1987. pb £5.95.

Bennett, Alan, *Two Kafka Plays: 'Kafka's Dick' and 'The Insurance Man'*. Faber, 1987. pb £4.95.

Benstock, Shari, *Women of the Left Bank: Paris 1900–1940*. Virago, 1987. pb £8.95.

Biles, Jack I., ed., *British Novelists Since 1900*. AMS, 1987. $40.

Billy, Ted, *Critical Essays on Joseph Conrad*. Hall, 1987. $32.50.

Bond, Edward, *Plays: Three*. Methuen, 1987. pb £3.95.

Bowker, Gordon, ed., *Malcolm Lowry: 'Under the Volcano'*. Macmillan, 1987. £20.

Brack, O. M., Jr, ed., *Twilight of Dawn: Studies in English Literature in Transition*. UAriz, 1987. $29.95.

Bradbury, Malcolm, *The Modern World: Ten Great Writers*. S&W, 1988. £12.95.

Bradbury, Malcolm, ed., *Modern British Short Stories*. Penguin, 1988. pb £4.95.

Brater, Enoch, *Beyond Minimalism: Beckett's Late Style in the Theatre*. OUP, 1987. £20.

Brook, Peter, *The Shifting Point: Forty Years of Theatrical Exploration 1946–1987*. Methuen, 1988. £14.95.

Brophy, Brigid, *'Baroque – 'n' Roll' and Other Essays*. HH, 1987. £10.95.

Buchan, John, *These for Remembrance: Memoirs of Six Friends Killed in the Great War*, ed. by Peter Vansittart. B&E, 1987. £9.95.

Burkhart, Charles, *The Pleasure of Miss Pym*. UTex, 1987.

Buttigieg, Joseph A., *A Portrait of the Artist in Different Perspective*. OhioU, 1987. £23.50.

Carens, James F., ed., *Critical Essays on Evelyn Waugh*. Hall, 1987. $37.50.

Carrière, Jean-Claude, *The Mahabharata*, trans. by Peter Brook. Methuen, 1988. pb £4.95.

Cassagrande, Peter, *Hardy's Influence on the Modern Novel*. Macmillan, 1987. £27.50.

Cave, Richard Allen, *New British Drama in Performance on the London Stage, 1970 to 1985*. Smythe, 1987. £16.

Cevasco, G. A., *The Sitwells: Edith, Osbert, Sacheverell*. Twayne, 1987. $19.95.

Chambers, Colin, and Mike Prior, *Playwrights' Progress: Patterns of Postwar British Drama*. AmberL, 1987. £11.95.

Chester, Gail, and Sigrid Nielsen, ed., *In Other Words: Writing as a Feminist*. Hutchinson, 1987. pb £5.95.

Chesterton, G. K., *The Annotated Innocence of Father Brown*, ed. by Martin Gardner. OUP, 1987. £12.95.

Chesterton, G. K., *The Essential G. K. Chesterton*, ed. by P. J. Kavanagh. OUP, 1987. pb £5.95.

Christopher, Joe R., *C. S. Lewis*. Twayne, 1987. $16.95.

Cohn, Ruby, ed., *Beckett: Waiting for Godot: A Casebook*. Macmillan, 1987. pb £6.95.

Conlon, D. J., ed., *G. K. Chesterton: A Half Century of Views*. OUP, 1987. £15.

Conrad, Joseph, *Chance*, ed. by Martin Ray. OUP, 1988. pb £3.50.

Conrad, Joseph, *Heart of Darkness*, ed. by Robert Kimbrough. Norton, 1988. £4.25.

Corrie, Joe, *Plays, Poems and Theatre Writings*, ed. by Linda Mackenney. 7:84 Pubns, 1985. hb £8.95, pb £4.95.

Couto, Maria, *Graham Greene: On the Frontier, Politics and Religion in the Novels*. Macmillan, 1988. £27.50.

Craig, Cairns, ed., *The History of Scottish Literature*. Vol. IV: Twentieth Century. AberdeenU, 1987. £16.50.

Crozier, Andrew, and Tim Longville, ed., *A Various Art*. Carcanet, 1987. £12.95.

Cunningham, Valentine, *British Writers of the Thirties*. OUP, 1988. £30.

Curtis, Anthony, and John Whitehead, ed., *Somerset Maugham: The Critical Heritage*. RKP, 1987. £25.

Dantanus, Ulf, *Brian Friel: A Study*. Faber, 1988. pb £4.95.

Davies, Andrew, *Other Theatres: The Development of Alternative and Experimental Theatre in Britain*. Macmillan, 1987. hb £20, pb £6.95.

Delany, Paul, *The Neo-Pagans: Friendship and Love in the Rupert Brooke Circle*. Macmillan, 1987. £16.95.

Donaghy, Henry J., *Graham Greene: An Introduction to his Writings*. Rodopi, 1986. Fl 27.50.

Draper, Michael, *H. G. Wells*. Macmillan, 1988. £18.

Dunbar, Andrea, *'Rita, Sue and Bob Too'; with 'The Arbor and Shirley'*, intro. by Rob Ritchie. Methuen, 1988. pb £4.50.

Eby, Cecil D., *The Road to Armageddon: The Martial Spirit in English Popular Literature 1870–1914*. DukeU, 1988. £25.

Edgar, David, *Entertaining Strangers*. Methuen, 1988. pb £4.50.

Elliot, Vivian, comp., *Dear Mr Shaw: Selections from Bernard Shaw's Postbag*. Bloomsbury, 1987. £14.95.

Ellis, David, and Howard Mills, *D. H. Lawrence's Non-Fiction: Art, Thought and Genre*. CUP, 1988. £22.50.

Ellis, Peter Beresford, *H. Rider Haggard: A Voice from the Infinite*. RKP, 1987. pb £8.95.

Erdinast-Vulcan, Daphna, *Graham Greene's Childless Fathers*. Macmillan, 1988. £25.

Esslin, Martin, *The Field of Drama*. Methuen, 1987. £14.95.

Finnegan, Seamus, *'North'; also, 'Act of Union'; 'Mary's Men'; 'Soldiers': Four Plays*. Boyars, 1987. pb £7.95.

Fletcher, Ian, *W. B. Yeats and his Contemporaries*. Harvester, 1987. £35.

Friedman, Alan Warren, Charles Rossman, and Dina Sherzer, ed., *Beckett Translating/Translating Beckett*. PSU, 1987. $24.95.

Gerard, David, *John Wain: A Bibliography*. Mansell, 1987. £40.

Gilbert, Sandra M., and Susan Gubar, *No Man's Land: The Place of the Woman Writer in the Twentieth Century*. Vol. I: *The War of the Words*. Yale, 1988. £12.95.

Gindin, James, *John Galsworthy's Life and Art: An Alien's Fortress*. Macmillan, 1987. £35.

Gissing, George, *Veranilda*, ed. by Pierre Coustillas. Harvester, 1987. £35.

Goodheart, Eugene, *Pieces of Resistance*. CUP, 1987. £25.

Graham, Kenneth, *Indirections of the Novel: James, Conrad and Forster*. CUP, 1988. £25.

Grant, Brian, ed., *The Quiet Ear: Deafness in Literature*. Deutsch, 1987. £9.95.

Gray, Frances, *Noel Coward*. Macmillan, 1987. pb £5.95.

Griffiths, Trevor, *Fatherland*. Faber, 1987. pb £3.95.

Gutierrez, Donald, *The Dark and Light Gods: Essays on the Self in Modern Literature*. Whitston, 1987. $22.50.

Harben, Niloufer, *Twentieth-Century History Plays: From Shaw to Bond*. Macmillan, 1988. £27.50.

Hardy, Thomas, *The Collected Letters of Thomas Hardy*. Vol. VI: *1920–1925*, ed. by Richard Little Purdy and Michael Millgate. Clarendon, 1987. £27.50.

Hardy, Thomas, *Figures in a Wessex Landscape: Thomas Hardy's Picture of English Country Life*, ed. by Joanna Cullen Brown. Allen, 1987. £16.95.

Harper, George Mills, *The Making of Yeats's 'A Vision': A Study of the Automatic Script*. Two vols. Macmillan, 1987. £70.

Harty, John, III, *Tom Stoppard: A Casebook*. Garland, 1988. $55.

Heller, Terry, ed., *The Delights of Terror: An Aesthetics of the Tale of Terror*. UIll, 1987. pb $10.95.

Herring, Phillip F., *Joyce's Uncertainty Principle*. Princeton, 1987. $32.

Herz, Judith Scherer, *The Short Narratives of E. M. Forster*. Macmillan, 1988. £27.50.

Heywood, Christopher, ed., *D. H. Lawrence: New Studies*. Macmillan, 1987. £27.50.

Hilton, Julian, *Performance*. Macmillan, 1987. hb £20, pb £6.95.

Hogg, James, ed., *Vitalism and Celebration: Anthony Johnson, William Oxley, Peter Russell: A Study of Three Europoets*. USalz, 1987.

Hollow, John, *Against the Night, the Stars: The Science Fiction of Arthur C. Clarke*. OhioU, 1987. pb £9.45.

Hyde, H. Montgomery, *Solitary in the Ranks: Lawrence of Arabia as Airman and Private Soldier*. Constable, 1987. pb £7.95.

Jackson, Holbrook, *The 1890s*, ed. by Malcolm Bradbury. Hutchinson, 1988. pb £6.95.

Jaffe, Jacqueline A., *Arthur Conan Doyle*. Twayne, 1987. $15.95.

Jellicoe, Ann, *Community Plays: How to Put Them On*. Methuen, 1987. pb £6.95.

Johnson, Deborah, *Iris Murdoch*. Harvester, 1987. hb £22.50, pb £7.95.

Joyce, James, *James Joyce's Letters to Sylvia Beach: 1921–1940*, ed. by Melissa Banta and Oscar A. Silverman. IndU, 1987. $25.

Keatley, Charlotte, *My Mother Said I Never Should*. Methuen, 1988. pb £2.95.

Kelley, Alice van Buren, *'To the Lighthouse': The Marriage of Life and Art*. Twayne, 1987.

Kelly, Richard, *Daphne du Maurier*. Twayne, 1987.

Kenner, Hugh, *Dublin's Joyce*. ColU, 1987. $15.

Kingsmill, Hugh, *Frank Harris*, ed. by Michael Holroyd. Biografia, 1987. £17.50.

Kipling, Rudyard, *The Complete Supernatural Stories of Rudyard Kipling*, ed. by Peter Haining. Allen, 1987. £12.95.

Kipling, Rudyard, *Debits and Credits*, ed. by Sandra Kemp. Penguin, 1987. pb £2.95.

Kipling, Rudyard, *A Diversity of Creatures*, ed. by Paul Driver. Penguin, 1987. pb £2.95.

Kipling, Rudyard, *Jungle Books*, ed. by Daniel Karlin. Penguin, 1987. pb £2.50.

Kipling, Rudyard, *Just So Stories*, ed. by Peter Levi. Penguin, 1987. pb £1.95.

Kipling, Rudyard, *Kim*, ed. by Edward W. Said. Penguin, 1987. pb £2.50.

Kipling, Rudyard, *Kipling's India: Uncollected Sketches*, ed. by Thomas Pinney. Macmillan, 1987. pb £6.95.

Kipling, Rudyard, *Kipling's Kingdom: His Best Indian Stories*, sel and intro. by Charles Allen. Joseph, 1987. £14.95.

Kipling, Rudyard, *Life's Handicap*, ed. by P. N. Furbank. Penguin, 1987. pb £2.95.

Kipling, Rudyard, *Limits and Renewals*, ed. by Phillip V. Mallett. Penguin, 1987. pb £2.95.

Kipling, Rudyard, *Plain Tales from the Hills*, ed. by David Trotter. Penguin, 1987. pb £2.50.

Kipling, Rudyard, *Puck of Pook's Hill*, ed. by Sarah Wintle. Penguin, 1987. pb £2.50.

Kipling, Rudyard, *Rewards and Fairies*, ed. by Roger Lewis. Penguin, 1987. pb £2.95.

Kipling, Rudyard, *Selected Stories*, ed. by Sandra Kemp. Dent, 1987. pb £3.95.

Kipling, Rudyard, *Traffics and Discoveries*, ed. by Hermione Lee. Penguin, 1987. pb £2.95.

Klaus, H. Gustav, ed., *The Rise of Socialist Fiction 1880–1914*. Harvester, 1987. £35.

Langbaum, Robert, *The Word from Below: Essays on Modern Literature and Culture*. UWisc, 1987. pb £12.30.

Laski, Marghanita, *Kipling's English History*. BBC, 1987. pb £5.95.

Lawrence, D. H., *The Letters of D. H. Lawrence*. Vol IV: *1921–1924*, ed. by Warren Roberts. CUP, 1987. £35.

Lawrence, D. H., *'Love among the Haystacks' and Other Stories*, ed. by John Worthen. CUP, 1987. hb £37.50, pb £12.95.

Lawrence, D. H., *Mr Noon*, ed. by Lindeth Vasey. CUP, 1987. pb £8.95.

Lawrence, D. H., *'The Prussian Officer' and Other Stories*, ed. by John Worthen. CUP, 1987. hb £35, pb £9.95.

Lawrence, D. H., *'St Mawr' and Other Stories*, ed. by Brian Finney. CUP, 1987. hb £35, pb £12.95.

Lawrence, D. H., *The White Peacock*, ed. by Andrew Robertson. CUP, 1987. pb £13.95.

Layman, Richard, and Matthew J. Bruccoli, ed., *Crime Wave*. Robinson, 1987. pb £5.95.

Leacroft, Richard, *The Development of the English Playhouse* (1973). Rev. edn. Methuen, 1988. pb £7.95.

Lehmann, John, *Christopher Isherwood: A Personal Memoir*. W&N, 1987. £12.95.

Lellenberg, Jon, ed., *The Quest for Sir Arthur Conan Doyle: Thirteen Biographers in Search of a Life*. SIU, 1987. $19.95.

Lenz, Bernd, *Factification: Agentenspiele wie in der Realität. Wirklichkeitsanspruch und Wirklichkeitsgehalt des Agentenromans*. CWU, 1987. pb DM 80.

Lester, John, *Conrad and Religion*. Macmillan, 1988. £27.50.

Lewis, Wyndham, *Men without Art*, ed. by Seamus Cooney. BSP, 1987. pb $12.50.

Linklater, Andro, *Compton Mackenzie: A Life*. C&W, 1987. £20.

Loiseaux, Elizabeth Bergmann, *Yeats and the Visual Arts*. Rutgers, 1987. $32.50.

Lovell, Terry, *Consuming Fiction*. Verso, 1987. pb £7.95.

McCartney, George, *Confused Roaring: Evelyn Waugh and the Modernist Tradition*. IndU, 1987. $19.50.

Manlove, C. N., *C. S. Lewis: His Literary Achievement*. Macmillan, 1987. £29.50.

Mayor, F. M., *The Rector's Daughter*, ed. by Janet Morgan. Virago, 1987. pb £3.95.

Mayor, F. M., *The Squire's Daughter*, ed. by Janet Morgan. Virago, 1987. pb £3.95.

Meyers, Jeffrey, ed., *The Legacy of D.H. Lawrence*. Macmillan, 1987. £27.50.

Meynell, Dame Alix, *Public Servant, Private Woman: An Autobiography*. Gollancz, 1988. £16.95.

Mikhail, E. H., ed., *The Abbey Theatre: Interviews and Recollections*. Macmillan, 1988. £29.50.

Miles, Rosalind, *The Female Form: Women Writers and the Conquest of the Novel*. RKP, 1987. £14.95.

Milligan, Ian, *'Howards End' by E. M. Forster*. MMG. Macmillan, 1987. pb £1.95.

Milton, Colin, *Lawrence and Nietzsche: A Study in Influence*. AberdeenU, 1987. £18.50.

Milward-Oliver, Edward, *The Len Deighton Companion*. Grafton, 1987. £12.95.

Minghella, Anthony, *'Whale Music' and Other Plays*. Methuen, 1987. pb £4.95.

Mitchell, Tony, comp., *File on Brenton*. Methuen, 1987. pb £3.95.

Modiano, Marko, *Domestic Disharmony and Industrialization in D. H. Lawrence's Early Fiction*. Uppsala, 1987.

Morris, Jane, *Jane Morris to Wilfrid Scawen Blunt*, ed. by Peter Faulkner. UExe, 1986. £15.

Ormond, Leonee, *J. M. Barrie*. SAP, 1987. pb £4.95.

Ormond, Leonee, *'St Joan' by George Bernard Shaw*. MMG. Macmillan, 1986. pb £1.95.

Orr, John, *The Making of the Twentieth Century Novel: Lawrence, Faulkner and Beyond*. Macmillan, 1987. £27.50.

Page, Norman, *E. M. Forster*. Macmillan, 1988. £18.

Palmer, Alan, and Veronica Palmer, *Who's Who in Bloomsbury*. Harvester, 1988. £40.

Paritt, George, *Fiction of the First World War: A Study*. Faber, 1988. pb £4.95.

Peach, Linden, *The Prose Writings of Dylan Thomas*. Macmillan, 1988. £27.50.

Pickering, Kenneth, *How to Study Modern Drama*. Macmillan, 1988. pb £4.95.

Powell, Violet, ed., *The Album of Anthony Powell's 'Dance to the Music of Time'*. T&H, 1987. £14.95.

Raban, Jonathan, *For Love and Money*. Collins Harvill, 1987. £11.50.

Radell, Karen Marguerite, *Affirmation in a Moral Wasteland: A Comparison of Ford Madox Ford and Graham Greene*. Lang, 1987. Sfr 49.50.

Rankin, Nicholas, *Dead Man's Chest: Travels After Robert Louis Stevenson*. Faber, 1987. £14.95.

Redington, Christine, ed., *Six T. I. E. Programmes*. Methuen, 1987. pb £4.95.

Reynolds, Mary T., *Joyce and Dante: The Shaping Imagination*. Princeton, 1987. pb $18.50.

Roberts, Peter, ed., *The Best of 'Plays and Players' 1953-1968*. Methuen, 1988. £14.95.

Rossen, Janice, *The World of Barbara Pym*. Macmillan, 1987. £27.50.

Sakellaridou, Elizabeth, *Pinter's Female Portraits: A Study of Female Characters in the Plays of Harold Pinter*. Macmillan, 1988. £27.50.

Salgādo, Gāmini, and G. K. Das, ed., *The Spirit of D. H. Lawrence: Centenary Studies*. Macmillan, 1988. £29.50.

Sammells, Neil, *Tom Stoppard: The Artist as Critic*. Macmillan, 1988. £27.50.

Schwarz, Daniel R., *Reading Joyce's 'Ulysses'*. Macmillan, 1987.

Sekine, Masaru, ed., *Irish Writers and the Theatre*. Smythe, 1987. £15.

Shaw, Bernard, *Collected Letters 1926-1950*, ed. by Dan H. Laurence. Reinhardt, 1988. £30.

Sillars, Stuart, *Art and Survival in First World War Britain*. Macmillan, 1988. £29.50.

Sim, Naomi, *Dance and Skylark: Fifty Years with Alastair Sim*. Bloomsbury, 1987. £12.95.

Singh, Caru Sheel, *Auguries of Evocation: British Poetry During and After the Movement*. APH, 1987. Rs 250.

Smith, Grahame, *The Achievement of Graham Greene*. Harvester, 1988. pb £9.95.

Stapledon, Olaf, and Agnes Miller, *Talking across the World: The Love Letters of Olaf Stapledon and Agnes Miller, 1913-1919*, ed. by Robert Crossley. UPNE, 1988. £18.

Stavert, Geoffrey, *From Bush Villas to Baker Street: The Unrevealed Life of Doctor Arthur Conan Doyle, the Creator of Sherlock Holmes*. Milestone, 1987. £9.95.

Sternlicht, Sanford, *John Galsworthy*. Twayne, 1987. $17.95.

Stevenson, Robert Louis, *Island Landfalls*, ed. by Jenni Calder. Canongate, 1987. pb £3.95.

Strachey, Lytton, *The Illustrated Queen Victoria*, ed. by Michael Holroyd. Bloomsbury, 1987. £13.95.

Sultan, Stanley, *Eliot, Joyce and Co*. OUP, 1987. £25.

Symons, Julian, *Makers of the New: The Revolution in Literature 1912-1939*. Deutsch, 1987. £12.95.

Taylor, C. P., *North: Six Plays*. Methuen, 1987. pb £5.95.

Thickstun, William R., *Visionary Closure in the Modern Novel*. Macmillan, 1988. £27.50.

Thurston, Carol, *The Romance Revolutions: Erotic Novels for Women and the Quest for a New Sexual Identity*. UIll, 1987. pb $9.95.

Tynan, Kathleen, *The Life of Kenneth Tynan*. W&N, 1987. £16.95.

Wandor, Michelene, *Look Back in Gender*. Methuen, 1987. pb £5.95.

Wells, H. G., *The Definitive 'Time Machine'*. IndU, 1987. pb $10.95.

Wells, H. G., *The Future in America*. Granville, 1987. hb £10.95, pb £5.95.

West, Rebecca, *Family Memories*, ed. by Faith Evans. Virago, 1987. £14.95.

West, Rebecca, *The Strange Necessity: Essays and Reviews*, ed. by G. Evelyn Hutchinson. Virago, 1987. pb £6.95.

West, Rebecca, Vita Sackville-West, and M. J. Farrell (Molly Keane), *'The Return of the Soldier'; 'All Passion Spent'; and 'Two Days in Aragon'*. Virago, 1987. £12.95.

White, Sidney Howard, *Alan Ayckbourn*. Twayne, 1984. £18.35.

Whitehead, John, *Maugham: A Reappraisal*. Vision, 1987. £18.95.

Whiteside, Anna, and Michael Issacharoff, ed., *On Referring in Literature*. IndU, 1987. pb $12.50.

Williams, David, *Peter Brook: A Theatrical Casebook*. Methuen, 1988. pb £8.95.

Williams, John, *Twentieth-Century British Poetry: A Critical Introduction*. Arnold, 1987. pb £4.95.

Wiliams, Merryn, *Six Women Novelists*. Macmillan, 1987. £18.

Williamson, Henry, *The Wet Flanders Plain*. Gliddon, 1987. £12.95.

Wilson, Jean Moorcroft, *Virginia Woolf: Life and London: A Biography of Place*. Woolf, 1987. £12.50.

Wisenthal, J. l., *Shaw's Sense of History*. Clarendon, 1988. £22.50.

Woolf, Virginia, *The Essays of Virginia Woolf*. Vol. II: *1912-1918*, ed. by Andrew McNeillie. Hogarth, 1987. £25.

Wykes, David, *A Preface to Orwell*. Longman, 1987. pb £7.50.

Chapter XVII. American Literature to 1900

Bercovitch, Sacvan, ed., *Reconstructing American Literary History*. Harvard, 1986. pb £7.25

Budd, Louis J., ed. *New Essays on 'The Adventures of Huckleberry Finn'*. CUP, 1985. hb £20, pb £6.95.

Budd, Louis J., and Edwin H. Cady, ed., *On Whitman: The Best from 'American Literature'*. DukeU, 1987. £31.85.

Burbick, Joan, *Thoreau's Alternative History: Changing Perspectives on Nature, Culture and Language*. UPenn, 1987. $24.95.

Cady, Edwin H., and Louis J. Budd. *On Mark Twain: The Best from 'American Literature'*. DukeU, 1987. £31.85.

Chai, Leon, *The Romantic Foundations of the American Renaissance*. CornU, 1987. $29.95.

Chevigny, Bell Gale, and Gari Laguardia, *Reinventing the Americas: Comparative Studies of Literature of the United States and Spanish America*. CUP, 1987. £30.

Dekker, George, *The American Historical Romance*. CUP, 1987. £30.

Elliott, Emory, ed., *Columbia Literary History of the United States*. ColU, 1988. $59.95.

Haas, Rudolf, ed., *Amerikanische Lyrik: Perspektiven und Interpretationen*. Schmidt, 1987. DM 86.

Higgins, Brian, ed., *Herman Melville: A Reference Guide 1931–1960*. Hall, 1987. $55.

Johnson, Courtney, Jr, *Henry James and the Evolution of Consciousness: A Study of 'The Ambassadors'*. MichSU, 1987. $15.

Kirkpatrick, D. L., *Reference Guide to American Literature*. Second edn. St James, 1987. £45.

Murphy, Brenda, *American Realism and American Drama, 1880–1940*. CUP, 1987. £25.

Myerson, Joel, *American Transcendentalists*. DLB Documentary Series. Gale, 1988. $95.

Newman, Benjamin, *Searching for the Figure in the Carpet in the Tales of Henry James: Reflections of an Ordinary Reader*. Lang, 1987. $39.

Rathbun, John W., and Monica M. Grecu, *American Literary Critics and Scholars, 1800–1850*. DLB Documentary Series. Gale, 1987. $92.

Rowe, Joyce A., *Equivocal Endings in Classic American Novels*. CUP, 1988. £20.

Shapiro, Ann R., *Unlikely Heroines: Nineteenth-Century American Women Writers and the Women Question*. Greenwood, 1987. £22.50.

Shulman, Robert, *Social Criticism and Nineteenth-Century American Fictions*. UMiss, 1987. $30.

Thomas, Brook, *Cross-Examinations of Law and Literature; Cooper, Hawthorne, Stowe and Melville*. CUP, 1987. £27.50.

Williams, Michael J. S., *A World of Words: Language and Displacement in the Fiction of Edgar Allan Poe*. DukeU, 1988. £28.05.

Wilson, James D., *A Reader's Guide to the Short Stories of Mark Twain*. Hall, 1987. $35.

Chapter XVIII. American Literature: The Twentieth Century

Algren, Nelson, *Somebody in Boots*. TMP, 1987. pb $8.95.

Anderson, Chris, *Style as Argument: Contemporary American Nonfiction*. SIU, 1987. hb $19.95, pb $10.95.

Anderson, Sherwood, *Winesburg, Ohio*. Pan, 1988. pb £3.50.

Arksey, Laura, Nancy Pries, and Marcia Reed, ed., *American Diaries: An Annotated Bibliography of Published American Diaries in Journals*. Vol. II: *Diaries Written from 1845 to 1980*. Gale, 1987. $98.

Armitage, Shelley, *John Held Jr., Ilustrator of the Jazz Age*. Syracuse, 1987. $37.50.

Ashbery, John, *April Galleons*. Carcanet, 1988. £8.95.

Ashbery, John, *Three Plays*. Carcanet, 1988. £10.95.

Ashbery, John, and James Schuyler, *A Nest of Ninnies*. Carcanet, 1987. £10.95.

Bald, Wambly, *On the Left Bank 1929–1933*, ed. by Benjamin Franklin V. OhioU, 1987. $19.95.

Bambara, Toni Cade, *The Salt Eaters*. WP, 1987. pb £4.95.

Barnett, Gene A., *Lanford Wilson*. TUSAS. Twayne, 1987. $21.95.

Benstock, Shari, *Women of the Left Bank: Paris, 1900–1940*. Virago, 1987. pb £8.95.

Bernstein, Aline, *An Actor's Daugther*. OhioU, 1987. pb $12.95.

Berstein, Aline, *The Journey Down*. OhioU, 1987. pb $12.95.

Bloom, Harold, ed., *Saul Bellow: Modern Critical Views*. ChelseaH, 1987. $24.50.

Bloom, Harold, ed., *Ralph Ellison: Modern Critical Views*. ChelseaH, 1987. $24.50.

Bloom, Harold, ed., *Norman Mailer: Modern Critical Views*. ChelseaH, 1986. $24.50.

Bloom, Harold, ed., *Thomas Pynchon: Modern Critical Views*. ChelseaH, 1986. $24.50.

Bloom Harold, ed., *Philip Roth: Modern Critical Views*. ChelseaH, 1987. $24.95.

Boch, Hedwig, and Albert Wertheim, ed., *Essays on the Contemporary American Novel*. Hueber, 1986. pb DM 42.

Bohlke, L. Brent, ed., *Willa Cather in Person: Interviews, Speeches, and Letters*. UNeb, 1987. £17.05.

Boxill, Roger, *Tennessee Williams*. Macmillan, 1987. £18.

Branden, Barbara, *The Passion of Ayn Rand*. Allen, 1987. £14.95.

Brinnin, John Malcolm, *Truman Capote: A Memoir*. S&J, 1987. £9.95.

Bruccoli, Matthew J., *Conversations with Ernest Hemingway*. UMissip, 1987. pb £11.50.

Burgess, Gelett, *Burgess Unabridged*. Archon, 1987. £15.30.

Cain, James M., ed., *Sixty Years of Journalism*. BGUP, 1987. hb $29.95, pb $12.95.

Caldwell, Erskine, *With All My Might*. Peachtree, 1987. $19.95.

Callahan, North, *Carl Sandburg: His Life and Works*. UPenn, 1987. £28.25.

Campbell, Jane, *Mythic Black Fiction: The Transformation of History*. UTenn, 1987. $16.95.

Capote, Truman, *A Capote Reader*. RandomH, 1987. $25.

Carpenter, Humphrey, *Geniuses Together: American Writers in Paris in the 1920s*. Unwin Hyman, 1987. £12.95.

Carroll, Joseph, *Wallace Stevens' Supreme Fiction: A New Romanticism*. LSU, 1988. £35.65.

Cather, Willa, *One of Ours*. Virago, 1987. pb £4.95.

Childs, John Steven, *Modernist Form: Pound's Style in the Early Cantos*. SusquehannaU, 1986. £19.50.

Clark, Michael, *Dos Passos' Early Fiction, 1912-1938*. AUP, 1987. £19.95.

Cowley, Malcolm, *Conversations with Malcolm Cowley*, ed. by Thomas Daniel Young. UMissip, 1987. pb £9.25.

Crane, David, *On Eliot's 'Four Quartets'*. NCP, 1987. £15.

Crawford, Robert, *The Savage and the City in the Work of T. S. Eliot*. Clarendon, 1987. £25.

Cronin, Gloria L., and Blaine H. Hall, *Saul Bellow: An Annotated Bibliography*. Second edn. Garland, 1987. $46.

Cunliffe, Marcus, ed., *American Literature Since 1900*. Sphere, 1987. £12.95.

Dahlberg, Edward, *'The Leafless American' and Other Writings*. McPherson, 1987. pb $10.

Darby, William, *Necessary American Fictions; Popular Literature of the 1950s*. BGUP, 1987. hb $35, pb $16.95.

Debusscher, Gilbert, ed., *American Literature in Belgium*. Rodopi, 1987. Fl 50.

Dekker, George, *The American Historical Romance*. CUP, 1987. £30.

Devlin, Albert J., ed., *Welty: A Life in Literature*. UMissip, 1987. £25.

Dick, Philip K., *The Collected Stories of Philip K. Dick*. Five vols. U-M, 1987. $125.

Dixon, Wheeler Winston, *The Cinematic Vision of F. Scott Fitzgerald*. UMIRes, 1986. $44.95.

Donald, David Herbert, *Look Homeward: A Life of Thomas Wolfe*. Bloomsbury, 1987. £16.95.

Dreiser, Theodore, *Selected Magazine Articles of Theodore Dreiser*, Vol. II, ed. by Yoshinobu Hakutani. Freell, 1987. £19.95.

Dreiser, Theodore, *'Sister Carrie'; 'Jennie Gerhardt'; and 'Twelve Men'*, ed. by Richard Lehan. LAm/CUP, 1987. £30.

DuBois, W. E. B., *Writings*, ed. by Nathan Huggins. LAm/CUP, 1987. £30.

Ellmann, Maud, *The Poetics of Impersonality: T. S. Eliot and Ezra Pound*. Harvester, 1988. £29.95.

Everman, Welch D., *Who Says This? The Authority of the Author, the Discourse, and the Reader*. SIU, 1988. $17.95.

Fante, John, *West of Rome*. BSP, 1987. pb £8.95.

Faulkner, William, *The Sound and the Fury*, ed. by David Minter. Norton, 1987. pb £4.95.

Fitzgerald, F. Scott, *The Crack-Up*. ND, 1987. pb $6.95.

Fleming, Robert E., *James Weldon Johnson*. Twayne, 1987. $19.95.

Ford, Hugh, *Four Lives in Paris*. NPP, 1987. $19.95.

Frewin, Leslie, *The Late Mrs. Dorothy Parker*. S&J, 1987. £14.95.

Gale, Steven H., ed., *Encyclopedia of American Humorists*. Garland, 1988. $75.

Gardner, John, *Stillness and Shadows*. S&W, 1987. £12.95.

Gates, Henry Louis, Jr, *Figures in Black: Words, Signs, and the 'Racial' Self*. OUP, 1987. £25.

Gelpi, Albert, *A Coherent Splendor: The American Poetic Renaissance, 1910–1950*. CUP, 1987. £35.

Gentry, Marshall Bruce, *Flannery O'Connor's Religion of the Grotesque*. UMissip, 1987. £20.20.

Gilman, Charlotte Perkins, *Herland*. WP, 1986. pb £1.95.

Glaspell, Susan, *Plays by Susan Glaspell*, ed. and intro. by C. W. E. Bigsby. CUP, 1987. pb £9.95.

Gonnard, Maurice, Sergio Perosa, and C. W. E. Bigsby, ed., *Cultural Change in the United States Since World War Two*. FreeU, 1986. Fl 60.

Gorak, Jan, *God the Artist: American Novelists in a Post-Realistic Age*. UIll, 1987. $21.95.

Gorman, Edward, ed., *The Black Lizard Anthology of Crime Fiction*. Black Lizard: CA, 1987. pb $8.95.

Haas, Rudolf, ed., *Amerikanische Lyrik: Perspektiven und Interpretationen*. Schmidt, 1987. DM 86.

Hamilton, Cynthia S., *Western and Hard-Boiled Detective Fiction in America*. Macmillan, 1987. £27.50.

Hardy, John Edward, *The Fiction of Walker Percy*. UIll, 1987. $24.95.

Hart, James D., *The Concise Oxford Companion to American Literature*. OUP, 1986. £19.50.

Hemingway, Ernest, *The Complete Short Stories of Ernest Hemingway: The Finca Vigia Edition*. Scribner, 1987. $22.50.

Hemingway, Ernest, *Dateline: Toronto. The Complete 'Toronto Star' Dispatches, 1920–1924*. Scribner, 1986. $19.95.

Hendrick, Willene, and George Hendrick, *Katherine Anne Porter*. Twayne, 1987. $17.95.

Hoennighauser, Lothar, *William Faulkner: The Art of Stylization in his Early Graphic and Literary Work*. CUP, 1987. £27.50.

Hoffman, Michael J., ed., *Critical Essays on Gertrude Stein*. Hall, 1986. $35.

Hohmann, Charles, *Thomas Pynchon' 'Gravity's Rainbow': A Study of its Conceptual Structure and of Rilke's Influence*. Lang, 1986. $48.05.

Holley, Margaret, *The Poetry of Marianne Moore: A Study in Voice and Value*. CUP, 1988. £27.50.

Hughes, Langston, *I Wonder as I Wander*. TMP, 1987. pb $9.95.

Hurston, Zora Neale, *Jonah's Gourd Vine*. Virago, 1988. pb £4.50.

Hurston, Zora Neale, *Spunk: The Selected Short Stories of Zora Neale Hurston*. Camden, 1987. pb £4.95.

Ickstadt, Heinz, Rob Kroes, and Brian Lee, ed., *The Thirties: Politics and Culture in a Time of Broken Dreams*. FreeU, 1987. hb Fl 65, pb Fl 37.50.

James, Henry, *The Complete Notebooks of Henry James: The Authoritative and Definitive Edition*, ed. by Leon Edel and Lyall H. Powers. OUPAm, 1987. $32.95.

James, Henry, *The Spoils of Poynton*, ed. by David Lodge. Penguin, 1987. pb £2.50.

Jarrell, Randall, *Pictures from an Institution*. Faber, 1987. pb £4.95.

Jay, Gregory S., ed., *Modern American Critics, 1920–1955*. DLB. Gale, 1987. $92.

Jeffers, Robinson, *Selected Poems*, ed. by Colin Falck. Carcanet, 1987. pb £6.95.

Jay, Gregory S., ed., *Modern American Critics, 1920–1955*. DLB. Gale, 1987. $92.

Jeffers, Robinson, *Selected Poems*, ed. by Colin Falck. Carcanet, 1987. pb £6.95.

Johnson, Courtney, Jr, *Henry James and the Evolution of Consciousness: A Study of 'The Ambassadors'*. MichSU, 1987. $15.

Johnston, Carol, *Thomas Wolfe: A Descriptive Bibliography*. UPitt, 1987. $65.

Joyce, Joyce Ann, *Richard Wright's Art of Tragedy*. UIowa, 1986. $14.95.

Keller, Lynn, *Re-making It New: Contemporary American Poetry and the Modernist Tradition*. CUP, 1988. £27.50.

Kellner, Bruce, ed., *The Harlem Renaissance: A Historical Dictionary for the Era*. Methuen, 1987. pb £12.95.

Kerman, Cynthia Earl, and Richard Eldridge, *The Lives of Jean Toomer: A Hunger for Wholeness*. LSU, 1987. £28.45.

Kesey, Ken, *Demon Box*. Methuen, 1987. pb £3.95.

Kroes, Rob, and Alessandro Portelli, ed., *Social Change and New Modes of Expression: The United States, 1910–1930*. FreeU, 1987. pb Fl 60.

Landesman, Jay, *Rebel Without Applause*. Bloomsbury, 1987. £12.95.

Laughlin, James, *Pound As Wuz: Essays and Lectures on Ezra Pound*. Graywolf, 1987. pb $9.50.

Lee, Brian, *American Fiction 1865–1940*. Longman, 1987. hb £15.95, pb £6.95.

Levitt, Morton P., *Modernist Survivors: The Contemporary Novel in England, the United States, France, and Latin America*. OSU, 1987. $27.50.

Lowell, Robert, *Collected Prose*, ed. and intro. by Robert Giroux. Faber, 1987. £17.50.

Lucas, Mark, *The Southern Vision of Andrew Lytle*. LSU, 1987. $22.50.

Lyndenberg, Robin, *Word Cultures: Radical Theory and Practice in William S. Burroughs' Fiction*. UIll, 1987. $24.95.

Lynn, Kenneth S., *Hemingway*. S&S, 1987. £16.

McCaffery, Larry, and Sinda Gregory, ed., *Alive and Writing: Interview with American Authors of the 1980s*. UIll, 1988. hb $22.50, pb $9.95.

McCarthy, Gerry, *Edward Albee*. Macmillan, 1987. £18.

McCarthy, Mary, *How I Grew*. W&N, 1987. £14.95.

McHale, Brian, *Postmodern Fiction*. Methuen, 1987. hb £25, pb £7.95.

Mackinon, Janice R., and Stephen R. Mackinon, *Agnes Smedley: The Life and Times of an American Radical*. Virago, 1988. £20.

Marable, Manning, *W. E. B. Dubois: Black Radical Democrat*. Twayne, 1986. hb $29.95, pb $13.95.

Martin, Reginald, *Ishmael Reed and the New Black Aesthetic Critics*. Macmillan, 1988. £25.

Matterson, Stephen, *Berryman and Lowell: The Art of Losing*. Macmillan, 1988. £25.

Meade, Marion, *Dorothy Parker: What Fresh Hell Is This?* Heinemann, 1988. £12.95.

Mencken, H. L., *'Ich Kuss Die Hand': The Letters of H. L. Mencken to Gretchen Hood*, ed. by Peter Dowell. UAla, 1986. £17.50.

Mencken, H. L., and Sara Mencken, *Mencken and Sara: A Life in Letters*, ed. by Marion Elizabeth Rodgers. McGraw-Hill, 1987. $22.95.

Merrill, James, *Recitative: Prose*, ed. by J. D. McClatchy. NPP, 1987. hb $25, pb $12.50.

Merrill, Robert, *Joseph Heller*. Twayne, 1987. $17.95.

Messerli, Douglas, *'Language' Poetries: An Anthology*. ND, 1987. pb $8.95.

Metcalf, Paul, *Where Do You Put the Horse?* Dalkey, 1987. $20.

Meyers, Jeffrey, *Manic Power: Robert Lowell and his Circle*. Macmillan, 1987. £16.95.

Middleton, David L., *Toni Morrison: An Annotated Bibliography*. Garland, 1987. $36.

Milbauer, Asher Z., and Donald G. Watson, ed., *Reading Philip Roth*. Macmillan, 1987. £27.50.

Miller, Arthur, *Conversations with Arthur Miller*, ed. by Matthew C. Roudané. UMissip, 1987. pb £10.95.

Miller, Henry, *Book of Friends: A Trilogy*. Capra, 1987. pb $9.95.

Miller, Russell, *Bare-faced Messiah: The True Story of L. Ron Hubbard*. Jospeh, 1987. £12.95.

Millgate, Michael, ed., *New Essays on 'Light in August'*. CUP, 1987. hb £20, pb £6.95.

Mizener, Arthur, *Scott Fitzgerald* (1972). T&H, 1987. pb £3.95.

Montgomery, John, *Kerouac at the 'Wild Boar'*. F&F, 1986. pb $16.95.

Montgomery, John, *The Kerouac We Knew*. F&F, 1987. pb $5.25.

Moore, Marianne, *The Complete Prose of Marianne Moore*, ed. by Patricia C. Willis. Faber, 1987. £30.

Newman, Robert D., *Understanding Thomas Pynchon*. USC, 1987. hb $19.95, pb $7.95.

Nolan, William F., ed., *Max Brand: Western Giant*. BGUP, 1986. hb $21.95, pb $9.95.

Norman, Frank, *Bang to Rights*. Hogarth, 1987. pb £3.95.

O'Brien, Tim, *Going after Cacciato*. Collins, 1988. pb £3.95.

O'Donnell, Patrick, *Passionate Doubts: Designs of Interpretation in Contemporary American Fiction*. UIowa, 1986. $19.95.

O'Neill, Eugene, *'As Ever, Gene': The Letters of Eugene O'Neill to George Jean Nathan*, ed. by Nancy L. Roberts and Arthur W. Roberts. FDU, 1987. £24.50.

Panichas, George A., and Claes G. Ryan, ed., *Irving Babbitt in our Time*. CUAP, 1986. $27.95.

Paz, Octavio, *On Poets and Others*, trans. by Michael Schmidt. Seaver, 1986. $16.95.

Pearce, Roy Harvey, *Gesta Humanorum: Studies in the Historicist Mode*. UMiss, 1987. $23.

Pieratt, Asa B., Jr., Julie Huffman-Klinkowitz, and Jerome Klinkowitz, ed., *Kurt Vonnegut: A Comprehensive Bibliography*. Archon, 1987. £31.05.

Platt, Charles, *Dream Makers: Science Fiction and Fantasy Writers at Work*. Xanadu, 1987. £9.95.

Poirier, Richard, *The Renewal of Literature: Emersonian Reflections*. Faber, 1987. £14.95.

Pound, Ezra, *Pound/Zukofsky: Selected Letters of Ezra Pound and Louis Zukofsky*, ed. by Barry Ahearn. Faber, 1987. £30.

Rehder, Robert, *The Poetry of Wallace Stevens*. Macmillan, 1988. £29.50.

Reynolds, Michael, *Hemingway's First War*. Blackwell, 1987. pb £7.95.

Root, Waverley, *The Paris Edition: The Autobiography of Waverley Root, 1927–1934*, ed. by Samuel Abt. NPP, 1987. $16.95.

Rosenthal, M. L., *The Poet's Art*. Norton, 1987. £10.95.

Saltzman, Arthur M., *The Fiction of William Gass: The Consolation of Language*. SIU, 1986. $19.95.

Salzman, Jack, ed., *American Studies; An Annotated Bibliography*. Three vols. CUP, 1987. £150.

Sanders, David, *John Dos Passos; A Comprehensive Bibliography*. Garland, 1987. $67.

Sarton, May, *Recovering: A Journal*. Norton, 1986. pb £4.95.

Schlueter, June, and James K. Flanagan, *Arthur Miller*. Ungar, 1987. $16.95.

Schuerer, Ernst, and Philip Jenkins, ed., *B. Traven: Life and Work*, PSU, 1987. $22.50.

Schwartz, Delmore, *The Ego Is Always at the Wheel: Bagatelles*. Carcanet, 1987. £6.95.

Selby, Hubert, Jr, *Last Exit to Brooklyn*. Paladin, 1987. pb £3.95.

Silliman, Ron, *The New Sentence*. Segue, 1987. pb $12.95.

Solomon, Carl, *Mishaps Perhaps*. CL, 1987. pb £2.50.

Sontag, Susan, *A Susan Sontag Reader*. Penguin, 1987. pb £5.95.

Sorrentino, Gilbert, *The Sky Changes*. NPP, 1987. pb $12.50.

Starr, Kevin, *Inventing the Dream: California through the Progressive Era*. OUPAm, 1987. $19.95.

Stein, Gertrude, *Mrs. Reynolds*. S&M, 1987. hb $15.95, pb $11.95.

Stern, Milton R., ed., *Critical Essays on F. Scott Fitzgerald's 'Tender Is the Night'*. Hall, 1986. $35.

Styron, William, *Conversations with William Styron*, ed. by James L. W. West III. UMissip, 1987. £15.85.

Sweeny, Mary K., *Walker Percy and the Postmodern World*. LUP, 1987. $8.95.

Taylor, Gordon O., *Studies in Modern American Autobiography*. Macmillan, 1987. pb £8.95.

Taylor, J. Golden, *et al.*, ed., *A Literary History of the American West*. TCUP, 1987. $79.50.

Teper Bender, Eileen, *Joyce Carol Oates, Artist in Residence*. IUP, 1987. hb $29.95, pb $9.95.

Tichi, Cecelia, *Shifting Gears: Technology, Literature, Culture in Modernist America*. UNC. hb $29.75, pb $12.70.

Toomer, Jean, *Cane*, ed. by Darwin T. Turner. Norton, 1988. pb £4.95.

Updike, John, *Forty Stories*. Penguin, 1987. pb £4.95.

Van Vechten, Carl, *Letters of Carl Van Vechten*, ed. by Bruce Kellner. Two vols. Yale, 1987. £22.50.

Wadlington, Warwick, *Reading Faulknerian Tragedy*. CornU, 1987. $29.95.

Wagner, Linda W., ed., *Ernest Hemingway: Six Decades of Criticism*. MichSU, 1987. pb $18.

Wagner-Martin, Linda, ed., *New Essays on 'The Sun Also Rises'*. CUP, 1987. hb £20, pb £6.95.

Warrick, Patricia S., *Mind in Motion: The Fiction of Philip K. Dick*. SIU, 1987. $18.95.

Watson, James G., *William Faulkner: Letters and Fictions*. UTex, 1987. $22.50.

Weidman, Jerome, *Praying for Rain: An Autobiography*. Reinhardt, 1987. £15.

Wenke, Joseph, *Mailer's America*. UPNE, 1987. £20.

Westarp, Karl-Heinz, and Jan Nordby Gretlund, ed., *Realist of Distances: Flannery O'Connor Revisited*. AarhusU, 1987. pb Dkr 122.

Whalen, Philip, *Two Novels by Philip Whalen*. Zephyr, 1987. pb £7.95.

Wharton, Edith, *A Backward Glance*. Century, 1987. pb £5.95.

Wharton, Edith, *Ethan Frome*. Penguin, 1987. pb £2.95.

Wilde, Alan, *Middle Grounds: Studies in Contemporary American Fiction*. UPenn, 1987. £23.70.

Williams, William Carlos, *The Collected Poems of William Carlos Williams*. Vol. I: *1909–1939*, ed. by A. Walton Litz and C. MacGowan. Carcanet, 1987. £18.95.

Wolfe, Thomas, *The Complete Short Stories of Thomas Wolfe*, ed. by Francis E. Skipp. Scribner, 1987. $24.95.

Wright, Richard, *Eight Men*. TMP, 1987. pb £9.95.

Chapter XIX. African, Caribbean, Indian, Australian, Canadian, New Zealand, and South Pacific Literatures in English

General

Durix, Jean-Pierre, *The Writer Written: The Artist and Creation in the New Literatures in English.* Greenwood, 1987. $29.95.

Niven, Alastair, ed., *Under Another Sky: The Commonwealth Poetry Prize Anthology.* Carcanet, 1987. pb £6.95.

Singh, Kirpal, ed., *The Writer's Sense of the Past.* SingaporeU, 1987. pb $18/S$28.

Stummer, Peter O., ed., *The Story Must Be Told: Short Narrative Prose in the New English Literatures.* K&N, 1986. pb DM 39.

Africa

Gikandi, Simon, *Reading the African Novel.* Currey, 1987. £8.95.

Maduakor, Obi, *Wole Soyinka: An Introduction to his Writing.* Garland, 1987. $35.

Schreiner, Olive, *Letters.* Vol. I: *1871–1899*, ed. by Richard Rive. Clarendon, 1988. £30.

The Caribbean

Dabydeen, Cyril, ed., *A Shapely Fire: Changing the Literary Landscape.* Mosaic, 1987. hb C$24.95, pb C$12.95.

Dabydeen, David, and Brinsley Samaroo, ed., *India in the Caribbean.* Hansib/CCS, UWarwick, 1987. hb £11.95, pb £8.95.

Habekost, Christian, ed., *Dub Poetry: Nineteen Poets from England and Jamaica.* Schwinn, 1987. pb.

Nightingale, Peggy, *Journey through Darkness: The Writing of V. S. Naipaul.* UQP, 1987. pb £16.95.

Saakana, Amon Saba, *The Colonial Legacy in Caribbean Literature.* Karnak, 1987. pb £4.95.

Thieme, John, *The Web of Tradition: Uses of Allusion in V. S. Naipaul's Fiction.* Hansib/Dangaroo, 1987. pb £6.95.

Indian

Blaise, Clark, and Bharati Mukherjee, *Days and Nights in Calcutta.* Penguin, 1986. pb £3.95.

Gupta, G. S. Balarama, ed., *Studies in Indian Fiction in English.* JIWE Pubns, 1987.

Jhabvala, Ruth Prawer, *Out of India: Selected Stories.* Murray, 1987. £10.95.

Kadare, Ismail, *Chronicle in Stone.* Serpent's Tail, 1987. £9.95.

Kali for Women, ed., *Truth Tales: Stories by Indian Women.* WP, 1987. pb £3.95.

Murti, K. V. Suryanarayana, *Kohinoor in the Crown: Critical Studies in Indian English Literature.* OrientalUP, 1987. £9.95.

Raine, Kathleen, *The English Language and the Indian Spirit: Correspondence between Kathleen Raine and K. D. Sethna*, ed. by K. D. Sethna. Sethna, 1986. Rs 35.

Raiziss, Sonia, *Chelsea*. ChelseaA, 1987. $6.
Ramanujan, A. K., *Second Sight*. OUPI, 1986. Rs 40.
Ray, Satyajit, *Stories*. S&W, 1987. £10.95.

Australia

Akerholt, May-Brit, *Patrick White*. Rodopi, 1988. pb.
Colmer, John, and Dorothy Colmer, ed., *Australian Autobiography*. PenguinA, 1987. pb A$12.95.
Giles, Fiona, ed., *From the Verandah*. PenguinA, 1987. pb A$14.95.
Harpur, Charles, *Stalwart the Bushranger*. Currency, 1987. pb
McGillick, Paul, *Jack Hibberd*. Rodopi, 1988. pb.
Thomson, Helen, ed., *Catherine Helen Spence*. UQP, 1987. pb £9.95.

Canada

Aitken, Johan Lyall, *Masques of Morality: Females in Fiction*. WPC, 1987. pb C$9/£7.95.
Benson, E., and L. W. Connolly, *English Canadian Theatre*. OUPC, 1987. pb C$9.95.
Bisztray, George, *Hungarian-Canadian Literature*. UTor, 1987. £13.
Cooley, Dennis, *The Vernacular Muse: The Eye and Ear in Contemporary Literature*. Turnstone, 1987. pb C$12.95.
Copoloff-Mechanic, Susan, *Pilgrim's Progress: A Study of the Short Stories of Hugh Hood*. ECW, 1988. pb C$15.
Darling, Michael, ed., *Perspectives on Mordecai Richler*. ECW, 1986. pb C$15.
Daymond, D., and L. Monkman, ed., *On Middle Ground*. MethuenC, 1987. pb C$19.95.
De Mille, James, *A Strange Manuscript Found in a Copper Cylinder*, ed. by Malcolm Parks. Carleton, 1986. pb C$9.95.
Duffy, Dennis, *Sounding the Iceberg: An Essay on Canadian Historical Novels*. ECW, 1986. pb C$14.
Filewood, Alan, *Collective Encounters: Documentary Theatre in English Canada*. UTor, 1988. pb £10.50.
Godard, Barbara, *Gynocritics/La Gynocritique*. ECW, 1985. pb C$15.
Hancock, Geoff, *Canadian Writers at Work*. OUPC, 1987. pb C$19.95.
Hjartarson, Paul, ed., *A Stranger to my Time: Essays by and about Frederick Philip Grove*. NeWest, 1987. pb C$11.95.
Howells, Coral Ann, *Private and Fictional Words: Canadian Women Novelists of the 1970s and 80s*. Methuen, 1987. pb £6.95.
Irvine, Lorna, *Sub/Version*. ECW, 1986. pb C$14.
Keefer, Janice Kulyk, *Under Eastern Eyes: A Critical Reading of Maritime Fiction*. UTor, 1988. pb £10.50.
Kent, David, ed., *Lighting Up the Terrain: The Poetry of Margaret Avison*. ECW, 1987. pb C$15.
Kroller, Eva-Marie, *Canadian Travellers in Europe 1851–1900*. UBC, 1987. £24.65.
Lecker, Robert, and Jack David, ed., *The Annotated Bibliography of Canada's Major Authors*, Vol. VII. ECW, 1987. pb C$28.
Lecker, Robert, J. David, and E. Quigley, ed., *Canadian Writers and their Works*. ECW, 1987. C$40.

McDougall, R., and G. Whitlock, ed., *Australian/Canadian Literatures in English: Comparative Perspectives*. MethuenA, 1987. pb.

McLuhan, Marshall, *Letters*, ed. by M. Molinaro, C. McLuhan, and W. Toye. OUPC, 1987. £25.

MacLulich, T. D., *Between Europe and America: The Canadian Tradition in Fiction*. ECW, 1988. pb C$15.

Mandel, Eli, *The Family Romance*. Turnstone, 1986. pb.

Mandel, Eli, and D. Taras, ed., *A Passion for Identity: An Introduction to Canadian Studies*. MethuenC, 1987. pb C$16.95.

Martin, W. R., *Alice Munro: Paradox and Parallel*. UAlberta, 1987.

Moss, John, ed., *Future Indicative: Literary Theory and Canadian Literature*. UOttawa, 1987. pb C$24.95.

Munro, Alice, *The Alice Munro Papers: First Accession*, ed. by J. Moore, J. Tenner, and A. Steele. UCalgary, 1986. pb C$15.

Munro, Alice, *The Alice Munro Papers: Second Accession*, ed. by J. Moore. UCalgary, 1987. pb C$15.

Norris, Ken, *The Little Magazine in Canada 1925-80*. ECW, 1984. pb C$15.

Pitt, David G., *E. J. Pratt: The Master Years 1927-1964*. UTor, 1988. £24.50.

Richardson, John, *Wacousta, or The Prophecy: A Tale of the Canadas*, ed. by Douglas Cronk. Carleton, 1987. pb C$12.95.

Ripley, Gordon, and A. Mercer, *Who's Who in Canadian Literature, 1987-88*. Reference, 1987. C$25.

Salloum, Sheryl, *Malcolm Lowry: Vancouver Days*. Harbour, 1987. pb C$9.95.

Staines, D., ed., *Leacock: A Reappraisal*. UOttawa, 1986. pb C$14.95.

Sproxton, Birk, ed., *Trace: Prairie Writers on Writing*. Turnstone, 1986. pb.

Stratford, Philip, *All the Polarities: Comparative Studies in Contemporary Canadian Novels in French and English*. ECW, 1986. pb C$15.

Twigg, Alan *Vancouver and its Writers*. Harbour, 1986. pb C$10.95.

York, Lorraine, *The Other Side of Dailiness: Photography in the Works of Alice Munro, Timothy Findley, Michael Ondaatje, Margaret Laurence*. ECW, 1988. pb C$15.

New Zealand and the South Pacific

Alpers, Anthony, *The World of the Polynesians Seen through their Myths and Legends, Poetry and Art* (1970). OUPNZ, 1987. pb NZ$27.95/£15.

Bock, Hedwig, and Albert Wertheim, ed., *Essays on Post-Colonial Fiction*. Hueber, 1986.

Corballis, Richard, and Simon Garrett, *Witi Ihimaera*. Longman P, 1984. pb NZ$6.50.

Coussy, Denise, Evelyne Labbé, Michel and Geneviève Fabre, *Les Littératures de langue anglaise depuis 1945: Grande-Bretagne, Etats-Unis, Commonwealth*. Nathan, 1988. pb Ffr 130.

Curnow, Allen, *Look Back Harder: Critical Writings 1935-1985*, ed. by Peter Simpson. AucklandU, 1987. pb NZ$32.50.

Durix, Jean-Pierre, *The Writer Written: The Artist and Creation in the New Literatures in English*. Greenwood, 1987. $29.95.

Hyde, Robin, *Passport to Hell*, ed. by D. I. B. Smith. AucklandU, 1986. pb NZ$21.95.

Jones, Lawrence, *Barbed Wire and Mirrors: Essays on New Zealand Prose.* UOtago, 1987. pb NZ$27.23.

Mansfield, Katherine, *The Stories of Katherine Mansfield*, ed. by Anthony Alpers. OUPNZ, 1984. NZ$54.95.

O'Sullivan, Vincent, *An Anthology of Twentieth Century New Zealand Poetry* (1970). OUPNZ, 1987. pb NZ$25.

Satchell, William, *The Toll of the Bush*, ed. by Kendrick Smithyman. AucklandU, 1985. pb NZ$16.50.

Simms, Norman, *Silence and Invisibility: A Study of the Literatures of the Pacific, Australia and New Zealand.* TCP, 1986. pb $16.

Sinclair, Keith, ed., *Tasman Relations: New Zealand and Australia, 1788–1988.* AucklandU, 1987. NZ$45.

Stone, R. J. C., *The Father and his Gift: John Logan Campbell's Later Years.* AucklandU, 1987. NZ$39.95.

Best Books and Articles

The best of 1986: listings by chapter of the best articles and books reviewed here in the opinion of our critics. Location of reviews and bibliographical details may be found through use of Index I immediately following these listings.

Chapter I.   Reference, Literary History, and Bibliography

Pollard, A. W., and G. R. Redgrave, comp., *A Short-Title Catalogue of Books Printed in England, Scotland, and Ireland and of English Books Printed Abroad 1475-1640*. Vol. I: *A–H*. Second edn begun by W. A. Jackson and F. S. Ferguson, completed by Katharine F. Pantzer. BibS.

Smith Margaret M., and Penny Boumelha, ed., *Index of English Literary Manuscripts*. Vol. III: *1700-1800*. Part I: *Addison-Fielding*. Mansell.

Chapter II.   Literary Theory

Bersani, Leo, *The Freudian Body: Psychoanalysis and Art*. ColU.

Derrida, Jacques, *Memoires: For Paul de Man*. ColU.

Dews, Peter, 'Adorno, Post-structuralism and the Critique of Identity' (*NLR*).

Felman, Shoshana, *Writing and Madness (Literature/Philosophy/Psycho-analysis)*. CornU.

Frow, John, *Marxism and Literary History*. Blackwell.

Gasché, Rodolphe, *The Tain of the Mirror: Derrida and the Philosophy of Reflection*. Harvard.

Huyssen, Andreas, *After the Great Divide: Modernism, Mass Culture, Post-modernism*. IndU.

Jacobus, Mary, *Reading Woman: Essays in Feminist Criticism*. Methuen.

Kaplan, Cora, *Sea Changes: Culture and Feminism*. Verso.

de Man, Paul, *The Resistance to Theory*. UMinn.

Miller, Nancy K., ed., *The Poetics of Gender*. ColU.

Rose, Jacqueline, *Sexuality in the Field of Vision*. Verso.

Todd, Jane Marie, 'The Veiled Woman in Freud's "Das Unheimliche" ' (*Signs*).

Chapter III.   English Language

Burchfield, R. W., ed., *A Supplement to the Oxford English Dictionary*. Vol. IV: *Se–Z*. Clarendon.

Harris, John, *Phonological Variation and Change: Studies in Hiberno-English*. CUP (1985).

Kastovsky, Dieter, and Aleksander Szwedek, ed., *Linguistics across Historical and Geographical Boundaries: In Honour of Jacek Fisiak on the Occasion of his Fiftieth Birthday*. 2 vols. MGruyter.

McIntosh, Angus, M. L. Samuels, and Michael Benskin, ed., *A Linguistic Atlas of Late Mediaeval English*. 4 vols. AberdeenU.

Ó Mathúna, Seán, *William Bathe, S.J., 1564-1614: A Pioneer in Linguistics*. SiHoLS. Benjamins.

Chapter IV.   Old English Literature

Bately, Janet M., ed., *The Anglo-Saxon Chronicle: A Collaborative Edition*. Vol. III: *MS A*. Brewer.

Clayton, Mary, 'Ælfric and the Nativity of the Blessed Virgin Mary' (*Anglia*).

Fausbøll, Else, ed., *Fifty-six Ælfric Fragments: The Newly-Found Copenhagen. Fragments of Ælfric's 'Catholic Homilies'. With Facsimiles*. UCophenhagen.

Kiernan, Kevin S., *The Thorkelin Transcripts of 'Beowulf'*. Anglistica. R&B.

Lapidge, Michael, 'The School of Theodore and Hadrian' (*ASE*).

Chapter V.   Middle English: Excluding Chaucer

Bennett, J. A. W., *Medieval English Literature*, ed. and completed by Douglas Gray. Clarendon.

Burnley, David, 'Christine de Pisan and the so-called *style clergial*' (*MLR*).

Field, Rosalind, 'The Heavenly Jerusalem in *Pearl*' (*MLR*).

Kenny, Anthony, ed., *Wyclif in his Times*. Clarendon.

Szittya, Penn R., *The Antifraternal Tradition in Medieval Literature*. Princeton.

Chapter VI.   Middle English: Chaucer

Benson, C. David, *Chaucer's Drama of Style: Poetic Variety and Contrast in the 'Canterbury Tales'*. UNC.

Burnley, David, 'Courtly Speech in Chaucer' (*PoeticaJ*).

Burnley, David, 'Curial Prose in England' (*Speculum*).

Hardman, Phillipa, 'Chaucer's Muses and his "Art Poetical" ' (*RES*).

Ramsey, R. Vance, 'Paleography and Scribes of Shared Training' (*SAC*).

Chapter VII.   The Sixteenth Century: Excluding Drama After 1550

Barkan, Leonard, *The Gods Made Flesh: Metamorphosis and the Pursuit of Paganism*. Yale.

Fumerton, Patricia, 'Exchanging Gifts: The Elizabethan Currency of Children and Poetry' (*ELH*).

Gilman, Ernest B., *Iconoclasm and Poetry in the English Reformation: Down Went Dagon*. UChic.

Heninger, S. K. Jr, 'Sequences, Systems, Models: Sidney and the Secularization of Sonnets', in *Poems in their Place: The Intertextuality and Order of Poetic Collections*, ed. by Neil Fraistat. UNC.

Maynard, Winifred, *Elizabethan Lyric Poetry and its Music*. Clarendon.

Schibanoff, Susan, 'Taking Jane's Cue: *Phyllyp Sparowe* as a Primer for Women Readers' (*PMLA*).

Stillman, Robert E., *Sidney's Poetic Justice: 'The Old Arcadia', its Eclogues, and Renaissance Pastoral Traditions*. AUP/BuckU.

Chapter VIII.   Shakespeare

Davies, H. Neville, 'Jacobean *Antony and Cleopatra*' (*ShakS*, 1985).

Everett, Barbara, 'Two Damned Cruces: *Othello* and *Twelfth Night*' (*RES*).

Gillies, John, 'Shakespeare's Virginian Masque' (*ELH*).

Miller, Jonathan, *Subsequent Performances*. Faber.

Rackin, Phyllis, 'Temporality, Anachronism, and Presence in Shakespeare's English Histories' (*RenD*).

Shakespeare, William, *The Complete Works*, ed. by Stanley Wells and Gary Taylor. Original-Spelling Edition. OUP.

Shakespeare, William, *'The Sonnets' and 'A Lover's Complaint'*, ed. by John Kerrigan. NPS. Penguin.

Chapter IX.   Renaissance Drama: Excluding Shakespeare

Berry, Herbert, *The Boar's Head Playhouse*. Folger/AUP.

Donaldson, Ian, 'Jonson's Magic Houses' (*E&S*).

Jones, Robert C., *Engagement with Knavery: Point of View in 'Richard III', 'The Jew of Malta', 'Volpone', and 'The Revenger's Tragedy'*. DukeU.

Leech, Clifford, *Christopher Marlowe: Poet for the Stage*, ed. by Anne Lancashire. AMS.

Chapter X.   The Earlier Seventeenth Century: Excluding Drama

Diehl, Huston, 'Into the Maze of Self' (*JMRS*).

Goldberg, Jonathan, *Voice Terminal Echo: Postmodernism and English Renaissance Texts*. Methuen.

Stocker, Margarita, *Apocalyptic Marvell: The Second Coming in Seventeenth-Century Poetry*. Harvester.

Watson, Graeme J., 'The Temple in "The Night"': Henry Vaughan and the Collapse of the Established Church' (*MP*).

Chapter XI.   Milton

Kerrigan, William, and Gordon Braden, 'Milton's Coy Eve: *Paradise Lost* and Renaissance Love Poetry' (*ELH*).

Revard, Stella P., ' "L'Allegro" and "Il Penseroso": Classical Tradition and Renaissance Mythography' (*PMLA*).

Teskey, Gordon, 'From Allegory to Dialectic: Imagining Error in Spenser and Milton' (*PMLA*).

Wittreich, Joseph, *Interpreting 'Samson Agonistes'*. Princeton.

Chapter XII.   The Later Seventeenth Century

Hopkins, David, *John Dryden*. CUP.

Kupersmith, William, *Roman Satirists in Seventeenth-Century England*. UNeb (1985).

Milhous, Judith, and Robert D. Hume, *Producible Interpretation: Eight English Plays 1675–1707*. SIU (1985).

Thickstun, Margaret Olofson, 'From Christiana to Stand-fast: Subsuming the Feminine in *The Pilgrim's Progress*' (*SEL*).

Weber, Harold, *The Restoration Rake-Hero: Transformations in Sexual Understanding in Seventeenth-Century England*. UWisc.

Zimbardo, Rose A., *A Mirror to Nature: Transformations in Drama and Aesthetics 1660–1732*. UKen.

Chapter XIII.   The Eighteenth Century

Agnew, Jean-Christophe, *Worlds Apart: The Market and the Theater in Anglo-American Thought, 1550–1750*. CUP.

Barrell, John, *The Political Theory of Painting from Reynolds to Hazlitt: 'The Body of the Public'*. Yale.

Castle, Terry, *Masquerade and Civilization: The Carnivalesque in Eighteenth-Century English Culture and Fiction*. Methuen.

Griffin, Dustin, *Regaining Paradise: Milton and the Eighteenth Century*. CUP.

Hulme, Peter, *Colonial Encounters: Europe and the Native Caribbean 1492-1797*. Methuen.

Chapter XIV.   The Nineteenth Century: Romantic Period

Barrell, John, *The Political Theory of Painting from Reynolds to Hazlitt: 'The Body of the Public'*. Yale.

Bidney, Martin, 'Solomon and Pharaoh's Daughter: Blake's Response to Wordsworth's Prospectus to *The Recluse*' (*JEGP*).

Bromwich, David, 'Romantic Poetry and the *Edinburgh* Ordinances' (*YES*).

Kaplan, Cora, *Sea Changes: Culture and Feminism*. Verso.

Neumann, Anne Waldron, 'Characterization and Comment in *Pride and Prejudice*' (*Style*).

Snyder, Robert Lance, 'De Quincey's Literature of Power: A Mythic Paradigm' (*SEL*).

Tanner, Tony, *Jane Austen*. Macmillan.

Turner, John, *Play and Politics in Wordsworth*. Macmillan.

Valente, Joseph, ' "Upon the Braes": History and Hermeneutics in *Waverley*' (*SIR*).

Chapter XV.   The Nineteenth Century: Victorian Period

Altick, Richard D., *Paintings from Books: Art and Literature in Britain, 1760-1900*. OSU.

Beetham, Margaret, ' "Healthy Reading": The Periodical Press in Late Victorian Manchester', in *City, Class and Culture*, ed. by Alan Kidd and Ken Roberts. ManU (1985).

Block, Ed Jr, 'Walter Pater, Arthur Symons, W. B. Yeats, and the Fortunes of the Literary Portrait' (*SEL*).

Bloom, Harold, ed. and intro., *Pre-Raphaelite Poets*. ChelseaH.

Bullen, J.B., *The Expressive Eye: Fiction and Perception in the Work of Thomas Hardy*. Clarendon.

Chase, Karen, 'The Kindness of Consanguinity: Family History in *Henry Esmond*' (*MLS*).

Clark-Beattie, Rosemary, 'Fables of Rebellion: Anti-Catholicism and the Structure of *Villette*' (*ELH*).

Cotsell, Michael, *The Companion to 'Our Mutual Friend'*. A&U.

Davis, Tracy C., 'The Employment of Children in the Victorian Theatre' (*NTQ*).

Dowling, Linda, *Language and Decadence in the Victorian Fin de Siècle*. Princeton.

Jacobson, Wendy S., *The Companion to 'The Mystery of Edwin Drood'*. A&U.

Jann, Rosemary, *The Art and Science of Victorian History*. OSU.

Kent, Christopher, 'The Editor and the Law', in *Innovators and Preachers*, ed. by Joel H. Wiener. Greenwood (1985).

Larson, Janet L., *Dickens and the Broken Scripture*. UGeo (1985).

Leighton, Angela, *Elizabeth Barrett Browning*. Harvester.

McGann, Jerome J., *The Beauty of Inflections: Literary Investigations in Historical Method and Theory*. Clarendon (1985).

Parry, Ann. 'The Grove Years 1868-1883' (*VPR*).

Peterson, Linda H., *Victorian Autobiography: The Tradition of Self-Interpretation*. Yale.

Shatto, Susan, ed., *Tennyson's 'Maud': A Definitive Edition*. Athlone.

Sinfield, Alan, *Alfred Tennyson*. Blackwell.

Tambling, Jeremy, 'Prison-bound: Dickens and Foucault' (*EIC*).

Thomson, Peter, ' "Weirdness that lifts and colours all": The Secret Self of Henry Irving', in *Shakespeare and the Victorian Stage*, ed. by Richard Foulkes. CUP.

Weintraub, Stanley, ed., *Bernard Shaw: The Diaries, 1885-97*. PSU.

Yeazell, Ruth Bernard, ed., *Sex, Politics, and Science in the Nineteenth-Century Novel*. JHU.

Chapter XVI.   The Twentieth Century

Barley, Tony, *Taking Sides: The Fiction of John le Carré*. OpenU.

Bishop, John, *Joyce's Book of the Dead*. UWisc.

Fishburn, Katherine, *The Unexpected Universe of Doris Lessing: A Study in Narrative Teachnique*. Greenwood.

Goorney, Howard, and Ewan MacColl, ed., *Agit-Prop to Theatre Workshop: Political Playscripts 1930-50*. ManU.

Herr, Cheryl, *Joyce's Anatomy of Culture*. UIll.

Hibberd, Dominic, *Owen the Poet*. Macmillan.

Kirkham, Michael, *The Imagination of Edward Thomas*. CUP.

Lidoff, Joan, 'Virginia Woolf's Feminine Sentence: The Mother-Daughter World of *To the Lighthouse*' (*L&P*).

Miller, Jonathan, *Subsequent Performances*. Faber.

O'Shea, Edward, *A Descriptive Catalogue of W. B. Yeats's Library*. Garland (1985).

Rubin, David, *After the Raj: British Novels of India Since 1947*. UPNE.

Scott, Paul, *My Appointment with the Muse: Essays, 1961-75*, ed. and intro. by Shelley C. Reece. Heinemann.

Stead, C. K., *Pound, Yeats, Eliot and the Modernist Movement*. Macmillan.

Tanner, Tony, 'Joseph Conrad and the Last Gentleman' (*CritQ*).

Wandor, Michelene, *Carry on Understudies*. RKP.

Yeats, W. B., *The Collected Letters of W. B. Yeats*. Vol. I: *1865-1895*, ed. by John Kelly, with assoc. ed. Eric Domville. Clarendon.

Chapter XVII.   American Literature to 1900

Beaver, Harold, *The Great American Masquerade*. Vision/B&N (1985).

Bryant, John, ed., *A Companion to Melville Studies*. Greenwood.

Myers, Gerald E., *William James: His Life and Thought*. Yale.

Poirier, Richard, *The Renewal of Literature: Emersonian Reflections*. RandomH.

Chapter XVIII.   American Literature: The Twentieth Century

Field, Andrew, *VN: The Life and Art of Vladimir Nabokov*. Crown.

Giles, Paul, *Hart Crane: The Contexts of 'The Bridge'*. CUP.

Hemenway, Robert E., *Zora Neale Hurston: A Literary Biography*. Camden.

Kayman, Martin A., *The Modernism of Ezra Pound: The Science of Poetry*. Macmillan.

Miller, Jeffrey, *Paul Bowles: A Descriptive Bibliography*. BSP.

Morris, Adalaide, 'A Relay of Power and of Peace: H.D. and the Spirit of the Gift' (*ConL*).

Rabaté, Jean-Michel, *Language, Sexuality, and Ideology in Ezra Pound's 'Cantos'*. Macmillan.

Stein, Gertrude, and Carl Van Vechten, *The Letters of Gertrude Stein and Carl Van Vechten*, ed. by Edward Burns. ColU.

Chapter XIX.   African, Caribbean, Indian, Australian, and Canadian Literatures in English

Africa

Clingman, Stephen R., *The Novels of Nadine Gordimer: History from the Inside*. A&U.

Gérard, Albert S., ed., *European-Language Writing in Sub-Saharan Africa*. AK.

Osofisan, Femi, 'The Alternative Tradition: An Insider's Postscript', in *European-Language Writing in Sub-Saharan Africa*, ed. by Albert S. Gérard. AK.

The Caribbean

Burnett, Paula, ed., *The Penguin Book of Caribbean Verse in English*. Penguin.

Dance, Daryl Cumber, ed., *Fifty Caribbean Writers: A Bio-Bibliographical Sourcebook*. Greenwood.

McCorkle, James, 'Re-mapping the New World: The Recent Poetry of Derek Walcott' (*ArielE*).

O'Connor, Teresa F., *Jean Rhys: The West Indian Novels*. ColU.

Thieme, John, ' "The World Turned Upside Down": Carnival Patterns in *The Lonely Londoners*' (*TSAR*).

India

Alexander, Meena, 'Romanticism and Renaissance' (*ArielE*).

Mitter, Partha, 'Art and Nationalism in India' (*LCrit*).

Ramachandran, C. N., 'In Search of the Text: A Comparative Study of Western and Eastern Concepts' (*LCrit*).

Summerfield, H., 'Holy Women and Unholy Men: Ruth Prawer Jhabvala Confronts the Non-Rational' (*ArielE*).

Australia

Goodwin, Ken, *A History of Australian Literature*. Macmillan.

Hergenhan, Laurie, ed., *The Australian Short Story: An Anthology from the 1890s to the 1980s*. UQP.

Jones, Dorothy, 'Mapping and Mythmaking: Women Writers and the Australian Legend' (*ArielE*).

Neilsen, Philip, ed., *The Penguin Book of Australian Satirical Verse*. PenguinA.

Canada

Lecker, Robert, *Robert Kroetsch*. Twayne.

Neuman, Shirley, and Smaro Kamboureli, ed., *A Mazing Space*. NeWest.

Index I. Critics

Authors such as Mary Jacobus and Terry Eagleton, who are both authors of criticism and subjects of discussion by critics, are listed in whichever index is appropriate for each reference; a page number in bold indicates a chapter or part of a chapter written by a contributor to the volume.

Index II. Authors and Subjects Treated

Authors such as Mary Jacobus and Terry Eagleton, who are both authors of criticism and subjects of discussion by critics, are listed in whichever index is appropriate for each reference; a page number in bold represents the main entry for a particular author; numbers in brackets e.g. 346(2) indicate the number of times the author or subject is referred to on a particular page. Under each author, subjects are grouped showing the author's relationship first with other authors and secondly with other subjects; the author's characteristics follow, and finally the works themselves are listed.

Amis, Martin, 480
Ammons, A.R.: *Sphere: The Form of Motion*, 580; *Tape for the Turn of the Year*, 580
Ammons, Elizabeth, 657
anachronism: in Shakespeare, 240
anagrams, 577
Anand, Mulk Raj, 497; *Private Life of an Indian Prince*, 737
Anantanarayanan: *The Silver Pilgrimage*, 737
anarchy: and Goodman, 680
Andersen, Hans Christian: and Atwood, 767; 'The Little Mermaid', 767; 'The Red Shoes', 767
Anderson, Jessica, 755, 755–6; *Tirra Lirra by the River*, 755–6
Anderson, Kay, 724
Anderson, Patrick, **772**
Anderson, Quentin, 587
Anderson, Sherwood, 512, **668**; *Death in the Woods*, 668
Andreas, 121, **127**
Andreas Capellanus: *De amore*, 144
Andrewes, Lancelot, 284, 285, 637; and Browne, 285; and T.S. Eliot, 544–5, 545; and W. Percy, 544–5
androgyny, 45; and Shakespeare, 232; and Mary Shelley, 368–9
'The Angel in the House', 387
Angelou, Maya, 608, 612; *I Know Why the Caged Bird Sings*, 705
Anger, Jane, 197
Anglo-American fiction: Canadian issues, 13
Anglo-Indian culture: and Kipling, 489, *see also* Indian culture
Anglo-Irish dialect: Joyce, 503
Anglo-Irish literature, 423, 475; Bowen, 523
Anglo-Saxon Chronicle, 94, 95, **135–6**, 136
Anglo-Saxon studies *see* Old English
Anselm: and Newman, 441
anthologies, 6–8
Anthony, Michael, 722
anthropology: and T.S. Eliot, 544; and Pym, 530
antimasque, 272–3, 273
Antin, David, 624–5
Antin, Mary: *The Promised Land*, 571
antinomianism, 4, 276, 577, 622
antiquarianism, 427; and Lawrence, 515
antisemitism: in America, 675; Chesterton, 495; Lawrence, 515–16;

and Pound, 647, *see also* Holocaust
apartheid: and South African literature, 721
apocalypse, 38; and Marvell, 282;
apocalyptic messianism, 622–3; in Beckett, 559; in Lawrence, 516
Apollinaire, Guillaume, 621
Apollonius of Rhodes: *Argonautica*, 294
Apollonius of Tyre, 180
Apuleius: and Shakespeare, 231; *The Golden Asse*, 231
Aquin, Hubert, 764
Aquinas, St Thomas, 139; and Milton, 288; and Spenser, 210–11
'The Arabian Nights': and Barth, 684; and Conrad, 485; 'The Tale of the Fisherman and the Jinn', 485
Arabic–English dictionaries, 68
Arac, Jonathan, 401, 404
Arbuthnot, John: *John Bull*, 344
archaeology: and Hardy, 415; in Victorian Britain, 427
Archer, William, 564
architecture: 18th C, 330(2); as image, in Emerson, 576
Arden, John, 554, **555**; *Serjeant Musgrave's Dance*, 554; (with D'Arcy), *The Island of the Mighty*, 555
Ariosto: Ludovico, 209
aristocracy, 462(2); and the novel, 396
Aristophanes, 344
Aristotle: and Arnold, 377; and Burke, 347
Armah, Ayi Kwei, 706, 711–12, **712**; *The Beautyful Ones Are Not Yet Born*, 712; *Two Thousand Seasons*, 706; *Why Are We So Blest?*, 706, 712
Armattoe, Raphael, 707
Arnheim, Rudolph, 648
Arnold, Matthew, 20, **377**, 423, 424, **430–1**, 434, 437, 443(2), 450(2); and Disraeli, 400; and Joyce, 499; and Newman, 441; and Wells, 492; and Wordsworth, 391; and religion, 422; criticism, 420; letters, 430; 'The Buried Life', 377; *Culture and Anarchy*, 400; *On the Study of Celtic Literature*, 423; 'The Study of Poetry', 431; 'The Terrace at Berne', 376; 'Thyrsis', 377; 'To A Republican Friend', 377
Arnold, Thomas: as historian, 427
Arnow, Harriette: *The Dollmaker*, 615
Aron, Jean-Paul, 26

Power, 720; *Serowe, Village of the Rain Wind*, 719

Head, Richard: with Kirkman, *The English Rogue*, 303

Heaney, Seamus, 528, **547–8**, 549; and the past, 549; 'In Memoriam Francis Ledwidge', 548; *Sweeney Astray*, 548

Hearne, Samuel, 762

Hearst, William Randolph, 575

Heath, W.L., **672–3**; *Ill Wind*, 672–3; *Violent Saturday*, 672

Hébert, Ann, 764

Hebrew: *see also* Jewish literature; Judaism

Hebrew loan words, 109

Hegel, Georg Wilhelm Friedrich, 20, 31, 35, 36, 502; and Coleridge, 355; and Derrida, 34; and Shakespeare, 44; *The Phenomonology of Spirit*, 34

hegemony, 51

Heidegger, Martin, 34, 35, 36, 37, 38, 39, 40, 44, 60, 443, 634, 651; and Derrida, 37, 40, 44; and Dickinson, 583; and Nietzsche, 37; and Pound, 644–5; and W.C. Williams, 655; 'Sein und Zeit', 37

Heine, Heinrich: and Shakespeare, 230

Heinemann, Margot, 275

Heinemann (publishers): and African literature, 705

'Helford, John' *see* H.D.

Heliodorus of Emesa: and Fielding, 350

Hellenism: Victorian, 380, *see also* classicism; Greek (classical) literature

Heller, Joseph, 610, **684**; *Catch-22*, 684; *Good As Gold*, 614; (with Speed Vogel), *No Laughing Matter*, 684

Hellman, Lillian, 697

Helwig, David: *Catchpenny Poems*, 773

Hemingway, Ernest, 512, 572, 614, 615, **663–5**; and Chandler, 672; and Farrell, 694; and Pound, 647; and journalism, 615; and time, 473; female characters, 616; posthumous works, 665; short stories, 664, 665; 'The Battler', 665; 'Cat in the Rain', 117, 665; *The Garden of Eden*, 663; *In Our Time*, 115, 615; 'The Snows of Kilimanjaro', 665; *The Sun Also Rises*, 665(2); 'A Way You'll Never Be', 665

Henry, Arthur: and Dreiser, 660–1

Henry, Prince of Wales, 273, 276

Henryson, Robert, 156; fables, 158

Henshaw, James Ene, 709

Henslowe, Philip: *The Sege of London*, 258

heraldry: and Joyce, 508

Herbert, George, 276, **279–81**; and Hopkins, 377; and C. Rossetti, 375–6; and Shakespeare, 233; allusions to, 280; postmodernist criticism, 22; rhetoric, 280; 'Affliction', 281; 'Employment', 280; 'The Forerunners', 280; 'The Holdfast', 281; 'Prayer' (I), 280; 'The Pulley', 280; *The Temple*, 196, 280(3)

hermeneutics, **39–41**; and deconstruction, 37; and T.S. Eliot, 634; and Schleiermacher, 355

hero, 427–8; Christian, 578; heroic myth, Dreiser, 661; woman as, OE, 123; in Kipling, 417; in Shaw, 564; in Tolson, 623

Herod: and Shakespeare, 241

Heron, Robert: on Burns, 338; *Memoir*, 338

Herr, Michael: *Dispatches*, 615–16

Herrick, Robert, 275(2), 276, **283**; and history, 283

Hersey, John, **674**; *Hiroshima*, 674

Herzfeld, George, 136

Hesse, Hermann, 473

Hewett, Dorothy: *The Man from Mukinupin*, 752

Heywood, Thomas, **269**; pageants, 273; *The Fair Maid of the West*, 256; *A Woman Killed with Kindness*, 269(2)

Hiberno-English *see* Irish English

Hickes, George, 121

Hickey, Raymond, 101

Hieron, Samuel: and Middleton, 270; sermons, 270

Higden, Ranulf: *Polychronicon*, 144

Higgins, Aidan, 477

Higgins, Bertram: ' "Mordecaius" Overture', 749

High Church: 18th C, 331

Hill, Aaron, 341

Hill, Christopher, 293

Hill, Donald, 442

Hill, Geoffrey, 549

Hill, Susan, 6

Hill, Thomas, 771

Hiller, Wendy, 564

Hilton, James, 480, **518–19**; *Goodbye,*